THE
AMERICAN
PEOPLE

The United States

CANADA

MAINE

MINNESOTA

WISCONSIN

MICHIGAN

IOWA

ILLINOIS

INDIANA

OHIO

PENNSYLVANIA

NEW YORK

VT

NH

MA

CT RI

NEW JERSEY

DELAWARE

MARYLAND

WEST VIRGINIA

VIRGINIA

KENTUCKY

MISSOURI

ARKANSAS

TENNESSEE

NORTH CAROLINA

SOUTH CAROLINA

MISSISSIPPI

ALABAMA

GEORGIA

LOUISIANA

FLORIDA

ATLANTIC OCEAN

Gulf of Mexico

CUBA

Cities and geographic labels:

nd Forks, Duluth, St. Paul, Minneapolis, oux Falls, Green Bay, Madison, Milwaukee, Grand Rapids, Lansing, Detroit, Cedar Rapids, Rockford, Chicago, Gary, Fort Wayne, Toledo, Cleveland, Akron, Des Moines, Omaha, ncoln, Peoria, Springfield, Indianapolis, Cincinnati, Wheeling, Columbus, Pittsburgh, Harrisburg, Philadelphia, Wilmington, Dover, Baltimore, WASHINGTON D.C., Annapolis, Rochester, Syracuse, Buffalo, Albany, Hartford, Bridgeport, New York City, Newark, Jersey City, Trenton, Providence, Worcester, Boston, Manchester, Concord, Montpelier, Burlington, Augusta, Lewiston, Portland

Kansas City, Kansas City, ka, Jefferson City, St. Louis, Springfield, Tulsa, Louisville, Frankfort, Lexington, Huntington, Charleston, Richmond, Newport News, Norfolk

Nashville, Knoxville, Mt. Mitchell 6,684 ft. (2,030 m), Winston-Salem, Greensboro, Raleigh, Charlotte

Memphis, Fort Smith, Little Rock, Pine Bluff, Huntsville, Greenville, Columbia, Charleston, Cape Fear

Shreveport, Meridian, Jackson, Birmingham, Montgomery, Columbus, Macon, Atlanta, Savannah

llas, Baton Rouge, New Orleans, Biloxi, Mobile, Tallahassee, Jacksonville

Tampa, St. Petersburg, Fort Lauderdale, Miami, Cape Canaveral

Cape Cod, LONG ISLAND, DELMARVA PENINSULA, Chesapeake Bay, Cape Hatteras, 35° North Latitude, 70° West Longitude

Lake Superior, Lake Michigan, Lake Huron, Lake Ontario, Lake Erie, St. Lawrence River, Bay of Fundy

ADIRONDACK MTS, ALLEGHENY MTS, APPALACHIAN MOUNTAINS, Blue Ridge Mts, PIEDMONT, CENTRAL PLAINS, OZARK PLATEAU, COASTAL PLAIN, FLORIDA PENINSULA, Lake Okeechobee, Mississippi Delta, Florida Keys, Straits of Florida, Tropic of Cancer

| | 0 | 100 | 200 Miles |
| | 0 | 100 200 | Kilometers |

PUERTO RICO (U.S.)

ATLANTIC OCEAN

20°N

San Juan

| 0 | 100 Miles |
| 0 | 100 Kilometers |

Student:

To help you make the most of your study time and improve your grades, we have developed the following supplement designed to accompany Nash/ Jeffrey et al.: *The American People: Creating a Nation and a Society*, Second Edition (Volume I):

Study Guide by Julie Roy Jeffrey and Peter Frederick
0-06-044738-9

You can order a copy at your local bookstore or call Harper & Row directly at 1-800-638-3030.

THE AMERICAN PEOPLE

Creating a Nation and a Society

Second Edition

VOLUME 1 • TO 1877

GENERAL EDITORS

GARY B. NASH
University of California, Los Angeles

JULIE ROY JEFFREY
Goucher College

JOHN R. HOWE
University of Minnesota

PETER J. FREDERICK
Wabash College

ALLEN F. DAVIS
Temple University

ALLAN M. WINKLER
University of Oregon

HarperCollins*Publishers*

Sponsoring Editor: Lauren Silverman

Project Editors: Jo-Ann Goldfarb, Betsy Feist

Art Direction: Kathie Vaccaro

Text Design: Function Thru Form, Inc.

Technical Art: Function Thru Form, Inc.

Cover Coordinator: Mary Archondes

Cover Design: A.G.T., Inc.

Cover Illustration/Photo: *The Quilting Party,* Abby Aldrich Rockefeller Folk Art Center, Williamsburg, Virginia

Photo Research: Elsa Peterson, Joan Scafarello

Production: Willie Lane

THE AMERICAN PEOPLE: Creating a Nation and a Society, Volume 1, Second Edition

Library of Congress Cataloging-in-Publication Data

The American people: creating a nation and a society/general
editors, Gary B. Nash. Julie Roy Jeffrey . . . [et al.]: Allen
Yarnell, administrative editor.—2nd ed.
   p. cm.
  Includes bibliograhical references.
  Contents: v. 1. To 1877—v. 2. Since 1865.
  ISBN 0-06-044736-2 (v. 1: student ed.).—ISBN 0-06-044737-0
(v. 2: student ed.)—ISBN 0-06-044740-0 (teacher ed.)
   1. United States—History.   I. Nash, Gary B.   II. Jeffrey, Julie
Roy.   III. Yarnell, Allen.
E178.1.A49355 1990b   89–24612
973—dc20   CIP

0-06-044736-2   (Student Edition)
0-06-044740-0   (Teacher Edition)
         93 9 8 7 6

CONTENTS IN BRIEF

CONTENTS

RECOVERING THE PAST

INNOVATIONS

MAPS

CHARTS

PREFACE

The Yoruba people of West Africa have an old saying, "However far the stream flows, it never forgets its source." Why, we wonder, do such ancient societies as the Yoruba find history so important, while modern American students question its relevance? This book aims to end such skepticism about the usefulness of history.

When we study our own history, that of the American people, we see a rich and extraordinarily complex human story. This country, whose written history began with a convergence of Native Americans, Europeans, and Africans, has always been a nation of diverse peoples—a magnificent mosaic of cultures, religions, and skin shades. This book explores how American society assumed its present shape and developed its present forms of government; how as a nation we have conducted our foreign affairs and managed our economy; how as individuals and in groups we have lived, worked, loved, married, raised families, voted, argued, protested, and struggled to fulfill our dreams and the noble ideals of the sacred texts of the American experiment.

Several ways of making the past understandable distinguish this book from most textbooks written in the last twenty years. The coverage of public events like presidential elections, diplomatic treaties, and economic legislation is integrated with the private human stories that pervade them. Within a chronological framework we have woven together our history as a nation, as a people, and as a society. When, for example, national political events are discussed, we analyze their impact on social and economic life at the state and local level. Wars are described not only as they unfolded on the battlefields and in the salons of diplomats, but also on the home front, where they are history's greatest motor of social change. The interaction of ordinary Americans with extraordinary events runs as a theme throughout the book.

Above all, we have tried to show the "humanness" of our history as it is revealed in people's everyday lives. The authors have often used the words of ordinary Americans to capture the authentic human voices of those who participated in and responded to epic events such as war, slavery, industrialization, and reform movements.

GOALS AND THEMES OF THE BOOK

Our primary goal is to provide students with a rich, balanced, and thought-provoking treatment of the American past. By this we mean a history that treats the lives and experiences of Americans of all national origins and cultural backgrounds, at all levels of society, and in all regions of the country. It also means a history that seeks connections between the many factors–political, economic, technological, social, religious, intellectual, and biological—that have molded and re-molded American society over four centuries. And finally it means a history that encourages students to think about how we have all inherited a complex past filled with both notable achievements and thorny problems. The only history befitting a democratic nation is one that inspires students to initiate a frank and searching dialogue with their past.

To speak of a dialogue about the past presumes that history is interpretive. Students should understand that historians are continually reinterpreting the past. New interpretations are often based on the discovery of new evidence, but more often new interpretations emerge because historians reevaluate old evidence in the light of new ideas that spring from the times in which they write and from their personal views of the world.

Through this book, we also hope to promote class discussions, which can be organized around eight questions that we see as basic to the American historical experience:

1. How have Americans developed a stable political system consistent with the fundamental principles of our nation's founding and flexible enough to address the extraordinary changes that have occurred in the last two centuries? To what degree have they fashioned a national democratic order consistent with those principles?

2. What forms has the tension between idealism—a sense of the special virtue of the American people and the importance of the common good—and individual self-interest, as expressed in the struggle for material gain and personal advancement, taken in the past?

3. What are the competing claims of liberty and authority—in families, schools, workplaces, communities, and nation? How have Americans argued and negotiated over the ways in which power and authority are justified, limited, and rightfully distributed?

4. What has been the character of the sporadic but recurring reform impulse in American society? To what extent has reform in the last two centuries been directed at more fully realizing the ideals of liberty, equality, and social justice in racial, gender, and social relations?

5. What has been the role of our nation in the world, and how has it expressed the tension between mission-oriented expansionism and isolationism?

6. In what ways have economic and technological changes affected the daily lives, work, family structure, leisure habits, and community relations of all Americans?

7. What has been the experience of the country's original inhabitants and newly arrived immigrant groups as they confronted the dominant culture, which often seemed to threaten their ethnic, racial, and religious heritage?

8. In what ways have Americans struggled for social unity and national identity amid cultural diversity and conflict?

In writing a history that revolves around these themes, we have tried to convey two dynamics that operate in all societies. First, we observe people continuously adjusting to new developments, such as industrialization and urbanization, over which they seemingly have little control; yet we realize that people are not paralyzed by history but are the fundamental creators of it. They retain the ability, individually and collectively, to shape the world in which they live and thus in considerable degree to control their own lives.

Second, we emphasize the connections that always exist among social, political, economic, and cultural events. Just as our individual lives are never neatly parceled into separate spheres of activity, the life of a society is made up of a complicated and often messy mixture of forces, events, and accidental occurrences. In this text, political and economic, technological and cultural factors are intertwined like strands in a rope.

STRUCTURE OF THE BOOK

Part Organization

The chapters of this book are grouped into six parts relating to major periods in American history. Each part begins with a brief *introductory essay* that outlines how the eight organizing questions described above are developed in the subsequent chapters. Each part also contains a *comparative chronology* summarizing the political and diplomatic, social and economic, and cultural and technological events of the period.

Chapter Structure

Every chapter begins with a *personal story* recalling the experience of an ordinary or lesser-known American. Chapter 1, for example, is introduced with the tragic account of Opechancanough, a Powhattan tribesman whose entire life of nearly ninety years was consumed by a struggle against the land, hunger, and alien values brought by Spanish and English newcomers. This brief anecdote serves several purposes. First, it introduces the overarching themes and major concepts of the chapter, in this case the meeting of three societies—Native American, European, and African—in the North American wilderness, each with different cultural values, life-styles, and aspirations. Second, the personal story launches the chapter in a way that facilitates learning—by engaging the student with a human account. Last, the personal story suggests that history was shaped by ordinary as well as extraordinary people. At the end of the personal story a *brief overview* links the biographical sketch to the chapter by elaborating the major themes of the chapter. Students should read this crucial transition paragraph carefully to enhance their comprehension of the material to come.

We aim to facilitate the learning process for students in other ways as well. Every chapter ends with pedagogical features to reinforce and expand the presentation. A *conclusion* briefly summarizes the main concepts and developments elaborated in the chapter and serves as a bridge to the following chapter. An annotated list of *recommended readings* provides supplementary sources for further study or research; novels contemporary to the period are often included. Finally, a *timeline* reviews the major events and developments covered in the chapter. Each graph, map, and illustration has been chosen to relate clearly to the narrative.

SPECIAL FEATURES

A distinctive feature of this book is the two-page *Recovering the Past* presented in each chapter. These RTPs, as the authors affectionately call them, introduce students to the fascinating variety of evidence—ranging from tax lists, folk tales, and diaries to tombstones, advertising, and house designs—that historians have learned to employ in reconstructing the past. Each RTP gives basic information about the source and its use by historians and then raises questions for students to consider as they study the example reproduced for their inspection.

In addition to the RTPs, we have provided other elements that will facilitate learning for students. The program of *color illustrations*—paintings, cartoons, photographs, maps, and charts—amplifies important themes while presenting visual evidence for student reflection and analysis.

THE SECOND EDITION

The second edition of *The American People* has benefited from both the helpful comments of scholars and the experience of teachers and students who used the first edition of the book. Some of the modifications are small, but others, like the reorganization of the chapters on the American Revolution and its aftermath and those on post–World War II America, are substantial.

Several changes in presentation strengthen the text. We have, for example, highlighted the central questions around which the book is organized by referring to these questions in the part and chapter introductions. New charts clarify and elaborate on points discussed in the narrative, while additional entries for each chapter's *Recommended Readings* will help students complete research projects.

New sections on technology, called *Innovations,* strengthen the analysis of economic and technological change contained in the text. In each section, an essay describes both the development and importance of a major innovation—such as the sewing machine, the bicycle, and the computer—and its impact on the lives and work of ordinary people as well as on those in positions of wealth and power. Several illustrations allow the student to visualize the innovation in its various stages of development.

To give the entire book a stronger chronological framework, we have revised the chapter *Timelines* and part-opening *Comparative Chronologies* and added specific dates to subheads in the text. Finally, we have incorporated the results of new scholarship throughout.

Supplemental Teaching and Learning Aids

Several companion volumes for both teachers and students enhance this comprehensive presentation of American history.

The two-volume set of readers, *Retracing the Past,* has been revised by Gary B. Nash and Ronald Schultz, of the University of Wyoming. The readings cover economic, political, and social history, with a special emphasis on the role of women, ethnic groups, and laborers. Two-thirds of the selections are new to this edition.

Authors Julie Roy Jeffrey and Peter J. Frederick have written the *Study Guide* and *Instructor's Manual* that accompany the text. Both supplements are based on ideas generated in the frequent "active learning" workshops held by the authors and both are tied closely to the text.

The *Study Guide* includes chapter outlines, significant themes and highlights, glossary, learning enrichment ideas, sample test questions, exercises for identification and interpretation, and geography exercises based on maps in the text.

The *Instructor's Manual* provides suggestions on how to generate lively class discussion and involve students in active learning. It also offers a file of exam questions and lists of resources, including films, slides, photo collections, records, and audiocassettes.

Two separate *test banks*—Volume I (Chapters 1–17), by Charles Cook, Houston Community College, and Volume II (Chapters 17–31), by J. B. Smallwood, North Texas State University—together contain over 3500 objective, conceptual, and essay questions. Both of these unusually comprehensive test banks have been thoroughly reviewed for accuracy and coverage.

The *Harper Test,* a highly acclaimed test-generation software system, offers a menu-driven program that allows instructors to add, delete, edit, scramble, and store items. It is available for both IBM-PC and Macintosh computers.

Mapping America: A Guide to Historical Geography, by Ken Weatherbie, Del Mar College, was prepared specifically for the new text edition in response to the increasing evidence of weak geography skills among today's college students. It contains 35 sequenced exercises corresponding to the map programs in the text, each culminating in a series of interpretive questions about the role of geographical factors in American history.

Available only to adopters of this text are the *Harper & Row Audio History Cassettes.* These two cassette packages, "Oral History: American Voices" and "Great Speeches: Words that Made History," feature the words and thoughts of Americans of the past, both celebrated and obscure, as set down in diaries, letters, interviews, and famous speeches.

Also available to adopters are *videocassettes* from highly acclaimed series like "Eyes on the Prize," "The American Experience," and David Frost's "The Modern Presidency."

The *Media Handbook,* a media resource guide tied directly to the concepts and features in *The American People,* Second Edition, contains a description of Harper & Row's comprehensive U.S. history media program along with probing discussion questions and instructor's notes.

Super Shell Student Software, a computerized study guide, written by Virginia Bellows of Tulsa Junior College and Donald Bellows of Oklahoma Junior College and produced at Oklahoma State University, includes Hypertext chapter outlines for key topics, diagnostic self-tests, and *flash cards,* for terminology and identification.

Also available to adopters are:

A set of over 50 *map transparencies* drawn from the text.

The American Adventure Telecourse, Beginnings to 1877, a series of 26 half-hour episodes corresponding to Volume One of *The American Experience,* accompanied by a *Student Telecourse Guide,* by John A. Trickle, Richland College.

Grades, Harper & Row's easy-to-use classroom management software.

Our aim has been to write a balanced and vivid history of the development of the American nation and its society. We have also tried to provide the support materials necessary to make teaching and learning enjoyable and rewarding. The reader will be the judge of our success. The authors and Harper & Row welcome your comments.

GBN, JRJ

ACKNOWLEDGMENTS

Over the years, as the first and second editions of this text were being developed, many of our colleagues read and criticized the various drafts of the manuscript. For their thoughtful evaluations and constructive suggestions, the authors wish to express their gratitude to the following reviewers:

Harry Baker, University of Arkansas at Little Rock
Michael Batinski, Southern Illinois University
Gary Bell, Sam Houston State University
Spencer Bennett, Siena Heights College
Jeffrey P. Brown, New Mexico State University
Professor David Brundage, University of California at Santa Cruz
Colin Calloway, University of Wyoming
D'Ann Campbell, Indiana University
Neil Clough, North Seattle Community College
Bruce Dierenfield, Canisius College
John Dittmer, DePauw University
Gordon Dodds, Portland State University
Richard Donley, Eastern Washington University
Bernard Friedman, Indiana University—Purdue University at Indianapolis
Bruce Glasrud, California State University, Hayward
Professor Richard Griswold-Castillo, San Diego State University
Colonel Williams L. Harris, The Citadel Military College
John S. Hughes, University of Texas—Austin
Donald M. Jacobs, Northeastern University
Delores Janiewski, University of Idaho, Mt. Holyoke
David Johnson, Portland State University
Monte Lewis, Cisco Junior College
William Link, University of North Carolina—Greensboro

Vern Mattson, University of Nevada at Las Vegas
John McCormick, Delaware County Community College
Norma Mitchell, Troy State University
William Morris, Midland College
Marian Morton, John Carroll University
Roger Nichols, University of Arizona
Paul Palmer, Texas A&I University
Al Parker, Riverside City College
Neva Peters, Tarrant County Junior College
James Prickett, Santa Monica College
Juan Gomez-Quinones, University of California, Los Angeles
George Rable, Anderson College
Leonard Riforgiato, Pennsylvania State University
Randy Roberts, Purdue University
Mary Robertson, Armstrong State University
David Robson, John Carroll University
Sylvia Sebesta, San Antonio College
David R. Shibley, Santa Monica College
Kathryn Sklar, Stanford University
James Smith, Virginia State University
John Snetsinger, California Polytechnic State University
Tom Tefft, Citrus College
John Trickell, Richland College
Donna Van Raaphorst, Cuyahoga Community College
Morris Vogel, Temple University
Jackie Walker, James Madison University

We'd also like to thank six colleagues for reviewing the second edition manuscript for accuracy and currency in the following areas:

Labor: David Brundage, University of California at Santa Cruz
Blacks: John Dittmer, DePauw University
Mexican-Americans: Juan Gomez-Quinones, University of California, Los Angeles

Hispanics: Richard Griswold del Castillo, San Diego State University
Native Americans: Frederick Hoxie, McNickle Center for Study of American Indians
Women: Kathryn Sklar, Stanford University

The following colleagues participated in focus groups held at the meetings of the Organization of American Historians in 1988 and 1989. The authors express their thanks for the many useful comments and suggestions provided in these meetings:

James Bradford, Texas A&M University
Bernard Friedman, Indiana University—Purdue University at Indianapolis
Bruce Glasrud, California State University, Hayward
Robert Haws, University of Mississippi

David Johnson, Portland State University
William Link, University of North Carolina
Sylvia McGrath, Stephen F. Austin University
Roger Nichols, University of Arizona, Tucson
Noel Pugash, University of New Mexico
Herbert Shapiro, University of Cincinnati

ABOUT THE AUTHORS

Gary B. Nash received his Ph.D. from Princeton University in 1964. He is currently Associate Director of the National Center for History in the Schools at the University of California, Los Angeles, where he teaches colonial and revolutionary American history. Among the books Nash has authored are *Quakers and Politics: Pennsylvania, 1681–1726* (1968); *Red, White, and Black: The Peoples of Early America* (1974, 1982); *The Urban Crucible: Social Change, Political Consciousness, and the Origins of the American Revolution* (1979); and *Forging Freedom: The Black Urban Experience in Philadelphia, 1720–1840* (1988). His scholarship is especially concerned with the role of common people in the making of history. He wrote Part One and served as a general editor of this book.

Julie Roy Jeffrey earned her Ph.D. in history from Rice University in 1972. Since then she has taught at Goucher College, offering the American history survey and historic preservation courses. Honored as an outstanding teacher, Jeffrey has been involved in faculty development activities and curriculum evaluation. Jeffrey's major publications include *Education for Children of the Poor* (1978); *Frontier Women: The Trans-Mississippi West, 1840–1880* (1979); and many articles on the lives and perceptions of nineteenth-century women. She wrote Parts Three and Four in collaboration with Peter Frederick and acted as a general editor of this book.

John R. Howe received his Ph.D. from Yale University in 1962. At the University of Minnesota his teaching interests include early American politics and relations between Native Americans and whites. His major publications include *The Changing Political Thought of John Adams* (1966) and *From the Revolution Through the Age of Jackson* (1973). His major research currently involves a manuscript entitled "The Transformation of Public Life in Revolutionary America." Howe wrote Part Two of this book.

Peter J. Frederick received his Ph.D. in history from the University of California at Berkeley in 1966. The innovative teaching of American history has been the focus of his career at San Francisco State College and California State College at Hayward, and since 1970 at Wabash College. His areas of research interest include nineteenth-century American social and intellectual history as well as black and Native American history. Frederick has written *Knights of the Golden Rule: The Intellectual as Christian Social Reformer in the 1890's.* He coordinated and edited all the Recovering the Past sections and coauthored Parts Three and Four of this book.

Allen F. Davis earned his Ph.D. at the University of Wisconsin in 1959. He is a professor at Temple University where he is the codirector of the Center for Public History. Davis is the author of *Spearheads for Reform: The Social Settlement and the Progressive Movement* and *American Heroine: The Life and Legend of Jane Addams* and coauthor of *Generations: Your Family in Modern American History.* Most recently he wrote *Philadelphia Stories,* and *One Hundred Years at Hull-House.* Davis wrote Part Five of this book.

Allan M. Winkler received his Ph.D. from Yale in 1974. He is presently teaching at Miami University of Ohio, where he chairs the History Department. His books include *The Politics of Propaganda: The Office of War Information, 1942–1945* (1978); *Modern America: The United States from the Second World War to the Present* (1985); and *Home Front U.S.A.: America during World War II* (1986). His research centers on the connections between public policy and popular mood in modern American history. He is currently studying American atomic energy policy. Winkler wrote Part Six of this book.

THE
AMERICAN
PEOPLE

PART ONE

A COLONIZING PEOPLE

1492   1776

America has always been a nation of immigrants, an elaborate cultural mosaic created out of the unending streams of people who for four centuries have flocked to its shores from every corner of the world. It is the colonial roots of this intermingling of people and cultures that provides an organizing framework for the first part of this book. America began with the convergence of people from the three continents of North America, Europe, and Africa. We examine the mingling of their values, institutions, and lifeways during the fifteenth and sixteenth centuries in Chapter 1, "Three Worlds Meet." Chapter 2, "Colonizing a Continent," explores five regions of settlement along the Atlantic seaboard. The interplay of religious idealism, economic opportunity, political experimentation, and social adaptation to the new environment are examined on the Chesapeake tobacco coast, in Puritan New England, in the French, Dutch, and English colonies from the St. Lawrence to the Hudson rivers, in proprietary Carolina, and in Quaker Pennsylvania.

The ability to grow from small and struggling settlements in the seventeenth century to thriving, more populous colonies in the early eighteenth century depended above all on exploiting the natural resources of North America. Chapter 3, "Mastering the New World," explores how colonists struggled against Native Americans to expand their land base and turned to slave labor in the southern colonies. While controlling Native Americans and African slaves, the colonists also had to master themselves as social and political tensions grew at the end of the seventeenth century. At the same time, French ambitions in North America challenged the territorial mastery of England's American colonies and involved them in another kind of conflict.

Chapter 4, "The Maturing of Colonial Society," traces the development of the colonies of England, Spain, and France in the first half of the eighteenth century. It stresses the increasingly complex yet unfinished character of colonial society, highlights its regional differ-

ences, and shows how economic growth, religious revival, and political maturation prepared the English colonists by 1750 for the epic events that would occur in the next generation. It was this fluidity of colonial society that made the Seven Years' War (1756–1763) and the subsequent coming of the American Revolution such a multifaceted and dynamic period, as Chapter 5, "Bursting the Colonial Bonds," spells out.

1

COMPARATIVE CHRONOLOGIES

Political and Diplomatic	Social and Economic	Cultural and Technological

Political and Diplomatic	Social and Economic	Cultural and Technological
1492 Spain completes expulsion of Moors 1493 Pope declares demarcation line in New World 1509–1547 Reign of Henry VIII in England 1519–1521 Cortés conquers Aztec empire	1492–1504 Columbus makes four voyages exploring New World 1497–1585 French and English explore North America 1498 Da Gama reaches India 1515–1565 Spanish explore southern parts of North America 1518–1530 European diseases decimate New World native populations 1521–1522 Magellan circumnavigates the earth	1500 Indian tribes of Southeast attain artistic peak 1508 First New World sugar mill established in West Indies 1517 Luther launches the Reformation 

1525

Political and Diplomatic	Social and Economic	Cultural and Technological
1532–1535 Pizarro conquers Inca empire 1558–1603 Reign of Elizabeth I in England 1565 Spanish found St. Augustine in Florida	1540–1542 Coronado explores the Southwest 1545–1560 Bonanza silver strikes made in Mexico and Bolivia 1550–1650 Price revolution in western Europe causes widespread distress	1530s Calvin calls for further religious reforms 1539 First printing press in New World established in Mexico City 1564 Jacques LeMoyne paints first scenes of Indian life in New World

1575

Political and Diplomatic	Social and Economic	Cultural and Technological
1585–1598 England colonizes Ireland 1588 Spanish armada attacks England 1603–1625 Reign of James I in England 1607 Virginia Company of London settles Jamestown 1620 Pilgrims establish colony at Plymouth 1624 Dutch settle New Netherland	1616–1621 Decimation of Native Americans in New England by European diseases 1617 First Virginia tobacco shipped to England 1619 First Africans brought to Virginia	1585 John White, member of Roanoke expedition, paints first scenes of Indian life in area of English settlement 1612–1613 John Rolfe's experiments with tobacco develop a hybrid suitable for export

1625

Political and Diplomatic	Social and Economic	Cultural and Technological
1625–1649 Reign of Charles I in England 1630 Puritans migrate to New England 1634 Settlement of Maryland begins 1642–1649 Civil war in England 1651 First navigation act 1660 Restoration of Stuart monarchy; Charles II installed 1663 Carolina granted charter 1664 English conquer New Netherland	1625–1660 Slavery becomes backbone of labor force in English Caribbean 1637 Pequot War in New England 1650–1670 Judicial and legislative decisions solidify racial lines in southern colonies 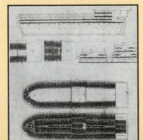	1636 Harvard College established 1642 Massachusetts passes basic literacy law 1643 Roger Williams compiles first American dictionary of an Indian language 1661 John Eliot's translation of the New Testament into Algonquian becomes first Bible printed in North America 1662 Half-Way Covenant in Massachusetts

Political and Diplomatic	Social and Economic	Cultural and Technological
1673–1683 French expand into Mississippi valley 1682 Quakers migrate to Pennsylvania under proprietary charter to William Penn 1682 LaSalle claims Louisiana for France 1688–1691 Revolts in American colonies inspired by overthrow of James II 1689–1697 King William's War 1702–1713 Queen Anne's War 1718 French settle New Orleans	1675–1677 King Philip's War in New England; war against Chesapeake tribes associated with Bacon's Rebellion 1690s South Carolinians begin rice cultivation 1690–1720 Most colonies enact slave codes 1692 Witchcraft hysteria and executions in Salem, Massachusetts 1697–1715 Colonial importations of slaves increase rapidly 1711–1715 Tuscarora and Yamasee wars in the Carolinas 1712 Slave revolt in New York City 1714–1720 Scots-Irish and German immigration begins 1715–1730 Volume of slave trade doubles	1690 First newspaper in colonies published (and quickly suppressed) in Boston 1693 William and Mary College founded 1701 Yale College founded 1721–1722 Inoculation against smallpox creates controversy in colonies 

1725

1732 Georgia founded as colony for English paupers and buffer against Spanish Florida 1744–1748 King George's War 1756–1763 Seven Years' War 1764 Pontiac's Rebellion 1764–1765 Sugar, Stamp, and Currency acts 1767 Townshend duties 1773 Tea Act and Boston Tea Party 1774 Coercive Acts and meeting of First Continental Congress	1734–1760 Great Awakening in different regions of colonies 1739 Stono Rebellion in South Carolina 1741 Hysteria over suspected slave plot in New York City 1759–1761 Cherokee War against the English 1761–1765 Depression hits most colonies	1747 Benjamin Franklin publishes *Poor Richard's Almanack* in Philadelphia 1749 Franklin invents lightning rod 1752 First American hospital established in Philadelphia Franklin's *Experiments and Observations in Electricity* published 1754 College of Philadelphia founded 1757 First streetlights in a colonial city installed in Philadelphia 1769 American Philosophical Society founded

1775

1775 Battles of Lexington and Concord Meeting of Second Continental Congress 1776 Thomas Paine publishes *Common Sense* Declaration of Independence	1775 Pennsylvania Abolition Society established 	1775 Postal system established by Continental Congress

1

Three Worlds Meet

In the late 1550s, a few years after Catholic King Philip II and Protestant Queen Elizabeth assumed the throne in Spain and England, respectively, Opechancanough was born in Tsenacommacah. In the Algonquian language, the word Tsenacommacah meant "densely inhabited land." Later English colonizers would rename this place Virginia after their monarch, the virgin Queen Elizabeth. Before he died in the 1640s, in the ninth decade of his life, Opechancanough had seen light-skinned, swarthy, and black-skinned newcomers from a half dozen European nations and African kingdoms swarm into his land. Like thousands of other Native Americans, he was witnessing the early moments of European expansion across the Atlantic Ocean.

Opechancanough was only an infant when Europeans first reached the Chesapeake Bay region. A small party of Spanish had explored the area in 1561, but they found neither gold nor silver nor anything else of value. Upon departing, they took with them the brother of one of the local chieftains, who was a member of Opechancanough's clan. They left behind something of unparalleled importance in the history of contact between the peoples of Europe and the Americas: a bacterial infection that spread like wildfire through a population that had no immunity against it. Many members of Opechancanough's tribe died, although their casualties were light compared with those of other tribes that caught the deadly European diseases.

In 1570, when Opechancanough was young, the Spanish returned and established a Jesuit mission near the York River. Violence occurred, and before the Spanish abandoned the Chesapeake in 1572, they put to death a number of captured Indians, including a chief who was Opechancanough's relative. The Native Americans learned that Europeans, even when they came bearing the crosses of their religion, were a volatile and dangerous people.

Opechancanough was in his forties when three ships of fair-skinned settlers disembarked in 1607 to begin the first permanent English settlement in the New World. For several months, he watched his half brother Powhatan, high chief of several dozen loosely confederated tribes in the region, parry and fence with the newcomers. Then Powhatan sent him to capture the English leader

F. Maij

John Smith and escort him to the Indians' main village. Smith was put through a mock execution but then released. He later got the best of Opechancanough, threatening him with a pistol, humiliating him in front of his warriors, and assaulting one of his sons, whom Smith "spurned like a dog."

Opechancanough nursed his wounds for years while Powhatan grew old and the English settlements slowly spread in the Chesapeake region. Then, in 1617, he assumed leadership of the Powhatan Confederacy. Two years later, a Dutch trader sold 20 Africans to the settlers after docking at Jamestown. Three years after that, Opechancanough led a determined assault on the English plantations that lay along the rivers and streams emptying into the bay. The Indians killed nearly one-third of the intruders. But they paid dearly in the retaliatory raids that the colonists mounted in succeeding years.

As he watched the land-hungry settlers swarm in during the next two decades, Opechancanough's patience failed him. Finally, in 1644, now in his eighties, he galvanized a new generation of warriors and led a final desperate assault on the English. It was a suicidal attempt, but the "great general" of the Powhatan Confederacy, faithful to the tradition of his people, counseled death over enslavement and humiliation. Though the warriors inflicted heavy casualties, they could not overwhelm the colonizers, who vastly outnumbered them. For two years, Opechancanough was kept prisoner by the Virginians. Nearly blind and "so decrepit that he was not able to walk alone," he was fatally shot in the back by an English guard in 1646.

Over a long lifetime, Opechancanough painfully experienced the meeting of people from three continents. His land was one of many that would be penetrated by Europeans over the next three centuries, as Christian civilization girdled the globe. On the Chespeake Bay, this clash of cultures formed the opening chapter of what we know as American history. That history, in turn, was one scene in a much broader drama of European colonization and exploitation of many indigenous cultures thousands of miles from the Old World. The nature of this violent intermingling of Europeans, Africans, and Native Americans is an essential part of early American history. But to understand how the destinies of red, white, and black people became intertwined in Opechancanough's land, we must look at the precontact history and cultural foundations of life in the homelands of each of them.

THE PEOPLE OF AMERICA BEFORE COLUMBUS

Thousands of years before the European voyages of discovery, the history of humankind in North America began. Nomadic bands from Siberia, hunting big game animals such as bison, caribou, and reindeer, began to migrate across a land bridge connecting northeastern Asia with Alaska. Geologists believe that this land bridge existed most recently between 28,000 and 12,000 years ago, when massive glaciers locked up much of the earth's moisture and left part of the Bering Sea floor exposed. Ice-free passage through Canada was possible only briefly at the beginning and end of this period, however. At other times melting glaciers flooded the land bridge and blocked foot traffic to Alaska. Paleo-anthropologists remain divided on the exact timing, but the main migration apparently occurred either about 12,000 to 14,000 or 25,000 to 28,000 years ago.

Hunters and Farmers

For thousands of years, these early hunters trekked southward and eastward, following vegetation and game. In time, they reached the tip of South America and the eastern edge of North America, thousands of miles from their Asian homeland. Thus did people from the "Old World" discover the "New World" thousands of years before Columbus.

Migration Routes from Asia to the Americas

Approximate dry land area during ice ages

Glaciers

Modern coastline

Archaeologists have excavated ancient sites of early life in the Americas, unearthing tools, ornaments, and skeletal remains that can be scientifically dated. In this way they have tentatively reconstructed the dispersion of these first Americans over an immense landmass. Although much remains unknown, this archaeological evidence suggests that as centuries passed and population increased, the earliest inhabitants evolved into separate cultures, organizing life and adjusting to a variety of environments in distinct ways. Europeans who rediscovered the New World thousands of years later would indiscriminately lump together the myriad societies they found. But by the 1500s, the "Indians" of the Americas were enormously diverse in the size and complexity of their societies, the languages they spoke, and their forms of social organization.

Archaeologists and anthropologists have charted several phases of "Native American" history. A long Beringian epoch ended about 14,000 years ago. From that time a rich archaeological record indicates that the hunters had developed a new technology. Big game hunters now flaked hard stones into spear points and chose "kill sites" where they slew whole herds of Pleistocene mammals. This more reliable food source allowed population growth, and nomadism began to give way to settled habitations or local migration within limited territories.

In another phase of evolution, the Archaic era, from about 10,000 to 2,500 years ago, great geological changes brought further adaptations to the land. As the massive glaciers of the Ice Age slowly retreated, a warming trend deprived vast areas from Utah to the highlands of Central America of sufficient water and turned them from grasslands into desert. The Pleistocene mammals could not survive more arid conditions, but human populations ably adapted. They learned to exploit new sources of food, especially plant life. In time a second technological breakthrough, the "agricultural revolution," occurred.

When Native Americans learned to "domesticate" plant life, they began the long process of transforming their relationship to the physical world. To learn how to harvest, plant, and nurture a seed was to gain partial control over natural forces that before had been ungovernable. Anthropologists believe that this process began independently in widely separated parts of the world—Africa, Asia, Europe, and the Americas—about 7,000 to 9,000 years ago. Though agriculture developed very slowly, everywhere it eventually brought dramatic changes in human societies.

Over the millennia, humans progressed from doorside planting of a few wild seeds to systematic clearing and planting of bean and maize fields. As the production of domesticated plant food ended dependence on gathering wild plants and pursuing game, sedentary village life began to replace nomadic existence. The increase in food supply brought about by agriculture triggered other major changes. As populations grew, large groups split off to form separate societies. Greater social and po-

Baskets were essential equipment for daily life, as well as an art form, in Native American societies.

litical complexity developed because not everyone was needed as before to secure the society's food supply. Men cleared the land and hunted game, while women planted, cultivated, and harvested crops. Many societies empowered religious figures, who organized the common followers, directed their work, and exacted tribute as well as worship from them. In return they were trusted to protect the community from hostile forces.

Everywhere in the Americas, regional trading networks formed. Along trade routes carrying commodities such as salt, obsidian rock for projectile points, and copper for jewelry also traveled technology, religious ideas, and agricultural practices. By the end of the Archaic period, about 500 B.C. (to use the Christian European method of dating), hundreds of independent, kin-based groups, like people in other parts of the world, had learned to exploit the resources of their particular area and to trade with other groups in their region.

Native Americans in 1600

The last epoch of pre-Columbian development, the post-Archaic phase, occurred during the 2,000 years before contact with Europeans. It involved a complex process of growth and environmental adaptation among many distinct societies—and crisis in some of them. In the American Southwest, for

One of the hundreds of symbolic mounds built by people of the Hopewell culture, this one, in the shape of a serpent, is near present-day Cincinnati.

example, the ancestors of the present-day Hopi and Zuni developed carefully planned villages composed of large terraced buildings, each with many rooms. By the time the Spanish arrived in the 1540s, the indigenous Pueblo people were using irrigation canals, check dams, and hillside terracing to bring water to their arid maize fields. In their agricultural techniques, their skill in ceramics, their use of woven textiles for clothing, and their village life, Pueblo society resembled that of peasant communities in many parts of Europe and Asia.

Far to the east were the mound-building societies of the Mississippi and Ohio valleys. When European settlers first crossed the Appalachian Mountains a century and a half after arriving on the continent, they were amazed to find hundreds of ceremonial mounds, some of them 70 feet high, and gigantic sculptured earthworks in geometric designs or in the shapes of huge humans, birds, or writhing serpents. Believing all "Indians" to be forest primitives, they reasoned that these were the remains of an ancient civilization that had found its way to North America—perhaps Phoenicians, survivors of the sunken islands of Atlantis, or the Lost Tribes of Israel spoken of in European mythology.

The mound-building societies of the Ohio valley declined about 1,000 years before Europeans reached the continent, perhaps because of attacks from other tribes or severe climatic changes that undermined agriculture. Several centuries later, another culture, based on intensive cultivation of beans, maize, and squash, began to flourish in the Mississippi valley. Its center, a city of perhaps 40,000, stood near present-day St. Louis. Great ceremonial plazas, flanked by a temple that rose in four terraces to a height of 100 feet, marked this first metropolis in America. This was the urban center of a far-flung "Mississippi" culture that radiated out to encompass thousands of villages from Wisconsin to Louisiana and from Oklahoma to Tennessee.

Several centuries before Europeans arrived in North America, the mound-building cultures of the continental heartlands began to decline. But their influence had already passed eastward to transform the woodlands societies along the Atlantic coastal plain. The numerous small tribes that settled from Nova Scotia to Florida never equaled the larger societies of the midcontinent in earthwork sculpture, architectural design, or development of large-scale agriculture. But they were far from the "savages" that the first European explorers described. They had added limited agriculture to their skill in exploiting natural plants for food, medicine, dyes, and flavoring and had developed food procurement strategies that used all the resources around them—cleared land, forests, streams, shore, and ocean.

Most of the eastern woodlands tribes lived in waterside villages. Locating their fields of maize near fishing grounds, they often migrated seasonally between inland and coastal village sites or situated themselves astride two ecological zones. In the Northeast, their birchbark canoes, light enough to be carried by a single man, gave them a means of trading and communicating over immense territories. In the Southeast, population was denser and social and political organization more elaborate.

As European exploration of the Americas drew near, the continent north of the Rio Grande contained perhaps 4 million people, of whom perhaps 500,000 lived along the eastern coastal plain and in the piedmont region accessible to the early European settlers. The colonizers were not coming to a "virgin wilderness," as they often described it, but to a land inhabited for thousands of years by people whose village existence in many ways resembled that of the arriving Europeans.

Contrasting World Views

Colonizing Europeans called themselves "civilized" and typically described the people they met in the Americas as "savage," "heathen," or "barbarian." But the gulf separating people in Europe and North America was not defined so much by how the two cultures extracted a food supply from the land, housed themselves, or organized family life as by how they viewed their relationship to the environment and defined social relations in their communities. In these areas, a wide difference in values existed. This created the potential for a dangerous conflict once the Atlantic Ocean that had separated two ancient civilizations had been transformed from a barrier to a bridge by a technological and scientific leap forward by western Europeans in the fifteenth century.

In the view of Europeans, the natural world was a resource designed for man's use. "Subdue the earth," read the first book of the Old Testament, "and have dominion over every living thing that moves on the earth." God ruled the cosmos, bringing floods, droughts, and earthquakes, but humans could reshape their physical surroundings into a productive and secure world. Man's relationship to the natural environment was a secular matter, even if God, in the sacred sphere, sometimes intervened.

Native Americans, in contrast, were "a people that are contented with Nature as they find her," as one colonist phrased it. In their ethos, every part of the natural environment was sacred. Rocks, trees, and animals all possessed spiritual power, and all were linked to form a sacred whole. To injure the environment, by overfishing or abusing it in any way, was to offend the spiritual power present throughout nature and hence to risk spiritual retaliation. In the villages of Europe, peasant people had similarly believed in spirits residing in trees and rocks, but such "superstition" was fading.

Regarding the soil as a resource to be exploited for man's benefit, Europeans believed that land should be privately possessed. Individual ownership of property became a fundamental concept, and an extensive institutional apparatus grew up to support it. Fences symbolized private property, inheritance became the mechanism for transmitting land from one generation to another within the same family, and courts gained the power to settle property disputes. Property was the basis not only of sustenance but also of independence, material wealth, political status, and personal identity. The social structure directly mirrored patterns of land ownership, with a land-wealthy elite at the apex of the social pyramid and a mass of propertyless individuals forming the broad base.

Native Americans also had concepts of property, and tribes recognized territorial boundaries. But they believed that land was invested with sacred qualities and should be held in common. As one German missionary to the Delaware Indians explained their view in the eighteenth century, the Creator "made the Earth and all that it contains for the common good of mankind. Whatever liveth on the land, whatsoever groweth out of the earth, and all that is in the rivers and waters . . . was given jointly to all and everyone is entitled to his share."

Communal ownership sharply limited social stratification in most tribal communities. Accustomed to wide disparities of wealth, Europeans often found this remarkable. Observing the Iroquois of the eastern woodlands in 1657, a French Jesuit noted with surprise that they had no almshouses because "their kindness, humanity and courtesy not only makes them liberal with what they have, but causes them to possess hardly anything except in common. A whole village must be without corn, before any individual can be obliged to endure privation." Not all Europeans were acquisitive, competitive individuals. The majority were peasants scratching a subsistence living from the soil, living in kin-centered villages with little contact with the outside world, and exchanging goods and labor through barter. But in Europe's urban centers a wealth-conscious, striving individual who celebrated wider choices and greater opportunities to enhance personal status was coming to the fore. In contrast, Native American traditions stressed the group rather than the individual. Holding land and other resources in common, Indian societies were usually more egalitarian and their members more concerned with personal valor than personal wealth.

Exceptions to this cultural system occurred in the highly developed and populous Aztec and Inca empires and, in North America, among a few tribes such as the Natchez. But on the eastern and western coasts of the continent and in the Southwest—the regions of contact in the sixteenth and seventeenth centuries—the European newcomers encountered a people whose cultural values differed strikingly from theirs.

European colonizers in North America also found disturbing the matrilineal organization of many tribal societies. Contrary to European practice, family membership among the Iroquois, for example, was determined through the female line. A typical family consisted of an old woman, her daughters with their husbands and children, and her unmarried granddaughters and grandsons. When a son or grandson married, he moved from this female-headed household to one headed by the matriarch of his wife's family. Divorce was also the woman's prerogative. If she desired it, she merely set her husband's possessions outside their dwelling door. Clans were composed of several matrilineal kin groups related by a blood connection on the mother's side. To Europeans this was a peculiar and dangerous reversal of their sexual hierarchy in which men, from time immemorial, had been supreme.

In Native American societies, women also held subordinate positions, but not nearly to the extent as among European women. For example, European women, with rare exceptions, were entirely excluded from political affairs. By contrast, in Native American villages, again to take the Iroquois example, designated men sat in a circle to deliberate and make decisions, but the senior women of the village stood behind them, lobbying and instructing. The village chiefs were male, but they were named

Indian Tribes During the Period of Early European Settlement

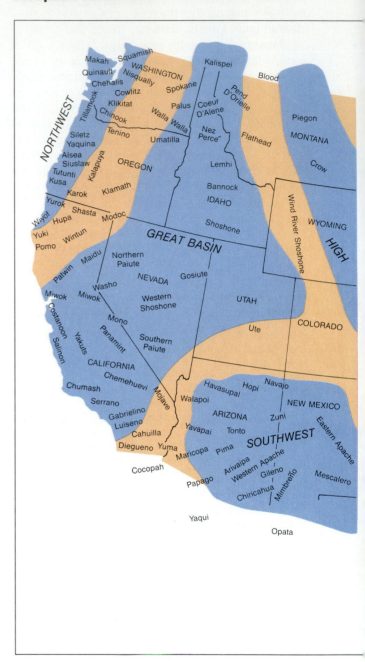

to their positions by the elder women of their clans. If they moved too far from the will of the women who appointed them, these chiefs were removed—or "dehorned."

The role of women in the tribal economy reinforced the sharing of power between male and female. Men were responsible for hunting, fishing, and clearing land, but women controlled the cultivation, harvest, and distribution of food. When the

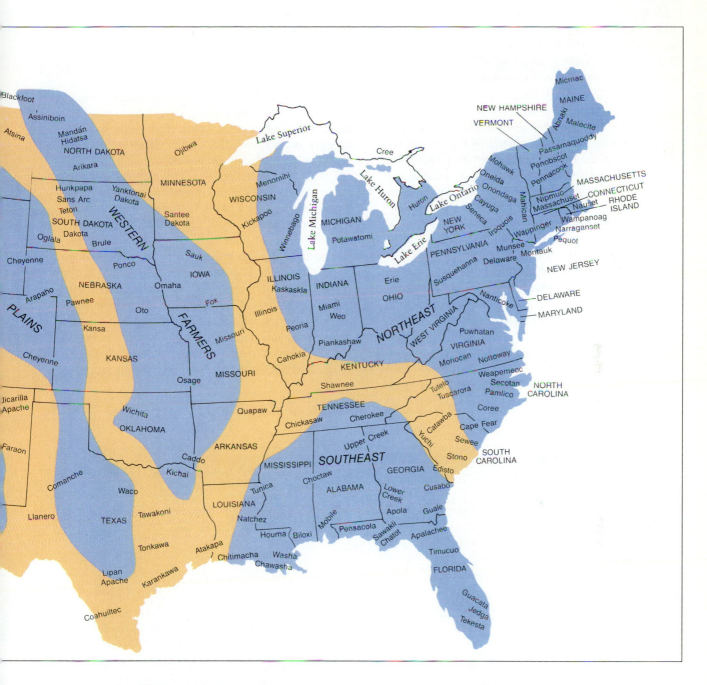

men were away on hunting expeditions, women directed village life. Europeans, imbued with the idea of male superiority and female subordination, perceived such a degree of sexual equality as another mark of the uncivilized nature of tribal society.

In the religious beliefs of Native Americans, the English saw a final cultural defect. Europeans built their religious life around the belief in a single god, written scriptures, an organized clergy, and churches. Most Native American societies, sharing no literary tradition, expressed their religious beliefs in a less structured way. Animated by a belief in a spirit power dwelling throughout nature (polytheism), they seemed to Europeans to worship the devil. European settlers, their fear and hatred of infidels intensified by the Protestant Reformation, saw a holy necessity to convert—or destroy—these enemies of their God.

ECOVERING THE PAST

ARCHAEOLOGICAL ARTIFACTS

The recovery of the past before there were extensive written records is the domain of archaeology. Virtually our entire knowledge of Indian societies in North America before the arrival of European colonizers is drawn from the work of archaeologists who have excavated the ancient living sites of the first Americans. Many Native Americans today strongly oppose this rummaging in the ancient ancestral places; they particularly oppose the unearthing of burial sites. But the modern search for knowledge about the past goes on.

Archaeological data has allowed us to overcome the stereotypic view of Native Americans as a primitive people whose culture was static for thousands of years before Europeans arrived in North America. This earlier view allowed historians to argue that the tremendous loss of Native American population and land accompanying the initial settlement and westward migration of white Americans was more or less inevitable. When two cultures, one dynamic and forward-looking and the other static and backward, confronted each other, historians have frequently maintained, the more advanced or "civilized" culture usually prevailed.

Much of the elaborate early history of people in the Americas is unrecoverable. But many fragments of this long human history are being recaptured through archaeological research. Particularly important are studies that reveal how Indian societies were changing during the few centuries immediately preceding the European arrival in the "New World." These studies give us a much better chance to interpret the seventeenth-century interaction of Native Americans and Europeans because they provide an understanding of Indian values, social and political organization, material culture, and religion as they existed when the two cultures first met.

A reconstructed view of Cahokia, the largest town in North America before European arrival; painted by Valerie Waldorf.

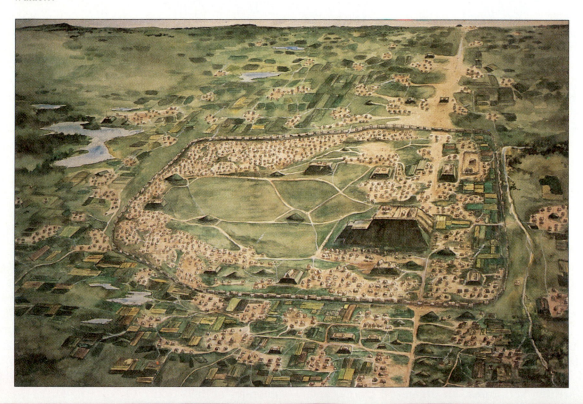

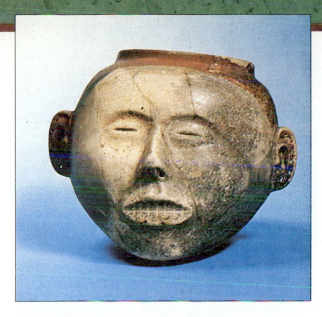

Pottery effigy vessels, in the shape of human heads.

One such investigation has been carried out over the last century along the Mississippi River near modern-day East St. Louis, Illinois. Archaeologists have found the center of a vast "Mississippi" culture that began about A.D. 600, reached its peak about 300 years before Columbus's voyages, and then declined. Cahokia is the name given to the urban center of a civilization that at its height dominated an area as large as New York State. At the center of Cahokia stood one of the largest earth constructions built by ancient man anywhere on the planet. Its base covering 15 acres, this gigantic earthen temple rises in four terraces to a height of 100 feet, as tall as a ten-story modern office building. The imaginary drawing shown here indicates some of the dozens of smaller geometric mounds discovered near this major temple. Notice the outlying farms, a sure sign of the settled (as opposed to nomadic) existence of the people who flourished ten centuries ago in this region. How does this depiction of ancient Cahokia change your image of Native American life before the arrival of Europeans?

By recovering artifacts from Cahokia burial mounds, archaeologists have pieced together a picture, still tentative, of a highly elaborate civilization along the Mississippi bottomlands. Cahokian manufacturers mass-produced salt, knives, and stone hoe blades for both local consumption and export. Cahokian artisans made sophisticated pottery, ornamental jewelry, metalwork, and tools. They used copper and furs from the Lake Superior region, black obsidian stone from the Rocky Mountains, and seashells from the Gulf of Mexico, demonstrating that the people at Cahokia were involved in long-distance trade. In fact, Cahokia may have been a crucial crossroads of trade and water travel in the heartland of North America.

The objects shown here, unearthed from graves by archaeologists, are an example of the culture of the Mississippi Mound Builders. The round-faced pottery bottles in the form of heads, each about 6 inches tall and wide, show a sense of humor in early Mississippi culture. Holes in the ears of the bottles and in the armpits and wrists of the woman once held thongs so that the objects could be hung or carried. Other objects, such as a kneeling woman found in Tennessee, for example, had holes under the arms for a similar purpose. What other conclusions about Cahokian culture can you draw from figures such as these? Are there archaeological sites in your area that contain evidence of Native American civilization?

The fact that some graves uncovered at Cahokia contain large caches of finely tooled objects while other burial mounds contain many skeletons unaccompanied by any artifacts leads archaeologists to conclude that this was a more stratified society than those the first settlers encountered along the Atlantic seaboard. Anthropologists believe that some of the Mississippi culture spread eastward before Cahokia declined, but much mystery still remains concerning the fate and cultural diffusion of these early Americans.

AFRICA ON THE EVE OF CONTACT

Half a century before Columbus reached the Americas, a Portuguese sea captain, Antam Gonçalves, made the first European landing on the west coast of sub-Saharan Africa. If he had been able to travel the length and breadth of the immense continent, he would have encountered a rich variety of African peoples and cultures. The notion of African "backwardness" and cultural impoverishment was a myth perpetuated after the slave trade had begun transporting millions of Africans to the New World. During the period of early contact with Europeans, Africa, like pre-Columbian America, was recognized as a diverse continent with a long history of cultural evolution.

The Kingdoms of Africa

The peoples of Africa, estimated at about 50 million in the fifteenth century when Europeans began making extensive contact with them, lived in vast deserts, grasslands, and tropical forests. As in Europe and the Americas at that time, most people tilled the soil. Part of their skill in farming derived from the development of iron production, which may have begun in West Africa while Europe was still in the Stone Age. More efficient iron implements increased agricultural productivity, which in turn spurred population growth. The pattern was repeated in other parts of the world—the Americas, Europe, the Far East, and the Middle East—when the agricultural revolution began.

By the time Europeans reached the west coast of Africa, a number of large empires had risen there. The first was the kingdom of Ghana. It embraced an immense territory between the Sahara and the Gulf of Guinea and stretched from the Atlantic Ocean to the Niger River.

The development of large towns, skillfully designed buildings, elaborate sculpture and metalwork depicting humans and animals, long-distance commerce, and a complex political structure marked the Ghanaian kingdom from the sixth to eleventh centuries. A thriving caravan trade with Arab peoples across the Sahara to Morocco and Algeria brought extensive Muslim influence by the end of this period. By the eleventh century the king of Ghana boasted an army of 200,000, maintained trading contacts as far east as Cairo and Baghdad, and was furnishing, through Muslim middlemen in North Africa, much of the gold supply for the Christian Mediterranean region.

An invasion of North African Muslim people beginning in the eleventh century introduced a period

West African Cultures and Slaving Forts

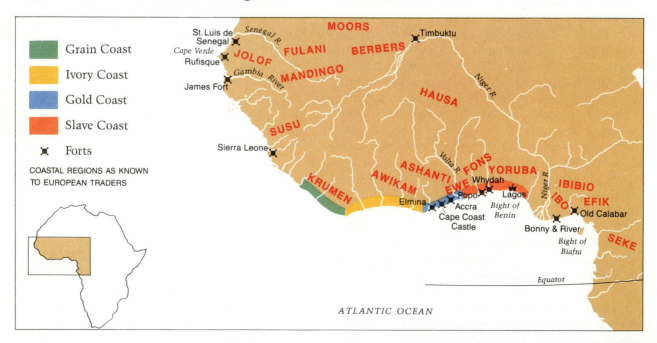

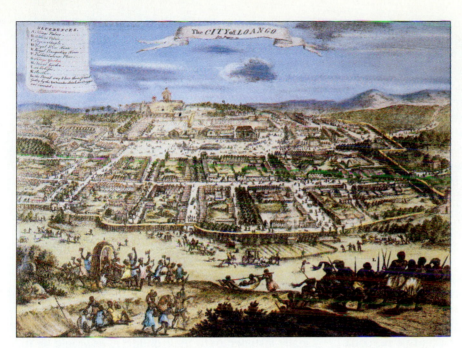

The city of Loanga, at the mouth of the Congo River on the west coast of Africa, was larger at the time of this drawing in the mid-eighteenth century than all but a few seaports in the British colonies in North America.

of religious strife that eventually destroyed the kingdom of Ghana. But in the same region arose the Islamic kingdom of Mali. Prospering through its control of the gold trade, Mali flourished until the fifteenth century. Its city of Timbuktu contained a distinguished faculty of scholars to whom North Africans and even southern Europeans came to study. Traveling there in the 1330s, the Arab geographer ibn-Battutu wrote admiringly of "the discipline of its officials and provincial governors, the excellent condition of public finance, and . . . the respect accorded to the decisions of justice and to the authority of the sovereign."

Lesser kingdoms such as Congo, Songhay, and Benin had also been growing for centuries before Europeans reached Africa by water. In their towns, rivaling those of Europe in size, lived people skilled in metalworking, weaving, ceramics, architecture, and aesthetic expression. Codes of law, regional trade, and effective political organization all developed by the fifteenth century. Finding their way to Africa south of the Sahara, Europeans encountered not a backward area but a densely settled region with an ancient history of long-distance trade and cultural exchange with other peoples.

Population growth and cultural development in Africa, as elsewhere in the world, proceeded at different rates. Ecological conditions and geography had much to do with this. Where soil was rich, rainfall was adequate, and minerals were abundant, as in western Sudan, population grew and cultures changed rapidly. Where inhospitable desert or impenetrable jungle ruled, societies remained small and changed at a crawl. Isolation from other cultures retarded development, while contact with other regions encouraged change. For example, cultural innovation accelerated in East African, Swahili-speaking societies facing the Indian Ocean after trading contacts began with the Eastern world in the ninth century. At about the same time, trans-Sahara traders from the Arab world began to spread Muslim influence in West Africa.

The African Ethos

The many peoples of Africa, who were to supply more than half of all the immigrants who crossed the ocean to the Western Hemisphere in the three centuries after Europeans began colonizing there, came from a rich diversity of cultures. But most of them shared certain ways of life that differentiated them from Europeans.

As in Europe, the family was the basic unit of social organization. Unlike Europe, however, African societies were organized in a variety of kinship and political systems. In many African societies, as in many Native American ones, the family was matrilineal. Property rights and political inheritance descended through the mother rather than the father. It was not the son of a chief who inherited his father's position but the son of the chief's sister. When a man married, his wife did not leave her family and take his name; the bridegroom left his family to join that of his bride.

West Africans believed in a supreme creator of the cosmos and in an assortment of lesser deities associated with natural forces such as rain, fertility, and animal life. Since these deities could intervene in human affairs, they were elaborately honored. Like most North American Indian societies, the peoples of West Africa held that spirits dwelt in the trees, rocks, and rivers around them, and hence they exercised care in the treatment of these natural objects.

In Africa ancestors were also worshiped, for they mediated between the Creator and the living of the earth. Since the dead played such an important role for the living, relatives held elaborate funeral rites to ensure the proper entrance of a deceased relative into the spiritual world. The more ancient an ancestor, the greater was this person's power to affect the living; thus the "ancient ones"

were devoutly worshiped. Deep family loyalty and regard for family lineage flowed naturally from this ancestor worship.

Social organization in much of West Africa by the time Europeans arrived was as elaborate as in fifteenth-century Europe. At the top of society stood the nobility and the priests, usually men of advanced age. Beneath them were the great masses of people. Most of them were farmers, but some worked as craftsmen, traders, teachers, and artists. At the bottom of society resided slaves. As in ancient Greece and Rome, they were "outsiders"—war captives, criminals, or sometimes persons who sold themselves into servitude to satisfy a debt. The rights of slaves were restricted, and their opportunities for advancement were narrow. Nevertheless, as members of the community, they were entitled to protection under the law and allowed the privileges of education, marriage, and parenthood. Their servile condition was not permanent, nor was it automatically fastened onto their children, as would be the fate of Africans enslaved in the Americas.

The art of sixteenth-century West Africa, much of it ceremonial, shows a high degree of aesthetic development. On the left is Gou, god of war, a metal sculpture from the Fon culture in Dahomey; on the right is a pair of antelope headdresses (worn by running a cord through holes in the base and tying them atop the head) carved of wood by the Bambara tribe of Senegambia.

EUROPE IN THE AGE OF EXPLORATION

In the ninth century, about the time that the Mound Builders of the Mississippi valley were constructing their urban center at Cahokia and the kingdom of Ghana was rising in West Africa, western Europe was an economic and cultural backwater. The center of political power and economic vitality in the "Old World" had shifted eastward to Christian Byzantium, which controlled Asia Minor, the Balkans, and parts of Italy. The other dynamic culture of this age had spread through the Middle East, spilled across North Africa, and penetrated Spain and West Africa south of the Sahara.

Over the next six centuries, an epic revitalization of western Europe occurred, creating the conditions that enabled its leading maritime nations vastly to extend their oceanic frontiers. Thence began a 400-year epoch of the militant expansion of European peoples and European culture into other continents. Only in the present century has this process of Europeanization been reversed, as colonized people have regained their autonomy and cultural identity through wars of national liberation.

The Rise of Europe

The rebirth of western Europe, which began around A.D. 1000, owed much to a revival of long-distance trading from Italian ports on the Mediterranean and the rediscovery of ancient knowledge that these contacts permitted. The once mighty cities of the Roman Empire had stagnated for centuries, but now Venice, Genoa, Pisa, and other Italian ports began trading with peoples facing the Adriatic, the Baltic, and the North Sea. These new contacts brought wealth and power to the Italian commercial cities, which gradually evolved into merchant-dominated city-states that freed themselves from the rule of feudal lords in control of the surrounding countryside.

While merchants led the emerging city-states, western Europe's feudal system was gradually weakening. For centuries, feudal lords, not kings, had exercised the normal powers of the state—the power to tax, wage war, and administer the law. In the thirteenth and fourteenth centuries, however, kings began to reassert their political authority and to undertake efforts to unify their realms. One of their primary goals was to curb the power of the great lords who dominated entire regions and to force lesser nobles into dependence on and obedience to the crown.

The Black Death that devastated western Europe and Africa in 1348 and 1349 promoted the unification of old realms into early modern states. The plague killed one-third of the population, a blow from which Europe did not recover demographically for centuries. The nobilities with which monarchs had to contend were reduced in size, for the plague defied class distinction. Ironically, feudal lords treated their peasants better for a time because their labor, tremendously reduced by the plague, became more valuable.

Early developments in England led to a distinctive political system. In 1215, the English aristocracy curbed the powers of the king when they forced him to accept the Magna Charta. On the basis of this charter, a parliament composed of elective and hereditary members eventually gained the right to meet regularly to pass money bills. Parliament was thus in a position to act as a check on the crown, an arrangement unknown on the Continent. During the sixteenth century, the crown and Parliament worked together toward a more unified state, with the English kings wielding less political power than their European counterparts.

Economic changes of great significance also occurred in England during the sixteenth century. Members of the landed class began to combine their estates in order to practice more intensive and profitable agriculture. In this process, they threw peasant farmers off their plots, turning many of them into wage laborers. The formation of this working class was the crucial first step toward industrial development.

Continental Europe lagged behind England in two respects. First, it was far less affected by the move to consolidate, or "enclose," land. Part of the explanation lies in the values of continental aristocrats, who regarded the maximization of profit as unworthy of gentlemen. French nobles could lose their titles for commercial activities. Second, continental rulers were less successful in engaging the interests of their nobilities, and these nobles never shared governance with their king, as did English aristocrats through their participation in Parliament. In France, a noble faction assassinated Henry III in 1589, and the nobility remained disruptive for nearly another century. In Spain, the bloody expulsion of the Muslims and the Jews in 1492 strengthened the monarchy's hold, but regional cultures and leaders remained strong. The continental monarchs would thus warmly embrace doctrines of royal absolutism developed in the sixteenth century.

The New Monarchies and the Expansionist Impulse

In the second half of the fifteenth century, ambitious monarchs coming to power in France, England, and Spain sought social order and political stability in their kingdoms. Louis XI in France, Henry VII in England, Isabella of Castile, and Ferdinand of Aragon all created armies and bureaucratic state machinery strong enough to quell internal conflict, such as the English War of the Roses, and to raise taxes sufficient to support their regimes. In these countries, and in Portugal as well, economic revival and the reversal of more than a century of population decline and civil disorder nourished the impulse to expand beyond known frontiers. This impulse was also fed by Renaissance culture. Ushering in a new more secular age, the Renaissance (Rebirth) encouraged freedom of thought, richness of expression, and an emphasis on human abilities. Beginning in Italy and spreading northward through Europe, the Renaissance peaked dramatically in the late fifteenth century when the age of exploration began.

The exploratory urge had two initial objectives: to circumvent Muslim traders by finding an eastward oceanic route to Asia and to tap at its source the African gold trade. Since the tenth century, Muslim middlemen in North Africa had brought the precious metal to Europe from Guinea. Now the possibility arose of bypassing these non-Christian traffickers. Likewise, Christian Europeans dreamed of eliminating Muslim traders from the commerce with Asia. Since 1291, when Marco Polo returned to Venice with tales of Eastern treasures—spices, silks, perfumes, drugs, and jewels—Europeans had bartered with the Orient. But the difficulties of the long eastward overland route through the Muslim world kept alive the hopes of Christian Europeans that an alternative water route existed. Eventually, Europe's mariners would find that they could voyage to Cathay by both eastward and westward water routes, but this took two more centuries to discover.

Portugal seemed the least likely of the rising nation-states to lead the expansion of Europe outside its continental boundaries, yet it forged into the lead at the end of the fifteenth century. A poor and insignificant country of only one million inhabitants, Portugal had gradually overcome Moorish control in the twelfth and thirteenth centuries and, in 1385, had wrenched itself free of domination by neighboring Castile. Led by Prince Henry the Navigator, for whom trade was secondary to the conquest of the Muslim world, Portugal breached the geographical unknown. In the 1420s, Henry began dispatching Portuguese mariners to probe the unknown Atlantic "sea of darkness." His intrepid sailors were aided by important improvements in navigation, mapmaking, and ship design, all promoted by the prince.

Portuguese captains operated at sea on three ancient Ptolemaic principles: that the earth was round, that distances on its surface could be measured by degrees, and that navigators could "fix" their position on a map by measuring the position of the stars. The invention in the 1450s of the quadrant, which allowed a precise measurement of star altitude necessary for determining latitude, represented a leap forward from the chart-and-compass method of navigation. Equally important was the design of a lateen-rigged caravel, adapted from a Moorish ship design. Its triangular sails permitted ships to sail with a contrary wind, allowing them to beat southward along the African coast—a feat the square-rigged European vessels could never perform.

By the 1430s, the ability of Prince Henry's captains to break through the limits of the world known to Europeans had carried them to Madeira, the Canaries, and the Azores, lying off the coasts of Portugal and northwestern Africa. These were soon developed as the first European agricultural plantations, located on the Continent's periphery. From there, the Portuguese sea captains pushed farther south.

By the time of Prince Henry's death in 1460, Portuguese mariners had reached the west coast of Africa, where they began a profitable trade in ivory, slaves, and, especially, gold. By 1500, they had captured control of the African gold trade monopolized for centuries by North African Muslims. The gleaming metal now traveled directly to Lisbon by sea rather than by camel caravan across the Sahara to North African Muslim ports such as Tunis and Algiers. In 1497, Vasco da Gama became the first European to sail around the Cape of Africa, allowing the Portuguese to colonize the Indian Ocean and as far east as the Spice Islands and Canton by 1513. By forcing trade concessions in the islands and

Oceanic Exploration in the Fifteenth and Sixteenth Centuries

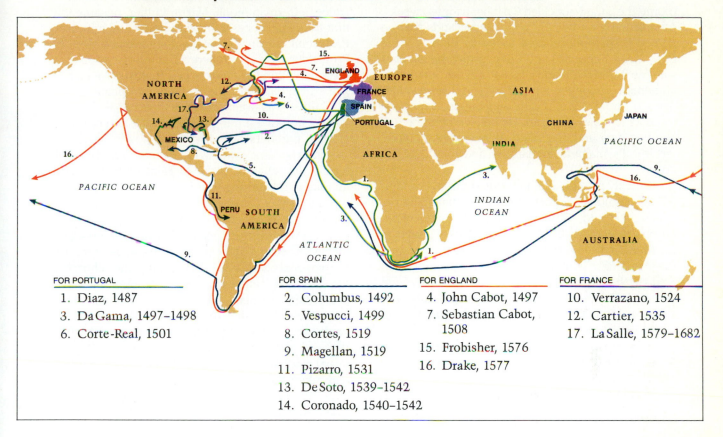

FOR PORTUGAL

1. Diaz, 1487
3. DaGama, 1497–1498
6. Corte-Real, 1501

FOR SPAIN

2. Columbus, 1492
5. Vespucci, 1499
8. Cortes, 1519
9. Magellan, 1519
11. Pizarro, 1531
13. DeSoto, 1539–1542
14. Coronado, 1540–1542

FOR ENGLAND

4. John Cabot, 1497
7. Sebastian Cabot, 1508
15. Frobisher, 1576
16. Drake, 1577

FOR FRANCE

10. Verrazano, 1524
12. Cartier, 1535
17. LaSalle, 1579–1682

coastal states of the East Indies, the Portuguese unlocked the fabulous Asian treasure houses that since Marco Polo's time had whetted the appetites of Europe's seagoing men.

Reaching the Americas

The marriage of Ferdinand and Isabella in 1469 united the independent states of Aragon and Castile and launched the Spanish nation into its golden age. Leading the way for Spain was an Italian sailor, Christopher Columbus. The son of a poor Genoese weaver, Columbus had married into a prominent family of Lisbon merchants and thus made important contacts at court.

Like many sailors, Columbus had listened to sea tales about lands to the west. He may have heard Icelandic sagas about the voyages of Leif Ericsson and other Norsemen to an unknown world five centuries before. Others speculated that the Atlantic Ocean stretched to India and eastern Asia. Could one reach the Indies by sailing west rather than by

sailing east around Africa, as the Portuguese were attempting? Columbus hungered to know.

For nearly ten years, Columbus failed to secure financial backing and royal sanction in Portugal for exploratory voyages. Many mocked his modest estimates of the distance westward from Europe to Japan. Finally, in 1492, Queen Isabella of Spain commissioned him, and he sailed west with three tiny ships manned by about 90 men.

Strong winds, lasting ten days, blew the ships far into the Atlantic. There they were becalmed. In the fifth week at sea—longer than any European sailors had been out of the sight of land—mutinous rumblings swept through the crews. But Columbus pressed on. On the seventieth day, long after Columbus had calculated he would reach Japan, a lookout sighted land. On October 12, 1492, the sailors clambered ashore on a tiny island in the Bahamas, which Columbus named San Salvador (Holy Savior). Grateful sailors "rendered thanks to Our Lord, kneeling on the ground, embracing it with tears of joy."

Believing he had reached Asia, Columbus explored the island-speckled Caribbean for ten weeks. After landing on heavily populated islands that he named Hispaniola (shared today by Haiti and the Dominican Republic) and Cuba (which he thought was the Asian mainland), he set sail for Spain with cinnamon, coconuts, a bit of gold, and several kidnapped natives. While homeward bound, he penned a report of his discoveries. He believed that he had reached Asia and described its hospitable people, fertile soils, magnificent harbors, and gold-filled rivers.

Quickly printed and distributed throughout Europe, Columbus's report brought him financing between 1494 and 1504 for three much larger expeditions to explore the newfound lands. Though at the time his discoveries seemed less significant than the Portuguese exploits in the South Atlantic, he led Spain to the threshold of a mighty empire. He reaped few rewards, however, dying unnoticed and penniless in 1506. To the end he believed that he had found the water route to Asia.

The expansion of Spain and Portugal into new areas of the world profoundly affected patterns of economic activity in Europe. Its commercial center now shifted away from the ports of the Mediterranean to the Atlantic ports facing the New World.

While Spanish and Portuguese explorations promised to stimulate the awakening economies of western Europe, the New World also beckoned as a field of religious contest. The European discovery of the heavily populated Americas offered an especially rewarding opportunity to convert to Christianity millions of people who were innocent of the Bible.

The Catholic-Protestant division within Christianity complicated Christian dreams of converting a "heathen" continent, however. The people of western Europe, at precisely the time they were unlocking the secrets of the new worlds to the east and west in the sixteenth century, were being torn by religious schisms that magnified the era's national rivalries.

Religious Conflict During the Reformation

At the heart of Europe's religious strife was a continental movement to cleanse the Christian church of corrupt practices and return it to the purer ways of "primitive" Christianity, as practiced by the early Christians. While criticism of the worldliness of the Catholic church mounted during the Renaissance, a German monk, Martin Luther, became the first to break successfully with Rome and initiate a Protestant reformation of theology and practice. As Protestant sects multiplied, a Catholic Reformation grew up within the church, and the two groups began a long battle for the souls of Europeans.

Luther was preparing for a legal career in 1505 when a bolt of lightning nearly struck him during a violent thunderstorm. Trembling with fear, he vowed to become a monk. But peace of mind eluded him in the religious order of Saint Augustine that he joined. Despairing that he could earn salvation through any of the age-old rituals of the church—prayer, the Mass, confession, pilgrimages to holy places, even crusades against Muslim infidels—Luther agonized and finally found a new understanding of personal salvation. Discarding the church's teaching that man could earn redemption by these prescribed "works," he reasoned that salvation came through an inward faith, or "grace," that God conferred on those he chose. Good works, Luther believed, did not earn grace but were only the external evidence of grace won through faith. Luther had taken the revolutionary step of rejecting the church's elaborate hierarchy of officials, who presided over the rituals intended to guide individuals along the path toward salvation.

Luther's doctrine of private "justification by faith" did not immediately threaten the church. But in 1517, he openly attacked the sale of "indulgences" for sins by which the pope raised money for the building of St. Peter's in Rome. By purchasing indulgences, individuals believed they could reduce their time (or that of a deceased relative) in purgatory. Luther drew up 95 arguments against this practice and called on Christians to practice true repentance. The spread of printing, invented less than 70 years before, allowed the rapid circulation of his ideas. The printed word—and the ability to read it—were to become revolutionary weapons throughout the world.

Luther's cry for reform soon inspired open revolt among Germans of all classes. He denounced five of the seven sacraments of the church, calling for a return to baptism and communion alone, the only sacraments prescribed by the Scriptures. He attacked the clergy for luxurious living and urged celibate prelates to marry. He attacked "the detestable tyranny of the clergy over the laity" and called for a priesthood of all believers. He rejected age-old rituals such as masses and pilgrimages. He

The Reformation, sparked by Martin Luther's protest, brought sweeping changes to western Europe in the sixteenth century and eventually played a part in migrations across the Atlantic. Lucas Cranach the Younger commemorates the Reformation's leaders in his Epitaph of the Burgomeisters of Myenburg.

urged people to seek faith individually by reading the Bible, which he translated into German and made widely available for the first time in printed form. Most dangerously, he called on the German princes to assume control over religion in their states. This directly challenged the authority of Rome and further undermined the functions of its clergy.

Building on Luther's redefinition of Christianity, John Calvin, a Frenchman, brought new intensity and meaning to the Protestant Reformation. In 1536, at age 26, he published a ringing appeal to every Christian to form a direct, personal relationship with God. By Calvin's doctrine, God had saved a few souls at random before Creation and damned the rest. Human beings were too depraved to know or alter this predestination, but good Christians must struggle to believe in their hearts that they were saved. Without mediation of ritual or priest but by "straight-walking," one was to behave as one of God's elect, the "saints." This radical theology, even more insistent on individual godliness than Luther's, also had profound social implications, for the highest and most privileged on earth might be damned to burn in hell, and the lowest of all might be saved. Elements in all classes throughout Europe were attracted to these ideas.

Calvin proposed reformed Christian communities structured around the elect few. To remake the corrupt world and follow God's will, communities of "saints" must control the state, rather than the other way around. Elected bodies of ministers and dedicated laymen, called presbyteries, were to govern the church, directing the affairs of society down to the last detail so that all, whether saved or damned, would work for God's ends.

Calvinism, as a fine-tuned system of self-discipline and social control, was first put into practice in the 1550s in the city-state of Geneva, near the French border of Switzerland. Here the brilliant and austere leader established what he intended to be a model Christian community. A council of 12 elders drove nonbelievers from the city, rigidly disciplined daily life, and stripped the churches of every appeal to the senses—images, music, incense, and colorful clerical costumes. Offenders great and small, from those committing violent acts to those guilty of minor lapses such as frivolous behavior on the Sabbath, were ferreted out and punished. Religious reformers from all over Europe flocked to the new holy community, and Geneva soon became the continental center of the reformist Christian movement and a haven for refugee Protestant leaders. The city, wrote John Knox of Scotland in 1556, "is the most perfect school of Christ that ever was in the earth since the days of the apostles."

Calvin's radical program converted large numbers of people to Protestantism throughout Europe. Like Lutheranism, it recruited most successfully among the privileged classes of merchants, landowners, lawyers, and the nobility and among the rising middle class of master artisans and shopkeepers.

Sixteenth-century monarchs regarded attacks on the Catholic church with horror. But many local princes adopted some version of the reformed faith, and Henry VIII of England inaugurated the Reformation in his realm. Blaming his wife Catherine for their failure to produce a male heir to the throne, Henry asked Pope Clement VII for permission to divorce and remarry. When the pope refused, Henry declared himself head of a Protestant (Anglican) church. Although the Anglican church retained many Catholic features, it moved further in a Protestant direction under Henry's son Edward. But when Mary, Henry's older Catholic daughter, came to the throne, she vowed to reinstate her mother's religion by suppressing Protestants. Her policy created Protestant martyrs, and many were relieved when she died in 1558, bringing Henry's younger Protestant daughter, Elizabeth, to the throne. During her long rule, Elizabeth helped to create an Anglican church that steered a middle course between the radicalism of Geneva and the Catholicism of Rome.

Because the Catholic princes of Europe vied for the title of most pious monarch of the Counter-Reformation, the English could not risk provoking them to try for the greatest prize—the restoration of Catholicism in England. This partly explains why the English were slow in colonizing the Americas in open defiance of Philip II. The Dutch were too involved in defending their independence from Spain to launch the colonial empire they would win in the next century. The French were slow to recognize the importance of transatlantic colonization partly because French kings feared draining a population still suffering the effects of the Black Death and partly because the civil wars of religion inhibited imaginative policymaking. However, conditions were quite different on the Iberian peninsula.

Catholicism in Spain and Portugal remained almost immune from the Protestant Reformation. So even while under attack, it swept across the Atlantic almost unchallenged during the century after Columbus's voyages. The massive native population of the Americas, in the eyes of the pope in Rome and the monarchs in Lisbon and Seville, must not only be rescued from heathenism but also protected from Protestantism.

THE IBERIAN CONQUEST OF AMERICA

From 1492 to 1518, Spanish and Portuguese explorers opened up vast parts of Asia and the Americas to European knowledge. Yet during this age of exploration, only modest attempts at settlement were made, mostly by the Spanish on the Caribbean islands of Cuba, Puerto Rico, and Hispaniola. The three decades after 1518, however, became an age of conquest. In some of the bloodiest chapters in recorded history, the Spanish nearly exterminated the native peoples of the Caribbean islands, toppled and plundered the great inland empires of the Aztecs and Incas in Mexico and Peru, discovered fabulous silver mines, and built a westward oceanic trade of enormous importance to all of Europe. The consequences of this short era of conquest proved to be immense for the entire world.

Portugal, meanwhile, restricted by one of the most significant lines ever drawn on a map, concentrated mostly on building an eastward oceanic trade to southeastern Asia. In 1493, to settle a dispute, the pope had demarcated Spanish and Portuguese spheres of exploration in the Atlantic. Drawing a north-south line 100 leagues (about 300 miles) west of the Azores, the pope confined Portugal to the European side of the line. One year later, in the Treaty of Tordesillas, Portugal obtained Spanish agreement to move the line 270 leagues farther west. Nobody knew at the time that a large part of South America, as yet undiscovered by Europeans, bulged east of the new demarcation line and therefore fell within the Portuguese sphere. In time, Portugal would develop this region, called Brazil, into one of the most profitable areas of the New World.

The Spanish Onslaught

Within a single generation of Columbus's death in 1506, Spanish conquistadores explored, claimed, and conquered most of South America (except Brazil), Central America, and the southern parts of North America from Florida to California. Led by audacious explorers and military leaders, they established the authority of Spain and Catholicism over an area that dwarfed their homeland in size and population. They were motivated by religion, growing pride of nation, and dreams of personal enrichment. "We came here," explained one Spanish footsoldier in Cortés's legion, "to serve God and the king, and also to get rich."

In two bold and bloody strokes, the Spanish overwhelmed the ancient civilizations of the Aztecs and Incas. In 1519, Hernando Cortés set out with 600 soldiers from coastal Veracruz and marched over rugged mountains to attack Tenochtitlan (modern-day Mexico City), the capital of Montezuma's Aztec empire. At its height, centuries before, the ancient city in the Valley of Mexico had contained perhaps 200,000 people. But in 1521, following two years of tense relations between the Spanish and Aztecs, it fell before Cortés's assault. The Spanish use of horses and firearms provided an important advantage, but the alliance of dissident natives oppressed by Montezuma's tyranny was indispensable in overthrowing the Aztec ruler. From the Valley of Mexico, the Spanish extended their dominion over the Mayan people of the Yucatán and Guatemala in the next few decades.

Before the arrival of Cortés in 1519, Tenochtilán was the capital and showplace of Montezuma's Aztec empire. The Spanish were astounded to see such a magnificent city, larger than any in Spain at the time. This modern rendering is based on archaeological evidence.

In the second conquest, the intrepid Francisco Pizarro, marching from Panama through the jungles of Ecuador and into the towering mountains of Peru with a mere 168 men, most of them not even soldiers, toppled the Inca empire. Like the Aztecs, the populous Incas lived in a highly organized social system. But also like the Aztecs, violent internal divisions had weakened them. This ensured Pizarro's success in capturing their capital at Cuzco in 1533. From there, Spanish soldiers marched farther afield, plundering other gold- and silver-rich Inca cities. Further expeditions into Chile, New Granada (Colombia), Argentina, and Bolivia in the 1530s and 1540s brought under Spanish control an empire larger than any in the Western world since the fall of Rome.

By 1550, Spain had overwhelmed the major centers of native population throughout the Caribbean, Mexico, Central America, and the west coast of South America. Spanish ships carried gold, silver, dyewoods, and sugar east across the Atlantic and transported African slaves, colonizers, and finished goods west. In a brief half century, Spain had exploited the advances in geographical knowledge and marine technology made by their Portuguese rivals and brought into harsh but profitable contact with each other the people of three continents. The triracial character of the Americas had now been established.

For nearly a century after Columbus's voyages, Spain enjoyed almost unchallenged dominion over the fabulous hemisphere newly revealed to Europeans. Greedy buccaneers of various nations snapped at the heels of homeward-bound Spanish treasure fleets with cargoes of silver, but this was only a nuisance. France made gestures of contesting Spanish or Portuguese control by planting small settlements in Brazil and Florida in the mid-sixteenth century, but they were quickly wiped out. England remained island-bound until the 1580s. Until the seventeenth century, only Portugal, which staked out important claims in Brazil in the 1520s, challenged Spanish domination of the New World.

In this woodcut, published in a German book in 1590, Theodore De Bry depicts Francisco Pizarro's conquest of Cuzco, the Inca capital.

The Great Dying

Spanish conquest of major areas of the Americas set in motion two of the most far-reaching processes in modern history. One involved microbes, the other precious metal. Spanish contacts with the natives of the Caribbean basin, central Mexico, and Peru in the early sixteenth century triggered the most dramatic and disastrous population decline ever recorded. The population of the Americas on the eve of European arrival had grown to an estimated 50 million or more. In some areas, such as central Mexico, the highlands of Peru, and certain Caribbean islands, population density exceeded that of most of Europe. But though they were less populous than the people of the Americas, the Europeans had one extraordinary biological advantage over them. They were members of a population that for centuries had been exposed to nearly every lethal parasite that infects humans on an epidemic scale in the temperate zone. Over the centuries, Europeans had built up immunities to these diseases. Such biological defenses did not eliminate smallpox, measles, diphtheria, and other afflictions, but they limited their deadly power.

In contrast, the people of the Americas had been geographically isolated from these diseases. Arriving Europeans therefore unknowingly encountered a huge component of the human race that was utterly defenseless against the "domesticated" infections the explorers, traders, and settlers carried inside their bodies.

The results were catastrophic. On Hispaniola, a population of about one million that had existed when Columbus arrived had only a few thousand survivors by 1530. Of some 25 million inhabitants of the Aztec empire prior to Cortés's arrival, about 90 percent were felled by disease within a half century. Demographic disaster also struck the populous Inca peoples of the Peruvian Andes. Smallpox "spread over the people as great destruction," an old Indian told a Spanish priest in the 1520s. "There was great havoc. Very many died of it. They could not stir, they could not change position, nor lie on one side, nor face down, nor on their backs. And if they stirred, much did they cry out. . . . And very many starved; there was death from hunger, [for] none could take care of [the sick]." Such terrifying sickness led many natives to believe that their gods had failed them and left them ready to

Spanish and Portuguese New World Conquests

Spanish
Portuguese
Disputed
(1555) Date city founded

Santa Fe (1609)
NEW SPAIN
Gulf of Mexico
St. Augustine (1565)
Havana (1515)
Mexico City (1521)
ATLANTIC OCEAN
Caribbean Sea
Demarcation line, Treaty of Tordesillas, 1494
Panama City (1519)
NEW GRENADA
Caracas (1567)
PACIFIC OCEAN
PERU
Lima (1535)
São Paulo (1554)
Rio de Janeiro (1555)
LA PLATA
Santiago (1541)
Buenos Aires (1535)
TO SPAIN   TO PORTUGAL

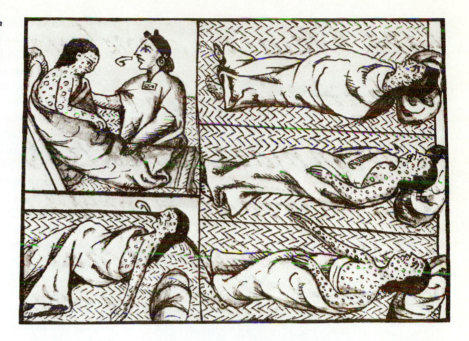

The devastating effects of smallpox on the Native American population were illustrated in this woodcut for a sixteenth-century book about Nueva España.

acknowledge the greater power of the Christian God that Spanish priests proclaimed.

In most areas where Europeans intruded in the hemisphere for the next three centuries, the catastrophe repeated itself. Whether Protestant or Catholic, whether French, English, Spanish, or Dutch, whether male or female, every newcomer from the Old World participated in the spread of disease that typically eliminated, within a few generations, at least two-thirds of the native population. Millions of Native Americans who never saw a European died of European diseases, which swept like wildfire through densely populated regions.

The enslavement and brutal treatment of the native people intensified the lethal effects of European diseases. After their spectacular conquests of the Incas and Aztecs, the Spanish enslaved thousands of native people and assigned them work regimens that severely weakened their resistance to disease. Some priests like Bartholme Las Casas waged lifelong campaigns to reduce the exploitation of the Indians, but they had only limited power to control the actions of their colonizing compatriots.

Silver, Sugar, and Their Consequences

The small amount of gold that Columbus brought home from his explorations of the West Indies raised hopes that this metal, which along with silver formed the standard of wealth in Europe, might be found in the transatlantic paradise. Some gold was gleaned from the Caribbean islands and later from Colombia, Brazil, and Peru. But though men pursued it fanatically to the far corners of the hemisphere, more than three centuries would pass before they found gold in windfall quantities on the North American Pacific slope and in the Yukon. It was silver that proved most abundant—so plenteous, in fact, that when bonanza strikes were made in Bolivia in 1545 and then in northern Mexico in the next decade, much of Spain's New World enterprise focused on its extraction. The Spanish empire in America, for most of the sixteenth century, was a vast mining community.

Native people, along with some African slaves, provided the labor supply for the mines. The Spaniards permitted the highly organized Indian societies to maintain control of their own communities but exacted from them huge labor drafts for mining. By imposing themselves at the top of a highly stratified social order that had previously been organized around tributary labor, the Spanish enriched themselves beyond the dreams of even the most visionary explorers. At Potosí, in Bolivia, 58,000 workers labored at elevations of up to 13,000 feet to extract the precious metal from a fabulous sugarloaf "mountain of silver." The town's population reached 120,000 by 1570, making it larger than any in Spain at the time. Thousands of other workers toiled in

Real Wages and Population in England, 1500–1700

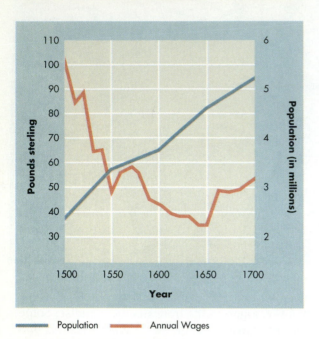

Population ——— Annual Wages ———

Sources: Walton and Shepherd, *The Economic Rise of Early America,* 1979; and Coleman, *The Economy of England, 1450-1750,* 1977.

the mines of Zacatecas, Taxco, and Guanajuato. By 1660, they had scooped up more than 7 million pounds of silver from the Americas, tripling the entire European supply.

The massive flow of bullion from the Americas to Europe triggered profound changes. It financed further conquests and settlement in Spain's American empire, spurred long-distance trading in luxury items such as silks and spices from the Far East, and capitalized agricultural development in the New World of sugar, coffee, cacao, and indigo. The bland diet of Europeans gradually changed as items such as sugar and spices, previously luxury articles for the wealthy, became accessible to ordinary people.

The enormous increase of silver in circulation in Europe after the mid-sixteenth century also caused a "price revolution." As the supply of silver increased faster than the volume of goods and services that Europeans could produce, the value of the metal declined. Put differently, prices rose. Between 1550 and 1600, they doubled in many parts of Europe and then rose another 50 percent in the next half century. Landowning farmers got more for

their produce, and merchants thrived on the increased circulation of goods. But artisans, laborers, and landless agriculture workers (the vast majority of the population) suffered because their wages did not keep pace with rising prices. Skilled artisans, lamented one of the first English immigrants to America, "live in such a low condition as is little better than beggary."

Overall, the price revolution brought a major redistribution of wealth and increased the number of people in western Europe living at the margins of society. It thus built up the pressure to emigrate to the Americas, Europe's new frontier. At the same time, rising prices stimulated commercial development. Expansion overseas fed expansion at home and intensified changes toward capitalist modes of production already under way in the sixteenth century.

While the Spaniards organized their overseas empire around the extraction of silver from the highlands of Mexico and Peru, the Portuguese staked their future on sugar production in the lowlands of Brazil. Spanish colonial agriculture supplied the huge mining centers, but the Portuguese, adapting techniques of cultivation worked out earlier on their Atlantic islands, produced sugar for the export market.

Whereas the Spanish mining operations rested primarily on the backs of the native labor force, the lowland Portuguese sugar planters scattered the indigenous people and replaced them with platoons of African slaves. By 1570, this regimented work force was producing nearly 6 million pounds of sugar annually; by the 1630s, output had risen to 32 million pounds per year. High in calories but low in protein, the sweet "drug food" revolutionized the tastes of millions of Europeans and caused the oceanic transport of millions of African slaves to the coast of Brazil and later to Colombia, Ecuador, and Peru.

From Brazil, sugar production jumped to the island-specked Caribbean. Here, in the early seventeenth century, England, Holland, and France challenged Spain and Portugal for the riches of the New World. Once they secured a foothold in the West Indies, Spain's enemies stood at the gates of the Hispanic New World empire. This ushered in a long period of conflict "beyond the line"—where European treaties had no force. Through contraband trading with Spanish settlements, piratical attacks on Spanish treasure fleets, and outright seizure of Spanish-controlled islands, the Dutch, French, and English in the seventeenth century gradually sapped the strength of the first European empire outside of Europe.

Spain's Northern Frontier

The crown jewels of Spain's New World empire were silver-rich Mexico and Peru, with the islands and coastal fringes of the Caribbean representing lesser, yet valuable, gemstones. Distinctly third in importance were the northern borderlands of New Spain—the present-day Sun Belt of the United States. The early Spanish influence in Florida, the Gulf region, Texas, New Mexico, Arizona, and California indelibly marked the history of the United States.

Spanish explorers began charting the southeastern region of North America in the early sixteenth century, beginning with Juan Ponce de León's expeditions to Florida in 1515 and 1521. For the next half century, Spaniards planted small settlements there. They traded some with the natives, but the area was chiefly important to the Franciscan priests who attempted to gather the local tribes into mission villages and convert them to Catholicism.

The Spanish made several attempts to bring the entire Gulf of Mexico region under their control. From 1539 to 1542, Hernando de Soto, a veteran of Pizarro's conquest of the Incas, led an expedition deep into the homelands of the Creeks and explored westward across the Mississippi to Arkansas. In 1559, Spaniards marched northward from Mexico in an attempt to establish their authority in the lower Gulf region. Everywhere they went, they enslaved Indians and used them as provision carriers. In 1565, they sought to secure Florida. Feeling threatened by a French settlement planted there, the Spanish built a fort at St. Augustine and evicted their French rivals. St. Augustine became the center of Spain's southeastern religious frontier. Florida would remain a Spanish possession for more than two centuries.

The Southwest became the second region of Spanish activity in North America. Francisco Vásquez de Coronado explored the region from 1540 to 1542, leading an expedition of several hundred Spanish soldiers and a baggage train of 1,300 friendly Indians, servants, and slaves. Coronado never found the Seven Cities of Cíbola, reported by earlier Spanish explorers to be fabulously decorated in turquoise and gold. But he opened much of Arizona, New Mexico, and Colorado to eventual Spanish control and probed as far north as the Great Plains. His interior explorations, together with the nearly simultaneous expedition of de Soto in the Southeast, established Spanish claims to the southern latitudes of North America and gave them contacts, often bloody, with the populous corn-growing Indian societies of the region.

The Southwest, like Florida, proved empty of the fabled golden cities. Hence, in the seventeenth century, the region chiefly interested Jesuit and Franciscan missionaries. The Spanish established presidios, or garrisons, such as those at Santa Fe (1609) and Albuquerque (1706), to control these vast regions and serve as trade centers. But the Catholic mission became the primary institution of the Spanish borderlands. In the eighteenth century, the Catholic missions reached northward, bringing most of the Indians of the California coast, from San Diego to the San Francisco Bay, under the control of the Spanish padres.

The Spanish missionary frontier operated differently, depending on the Indian cultures encountered. In Florida and California, where the native people lived in small, often seminomadic tribes, the Spanish used persuasion mixed with force to gather them within the sound of the mission bell. Setting the Indians to agricultural labor, the Spanish attempted slowly to convert them to European ways of life.

In New Mexico, however, missionaries made no attempt to uproot Pueblo people and contain them within the mission walls. The natives they encountered had lived in settled villages and practiced agriculture for centuries, so here the Spanish aimed to graft Catholicism onto Pueblo culture by building churches on the edges of ancient native villages. When they attempted to do more than overlay Indian culture with a veneer of Catholicism, they encountered fierce resistance. Such was the case in Popé's revolt in 1680. For five years, the Spanish padres had tried to root out traditional Pueblo religious practices. In response, a Pueblo leader named Popé led an Indian uprising that destroyed most of the churches in New Mexico and for more than a decade drove the Spanish from the region. Spaniards and Indians declared a kind of cultural truce: the Spaniards agreed to allow certain Pueblo rituals in return for nominal acceptance of Christianity.

ENGLAND LOOKS WEST

By the time England awoke to the promise of the New World, the two Iberian powers were firmly entrenched there. But by the late sixteenth century, the conditions necessary to propel England overseas had ripened. During the seventeenth century, the English, as well as the Dutch and French, began overtaking their southern European rivals. The first challenge came in the Caribbean, where between 1604 and 1640 the English planted several small colonies producing tobacco and later sugar. Few guessed that some secondary and relatively unproductive settlements also being planted on the North American mainland would in time be among England's most prized possessions.

England Challenges Spain

England was the most backward of the European nations facing the Atlantic in exploring and colonizing the New World. Although far more numerous than the Portuguese, the English in the fifteenth century had little experience with long-distance trade and few contacts with cultures beyond their island aside from the French, against whom they had waged the Hundred Years' War (1337–1453). Only the voyages of John Cabot (the Genoa-born Giovanni Caboto) gave England any claim in the New World sweepstakes. But Cabot's voyages to Newfoundland and Nova Scotia a few years after Columbus's first voyage—the first northern crossing of the Atlantic since the Vikings—were never followed up.

At first, England's interest in the far side of the Atlantic centered primarily on fish. This high-protein food, basic to the European diet, was the gold of the North Atlantic. The early North Atlantic explorers found the waters off Newfoundland and Nova Scotia teeming with fish, not only the ordinary cod but also the delectable salmon. But it was the fishermen of Portugal, Spain, and France, more than those of England, who began making annual spring trips to the offshore fisheries in the 1520s. Not until the end of the century would the French and English drive Spanish and Portuguese fishermen from the Newfoundland Banks.

Exploratory voyages along the eastern coast of North America hardly interested the English. It was for the French that Cartier and Verrazano sailed between 1524 and 1535. Looking for straits westward to India, through the northern landmass, which was still thought to be a large island, they made contact with many Indian tribes and charted the coastline from the St. Lawrence River to the Carolinas. They established the northern latitudes as a suitable place for settlement but found nothing of immediate value to take home. The time had not yet arrived when Europeans would leave their homelands to resettle in America rather than go there merely to extract its riches.

Changes occurred in the late sixteenth century, however, that propelled the English overseas. The rising production of woolen cloth, a mainstay of the English economy, had sent merchants scurrying for new markets after 1550. Their success in establishing trading companies in Russia, Scandinavia, the Middle East, and India vastly widened England's commercial orbit and raised hopes that still other spheres could be developed. At the same time, population growth and rising prices depressed the existence of ordinary people and made them look to the transoceanic frontier for new opportunities.

Queen Elizabeth, who ruled from 1558 to 1603, followed a cautious policy that did not include the promotion of overseas colonies. She favored Protestantism partly as a vehicle of national independence. Ambitious and talented, she had to contend with Philip II, king of Spain and her fervently Catholic brother-in-law, whose long reign nearly coincided with hers. Regarding Elizabeth as a Protestant heretic, Philip plotted incessantly against her. The pope added to Catholic-Protestant tensions in England by excommunicating Elizabeth in 1571 and absolving her subjects from paying her allegiance. This, in effect, gave them religious license to overthrow her.

The smoldering conflict between Catholic Spain and Protestant England broke into open flames in 1587. Two decades before, Philip II had sent 20,000 Spanish soldiers into his Netherlands provinces to suppress Protestantism. Then, in 1572, he had helped to arrange the massacre of thousands of French Protestants. By the 1580s, Elizabeth was providing covert aid to the Protestant Dutch revolt against Catholic rule. Philip vowed to crush the rebellion and decided as well to launch an attack on England in order to wipe out this growing center of Protestant power.

Elizabeth fed the flames of the international Catholic-Protestant conflict in 1585 by sending 6,000 English troops to aid the Dutch Protestants. Three

Under the leadership of Elizabeth I, here displayed in royal finery and resting her hand on the globe, England challenged and ultimately overturned Spain's domination of worldwide sea trade.

years later, Philip dispatched a Spanish armada of 130 ships carrying 30,000 men and 2,400 artillery pieces. Sails blazing with crusader's crosses, the fleet set forth to conquer Elizabeth's England. For two weeks in the summer of 1588, a sea battle raged off the English coast. A motley collection of smaller English ships, with the colorful sea dog Francis Drake in the lead, defeated the Armada, sinking many of the lumbering Spanish galleons and then retiring as the legendary "Protestant wind" blew the crippled Armada into the North Sea.

The Spanish defeat prevented a crushing Catholic victory in Europe and brought a temporary stalemate in the religious wars. It also solidified Protestantism in England and brewed a fierce na-

tionalistic spirit there. Shakespeare's love of "this other Eden, this demi-paradise" spread among the people; and with Spanish naval power checked, both the English and the Dutch found the seas more open to their rising maritime and commercial interests.

The Westward Fever

In the last decades of the sixteenth century, the idea of overseas expansion captured the imagination of important elements of English society. Urging them on were two Richard Hakluyts, uncle and nephew. In the 1580s and 1590s, they devoted themselves to advertising the advantages of colonizing on the far side of the Atlantic. For nobles at court, colonies offered new baronies, fiefdoms, and estates. For merchants, the New World promised exotic produce to sell at home and a new outlet for English cloth and other goods. For the militant Protestant clergy, there awaited a continent filled with heathen people to be saved from both savagery and Catholicism. For the commoner, opportunity beckoned in the form of bounteous land, almost for the taking. In a number of pamphlets the Hakluyts publicized the idea that the time was ripe for England to break the Iberian monopoly on the riches of the New World.

England mounted its first attempts at colonizing, however, in Ireland. In the 1560s and 1570s, the English gradually extended their control over the country through brutal military conquest. Ireland became a turbulent frontier for thousands of career-hungry younger sons of gentry families as well as landless commoners. Many of the leaders first involved in New World colonizing had served in Ireland, and many of their ideas of how to deal with a "savage" and "barbaric" people stemmed from their Irish experience.

The first English attempts at overseas settlement were small, feeble, and ill-fated. Whereas the Spanish encountered unheard-of wealth and scored epic victories over ancient and populous civilizations, the English at first met only failure in relatively thinly settled lands. Beginning in 1583, they mounted several unsuccessful attempts to settle Newfoundland. Other settlers, organized by Walter Raleigh, planted a settlement from 1585 to 1588 at Roanoke Island, off the North Carolina coast. They apparently perished in attacks by a local tribe after killing a tribal leader and displaying his head on a pike. Small groups of men sent out to establish a tiny colony in Guiana, off the South American coast, failed in 1604 and 1609, and another group that set down in Maine in 1607 lasted only a year. Even the colonies founded in Virginia in 1607 and Bermuda in 1612, although they would flourish in time, floundered badly for several decades.

English merchants, sometimes supported by gentry investors, undertook these first tentative efforts. They risked their capital hoping that small-scale ventures in North America might produce the profits of their other overseas commercial ventures. They had little backing from the government, in subsidies, ships, or naval protection, though they had the blessing of their queen. The Spanish and Portuguese colonizing efforts were national enterprises, sanctioned, capitalized, and coordinated by the crown. The English colonies were private ventures, organized and financed by small partnerships of merchants who pooled their slender resources.

Not until these first merchant adventurers solicited the wealth and support of the prospering middle class of English society could colonization succeed. This support grew steadily in the first half of the seventeenth century, but even then, investors were drawn far more to the quick profits promised in West Indian tobacco production than to the uncertainties of mixed farming, lumbering, and fishing on the North American mainland. In the 1620s and 1630s, most of the English capital invested overseas went into establishing tobacco colonies in the flyspeck Caribbean islands of St. Christopher (1624), Barbados (1627), Nevis (1628), Montserrat (1632), and Antigua (1632).

Apart from the considerable financing required, the vital element in launching a colony was a suitable body of colonists. About 80,000 streamed out of England between 1600 and 1640, as economic, political and religious developments pushed them from their homeland at the same time that dreams of opportunity and adventure pulled them westward. In the next 20 years, another 80,000 departed.

Economic difficulties in England prompted many to try their luck in the New World. The changing agricultural system, combined with population growth and the unrelenting increase in prices caused by the influx of New World silver, produced a surplus of unskilled labor, squeezed many small producers, and spread poverty and crime. By the late 1500s, the roads, wrote Richard Hakluyt, were swarming with "valiant youths rusting and hurtful for lack of employment," and the prisons were "daily pestered and stuffed full of them." A generation later, beginning in 1618, the renewed European religious wars between Protestants and Catholics devastated the continental market for English woolen cloth, bringing unemployment and desperate conditions to the textile regions. Probably half the households in England lived on the edge of poverty, struggling for survival and subject to a punishing economic system in which they had no voice. "This land grows weary of her inhabitants," wrote John Winthrop of East Anglia, "so as a man, which is the most precious of all creatures, is near more vile among us than a horse or a sheep."

Religious persecution and political considerations intensified the pressure to emigrate from England in the early seventeenth century. How this operated in specific situations will be considered in the next chapter. The largest number of emigrants went to the West Indies. The North American mainland colonies attracted perhaps half as many, and the Irish plantations in Ulster and Munster still fewer. For the first time in their history, large numbers of English people were abandoning their island homeland to carry their destinies to new frontiers.

Anticipating North America

English settlers approaching the North American coast, from the Roanoke settlers in 1585 to the Puritans who flocked to Massachusetts Bay in the 1630s, knew that Spain dominated the New World. But since they chose to settle on the middle part of the Atlantic seaboard, which the Spanish regarded as useless, it was the native occupiers of the land who most concerned the newcomers. What did the English know of these people whom Columbus, thinking he had reached India, mistakenly called Indians? How would they receive the English, and how would the colonizers obtain the possession of the land along the coast?

The early settlers were far from uninformed about the indigenous people of the New World. Beginning with Columbus's first description of the New World, published in several European cities in 1493 and 1494, reports and promotional accounts circulated among the participants in early voyages of discovery, trade, and settlement. This literature became the basis for anticipating the world that had been discovered beyond the setting sun.

Colonists who read or listened to these accounts probably held a split image of the native people. On the one hand, the Indians were depicted as a gentle people who eagerly received Europeans. Columbus had written of the "great amity towards us" that he encountered in San Salvador in 1492 and had described the Arawaks there as "a loving people" who "were greatly pleased and became so entirely our friends that it was a wonder to see." Verrazano, the first European to touch the eastern edge of North America, wrote optimistically about the native people in 1524. The natives, graceful of limb and tawny-colored, he related, "came toward us joyfully uttering loud cries of wonderment, and showing us the safest place to beach the boat."

This positive image of the Native Americans reflected both the friendly reception that Europeans often actually received and the European vision of the New World as an earthly paradise where war-torn, impoverished, or persecuted people could build a new life. The strong desire to trade with the native people also encouraged a favorable view because only a friendly Indian could become a suitable partner in commercial exchange.

A counterimage, of a savage, hostile Indian, however, also entered the minds of settlers coming to North America. Like the positive image, it originated in the early travel literature. As early as 1502, Sebastian Cabot had paraded in England three Eskimos he had kidnapped on an Arctic voyage. They were described as flesh-eating savages and "brute beasts" who "spake such speech that no man could understand them." Many other accounts portrayed the New World natives as crafty, brutal, loathsome halfmen, who lived, as Amerigo Vespucci put it, without "law, religion, rulers, immortality of the soul, and private property."

The English had another reason for believing that all would not be friendship and amiable trading when they came ashore. For years they had read accounts of the Spanish experience in the Caribbean, Mexico, and Peru—and the story was not pretty. Many books described in gory detail the wholesale violence that occurred when Spaniard met Mayan, Aztec, or Inca. Accounts of Spanish cruelty, even genocide, were useful to Protestant pamphleteers, who labeled the Catholic Spaniards "hellhounds and wolves." Immigrants embarking for North America wondered if similar violent confrontations did not await them.

Another factor nourishing negative images of the Indian stemmed from the Indians' possession of the land necessary for settlement. For Englishmen, rooted in a tradition of the private ownership of property, this presented moral and legal, as well as practical, problems. As early as the 1580s, George Peckham, an early promoter of colonization, had admitted that the English doubted their right to take the land of others. In 1609, Anglican minister Robert Gray wondered, "By what right can we enter into the land of these savages, take their rightful inheritance from them, and plant ourselves in their places, being unwronged or unprovoked by them?"

The problem could be partially solved by arguing that English settlers did not intend to take the Indians' land but wanted only to share it with them.

In return, they would offer the natives the advantages of a more advanced culture and, most important, the Christian religion. This argument was heard repeatedly in succeeding generations. As the governing council in Virginia put it in 1610, the settlers "by way of merchandizing and trade, do buy of [the Indians] the pearls of earth, and sell to them the pearls of heaven."

A more ominous argument arose to justify English rights to native soil. By denying the humanity of the Indians, the English, like other Europeans, claimed that the native possessors of the land disqualified themselves from rightful ownership of it. "Although the Lord hath given the earth to children of men," one Englishman reasoned, "the greater part of it [is] possessed and wrongfully usurped by wild beasts and unreasonable creatures, or by brutish

savages, which by reason of their godless ignorance and blasphemous idolatry, are worse than those beasts which are of the most wild and savage nature."

Defining the Native Americans as "savage" and "brutish" did not give the English arriving in Opechancanough's land the power to dispossess his people of their soil, but it armed them with a moral justification for doing so when their numbers became sufficient. Few settlers arriving in North America doubted that their technological superiority would allow them to overwhelm the indigenous people. For their part, people like Opechancanough probably perceived the arriving Europeans as impractical, irreligious, aggressive, and strangely intent on accumulating material wealth.

CONCLUSION

Converging Worlds

The English migrants who began arriving on the eastern edge of North America in the early seventeenth century came late to a New World that other Europeans had been colonizing for more than a century. The first English arrivals, the immigrants to Virginia, were but a small advance wave of the large, varied, and determined fragment of English society that would flock to the western Atlantic frontier during the next few generations. Like Spanish, Portuguese, and French colonizers before them, they would establish new societies in the newfound lands in contact with the people of two other cultures—one made up of ancient inhabitants of the lands they were settling and the other composed of those brought across the Atlantic against their will. We turn now to the richly diverse founding experience of the English latecomers in the seventeenth century.

Recommended Reading

The rich pre-Columbian history of the Americas is surveyed in Kenneth Macgowan and Joseph A. Hester, Jr., Early Man in the New World (1962), Jesse Jennings, The Prehistory of North America (1968), and Dean Snow, The Archaeology of North America: American Indians and Their Origins (1980). Another fascinating analysis is Marshall Sahlins, Stone Age Economics (1972).

Excellent introductions to early African history include Basil Davidson, The African Genius (1969), and J. D. Fage, A History of West Africa, 4th ed. (1969).

W. H. McNeil, in The Rise of the West (1963), presents a fine overall treatment of European development in the early modern period. Europe in the Age of Exploration can be studied in Ralph Davis, The Rise of the Atlantic Economies (1973); J. H. Parry, The Age of Reconnaissance (1963); Carlo M. Cipolla, Guns, Sails, and Empire: Technological Innovations and the Early Phases of European Expansion (1966); and Eric Wolf, The People Without History (1983).

A fine corrective to the much romanticized and often distorted story of the Spanish and Portuguese conquest of the Americas is James Lockhart and Stuart B. Schwartz, Early Latin America (1983). Also valuable are J. H. Elliott, Imperial Spain, 1469–1716 (1963); J. H. Parry, The Spanish Seaborne Empire (1966); Charles Gibson, Spain in America (1966); and C. R. Boxer, The Portuguese Seaborne Empire, 1415–1825 (1972).

The shape of English society as overseas colonization began is detailed in Carl Bridenbaugh, Vexed and Troubled Englishmen, 1500–1642 (1968); Peter Laslett, The World We Have Lost (1971); C. R. Elton, England Under the Tudors (1955); A. G. Dickens, The English Reformation (1964); and Peter Clark and Paul Slack, eds., Crisis and Order in English Towns, 1500–1700 (1972). England's belated intervention in the Americas is followed in A. L. Rowse, The Expansion of Elizabethan England (1955); Nicholas P. Canny, The Elizabethan Conquest of Ireland (1976); David B. Quinn, England and the Discovery of America, 1481–1620 (1974); and David B. Quinn, North America from Earliest Discovery to First Settlements (1977).

TIME LINE

	Pre-Columbian epochs
12,000 B.C.	Beringian epoch ends
6,000 B.C.	Paleo-Indian phase ends
500 B.C.	Archaic era ends
500 B.C.–A.D. 1500	Post-Archaic era in North America Kingdoms of Ghana, Mali, Songhay in Africa
1420s	Portuguese sailors explore west coast of Africa
1492	Christopher Columbus lands on Caribbean islands Spanish expel Moors (Muslims)
1494	Treaty of Tordesillas
1497–1585	French and English explore northern part of the Americas
1498	Vasco da Gama reaches India after sailing around Africa
1513	Portuguese explorers reach China
1515–1565	Spanish explore Florida and southern part of North America
1520s	Luther attacks Catholicism
1521	Cortés conquers the Aztecs
1530s	Calvin calls for religious reform
1533	Pizarro conquers the Incas
1540–1542	Coronado explores the Southwest
1558	Elizabeth I crowned queen of England
1585	Roanoke Island settlement
1588	English defeat the Spanish armada
1603	James I succeeds Elizabeth I
1607	English begin settlement at Jamestown, Virginia
1680	Popé's revolt in New Mexico

2

Colonizing a Continent

By 1637, after five years in New England, John Mason knew both the prospects and perils of England's new overseas frontier. In his early thirties, Mason had emigrated from southeastern England. He was part of the flock of John Warham, a Puritan minister from the village of Dorchester. In Massachusetts, the group commemorated their origins by giving the name Dorchester to the area assigned to them. Here, 6 miles south of Boston, they built a crude church, assigned town lots and outlying farms, and began the work of serving their God in the wilderness of North America.

Like many Puritans, Mason had thrilled at the sight of southern New England's game-filled forests and fish-filled streams, the fields cleared and tilled by Algonquian agriculturalists, the lush meadows available for grazing stock. Though the winters were inhospitable, it seemed this might be the Promised Land where Puritan refugees could plant their New World Zion. But Mason also recognized that these lands were not vacant. From the earliest days of the Pilgrim settlers at Plymouth in 1620, it was evident that the native occupiers of the region, whose claim went back a hundred generations, stood in the way of the Puritan "errand into the wilderness."

In the fall of 1636, Mason followed many of his Dorchester friends out of Massachusetts. In search of better land and restless with the political squabbling in the Massachusetts Bay Colony, the Dorchester settlers set out for the Connecticut River, 100 miles to the west. For 14 days, nipped by the frost of late autumn, they trekked wearily along Indian paths, carrying their meager possessions. At their journey's end, they founded the town of Windsor, on the west bank of the Connecticut.

Six months later, when his new village was no more than a collection of crude lean-tos, militia captain John Mason marched south against the Pequots. He owed his officership to military experience in the Netherlands, where thousands of English soldiers had gone in the 1620s to help the Protestant Dutch break the yoke of Catholic Spain in the Lowlands. Now he commanded several hundred men whom the fledgling Connecticut River towns had dispatched to drive the Pequots from the area. In the years before the English arrival, the powerful Pequots had formed a network of tributary tribes. Finding it impossible to placate the English as

they swarmed into the Connecticut River valley, the Pequots chose resistance.

At dawn on May 26, 1637, Captain Mason and his troops approached a Pequot village on the Mystic River. Supported by Narragansett allies, the English slipped into the town. After a few scuffles in the half-light, Mason cried out, "We must burn them," and his men began torching the Pequot wigwams. Then they rushed from the fortified village. As flames engulfed the huts, the Pequots fled the inferno, only to be cut down with musket and sword by the English soldiers, who had ringed the community. Most of the terrified victims were noncombatants—old men, women, and children—for the Pequot warriors were preparing for war at another village about 5 miles away.

Before the sun rose, a major portion of the Pequot tribe had been exterminated. The resistance of the others crumbled when they learned the fate of their families. "It was a fearful sight to see them thus frying in the fire," wrote one Puritan, "and horrible was the stink and scent thereof; but the victory seemed a sweet sacrifice, and they gave the praise thereof to God, who had wrought so wonderfully for them." Mason himself wrote that God had "laughed at his enemies and the enemies of his people, . . . making them as a fiery oven."

aptain John Mason was a God-fearing Puritan and a man highly esteemed by his fellow colonists. His actions at the Mystic River, just seven years after the great Puritan migration to New England began in 1630, testify that the European colonization of America involved a violent confrontation of two cultures. We often speak of the "discovery" and "settlement" of North America by English and other European colonists. But the penetration of the eastern edge of what today is the United States might more accurately be called "the invasion of America."

Yet mixed with violence was utopian idealism. In the New World, Puritans—and countless waves of immigrants who followed them—sought both spiritual and economic renewal. Settlement in America represented a chance to escape European war, despotism, material want, and religious corruption. The New World was a place to rescue humankind from the ruins of the Old World. This chapter reconstructs the manner of settlement and the character of immigrant life in five areas of early colonization: the Chesapeake Bay, southern New England, the St. Lawrence to the Hudson rivers, the Carolinas, and Pennsylvania. A comparison of these various colonies will show how the colonizers' backgrounds, ideologies, goals, and modes of settlement produced distinctly different societies along the Atlantic seaboard in the seventeenth century.

THE CHESAPEAKE TOBACCO COAST

In 1585, England gained a first foothold in a hemisphere dominated by Spanish and Portuguese colonizers. A reconnaissance expedition organized by Walter Raleigh, one of Queen Elizabeth's favorite courtiers, scouted the Carolina coast, surveyed Roanoke Island in Albemarle Sound, and then hastened homeward carrying two natives and a string of tales about rich soil, friendly Indians, and mineral wealth. A second voyage in 1585 and a third in 1587, composed of 91 men, 17 women, and 9 children, planted a small colony on Roanoke Island. But the enterprise failed. The voyages to Roanoke were too small and poorly financed to establish successful settlements. They served only as tokens of England's rising challenge to Spain in North America and as a source of valuable information for colonists later settling the area.

The Roanoke colony also failed resoundingly as the first sustained contact between English and Native American peoples. Although one member of the first expedition reported that "we found the people

most gentle, loving, and faithful, void of all guile and treason," relations with the local tribes quickly soured and then turned violent. Charges flew back and forth, the English believing that the local Indians had stolen a silver cup and the Indians angered by English raids on their winter supply of corn. Aware of their numerical disadvantage and afraid of a co-ordinated attack against them, the English turned their muskets on a local leader to intimidate the natives with their superior technology. In 1591, when a relief expedition reached Roanoke, none of the settlers could be found. It is likely that in spite of their Iron Age weaponry, these "lost colonists" of Roanoke succumbed to Indian attacks. It was an ominous beginning for England's overseas ambitions.

Jamestown

In 1607, a generation after the first Roanoke expedition, a group of merchants established the first permanent colony in North America at Jamestown, Virginia. Under a charter from James I, they operated as a joint-stock company, an early form of a modern corporation that allowed them to sell shares of stock in their company and use the pooled investment capital to outfit and supply overseas expeditions. Although the king's charter to the Virginia Company of London began with a concern for bringing Christian religion to native people who "as yet live in darkness and miserable ignorance of the true knowledge of God," most of the settlers probably agreed with Captain John Smith, who emerged as their strongest leader. "We did admire," he wrote, "how it was possible such wise men could so torment themselves with such absurdities, making religion their colour, when all their aim was profit."

Profits in the early years proved elusive, however. Expecting to find gold and other minerals, anticipating a rewarding trade with Indians for beaver and deer skins, and, best of all, hoping to discover the fabled passage through the North American continent to China, the original investors and settlers received a rude shock. Rather than duplicating the remarkable success of the Spanish and Portuguese in Mexico, Peru, and Brazil, the early Virginia colonists died miserably of dysentery, malaria, and malnutrition. More than 900 settlers, mostly men, arrived in the colony between 1607 and 1609; only 60 survived.

Seeking occupational diversity, the Virginia Company sent French silk artisans, Italian glassmakers, and Polish potash burners to Jamestown. But one-third of the first three groups of immigrants were gold-seeking adventurers with unroughened hands, a proportion of gentlemen six times as great as in the English population. Many others were unskilled servants, some with criminal backgrounds, who "never did knowe what a days work was," observed John Smith. Both types adapted poorly to wilderness conditions, leaving Smith begging for "but thirty carpenters, husbandmen, gardeners, fishermen, and blacksmiths" rather than "a thousand such gallants as were sent to me, that would do nothing but complain, curse and despair, when they saw . . . all things contrary to the report in England."

The Jamestown colony, in addition to its unproductive mix of settlers, was hampered by the common assumption that Englishmen could exploit the Indians of the region. Cortés and Pizarro had conquered the mighty Aztec and Inca empires with a few hundred soldiers and then turned the labor of thousands of natives to Spanish advantage. Why, the early settlers mused, should it not be so in Virginia?

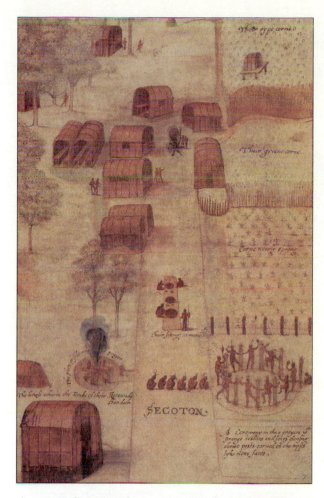

As seen in this sixteenth-century watercolor by John White, a member of the expedition to Roanoke Island, the natives who inhabited the village of Secotan lived much like English or Irish peasants.

But in the Chesapeake the English found that the indigenous peoples were not densely settled and could not easily be subjugated. Contrary to expectations, no wealthy Indian empire lay waiting to be conquered. Nor could the Virginians mold the 20,000 Powhatan Indians of the region into a servile labor force because, unlike the Spanish, the English settlers brought neither an army of conquistadores nor an army of priests to subdue the natives.

Instead, relations with some 40 small tribes, grouped into a confederacy led by the able Powhatan, turned bitter almost from the beginning. Powhatan brought supplies of corn to the sick and starving Jamestown colony during the first autumn. However, John Smith, whose military experience in eastern Europe had schooled him in dealing with

No one knows exactly what the Jamestown settlement looked like in its early years; this twentieth-century mural by Sidney King is a conjectural rendering based on archaeological evidence.

Early Chesapeake Settlement

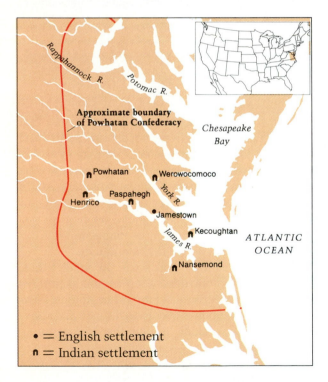

• = English settlement
ᴨ = Indian settlement

people he regarded as "barbarians," raided Indian corn supplies and tried to cow the local tribes by shows of force. In response, Powhatan withdrew from trade with the English and sniped at their flanks. Many settlers died in the "starving times" of the first years.

Despite these early failures, merchants of the Virginia Company of London poured more money and settlers into the venture. Understanding the need for ordinary farmers who could raise the food necessary to sustain the colony, they reorganized the company in 1609. They enticed many new settlers by promising free land at the end of seven years' labor for the company. In 1618, they sweetened the terms by offering 50 acres of land outright to anyone journeying to Virginia. To thousands of people on the margins of English society, such an offer seemed irresistible. More than 9,000 crossed the Atlantic between 1610 and 1622 to begin life anew in Virginia. Yet only 2,000 remained alive at the end of that period. "Instead of a plantation," wrote one English critic, "Virginia will shortly get the name of a slaughter house."

Sot Weed and Indentured Servants

The promise of free land lured a steady stream of settlers to Virginia, even though the colony proved a burial ground for most immigrants within a few years of arrival. Also crucial to the continued migration was the discovery that tobacco grew splendidly in Chesapeake soil. Frenchmen had first brought tobacco from Florida to Portugal in the 1560s. But it was Francis Drake's boatload of the "jovial weed" (so named for its intoxicating effect), procured in the West Indies in 1586, that popularized it among the upper class and launched a long history of addiction among Europeans.

Even James I's denunciation of smoking as "loathsome to the eye, hateful to the nose, harmful to the brain, and dangerous to the lungs" failed to halt the smoking craze. It proved to be Virginia's salvation. The planters shipped the first crop in 1617, and thereafter tobacco cultivation spread rapidly. Commanding the handsome price of 3 shillings per pound in England, tobacco allowed a profit sufficient for settlers to plant it even in the streets and marketplace of Jamestown. By 1624, Virginia was exporting 200,000 pounds of the "stinking weed"; by 1638, though the price had plummeted, the crop exceeded 3 million pounds. Tobacco became to Virginia in the 1620s what sugar was to the West Indies and silver to Mexico and Peru. In London, men gibed that Virginia was built on smoke.

While launching Virginia on an era of sustained growth, the cultivation of tobacco also obliged Virginia's planters to find a reliable supply of cheap labor. The "sot weed" required intensive care through the various stages of planting, weeding, thinning, suckering, worming, cutting, curing, and packing. To fill their need, planters recruited immigrants in England and Ireland and a scattering from Sweden, Portugal, Spain, Germany, and even Turkey and Poland. Such people, called indentured servants, willingly sold a portion of their working lives in exchange for free passage across the Atlantic. About four of every five seventeenth-century immigrants to Virginia—and later Maryland—came in this status. Nearly three-quarters of them were male, and most of them were between 15 and 24 years old.

Many of the indentured servants came from the armies of the unemployed. Others were orphans, political prisoners, or common criminals swept out of the jails and given a choice of transportation or the gallows. Some were of the "middling sort," younger sons unlikely to inherit a father's farm or shop, or young men eager to leave behind an unfortunate marriage. Others were drawn simply by the prospect of adventure in a "strange new land." But overwhelmingly, indentured servants had occupied the lower rungs of the social ladder in their place of origin.

Life for indentured servants often turned into a nightmare. Only a handful, perhaps one in 20, realized the dream of achieving freedom and acquiring land. If malarial fevers or dysentery did not quickly kill them, servants often succumbed to the brutal work routine harsh masters imposed. Even by the middle of the seventeenth century, when the "starving times" were only a memory, about half died during the first few years of "seasoning." Masters bought and sold their servants as property, gambled for them at cards, and worked them to death since there was little motive for keeping them alive beyond their term of labor. "My Master Adkins," wrote one servant in 1623, "hath sold me for

The Virginia Company of London tried hard to recruit settlers through promotional pamphlets that promised abundant opportunity (top left); by 1650, a more sober view of life in Virginia led to precise instructions on what immigrants coming to the colony should bring (bottom left).

NOVA BRITANNIA.

OFFERING MOST

Excellent fruites by Planting in VIRGINIA.

Exciting all such as be well affected to further the same.

LONDON

Printed for SAMVEL MACHAM, and are to be sold at his Shop in Pauls Church-yard, at the Signe of the Bul-head.
1609.

To the worthy Gentlemen, Adventurers and Planters in *VIRGINIA*.

My loving Friends:

 Thought it convenient heere briefly to minde you of those Necessaries, that if wanted there, would greatly prove your prejudice, and render you obnoxious to many evils, which are these.

Necessaries for Planters.

For Aparell: Provide each man 1. Monmouth Cap, 1.Wastcoat, 1. Suit of Canvase, Bands, Shirts, Shooes, Stockings, Canvase to make sheets, with Bed and Bolster to fill in Virginia, 1. Rugge, and Blankets.

For Armes: Provide 1. Suit of compleat light Armour, and each man 1. Sword, 1. Musket or Fowling Peece, with Powder and Shot convenient.

For Houshold stuffe: Provide one great Iron Pot, large and small Kettles, Skellets, Frying pannes, Gridiron, Spit, Platters, Dishes, Spoons, Knives, Sugar, Spice, Fruit, and Strong water at Sea for sicke men.

For Tools: Provide Howes broad and narrow, Axes broad and narrow, Handsawes, two-band-sawes, whipsawes, Hammers, Shovels, Spades, Augors, Piercers, Gimlets, Hatchets, Handbills, Frowes to cleave pale, Pickaxes, Nayls of all sorts, 1. Grindstone, Nets, Hooks, Lines, Plowes: All which accommodation wherewith each to be well furnished, together with his Transportation.

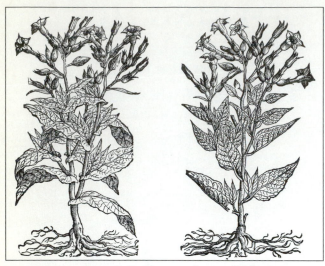

At first more a curiosity than a cash crop, "Taboco, or Henbane of Peru" was included in a history of plants published in 1633. By that year, it had become the mainstay of the Chesapeake's economy.

£150 like a damned slave." When servants neared the end of their contract, masters found ways to add time and were backed by courts controlled by the planter class.

Contrary to English custom, masters often put women servants to work at the hoe. Sexual abuse by masters was common. Servant women paid dearly for illegitimate pregnancies. The courts fined them heavily and ordered them to serve an extra year or two to repay the time lost during pregnancy and childbirth. They also deprived mothers of their illegitimate children, indenturing them out at an early age. For many servant women, marriage was the best release from this hard life. Many willingly accepted the purchase of their indenture by any man who suggested marriage.

Expansion and Indian War

As Virginia's population increased, spurred by the growth of tobacco production, violence mounted between white colonizers and the Powhatan tribes. In 1614, the sporadic hostility that had marred relations in the early years ended temporarily with the arranged marriage of Powhatan's daughter, the fabled Pocahontas, to planter John Rolfe. However, the profitable cultivation of tobacco created an intense demand for land. As more and more settlers pushed up the rivers that flowed into Chesapeake Bay, the local tribes worried that the previous abrasive and sometimes bloody contact might become a disastrous one.

In 1617, when Powhatan retired, the leadership of the Chesapeake tribes fell to Opechancanough. This proud and talented leader began building military strength for an all-out attack on his English enemies. The English murder of Nemattanew, a Powhatan war captain and religious prophet, triggered a fierce Indian assault on Good Friday in 1622 that dealt Virginia a staggering blow. More than one-quarter of the white population fell before the marauding tribesmen; the casualties in cattle, crops, and buildings were equally severe.

The devastating attack led to the bankruptcy of the Virginia Company. As a result, the king annulled its charter in 1624, and established a royal government, which allowed the elected legislative body established in 1619 to continue lawmaking in concert with the royal governor and his council.

The Indian assault of 1622 fortified the determination of the surviving planters to pursue a ruthless new Indian policy. John Smith, writing from England two years later, noted the grim satisfaction that had followed the Indian attack. Many, he reported, believed that it "will be good for the plantation, because now we have just cause to destroy them by all means possible." Bolstered by instructions from London to "root out [the Indians] from being any longer a people," the Virginians adopted a policy of annual military expeditions against the native villages west and north of the settled areas. The "flood of blood," as the English poet John Donne called it, in 1622 cost the colony dearly and doomed the Virginia Company of London. Yet it justified a policy of "perpetual enmity," even though several leaders admitted that the Indians had attacked in 1622 because of "our own perfidious dealing with them."

Population growth after 1630 and the recurrent need for fresh acreage by settlers who planted soil-exhausting tobacco intensified the pressure on Indian land. The tough, ambitious planters soon encroached on Indian territories, provoking war in 1644 and again in 1675. In each of these conflicts, the colonizers proved superior. Greatly outnumbering their opponents, they reduced the native population of Virginia to less than 1,000 by 1680. The Chesapeake tribes, Virginians came to believe, had little to contribute to the goals of English colonization; they were merely obstacles to be removed from the path of English settlement.

Proprietary Maryland

By the time Virginia had achieved commercial success in the 1630s, another colony on the Chesapeake took root. Rather than hoping for profit, the founder sought to establish a religious refuge for Catholics and a New World version of the English manorial countryside.

George Calvert, an English nobleman, designed and promoted Virginia's Chesapeake neighbor. Closely connected to the royal family, he had received a huge grant of land in Newfoundland in 1628, just three years after James I had elevated him to the peerage as Lord Baltimore. In 1632, Charles I, James's son, prepared to grant him a more hospitable domain of 10 million acres. He named it Terra Maria after the king's Catholic wife, Queen Henrietta Maria. In English it became Maryland.

Catholics were an oppressed minority in England, and Lord Baltimore planned his colony as a place where they could start anew without fear of harassment. But knowing that he needed more than a small band of Catholic settlers, the proprietor planned to invite others as well. Catholics would never form a majority in his colony. They were quickly overwhelmed by Protestants who jumped at the offer of free land with only a modest yearly fee to the proprietary family (a "quitrent") of 2 shillings per 100 acres.

Calvert died while the charter for his colony was being drawn up in 1632, leaving his 26-year-old son, Cecilius, to carry out his plans. The charter guaranteed the proprietor control over all branches of government, but young Calvert learned that his colonists could not be satisfied with fewer political liberties than they enjoyed at home or could find in other colonies. Hence the Lords Baltimore were obliged to give up their charter-given right to initiate all colonial laws, subject only to the advice and consent of the people.

In land policy, Calvert's heirs found it impossible to carry out his plan for establishing feudalism in the woodlands of eastern North America. Arriving in 1634, immigrants blithely ignored his design of 6,000-acre manors for his relatives and 3,000-acre manors for lesser aristocrats, each to be ruled by provincial nobles and worked by flocks of serflike tenants. The newcomers took up their free land, imported as many indentured servants as they could afford, maintained generally peaceful relations with local Indian tribes, began to grow tobacco on scat-

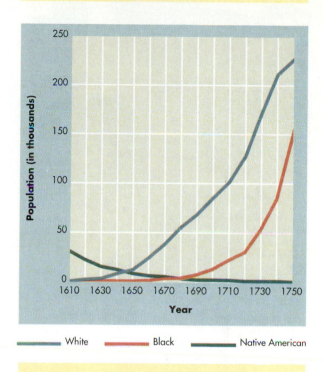

Population of the Chesapeake Colonies, 1610–1750

White Black Native American

Source: U.S. Bureau of the Census.

tered riverfront plantations like their Virginia neighbors, and governed themselves locally as much as possible. In time, they created their own social hierarchy, not with assigned social roles but with status determined by the ability of some to rise above others in the competitive tobacco economy. Although Maryland grew slowly at first—in 1650 it had a population of only 600—it developed rapidly in the second half of the seventeenth century. By 1700, its population of 33,000 was half that of Virginia's.

Daily Life on the Chesapeake

Though immigrants to the Chesapeake Bay region dreamed of bettering the life they had known in England, existence for most of them was dismally difficult. Only a minority could expect to marry and raise a family because marriage had to be deferred until after the indenture was completed, and there

Tobacco production involved indentured servants and slaves in a multistage work process as they planted, topped, suckered, cut, cured, stripped, and prized (packed into hogsheads) the leaf. Some of the stages are pictured here in a London book, The Culture of Tobacco.

Such conditions produced complex families, full of stepchildren and stepparents, half sisters and half brothers. In the common case of marriage between a widow and a widower, each with children from a previous marriage, the web of family life became particularly complex, and the tensions attending child rearing unusually thick.

The household of Robert Beverley of Middlesex County illustrates the tangled family relationships in this death-filled society. When Beverley married Mary Keeble in 1666, she was a 29-year-old widow who had borne seven children during her first marriage. At least four of them were still alive to join the household of their mother's new husband. They gained five half brothers and half sisters during their mother's 12-year marriage to Beverley. When Mary Keeble Beverley died at age 41, her husband quickly remarried a recent widow, Katherine Hone. Beverley's second wife brought her son into the household and in the next nine years produced four more children with Beverley before his death in 1687. Thus between 1666 and 1687, Beverley had married two widows who bore him nine children and had been stepfather to the eight children his two wives had produced with previous husbands. Not one of these 17 children, from an interlocking set of four marriages, reached adulthood with both a living mother and father.

Plagued by such mortality, the Chesapeake remained, for most of the seventeenth century, a land of immigrants rather than a land of settled families. Social institutions such as churches and schools took root very slowly amid such fluidity. The large number of indentured servants further increased the instability of community life. Strangers in a household, they served their time and moved on. Other strangers, purchased as they clambered off boats fresh from England, replaced them.

The fragility of life in the tobacco-growing Chesapeake world showed clearly in the region's architecture. As in most New World colonies, the settlers at first erected only primitive huts and shanties, hardly more than windbreaks. After establishing crops, planters improved their habitats but still built ramshackle, one-room dwellings. "Their houses," it was observed in 1623, "stand scattered one from another, and are only made of wood . . . so as a firebrand is sufficient to consume them all." Even as Virginia and Maryland matured, cheaply built and cramped houses, usually no larger than 16 by 24 feet, remained the norm. Life was too uncertain, the

were three times more men than women. Once made, marriages were fragile. Either husband or wife was likely to succumb to disease within about seven years. The vulnerability of pregnant women to malaria frequently terminated marriages in the first few years, and death claimed half the children born before they reached adulthood. Few children could expect to have both parents alive while growing up. Grandparents were almost unknown.

In a society so numerically dominated by men, widowed women were prized and remarried quickly.

tobacco economy too volatile, and the desire to invest every available shilling in field labor too great for men to build grandly. In England, solidly framed buildings erected on stone foundations had become the rule several centuries before. But throughout the Chesapeake, settlers erected "earthfast" flimsy cabins and houses directly on the ground or on posts.

Even by the early eighteenth century, most Chesapeake families were "pigg'd lovingly together," as one planter said, in a crude house without interior partitions. Eating, dressing, working, and loving all took place with hardly a semblance of privacy. For nearly two centuries, most ordinary Virginians and Marylanders lived in such quarters. "Like a flock of sheep in a fold," an eighteenth-century traveler described the family he bedded down with, 16 to a room, on the Virginia frontier. Even prosperous planters did not begin constructing fully framed, substantial homesteads until a century after the colony was founded.

The crudity of life also showed in the household possessions of the Chesapeake colonists. Struggling farmers and tenants were likely to own only a straw mattress, a simple storage chest, and the tools necessary for food preparation and eating—a mortar and pestle to grind corn, knives for butchering, a pot or two for cooking stews and porridges, wooden trenchers and spoons for eating. Most ordinary settlers owned no chairs, no dressers, no plates or silverware. Among middling planters the standard of living was raised only by possession of a flock mattress, coarse earthenware for milk and butter, a few pewter plates and porringers, a frying pan or two, and a few rough tables and chairs.

Even one of Virginia's wealthiest planters, the prominent Robert Beverley, had "nothing in and about his house but what was necessary . . . good beds . . . but no curtains, and instead of cane chairs, he hath stools made of wood." To be near the top of Chesapeake society meant to enlarge one's living space to three or four rooms, to sleep more comfortably, to sit on chairs rather than squat on the floor, and to acquire such ordinary decencies as chamber pots, candlesticks, bed linen, a chest of drawers, and a desk. But only the affluent few could boast luxury items such as clocks, window curtains, punch bowls, wine glasses, and imported furniture. Four generations elapsed in the Chesapeake settlements before the frontier quality of life slowly gave way to more refined living.

MASSACHUSETTS AND ITS OFFSPRING

While some English settlers in the reign of James I (1603–1625) scrambled for wealth on the Chesapeake, others in England were seized by the spirit of religion. They looked to the wilds of North America as a place to build a tabernacle to God. The society they fashioned aimed at unity of purpose and utter dedication to reforming the corrupt world. American Puritanism would powerfully affect the nation's history, especially in planting the seeds of a belief in America's special mission in the world. Yet the "New England way" only partially prefigured the pathways of American development because Puritanism represented a visionary attempt to banish diversity on a continent where the arrival of streams of immigrants from around the globe was destined to become a primary phenomenon.

Puritanism in England

England had been officially Protestant since 1558. Many English in the late sixteenth century, however, thought the Church of England was still ridden with Catholic elements. Detesting such remnants of Catholicism as vestments and rituals that lingered on in the reign of Elizabeth (1558–1603), some voices demanded the end of every taint of "the Bishop of Rome and all his detestable enormities." Because they wished to purify the Church of England, they were dubbed Puritans.

The people attracted to the Puritan movement were not only religious reformers but also men and women who hoped to find in religion an antidote to the changes sweeping over English society. Many feared for the future as they witnessed the growth of turbulent cities, the increase of wandering poor, rising prices, and accelerating commercial activity. In general, they disapproved of the growing freedom from the restraints of gentry-dominated medieval institutions such as the church, guilds, and local government.

The concept of the individual operating as freely as possible, maximizing both opportunities and personal potential, is at the core of our modern system of beliefs and behavior. But many in England cringed at the crumbling of traditional restraints of individual action. They worried that individualistic behavior would undermine the notion of community—

the belief that people were bound together by reciprocal rights, obligations, and responsibilities. Especially they decried the "degeneracy of the times," which they saw in the defiling of the Sabbath by maypole dancing, card playing, fiddling, bowling, and all the rest of the roistering and erotic behavior reflected in Shakespeare's dramatic portrayals of "Merrie England." Puritans vowed to reverse the march of disorder, wickedness, and disregard for community by imposing a new discipline. They intended not only to purify the Church of England but to reform society as well.

One part of their plan was a social ethic stressing work as a primary way of serving God. Derived from the Calvinist concept of "calling," this emphasis on work made the religious quest of every member of society equally worthy. The labor of a mason was just as valuable in God's sight as that of a merchant, and so was his soul. The "work ethic" would banish idleness and impart discipline throughout the community. Second, Puritans organized themselves into religious congregations where each member hoped for personal salvation but also supported all others in their quest. Third, Puritans assumed responsibility for the "unconverted" people around them. They were convinced that others who could not find Christian truth in their hearts might have to be coerced and controlled, as in Calvin's Geneva. Religious reform and social vision were in this way interlocked.

We think of the churches of the colonial South as handsome, steepled, red brick buildings, but this clapboard church is typical of the rudimentary buildings erected by early colonists in the Chesapeake region.

When King James VI of Scotland succeeded the childless Elizabeth as James I of England in 1603, he spoke stridently for the divine right of the monarch and his own role as head of the church. Claiming responsibility only to God, James collided with the rising power of the Puritans. They had occupied the pulpits in hundreds of churches, gained control of several colleges at Oxford and Cambridge, and recruited large numbers to their cause. Translating their religious appeal into political power, the Puritans obtained many seats in Parliament and aggressively challenged the king's power. James responded by harassing them, removing dozens of Puritan ministers from their pulpits, and threatening many others. "I will harry them out of the land," he vowed, "or else do worse."

When Charles I succeeded to the throne in 1625, the situation worsened for Puritans. Determined to strengthen the monarchy and stifle dissent, the king summoned a new Parliament in 1628 and one year later adjourned this venerable body (which was the Puritans' main instrument of reform) when it would not accede to royal demands. The king then appointed William Laud, the bishop of London, to high office and turned him loose on the Puritans, whom Laud called "wasps" and "the most dangerous enemies of the state."

By 1629, when the king began ruling without Parliament, many Puritans were turning their eyes outward to Northern Ireland, Holland, the Caribbean islands, and, especially, North America. They were convinced that God intended them to carry their religious and social reforms beyond the reach of persecuting authorities. The state of the economy added to their discouragement about their homeland, for England was suffering a depression in the cloth trades, most severely in Puritan strongholds. To some distant shore, many Puritans decided, they would transport a fragment of English society and carry out the completion of the Protestant Reformation. As they understood history, God had assigned them a special task in his plan for the redemption of humankind.

Puritan Predecessors in New England

Puritans were not the first Europeans to reach the shores of New England. Fishermen of various European nations had been working the fishing banks off Newfoundland and drying the cod they caught on the coast of Cape Cod and Maine since the early 1500s. They frequently made contact with the Algonquian-speaking tribes of the area. A short-lived attempt at settlement on the coast of Maine had also been made in 1607. Seven years later, the aging Chesapeake war dog, John Smith, hired to hunt whales off the North American coast, coined the term "New England" after visiting the area. In his *Description of New England,* published in 1616, he excited considerable interest in "the Paradise of these parts."

No permanent settlement took root, however, until the Pilgrims arrived in Plymouth in 1620. Unlike the Puritans who followed, these humble Protestant farmers did not expect to convert a sinful world. Rather, they wanted to be left alone to realize their radical vision of a pure and primitive life. Rather than reform the Church of England, they left it and hence were called Separatists. They had first fled from England to Amsterdam in 1608, then to Leyden when they found the commercial capital of Holland too corrupt, and finally, in 1620, to North America.

When they arrived at the northern tip of Cape Cod in November of that year, the Pilgrims were weakened from the stormy nine-week voyage and ill-prepared for the harsh winter ahead. Misled by John Smith's glowing report of a fertile country at the same latitude as southern France, they discovered instead a severe climate and a rockbound coast. By the following spring, half of the *Mayflower* passengers were dead, including 13 of the 18 married women.

The survivors, led by the staunch William Bradford, settled at Plymouth. Squabbles soon erupted with local Indians, whom Bradford considered "savage and brutish men, which range up and down, little otherwise than the wild beasts." In 1622, they found themselves nearly overwhelmed by the arrival of 60 non-Pilgrims, sent out by the London Company, which had helped the Pilgrims finance their colony. For two generations, the Pilgrims tilled the soil and fished while trying to keep intact their religious vision. But with the much larger Puritan migration that began in 1630, the Pilgrim villages nestled on the shores of Cape Cod Bay became a backwater of the thriving, populous Massachusetts Bay Colony, which absorbed them in 1691.

Errand into the Wilderness

In 11 ships, 1,000 Puritans set out from England in 1630 for the Promised Land. They were the vanguard of a movement that by 1642 had brought about 18,000 colonizers to New England's shores. Led by John Winthrop, a talented Cambridge-educated member of the English gentry, they operated under a charter from the king to the Puritan-controlled Massachusetts Bay Company. The Puritans set about building their utopia with the characteristic fervor of people convinced they are carrying out a divine task.

Their intention was to establish communities of pure Christians who collectively swore a covenant with God to work for his ends. To accomplish this, the Puritan leaders agreed to employ severe means. Their historic mission was too important, they believed, to allow the luxury of diversity of opinion in religious matters. Likewise, participation in government must be limited to church members. Civil and religious transgressors must be rooted out and severely punished. Their emphasis was on homogeneous communities where the good of the group outweighed individual interests. "We must delight in each other, make others' conditions our

John Winthrop was one of the lesser gentry who joined the Puritan movement and in the 1620s looked westward for a new life. Always searching himself as well as others for signs of weakness, Winthrop was one of the Massachusetts Bay Colony's main leaders for many years.

own, rejoice together, mourn together, labor and suffer together," counseled Winthrop.

To realize their utopian goals, the Puritans willingly gave up freedoms that their compatriots sought. An ideology of rebellion in England, Puritanism in America became an ideology of control. Much was at stake, for as Winthrop reminded the first settlers, "we shall be as a city upon a hill [and] the eyes of all people are upon us." That visionary sense of mission would help to shape a distinctive American self-image in future generations.

As in Plymouth and Virginia, the first winter tested the strongest souls. More than 200 of the first 700 settlers perished, and 100 others, disillusioned and sickened by the forbidding climate, returned to England the next spring. But Puritans kept coming. They "hived out" along the Back Bay of Boston, the port capital of the colony, along the rivers that emptied into the bay, south into what became Connecticut and Rhode Island a few years later, and north along the rocky Massachusetts coast.

Motivated by their militant work ethic and sense of mission, led by men experienced in local government, law, and the uses of exhortation, the Puritans thrived almost from the beginning. The early leaders of Virginia were soldiers of fortune or roughneck adventurers with predatory instincts, men who had no families or had left them at home. The ordinary Chesapeake settlers were mostly young men with little stake in English society who sold their labor to cross the Atlantic. In Massachusetts, the early leaders were university-trained ministers, experienced members of the lesser gentry, and men with a compulsion to fulfill what they knew was God's prophecy for New England. Most of the ordinary settlers came as freemen in families. Trained artisans and farmers from the middling rank of English society, they established tightknit communities in which, from the outset, the brutal exploitation of labor rampant in the Chesapeake had no place.

An Elusive Utopia

The Massachusetts Bay Colony flourished at first. The Puritans built a sound economy based on agriculture, fishing, timbering, and trading for beaver furs with local Indians. Even before leaving England, the directors of the Massachusetts Bay Company transformed their commercial charter into a rudimentary government and transferred the charter to New England. Once there, they laid the foundations of self-government. Free male church members annually elected a governor and deputies from each town who formed one house of a colonial legislature. The other house was composed of the governor's assistants, later to be called councillors. Consent of both houses was required to pass laws.

The Puritans also established the first printing press in the English colonies and planted the seed of a university, Harvard College, which opened its doors in 1636 for the training of prospective clergymen. The Puritan leaders also launched a brave attempt in 1642 to create a tax-supported school system so that all children might gain "the ability to read and understand the principles of religion and the capital laws of this country." In 1647, the government ordered every town with 50 families to establish an elementary school and every town with 100 families a secondary school as well, open to all who wished to take advantage of this education.

In spite of these accomplishments, the Puritan colony suffered many of the tensions besetting people bent on perfecting the human condition. Also, its inhabitants proved no better than their less religious countrymen on the Chesapeake in reaching an accommodation with the Native Americans. Surrounded by seemingly boundless land, the Puritans found it difficult to stifle acquisitive instincts and to keep families confined in compact communities. Restless souls looked to more distant valleys. "An over-eager desire after the world," wrote an early leader, "has so seized on the spirits of many as if the Lord had no farther work for his people to do, but every bird to feather his own nest." Others, remaining at the nerve center in Boston, agitated for broader political rights and even briefly ousted Winthrop as governor in 1635, when the colony's clergy backed the stiffnecked Thomas Dudley. After a few years, Governor Winthrop wondered if the Puritans had not gone "from the snare to the pit."

Winthrop's troubles multiplied in 1633 when Salem's Puritan minister, Roger Williams, began to voice disturbing opinions on church and government policies. Now the colony's leaders faced a contentious and visionary young man who argued that the Massachusetts Puritans were not truly pure because they would not completely separate themselves from the polluted Church of England (which most Puritans still hoped to reform). Williams also denounced mandatory worship, which he said "stinks in God's nostrils," and argued that government officials should not interfere with religious

Early New England

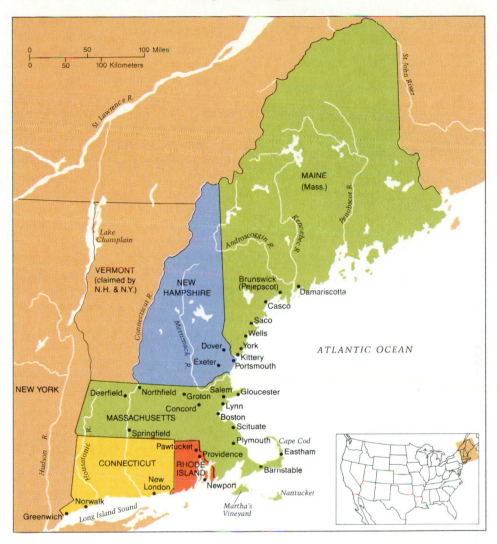

matters but confine themselves to civil affairs. Later to be celebrated as the earliest spokesman for the separation of church and state, Williams seemed in 1633 to strike at the heart of the Bible commonwealth, whose leaders regarded civil and religious affairs as inseparable. Williams also charged the Puritans with illegally intruding on Indian land.

Winthrop and others spent two years plying Williams alternately with sweet reason and threats, but they could not quiet the determined young man. Convinced that he would split the colony into competing religious groups and undermine authority, the magistrates vowed to deport him to England. Warned by Winthrop, Williams fled southward through winter snow with a small band of followers

to found Providence, a settlement on Narragansett Bay in what would become Rhode Island.

Even as they were driving Williams out, the Puritan authorities confronted another threat. This time it was a woman of extraordinary talent and intellect. Anne Hutchinson was as devoted a Puritan as any who came to the colony. Arriving in 1634 with her husband and seven children, she gained great respect among Boston's women as a practiced midwife, healer, and spiritual counselor. She soon began to discuss religion, suggesting that the "holy spirit" was absent in the preaching of some ministers. Before long Hutchinson was leading a movement labeled antinomianism, an interpretation of Puritan doctrine that stressed the mystical nature of God's free gift of grace while discounting the efforts the individual could make to gain salvation.

By 1636, Boston was dividing into two camps, those who followed the male clergy and those who cleaved to the theological views of a gifted though untrained woman with no official standing. Her followers included most of the community's malcontents—merchants who chafed under the price controls the magistrates imposed in 1635, young people resisting the rigid rule of their elders, women disgruntled by male authority, and artisans who resented wage controls designed to arrest growing inflation. Hutchinson doubly offended the male leaders of the colony because she boldly stepped outside the subordinate position expected of women. "The weaker sex" set her up as "a priest" and "thronged" after her, wrote one male leader. Another described a "clamour" in Boston that "New England men [should] usurp over their wives and keep them in servile subjection."

Determined to remove this nettle from their sides, the clergy and magistrates put Hutchinson on trial in 1637. After two long interrogations, they convicted her of sedition and contempt in a civil trial and banished her from the colony "as a woman not fit for our society." Six months later, the Boston church excommunicated her for preaching 82 erroneous theological opinions. She had "highly transgressed and offended and troubled the church," intoned the presiding clergyman, and "therefore in the name of our Lord Jesus Christ, I do cast you out and deliver you up to Satan and account you from this time forth to be a heathen and a leper." In the last month of her eighth pregnancy, Hutchinson, with a band of supporters, followed the route of Roger Williams to Rhode Island, the catch basin for Massachusetts Bay's dissidents.

But ideas proved harder to banish than people. The magistrates could never enforce uniformity of belief. Neither could they curb the appetite for land. Growth, geographic expansion, and commerce with the outside world all eroded the ideal of integrated, self-contained communities filled with religious piety. Leaders never wearied of reminding Puritan settlers that "the care of the public must oversway all private respects." But they faced the nearly impossible task of containing land-hungry immigrants in an expansive region. By 1636, groups of Puritans had swarmed not only to Rhode Island but also to Hartford and New Haven, where Thomas Hooker and John Davenport led new Puritan settlements in what became Connecticut.

New Englanders and Indians

The charter of the Massachusetts Bay Company proclaimed that the "principal end of this plantation" was "to win and incite the natives to the knowledge and obedience of the only true God and Saviour of mankind and the Christian faith." But the instructions that Governor John Winthrop carried from England reveal other Puritan thoughts about the native inhabitants. According to Winthrop's orders, all men were to receive training in the use of firearms, a reversal of the sixteenth-century English policy of disarming the citizenry in order to quell public disorders. Also, Indians were prohibited from entering Puritan towns, and any colonist selling arms to an Indian or instructing one in their use was to be deported.

Only sporadic conflict with local tribes occurred at first because disease had catastrophically struck the Native American population of southern New England, which may have numbered as many

New England's leaders were always troubled by their difficult relations with the native inhabitants of the region, and histories of these tensions, like this one published in Boston and London in 1677, often appeared after Indian wars.

THE

Present State

OF

New - England.

BEING A

NARRATIVE

Of the Troubles with the

INDIANS

IN

NEW-ENGLAND, from the first planting thereof in the year 1607, to this present year 1677: But chiefly of the late Troubles in the two last years 1675, and 1676.

To which is added a Discourse about the War with the PEQUODS in the year 1637.

By *W. Hubbard* Minister of *Ipswich.*

And the Lord said unto Moses, Write this for a Memorial in a Book, and rehearse it in the ears of Joshua; for I will utterly put out the Remembrance of Amalek from under heaven, Exod. 17. 14.

LONDON:

Printed for *Tho. Parkhurst* at the *Bible* and *Three Crowns* in *Cheapside,* near *Mercers-Chappel,* and at the *Bible* on *London-Bridge.* 1677.

as 125,000 in 1600, and left much of their land vacant. English fishermen, stopping along the coast in 1616, triggered an outbreak of respiratory viruses or smallpox among a population with no immunity against European microbes. Entire towns of Indians died in an epidemic that wiped out at least half the population. Five years later, an Englishman exploring the area wrote that the Indians "died on heapes, as they lay in their houses" and described walking through a forest where human skeletons covered the ground.

When smallpox returned in 1633, killing thousands more natives, it again relieved pressure for land. The Puritans saw the disease as proof that God had intervened on their side, just when a flood of new settlers was causing trouble over rights to land. "Without this remarkable and terrible stroke of God upon the natives," reported the Charlestown settlers, "[we] would with much more difficulty have found room, and at far greater charge have obtained and purchased land." Many surviving Indians welcomed the Puritans because they now had surplus land and through trade hoped to gain English protection against tribal enemies to the north.

The settler pressure for new land, however, soon reached into areas untouched by disease. When land hunger mingled with the Puritan sense of mission, it proved an explosive mix. To a people charged with messianic zeal, the heathen Indians represented a mocking challenge to the building of a religious commonwealth that would "shine as a beacon" back to decadent England. How could order and discipline be brought to their New Jerusalem unless its native inhabitants were tamed and "civilized"? If the natives could not be converted to civility and Christianity, the Puritans would have demonstrated their failure to control the land to which God had directed them. God, they knew, would answer this failure with his wrath.

Making the "savages" of New England strictly accountable to the ordinances that governed white behavior was part of this quest for fulfilling their mission. In this the Puritans succeeded with the smaller, disease-ravaged tribes of eastern Massachusetts. But their attempts to control the stronger Pequots led to the bloody war in 1637 in which John Mason was a leader. The Puritan victory in that war assured English sovereignty over all the tribes of southern New England except the powerful Wampanoags and Narragansetts of Rhode Island and removed the last obstacle to expansion into the Connecticut River valley. Missionary work, led by John

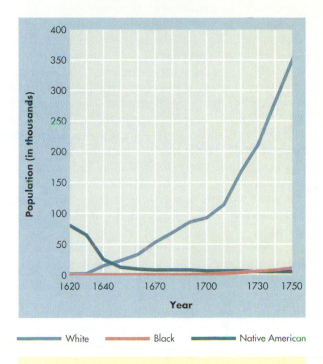

Population of the New England Colonies, 1620–1750

Source: U.S. Bureau of the Census.

Eliot, began among the remnant tribes in the 1640s. After a decade of effort, about 1,000 Indians had been settled in four "praying villages," learning to live according to the white man's ways.

The Web of Village Life

The village was the vital center of Puritan life. Unlike the Chesapeake tobacco planters, who dispersed along the streams and rivers of their area, the Puritans established small, tightly settled villages. Most pursued "open field" agriculture, trudging out from the village each morning to farm narrow strips of land that radiated out from the town. They grazed their cattle on common meadow and cut firewood on common woodland. Such a system recreated agricultural life in many parts of England.

In other towns, Puritans employed the "closed field" system of self-contained farms that they had known at home. But in either system, families lived close together in compact towns built around a common, where the meetinghouse and tavern were located. These small, communal villages kept families in close touch so that each could be alert not only to its own transgressions but also to those of its neighbors. "In a multitude of counsellors is safety," Puritan ministers were fond of advising, and the little villages of 50 to 100 families perfectly served the need for moral surveillance, or "holy watching."

Determined to achieve godliness and communal unity, Puritans also prohibited single men and women from living by themselves, for this would put individuals beyond patriarchal authority and group observation. Left to themselves, men and women would stray from the path, for, as Thomas Hooker put it, "every natural man and woman is born full of sin, as full as a toad of poison." In Virginia, the planters counted the absence of restraint as a blessing. In New England, it was feared as the Devil.

At the center of every Puritan village stood the meetinghouse. These plain wooden structures, sometimes called "Lord's barns," gathered within them every soul in the village, not just once but twice a week—on the Lord's day and during midweek as well. No man stood higher in the community than the minister. He was the spiritual leader in these small, family-based, community-oriented settlements, which viewed life as a Christian pilgrimage.

The unique Puritan mixture of strict authority and incipient democracy, of hierarchy and equality, can be seen in the way the Massachusetts town distributed land and devised local government. Each town was founded by a grant of the colony's General Court, sitting in Boston. Only groups of Puritans who had signed a compact signifying their unity of purpose received settlement grants. "We shall by all means," read the town of Dedham's covenant, "labor to keep off from us such as are contrary minded, and receive only such unto us as may be probably of one heart with us."

After receiving a grant, townsmen met to parcel out land. They awarded individual grants according to the size of a man's household, his wealth, and his usefulness to the church and town. Such a system perpetuated existing differences in wealth and status. Yet some towns wrote language into their convenants that to the modern ear has an almost socialistic ring. "From each according to his ability

The similarity in settlement patterns between England and New England is seen in a modern rendering of early seventeenth-century Rowley, Massachusetts (left), and a plan of Chelmsford, Essex, in 1591 (right).

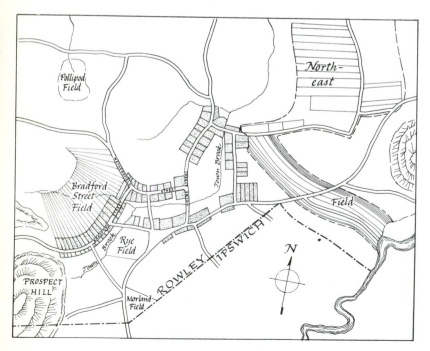

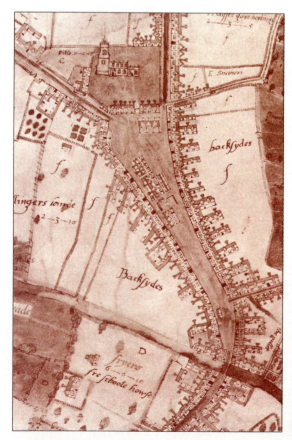

to each as need shall require," read one. It was not socialism that the Puritans had in mind. Rather, they believed that the community's welfare transcended individual ambitions or accomplishments and that unity demanded limits on the accumulation of wealth. Every family should have enough land to sustain it, and prospering men were expected to use their wealth for the community's benefit, not for conspicuous consumption. Repairing the meeting-house, building a school, aiding a widowed neighbor—such were the proper uses of wealth.

Having felt the sting of centralized power in church and state, Puritans emphasized local exercise of authority. Until 1684, only male church members could vote, and as the proportion of males who were church members declined, so did the proportion of men who could vote. These voters elected selectmen, who allocated land, passed local taxes, and settled disputes. Once a year, all townsmen gathered for the town meeting, called later by Thomas Jefferson "the wisest invention ever devised by the wit of man for the perfect exercise of self-government." At the town meeting, the citizens selected town officers for the next year and decided matters large and small: Should the playing of football in the streets be prohibited? Might Widow Thomas be allowed £10 for a kidney stone operation for her son? What salary should the schoolteacher be paid?

The appointment of many citizens to minor offices—surveyors of hemp, informers about deer, purchasers of grain, town criers, measurers of salt, fence viewers, and many others—bred the tradition of local government. Complaints about officialdom rarely grew into political bitterness in such a system. All officeholders were annually subject to electoral approval, and about one out of every ten adult males in many towns was selected each year for some office, large or small. In New England, nobody could acquire a reputation for sobriety and industry without finding himself elected to a local post.

The predominance of families also lent cohesiveness to Puritan village life. Strengthening this family orientation was the remarkably healthy environment of the Puritans' "New Israel." While the germs carried by English colonizers devastated neighboring Indian societies, the effect on the newcomers of entering a new environment was the opposite. The low density of settlement prevented infectious diseases from spreading, and the isolation of the New England villages from the avenues of Atlantic commerce, along which diseases as well as cargo flowed, minimized biological hazards in the seventeenth century.

The result was a spectacular natural increase in the population and a life span unknown in Europe. At a time when the population of western Europe was barely growing—deaths almost equaled births—the population of New England, discounting new immigrants, doubled every 27 years. The difference was not a higher birthrate. New England women typically bore about seven children during the course of a marriage, but this barely exceeded the European norm. The crucial factor was that chances for survival after birth were far greater than in England because of the healthier climate and better diet. In most of Europe, only half the babies born lived long enough to produce children themselves. Life expectancy for the population at large was less than 40 years. In New England, nearly 90 percent of the infants born in the seventeenth century survived to marriageable age, and life expectancy exceeded 60 years—longer than for the American population as a whole at any time until the early twentieth century. About 25,000 people immigrated to New England in the seventeenth century, but by 1700 they had produced a population of 100,000. By contrast, some 75,000 immigrants to the Chesapeake colonies had yielded a population of about 70,000 by the end of the century.

Women played a vital role in this family-centered society. In the household economies of the Puritan villages, the woman was not only wife, mother, and housekeeper but also custodian of the vegetable garden; processor of salted and smoked meats, dairy products, and preserved vegetables; and spinner, weaver, and clothesmaker.

The presence of women and a stable family life strongly affected New England's regional architecture. As communities formed, the Puritans converted early economic gains into more substantial housing rather than investing in bound labor as in the Chesapeake colonies, where family formation was retarded and the economy unstable. Well-constructed one-room houses with sleeping lofts quickly replaced the early "wigwams, huts, and hovels." Families then added parlors and lean-to kitchens as soon as they could. Within a half century, New England immigrants accomplished a general rebuilding of their living structures, while the Chesapeake lagged far behind.

A final binding element in Puritan communities was the stress on literacy and education, eventually to become a hallmark of American society. Placing

RECOVERING THE PAST

HOUSES

Homesteading is central to our national experience. For 300 years after the founding of the first colonies, most Americans were involved in taming and settling the land. On every frontier, families faced the tasks of clearing the fields, beginning farming operations, and building shelter for themselves and their livestock. The kinds of structures they built depended on available materials, their resources and aspirations, and their notions of a "fair" dwelling. The plan of a house and the materials used in its construction reveal much about the needs, resources, priorities, and values of the people who built it.

By examining archaeological remains of early ordinary structures and by studying houses that are still standing, historians are reaching new understandings of the social life of pioneering societies. Since the 1960s, archaeologists and architectural historians have been studying seventeenth-century housing in the Chesapeake Bay and New England

regions. They have discovered a familiar sequence of house types—from temporary shanties and lean-tos to rough cabins and simple frame houses to larger and more substantial dwellings of brick and finished timber. This hovel-to-house-to-home pattern existed on every frontier, as sodbusters, gold miners, planters, and cattle raisers secured their hold on the land and then struggled to move from subsistence to success.

What is unusual in the findings of the Chesapeake researchers is the discovery that the second phase in the sequence—the use of temporary, rough-built structures—lasted for more than a century. While many New Englanders had rebuilt and extended their temporary clapboard houses into timberframed, substantial dwellings by the 1680s, Chesapeake settlers continued to construct small, rickety buildings that had to be repaired continually or abandoned altogether every 10 to 15 years.

The William Boardman house, built around 1687, is an example of the "orderly, fair, and well-built" houses of late-seventeenth-century Massa-

William Boardman house, Saugus, Massachusetts, c. 1687

William Boardman house, floor plan

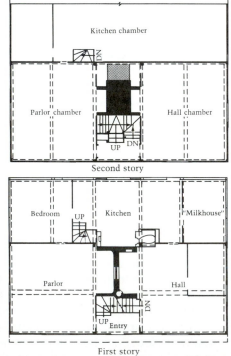

Kitchen chamber

Parlor chamber

Hall chamber

UP DN

Second story

Bedroom UP Kitchen "Milkhouse"

Parlor Hall

UP Entry DN

First story

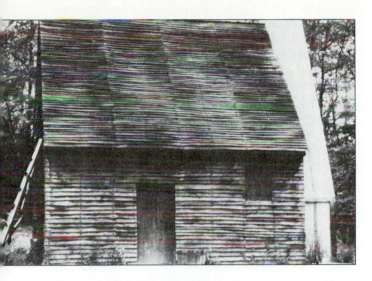

Reconstructed Chesapeake planter's house, typical of such structures in the seventeenth century.

chusetts. Its plan shows a typical arrangement of space: the hall, used for cooking, eating, working, and socializing; the parlor; a sleeping room for the parents; and a lean-to for kitchen chores and activities such as dairying. The great central chimney warmed the main downstairs room. Upstairs were two rooms used for both storage and sleeping. As you examine the exterior of the building, note the materials that have been used and the arrangement and treatment of windows, doors, and chimney. What impression of the Boardman family might visitors have as they approached the house? What kind of privacy and comfort did the house provide for family members?

The second house is a typical reconstructed tobacco planter's house. It has some of the same features as the Boardman house, for both are products of an English building tradition. But there are some major differences between the two. In the Chesapeake house, the chimney is not built of brick but of mud and wood; there is no window glass, only small shutters. The exterior is rough, unfinished planking. The placement of doors and windows and the overall dimensions indicate that this house has only one room downstairs and a loft above. The builders of this house clearly enjoyed less privacy and comfort than the Boardmans.

Historians have puzzled over this contrast between the architecture of the two regions. Part of the explanation may lie in the different climatic conditions and different immigration patterns of New England and the Chesapeake. In the southern region, disease carried off thousands of settlers in the early decades. The imbalance of men and women produced a stunted and unstable family life, hardly conducive to an emphasis on constructing fine homes. In New England, good health prevailed almost from the beginning, and the family was at the heart of society. It made more sense, in this environment, to make a substantial investment in larger and more permanent houses. Some historians argue, moreover, that the Puritan work ethic impelled New Englanders to build solid homes—a compulsion unknown in the culturally backward, "lazy" South.

Archaeological evidence combined with data recovered from land, tax, and court records, however, suggests another reason for the impermanence of housing in the Chesapeake region. Living in a labor-intensive tobacco world, it is argued, planters large and small economized on everything possible in order to buy as many indentured servants and slaves as they could. Better to live in a shanty and have ten slaves than to have a handsome dwelling and nobody to cultivate the fields. As late as 1775, the author of *American Husbandry* calculated that in setting up a tobacco plantation, five times as much ought to be spent on purchasing 20 black fieldhands as on the "house, offices, and tobacco-house."

Only after the Chesapeake region had emerged from its prolonged era of mortality and gender imbalance and a mixed economy of tobacco, grain, and cattle had replaced the tobacco monoculture did the rebuilding of the region begin. Excavated house sites indicate that this occurred in the period after 1720. New research is revealing that the phases of home building and the social and economic history of a society were closely interwoven. What do houses today reveal about the resources, economic livelihood, priorities, and values of contemporary Americans? Do class and regional differences in house design continue?

religion at the center of their lives, Puritans emphasized the ability to read catechisms, psalmbooks, and especially the Bible. Literacy could instill the basic precepts of life in all. "Thy life to mend, this book attend" went one verse in a children's schoolbook. In literacy Puritans saw guarantees that they would not succumb to the savagery they perceived all around them in the new land. They also trusted that through education they could preserve the central values of their struggle to redeem humankind in the North American wilderness.

An event in England in 1642 affected the future development of the New England colonies. King Charles I pushed his people into revolution by violating the country's customary constitution and trying to continue the reformation in the Anglican church. The ensuing civil war climaxed with the trial and beheading of the king in 1649. Thereafter, during the so-called Commonwealth period (1649–1660), Puritans had the opportunity to complete the reform of English religion and society. Migration to New England abruptly ceased.

The 20,000 English immigrants who had come to New England by 1649 were scattered from Maine to Long Island. Governor Winthrop of Massachusetts lamented the dispersion, and Roger Williams condemned the "depraved appetite" for new and better land. Yet, in a terrain so rock-strewn that its pastures were said to produce Yankee sheep with sharpened noses, it was natural that men should seek better plow land.

To combat dispersion, Puritan leaders established a broad intercolony political structure in 1643 called the Confederation of New England. Designed to coordinate government among the various Puritan settlements (Rhode Island was pointedly excluded) and especially to provide greater defense against the French, the Dutch, and the Indians, the pact bound together Massachusetts, Plymouth, the small colony of New Haven, and the river towns of Connecticut. This first American attempt at federalism functioned fitfully for a generation, though Massachusetts, the strongest and largest member, often refused to abide by group decisions when they ran counter to its objectives.

Although the Puritans fashioned stable communities, developed the economy, and constructed effective government, their leaders, as early as the 1640s, complained that the founding vision of Massachusetts Bay was faltering. Material concerns seemed to transcend religious commitment; the individual prevailed over the community. In 1638, the General Court declared a day of humiliation and prayer to atone for the colony's "excess idleness and contempt of authority." A generation later, the synod of 1679—a convention of Puritan churches—cried out that "the church, the commonwealth and the family are being destroyed by self-assertion." By this time, Puritans rarely mentioned the work of salvaging western Protestantism by example. Instead, they concentrated on keeping their children on the straight and narrow road.

Frequent complaints about moral laxness notwithstanding, New England had achieved economic success and political stability by the end of the seventeenth century. Towns functioned efficiently, poverty was uncommon, public education had been mandated, and family life was stable. If social diversity increased and the religious zeal of the founding generation waned, that was only to be expected. One second-generation Bay colonist put the matter bluntly. His minister had noticed his absence in

Primers such as this served to instill religious values as well as literacy in the Puritan colonies.

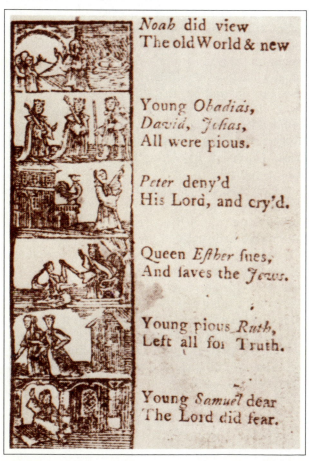

church and found him late that day at the docks, unloading a boatload of cod. "Why were you not in church this morning?" asked the clergyman. Back came the reply: "My father came here for religion, but I came for fish."

FROM THE ST. LAWRENCE TO THE HUDSON

The New Englanders were not the only European settlers in the northern region, for both France and Holland created colonies there. At the same time that Jamestown was founded, the French repeated their attempt to settle Canada, more successfully than in the 1540s. Henry IV, the first strong French king in half a century, sent Samuel de Champlain to explore deep into the territory. He established a small settlement in Port Royal, Acadia (later Nova Scotia), in 1604, and another at what would become the capital of New France, Quebec, in 1608. Already established French fish-drying stations in Newfoundland had initiated trading with Indians for furs, and Champlain's settlers hoped for easy profits on beaver. But the holders of the fur monopoly in France did not encourage emigration to the colony because settlement would reduce the forests from which the furs were harvested. New France therefore remained so lightly populated that English marauders easily seized and held Quebec from 1629 to 1632.

In 1609, Champlain allied with the Algonquian Indians of the St. Lawrence region in attacking their enemies the Iroquois to the south, earning their eternal enmity. The Iroquois traded furs to the Dutch on the Hudson River for European goods, and when they exhausted the furs of their own territory, they turned north, determined to destroy the French-allied Hurons of the Great Lakes region and seize their rich forests. In the 1640s and 1650s, the Iroquois smashed the Hurons and the French Jesuit missions among them. That ended all commerce in New France for a time and menaced Quebec and Montreal. The bitterness bred in these years colored future colonial warfare, driving the Iroquois to ally with the English against the French. But for the time being, in the mid-seventeenth century, the English remained free of pressure from the beleaguered French colonists, who numbered only about 400.

By the mid-seventeenth century, the Chesapeake and New England regions each contained about 50,000 settlers. Between them lay the mid-Atlantic area controlled by the Dutch, who had planted a small colony named New Netherland at the mouth of the Hudson River in 1624 and in the next four decades had extended their control to the Connecticut and Delaware river valleys. To the south of the Chesapeake lay a vast territory where only the Spanish, on their mission frontier in Florida, challenged the power of Native American tribes.

These two areas, north and south of the Chesapeake, became strategic zones of English colonizing activity after the end of England's civil war in 1660 brought the reinstallation of the English monarchy. Commercial rival of the Dutch and religious and economic enemies of the Spanish, England moved to cement its claims on the North American coast.

England Challenges the Mighty Dutch

Although for generations they had been the Protestant bulwarks in a mostly Catholic Europe, England and Holland became bitter commercial rivals in the mid-seventeenth century. By the time the Puritans arrived in New England, the Dutch had become the mightiest carriers of seaborne commerce in western Europe. By one contemporary estimate, Holland owned 16,000 of Europe's 20,000 merchant ships. The Dutch had also muscled in on Spanish and Portuguese transatlantic commerce, trading illegally with Iberian colonists who gladly violated their government's commercial policies in order to obtain cloth and slaves more cheaply.

By 1650, the Dutch had temporarily overwhelmed the Portuguese in Brazil, and soon their vast trading empire reached the East Indies, Ceylon, India, and Formosa. The best shipbuilders, mariners, and businessmen in western Europe, they validated the dictum of Sir Walter Raleigh that "whosoever commands the sea commands the trade; whosoever commands the trade of the world commands the riches of the world, and consequently the world itself."

In North America, the Dutch West India Company's New Netherland colony was small but profitable. Agents fanned out from Fort Orange (Albany) and New Amsterdam (New York City) into the Hudson, Connecticut, and Delaware river valleys. There they established a lucrative fur trade with local tribes by hooking into the sophisticated trading network of the Iroquois Confederacy, which stretched to the Great Lakes. The Iroquois welcomed the

Dutch presence. The newcomers were few in number, they did not have voracious appetites for land, and they were willing to exchange desirable goods for the pelts of animals that were abundant in the vast Iroquois territory. At Albany, the center of the Dutch-Iroquois trade, relations remained peaceful and profitable for several generations because both peoples admirably served each other's needs.

Although the Dutch never settled more than 10,000 people in their mid-Atlantic colonies, their commercial and naval powers were impressive. The Virginians learned as much in 1667 when brazen Dutch raiders captured 20 tobacco ships on the James River and confiscated virtually the entire tobacco crop for that year.

By 1650, England was ready to challenge Dutch maritime supremacy. Three times between 1652 and 1675, war broke out between the two Protestant competitors for control of the emerging worldwide capitalist economy. In the second and third wars, the Dutch colony on the Hudson River became an easy target for the English. They captured it in 1664 and then, after it fell to the Dutch in 1673, recaptured it almost immediately. By 1675, the Dutch had been permanently dislodged from the North American mainland. But they remained mighty commercial competitors of the English in Europe, Africa, the Far East, and the Caribbean.

New Netherland, where from the beginning Dutch, French Huguenots, Walloons from present-

Restoration Colonies: New York, the Jerseys, Pennsylvania, and the Carolinas

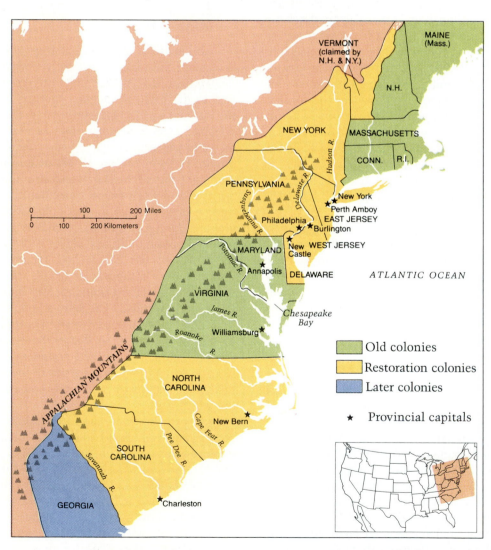

day Belgium, Swedes, Portuguese, Finns, English, refugee Portuguese Jews from Brazil, and Africans had commingled in a babel of languages and religions, now became New York. It was so named because Charles II made a proprietary grant of the territory, along with the former Dutch colonies on the Delaware River, to James, duke of York, his brother and heir to the English throne.

Under English rule, the former Dutch colonists retained much of their ethnic identity for several generations. They spoke their native language, worshiped in their Dutch Reformed Calvinist churches, and perpetuated Dutch architecture. In time, however, English immigrants overwhelmed the Dutch, and gradual intermarriage between the Dutch, the Huguenots, and the English—the three main groups—diluted ethnic loyalties. But New York retained its polyglot, religiously tolerant character, and its people never allowed religious concerns or utopian plans to interfere with the pragmatic conduct of business.

PROPRIETARY CAROLINA: A RESTORATION REWARD

In 1663, three years after he was restored to the throne taken from his father, Charles II granted a vast territory named Carolina to a group of men who had supported him when he was in exile. Its boundaries extended from ocean to ocean and from Virginia to central Florida. Within this miniature empire, eight proprietors, including several involved in Barbados sugar plantations, gained large powers of government and semifeudal rights to the land. For settling their royal reward, they constructed a system of government with both feudal and modern features. To lure settlers, they promised religious freedom and offered land free for the asking. Onto this generous land offer they grafted plans for a semimedieval government that provided themselves, their deputies, and a small number of noblemen with a monopoly of political power.

The architects of Carolina, which included the brilliant young John Locke, were reacting to a generation of violence and radical social experiments during the English civil war (1642–1649). They intended their design for Carolina to bring social and political stability to the southern wilds of North America. A hereditary aristocracy of wealthy manor lords, they thought, would check boisterous small landholders.

However, the reality of settlement in Carolina bore faint resemblance to what the planters envisaged. The rugged sugar and tobacco planters who streamed in from Barbados and Virginia, where depressed economic conditions made a new beginning in Carolina seem attractive, claimed their 150 acres of free land (and additional acreage for each family member or servant they brought). But they ignored proprietary regulations about settling in compact rectangular patterns and reserving two-fifths of every county for an appointed nobility. In government they also did as they pleased. Meeting in assembly for the first time in 1670, they refused to accept the proprietors' Fundamental Constitutions of 1667 and ignored the orders of the governor appointed in London. In shaping local government, the planters were guided mostly by their experience in the slave society of Barbados, whence most of them had come.

The Indian Debacle

Carolina was the most elaborately planned colony in English history but the least successful in achieving amicable relations with the natives. The proprietors in London had intended otherwise. Mindful of the violent encounters that had plagued other settlements, they projected a well-regulated Indian trade limited to their appointed agents. But the aggressive settlers from the West Indies and the Chesapeake openly flouted proprietary policy. Those from Barbados, accustomed to exploiting African slave labor, saw that if the major tribes of the Southeast—the Cherokees, Creeks, and Choctaws— could be drawn into trade, the planters might reap vast wealth. The Spanish in Florida had done little to tap this potential gold mine; their main goal was to protect their territorial claim by establishing missions that gathered local Indians into a sedentary, agricultural life.

It was not the beaver that beckoned in the Indian trade, as in the North, but the deerskin, much desired in Europe for making warm and durable clothing. In the villages of the southeastern tribes, where natives farmed as well as hunted, the Carolina colonies found a people eager to obtain European trade goods. But what began as a trade for the skins of deer soon became a trade for the skins of Indians. To the consternation of the London proprietors, capturing Indians for sale in New England and the West Indies became the cornerstone of commerce in Carolina in the early years.

The Indian slave trade plunged Carolina into a series of wars. Local planters and merchants selected a tribe, armed it, and rewarded it handsomely for bringing in captives from another. Even strong tribes that allied for trade with the Carolinians found that after they had used English guns to enslave their weaker neighbors, they themselves were sometimes scheduled for elimination. The colonists justified the policy by claiming that "thinning the barbarous Indian natives" was necessary to make room for white settlement. The "thinning" was so thorough that by the early eighteenth century, the two main tribes of the coastal plain, the Westos and the Savannahs, were nearly extinct.

Early Carolina Society

Carolina's fertile land and warm climate convinced many that it was "a Country so delicious, pleasant, and fruitful that were it cultivated doubtless it would prove a second Paradize." Into the country came Barbadians, Swiss, Scots, Irish, French Huguenots, English, and even migrants from New England, New York, and New Jersey. But far from creating paradise, this ethnically and religiously diverse people clashed abrasively in an atmosphere of fierce competition, brutal race relations, and stunted social institutions.

For the land-hungry white cattle raisers and rice growers of coastal South Carolina, the Indian slave trade had no direct benefits, since the profits flowed entirely to the merchants of Charleston, the main port and seat of government. They reaped important secondary advantages, however. As the Indian population of the coastal region fell sharply, expansion

from the initial settlements around Charleston became easier. Along the twisting rivers that flowed to the coast, planters staked out claims and experimented with a variety of exotic crops, including sugar, indigo, tropical fruits, tobacco, and rice. It was this last that, after much experimentation, proved to be the staple crop upon which a flourishing economy could be built.

The cultivation of rice required backbreaking labor to drain the swampy lowlands, build dams and levees, and hoe, weed, cut, thresh, and husk the crop. Since many of the early settlers had experience with African slaves in Barbados, their early reliance on slave labor came naturally to them. On widely dispersed plantations, black labor came to predominate. In 1680, four-fifths of South Carolina's population was white. But by 1720, when the colony had grown to 18,000, blacks outnumbered whites two to one.

As in Virginia and Maryland, the low-lying areas of coastal Carolina were so disease-ridden that population grew only slowly in the early years. "In the spring a paradise, in the summer a hell, and in the autumn a hospital," remarked one traveler. Malaria and yellow fever, especially dangerous to pregnant women, were the twin killers that retarded population growth, while the scarcity of women further limited natural increase. Like the West Indies, the rice-growing region of Carolina was at first more a place to accumulate a fortune than to raise a family.

In the northern part of Carolina, mostly pine barrens along a sandy coast, a different kind of society emerged. Populated largely by small tobacco farmers from Virginia seeking free land, the Albemarle region developed a mixed economy of livestock grazing, tobacco and food production, and

This painting of Mulberry Plantation in South Carolina shows the mansion house, built in 1708, and rows of slave huts constructed in an African style.

the mining of the pine forests for naval stores—turpentine, resin, pitch, tar, and lumber. In 1701, North and South Carolina became separate colonies, but their distinctiveness had emerged before that. Slavery took root only slowly in North Carolina, which was still 85 percent white in 1720. A land of struggling white settlers (called "Lubberland" by one prosperous Virginia planter), its healthier climate and settlement by families rather than by single men with servants and slaves gave it a greater potential for sustained growth. But in both North and South Carolina, several factors inhibited the growth of a strong corporate identity: the pattern of settlement, the ethnic and religious diversity, and the lack of shared assumptions about social and religious goals.

THE QUAKERS' PEACEABLE KINGDOM

Of all the utopian dreams imposed on the North American landscape in the seventeenth century, the most remarkable was that of the Quakers. During the English civil war, the Society of Friends, as the Quakers called themselves, had sprung forth as one of the many radical sects searching for a more just society and a purer religion. Their visionary ideas and their defiance of civil authority cost them dearly in fines, brutal punishment, and imprisonment. After Charles II and Parliament stifled radical dissent in the 1660s, they too sent many converts across the Atlantic. In America they swam against the tide, attempting to perfect social relations among religiously and ethnically diverse people. The reformist imprint they placed on the larger society is still vibrant today in spite of their small number. Moreover, the society they founded in Pennsylvania foreshadowed more than any other colony the future religious and ethnic pluralism of the United States.

The Early Friends

Like their Puritan cousins, the Quakers regarded the English Protestant church (called the Church of England) as corrupt and renounced its formalities and rituals, which smacked of Catholicism. But they carried the Puritan revolt against the Church of England to the extreme. They foreswore all church officials and institutions, persuaded that every believer could find grace through the "inward light," a spark of redemption that resided in every

man and woman, unaided by priests, ministers, liturgy, or other human devices. By discarding the ideas of original sin and eternal predestination, they offered a radically liberating alternative to the reigning Calvinist doctrine.

Quakers were persecuted in England after their movement, led by George Fox and Margaret Fell, gathered momentum in the 1650s. Other Protestants regarded them as dangerous fanatics, for the Quakers' egalitarian doctrine of the light within elevated all lay persons to the position of the clergy and denied the primary place accorded the Scriptures. Such views threatened the stability of the organized church in the eyes of many.

Equally threatening was the Quakers' social radicalism. They refused to observe the customary marks of deference, such as doffing one's hat to a superior, believing that in God's sight no social distinctions existed. They used the familiar *thee* and *thou* instead of the formal and deferential *you,* they resisted taxes supporting the Church of England, and they refused to sign witnesses' oaths on the Bible, regarding this as profane. They also shocked a world conditioned to violence by renouncing the use of force in human affairs. Their pacifism carried them into a refusal to perform militia service. Garbing themselves in plain black cloth and practicing civil disobedience, the Quakers presented a threat to social hierarchy and order in every community they entered.

By conferring on women a more equal place than anywhere in the English-speaking world, the Quakers also affronted traditional views. They insisted on the spiritual equality of the sexes and the right of women to participate in church matters on an equal, if usually separate, footing with men. The Puritans had granted spiritual equality to women but excluded them from preaching, electing ministers, admitting others to membership, and other churchly functions. They had excommunicated Anne Hutchinson with the words, "You have stepped out of your place, you have rather been a husband than a wife, and a preacher than a hearer."

Quaker leader George Fox renounced such discrimination. "Now Moses and Aaron and the 70 elders did not say to those assemblies of women: 'we can do our work ourselves and you are more fit to be at home to wash the dishes,' but they did encourage them in the work and service of God." Quaker leaders urged women to preach and to establish separate women's meetings. Among Quakers who fanned out from England to preach the doctrine of the "inward light," 26 of the first 59 to cross the Atlantic were women. All but four of them were unmarried or without their husbands and therefore living, traveling, and ministering outside the bounds of male authority.

Intensely committed to converting the rest of the world to their beliefs, the Quakers ranged westward to North America and the Caribbean in the 1650s and 1660s. Nearly everywhere they were reviled, mutilated, imprisoned, and deported. Puritan Massachusetts warned them that their liberty in that colony consisted of "free liberty to keep away from us and such as will come to be gone as fast as they can, the sooner the better." Hungering to serve in what they called "the Lamb's War" (the crusade of the meek), the Quakers vowed to test the Puritans' resolve and kept coming.

The Bay Colony magistrates were desperate to eliminate this dangerous threat to religious conformity and civil authority. Finally, in 1659, they hanged two Quaker men on the Boston Common and went through the motions of hanging Mary Dyer, an old woman who had followed Anne Hutchinson a quarter century before. Escorted from the colony, Mary Dyer returned the next year to defy the Massachusetts ban. Undaunted, she met her death at the end of a rope.

Early Quaker Designs

By the 1670s, the English Quakers were looking for a place in the New World to carry out their millennial dreams. In England, royal fears of a Catholic conspiracy led to severe religious repression of all dissenting groups in the late 1670s. Thousands of Quakers were jailed and fined heavily for practicing their faith.

Emerging as their leader in this dark period was William Penn, whose background made him an unlikely Quaker. Penn was the son of Admiral Sir William Penn, who by capturing Jamaica from the Spanish in 1654 had placed in English hands one of the most productive sugar-growing sites in the world. Young William had been groomed for life in the English aristocracy. But when sent to Oxford, he found it a "hellish darkness and a debauchery." He rebelled against his parents' designs for him in one of the professions; then, at age 23, he was converted by a spellbinding speech about the power of the Quaker inward light.

After joining the Society of Friends in 1666, Penn devoted himself to their cause. He defended Quakers

arrested for religious nonconformity and trekked through England, Ireland, Holland, and Germany spreading the Quaker faith. In 1674, Penn joined other Friends in establishing their own colony, between the Hudson and Delaware rivers.

The area south of New York had originally been part of the Dutch New Netherland colony, but it was only sparsely settled. Following the English capture of New Netherland in 1664, Charles II granted the area, divided into two large tracts called West and East Jersey, as a royal gift to Lord John Berkeley and Sir George Carteret. Little interested in managing his half of the 4,600-square-mile territory, Berkeley sold his rights to West Jersey to a group of Quakers in 1674. William Penn was among them.

One of England's most active pamphleteers on the side of religious toleration and parliamentary rights in the 1670s, Penn now helped fashion an extraordinarily liberal constitution for the budding Quaker colony. Legislative power and the authority to constitute courts were vested in an assembly chosen annually by virtually all free males in the colony. Election of justices of the peace and local officeholders was also mandated. Settlers were guaranteed freedom of religion and trial by jury. As Penn and the other trustees of the colony explained, "We lay a foundation for [later] ages to understand their liberty as men and Christians, that they may not be brought in bondage, but by their own consent; for we put the power in the people."

The last phrase, summing up the document, would have shocked anyone of property and power in England or America at the time. Most regarded "the people" as ignorant, dangerous, certain to bring society to a state of anarchy if entrusted with the right to rule themselves. Nowhere in the English world had ordinary citizens, especially those who owned no land, enjoyed such extensive privileges. Nowhere had a popularly elected legislature received such broad authority.

Despite these idealistic plans, West Jersey sputtered at first. Only 1,500 immigrants arrived in the first five years, and the colony for several decades was caught up in legal complications caused by the tangled claims to the land and government. The focus of Quaker hopes lay across the Delaware River, where in 1681 Charles II granted William Penn a vast territory, almost as large as England itself. The grant extinguished a large royal debt to Penn's father, but the crown also benefited by getting the pesky Quakers out of England. To the Quakers' great fortune, the territory granted to Penn, the last unassigned segment of the eastern coast of North America, was also one of the most fertile.

Pacifism in a Militant World: Quakers and Indians

On the day Penn received his royal charter for Pennsylvania, he wrote a friend, "My God that has given it to me will, I believe, bless and make it the seed of a nation." The nation that Penn envisioned was unique among colonizing schemes. Penn intended to make his colony an asylum for the persecuted, a refuge from arbitrary state power. Puritans strove to nurture social homogeneity and religious uniformity, excluding all not of like mind. In the Chesapeake and Carolina colonies, aggressive, unidealistic men sought to exploit the region's resources. But Penn dreamed of inviting to his sylvan woods people of all religions and national backgrounds and blending them together in peaceful coexistence. His state would claim no authority over the consciences of its citizens nor demand military service of them.

The Quakers who began streaming into Pennsylvania in 1682 quickly absorbed earlier Dutch, Finnish, and Swedish settlers. Primarily farmers, they fanned out from the capital city of Philadelphia. They participated in the government by electing representatives, who initiated laws (which also required the approval of the proprietary governor, Penn's appointee, and his council). Like colonists elsewhere, they avidly acquired land, purchasing it from Penn at reasonable rates. But unlike other colonizers, the Quakers practiced pacifism, holding the ethic of love and nonresistance embodied in the Sermon on the Mount as literally binding on them.

Even before arriving, Penn laid the foundation for peaceful relations with the Delaware tribe inhabiting his colony. He wrote to the Delaware chiefs: "The king of the Country where I live, hath given me a great Province; but I desire to enjoy it with your Love and Consent, that we may always live together as Neighbors and friends." In this single statement Penn dissociated himself from the entire history of European colonization in the New World and from the widely held negative view of Indians. Recognizing the Indians as the rightful owners of the land included in his grant, Penn pledged not to sell one acre until he had first purchased it from local chiefs. He also promised strict regulation of the Indian trade and a ban on the sale of alcohol. Voltaire was later moved to write, although not

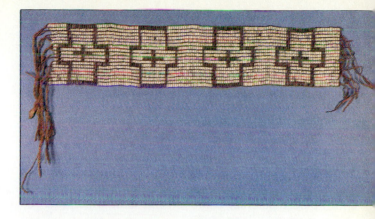

Just as a deed finalized a land exchange to Europeans, the wampum belt signified an agreement to the Indians. This Lenape belt, made of leather and simple shell beads, is said to have been given to William Penn at the signing of the Treaty of Shackamaxon in 1683.

with strict accuracy, that this was "the only league between those [Indian] nations and the Christians that was never sworn to, and never broken."

The Quaker accomplishment is sometimes disparaged with the claim that there was little competition for land in eastern Pennsylvania between the natives and the newcomers. However, a comparison between Pennsylvania and South Carolina, both established after the restoration of Charles II to the English throne in 1660, shows the power of pacifism. A quarter century after initial settlement, Pennsylvania had a population of about 20,000 whites. Penn's peaceful policy had so impressed Native American tribes that Indian refugees began migrating into Pennsylvania from all sides. During the same 25 years, South Carolina had grown to only about 4,000 whites, but the area had become a cauldron of violence. Carolinians spread arms through the region to facilitate slave dealing, shipped some 10,000 members of local tribes off to New England and the West Indies as slaves, and laid waste to the Spanish mission frontier in Florida.

As long as the Quaker philosophy of pacifism and friendly relations with the Delawares and Susquehannocks held sway, interracial relations in the Delaware River valley contrasted sharply with those in other parts of North America. Long after Penn left his colony in 1701, the native people cherished in tradition his fair treatment and genuine regard for them. Ironically, the Quaker policy of toleration, liberal government, and exemption from military service attracted to the colony, especially in the eighteenth century, thousands of immigrants whose land hunger and disdain for Indians undermined Quaker trust and friendship. Germans and Scots-

Irish flooded in, swelling the population to 31,000 by 1720. Neither of these groups shared Quaker idealism about racial harmony. Driven from their homelands by hunger and war, they cared only about tilling the soil in Pennsylvania. Pressing inland, they encroached on the lands of the local tribes, sometimes encouraged by the land agents of Penn's heirs. This created conflict with the natives who had sought sanctuary in Pennsylvania. By the mid-eighteenth century, a confrontation of displaced persons, some red and some white, was occurring in Pennsylvania.

Building the Peaceable Kingdom

Although Pennsylvania came closer to matching its founder's goals than any other European colony, Penn's dream of a society that banished violence, religious intolerance, and arbitary authority never completely materialized. Nor was he able to convince people to settle in compact villages, which he believed necessary for his "holy experiment." The plain Quaker farmers scattered across the countryside and built simple farmsteads. Instead of agricultural villages with meetinghouses at their centers, as in New England, they created open country networks without any particular centers or boundaries. Yet a sense of common endeavor persisted.

While Penn's official settlement policies carried "no more weight than the East Wind," Quaker farmers prized family life and emigrated almost entirely in kinship groups. At first, people from the same region clustered together—the Welsh in "the Welsh tract," the Rhinelanders in Germantown, the Cheshire immigrants in Chester County. In time, intermarriage and sale of land to newcomers created a patchwork of national and religious groups across Pennsylvania's countryside. The Quakers maintained their distinctive identity, however, allowing marriage only within their society, carefully providing land for their offspring, and guarding against too great a population increase (which would cause too rapid a division of farms) by limiting the size of their families.

Settled by religiously dedicated farming families and favored by rich grainlands, Pennsylvania's countryside blossomed. The colony avoided the "starving period" known in other areas and achieved economic success from the beginning. The colony's port capital of Philadelphia also grew rapidly. By 1700, it had overtaken New York City in population, and a half century later it was the largest city in the

colonies, bustling with a wide range of artisans, merchants, and professionals.

The Limits of Perfectionism

In spite of commercial success and peace with Native Americans, not all was harmonious in early Pennsylvania. Promotional literature described a "precious harmony" in meetings of the legislature and a "heavenly authority" that bound settlers in common purpose. But in reality, political affairs were often turbulent.

In part, dissension arose because of Pennsylvania's weak leadership. Penn was a much-loved proprietor, but he did not tarry long in his colony to guide its course. He returned to England in 1684, visited his colony briefly in 1700, and then left forever. The leadership vacuum he left was never filled.

A more important cause of disunity resided in the Quaker attitude toward authority. In England, balking at authority was almost a daily part of Quaker life. To be a Quaker was to refuse to bear arms, to disobey the law prohibiting nonconformists to hold religious services, to deny the Bible as revealed truth, to reject the traditional role assigned women, and to violate social custom obliging inferiors to defer to their superiors. The Quaker was the supremely "inner-directed" person, fired by an apocalyptic view of the world and bound to other Quakers by decades of persecution.

In Pennsylvania, the absence of persecution eliminated a crucial binding element. In their own colony, Quakers had no need to cling together in mutual defense. The factionalism that developed among them demonstrated that people never unify so well as when under attack. Rather than looking inward and banding together, they looked outward to an environment filled with opportunity. Their squabbling filled Penn with dismay. Why, he asked, were his settlers so "governmentish, so brutish, so susceptible to scurvy quarrels that break out to the disgrace of the Province?"

Pennsylvania proved to be different from other colonies in several but not all respects. The Quaker immigrants were just as eager to acquire land and build an estate as their Puritan counterparts. In fact, Quaker industriousness and frugality led to such material success that after a generation, social radicalism and religious evangelicalism began to fade. As in other colonies, settlers discovered the door to prosperity wide open and surged across the threshold.

PENNS TREATY with the INDIANS, made 1681 with out an Oath, and never broken. The foundation of Religious and Civil LIBERTY, in the U.S. of AMERICA.

Edward Hicks's Penn's Treaty with the Indians *was painted in the nineteenth century and is a romanticized version of the Treaty of Shackamaxon by which the Lenape Indians ceded the site of Philadelphia to Penn. The treaty was actually made in 1682, but Hicks was correct in implying that the Lenape held Penn in high regard for his fair treatment of them.*

Where Pennsylvania differed from New England and the South was in its relations with Native Americans, at least for the first few generations. It also departed from the Puritan colonies in its immigration policy. Pennsylvania, it is said, was the first community since the Roman Empire to allow people of different national origins and religious persuasions to live together under the same government on terms of near equality. English, Highland Scots, French, Germans, Irish, Welsh, Swedes, Finns, and Swiss all settled in Pennsylvania. This ethnic mosaic was further complicated by a medley of religious groups, including Mennonites, Lutherans, Dutch Reformed, Quakers, Baptists, Anglicans, Presbyterians, Catholics, Jews, and a sprinkling of mystics. Their relations may not always have been friendly, but few attempts were made to discriminate against dissenting groups. Pennsylvanians thereby laid the foundations for the pluralism that was to become the hallmark of American society.

CONCLUSION
The Achievement of New Societies

Nearly 200,000 immigrants who had left their European homelands reached the coast of North America in the seventeenth century. Coming from a variety of social backgrounds and spurred by different motivations, they represented the rootstock of distinctive societies that would mature in the North American colonies of England, France, Holland, and Spain. For three generations, North America served as a social laboratory for religious and social visionaries, political theorists, fortune seekers, social outcasts, and most of all, ordinary men and women seeking a better life than they had known in their European homelands.

Nearly three-quarters of them came to the Chesapeake and Carolina colonies. Most of them found this region a burial ground rather than an arena of opportunity. Disease, stunted family life, and the harsh work regimen imposed by the planters who commanded the labor of the vast majority ended the dreams of most who came. Yet population inched upward, and the bone and sinew of a workable economy formed. In the northern colonies, to which the fewest immigrants came, life was more secure. Organized around family and community, favored by a healthier climate, and motivated by religion and social vision, the Puritan and

Quaker societies thrived. Utopian expectations were never completely fulfilled. But nowhere else in the Western world at that time could they even have been attempted. What did succeed was the rooting of agricultural life based on family farms and the establishment of locally oriented political institutions marked by widespread participation. Thus, as the seventeenth century progressed, the scattered settlements along the North American coast, largely isolated from one another, as well as a few inland French and Spanish settlements, pursued their separate paths of development.

Recommended Reading

The early settlement of the Chesapeake is the subject of much exciting recent research. Among the older treatments, the soundest is Wesley F. Craven, The Southern Colonies in the Seventeenth Century (1949). Newer works include Edmund S. Morgan, American Slavery, American Freedom: The Ordeal of Colonial Virginia (1975); Thad W. Tate and David L. Ammerman, eds., The Chesapeake in the Seventeenth Century (1979); David B. Quinn, ed., Early Maryland in a Wider World (1982); Gloria L. Main, Tobacco Colony: Life in Early Maryland (1982); and Darrett B. Rutman and Anita H. Rutman, A Place in Time: Middlesex County, Virginia, 1650–1750 (1984).

A good introduction to English Puritanism is Christopher Hill, Society and Puritanism in Pre-Revolutionary England, 2d ed. (1967). Perry Miller's Errand into the Wilderness (1956) introduces the intellectual history of New England's leaders. For information on the Puritans in their early New England communities, consult David G. Allen, In English Ways (1981); John Demos, A Little Commonwealth (1970); Kenneth Lockridge, A New England Town (1970); Philip Greven, Jr., Four Generations (1970); Stephen Innes, Labor in a New Land (1983); and Darrett B. Rutman, Winthrop's Boston (1965). Illuminating biographies of early Puritan leaders are Edmund S. Morgan, The Puritan Dilemma: The Story of John Winthrop (1958); Richard S. Dunn, Puritans and Yankees (1962); and Robert Middlekauff, The Mathers (1971). For rich analyses of Puritan-Indian relations, see Neal Salisbury, Manitou and Providence (1982); William Cronon, Changes in the Land: Indians, Colonists, and the Ecology of New England (1983); Francis Jennings, The Invasion of America

(1975); Karen Ordahl Kupperman, Settling with the Indians, (1981); and James Axtell, The Invasion Within (1985).

Proprietary New York and Carolina are treated in Robert C. Ritchie, The Duke's Province (1977); Allen W. Trelease, Indian Affairs in Colonial New York (1960); Michael Kammen, Colonial New York (1975); M. Eugene Sirmans, Colonial South Carolina (1966); Verner Crane, The Southern Frontier, 1670–1732 (1929); and Robert M. Weir, Colonial South Carolina (1983).

Quaker Pennsylvania is the subject of Frederick B. Tolles, Meeting House and Counting House: The Quaker Merchants of Colonial Philadelphia (1948), and Gary B. Nash, Quakers and Politics (1968).

On indentured servitude, which played such an important role in the early colonies, see David Galenson, White Servitude in Colonial America (1981), and Sharon V. Salinger, "To Serve Well and Faithfully": Labor and Indentured Servitude in Pennsylvania (1987).

TIME LINE

1590 Roanoke Island colony fails

1607 Jamestown settled

1616–1621 Native American population in New England decimated by European diseases

1617 First tobacco crop shipped from Virginia

1619 First Africans arrive in Jamestown

1620 Pilgrims land at Plymouth

1622 Powhatan tribes attack Virginia settlements

1624 Dutch colonize mouth of Hudson River

1630 Puritan migration to Massachusetts Bay

1632 Maryland grant to Lord Baltimore (George Calvert)

1633–1634 Native Americans in New England again struck by European diseases

1635 Roger Williams banished to Rhode Island

1636 Anne Hutchinson exiled to Rhode Island

1637 New England wages war against the Pequot tribe

1642–1649 English Civil War ends great migration to New England

1643 Confederation of New England

1659 Two Quaker men hanged on Boston Common

1660 Restoration of King Charles II in England

1663 Carolina charter granted to eight proprietors

1664 English capture New Netherland and rename it New York
Royal grant of the Jersey lands to proprietors

1681 William Penn receives Pennsylvania grant

3

Mastering the New World

Anthony Johnson, an African, arrived in Virginia in 1621 with only the name "Antonio." Caught as a young man in the Portuguese slave-trading net, he had passed from one trader to another in the New World until he reached Virginia. There he was purchased by Richard Bennett and sent to work at Warrasquoke, Bennett's tobacco plantation situated on the James River. In the next year, Antonio was brought face to face with the world of triracial contact and conflict that would shape the remainder of his life. On March 22, 1622, the Powhatan tribes of tidewater Virginia fell upon the white colonizers in a determined attempt to drive them from the land. Of the 57 persons on the Bennett plantation, only black Antonio and four others survived.

Antonio—anglicized to Anthony—labored on the Bennett plantation for some 20 years, slave in fact if not in law, for legally defined bondage was still in the formative stage. During this time he married Mary, another African trapped in the labyrinth of servitude, and fathered four children. In the 1640s, Anthony and Mary Johnson gained their freedom after half a lifetime of servitude. Probably at this point they chose the surname Johnson to signify their new status. Already past middle age, the Johnsons began carving out a niche for themselves on Virginia's eastern shore. By 1650, they owned 250 acres, a small herd of cattle, and two black servants. In a world in which racial boundaries were not yet firmly marked, the Johnsons had entered the scramble of small planters for economic security.

By schooling themselves in the workings of the English legal process, carefully cultivating white patronage, and working industriously on the land, the Johnsons gained their freedom, acquired property, established a family, warded off contentious neighbors, and hammered out a decent existence. But by the late 1650s, as the lines of racial slavery tightened, the customs of the country began closing in on Virginia's free blacks.

In 1664, convinced that ill winds were blowing away the chances for their children and grandchildren in Virginia, the Johnsons began selling their land to white neighbors. The following spring, most of the clan moved north to Maryland, where they rented land and again took up farming and cattle raising. Five years later,

Anthony Johnson died, leaving four children and his wife. The growing racial prejudice of Virginia followed Johnson beyond the grave. A jury of white men in Virginia declared that because Johnson "was a Negroe and by consequence an alien," the 50 acres he had deeded to his son Richard before moving to Maryland should be awarded to a local white planter.

Johnson's children and grandchildren, born in America, could not duplicate the modest success of the African-born patriarch. By the late seventeenth century, people of color faced much greater difficulties in extricating themselves from slavery. When they did, they found themselves forced to the margins of society. Anthony's sons never rose higher than tenant farmer or small freeholder. John Johnson moved farther north into Delaware in the 1680s, following a period of great conflict with Native Americans in the Chesapeake region. Members of his family married local Indians and became part of a triracial community that has survived to the present day. Richard Johnson stayed behind in Virginia. When he died in 1689, just after a series of colonial insurrections connected with the overthrow of James II in England, he had little to leave his four sons. They became tenant farmers and hired servants, laboring on plantations owned by whites. By now, in the early eighteenth century, slave ships were pouring Africans into Virginia and Maryland to replace white indentured servants, the backbone of the labor force for four generations. To be black had at first been a handicap. Now it became a fatal disability, an indelible mark of degradation and bondage.

astering the North American environment involved several processes that would echo down the corridors of American history. Prominent among them were the molding of an African labor force and the gradual subjection of Native American tribes who contested white expansion. Both developments occurred in the lifetimes of Anthony and Mary Johnson and their children. Both involved a level of violence that made this frontier of European expansion not a zone of pioneer equality and freedom but one of growing inequality and servitude.

This chapter surveys the fluid, conflict-filled era from 1675 to 1715, a time when five overlapping struggles for mastery occurred. First, in determining to build a slave labor force, the colonists struggled to establish their mastery over resistant African captives. Second, the settlers sought mastery over Native American tribes, both those that stood in the way of white expansion and those that were their trading and military partners. Third, the colonists resisted the attempts of English imperial administrators to bring them into a more dependent relationship. Fourth, within colonial societies, emerging elites struggled to establish their claims to political and social authority. Finally, the colonizers, aided by England, strove for mastery over French, Dutch, and Spanish contenders in North America.

BLACK BONDAGE

For almost four centuries after Columbus's voyages to the New World, European colonizers forcibly transported Africans out of their homelands and used their labor to produce wealth in their colonies. Estimates vary widely, but the number of Africans brought to the New World was probably not less than 12 million. Millions more lost their lives while being marched from the African interior to coastal trading forts or during the passage across the Atlantic. Of all the immigrants who peopled the New World between the fifteenth and eighteenth centuries, the Africans were by far the most numerous, probably outnumbering Europeans two to one.

European slave traders carried a large majority of the slaves to the West Indies, Brazil, and Spanish America. Fewer than one out of every 20 reached North America, which remained a fringe area for slave traders until the eighteenth century. Yet those who came to the American colonies, about 10,000 in the seventeenth century and 350,000 in the eighteenth, profoundly affected the destiny of American society. In a prolonged period of labor scarcity, their labor and skills were indispensable to colonial economic development. Their African culture mixed continuously with that of their European masters. And the race relations that grew out of slavery so deeply marked society that the problem of race has continued ever since to be the "American dilemma."

The Slave Trade

The African slave trade did not begin as a part of the colonization of the Americas but rather as an attempt to fill a labor shortage in the Mediterranean world. As early as the eighth century, Arab and Moorish traders had driven slaves across Saharan caravan trails for delivery to Mediterranean ports. Seven centuries later, Portuguese merchants became the first Europeans involved in the slave trade. Reaching the west coast of Africa by water, they began buying slaves captured by other Africans and transporting them home by ship. These slaves were mostly criminals consigned to bondage in their own society or unfortunate individuals captured in tribal wars.

Origins and Destinations of African Slaves, 1526–1810

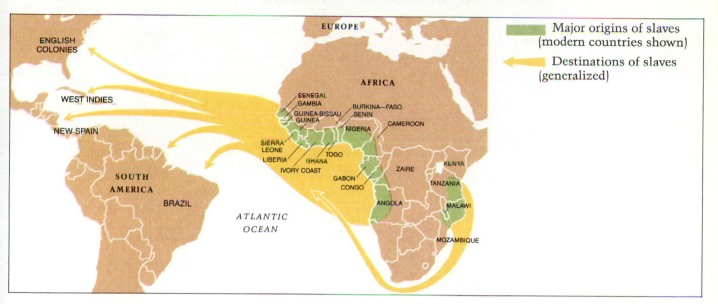

More than anything else, sugar transformed the African slave trade. For centuries, sugarcane had been grown in the Mediterranean countries to sweeten the diet of the wealthy. As its popularity grew, the center of production shifted to Portuguese Madeira, an island off the coast of Africa. Here in the sixteenth century, a European nation for the first time established an overseas colony organized around slave labor. From Madeira the cultivation of sugar spread to Portuguese Brazil and Spanish Santo Domingo. By the seventeenth century, with Europeans developing a taste for sugar almost as insatiable as their craving for tobacco, they vied fiercely for possession of the tiny islands dotting the Caribbean and for control of the trading forts on the West African coast. African kingdoms, eager for European trade goods, warred against each other in order to supply the "black gold" demanded by white ship captains.

Many European nations competed for trading rights on the West African coast. In the seventeenth century, when about 1 million Africans were brought to the New World, the Dutch replaced the Portuguese as the major supplier. The English, meanwhile, hardly counted in the slave trade. Not until the 1690s, when they began their century-long rise to maritime greatness, did the English challenge the Dutch. But by the 1790s, the English were the foremost slave-trading nation in Europe.

In the eighteenth century, European traders carried at least 6 million Africans to the Americas, probably the greatest forced migration in history. By this time African slave labor figured so importantly in the colonial world that one Englishman called slavery "the strength and the sinews of this western world."

Even the most vivid accounts of the slave trade cannot convey the pain and demoralization that accompanied the initial capture and subsequent march to slave-trading forts on the West African coast or the dreaded passage across the Atlantic. Olaudah Equiano, an eighteenth-century Ibo from what is now Nigeria, described how raiders from another tribe kidnapped him and his younger sister when he was only 11 years old. He passed from one trader to another while being marched to the coast. Many slaves attempted suicide or died from exhaustion or hunger on these forced marches. But Equiano survived. Reaching the coast, he encountered the next humiliation, confinement in barracoons, fortified enclosures on the beach where a surgeon from an English slave ship inspected him. Equiano was terrified by the light skins, language, and long hair of the English and was convinced that he "had got into a world of bad spirits and that they were going to kill me."

More cruelties followed. European traders often branded the African slaves they purchased with a

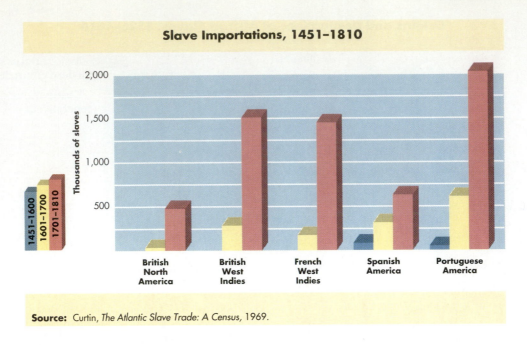

Slave Importations, 1451–1810

Thousands of slaves

1451–1600 | 1601–1700 | 1701–1810

British North America | British West Indies | French West Indies | Spanish America | Portuguese America

Source: Curtin, *The Atlantic Slave Trade: A Census,* 1969.

hot iron to indicate which company had procured them. The next trauma came with the ferrying of slaves in large canoes to the ships anchored in the harbor. An English captain recounted the desperation of Africans who were about to lose touch with their ancestral homeland and embark upon a vast unknown ocean. "The Negroes are so loath to leave their own country, that they have often leaped out of the canoes, boat and ship, into the sea, and kept under the water till they were drowned."

Conditions aboard the slave ships were miserable, even though the traders' goal was to deliver alive as many slaves as possible to the other side of the Atlantic. Equiano recounted the scene below decks, where manacled slaves crowded together like corpses in coffins. "With the loathsomeness of the stench, and crying together, I became so sick and low that I was not able to eat, nor had I the least desire to taste anything." The refusal to take food was so common that ship captains devised special techniques to cope with slaves who were determined to starve themselves to death rather than reach the New World in chains. Slavers flogged their captives brutally and applied hot coals to their lips. If this did not suffice, they employed a specially devised mouth wrench to pry apart the jaws of resistant Africans for forced feeding.

The Atlantic passage usually took four to eight weeks. It was so physically depleting and psychologically wrenching that one of every seven captives died en route. Many others arrived in the Americas deranged or near death. In all, the relocation of any African may have averaged about six months from the time of capture to the time of arrival at the plantation of a colonial buyer. During this protracted personal crisis, the slave was completely cut off from the moorings of a previous life—language, family and friends, tribal religion, familiar geography, and status in a local community. Still facing these victims of the European demand for cheap labor was adaptation to a new physical environment, a new language, a new work routine, and a life of unending bondage for themselves and their children.

The Southern Transition to Black Labor

Although they were familiar with Spanish, Dutch, Portuguese, and French use of black slaves, English colonists on the mainland of North America turned only slowly to Africa to solve their labor problem. Like other Europeans, they first regarded Native Americans as the obvious source of labor. But European diseases ravaged native societies, and Indians, more at home in the environment than the white colonizer, proved difficult to subjugate. Indentured white labor proved the best way to meet the demand for labor during most of the seventeenth century. Beginning in 1619, a small number of Af-

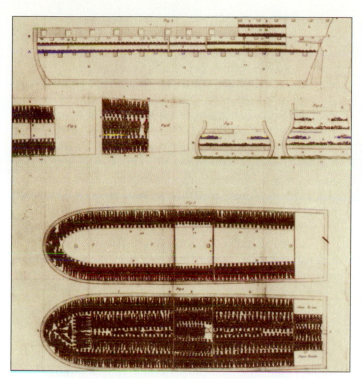

Diagrams such as this, useful to captains wishing to take advantage of "tight packing," were printed as late as the nineteenth century.

One of the most dehumanizing aspects of slavery was the auctioning of newly arrived Africans at dockside.

ricans entered Virginia and Maryland to labor in the tobacco fields alongside white servants. But as late as 1671, when some 30,000 slaves toiled in English Barbados, fewer than 3,000 served in Virginia. They were still outnumbered there at least three to one by white indentured servants.

The transformation of the southern labor force from one in which many whites and a few black servants labored side by side to one in which black slaves performed most of the field labor began only in the last quarter of the seventeenth century. Three reasons explain this shift. First, the rising commercial power of England, at the expense of the Spanish and Dutch, swelled English participation in the African slave trade. Beginning in the 1680s, southern planters could purchase slaves more readily and cheaply than before. Second, the supply of white servants from England began drying up. Those who did arrive fanned out among a growing number of colonies. Finally, white servant unrest and a growing population of ex-servants who were landless, discontented, and potential challengers to established white planters led the southern elite to welcome a more pliable labor force. Consequently, by the 1730s, the number of white indentured servants had dwindled to insignificance. Black hands, not white, tilled and harvested Chesapeake tobacco and Carolina rice. Nothing had greater priority in start-

ing a plantation than procuring slave labor. "If any one designs to make a plantation in this province," wrote Thomas Nairne from South Carolina in 1710, "the first thing to be done is, after having cut down a few trees, to split palisades or clapboards and therewith make small houses or huts to shelter the slaves."

In enslaving Africans, English colonists merely copied their European rivals in the New World. Making it all the more natural for American planters to adopt this labor system was the precedent their countrymen had set in the English West Indies. From the 1630s onward, the English imported Africans in droves in Barbados, Jamaica, and the Leeward Islands. Through brutal repression, they molded them into a sugar-producing slave labor force. Human bondage would later become the subject of intense moral debate. But in the seventeenth century, all but a few whites readily accepted it.

Slavery in the Northern Colonies

Slavery never became the foundation of the northern colonial work force, for labor-intensive crops such as sugar and rice would not grow in colder climates. On the smaller family farms, household labor and occasional hired hands sufficed. Only in the cities, where slaves worked as artisans and domestic servants, and in a few scattered rural areas did slavery take substantial root.

Although the northern colonists employed few slaves, their economies were becoming enmeshed in the commercial network of the Atlantic basin, which depended on slavery and the slave trade. New England's merchants eagerly pursued profits in the slave trade as early as the 1640s, when their ships began supplying Barbados with Africans. By 1676, New England slavers were packing their holds with slaves from Madagascar, off the coast of East Africa, and transporting them 6,000 miles to the western side of the Atlantic. Rhode Island became so involved in the dirty business that by 1750 half the merchant fleet of Newport reaped profits from carrying human cargo. In New York and Philadelphia, building and outfitting slave vessels proved profitable.

New England's involvement in the international slave trade deepened with the growth of its seaports as centers for the distilling of rum—the "hot, hellish and terrible liquor." Made from West Indian sugar, rum became one of the principal commodities traded for slaves on the African coast. As the number of slaves to be fed in the Caribbean multiplied— from about 50,000 in 1650 to 500,000 in 1750—the West Indies became a favorite market for the codfish hauled in by new England's extensive fishing fleet. Wheat from the middle colonies and barrel staves and hoops from North Carolina also fed into the slave-based West Indies economy. Hence, as the plantation South became most directly involved in an international system of racial exploitation, every other North American colony also participated in it.

The System of Bondage

The first Africans brought to the American colonies came as bound servants. They served for a number of years; then, like Anthony and Mary Johnson, many of them eventually gained their freedom. Once released, they could own land, hire out their labor, and move as they pleased. Their children, like those of white indentured servants, were born free. Gradually during the seventeenth century, Chesapeake planters began to draw tighter lines around the activities of black servants. By the 1640s, Virginia forbade blacks, free or bound, to carry firearms. In the 1660s, marriages between white women and black servants were called "shameful matches" and "the disgrace of our Nation." Bit by bit, white

settlers strengthened the association between black skin and slave status.

By the mid-seventeenth century, most white colonists were convinced that perpetual bondage was the appropriate status for black servants. By the end of the century, when incoming Africans increased from a trickle to a torrent, even the small number of free blacks found themselves pushed to the margins of society. Slavery, which had existed for centuries in many societies as the lowest social status, was becoming in the Americas a racial caste reserved for those with black skin. Step by step, white society transformed the black servant from human being to chattel.

In this dehumanization of Africans, which the English largely copied from their colonial rivals, the key step was instituting hereditary lifetime service. Once servitude became perpetual, relieved only by death, the elimination of all other privileges followed quickly. When the slave condition of the mother legally fell upon the black infant (not the case in other forms of slavery, such as in Africa), slavery became self-perpetuating, passing automatically from one generation to the next.

Slavery existed not only as a system of forced labor but also as a pattern of human relationships eventually legitimated by law. By the early eighteenth century, most provincial legislatures were enacting laws for controlling black rights and activities. Borrowed largely from the statute books of England's Caribbean colonies, these "black codes" forced Africans into an ever more limited world. Slaves were forbidden to testify in court, engage in commercial activity, hold property, participate in the political process, congregate in public, travel without permission, or engage in legal marriage or parenthood. Nearly stripped of human status, they became defined as a form of property. Restraints on the master's freedom to deal with his slave property in any way he saw fit gradually disappeared.

Eliminating all slave rights had both pragmatic and psychological dimensions. Every black man and woman in chains was a potential rebel. So the rapid increase in the slave population brought anxious demands to bring slaves under strict control. The desire to stifle black rebelliousness mingled with a need to justify brutal behavior toward slaves by defining them as less than human. "The planters," wrote one Englishman in Jamaica, "do not want to be told that their Negroes are human creatures. If they believe them to be of human kind, they cannot regard them as no better than dogs or horses."

Defining slaves in nonhuman terms involved one of the great paradoxes of modern history. Many Old World immigrants imagined the Americas as a liberating and regenerating arena. Yet the opportunity to exploit its resources led to a historic world process by which masses of people were wrenched from their homelands and forced into a system of slavery that could be maintained only by increasing intimidation and brutality.

SLAVE CULTURE

The basic struggle for Africans toiling on plantations 5,000 miles from their homes was to create strategies for living as satisfactorily as possible despite horrifying treatment. The master hoped to convert the slave into a mindless drudge who obeyed every command and worked efficiently for his profit. But the attempt to cow slaves rarely succeeded completely. Masters could set the external boundaries of existence for their slaves, controlling physical location, work roles, diet, and shelter. But the authority of the master class impinged far less on how slaves established friendships, fell in love, formed kin groups, raised children, worshiped their gods, buried their dead, and organized their leisure time.

In these aspects of daily life, slaves in America drew on their African heritage to shape their existence to some degree. In doing so, they laid the foundations for an Afro-American culture. At first, this culture had many variations because slaves came from many areas in Africa and lived under different conditions in the colonies. But common elements emerged, led by developments in the South, where about 90 percent of American slaves labored in the colonial period.

The Growth of Slavery

In contrast to other areas of the New World, in North America Africans reached a relatively healthy environment. The West Indies became a graveyard for both whites and blacks. In South America, tropical diseases swept away slaves like leaves in a windstorm. In the southern American colonies, where the ghastly mortality of the early decades had subsided by the time Africans were arriving in large numbers, their chances for survival were much better. A simple comparison makes the point. Colonizers in Virginia and Jamaica each owned about 200,000 slaves in 1775. But to attain that number, more than three times as many Africans had been imported into Jamaica as into Virginia during the eighteenth century. This environmental advantage, combined with a more even sex ratio, led to a natural increase in the American slave population that was unparalleled elsewhere.

In 1675, about 4,000 slaves were scattered across Virginia and Maryland. Most were men. They toiled with their masters and a larger number of white indentured servants, clearing the land, planting, hoeing, and harvesting tobacco. A half century later, with the decline of white servitude, 45,000

This eighteenth-century watercolor depicts slaves in South Carolina dancing the "juba," a West African dance. The gourdlike banjo and the twisted leather drumsticks are of African design, reflecting the cultural heritage of Africa transplanted to the American colonies.

slaves labored on Chesapeake plantations. By 1760, when their number exceeded 185,000, the Chesapeake plantations relied almost entirely on black labor.

Although slave codes severely restricted the lives of slaves, the possibility for family life increased as the southern colonies matured. Larger plantations employed dozens and even hundreds of slaves, and the growth of roads and market towns permitted them greater opportunities to forge relationships beyond their own plantation. By the 1740s, a growing proportion of Chesapeake slaves were American-born, had established families, and lived in plantation outbuildings where from sundown to sunup they could fashion personal lives of their own.

In South Carolina, African slaves drew on agricultural skills they had practiced on the other side of the Atlantic and made rice the keystone of the coastal economy by the early eighteenth century. Their numbers increased rapidly, from about 4,000 in 1708 to 90,000 by 1760. Working mostly on large plantations in swampy lowlands, they endured the most life-sapping conditions on the continent. But in the coastal low country they outnumbered whites three to one by 1760 and hence were able to maintain more of their African culture than slaves in the Chesapeake. South Carolina, one European observed in 1737, "looks more like a negro country than like a country settled by white people." Many slaves spoke Gullah, a "pidgin" or mixture of several African languages. They often gave African names to their children, names like Cudjoe, Cuffe, Quashey, and Phibbi. And they kept alive their African religious customs.

In the northern colonies, where no labor shortage existed and the climate did not allow the cultivation of staple crops, slaves made up less than 10 percent of the population. They typically worked as artisans, farmhands, or personal servants. Mingled among them were occasional Indian slaves. Whereas about two-thirds of all southern slaves worked on plantations with at least ten of their fellows by the 1720s, in the North the typical slave labored alone or with only a few others. Living in the same house as the master, slaves adapted to European ways much faster than in the South, where the slave quarters were places for perpetuating African folkways. Slavery was also less repressive in the North than in the South. Slaves were more widely dispersed among the white population, and black-white contact was so extensive that African culture faded more quickly.

Slavery spread more extensively in the northern ports than across the countryside. Artisans found it profitable to invest in slaves whom they could work on a year-round basis. Ship captains purchased them for maritime labor. And an emerging urban elite of merchants, lawyers, and landlords displayed their wealth and status by employing slaves as liveried coachmen and house servants. By the beginning of the eighteenth century, more than 40 percent of New York City's households owned slaves. Even in Quaker Philadelphia, slaveholding increased sharply in the eighteenth century. Struggling white artisans resented slave workers for undercutting their wages, and the white citizenry felt threatened by potential black arsonists and rebels. Yet where labor demand was high, the desire for lifelong servants, who could be purchased for a mere two years of a free white laborer's wages, outweighed these reservations.

Resistance and Rebellion

While struggling to adapt to bondage in various regions of British America, slaves also resisted and rebelled in ways that constantly reminded their masters that slavery's price was eternal vigilance. Slave owners preferred to interpret rebelliousness as evidence of the "barbarous, wild savage natures" of Africans, as a South Carolina law of 1712 phrased it. Some planters, like Virginia's Landon Carter, believed that "slaves are devils and to make them free is to set devils free." But from the African point of view, the struggle against enslavement was essential to maintaining meaning and dignity in a life of degrading toil.

"Saltwater" Africans fresh from their homelands often resisted slavery fiercely. "You would really be surprised at their perseverance," wrote one observer. "They often die before they can be conquered." Commonly this initial resistance took the form of escaping to the frontier to began renegade settlements, to Indian tribes in the interior that sometimes offered refuge, or to Spanish Florida. Open rebellions, such as those in New York City in 1712 and at Stono, South Carolina, in 1739, mostly involved newly arrived slaves.

There was no North American parallel, however, for the massive slave uprisings that erupted periodically in the West Indies and Brazil. Nor was there an American parallel to the semistates in the South Atlantic sugar world, where runaway slaves built their own communities and resisted periodic assaults by colonial troops. Slaves had far better

The physical appearance of Africans captured the imaginations of some American artists. John Singleton Copley's Head of a Negro (left) *and John Greenwood's* Jersey Nanny (right) *depicted two slaves in the eighteenth century.*

chances to mount successful rebellions in these areas because they vastly outnumbered their masters and, in the case of Brazil, could flee to the rugged interior to join unconquered Indian tribes. "The greater number of blacks which a frontier has," remarked one colonist, "and the greater the disproportion is between them and her white people, the more danger she is liable to."

In North America, slaves rarely outnumbered whites except in South Carolina, and the master class tried to cultivate tension between local Indians and slaves so that they would be "a check upon each other," as one worried planter explained. When rebellion did occur, white colonizers stopped at nothing to quell it. They tried to intimidate all slaves by torturing, hanging, dismembering, and even burning captured rebels at the stake. After a rumored uprising was disclosed near Charleston, South Carolina, in 1740, for example, city officials tortured and hanged 50 blacks. Their decapitated heads, impaled on posts, gave warning to other potential insurrectionists. In New York City a year later, officials responded to a rumored insurrection by hanging 18 slaves and 4 whites and burning 13 other slaves at the stake.

Open rebelliousness often gave way to more subtle forms of resistance as slaves learned English, adjusted to the routines of shop, farm, and plantation, and began forming families. Dragging out the job, shamming illness, pretending ignorance, and breaking tools were strategies for avoiding physical exhaustion and also indirect forms of opposing slavery itself.

Slaves resisted more directly through truancy, arson directed against the master's barns and houses, crop destruction, pilfering to supplement their food supply, and direct assaults on masters, overseers, and drivers. Slave masters extracted labor and obedience from their slaves in an overall sense. If they had not, the slave system would have collapsed. But they did so only with difficulty. Masters learned that to push slaves too hard could be costly. One South Carolina planter drove his slaves late into the night cleaning and barreling a rice crop in 1732. When he awoke in the morning, he found his barn, with the entire harvest in it, reduced to ashes.

Black Religion and Family

Resistance and rebellion represented attacks on the institution of slavery. But the balance of power was always massively stacked against the slaves. Only the most desperate were willing to challenge the system directly. Of greater importance was the struggle of Afro-Americans to find meaning and worth in their existence, no matter how brutal and discouraging the slave system that manacled them,

In this quest, religion and family played a central role—one destined to continue far into the post-slavery period.

Africans brought a complex religious heritage to the New World. No amount of desolation or physical abuse could wipe out these deeply rooted beliefs. People enduring the daily travail that accompanied slavery typically turned for relief to their deepest emotional sources. Coming from cultures where the division between sacred and secular activities was less clear than in Europe, slaves made religion central to their existence. The black Christianity that emerged in the eighteenth century blended African religious practices with the religion of the master class. It laid the foundations for the black church that later became the central institution in Afro-American life.

Slave masters were not eager to see their slaves exposed to Christianity because of its potentially dangerous notions of brotherhood and its prohibition against enslaving other Christians. Yet Christianity's emphasis on meekness and obedience might restrain black rebelliousness. Gradually in the eighteenth century, slaves gained exposure to Christianity. They used it both to light the spark of resistance and to find comfort from oppression.

The religious revival that began in the 1720s in the northern colonies and spread southward thereafter made important contributions to Afro-American religion. Evangelicalism stressed personal rebirth, used music and body motion, and caught individuals up in an intense emotional experience. The dancing, shouting, rhythmic clapping, and singing that came to characterize slaves' religious expression represented a creative mingling of West African and Christian religions.

Besides religion, the slaves' greatest refuge from their dreadful fate lay in their families. In West Africa, all social relations were centered in kinship lines, which stretched backward to include dead ancestors. Torn from their native societies, slaves placed great importance on rebuilding extended kin groups.

Most English colonies prohibited slave marriages. But in practice, domestic life was an area in which slaves and masters struck a bargain. Masters found that slaves would work harder if they were allowed to form families. Moreover, family ties stood in the way of escape or rebellion, for few slaves wanted to leave loved ones at the mercy of an angry master. For their part, slaves valued family life so highly that they were willing to risk almost everything to secure the right to marry and parent children.

Slaves fashioned a family life only with difficulty, however. The general practice of importing three male slaves for every two females stunted family formation. Female slaves, much in demand, married in their late teens, but males usually had to wait until their mid- to late twenties. As natural increase swelled the slave population in the eighteenth century, however, the sex ratio became more even.

The sale of either husband or wife could abruptly sever their fragile union. Broken marriages were frequent, especially when a deceased planter's estate was divided among his heirs or his slaves were sold to his creditors to satisfy debts. Young children usually stayed with their mothers until about age 8; then they were frequently torn from their families through sale, often to small planters needing only a hand or two. Few slaves escaped separation from family members at some time during their lives.

White male exploitation of black women represented another assault on family life. How many black women were coerced or lured with favors into sexual relations with white masters and overseers cannot be known. But the sizable mulatto (racially mixed) population at the end of the eighteenth century indicates that the number was large. Interracial liaisons, frequently forced, were widespread, especially in the Lower South. In 1732, the *South-Carolina Gazette* called racial mixing an "epidemical disease." It was a malady that had traumatic effects on slave attempts to build stable relationships.

Not all interracial relationships were cruel. In some cases, black women sought the liaison to gain advantages for themselves or their children. These unions nonetheless threatened both the slave community and the white plantation ideal. They bridged the supposedly unbridgeable gap between slave and free society and produced children who plagued whites because they did not fit into the separate racial categories that the colonists wished to maintain.

Despite such obstacles, slaves fashioned intimate ties as husband and wife, parent and child. If monogamous relationships did not last as long as in white society, much of the explanation lies in the conditions of slave life: the shorter life span of Afro-Americans, the shattering of marriage through sale of one or both partners, and the call of freedom that impelled some slaves to run away.

While slave men struggled to preserve their family role, many black women assumed a position in the family that differed from that of white women. Plantation mistresses usually worked hard in helping to manage estates, but nonetheless the ideal grew that they should remain in the house to guard white virtue and set the standards for white culture. In contrast, the black woman remained indispensable to both the work of the plantation and the functioning of the slave quarters. She toiled in the fields and worked in the slave cabins. Paradoxically, black women's roles, which required constant labor, made them more equal to men than was the case of women in white society.

Above all, slavery was a set of power relationships designed to extract the maximum labor from its victims. Hence it regularly involved cruelties that filled family life with tribulation. But slaves in America were unusually successful in establishing families because they lived in a healthier environment, toiled in less physically exhausting circumstances than slaves on sugar and coffee plantations, and were better clothed, fed, and treated than Africans in the West Indies, Brazil, and other parts of the hemisphere. In these more tropical areas, plantation owners imported large numbers of male slaves, literally worked them to death, and then purchased replacements from Africa. Family life in the American colonies brimmed over with uncertainty and sorrow, but slaves nonetheless made it the greatest monument to their will to endure captivity and eventually gain their freedom.

THE STRUGGLE FOR LAND

In the same period that slavery gained a permanent foothold in North America, both New England and Virginia fought major wars against Native Americans. The desire for land, a cause of both wars, produced a similar conflict somewhat later in South Carolina. The conflicts brought widespread destruction to the towns of both colonizers and Indians, inflicted heavy human casualties, and left a legacy of bitterness on both sides. For the coastal tribes, it was a disastrous time of defeat and decline. For the colonists, the wars contributed to the turbulence of the late seventeenth and early eighteenth centuries. Sometimes they even overlapped, as in Virginia, with a struggle within white society for social and political control.

King Philip's War in New England

Following the Pequot War of 1637 in New England, the Wampanoags and Narragansetts, whose fertile land lay within the boundaries of Plymouth and Rhode Island, attempted to maintain their distance from the New England colonists. But the New Englanders coveted Indian territories. As they quarreled among themselves over provincial boundaries, they gradually reduced the Indians' land base.

By the 1670s, when New England's population had grown to about 50,000, younger Indians began brooding over their situation. Their leader, Metacomet (named King Philip by the English), was the son of Massasoit, the Wampanoag who had allied himself with the first Plymouth settlers in 1620. Metacomet had watched his older brother preside over the deteriorating position of his people after their father's death in 1661. A year later, Metacomet's brother died mysteriously while Plymouth officials questioned him about a rumored Indian con-

The Wampanoags led New England tribes in a tenacious campaign of resistance against the white settlers. Paul Revere engraved this picture of the Wampanoag chief Metacomet, called King Philip by the English.

spiracy. As the Wampanoag leader, Metacomet faced one humiliating challenge after another.

In 1671, Plymouth forced Metacomet to surrender a large stock of guns and accept a treaty of submission acknowledging Wampanoag subjection to English law. Convinced that more setbacks would follow and humiliated by the discriminatory treatment of Indians brought before English courts, Metacomet began recruiting for a resistance movement.

The triggering incident of King Philip's War was the trial of three Wampanoags who were dragged before a Puritan court for an act of tribal revenge against John Sassamon, a Christianized Indian educated at Harvard. Sassamon was a man caught between two cultures. Though he had fled white society after his college years; he warned the Plymouth government in 1675 that the Wampanoags were preparing a general attack on the English settlements. When Sassamon was found murdered shortly afterward, Plymouth officials produced an Indian who claimed he had witnessed the murder and could identify the felons. As a result, three Wampanoags swung at the end of English ropes in June 1675.

The execution of the three tribesmen was the catalyst, but the root cause of the war that erupted was the rising anger of the young Wampanoag males. As would happen repeatedly in the next two centuries as Americans pushed westward, these younger Native Americans refused to imitate their fathers, who had watched the colonizers erode their land base and compromise their sovereignty. Rather than put themselves under white authority, they attempted a pan-Indian offensive against an intruder with far greater numbers and a much larger arsenal of weapons. For the young tribesmen, revitalization of their ancient culture through war became as important a goal as defeating the enemy.

In the summer of 1675, the Wampanoags unleashed daring hit-and-run attacks on villages in the Plymouth colony. By autumn, many New England tribes, including the powerful Narragansetts, had joined King Philip's warriors. Towns all along the frontier reeled under Indian attacks. "We were too ready to think that we could easily suppress that flea," confessed John Eliot, who had worked to convert the Indians to Christianity, "but now we find that all the craft is in catching them, and that in the meantime they give us many a sore nip." By the time the first snow fell in November, mobile Indian warriors had laid waste to the entire upper Connecticut River Valley.

By March 1676, King Philip's forces were attacking less than 20 miles from Boston and Providence. Assumptions about English military superiority faded. Desperate to reverse the course of the war, New England officials passed America's first draft laws. Evasion was widespread, however, with eligible men—all those between 16 and 60—"skulking from one town to another." Political friction among the New England colonies also hampered a united counteroffensive.

King Philip's offensive faltered in the spring of 1676. Food shortages and disease sapped Indian strength, and the powerful Mohawks, with their own advantages in the fur trade to protect, refused to support the New England tribes. By summer, groups of Indians were surrendering, while some moved westward seeking shelter among other tribes. King Philip fell in a battle near the Wampanoag village in Rhode Island where the war began. The head of this "hell-hound, fiend, serpent, caitiff and dog," as one colonial leader branded him, was carried triumphantly back to Plymouth, where it remained on display for 25 years.

At war's end, several thousand colonists and perhaps twice as many Indians lay dead. Of some 90 Puritan towns, 52 had been attacked and 13 completely destroyed by the "tawny serpents." Some 1,200 homes lay in ruins, and 8,000 cattle were dead. The estimated cost of the war exceeded the value of all personal property in New England. Not for 40 years would the frontier advance beyond the line it had reached in 1675. Indian towns were devastated even more completely, including several of those inhabited by "praying Indians" who had converted to Christianity and allied with the whites. An entire generation of young men had been nearly annihilated. Many of the survivors, including Metacomet's wife and son, were sold into slavery in the West Indies.

Bacon's Rebellion Engulfs Virginia

While New Englanders fought local tribes in 1675 and 1676, the Chesapeake colonies became locked in a struggle involving both a war between the red and white populations and civil war within the colonizers' society. Before it ended, hundreds of whites and Indians lay dead in Virginia and Maryland, Virginia's capital of Jamestown lay smoldering, and English troops were crossing the Atlantic to suppress what the king labeled an outright rejection of his authority. This deeply tangled conflict was called Bacon's Rebellion after the head-strong Cambridge-educated planter Nathaniel Bacon, who arrived in Virginia at age 28.

Bacon and many other ambitious young planters detested the Indian policy of Virginia's royal governor, Sir William Berkeley. In 1646, at the end of the second Indian uprising against the Virginians, the Powhatan tribes had accepted a treaty granting them exclusive rights to territory north of the York River, beyond the limits of white settlement. Stable Indian relations suited the established planters, some of whom traded profitably with the Indians, but became obnoxious to new settlers arriving in the 1650s and 1660s. Nor did it please the white indentured servants who had served their time and were hoping to find cheap frontier land.

Land hunger and dissatisfaction with declining tobacco prices, rising taxes, and lack of opportunity erupted into violence in the summer of 1675. A group of frontiersmen used an incident with a local tribe as an excuse to attack the Susquehannocks, whose rich land they coveted. Governor Berkeley denounced the attack, but few supported his position. He faced, he said, "a people where six parts of seven at least are poor, indebted, discontented, and armed."

Although badly outnumbered, the Susquehannocks prepared for war. Virginians girded themselves for the southern version of what they heard was occurring in New England. Rumors swept the colony that the Susquehannocks were offering large sums to western Indian nations to join in attacking the colonists. Some even said that King Philip had formed a confederacy with the Chesapeake tribes.

Thirsting for revenge, the Susquehannocks attacked during the winter of 1675–1676 and killed 36 Virginians. That spring, the hot-blooded Nathaniel Bacon became the frontiersmen's leader. Joined by hundreds of runaway servants and some slaves, he launched a campaign of indiscriminate warfare on friendly and hostile Indians alike. When Governor Berkeley refused to sanction these attacks, Bacon ignored his authority. The governor then declared Bacon a rebel and sent out 300 militiamen to drag him to Jamestown for trial. Bacon headed into the wilderness for "a more agreeable destiny" and recruited more followers, including many substantial planters. Frontier skirmishes with Indians had turned into civil war.

During the summer of 1676, Bacon's and Berkeley's troops maneuvered around each other, while Bacon's men continued their forays against local Indian tribes. In one bold move, Bacon and his followers captured the capital at Jamestown. They razed the statehouse, church, and other buildings and put Governor Berkeley to flight across Chesapeake Bay.

Virginians at all levels had chafed under Berkeley's rule. High taxes, an increase in the governor's powers at the expense of local officials, and the monopoly that Berkeley and his friends held on the Indian trade were especially unpopular. This opposition surfaced in the summer of 1676 as Berkeley's and Bacon's troops pursued each other through the wilderness. Berkeley tried to rally public support by holding new assembly elections and extending the vote to all freemen, whether they owned property or not. The new assembly promptly turned on the governor, passing a set of reform laws intended to make government more responsive to the common people and to end rapacious officeholding. The assembly also made legal the enslavement of Native Americans.

Time was on the governor's side, however. Having crushed the Indians, Bacon's followers began drifting home to tend their crops. Meanwhile, Berkeley's reports of the rebellion brought the dispatch of 1,100 royal troops from England. By the time they arrived, in January 1677, Nathaniel Bacon lay dead of swamp fever and most of his followers had melted back into the frontier. After Bacon's death in October 1676, Berkeley rounded up 23 rebel leaders and hanged them without benefit of civil trial.

Royal investigators who arrived in 1677 remarked on the genocidal mentality of Bacon's followers, whom they denounced as the "inconsiderate sort of men who so rashly and causelessly cry up a war and seem to wish and aim at an utter extirpation of the Indians." Even a royal governor could not restrain such men, bent on pursuing their hopes of land ownership and independence. To them, Indians were only "wolves, tigers, and bears," as Bacon charged, "which daily destroyed our harmless and innocent lambs."

The hatred of Indians bred into white society during the war became a permanent feature of Virginia life. A generation later, in 1711, the legislature spurned the governor's plea for quieting the Indian frontier with a program of educational missions and regulated trade. Instead, the legislators voted military appropriations of £20,000 "for extirpating all Indians without distinction of Friends or Enemys." The remnants of the once populous Powhatan Con-

TOMBSTONES

Historians have used funeral orations, gravestone designs and inscriptions, and handbooks on how to die to gain insight into early American culture. Tombstone markings—"graven images," they have been called—provide a particularly fascinating body of evidence. At first, Puritans in New England marked their graves only with wooden rails and posts. But in the 1670s, carved headstones filled with symbolic images began to appear, and they became a regular feature of New England graveyards after that. Hardly any Puritan family thereafter, one historian noted, was "ready to commit its loved ones to the cold earth without an appropriate cluster of symbols hovering protectively over the grave." How the symbols carved on tombstones changed tells much about how people's attitudes and values shifted. "There is no better place in all New England to stand face to face with the past," it has been said, "than in the old burying grounds."

The tombstone shown here shows vividly the intensity with which Puritans faced death. To die was to be called to final account by a just and merciful God, and the way one died gave evidence of one's self-discipline and faith. The scrolled pediment on this gravestone signifies the doorway between earthly life and spiritual rebirth through which Joseph Tapping's relatives hoped he passed. The grim winged skull represents the soul of the dying man in transition. This death's-head motif was widely used on seventeenth-century gravestones. It conveys much of the Puritans' intense concern that life is transitory (note the hourglass) and that salvation is not automatically granted to those who believe in Christ. This emphasis on life as a preparation for afterlife is reinforced by the Latin mottoes on the right side of the stone: *Vive memor loethi* ("Live mindful of death") and *Fugit hora* ("The hour flies"). At bottom center of the stone is an image of Time fending off Death as Death tries to snuff out the candle of Life. Note Father Time's symbols— the hourglass and scythe—in the background.

The Puritans' fixation on death has also been noted in the elaborate and expensive funerals they often conducted and in the content of funeral sermons and handbooks on how to die well. In a popular book on advice for the young, *Token for Children,* published first in England in 1671 and in an American edition in 1700, James Janeway described the "Joy and holy Triumph" of a 12-year-old girl's death. As a model of faith in God's mercy, without yielding to pride or certainty of salvation in her last hours, this young girl

> spake with a holy Confidence in the Lord's Love to her Soul, and was not in the least daunted when she spake of her Death, but seemed greatly delighted in the Apprehension of her nearness to her Father's House: And it was not long before she was fill'd with Joy unspeakable in believing.

Also obsessed with death, but with a less joyful view, was Michael Wigglesworth's *Day of Doom* (1662), an account of the Judgment Day in verse intended to reinvigorate Puritan spirituality. *Day of Doom* was New England's first best-seller. The verses reprinted here may suggest why.

By the second quarter of the eighteenth century, attitudes toward death were changing, as the grave-

Joseph Tapping headstone, Boston, 1678

stone iconography after about 1730 attests. The epitaphs stressing mortality appeared much less frequently, and the ever-present foreboding death's-head, shovels, and hourglass symbols of the seventeenth century began to be replaced by smiling cherubs, angels, natural objects, and sentimentalized willow and urn motifs.

Note the details shown here from an eighteenth-century gravestone compared to those on the Tapping stone. A winged image of Mrs. Betsy Shaw (Plymouth, Massachusetts, 1795) optimistically represents the flight of her soul heavenward. This romantic design tells us much about the secularization of New England society and the passing of the early Puritans' intense seriousness about their godly mission in America to redeem humankind. As the funerary handiwork of stonecarvers reveals, the Puritans' early providential self-image had been transformed. Less piety and morbid introspection, more worldliness and individual hopefulness had spread through the Puritan Holy Commonwealth.

Betsy Shaw headstone, Plymouth, 1795

Can you point out how these changes are reflected on the Shaw and Tapping gravestones? What do the markings, inscriptions, and design of tombstones in cemeteries near you reveal about the changing experience and values of later Americans?

Michael Wigglesworth (1662)

56

Now it comes in, and every sin
  unto men's charge doth lay;
It judgeth them and doth condemn,
  though all the world say nay.
It so stingeth and tortureth,
  it worketh such distress,
That each man's self against himself
  is forced to confess.

57

It's vain moreover for men to cover
  the least iniquity;
The Judge hath seen, and privy been
  to all their villainy.
He unto light and open sight
  the work of darkness brings;
He doth unfold both new and old,
  both known and hidden things.

58

All filthy facts and secret acts,
  however closely done
And long concealed, are there revealed
  before the mid-day sun.
Deeds of the night, shunning the light,
  which darkest corners sought,
To fearful blame and endless shame
  are there most justly brought.

59

And as all facts and grosser acts,
  so every word and thought,
Erroneous notions and lustful motion,
  are unto judgment brought,
No sin so small and trivial
  but hither it must come,
Nor so long past, but now at last
  it must receive a doom. . . .

188

The Judge is strong; doers of wrong
  cannot his power withstand.
None can be flight run out of sight
  nor 'scape out of his hand.
Sad is their state, for advocate
  to plead their cause there's none—
None to prevent their punishment,
  or misery bemoan.

189

O dismal day! wither shall they
  for help and succor flee?
To God above, with hopes to move
  their greatest enemy?
His wrath is great, whose burning heat
  no floods of tears can slake:
His word stands fast, that they be cast
  into the burning lake.

federacy lost their last struggle for the world they had known. Now they moved farther west or submitted to a life on the margins of white society as tenant farmers, day laborers, or domestic servants.

After Bacon's Rebellion, an emerging planter aristocracy annulled most of the reform laws of 1676. But the war relieved much of the social tension among white Virginians. Newly available Indian land created fresh opportunities for small planters and former servants. Equally important, Virginians with capital to invest were turning from the impoverished rural villages of England and Ireland to the villages of West Africa to supply their labor needs. This halted the influx of poor white servants who, once free, had formed a discontented mass at the bottom of Chesapeake society. A racial consensus, uniting whites of different ranks in the common pursuit of a prosperous, slave-based economy, began to take shape.

North and south of Virginia, Bacon's Rebellion caused insurrectionary rumblings. Many of Bacon's compatriots took refuge after his death in North Carolina's Albemarle County, the "backside of Virginia." There they joined dissident tobacco farmers, who were distressed by recent Indian uprisings, export duties on tobacco, and quitrents controlled by a mercenary elite. Led by George Durant and John Culpeper, they drove the governor from office and briefly seized the reins of power.

In Maryland, Protestant settlers chafed under high taxes, quitrents, and officeholders regarded as venal, Catholic, or both. Declining tobacco prices and a fear of Indian attacks increased their touchiness. A month after Bacon razed Jamestown, insurgent small planters tried to seize the Maryland government. Two of their leaders were hanged for the attempt. In 1681, Josias Fendall and John Coode, "two rank Baconists" according to Lord Baltimore, led another abortive uprising. After their attempt to kidnap the Catholic proprietor failed, Fendall was executed and Coode banished from the colony.

In all three southern colonies, the volatility of late-seventeenth-century life owed much to the region's peculiar social development. Where family formation was retarded by imbalanced sex ratios and fearsome mortality, and where geographic mobility was high, little social cohesion or attachment to community could grow. Missing in the southern colonies were the stabilizing power of mature local institutions, a vision of a larger purpose, and the presence of experienced and responsive political leaders.

AN ERA OF INSTABILITY

A dozen years after the major Indian wars in New England and Virginia, a series of insurrections and a major witchcraft incident rumbled through colonial society. The rebellions were triggered by the Revolution of 1688, known to Protestants in England thereafter as the Glorious Revolution because it ended forever the notion that kings ruled by a God-given "divine right" and marked the last serious Catholic challenge to Protestant supremacy. But these colonial disruptions also signified a struggle for social and political dominance in the expanding colonies, as did the Salem witchcraft trials in Massachusetts.

Organizing the Empire

From the earliest attempts at colonization, the English assumed that overseas settlements existed to promote the national interest at home. According to this mercantilist theory, colonies served as outlets for English manufactured goods, provided foodstuffs and raw materials, stimulated trade (and hence promoted a larger merchant navy), and contributed to the royal coffers by paying duties on exported commodities such as sugar and tobacco. Colonies benefited by the military protection and guaranteed markets provided by England.

England proceeded slowly in the seventeenth century to regulate its colonies and mold them into a unified empire. A first small step was taken in 1621, when the king's council forbade tobacco growers to export their crop to anywhere but England. Three years later, when the Virginia Company of London plunged into bankruptcy, the crown made Virginia a royal colony, the first of many. However, not until 1651, when the colonists traded freely with the commercially aggressive Dutch, did Parliament consider regulating colonial affairs. It passed a navigation act requiring that English or colonial ships, manned by English or colonial sailors, carry all goods entering England, Ireland, and the colonies, no matter where those goods originated. These first steps toward a regulated empire were also the first steps to place England's power behind national economic development.

In 1660, after the monarchy was restored, Parliament passed a more comprehensive navigation act that listed colonial products (tobacco, sugar, indigo, dyewoods, cotton) that could be shipped only to England or to other English colonies. Like its predecessor, the act took dead aim at Holland's domination of Atlantic commerce while increasing England's revenues by imposing duties on the enumerated articles. In the following decades, other navigation acts closed loopholes in the 1660 law and added other enumerated articles. Nevertheless, this regulation bore lightly on the colonists because the laws lacked enforcement mechanisms.

After 1675, international competition and war led England to impose greater imperial control. That year marked the establishment of the Lords of Trade, a committee of the king's privy council vested with power to make and enforce decisions regarding the management of the colonies. Chief among their goals was the creation of more uniform governments in North America and the West Indies that would answer to the crown's will. Although this movement toward the central administration of empire often sputtered, the trend was unmistakable, especially to colonists who felt the sting of royal customs agents sent to enforce the navigation acts. England was becoming the shipper of the world, and its state-regulated policy of economic nationalism, duplicating that of the Dutch, was essential to this rise to commercial greatness.

The Glorious Revolution in New England

When Charles II died in 1685, his brother, the duke of York, assumed the throne as James II. This set in motion a train of events that nearly led to civil war. Like his brother, James II professed the Catholic faith. But unlike Charles II, who had disclosed this only on his deathbed, the new king announced his faith immediately upon assuming the throne. Consternation ensued. Protestant England recoiled when James issued the Declaration of Indulgence, which granted liberty of worship to all. Although religious toleration is cherished today, it was unacceptable to most English Protestants 300 years ago. Belief that the declaration was primarily a concession to Catholics hardened when the king began creating Catholic peerages to fill the House of Lords, appointed Catholics to high government posts, including command of the English navy, and demanded that Oxford and Cambridge open their doors to Catholic students. In 1687, the king dismissed a resistant Parliament. When his wife, believed to be too old for further childbearing, gave birth to a son in 1688, a Catholic succession loomed.

The center of government and official news in colonial New England was Boston's town house, built in 1657. Note the stocks and whipping post at lower left.

Convinced that James was trying to seize absolute power and fearing a Catholic conspiracy, a group of Protestant leaders secretly plotted the king's downfall. In 1688, led by the earl of Shaftesbury, they invited William of Orange, a prince of the Netherlands, to invade England and take the throne with his wife, Mary, James's Protestant daughter. James abdicated rather than fight. It was a bloodless victory for Protestantism, for parliamentary power and the limitation of kingly prerogatives, and for the propertied merchants and gentry of England who stood behind the revolt.

The response of New Englanders to these events stemmed from their previous experience with royal authority and their fear of "papists." New England became a prime target for reform when the administrative reorganization of the empire began in 1675, for an independent spirit and widespread evasion of commercial regulations had prevailed there for two generations. In 1684, Charles II had annulled the Massachusetts charter. Two years later, James II appointed Sir Edmund Andros, a crusty professional soldier and former governor of New York, to rule over the newly created Dominion of New England that soon gathered under one government the colonies of New Hampshire, Massachusetts, Connecticut, Plymouth, Rhode Island, New York, New Jersey, and part of Maine. Puritans were now forced to swallow the bitter fact that they were subjects of London bureaucrats who cared more about shaping a disciplined empire than about the special religious vision of one group of overseas subjects.

At first, New Englanders accepted Andros, though coolly. But he soon earned their hatred by invading freedoms they had come to cherish. He imposed taxes without legislative consent, ended trial by jury, abolished the General Court of Massachusetts (which had met annually since 1630), muzzled Boston's town meeting, and challenged the validity of all land titles. He mocked the Puritans by converting a Boston Puritan church into an Anglican chapel and holding services there on Christmas Day. In Puritan nostrils, this gesture stank of popery. Adding to Puritan outrage, Andros rejected their practice of suppressing religious dissent.

When news reached Boston in April 1689 that William of Orange had landed in England, ending James II's hated Catholic regime, Bostonians streamed into the streets to the beat of drums. They imprisoned Andros, a suspected papist, and overwhelmed the fort in Boston harbor, which held most of the governor's small contingent of red-coated royal troops. Andros escaped, disguised in women's clothing, but was quickly recaptured. Boston's ministers, along with merchants and former magistrates, led the rebellion, but city folk of the lower orders supplied the footsoldiers. For three years, an interim government ruled Massachusetts while the Bay colonists awaited a new charter and a royal governor.

Although Bostonians had dramatically rejected royal authority, which to them represented the "bloody Devotees of Rome" as well as arbitrary power, no internal revolution occurred. However, growing social stratification and the emergence of a political elite led to some disturbing effects. Some citizens challenged the traditional view that those at the top of society were the true guardians of the public interest. They argued that men of modest means but common sense might better be trusted with power. *Anarchy* was the word chosen by Samuel Willard, minister of Boston's Third Church, to tar the popular spirit he saw unloosed in Boston in the aftermath of Andros's ouster. But such egalitarian rumblings came to little.

Leisler's Rebellion in New York

In New York, the Glorious Revolution was similarly bloodless at first but far more disruptive. It was not necessary to overthrow royal government when news arrived of James II's abdication. It simply melted away. When a local militia captain, the German-born Jacob Leisler, appeared at Fort James at the lower tip of Manhattan, Governor Francis Nicholson made only a token show of resistance before quietly stepping down. Displacing the governor's "popishly affected dogs and rogues," Leisler established an interim government and ruled with an elected Committee of Safety for 13 months until a governor appointed by King William arrived.

Leisler's government enjoyed popularity among small landowners and urban laboring people. Most of the upper echelon, however, detested him. They remembered that he had come to New Amsterdam in 1660 as a common footsoldier of the Dutch West India Company and three years later had leapfrogged into the merchant class by marrying a wealthy widow. After the English took over the Dutch colony in 1664, he was often at odds with New Yorkers of the upper rank. "Up jump into the saddle hott brain'd Capt. Leisler," sneered one aristocrat after Leisler's takeover. Thereafter the Leislerians were often labeled as people of "mean birth, and sordid education and desperate fortunes."

Much of this antipathy originated in the smoldering resentment lower- and middle-class Dutch inhabitants felt toward the town's English elite. Many Dutch merchants had readily adjusted to the English conquest of New Netherland in 1664, and many incoming English merchants had married into Dutch families. But beneath the upper class, where economic success softened ethnic friction, incidents of Anglo-Dutch hostility were common. The feeling rose in the 1670s and 1680s among ordinary Dutch families that the English were crowding them out of the society they had built.

The Glorious Revolution provided a spark to ignite this smoldering social conflict. Leisler shared Dutch hostility toward New York's English elite, and his sympathy for the common people, mostly Dutch, earned him the hatred of the city's oligarchy. Leisler freed imprisoned debtors, planned a town-meeting system of government for New York City, and replaced merchants with artisans in important official posts. By the autumn of 1689, Leislerian mobs were attacking the property of some of New York's wealthiest merchants. Two merchants, refusing to recognize Leisler's authority, were jailed.

Leisler's opponents, accustomed to controlling government, were horrified at the power of what they called the "rabble," the "tumultuous multitude." They believed that ordinary people had no right to rebel against authority or to exercise political power. When a new English governor arrived in 1691, the anti-Leislerians embraced him and charged Leisler and seven of his assistants with treason for assuming the government without royal instructions.

In the ensuing trial, Leisler and Jacob Milbourne, his son-in-law and chief lieutenant, were convicted of treason by an all-English jury and hanged. Leisler's popularity among the artisans of the city was evident when his wealthy opponents could find no carpenter in the city who would furnish a ladder to use at the scaffold. After his execution, peace gradually returned to New York, but for years provincial and city politics reflected the deep rift between Leislerians and anti-Leislerians.

Southern Rumblings

The Glorious Revolution also focused dissatisfactions in several southern colonies. Since Maryland was ruled by a Catholic proprietary family, the Protestant majority predictably seized on word of the Glorious Revolution and used it for their own purposes. Lord Baltimore had returned to England in 1684. In 1688, when his instructions to his colony to honor William and Mary were delayed, leading officials and planters formed a Protestant Association. Seizing control of the government in July 1689, they vowed to cleanse Maryland of its popish hue and to reform a corrupt customs service, cut taxes and fees, and extend the rights of the representative assembly. John Coode, formerly a fiery Anglican minister who had been involved in a brief rebellion in 1681, assumed the reins of government and held them until the arrival of Maryland's first royal governor in 1692.

In neighboring Virginia, the wounds of Bacon's Rebellion were still healing when word of the Glorious Revolution arrived. The fact that Virginia lived under the governorship of the Catholic Lord Howard of Effingham, who had installed a number of Catholic officials, made it easy for rumors to spread that a Catholic conspiracy was hatching. News of the revolution in England led a group of planters, who had suffered a prolonged drop in tobacco prices, to attempt an overthrow of the governor. The uprising quickly faded when the governor's council asserted itself and took its own measures to remove Catholics from positions of authority.

The Glorious Revolution brought political changes to several colonies. The Dominion of New England was shattered. While Connecticut and Rhode Island were allowed to elect their own governors, Massachusetts and New Hampshire became royal colonies with governors appointed by the king. In Massachusetts, a new royal charter in 1691 eliminated church membership as a voting requirement. The Maryland proprietorship was abolished (to be restored in 1715 when the Baltimore family became Protestant), and Catholics were barred from office. Everywhere the liberties of Protestant Englishmen were celebrated.

The Social Basis of Politics

Although the colonial insurrections associated with the Glorious Revolution sought primarily to overthrow arbitrary royal governors and foil papist plots (most of them imaginary), they revealed social and political tensions that accompanied the transplanting of English society to the North American wilderness. Still hardly beyond the frontier stage, the immature societies along the coast were fluid and competitive. They lacked the stable political systems and acknowledged leadership class thought necessary for maintaining social order.

The colonial elite tried, of course, to foster social and political stability. The best insurance of this, they believed, was the maintenance of a stratified society where children were subordinate to parents, women to men, servants to masters, and the poor to the rich. Only well-knit societies had coherence and balance, the upper echelon believed. Amid the barbarizing conditions of the New World, where anarchy lurked just beyond every threshold, it was especially vital to reproduce the social arrangements of the Old World.

Hence, in every settlement leaders tried to maintain a system of social gradations and subordination. Puritans did not file into church on Sundays and occupy the pews in random fashion. Rather, the seats were "doomed," or assigned according to customary yardsticks of respectability—age, parentage, social position, wealth, and occupation. Even in fluid Virginia, lower-class persons were haled before courts for horse racing because this was a sport by law reserved for men of social distinction.

This social ideal proved difficult to maintain on North American soil, however. Regardless of previous rank, settlers rubbed elbows so frequently and faced such raw conditions together that those without pedigrees often saw little reason to defer to men of superior rank. "In Virginia," explained John Smith, "a plain soldier that can use a pickaxe and spade is better than five knights." Colonists everywhere learned that basic lesson. They gave respect not to those who claimed it by birth but to those who earned it by deed.

Adding to the difficulty of reproducing a traditional social order in the colonies was the social fluidity in frontier society. A native elite gradually formed, but it had no basis, as in Europe, in legally defined and hereditary social rank. Planters and merchants, accumulating large estates, aped the English gentry by cultivating the arts, building fine houses, and acquiring symbols of respectability such as libraries, coaches, and racehorses. Yet their place was rarely secure. In the race to drag wealth from the resource-rich environment, new competitors nipped constantly at their heels.

Amid such social flux, the elite could never command general allegiance to the ideal of a fixed social structure. Ambitious men on the rise such as Nathaniel Bacon and Jacob Leisler, and thwarted men below them who followed their lead, rose up against the constituted authorities, though they almost certainly would not have dared to do so in their homelands. When they gained power during the Glorious Revolution, in every case only briefly, the leaders of these uprisings linked themselves with a tradition of English struggle against tyranny and oligarchical power. They vowed to make government more responsive to the ordinary people, who composed most of their societies.

In both North and South this earned parvenu leaders the epithet "Masaniello" after the peasant fish seller of Naples who in 1647 had mobilized ordinary people against exploitation by the rich. Masaniello briefly controlled the city, momentarily stood the political order on its head, and became an Italian Robin Hood. In America, Bacon's Rebellion was likened to Masaniello's revolt by the royal governor. In New York, Leisler was labeled a local Masaniello by his wealthy enemies. In Maryland, John Coode proudly called himself a Chesapeake Masaniello. The comparisons were far from exact, but references to the Italian folk hero indicate that colonists from all ranks recognized that social relations in their competitive and open society were subject to violent alterations that violated the ideal of a fixed, orderly social system.

Witchcraft in Salem

The greatest internal conflict of the late seventeenth century did not come as a part of the Glorious Revolution in America but was indirectly nourished by the governmental instability associated with it. In Massachusetts, the deposing of Andros left the colony in political limbo for three years, and this allowed what might have been a brief outbreak of witchcraft in the little community of Salem to escalate into a bitter and bloody battle that the provincial government, caught in transition, reacted to only belatedly.

Witch hangings were numerous in Europe as well as the colonies; this woodcut appeared in England's Grievance Discovered (1655), a book on injustices in England's coal industry.

On a winter's day in 1692, 9-year-old Betty Parris and her 11-year-old cousin Abigail Williams began to play at magic in the kitchen of a small house in Salem, Massachusetts. They enlisted the aid of Tituba, the slave of Betty's father, Samuel Parris, the minister of the small community. Tituba told voodoo tales handed down from her African past and baked "witch cakes." The girls soon became seized with fits and began making wild gestures and speeches. Soon other young girls in the village were behaving strangely. Village elders extracted confessions that they were being tormented by Tituba and two other women, one a decrepit pauper, the other a disagreeable hag.

What began as the innocent play of young girls turned into a ghastly rending of a farm community capped by the execution of 20 villagers accused of witchcraft. The incident displayed, in exaggerated form, the tensions that beset the lives of obscure, ordinary individuals in England's late seventeenth-century colonies.

Belief in the supernatural, and in witchcraft, was ancient. For centuries throughout western Europe, people had believed that witches followed Satan's bidding and could spread his evil to anyone he designated. Communities had accused and sentenced women more often than men to death for witchcraft. In the seventeenth century, people still took literally the biblical injunction "Thou shalt not suffer a witch to live." In Massachusetts, more than 100 people, mostly older women, had been accused of witchcraft before 1692, and more than a dozen had been hanged.

In Salem, the initial accusations against three older women quickly multiplied. Within a matter of weeks, as fear gripped the town, dozens had been charged with witchcraft, including several prominent members of the community. But formal prosecution of the accused witches could not proceed because neither the new royal charter of 1691 nor the royal governor to rule the colony had yet arrived. For three months, while charges spread, local authorities could only send the accused to jail without trial. When Governor William Phips arrived from England in May 1692, he ordered a special court to try the accused, but by now events had careened out of control. All through the summer the court listened to testimony. By September it had condemned about two dozen villagers. The authorities hanged 19 of them on barren "Witches Hill" outside the town, and 80-year-old Giles Corey was crushed to death under heavy stones. The trials rolled on

into 1693, but by then colonial leaders, including many of the clergy, recognized that a feverish fear of one's neighbors, rather than witchcraft itself, had possessed the little village of Salem.

Many factors contributed to the hysteria. Among them were generational strife, old family animosities, tensions between agricultural Salem Village and the nearby commercial center called Salem Town, and even an outbreak of food poisoning that may have caused hallucinogenic behavior. Probably nobody will ever fully understand the underlying causes, but the fact that the accusations of witchcraft kept spreading suggests the anxiety of this tumultuous era, marked by war, economic disruption, the political takeover of the colony by Andros and then his overthrow, and the erosion of the early generation's utopian vision.

CONTENDING FOR A CONTINENT

At the end of the seventeenth century, following an era of Indian wars and internal upheaval, the colonists for the first time confronted an extended period of international war. The long incipient struggle for mastery of the New World among four contending European powers—Holland, Spain, France, and England—now became more overt. North America was less an arena of armed rivalry among the European powers than the sugar-rich islands of the Caribbean. Nonetheless, the global struggle for control of land and sea that erupted late in the seventeenth century—the beginning of nearly 100 years of conflict—reached to the doorsteps of those who thought that in immigrating to North America they had left war behind.

Anglo-French Rivalry

In 1661, the French king, Louis XIV, ushered in a new era for New France. Determined to make his country the most powerful in Europe, the king regarded North America and the Caribbean with renewed interest. New France's timber resources would build the royal navy, its fish would feed the growing mass of slaves in the French West Indies, and its fur trade, if greatly expanded, would fill the royal coffers.

Under the leadership of able governors such as Count Frontenac, New France grew in population, economic strength, and ambition in the late seventeenth century. In the 1670s, Louis Jolliet and

Father Jacques Marquette, a Jesuit priest, explored an immense territory watered by the Mississippi and Missouri rivers, previously unknown to Europeans. A decade later, military engineers and priests began building forts and missions, one complementing the other, throughout the Great Lakes region and the Mississippi valley.

Visions of a mighty inland empire grew in the 1680s when René Robert de La Salle canoed down the Mississippi all the way to the Gulf of Mexico and planted a settlement in Texas at Matagorda Bay. The dream of connecting Canada and Louisiana by a chain of forts and trading posts would not be realized for another half century. But it was the French, with a colonial population of only 12,000, rather than the English, with colonies inhabited by 200,000, whom the Indian tribes permitted to settle in the interior of North America.

The growth of French strength and ambitions brought New England and New France into deadly conflict for a generation beginning in the late seventeenth century. Religious hostility overlaid commercial rivalry. Protestant New Englanders regarded Catholic New France as a satanic challenge to their divinely sanctioned mission. When the European wars began in 1689, precipitated by Louis XIV's territorial aggression in western and central Europe, armed conflict between England and France quickly extended into every overseas theater where the two powers had colonies. In North America, the battle zone was New York, New England, and eastern Canada.

In two wars, from 1689 to 1697 and 1702 to 1713, the English and French, while fighting in Europe, also sought to oust each other from the New World. The zone of greatest importance was the Caribbean, where slaves produced huge sugar fortunes. Both home governments understood that the importance of the North American colonies lay chiefly in supplying the timber and fish necessary to sustain the sugar-producing tropical economy of the West Indies. In the North American zone, problems of weather, disease, transport, and supply were so great that only irregular warfare was possible.

The English struck three times at the centers of French power—Port Royal, which commanded the access to the St. Lawrence River, and Quebec, the administrative center of New France. In 1690, during King William's War (1689–1697), their small flotilla captured Port Royal, the hub of Acadia (which was returned to France at the end of the war). The English assault on Quebec, however, failed disastrously. In Queen Anne's War (1702–

1713), New England attacked Port Royal three times before finally capturing it in 1710. A year later, when England sent a flotilla of 60 ships and 5,000 men to conquer Canada, the land and sea operations foundered before reaching their destinations.

With European-style warfare miserably unsuccessful in America, both England and France attempted to subcontract military tasks to their Indian allies. Here was a new aspect of the meeting of cultures—the use of Native Americans as mercenaries in an international conflict. This policy occasionally succeeded, especially with the French, who gladly sent their own troops into the fray alongside Indian partners. The French and Indians wiped out the frontier outpost of Schenectady, New York, in 1690; razed Wells, Maine, and Deerfield, Massachusetts, in 1703; and battered other towns along the New England frontier during both wars. In retaliation, the Iroquois, supplied by the English, stung several French settlements and left New France "bewildered and benumbed" after a massacre near Montreal in 1689. Assessing their own interests and too powerful to be dictated to by either France or England, the Iroquois sat out the second war in the early eighteenth century. Convinced that neutrality served their purposes better than acting as mercenaries for the English, they held to the principle that "we are a free people uniting ourselves to whatever sachem [chief] we wish."

The Results of War

The Peace of Utrecht in 1713, which ended the war, capped the century-long rise of England and the decline of Spain in the rivalry for the sources of wealth outside Europe. England, the big winner, received Newfoundland and Acadia (renamed Nova Scotia), and France recognized English sovereignty over the fur-rich Hudson Bay territory. France retained Cape Breton Island, controlling the entrance to the St. Lawrence River. In the Caribbean, France yielded St. Kitts and Nevis to England. In Europe, Spain lost its provinces in Italy and the last of its holdings in the Netherlands to the Austrian Hapsburgs. Spain also surrendered Gibraltar and Minorca to the English and awarded England the lucrative privilege of supplying the Spanish empire in America with African slaves, a favor formerly enjoyed by the French Senegal Company.

The French were the big losers in these wars, but they did not abandon their ambitions in the New World. Soon after Louis XIV died in 1715, the Regency government of the duke of Orleans tried to regain lost time in America by mounting a huge expedition to settle Louisiana. Because the state deported many undesirables to the colony and because the French aristocracy destroyed by wild speculation the stock that financed the project, few French immigrants joined the settlement of New Orleans thereafter. French colonies expanded only in the Caribbean, where by 1750 the islands of Hispaniola, Martinique, and Guadeloupe counted 46,000 whites and 250,000 slaves. While the islands enriched a few, they strengthened the empire little since slaves could not be armed and the islands were expensive to defend.

At the Peace of Utrecht, Spain retained a vast empire in America. When France decided in 1762 that Louisiana was not worth the expense, Spain gladly accepted it and tried to make it a buffer against the British Americans migrating westward toward New Spain. Spain's policy was not so much to expand its colonial empire as to preserve what it had by keeping others away from it. Neither France nor Spain, as it happened, was able to develop a policy that would halt the expansion of British America.

Though England had rebuffed France after a generation of war, New England suffered grievously. In time Nova Scotia would provide a new frontier for Puritan farmers. But the two wars between 1689 and 1713 struck hard at New England's economy. Massachusetts bore the brunt of the burden. Probably one-fifth of all able-bodied males in the colony participated in the Canadian campaigns, and of these about one-quarter never lived to tell of the terrors of New England's first major experience with international warfare. At the end of the first war in 1697, one leader bemoaned that Massachusetts was left "quite exhausted and ready to sink under the calamities and fatigue of a tedious consuming war." The war debt was £50,000 sterling in Massachusetts alone, a greater per capita burden than the national debt today.

At the end of the second conflict in 1713, war widows were so numerous that the Bay Colony faced its first serious poverty problem. In addition, wartime taxes had "much impoverished and enfeebled" the people, and price inflation had eaten deeply into the pocketbooks of most working families. Pamphleteers in New England's principal port wrote of "the present melancholy circumstances" and "the distressed state of the Town of Boston."

The colonies south of New England remained on the sidelines during most of the war. But war at sea between European rivals affected even those who sat out the land war. In Queen Anne's War, New York lost one of its best grain markets when Spain, allied with France, outlawed American foodstuffs in its West Indian colonies. The French navy plucked off nearly 30 New York merchant vessels, about one-quarter of the port's fleet, and disrupted the vital sea lanes between the mainland and the Caribbean, to the detriment of Philadelphia's grain merchants as well.

One lesson of war, to be repeated many times in succeeding generations, was that the burdens and rewards fell unevenly on the participants. Some low-born men could rise spectacularly. William Phips, the twenty-sixth child in his family, had been a poor sheep farmer and ship's carpenter in Maine who seemed destined to go nowhere. Then he won a fortune by recovering a sunken Spanish treasure

A seventeenth-century French engraving depicts a frontier settlement in what is now Texas. Note the military presence, always strong in French Louisiana.

ship in the West Indies in 1687. For that feat he was given command of the expedition against Port Royal in 1690. Victory there catapulted him to the governorship of Massachusetts in 1691, and thereafter his status was secure.

Other men, already rich, multiplied their wealth. Andrew Belcher of Boston, who had grown wealthy on provisioning contracts during King Philip's War in 1675 and 1676, combined patriotism with profit in King William's and Queen Anne's wars by supplying warships and outfitting the New England expeditions to Canada. As one of the favored recipients of the fruits of war, Belcher became a local titan, riding through Boston's crooked streets in London-built coaches, erecting a handsome mansion on State Street, and purchasing slaves to symbolize his rise to the pinnacle of New England society.

Most men, especially those who did the fighting, gained little, however, and many lost all. It was from the ranks of the least securely placed New Englanders—indentured servants, apprentices, recently arrived immigrants, unskilled laborers, fishermen, and ordinary farmers—that most troops were recruited or pressed involuntarily into service. Once in the army or navy, they died in proportions that seem staggering today. Fervent antipopery, dreams of glory, and promises of plunder from the commercial centers of French Canada lured most of them into uniform. Having achieved no place on the paths leading upward, they grasped at straws. A hefty percentage of those who sailed in the naval expeditions against Port Royal or plodded overland to attack Montreal and Quebec never lived even to collect their meager wages. None found the advertised booty, which turned out to be only a sugarplum dangled by military recruiters.

CONCLUSION

Controlling the New Environment

By the second decade of the eighteenth century, the 12 English colonies on the eastern edge of North America had secured footholds in the hemisphere and erected the basic scaffolding of colonial life. With the aid of England, they had ousted the Dutch from their mid-Atlantic perch. They had fought the French to a draw and held their own against the Spanish. The coastal Indian tribes were reeling from disease and a series of wars that secured the colonists' land base along 1,000 miles of coastal plain. Though never controlling the powerful Indian tribes of the interior, the colonists had established a profitable trade with them. The settlers had overcome a scarcity of labor by copying the other European colonists in the hemisphere, who had linked the west coast of Africa to the New World through the ghastly trade in human flesh. Finally, the colonists had engaged in insurrections against what they viewed as arbitrary and tainted governments imposed by England.

The embryo of British America carried into the eighteenth century contained peculiarly mixed features. Still physically isolated from Europe, the colonists developed of necessity a large measure of self-reliance. Slowly, they began to identify themselves as the permanent inhabitants of a new land rather than transplanted English, Dutch, or Scots-Irish. Viewing land and labor as the indispensable elements of a fruitful economy, they learned to exploit without apologies the land of one dark-skinned people and the labor of another. Yet even as they attained a precarious mastery in a triracial society, they were being culturally affected by the very people whose land and labor they had laid claim to. Although utopian visions of life in America still reverberated in the heads of some, most colonists had awakened to the reality that life in the New World was a puzzling mixture of unpredictable opportunity and sudden turbulence, unprecedented freedom and debilitating wars, racial intermingling and racial separation. It was a New World in much more than geographic sense, for the people of three cultures who now inhabited it had remade it; and, while doing so, they were remaking themselves.

Recommended Reading

The Atlantic slave trade, which spanned four centuries, is explored in Philip Curtin, The Atlantic Slave Trade *(1969); Martin Kilson and Robert I. Rotberg, eds.,* The African Diaspora *(1976); and Basil Davidson,* The African Slave Trade *(1961).*

The origins and early history of slavery in the Americas, long controversial topics, are studied in Frank Tannenbaum, Slave and Citizen *(1956); Carl N. Degler,* Neither Black nor White: Slavery and Race Relations in Brazil and the United States *(1971); H. Hoetink,* Slavery and Race Relations in the Americas *(1973); David B. Davis,* The Problem of Slavery in Western-Culture *(1966); and Richard S. Dunn,* Sugar and Slaves *(1972).*

For slavery in the American colonies, a fine introduction is Ira Berlin, "Time, Space, and the Evolution of Afro-American Society in British Mainland America," American Historical Review, *85 (1980). Other valuable studies include Peter H. Wood,* Black Majority *(1974); Gerald Mullins,* Flight and Rebellion *(1972): Winthrop D. Jordan,* White over Black *(1968); and Daniel C. Littlefield,* Rice and Slaves *(1981).*

Relations between colonizers and Native Americans after the founding period are examined in James Axtell, The European and the Indian *(1981); Wilcomb Washburn's history of Bacon's Rebellion,* The Governor and the Rebel *(1957); Douglas Leach,* Flintlock and Tomahawk: New England in King Philip's War *(1958); Francis Jennings,* The Invasion of America *(1975), and* The Ambiguous Iroquois Empire *(1984); J. Leitch Wright,* The Only Land They Knew: The Tragic Story of the American Indians in the Old South *(1981); A. H. Johns,* Storms Brewed in Other Men's Worlds: The Confrontation of Indians, Spanish, and French in the Old Southwest *(1975); Oakah L. Jones, Jr.,* Los Paisanos: Spanish Settlers on the Northern Frontier of New Spain *(1979); and Gary B. Nash,* Red, White, and Black *(1974, 1982).*

For the Glorious Revolution in America and the era of instability at the end of the seventeenth century, consult David Lovejoy, The Glorious Revolution in America *(1972), Jerome Reich,* Leisler's Rebellion *(1953); Paul Boyer and Steven Nissenbaum,* Salem Possessed: The Social Origins of Witchcraft *(1974); and Carol F. Karlsen,* The Devil in The Shape of a Woman *(1987).*

TIME LINE

1600–1700 Dutch monopolize slave trade

1619 First Africans imported to Virginia

1637 Pequot War in New England

1640s New England merchants enter slave trade
Virginia forbids blacks to carry firearms

1650–1670 Judicial and legislative decisions in Chesapeake colonies solidify racial lines

1660 Parliament passes first Navigation Act

1664 English conquer New Netherland

1673–1685 French expand into Mississippi valley

1675–1677 King Philip's War in New England

1676 Bacon's Rebellion in Virginia

1682 La Salle sails down Mississippi River and claims Louisiana for France

1684 Massachusetts charter recalled

1686 Dominion of New England

1688 Glorious Revolution in England, followed by accession of William and Mary

1689 Overthrow of Governor Andros in New England
Leisler's Rebellion in New York

1689–1697 King William's War

1690s Transition from white indentured to black slave labor begins in Chesapeake

1692 Witchcraft hysteria in Salem

1702–1713 Queen Anne's War

1713 Peace of Utrecht

4

The Maturing of Colonial Society

As a youth, Devereaux Jarratt knew only the isolated life of the small southern planter. Born in 1733 on the Virginia frontier, he was the third son of an immigrant yeoman farmer. In New Kent County, where Jarratt grew up, class status showed in a man's dress, his leisure habits, his house, even in his religion. A farmer's "whole dress and apparel," Jarratt recalled later, "consisted in a pair of coarse breeches, one or two shirts, a pair of shoes and stockings, an old felt hat, and a bear skin coat." In a maturing colonial society that was six generations old by the mid-eighteenth century, such simple folk stepped aside and tipped their hats when prosperous neighbors went by. "A periwig, in those days," recollected Jarratt, "was a distinguishing badge of gentle folk—and when I saw a man riding the road, near our house, with a wig on, it would so alarm my fears . . . that, I dare say, I would run off, as for my life."

As the colonies grew rapidly after 1700, economic development brought handsome gains for some, opened modest opportunities for many, but produced disappointment and privation for others. Jarratt remembered that his parents "neither sought nor expected any title, honors, or great things, either for themselves or their children. They wished us all brought up in some honest calling that we might earn our bread, by the sweat of our brow, as they did." But Jarratt was among those who advanced. His huge appetite for learning was apparent to his parents when as a small child he proved able to repeat entire chapters of the Bible before he had learned to read. That earned him some schooling. But at age 8, when his parents died, he had to take his place behind the plow alongside his brothers. Then, at 19, Jarratt was "called from the ax to the quill" by a neighboring planter's timely offer of a job tutoring his children.

Tutoring put Jarratt in touch with the world of wealth and status. Gradually he advanced to positions in the households of wealthy Virginia planters. His modest success also introduced him to the world of evangelical religion. In the eighteenth century, an explosion of religious fervor dramatically reversed the growing secularism of the settlers. Jarratt first encountered evangelicalism in the published sermons of George Whitefield, an English clergyman.

But it was later, at the plantation of John Cannon, "a man of great possessions in lands and slaves," that he personally experienced conversion under the influence of Cannon's wife.

Jarratt later became a clergyman in the Anglican church, which was dominated in the South by wealthy and dignified planters. But he never lost his religious zeal and desire to carry religion to the common people. In this commitment to spiritual renewal, he participated in the first mass religious movement to occur in colonial society.

Colonial North America in the first half of the eighteenth century was a thriving, changing set of regional societies that had developed from turbulent seventeenth-century beginnings. New England, the mid-Atlantic colonies, the Upper and Lower South, New France, and the northern frontier of New Spain were all distinct regions. Even within regions, diversity increased in the eighteenth century as incoming streams of immigrants, mostly from Africa, Germany, Ireland, and France added new pieces to the emerging American mosaic.

Despite their bewildering diversity and lack of cohesion, the colonies along the Atlantic seaboard were affected similarly by population growth and economic development. Everywhere except on the frontier, class differences grew. A commercial orientation spread from north to south, especially in the towns, as local economies matured and forged links with the network of trade in the Atlantic basin. The exercise of political power of elected legislative assemblies and local bodies produced seasoned leaders, a tradition of local autonomy, and a widespread belief in a political ideology stressing the liberties that freeborn Englishmen should enjoy. All regions experienced a deep-running religious awakening that was itself connected to secular changes. All of these themes will be explored as we follow the way that scattered frontier settlements developed into mature provincial societies.

AMERICA'S FIRST POPULATION EXPLOSION

In 1680, some 150,000 colonizers clung to the eastern edge of North America. By 1750, they had swelled sevenfold to top 1 million. This growth rate, never experienced in Europe, staggered English policymakers. Perceptive observers understood that the gap between the population of England and its American colonies was closing rapidly. Benjamin Franklin's prediction in 1751—that before his grandchildren died, the colonies would outstrip the mother country in population—proved correct.

The population boom was fed from both internal and external sources. Among the white colonial population, a high marriage rate, large families, and lower mortality than in Europe prevailed by the 1720s. Natural increase accounted for much of the population boom in all the colonies and nearly all of it in New England, where immigrants arrived only in a trickle in the eighteenth century. The black population also began to increase naturally by the 1720s. American-born slaves, forming families and producing as many children as white families, soon began to outnumber slaves born in Africa.

The New Immigrants

While expanding through natural increase, the colonial population also received waves of new immigrants. They were not English, however. The last sizable group of settlers from England had arrived at the end of the seventeenth century. The eighteenth-century newcomers, who far outnumbered those emigrating before 1700, came overwhelmingly from Germany, Switzerland, Ireland, and Africa, and they were mostly indentured servants and slaves. Africans, who numbered about 15,000 in 1690, grew to 80,000 in 1730 and 325,000 in 1760. By the last date, when they composed one-fifth of the colonial population, their numbers were growing far more from natural increase than from importation. Of all the groups arriving in the eighteenth century, the Africans were the largest.

Population of European Colonies in North America, 1680–1770

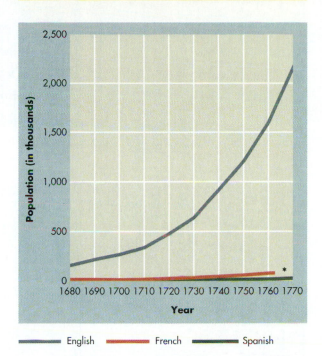

* France's North American colonies in Canada and Louisiana ceded to England and Spain, respectively, in 1763.

German-speaking settlers, about 90,000 strong, flocked to the colonies in the eighteenth century. Many were Protestant farmers of Swiss and French extraction, fleeing "God's three arrows"—famine, war, and pestilence. Drifting down the Rhine to Rotterdam, they crowded onto ships and began the long voyage to America. Once in the colonies, they hurried to areas where promoters promised them cheap and fertile land, low taxes, and freedom from military duty. Most settled between New York and South Carolina, with Pennsylvania claiming the largest number of them. Coming mostly in families, they turned much of the mid-Atlantic hinterland into a German-speaking region. Place names still mark their zone of settlement: Mannheim, New Berlin, and Herkimer, New York; Bethlehem, Ephrata, Nazareth, and Hanover, Pennsylvania; Hagerstown and Frederick, Maryland; Mecklenberg and New Hanover, North Carolina.

Outnumbering the Germans were the Protestant Scots-Irish. Several thousand from Northern Ireland arrived each year after the Peace of Utrecht in 1713 reopened the Atlantic sea lanes. Mostly poor farmers, they streamed into the same backcountry areas where Germans were settling, though more of them followed the mountain valleys south into the Carolinas and Georgia. Occasionally mingling with the Germans, these Ulster families washed over the ridges of Appalachia until their appetite for land brought them face to face with the ancient occupiers of the land. No major Indian wars occurred between 1715 and 1754, but the frontier bristled with tension as the new settlers pushed westward.

In the enormous population growth occurring after 1715, the region southward from Pennsylvania witnessed the most spectacular increase. New England nearly tripled in population, but the middle and southern colonies quadrupled, though in the South the fast-growing slave population accounted for much more of the growth than in the mid-Atlantic. Pennsylvania, with its fertile lands and open door policy, grew fastest of all. Between 1720 and 1760, its population mushroomed from 30,000 to 180,000. Virginia, with a population of nearly 340,000 by 1760, remained by far the largest colony.

New Classes of Newcomers

The social background of these new European immigrants differed substantially from their seventeenth-century predecessors. The early settlers included a number of men from the upper levels of the English social pyramid: university-trained Puritan ministers, sons of wealthy gentry, and merchants. In the eighteenth century, few such men arrived.

The seventeenth-century immigrants had also included many from the middle rungs of the English social ladder—yeomen farmers, skilled craftsmen, and shopkeepers. They formed the backbone of the provincial churches and participated actively in community politics. Through "shipboard mobility" they moved up a notch or two on the western side of the Atlantic. Many lived to see their sons enter the professions or embark on a mercantile career in a society with plenty of room at the top. Such people came rarely in the eighteenth century, for religious persecution had waned in England, and material conditions had improved.

Slaves and indentured servants made up most of the incoming human tide after 1713. The traffic in servants became a regular part of the commerce linking Europe and America. Shipowners made their

German Settlements, 1775

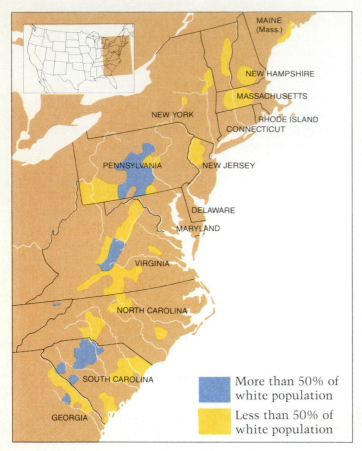

More than 50% of white population

Less than 50% of white population

Scots-Irish Settlements, 1775

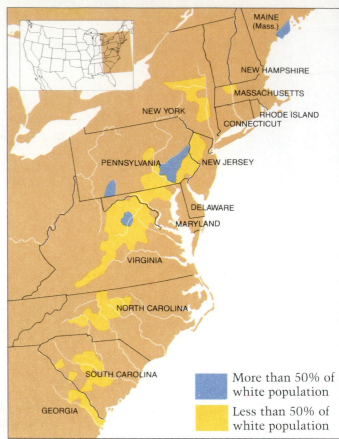

More than 50% of white population

Less than 50% of white population

profits fetching sugar, fish, furs, rice, tobacco, and forest products eastward. On the westbound voyages, plenty of room remained for human cargo after loading the less bulky textiles and manufactured products desired by colonists.

Shipboard conditions for servants worsened in the eighteenth century and were hardly better than aboard the slave ships. The wretchedness of the passage can be judged by the attempt at reform in the 1720s when the British government required an increase in horizontal space to 6 feet by 18 inches per passenger, with no allowance for children.

Such attempts to reduce "tight packing" did little to improve shipboard life. Crammed between decks in stifling air, servants suffered from smallpox and fevers, rotten food, impure water, cold, and lice. "Children between the ages of one and seven seldom survive the sea voyage," bemoaned one German immigrant, "and parents must often watch their offspring suffer miserably, die, and be thrown into the ocean." One expedition of 3,000 Palatinate immi-

grants in 1717 lost 470 en route; on another, 250 succumbed shortly after reaching port. "I never see such parcels of poor wretches," one Virginia observer remarked of an incoming troop of servants in 1758, "some almost naked and what had clothes was as black as chimney sweepers and almost starved." The misery would be repeated thousands of times in the next two centuries. The shipboard mortality rate of about 15 percent in the colonial era made this the most unhealthy of all times to seek American shores.

Like indentured servants in the seventeenth century, the servant immigrants who poured ashore after 1715 came mostly from the lower ranks of society. As earlier, some were petty criminals, political prisoners, and the castoffs of the cities. Yet they were bold and ambitious souls. "Men who emigrate," an Englishman commented, "are from the nature of their circumstances, the most active, hardy, daring, bold and resolute spirits, and probably the most mischievous also."

A Land of Opportunity?

Once ashore, most indentured servants, especially males, found the labor system harsh. Merchants sold them, one shocked Britisher reported in 1773, "as they do their horses, and advertise them as they do their beef and oatmeal." Facing cruel treatment, thousands of servants ran away. Advertisements for them filled the colonial newspapers alongside notices for escaped slaves. Servants knew the penalties if they were caught: whipping and additional service, usually reckoned at twice the time lost to the master but sometimes calculated at a 5 to 1 or 10 to 1 ratio, as in Pennsylvania and Maryland. When war came in the mid-eighteenth century, hundreds of servants fled to the British army, not known for its kindly treatment of soldiers but preferable in many servants' eyes to four or five years under a harsh colonial master.

The goal of every servant was to secure a foothold on the ladder of opportunity. "The hope of buying land in America," a New Yorker noted, "is what chiefly induces people into America." However, many servants died before serving out their time. Others won freedom only to toil for years as poor day laborers and tenant farmers. Only a small proportion achieved the dream of becoming independent landholders. The indentured servants in the seventeenth-century Chesapeake world suffered fearful mortality rates, but those who survived often rose in society. Among the eighteenth-century servants, ironically, the chances of living long enough to complete the labor contract were much better, but the opportunity to climb into the propertied ranks became less favorable. The chief beneficiaries of the system of bound white labor were not the laborers but their masters.

Africans in Chains

Among the thousands of ships crossing the Atlantic in the eighteenth century, the ones fitted out as seagoing dungeons for slaves were the most numerous. The slave trade to the southern colonies after the Peace of Utrecht expanded so sharply that within two generations what had been a society with many slaves became a society built on slavery. From 1690 to 1715, annual importations rarely exceeded 1,000, but in the next 15 years the number probably doubled. The generation after 1730 witnessed the largest influx of African slaves in the colonial period, averaging about 5,000 a year. In the entire period from 1700 to 1775, more than 350,000 African slaves entered the American colonies.

Most of these miserable captives were auctioned off to southern planters. Some, however, landed in the northern cities, especially New York and Philadelphia. Merchants sold them there to artisans, farmers, and upper-class householders seeking domestic servants.

Even as the traffic in slaves peaked, religious and humanitarian opposition to slavery arose. A few individuals, mostly Quaker, had objected to slavery on moral grounds since the late seventeenth century. But the idea grew in the 1750s that slavery contradicted the Christian concept of brotherhood

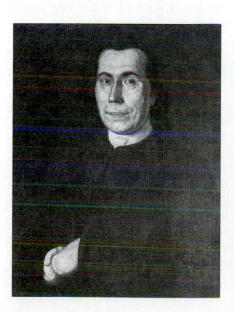

The communalistic Moravian immigrants who came to Pennsylvania in the 1740s dedicated themselves, like the Quakers, to peaceful relations with the Indians. The Prussian John Jacob Schmick and his Norwegian wife Johanna were missionaries to the Delaware tribe.

New-Providence Township, Philadelphia County, December 19th, 1772.

RUN AWAY from the subscriber, living in the aforesaid township, on Monday the fourteenth instant, an indented Irish servant man named BARNABAS KELLY, about five feet three inches high, and twenty one years of age, his left eye blind and is near-sighted with the other, has long black hair which he wears tied behind: Had on an old great coat, and a blue cut velvet jacket without buttons, a red outside jacket, and a white linen one without sleeves, an old pair of leather breeches, black stockings, and a pair of new shoes with strings. He took with him about Four or Five Pounds in money, and his own and his master's part of his indentures; also a grey HORSE, which trots mostly and paces a little. Whoever will take up the said servant, and secure him in any gaol, so that I may get him again, shall have FORTY SHILLINGS, and FORTY SHILLINGS more for the horse, and reasonable charges, paid by
EDWARD ROBERTS.

TO BE SOLD, The TIME of an *IRISH* SERVANT GIRL, WHO has about three years to serve. Enquire of the Printers.

Like slaves, indentured servants often fled the harsh conditions under which they labored. Advertisements for the recovery of runaway servants (left) filled the colonial newspapers. No explanation is given for the sale of the servant girl's time (right). Was her performance unsatisfactory? Did her master unexpectedly need cash?

and the Enlightenment notion of the natural equality of all humans. Abolitionist sentiment was also fed by the growing belief that the master's authority "depraved the mind," as the Quaker John Woolman argued. An introspective tailor from New Jersey, Woolman dedicated his life in the 1750s to a crusade against slavery. He traveled thousands of miles on foot through the colonies to convince every Quaker slaveholder of his or her wrongdoing. Only a few hundred masters freed their slaves in the mid-eighteenth century, but men such as Woolman had nevertheless planted the seeds of abolitionism.

BEYOND THE APPALACHIANS

By the mid-eighteenth century, the American colonists, though increasing rapidly in number, still occupied only a narrow strip of coastal plain in eastern North America. Of about 1.2 million settlers and slaves in 1750, only a tiny fraction lived farther than 100 miles from the shores of the Atlantic. But between them and the Pacific Ocean lay rich soils in the river valleys of the Ohio and Mississippi and beyond that a vast domain that they had not even

imagined. Beginning in the 1750s, westward-moving colonists in pursuit of more land would encounter four other groups already established to their west: the populous interior Native American tribes and smaller groups of French-Americans, Spanish-Americans, and Afro-Americans. Changes already occurring among these groups would affect settlers breaching the Appalachian barrier and, in the third quarter of the eighteenth century, would even reach eastward to the original British settlements.

Cultural Changes Among Interior Tribes

During the first half of the eighteenth century, the inland tribes proved their capacity to adapt to the contending European colonizers in their region while maintaining their political independence. Yet extensive contact with the French, Spanish, and English slowly transformed Indian ways of life in a manner that boded ill for the future.

The introduction of European trade goods, especially iron implements, textiles, firearms and ammunition, and alcohol, inescapably changed Indian lifeways. Subsistence hunting, limited to satisfying tribal food requirements, turned into commercial hunting, restricted only by the quantity of trade goods desired. Indian males spent far more time away from the villages trapping and hunting, and the increased importance of this activity to tribal life undermined the matrilineal basis of society. Women were also drawn into the new economic activities. Once killed, the beaver, marten, and fox had to be skinned and the pelts then scraped, dressed, trimmed, and sewed into robes. Among some tribes, the trapping, preparation, and transporting of skins became so time-consuming that they had to procure food resources from other tribes.

Involvement in the fur trade also altered the spiritual ethos that had long governed hunting. Native Americans had traditionally believed that the destinies of humans and animals were closely linked, for both inhabited a spiritual world governed by a Great Creator. This imposed obligations on both hunters and animals. The hunter knew that he must never kill more animals than he needed and must treat their bodies with respect. The animals in return must not resist capture. When trappers and hunters declared all-out war on the beaver and other fur-bearing animals to provide pelts for the European traders who offered attractive trade goods, they began to ignore the age-old custom of merging sympathetically with the environment.

The fur trade also heightened intertribal tensions, often to the point of war. Conflict between tribes long preceded the arrival of Europeans, but trade frequently flowed between cooperating tribes. As settlers of different nationalities competed for client tribes in the fur trade, however, the tribes were sucked into their patron's rivalry. Also, tribes became accustomed to certain trade articles. When furs became depleted in their hunting grounds, they could maintain their trade only by conquering more remote tribes with fertile hunting grounds or by forcibly intercepting the furs of other tribes as they were carried to European trading posts. The introduction of European weaponry, which Indians quickly mastered, further intensified intertribal conflict.

Tribal political organization among the interior tribes also changed in the eighteenth century. Most tribes had earlier been loose confederations of villages and clans, each exercising local autonomy. The Creek, Cherokee, and Iroquois gave primary loyalty to the village, not to the tribe or confederacy. But trade, diplomatic contact, and war with Europeans required more coordinated policies. To deal effectively with traders and officials, the villages gradually adjusted to more centralized leadership.

Cherokee political organization in the eighteenth century illustrates the changes overcoming tribal societies. Early in the century, the nearly autonomous village formed the basic unit of political authority. But tension with Creek neighbors and intermittent hostilities with English traders and settlers pressed home the need for coordinated decision making. By 1750, the Cherokee had formed an umbrella political organization that under the leadership of Chief Old Hop gathered together the fragmented authority of the villages and formed a more centralized tribal "priest state." When even this proved inadequate, warriors began to assume the dominant role in tribal councils, replacing the civil chiefs. By this process the Cherokee reorganized their political structure so that dozens of scattered villages could amalgamate their strength.

While incorporating trade goods into their material culture and adapting their economies and political structures to new situations, the interior tribes held fast to tradition in many ways. Unimpressed with most settler practices, they saw little reason to replace what they valued in their own culture. When they observed the colonists' systems of law and justice, religion, education, family organization, and child rearing, Native Americans often concluded that their own ways were superior.

The Indians' refusal to accept the superiority of white culture frustrated English missionaries, eager to win Native Americans from "savage" ways. Some colonists understood that the white behavior observed by natives cast doubts on the notion that Indians were of an inferior race. A Carolinian admitted that "they are really better to us than we are to them. We look upon them with scorn and disdain, and think them little better than beasts in human shape, though if well examined, we shall find that, for all our religion and education, we possess more moral deformities and evils than these savages do."

Despite maintaining many cultural practices, the interior Indian tribes suffered from the commercial, diplomatic, and military contact with the British colonizers. Decade by decade, the fur trade spread epidemic diseases, raised the level of warfare, depleted their lands of game animals, and drew the Native Americans into a market economy where their trading partners gradually became trading masters.

France's Inland Empire, 1600–1720

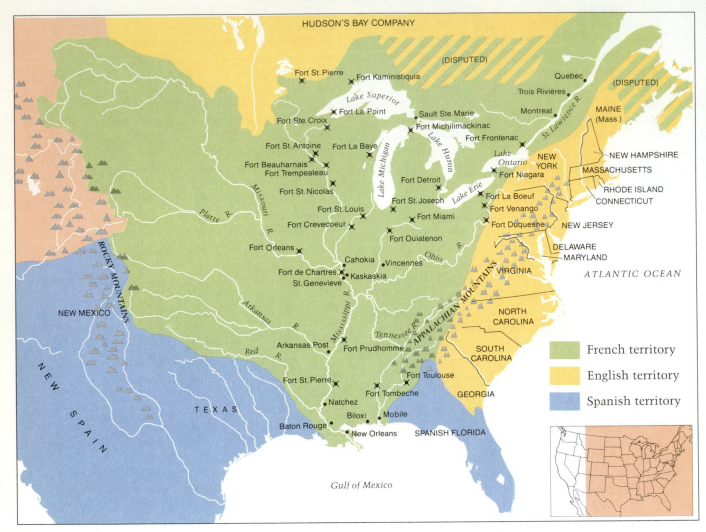

French territory

English territory

Spanish territory

France's Inland Empire

While the powerful Iroquois, Cherokee, Creek, and Choctaw tribes interacted with British colonists to their east, they also dealt with a growing French presence to their west. Between 1699 and 1754, the French developed a system of small forts, trading posts, and agricultural villages throughout the central area of the continent. The aim was to connect French Canada to the Gulf of Mexico and hence keep the settlers in the English colonies pinned to the seaboard. French success in this vast region hinged partly on shrewd dealing with the Indian tribes, which by their numbers retained sovereignty over the land but gradually succumbed to French dis-

eases, French arms, and French-promoted intertribal wars. At the same time, however, because France's interior empire was organized primarily as a military and trading operation, soldiers, fur traders, and other men arriving without wives often exploited or married Indian women. French Louisiana had more mixed-race children and more white and black men who lived with Native Americans than any Anglo-American colony.

In 1718, the few hundred early French pioneers of the interior were suddenly inundated when France settled New Orleans at great cost by transporting almost 7,000 whites and 5,000 African slaves to the mouth of the Mississippi River. Disease rapidly whittled down these numbers, and an uprising of the powerful Natchez tribe in 1729 discouraged further French immigration. Most of the survivors settled around the little town of New Orleans in long, narrow plantations stretching from the Mississippi River to the endless cypress swamps. Slaves made wood products from cypress and pine for the West Indies and produced indigo, rice, and other crops for France. New Orleans merchants also received wheat from the little farming villages taking root in Illinois; bear oil and tobacco from settlements around the western post of Natchitoches; beef from herds in the Mobile valley; produce from the small upriver German village, Les Allemandes; and tens of thousands of deer skins and other pelts delivered annually by Indians for trade goods. In its economy and society, New Orleans much resembled early Charleston, South Carolina.

What distinguished the people of New Orleans from those of Charleston, however, was that the French knew nothing of representative political institutions. Ruled by a governor, a commissary and chief judge, and a small appointed council, the people had no elections or assembly, no newspapers or taxes. Since the French king paid dearly to keep the town's troops supplied, he would share power with no one, although he granted planters many favors. A midcentury English observer noted that "the planter is considered as a Frenchman venturing his life, enduring a species of banishment, and undergoing great hardships for the benefit of his country, for which reason he has great indulgence shown." This could not have been said of English planters in Georgia, South Carolina, or Virginia.

From its first introduction in Louisiana in 1719, French plantation slavery grew so that by 1765, blacks outnumbered whites. Most slaves and a majority of whites lived in the New Orleans area. The conditions of life for slaves differed little from the southern English colonies. In Louisiana, slaves also lived in simple cabins and worked under the sun and the lash in a master's fields and swamps. But the French had a paternalistic black legal code that gave slaves some protection in courts. When the Spanish took over the colony in 1769, they instituted their law guaranteeing slaves the right to buy freedom with money earned in their free time. Soon a large free black class emerged, headed by substantial people like Simon Colfat, who ran various enterprises, helped other slaves pay for their freedom, and headed the company of free black militia. When Americans acquired the colony in 1803, they suppressed freedom purchase and discouraged manumission.

Most blacks who lived outside the British colonies labored in New Orleans, but a few could be found pioneering elsewhere beyond the Appalachians. By the early eighteenth century, slaves who escaped Spanish, French, or English masters formed bands in the interior that allied them with Indian tribes. The Spanish settlers in Texas and California carried a few blacks with them. A supreme expression of the range of possibilities occurred just before the American Revolution when a free black of West Indian parentage, Jean-Baptiste Point Du Sable, with his Potawatomi wife Kittihawa, set down the first settlement in what was to become Chicago. A few years later, the British army arrested Point Du Sable and his fellow pioneers as sympathizers with the American rebels.

Spain's America

In the first half of the eighteenth century, the Spanish still possessed by far the largest American empire. Even as Spanish power declined in Europe, it spread in America. Spain strengthened its Florida military posts to challenge English settlement of the Carolinas and French settlement of the Mississippi valley. Also to counter the French, the Spanish established permanent military posts in Texas and New Mexico for the first time. Popé's insurrection in 1680, described in Chapter 1, had taught Spaniards a lesson, and they never dared establish the system of exploiting Indian labor that prevailed in much of Spanish America. But surviving Hispanics, mestizos, and Indians began to increase in number and were joined by new Spanish settlers and African slaves. Nevertheless, at the end of the eighteenth century, fewer than 50,000 Spanish and Hispanicized people of color inhabited Texas, New Mexico, and California.

As in New France, racial intermixture and social fluidity were more extensive in New Spain than in the English colonies. Precise counts of the various elements of society in these Spanish areas are rare because the Spanish never defined racial groups as distinctly as the English. The word *Spaniard* on a census might mean a white immigrant from Mexico or a part-Indian person who "lived like a Spaniard." Social mobility was considerable because the crown was willing to raise even a common person to the status of *hildago* (minor nobleman) as an inducement to settle in New Spain's remote northern frontier. Most of the immigrants became small ranchers, producing livestock, corn, and wheat for export to other Spanish provinces to the south.

The Native Americans of New Mexico were unusually successful in resisting Spanish domination. An early nineteenth-century Spanish investigator explained part of the reason by describing the *kivas* maintained by Pueblo people. These were "like impenetrable temples, where they gather to discuss mysteriously their misfortunes or good fortunes, their happiness or grief. The doors of these *estufas* are always closed to us." Through this secrecy, the Pueblos clung to their traditions better than most tribes.

The tribes of California were less successful in maintaining cultural cohesion. In the 1770s, the Spanish rapidly completed their western land and sea routes from San Diego to the new port of Yerba Buena (San Francisco) to block Russian settlement south of their base in northern California. The Spanish pioneers were Franciscan missionaries, accompanied by soldiers provided by the crown. The priests would choose a good location and then attract a few Indians to baptism by gifts and preaching. The priests settled "neophytes" next to the mission, which they helped to build. When their relatives came to visit, priests induced them to stay as well. These Indians lived under an increasingly harsh regimen until they were reduced to a condition of virtual slavery. The California mission, with its extensive and profitable herds and grain crops, theoretically belonged to the Indian converts, but they did not enjoy the profits. Priests even hired them out to immigrant Spaniards. Ironically, the spiritual motives of the priests resulted in the same reduction and degradation of tribal Americans as elsewhere.

A LAND OF FAMILY FARMS

Population growth and economic development gradually transformed the landscape of eighteenth-century British America. Three variations of colonial society emerged: the farming society of the North, the plantation society of the South, and the urban society of the seaboard commercial towns. Although they shared some important characteristics, each was distinct.

Northern Agricultural Society

In the northern colonies, especially New England, tightknit farming families, organized in communities of several thousand people, dotted the landscape by the mid-eighteenth century. New Englanders staked their future on a mixed economy. They cleared forests for timber used in barrels, ships, houses, and barns. They plumbed the offshore waters for fish that fed both local populations and the ballooning slave population of the West Indies. And they cultivated and grazed as much of the thin-soiled, rocky hills and bottomlands as they could recover from the forest.

The farmers of the middle colonies—Pennsylvania, Delaware, New Jersey, and New York—set their wooden plows to much richer soils than New Englanders did. They enjoyed the additional ad-

A proud and prosperous Rhineland immigrant, Martin Van Bergen, had this mural painted over the mantelpiece of his New York farmhouse, giving us a rare view of a colonial farm.

vantage of settling an area cleared by native Americans who had relied more on agriculture than New England tribes. Thus favored, mid-Atlantic farm families produced modest surpluses of corn, wheat, beef, and pork. By the mid-eighteenth century, New York and Philadelphia ships were carrying these foodstuffs not only to the West Indies, always a primary market, but also to areas that could no longer feed themselves—England, Spain, Portugal, and even New England.

In the North, the broad ownership of land distinguished farming society from every other agricultural region of the Western world. Although differences in circumstances and ability led gradually toward greater social stratification, in most communities the truly rich and abjectly poor were few and the gap between them small compared to European society. Most men other than indentured servants lived to purchase or inherit a farm of at least 50 acres. With their family's labor they earned a decent existence and provided a small inheritance for each of their children. Settlers valued land highly, for freehold tenure ordinarily guaranteed both economic independence and political rights.

Amid widespread property ownership, a rising population pressed against a limited land supply by the eighteenth century, especially in New England. Family farms could not be divided and subdivided indefinitely, for it took at least 50 acres (of which only a quarter could usually be cropped) to support a single family. In Concord, Massachusetts, for example, the founders had worked farms averaging about 250 acres. A century later, in the 1730s, the average farm had shrunk by two-thirds, as farm owners struggled to provide an inheritance for the three or four sons that the average marriage produced.

The decreasing fertility of the soil compounded the problem of dwindling farm size. When land had been plentiful, farmers planted crops in the same field for three years and then let it lie fallow in pasturage seven years or more until it regained its fertility. But on the smaller farms of the eighteenth century, farmers had reduced fallow time to only a year or two. Inevitably, such intense use of the soil reduced crop yields, forcing farmers to plow marginal land or shift to livestock production. Such was the process that led Jaret Eliot, New England's first agricultural essayist, to refer to "our old land which we have worn out."

The diminishing size and productivity of family farms forced many New Englanders to move to the frontier or out of the area altogether in the eighteenth century. "Many of our old towns are too full of inhabitants for husbandry, many of them living on small shares of land," bemoaned one Yankee. In Concord, one of every four adult males migrated from town every decade from the 1740s on, and in many towns out-migration was even greater. Some drifted south to New York and Pennsylvania. Others sought opportunities as artisans in the coastal towns or took to the sea. More headed for the colony's western frontier or north into new Hampshire and the eastern frontier of Maine. Several thousand New England families migrated even farther north, to the Annapolis valley of Nova Scotia. Throughout New England after the early eighteenth century, most farmers' sons knew that their destiny lay elsewhere.

Wherever they took up farming, northern cultivators engaged in agricultural work routines that were far less intense than in the South. The growing season was much shorter, and the cultivation of

RECOVERING THE PAST

TAX RECORDS

In recent years, historians have borrowed methods of analysis from economics and sociology to study social and economic patterns, divisions of wealth within society, the degree of mobility between social ranks, and the pattern of recruitment of elite groups. Understanding how to use quantitative indicators is important because social changes, working silently beneath the surface of public events and involving masses of people, often bring about political tensions that culminate in protest, reform, and sometimes revolution.

In colonial America, contemporary opinion varied widely on how much equality and opportunity existed. Writing from Philadelphia in 1756, a recent German immigrant, Gottlieb Mittelberger, exclaimed, "Even in the humblest or poorest houses, no meals are served without a meat course." Yet the Quaker John Smith noted in his diary, "It is remarkable what an increase of the number of beggars there is about this town this winter." Thomas Hutchinson, one of Boston's wealthiest merchants, believed in 1768 that "in some towns you see scarce a man destitute"; yet in that very year, hundreds of indigent Massachusetts people were wandering into Boston in search of work, and magistrates were dispensing poor relief to approximately one out of every ten adults in the town.

To go beyond such contradictory literary sources, historians have turned to previously unexamined sources such as tax lists and probate records to gain a more precise and verifiable picture of how the structure of wealth and opportunity was changing in eighteenth-century America. These sources are often incomplete and difficult to interpret. But when used cautiously and subjected to modern techniques of statistical analysis, they can provide insights into changes in the lives of colonial Americans before the Revolution.

Tax records are among the most accessible and useful sources for studying the social structure. A tax assessor's list gives a snapshot of a community's social profile by indicating how much taxable wealth each inhabitant possessed. The list usually included land, houses and barns, rental property, horses and cattle, and servants and slaves. By comparing a series of lists for a single community, historians have been able to measure the

Tax List, Upper Delaware Ward, 1767

Leonard Hammond			Thomas Thompson	4
1 Negro	£8		Robert Waln merchant	
William Hodge, merchant			Dwelling—£80	48
6 Negroes, 1 horse	24–13		3 Negroes, 1 horse	12–13
£18 of Edward Gallean—Southwark	10–16		£30 of Isaac Cathrell	19
£18 of Robt Willson—Southwark	10–16		£30 of Zachariah Martin	19
£18 of William Gordon—Southwark	10–16		£15 of	9
£18 of Patrick McGavock—Southwark	10–16		£40 of Catherine Hesbruck	24
3 acres of meadow—Moyamensin	2–5		£12 of Philip Leary	7
half a house—Frankford Road	8		. . .	
	78–2			255
Arthur Barnes mariner	5		Isaac Catherall cooper	5
William Coon cordwainer	3		Mary McCulloch	3
Joseph Norris ship carpenter	4		William Pollard merchant	10
John Clinton	3		Martha Green	15
Thomas Vaughan	3		John Pearson cordwainer	2
Tobias Barthson for George Vanlears				
Estate			Stephen Hutchins	3
£20 of Tobias Barthson in No. Lib.	12		Benjamin Worthington	10
£5–10 of Elizabeth Arins in No. Lib.	3–6		A small shop £15–9	
	15–6		William Howard	2
Thomas Brice mariner	5			
Edward Beach cooper				
2 Negroes, 1 horse	8–13			
2 Servants	3			

degree and pace of change for a number of important social indicators: the proportion of residents owning no land, the changing size of farms and urban properties, the concentration of wealth, and the ownership of indentured servants and slaves.

Two tax-list fragments are reproduced here. One is for a street in Upper Delaware Ward in Philadelphia. It was drawn up to determine the taxes residents owed the colonial government to enable it to meet expenses of the Seven Years' War. The assessment was, of course, expressed in pounds and shillings. As you look through the list, you can see that some residents, like William Hodge, had several tenants. Edward Gallean, who rented one of Hodge's houses, paid him £18 for property in Southwark. If you rank the residents in order of their wealth, you can determine the gap between the richest and poorest taxpayers and can see how many people fall into various wealth categories. The list also gives occupations for some of the taxpayers, thus allowing you to make some inferences about the connection between occupation and wealth. It also shows who owns slaves and the number of women who lived on their own.

The second fragment is from rural Chester Country, a few miles outside Philadelphia. Even though the categories (land, servants, Negroes, cattle, horses, sheep, mills, etc.) are different, by comparing this information with that for Upper Delaware Ward, you can draw some conclusions about the composition of a rural community and the ways its social structure differed from that of the city. Is wealth more concentrated in the city or the country? Are the gaps between rich and poor similar in both places? Where did slavery appear more common? What generalizations can be made about economic equality and opportunity for eighteenth-century Americans?

Assessor's Return, Chester County, Pennsylvania, 1759

Name	Land	Sow'd	Servants	Negroes	Ages	Cattle	Horses	Sheep	Mills	Pounds	Shillings	Pence
Burnett James	200	12	—	—	—	7	4	8	—	1	17	9
Barnard Isaac	160	5	—	1	16	5	2	6	—	1	8	—
Connaly Edward	7	—	—	—	—	2	2	—	—	—	5	—
Carter Jacob Stiller	66	6	—	—	—	3	2	4	—	—	10	—
Carter Joseph	66	—	—	—	—	2	4	—	1	—	13	—
Crage James	50	6	—	—	—	3	2	9	—	—	12	—
Carter Joseph Smith	150	10	—	—	—	4	3	—	—	1	7	—
Cambel John	50	6	—	—	—	2	2	6	—	—	11	—
Chamberlin Joseph	200	—	—	—	—	—	—	—	—	1	7	—
Chamberlin Isaac	141	16	—	—	—	2	2	6	—	1	5	—
Carter Samuel	90	8	—	—	—	2	3	—	—	—	15	—
Caldwell Margrat	100	—	—	—	—	1	—	—	—	—	12	6
Dinge Christopher	120	15	—	—	—	4	3	7	—	1	4	—
Dutton Joseph Mill Wright	68	4	—	—	—	1	1	4	—	—	9	9
Darragh John	100	10	—	—	—	2	1	4	—	—	18	—
Dutton Kingsman	6	5	—	—	—	1	1	—	—	—	3	6
Dutton Richard	200	12	1	—	—	5	3	8	—	1	19	—
Eleson Jared	100	6	—	—	—	1	1	—	—	—	14	9
Farra Oliver	—	—	—	—	—	2	1	—	—	—	2	6
Gillieson John	50	—	—	—	—	4	2	—	—	1	Free Man	
Griffith William	150	10	—	—	—	3	2	6	—	1	2	—
Harclay Thomas	100	11	—	—	—	—	—	—	—	—	14	—
Johnson James	—	—	—	—	—	1	1	—	—	—	5	—
Linn Hugh	100	7	—	—	—	4	2	6	—	—	17	6
Lindsay James	150	10	—	—	—	6	3	12	—	1	9	—
Martin Abraham	200	12	1	—	—	5	3	8	—	1	19	—
Myer Henry	100	9	—	—	—	3	3	—	—	—	18	3
McCloskey Joseph	130	10	—	—	—	2	2	2	—	1		1
McMinn John	50	8	—	—	51	—	—	—	—	—	12	—
Noblet William	100	—	—	—	47	4	2	—	—	—	11	9
Peters William	300	20	1	4	36	9	4	14	2	3	13	9
Pike Abraham	29	10	—	—	12	2	2	—	2	—	7	6
Perkins John a house and Garden	—	—	—	—	—	—	—	—	—	—	3	9
Richards Edward	—	—	—	1	30	2	—	6	—	—	7	6
Reed John	—	9	—	—	—	2	1	—	—	—	2	—
Richards Jacob	170	13	—	—	—	6	4	7	—	1	12	9
Richards John	80	—	—	—	—	—	—	—	—	1	Free Man	
Richards Jonathan	130	8	—	—	—	5	1	4	—	1	1	—
Ratten John	100	8	—	—	—	3	2	5	—	—	16	—
Shelley Nathan	—	—	—	—	—	1	—	—	—		Poor	
Smith Richard	100	3	—	—	—	2	1	2	—	—	12	—
Thomson William	100	8	—	—	—	2	2	2	—	—	18	—
Tayler Elizabeth	125	—	—	—	—	—	—	—	1	—	15	—
Withrow Alexander	—	—	—	—	—	2	1	—	—	—	5	—
Withrow William	—	—	—	—	—	2	1	—	—	—	5	—
Phillip Taylers Children	180	—	—	—	—	—	—	—	—	1	3	—

INMATES

Name	Land	Cattle	Horses	Pounds	Shillings	Pence
John Bean	—	—	—	—	3	6
Samuel Farra	—	1	1	—	5	—
John Farra	—	2	—	—	4	—
Jacob Pike	—	1	1	—	5	—

cereal crops required incessant labor only during spring planting and autumn harvesting. This less burdensome work rhythm led many northern cultivators to fill out their calendars with intermittent work as clockmakers, shoemakers, carpenters, and weavers.

Changing Values

Boston's weather on April 29, 1695, began warm and sunny, noted the devout merchant Samuel Sewall in his diary. But by afternoon thunder, lightning, and hailstones "as big as pistol and musket bullets" pummeled the town. Sewall dined that evening with Cotton Mather, New England's most prominent Puritan clergyman. Mather wondered why "more ministers houses than others proportionally had been smitten with lightning." The words were hardly out of his mouth before hailstones began to shatter the windows of Sewall's house, "flying to the middle of the room or farther." Sewall and Mather fell to their knees and broke into prayer together "after this awful Providence."

These two third-generation Massachusetts Puritans understood that God was angry with them as leaders of a people whose piety and moral rectitude were being overtaken by worldliness. Even if farms were getting smaller and open land scarcer, growth and success had undermined early utopian dreams and made Massachusetts "sermon-proof," as one dejected minister put it.

In other parts of the North, the expansive environment and the Protestant emphasis on self-discipline and hard work were also breeding qualities that would become hallmarks of American culture: an ambitious outlook, individualistic behavior, and a love of material things. In Europe, most tillers of the soil expected little from life. With no frontier lands ripe for exploitation, impoverished peasant farmers viewed life not as a quest for achievement but as a perpetual struggle against famine and disease. In America, starvation was almost unknown, and few obstacles held people back from uncharted expanses of land once they had overwhelmed the Native Americans. "Every man," one colonist remarked, "expects one day or another to be upon a footing with his wealthiest neighbor."

Commitment to religion, family, and community did not disappear in the eighteenth century. But fewer men and women saw daily existence as a preparation for the afterlife. They began to regard land not simply as a source of livelihood but as a commodity to be bought and sold for profit. "Every man is for himself," sighed a Philadelphia leader only a generation after Penn had planted his "holy experiment." A few decades later, a New Yorker wrote that "the only principle of life propagated among the young people is to get money, and men are only esteemed according to what they are worth, that is, the money they are possessed of."

A slender almanac, written by the twelfth child of a poor Boston candlemaker, captured the new outlook with wit and charm. Born in 1706, Benjamin Franklin had climbed the ladder of success spectacularly. Running away from a harsh apprenticeship to an older brother when he was 16, he abandoned a declining Boston for a rising Philadelphia. By 23, he had learned the printer's trade

Boston-born Benjamin Franklin's wit and pragmatic wisdom made his Poor Richard's Almanack *the most widely read book in the colonies after the Bible.*

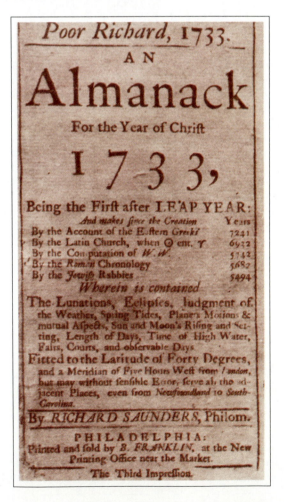

and was publishing the *Pennsylvania Gazette.* Three years later, he began *Poor Richard's Almanack,* next to the Bible the most widely read book in the colonies.

Franklin spiced his annual almanac—the ordinary person's guide to weather and useful information—with quips, adages, and homespun philosophy. Eventually this homely material added up to a primer for success published in 1747 as *The Way to Wealth.* "The sleeping fox gathers no poultry" and "Lost time is never found again," advised Poor Richard, emphasizing that time is money. "It costs more to maintain one vice than to raise two children," he counseled, advocating not morality but practicality. "Sloth makes all things difficult but industry all easy," he assured his readers. Ever cocky, Franklin caught the spirit of the rising secularism of the eighteenth century. He embodied the growing utilitarian doctrine that the good is whatever is useful and the notion that the community is best served through individual self-improvement and accomplishment.

Women in Northern Colonial Society

In 1662, Elnathan Chauncy, a Massachusetts schoolboy, copied into his writing book that "the soul consists of two portions, inferior and superior; the superior is masculine and eternal; the feminine inferior and mortal." This lesson had been taught for generations on both sides of the Atlantic. It was part of a larger conception of a world, of God's design, that assigned degrees of status and stations in life to all persons. In such a world, the place of women was, by definition, subordinate to that of men. From infancy, women were taught to be modest, patient, compliant. Regarded by men as weak of mind and large of heart, they existed for and through men. As daughters they were subject to their fathers, as wives to their husbands. John Winthrop reflected the common view that such submission was natural and hence "a true wife accounts her subjection her honor."

European women usually accepted these narrowly circumscribed roles. Few complained, at least openly, that their work was generally limited to housewifery and midwifery. They remained silent about exclusion from the early public schools and laws that transferred to their husbands any property or income they brought into a marriage. Nor could women speak in church or participate in governing it, and they had no legal voice in political affairs.

Most women did not expect to choose a husband for love; parental guidance prevailed in a society in which producing legal heirs was the means of transmitting property. Once wed, women expected to remain so until death, for they could rarely obtain a divorce.

On the colonial frontier, women's lives changed in modest ways. In Europe, about one of ten women did not marry. But in the colonies, where men outnumbered women for the first century, a spinster was almost unheard of, and widows remarried with astounding speed. "A young widow with 4 or 5 children, who among the middling or inferior ranks of people in Europe would have little chance for a second husband," observed one Englishman, "is in America frequently courted as a sort of fortune." *Woman* and *wife* thus became nearly synonymous.

A second difference concerned property rights. Single women and widows in the colonies, as in England, could make contracts, hold and convey property, represent themselves in court, and conduct business. Under English common law, a woman forfeited these rights, as well as all property, when she married. In the colonies, however, legislatures and courts gave wives more control over property brought into marriage or left at their husbands' death. They also enjoyed broader rights to act for and with their husbands in business transactions. In addition, young colonial women slowly gained the right of consenting to a marriage partner—a right that came by default to the thousands of female indentured servants who completed their labor contracts and had no parents within 3,000 miles to dictate to them.

While colonial society did not encourage or reward female individuality and self-reliance, women acted in competent and complementary ways. Women had limited career choices and rights but broad responsibilities. Moreover, the work spaces and daily routines of husband and wife overlapped and intersected far more than today. A farm wife helped with planting and harvesting, milked cows, made candles and soap, butter and cheese, smoked meat, made cloth, and sometimes marketed farm products. The merchant wife kept shop, handled accounts when her husband voyaged abroad, and helped supervise the servants and apprentices. "Deputy husbands" and "yoke mates" were revealing terms used by New Englanders to describe eighteenth-century wives.

Women also figured importantly in neighborhood life. Within female networks, dictated by custom rather than by law, older women shaped the behavior of young women, aided the needy, and subtly affected menfolk, who held the formal reins of authority. In church life, where they outnumbered men, women worked privately in their families to promote religion in outlying areas, to seat and unseat ministers, and to influence the community's moral life. Periodically they appeared as visionaries and mystics. Schooled to believe that they were inferior and subordinate, women nonetheless operated within their families and localities to shape the world around them.

As midwives, women held vital responsibilities. Until the late eighteenth century, the "obstetrick art" was almost entirely in women's hands. Midwives such as Anne Hutchinson counseled pregnant women, delivered babies, supervised postpartum recovery, and participated in ceremonies of infant baptism and burial. Mrs. Phillips, an immigrant to Boston in 1719 who delivered more than 3,000 infants in her 42-year career, was a familiar figure as she hurried through the streets to attend the lying-in of about 70 women each year. Since colonial women were pregnant or nursing infants for about half of the years between 20 and 40 and because childbirth was a recurring and dangerous crisis, the circle of female friends and relatives who attended childbirth created strong networks of mutual assistance.

In her role as wife and mother, the eighteenth-century northern woman differed somewhat from her English counterpart. Whereas English women married in their mid-twenties, American women typically took husbands a few years earlier. This head start increased their childbearing years. Hence the average colonial family included five children (two more typically died in infancy), whereas the English family contained fewer than three. Gradually, as the coastal plain filled up in the eighteenth century and older family farms were divided and subdivided among descendants of the early settlers, marriage age crept up and the number of children per family inched down.

Northern childbearing patterns differed considerably. In the seventeenth century, stern fathers dominated Puritan family life, and few were reluctant to punish unruly children. "Better whip'd than damn'd," advised Cotton Mather, the minister who served as the Puritan conscience of New England. Many parents believed that breaking the young child's will created a pious and submissive personality. In Quaker families, however, mothers played a more active role in child rearing. More permissive, they relied on tenderness and love rather than guilt to mold their children. Attitudes toward choosing a marriage partner also separated early Puritan and Quaker approaches to family life. Puritan parents usually arranged their children's marriages but allowed them the right to veto. Young Quaker men and women made their own matches, subject to parental veto.

Despite this initial diversity in child rearing, the

Childbirth was an oft-repeated event in the lives of most colonial wives. In this portrait of the Cheney family, the older woman is a nanny or mother-in-law; the younger women holding a baby is Mr. Cheney's second wife.

father-dominated family of New England gradually declined in the eighteenth century. In its place rose the mother-centered family, in which affectionate parents encouraged self-expression and independence in their children. This "modern" approach, on the rise in Europe as well, brought the colonists closer to the parenting methods of the coastal Native Americans, who initially had been widely disparaged for their lax methods of rearing their young.

THE PLANTATION SOUTH

Between 1680 and 1750, the white tidewater settlements of the southern colonies made the transition from a frontier society marked by a high immigration rate, a surplus of males, and an unstable social organization to a settled society composed mostly of native-born families. After 1715, Scots-Irish and German immigrants flooded into the backcountry of Virginia, the Carolinas, and Georgia, this last intended as a debtors' haven but designed in 1732 as a buffer between Spanish Florida and the Carolinas. But between the piedmont region and the ocean, a mature southern culture took form.

The Tobacco Coast

Tobacco production in Virginia and Maryland expanded rapidly in the seventeenth century, with exports reaching 25 million pounds annually during the 1680s. But war in Europe and the Americas for the two decades bridging the turn of the century drove up transportation costs and dampened the demand for tobacco. Stagnation in the tobacco market lasted from the mid-1680s until about 1715.

Yet it was in this period that the Upper South underwent a profound social transformation. First, slaves replaced indentured servants so rapidly that by 1730 the unfree labor force was overwhelmingly black. Second, the planters responded to the dull tobacco market by diversifying their crops. They shifted some of their tobacco fields to grain, hemp, and flax; increased their herds of cattle and swine; and became more self-sufficient by developing local industries to produce iron, leather, and textiles. By the 1720s, when a profitable tobacco trade with France created a new period of prosperity, their economy was much more diverse and resilient than a generation before.

Third, the structure of the population changed rapidly. Black slaves grew from about 7 percent to 35 percent of the region's population between 1690 and 1750, and the drastic imbalance between white men and women disappeared. Families rather than single men now predominated. The earlier frontier society of white immigrants who mostly lived short and unrewarding lives as indentured servants grew into an eighteenth-century plantation society of native-born freeholder families.

Notwithstanding the influx of Africans, slave-owning was far from universal. As late as 1750, a majority of families owned no slaves at all. Among slave owners, not more than one-tenth held more than 20 slaves. Nonetheless, the common goal was the large plantation where black slaves made the earth yield up profits to support an aristocratic life for their masters. One Virginia minister observed that "the custom of the country is such that without slaves a man's children stand but a poor chance to marry in reputation."

The Chesapeake planters who acquired the best land and accumulated enough capital to invest heavily in slaves created a gentry life style that set them apart from ordinary farmers such as Devereaux Jarratt's father. By the eighteenth century, the development of the northern colonies had produced prosperous farmers worth several thousand pounds. But such wealth paled by comparison with the estates of men such as Charles Carroll of Maryland and Robert "King" Carter and William Byrd of Virginia. These Chesapeake planters counted their slaves by the hundreds, their acres by the thousands, and their fortunes by the tens of thousands of pounds.

Ritual display of wealth marked southern gentry life. Racing thoroughbred horses and gambling on them recklessly, sometimes for purses of £100 (at a time when a laboring man earned £40 per year) became common sport for young gentlemen, who had often been educated in England. Planters began to construct stately brick Georgian mansions, some designed by imported English architects. These "great houses," similar in style to the houses of English gentry, were filled with imported furniture, attended by liveried black slaves, and graced by formal gardens and orchards.

Some observers saw the cultivated aristocratic life style as a veneer. "If a [man] has Money, Negroes, and Land enough," scoffed a Scottish newcomer, "he is a complete Gentleman. These hide all his defects, usher him into the best of company, and draw upon him the smiles of the fair Sex." Affected or not, the emerging Chesapeake planter elite con-

The distribution of cultivated fields, dwellings, and commercial buildings in the tidewater landscape created "communities" without towns (rendered from historical and archaeological evidence).

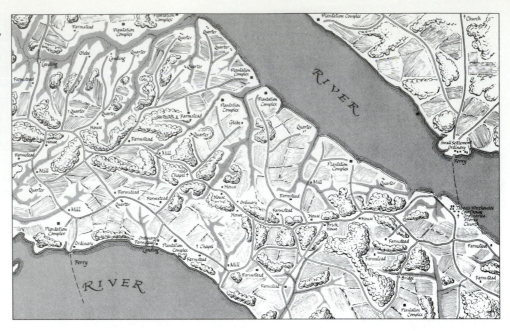

trolled the county courts, officered the local militia, ruled the parish vestries of the Anglican church, and made law in their legislative assemblies. To their sons they passed the mantle of political and social leadership.

For all their social display, southern planter squires were essentially agrarian businessmen. They spent their days obtaining credit, dealing in land and slaves, scheduling planting and harvesting routines, conferring with overseers, disciplining slaves, and arranging leases with tenants. Cultivating tobacco was a particularly demanding enterprise and a highly personal one. Whereas other staple crops such as wheat and corn required intensive labor only during the planting and harvesting seasons, tobacco demanded the planter's attention throughout the year as the crop moved through the many stages of planting, transplanting, topping, cutting, curing, and packing. A planter's reputation rose and fell with the quality of his crop, and so personalized was the culture of tobacco that planters stamped their hogsheads of leaf with their initials or emblem. "Question a planter on the subject," explained one observer, "and he will tell you that he cultivates such or such a kind [of tobacco], as for example, Colonel Carter's sort, John Cole's sort' or [that of] some other leading crop master."

Planters' wives also shouldered many responsibilities. They superintended cloth production and the processing and preparation of food while ruling over households crowded with children, slaves, and visitors. An aristocratic veneer gave the luster of gentility to plantations from Maryland to North Carolina, but it could not disguise the fact that these were large working farms, often so isolated from each other that the planter and his wife lived a "solitary and unsociable existence," as one phrased it. With only infrequent contact with the outside world, they learned to be independent as they managed their own little communities of servants, slaves, and family members. Patriarchs on their estates, southern planters were "haughty and jealous of their liberties, impatient of restraint, and can scarcely bear the thought of being controlled by any superior power," noted Andrew Burnaby, a mid-eighteenth-century visitor.

The Rice Coast

The plantation economy of the Lower South in the eighteenth century rested on the production of rice and indigo. Rice exports surpassed 1.5 million pounds per year by 1710 and reached 80 million pounds by the eve of the Revolution. Indigo, a blue dye obtained from plants for use in textiles, became a staple crop in the 1740s after Eliza Lucas Pinckney, a wealthy South Carolina planter's wife, experimented successfully with its cultivation. Within a

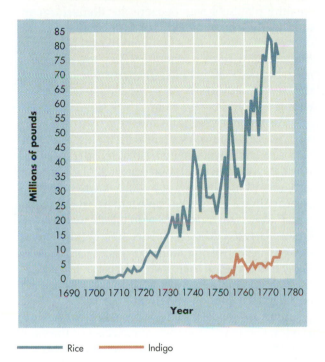

Rice and Indigo Exports from South Carolina and Georgia, 1698–1775

— Rice   — Indigo

Source: U.S. Bureau of the Census.

brought together people of all classes. They came to settle debts, dispute land boundaries, sue and be sued. When court was over, a multitude lingered on, drinking, gossiping, and staging horse races, cockfights, wrestling matches, footraces, and fiddling contests. Competition and assertiveness lay at the heart of all these demonstrations of male personal prowess.

The church, almost always Anglican in the South before 1750, also became a center of community gathering. Philip Fithian described the animated socializing before worship, men "giving and receiving letters of business, reading advertisements, consulting about the price of tobacco and grain, and settling either the lineage, age, or qualities of favourite horses." Then, as the hour of service approached, people filed into church. Reaffirming the social gradation of their rank-conscious society, the lower and middling planters entered first. They stood attentively until the wealthy gentry, striding in together "in a body," took their pews at the front. After church, socializing continued, with young people strolling together and older ones extending invitations to Sunday dinner. The pious Sabbath atmosphere perpetuated in New England was little in evidence.

The Backcountry

While the southern gentry matured along the tobacco and rice coasts, settlers poured into the upland backcountry. As late as 1730, only hunters and Indian fur traders had known this vast expanse of hilly red clay and fertile limestone soils, stretching from Pennsylvania to Georgia. Over the next four decades, it attracted some 250,000 inhabitants, nearly half the southern white population.

Thousands of land-hungry German and Scots-Irish settlers spilled into the interior valleys running along the eastern side of the Appalachians. They squatted on land, lived tensely with neighboring Indians in a region where boundaries were shadowy, and created a subsistence society of small farms. Gradually acquiring slaves, this "mixed medley from all countries and the off scouring of America," as one colonist described them, pursued mixed farming and cattle raising. Their enclaves remained isolated from the coastal region for several generations, which helped these pioneers cling fiercely to the folkways they had known on the other side of the Atlantic.

generation, indigo production had spread into Georgia. It soon ranked among the leading colonial exports.

The expansion of rice production transformed the swampy coastal lowlands. In the rice-producing region radiating out from Charleston, planters imported thousands of slaves after 1720; by 1740, they composed nearly 90 percent of the region's inhabitants. White population declined as wealthy planters left their estates in the hands of resident overseers. They wintered in cosmopolitan Charleston and summered in Newport, Rhode Island, their refuge from seasonal malaria along the rice coast. Rice converted the eighteenth-century Carolina coast into a tropical plantation regime similar to that of the sugar-producing West Indies. At midcentury, a shocked New England visitor described it as a society "divided into opulent and lordly planters, poor and spiritless peasants, and vile slaves."

Throughout the plantation South, the courthouse became a central gathering place. Court day

The crudity of backcountry life appalled many visitors from the more refined seaboard. In 1733, William Byrd described a large Virginia frontier plantation as "a poor, dirty hovel, with hardly anything in it but children that wallowed about like so many pigs." Charles Woodmason, a stiff-necked Anglican minister who spent three years tramping between settlements in the Carolina upcountry, could hardly find words to express his shock. "Through the licentiousness of the people," he wrote, "many hundreds live in concubinage—swopping their wives as cattle and living in a state of nature more irregularly and unchastely than the Indians."

What Byrd and Woodmason were really observing was the poverty of frontier life and the lack of schools, churches, and towns. Most families plunged into the backcountry with only a few crude household possessions and farm tools, perhaps a pair of oxen, a few chickens and swine, and the clothes on their backs. They lived in rough-hewn log cabins—"cold cabins, unfloored and almost open to the sky," Woodmason observed—and planted their corn, beans, and wheat between the stumps of trees they had felled. Women toiled alongside men, in the fields, forest, and homestead. For a generation, these settlers endured a poor diet, endless work, and meager rewards.

By the 1760s, the southern backcountry began to emerge from the frontier stage. Small marketing towns such as Camden, South Carolina; Salisbury, North Carolina; Winchester, Virginia; and Fredericktown, Maryland, became centers of craft activity, church life, and local government. Farms began producing surpluses for shipment east. Density of settlement increased, creating a social life known for harvest festivals, logrolling contests, horse races, wedding celebrations, dances, and prodigious drinking bouts during which hard cider, whiskey, and apple and peach brandy flowed freely. Class distinctions remained narrow compared with the older seaboard settlements, but many backcountry settlements acquired the look of permanence.

Family Life in the South

As the South emerged from the early era of withering mortality and stunted families, male and female roles gradually became more physically and functionally separated. In most areas, the white gender ratio reached parity by the 1720s. Women lost the leverage in the marriage market that scarcity had provided earlier. With the growth of slavery, the work role of white women also changed. The wealthy planter's wife became the domestic manager in the "great house." In a description of his daughters' daily routine, William Byrd II pointed to the emerging female identity: "They are every day up to their elbows in housewifery, which will qualify them effectually for useful wives and if they live long enough for notable women."

The balanced sex ratio and the growth of slavery also brought changes for southern males. The planter's son had always been trained to operate in the world beyond the plantation-house doors. Learning horsemanship, the use of a gun, and the rhythms of agricultural life was as important a part of a young man's education as lessons with tutors such as Devereaux Jarratt. Ordering and disciplining slaves also became a part of the southern youth's education. Many had slaves of their own before reaching adulthood. Some planters worried that this would lead, as Thomas Jefferson would later write, to "odious peculiarities" in the character of southern men since slavery involved "a perpetual exercise of the most boisterous passions" by white masters "nursed, educated, and daily exercised in tyranny." But bred to command, southern planters' sons also developed a self-confidence and authority that propelled many of them into leadership roles during the American Revolution.

On the small farms of the tidewater region and throughout the back settlements, women's roles closely resembled those of northern women. Women labored in the fields alongside their menfolk. "She is a very civil woman," noted an observer of a southern frontierswoman," and shows nothing of ruggedness or immodesty in her carriage; yet she will carry a gun in the woods and kill deer and turkeys, shoot down wild cattle, catch and tie hogs, knock down beeves with an ax, and perform the most manful exercises as well as most men in those parts."

Marriage and family life were also more informal in the backcountry. With vast areas unattended by ministers of any religion and courthouses out of reach, most couples married or "took up" with each other in matches unsanctioned by state or church. The arrival of an itinerant clergyman on horseback typically brought forth dozens of couples living in common-law marriage who asked to have vows performed and their children legitimized by baptism.

Respectable clergymen saw the frontier settlers living in lascivious abandon. But the poor upcountry hunters and farmers were really only the first of many generations of pioneers who made do as best they could on the forest's edge, where the institutions of settled society had not yet arrived.

THE URBAN WORLD OF COMMERCE AND IDEAS

Only about 5 percent of the eighteenth-century colonists lived in towns as large as 2,500, and none of the commercial centers boasted a population greater than 16,000 in 1750 or 30,000 in 1775. Yet the urban societies were at the leading edge of social change. Almost all the alterations associated with the advent of "modern" life occurred first in the seaport towns and radiated outward to the villages, farms, and plantations of the hinterland. In the seaboard centers, the transition first occurred from a barter to a commercial economy, from a social order based on assigned status to one based on achievement, from rank-conscious and deferential politics to participatory and contentious politics, and from small-scale craftsmanship to factory production. In addition, the cities were the centers of intellectual life and the conduits through which European ideas flowed into the colonies.

Sinews of Trade

In the half century after 1690, Boston, New York, and Philadelphia blossomed from urban villages into thriving commercial centers. This urban growth accompanied the development of the agricultural interior, to which the seaports were closely linked. As the colonial population rose and spread geographically, minor seaports such as Newport, Providence, Baltimore, Annapolis, Norfolk, and Charleston gathered 10,000 or more inhabitants.

Trade was indispensable to colonial economic life, and cities were trade centers. Through them flowed colonial export staples such as tobacco, rice, wheat, timber products, and fish as well as the imported goods that colonists needed. The imports included manufactured and luxury goods from England such as glass, paper, iron implements, and cloth; wine, spices, coffee, tea, and sugar from other parts of the world; and the human cargo to fill the labor gap.

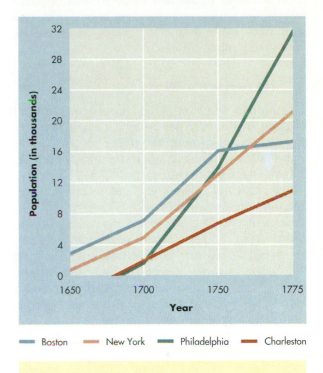

Urban Population Growth, 1650–1775

Legend: Boston, New York, Philadelphia, Charleston

Source: Nash, *The Urban Crucible*, 1979.

By the eighteenth century, the American economy was integrated into an Atlantic basin trading system that connected Great Britain, western Europe, Africa, the West Indies, and Newfoundland. In the commercial seaports, the pivotal figure was the merchant. He linked producers and consumers, coordinating a commercial network that reached from the coastal city to the interior villages, plantations, and frontier trading posts and stretched outward across the Atlantic. Frequently engaged in both retail and wholesale trade, the merchant was also moneylender (for no banks yet existed), shipbuilder, insurance agent, land developer, and often coordinator of artisan production.

The colonists could never produce enough exportable raw materials to pay for the imported goods they craved, so they had to earn credits in England by supplying the West Indies and other areas with foodstuffs and timber products. They also accumulated credit by providing shipping and distributional services. New Englanders became the most ambitious participants in the carrying trade. Sailing from Boston, Salem, Newport, and Providence, Yankee merchant seamen, manning Yankee-built ships, dominated the traffic along the Atlantic seaboard, the Caribbean trade, and the transatlantic commerce. A much higher proportion of New England's population made its living in maritime enterprise than in any other colonial region.

The Artisan's World

Though merchants stood first in wealth and prestige in the colonial towns, artisans were far more numerous. About two-thirds of urban adult males, slaves excluded, labored at handicrafts. By the mid-eighteenth century, the colonial cities contained scores of specialized "leather apron men," not only the proverbial butcher, baker, and candlestick maker but also carpenters and coopers (who made barrels); shoemakers and tailors; silver-, gold-, pewter-, and blacksmiths; mast and sail makers; masons, plasterers, weavers, potters; and many more. Handicraft specialization increased as the cities matured, but every artisan worked with hand tools, usually in small shops.

Work patterns for artisans were irregular, dictated by weather, hours of daylight, erratic delivery of raw materials, and shifting consumer demand. When ice blocked northern harbors, mariners and dockworkers endured slack time. If prolonged rain delayed the slaughter of cows in the country or made impassable the rutted roads into the city, the tanner and the shoemaker laid their tools aside. The hatter depended upon the supply of beaver skins, which could stop abruptly if disease struck an Indian tribe or war disrupted the fur trade. Every urban artisan knew "broken days," slack spells, and dull seasons. Ordinary laborers dreaded winter, for it was a season when cities had "little occasion for the labor of the poor," and firewood to heat a small house could cost several months' wages.

Urban artisans took fierce pride in their crafts. While deferring to those above them, they saw themselves as the backbone of the community, contributing essential products and services. "Our professions rendered us useful and necessary members of our community," the Philadelphia shoemakers asserted; "proud of that rank, we aspired to no higher." This self-esteem and desire for community recognition sometimes jostled with the upper-class view of artisans as mere mechanics, part of the "vulgar herd."

In striving for respectability, artisans placed a premium on achieving economic independence.

Every craftsman began as an apprentice, spending five or more teenage years learning the "mysteries of the craft" in the shop of a master "mechanick." After fulfilling his contract, the young artisan became a "journeyman." He sold his labor to a master craftsman and frequently lived in his house, ate at his table, and sometimes married his daughter. The journeyman hoped to complete within a few years the three-step climb from servitude to self-employment. After setting up his own shop, he could control his work hours and acquire the respect that came from economic independence. In trades requiring greater organization and capital, such as distilling and shipbuilding, the rise from journeyman to master proved impossible for many artisans. Nonetheless, the ideal of the independent craftsman prevailed.

In good times, urban artisans fared well. They expected to earn "a decent competency" and eventually to purchase a small house. In Philadelphia, about half the artisans living in the first half of the eighteenth century left personal property worth between £50 and £200 sterling, signifying a comfortable standard of living. Another quarter left more than £200, often including slaves and indentured servants. New England's artisans did not fare so well, for their economy was weaker in the eighteenth century. But in all cities, artisans took pride in their life of productive labor. "The meanest [of them] thinks he has a right of civility from the greatest" person in the city, wrote one city dweller.

The careers of two immigrant families in Philadelphia demonstrate how differently urban artisans fared. Francis Richardson, a Quaker mariner from England, emigrated in the 1680s. He acquired land in Penn's colony, bought several slaves, and at his death in 1688 left his family in comfortable circumstances. Richardson's widow married a Quaker merchant, and when her son, Francis, Jr., grew up, he learned the silversmith's trade. Francis, Jr., married the daughter of a wealthy Bucks County landowner and passed on to his sons, Francis and Joseph, a place among the Philadelphia Quaker elite when he died in 1729. Francis III practiced silversmithing like his father, but his assets launched him on mercantile and real estate ventures that allowed him to retire to a country estate at age 54 and spend the remainder of his life in philanthropic and civic affairs. The Richardsons had risen from mariner to country gentleman, from subsistence to affluence, in three generations.

César Ghiselin, a French Huguenot, also came

to Philadelphia in the 1680s. Establishing himself as a silversmith, he prospered modestly, ranking just below Francis Richardson, Jr., on the city tax list in 1709. Nine years later, he moved to Maryland, but he returned to the Quaker city in 1728 after his wife's death. When he died in 1733, he left a considerable estate. But then the family fortunes collapsed. César's sons, Nicholas and William, made inauspicious marriages, and though one of them carried on his father's silversmithing trade, they could not maintain their father's gains. William's son, named César after his grandfather, became a barber in Philadelphia. By the bitter winter of 1761, his family was receiving poor relief. The grandson of the first Francis Richardson served on the committee that distributed blankets and firewood to the grandson of the first César Ghiselin. The Ghiselins had declined from silversmith to barber and from middle class to near poverty in three generations.

Working under supervision was thought of as a temporary status by most artisans, who aspired to self-employment. In a high-capital industry such as shipbuilding, most did not attain the status of master, however.

These two vignettes remind us that in colonial cities, success was far from automatic, even for those following all of Poor Richard's advice about hard work and frugal living. Nor did urban growth and economic expansion guarantee success. An advantageous marriage, luck in avoiding illness, and the size of an inheritance were often the critical factors in whether an artisan moved up or down the ladder of success.

Urban Social Structure

Population growth, economic development, and a series of wars that punctuated the period from 1690 to 1765 altered the urban social structure. Stately townhouses rose as testimony to the fortunes acquired in trade, shipbuilding, war contracting, and urban land development. This last may have been the most profitable of all. "It is almost a proverb," a Philadelphian observed in the 1760s, "that every great fortune made here within these 50 years has been by land." Some merchants amassed fortunes. A merchant's estate of £2,000 sterling was counted impressive in the early eighteenth century. Two generations later, some commercial titans had become America's first millionaires by accumulating estates of £10,000 to £20,000 sterling.

The rise of Thomas Hancock, upon whose fortune his less commercially astute nephew, John Hancock, would later construct a shining political career, provides a glimpse of how war could catapult an enterprising trader to affluence. Hancock, a minister's son, became a bookseller in Boston. An opportune marriage to the daughter of a prosperous merchant provided a toehold in commerce and enough capital to invest in several vessels. By 1735, Hancock had made enough money, much of it from smuggling tea, to build a mansion on Beacon Hill.

When war broke out with Spain in 1739, Hancock used his connections with the governor to obtain lucrative supply contracts for military expeditions to the Caribbean and Nova Scotia. He also invested heavily in privateers, who engaged in private warfare against enemy shipping and auctioned the enemy vessels they overpowered. When peace returned in 1748, all Boston witnessed what war had done for a well-connected merchant. The man who had sold books from a tiny shop on Drawbridge Street 15 years before now imported a four-horse chariot from London with the interior lined in scarlet and the doors emblazoned with a heraldic shield.

Alongside urban wealth grew urban poverty. From the beginning, every city had its disabled, orphaned, and widowed who required aid. But after 1720, poverty marred the lives of many more city dwellers. Many were war widows with numerous children and no means of support. Others were rural migrants seeking opportunities in the city. Some were recent immigrants, who found fewer chances for employment than earlier. Boston was hit especially hard. Its economy stagnated in the 1740s, and the taxpayers strained under the burden of paying for heavy war expenditures. The overseers of the poor groaned that their relief expenditures were double the outlays of any town of equal size "upon the face of the whole earth."

Burdened with mounting poor taxes, cities devised new ways of helping the needy. Rather than support the impoverished in their homes with "outrelief" payments, officials built large almshouses where the poor could be housed and fed more economically. Many of the indigent preferred "to starve in their homes," rather than leave their neighborhoods to suffer the discipline and indignities of the poorhouse. Boston's poor women also resisted laboring in the linen factory that was built in 1750 to enable them to contribute to their own support through spinning and weaving. Despite the warnings of Boston's ministers that "if any would not work, neither should they eat," they refused to leave their children at home to labor in America's first textile factory.

The increasing gap between the wealthy and the poor in the colonial cities was recorded in the eighteenth-century tax lists. The top 5 percent of taxpayers increased their share of the cities' taxable assets from about 30 percent to 50 percent between 1690 and 1770. The bottom half of the taxable inhabitants saw their share of the wealth shrink from about 10 percent to 4 percent. The urban middle classes, except in Boston, continued to make gains. But the growth of princely fortunes amid increasing poverty made some urban dwellers reflect that the conditions of the Old World seemed to be reappearing in the New.

The Entrepreneurial Ethos

As the cities grew, new values took hold. In the older, medieval, "corporate" view of society, economic life ideally operated according to what was equitable, not what was profitable. Citizens usually

agreed that government should provide for the general welfare by regulating prices and wages, setting quality controls, licensing providers of service such as tavernkeepers and ferrymen, and supervising public markets where all food was sold. Such regulation seemed natural because a community was defined not as a collection of individuals, each entitled to pursue separate interests, but as a single body of interrelated parts where individual rights and responsibilities formed a seamless web.

In America, as in Europe, new ideas about economic life gathered support. The subordination of private interests to the commonweal became viewed as a lofty but unrealistic ideal. Prosperity required the encouragement of acquisitive appetites rather than self-denial, for ambition would spur economic activity as more people sought more goods. According to the new view, if people were allowed to pursue their own material desires com-

Wealth Distribution in Colonial America
Percentage of wealth held by the richest 10% and the poorest 30% of the population in two cities and one rural area

Year	Richest 10%	Poorest 30%
Boston		
1684–1699	41.2	3.3
1700–1715	54.5	2.8
1716–1725	61.7	2.0
1726–1735	65.6	1.9
1736–1745	58.6	1.8
1746–1755	55.2	1.8
1756–1765	67.5	1.4
1766–1775	61.1	2.0
Philadelphia		
1684–1699	36.4	4.5
1700–1715	41.3	4.9
1716–1725	46.8	3.9
1726–1735	53.6	3.7
1736–1745	51.3	2.6
1746–1755	70.1	1.5
1756–1765	60.3	1.1
1766–1775	69.9	1.0
Chester County, Pennsylvania		
1693	23.8	17.4
1715	25.9	13.1
1730	28.6	9.8
1748	28.7	13.1
1760	29.9	6.3
1782	33.6	4.7

Source: Nash, *The Urban Crucible*, 1979.

petitively, they would collectively form a natural, impersonal market of producers and consumers that would operate to everyone's advantage.

As the colonial port towns took their places in the Atlantic world of commerce, merchants became accustomed to making decisions according to the emerging commercial ethic that rejected traditional restraints on entrepreneurial activity. If wheat fetched 8 shillings a bushel in the West Indies but only 5 in Boston, a grain merchant felt justified in sending all he could purchase from local farmers to the more distant buyer. Indifferent to individuals and local communities, the new transatlantic market responded only to the invisible laws of supply and demand.

The underlying tension between the new economic freedom and the older concern for the public good erupted only with food shortages or galloping inflation. Since the American colonies experienced none of the punishing famines that plagued Europe in this period, such crises occurred rarely, usually during war, when demand for provisions rose sharply.

Such a moment struck in Boston during Queen Anne's War. Merchant Andrew Belcher contracted to ship large quantities of wheat to the Caribbean, where higher prices would yield greater profit than in Boston. Ordinary neighbors, threatened with a bread shortage and angered that a townsman would put profit ahead of community needs, attacked one of Belcher's grain-laden ships in 1710. They sawed through the rudder and tried to run the vessel aground in order to seize the grain. Invoking the older ethic that the public welfare outweighed private interests, they took the law into their own hands. Even the grand jury, composed of substantial members of the community, hinted its approval of the violent action against Belcher by refusing to indict the rioters.

The two conceptions of community and economic life rubbed against each other for many decades. Urban merchants, shopkeepers, land speculators, and ambitious artisans—participants in England's rising commercial empire—cleaved more and more to the new economic formulas, although they continued to voice respect for the old precepts of the corporate community. The clergy continued to preach the traditional message: "Let no man seek his own, but every man another's wealth." But by the mid-eighteenth century, the pursuit of a profitable livelihood, not the social compact of the community, animated most city dwellers.

The American Enlightenment

Ideas about not only economic life but also the nature of the universe and improving the human condition reached across the Atlantic to the colonies. In the eighteenth century, an American version of the European intellectual movement called the Enlightenment occurred, and the cities became centers for disseminating these new ideas.

European thinkers, in what is called the Age of Reason, rejected the pessimistic Calvinist concept of innate human depravity, replacing it with the optimistic notion that a benevolent God had blessed humankind with the supreme gift of reason. Thinkers like John Locke, in his influential *Essay Concerning Human Understanding* (1689), argued that God had not predetermined the content of the human mind but furnished it with the capacity to acquire knowledge. All Enlightenment thinkers prized this acquisition of knowledge, for it allowed humankind to improve its condition. As the great scientific thinker Isaac Newton demonstrated, systematic investigation could unlock the secrets of the physical universe. Moreover, scientific knowledge could be applied to human institutions in order to improve society.

Though only a small number of educated colonists read the Enlightenment authors, they began in the eighteenth century to make significant contributions to the advancement of science. Naturalists such as John Bartram of Philadelphia ranged the eastern part of the continent gathering and describing American plants as part of the transatlantic attempt to classify all plant life into one universal system of classification. Professor John Winthrop III of Harvard made an unusually accurate measurement of the earth's distance from the sun. Standing above them all was Benjamin Franklin, whose spectacular (and dangerous) experiments with electricity, whose properties were just becoming known, earned him an international reputation.

Franklin's true genius as a figure of the Enlightenment came, however, in his practical application of scientific knowledge. Among his inventions were the lightning rod, which nearly ended the age-old danger of fires when lightning struck wooden buildings; bifocal spectacles; and an iron stove that heated rooms—in an age when firewood was a major item in the household budget—far more efficiently than the open fireplace commonly used. Franklin also made his adopted home of Philadelphia a center of the American Enlightenment. He played a leading

BENJAMIN FRANKLIN'S LIGHTNING ROD

In 1746, Benjamin Franklin, already a successful printer and civic organizer, began experimenting with electricity. That year, a Dutchman Pieter van Musschenbroek had learned how to condense electricity in a glass bottle (called a Leyden jar) and to produce electrical sparks by attaching a conductor to the two sides of the bottle. Throughout Europe, amateur scientists began to play with this device, but nobody really understood the source or the nature of the mysterious electrical "fluid."

By 1748, Franklin had constructed a number of experiments in his house in Philadelphia for producing brilliant sparks from Leyden jars. His *Experiments and Observations on Electricity* was published in London in 1751, putting his name on the lips of scientists all over Europe. Far more important than Franklin's household experiments, however, was his development of the technical means to test what many already believed—that lightning produced by thunderstorms was a form of electricity. Franklin reasoned that a common kite could give him access to the electrical charges in clouds. He stretched a large silk handkerchief across two crossed sticks of wood, fitted the kite with a tail, and attached a "sharp-pointed wire" to the top. To the end of the twine by which he held the kite aloft, Franklin fastened a metal key, and to that a silk ribbon that he held in his hand. "As soon as any of the thunder-clouds come over the kite," Franklin wrote, "the pointed wire will draw the electric fire from them, and the kite, with all the twine, will be electrified. . . . And when the rain has wet the kite and twine, so that it can conduct the electric fire freely, you will find it stream out plentifully from the key on the approach to your knuckle." Franklin claimed that the similar appearance and behavior of lightning sparks and electrical ones proved that the "fluid" streaming from the key was the same as the electricity produced in Leyden jars. His experiment constituted a breakthrough of one of the most formidable barriers of the unknown and opened up an entirely new field of controlled study. After the kite experiment was publicized in Europe, Franklin's achievements catapulted him to the forefront of the world's scientists and earned him the Copley Medal of the Royal Society of London, one of the most advanced scientific bodies in the world.

Franklin personified the eighteenth-century Enlightenment in his desire to understand the laws

Benjamin Franklin, 1762. Franklin installed the pair of balls at left in his study, the upper one connected to a lightning rod atop his house, the lower one grounded. During a lightning storm they would ring, to the delight of Franklin's guests.

This simulated destruction of a church by lightning was used in an Austrian book on electricity published in 1787. A demonstrator could show that a discharge of electricity from a Leyden jar could be carried harmlessly to the ground with a lightning rod rather than destroy the church by fire caused by lightning.

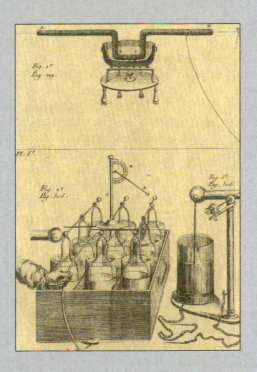

Franklin's first book on electricity, published in London in 1751, gained him international fame. The book went through many editions in Europe and America, with later editions including contributions from his correspondents and illustrations like the one above (from a French edition in 1773), which shows an assembly of Leyden jars, the first condensers, and an electrometer for measuring current.

that govern the natural world and in his determination to use these ideas, or what we would call scientific theory, to harness nature. In his experiments he encountered one of the most destructive natural forces, for electricity, in the form of lightning, destroyed buildings and ships with awful regularity. But once Franklin had learned the properties of electricity and had established that lightning was a form of it, it became relatively easy to contrive a metal rod, coated to prevent rusting, that would "throw off" the electricity and render it harmless. By 1753, convinced that he had mastered the theory of electricity and lightning, Franklin published a practical essay, "How to Secure Houses &c. from Lightning," in his best-selling *Poor Richard's Almanack*. Here he explained a natural phenomenon that had always terrified people, and he provided the world with a relatively simple and inexpensive device to protect lives and property. Soon lightning rods shot up on houses and barns all over the American colonies. Farmers, homeowners, mariners, and church wardens could soon rest easier, knowing that their barns, houses, ships, and churches were safe. What had seemed to be the wrathful work of an angry God now became a force within the power of human beings to control. If the power of lightning could be harnessed by the son of a Boston candle-maker far from the centers of learning in Europe, what other forces of nature might be understood and brought under rein?

role in founding America's first circulating library in 1731, an artisans' debating club for "mutual improvement" through discussion of the latest ideas from Europe, and an intercolonial scientific association that would emerge in 1769 as the American Philosophical Society. Though most colonists were not educated enough to participate actively in the American Enlightenment, the efforts of men such as Franklin exposed thousands, especially in the cities, to new currents of thought. This led to the growing sense that the colonists, blessed by their abundant environment, might truly inhabit the part of the world where the Enlightenment ideal of achieving a perfect society might be fulfilled.

THE GREAT AWAKENING

Many of the social, economic, and political changes occurring in the eighteenth-century colonies converged in the Great Awakening, the first of many religious revivals that would sweep American society during the next two centuries. The timing, as well as the religious and social character of the Awakening, varied from region to region. But everywhere this quest for spiritual renewal challenged old sources of authority and produced patterns of thought and behavior that helped fuel a revolutionary movement in the next generation.

Fading Faith

Colonial America in the early eighteenth century remained an overwhelmingly Protestant culture. The Puritan, or Congregational, church dominated all of New England except Rhode Island. Anglicanism held sway in much of New York and throughout the South except the backcountry. In the mid-Atlantic and in the back settlements, a polyglot of German Mennonites, Dunkers, Moravians, and Lutherans; Scots-Irish Presbyterians; and English Baptists and Quakers mingled.

Yet these diverse groups commanded the allegiance of only about one-third of the colonists. Those who went to no church at all remained the majority. In many areas, ministers and churches were simply unavailable. In Virginia, the most populous colony, only 60 clergymen in 1761 served a population of 350,000—one parson for every 5,800 people.

In the eighteenth century, most colonial churches were voluntary or gathered ("congre-

gated") groups, formed for reasons of conscience, not because of government compulsion. Catholics, Jews, and nonbelievers could not vote or hold office. But the persecution of Quakers and Catholics had largely passed, and some dissenting groups by 1720 had gained the right to use long-obligatory church taxes to support their own congregations.

The clergy often administered their congregations with difficulty. Anglicans and several German sects maintained close ties to mother churches across the Atlantic, while other denominations attempted to centralize authority. However, most efforts to tighten organization and discipline were ineffective. For example, Anglican ministers had to be ordained in England and make regular reports to the bishop of London. But once installed in Chesapeake parishes, Anglican priests faced wealthy planters who controlled the vestry (the local church's governing body), set the minister's salary, and drove out ministers who challenged them too forcefully. In Connecticut, the Saybrook Platform of 1708 created a network, or "consociation," of Congregational churches, but individual churches still preserved much of their autonomy.

Though governing their churches frustrated many clergymen, religious apathy was a far more pressing problem in the early eighteenth century. As early as the 1660s, the Congregational clergy of New England had attempted to return wandering sheep to the fold by adopting the Half-Way Covenant. It specified that children of church members, if they adhered to the "forms of godliness," might join the church even if they could not demonstrate that they had undergone a conversion experience. They could not, however, vote in church affairs or take communion.

Adopted in 1662, this compromise kept in the church many children of the founders, and they in turn could pass church membership on to their children. Some ministers took other measures to increase their flocks. Solomon Stoddard, for 60 years patriarch of the Congregational church in Northampton, Massachusetts, gave communion to every professing Christian and used an emotional style of preaching to reap annual "harvests" of souls.

Despite compromises and innovations, most church leaders saw creeping religious apathy when they surveyed their towns. An educated clergy, its energies often drained by doctrinal disputes within denominations, appealed too much to the mind and not enough to the heart. In such a state, as one Connecticut leader remembered it, "the spirit of God appeared to be awfully withdrawn."

The Awakeners' Message

The Great Awakening was not a unified movement but rather a series of revivals that swept different regions between 1720 and 1760 with varying degrees of intensity. The first stirrings came in the 1720s in New Jersey and Pennsylvania. Theodore Frelinghuysen, a Dutch Reformed minister, excited his congregation through emotional preaching. Avoiding theological abstractions, he concentrated on arousing a need to be "saved" among his parishioners. A neighboring Presbyterian, Gilbert Tennent, soon took up the Dutchman's techniques, with similar success.

From New Jersey the Awakening spread to Pennsylvania in the 1730s, especially among Presbyterians, and then broke out in the Connecticut River valley. There it was led by Jonathan Edwards, who had succeeded his grandfather, Solomon Stoddard, in Northampton's church. Edwards later became a philosophical giant in the colonies. But as a young man, he gained renown by lambasting his parishioners and warned them of the fate of "sinners in the hands of an angry God." "How manifold have been the abominations of your life!" Edwards preached. "Are there not some here that have debased themselves below the dignity of human nature, by wallowing in sensual filthiness, as swine in the mire . . . ?" Edwards paraded one sin after another before his trembling congregants: "God and your own consciences know what abominable lasciviousness you have practised in things not fit to be named, when you have been alone; when you ought to have been reading, or meditating, or on your knees before God in secret prayer."

After cataloging his parishioners' sins, Edwards drew such graphic pictures of the hell awaiting the unrepentant that his Northampton neighbors were soon preparing frantically for the conversion experience by which they would be "born again." Edwards's *Faithful Narrative of the Surprizing Work of God* (1736), which described his town's awakening, was the first published revival narrative. This literary form would be used many times in the future to fan the flames of evangelical religion.

In 1739, these regional brushfires of evangelicalism began to spread. Instrumental in drawing together the separate local revivals and in inspiring a more scorching religious enthusiasm was a 24-year-old Anglican priest from England named George Whitefield. Inspired by John Wesley, the founder of English Methodism, Whitefield became a master of emotional open-air preaching.

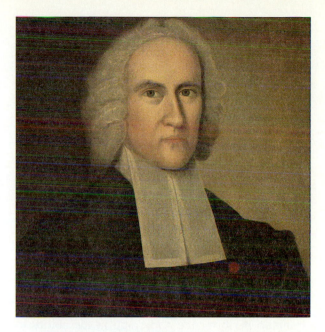

Jonathan Edwards (1703–1758) was the first major philosopher in the American colonies. A leader of the Great Awakening in Massachusetts, he was ousted by his congregation for reprimanding the children of church members for reading The Midwife Rightly Instructed, *an obstetrical guide that was as close as curious children could come to learning about sex.*

George Whitefield, who first toured the American colonies in 1739 and 1740, sent thousands of souls "flying to Christ" with his emotional sermons.

Whitefield made seven barnstorming tours along the American seaboard, the first in 1739 and 1740. Thousands turned out to see him, and with each success his fame and influence grew. In the cities, people fought for places in the churches when he spoke and gathered by the thousands in open fields to hear his message. Even in sedate Philadelphia, he turned skeptics into true believers, "so that one could not walk thro' town, in an evening," claimed the unreligious Benjamin Franklin, "without hearing psalms sung in different families of every street." In Boston, Whitefield preached to 19,000 in three days. Then, at a farewell sermon, he left 25,000 writhing in fear of damnation. In his wake came American preachers, mostly young men like Devereaux Jarratt, whom he had inspired.

Some of Whitefield's appeal lay in his genius for dramatic performance and some in his ability to simplify theological doctrine and focus people's attention on one facet of religious life, the conversion experience. In electrifying performances, he cast away the conventional written sermons in favor of spontaneous preaching. Using wild body movements and his magnificent voice, he filled thousands with the desire to "fly to Christ."

The appeal of the Awakeners lay not only in the medium but also in the message. They preached that the established, college-trained clergy was too intellectual and tradition-bound to bring faith and piety to a new generation. Congregations were dead, Whitefield declared, "because dead men preach to them." "The sapless discourses of such dead drones," cried another Awakener, were worthless. The fires of Protestant belief could be reignited only if individuals assumed responsibility for their own conversion.

An important form of individual participation was "lay exhorting." In this personal religious testimony, any person—young or old, female or male, black or white—might spontaneously recount a conversion experience and preach "the Lord's truth." This horrified most established clergymen. Lay exhorting shattered the trained clergy's monopoly on religious discourse and gave new importance to the oral culture of common people, whose spontaneous outpourings contrasted sharply with the controlled literary culture of the gentry. Through lay exhorting, ordinary men and women, and even children, servants, and slaves, crossed class lines and defied assigned roles.

How religion, social change, and politics became interwoven in the Great Awakening can be seen by examining two regions swept by revivalism. Both Boston, the heartland of Puritanism, and interior Virginia, a land of struggling small planters and slave-rich aristocrats, experienced the Great Awakening, but in different ways and at different times.

The Urban North

In Boston, revivalism ignited in the midst of political controversy. Since 1739, the citizens had argued strenuously about remedies for the severe depreciation of the province's paper currency, which had been issued for years to finance military expeditions against French Canada. The English government insisted that Massachusetts retire all paper money by 1741. Searching for a substitute circulating medium, one group proposed a land bank to issue private bills of credit backed by land. Another group proposed a silver bank to distribute bills of credit backed by silver. Controversy over the land and silver banks swept politics in 1740 and 1741, pitting large merchants, who preferred the fiscally conservative silver bank, against local traders, artisans, and the laboring poor, who preferred the land bank.

Whitefield's arrival in Boston coincided with the currency furor. He first preached shortly after leading merchants announced they would not accept land bank bills for payment. His stay in Boston overlapped with attacks on these merchants as "gripping and merciless usurers" who "heaped up vast estates" at the expense of the common people. At first, Boston's elite applauded Whitefield's ability to call the masses to worship. The master evangelist, it seemed, might restore social harmony by redirecting people from earthly matters such as the currency dispute to concerns of the soul.

When Whitefield left Boston in 1740, he was succeeded by others who were more critical of the "unconverted" clergy and the self-indulgent accumulation of wealth. Among them was James Davenport, who arrived in 1742. His great-grandfather had been a founder of New Haven, and his father was a respected Congregational minister in Connecticut. But the 25-year-old Davenport, who had been inspired by Whitefield, appeared anything but respectable to the elite.

Finding every church closed to him, even those whose clergy had embraced the Awakening, Davenport preached daily on Boston Common, aroused religious ecstasy among thousands, and stirred up feeling against Boston's leading figures. Respectable people grew convinced that revivalism had gotten out of hand, for by this time ordinary people were verbally attacking opponents of the land bank in the streets as "carnal wretches, hypocrites, fighters against God, children of the devil, cursed Pharisees." A revival that had begun as a return to religion among backsliding Christians had overlapped with political affairs. Hence it threatened polite culture, which stressed order and discipline from ordinary people.

The Rural South

The Great Awakening was ebbing in New England and the middle colonies by 1744, although aftershocks continued for years. But in Virginia, where the initial religious earthquake was barely felt, tremors of enthusiasm rippled through society from the mid-1740s onward. As in Boston, the Awakeners challenged and disturbed the gentry-led social order.

Whitefield stirred some religious fervor during his early trips through Virginia. Traveling "New Light" preachers, led by the brilliant orator Samuel Davies, were soon gathering large crowds both in the backcountry and in the traditionally Anglican parishes of the older settled areas. By 1747, worried Anglican clergyman convinced the governor to issue a proclamation restraining "strolling preachers." As in other colonies, Virginia's leaders despised traveling evangelists, for like lay exhorters, these roving Awakeners conjured up a world without properly constituted authority. As one critic put it in 1745, the wandering preachers "have turned the world upside down." When the Hanover County court gave the fiery James Davenport a license to preach in 1750, the governor ordered the suppression of all circuit riders.

New Light Presbyterianism, which challenged the religious monopoly of the gentry-dominated Anglican church, continued to spread in the 1750s. The evangelical cause advanced further with the rise of the Baptists in the 1760s. Renouncing finery, attacking ostentatious display, and addressing each other as "brother" and "sister," the Baptists reached out to thousands of unchurched people. Like northern revivalists, they focused on the conversion experience. Many of their preachers were uneducated farmers and artisans who called themselves "Christ's poor." They stressed equality in human affairs and insisted that heaven was always more

populated by the humble poor than by the purse-proud rich. Among the poorest of all, Virginia's 140,000 slaves in 1760, the evangelical message penetrated deeply.

The insurgent Baptist movement in rural Virginia became both a quest for a personal, emotionally satisfying religion among ordinary folk and a rejection of the gentry's social values. It brought from the established pulpits the same denunciations that had been voiced earlier in urban New England. In both regions, social changes had weakened the cultural authority of the upper class and, in the context of religious revival, produced a vision of a society drawn along more equal lines.

Legacy of the Awakening

By the time George Whitefield returned to America for his third tour in 1745, the revival had burned out in the North. Its effects, however, were long-lasting. The Awakening promoted religious pluralism and nourished the idea that all denominations were equally legitimate; none had a monopoly on the truth. Whitefield had anticipated this tendency when he sermonized: "Father Abraham, whom have you in heaven? Any Episcopalians? And the answer came back, No! Any Presbyterians? No! Any Independents or Methodists? No, no, no! Whom have you there? And the final answer came down from heaven, We don't know the names here. All who are here are Christians."

By legitimizing the dissenting Protestant groups that had sprung up in seventeenth-century England, the Great Awakening gave competing Protestant churches, which had rubbed abrasively for generations, a theory for living together in relative harmony. From this framework of denominationalism came a second change—the separation of church and state. Once a variety of churches gained legitimacy, it was impossible for any one church to claim special privileges. In the seventeenth century, Roger Williams had tried to sever church and state because he believed that ties with civil bodies would corrupt the church. But during the Awakening, groups such as the Baptists and the Presbyterians in Virginia constituted their own religious bodies and broke the Anglican monopoly as *the* church in the colony. This undermining of the church-state tie would be completed during the Revolutionary era.

A third effect of the revival was to bolster the view that diversity within communities, for better or worse, could not be prevented. Almost from the beginning, Rhode Island, the Carolinas, and the middle colonies had recognized this. But homogeneity had been prized elsewhere, especially in Massachusetts and Connecticut. In these colonies, the Awakening split Congregational churches into New Lights and Old Lights, and mid-Atlantic Presbyterian churches were similarly beset by schisms. In hundreds of rural communities by the 1750s, two or three churches existed where only one had stood before. People learned that the fabric of community could be woven from threads of many hues.

New eighteenth-century colonial colleges reflected the religious pluralism symbolized by the Great Awakening. Before 1740 there existed only three. Puritans had founded Harvard in 1636 and Yale in 1701 to provide new England with educated ministers, and Anglicans had chartered William and Mary in 1693. To these small seats of higher education were added six new colleges between 1746 and 1769.

In spite of ties to particular denominations, none of the new colleges were controlled by an established church, all had governing bodies composed of men of different faiths, and all admitted students regardless of religion. Eager for students and funds, they made nonsectarian appeals and constructed classical curricula mixed with natural sciences and natural philosophy.

Last, the Awakening nurtured a subtle change in values that crossed over into politics and daily life. Especially for ordinary people, the revival experience created a new feeling of self-worth. People assumed new responsibilities in religious affairs and became skeptical of dogma and authority. Many of them, especially among the fast-growing Baptists, decried the growing materialism and deplored the new acceptance of self-interested behavior. He who was "governed by regard to his own private interest," Gilbert Tennent preached, was "an enemy to the public," for in true Christian communities "mutual love is the band and cement." By learning to oppose authority and to take part in the creation of new churches, thousands of colonists unknowingly rehearsed for revolution.

Yale College, founded in 1701, was one of only three institutions of higher learning in the colonies before the Great Awakening.

| Colonial Colleges | | | |
Name	Colony	Founding Date	Denominational Affiliation
Harvard College	Massachusetts	1636	Congregational
College of William and Mary	Virginia	1693	Anglican
Yale College	Connecticut	1701	Congregational
College of New Jersey (Princeton)	New Jersey	1746	Presbyterian
College of Philadelphia (University of Pennsylvania)	Pennsylvania	1754	Secular
King's College (Columbia)	New York	1754	Anglican
College of Rhode Island (Brown)	Rhode Island	1764	Baptist
Queen's College (Rutgers)	New Jersey	1766	Dutch Reformed
Dartmouth College	New Hampshire	1769	Congregational

POLITICAL LIFE

"Were it not for government, the world would soon run into all manner of disorders and confusions," wrote a Massachusetts clergyman early in the eighteenth century. "Men's lives and estates and liberties would soon be prey to the covetous and the cruel," and every man would be "as a wolf" to his neighbors. Few colonists, wherever they lived, would have disagreed. On both sides of the Atlantic, people believed that government protected life, liberty, and property.

A much less easily resolved matter was how political power should be divided—in England, between the English government and the American colonies, and within each colony. American colonists naturally drew heavily on inherited political ideas and institutions. These were almost entirely English because English charters sanctioned settlement, English governors ruled the colonies, and English common law governed the courts. But in a new environment, where they met unexpected circumstances, the colonists modified familiar political forms to suit their needs.

Structuring Colonial Governments

As in all societies, determining the source of political authority was fundamental. In England, the notion of the God-given supreme authority of the monarch was crumbling even before the planting of the colonies. In its place arose the belief that stable and enlightened government depended on balancing the interests of monarchy, aristocracy, and democracy. Each of these pure forms of government would degenerate into oppression if unleavened by the other two. Monarchy, the rule of one, would become despotism. Aristocracy, the rule of the few, would turn into corrupt oligarchy. Democracy, the rule of the many, would descend into anarchy or mob rule. The Revolution of 1688 in England, by thwarting the king's pretensions to greater power, seemed to most colonists a vindication and strengthening of a carefully balanced political system.

In colonial governments, political balance was achieved somewhat differently. The governor was the king's agent or, in proprietary colonies, the agent of the king's delegated authority. The council, composed of wealthy appointees of the governor in most colonies, was a pale equivalent of the English House of Lords. The assembly, elected by white male freeholders, functioned as a replica of the House of Commons. "The concurrence of these three forms of government," wrote a Bostonian in 1749, "seems to be the highest perfection that human civil government can attain to."

Bicameral legislatures developed in most of the colonies in the seventeenth century. The lower houses, or assemblies, represented the local interests of the people at large. The upper houses, or councils (which usually also sat as the highest courts), represented the nascent aristocracy. Except in Rhode Island and Connecticut, every statute required the governor's assent, and all colonial laws required final approval from the king's privy council. This royal check on colonial lawmaking operated imperfectly, however. Laws took months to reach England, and months more passed before word of their final approval or rejection returned. In the meantime, the laws set down in the colonies took force.

Behind the formal structure of politics stood the rules governing who could participate in the political process. In England since the fifteenth century, the ownership of land had largely defined electoral participation (women and non-Christians were uniformly excluded). Only those with property sufficient to produce an annual rental income of 40 shillings could vote or hold office. The colonists closely followed this principle, except in Massachusetts, where it took until 1691 to break the requirement of church membership for suffrage. As in England, the poor and propertyless were excluded, for they lacked the "stake in society" that supposedly transformed unpredictable, ignorant creatures into thoughtful and responsible voters.

Whereas in England the 40-shilling freehold requirement was intended to restrict the size of the electorate, in the colonies, because of the cheapness of land, it conferred the vote on a large proportion of adult males. Between 50 and 75 percent of the adult free males could vote in most colonies. As the proportion of landless colonists increased in the eighteenth century, however, the franchise slowly became more limited.

Colonial Foundations of the American Political System

1606 Virginia companies of London and Plymouth granted patents to settle lands in North America.

1619 First elected colonial legislature meets in Virginia.

1634 Under a charter granted in 1632, Maryland's proprietor is given all the authority "as any bishop of Durham" ever held—more than the king possessed in England.

1635 The council in Virginia deports Governor John Harvey for exceeding his power, thus asserting the rights of local magistrates to contest authority of royally appointed governors.

1643 The colonies of Massachusetts, Plymouth, Connecticut, and New Haven draw up articles of confederation and form the first intercolonial union, the United Colonies of New England.

1647 Under a charter granted in 1644, elected freemen from the Providence Plantations draft a constitution establishing freedom of conscience, separating church and state, and authorizing referenda by the towns on laws passed by the assembly.

1677 The Laws, Concessions and Agreements for West New Jersey provide for a legislature elected annually by virtually all free males, secret voting, liberty of conscience, election of justices of the peace and local officeholders, and trial by jury in public so that "justice may not be done in a corner."

1689 James II deposed in England in the Glorious Revolution, and royal governors, accused of abusing their authority, ousted in Massachusetts, New York, and Maryland.

1701 First colonial unicameral legislature meets in Pennsylvania under the Frame of Government of 1701.

1735 John Peter Zenger, a New York printer, acquitted of seditious libel for printing attacks on the royal governor and his faction, thus widening the freedom of the press.

1754 First congress of all the colonies meets at Albany (with seven colonies sending delegates) and agrees on a Plan of Union (which is rejected by the colonies and the English government).

1765 The Stamp Act Congress, the first intercolonial convention called outside England's authority, meets in New York.

Though voting rights were broadly based, most men assumed that only the wealthy and socially prominent were entitled to hold positions of political power. Lesser men, it was held, ought to defer to their betters. Balancing this elitist conception of politics, however, was the notion that the entire electorate should periodically judge the performance of those they entrusted with political power and reject those who represented them inadequately. Unlike the members of the English House of Commons, who by the seventeenth century thought of themselves as representing the entire nation, the colonial representatives were expected to reflect the views of those who elected them locally. Believing this, their constituents judged them accordingly.

When were citizens entitled to defy those who ruled them? The answer to this vexing question followed English precedent: the people were justified in badgering their leaders, protesting openly, and, in extreme cases of abuse of power, assuming control in order to rectify the situation. The uprisings in the colonies associated with England's Glorious Revolution represented such moments when the deferential mass transformed itself into a purposeful crowd in order to overthrow those who trampled on their traditional English liberties.

The Crowd in Action

What gave special power to the common people when they assembled to protest oppressive authority was the general absence of effective police power. In the countryside, where most colonists lived, only the county sheriff, with an occasional deputy, insulated civil leaders from angry farmers. In the towns, police forces were still unknown. Only the sheriff, backed up by the night watch, safeguarded public order. As late as 1757, the night watch of New York was described as a "parcell of idle, drinking vigilant snorers, who never quelled any nocturnal tumult in their lives." In theory, the militia stood ready to suppress public disturbances, but both urban and rural crowds usually included many of the very people who composed the militia.

Since agencies of law enforcement were weak, the potential for political action outside formal legislative channels was never so great as in the colonial period. Crowd action, frequently effective, gradually achieved a kind of legitimacy. The assembled people became perceived as the watchdog of government, ready to chastise or drive from office those who violated the collective sense of what was right and proper.

Boston's impressment riot of 1747 vividly illustrates the people's readiness to defend their inherited privileges and the weakness of law enforcement. It began when Commodore Charles Knowles brought his Royal Navy ships to Boston for provisioning—and to replenish the ranks of mariners thinned by desertion. When Knowles sent press gangs out on a chill November evening with orders to fill the crew vacancies from Boston's waterfront population, they scooped up artisans, laborers, servants, and slaves, as well as merchant seamen from ships riding at anchor in the harbor.

But before the press gangs could hustle their victims back to the British men-of-war, a crowd of angry Bostonians seized several British officers, surrounded the governor's house, and demanded the release of their townsmen. When the sheriff and his deputies attempted to intervene, the mob mauled them. The militia, called to arms by the governor to "suppress the mob by force, and if need be to fire upon 'em with ball," refused to respond. By dusk, a crowd of several thousand defied the governor's orders to disperse, stoned the windows of the governor's house, and dragged a royal barge from one of the British ships into the courtyard of his house, where they burned it amid cheers.

Enraged by the defiant Bostonians, Commodore Knowles threatened to bombard the town. Determined negotiations conducted during several days of further tumult averted a showdown. Finally, Knowles released the impressed Bostonians. After the riot, a young politician named Samuel Adams defended Boston's defiance of royal authority. The people, he argued, had "a natural right" to band together against press gangs that deprived them of their liberty. Local magnates who supported the governor in this incident were labeled "tools to arbitrary power."

The Growing Power of the Assemblies

Incidents such as the impressment riot of 1747 demonstrated the touchiness of England's colonial subjects. But a more gradual and restrained change—the growing ambition and power of the legislative assemblies—was far more important. For most of the seventeenth century, royal and proprietary governors had exercised greater power in relation to the elected legislatures than did the king in relation to Parliament. The governors could dissolve the lower houses and delay their sitting, control the election of their speakers, and in most col-

When frontier farmers marched on Philadelphia in 1763 to demand more protection on the frontier, a miniature civil war almost broke out. Philadelphians had little use for the "Paxton Boys," who had murdered 20 harmless Christian Indians in retaliation for frontier raids.

onies initiate legislation with their appointed councils. Colonial governors also had authority to appoint and dismiss judges at all levels of the judiciary and to create chancery courts, which sat without juries. Governors also controlled the expenditure of public monies and had authority to grant land to individuals and groups, which they sometimes used to confer vast estates on their favorites.

By the 1730s, royal governments had replaced many of the proprietary governments. In the seventeenth century, Virginia, Massachusetts, and New York had become royal colonies, with governors appointed by the crown. In the eighteenth century, royal government came to New Jersey (1702), South Carolina (1719), and North Carolina (1729).

Many of the royal governors were competent military officers or bureaucrats, but often they were simply recipients of patronage posts. They were rewarded for whom they knew, not what they had done or might accomplish. A few were psychologically damaged, like Sir Danvers Osborn, who committed suicide a week after arriving in New York in 1753. Many were corrupt. Some governors never took up their posts at all, preferring, like the earl of Orkney, Virginia's royal governor from 1705 to 1737, to pocket the salary and pay a part of it to other men who went to the colony as lieutenant

governors. But most governors were not crazy, corrupt, or absent; they were merely mediocre.

In the eighteenth century, elected colonial legislatures challenged the swollen executive powers of these colonial governors. The governors lacked the extensive patronage power that in England enabled ministers of government to manipulate elections and buy off opposition groups. They could therefore contest but not prevent encroachments on their power. Bit by bit, the representative assemblies won new rights—to initiate legislation, to elect their own speakers, to settle contested elections, to discipline their membership, and to nominate provincial treasurers who controlled the disbursement of public funds. The most important gain of all was acquiring the "power of the purse"—the authority to initiate money bills, which specified how much money should be raised by taxes and how it should be spent.

Originally thought of as advisory bodies, the elected assemblies gradually transformed themselves into governing bodies reflecting the interests of the electorate. The Glorious Revolution had eroded royal power in England in the late seventeenth century. Thereafter, colonial executive power, an extension of royal power in the colonies, also gave ground to the ambitious legislative assemblies. Governors complained bitterly about the "levelling spirit" and "mutinous and disorderly behavior" of the assemblies, but they could not stop their rise.

Local Politics

Binding elected officeholders to their constituents became an important feature of the colonial political system. In England, the House of Commons was filled with representatives from "rotten boroughs," ancient places left virtually uninhabited by population shifts, and with men whose vote was in the pocket of the ministry because they had accepted crown appointments, contracts, or gifts. The American assemblies, by contrast, contained mostly representatives sent by voters who instructed them on particular issues and held them accountable for serving local interests.

Royal governors and colonial grandees who sat as councillors often deplored this localist, popular orientation of the people's representatives. The assemblies, sniffed one aristocratic New Yorker, were crowded with "plain, illiterate husbandmen [small farmers], whose views seldom extended farther than the regulation of highways, the destruction of wolves, wildcats, and foxes, and the advancement of the other little interests of the particular counties which they were chosen to represent." In actuality, the voters mostly sent merchants, lawyers, and substantial planters and farmers to represent them in the lower houses, and by the mid-eighteenth century in most colonies, these men had formed political elites. But it was true that they represented the local interests of their constituents. They prided themselves on doing so, for they saw themselves as bulwarks against oppression and arbitrary rule, which history taught them were most frequently imposed by monarchs and their appointed agents.

Local government was usually more important to the colonists than provincial government. In the North, local political authority generally rested in the towns. The New England town meeting decided a wide range of matters. In making decisions, the meeting strived for consensus, searching and arguing until it could express itself as a single unit. "By general agreement" and "by the free and united consent of the whole" were phrases denoting a decision-making process that sought participatory assent rather than a democratic competition among differing interests and points of view.

In the South, the county constituted the primary unit of government. No equivalent of the town meeting existed for placing local decisions before the populace. The planter gentry ruled the county courts and the legislature, while substantial farmers served in minor offices such as road surveyor and deputy sheriff. At court sessions, usually convened four times a year, deeds were read aloud and then recorded, juries impaneled and justice dispensed, elections held, licenses issued, and proclamations read aloud. On election days, gentlemen treated their neighbors (on whom they depended for votes) to "bumbo," "kill devil," and other alcoholic treats. By the mid-eighteenth century, a landed squirearchy of third- and fourth-generation families had achieved political dominance.

The Spread of Whig Ideology

Whether in local or provincial affairs, a political ideology called Whig or "republican" had spread widely by the mid-eighteenth century. The canons of this body of thought, inherited from England, flowed from the belief that concentrated power was historically the enemy of liberty and that too much power lodged in any person or group inevitably produced corruption and tyranny. The best defenses against concentrated power were balanced government, elected legislatures adept at checking executive authority, prohibition of standing armies (almost always controlled by tyrannical monarchs to oppress the people), and vigilance by the people in watching their leaders for telltale signs of corruption.

Much of this Whig ideology reached the people through the newspapers that began appearing in the seaboard towns in the early eighteenth century. The first was the *Boston News-Letter,* founded in 1704. By 1763, some 23 papers circulated in the colonies. Though limited to a few pages and published only once or twice a week, the papers passed from hand to hand and were read aloud in taverns and coffeehouses. In this way, their contents probably reached most households in the towns and a substantial minority of farmsteads in the countryside.

By the 1730s, newspapers had become an important conduit of Whig ideology. Many of them reprinted material from English Whig writers who railed against corruption and creeping despotism in the reign of George II (1727–1760). Particularly popular were the essays of John Trenchard and Thomas Gordon, whose *Cato's Letters* and *Independent Whig* found their way into the private libraries of many colonists and were widely reprinted in the newspapers.

The new power of the press and its importance in guarding the people's liberties against would-be tyrants, such as abrasive royal governors, was vividly illustrated in the Zenger case in New York. Young John Peter Zenger, a printer's apprentice, had been hired in 1733 by the antigovernment faction of Lewis Morris to start a newspaper that would publicize the tyrannical actions of Governor William Cosby. In Zenger's *New-York Weekly Journal,* the Morris faction fired salvos at Cosby's interference with the courts and his alleged corruption in giving important offices to his henchmen. New Yorkers believed, said one essay published by Zenger, "that their LIBERTIES and PROPERTIES are precarious, and that SLAVERY is like to be tailed on them and their posterity if some things past are not amended."

This and other bruising indictments of the governor led to Zenger's arrest for seditious libel. He was rescued from an early end to his career by the brilliant defense of Andrew Hamilton, a Philadelphia lawyer hired by the Morris faction to convince the jury that Zenger was innocent of everything but trying to inform the people of attacks on their liberties. Although the jury acquitted Zenger, the libel laws remained very restrictive. But the acquittal did reinforce the notion that the government was the people's servant, and it brought home the point that public criticism could keep people with political authority responsible to the people they ruled. Such ideas about liberty and corruption, raised in the context of local politics, would shortly achieve a much broader significance.

CONCLUSION

America in 1750

The American colonies, robust and expanding, matured rapidly between 1700 and 1750. Transatlantic commerce linked them closely to Europe, Africa, and other parts of the New World. Churches, schools, and towns—the visible marks of the receding frontier—appeared everywhere. A balanced sex ratio and stable family life had been achieved throughout the colonies. Seasoned political leaders and familiar political institutions functioned from Maine to Georgia.

Yet the sinew, bone, and muscle of American society had not yet fully knit together. The polyglot population, one-fifth of it bound in chattel slavery and its Native American component still unassimilated and uneasily situated on the frontier, was a kaleidoscopic mixture of ethnic and religious groups. Its economy, while developing rapidly, showed weaknesses, particu-larly in New England, where land resources had been strained. The social structure reflected the colonizers' emergence from a frontier stage, but the consolidation of wealth by a landed and mercantile elite was matched by pockets of poverty appearing in the cities and some rural areas. Full of strength yet marked by awkward incongruities, colonial Americans in 1750 approached an era of strife and momentous decisions.

Recommended Reading

James A. Henretta and Gregory Nobles provide a good introduction to the growth and development of eighteenth-century colonial society in Evolution and Revolution: American Society: 1620–1820 *(1986). On immigration and immigrant groups, see Stephanie G. Wolf,* Urban Village: Population, Community, and Family Structure in Germantown, Pennsylvania *(1977); Jon Butler,* The Huguenots in Colonial America *(1983); Ned Landsman,* Scotland and Its First American Colony *(1985); and Bernard Bailyn,* Voyagers to the West *(1986).*

On the development of the northern colonies, rich material can be found in Richard Bushman, From Puritan to Yankee *(1967); Christopher M. Jedrey,* The World of John Cleaveland *(1979); Laurel T. Ulrich,* Good Wives *(1982); Sung Bok Kim,* Landlord and Tenant in the Colony of New York (*1976*); *and James Lemon,* The Best Poor Man's Country (*1972*).

The transformation of eighteenth-century southern society is the subject of Paul G. E. Clemens, *The Atlantic Economy and Colonial Maryland's Eastern Shore (1980); Carville Earle,* The Evolution of a Tidewater Settlement System (*1975*); *Rhys Isaac,* The Transformation of Virginia (*1982*); *Allan Kulikoff,* Tobacco and Slaves (*1986*); *T. H. Breen,* Tobacco Culture: The Mentality of the Great Tidewater Planters on the Eve of the Revolution (*1985*); *Daniel B. Smith,* Inside the Great House (*1980*); *and Mechal Sobel,* The World They Made Together: Black and White Values in Eighteenth-Century Virginia (*1987*).

Much can be learned about commercial and intellectual life in the cities from Bernard Bailyn, *The New England Merchants in the Seventeenth Century (1955); Gary M. Walton and James F. Shepherd,* The Economic Rise of Early America (*1979*); *J. E. Crowley,* This Sheba Self: The Conceptualization of Economic Life in Eighteenth-Century America (*1974*); *and Gary B. Nash,* The Urban Crucible (*1979*). Henry May addresses the American Enlightenment in *The American Enlightenment (1976).*

Excellent treatments of religious life and the Great Awakening include Perry Miller, *From Colony to Province (1953); Alan Heimert,* Religion and the American Mind (*1966*); *Edwin Gaustad,* The Great Awakening in New England (*1957*); *Harry S. Stout,* The New England Soul: Preaching and Religious Life in Colonial New England (*1986*); *Patricia Tracy,* Jonathan Edwards, Pastor (*1979*); *and Patricia Bonomi,* Under the Cope of Heaven: Religion, Society, and Politics in Colonial America (*1986*).

The maturing colonial political systems involved many variations, which can be followed in Bernard Bailyn, *The Origins of American Politics (1968); Charles Sydnor,* American Revolutionaries in the Making (*1965*); *Jack P. Greene,* The Quest for Power (*1963*); *Edward M. Cook, Jr.,* The Fathers of the Towns (*1976*); *and Patricia Bonomi,* A Factious People: Politics and Society in Colonial New York (*1977*).

TIME LINE

1662 Half-Way Covenant in New England

1685–1715 Stagnation in tobacco market

1704 *Boston News-Letter,* first regular colonial newspaper, published

1713 Beginning of Scots-Irish and German immigration

1715–1730 Volume of slave trade doubles

1718 French settle New Orleans

1720s Black population begins to increase naturally

1734–1736 Great Awakening begins in Northampton, Massachusetts

1735 Zenger acquitted of seditious libel in New York

1739–1740 Whitefield's first American tour spreads Great Awakening
Slaves compose 90 percent of population on Carolina rice coast

1740s Indigo becomes staple crop in Lower South

1747 Benjamin Franklin publishes first *Poor Richard's Almanack*
Impressment riot in Boston

1760 Africans compose 20 percent of American population

1760s–1770s Spanish establish California mission system

1769 American Philosophical Society founded at Philadelphia

5

Bursting the Colonial Bonds

In 1758, when he was 21 years old, Ebenezer MacIntosh of Boston laid down his shoemaker's awl and enlisted in the Massachusetts expedition against the French on Lake Champlain. The son of a poor Boston shoemaker who had fought against the French in a previous war, MacIntosh had known poverty all his life. Service against the French offered the hope of plunder or at least an enlistment bounty worth half a year's wages. One among thousands of colonists who fought against the "Gallic menace" in the Seven Years' War, MacIntosh contributed his mite to the climactic Anglo-American struggle that drove the French from North America.

But a greater role lay ahead for the poor Boston shoemaker. Two years after the Peace of Paris in 1763, England imposed a stamp tax on the American colonists. In the massive protests that followed, MacIntosh emerged as the street leader of the Boston crowd. In two nights of the most violent attacks on private property ever witnessed in America, a Boston crowd nearly destroyed the houses of two of the colony's most important officials. On August 14, they tore through the house of Andrew Oliver, a wealthy merchant and the appointed distributor of stamps for Massachusetts. Twelve days later, MacIntosh led the crowd in attacking the mansion of Thomas Hutchinson, a wealthy merchant who served as lieutenant governor and chief justice of Massachusetts. "The mob was so general," wrote the governor, "and so supported that all civil power ceased in an instant."

For the next several months, the power of the poor Boston shoemaker grew. Called "General" MacIntosh and "Captain-General of the Liberty Tree" by his townspeople, he soon sported a militia uniform of gold and blue and a hat laced with gold. Two thousand townsmen followed his commands on November 5, when they marched in orderly ranks through the crooked streets of Boston to demonstrate their solidarity in resisting the hated stamps.

Five weeks later, a crowd publicly humiliated stamp distributor Oliver. Demanding that he announce his resignation before the assembled citizenry, they marched him across town in a driving December rain. With MacIntosh at his elbow, he finally reached the "Liberty Tree," which had become a symbol of resistance to

England's new colonial policies. There the aristocratic Oliver ate humble pie. He concluded his resignation remarks with bitter words, hissing sardonically that he would "always think myself very happy when it shall be in my power to serve the people."

"To serve the people" was an ancient idea embedded in English political culture, but it assumed new meaning in the American colonies during the epic third quarter of the eighteenth century. Few colonists in 1750 held even a faint desire to break the connection with England, and fewer still might have predicted the form of government that 13 independent states in an independent nation might fashion. Yet in a whirlwind of events, 2 million colonists moved haltingly toward a showdown with mighty England. Little-known men like Ebenezer MacIntosh as well as his well-known and historically celebrated townsmen Samuel Adams, John Hancock, and John Adams were part of the struggle. Collectively, ordinary persons such as MacIntosh influenced—and in fact sometimes even dictated—the revolutionary movement in the colonies. Though we read and speak mostly of a small group of "founding fathers," the wellsprings of the American Revolution can be fully discovered only among a variety of people from different social groups, occupations, regions, and religions.

133

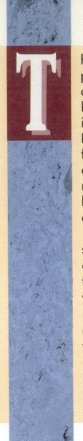

his chapter addresses the tensions in late colonial society, the imperial crisis that followed the Seven Years' War (in the colonies often called the French and Indian War), and the tumultuous decade that led to the "shots heard around the world" fired at Concord Bridge in April 1775. It portrays the origins of a dual American Revolution. Ebenezer MacIntosh, in leading the Boston mob against crown officers and colonial collaborators who tried to implement a new colonial policy after 1763, helped set in motion a revolutionary movement to restore ancient liberties thought by the Americans to be under deliberate attack in England. This movement eventually escalated into the War of American Independence.

But MacIntosh's Boston followers were also venting years of resentment at the accumulation of wealth and power by Boston's aristocratic elite. Behind every swing of the ax, every shattered crystal goblet and splintered mahogany chair, lay the fury of a Bostonian who had seen the city's conservative elite try to dismantle the town meeting, had suffered economic hardship, and had lost faith that opportunity and just relations still prevailed in his town. This sentiment, which called for the reform of a colonial society that had become corrupt, self-indulgent, and elite-dominated, fed an idealistic commitment to reshape American society even while severing the colonial bond. As distinguished from the War for Independence, this was the American Revolution.

THE CLIMACTIC SEVEN YEARS' WAR

After a brief period of peace following King George's War (1744–1748), France and England fought the fourth, largest, and by far most significant of the wars for empire that had begun in the late seventeenth century. Known variously as the Seven Years' War, the French and Indian War, and the Great War for Empire, this global conflict in part represented a showdown for control of North America between the Atlantic Ocean and the Mississippi River. In North America, the Anglo-American forces ultimately prevailed in the Seven Years' War. This victory dramatically affected the lives of the great variety of people living in the huge region east of the Mississippi—English, German, and Scots-Irish settlers in the Engish colonies; French and Spanish colonizers in Canada, Florida, and interior North America; African slaves in a variety of settlements; and, perhaps most of all, the powerful Native American tribes of the interior.

War and the Management of Empire

After the Glorious Revolution of 1688, England began constructing a more coherent imperial administration. In 1696, a professional Board of Trade replaced the old Lords of Trade; the Treasury strengthened the customs service; and Parliament created overseas vice-admiralty courts, which functioned without juries to prosecute smugglers who evaded the trade regulations set forth in the Navigation Acts. Royal governors received greater powers and more detailed instructions and came under more insistent demands from the Board of Trade to enforce British policies. England was quietly installing the machinery of imperial management and a corps of colonial bureaucrats.

The best test of an effectively organized state was its ability to wage war. Four times between 1689 and 1763, England matched its strength against France, its archrival in North America and the Caribbean. These wars of empire had tremendous consequences for all involved—the home governments, their colonial subjects, and the Indian tribes that were drawn into the bloody conflicts.

We have already seen (in Chapter 3) how the Peace of Utrecht that ended Queen Anne's War (1702–1713) brought victor's spoils of great importance to England. The generation of peace that followed the Peace of Utrecht was really only a time-out between wars. Both England and France used the years until 1739 to strengthen their war-making capacity, to which productive and efficiently governed New World colonies made important contributions. Though known as a period of "salutary neglect," this was actually an era when king and Parliament increased their control over colonial affairs.

Parliament had already begun playing a more active role after the reign of Queen Anne (1702–1714) and continued to do so when weak, German-speaking King George I came to the throne. Concerned mainly with economic regulation, Parliament added new articles such as furs, copper, hemp, tar, and turpentine to the list of items produced in America that had to be shipped to England before being exported to another country. Parliament also curtailed colonial production of articles important to England's economy: woolen cloth in 1699, beaver hats in 1732, finished iron products in 1750. Most important, Parliament passed the Molasses Act in 1733. Attempting to stop the trade between New England and the French West Indies, where Yankee traders exchanged fish, beef, and pork for molasses to convert into rum, Parliament imposed a prohibitive duty of 6 pence per gallon on molasses imported from the French islands. This turned many of New England's largest merchants and distillers into smugglers and schooled them for a generation, along with their ship captains, crews, and allied waterfront artisans, in defying royal authority.

The generation of peace ended abruptly in 1739 when England declared war on Spain. The immediate cause of hostilities was the ear of an English sea captain, Robert Jenkins. He had been deprived of that appendage eight years before by Spanish authorities, who charged him with smuggling in the Spanish colonies. With encouragement from his government, Jenkins publicly displayed his severed ear in 1738 as a way of whipping up war fever against Spain, which English policymakers wanted to chasten for transferring certain commercial privilges from England to France.

The real cause of the war, however, was England's determination to continue its drive toward commercial domination of the Atlantic basin. Five years after the war with Spain began in 1739, it merged into a much larger conflict between England and France, in Europe called The War of Austrian Succession, that lasted until 1748. The scale of King George's War (1744–1748) far exceeded previous conflicts. As military priorities became paramount, the need increased for discipline within the empire. In addition, unprecedented military expenditures brought pressure to enlarge colonial revenues. England asked its West Indian and American colonies to share in the costs of defending—and extending—the empire and to tailor their behavior to the needs of the home country.

Outbreak of Hostilities

The tension between English and French colonists in North America, which reached back to the early seventeenth century, was intensified by the spectacular growth of the English colonies: from a 0.25 million in 1700 to 1.25 million in 1750 and to 1.75 million in the next decade. Three-quarters of the increase came in the colonies south of New York. Such growth propelled thousands of land-hungry settlers toward the mountain gaps in the Appalachians in search of farmland.

Promoting this westward rush were eastern merchants and speculators. Fur traders in their employ penetrated a French-influenced region, where they offered better prices and higher-quality goods than the French. In the 1740s and 1750s, speculators formed land companies to capitalize on the population explosion. Many of the future leaders of the Revolution were heavily involved in companies that raced to establish claims to millions of acres of western land. The farther west the settlement line moved, the closer it came to the western trading empire of the French and their Indian allies.

Colonial penetration of the Ohio valley in the 1740s established the first English outposts in the continental heartland. This challenged the French where their interest was vital. While the English controlled most of the eastern coastal plain of North America, the French had nearly encircled them to the west by building a chain of trading posts and forts along the St. Lawrence River, through the Great Lakes, and southward into the Ohio and Mississippi valleys all the way to New Orleans.

Challenged by the English, the French resisted. They attempted to block further English expansion by constructing new forts in the Ohio valley and by prying some tribes loose from their new English connections. The English, a French emissary warned a western tribe in the 1750s, "are much less anxious to take away your peltries than to become masters of your lands, and your blindness is so great that you do not perceive that the very hand that caresses you will scourge you like negroes and slaves, so soon as it will have got possession of your lands."

By 1755, the French had driven the English traders out of the Ohio valley and established forts as far east as the forks of the Ohio River, near present-day Pittsburgh. It was there, at Fort Duquesne, that the French smartly rebuffed an ambitious young Virginia militia colonel named George Washington, dispatched by his colony's government to expel them from the region.

Men in the capitals of Europe, not in the colonies, made the decision to force a showdown in the interior of North America. England's powerful merchants, supported by American clients, had been emboldened by English success in the previous war against the French. Now they argued that the time was ripe to destroy the French overseas trade. Convinced, the English ministry ordered several thousands troops to America in 1754; in France, 3,000 regulars embarked to meet the English challenge.

With war looming, the colonial governments attempted to coordinate their efforts. Representatives of seven colonies met with 150 Iroquois chiefs at Albany, New York, in June 1754. The twin goals were to woo the powerful Iroquois out of their neutrality and to perfect a plan of colonial union. Both failed. The Iroquois left the conference with 30 wagonloads of gifts but made no firm commitment to fight against the French. Benjamin Franklin designed a plan for an intercolonial government that would manage Indian affairs and defense and have the power to pass laws and levy taxes. But even the clever woodcut displayed in the *Pennsylvania Gazette* that pictured a chopped-up snake with the insignia "Join or Die" failed to overcome the long-standing jealousies that had thwarted previous attempts at intercolony cooperation. "Everyone cries a union is necessary," sighed Franklin, "but when they come to the manner and form of the union, their weak noodles are perfectly distracted."

With his British army and hundreds of American recruits, General Edward Braddock slogged his way across Virginia in the summer of 1755, cutting a road through forests and across mountains at a few miles a day. A headstrong professional soldier who regarded his European battlefield experience as suf-ficient for war in the American wilderness, Braddock had contempt for the woods-wise French regiments and their stealthy Indian allies.

As Braddock neared Fort Duquesne, the entire French force and the British suddenly surprised one another in the forest. The French had 218 soldiers and militiamen and 637 Indian allies, while Braddock commanded twice that many men but few Indians. The initial bloody melee was a standoff. Then the French redeployed their Indian allies along both sides of the road in the trees. They poured murderous fire into Braddock's tidy lines of men, who could not see their enemies. Just before he fell, mortally wounded (perhaps by one of his own angry men), Braddock presumably learned that Indians were essential allies and were fully capable of pitched battle. Two-thirds of the British and Americans were killed or wounded, and Washington, his uniform pierced by four bullets, had two horses shot from beneath him. Although they had 1,000 men in reserve down the road, the Anglo-American force beat a hasty, ignominious retreat.

Throughout the summer, French-supplied Indian raiders put the torch to the Virginia and Pennsylvania backcountry. "The roads are full of starved, naked, indigent multitudes," observed one officer. One French triumph followed another during the next two years. The victory over Braddock's army had brought almost every tribe north of the Ohio River to the French side. Never was disunity within the English colonies so painfully evident. With its Indian allies, French Canada, only 70,000 inhabitants strong, had badly battered a million and a half colonists supported by the British army.

The turning point in the war came after the energetic William Pitt became England's prime minister in 1757. Proclaiming, "I believe that I can save this nation and that no one else can," he abandoned Europe as the main theater of action against the French and threw his nation's military might into the American campaign.

The forces dispatched by Pitt to America dwarfed all preceding commitments. About 23,000 British troops landed in America in 1757 and 1758, and the huge naval fleet that arrived in the latter year included 14,000 mariners. But even forces of this magnitude, when asked to engage the enemy in the forests of North America, were not necessarily sufficient to the task without Indian support, or at least neutrality. "A doubt remains not," proclaimed one English official in the colonies, "that the prosperity of our colonies on the continent will stand or fall with our interest and favour among them."

Tribal Strategies

Anglo-American leaders knew that in a war fought mainly in the northern colonies, the support of the Iroquois Confederacy and their tributary tribes was crucial. Iroquois allegiance could be secured in only two ways, through purchase or by a demonstration of power that would convince the tribes that the English would prevail with or without their assistance. The Iroquois understood that their interest lay in playing off one European power against the other. "To preserve the balance between us and the French," wrote a New York politician, "is the great ruling principle of modern Indian politics."

The first English strategem for securing Iroquois support failed in 1754 when colonial negotiators heaped gifts on the Iroquois chiefs at the Albany Congress but received in return only tantalizing half promises of support against the French. The second alternative fizzled because the English proved militarily inferior to the French in the first three years of the war. Hence, the westernmost of the Iroquois Six Nations, the Seneca, fought with the French in the campaigns of 1757 and 1758, while the Delaware, a tributary tribe, harassed the Pennsylvania frontier.

In 1758, the huge English military buildup began to produce victories. The largest army ever assembled in America, some 15,000 British and American soldiers, including the Bostonian Ebenezer MacIntosh, suffered terrible casualties and withdrew from the field after attempting to storm Fort Ti-

The storming of Quebec in 1759 was the decisive blow in England's campaign to end French domination of Canada and the lands west of the Appalachians.

conderoga on Lake Champlain in June 1758. Then the tide turned. Troops under Sir Jeffrey Amherst captured Louisbourg, on Cape Breton Island, and Fort Duquesne fell to an army of 6,000 led by General John Forbes. The resolute Pitt had mobilized the fighting power of the English nation and put more men in the field than existed in all of New France. The colonists, in turn, had put aside intramural squabbling long enough to overwhelm the badly outnumbered French.

The victories of 1758 finally moved the Iroquois away from neutrality. Added incentive to join the Anglo-American side came when the English navy bottled up French shipping in the St. Lawrence River, cutting the Iroquois off from French trade goods. By early 1759, foreseeing that the French were going down to defeat in North America, the Iroquois pledged 800 warriors for an attack on Fort Niagara, the strategic French trading depot on Lake Ontario. As always, their policy had been to assess the shifting military balance between rival European powers and to formulate their strategy accordingly.

Even dramatic Anglo-American victories did not always guarantee Indian support. In the South, backcountry skirmishes with the Cherokee from Virginia to South Carolina turned into a costly war from 1759 to 1761. In 1760, the Cherokee mauled a British army of 1,300 under Amherst. The following summer, a much larger Anglo-American force invaded Cherokee country, burning towns and food supplies. By this time, English control of the sea had interrupted the Indians' supply of French arms. Struggling against food shortages, lack of ammunition, and a smallpox epidemic, the Cherokee finally sued for peace.

Other Anglo-American victories in 1759, the "year of miracles," decided the outcome of the bloodiest war yet known in the New World. The capture of Fort Niagara, the critical link in the system of forts that joined the French inland empire with the Atlantic, was followed by the conquest of sugar-rich Martinique in the West Indies. The culminating stroke came with a dramatic victory at Quebec. Led by 32-year-old General James Wolfe, 5,000 troops scaled a rocky cliff and overcame the French on the Plains of Abraham. The capture of Montreal late in 1760 completed the shattering of French power in North America. The theater of operations shifted to the Caribbean, where fighting continued, as in Europe, for three years longer. But in the American colonies, the old English dream of ridding the continent of the "Gallic menace" had finally come true.

Consequences of War

For the interior Indian tribes, the Treaty of Paris ending the Seven Years' War in 1763 dealt a harsh blow. Unlike the coastal Native Americans, whose population and independence had ebbed rapidly through contact with the colonizers, the inland tribes had maintained their strength and sometimes even grown more unified through relations with settlers. Although they came to depend on European trade goods, Native Americans had turned this commercial connection to their advantage so long as more than one source of trade goods existed.

The Indian play-off system ended with the French defeat. By the terms of the Treaty of Paris, France ceded Canada and all territory east of the Mississippi, except for New Orleans, to England. To Spain went New Orleans and France's trans-Mississippi empire. Spain yielded Florida to England. For the interior tribes, only one source of trade goods remained. Two centuries of European rivalry for control of eastern North America ended abruptly. Iroquois, Cherokee, Creek, and other interior peoples were now forced to adjust to this reality.

After concluding peace with the French, the English government launched a new policy in North America designed to separate Native Americans and colonizers by creating a racial boundary roughly following the crestline of the Appalachian Mountains from Maine to Georgia. The Proclamation of 1763 ordered the colonial governors to reserve all land west of the line for Indian nations. White settlers already living beyond the Appalachians were charged to withdraw to the east.

Though well intended, this attempt to legislate interracial accord failed completely. Even before the proclamation was issued, the Ottawa chief Pontiac, concerned that the elimination of the French threatened the old treaty and gift-giving system, had gathered together many of the northern tribes that had aided the French assaults on the English forts during the Seven Years' War. Although Pontiac's pan-Indian movement to drive the British out of the Ohio valley collapsed in 1764, it served notice that the interior tribes would not passively watch the invasion of their lands after the French withdrawal from North America.

The English government could sternly command colonial governors to observe the Proclamation of 1763, but it could not enforce its policy. Staggering under an immense wartime debt, England decided to maintain only small army garrisons in America to regulate the interior. Nor could royal governors stop land speculators and settlers from privately purchasing land from trans-Appalachian tribes or from simply encroaching on their land. Under such circumstances, the western frontier seethed with tension after 1763.

While the Seven Years' War marked an epic victory of Anglo-American arms over the French and redrew the map of North America, it also had important social and economic effects on colonial society. The war convinced the colonists of their growing strength, yet left them debt-ridden and weakened in manpower. The wartime economy spurred economic development and poured British capital into the colonies, yet rendered them more vulnerable to cyclic fluctuations in the British economy.

Military contracts, for example, brought prosperity to most colonies during the war years. Huge orders for ships, arms, uniforms, and provisions enriched northern merchants and provided good prices for farmers as well. Urban artisans enjoyed full employment and high wages, as tailors' needles flashed to meet clothing contracts, shoemakers stitched for an unprecedented demand for shoes, and bakers found armies clamoring for bread. Privateers—privately outfitted ships licensed by colonial governments to attack enemy shipping—enriched the fortunate few. On a single voyage in 1758, John MacPherson snared 18 French ships. The prize money was lavish enough to allow this son of a Scottish immigrant to pour £14,000 into creating a country estate outside Philadelphia, to which he retired in splendor.

The war, however, required heavy taxes and took a huge human toll. Privateering carried many fortune seekers to a watery grave, and the wilderness campaigns from 1755 to 1760 claimed thousands of lives. Garrison life brought wracking fevers (which claimed more victims than enemy weapons), and battlefield medical treatment was too primitive to save many of the wounded. Boston's Thomas Hancock accurately predicted at the beginning of the war that "this province is spirited to [send] every third man to do the work of the Lord." But the Lord's work was expensive. Thomas Pownall, assuming the governorship of Massachusetts in August 1757, found not the "rich, flourishing, powerful, enterprizing" colony he expected but a province "ruined and undone."

The magnitude of the human losses in Boston indicates the war's impact. The wartime muster lists show that nearly every working-class Bostonian tasted military service at some point during the long war. When peace came, Boston had a deficit of almost 700 men in a town of about 2,000 families. The high rate of war widowhood produced a feminization of poverty and required expanded poor relief for the maintenance of husbandless women and fatherless children.

Peace ended the casualties but also brought depression. The British forces in the American theater numbered about 40,000 at the conclusion of the North American campaigns. With their departure for the Caribbean in 1760, the economy slumped badly, especially in the coastal towns. "The tippling soldiery that used to help us out at a dead lift," mused a New York merchant, "are gone to drink [rum] in a warmer region, the place of its production."

The greatest hardships after 1760 fell on laboring people, although even some wealthy merchants went bankrupt. Those with the smallest wages had the thinnest savings to cushion them against hard times. How quickly their security could evaporate showed in Philadelphia, where early in the contractionary cycle many poor people, unable to pay their property taxes, were "disposing of their huts and lots to others more wealthy than themselves." The economic security of the middle sector of society also slipped, as established craftsmen and shopkeepers were caught between rising prices and reduced demand for their goods and services. A New York artisan expressed a common lament in 1762. Thankfully, he still had employment, he wrote in the *New-York Gazette*. But despite every effort at unceasing labor and frugal living, he had fallen into poverty and found it "beyond my ability to support my family . . . [which] can scarcely appear with decency or have necessaries to subsist." His situation, he added, "is really the case with many of the inhabitants of this city."

In spite of its heavy casualties and economic repercussions, the Seven Years' War paved the way, though not foreseen at the time, for a far larger conflict in the next generation. The legislative assemblies, for example, which had been flexing their muscles at the expense of the governors in earlier decades, accelerated their bid for political power. During wartime, knowing that their governors must obtain military appropriations, they extracted concessions as the price for raising revenues. The war also trained a new group of military and political leaders. In carrying out military operations on a scale unknown in the colonies and in shouldering heavier political responsibilities, men such as George Washington, Samuel Adams, Benjamin Franklin, Patrick Henry, and Christopher Gadsden acquired the experience that would serve them well in the future.

The Seven Years' War, in spite of the severe costs, left many of the colonists with a sense of buoyancy. New Englanders rejoiced at the final victory over the "Papist enemy of the North." Frontiersmen, fur traders, and land speculators also celebrated the French withdrawal, for the West now appeared open for exploitation. This "Garden of the World," trumpeted a Boston almanac publisher, was larger than France, Germany, and Poland combined, "and all well provided with rivers, a very fine wholesome air, a rich soil, . . . and all things necessary for the conveniency and delight of life." A new frontier now seemed to await those whom opportunity had passed by on the crowded seaboard.

The colonists also felt a new sense of their identity after the war. Surveying a world free of French and Spanish threats, they could not help but reassess the advantages and disadvantages of subordination to England. The colonists would soon discover, a French diplomat predicted at the war's end, "that they stand no longer in need of your protection. You will call on them to contribute towards supporting the burden which they have helped to bring on you; they will answer you by shaking off all dependence."

THE CRISIS WITH ENGLAND

George Grenville became the chief minister of England's 25-year-old king, George III, at the end of the Seven Years' War. He inherited a national debt that had billowed from £75 million to £145 million during the war and a nation of wearied taxpayers. To reduce the debt, Grenville proposed new taxes in England and others in America, where the colonists were asked to bear their share of running the empire. Grenville's particular concern was financing the 10,000 British regulars left in North America after 1763 to police French-speaking Canada and the frontier and to remind the unruly American subjects that they were still beholden to the crown. Grenville's revenue program initiated a rift between England and its colonies that a dozen years later would culminate in revolution.

RECOVERING THE PAST

HOUSEHOLD INVENTORIES

Historians use probate records to examine social changes in American society. They include wills, the legal disposition of estates, and household inventories taken by court-appointed appraisers that detail the personal possessions left at death. Inventories have been especially valuable in tracing the transformation of colonial communities.

Like tax lists, inventories can be used to show changes in a community's distribution of wealth. But they are far more detailed than tax lists, providing a snapshot of how people lived at the end of their life. Inventories list and value almost everything a person owned—household possessions, equipment, books, clothes and jewelry, cash on hand, livestock and horses, crops and stored provisions. Hence through inventories we can measure the quality of life at different social levels. We can also witness how people made choices about investing their savings—in capital goods of their trade such as land, ships, and equipment; in personal goods such as household furnishings and luxury items; or in real property such as land and houses.

Studied systematically (and corrected for biases, which infect this source as well as others), inventories show that by the early 1700s, ordinary householders were improving their standard of living. Finished furniture such as cupboards, beds, tables, and chairs turn up more frequently in inventories. Pewter dinnerware replaces wooden bowls and spoons, bed linen makes an appearance, and books and pictures are sometimes noted.

Among an emerging elite before the Revolution, much more fashionable articles of consumption appear. The partial inventory of Robert Oliver, a wealthy merchant and officeholder living in a Boston suburb, is reproduced here. You can get some idea of the dignified impression Oliver wished to make by looking at his furniture and dishes and by noticing that he owned a mahogany tea table, damask linen, and a bed with curtains. The inventory further suggests the spaciousness of Oliver's house and shows how he furnished each room.

It is helpful when studying inventories to categorize the goods in the following way: those that are needed to survive (basic cooking utensils, for example); those that make life easier or more comfortable (enough plates and beds for each member of the family, for example); and those that make life luxurious (slaves, silver plates, paintings, mahogany furniture, damask curtains, spices, wine, and so forth). Oliver had many luxury goods as well as items that contributed to his use of leisure time and his personal enjoyment. Which items in his inventory do you think were needed only to survive comfortably? Which were luxuries? What other conclusions can you draw about the life style of rich colonial merchants like Oliver?

Beyond revealing a growing social differentiation in colonial society, the inventories help the historian understand the reaction during the Great Awakening to what many ordinary colonists regarded as sinful pride and arrogance displayed by the elite. By the 1760s, this distrust of affluence among simple folk had led to outright hostility toward men who surrounded themselves with the trappings of aristocratic life. Even the ambitious young John Adams, a striving lawyer, was shocked at what he saw at the house of a wealthy merchant in Boston. "Went over the House to view the Furniture, which alone cost a thousand Pound sterling," he exclaimed. "A seat it is for a noble Man, a Prince. The Turkey Carpets, the painted Hangings, the Marble Tables, the rich Beds with crimson Damask Curtains . . . are the most magnificent of any Thing I have ever seen."

Such a description takes on its fullest meaning only when contrasted with what inventories tell us about life at the bottom of society. The hundreds of inventories for Bostonians dying in the decade before the American Revolution show that fully half of them died with less than £40 personal wealth and one-quarter with £20 or less. The inventories and wills of Jonathan and Daniel Chandler of Andover, Massachusetts, show the material circumstances of less favored Americans who suffered from the economic distress afflicting New England since the 1730s. Note that Daniel Chandler, like Ebenezer MacIntosh, was a shoemaker. How do the possessions of these brothers compare with Oliver's partial inventory? An examination of these contrasting inventories helps explain the class tension that figured in the Revolutionary experience.

Household Inventory of Jonathan Chandler (d. 1745)

Cash	£ 18
Gun	1
Psalmbook	8 p
	£ 19
	£ 5
Debts	£ 14
Total	

Household Inventory of Daniel Chandler (d. 1752), Shoemaker

Bible	
Shoe knife	
Hammer	Total £ 12
Last (shoe shaper) }	
Various notes }	

Household Inventory of Robert Oliver, Wealthy Merchant

Dorchester Jan.ʸ 11ᵗʰ 1763.

Inventory of what Estates Real & Personall, belonging to Coll:° Robert Oliver [Esquire] late of Dorchester Deceased, that has been Exhibited to us the Subscribers, for Apprizement. Viz.!

In the Setting Parlour Viz.!

a looking Glass		£ 4. —. —
a Small Ditto		0. 6. 0
12 Metzitens pictures Glaz'd	@ 6/	3. 12. —
8 Cartoons D:° Ditto		4. —. —
11 small Pictures		—. 4. —
4 Maps		—. 10. —
1 Prospect Glass		—. 10. —
2 Escutchons Glaz'd		—. 4. —
1 pair small hand Irons		—. 6. —
1 Shovel & Tongs		—. 8. —
1 Tobacco Tongs		—. 1. —
1 pair Bellowes		—. 2. —
1 Tea Chest		—. 2. —
2 Small Waters		—. 1. —
1 Mehogony Tea Table		1. —. —
8 China Cups & Saucers		—. 2. —
1 Earthen Cream Pott		—. —. 1
1 Ditto. Sugar Dish		—. —. 4
1 Black Walnut Table		1. —. —
1 Black Ditto Smaller		0. 6. —
1 Round painted Table		0. 1. —
7 Leather Bottom Chairs	@ 6/	2. 2. —
1 Arm:ᵈ Chair Common		1. 3. —
1 Black Walnut Desk		1. 12. —
1 pair Candlesticks snuffers & Stand Base Mettle		—. 4. —
6 Wine Glasses 1 Water Glass		—. 1. —
a parcell of Books		1. —. —
a Case with Small Bottles		0. 4. —
		22. 1. 5

In the Marble Chamber Viz.!

1 Bedstead & Curtains Compleat		£ 8. —. —
1 feather Bed, Bolster & 2 pillows		8. —. —
1 Chest of Drawers		2. 8. —
1 Buroe Table		1. —. —
6 Chairs Leather'd Bottoms	@ 6/	1. 16. —
1 Small dressing Glass		—. 6. —
1 Small Carpett		1. —. —

(continued)

1 White Cotton Counterpin		—. 18. —
1 pair Blanketts		1. 12. —
1 pair holland Sheets		1. 4. —
3 pair Dowlases D:° New	12ˢ/p:ʳ	1. 16. —
3 pair & 1 Ditto Coarser	4/	0. 14. —
3 pair Cotton & Linnen D:°	3/	0. 9. —
4 pair Servants Ditto	2/	0. 8. —
4 Coarse Table Cloths	1/	0. 4. —
10 Ditto Kitchen Towels	1/	0. 1. —
5 Diaper Table Cloths	12/	3. —. —
6 Damask Table Cloths	@ 18/	5. 8. —
4 N: England Diaper D:°	3/	0. 12. —
4 pair Linnen pillow Cases	2/	0. 8. —
5 Coarser Ditto	1/	0. 5. —
6 Diaper Towels	6ᵈ	0. 3. —
7 Damask Ditto	2/	0. 14. —
2 doz.ⁿ & 9 Damask Napkins	@ 24 doz.ⁿ	3. 6. —
1 Gauze Tea Table Cover		0. 1. —
		£ 43. 13. 0

In the Entry & Stair Case Viz.!

17 pictures	£ 0. 10. —
	0. 10. 0

In the Kitchen Chamber Viz.!

a Bedstead & Curtains Compleat	£ 4. —. —
a Bed Bolster & 2 pillows	5. —. —
a Under Bed & 1 Chair	0. 1. —
2 Rugs & 1 Blankett @ 6/	0. 18. —
	09. 19. 0

In the Dining Room Viz.!

1 pair of andirons	£ 0. 3. —
7 Bass Bottoms Chairs	0. 7. —
1 Large Wooden Table	0. 3. —
1 Small Ditto Oak	0. 1. —
1 Small looking Glass	0. 6. —
1 Old Desk	0. 6. —
1 Case with 2 Bottles	0. 2. —
1 Warming pan	0. 12. —
	2. 0. 0

Sugar, Currency, and Stamps

In 1764, Grenville pushed through Parliament several bills that in combination pressed hard against the economic system of the colonies. First came the Revenue Act (or Sugar Act) of 1764. While reducing the tax on imported French molasses from 6 to 3 pence per gallon, it added a number of colonial products to the list of commodities that could be sent only to England. It also required American shippers to post bonds guaranteeing observance of the trade regulations before loading their cargoes. Finally, it strengthened the vice-admiralty courts, where violators of the trade acts were prosecuted.

Many of the colonial legislatures grumbled about the Sugar Act because a strictly enforced duty of 3 pence per gallon on molasses pinched more than the loosely enforced 6-pence duty. But only New York objected that *any* tax by Parliament to raise revenue (rather than to control trade) violated the rights of overseas English subjects who were unrepresented in Parliament.

On the heels of the Sugar Act came the Currency Act. In 1751, Parliament had forbidden the New England colonies to issue paper money as legal tender, and now it extended that prohibition to all the colonies. In a colonial economy chronically short of hard cash, this constricted trade.

The move to tighten up the machinery of empire confused the colonists because many of the new regulations came from Parliament, which had heretofore been content to allow the king, his ministers, and the Board of Trade to run overseas affairs. In a world where history taught that power and liberty were perpetually at war, generations of colonists had viewed Parliament as a bastion of English liberty, the bulwark against despotic political rule. The Parliament on which colonial legislatures had modeled themselves now began to seem like a violator of colonial rights.

In protesting new parliamentary regulations, colonial leaders were hobbled by uncertainty concerning where Parliament's authority began and ended in administering the colonies. The colonists had always implicitly accepted parliamentary power overseas because it was easier to evade distasteful trade regulations than to contest this power. But the exact limits of that authority were vague.

After Parliament passed the Sugar Act in 1764, Grenville announced his intention to extend to America the stamp duties that had already been imposed in England. However, he gave the colonies a year to suggest alternative ways of raising revenue.

The colonies objected strenuously to the proposed stamp tax, but none provided another plan. Knowing that colonial property taxes were slight compared to those in England, Grenville dismissed the petitions that poured in from the colonies and drove the bill through Parliament. The Stamp Act, effective November 1765, required revenue stamps on every newspaper, pamphlet, almanac, legal document, liquor license, college diploma, pack of playing cards, and pair of dice.

Colonial reaction to the Stamp Act ranged from disgruntled submission to mass defiance. The breadth of the reaction shocked the British government—and many Americans as well. Lieutenant Governor Hutchinson of Massachusetts believed that "there is not a family between Canada and Pensacola that has not heard the name of the Stamp Act and but very few . . . but what have some formidable apprehensions of it." In many cases, resistance involved not only discontent over England's tightening of the screws on the American colonies but also internal resentments born out of the play of local events. Especially in the cities, the defiance of authority and destruction of property by people from the middle and lower ranks redefined the dynamics of politics, setting the stage for a ten-year internal struggle for control among the various social elements alarmed by the new English policies.

Stamp Act Riots

The Virginia House of Burgesses was the first legislature to react to the news of the Stamp Act, which arrived in April 1765. Virginians were already on edge because a severe decline in tobacco prices and heavy war-related taxes had mired most planters in debt. In late 1764, the burgesses had strenuously objected to the proposed stamp tax, citing the economic hardship it would cause and arguing that it was their "inherent" right to be taxed only by their own consent.

The Stamp Act enraged a group of Virginia's young burgesses. In May 1765, led by 29-year-old Patrick Henry, a fiery lawyer newly elected from a frontier county, the House of Burgesses debated seven strongly worded resolutions. Old-guard burgesses regarded some of them as treasonable. The legislature finally adopted the four more moderate resolves, including one proclaiming Virginia's right to impose taxes. But they rejected the other resolves, which declared it "illegal, unconstitutional, and unjust" for anybody outside Virginia to lay taxes; asserted that Virginians did not have to obey

From the time of his election to the Virginia House of Burgesses at the age of 29, Patrick Henry was an outspoken proponent of American rights. In this portrait, he pleads a case at a county courthouse crowded with local planters.

any externally imposed tax law; and labeled as "an enemy to this, his Majesty's colony" anyone denying Virginia's exclusive right to tax its inhabitants.

Since many burgesses had left for home before Henry introduced his resolutions, less than a quarter of Virginia's legislators voted for the four moderate resolves. But within a month, all seven resolutions were broadcast in the newspapers of other colonies. Henry and the aggressive young burgesses had hurled words of defiance at Parliament for other colonies to reflect on and match.

Governor Francis Bernard of Massachusetts called the Virginia resolves "an alarm bell for the disaffected." The events in Boston in August 1765 amply confirmed his view. On August 14, Bostonians awoke to find an effigy of stamp distributor Andrew Oliver, dressed in rags, hanging from an elm tree in the south end of town. When the sheriff tried to remove it at the order of Lieutenant Governor Thomas Hutchinson, Oliver's brother-in-law, a hostile crowd intervened. In the evening, working men began gathering for a mock funeral. Led by Ebenezer MacIntosh, they cut down Oliver's effigy and boisterously carried it through the streets. Then they leveled Oliver's new brick office on the wharves, rumored to be the distribution point for the hated stamps.

As night fell, the crowd reduced Oliver's luxurious mansion to a shambles. The stamp distributor promptly asked to be relieved of his commission. Twelve days later, MacIntosh led the crowd again in an all-night bout of destruction of the handsomely appointed homes of two British officials and Hutchinson, a haughty man, who was as unpopular with the common people as his great-great-grandmother, Anne Hutchinson, had been popular. Military men "who have seen towns sacked by the enemy," one observer reported, "declare they never before saw an instance of such fury."

In attacking the property of men associated with the stamp tax, the Boston crowd under MacIntosh demonstrated its opposition to parliamentary policy. But the crowd was also expressing hostility toward a local elite that for years had disdained lower-class political participation and had publicly denounced the working poor for their supposed lack of industry and frugality. For decades, ordinary Bostonians had aligned politically with the Boston "caucus," which led the colony's "popular party" against conservative aristocrats such as Hutchinson and Oliver. They had also read in the *Boston Gazette* that the new parliamentary legislation had been proposed by "mean mercenary hirelings among yourselves, who for a little filthy lucre would at any time

City Plan of Boston, 1772

Charlestown

Charles River

NORTH
BATTERY

North
Writing
School

Christ
Church

North Grammar School

New North Meeting

Second
Baptist
Meeting

Bennet Street Meeting
(Mather's Church)

Mill Pond

First Baptist
Meeting

Old North Meeting

New Brick Meeting

West Church

OLD WHARF

Manifesto
Church

The Harbor

Writing
School

Faneuil Hall

Powder House

Beacon
Hill

QUEEN STREET

WHARF

LONG

Prison and courthouse

KING STREET

Almshouse

King's
Chapel

First
Church

Town House

OLD WHARF

Bridewell

STREET

Friends Meeting

Workhouse

South
Grammar

School Street Meeting

Town Granary

Province
House

Old South Meeting

SOUTH
BATTERY

Common

THE MALL

South
Writing
School

MARLBOROUGH

Fort
Hill

Trinity Church

Irish
Meeting

NEWBURY

STREET

New Baptist Meeting

Hollis Street
Meeting

Boston
Neck

Public buildings

Churches

Houses and commercial buildings

betray every right, liberty, and privilege of their fellow subjects."

But the "rage-intoxicated rabble" had suddenly broken away from the leaders of the popular party and gone farther than they had intended. Thomas Hutchinson was one of their main targets. Characterized in the diary of a young lawyer named John Adams as "very ambitious and avaricious," Hutchinson was chief among the "mean mercenary hirelings" in the popular view. In the aftermath of the destruction of his house—what Governor Bernard called "a war of plunder, of taking away the distinction between rich and poor"—the more cautious political leaders knew that they would have to struggle to regain control of the protest movement.

Violent protest against the Stamp Act also wracked New York and Newport, Rhode Island. Leading the resistance were groups calling themselves the Sons of Liberty, composed mostly of artisans, shopkeepers, and ordinary citizens. Protest took a more dignified form at the Stamp Act Congress, called by Massachusetts and attended by representatives of nine colonies, who met in New York in October 1765. English authorities branded this first self-initiated intercolonial convention a "dangerous tendency." The delegates formulated 12 restrained resolutions that accepted Parliament's right to legislate for the colonies but denied its right to tax them directly.

All over America by late 1765, effigy-burning crowds had convinced stamp distributors to resign their commissions. The colonists defied English authority even more directly by forcing most customs officers and court officials to open the ports and courts for business after November 1 without using the hated stamps required after that date. This often took months of pressure, sometimes accompanied by mob action, but the Sons of Liberty, often led by new faces in local politics, ultimately got their way by going outside the law.

In March 1766, Parliament debated the surprising American reaction to the Stamp Act. Lobbied by many merchant friends of the Americans, Parliament voted to repeal it. Some members warned that to retreat before colonial defiance of the law would ultimately be fatal. But the legislators bowed to expediency. They satisfied themselves with passing the Declaratory Act, which asserted Parliament's power to enact laws for the colonies in "all cases whatsoever." The crisis had passed. Yet nothing was really solved. Americans had begun to recognize a grasping government trampling its subjects' rights. The Stamp Act, one New England clergyman foresaw, "diffused a disgust through the colonies and laid the basis of an alienation which will never be healed."

In the course of challenging parliamentary authority, the Stamp Act resisters politicized their communities as never before. The established leaders, generally cautious in their protests, were often displaced by those beneath them on the social ladder. Men such as New York ship captains Alexander McDougall and Isaac Sears mobilized common citizens and raised political consciousness, employing

This wood engraving, published in 1829 in a history of the United States, recalls a New Hampshire riot in which townspeople lynched and stoned a stamp master in effigy.

mass demonstrations and street violence to humble stamp distributors and force open the courts and seaports. Scribbled John Adams in his diary: "The people have become more attentive to their liberties, . . . and more determined to defend them. . . . Our presses have groaned, our pulpits have thundered, our legislatures have resolved, our towns have voted; the crown officers have everywhere trembled, and all their little tools and creatures been afraid to speak and ashamed to be seen."

An Uncertain Interlude

Ministerial instability in England hampered the quest for a coherent, workable American policy. Attempting to be a strong king, George III chose ministers who commanded little respect in Parliament. This led to strife between Parliament and the king's chief ministers; that in turn led to a shuffling of chief ministers and to a chaotic political situation at the very time that the king was attempting to overhaul the administration of the empire.

To manage the colonies more effectively, the Pitt-Grafton ministry that the king had appointed in 1767 obtained new laws to reorganize the customs service, establish a secretary of state for American affairs, and install three new vice-admiralty courts in the port cities. Still hard pressed for revenue—for at home the government faced severe unemployment, tax protests, and riots over the high price of grain—the ministry also pushed through Parliament the Townshend duties on paper, lead, painters' colors, and tea. A final law suspended New York's assembly until that body ceased its noncompliance with the Quartering Act of 1765, which required public funds for support of British troops garrisoned in the colony since the end of the Seven Years' War.

Colonial reaction to the Townshend Acts, centered in Massachusetts, was more restrained than in 1765. New York buckled under to the Quartering Act rather than see its assembly suspended. But the Massachusetts House of Representatives sent a circular letter to each colony objecting to the new Townshend duties, small though they were. Written by Samuel Adams, the letter attacked as unconstitutional the plan to underwrite salaries for royal officials in America from customs duties. Under instructions from England, Governor Bernard dissolved the legislature after it refused to rescind the circular letter. "The Americans have made a discovery," declared Edmund Burke before Parliament, "that we mean to oppress them; we have made a

discovery that they intend to raise a rebellion. We do not know how to advance; they do not know how to retreat."

While most of the colonists only grumbled and petitioned, Bostonians protested stridently. In the summer of 1768, after customs officials seized a sloop owned by John Hancock for a violation of the trade regulations, an angry crowd mobbed them. They fled to a British warship in Boston harbor and remained there for months. The newspapers hounded overeager revenue officers who extracted money for the maintenance of "swarms of officers and pensioners, and an enormous train of underlings and dependents"; they also warned of new measures designed "to suck the life blood" from the people and predicted that troops would be sent "to dragoon us into passive obedience." In many minds the belief grew that the English were plotting "designs for destroying our constitutional liberties."

Troops indeed came. The attack on the customs officials brought a resolute response from England, where the government regarded the Bostonians' action as insubordinate and selfish. The ministry dispatched two regiments from England and two more from Nova Scotia. The intention was to bring the Bostonians to a proper state of subordination and make them an example to the rest of the colonies. Now cries went up against maintaining standing armies in peacetime, but radical Bostonians who proposed force to prevent the troops from landing got little support from delegates called to a special provincial convention. On October 1, 1768, red-coated troops marched into Boston without resistance.

After the troops occupied Boston, the colonists' main tactic of protest against the Townshend Acts became economic boycott. First in Boston and then in New York and Philadelphia, merchants and consumers adopted nonimportation and nonconsumption agreements. They pledged neither to import nor to use British articles. These measures promised to bring the politically influential English merchants to their aid, for half of British shipping was engaged in commerce with the colonies, and one-quarter of all English exports were consumed there.

Many colonial merchants, however, especially those tied to the government's interest, had no intention of being bound by a community compact that had no force in law. They had to be persuaded otherwise by street brigades, usually composed of artisans who warmly supported nonimportation as a boon to home manufacturing. Crowd action welled up again in the seaports, as determined patriot bands attacked the homes and warehouses of of-

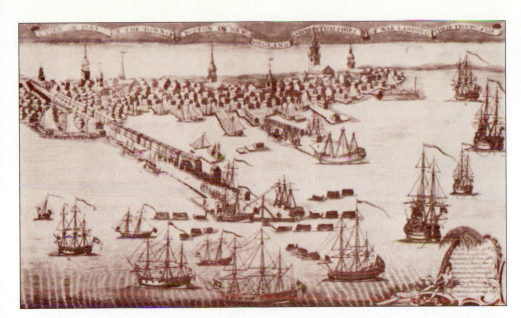

The occupation of Boston by British troops in 1768 never quelled disorder as King George III had hoped. In this engraving by Paul Revere, the troops are debarking at the Long Wharf.

fending merchants and "rescued" incoming contraband goods seized by zealous customs officials. When the southern colonies also adopted nonimportation agreements in 1768, a new step toward intercolonial union had been taken.

England's attempts to discipline its American colonies and oblige them to share the costs of governing an empire lay in shambles by the end of the 1760s. The employment of troops to restore order undermined the respect for the mother country on which colonial acceptance of its authority ultimately depended. American newspapers denounced new extensions of British authority. Colonial governors quarreled with their legislatures. Customs officials met with determined opposition and were widely accused of arbitrary actions and excessive zeal in enforcing the Navigation Acts. The Townshend duties had failed miserably, yielding less than £21,000 by 1770 while costing British business £700,000 through the colonial nonimportation movement.

In London, on March 5, 1770, Parliament repealed all the Townshend duties except the one on tea (which the new minister of state, Lord North, explained was retained "as a mark of the supremacy of Parliament and an efficient declaraction of their right to govern the colonies"). On that same evening in Boston, British troops fired on an unruly crowd of heckling citizens. For months, Bostonians had been baiting the "lobsterbacks," as they dubbed the red-coated British soldiers. They hated them for competing with townspeople for menial jobs when off duty, as well as for their military presence. On this evening, a taunting crowd had first hurled insults and snowballs and then surged toward a sentry. After a squad of redcoats joined the sentry, someone cried, "Fire!" When the smoke cleared, five bloody bodies, including that of Ebenezer MacIntosh's brother-in-law, stained the snow-covered street. Bowing to furious popular reaction, Thomas Hutchinson, recently appointed governor, ordered the British troops out of town and arrested the commanding officer and the soldiers involved. They were later acquitted, with two young patriot lawyers, John Adams and Josiah Quincy, Jr., providing a brilliant defense.

In spite of the potential of the "Boston massacre" for galvanizing the colonies into further resistance, opposition to English policies, including economic boycotts, subsided in 1770. Popular leaders such as Samuel Adams in Boston and Alexander McDougall in New York, who had made names for themselves as the standard-bearers of American liberty, had few issues left to exploit. They were further handicapped by the end of the depression that had previously helped sow discontent. Yet the fires of revolution had been not extinguished but merely damped.

The Growing Rift

From 1770 to 1772, relative quiet descended over the colonies. Not until June 1772 did England provide another inflammatory issue. Then, by an-

Paul Revere was not only a noted silversmith and political activist but also a man who put art to work in the cause of Revolutionary politics. This engraving became known throughout the colonies and convinced many people to involve themselves in what had been mainly New England's cause.

nouncing that it would pay the salaries of the royal governor and superior court judges in Massachusetts rather than allow the provincial legislature to continue supporting these positions, the crown created a new furor. Even though the measure saved the colony money, it was seen as a dangerous innovation because it undermined a right set forth in the colony's charter and hence was interpreted as a design to impose a despotic government on the colony. Judges paid from London, it was assumed, would respond to London.

Boston's town meeting protested loudly and created a Committee of Correspondence "to state the rights of the colonists . . . and to communicate and publish the same to the several towns and to

the world." Crown supporters called the committee "the foulest, subtlest, and most venomous serpent ever issued from the egg of sedition." By the end of 1772, another 80 towns in Massachusetts had created committees. In the next year, all but three colonies established Committees of Correspondence in their legislatures.

Samuel Adams was by now the leader of the Boston radicals, for the influence of laboring men like Ebenezer MacIntosh had been quietly reduced. Adams was an experienced caucus politicker, a skilled political journalist, and a man with deep roots among the laboring people despite his Harvard degree. He organized the working ranks through the taverns, clubs, and volunteer fire companies and also secured the support of wealthy merchants such as John Hancock, whose ample purse financed patriotic celebrations and feasts that kept politics on everyone's mind and helped to build interclass bridges. In England, Adams became known as one of the most dangerous firebrands in America.

In 1772, a band of Rhode Island colonists gave Adams new material to work with when they attacked a royal warship. The British commander of the *Gaspee* was roundly hated for hounding the fishermen and small traders of Narragansett Bay. When his ship ran aground while pursuing a suspected smuggler, Rhode Islanders took their revenge. Clambering aboard the stranded vessel, they burned it to the water's edge. Adding insult to injury, a Rhode Island court convicted the *Gaspee*'s captain of illegally seizing what he was convinced was smuggled sugar and rum. The government in London reacted with cries of high treason. Finding the lips of Rhode Islanders sealed regarding the identity of the arsonists, an investigating committee could do little. The event was tailor-made for Samuel Adams, who used it to "awaken the American colonies, which have been too long dozing upon the brink of ruin."

In early 1773, Parliament's passage of the Tea Act precipitated the final plunge into revolution. The act allowed the East India Company, which was on the verge of bankruptcy, to ship its tea directly to America. By eliminating English middlemen and English import taxes, this provided Americans with the opportunity to buy their tea cheaply from the company's agents in the colonies. Even with the small tax to be paid in the colonies, Indian tea would now undersell smuggled Dutch tea. The Americans would get inexpensive tea, the crown would derive a modest revenue, and the East India Company would obtain a new lease on life. The company soon had 600,000 pounds of tea in 2,000 chests ready for shipment to America.

Parliament monumentally miscalculated the American response. For several years, merchants in Philadelphia and New York had been flagrantly smuggling Dutch tea. As a consequence, imports of English tea in the two seaports plummeted from 500,000 pounds in 1768 to a mere 650 pounds in 1772. The merchants bitterly denounced the new act for giving the East India Company a monopoly on the American tea market. Other monopolies would follow, they predicted, and middlemen of all kinds would be eliminated. The colonists also objected that the government was shrewdly trying to gain implicit acceptance of Parliament's taxing

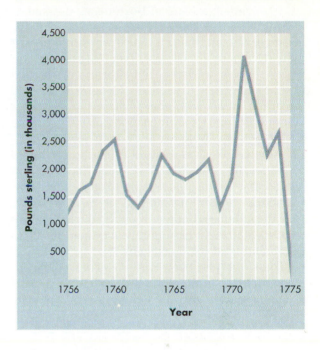

British Exports to North America, 1756–1775

Source: U.S. Bureau of the Census.

power by offering tea at a new reduced rate. When Americans drank the taxed tea, they would also be swallowing the English right to impose taxes.

The colonists quickly demonstrated that their principles were not entirely in their pocketbooks. Mass meetings in the port towns soon forced the resignation of the East India Company's agents, and citizens vowed to stop the obnoxious tea at the water's edge.

Governor Hutchinson of Massachusetts brought the tea crisis to a climax. He decided that to yield once more to popular pressure would forever cripple English sovereignty in America. The popular party led by Samuel Adams had been urging the citizenry to demonstrate that they were not yet prepared for the "yoke of slavery" by sending the tea back to England. Hutchinson's refusal to grant the tea ships clearance papers to return to England with their cargoes finally led to dramatic action. Buoyed by resolutions from surrounding towns, 5,000 Bostonians packed Old South Church on December 16, 1773. The meeting noisily passed resolutions urging the governor to clear the ships. But Hutchinson was not swayed by the Bostonians' determination to resist what they regarded as another affront to their liberties. "This meeting," despaired Samuel Adams, "can do no more to save the country."

At nightfall, a band of Bostonians, dressed as Indians, boarded the tea ships, broke open the chests of tea, and flung £10,000 worth of the East India Company's property into Boston harbor. George Hewes, a 31-year-old shoemaker, recalled how he had garbed himself as a Mohawk, blackened "face and hands with coal dust in the shop of a blacksmith," and joined men of all ranks in marching stealthily to the wharves to do their work.

Now the die was cast. Lord North, the king's chief minister, called the Bostonians "fanatics" and argued that the dispute was no longer about taxes but about whether England had any authority at all over the colonies. George III put it succinctly: "We must master them or totally leave them to themselves and treat them as aliens."

Thoroughly aroused, Parliament passed the Coercive Acts, a set of stern laws, which Bostonians promptly labeled the "Intolerable Acts." The acts

Public sentiment against the importation of tea and other British goods often found expression in a coat of tar and feathers applied to the bare skin of the offending importer. Note the symbols in The Bostonians Paying the Excise-Man: *the Liberty Tree with a hangman's noose and the overturned copy of the Stamp Act. In the background, Bostonians dump chests of tea into the harbor.*

closed the port of Boston to all shipping until the colony paid for the destroyed tea. They declared British soldiers and officials immune from local court trials for acts committed while suppressing civil disturbances. To hamstring the colony's truculent political assemblies, Parliament amended the Massachusetts charter to transform the council from an upper legislative chamber, elected by the lower house, to a body appointed by the governor. This stripped the council of its veto power over the governor's decisions.

The act also struck at local government by authorizing the governor to prohibit all town meetings except for one annual meeting in each town to elect local officers of government. Finally, General Thomas Gage, commander in chief of British forces in America, replaced Thomas Hutchinson as governor. "This is the day, then," declared Edmund Burke in the House of Commons, "that you wish to go to war with all America, in order to conciliate that country to this."

The English plan to strangle Massachusetts into submission and hope for acquiescence elsewhere in the colonies proved popular in England. Earlier, the colonies had gained supporters in Parliament for their resistance to what many regarded as attacks on their fundamental privileges. Now this support evaporated. After a decade of debating constitutional rights and mobilizing sentiment against what many believed was a systematic plot to enslave freeborn citizens, the Americans found their maneuvering room severely narrowed.

When the Intolerable Acts arrived in May 1774 aboard the *Harmony,* Boston's town meeting reacted belligerently. It dispatched a circular letter to all the colonies urging an end to trade with England. This met with faint support. But a second call, for a meeting in Philadelphia of delegates from all colonies, received a better response. The Continental Congress, as it was called, now began to transform a ten-year debate conducted by separate colonies into a unified American cause.

Fifty-five delegates from all the colonies except Georgia converged on Carpenter's Hall in Philadelphia in September 1774. The discussions centered not on how to prepare for a war that many sensed was inevitable, but on how to resolve differences that most delegates feared were irreconcilable. Overcoming sectional prejudices and hostilities was as important as the formal debates. New Englanders were especially eyed with suspicion for their reputed intolerance and self-interest. "We have numberless prejudices to remove here," wrote John Adams from Philadelphia. "We have been obliged to keep ourselves out of sight, and to feel pulses, and to sound the depths; to insinuate our sentiments, designs, and desires by means of other persons, sometimes of one province, and sometimes of another."

The Continental Congress was by no means a unified body. Some delegates, led by cousins Samuel and John Adams from Massachusetts and Richard Henry Lee and Patrick Henry of Virginia, argued for outright resistance to Parliament's Coercive Acts. Moderate delegates from the middle colonies, led by Joseph Galloway of Pennsylvania and James Duane of New York, urged restraint and further attempts at reconciliation. After weeks of debate, the delegates agreed to issue a restrained Declaration of Rights and Resolves. It attempted to define American grievances and to justify the colonists' defiance of English policies and laws by appealing to the "immutable laws of nature, the principles of the English constitution, and the several [colonial] charters and compacts" under which they lived. More concrete was the Congress's agreement on a plan of resistance. If England did not rescind the Intolerable Acts by December 1, 1774, a ban on all imports and exports between the colonies and Great Britain, Ireland, and the British West Indies would take effect. Some exceptions were made for the export of southern staple commodities in order to keep reluctant southern colonies in the fold.

By the time the Congress adjourned in late October, leaders from different colonies had learned of one another's conditions, measured one another's rhetoric and temperament, and transformed what had been primarily Boston's cause into a national movement. "Government is dissolved [and] we are in a state of nature," Patrick Henry argued dramatically. "The distinctions between Virginians, Pennsylvanians, New Yorkers, and New Englanders are no more. I am not a Virginian, but an American."

Many of Henry's fellow delegates were a long way from converting their provincial identities to a national one, but in adjourning, the Congress agreed to reconvene in May 1775.

Even before the Second Continental Congress met, the fabric of government had been badly torn in most colonies. Revolutionary committees, conventions, and congresses, entirely unauthorized by law, were replacing legal governing bodies. Assuming authority in defiance of royal governors, who suspended truculent legislatures in many colonies, they often operated on instructions from mass meetings where the legal franchise was ignored. These extralegal bodies created and armed militia units, bullied merchants and shopkeepers refusing to conform to popularly authorized boycotts, levied taxes, operated the courts, and obstructed the work of English customs officials. By the end of 1774, all but three colonies defied their own charters by appointing provincial assemblies without royal authority. In the next year, this independently created power became evident in the nearly complete cessation of trade with England.

The Final Rupture

The final spark to the revolutionary powder keg was struck in early 1775. General Gage had assumed the governorship of Massachusetts 11 months earlier and occupied Boston with 4,000 troops—one for every adult male in the town. In April 1775, the government in London ordered Gage to arrest "the principal actors and abettors" of insurrection in Massachusetts. As a first step, he sent 700 redcoats out of Boston under cover of night to seize colonial arms and ammunition in nearby Concord. But Americans learned of the plan. When the troops reached Lexington at dawn, 70 "Minutemen"—townsmen available on a minute's notice—occupied the village green. In the skirmish that ensued, 18 Massachusetts farmers fell, 8 of them mortally wounded.

Not only Bostonians took action against the Tea Act. This Philadelphia broadside from "The Committee for Tarring and Feathering," issued several weeks before the Boston Tea Party, exhorts pilots on the Delaware River to watch for an arriving tea ship.

Marching 6 miles west, the British entered Concord, where another firefight broke out. Withdrawing, the redcoats made their way back to Boston, harassed by militiamen firing from farmhouses and barns and from behind stone walls. Before the bloody day ended, 273 British and 95 Americans lay dead or wounded. News of the bloodshed swept through the colonies. Within weeks, thousands of men besieged the British troops in Boston. One colonist reported that wherever one traveled, "you see the inhabitants training, making firelocks, casting mortars, shells, and shot."

The outbreak of fighting vastly altered the debates of the Second Continental Congress, which assembled in Philadelphia in May 1775. The Congress had the same slim powers as its predecessor, but it acquired awesome new responsibilities. Many delegates knew one another from the earlier Congress. But fresh faces appeared, including Boston's wealthy merchant, John Hancock; a tall, young planter-lawyer from Virginia, Thomas Jefferson; and the much-applauded Benjamin Franklin, who had arrived from London only four days before the Congress convened.

The Congress had no power to legislate or command; it could only request and recommend. Delegate John Adams worried that such a body could form a constitution "for a great empire," while "at the same time they have a country of 1,500 miles to fortify, millions to arm and train, a naval power to begin, an extensive commerce to regulate, numerous tribes of Indians to negotiate with, a standing army of 27,000 men to raise pay, victual, and officer."

Another 14 months elapsed before the Congress issued a formal declaration of independence, but the war with England—and a civil war in America—had already begun. Meeting in the statehouse in Philadelphia, where the king's arms hung over the entrance and the inscription on the tower bell read "Proclaim liberty throughout the land unto all the inhabitants thereof," the Second Congress set to work. It authorized a continental army of 20,000 and, partly to cement Virginia to the cause, chose George Washington as commander in chief. It issued a "Declaration of Causes of Taking-up Arms," sent the king an "Olive Branch Petition" humbly begging him to remove the obstacles to reconciliation, made moves to secure the neutrality of the interior Indian tribes, issued paper money, erected a postal system, and approved plans for a military hospital.

While debate continued over whether the colonies ought to declare themselves independent, military action grew hotter. The hotheaded Ethan Allen and his Green Mountain boys from eastern New York captured Fort Ticonderoga, controlling the Champlain valley, in May 1775. On New Year's Day in 1776, the British shelled Norfolk, Virginia. In March 1776, Washington's army forced the British to evacuate Boston. Yet many members of the Congress dreaded a final rupture and still hoped for reconciliation with England. Such hopes crumbled at the end of 1775 when news arrived that the king, rejecting the Olive Branch Petition, had dispatched 20,000 additional British troops to quell the American insurrection and had proclaimed the colonies in "open and avowed rebellion." Those fatal words made all the Congress's actions treasonable and turned all who obeyed them into traitors.

By the time Thomas Paine's hard-hitting pamphlet *Common Sense* appeared in Philadelphia on January 9, 1776, members of the Congress were talking less gingerly about independence. Paine's blunt words and compelling rhetoric smashed through the remaining reserve. "O ye that love mankind! Ye that dare oppose not only the tyranny, but also the tyrant, stand forth!" wrote Paine. Within weeks the pamphlet was in bookstalls all over the colonies. "The public sentiment which a few weeks before had shuddered at the tremendous obstacles, with which independence was envisioned," declared Edmund Randolph of Virginia, now "overleaped every barrier."

The Continental Congress continued to debate independence during the spring of 1776, even as the war became bloodier. While the delegates talked, men under arms acted. The army that Washington had gathered in Massachusetts forced the British to evacuate Boston in March. Several months later, an American assault on Quebec failed. England embargoed all trade to the colonies and ordered the seizure of American ships. That convinced the Congress to declare its ports open to all countries. "Nothing is left now," Joseph Hewes of North Carolina admitted, "but to fight it out." It was almost anticlimactic when Richard Henry Lee introduced his congressional resolution on June 7 calling for a declaration of independence. After two days of debate, the Congress ordered a committee chaired by Jefferson to begin drafting the document.

Though it would become revered as the new nation's birth certificate, the declaration was not a highly original statement. It drew heavily on the addresses that the Congress had been issuing to justify American resistance, and it presented a theory of government that was embedded in the scores of pamphlets that had issued from the colonial presses over the previous decade. The ringing phrases that "all men are created equal, that they are endowed by their Creator with certain unalienable Rights, that among these are Life, Liberty and the pursuit of Happiness" were familiar in the writing of many pamphleteers, including John Adams, Thomas Paine, and James Wilson.

Jefferson's committee brought its handiwork before the Congress on June 28. The proposals were read and ordered "to lie on the table" until the following Monday, July 1. "This morning is assigned for the greatest debate of all," noted John Adams, when the Congress reconvened. "May Heaven prosper the new-born republic, and make it more glorious than any former republics have been." At the end of the day, nine colonies voted to adopt the declaration, two voted against, one delegation split, and one abstained. The next day, July 2, twelve delegations voted yes, with New York's abstaining, thus allowing the Congress to say that the vote for independence was unanimous. Two days more were spent cutting and polishing the document. The major change was the elimination of a long argument blaming the king for slavery in America.

On July 4, Congress sent the Declaration of Independence to the printer. Four days later, Philadelphians thronged to the statehouse to hear it read aloud. They huzzahed the reading, tore the king's arms from above the statehouse door, and later that night, amid cheers, toasts, and clanging church bells, hurled this symbol of more than a century and a half of colonial dependency to England into a roaring bonfire.

THE IDEOLOGY OF REVOLUTIONARY REPUBLICANISM

In the years after 1763, the colonists responded to a variety of ideas that gave meaning to the events and conditions they were experiencing. Most of these ideas were formally expressed, in hundreds of newspaper articles and pamphlets, by educated lawyers, clergymen, merchants, and planters, but some came from the middling and lower ranks of society in the form of broadsides, appeals in the newspapers, and even street demonstrations in which ordinary people carried out ideologically laden rituals of humiliation against their enemies such as tarring and feathering and burnings in effigy. Gradually, the colonists pieced together a political ideology, borrowed partly from English political

thought, partly from the theories of the Enlightenment, and partly from their own experiences. Historians call this new ideology "revolutionary republicanism." But it is important to understand that because the colonists varied widely in interests and experiences, there was never a single coherent ideology to which they all subscribed.

A Plot Against Liberty

Many American colonists subscribed to the notion advanced by earlier English Whig writers that corrupt and power-hungry men were slowly extinguishing the lamp of liberty in England. The so-called "country" party represented by these Whig pamphleteers proclaimed itself the guardian of the true principles of the English constitution and opposed the "court" party representing the king and his appointees.

When the king's ministers began a new program for disciplining the empire after 1763, American Whig writers were intellectually prepared to view the new laws and policies as attacks on such traditional English liberties as balanced government, representative rights, and disestablishment of standing armies in peacetime. Even Parliament, traditionally the preserver of the people's rights against tyrannical executive power, seemed to threaten a despotism of its own in its alliance with the monarchy. Every ministerial policy and parliamentary act in the decade after the Stamp Act appeared as a subversion of English liberties. Most Americans regarded resistance to such blows against liberty as wholly justified.

The belief that England was carrying out "a deep-laid and desperate plan of imperial despotism . . . for the extinction of all civil liberty," as the Boston town meeting expressed it in 1770, spread rapidly in the next few years. By 1774, John Adams was writing of "the conspiracy against the public liberty [that] was first regularly formed and begun to be executed in 1763 and 1764." From London, America's favorite writer, Benjamin Franklin, described the "extreme corruption prevalent among all orders of men in this old rotten state." Another pamphleteer reached the conclusion that England was no longer "in a condition at present to suckle us, being pregnant with vermin that corrupt her milk and convert her blood and juices into poison."

Among many Americans, especially merchants, the attack on constitutional rights blended closely with the threats to their economic interests contained in the tough new trade policies. Merchants

Liberty always had to struggle against power, as American colonists saw it; in this cartoon, England (power) forces Liberty (America in the form of a woman) to drink the "Bitter Draught" of tea. Uncompliant, America spits the tea into England's face while another corrupt Englishman peeks under her petticoat.

perceived a coordinated attack on their "lives, liberties, and property," as they frequently phrased it. If a man was not secure in his property, he could not be secure in his political citizenship, for it was property that allowed a man the independence to shape his identity.

The continuing crisis over the imperial relationship by itself inspired many colonists to resist impending tyranny. But the revolutionary mentality of others was also nourished by a belief that an opportunity was at hand to revitalize American society. They believed that the colonies had been undergoing a silent transformation and that the growing commercial connection with the decadent and corrupt mother country had injected deadly fluids into the American bloodstream. They worried about the luxury and vice they saw around them and came to believe that resistance to England would return American society to a state of civic virtue, spartan living, and godly purpose.

The fervent support of the patriot movement by much of the colonial clergy, especially in New England, and the clergy's importance in writing protest pamphlets helped give a high-toned moral character to colonial protest. As in most revolutionary movements, the notion of moral regeneration, of a society-wide rebirth through battle against a corrupt enemy, ennobled the cause. Such appeals resonated most strongly in New England, where even so secular a man as John Adams groaned at the "universal spirit of debauchery, dissipation, luxury,

effeminacy and gaming." But they also inspired people in areas that had been affected a generation before by the Great Awakening.

The growth of a revolutionary spirit among common people also owed much to the plain style of polemical writers such as Thomas Paine and Patrick Henry. Paine's *Common Sense* transformed the terms of the imperial argument by attacking monarchy itself. Its astounding popularity—it went through 25 editions in 1776 and sold more copies than any printed piece in colonial history—stemmed not only from its argument but also from its style. Paine wrote for the common people, assuming their knowledge of nothing more than the Bible. Using biblical imagery and plain language, he appealed to their Calvinist heritage and their belief in their providential destiny. After savagely attacking the king, whom he called "a royal brute," Paine appealed to millennial yearnings: "We have it in our power to begin the world over again. The birthday of a new world is at hand," if only the Americans would stand up for liberty, the goddess whom "Europe regards . . . like a stranger, and England hath given . . . warning to depart."

Paine avoided the elaborate legalistic style of most of the pamphlets written by lawyers and clergymen in the preceding decade. His language could be understood on the docks, in the taverns, on the streets, and in the farmyards. Many Whig leaders found his pungent language and egalitarian call for ending hereditary privilege and concentrated power too strong. They denounced the disheveled immigrant with "genius in his eyes" as "a crack-brained zealot for democracy" and a dangerous man who appealed to "every silly clown and illiterate mechanic." But thousands who read or listened to *Common Sense* were radicalized by it.

Rejecting Monarchy

The rejection of monarchy was one basic component of the republican faith that emerged in the prerevolutionary decade. "The word *republic*," explained Thomas Paine, "means the public good of the whole, in contra-distinction to the despotic form which makes the good of the sovereign, or of one man, the only object of government." The American people did not easily turn away from the English monarchy. Up to the moment of independence, they had celebrated England's "mixed and balanced" government with its combination of king, Lords, and Commons. They had thought England's limited monarchy, when properly administered, the safest and most stable form of government ever devised. America's problems with England had arisen not because of the monarchy but because the king and Parliament, corrupted by their own power, had turned their backs on the English constitution and attacked the liberties it was intended to protect.

Only at the very end of the imperial crisis, after they had already repudiated Parliamentary authority, did the colonists attack the king. It was Paine's unsparing rejection of monarchy, his denial that it was in any way compatible with liberty, that made his pamphlet *Common Sense* so radical. "Of more worth is one honest man to society, and in the sight of God," he scoffed, "than all the crowned ruffians that ever lived." Americans were not accustomed to using such language in reference to the king.

In rejecting monarchy, the American people also rejected the system of hierarchical authority on which the monarchy was based. They set aside the belief that political authority grew out of gov-

In Common Sense, *Thomas Paine dared to articulate, in plain but muscular language, the thoughts of rebellion and independence that others had only alluded to.*

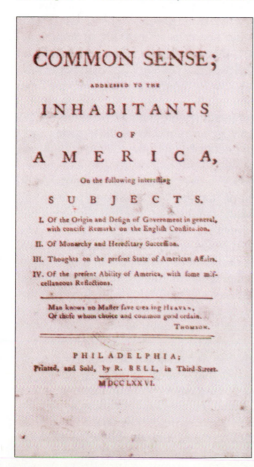

ernmental power and the doctrine that in return for the king's protection, the people owed him loyalty and obedience. Therein lay much of the true radicalism of their republican faith.

Balancing Liberty and Power

Revolutionary republicanism emphasized not the benefits of governmental power but its dangers. Political power—the ability to influence and control others—was understood to entice people and ultimately to corrupt them. Those possessing power inevitably used it for their own advantage rather than for the general good. Given human nature, this was unavoidable, for power charmed even the best-intentioned.

In the republican world view, liberty was seen as the opposite of power: freedom from the controlling influence of others and the ability to govern one's own life. Republicanism assumed that liberty and power were in perpetual conflict in human affairs, because power was expansive and always threatening to grow at liberty's expense. The Revolutionary generation believed that this tension between power and liberty was the central theme of human history. Their recent experience with England burned the lesson indelibly into their minds. Thus their overriding concern in thinking about politics and government was to find ways of controlling power and maximizing liberty.

The revolutionaries acknowledged that excessive liberty could degenerate into political chaos. History and their own experience, however, told them that trouble arose most often not from excessive liberty but from too much governmental power. "It is much easier to restrain the people from running into licentiousness," went the common refrain, "than power from swelling into tyranny and oppression."

Given the dangers of governmental power and the need to limit it, how could political order be maintained? The Revolutionary generation offered an extraordinary answer to that question. Order was not to be imposed from above through such traditional agencies of control as monarchies, centralized governments, or standing armies. In republican systems, political order flowed upward from the responsible, self-regulated behavior of the people, especially from their willingness to put the public good before their own private interests. In a republic, explained one pamphleteer, "each individual gives up all private interest that is not consistent with the general good." The term for this extraordinary self-denial was "public virtue." It formed the core of the Revolution's republican faith.

In placing responsibility for political order with the people and counting on them to act for the good of the whole, Americans made a revolutionary change in the location of authority. Some seventeenth-century visionaries had talked of placing "the power in the people"—but now a nation was being founded on such a principle. The dangers in redefining so radically the location of authority was obvious. If the people proved unworthy, as some believed they would, chaos would ensue. If the attempt was made, warned one alarmed soul, "the bands of society would be dissolved, the harmony of the world confused, and the order of nature subverted." A strong incentive toward Loyalism lurked in such concerns.

Few patriots were so naive as to believe that the American people were uncompromisingly virtuous. But during the first years of war, when Revolutionary enthusiasm ran high, most Americans believed that public virtue was sufficiently widespread to support republican government. Religion and education could instruct citizens in virtuous behavior. More than that, the American people would learn virtue by its practice. The Revolutionary struggle would serve as a "furnace of affliction," refining the American character as it tested and strengthened people's capacity for virtuous behavior. It was an extraordinarily hopeful but risk-filled undertaking.

Republicanism posed another problem for the Revolutionary generation. Republics, given their lack of strong, central government, were understood to be vulnerable to internal decay and external attack. The concern over internal decay centered on the problem of "faction," or organized political interests. History taught that internal divisions had destroyed every republic in the past. Faction was the "mortal disease under which popular governments have everywhere perished." In a monarchy, the crown, the army, or the church might control factional disputes and maintain order. In a republic, however, no such agencies of control existed, and factional conflict, once begun, could easily spin out of control.

The only way to master the demon was to avoid its causes, and that was possible only where societies were small and homogeneous, free of serious economic, social, or religious conflicts. It was impossible to measure exactly how much internal division a republic could tolerate. Some people worried that the larger colonies, such as New York and Pennsylvania, were already too diverse, but most assumed that the familiar colonial boundaries could safely be used to separate one republican state from another. Few Americans during the early years of independence believed that a single, unified continental republic was possible. The nation would have to be organized differently, as a confederation of individual republican states. The problem of faction and its control would trouble American politics throughout the years of the nation's founding.

Debate over Political Equality

Political equality was the other great principle at the heart of the nation's republican faith. No doctrine was more fundamental—or, as things soon proved, more controversial. Republicanism's rejection of monarchy and its emphasis on individual liberty were accompanied by the belief that republican citizens must watch over their governments in order to protect their own rights. That meant that every citizen must have a political voice. Virtually everyone agreed that republican governments had to be grounded in popular consent, that frequent elections were needed, and that public officials should be accountable to the people.

The doctrine of political equality, however, would generate sharp debate. As the Revolution approached, some Americans took the principle literally, arguing that no one should have more political power than anyone else. This position found its greatest support among groups largely outside the political process—farmers and tenants in the interior, workers and artisans in the coastal towns and cities.

Republican equality, however, meant something quite different to other revolutionaries. More cautious patriots talked about order as well as liberty, arguing that each was essential to the other and that both depended on the leadership of persons wise in the ways of politics and experienced in government. While rejecting European-like aristocracies and their legally established privileges and political power, conservative republicans emphasized the importance of what they called an "aristocracy of talent"—that is, of ability, wisdom, and public virtue. That argument was voiced most frequently by individuals and groups who already enjoyed political power—merchants, planters, large commercial farmers. They saw no need to alter radically the existing political system.

THE TURMOIL OF REVOLUTIONARY SOCIETY

The long struggle with England over colonial rights between 1764 and 1776 did not occur in a unified society. Social and economic change, which accelerated in the late colonial period, brought deep unrest and calls for reform from many quarters. By the end of the Seven Years' War, faith in the internal social systems of the colonies had waned among many colonists, just as allegiance to the mother country and to the British mercantile system had worn thin.

Many of the colonists who struggled for security in the aftermath of the Seven Years' War hoped that migration to frontier land would improve their fortunes. A flood of new immigrants from Ireland and Germany after the Treaty of Paris in 1763 added to the pressure to reach the trans-Appalachian river valleys. However, the western option involved much violence with Indian tribes unreceptive to encroaching settlers. So most colonists chose to work out their destinies at home or in other communities along the coastal plain to which they migrated in search of opportunity.

As agitation against English policy intensified, previously acquiescent people took a more active interest in politics. In this charged atmosphere, the constitutional struggle with England spread quickly over its original boundaries into uncharted territory. Groups emerged—slaves, urban laboring people, backcountry farmers, evangelicals, women—who enunciated goals of their own that were sometimes only loosely connected to the struggle with England. The stridency and potential power of these groups raised for many upper-class leaders the frightening specter of a radically changed society. Losing control of the protests they had initially led, many of them would abandon the resistance movement against England.

Urban People

Although the cities contained only about 5 percent of the colonial population, they formed the vital cores of revolutionary agitation. As centers of communications, government, and commerce, they led the way in protesting English policy, and they soon contained the most politicized citizens in America. Local politics could be rapidly transformed as the struggle against England became enmeshed with calls for internal reform.

As marketgoers and consumers, urban women played a crucial role in applying economic pressure on England during the pre-Revolutionary decade. This British cartoon, published in 1775, derisively depicts a group of North Carolina ladies signing an antitea agreement.

In Philadelphia, for example, craftsmen had usually acquiesced in politics to the merchant and lawyer politicos before the Seven Years' War. But economic difficulties in the 1760s and 1770s led them to band together within their craft and their community. Artisans played a central role in forging a nonimportation agreement in 1768, calling public meetings, publishing newspaper appeals, organizing secondary boycotts against foot-dragging merchants, and ferreting out and tarring and feathering opponents to their policies. Cautious merchants complained that mere artisans had "no right to give their sentiments respecting an importation" and called the craftsmen "a rabble." But artisans, casting off their customary deference, forged ahead.

By 1772, artisans were filling elected municipal positions and insisting on their right to participate equally with their social superiors in nominating assemblymen and other important officeholders. They also began lobbying for reform laws. The craftsmen called for elected representatives to be more accountable to their constituents. Genteel Philadelphians muttered, "It is time the tradesmen were checked—they ought not to intermeddle in state affairs—they will become too powerful."

By 1774, working-class intermeddling in state affairs had taken a bold new step—the de facto assumption of governmental powers by committees called into being by the people at large. Craftsmen had first clothed themselves in such extralegal authority in policing the nonimportation agreement in 1769. Five years later, in response to the Intolerable Acts, they put forward a radical slate of candidates for a committee to enforce a new economic boycott. Their ticket drubbed one nominated by the city's conservative merchants.

The political mobilization and heightened consciousness of laboring Philadelphians continued as the impasse with England reached a climax in 1775. Many pacifist Quaker leaders of the city had abandoned politics by this time, and other conservative merchants had also concluded that mob rule had triumphed. Into the leadership vacuum stepped a group of radicals from the middling ranks: the fiery Scots-Irish doctor, Thomas Young, who had agitated in Boston and Albany before migrating to Philadelphia; Timothy Matlack, a hardware retailer who was popular with the lower class for matching his prize bantam cocks against those of New York's aristocratic James Delancy; James Cannon, a young schoolteacher; Benjamin Rush, whose new medical practice took him into the garrets and cramped rooms of the city's poor; and Thomas Paine, a recent immigrant seeking something better in America than he had found as an ill-paid excise officer in England.

The political support of the new radical leaders was centered in the 31 companies of the Philadelphia militia, composed mostly of laboring men, and in the extralegal committees now controlling the city's economic life. Their leadership helped to overcome the conservatism of the regularly elected Pennsylvania legislature, which was resisting the movement of the Continental Congress toward independence. In addition, the new radical leaders demanded internal reforms: opening up opportunity; curbing the accumulation of wealth by "our great merchants" who were "making immense fortunes at the expense of the people"; abolishing the property requirement for voting; allowing militiamen to elect their officers; and imposing stiff fines, to be used for the support of the families of poor militiamen, on men who refused militia service.

Philadelphia's radicals never controlled the city. They always jostled for position with prosperous artisans and shopkeepers of more moderate views and with cautious lawyers and merchants. But mobilization among artisans, laborers, and mariners, in other cities as well as Philadelphia, became part of the chain of events that led toward independence. Whereas most of the patriot elite fought only to change English colonial policy, the populace of the cities also struggled for internal reforms and raised notions of how an independent American society might be reorganized.

Women also played a vital role in the urban crucibles of revolutionary activity. They signed nonimportation agreements, harassed noncomplying merchants, and helped organize "fast days" when communities prayed for deliverance from English oppression. But the women's most important role was in facilitating the economic boycott of English goods. The success of the nonconsumption pacts depended on substituting homespun cloth for English textiles on which colonists of all classes had always relied. From Georgia to Maine, women and children began spinning yarn and weaving cloth. "Was not every fireside, indeed a theatre of poli-

Benjamin Rush, a young Philadelphia doctor, was one of the Revolutionary radicals who wanted to reform American society as well as win independence. Among the reforms Rush promoted were abolishing slavery and establishing free public schools.

tics?" John Adams remembered after the war. Towns often vied patriotically with each other in the manufacture of cotton, linen, and woolen cloth, the women staging open-air spinning contests to publicize their commitment. In 1769, the women of tiny Middletown, Massachusetts, set the standard by weaving 20,522 yards of cloth, about 160 yards each.

After the Tea Act in 1773, the interjection of politics into the household economy increased as patriotic women boycotted their favorite drink. Newspapers carried recipes for tea substitutes and recommendations for herbal teas. In Wilmington, North Carolina, women paraded solemnly through the town and then made a ritual display of their patriotism by burning their imported tea. Many women could agree with one Rachel Wells: "I have done as much to carry on the war as many that set now at the helm of government."

Protesting Farmers

In most of the agricultural areas of the colonies, where many settlers made their livelihoods, passions concerning English policies were aroused only slowly. After about 1740, farmers had benefited from a sharp rise in the demand for foodstuffs in England, southern Europe, and the West Indies. Rising prices and brisk markets brought a higher standard of living to thousands of rural colonists, especially south of New England. Living far from harping English customs officers, impressment gangs, and occupying armies, the colonists of the interior had to be drawn gradually into the resistance movement by their urban cousins. Even in Concord, Massachusetts, only a dozen miles from the center of colonial agitation, townspeople found little to protest in English policies until England closed the port of Boston in 1774. They concerned themselves with local issues—roads, schools, the location of churches—but rarely with the frightful offenses to American liberty that Bostonians perceived.

Yet some parts of rural America seethed with social tension in the prewar era. The dynamics of conflict, shaped by the social development of particular regions, eventually became part of the momentum for revolution. In three western counties of North Carolina and in the Hudson River valley of New York, for example, widespread civil disorder marked the pre-Revolutionary decades. The militant rhetoric and tactics small farmers used to combat exploitation formed rivulets that fed the main stream of revolutionary consciousness.

For years, the small farmers of western North Carolina had suffered exploitation by corrupt county court officials appointed by the governor and a legislature dominated by eastern planter interests. Sheriffs and justices, allied with land speculators and lawyers, seized property when farmers could not pay their taxes and sold it, often at a fraction of its worth, to their cronies. The legislature rejected western petitions for lower taxes, paper currency, and lower court fees. In the mid-1760s, frustrated at getting no satisfaction from legal forms of protest, the farmers formed associations of so-called Regulators that forcibly closed the courts, attacked the property of their enemies, and whipped and publicly humiliated judges and lawyers. When their leaders were arrested, the Regulators stormed the jails and released them.

In 1768 and again in 1771, Governor William Tryon led troops against the Regulators. Bloodshed was averted on the first occasion, but on the second, at the Battle of Alamance, two armies of more than 1,000 opened fire on each other. Nine men died on each side before the Regulators fled the field. Seven leaders were executed in the ensuing trials. Though the Regulators lost on the field of battle, their protests became part of the larger revolutionary struggle. They railed against the self-interested behavior of a wealthy elite and asserted the necessity for people of humble rank to throw off deference and assume political responsibilities.

Rural insurgency in New York flared up in the 1750s, subsided, and then erupted again in 1766. The conditions under which land was held precipitated the violence. The Hudson River valley had long been controlled by a few wealthy families with enormous landholdings, which they leased to small tenant farmers. The Van Rensselaer manor totaled a million acres, the Phillipses' manor nearly half as much. Hundreds of tenants with their families paid substantial annual rents for the right to farm on these lands, which had been acquired as virtually free gifts from royal governors. When tenants resisted rent increases or purchased land from Indians who swore that manor lords had extended the boundaries of their manors by fraud, the landlords began evicting their leaseholders.

As the wealthiest men of the region, the landlords had the power of government, including control of the courts, on their side. Organizing themselves and going outside the law became the tenants' main strategy, as with the Carolina Regulators. By 1766, while New York City was absorbed in the

Stamp Act furor, tenants led by William Prendergast began resisting sheriffs who tried to evict tenants from lands they claimed. The militant tenants threatened landlords with death and broke open jails to rescue their friends. British troops from New York were used to break the tenant rebellion. Prendergast was tried and sentenced to be hanged, beheaded, and quartered. Although he was pardoned, the bitterness of the Hudson River tenants endured through the Revolution when most of them, unlike the Carolina Regulators, fought with the British because their landlords had joined the patriot cause.

Steps on the Road to Revolution

1763 Treaty of Paris ends Seven Years' War between England and France; France cedes Canada to England.
Proclamation of 1763 forbids white settlement west of Appalachian Mountains.

1764 Sugar Act sets higher duties on imported sugar, lower duties on molasses, and enlarges the power of vice-admiralty courts.
Currency Act prohibits issuance of paper money by colonies.

1765 Stamp Act requires printed documents to affix revenue-raising stamps purchased from British-appointed stamp distributors.
Stamp Act Congress meets in New York.
Quartering Act requires colonies to furnish British troops with housing and certain provisions.
Sons of Liberty formed in New York City and thereafter in many towns.

1766 Declaratory Act asserts Parliament's sovereignty over the colonies after repealing Stamp Act.
Rent riots by New York tenant farmers.

1767 Townshend Revenue Acts impose duties on tea, glass, paper, paints, and other items.
South Carolina Regulators organize in backcountry.

1768 British troops sent to Boston.

1770 British troops kill four and wound eight American civilians in Boston Massacre.

1771 Battle of Alamance pits frontier North Carolina Regulators against eastern militia led by royal governor.

1772 British schooner *Gaspee* burned in Rhode Island.
Committee of correspondence formed in Boston and thereafter in other cities.

1773 Tea Act reduces duty on tea but gives East India Company right to sell directly to Americans.
Boston Tea Party dumps £10,000 of East India Company tea into Boston harbor.

1774 Coercive Acts close port of Boston, restrict provincial and town governments in Massachusetts, and send additional troops to Boston.
Quebec Act attaches trans-Appalachian interior north of Ohio River to government of Quebec.
First Continental Congress meets and forms Continental Association to boycott British imports.

1775 Battles of Lexington and Concord cause 93 American and 272 British casualties; Americans take Fort Ticonderoga.
Second Continental Congress meets and assumes many powers of an independent government.
Dunmore's Proclamation in Virginia promises freedom to slaves and indentured servants fleeing to British ranks.
Prohibitory Act embargoes American goods.
George III proclaims Americans in open rebellion.

1776 Thomas Paine publishes *Common Sense*.
British troops evacuate Boston.
Declaration of Independence.

CONCLUSION
Forging a Revolution

The colonial Americans who lived in the third quarter of the eighteenth century participated in an era of political tension and conflict that changed the lives of nearly all of them. The Seven Years' War removed French and Spanish challengers and nurtured the colonists' sense of separate identity. Yet it left them with difficult economic adjustments, heavy debts, and growing social divisions. The colonists heralded the Treaty of Paris in 1763 as the dawning of a new era, but it led to a reorganization of England's triumphant yet debt-torn empire that had profound repercussions in America.

In the pre-Revolutionary decade, as England and the colonies moved from crisis to crisis, a dual disillusionment penetrated ever deeper into the colonial consciousness. Pervasive doubt arose concerning both the colonies' role, as assigned by England, in the economic life of the empire and the sensitivity of the government in London to the colonists' needs. At the same time, the colonists began to perceive British policies—instituted by Parliament, the king, and his advisers—as a systematic attack on the fundamental liberties and natural rights of British subjects in America.

The fluidity and diversity of colonial society and the differing experiences of Americans during and after the Seven Years' War evoked varying responses to the disruption that accompanied the English reorganization of the empire. In the course of resisting English policy, many previously inactive groups entered public life to challenge gentry control of political affairs. Often occupying the most radical ground in the opposition to England, they simultaneously challenged the growing concentration of economic and political power in their own communities.

When the Congress turned the 15-month undeclared war into a formally declared struggle for national liberation in July 1776, it steered its compatriots onto turbulent and unknown seas. Writing to his wife Abigail from his Philadelphia boardinghouse, the secularized Puritan John Adams caught some of the peculiar blend of excitement and dread that thousands shared. "You will think me transported with enthusiasm but I am not. I am well aware of the toil and blood and treasure that it will cost us to maintain this Declaration, and support and defend these States. Yet through all the gloom I can see the rays of ravishing light and glory. I can see that the end is more than worth all the means. And that posterity will triumph in that day's transactions, even although we should rue it, which I trust in God we shall not."

Recommended Reading

Further knowledge of the long, exhausting wars of empire that embroiled the colonies for four generations before 1763 can be derived from Douglas E. Leach, Arms for Empire *(1973);* William Eccles, The Canadian Frontier, rev. ed. *(1983);* David H. Corkran, The Cherokee Frontier *(1962); and* Lawrence H. Gipson, The British Empire Before the American Revolution, *15 vols. (1936–1970).*

The administration of the British Empire and the advent of the Seven Years' War are addressed in Michael Kammen, Empire and Interest *(1970);* Ian R. Christie, Crisis of Empire *(1966);* Jack M. Sosin, Whitehall and the Wilderness *(1961);* Howard Peckham, Pontiac and the Indian Uprising *(1947);* John R. Alden, John Stuart and the Southern Colonial Frontier *(1944); and* Francis Jennings, Empire of Fortune: Crown, Colonies, and Tribes in the Seven Years' War in America *(1988).*

For different points of view on the origins of the American Revolution, see John Brewer, Party Ideology and Popular Politics at the Accession of George III *(1976);* Bernard Bailyn, The Ideological Origins of the American Revolution *(1967);* Gary B. Nash, The Urban Crucible *(1979);* Edmund S. Morgan and Helen M.

Morgan, The Stamp Act Crisis *(1953); Joseph A. Ernst,* Money and Politics in America, 1755–1775 *(1973); David Ammerman,* In the Common Cause *(1974); and Pauline Maier,* From Resistance to Rebellion *(1972). Merrill Jensen gives a comprehensive view in* The Founding of a Nation *(1968).*

Rich local studies of the Revolutionary crisis include Robert Gross, The Minutemen and Their World *(1976); Dirk Hoerder,* Crowd Action in Revolutionary Massachusetts *(1977); Eric Foner,* Tom Paine and Revolutionary America *(1976); Edward Countryman,* A People in Revolution *(1981); and Steven Rossman,* Arms, Country, and Class: The Philadelphia Militia and the "Lower Sort" During the American Revolution *(1987). Excellent essays on various aspects of the coming of the Revolution can be found in Stephen G. Kurtz and James H. Hutson, eds.,* Essays on the American Revolution *(1973); Alfred F. Young, ed.,* The American Revolution *(1976); and Jeffrey J. Crow and Larry E. Tise, eds.,* The Southern Experience in the American Revolution *(1978).*

TIME LINE

1696	Parliament establishes Board of Trade
1701	Iroquois set policy of neutrality
1702–1713	Queen Anne's War
1713	Peace of Utrecht
1733	Molasses Act
1744–1748	King George's War
1754	Albany conference
1755	Braddock defeated by French and Indian allies
1756–1763	Seven Years' War
1759	Wolfe defeats the French at Quebec
1759–1761	Cherokee War against the English
1760s	Economic slump
1763	Treaty of Paris ends Seven Years' War Proclamation line limits westward expansion
1764	Sugar and Currency acts Pontiac's Rebellion in Ohio valley
1765	Colonists resist Stamp Act Virginia House of Burgesses issues Stamp Act resolutions
1766	Declaratory Act Tenant rent war in New York Slave insurrections in South Carolina
1767	Townshend duties imposed
1768	British troops occupy Boston
1770	"Boston Massacre" Townshend duties repealed (except on tea)
1771	North Carolina Regulators defeated
1772	*Gaspee* incident in Rhode Island
1773	Tea Act provokes Boston Tea Party
1774	"Intolerable Acts" First Continental Congress meets
1775	Second Continental Congress meets Battles of Lexington and Concord
1776	Thomas Paine publishes *Common Sense* Declaration of Independence

PART TWO

A REVOLUTIONARY PEOPLE

1775 1828

The American Revolution not only marked an epic military victory over the powerful mother country but also set the course of national development in ways that still affect American society. Members of the Revolutionary generation were inspired by the idea that once they were free from England, they would build a model society based on principles of freedom and equality. Even as the battle for independence raged, they embarked on the task of building new forms of government and transforming their social, religious, and economic lives. This attempt to construct a *novus ordo seclorum,* a new order of the ages, continued beyond the Revolutionary era and continues yet today.

Chapter 6, "A People in Revolution," traces the impact of the Revolutionary call to arms on the various groups—male and female, white, black, and Native American—that made up American society and traces the exhilarating yet divisive efforts to fashion a new, republican political order. Chapter 7, "Consolidating the Revolution," examines the critical years of the 1780s, when the new nation struggled to forge national unity following the Revolutionary War and to find security in a hostile Atlantic world. Out of that struggle and the continuing competition for political power in the states emerged a great debate over the country's governmental structure. That debate led to the replacement of the Articles of Confederation with a new constitution, which in turn helped to create a stronger government. Learning to live under the new constitution during the 1790s is the focus for Chapter 8, "Creating a Nation." During those tumultuous years, charged with the reverberations of the French Revolution and fierce disagreements about the government's role in economic affairs, Federalists and Jeffersonians battled for control of the new government and the chance to shape the nation's future.

Chapters 9 and 10, overlapping in time, should be considered as a pair. Chapter 9, "Politics and Society in the Early Republic," delves into the political and diplomatic developments of the first three decades of the nineteenth century, when the young nation expanded rapidly beyond the Appalachians,

acquired vast new territories, fought a series of wars with Indian tribes and a second war against England, and moved toward a new party system, all under the presidencies of three Virginia Democratic-Republicans—Jefferson, Madison, and Monroe—and one New Englander, John Quincy Adams. Chapter 10, "The Preindustrial Republic," examines the underlying social and economic changes occurring in the early decades of the republic by exploring regional patterns of life and the experiences of various social groups on the brink of industrialization. It also investigates efforts by the American people in the areas of education, women's rights, and slavery to perfect their republican society in keeping with the lofty principles of the Revolution.

Political and Diplomatic	Social and Economic	Cultural and Technological

1775

Political and Diplomatic

1776 Cherokee War
Declaration of Independence
British evacuate Boston and occupy New York
1777 Burgoyne defeated at Saratoga
Washington's army encamps at Valley Forge
1778 Treaty of alliance with France
British peace commission fails
1779 Sullivan's expedition against the Iroquois
1780 British capture Charleston
1781 Cornwallis surrenders at Yorktown
Articles of Confederation ratified
Robert Morris named superintendent of finance
1782 British evacuate Savannah and Charleston
1783 Treaty of Paris with Great Britain ends Revolutionary War

Social and Economic

1775 Lord Dunmore's proclamation
Philadelphians organize first antislavery society

1780 Pennsylvania begins gradual abolition of slavery
1781 Bank of North America
1783 Massachusetts Supreme Court abolishes slavery
1784 *Empress of China* sails to Canton
Treaty of Fort Stanwix

Cultural and Technological

1776 Thomas Paine publishes *Common Sense*
Adam Smith publishes *Wealth of Nations*
1780 American Academy of Arts and Sciences
1781 Massachusetts Medical Society
New Jersey Society for Promoting Agriculture
1782 Crèvecoeur, *Letters from an American Farmer*
First Catholic parochial school established in Philadelphia
1783 Noah Webster's *Spelling Book*
1784 Jefferson's *Notes on Virginia*

1785

Political and Diplomatic

1785 Congress adopts Land Ordinance
Jay-Gardoqui negotiations
1786 Annapolis convention
1786–1787 Shays's Rebellion
1787 Northwest Ordinance
Constitutional Convention in Philadelphia
1788 Constitution ratified
1789 George Washington inaugurated
French Revolution begins
1790 Congress adopts Hamilton's funding and assumption program
Hamilton's Reports on the Public Credit
1791 Bill of Rights becomes part of Constitution
First U.S. Bank established
1792 Washington reelected
1793 Democratic-Republican societies founded
Washington issues Neutrality Proclamation
First Fugitive Slave Act
Citizen Genêt affair
1794 Whiskey Rebellion

Social and Economic

1785 Treaty of Hopewell
1786 Virginia statute of religious freedom
1787 Free African School established in New York City
1789 Treaty of Fort Harmar
1790 Non-intercourse Act regulates treaty making by states
Samuel Slater's cotton mill
1792 New York Stock Exchange established
1793 Yellow fever epidemic hits Philadelphia
1794 Battle of Fallen Timbers
Richard Allen establishes Bethel African Methodist Episcopal Church

Cultural and Technological

1787 John Fitch launches first American steamboat
Federalist Papers published
Joel Barlow, *Vision of Columbus*
1789 State University of North Carolina begins instruction
Thanksgiving first celebrated as national holiday
1790 Roman Catholic episcopate created
First federal patent issued
1790s Second Great Awakening begins

1791 Anthracite coal discovered in Pennsylvania
First macadam road opens in Pennsylvania
Franklin's *Autobiography* published in France
1793 Eli Whitney perfects cotton gin
1794 Charles Willson Peale establishes Philadelphia Museum

Political and Diplomatic	**Social and Economic**	**Cultural and Technological**

1795

Political and Diplomatic

1795 Jay's Treaty with Great Britain
1796 John Adams elected president
1797 XYZ affair
1798 Undeclared naval war with France
Alien and Sedition Acts; Naturalization Act
Virginia and Kentucky Resolutions
1800 Capital moves to Washington, D.C.
1801 Thomas Jefferson elected president
John Marshall named chief justice
1803 *Marbury* v. *Madison*
Louisiana Purchase
1803–1806 Louis and Clark expedition
1804 Jefferson reelected

Social and Economic

1795 Treaty of Greenville
1796 Congress establishes Indian factory system

1800 Gabriel Prosser's Rebellion

Cultural and Technological

1799 Nathaniel Bowditch, *Practical Navigator*

1800 Library of Congress established

1805

Political and Diplomatic

1806 Non-Importation Act
1807 Embargo Act
Chesapeake-Leopard affair
1808 James Madison elected president
1809 Non-Intercourse Act
1810 Macon's Bill No. 2
1812 West Florida annexed
Madison reelected
War declared against Britain
1814 Treaty of Ghent ends War of 1812
1814–1815 Hartford Convention

Social and Economic

1807 Congress prohibits slave trade
1808 John Jacob Aster founds American Fur Company
1809 Tecumseh forms confederation
1811 Battle of Kithtippecanoe
1813 Boston Manufacturing Company formed at Waltham, Massachusetts
Battle of the Thames
1814 Jackson defeats Creek Indians at Horseshoe Bend

Cultural and Technological

1805–1809 Pike explores the West
1807 Robert Fulton launches steamboat *Clermont*
Cast-iron plow patented
1811 Construction begins on Cumberland Road
1812 Benjamin Rush, *Diseases of the Mind*
1814 Francis Scott Key writes "The Star Spangled Banner"

1815

Political and Diplomatic

1816 Second U.S. Bank
First protective tariff
Monroe elected president
1819 *McCulloch* v. *Maryland*
Spain cedes East Florida
1820 Missouri Compromise
Monroe reelected
1822 Diplomatic recognition of Latin American republics
1823 Monroe Doctrine
1824 Henry Clay's "American System"
John Quincy Adams elected president
Gibbons v. *Ogden*

Social and Economic

1815 Battle of New Orleans
1817 American Colonization Society established
1818 First Seminole War
1819–1821 Financial panic and depression
1824 Bureau of Indian Affairs created
Female weavers strike at Pawtucket, Rhode Island
1825 Erie Canal opens
Robert Owen begins New Harmony
1826 Sequoyah devises Cherokee alphabet
1827 Cherokee constitution

Cultural and Technological

1821 James Fenimore Cooper, *The Spy*
Emma Willard founds New York Female Seminary at Troy, New York

6

A People in Revolution

Among the Americans wounded and captured at the Battle of Bunker Hill in the spring of 1775 was Lieutenant William Scott of Peterborough, New Hampshire. Asked by his captors how he had come to be a rebel, "Long Bill" Scott replied:

The case was this Sir! I lived in a Country Town; I was a Shoemaker, & got [my] living by my labor. When this rebellion came on, I saw some of my neighbors get into commission, who were no better than myself. . . . I was asked to enlist, as a private soldier. My ambition was too great for so low a rank. I offered to enlist upon having a lieutenant's commission, which was granted. I imagined my self now in a way of promotion. If I was killed in battle, there would be an end of me, but if my Captain was killed, I should rise in rank, & should still have a chance to rise higher. These Sir! were the only motives of my entering into the service. For as to the dispute between Great Britain & the colonies, I know nothing of it; neither am I capable of judging whether it is right or wrong.

People fought in America's Revolutionary War for many reasons: fear, ambition, principle. We have no way of knowing whether Long Bill Scott's motives were typical. Certainly many Americans knew more than he about the colonies' struggle with England. But many did not.

In the spring of 1775, the Revolutionary War had just begun. So, as it turned out, had Long Bill's adventures. When the British evacuated Boston a year later, Scott was taken prisoner and transported to Halifax, Nova Scotia. After more than a year's captivity, he managed to escape, secure passage on a ship, and make his way home to fight once more. He was recaptured in November 1776 near New York City, when its garrison fell to a surprise British assault. Again Scott escaped, this time by swimming the Hudson River at night with his sword tied around his neck and his watch pinned to his hat.

During the winter of 1777, he returned to New Hampshire to recruit his own militia company. It included two of his eldest sons. In the fall, he joined in the defeat of Burgoyne's army near Saratoga, New York, and later took part in the fighting around Newport, Rhode Island. When his light infantry company was ordered to Virginia in early 1778, Scott's health broke, and he was permitted to resign from the army. After only a few months of recuperation, however, he was at it again. During the last year of the war, he served as a volunteer on a navy frigate.

For seven years, the war held Scott in its harsh grasp. Scott's oldest son died of camp fever after six years of service. In 1777, Long Bill sold his New Hampshire farm, to meet family expenses. The note he took in exchange turned into a scrap of paper when the dollar of 1777 became worth less than 2 cents by 1780. He lost a second farm, in Massachusetts, when his military pay depreciated similarly. After his wife died, he helplessly turned their youngest children over to his oldest son and set off to beg a pension or job from the government. When his son begged Scott for help, he could only recommend that the children be turned over to the town of Peterborough for support.

Long Bill's saga was still not complete. In 1792, he gained notoriety by rescuing eight people when their boat capsized in New York harbor. Two years later, he landed a job as deputy storekeeper for the military garrison at West Point. In 1795, General Benjamin Lincoln took Scott with him to the Ohio country, where they negotiated with the Indians and surveyed land that was opening for white settlement. At last he had a respectable job and even a small government pension for his nine wounds. But trouble would still not let him go. While surveying on the Black River near Sandusky, Scott and his colleagues contracted "lake fever." Though ill, he guided part of the group back to Fort Stanwix in New York, then returned for the others. It was his last heroic act. A few days after his second trip, on September 16, 1796, he died.

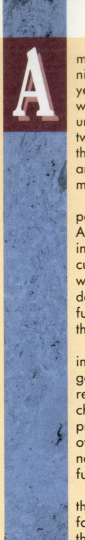

American independence and the Revolutionary War that accompanied it were not as hard on everyone as they were on Long Bill Scott, yet together they transformed the lives of countless Americans. The war lasted for seven years, longer than any other of America's wars until Vietnam nearly two centuries later. And unlike the nation's twentieth-century contests, it was fought on American soil, among the American people. It called men by the thousands from shops and fields, disrupted families, killed civilians, spread diseases, and made a shambles of the economy.

While carrying on this struggle for independence, the American people also mounted a political revolution of profound importance. Approaches to politics, government, and elections were transformed in keeping with republican principles and the rapidly changing circumstances of political life. What did republican liberty mean? How was governmental power to be organized and controlled? How democratic should American politics be? These were among the fundamental questions with which the American people wrestled at the nation's beginning.

Faced with the twin pressures of war and revolution, people turned increasingly to politics to solve their problems and achieve their goals. As the tempo of political activity increased, they clashed repeatedly over such explosive issues as slavery, the separation of church and state, paper money and debt relief, the regulation of prices, and the toleration of political dissent. They argued as well over the design of new state constitutions and the shape of a new national government. Seldom has America's political agenda been fuller or more troubled.

The American Revolution dominated the lives of all who lived through it. But it had different consequences for men than for women, for black slaves than for their white masters, for Native Americans than for frontier settlers, for overseas merchants than for urban workers, for northern businessmen than for southern planters. Our understanding of the Revolutionary experience out of which our nation emerged must begin with the Revolutionary War, for liberty came at a high cost.

THE WAR FOR AMERICAN INDEPENDENCE

On the afternoon of October 19, 1781, near the Virginia hamlet of Yorktown, Lord Charles Cornwallis, commander of His Majesty's army in the southern states, surrendered to General George Washington. His decision followed nearly three weeks of close, bitter fighting. While a military band played "The World Turned Upside Down" and hundreds of civilians looked on, nearly 7,000 British troops laid down their arms.

Learning the news of Yorktown a month later, Lord North, the king's chief minister, exclaimed, "Oh, God! It is all over." On February 27, 1782, the House of Commons voted against further support of the war, and the next month, Lord North resigned. In Philadelphia, citizens poured into the streets to celebrate while the Congress assembled for a solemn ceremony of thanksgiving. Sporadic fighting continued for another year; not until November 1782 were the preliminary articles of peace signed. But everyone knew after Yorktown that the war was over. Americans had won their independence.

Creating an Independent Government

America's military victory over mighty England was all the more remarkable given the weak national government that directed the war effort. For six years, the American cause depended on the inadequately empowered and uncertain Continental Congress. It operated under a document called the Articles of Confederation that was not ratified until seven months before Yorktown.

Prior to independence, the colonies had repeatedly quarreled over territory, settlers, control of the fur trade, and commercial advantage within the British Empire. The crisis with England, however, forced them together, first to protest England's efforts at imperial reform and then to carry on the war. The Continental Congress was the first embodiment of that union. The First Continental Congress met for only seven weeks and limited itself to sending resolutions of protest to England and calling on the people to support the Continental Association. It functioned, in short, as a temporary assembly.

The Second Continental Congress, however, meeting in May 1775, in the midst of a war crisis, began to exercise some of the most basic responsibilities of a sovereign government: raising an army and conducting diplomatic relations. Its powers, though, were unclear, its legitimacy uncertain. While hopes of reconciliation with England remained, these limitations posed no serious problems. But as independence and the prospects of an extended war loomed, pressure grew to establish the Congress on a sounder footing. On June 20, 1776, shortly before independence was declared, Congress appointed a committee, chaired by John Dickinson of Pennsylvania, to draw up a plan of perpetual union. So urgent was the crisis that the committee responded in exactly a month's time, and debate on its proposed Articles of Confederation quickly began.

While the war erupted around them, the delegates struggled with the new and difficult problem of creating a permanent government. They promptly clashed over whether to form a strong, consolidated regime or a loosely joined confederation of sovereign states. Those differences sharpened as the discussion proceeded.

The Dickinson draft outlined a government of considerable power. Each state was to retain "the sole and exclusive regulation and government of its internal police," but only in "matters that shall not interfere with the Articles of Confederation." The only unqualified restriction on the Congress was that it might never impose taxes or duties except in managing the post office. Dickinson's proposals, however, met determined opposition. North Carolina's Thomas Burke, fearful of the centralizing tendencies of the war, insisted that the Congress be subordinate to the states.

As finally approved, the Articles fell between Dickinson's and Burke's positions. Article 9 gave the Congress sole authority to regulate foreign affairs, declare war, mediate boundary disputes between the states, manage the post office, and administer relations with Indians living outside state boundaries. The Articles also stipulated that the inhabitants of each state were to enjoy "the privileges and immunities" of the citizens of every other state. Embedded in that clause was the basis for national, as distinguished from state, citizenship. Given the experience out of which it came, the Articles were surprisingly strong. Their strength evidenced the desperate crisis the American people faced.

At the same time, the Articles sharply limited what the Congress could do and reserved broad governing powers to the states. For example, the Congress could not raise troops on its own but only set quotas for each of the states. Nor could it tax unless the states gave unanimous consent. Article 2 of the Articles stipulated that each of the states was to "retain its sovereignty, freedom and independence, and every power, jurisdiction, and right which is not by this confederation expressly delegated to the United States in Congress assembled." Nor could the puny powers that were given to the Congress be easily enlarged, since the Articles could be amended only by the unanimous agreement of the 13 states.

Though the Congress sent the Articles to the states for approval in November 1777, they were not ratified until March 1781. Several reasons explain the delay. They required the approval of all 13 states, and that was hard to obtain. The biggest impediment to ratification, however, was disputes over the control of lands west of the Appalachian Mountains. The controversy pitted states such as Virginia, South Carolina, and New York, which had western claims tracing back to their colonial charters, against states such as Maryland and New Jersey, which had none. Representatives of the six "landless" states argued that Trans-Appalachia should be common property because it was being "wrested from the common enemy by the blood and treasure of the thirteen states." In December 1778, the Maryland assembly announced that it would not ratify the Articles until all the western lands had been ceded to the Congress. It was the most powerful trump card that landless Maryland could play.

Land speculators, such as the Indiana and Illinois-Wabash companies, also worked actively for state cession, hoping that the Congress would honor their land purchases from interior tribes such as the Shawnee and the Miami.

For several years, ratification hung in the balance while politicians and speculators jockeyed for advantage. A breakthrough finally came in February 1780, when New York offered to transfer its western claims to the Congress. Virginia, however, held out, and its lands were so vast that no solution was possible unless they were ceded as well. In September, the Virginia assembly agreed to turn over its western claims, but only on condition that the Congress not recognize any of the Indian purchases

that the land companies had made. The speculators were furious, but their efforts to raise support by distributing stock to influential congressmen were in vain.

In early 1781, the Maryland assembly accepted Virginia's conditions and approved the Articles. Ratification was now assured. In September 1783, the Congress finally agreed to Virginia's condition, and in 1784 the actual transfer of land occurred.

The war did not wait during the struggle over ratification. The Congress did the best it could, using the unratified Articles as a guide. Events, however, quickly proved the inadequacy of the powers allotted to the Congress, since it could do little more than pass resolutions and ask the states for support. If they refused, as they frequently did, the Congress could only protest and urge cooperation. Its ability to function was further limited by the stipulation that each state's delegation cast but one vote. On

Western Land Claims Ceded by the States, 1782–1802

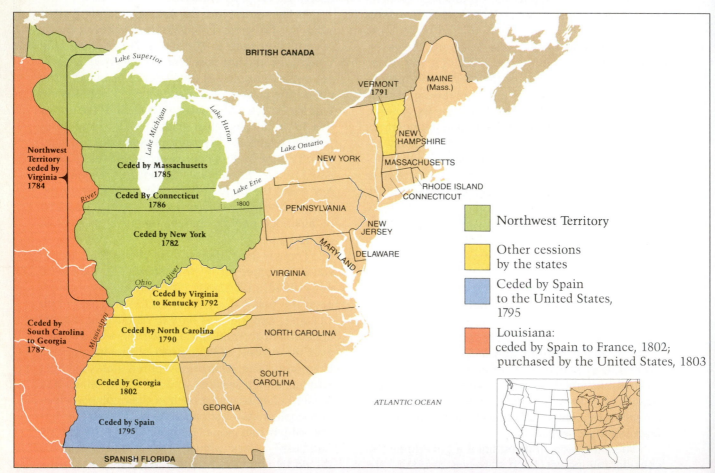

Europeans were fascinated by news of the colonies' rebellion against England. Here a French artist offers a dramatic portrayal of the fateful encounter at Lexington in April 1775.

a number of occasions, disagreements within state delegations prevented them from voting at all. That could paralyze the Congress, since most important decisions required a nine-state majority.

During the war, Washington repeatedly criticized the Congress for its failure to support the army adequately. In 1778, acknowledging its own ineffectiveness, the body temporarily granted Washington extraordinary powers and asked him to manage the war on his own. The Congress did, of course, survive because the states realized that disaster would follow its collapse and because enough of its members were determined to see things through. But it struggled continuously just to keep the war going.

The War in the North

As we know, the war began in Massachusetts in 1775. Within a year, the center of fighting shifted to the middle states. After 1779, the South was the primary theater. Why did this geographic pattern develop, what was its significance, and why did the Americans win?

For a brief time following Lexington and Concord, British officials thought of launching forays out from Boston into the surrounding countryside. They soon reconsidered, however, for the growing size of the continental army and the absence of significant Loyalist strength in the New England region urged caution. Even more important, the Americans' successful emplacement of artillery on the strategic Dorchester Heights overlooking the city made its continued occupation untenable. On March 7, 1776, the British commander, General William Howe, decided to evacuate.

People worried that Howe would set fire to the city as he departed. Fearing retaliation against Loyalist property and wishing not to destroy any lingering hopes of reconciliation, Howe spared the city from the torch. The town had been treated badly enough. British officers had taken over the homes of John Hancock, James Bowdoin, and others. Dragoons had used the Old South Meeting House as a riding school, after tearing out the pews. The West Street and Hollis Street churches had served as barracks, and the Old North Church had been demolished for firewood. All around lay trampled gardens, uprooted trees, and filth. The city, one resident lamented, was not "that agreeable place it once was. Almost everything here, appears Gloomy and Melancholy."

For a half dozen years after Boston's evacuation, British ships prowled the New England coast, attacking American commerce, confiscating supplies, and destroying towns. Yet away from the coast there was little fighting at all. Most New Englanders had reason to be thankful for their good fortune.

RECOVERING THE PAST

MILITARY MUSTER ROLLS

In almost all of America's wars, patriotism has run high, and bombastic rhetoric has inspired citizens to arms. The American Revolutionary War was no exception. But people fought for other than patriotic reasons, as the account of "Long Bill" Scott makes clear. It is always difficult to assess human motivations in something as complex as war. If we knew which Americans bore arms, however, it would help us understand why people fought and perhaps even understand what the war meant to them.

As we see in this chapter, the social composition of the Revolutionary army changed markedly as the war went along. At the beginning, men from all walks of life and every class fought in defense of American liberty. Within a short time, however, that began to change. As the war lengthened and its costs increased, men who could afford to do so hired substitutes or arranged to go home, while men of less wealth and influence increasingly carried the burden of fighting. Many of them did so out of choice, for the army promised adventure, an escape from the tedium of daily life, a way to make a living, and even, as for "Long Bill" Scott, the chance to rise in the world. And so thousands of poorer men hired out to defend American liberty. Such a decision, of course, was more attractive to them because other opportunities were limited.

One source for studying the social history of the Revolutionary War is the muster rolls and enlistment lists of the continental army and the state militias. Although eighteenth-century records are imperfect by modern standards, recruiting officers did keep track of the men they signed up so that bounties and wages could be paid accurately. These lists usually give the recruit's name, age, occupation, place of birth, residence, and length of service.

Such lists exist for some of America's earliest wars. The muster rolls for New York City and Philadelphia during the Seven Years' War, for example, show that these two cities contributed 300 and 180 men per year, respectively, to the war effort. Most of the enlistees were immigrants—about 90 percent of New York's recruits and about 75 percent of Philadelphia's. Their occupations—mariner, laborer, shoemaker, weaver, tailor—indicate that they came primarily from the lowest ranks of the working class. Many were former indentured servants, and many others were servants running away from their masters to answer the recruiting sergeant's drum. In these Middle Atlantic port towns, successful, American-born artisans left the bloody work of bearing arms against the French to those beneath them on the social ladder. Enlistment lists for Boston, however, reveal that soldiers from that city were drawn from higher social classes.

A comparison of the Revolutionary War muster rolls from different towns and regions provides a view of the social composition of the Revolutionary army and how it changed over time. It also offers clues to social conditions in different regions during the war and how they might have affected military recruitment.

The lists shown here of Captain Wendell's and Captain White's companies from New York and Virginia give "social facts" on 81 men. What kind of group portrait of these units can you draw from the data? Some occupations, such as tanner, cordwainer, and chandler, may be unfamiliar, but they are defined in standard dictionaries. How many of the recruits come from middling occupations (bookkeeper, tobacconist, shopkeeper, and the like)? How many are skilled artisans? How many are unskilled laborers? What proportions are foreign and native-

New York Line—1st Regiment

CAPTAIN JOHN H. WENDELL'S COMPANY, 1776–1777

MEN'S NAMES	AGE	OCCUPATION	PLACE OF BIRTH	PLACE OF ABODE
Abraham Defreest	22	Yeoman	N. York	Claverack
Benjamin Goodales	20	do [ditto]	Nobletown	do
Hendrick Carman	24	do	Rynbeck	East Camp
Nathaniel Reed	32	Carpenter	Norwalk	Westchester
Jacob Crolrin	29	do	Germany	Bever Dam
James White	25	Weaver	Ireland	Rynbeck
Joseph Battina	39	Coppersmith	Ireland	Florida
John Wyatt	38	Carpenter	Maryland	
Jacob Reyning	25	Yeoman	Amsterdam	Albany
Patrick Kannely	36	Barber	Ireland	N. York
John Russell	29	Penman	Ireland	N. York
Patrick McCue	19	Tanner	Ireland	Schohary
James J. Atkson	21	Weaver	do	Stillwater
William Burke	23	Chandler	Ireland	N. York

MEN'S NAMES	AGE	OCCUPATION	PLACE OF BIRTH	PLACE OF ABODE
Wᵐ Miller	42	Yeoman	Scotland	Claverack
Ephraim H. Blancherd	18	Yeoman	Ireland	White Creek
Francis Acklin	40	Cordwainer	Ireland	Claverack
William Orr	29	Cordwainer	Ireland	Albany
Thomas Welch	31	Labourer	N. York	Norman's Kill
Peter Gasper	24	Labourer	N. Jersey	Greenbush
Martinis Rees	19	Labourer	Fishkill	Flatts
Henck Able	24	do	Albany	Flatts
Daniel Spinnie	21	do	Portsmouth	
Patrick Kelly	23	Labourer	Ireland	Claverack
Richᵈ James Barker	12	do	America	Rynbeck
John Patrick Cronkhite	11			Claverack
William Dougherty	17		Donyal, Ireland	Schᵗʸ

born? Analyze the ages of the recruits; what does that tell you about the kind of fighting force that was assembled? How do the New York and Virginia companies differ in terms of these social categories and occupations? How would you explain these differences?

To extract the full meaning of the soldiers' profile, you would have to learn more about the economic and social conditions prevailing in the communities from which these men were drawn. But already you have glimpsed how social historians are trying to go beyond the history of military strategy, tactics, and battles to understand the "internal" social history of the Revolutionary War.

How would social historians describe and analyze a more recent American war? What would a social profile of soldiers who fought in Vietnam, including their age, region, race, class, extent of education, and other differences, suggest to a social historian of this recent war?

Virginia Line—6th Regiment

CAPTAIN TARPLEY WHITE'S COMPANY, DECEMBER 13TH 1780

NAMES	AGE	TRADE	WHERE BORN STATE OR COUNTRY	TOWN OR COUNTY	PLACE OF RESIDENCE STATE OR COUNTRY	TOWN OR COUNTY
Wm Balis, Serjt	25	Baker	England	Burningham	Virg.	Leesburg
Arthur Harrup. "	24	Carpenter	Virg.	Southampton	"	Brunswick
Charles Caffatey "	19	Planter	"	Caroline	"	Caroline
Elisha Osborn "	24	Planter	New Jersey	Trenton	"	Loudon
Benj Allday	19	"	Virg.	Henrico	"	Powhatan
Wm Edwards Senr	25	"	"	Northamberland	"	Northumberland
James Hutcherson	17	Hatter	Jersey	Middlesex	"	P. Williams
Robert Low	31	Planter	"	Powhatan	"	Powhatan
Cannon Row	18	Planter	Virg.	Hanover	Virg.	Louisa
Wardon Pulley	18	"	"	Southampton	"	Hallifax
Richᵈ Bond	29	Stone Mason	England	Cornwell	"	Orange
Tho Homont	17	Planter	Virg.	Loudon	"	Loudon
Tho Pope	19	Planter	"	Southampton	"	Southampton
Tho Morris	22	Planter	"	Orange	"	Orange
Littlebury Overby	24	Hatter	"	Dinwiddie	"	Brunwick
James [Pierce]	27	Planter	"	Nansemond	"	Nansemond
Joel Counsil	19	Planter	"	Southampton	"	Southampton
Elisha Walden	18	Planter	"	P. William	"	P. William
Wm Bush	19	S Carpenter	"	Gloucester	"	Gloucester
Daniel Horton	22	Carpenter	"	Nansemond	"	Nansemond
John Soons	25	Weaver	England	Norfolk	"	Loudon
Mora Lumkin	18	Planter	Virg.	Amelia	"	Amelia
Wm Wetherford	27	Planter	"	Goochland	"	Lunenburg
John Bird	16	Planter	"	Southamton	"	Southamton
Tho Parsmore	22	Planter	England	London	"	Fairfax
Josiah Banks	27	Planter	Virg.	Gloucester	"	Gloucester
Richᵈ Roach	28	Planter	England	London	"	Culpeper
Joseph Holburt	33	Tailor	"	Middlesex	"	Fredericksbᵍ
Henry Willowby	19	Planter	Virg.	Spotsylvania	"	Spotsylvania
Thos Pearson	22	Planter		Pennsylvany	"	Loudon
Jno Scarborough	19	Planter	Virg.	Brunswick	"	Brunswick
Chas Thacker	21	Planter	"	"	"	"
Nehemiah Grining	20	Planter	Virg.	Albemarle	Virg.	Albemarle
Ewing David	19	Planter	"	King Wᵐ	"	Brunswick
Isaiah Ballance	17	Shoemaker	"	Norfolk	"	Norfolk
Wm Alexander	20	Planter	Virg.	Northumbⁱᵈ	Virgᵃ	Nothumbⁱᵈ
Wm Harden	26	Planter	"	Albemarle	"	Albemarle
John Ward	20	Sailor	England	Bristol	"	Nothumbⁱᵈ
Daniel Cox	19	Planter	Virg.	Sussex	"	Sussex
George Kirk	21	Planter	"	Brunswick	"	Brunswick
John Nash	19	Planter	"	Nothumlⁱᵈ	"	Northumⁱᵈ
Wm Edwards, Jr.	19	Planter	"	Northumⁱᵈ	"	Northumⁱᵈ
John Fry	20	Turner	"	Albemarle	"	Albemarle
Jno Grinning	25	Hatter	"	"	"	"
Daniel Howell	30	Planter	"	Loudon	"	Loudon
Milden Green	25	Planter	"	Sussex	"	Sussex
Matthias Cane	32	Planter	"	Norfolk	"	Norfolk
Wm Mayo	21	Joiner	"	Dinwiddie	"	Dinwiddie
Jas Morgan	25	Shoemaker	England	Shropshire	"	Stafford
Mathew Carson	19	Planter	Pennsylvania	York	"	Berkly
Wm B[rown]	22	Planter			"	
Richᵈ Loyd	42	Planter	Virg.	Surry	"	Surry
Abram Foress	33	Planter	"	Gloster	"	Gloster
Wm White	19	Planter	"	"	"	"

175

After evacuating Boston, British officials established their military headquarters in New York City. Their decision was strategically sound, for New York was more centrally located and had served as headquarters for British forces during the Seven Years' War. Moreover, its harbor was spacious and overlooked the mouth of the Hudson River, the major water route northward into the interior. Control of New York would, in addition, ensure access to the abundant grain and livestock of the Middle Atlantic states. Finally, Loyalist sentiment ran wide and deep among the inhabitants of the city and its environs. Both politically and militarily, New York offered advantages that Boston did not.

In the summer of 1776, Washington moved his troops south from Boston, determined to challenge the British for control of Manhattan. It proved a terrible mistake. Outmaneuvered and badly outnumbered, he suffered defeat, first at the Battle of Long Island and then in Manhattan itself. By late October, the city was firmly in British hands. It would remain so until the war's end.

In the fall of 1776, King George III instructed his two chief commanders in North America, the brothers General William and Admiral Richard Howe, to make a final effort at reconciliation with the colonists. They carried authority to pardon all Americans who acknowledged allegiance to the king and to negotiate with any colony that dissolved its revolutionary committees. In early September, the Howes met on Staten Island, in New York harbor, with three delegates from the Congress. The outcome was not long in doubt, for when the Howes demanded revocation of the Declaration of Independence before negotiations could begin, the Americans walked out. It was clear from that point on that the war would be long and difficult.

For the next two years, the war swept back and forth across New Jersey and Pennsylvania. Reinforced by German mercenaries hired in Europe, the British moved virtually at will. Neither the state militias nor the continental army, weakened by losses, low morale, and inadequate supplies, offered serious opposition. At Trenton in December 1776 and again at Princeton the following month, Washington surprised the British and scored victories that prevented the Americans' collapse. For the rebels, however, survival remained the primary goal.

American efforts during the first year of the war to invade Canada and bring that British colony into the rebellion also fared badly. In November 1775, American forces under General Richard Montgom-

ery had taken Montreal. But the subsequent assault against Quebec ended with almost 100 Americans killed or wounded and more than 300 taken prisoner. The American cause, Washington realized, could not survive many such losses.

At New York, Washington had learned the painful lesson that his troops were no match for the British in frontal combat and had realized that if the continental army was defeated and scattered, American independence would almost certainly be lost. Above all, the army must be preserved. Thus he adopted a strategy of caution and delay. He would harass the British, make the war as costly for them as possible, and protect the civilian population as best he could. But above all, he would avoid major battles. For the remainder of the war, Washington's posture was primarily defensive and reactive.

As a consequence, the war's middle years turned into a deadly chase that neither side proved able to win. In September 1777, the British took Philadelphia, sending the Congress fleeing into the countryside, but then failed to press their advantage. British commanders repeatedly hesitated to act, either reluctant to move through the hostile countryside or uncertain of their instructions. Offsetting British domination of the Middle Atlantic region was the American victory at Saratoga, New York, where 5,700 British soldiers under General Burgoyne surrendered in October 1777.

The War Moves South

As the war in the North bogged down in a costly stalemate, British officials adopted another strategy: invasion and pacification of the South. From the war's beginning, British officials had talked about a southern campaign. When rapid victory in the middle states failed to materialize, a southern strategy seemed increasingly attractive. Royal officials in the South encouraged the idea with reports that thousands of Loyalists would rally to the British standard. The southern coastline with its numerous rivers, moreover, offered maximum advantage to British naval strength. Then there were the slaves, that vast but imponderable force in southern society. If they could be lured to the British side, the balance might tip in Britain's favor. In any case, the threat of slave rebellion would weaken white southerners' will to resist. Persuaded by these arguments, British policymakers made the southern states the primary theater of military operations during the final years of the war.

Military Operations in the North, 1776–1780

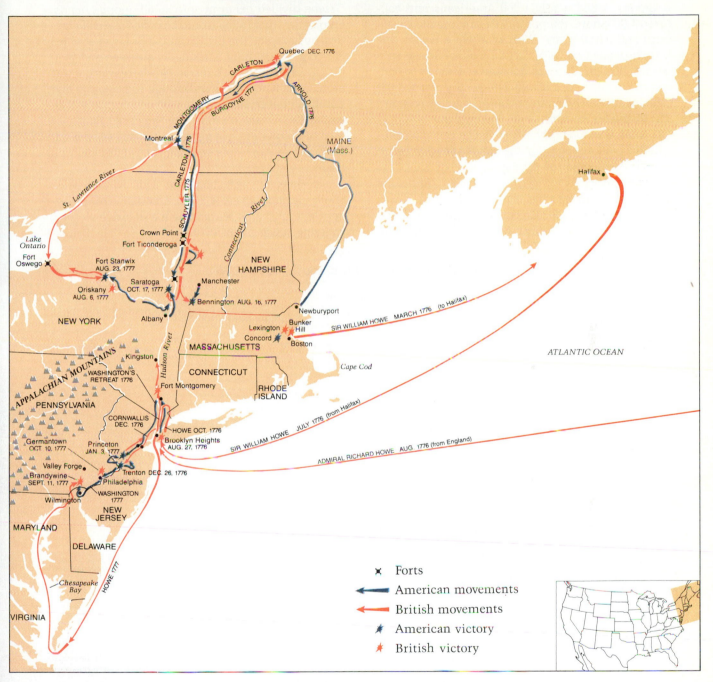

Georgia—small, isolated, and largely defense-less—was the initial target. In December 1778, Sa-vannah, the state's major port, fell before a seaborne attack of 3,500 men. For nearly two years, the Revolution in the state virtually ceased. Encouraged by their success, the British turned to the Carolinas, with equally impressive results. On May 12, 1780,

Charleston surrendered after a month's siege. At a cost of only 225 casualties, the British captured the entire 5,400-man American garrison. It was the costliest American defeat of the war.

After securing Charleston, the British quickly extended their control north and south along the coast. At Camden, South Carolina, the British commander, Cornwallis, aided by a corps of mounted dragoons, killed nearly 1,000 Americans and captured 1,000 more, temporarily destroying the southern continental army. With scarcely a pause, the British pushed on into North Carolina. These successes, however, proved deceptive. Though in control of the coast, British officers quickly learned the difficulty of extending their control into the interior. The distances were too large, the problems of supply too great, the reliability of Loyalist troops too problematic, and support for the Revolutionary cause among the people too strong.

In October 1780, Washington sent Nathanael Greene south to lead the continental forces. It was a fortunate choice, for Greene knew the region and the kind of war that had to be fought. Determined,

like Washington, to avoid large-scale encounters, Greene divided his army into small, mobile bands. Employing what today would be called guerrilla tactics, he harassed the British and their Loyalist allies at every opportunity, striking by surprise and then disappearing into the interior. Nowhere was the war more fiercely fought than through the Georgia and Carolina countryside. Neither British nor American authorities could restrain the violence. Bands of private marauders, roving the land and seizing advantage from the war's confusion, compounded the chaos.

In time, the tide began to turn. At Cowpens, South Carolina, in early 1781, American troops under General Daniel Morgan won a decisive victory, suffering fewer than 75 casualties to 329 British

Military Operations in the South, 1778–1781

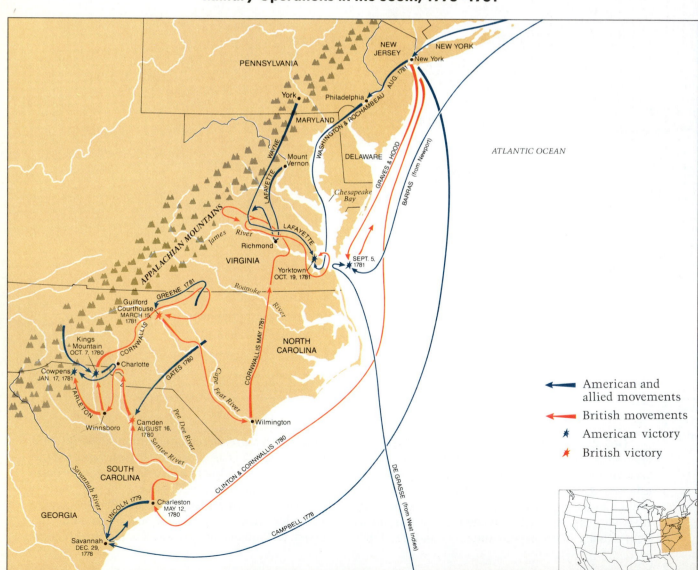

deaths and taking 600 men prisoner. In May, at Guilford Court House in North Carolina, Cornwallis won, but at a cost that forced his retreat to safety at Wilmington, near the sea.

In April 1781, convinced that British authority could not be restored in the Carolinas while Virginia remained a supply and staging area for the rebels, Cornwallis moved north out of the Carolinas. With a force of 7,500, he raided deep into Virginia. In June, his forces sent Governor Jefferson and the Virginia legislature fleeing from Charlottesville into the mountains. But again Cornwallis found the costs of victory high, and again he turned toward the coast for protection and resupply. This time his goal was Yorktown, where he arrived on August 1.

As long as the British fleet controlled the waters of Chesapeake Bay, his position was secure. That advantage, however, did not last. In 1778, the French government, still smarting from its defeat by England in the Seven Years' War and buoyed by the American victory at Saratoga in 1777, had signed a treaty of alliance with the American Congress, promising to send its naval forces into the war. Initially, the French concentrated their fleet in the West Indies, where they hoped to seize some of the rich British sugar islands. After repeated American urging, however, the French finally sailed north, and on August 30, 1781, the French admiral, Comte de Grasse, arrived off Yorktown. Reinforced by a second French squadron from the North, De Grasse established clear naval superiority in the region.

As Washington had foreseen, French entry into the war turned the tide decisively. Cut off from the sea and caught on a peninsula between the York and James rivers by 17,000 French and American troops, Cornwallis's fate was sealed. On October 17, 1781, he opened negotiations for surrender.

Native Americans in the Revolution

The Revolutionary War involved more than Englishmen and colonists, for it drew in countless Native Americans as well. It could hardly have been otherwise, for the lives of all three peoples had been intimately connected since the first white settlements more than a century and a half before.

By the time of the Revolution, the coastal tribes were mostly gone, victims of white settlement and the ravages of European diseases. In the interior, however, between the Appalachian Mountains and the Mississippi River, powerful tribes remained. The Iroquois Six Nations, formed into a confederation numbering 15,000 people, controlled the area from

Lord Cornwallis surrenders his sword to General Washington and Count de Rochambeau at Yorktown in October 1781, signaling the formal cessation of hostilities.

Albany, New York, to the Ohio country. Their size, location, and fighting ability enabled them to dominate the "western" tribes of the Ohio valley—the Shawnee, Delaware, Wyandotte, and Miami. In the Southeast, five tribes—the Choctaw, Chickasaw, Seminole, Creek, and Cherokee—dominated the interior. These 60,000 people occupied a vast region bounded by the Carolinas, the Ohio and Mississippi rivers, and the Gulf of Mexico.

When the Revolutionary War began, British and American officials urged neutrality on the Indians. The British, expecting the conflict to be short, wished to disrupt the interior as little as possible. The Americans worried about Indian attacks from the west while facing British power along the coast. The Native Americans were too important militarily to ignore. Both the British and the Americans feared the other would be first to recruit them. By the spring of 1776, both sides were actively seeking Indian alliances.

Recognizing their immense stake in the conflict, Native Americans up and down the interior debated their options. Alarmed by the westward advance of

Indian Battles, 1775–1783

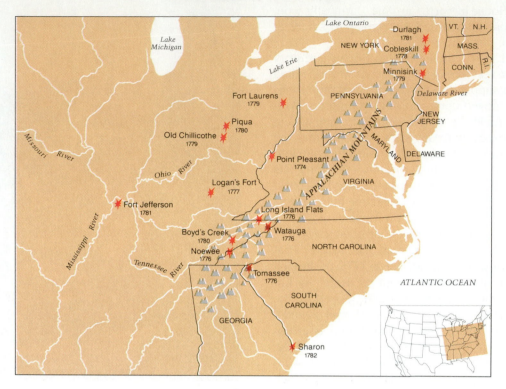

white settlement from Virginia and the Carolinas and eager to take advantage of the colonists' troubles, a band of Cherokee, led by the warrior Dragging Canoe, launched a series of raids in July 1776 against white settlements in what is today eastern Tennessee. The American response was quick and devastating. Fearing a general uprising, the Virginia and Carolina militias laid waste a group of Cherokee towns. Thomas Jefferson expressed satisfaction at the outcome. "I hope that the Cherokees will now be driven beyond the Mississippi," he wrote, "and that this in the future will be declared to the Indians the invariable consequence of their beginning a war. Our contest with Britain is too serious, and too great to permit any possibility of [danger] . . . from the Indians."

During the winter of 1780–1781, American militias once more ravaged Cherokee towns. Though the Cherokees raided sporadically throughout the war, they never again mounted a sustained military effort against the patriots. Seeing what had become of their neighbors, the Creek stayed aloof. Their time for resistance would come in the early nineteenth century, when white settlers began to push aggressively onto their lands.

The Devastation of the Iroquois

To the northeast, a similar but even more deadly scenario unfolded. At a council in Albany, New York, in August 1775, representatives of the Iroquois Six Nations listened while American commissioners urged them to remain at home and keep the hatchet buried deep. Little Abraham, a Mohawk leader, returned the tribes' answer. "The determination of the Six nations," he declared, "[is] not to take any part; but as it is a family affair, to sit still and see you fight it out." The Iroquois would remain neutral as long as neither side sent troops across their land. Their neutrality did not last long.

As the war spread throughout the Northeast in 1776, American troops raided deep into Mohawk territory west of Albany. Alarmed, the British argued with words, rum, and trade goods for Iroquois involvement against the rebels. At the Oswego Council in the summer of 1777, most of the Iroquois abandoned neutrality and joined the struggle against the Americans. They did so at the urging of Joseph Brant, a Mohawk warrior who had visited England several years before and argued England's value as an ally against American expansion.

It was a fateful decision for Indians and whites alike. Over the next several years, the Iroquois and their English allies devastated large areas in central New York and Pennsylvania, destroying property, terrorizing the inhabitants, and disrupting the entire region. An officer of the Pennsylvania militia reported somberly, "Our country is on the eve of breaking up. There is nothing to be seen but disolation, fire & smoak."

The Americans' revenge came swiftly. During the summer of 1779, General John Sullivan led a series of raids into Iroquois country, burning the Iroquois villages, killing men, women, and children, destroying fields of corn, and cutting down orchards. His motto for the campaign was blunt: "Civilization or death to all American savages." Two of the Iroquois nations, the Oneida and the Tuscarora, had allied with the Americans, and their villages were spared. The British and other Iroquois tribes, however, destroyed them in turn. The Iroquois recovered sufficiently to conduct punishing counter-raids during the final years of the war, but their losses in human lives and property were great.

Mohawk chief Joseph Brant (Tayadaneega) *played a major role in the Iroquois's decision to enter the war on the side of Britain.*

At the peace talks, the British entirely ignored the Indians' interests. No compensation for their losses was provided, nor any guarantees of their land, for the boundary of the United States was set far to the west, at the Mississippi. Most of the Indians had had good reason for choosing England as their ally. England had provided them with trade goods, gifts, and arms. England, moreover, had offered them protection against the expansionist Americans, as the Proclamation Line of 1763 had demonstrated. England, however, lost the war and so, as a consequence, did their Indian allies.

Negotiating Peace

In September 1781, formal peace negotiations got under way in Paris between the British commissioner, Richard Oswald, and the American emissaries, Benjamin Franklin, John Adams, and John Jay. The negotiations were complicated by the fact that several European countries, seeking opportunity to weaken Great Britain, had become involved. France had entered the war in February 1778. Eight months later, Spain declared war on England, though it declined to recognize American independence. Between 1780 and 1782, Russia, the Netherlands, and six other European countries joined in a League of Armed Neutrality aimed at protecting their maritime trade against British efforts to control it. Thus America's Revolutionary War had quickly become internationalized. It could hardly have been otherwise, given England's centrality to the European balance of power and the historical interest of the major European powers in North America.

The American commissioners quickly discovered how complicated peacemaking could be. Franklin, Adams, and Jay carried instructions from the Congress obligating them to follow the advice and counsel of Vergennes, the French foreign minister. The Congress, recognizing American dependence on French economic and military support, had agreed to this under pressure from its French ally.

As the treaty talks began, the American commissioners learned to their distress that Vergennes was prepared to let the exhausting war continue in order to weaken England further and tighten America's dependence on France. Even more alarming, while reaffirming his commitment to American independence, Vergennes suggested that the new nation's western boundary ought to be set no farther inland than the crest of the Appalachian Mountains.

John Jay, John Adams, and Benjamin Franklin (the three figures on the left) meet with the British commissioners to negotiate preliminary conditions of peace in this unfinished painting by Benjamin West.

In addition, he hinted that the British might retain the territories they controlled at the war's end. That threatened to leave New York City and other coastal enclaves in British hands.

In the end, the American commissioners ignored their instructions and, without a word to Vergennes, arranged a provisional peace agreement with the British emissaries. It was fortunate that they did so, for the British were prepared to be generous. In the Treaty of Paris, signed in September 1783, England agreed to recognize American independence and set the western boundary of the United States at the Mississippi River. Moreover, Britain promised that U.S. fishermen would have the "right" to fish the waters off Newfoundland and that British forces would evacuate American territory "with all convenient speed" once hostilities had ceased. In return, the Congress agreed to recommend that the states restore the rights and property of the Loyalists. Both sides agreed that prewar debts owed the citizens of one country by the citizens of the other would remain valid. Each of these issues would trouble Anglo-American relations in the decades ahead, but for the moment it seemed a splendid outcome to a long and difficult struggle.

The Ingredients of Victory

How were the weak and disunited American states able to defeat Great Britain, the most powerful nation in the Atlantic world? Certainly the Dutch and French loans, war supplies, and military forces were crucially important. More decisive, though, was the American people's determination not to submit. Often the Americans were disorganized and uncooperative. Repeatedly, it seemed that the war effort was about to collapse as continental troops drifted away, state militias refused to march, and military supplies failed to materialize. Neither the Congress nor the states, which often squabbled, provided consistent direction to the struggle. Yet as the war progressed, the people's estrangement from England and their commitment to the "glorious cause" increased. To subdue the colonies, England would have had to occupy the entire eastern third of the continent, and that it could not do.

Even though state militias frequently refused to go beyond their own state borders and after the first months of the war engaged in relatively few battles, they provided a vast reservoir of manpower to control the countryside, intimidate Loyalists, and harass British forces. All of this occupied British troops that would otherwise have been free to engage the continental army.

The American victory owed much as well to the administrative and organizational talents of Washington. Against massive odds, he held the continental army together, often only by the force of his will. Facing inadequate supplies, low pay, high rates of turnover among the troops, ineffective support from the Congress, and lack of cooperation from the states, he contrived a military force capable of winning selected encounters and, more important, of surviving over time. Had he failed, the Americans could not possibly have defeated the British.

In the end, however, it is as accurate to say that Britain lost the war as that the United States won it. With vast economic and military resources, Britain enjoyed clear military superiority over the American states. Its troops were more numerous, better armed and supplied, and more professionally trained. Until the closing months of the contest, Britain enjoyed naval superiority as well. As a consequence, its forces could move up and down the coast virtually at will.

England, however, could not capitalize sufficiently on its advantages. It proved too difficult to extend command structures and supply routes across several thousand miles of ocean. Because information flowed erratically back and forth across the water, strategic decisions made in London were often based on faulty or outdated intelligence. Given the difficulties of supply over such distances, British troops often had to live off the land. This reduced their mobility and increased the antagonism of the Americans whose crops and animals they commandeered.

In addition, British leaders were often overly cautious. Burgoyne's attempt in 1777 to isolate New England by invading from Canada failed because Sir William Howe decided to attack Philadelphia rather than move northward up the Hudson River to join him. Thus ended England's hope of dividing the new nation in two and forcing an early surrender. Similarly, neither Howe nor Cornwallis pressed his advantages in the central states during the middle years of the war, when more aggressive action might have defeated and scattered the continental force.

British commanders also generally failed to adapt their battlefield tactics to the realities of the American war. This was perhaps their greatest shortcoming. They continued to fight in the European style, during specified times of the year and using set formations of troops deployed in formal battlefield maneuvers. The War for American Independence required different tactics. Much of the terrain was rough and wooded and thus better suited to the use of smaller units and irregular troops. Washington and Greene were more flexible, often employing a patient strategy of raiding, harassment, and strategic retreat. Behind this strategy lay a willingness, grounded in necessity, to allow England control of considerable territory, especially along the coast. But it was based as well on the conviction that popular support for the Revolutionary cause

would persist and that over time the costs of subduing the colonial rebellion would be greater than the British government could bear. As a much later American war in Vietnam would also reveal, a guerrilla force can win if it does not lose; a regular army loses if it does not consistently win.

The American strategy proved sound. As the war dragged on and its costs escalated, Britain's will began to waver. After France and Spain entered the conflict, Britain's problems increased, for its government then had to worry about Europe, the Caribbean, and even the Mediterranean as well as North America. Unrest in Ireland and massive London riots prevented England from sending more troops to North America. All told, the drain on the nation's resources was immense. As the cost in money and lives increased and prospects of victory diminished, political support for the war eroded. With the defeat at Yorktown, it collapsed. Britain's effort to hold onto its 13 North American colonies had failed.

THE EXPERIENCE OF WAR

In terms of total loss of life and destruction of property, the Revolutionary War pales by comparison with America's more recent wars. How destructive, we might ask, could a war have been in which Benjamin Franklin urged the widespread use of bows and arrows? "Nothing terrifies enemies more," Franklin explained, "than the deadly silent flight of a volley of arrows." Yet modern comparisons are misleading, for, in relative terms, the War for American Independence was both terrifying to the people caught up in it and destructive of lives and property.

Recruiting an Army

No one, of course, was affected more directly than the combatants. Estimates vary, but on the American side as many as 250,000 men may at one time or another have borne arms. That would amount to about one out of every two or three adult males. Before the war's end, Concord, Massachusetts, had provided 875 soldiers, more than $2\frac{1}{2}$ times its eligible male population on the eve of the war. Concord's experience was not unique.

Tens of thousands served in the state militias. Each of the colonies had required adult males between the ages of 15 and 60 to enroll in their local militia company, attend the monthly drill, and turn

The American rifleman, even as idealized in this engraving, lacked the pomp and formality—and often the discipline—of the British soldier.

alists (those who supported England) than by mustering the local company and seeing who turned out?

During the first year of the war, when enthusiasm ran high, men of all ranks—rich and middle-class as well as poor—volunteered to fight the British. But as the war proceeded, its personal costs increased and community quotas grew; its social character changed. Initially fought by volunteers, the war soon became a battle by conscripts. Eventually it was transformed, as wars so often are, into a poor man's fight. Middle- and upper-class men increasingly hired substitutes to replace them, and communities such as Concord filled their quotas with strangers lured by the promise of enlistment bonuses. For Concord, as for countless communities across the states, the Revolution became a war by proxy. This social transformation was even more evident in the continental army, where terms were longer, discipline stiffer, and battlefields more distant from the soldiers' homes.

For the poor and the jobless, whose ranks the war rapidly expanded, bonus payments and the promise of board and keep proved attractive. But often the bonuses failed to materialize, and pay was long overdue. Moreover, life in the camps was harsh, and soldiers frequently heard from their wives about their families' distress at home. Faced with such trials, soldiers often became disgruntled and insubordinate. As the war progressed, Washington imposed harsher discipline on the continental troops in an effort to hold them in line.

Occasionally frustration and despair spilled over into open revolt. Sergeant Samuel Glover of the North Carolina line learned in 1779 what the costs of such behavior were. He was executed for leading a group of soldiers, unpaid for 15 months, that, in Glover's words, "demanded their pay, and refused to obey the commands of their superior officer, and would not march until they had justice done them." His widow later apologized to the North Carolina assembly for her husband's conduct but begged leave to ask, "What must the feeling of the man be who fought at Brandywine, at Germantown, and at Stony Point and did his duty, and when on another march in defense of his country, with poverty staring him full in the face, he was denied his pay?" Poor soldiers, she explained to the assembly, were "possessed of the same attachment and affection for their families as those in command."

Throughout the war, soldiers suffered from severe shortages of supplies. At Valley Forge during

out when called. At the time of independence, however, the militia in most of the states was not an effective fighting force. This was especially true in the South, where Nathanael Greene complained that the men came "from home with all the tender feelings of domestic life" and were not "sufficiently fortified . . . to stand the shocking scenes of war, to march over dead men, [or] to hear without concern the groans of the wounded." Fighting, Greene knew, was neither pleasant nor heroic.

The militia did serve as a convenient recruiting system. Men were already enrolled, and arrangements were in place for calling them into the field on short notice. This was of special importance during the early months of the war, before the continental army took shape. Given its grounding in local community life, the militia also served to legitimate the war among the people and secure their commitment to the Revolutionary cause. What better way, as well, to separate the Patriots (those who supported the cause of independence) from the Loy-

the terrible winter of 1777–1778, men hobbled about without shoes or coats. From the midst of that winter's gloom, Washington wrote, "There are now in this army 4000 men wanting blankets, near 2000 of which have never had one, altho' some of them have been 12 months in service." "I am sick, discontented, and out of humour," declared one despairing soul. "Poor food, hard lodging, cold weather, fatigue, nasty cloathes, nasty cookery, vomit half my time, smoaked out of my senses. The Devil's in't, I can't Endure it. Why are we sent here to starve and freeze?"

The states possessed food and clothing enough but were often reluctant to strip their own people of wagons and livestock, blankets and shoes for use elsewhere. Moreover, mismanagement and difficulties in transportation stood in the way. Neither the state governments nor the Congress had the ability to administer a war effort of such magnitude. Wagon transport was slow and costly, and the presence of the British fleet made water transportation along the coast perilous. Though many individuals served honorably as supply officers, others took advantage of the army's distress. Washington commented bitterly on the "speculators, various tribes of money makers, and stock-jobbers of all denominations" whose "avarice and thirst for gain" threatened the country's ruin.

The Casualties of Combat

Even though the weaponry of the eighteenth century was limited in range and firepower, it killed and maimed when it hit. Medical treatment, whether for wounds or diseases (such as smallpox, dysentery, and typhus) that raged through the camps, did little to help. Casualties poured into hospitals, overcrowding them beyond capacity. Dr. James Tilton, the prescribing physician at Princeton, commented after the battles of Brandywine and Red Bank that with the "sick & wounded, flowing promiscuously without restraint into the hospital, it soon became infectious and was attended with great mortality." Dr. Jonathan Potts, the attending physician at Fort George in New York, reported that "we have at present upwards of one thousand sick crowded into sheds & labouring under the various and cruel disorders of dysentaries, bilious putrid fevers and the effects of a confluent smallpox; to attend to this large number we have four seniors and four mates, exclusive of myself."

Surgeons, operating without anesthetics and with the crudest of instruments, as readily threatened life as preserved it. Few understood the causes and treatment of infection. Doctoring consisted mostly of bleeding, blistering, vomiting (which was "deemed of excellent use, by opening and squeezing all the glands of the body, & then shaking from the nervous system, the contaminating poison"), and laxatives. Mercury, a highly toxic chemical, was a commonly administered drug. One doctor had "no hesitation in declaring . . . that we lost no less than from 10 to 20 of camp diseases, for one by weapons of the enemy."

How many soldiers actually died we do not know, for no one kept accurate records. But the most conservative estimate runs to over 25,000, a higher percentage of the total population than for any other American conflict except the Civil War. About 12 percent of American soldiers died of wounds or disease, a rate virtually the equivalent of the Civil War and higher than any of America's other conflicts. For the Revolutionary War soldier, death was real and imminent.

The death that soldiers dispensed to each other on the battlefield was also intensely personal. Because of the limits of the weaponry—the effective range of muskets was little more than 100 yards—combat was typically at close quarters. That meant that soldiers came virtually face to face with the men they killed. According to eighteenth-century military conventions, armies formed on the battlefield in ranks and fired in unison. After massed volleys, the lines often closed for hand-to-hand combat with knives and bayonets. Such encounters were powerfully etched in the memory of individuals who survived them. The partisan warfare in the South, with its emphasis on ambush and small group actions and its cyclic patterns of revenge and counterrevenge, personalized combat even more. British officers, used to more distanced and dispassionate styles of warfare, were shocked at the ferocity with which Americans often fought. One attributed to the American troops "a sort of implacable ardor and revenge, which happily are a good deal unknown in the prosecution of war in general."

The American fervor in battle is also largely explained by the fact that this was in part a civil war. Not only did Englishmen fight Americans, but American Loyalists and Patriots fought each other as well. As many as 50,000 colonists fought for the king and engaged in some of the war's bitterest encounters. They figured importantly in Burgoyne's invasion from Canada and in the attacks on Savannah and Charleston. Benedict Arnold led a force of Loyalists on raids through the Connecticut and James river valleys, and Loyalist militia joined Indian allies in destructive sweeps through central New York, Pennsylvania, and the backcountry of the Carolinas and Kentucky. Throughout America, communities and families divided against each other. The war's violent temper reflected this civil conflict.

Moreover, the war was fought in the midst of American society. When war came to a locality, soldiers found themselves fighting for the survival of their family and community. Finally, Americans believed fervently in the Revolutionary cause. The struggle, as they understood it, was between irreconcilable principles—their own liberty and the tyranny that Britain threatened. In such a crusade, against such a foe, nothing was to be spared that might bring victory.

Civilians and the War

Noncombatants also suffered the reality of war, most of all in the most densely settled areas along the coast. England focused its military efforts there because the coastal communities were the political, economic, and cultural centers of American life. Moreover, along the coast, England could bring its naval power directly to bear. At one time or another, British troops occupied every major port—Boston for a year at the war's start, New York from 1777 to 1783, Philadelphia over the winter and spring of 1777–1778, Charleston in 1780–1781, and Savannah two years before. The resulting disruptions of urban life were profound.

The chaos in New York was typical. In September 1776, a fire consumed 500 houses, nearly a quarter of the city's dwellings. Most were not rebuilt until well after the war was over. About half the town's inhabitants fled when the British occupation began and were replaced by an almost equal number of Loyalists who streamed in from the surrounding countryside. Ten thousand British and German troops added to the crowding. The growing numbers of poor erected makeshift shelters of sailcloth and timbers. "Canvass Town" was the name people gave to the region stretching along Broadway. At the war's end, an American officer somberly reported what he found as his troops entered the city: "Close on the eve of an approaching winter, with an heterogeneous set of inhabitants, composed of almost ruined exiles, disbanded soldiery, mixed foreigners, disaffected Tories, and the refuse of the British army, we took possession of a ruined city."

In Philadelphia, the occupation was shorter and the disruptions were less severe, but the shock of invasion was no less real. Elizabeth Drinker, living alone after local Patriots had exiled her Quaker husband, found herself the unwilling landlady of a British officer, Major Crammond, and his friends. The major's presence may have protected her from the plundering that went on all around. She was, however, constantly anxious, confiding to her journal, "I often feel afraid to go to Bed." During the occupation, British soldiers frequently took what they wanted, tore down fences for their campfires, and confiscated food to supplement their own tedious fare. Even the Loyalists commented on the "dreadful consequences" of occupation.

More than the ports was at risk, however, for the entire coastal plain lay open to British attack. Landing parties descended without warning to capture supplies or terrorize inhabitants. Charlestown, Massachusetts, was almost entirely consumed by shelling and fire during the Battle of Bunker Hill. In 1780 and 1781, the British mounted a sustained, punitive attack along the Connecticut coast in an effort to divert American troops from the defense of Virginia. Over 200 buildings in Fairfield were burned, and much of nearby Norwalk was destroyed.

The southern coast was even more vulnerable to attack. From 1779 to 1781, the Virginia tidewater region lay open to the British. In December 1780, Benedict Arnold ravaged the James River valley, uprooting tobacco, confiscating slaves, and creating panic among the white population. Similar devastation befell the coasts of Georgia and the Carolinas.

These relentless British attacks sent civilians fleeing into the interior. During the first years of the war, the port cities lost nearly half their population, while inland communities strained to cope with the thousands of migrants who streamed into them. So many refugees had crowded into Concord by July 1775 that they decided to hold a Boston town meeting there! By March 1776, Concord's population had grown by 25 percent, creating major problems of housing, social order, and public health. Communities to the north of New York City absorbed even larger numbers of refugees from the British-occupied city and its surrounding counties.

Not all the traffic was inland, away from the coast. In western New York, Pennsylvania, Virginia, and the Carolinas, numerous frontier settlements

In September 1776, as American troops fought unsuccessfully for control of New York, nearly a quarter of the city was destroyed by fire. Not until the war ended did reconstruction and cleanup of the ruins begin.

collapsed in the face of British and Indian attack. By 1783, the white population along the Mohawk River west of Albany, New York, had declined from 10,000 to 3,500. According to one observer, after nearly five years of warfare in Tryon County, 12,000 farms had been abandoned, 700 buildings burned, hundreds of thousands of bushels of grain destroyed, nearly 400 women widowed, and perhaps 2,000 children orphaned. On July 3, 1778, Sir John Butler led Loyalists and Indians in a brutal sweep through the Wyoming Valley in northeastern Pennsylvania, while at Cherry Valley, New York, 40 survivors of a Loyalist and Indian attack were massacred after they had surrendered.

Wherever the armies went, they generated a swirl of refugees, who spread vivid tales of the war. This refugee traffic, added to the constant movement of soldiers back and forth between army and civilian life, brought the war home even to people who did not experience it at first hand.

Disease followed the armies like an avenging angel, ravaging civilians and soldiers alike. And wherever they went, the armies lived off the land, commandeering the supplies they needed. During the desperate winter of 1777–1778, in an effort to protect the surrounding population, Washington issued an order prohibiting his troops from roaming more than a half mile from camp. In New Jersey, Britain's German mercenaries generated special fears among the citizenry. The Patriot press was filled with lurid stories of attacks on American civilians, especially women.

In April 1777, a committee of the Congress, appointed to inquire into the conduct of British troops, took affidavits from women who had suffered rape. The committee reported that it had "authentic information of many instances of the most indecent treatment, and actual ravishment of married and single women; but, such is the nature of that most irreparable injury that the persons suffering it, though perfectly innocent, look upon it as a kind of reproach to have the facts related and their names known." Whether the report had any effect is unknown.

The Loyalists

None among the American people suffered greater losses than those who remained loyal to the crown. On September 8, 1783, Thomas Danforth, formerly a lawyer from Cambridge, Massachusetts, appeared in London before the King's Commission of Enquiry into the Losses and Services of the American Loyalists. Danforth was there to seek compensation for losses he had suffered at the hands of the American revolutionaries. Like other Loyalists who appealed to the commission, Danforth began by explaining the consequences of his loyalty to the crown. "Having devoted his whole life . . . in preparing himself for future usefulness," he began,

> . . . now he finds himself near his fortieth year, banished under pain of death, to a distant country, where he has not the most remote family connection . . . cut off from his profession—from every hope of importance in life, and in a great degree from social enjoyments. And where . . . he shall be unable . . . to procure common comforts and conveniences, in a station much inferior to that of a menial servant, without the assistance of government.

The commission's response is unknown, but many of the several thousand Loyalists who appeared before it were reimbursed for about one-third of their losses. Though more than most Loyalist refugees could expect, this was meager compensation for what they had endured—the confiscation of house and property, expulsion from their native land, ostracism and attack by former neighbors, and the trauma of relocation in a distant and unfamiliar land.

How many colonists remained loyal to England can only be estimated because complete records were not kept. We do know that tens of thousands left from New York, Charleston, and Savannah at the end of the war. At least as many slipped away to England, Canada, or the West Indies while the fighting was still under way. Additional thousands stayed on in the new nation and struggled to rebuild their lives. Many more wished in their hearts that independence had never come but, out of prudence or fear, kept their views to themselves and tried to stay out of trouble.

Though no count can be exact, as many as 80,000 men, women, and children may have departed from the new nation, while several hundred thousand more remained in the United States. These

Loyalists, or Tories, as the Patriots called them, often suffered the indignities of tarring, feathering, and public humiliation for their loyalty to England.

are substantial numbers when set against the total American population, black and white, of about 2.5 million. The incidence of loyalism differed dramatically from region to region. There were fewest Loyalists in New England and most in and around New York City, where British authority was most stable.

Why did so many Americans remain loyal, often at the cost of personal danger and loss? Some, appointed to office in the king's name, had a special incentive to loyalism. Customs officers, members of the governors' councils, and Anglican clergymen often remained with the crown. Loyalism was common as well among groups especially dependent on British authority—for example, settlers on the Carolina frontier who believed themselves mistreated by the politically dominant planter elite along the coast; ethnic minorities, such as the Germans in the middle states, who feared domination by the Anglo-American majority; or tenants on some of the large estates along the Hudson River, who had struggled for years with their landlords over the terms of their leaseholds.

For many colonists, the prospect of confronting English military power, however justified they believed the American protest to be, was sufficiently daunting. Others doubted the ability of a new, weak nation to survive in an Atlantic world dominated by competing empires, even if independence could be won.

Samuel Seabury explained the principled basis of his loyalism. "Every person," he wrote in 1775, "owes obedience to the laws of the government . . . and is obliged in honour and duty to support them. Because if *one* has a right to disregard the laws of the society to which he belongs, *all* have the *same* right; and then government is at an end. . . . And you are so far from being bound in honour to obey *any* determinations of the Congress, which interfere with the laws of the government, that you are really bound in honour to *oppose* them."

William Eddis wondered what kind of society independence would bring when Revolutionary crowds showed no respect for the rights of Loyalist dissenters such as he. "If I differ in opinion from the multitude," he asked, "must I therefore be deprived of my character, and the confidence of my fellow-citizens; when in every station of life I discharge my duty with fidelity and honour?" Whatever their motives, the Loyalists believed themselves advocates of reason and the rule of law in the midst of revolutionary passion. Tens of thousands of Americans believed strongly enough in their position to sacrifice home, community, and personal safety on its behalf.

Many who faced exile successfully established new lives in other parts of the empire. The majority settled in the Maritime Provinces of Canada. But even under the best of circumstances, forced resettlement was traumatic. Most of the several thousand or so who made it to England met something other than a warm and grateful reception. Try as they might to be English, they quickly discovered that they were not; and so, along with Thomas Danforth, they remained on the fringes of English society, their financial affairs troubled, their futures uncertain.

Loyalists came from all social classes but were most numerous among the upper and middle ranks of society, where individuals were most likely to have direct political and social connections with English officials and to fear the social consequences of revolution. In localities where they were numerous, their departure opened positions of social and political leadership and increased the tempo of social change. More generally, given their adherence to monarchical government and its values of hierarchy and subordination, their loss weakened the forces of social conservatism in America and facilitated the progress of revolutionary reform.

Blacks and the Revolution

American blacks were deeply involved in the Revolution. In fact, the conflict provoked the largest slave rebellion in American history prior to the Civil War. Once the war was under way, blacks found a variety of ways to turn events to their own advantage. For some, this meant applying Revolutionary principles to their own lives and calling for their personal freedom. For others, it meant seeking liberty behind English lines or in the continent's interior. Thousands of American blacks found their lives changed.

During the pre-Revolutionary decade, as their white masters talked excitedly about liberty, the dignity of humankind, and the nobility of opposing despotism, increasing numbers of black Americans questioned their own oppression. In the North, some slaves petitioned legislatures to set them free. In the South, pockets of insurrection appeared. In 1765, more than 100 South Carolina slaves fled to the interior, where they tried to establish a colony of their own. The next year, slaves paraded through the streets of Charleston, chanting, "Liberty, liberty!"

In November 1775, Lord Dunmore issued a proclamation offering freedom to all Virginia slaves and servants, "able and willing to bear arms," who would leave their masters and join the British forces in Norfolk. Within weeks, 500 to 600 slaves had responded. Among those who demonstrated their commitment to freedom by traveling through the hostile, Patriot-controlled countryside was Thomas Peters, from Wilmington, North Carolina.

Kidnapped from the Yoruba tribe in what is now Nigeria and brought to America by a French slave trader, Peters was sold in Louisiana about 1760. He

During the Revolutionary War, James Armistead Lafayette, a Virginia slave, served as a spy against the British for the French general, Lafayette. In recognition of his service, the Virginia General Assembly granted him his freedom in 1786.

resisted enslavement so fiercely that his master sold him into the English colonies. By 1770, Peters belonged to William Campbell, an immigrant Scots planter on North Carolina's Cape Fear River. Here Peters toiled while the storm brewed between England and the colonies.

Peters's plans for his own declaration of independence may have ripened as a result of the rhetoric of liberty he heard around his master's house, for William Campbell had become a leading member of Wilmington's Sons of Liberty and talked much about inalienable rights. By mid-1775, the Cape Fear region, like most areas from Maryland to Georgia, buzzed with rumors of slave uprisings. Importations of new slaves were banned, and patrols were dispatched to disarm all blacks in the area. In July, the state's Revolutionary government imposed martial law when the British commander of Fort Johnston at the mouth of the Cape Fear River near Wilmington gave "encouragement to Negroes to elope from their masters." Four months later, Dunmore issued his dramatic proclamation.

Thomas Peters struck his blow for freedom in March 1776, when 20 British ships entered the Cape Fear River and disembarked royal troops, who quickly established control over the surrounding countryside. Peters seized the moment to redefine himself as a man instead of William Campbell's property and escaped. During the war, he fought with the British-officered Black Pioneers.

How many American blacks such as Peters sought liberty behind British lines is unknown, but as many as 20 percent may have done so. In dramatic contrast to their white masters, blacks saw in England the promise of freedom, not tyranny. As the war dragged on, English commanders pressed blacks into service, usually in support roles but also as combatants. From the Virginia slaves who responded to Dunmore's proclamation, a regiment of black soldiers was formed and marched into battle, their chests covered with sashes on which was emblazoned "Liberty to Slaves." Some of the blacks who joined England and fought for their freedom achieved it. At the war's end, several thousand were evacuated with the British to Nova Scotia, where they established their own settlements. Their reception by the white inhabitants there, however, was generally hostile. By the end of the century, most had left Canada to found the free black colony of Sierra Leone on the west coast of Africa. Thomas Peters was a leader among them.

Many of the slaves who fled behind English lines, however, never won their freedom. At the end of the war, as the British prepared to evacuate the port cities, blacks from the surrounding countryside crowded in, begging to be taken away. Against their appeals for liberty, British commanders had to balance the terms of the peace treaty, which stipulated that the British were to evacuate "with all convenient Speed and without causing any destruction or carrying away any Negroes or other Property of the American Inhabitants." In the end, hundreds of slaves were returned to their American owners. Several thousand others, their value as fieldhands too great to be ignored, were transported to the West Indies and the harsher slavery of the sugar plantations. It was evident that England had not entered the war to abolish slavery.

Other blacks chose not to flee behind British lines but took advantage of the war's confusion to drift away into the towns or country-side in pursuit of a new life. Some sought refuge among the Indians, though not always with success. The Seminoles of Georgia and Florida generally welcomed black run-aways and through intermarriage absorbed them into tribal society. The blacks' reception by the Cherokees and Creeks, however, was more uncertain. Some were taken in, but others were returned to their white owners in return for bounties, while still others were held in slavelike conditions by new Indian masters. Numerous other blacks made their way north, following rumors that slavery had been abolished there. Whatever their destination, thousands of American blacks acted to throw off the bonds of slavery.

Fewer blacks fought on the American side than on England's, in part because neither the Congress nor the states were eager to see blacks armed. Faced with the increasing need for troops, however, the Congress and each of the states except Georgia and South Carolina relented and pressed blacks into service. Of the blacks who served the Patriot cause, many received the freedom they were promised. The patriotism of countless others, however, went unrewarded.

THE REVOLUTION AND THE ECONOMY

The Revolutionary War altered people's lives in ways that reached beyond the sights and sounds of battle. Before the war was over, major sectors of the American economy fell into disarray. Even had England allowed the colonies to leave the empire in peace, the economic consequences of independence would have been severe, for the American economies had taken shape under England's imperial system. Independence broke those historic ties of dependence, bringing important gains in economic freedom. The new nation however, now faced the daunting challenge of surviving in an Atlantic world divided into competing and often warring empires.

England, of course, did not let the colonies go without a fight, and so the American people experienced the economic shocks of warfare as well—destruction of property, loss of human life, diversion of productive labor into the army, rampant inflation, and collapse of the monetary system. No other American war has been more economically disruptive.

In time recovery would come. By the 1790s, the nation's economy would enter a new and more dramatic phase of development. That future, however, was not evident amid the chaos of the war years.

The Interruption of Trade

Waterborne commerce—across the ocean to England and Europe, along the North American coast, and down to the West Indies—had long been the lifeblood of the colonial economy. It carried away America's agricultural exports and brought back manufactured goods. It provided jobs for sailors and ship captains, carpenters and sailmakers, lumbermen and provisioners. During the imperial crisis, nonimportation had temporarily interrupted this trade. Independence and the war halted it.

Gone after 1776 were the familiar overseas markets in England and the British West Indies for such

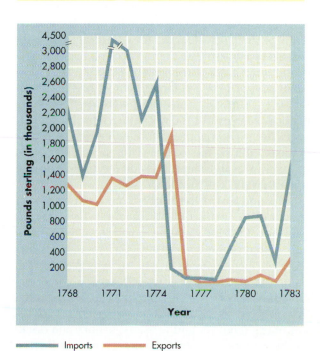

Exports and Imports, 1768–1783

Pounds sterling (in thousands)

4,500 / 3,000 / 2,800 / 2,600 / 2,400 / 2,200 / 2,000 / 1,800 / 1,600 / 1,400 / 1,200 / 1,000 / 800 / 600 / 400 / 200

Year: 1768, 1771, 1774, 1777, 1780, 1783

Imports — Exports

Source: U.S. Bureau of the Census.

staple exports as New England fish, Pennsylvania wheat, and Chesapeake tobacco. Gone were most of the English manufactured goods that had dominated American imports. Gone were the business connections with English bankers, wholesalers, and insurance brokers who had supported American commerce. Gone as well was the protection of the British fleet, for it was now the enemy blockading the coast, attacking coastal towns, and sweeping American merchantmen from the sea.

The end of British mercantile restrictions meant that American merchants could now deal directly with Europe, Africa, and the French and Dutch West Indies. And though England's naval blockade was effective, it was not complete. The Atlantic was too vast to police, even by England's massive fleet.

A certain amount of trade with England actually continued during the war, because American buyers could always be found for English goods. In 1782, Jonathan Amory, a Boston merchant, advised his brother, who had remained in London as agent for the family business, that "English goods . . . are prohibited by Congress; yet I think they might be so managed that by Invoice and mixed with Holland goods, there would be but little difficulty, and English goods sell best." For some merchants, this illicit trade proved highly profitable.

In addition, some merchants and ship captains found profit in privateering, the chartering of private vessels by state or Congress to prey on English merchantmen. Elias Derby of Salem, Massachusetts, became one of New England's richest merchants in this way. The risks, however, were high, and the majority of ventures did not return a profit. On balance, American overseas commerce declined dramatically during the war, and the heightened costs of insurance and shipping reduced profits on the trade that did get through.

Up and down the coast, communities whose livelihoods depended on the sea felt the war's impact. New England's fishing industry, once a central part of that region's economy, was decimated. Formerly thriving fishing centers, such as Wellfleet on Cape Cod, never recovered, and larger commercial communities, such as Newburyport, Massachusetts, just up the coast from Boston, struggled to survive. Countless laborers and artisans, sailors and dockworkers were cut adrift. Many moved to Boston seeking work or inland seeking land. Others stayed where they were, struggling to survive and wondering what prospects independence would open to them.

Boom and Depression in Agriculture

Independence and the war wreaked havoc on the lives of the majority of Americans who worked the land for their living. No area was harder hit than the Chesapeake. With the loss of English markets, tobacco production dropped precipitously, and a deep depression settled over the region. Not until 1790 would tobacco exports regain their prewar level. South Carolina's rice continued to command a good price in Europe when it could be slipped through the British blockade. It remained an important export until cotton supplanted it early in the nineteenth century. The production of indigo, the state's second most valuable export commodity, however, virtually ceased. To the north, Pennsylvania's once thriving overseas trade in wheat and corn declined, and New England farmers staggered under the loss of their lucrative West Indies provisioning trade.

Armies and navies, of course, have to eat. British and French as well as American troops sharply increased the demand for agricultural produce. As a consequence, farmers often prospered while the armies were nearby. At one point early in the war, the Congress called on New England farmers for 1,000 head of cattle weekly for the army's use. When the fighting shifted to the South, however, New England agriculture slipped into a decadelong depression.

As the war went on, farmers often received payment in continental dollars that depreciated before they could be spent or in other kinds of governmental IOUs that carried only the most distant prospect of redemption. When things got truly difficult, military commanders simply seized the corn, hay, livestock, and wagons they needed.

Agricultural productivity declined as well. The cost of agricultural labor escalated as men were called into the army and as large numbers of southern slaves slipped behind British lines or ran away. Few farmers had money to replace the property that was confiscated or destroyed. Throughout the colonial period, American farmers had increased production by bringing new acreage under cultivation as worn-out land declined in productivity. During the war, crop acreage actually decreased.

Some farmers tried to survive by withholding their produce from local markets until prices rose, by shifting from field crops to the more lucrative production of livestock, or by supplementing their incomes by smithing and cabinetmaking. During the war, farm women increased their already essential contributions to family incomes by making shirts, blankets, and other goods. In spite of the best efforts, however, the average real worth per farm, as measured by the combined value of farm implements, livestock, and crops, declined. When the war ended, farmers and planters almost unanimously lamented their heavy debts and the uncertainty of their future. In 1785, an English traveler visiting a Rhode Island farm found 11 people struggling for a living on 76 acres of land. The farmers here, he observed, "are miserably poor and in debt." For agriculturalists everywhere, independence and the war took a heavy toll. As we shall see, their frustrations soon boiled over in state politics.

Manufacturing and Wartime Profits

The war's impact on American manufacturing was uneven. New England shipbuilding was hardest hit. On the eve of independence, New England's booming shipyards had constructed nearly half the merchant tonnage carrying cargo within England's Atlantic empire. During the war, shipbuilding virtually ceased. For the ropemakers, shipwrights, blacksmiths, and sailors in towns like Boston and Newburyport, Massachusetts, the results were disastrous. The construction of a few ships under contract from the Congress or state governments offered some relief, but there were not many of them, and they were often delayed by insufficient funds.

At the same time, the war stimulated other manufactures. With British goods excluded, American producers moved to take up the slack. Patriotism as well as necessity argued for the use of domestic goods. (The familiar slogan "Buy American" has a long tradition!) Wearing homespun signified commitment to the Revolutionary cause. Women spun more thread, wove more cloth, and fashioned it into clothing appropriate for republican citizens.

It was hard to increase production however, for artisans and craftsmen, working at home or in small shops, fabricated virtually everything by hand. In Pennsylvania, skilled gunsmiths could produce no more than 50 muskets a year, for each part had to be made and fitted individually. With so many men in the army, the cost of labor escalated, a problem intensified by the wartime cutoff of immigration. And though the country's shops and mills were widely scattered across the land, they were most numerous in the coastal areas, where the war's destruction was heaviest.

There were, of course, profits to be made, especially by opportunistic merchants with the right political connections. The largest returns came from government contracting. Too often the search for profits shaded over into outright profiteering. An "insatiable thirst for riches," lamented George Washington in 1779, "seems to have got the better of every order of men." Members of the military were not immune from the temptation. General Henry Knox, commander of the continental artillery, observed to a friend that he was "exceedingly anxious to effect something in these fluctuating times, which may make . . . [me] lazy for life."

Then as now, the boundaries between individuals' private interests and their public responsibilities were often hazy. Silas Deane capitalized on his position as congressional purchasing agent in France by using public money to arrange lucrative trading ventures of his own. The Congress finally called the unscrupulous Deane to account, but many others acted much the same while charting their course more carefully.

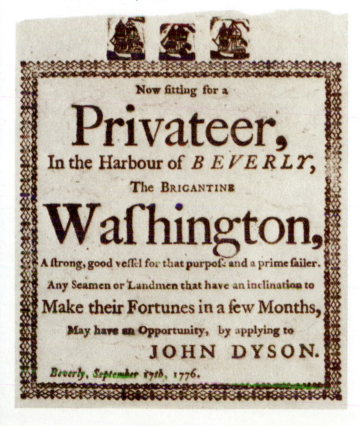

The lure of adventure and hope for quick profits enticed countless young men into dangerous but exciting service aboard American privateers.

Now fitting for a

Privateer,

In the Harbour of *BEVERLY*,

The BRIGANTINE

Wasington,

A strong, good vessel for that purpose and a prime sailer.

Any Seamen or Landmen that have an inclination to

Make their Fortunes in a few Months,

May have an Opportunity, by applying to

JOHN DYSON.

Beverly, September 17th, 1776.

Robert Morris, an eminent Philadelphia merchant, insisted on his right to continue his private ventures after he became treasurer of the Congress, and the Congress agreed. Explained Morris to one of his associates, "You may depend that the pursuit of . . . [our] plan deserves your utmost exertion & attention so far as your mind is engaged in making money, for there never has been so fair an oppert'y of making a large fortune since I have been conversant in the world." At the same time, the public benefited immeasurably from Morris's services, for he worked mightily to stabilize congressional finances and at several critical moments committed his own sizable fortune to support the Congress's tottering credit.

When peace returned in 1783, America's manufacturing boom collapsed as the demand for war material dropped and long-excluded English goods flooded the market, driving the cruder American goods from the stores. American merchants welcomed the renewal of English trade but artisans, who found their livelihoods endangered by English competition, were alarmed.

Financial Chaos

The Revolution left American finances in a state of chaos that would take more than a decade to repair. The war required unprecedented governmental expenditures. Faced with the uncontrollable escalation of costs, the Congress and the states did what colonial governments had done before and American governments have done ever since: they printed money. In the first year of the war, they together issued more than $400 million in various kinds of paper. By war's end, they had pumped additional millions into the economy in payment for military supplies and wages. Nothing supported the paper's value but the citizens' willingness to accept it in their dealings with the government and each other.

That willingness rapidly disappeared as the flood of paper expanded and efforts lagged to draw it in through taxation. The result was a headlong collapse of the currency's value. Congressional bills of credit that in 1776 were pegged against gold at the ratio of 1.5 to 1 had slipped five years later to 147 to 1. State currencies depreciated even more alarmingly. In 1780, most states called in their old depreciated money and issued new currency, hop-

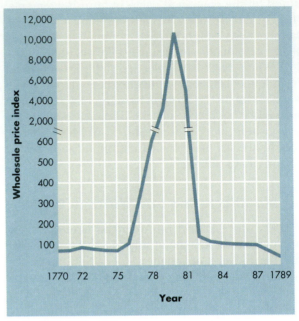

Wholesale Price Index, 1770–1789

Year

Note: 1850–1859 = 100

Source: U.S. Bureau of the Census.

ing that this would bring stability. New York pegged the exchange rate at 128 to 1, Virginia at nearly ten times that.

The situation offered ample opportunity for unscrupulous speculators to reap illicit profits. For most Americans, however, the flood of depreciated paper proved disastrous. What was one to do when goods and wages had no consistent value, when the idea of saving made no sense, and when even the incentive to work disappeared? James Lovell observed uneasily that "sailors with clubs parade" the streets of Boston "instead of working for paper." How could individuals make plans or conduct their business under such conditions? Often they could not. The accompanying upward spiral of price inflation was staggering. In Massachusetts, a bushel of corn that sold for less than a dollar in 1777 went for nearly $80 two years later, while in Maryland the price of wheat increased several thousandfold. In Boston, a crowd of women, angered by the escalating costs of food and other necessities, tossed a merchant suspected of monopolizing commodities into a cart and dragged him through the city's streets while "a large concourse of men stood amazed."

With property values in disarray, it seemed at times as if the foundations of society were coming unhinged. John Witherspoon remarked to a friend that his son-in-law had sold his furniture before leaving Virginia to come to Philadelphia. The continental bills of credit that he received for it soon depreciated to nothing. His loss was virtually complete. Thomas Paine described the situation in 1777 to Elbridge Gerry. "The war," he wrote, "has thrown property into channels where before it never was. . . . Monies in large sums . . . enable . . . [profiteers] to roll the snow ball of monopoly and forestalling; and . . . while these people are heaping up wealth . . . the remaining part are jogging on in their old way, with few or no advantages."

The poor suffered most. During the best of times, they lived at the margins of subsistence. More than others, they were vulnerable to losses in the purchasing power of wages or military pay. The poor, however, were not alone. Farmers and merchants, planters and artisans faced increasing debt and uncertainty. Rarely has the American economy been in such disarray as at the nation's founding.

THE FERMENT OF REVOLUTIONARY POLITICS

The Revolution also transformed the content of American political thought, patterns of political behavior, and the structure and operations of government. The result was a new political order independent of British authority, struggling to define the republican principles on which it was based and driven by the clash of social and economic interests.

Politicizing the People

Under the pressure of Revolutionary events, politics absorbed people's attention and energies as never before. The intense politicization was evident in the flood of printed material that streamed from American presses, generating controversy and heightening political awareness. Newspapers multiplied in number and gave vastly more attention to American news than they had before the Revolution began. Between 1750 and 1783, more than 1,500 pamphlets debated the imperial crisis, while countless others argued over what republicanism was to mean in state and nation. Declared one contemporary in amazement, it was

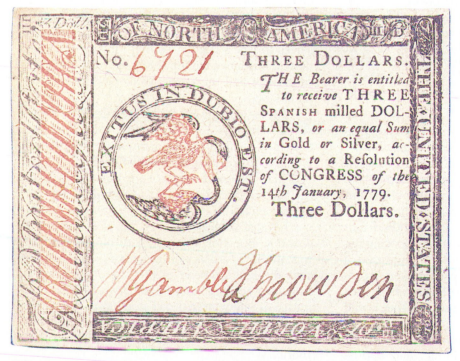

Lacking sufficient gold and silver to cover the escalating costs of war, Congress printed massive amounts of paper money, which rapidly depreciated in value.

In celebration of American independence, Patriots and their slaves toppled the statue of King George III that stood at Bowling Green in New York City.

a spectacle . . . without a parallel on earth. . . . Even a large portion of that class of the community which is destined to daily labor have free and constant access to public prints, receive regular information of every occurrence, [and] attend to the course of political affairs. Never . . . were [political pamphlets] . . . so cheap, so universally diffused, so easy of access.

Pulpits rocked with political exhortations as well. Religion and politics had never been sharply separated in colonial America, but the Revolution intensified their connection. America's separation from Great Britain fanned millennialist beliefs that God intended America as the place of Christ's Second Coming and that independence foretold that glorious day. Even Americans of less apocalyptic persuasions thought of America as a New Israel, a covenanted people specially chosen by God to preserve liberty in a threatening world. Samuel Adams called on Bostonians to create a society that would be a "Christian Sparta."

In countless recruiting and election day sermons, Congregational, Presbyterian, and Baptist clergy exhorted the American people to repent the sins that had caused God to visit English tyranny upon them and urged them to rededicate themselves to God's law by fighting for American freedom. It was language that everyone nurtured in Puritan piety and the Great Awakening instinctively understood.

The belief that God sanctioned their Revolution strengthened the resolve of Americans. It also encouraged them to equate national interest with divine intent and thus offered justification for whatever they believed necessary to do. This was not the last time that Americans would make that dangerous equation.

Loyalist Anglican clergy, such as Maryland's Jonathan Boucher, also mingled religion and politics, warning parishioners of their obligation to support the king as head of the church. During the months preceding independence, as the local Committee of Safety interrupted worship to harass him, Boucher carried a loaded pistol into the pulpit while he preached obedience and submission to royal authority.

Belief in the momentous importance of what they were doing intensified politics for the Revolutionary generation. John Adams, in a letter from Philadelphia to his wife, Abigail, as the Congress moved toward its fateful declaration, exalted independence as "the greatest question . . . which ever was debated in America, and a greater, perhaps, never has nor will be debated among men." This, he continued,

> will be the most memorable epocha in the history of America. . . . It ought to be commemorated as the day of deliverance, by solemn acts of devotion to God Almighty. It ought to be solemnized with pomp and parade, with shows, games, sports, guns, bells, bonfires, and illuminations, from one end of this continent to the other, from this time forward for evermore.

As independence was declared, people in towns and hamlets throughout the land raised toasts to the great event: "Liberty to those who have the spirit to preserve it." "May the Crowns of Tyrants be crowns of thorns." And "May Liberty expand sacred wings, and, in glorious effort, diffuse her influence o'er and o'er the globe."

They called themselves the Patriots of '76, a generation of Americans fused together by the searing experience of rebellion, war, and nation building. They believed themselves accountable for the fate of human liberty. Small wonder that they took politics so seriously or argued so passionately over Revolutionary affairs.

Mobilizing the People

The intensification of political life was evident in electoral behavior. In some states, nearly twice as many voters cast ballots as before. Elections were now more frequently contested and more often turned on issues of Revolutionary policy than on candidates' personality or social standing. Archibald Stuart of Virginia observed disapprovingly that "competition for seats in the House runs higher than ever it did under the old government."

Even more dramatic evidence of America's expanding Revolutionary politics appears in the array of extralegal committees and spontaneous gatherings that erupted across the states during the 1770s and 1780s. Electoral politics simply could not contain the political energies or resolve the political conflicts generated by the Revolution, and so people devised more direct forms of political action.

Earlier in the imperial crisis, people had frequently gathered "out of doors," that is, outside the regular processes of politics and government, to organize protests against measures like the Stamp Act (see Chapter 5). That practice accelerated as people formed committees and held meetings, sometimes with the approval of state authorities and sometimes without, to enforce nonimportation, regulate prices and wages, intimidate Loyalists, levy taxes, administer justice, and, as one individual protested, even direct "what we shall eat, drink, wear, speak, and think"—all on behalf of the Revolution.

More radical republicans celebrated such ac-

Ordinary men and women took to the streets in political rallies such as this mock parade of 1780 in Philadelphia, in which Benedict Arnold, an American general who deserted to the British, was burned in effigy.

tivity as the most direct and most legitimate expression of the popular will. More conservative republicans, however, believed that such behavior threatened political stability. Direct action by the people had been necessary in the struggle against England. But why such restlessness now when the threat of tyranny had disappeared and republican governments were in place? Even Thomas Paine was concerned. "It is time to have done with tarring and feathering," he wrote in 1777. "I never did and never would encourage what may properly be called a mob, when any legal mode of redress can be had."

This sudden and dramatic expansion of popular politics resulted naturally from the momentous process of rebellion and war. People took seriously all the talk about liberty, natural rights, and government by consent and applied those principles to their own lives. The outcome was a growing demand for access to the political process by artisans, workingmen, and farmers, people formerly on the margins of political life. In addition, Patriot leaders, recognizing the need for broad popular support, worked hard to organize committees of safety and correspondence as ways of stimulating popular participation.

The expanded activities of the new state governments also stimulated political participation. Independence freed those governments from the restraints of English law and administrative control, and the war vastly expanded their activities. As the fighting continued, the states had to tax and spend on an unprecedented scale, raise troops by the thousands for the militia and the continental army, control the Tories, regulate prices and wages, establish a stable money supply, and deal with the powerful issues of slavery and the relationship between church and state. It was a large and explosive political agenda.

The Limits of Citizenship

Revolutionary politics, however, was not open to everyone, for lawmakers imposed limits on who could claim the rights of republican citizenship. Those limits almost entirely excluded blacks and Native Americans.

Most Native Americans lived outside the boundaries of white society and politics, by mutual choice. The Revolution did nothing to change that. By the

standards of white society, Native Americans continued to be regarded as "uncivilized" and "savage," their systems of politics primitive and anarchic. After all, they had no written codes of law or legislative assemblies as "civilized" people did. Moreover, Native Americans had almost unanimously chosen to support England in the great struggle.

The Revolutionary generation admired Native Americans' reputation for bravery and their image as uncorrupted "children of nature." This appealed to white Americans' sense of their own innocence and virtue. The Indian woman became the earliest model for Columbia, the figure devised to represent the new American republic. Few people, however, thought seriously of including Native Americans in political life. The differences of culture and behavior were too great. Moreover, the tribes occupied the interior lands, lying between the Appalachians and the Mississippi, that the American people coveted. Obtaining that land would be easier if Indians could be dealt with as separate, dependent nations.

Nor did the Revolutionary generation seriously consider incorporating blacks into the political community. Certainly not black slaves, for they lacked the most essential attributes of republican citizenship—personal autonomy and political independence. Freedom and liberty, the watchwords of republicanism, had no relevance for people who were physically and legally enslaved.

But what of the growing number of free blacks in the northern states and the Chesapeake area? Unlike Native Americans, most free blacks lived within the boundaries of white society and were subject to the actions of state governments. In some states, such as Pennsylvania, New York, and North Carolina, blacks did occasionally vote. This was sometimes the inadvertent result of haste in constitution writing. The first draft of the Massachusetts constitution explicitly excluded blacks and mulattoes from the vote. When it was made public, Reverend William Gordon voiced his protest. "Would it not be ridiculous, inconsistent and unjust to exclude freemen from voting . . . though otherwise qualified, because their skins are black, tawny or reddish? Why not [be] disqualified for being long-nosed, short-faced, or higher or lower than five feet nine? A black, tawny or reddish skin is not so unfavorable a hue to the genuine son of liberty as a tory complexion." In the end, Massachusett's constitution made no mention of race, and during the 1780s a few blacks did cast ballots.

If black participation in the North was scattered and temporary, in the South it was altogether absent. Nor could blacks count on such basic rights of citizenship as protection of their persons and property before the law. No matter that most state constitutions explicitly guaranteed such rights. Blacks remained almost entirely without political voice, except in the petitions against slavery and mistreatment that they frequently pressed upon the state regimes.

Republican Women

The boundaries of republican politics were not even broad enough to include all white Americans. Only persons with property could vote because ownership of property was believed necessary to ensure a person's commitment to the local community and to support the independence of judgment that republican citizenship required. Most states reduced property requirements for the franchise, but nowhere were they abolished altogether. Even in Pennsylvania and Vermont, where political reform carried furthest, servants, dependent sons, and persons too poor to pay taxes could not vote.

Even more significant, republican citizenship did not encompass women. Except on scattered occasions, women had neither voted nor held public office during the colonial period. Nor, with rare exceptions, did they do so in Revolutionary America. The New Jersey constitution in 1776 opened the franchise to "all free inhabitants" meeting property and residency requirements. During the 1780s, a number of property-owning women participated in local elections. In 1790, the New Jersey assembly adopted an election law that explicitly referred to voters as "he or she," thus legitimating what had become common practice.

The experiment, however, did not last long. One political leader thought it "perfectly disgusting" to watch female voters cast their ballots. "It is evident," he asserted, "that women, generally, are neither by nature, nor habit, nor education . . . fitted to perform this duty with credit to themselves, or advantage to the public." In 1807, the New Jersey assembly concurred, passing a bill specifically disenfranchising women. Its author, John Condict, had several years earlier narrowly escaped defeat when a number of women voted for his opponent. In no other state did women even temporarily secure the vote.

Abigail Adams, like many women of the Revolutionary generation, protested the contradiction in men's subordination of women while they extolled the principles of liberty and equality.

Most women did not press for political equality, for the idea flew in the face of long-standing social convention, and its advocacy exposed a person to public ridicule. But some women did make the case, most often with each other or their husbands. "I cannot say, that I think you are very generous to the ladies," Abigail Adams chided her husband John. "For whilst you are proclaiming peace and good will to men, emancipating all nations, you insist upon retaining an absolute power over all wives." John consulted Abigail on many things but turned this admonition quickly aside. Not until the twentieth century would the female half of the American people secure that most basic attribute of republican citizenship, the vote.

Even though denied a formal political voice, women developed a new relationship to the public realm during the Revolution. Prior to independence, most women had accepted the principle that political debate fell outside the feminine sphere. Women, however, felt the urgency of the Revolutionary crisis as much as men. "How shall I impose a silence upon myself," wondered Anne Emlen in 1777, "when the subject is so very interesting, so much engrossing conversation—& what every member of the community is more or less concerned in?"

Not all women asked, as did she, for "divine prudence, which may prove a stay to my mind & a bridle to my tongue." With increasing frequency, women wrote and spoke to each other about public events, especially as they affected their own lives. Declared Eliza Wilkerson of South Carolina during the British invasion of 1780, "None were greater politicians than the several knots of ladies, who met together. All trifling discourses of fashions, and such low chat was thrown by, and we commenced perfect statesmen."

As the war progressed, increasing numbers of women ventured their opinions publicly. A few, such as Esther DeBerdt Reed of Philadelphia, published essays explaining women's urgent need to contribute to the Patriot cause. In her 1780 broadside "The Sentiments of an American Woman," she declared that women were determined to do more than offer "barren wishes" for the Revolution's success. Instead, they wanted to be "useful," like "those heroines of antiquity, who have rendered their sex illustrious." Anyone denying women that opportunity, she insisted, was not "a good citizen."

Reed called on women to renounce "vain ornament" as they had earlier renounced tea and English finery. The money no longer spent on clothing and hairstyles would be "the offering of the Ladies" to Washington's army. Within two weeks, a group of middle- and upper-class Philadelphia women outlined an organization whose purpose was nothing less than the mobilization of the nation's entire female population. The project never materialized, but in several places women traveling in pairs canvassed neighborhoods, requesting offerings from "each woman and girl without any distinction." In Philadelphia, they collected $300,000 in continental currency from over 1,600 individuals. Refusing Washington's proposal that the money be mixed with general funds in the national treasury, they insisted on using it to purchase materials for shirts so that each soldier might know he had received a contribution specifically from the women.

In the Revolutionary context, traditional female roles took on new political meanings. With English imports cut off and the army badly in need of clothing, spinning and weaving assumed increased importance. Often coming together as Daughters of Liberty, women made shirts, stockings, and other items of clothing. Charity Clarke, a New York teenager who knitted "stockens" for the soldiers, acknowledged that she "felt Nationaly." Though "heroines may not distinguish themselves at the head of an army," she informed an English cousin, women

The outpouring of political broadsides issuing from American presses during the Revolutionary War gave evidence of women's activism as well as men's. This notice, dated 1770, calls for "tea-drinking ladies of New York" to reject the imported brew.

could still contribute to America's defense. A "fighting army of amazons . . . armed with spinning wheels" would emerge in America. "Though this body is not clad with silken garments," she concluded, "these limbs are armed with strength, the soul is fortified by virtue, and the love of liberty is cherished within this bosom."

Finally, the most traditional of female roles, the care and nurture of children, also took on political overtones during the Revolutionary era. How could the republic be sustained once independence had been won? Only by a rising generation of republican citizens schooled in the principles of public virtue and ready to assume the task. How would they be prepared? During their earliest years by their republican mothers, the women of the Revolution.

In a variety of ways, women developed new connections with the public realm during the Revolutionary years. Those connections remained limited, for the assumption that politics and government belonged to men did not die easily. But challenges to that assumption would come, and when they did, women found guidance in the principles that the women of the Revolution had helped to define.

REVOLUTIONARY POLITICS IN THE STATES

While the struggle for independence continued, revolutionary politics centered in the states, for the state governments were most active in people's lives. The Congress, lacking both authority and the power to govern effectively, and elected indirectly by state legislatures rather than directly by the people, seemed to most Americans remote and largely irrelevant. Not until a new central government began to operate under the national constitution of 1788 would popular politics begin to develop at the national level.

Revolutionary politics took different forms in different states, depending on the impact of the war, the extent of Loyalism, patterns of social conflict, and the disruptions of economic change. In some states, Pennsylvania and Vermont, for example, political change ran deep, while in others, such as Connecticut and Virginia, change was more muted. In each of the states, though, citizens struggled with a bewildering and often intractable array of issues. Defining republican liberty, controlling governmental power, deciding who would share political power, finding a balance between individual liberty

and public order—these were the problems with which people wrestled. Nothing revealed more clearly the clash of ideology and interest than the struggle over new state constitutions.

Creating Republican Governments

With the decision for independence, no legally established governments existed in any of the 13 states, for the colonial regimes drew their legitimacy from their royal charters. Now those charters and the royal authority that supported them had been cast aside. Americans knew that fashioning new republican governments of their own would be difficult. One person thought it the "most difficult and dangerous business" they had to do.

When independence finally came, they set about the business of government making in earnest. Connecticut and Rhode Island continued under their colonial charters, simply deleting all references to the British crown. The other 11 states, however, set their charters aside and started anew. Within two years, all but Massachusetts had completed the task. By 1780, it had done so as well.

The work was not easy, for the American people had no experience with government making on such a scale. And these neophytes had to rebuild their governments while embroiled in war. Moreover, they were sharply divided over the kind of government they wished to create. In the debates over the new state constitutions, political divisions that had been simmering during the prewar decades burst through the surface of political life.

Given the promptings of republican theory and their own recent experience with England, the Revolutionary generation began with two overriding concerns: to limit the powers of government and to hold government officials accountable. The only certain way of accomplishing these goals was by creating a fundamental law, in the form of a written constitution, that could serve as a standard for regulating governmental behavior.

In most states, the provincial congresses, extralegal successors to the defunct colonial assemblies, wrote the first constitutions. This seemed easiest, for the congresses had been elected by the people and were regarded as representing the popular will. As the process went along, however, people became increasingly uneasy. Constitutions were intended to define and control government, but if government-like bodies wrote the documents, they could change them as well. If they could do that,

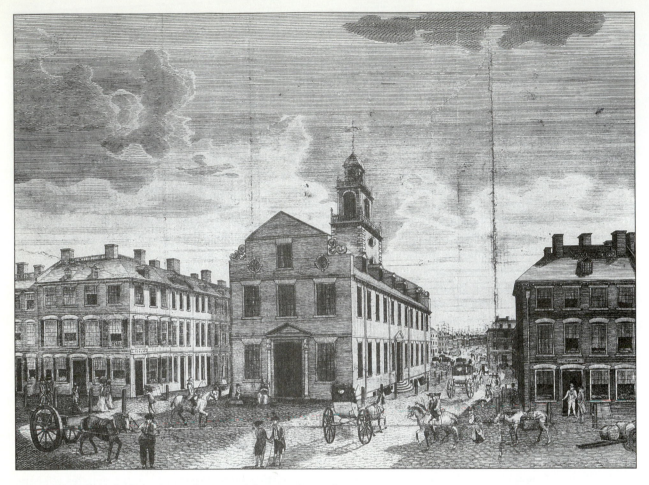

Massachusetts was the first state to elect a special convention to draw up a new constitution. The new government met in the old colonial statehouse, along with the town officials, courts, and the Merchants' Exchange.

what would guarantee against the abuse of governmental power? Some way had to be found of grounding the constitutions directly in the people's sovereign will.

Massachusetts was the first state to perfect the new procedures. In 1778, its citizens rejected a proposed constitution, in part because the provincial congress had drawn it up. A year later, the congress asked the voters to elect a special constitutional convention for the sole purpose of preparing a new and more satisfactory document. Elections were held, the convention did its work, and the resulting constitution was returned to the people for ratification, this time successfully.

Through trial and argumentation, the Revolu-

tionary generation worked out a practical understanding of what a constitution was and how it should be developed. In the process, it established some of the most basic doctrines of American constitutionalism: that sovereignty resides in the people; that written constitutions, produced by specially elected conventions and then ratified by the people, embody their sovereign will; and that government comes into being only after a constitution has been created and functions according to its terms. No doctrines have been more important to the preservation of American liberty.

The new state constitutions redefined American government in fundamental and lasting ways. For one thing, the new governments were considerably more democratic than the colonial regimes had been. Gone were the crown's appointed officials: governors, councillors, and customs officers. Most officials were now elected, many of them annually rather than every two or three years as before.

Just as important, most of the new constitutions sharply reduced the governors' powers and increased the powers of the assemblies. "The executive power," warned one commentator, "is ever restless, ambitious, and grasping at increases." He had in mind both the king and the royally appointed colonial governors. Above all, the documents sharply reduced the governors' powers of appointment. "He who has the giving of . . . places in the government," went the common refrain, "will always be master."

The assemblies absorbed most of the powers stripped from the governors. Not only were the assemblies more powerful, but they were larger and more representative as well. Reflecting the spirit of republican reform as well as the demands of farmers and artisans for a larger voice in public affairs, the assemblies grew in size by half or more.

Changes in attitudes toward representation further reduced the distance between government and citizens. Prior to the Revolution, most voters believed that assemblymen, once elected, should have considerable independence. This reflected the prevailing notion that public office was primarily the domain of the "better sort"—persons of wealth and experience who knew best what to do.

The Revolution transformed the relationship between rulers and ruled. Inspired by republican beliefs and concerned increasingly about governmental power, people came to view their representatives not as independent agents acting on their behalf but as direct extensions of the people's will. Vigilance, even outright suspicion of officials' behavior, became the hallmark of the true republican.

Different Paths to the Republican Goal

Constitution making generated considerable controversy, for there was strong disagreement about how democratic the new governments should be. Conservatives such as James Duane of New York, wanted the new governments to resemble the colonial regimes, allowing only for the most necessary republican changes. More radical republicans, how-

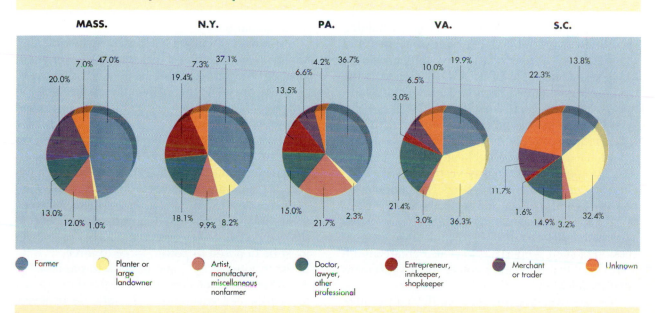

Occupational Composition of Several State Assemblies in the 1780s

MASS. — 47.0%, 7.0%, 20.0%, 13.0%, 12.0%, 1.0%

N.Y. — 37.1%, 7.3%, 19.4%, 18.1%, 9.9%, 8.2%

PA. — 36.7%, 4.2%, 6.6%, 13.5%, 15.0%, 21.7%, 2.3%

VA. — 19.9%, 10.0%, 6.5%, 3.0%, 21.4%, 3.0%, 36.3%

S.C. — 13.8%, 22.3%, 11.7%, 1.6%, 14.9%, 3.2%, 32.4%

Legend: Farmer • Planter or large landowner • Artist, manufacturer, miscellaneous nonfarmer • Doctor, lawyer, other professional • Entrepreneur, innkeeper, shopkeeper • Merchant or trader • Unknown

Source: Main, *Political Parties Before the Constitution*, 1973.

ever, sought to redistribute political power and build the principle of political equality into the very structure of the new regimes. Two examples, Pennsylvania and Massachusetts, illustrate how different the outcomes could be.

In Pennsylvania, a coalition of western farmers, Philadelphia artisans and shopkeepers, and radical leaders such as Thomas Paine, Timothy Matlack, and Thomas Young pushed through the most democratic state constitution of all. Drafted less than three months after independence, during the most intense period of republican reform, it rejected the familiar English model of a mixed and balanced government consisting of two legislative houses and an independent executive. Such complexity, radicals argued, had always protected the power of monarchs and aristocrats and robbed the people of their liberties. Republican governments, by contrast, should be simple, easily understood, and directly responsive to the people.

The architects of Pennsylvania's constitution provided for a single, all-powerful legislative house, its members elected annually, its debates open to the public. There was to be no governor. Legislative committees would assume executive duties. A truly radical assumption underlay this design: that only the "common interest of society" and not "separate and jarring private interests" should be represented in public affairs. There should therefore be neither separate governor nor upper legislative house to balance against the popular will. Property-holding requirements for public office were abolished, and the franchise was opened to every white male over 21 who paid taxes. The bill of rights introducing the document guaranteed every citizen religious freedom, trial by jury, and freedom of speech.

The most radical proposal of all called for the redistribution of property within the state as a step essential to preserving republican liberty. "An enormous proportion of property vested in a few individuals," declared the proposed constitution, "is dangerous to the rights, and destructive of the common happiness of mankind; and therefore every free state hath a right by its laws to discourage the possession of such property." No clause created more alarm, and Pennsylvania's conservatives just managed to defeat it.

Debate over the constitution divided the state deeply. Opponents, led by men of wealth, condemned the document's supporters as "coffee-house demagogues" and "political upstarts" and accused them of wanting a "tyranny of the people." The constitution's proponents—tradesmen, farmers, and other small producers—shot back that their critics were "the rich and great men and the wise men, the lawyers and doctors," who thought they had no "common interest with the body of the people."

In 1776, the radicals had their way, for the Pennsylvania constitution—together with its counterparts in Vermont and Georgia—represented the most radical thrust of Revolutionary republicanism. Its guiding principle, declared Thomas Young, one of the constitution's most ardent supporters, was that "the people at large [are] the true proprietors of governmental power." The struggle for control of the Revolution in Pennsylvania was not over, for in 1790 a considerably more moderate document would replace this one. For the moment, however, the lines of political power had been decisively redrawn in Pennsylvania.

In Massachusetts, constitution making followed a different path. There the disruptions of the war were less severe and the continuity of political leadership and control much greater. Though the Revolution brought western farmers and Boston artisans into state politics, it did not dramatically alter the balance of political power. As a consequence, the new Massachusetts constitution embodied a more cautious vision of what republican government should be.

The main architect of the constitution, John Adams, readily admitted that the new government must be firmly grounded in the people. "All power," he wrote, "residing originally in the people and being derived from them, the several magistrates and officers of government . . . are their subordinates and agents, and are at all times accountable to them." No principle was more fundamental to America's new republican faith. Yet Adams urged moderation in forming the new government. He saw danger in reckless experimentation. A balance between two legislative houses and an independent executive were essential to preserve liberty, for "power must be opposed to power, force to force, . . . interest to interest, . . . and passion to passion."

Adams had something else in mind in arguing for a balanced government. Society, he believed, was inescapably divided between "democratic" and "aristocratic" forces. Believing that each was dan-

As the role of government changed and political involvement by the citizens increased, state capitols, such as Pennsylvania's statehouse (later called Independence Hall), became the focus of intense political activity.

gerous if dominant, Adams sought to isolate them in separate legislative houses where they could guard against each other. The assembly, he explained, should be "an exact portrait, in miniature" of the people; it should "think, feel, act, and reason" like them. The senate, by contrast, should constitute a "natural aristocracy" of wealth, talent, and good sense. Following Adams's advice, the Massachusetts convention provided for a popular, annually elected assembly and a senate based on wealth, its members apportioned according to the amount of taxes paid in special senatorial districts. Since the senators' function was to balance the popular excesses of the assembly and look after the interests of property and social position, they were required to own three times as much property as assemblymen were. The Massachusetts constitution also provided for an independent governor with the power to veto legislation, make appointments, serve as commander in chief of the militia, and oversee state expenditures.

On March 2, 1779, the convention sent the document to the town meetings for approval. Farmers of the interior and artisans and working people of Boston attacked it as too "aristocratic," too much like the old colonial regime. The citizens of Richmond feared that the property requirement for the franchise would "exclude many good members of society." Only "misbehavior" or "vicious conduct" should deprive a person of the "free liberty to vote." Given the impact of the war on ordinary people's lives and the increasing number of the poor, warned the citizens of Dorchester, disfranchisement under the proposed constitution "may increase in such proportion, that one half the people of this commonwealth will have no choice in any branch of the general court."

The inhabitants of Petersham feared that with a strong governor, "the rich and powerful men . . . will act in competition with each other and spread the corruption that naturally flows from bribery and undue influence." A "republican monarch," they protested, should have no place in the new system. Controversy erupted as well over the senate's special character as the defender of property and social standing.

No complete tally of the towns' responses was ever taken. But when the convention reconvened in July 1779, it declared the constitution approved, and it went into effect the following year. In spite of the many objections, it was enough for the moment simply to have a new, republican government in place.

Separating Church and State

Another issue generating political controversy was the explosive question of the proper relationship between church and state in a republican order. In most of the colonies prior to the Revolution, one religious group had enjoyed the benefits of endorsement by the government and public tax support for its clergy. At the time of independence, these religious establishments were no longer as restrictive as they once had been. In each of the colonies, "dissenting" groups such as the Methodists and the Baptists were increasing in numbers, especially among the lower classes of city and countryside. Though authorities did not encourage them, they did allow them to function. As the dissenters pointed out, however, toleration was not the same as religious freedom, for that required the complete separation of church and state and the guarantee that conscience, not compulsion, would govern religious life.

With independence, pressure built for severing church and state completely. Republican theory warned that such alliances had been instruments of oppression throughout history and urged voluntary choice as the only safe basis for religious association. Even before independence, Rhode Island, New Jersey, Pennsylvania, and Delaware had established full religious liberty. In five additional states, the Anglican church collapsed when English support was withdrawn.

In Massachusetts, Connecticut, and New Hampshire, the Congregationalists fought to retain their long-established privileges. To separate church and state, they argued, was to invite infidelity and disorder. Isaac Backus, the most outspoken of New England Baptists, challenged that assumption. Building a drumfire of criticism against the Congregational order, he protested that "many, who are filling the nation with the cry of *liberty* and against oppressors are at the same time themselves violating that dearest of all rights, *liberty of conscience*."

Massachusetts's new constitution guaranteed everyone the right to worship God "in the manner and season most agreeable to the dictates of his own conscience." But as Backus pointed out, it also empowered the legislature to require towns to lay taxes for "the public worship of *God,* and for the support and maintenance of public protestant teachers of piety, religion, and morality."

This nineteenth-century print says it gives "A Correct View of the Old Methodist Church in John Street, New York. The first erected in America. Founded A.D. 1768." Methodists and Baptists were among the "dissenting" groups pressing for full religious freedom.

The citizens of Granville protested as well, denying that the people "have a right to invest their legislature with a power to interfere in matters that properly belong to the Christian Church." During the decades following independence, New England's Congregational establishment continued to weaken. But not until the early nineteenth century—in Massachusetts not until 1833—were the laws linking church and state finally repealed.

In Virginia, the Baptists pressed their cause against the Protestant Episcopal church, successor to the Church of England. Fighting to retain their special privileges, the Episcopalians proposed in 1784 a "general tax assessment" to be distributed among all Christian churches. Even that cautious proposal failed. In 1786, the adoption of Thomas Jefferson's Bill for Establishing Religious Freedom, rejecting all connections between church and state and removing all religious tests for public office, finally settled the issue. Three years later, that statute served as a model for the First Amendment to the new federal Constitution.

Even most supporters of religious freedom, however, were not prepared to extend it universally, limiting it typically to "Christians" or "Protestants." The people of Northbridge, Massachusetts, while opposing the Congregational establishment, wanted to prevent "Roman Catholics pagons or Mahomitents from having any seat in government, from which the People of God have so much suffred in past ages." Legal disestablishment did not end religious discrimination. But it did implant firmly the principle of religious liberty in American constitutional law.

Loyalists and the Public Safety

Emotions ran high between Patriots and Loyalists in Revolutionary America. "The rage of civil discord," lamented one individual, "hath advanced among us with an astonishing rapidity. The son is armed against the father, the brother against the brother, family against family." The security, perhaps the very survival of the republic required stern measures against counterrevolutionaries. Security, however, was not the only motive at work, for the Patriots were also determined to exact revenge on those whose "disloyalty" threatened the Revolutionary cause.

During the war, each of the states passed a series of laws to control the Loyalist menace. In 1778, the Georgia assembly declared 117 persons guilty of treason, banished them from the state upon pain of death, and declared their possessions subject to seizure and sale. Four years later, the assembly extended the act to anyone "deemed responsible" for committing "murder, rapine, and devastation" during the recent British occupation.

In 1776, the Connecticut assembly passed a remarkably punitive law threatening anyone who criticized either the assembly or the Continental Congress with immediate fine and imprisonment. In every state, individuals whose Revolutionary fervor was suspect were publicly forced to forswear loyalty to the crown and pledge allegiance to the new regime. Those who refused lost both the vote and the protection of the law. Probably not more than a few dozen Tories died at the hands of the Revolutionary regimes, but many others died in combat, and thousands found their livelihoods destroyed, their families ostracized, and themselves subject to physical attack.

Punishing Loyalists—or persons accused of loyalism—was a popular activity, especially since Loyalists were most numerous among the upper classes. Yet for many of the more conservative Patriots, troublesome questions surfaced. How safe would anyone's property be if some people's property was confiscated and sold? Did not American liberty rest on the principle that property rights were fundamental to all others? And were not everyone's rights threatened when the rights of some were disregarded, especially when it was often difficult to tell who actually was a Loyalist and who was not?

The continuing eruption of mob activity was equally disturbing. Some Patriots tried to distinguish between "public mobs," which punished enemies of the people, and "private mobs," which took advantage of public commotion to settle personal scores. The distinction, however, was not easily sustained. Caught up in the Revolution's turmoil, many argued that the Loyalists had put themselves outside the protection of American law. Others worried about the implications of setting aside the protections of the law, even for Loyalists. Republics, after all, were supposed to be "governments of law, and not of men." Once that distinction disappeared, no one would be safe.

After the war ended and passions cooled, most states repealed their anti-Tory legislation. In the midst of the Revolution, however, no issue raised more clearly the troubling question of how to balance individual liberty against the needs of public security. That question would return to trouble the nation in the future.

Slavery Under Attack

The place of human slavery in a republican society also vexed the Revolutionary generation. During the several decades preceding the imperial crisis, the trade in human chattels had flourished. Though several northern colonies abolished the slave trade, the 1760s witnessed the largest importations of slaves in colonial history.

The Revolution halted that trade almost completely. Once the war ended, southern planters sought to replace their lost slaves. In South Carolina and Georgia, the traffic continued well into the nineteenth century. Elsewhere, however, the revival was of short duration. Revolutionary principles, reduced need for fieldhands in the depressed tobacco economy, continuing natural increase in the slave population, and post-Revolutionary anxiety over black rebelliousness argued for the slave trade's extinction. By 1790, every state except South Carolina and Georgia had outlawed slave importations.

The consequences would be profound in the nineteenth century when the demand for slave labor, fueled by the soaring expansion of cotton agriculture, created an internal slave trade between the old colonial Chesapeake region and the boom areas of Mississippi and Alabama. That forced migration would affect the lives of thousands of black Americans and exacerbate sectional tensions between North and South.

Just as important, termination of the slave trade reduced the infusion of new Africans into the black population. This meant that over time an ever higher proportion of blacks were American-born and had no personal recollection of the African homeland, thus speeding the process of cultural transformation by which Africans became Afro-Americans.

The institution of slavery itself also came under attack during the Revolutionary era, with immense consequences for both blacks and the nation's future. Public criticism of slavery began even before independence. As the crisis with England heated up, catchwords such as *liberty* and *tyranny,* employed by colonists protesting British policies, reminded citizens that one-fifth of the colonial population was in chains. Writers on both sides of the imperial argument pointed out the contradiction of building a society on slave labor while protesting Britain's violation of human rights. Samuel Hopkins, a New England clergyman, chided his compatriots for "making a vain parade of being advocates for the liberties of mankind, while . . . you at the same time are continuing this lawless, cruel, inhuman, and abominable practice of enslaving your fellow creatures." Independence brought intensified attacks.

In South Carolina and Georgia, where blacks outnumbered whites more than two to one, slavery escaped significant challenge. Committed to the doctrine of racial superiority and fearing the black majority, whites shuddered at the prospect of black freedom. Moreover, slave labor remained essential to the rice economy. In response to the dangers generated by the war, whites wound the local slave codes even tighter.

In Virginia and Maryland, by contrast, whites argued openly over slavery's incompatibility with republicanism, and change did occur. The depression in the tobacco economy made the debate easier. Though neither state abolished slavery, both passed laws making it easier for owners to free their slaves. Moreover, increasing numbers of blacks petitioned for their own freedom, purchased it from their masters, or simply fled. By 1800, more than one of every ten blacks in the Chesapeake region was free, a dramatic increase over 30 years before.

The majority lived and worked in Baltimore, Richmond, and other towns, where they formed communities that became centers of an expanding Afro-American society and culture and havens for runaway slaves from the countryside. For blacks in the Chesapeake region, the conditions of life slowly changed for the better.

The most dramatic breakthroughs occurred in the North. There slavery was either abolished or put on the road to extinction. Abolition was easier in the North because there were fewer slaves. In most areas, they constituted no more than 4 percent of the population. Slavery thus did not have the economic or social importance that it did in the South.

Northern blacks joined in the attack on slavery. Following independence, they frequently petitioned the state assemblies for their freedom. "Every Principle from which America has acted in the course of their unhappy difficulties with Great Britain," declared one group of Philadelphia blacks, "pleads stronger than a thousand arguments in favor of our petition."

Pennsylvania acted first, in response to both black initiatives and the promptings of radical leaders in the state government. In 1780, the Pennsylvania assembly passed a law stipulating that all newborn blacks were to be free when they reached age 28. It was a cautious but decisive step. In the decades ahead, other northern states adopted similar policies of gradual emancipation.

Opposition to slavery was not necessarily accompanied by a commitment to racial equality. Even as freemen, blacks continued to encounter pervasive discrimination. Still, remarkable progress had been made. Prior to the Revolution, slavery had been an accepted fact of northern life; after the Revolution, it no longer was. The change made a vast difference in the lives of countless black Americans.

The abolition of slavery in the North also increased the sectional divergence between North and South. The consequences of that divergence would become more apparent in the nineteenth century. In addition, there now existed a coherent and publicly proclaimed antislavery argument, one closely linked in Americans' minds with the nation's founding. The first antislavery organizations had been created as well. Although another half century would pass before antislavery became a force in national political life, the groundwork for slavery's final abolition had been laid.

Politics and the Economy

Revolutionary politics also had to deal with the economic disruptions of independence and war. Price and wage inflation, skyrocketing taxation, mushrooming private and public debt—all demanded attention. As the war progressed, state governments increased their spending dramatically, and the public debt soared. Managing this debt during the war and struggling to reduce it afterward posed a continuing dilemma.

That dilemma centered on heated debates over whether the debt should be funded at face value or at some reduced rate. In support of full value were the states' major creditors—merchants and other persons of wealth—who had loaned the states money and had bought up large amounts of securities at deep discounts. These people spoke earnestly of upholding the public honor and giving fair return to those who had committed their own resources at critical moments to the cause.

The issue of taxation, seared into Americans' consciousness by their troubles with England, generated even more heated controversy. No governmental power more alarmed the Revolutionary generation, for none offered greater potential for abuse. As the costs of the war mounted, so did the tax burden. Between 1774 and 1778, Massachusetts levied a total of £408,976 in taxes, a dramatic increase over colonial days. Between 1783 and 1786, as the state struggled to reduce its accumulated debt, assessments jumped again, to £662,476. Taxes, complained one anguished soul, equaled nearly one-third of the inhabitants' incomes. And Massachusetts was not unique.

As taxes rose, so did clashes over tax policy. Farmers, artisans, and others of modest means argued that taxes should be payable in depreciated paper money or government securities rather than only in specie, as some state laws required. Most of them had no gold or silver coin and thus faced the prospect of having their property foreclosed when they could not meet their tax obligations. Government officials protested that to allow payment in depreciated paper was to deprive the governments of badly needed revenue.

People also argued over how the staggering tax burden should be apportioned. In the New York assembly, men of property urged continuing dependence on the poll tax, a uniform assessment levied on all males 16 years of age and older. Working people, however, protested the inequity of a tax that fell on everyone equally, arguing that taxes should bear some relationship to people's ability to pay. As the demand for public revenue increased, pressure for taxing property rather than people grew. The change, however, was bitterly contested.

Merchants and shopkeepers argued that agricultural property—land, crops, livestock—should bear the primary burden of taxation. Farmers replied that commercial goods such as ships, store inventories, and money on loan should carry the load. The stakes were high for everyone.

Controversy swirled around the states' efforts to control soaring prices as well. Each of the states experimented with price controls at one time or another. Seldom were such efforts effective; always they generated political storms.

In general, the poor and those not yet integrated into the market economy supported price controls. Faced with escalating prices, they had difficulty simply making ends meet. Such people, moreover, continued to believe that buying and selling had moral and social dimensions, for they involved intensely personal, face-to-face negotiations among neighbors. These notions of a "moral economy" were guided by the doctrine of a "just price," a price not determined by the attempt to maximize profit but one deemed fair to buyer and seller alike. Government had a responsibility to regulate prices for the public good. In keeping with these principles, a crowd in New Windsor, New York, in 1777 seized a shipment of tea bound for Albany and sold it for what they deemed a fair price.

Merchants, shopkeepers, and others caught up in the commercial economy, however, looked at things differently. For them, the exchange of goods and services was primarily an economic transaction and should be controlled only by the laws of supply and demand. "It is contrary to the nature of commerce," declared Benjamin Franklin, "for government to interfere in the prices of commodities." Attempts to regulate prices only created a disincentive to labor, which was "the principal part of the wealth of every country."

The economic agenda of Revolutionary politics proved both divisive and intractable. There were no ready solutions to the problems of debt, taxation, and price control. Such issues often defied understanding, lay beyond the reach of state action, and exceeded the capacity of politics for compromise and resolution. Thus they continued on the public agenda through the 1780s, heightening political tensions.

CONCLUSION

The Crucible of Revolution

Independence and war together redrew the contours of American life and changed the destinies of the American people. Though the Revolutionary War ended in victory, liberty had its costs. Lives were lost, property was destroyed, local economies were deranged. The war changed relationships between Indians and whites, for it left the Iroquois and Cherokee severely weakened and opened the floodgates of western expansion. For black Americans, the Revolution had paradoxical results. It produced an ideology that decried slavery of all sorts and marked the first general debate over abolishing the oppressive institution. Yet the Revolutionary generation took steps to eradicate slavery only where it was least important, in the North, while guaranteeing its future in the South where it was most important.

By 1783 a new nation had come into being where none had existed before, a nation based not on age-encrusted principles of monarchy and privilege but on the doctrines of republican liberty. That was the greatest change of all. The political transformations set in motion, however, were the subjects of angry disputes whose outcomes could only be dimly foreseen. Thomas Paine put the matter succinctly: "The answer to the question, can America be happy under a government of her own, is short and simple —as happy as she pleases; she hath a blank sheet to write upon." The years immediately ahead would determine whether the republican experiment, launched with such hopefulness in 1776, would succeed.

Recommended Reading

Standard accounts of the Revolutionary War can be found in Don Higginbotham, The War of American Independence *(1971), and Robert Middlekauff,* The Glorious Cause *(1982). In A* People Numerous and Armed *(1976), John Shy deals with the social dimensions of military conflict, while Charles Royster,* A Revolutionary People at War *(1979), explains how the continental army embodied the Revolution's social and ideological goals. Richard Morris,* The Peacemakers: The Great Powers and American Independence *(1965) and Jonathan Dull, A Diplomatic History of the American Revolution (1985), offer skillful discussions of Revolutionary War diplomacy.*

The most vivid description of Native American involvement in the Revolution can be found in Anthony Wallace, The Death and Rebirth of the Seneca *(1969). James O'Donnell discusses the situation in the Southeast in* Southern Indians in the American Revolution *(1973). Several books offer starting points for further examination of the tangled history of slavery, race, and the Revolution: Winthrop Jordan,* White over Black: American Attitudes Toward the Negro, 1550–1812 *(1968); Duncan MacLeod,* Slavery, Race, and the American Revolution *(1974); Ira Berlin and Ronald Hoffman, eds.,* Slavery and Freedom in the Age of the American Revolution *(1983); and Jeffrey Crow,* The Black Experience in Revolutionary North Carolina *(1977).*

Three excellent books examine the Revolutionary experience of women: Linda Kerber, Women of the Republic *(1980); Mary Beth Norton,* Liberty's Daughters *(1980); and Joy Buel and Richard Buel,* The Way of Duty: A Woman and Her Family in Revolutionary America *(1984). Robert Calhoon,* The Loyalists in Revolutionary America, 1760–1781 *(1973), and Mary Beth Norton,* The British-Americans: The Loyalist Exiles in England, 1774–1789 *(1972), deal with the experiences of Loyalist Americans. Robert Gross,* The Minutemen and Their World *(1976), offers a vivid portrayal of the Revolution's impact on the daily lives of ordinary people in Concord, Massachusetts. The essays in Jeffrey Crow and Larry Tise, eds.,* The Southern Experience in the American Revolution *(1978), offer similar insights for the South. See also Bar-*

bara Smith, After the Revolution: The History of Everyday Life in the Eighteenth Century (1985). Thomas Doerflinger, A Vigorous Spirit of Enterprise (1986), describes the Revolution's economic impact on Philadelphia.

For further information about the ideology of Revolutionary republicanism, see Bernard Bailyn, The Ideological Origins of the American Revolution (1967), and Morton White, The Philosophy of the American Revolution (1978).

State constitution making is discussed in many of the books listed, but see especially Gordon Wood, The Creation of the American Republic, 1776–1787 (1969), and Willi Paul Adams, The First American Constitutions (1980). The writing on Revolutionary state politics is rich and exciting. Among the most important books are Ronald Hoffman, A Spirit of Dissension: Economics, Politics and the Revolution in Maryland (1973); Edward Countryman, A People in Revolution: The American Revolution and Political Society in New York, 1760–1790 (1981); and Eric Foner, Tom Paine and Revolutionary America (1976).

Among many readable biographical accounts are Pauline Maier, The Old Revolutionaries: Political Lives in the Age of Samuel Adams (1980); Norman Risjord, Representative Americans: The Revolutionary Generation (1980); Fawn Brodie, Thomas Jefferson: An Intimate History (1974); Gerald Stourzh, Alexander Hamilton and the Idea of Republican Government (1970); Claude Lopez and Eugenia Herbert, The Private Franklin: The Man and His Family (1975); Peter Shaw, The Character of John Adams (1976); and Marcus Cunliffe, George Washington: Man and Monument (1958).

TIME LINE

1775 Lord Dunmore's proclamation to slaves and servants in Virginia
Iroquois Six Nations pledge neutrality
Continental Congress urges "states" to establish new governments

1776 British evacuate Boston and seize New York City
Declaration of Independence
Eight states draft constitutions
Cherokee raids and American retaliation

1777 British occupy Philadelphia
Most Iroquois join the British
Americans win victory at Saratoga
Washington's army winters at Valley Forge

1778 War shifts to the South
Savannah falls to British
French treaty of alliance and commerce

1779 Massachusetts state constitutional convention
Sullivan destroys Iroquois villages in New York

1780 Massachusetts constitution ratified
Charleston surrenders to British
Pennsylvania begins gradual abolition of slavery

1780s Virginia and Maryland debate abolition of slavery
Destruction of Iroquois Confederacy

1781 Cornwallis surrenders at Yorktown
Articles of Confederation ratified by states

1783 Peace Treaty with England signed in Paris
Massachusetts Supreme Court abolishes slavery
King's Commission on American Loyalists begins work

7

Consolidating the Revolution

Timothy Bloodworth of New Hanover County, North Carolina, knew what the American Revolution was about, for he had experienced it firsthand. A man of humble origins, Bloodworth had known poverty as a child. Lacking any formal education, he had worked hard and successfully during the middle decades of the eighteenth century as an innkeeper and ferry pilot, self-styled preacher and physician, blacksmith and farmer. By the mid-1770s, he owned nine slaves and 4,200 acres of land, considerably more than most of his neighbors.

His unpretentious manner and commitment to political equality earned Bloodworth the confidence of his community. In 1758, at the age of only 22, he was elected to the North Carolina colonial assembly. Over the next three decades, he remained deeply involved in North Carolina's political life.

When the colonies' troubles with England drew toward a crisis, Bloodworth spoke ardently of American rights and mobilized support for independence. In 1775, he helped form the Wilmington Committee of Safety. Filled with Revolutionary fervor, he urged forward the process of republican political reform and, as commissioner of confiscated property for the district of Wilmington, pressed the attack on local Loyalists.

In 1784, shortly after the war ended, the North Carolina assembly named Bloodworth one of the state's delegates to the Confederation Congress. There he learned for the first time about the problems of governing a new nation. As the Congress struggled through the middle years of the 1780s with the relentless problems of foreign trade, war debt, and control of the trans-Appalachian interior, Bloodworth shared the growing conviction that the Articles of Confederation were too weak. He supported the Congress's call for a special convention to meet in Philadelphia in May 1787 for the purpose of considering matters necessary "to render the constitution of the federal government adequate to the exigencies of the Union."

Like thousands of Americans, Bloodworth eagerly awaited the convention's work. And like countless Americans, he was stunned by the result, for the proposed constitution seemed to him designed not to preserve republican liberty but to endanger it.

Once again sniffing political tyranny on the breeze, Bloodworth resigned his congressional seat in August 1787 and hurried back to North Carolina to help organize opposition to the proposed constitution. Over the next several years, he worked tirelessly for its defeat.

Opposing the proposal to grant Congress the power of taxation, Bloodworth protested, "We cannot consent to the adoption of a Constitution whose revenues lead to aristocratic tyranny, or monarchical despotism, and open a door wide as fancy can point, for the introduction of dissipation, bribery and corruption to the exclusion of public virtue." Had Americans so quickly forgotten the dangers of consolidated power, he wondered? Were they ready to turn their backs on their brief experiment in republicanism?

A national government as strong as the one described in the proposed constitution, he feared, would gobble up the states, remove power from the people's control, and destroy individual liberties. Alarmed by the provision that Congress "may at any time by law make or alter" state regulations concerning elections and by the absence of explicit guarantees of trial by jury, Bloodworth demanded the addition of a federal bill of rights to protect individual liberties. Echoing the language of Revolutionary republicanism, he warned on the floor of the North Carolina ratifying convention, "Without the most express restrictions, Congress may trample on your rights. Every possible precaution should be taken when we grant powers. Rulers are always disposed to abuse them."

Bloodworth also feared the sweeping authority Congress would have "to make all laws which shall be necessary and proper for carrying into execution . . . all other powers vested . . . in the government of the United States." That language, he insisted, threatened "to sweep off all the constitutions of the states. . . . It will produce an abolition of the state governments. Its sovereignty absolutely annihilates them."

In North Carolina, the arguments of Bloodworth and his Anti-Federalist colleagues carried the day. By a vote of 184 to 84, the ratifying convention declared that a bill of rights "asserting and securing from encroachment the great Principles of civil and religious Liberty, and the unalienable rights of the People" must be approved before North Carolina would concur. The convention was true to its word. Not until November 1789—well after the new government had gotten under way and Congress had forwarded a national bill of rights to the states for approval—did North Carolina, with Timothy Bloodworth's cautious endorsement, finally enter the new union.

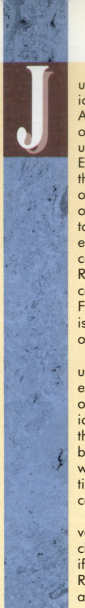

Just as Timothy Bloodworth knew the difficulties of achieving American independence, he learned as well the problems of preserving American liberty once independence had been won. As a member of the Confederation Congress, Bloodworth confronted the continuing vestiges of colonialism—the hostile, patronizing attitudes of England and France, their imperial ambitions in North America, and the republic's ongoing economic dependence on Europe. He also observed the Congress's continuing inability to reduce the war debt, open foreign ports to American commerce, and persuade the states to cooperate in a common tariff policy against England. As a southerner, Bloodworth was equally alarmed by the willingness of a congressional majority to forgo free navigation of the Mississippi River, deemed essential for development of the southern backcountry, in exchange for northern commercial advantages in Europe. Finally, he worried about political turmoil in the states as intractable issues of taxation, debt, and paper money led discontented citizens openly to challenge public authority.

By 1786, Bloodworth, like countless other Americans, was caught up in an escalating debate over reform of the Articles of Confederation and the very future of America's republican experiment. On one side of the debate were the Federalists, who believed that America's experiment in republicanism was in danger of collapse, that the Articles were fatally deficient, and that they had to be replaced by a new, much stronger national government. On the other side were the Anti-Federalists, committed to retaining America's traditional localism and still deeply impressed by the dangers posed by consolidated power to individual liberties.

That debate came to a focus in the momentous Philadelphia convention of 1787, which produced not reform but revolutionary change in national government, and in the state struggles over ratification that followed. With ratification of the new Constitution, the Revolutionary era came to an end, and the American people opened a portentous new chapter in their history.

STRUGGLING WITH THE PEACETIME AGENDA

As the war ended, difficult problems of demobilizaton and adjustment to the conditions of independence troubled the new nation. Whether the Confederation Congress could effectively deal with the problems of the postwar era remained unclear.

Demobilizing the Army

Demobilizing the army presented the Confederation government with some difficult moments,

for when the fighting stopped, many of the troops refused to disband and go home until the Congress redressed their grievances. Trouble first arose in early 1783 among the officers at the continental army camp in Newburgh, New York. In January, they sent a delegation to the Congress to complain about arrears in pay, unsettled food and clothing allowances, and failure to make provision for the lifetime pensions that the Congress had promised them during the dark days of 1780. The Congress responded by calling for the army to be decommissioned. Almost immediately, an anonymous address circulated among the officers, attacking the "coldness and severity" of the Congress, calling on the officers to assemble and draw up a "last remonstrance," and hinting darkly at more direct action if their grievances were not met.

Several members of the Congress encouraged the officers' mutterings, hoping the crisis would add urgency to their own calls for a strengthened central government. Most, however, found this challenge to the Congress's authority alarming. Washington was disturbed as well and moved quickly to calm the situation. Promising that the Congress would treat the officers justly, he counseled patience and urged his comrades not to tarnish the victory they had so recently won. His efforts succeeded, for the officers reaffirmed their confidence in the Congress and agreed to disband.

The officers were not the only ones to take action. In June, several hundred disgruntled continental soldiers and Pennsylvania militiamen gathered to express their frustrations in front of Independence Hall, where both the Congress and Pennsylvania's executive council were meeting. When the state authorities would not guarantee the Congress's safety, it fled in confusion to Princeton, New Jersey. Once there, it eased the tension by issuing the soldiers three months' pay and furloughing them until they could be fully discharged. By

early November, the crisis was over, but the Congress's authority had been seriously challenged.

During the mid-1780s, the Congress shuffled between Princeton and Annapolis, Trenton and New York, its transiency visible evidence of its steadily eroding position. A hot-air balloon, scoffed the *Boston Evening Herald,* would "exactly accommodate the itinerant genius of Congress," since it could then "float along from one end of the continent to the other . . . and when occasion requires . . . suddenly pop down into any of the states they please." The Congress had been criticized before, but never so mockingly.

Opening the West

The Congress was not without important accomplishments during the postwar years. Most notable were the two great land ordinances of 1785 and 1787. The first provided for the systematic survey and sale of the region west of New York and Pennsylvania and north of the Ohio River. The area was to be laid out in townships 6 miles square, which were in turn to be subdivided into lots of 640 acres each. Thus began the rectangular grid pattern of land survey and settlement that to this day characterizes the nation's Midwest and distinguishes it

Old Northwest Survey Patterns

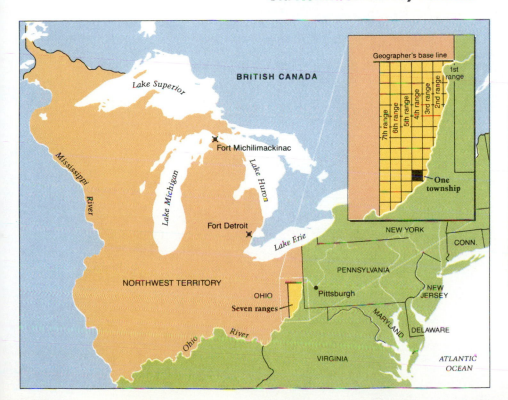

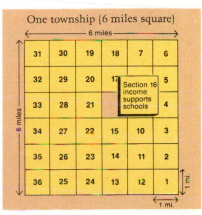

One township (6 miles square)

so markedly from the irregular settlement patterns of the older colonial areas to the east.

Two years later, the Congress passed the Northwest Ordinance. It provided for the political organization of the same interior region, first with appointed officials, then with popularly elected assemblies and congressionally appointed governors, and ultimately as new states to be incorporated into the Union "on an equal footing with the original states in all respects whatsoever." Together these two pieces of legislation provided the legal mechanism for the nation's dramatic territorial expansion during the nineteenth century.

The Congress was able to pass these bills because they served so many people's interests. They opened land to settlers and profits to speculators, and the income from land sales promised to help reduce the national debt. Officials determined that the Northwest Ordinance, moreover, permitted slave owners already living north of the Ohio River to retain their slaves but prohibited the importation of new slaves into the region. This made the area more attractive to white farmers from the Northeast who worried about their ability to compete with slave labor and were disinclined to live among blacks. Southern delegates in the Congress accepted the restriction because their constituents could look forward to slavery's expansion south of the Ohio. During the 1780s, the country's interior seemed large enough to accommodate everyone's needs.

Areas of White Settlement and Frontier in 1787

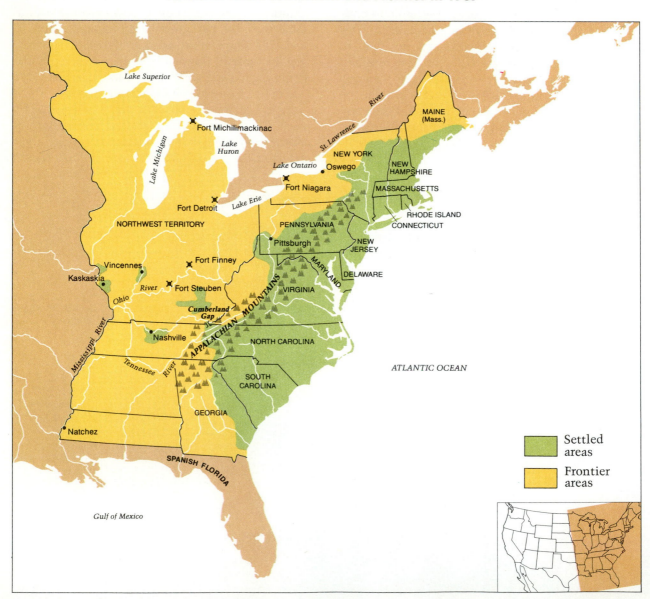

"Utmost Good Faith" Clause from the Northwest Ordinance (1787)

The following articles shall be considered as articles of compact between the original States and the people and States in the said territory and forever remain unalterable, unless by common consent, to wit:

The utmost good faith shall always be observed towards the Indians; their land and property shall never be taken from them without their consent; and, in their property, rights, and liberty, they shall never be invaded or disturbed, unless in just and lawful wars authorized by Congress, but laws founded in justice and humanity, shall from time to time be made for preventing wrongs being done to them, and for preserving peace and friendship with them.

Despite its success in providing the legal framework for settlement of the trans-Appalachian frontier, however, many Americans doubted that the Congress could successfully promote the nation's territorial growth. It had neither secured removal of the British troops from the western posts after 1783 nor guaranteed free navigation of the Mississippi. Nor could it clear the tribes of the Ohio region out of the white settlers' way.

During the immediate postwar years, the Congress operated as if the Native Americans of the interior were "conquered" peoples. As allies of England, they had lost the war and thus came under the American government's control. The Treaty of Paris, American officials insisted, gave the United States political sovereignty over the tribes south of the Great Lakes and east of the Mississippi as well as ownership of their land.

The conquest theory was fully consistent with white attitudes about Indian separateness and inferiority. Even the most sympathetic whites believed that before Native Americans could join white society, they would have to become "civilized" and "Christianized"—in other words, cease being Indian. Actually, most whites gave little thought in incorporating Native Americans into white society, even in the distant future. George Washington bluntly expressed the prevailing view. "The gradual extension of our settlements," he explained, "will as certainly cause the savage as the wolf to retire; both being beasts of prey though they differ in shape."

For a few years the conquest strategy seemed to work. During the mid-1780s, the Congress negotiated several important land treaties with the interior tribes. The Revolutionary War had cost the Iroquois dearly. Their confederation, divided and defeated, lay in ruins. Some Iroquois fled into Can-

ada. Pressed by the Congress and the New York government, those who remained rapidly deeded away most of their land. At the Treaty of Fort Stanwix in 1784, the first congressional treaty with an Indian tribe, the Six Nations made peace, ceded their western lands to the United States, and retreated to small reservations. By the 1790s, little remained of the once extensive Iroquois domain but a few islands in a spreading sea of white settlement. On those islands—"slums in the wilderness," they have been called—the Iroquois struggled for survival against disease and poverty, their traditional lifeways gone, their self-confidence broken.

The Iroquois were not the only tribes to lose their land. In January 1785, representatives of the Wyandotte, Chippewa, Delaware, and Ottawa tribes relinquished claim to most of present-day Ohio.

The treaties with the Indians, however, did not hold because they were often exacted under the threat of force and were typically accepted by few tribal leaders. At Fort Stanwix, for example, negotiations were held at gunpoint, and hostages were taken to coerce the Indian delegates. Native Americans regarded the attitude of the Congress's commissioners as insulting and arbitrary. Some of the disgusted delegates, including the Mohawk chief Joseph Brant, left before the agreement was signed. As Brant remarked before his departure, "We are sent in order to make peace and . . . are not authorized to stipulate any particular cession of land." Two years later, the Iroquois openly repudiated the treaty, asserting that they were still sovereigns of their own soil and "equally free as . . . any nation under the sun."

The Revolution, moreover, left behind a legacy of bitterness for both Indians and whites: for Indians because they had suffered betrayal and defeat, for white Americans because the Indians had sided with

England and thus threatened the success of the Revolutionary cause. This bitterness would trouble Indian-white relations for years to come.

By the mid-1780s, tribal groups both above and below the Ohio River were actively resisting white expansion onto their land. In the summer of 1786, the Creek resumed hostilities in the backcountry of Georgia, while north of the Ohio, the Shawnee, Delaware, Wyandotte, and Miami moved to strengthen their Western Confederacy and prepare for the defense of their common homeland. That fall, the confederacy rejected the whites' conquest theory, declared the Treaty of Fort Stanwix invalid, asserted that the Ohio River was the proper boundary between them and the United States, and insisted on a new treaty between the combined tribes of the confederacy and the United States. When white settlers continued to press into the region, Native Americans launched a series of devastating raids, virtually halting white settlement. By 1786, the entire region from the Great Lakes to the Gulf of Mexico was embroiled in warfare. With the continental army disbanded and the nation in no position to raise a new one, there was little that Congress could do.

The Congress's inability to open up the interior alarmed many Americans—speculators threatened with the loss of their investments, farmers wanting to leave the crowded lands of the east, Revolutionary soldiers eager to start afresh on the rich soil of Kentucky and Ohio, and leaders such as Thomas Jefferson who believed that republican liberty depended on an expanding nation of yeoman farmers. With the Confederation Congress unable to act effectively, each of these groups found reason to question its adequacy.

Settling the interior, the indispensable land reserve for the fast-growing nation, involved relations with other nations. Here, too, the Congress proved ineffective.

In June 1784, Spain—still in possession of Florida, the Gulf Coast, and the trans-Mississippi West—closed the outlet of the Mississippi River at New Orleans to American shipping. Spain's action raised a storm of protest, especially among settlers in the West, who counted on the interior river system to float their produce downstream to outside markets. Land speculators from Virginia to South Carolina were aroused as well, for closure of the Mississippi would discourage development of the southern backcountry. Rumors spread that Spanish agents were urging backcountry American settlers to seek affiliation with Spain. Washington commented un-

easily that the settlers there were "on a pivot. The touch of a feather," he feared, "would turn them away."

For more than a year, Foreign Secretary John Jay negotiated with the Spanish ambassador to the United States, Don Diego de Gardoqui, in an effort to reopen that vital commercial outlet. When Gardoqui held firm, Jay switched tactics and offered to relinquish American claims to free transit of the Mississippi in return for a new commercial treaty opening Spanish ports to American shipping. The northern states, excited at the prospect of Spanish trade, supported the bargain, but the southern states, angry at Jay's betrayal of their interests, refused. Thus stalemated, the Congress could take no action at all.

The symbolic figure of Columbia, often presented in the form of an Indian maiden embodying the innocence and freedom of the new republic, first became popular during the Revolution. This began to change as Americans moved west across the Appalachians. By the time this French engraving appeared in the early nineteenth century, Columbia was usually garbed in classical attire and had lost her Indian headdress.

L'AMÉRIQUE.

Wrestling with the National Debt

The Congress's inability to deal effectively with the massive war debt offered further evidence of the Confederation government's weakness. No one knew how large the public debt actually was at the war's end, but it probably stood at about $35 million. Much of it was held abroad by French and Dutch bankers. Not only was the Congress unable to make regular payment against the loan's principal, but it had to borrow additional money abroad simply to pay the accumulating interest. At home, things were no better. In response to the incessant demands of its creditors, the government could only delay and try to borrow more.

In 1781, the Congress had appointed Robert Morris, a wealthy and influential Philadelphia merchant, superintendent of finance and had given him broad authority to deal with the nation's troubled affairs. Morris persuaded the states to stop issuing paper money and obtained a demand from the Congress that they pay their requisitions in specie. In addition, he arranged for the Congress to charter the Bank of North America and take steps to make federal bonds more attractive to investors.

Though Morris made considerable progress, the government's finances remained shaky. Lacking the power to tax, the Congress continued to depend on the states' willingness to honor their obligations. This arrangement proved unworkable. In February 1781, New Jersey flatly refused to make payment on a new congressional requisition. In October, desperate for resources, the Congress requested an additional $8 million from the states. Two and a half years later, less than $1.5 million of it had come in. Late in 1783, Morris overdrew his personal account in Europe in an effort to find money for the army's demobilization. In January 1784, he resigned, partly in despair over the government's financial situation and partly to recoup his personal fortunes.

By 1786, total federal revenue amounted to no more than $370,000 a year, not a sufficient amount, as one official lamented, to provide for "the bare maintenance of the federal government [even] on the most economical establishment, and in a time of profound peace." "The crisis has arrived," declared a congressional committee in February 1786, when Americans

> must decide whether they will support their rank as a nation, by maintaining the public faith at home and abroad; or whether, for want of . . . a general revenue . . . they will hazard not only the existence of the

Union, but of the great and invaluable privileges for which they have so arduously and so honorably contended.

Not all Americans were alarmed. Some pointed out approvingly that several state governments, having brought their own public debt under control, were beginning to assume responsibility for portions of the national debt. Others, however, saw in that fact additional evidence of the Congress's weakening condition and wondered how a government unable to maintain its credit could long endure.

Surviving in a Hostile World

The Congress's difficulties in countering Spain's decision to close the Mississippi River to American commerce and in dealing with its creditors abroad pointed to a broader problem in American foreign relations. Even after the United States had formally won independence, England, France, and Spain continued their diplomatic domination of the new republic.

Independence and the war had dramatically transformed America's relationships with the outside world. England, once the nurturing "mother country," had become a tyrannical parent bent on enslaving its colonial children. Just as bewildering,

---

Philadelphia, Sept. 22, 1779.

TAXATION ROYAL TYRANNY,

Or the errors of the American Congreſs demonſtrated by a geometrical axiom.

SUPPOSE the congreſs emitted two years ago thirteen millions, but now the emiſſions amount to one hundred and eighty millions of congreſs paper dollars.

At two years ago one million was worth twenty millions of this day's congreſs paper dollars; then it geometrically follows, that the ſaid one hundred and eighty millions is worth no more than nine millions was two years ago, and by ſuch depreciation the congreſſal government can never get in debt; conſequently there is no need of a tax; for one hundred and eighty millions divided by twenty quotes nine millions only; *ergo* ſaid congreſſal government have gained by ſaid depreciation four millions of congreſſal paper dollars. If the beſt man in congreſs has any ſtronger demonſtration for tax, I hope he will produce them; if he has not I make no doubt, but he will defend theſe as ſufficient proofs of his congreſſal errors, or honeſtly give up the argument of taxation. " This point being eſtabliſhed, the next queſtion is whether the natural wealth, value and reſource of the" profits of the confiſcated crown land and king's quit rents will be equal to the debt. To this congreſs ſay nothing. VOX POPULI.

The outcry against currency depreciation shown in this newspaper attack in 1779 continued into the early 1780s when Robert Morris convinced the states to stop printing money.

RECOVERING THE PAST

INDIAN TREATIES

During the 1780s, the new American government contracted its first treaties with Native Americans of the trans-Appalachian interior, including the Wyandotte, the Delaware, and the Cherokee. The treaties were necessary to complete the peacemaking process at the end of the Revolutionary War since most of the interior tribes had sided with England. The treaties were also intended to open Trans-Appalachia to white settlement.

The treaty texts, like the agreement between the Congress and the Cherokee signed at Hopewell in 1785, presented here, tell us a great deal about the issues that lay at the center of Indian-white relations during the 1780s. What major issues did the treaty of 1785 attempt to resolve? Why were these issues important to the Congress and the Native Americans?

A careful reading of the treaty language can tell us a great deal as well about the attitudes and values that white negotiators brought to the treaty-making process and provide hints of how that process functioned. Which phrases in the treaty reveal how the Congress's negotiators viewed their Cherokee counterparts? From the evidence of the treaty text, how would you characterize the treaty negotiations?

Most of the treaties arranged during the 1780s failed to last, and by the end of the decade Trans-Appalachia, both north and south of the Ohio River, was embroiled in Indian-white warfare. Why did these agreements prove so fragile?

Treaty with the Cherokee, 1785.

Articles concluded at Hopewell, on the Keowee, between Benjamin Hawkins, Andrew Pickens, Joseph Martin, and Lachlan M'Intoch, Commissioners Plenipotentiary of the United States of America, of the one Part, and the Head-Men and Warriors of all the Cherokees of the other.

The Commissioners Plenipotentiary of the United States, in Congress assembled, give peace to all the Cherokees, and receive them into the favor and protection of the United States of America, on the following conditions:

ARTICLE I.

The Head-Men and Warriors of all the Cherokees shall restore all the prisoners, citizens of the United States, or subjects of their allies, to their entire liberty: They shall also restore all the Negroes, and all other property taken during the late war from the citizens, to such person, and at such time and place, as the Commissioners shall appoint.

ARTICLE II.

The Commissioners of the United States in Congress assembled, shall restore all prisoners taken from the Indians, during the late war, to the Head-Men and Warriors of the Cherokees, as early as is practicable.

ARTICLE III.

The said Indians for themselves and their respective tribes and towns do acknowledge all the Cherokees to be under the protection of the United States of America, and of no other sovereign whosoever.

ARTICLE IV.

The boundary allotted to the Cherokees for their hunting grounds, between the said Indians and the citizens of the United States, within the limits of the United States of America, is, and shall be the following . . . [see map].

ARTICLE V.

If any citizen of the United States, or other person not being an Indian, shall attempt to settle on any of the lands westward or southward of the said boundary which are hereby allotted to the Indians for their hunting grounds, or having already settled and will not remove from the same within six months after the ratification of this treaty, such person shall forfeit the protection of the United States, and the Indians may punish him or not as they please. . . .

ARTICLE VI.

If any Indian or Indians, or person residing among them, or who shall take refuge in their nation, shall commit a robbery, or murder, or other capital crime, on any citizen of the United States, or person under their protection, the nation, or the tribe to which such offender or offenders may belong, shall be bound to deliver him or them up to be punished according to the ordinances of the United States; Provided, that the punishment shall not be greater than if the robbery or murder, or other capital crime had been committed by a citizen on a citizen.

ARTICLE VII.

If any citizen of the United States, or person under their protection, shall commit a robbery or murder, or other capital crime, on any Indian, such offender or offenders shall be punished in the same manner as if the murder or robbery, or other capital crime, had been committed on a citizen of the United States; and the punishment shall be in presence of some of the Cherokees, if any shall attend at the time and place. . . .

ARTICLE VIII.

It is understood that the punishment of the innocent under the idea of retaliation, is unjust, and shall not be practiced on either side, except where there is a manifest violation of this treaty; and then it shall be preceded first by a demand of justice, and if refused, then by a declaration of hostilities.

ARTICLE IX.

For the benefit and comfort of the Indians, and for the prevention of injuries or oppressions on the part of the citizens or Indians, the United States in Congress assembled shall have the sole and exclusive right of regulating the trade with the Indians, and managing all their affairs in such manner as they think proper. . . .

ARTICLE XI.

The said Indians shall give notice to the citizens of the United States, of any designs which they may know or suspect to be formed in any neighboring tribe, or by any person whosoever, against the peace, trade or interest of the United States.

ARTICLE XII.

That the Indians may have full confidence in the justice of the United States, respecting their interests, they shall have the right to send a deputy of their choice, whenever they think fit, to Congress.

ARTICLE XIII.

The hatchet shall be forever buried, and the peace given by the United States, and friendship reestablished between the said states on the one part, and all the Cherokees on the other, shall be universal; and the contracting parties shall use their utmost endeavors to maintain the peace given as aforesaid, and friendship re-established.

In witness of all and every thing herein determined, between the United States of America and all the Cherokees, we, their underwritten Commissioners, by virtue of our full powers, have signed this definitive treaty, and have caused our seals to be hereunto affixed.

Done at Hopewell, on the Keowee, this twenty-eighth of November, in the year of our Lord one thousand seven hundred and eighty-five.

Benjamin Hawkins,
And'w Pickens,
Jos. Martin,
Lach'n McIntosh,

Koatohee, or Corn Tassel of Toquo, his x mark,
Scholauetta, or Hanging Man of Chota, his x mark,
Tuskegatahu, or Long Fellow of Chistohoe, his x mark,
Ooskwha, or Abraham of Chilkowa, his x mark,
Kolakusta, or Prince of Noth, his x mark,
Newota, or the Gritzs of Chicamaga, his x mark,
Konatota, or the Rising Fawn of Highwassay, his x mark,
Tuckasee, or Young Terrapin of Allajoy, his x mark,
Toostaka, or the Waker of Oostanawa, his x mark,
Untoola, or Gun Rod of Seteco, his x mark,
Unsuokanail, Buffalo White Calf New Cussee, his x mark,
Kostayeak, or Sharp Fellow Wataga, his x mark,
Chonosta, of Cowe, his x mark,
Chescoonwho, Bird in Close of Tomotlug, his x mark,
Tuckasee, or Terrapin of Hightowa, his x mark,
Chesetoa, or the Rabbit of Tlacoa, his x mark. . . .
Witness:
Wm. Blount,
Sam'l Taylor, Major.,
John Owen,
Jess. Walton,
Jno. Cowan, capt. comm'd't,
Thos. Gregg,
W. Hazzard,
James Madison,
Arthur Cooley,
    Sworn interpreters.

Source: Charles Kapple, ed., *Indian Affairs: Laws and Treaties* (Washington, D.C.: G.P.O., 1904–1941), vol. 2, pp. 8–11.

France, long the mortal enemy of England and the colonies alike, had been a helpful ally. Yet France was at best a strange and uncomfortable friend. With an empire of its own, France was no more sympathetic to colonial rebellions than England. Moreover, the French king and aristocracy regarded republicanism as subversive. French aid had been essential to achieving American independence, but France's efforts to manipulate the peace process for its own interests offered Americans a hard lesson in the realities of power diplomacy.

Independence did not end European imperial ambitions in North America. France had lost its North American possessions following the Seven Years' War, but before the century was over, it would gain title to most of the continent beyond the Mississippi River. England's Union Jack continued to fly over eastern Canada just north of the American border. English troops, moreover, retained possession of strategic outposts on American soil—at Detroit, Michilimackinac, and Niagara. Spain was no longer as powerful as before but, as the Jay-Gardoqui affair made evident, still conjured up grim memories of past New World conquests.

The reason for America's diplomatic troubles was clear: the country was new, weak, and republican in a world dominated by strong, monarchic governments. Nothing revealed more starkly the difficulties of national survival than the Congress's largely futile efforts to rebuild America's overseas commerce.

A flourishing overseas trade, across the Atlantic to markets in England and down the coast to the Caribbean, had been the foundation of colonial economic prosperity. As we have seen, the Revolutionary War brought American commerce virtually to a halt. Once the war was over, American traders sought eagerly to rebuild their overseas trade. It proved a difficult task because the Congress could give them little support.

When the war ended, familiar English goods flooded American markets. Few American goods, however, flowed the other way. John Adams learned why. In 1785, he arrived in London as the first American minister to England. The Congress had assigned him the task of negotiating a commercial treaty, but he soon discovered the unlikelihood of accomplishing that. After endless rebuffs and delays, he wrote home in frustration that England had no intention of opening the empire's ports to American shipping. English officials reminded him that Americans had desired independence and must now live with its

British and Spanish Possessions in Eastern North America, 1783

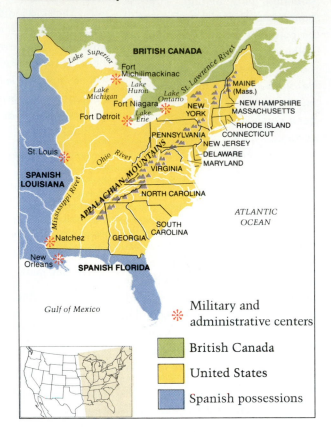

consequences. They pointed out, moreover, that British goods could command the American market without England's needing to grant any concessions in return.

During the mid-1780s, Americans had some success in their search for new commercial arrangements; progress, however, was slow. After the war, while England remained intractable, France and Spain gradually withdrew the special trading privileges they had extended and returned to their policy of mercantile restrictions. Though the New York merchant ship *Empress of China* made the first American voyage to China in 1784 and others soon followed, the successful development of that trade would not come until the nineteenth century.

In an effort to overcome its diplomatic weakness and rebuild American commerce, the Congress tried to secure the states' cooperation in a program of economic recovery. In 1784, however, it failed to obtain authorization from the states to regulate foreign commerce; each state wanted to channel its own trade for its own advantage. As a result, the Congress was unable to negotiate satisfactory commercial agreements abroad, and overseas trade continued to languish, deepening economic hardship in coastal communities.

In Philadelphia, for example, only 13 ships were built in 1786, one-third as many as just two years before. By the late 1780s, the per capita value of American exports had fallen a startling 30 percent from two decades earlier. No wonder that merchants and artisans, carpenters and shopkeepers, sailors and dockworkers—all dependent on shipbuilding and overseas commerce—suffered. In an Atlantic world divided into exclusive, imperial trading spheres, the United States stood outside and alone, lacking both the political unity and the economic power to protect its interests.

POLITICAL TUMULT IN THE STATES

As the Confederation Congress struggled to chart the nation's course, controversy again embroiled state politics. Two issues carried over from the Revolutionary agenda came together with particularly explosive force: problems of debt relief and paper money on the one hand and continuing arguments over political equality and the sharing of political power on the other.

The Limits of Republican Experimentation

For several years following 1783, the hectic tempo of state politics abated, in part because Americans, exhausted by the war's ordeal, turned their energies toward solving the problems of their personal lives. Other factors were at work as well. The mobilizing crusade against England was over, and the initial surge of republican reform, codified in the new state constitutions, had subsided. In a pattern to recur frequently in American history, the postwar era witnessed growing social and political conservatism.

Popular voting declined, and leadership in the state governments fell increasingly to people convinced that republican experimentation had gone too far, that order had to balance liberty, and that the "better sort" of men, not democratic newcomers, should be in charge. The repeal of anti-Tory legislation and the occasional reappearance of Loyalists in public life provided evidence of the changing political climate. In 1786, the Connecticut assembly invited exiled Loyalists to return home,

apparently hoping that their skills and experience would contribute to economic recovery.

Just as dramatic was the replacement in 1790 of the radical Pennsylvania constitution of 1776 that established a single legislative house designed to give maximum voice to the people. The new, more conservative document provided for a strong governor with power to veto legislation and control the militia and a senate intended to balance the more democratic assembly. Gaining a majority in the assembly by 1786, the conservatives dismantled much of the radicals' program, repealing the revolutionary test oaths and thus reenfranchising thousands of conservatives, stopping the issuance of paper money, and rechartering the Bank of North America. Thus ended Pennsylvania's distinctive experiment in radical republicanism.

Shays's Rebellion

In Pennsylvania, the conservative shift in politics and public policy generated little opposition, either from farmers in the west or artisans in Philadelphia. In other states, however, popular opposition to hard money and high-tax policies provoked vigorous protest. Nowhere was the situation more volatile than in Massachusetts. The controversy that erupted there in 1786 echoed strongly of equal rights and popular consent, staples of the rhetoric of 1776. The crisis was triggered by debt, paper money, and taxation—problems still festering from the Revolution.

The war vastly expanded the burden of debt among Massachusetts' citizens. By the mid-1780s, increasing numbers of people had to borrow money just to pay their taxes or support their families, while others borrowed to speculate in western land or government securities. Because there were no commercial banks in the state, people borrowed from each other in a complicated pyramid of credit and debt. At the top were the wealthiest merchants, who borrowed and loaned the largest amounts. Below them stretched descending layers of debtors and creditors. The top of the credit pyramid was located in the commercial regions along the coast. Its base lay in the less commercialized regions of the interior. The network was not only complicated but unstable, for if creditors at any level called in their loans, trouble could quickly spiral through the entire system.

A crisis began to build shortly after the war's end. As peace returned, English goods once again flooded the American market. Strong domestic demand encouraged American importers to borrow heavily in England and expand their purchases, which they sold to retailers at a handsome profit. Some of those profits they loaned to the retailers so they could sell even more goods. The retailers in turn extended credit to their customers.

The system held together reasonably well for several years, but the flood of English goods eventually glutted the American market and forced prices down. By 1785, a number of English banking houses, heavily overcommitted in the American trade, were in trouble. In an effort to survive, they called in their American loans. American merchants in turn tried to collect the debts due them, sending a credit crisis surging through the economy.

The crisis was most acute at the bottom of the credit pyramid, among the small farmers and laboring people of country and town. Caught in a tightening bind, they turned to their state governments for relief, asking for "stay laws" suspending the collection of private debts. If not granted relief, they faced the certain foreclosure and loss of shops and farms. They also pressed for new issues of paper money so that they would have something with which to pay both private debts and public taxes.

The largest creditors, however, most of whom lived in commercial areas along the coast, fought these relief proposals. They opposed stay laws because they wanted to be able to call in their outstanding loans. They argued against new paper money out of fear that it would depreciate and further confound economic affairs. Sound commerce, they argued, demanded a stable, specie-based money supply.

By 1786, heavy private debt and a lingering agricultural depression had made many Massachusetts farmers desperate. In words that echoed the colonial protests of the 1760s, they petitioned the Massachusetts assembly for relief. Their appeals, however, fell on deaf ears, for commercial and creditor interests now controlled the government. The farmers' call for new paper money was quickly rejected. In response to their appeal for tax relief, the government passed a law calling for the full and rapid repayment of the state debt and levying a heavy new round of taxes. No matter that the citizens of interior towns complained bitterly of "the great difficulty we labor under in regard to paying our taxes" or that Peter Wood, tax collector for the town of Marlborough, reported that "there was not . . . the money in possession or at command among the people . . . to discharge taxes" or that between 1784 and 1786, fully 29 towns declared an inability to meet their obligations.

As frustrated citizens had done before and would do again when the law proved unresponsive to their needs, Massachusetts farmers stepped outside the law and took matters into their own hands. A Hampshire County convention of 50 towns condemned the state senate, lawyers, court fees, and the tax system. It advised against violence, but mobs soon began to form.

The county courts drew much of the farmers' wrath because they issued the writs of property foreclosures that the state and private creditors demanded. On August 31, 1786, armed men prevented the county court from sitting at Northampton, and on September 5, angry citizens closed down the court at Worcester. When farmers threatened similar actions elsewhere, an alarmed Governor James Bowdoin dispatched 600 militiamen to protect the Supreme Court, then on circuit at Springfield.

About 500 insurgents had gathered near there under the leadership of Daniel Shays, a popular Revolutionary War captain recently fallen on hard times. A "brave and good soldier," Shays had mustered out of the army in 1780 and returned home, tired and frustrated, to await payment for his military service. Like thousands of others, he had a long wait. In the meantime, his farming went badly, his debts accumulated, and, as he later recalled, "the spector of debtor's jail always hovered close by." Most of the men who gathered around Shays were debtors and veterans also.

Worried about a possible raid on the federal arsenal at Springfield and encouraged by the Massachusetts delegates to take the affair seriously, the continental Congress authorized 1,300 troops, ostensibly for service against the Indians but actually to be ready for use against Shays and his rebels. For a few weeks, Massachusetts seemed poised on the brink of civil war.

In late November, the insurrection collapsed in eastern Massachusetts, but things were far from over in the west. When several insurgent groups refused to disband at the governor's command, Bowdoin called out a force of 4,400 men, financed and led by worried eastern merchants. On January 26, 1787, Shays led 1,200 men toward the federal arsenal. Frightened by the siege, its defenders opened fire, killing four of the attackers and sending the Shaysites into retreat.

Over the next several weeks, the militia chased

An unknown artist provided in 1787 the only contemporary image of General Daniel Shays and Colonel Jacob Shattuck, leaders of the Massachusetts farmers' rebellion against foreclosures and heavy taxes.

the remnants of Shays's followers across the state and sent Shays himself fleeing into Vermont for safety. By the end of February, the rebellion was over. In March, the legislature pardoned all but Shays and three other leaders; in another year, they too had been forgiven.

Similar challenges to public authority, fired by personal troubles and frustration over unresponsive government, erupted in at least six states. In Maryland in June 1786, a "tumultuary assemblage of the people" rushed into the Charles County courthouse and closed it down. Like the Massachusetts rebels, they demanded new paper money and the suspension of debt proceedings. In Cecil County, farmers circulated unsigned handbills threatening state officers if they seized people's property for unpaid taxes. The governor condemned the "riotous and tumultuous" proceedings and warned against further "violence and outrages." In South Carolina in May 1785, sheriffs were "threatened in the execution of their duty" as they attempted to foreclose several properties. In one incident, Colonel Hezekiah Mayham, "being served by the sheriff with a writ, obliged him to eat it on the spot." Warned Judge Aedanus Burke, not even "5,000 troops, the best in America or Europe, could enforce obedience" to the court. Across the nation, state politics was in turmoil.

TOWARD A NEW NATIONAL GOVERNMENT

By 1786, belief was spreading among members of the Congress and other political and commercial leaders that the nation was in crisis and that the recent experiment in republicanism was foundering. Explanations for the crisis and prescriptions for its resolution varied, but attention focused increasingly on the inadequacies of the Articles of Confederation. Within two years, following a raucous political struggle, a new and far more powerful constitution replaced the Articles. That outcome changed forever the course of American history.

The Rise of Federalism

The supporters of a stronger national government called themselves Federalists (leading their opponents to adopt the name Anti-Federalists). Led by men such as Washington, Hamilton, Madison, and Jay, they believed that the nation was in the midst of a social and political crisis that threatened its very survival. "Our affairs seem to lead to some crisis, some revolution," wrote Jay. Such men had never been comfortable with the more radical aspects of the Revolution. While supporting the principles of moderate republicanism, they continued to believe in an aristocracy of talent and to place high value on social order and the rights of property.

They were now persuaded that social and political change had been carried too far, "natural" distinctions among the people were being ignored, and the bases of social and political stability were in danger of collapse. The Revolution, Jay lamented, "laid open a wide field for the operation of ambition," especially for "men raised from low degrees to high stations and rendered giddy by elevation." It was time, he insisted, to find better ways of protecting "the worthy against the licentious."

The Federalist leaders feared for their own social and political security. But they were also concerned about the collapse of the orderly world they believed essential to the preservation of republican liberty. In 1776, American liberty had needed protection against English power. Danger now, however, came from too much liberty threatening to degenerate into license. "We have probably had too good an opinion of human nature in forming our Constitution," wrote Washington. "Experience has taught us, that men will not adopt and carry into execution measures the best calculated for their own good, without the intervention of a coercive power." In the Federalists' minds, power no longer stood as liberty's antagonist but as its guarantor. What America needed was "a strong government, ably administered."

The Federalists regarded Shays's uprising in Massachusetts and similar outbursts elsewhere not as evidence of genuine social distress but as threats to social and political order. Though they were reassured by the speed with which the Shaysites were dispatched, that episode persuaded them of the need for a stronger national government managed by the "better sort."

Congressional inability to handle the national debt, establish public credit, and restore overseas trade also troubled the Federalists. Sensitive to America's economic and military weakness, smarting from French and English arrogance, and aware of continuing Anglo-European designs on North America, the Federalists discussed the need for a new national government capable of extending American trade, spurring economic recovery, and protecting national interests.

Beyond that, the Federalists shared a vision of an expanding commercial republic, its people spreading across the rich lands of the interior, its merchant ships connecting America with the markets of Europe and beyond. That vision, so rich in national promise, seemed also at risk.

The Grand Convention

The first step toward governmental reform came in September 1786, when delegates gathered in Annapolis, Maryland, to discuss ways of promoting interstate commerce. Nine states had agreed to attend, but only five were actually represented. Persuaded that it was useless to continue with so few in attendance but determined to press ahead with reform, the delegates prepared an address to the states. Written by the ardent nationalist Alexander Hamilton, it called for a new convention to gather in Philadelphia in May 1787. In February, the Confederation Congress cautiously endorsed the idea of a convention to revise the Articles of Confederation. Before long, however, it became clear that more dramatic changes were in store.

During May, delegates representing every state except Rhode Island, began assembling in Philadelphia. Eventually 55 delegates would participate in the convention's work, though the usual attendance was between 30 and 40. The city bustled with excitement as they gathered, for the Grand Convention's roster read like an honor roll of the Revolution. From Virginia came the distinguished lawyer George Mason, chief author of Virginia's trailblazing bill of rights, and the already legendary George Washington. Proponents of the convention had held their breath as Washington considered

Shays's rebellion generated considerable alarm throughout Massachusetts. Grateful citizens of Springfield commissioned Paul Revere to make this silver punch bowl for General William Shepard, who was credited with defeating the insurgents.

James Madison of Virginia worked tirelessly between 1786 and 1788 to replace the Articles of Confederation with a new and more effective national constitution.

whether or not to attend. His presence vastly increased the prospects of success. James Madison was there as well. No one, with perhaps the single exception of Alexander Hamilton, was more committed to nationalist reform. Certainly no one had worked harder to prepare for the convention than he. Poring over treatises on republican government and natural law his friend Thomas Jefferson sent from France, Madison brought to Philadelphia his own design for a new national government. That design, presented in the convention as the Virginia Plan, would serve as the basis for the new constitution. Nor did anyone rival the diminutive Madison's contributions to the convention's work. Tirelessly he took the convention floor to argue the nationalist cause or buttonholed wavering delegates to strengthen their resolve. In addition, he somehow found the energy to keep extensive notes in his personal shorthand. Those notes constitute our essential record of the convention's proceedings.

Two distinguished Virginians were conspicuously absent. Thomas Jefferson was abroad serving as minister to France, and the old patriot Patrick Henry, long one of Madison's political foes and an ardent champion of state supremacy, feared what the convention might do and wanted no part of it.

From Pennsylvania came the venerable Franklin, too old to contribute significantly to the debates but able still, at several key moments, to call quarreling members to account and to reinspire them in their work. His colleagues from Pennsylvania included the erudite Scots lawyer James Wilson, whose nationalist sympathies had been inflamed when a democratic mob, resentful of privileged lawyers and merchants, attacked his elegant townhouse in 1779. Robert Morris, probably then the richest man in America, was there too. Massachusetts was ably represented by Elbridge Gerry and Rufus King, while South Carolina sent John Rutledge and Charles Pinckney. Roger Sherman led Connecticut's delegation.

The New York assembly sent a deeply divided delegation. Long a personal and ideological enemy of Alexander Hamilton and determined to protect both New York's autonomy and his own political power, Governor George Clinton saw to it that several Anti-Federalist skeptics also made the trip to Philadelphia.

They were no match for Hamilton. Born in the Leeward Islands, "the bastard brat of a Scots-peddlar" and a strong-willed woman with a troubled marriage, Hamilton used his immense intelligence and ingratiating charm to rise rapidly in the world. Sent to New York by some wealthy sponsors, he quickly established himself as a favorite of the city's mercantile community. In 1777, while still in his early twenties, he became Washington's wartime aide-de-camp. That relationship served Hamilton well for the next 20 years. Returning from the war, Hamilton wooed and won the wealthy Elizabeth Schuyler, thereby securing his personal fortunes and strengthening his political support. With Madison, Hamilton had promoted the abortive Annapolis convention. At Philadelphia, he was determined to drive his nationalist vision ahead.

Meeting in Independence Hall, where the Declaration of Independence had been proclaimed little more than a decade before, the convention elected Washington its presiding officer, adopted rules of procedure, and, after spirited debate, voted to close the doors and conduct the convention's business in secret.

Debate focused first on the Virginia Plan, introduced by Edmund Randolph on May 29. It outlined a new, truly national government and effectively set the convention's agenda. According to its provisions, there would be a bicameral congress, with the lower house elected by the people and the upper house, or senate, elected by the lower house from nominees proposed by the state legislatures. The plan also proposed a president chosen by the congress, a national judiciary, and a council of re-

vision, whose task was to review the contitutionality of legislation.

The smaller states quickly objected to the Virginia Plan's provision for proportional rather than equal representation for the states. On June 15, William Paterson introduced a counterproposal, the New Jersey Plan. It urged retention of the Articles as the basic structure of government but conferred on the congress the long-sought powers to tax and regulate foreign and interstate commerce, as well as authority to appoint a veto-less executive and a supreme court. After three days of heated debate, by a vote of seven states to three, the delegates adopted the Virginia Plan as the basis for further discussions. It was now clear that the convention would set aside the Articles of Confederation for a much stronger national government. For the next four months, the convention struggled to shape and define that new government.

At times it seemed that the Grand Convention would collapse under the weight of its own disagreements and the oppressive summer heat. How could the sharply conflicting interests of large and small states be reconciled? How should the balance of power between the national and state governments be cast? And what, if anything, would the convention say about slavery and the slave trade, issues on which northerners and southerners, antislavery and proslavery advocates so passionately disagreed? Finally, the delegates wrangled over the knotty problem of how to fashion an executive branch strong enough to govern but not so strong as to endanger republican liberty.

At one extreme was Hamilton's audacious proposal, made very early in the convention's deliberations, for a congress and president elected for

This painting by Thomas Rossiter, done in the early nineteenth century, provides an imaginative portrayal of the Philadelphia convention, with George Washington presiding and a rising sun, symbolic of the new nation, in the background.

life and a national government so powerful that the states would survive as little more than administrative agencies. Finding his plan under vigorous attack and his influence among the delegates rapidly eroding, a disillusioned Hamilton withdrew from the convention in late June. He would return a month later but make few additional contributions.

At the other extreme stood the ardent Anti-Federalist Luther Martin of Maryland. Rude and unkempt, Martin voiced his uncompromising opposition to anything that threatened state sovereignty or smacked of aristocracy. Increasingly isolated by the convention's nationalist inclinations, Martin also returned home, in his case to warn of the convention's direction.

By early July, with tempers frayed and frustrated over the apparent deadlock, the delegates agreed to recess, ostensibly in recognition of Independence Day but actually to enable Franklin, Roger Sherman of Connecticut, and others to mount a final effort at compromise. All agreed that only a bold stroke could save the gathering from collapse.

That stroke came on July 12, as part of what has become known as the Great Compromise. The reassembled delegates settled one major point of controversy by agreeing that representation in the lower house should be based on the total of each state's white population plus three-fifths of its black population. Though blacks were not accorded citizenship and could not vote, the southern delegates argued that they should be fully counted for this purpose. Delegates from the northern states, where relatively few blacks lived, did not want them counted at all, but the bargain was struck. As part of this compromise, the convention agreed that direct taxes would also be apportioned on the basis of population and that blacks would be counted similarly in that calculation as well. On July 16, the convention accepted the principle that each state should have an equal vote in the senate. Thus the interests of both large and small states were effectively accommodated.

The convention then submitted its work to a committee of detail for drafting in proper constitutional form. That group reported on August 6, and for the next month the delegates hammered out the exact language of the document's seven articles. On several occasions, differences seemed so great that it was uncertain whether the convention could proceed. In each instance, however, agreement was reached, and the discussion continued.

Determined to give the new government the stability the state governments lacked, the delegates created an electoral process designed to bring only persons of standing and experience into national office. An electoral college of wise and experienced leaders would meet to choose the president. The process functioned exactly that way during the first several presidential elections.

Selection of the new Senate would be similarly indirect, for its members were to be named by the state legislatures. (Not until 1913, when the Seventeenth Amendment to the Constitution was ratified, would the people elect their senators.) Even the House of Representatives, the only popularly elected branch of the new government, was to be filled with persons of standing and wealth, for the Federalists were confident that only familiar and experienced leaders would be able to attract the necessary votes.

The delegates' final set of compromises touched the fate of black Americans. At the insistence of southerners, the convention agreed that the slave trade would not formally end for another 20 years. The delegates never used the words *slavery* or *slave trade* but spoke more vaguely about not prohibiting "the migration or importation of such persons as any of the states now existing shall think proper to admit." Their meaning, however, was entirely clear.

Despite Gouverneur Morris's impassioned charge that slavery was "a nefarious institution" that would bring "the curse of Heaven on the states where it prevails," the delegates firmly rejected a proposal to abolish slavery, thereby tacitly acknowledging slavery's legitimacy. More than that, they guaranteed slavery's protection, writing in Section 2 of Article 4 of the Constitution "No person held to service or labour in one state, . . . [and] escaping into another, shall, in consequence of any law . . . therein, be discharged from such service, but shall be delivered up on claim of the party to whom such service or labour may be due." The delegates thus provided federal sanction for the capture and return of runaway slaves. This fugitive slave clause would return to haunt northern consciences in the years ahead, but at the time it seemed a small price to pay for sectional harmony and a new government. Northern accommodation to the demands of the southern delegates was eased, moreover, by knowledge that southerners in the Confederation Congress had just agreed to prohibit new slaves from entering the Northwest Territory.

The document that emerged from the Philadelphia Convention, then, represented compromises between large states and small, as well as North and South. Some of those compromises came at the expense of black Americans, who had no voice in the Constitution's drafting or ratification.

Although the Constitution called for shared responsibilities between the central government and the states, it shifted the balance in the national government's favor. Congress would now have authority to levy and collect taxes, regulate commerce with foreign nations and between states, devise uniform rules for naturalization, administer national patents and copyrights, and control the federal district in which it would eventually be located. Restrictions on the government's authority were limited and specific. Conspicuously missing was any statement reserving to the states all powers not explicitly conferred on the central government, which had been a crippling limitation of the Articles. On the contrary, the Constitution contained a number of clauses bestowing general grants of power on the new government. Section 8 of Article 1, for example, contained phrases granting Congress authority to "provide for the . . . general welfare of the United States" as well as "to make all laws . . . necessary and proper for carrying into execution . . . all . . . powers vested by this Constitution in the government of the United States." Later generations would call these phrases "elastic clauses" and would use them to expand the government's activities. A final measure of the Federalists' determination to make the new government supreme over the states was the assertion in Article 6 that the Constitution and all laws passed under it were to be regarded as "the supreme Law of the Land."

When the convention had finished its business, 3 of the 42 remaining delegates refused to sign the document. The other 39, however, affixed their names and forwarded it to the Confederation Congress along with their request that it be sent on to the states for approval. On September 17, the Grand Convention adjourned.

Federalists versus Anti-Federalists

Ratification presented the Federalists with more difficult problems than they had faced at Philadelphia. Now the debate moved into the open and shifted to the states, where sentiment was sharply divided and the situation was more difficult to control. The Federalists had thought carefully about securing ratification. Recognizing the unlikelihood

of gaining quick agreement from all 13 states, they provided that the Constitution should go into effect when any nine agreed to it. Other states could then enter the Union as they were ready. They arranged for ratification by specially elected conventions rather than the state assemblies, since under the Constitution the assemblies would lose substantial amounts of power. Ratification by convention was also more constitutionally sound, since it would give the new government its own grounding in the people and free it from dependence on the states.

When the convention reported its work to the Confederation Congress, opponents attempted to censure it for exceeding its authority. But after a few days' debate, the Congress dutifully forwarded the document to the states for consideration. Word of the dramatic changes being proposed spread rapidly. In each state, Federalists and Anti-Federalists, the latter now actively opposing the Constitution, prepared to debate the new articles of government.

Mercy Otis Warren, Massachusetts Patriot and historian, joined in the debate over the new constitution in this volume published in 1788.

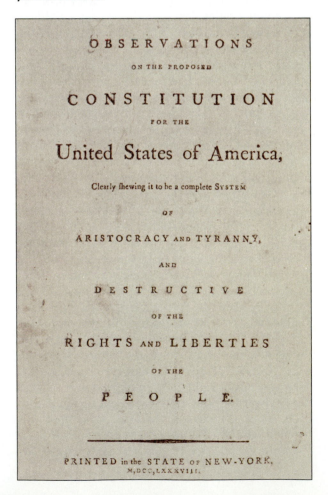

The federal ship **Hamilton** *formed the centerpiece of a grand procession in New York City celebrating the successful ratification of the new constitution.*

Federalist and Anti-Federalist strength differed from place to place, but in most of the states, opposition to the Constitution was widespread and vocal. Some critics feared that a stronger central government would threaten state interests or their own political power. Others, like Timothy Bloodworth, charged the Federalists with betraying Revolutionary republicanism. Like all "vigorous" and "energetic" governments, they warned, the new one would be corrupted by its own power. Far from the watchful eyes of the citizenry, its officials would behave as power wielders always had. American liberty, so recently preserved at such a high cost, would once again come under attack.

The Anti-Federalists were aghast at the Federalists' vision of an expanding "republican empire." "The idea of . . . [a] republic, on an average of 1000 miles in length, and 800 in breadth, and containing 6 millions of white inhabitants all reduced to the same standards of morals, . . . habits . . . [and] laws," exclaimed one critic incredulously, "is itself an absurdity, and contrary to the whole experience of mankind." Such an attempt would guarantee factional conflict and disorder. The Anti-Federalists continued to believe that republican liberty could be preserved only in simple, homogeneous societies, where faction was absent and public virtue guided citizens' behavior.

Nor did the Anti-Federalists believe that the proposed separation of executive, legislative, and judicial powers or the balancing of state and national governments would prevent power's abuse. Government, they insisted, must be kept simple, for complexity only confused the people and provided a cloak for the free play of selfish ambition.

Federalist spokesmen moved quickly to counter the Antis' criticism. The Federalists' most important effort was a series of essays penned by James Madison, Alexander Hamilton, and John Jay and published in New York under the pseudonym Publius.

The *Federalist Papers,* as they were called, were written to promote ratification in New York but were quickly reprinted by Federalists elsewhere.

Madison, Hamilton, and Jay moved systematically through the proposed constitution, explaining its virtues and responding to the Anti-Federalists' attacks. In the process, they described a political vision fundamentally different from that of their Anti-Federalist opponents.

No difference was more dramatic than the Federalists' discussion of governmental power. Power, the Federalists now argued, was not the enemy of liberty but its guarantor. Nothing was more dangerous than the "mischievous effects of unstable government." Where government was not "energetic" and "efficient" (these were favorite Federalist words), demagogues and disorganizers did their work. It is far better, Hamilton wrote in *Federalist* No. 26, "to hazard the abuse of . . . confidence than to embarrass the government and endanger the public safety by impolitic restrictions of . . . authority."

Federalists found it difficult to counter the Anti-Federalists' warning that a single, extended republic encompassing the country's economic and social diversity would lead inevitably to factional warfare and the end of republican liberty. Again, the Anti-Federalists drew on a basic theme of Revolutionary republicanism. The authors of the *Federalist Papers* responded by turning the classic republican argument on its head. Factional divisions, they explained, could never be avoided, even in the smallest societies, because they were the inevitable by-products of economic and social development. Faction, moreover, was the necessary accompaniment of human liberty. Wrote Madison in *Federalist* No. 10: "Liberty is to faction what air is to fire, an aliment without which it instantly expires." To suppress faction was to destroy liberty itself.

Earlier emphasis on public virtue, the Federalists explained, had been naive, for most people did not place the public good ahead of their own interests. Politics had to heed this harsh fact and provide for peaceful compromise among conflicting interests. That could best be accomplished by expanding the nation so that it included innumerable factions. Out of the clash and accommodation of social and economic interests would emerge public order and the best possible approximation of the public good.

The Federalists' argument established the basic rationale for modern democratic politics, but it left the Antis sputtering in frustration. Where in the Federalists' scheme was that familiar abstraction, the public good? Who would look after it? What place was there for public virtue in a system built on the notion of competing factional interests? In such a free market of competition, the Anti-Federalists warned, only the wealthy and powerful would benefit, while ordinary folk would suffer.

The Anti-Federalists accused their opponents of elitism as well, of wishing to join the government to wealth and privilege. Not all the Antis were democrats. Many of their leaders held slaves, and their appeals to local authority did not always mean support for political equality. Yet given their warnings against wealth and power and their distrust of centralization, the Anti-Federalists were more consistently sympathetic to democratic principles than were their Federalist opponents. Certainly they believed more firmly that for government to be safe, it must be tied intimately to the people.

As the ratification debate revealed, the Federalists and Anti-Federalists held sharply contrasting visions of the new republic. The Antis remained much closer to the original republicanism of 1776, with its suspicion of power and wealth, its emphasis on the primacy of local government, and its fears of national development. They envisioned a decentralized republic filled with self-reliant citizens whose ambitions were limited, whose activities were guided by public virtue, and whose destiny was determined primarily by what happened in the states rather than the nation. Anxious about what the future might bring, they wanted to keep their world much as it was.

The Federalists, arguing that America's situation had changed dramatically since 1776, em-

Ratification of the Constitution

Votes at state-ratifying convention

State	Date	For	Against
Delaware	December 1787	30	0
Pennsylvania	December 1787	46	23
New Jersey	December 1787	38	0
Georgia	January 1788	26	0
Connecticut	January 1788	128	40
Massachusetts	February 1788	187	168
Maryland	April 1788	63	11
South Carolina	May 1788	149	73
New Hampshire	June 1788	57	47
Virginia	June 1788	89	79
New York	July 1788	30	27
North Carolina	November 1789	194	77
Rhode Island	May 1790	34	32

braced the idea of nationhood and looked forward with anticipation to the development of a rising "republican empire" based on commercial development and led by men of wealth and talent. Both Federalists and Anti-Federalists claimed to be heirs of the Revolution, yet they differed dramatically on what the Revolution had meant.

The Struggle for Ratification

No one knows with certainty what most Americans thought of the proposed constitution. Probably no more than several hundred thousand participated in the elections for the state ratifying conventions, and many of the delegates carried no binding instructions from their constituents on how they should vote. No national plebiscite on the Constitution was ever taken. A majority of the people probably opposed the document, out of either indifference or alarm. Fortunately for the Federalists, they did not have to persuade most Americans; they needed only secure majorities in nine of the state ratifying conventions, a much less formidable task.

They set about it with determination. As soon as the Philadelphia convention adjourned, its members hurried home to organize the ratification movement in their states. In Delaware and Georgia, New

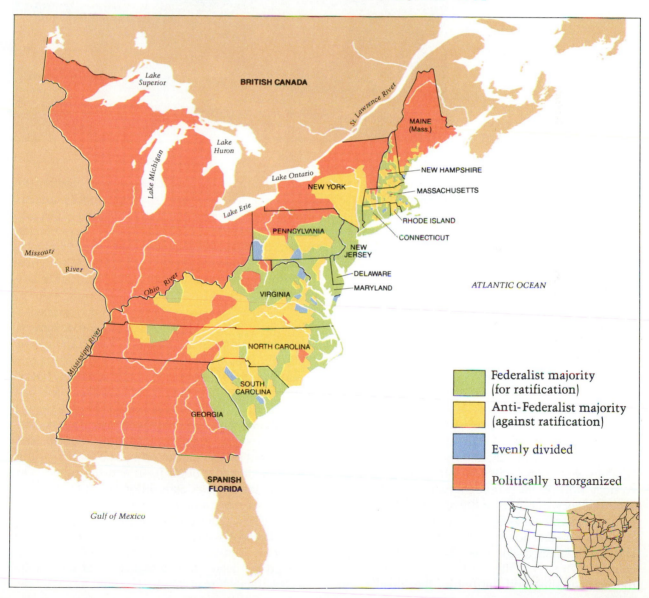

Federalist and Anti-Federalist Areas, 1787–1790

Legend:
- Federalist majority (for ratification)
- Anti-Federalist majority (against ratification)
- Evenly divided
- Politically unorganized

Soon after the Revolution, Americans set about trying to create a national identity to replace regional and local allegiances. The female Columbia, representing Liberty, became the personification of the young republic. In this painting by Samuel Jennings, she carries a liberty cap on a pole.

Jersey and Connecticut, where the Federalists were confident of their strength, they pressed quickly for ratification. Where the outcome was uncertain, as in New York and Virginia, they delayed, hoping that word of ratification elsewhere would work to their benefit.

It took less than a year from the time the document left Congress to secure approval of the necessary nine states. Delaware, Pennsylvania, and New Jersey ratified first, in December 1787. Approval came a month later in Georgia and Connecticut. Massachusetts was next to ratify, but only after considerable political maneuvering. When the Massachusetts convention gathered in Boston on January 9, the Anti-Federalists enjoyed a solid majority. In an effort to woo Anti-Federalist delegates and persuade the uncommitted, Federalist leaders agreed to forward a set of amendments describing a federal "bill of rights" along with notice of ratification. The strategy worked, for it brought Samuel Adams and John Hancock into line, and with them the crucial convention votes that they controlled.

Maryland and South Carolina were the seventh and eighth states to approve. That left New Hampshire and Virginia as the most likely candidates for the honor of being ninth and putting the Constitution over the top. In both states there was determined opposition. The New Hampshire convention met on February 13. Sensing that they lacked the necessary votes, the Federalists arranged to adjourn until mid-June and began working feverishly to build support. When the convention reconvened, it took but three days to secure a Federalist majority. New Hampshire ratified on June 21.

Two massive gaps in the new Union remained— Virginia and New York. Clearly, the government could not endure without them. In Virginia, Madison gathered support by promising that the new Congress would immediately consider a federal bill of rights. Other Federalists tried to weaken the opposition by spreading the rumor that Patrick Henry, most influential of the Anti-Federalist leaders, had changed sides. Henry vehemently denied the charge, but his eloquence proved no match for the careful politicking of Madison and the others. On June 25, the Virginia convention voted to ratify by the narrow margin of ten votes.

The New York convention met on June 17 at Poughkeepsie, with the Anti-Federalist followers of Governor Clinton firmly in command. Hamilton worked for delay, hoping that news of the results in New Hampshire and Virginia would turn the tide.

For several weeks, approval hung in the balance while the two sides maneuvered for support. On July 27, approval squeaked through, 30 to 27. That left two states still uncommitted. North Carolina (with Timothy Bloodworth's cautious approval) finally ratified in November 1789. Rhode Island did not enter the Union until May 1790, more than a year after the new government had gotten under way.

The Social Geography of Ratification

A glance at the geographic pattern of Federalist and Anti-Federalist strength in the states indicates how different were their sources of political support. Federalist strength was concentrated in areas along the coast and navigable rivers and was strongest of all in cities and towns. The centers of Anti-Federalist support lay away from the coast, in the interior of New England, upstate New York, the Virginia piedmont and southside, and the western regions of the Carolinas. Georgia was an exception to this pattern.

The eagle became another symbol of the new nation and soon appeared on water pitchers, whiskey bottles, flags, newspaper mastheads, and fabrics of all kinds.

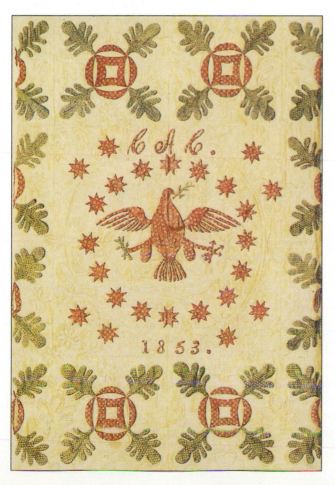

Unable alone to subdue the Creek Indians on their frontier and hoping desperately for help from a strengthened central government, Georgians favored the Constitution.

Merchants and businessmen supported the Constitution most ardently. Enthusiasm also ran high among urban laborers, artisans, and shopkeepers—surprising given the Anti-Federalists' criticism of wealth and power and their emphasis on political equality. City artisans and workers, after all, had been in the vanguard of political reform during the Revolution. But in the troubled circumstances of the late 1780s, they worried about their livelihoods and believed that a stronger government could better promote overseas trade and protect American artisans from foreign competition.

On July 4, 1788, a grand procession celebrating the Constitution's ratification wound through the streets of Philadelphia. Seventeen thousand strong, it graphically demonstrated working-class support for the Constitution. At the head of the line marched lawyers, merchants, and others of the city's elite, but close behind came representatives of virtually every trade in the city, from ship's carpenters to shoemakers, each with its own floats, flags, and mottoed banners. "May commerce flourish and industry be rewarded," declared the mariners and shipbuilders. "May the federal government revive our trade," exclaimed the bakers. "May industry ever be encouraged," urged the porters. "Homebrewed is best," insisted the maltsters.

For the moment, declared Benjamin Rush in amazement, "rank . . . forgot all its claims. Hand in hand marched merchants and seamen, shopkeepers and artisans." Within a few years, political disputes would again divide them. For the time being, however, people of all ranks joined in celebrating the new Constitution.

The Constitution found support as well in the countryside, especially among commercial farmers and southern planters eager for profit and anxious about overseas markets. But Federalist enthusiasm waned and Anti-Federalist sentiment increased in the interior. Among most ordinary farmers living outside the market economy and immersed in their own localities, the republicanism of 1776 outweighed their interests in national affairs. They found the Federalist vision of an "American empire" both strange and alarming.

Why were the Federalists finally successful? The political cards certainly seemed to be stacked against them. The Anti-Federalists had only to de-

The flag became another icon, though it had to be adapted frequently as new states entered the Union.

fend the status quo, arouse people's deep-seated fears of central government, and play on their local loyalties. The Federalists, by contrast, had to explain how republicanism had suddenly become compatible with national power and expansion. Moreover, they faced the complicated political task of coordinating ratification in the various states.

The Federalists' task was simplified by the widespread perception that the Articles needed strengthening. In light of the obvious troubles of the Confederation, the Federalists could argue that the

Revolution was doomed to failure unless dramatic action was taken.

Most of all, however, the Federalists succeeded because of their determination and political skill. Most of the Revolution's major leaders were Federalists. Time and again these heroes spoke out for the Constitution in the state ratifying debates, and time and again their support proved decisive. Their experience as army officers and as members of the Continental and Confederation congresses caused them to identify with the nation and what it might become. They brought their vision to the ratification process and asked others to share it.

Nor were they above tough political maneuvering. In New York, the Federalists warned darkly that if opposition persisted, they would carry the city and its surrounding counties out of the state and ratify on their own. In Pennsylvania, Federalist leaders in the assembly sent out a gang of supporters to round up two Anti-Federalist assemblymen who were desperately trying to leave town in order to deprive the assembly of a quorum and thus prevent it from calling for a state ratifying convention. The Federalists retrieved their hapless opponents, plunked them down in their seats, counted a quorum, and moved ratification on its way. Altogether, it was an impressive political performance. With their success, the Federalists turned the American republic in a new and fateful direction.

CONCLUSION
Completing the Revolution

Only five years had passed between England's acknowledgment of American independence in 1783 and ratification of the new national Constitution, yet to many Americans it seemed far longer. By war's end, the difficulties of sustaining American liberty were evident. The experience of the next half decade added to them. Whether struggling to survive in a hostile Atlantic environment or trying to cope with economic distress

and political turmoil at home, Americans continued to argue about their experiment in republicanism and to wonder whether it would actually work.

At the same time, the American people retained an immense reservoir of optimism about the future. Had they not defeated mighty England? Was not their revolution destined to change the course of history and preserve liberty for all humanity? Did not the wonderfully rich

interior contain the promise of economic and social opportunity for all? Most Americans, still filled with the enthusiasm of their new beginning, answered yes. Much would depend, of course, on their new constitution and the government soon to be created under it. As the ratification debate subsided and Congress prepared for the transition, the American people looked eagerly and anxiously ahead.

Among the major works dealing with the Articles of Confederation and the 1780s are Merrill Jensen, *The New Nation: A History of the United States During the Confederation, 1781–1789* (*1950*); *H. James Henderson,* Party Politics in the Continental Congress (*1974*); *Jack Rakove,* The Beginnings of National Politics: An Interpretive History of the Continental Congress (*1979*); *and Peter Onuf,* The Origins of the Federal Republic (*1983*).

The literature on the Philadelphia convention and the new constitution is extensive and important. Gordon Wood explains the Federalists' drive for a stronger national government and relates the new constitution to the Revolution in The Creation of the American Republic, 1776–1787 (*1969*). *For discussions of the Grand Convention, see Richard Morris,* Witnesses at the Creation: Hamilton, Madison, Jay and the Constitution (*1985*); *Christopher Collier and James Collier,* Decision in Philadelphia (*1986*); *Charles Mee,* The Genius of the People: The Constitutional Convention of 1787 (*1987*); *and J. Jackson Barlow et al.,* The American Founding: Essays on the Formation of the Constitution (*1988*). *Forrest McDonald explains the ideas that guided the Philadelphia convention in* Novus Ordo Seclorum: The Intellectual Origins of the Constitution (*1985*). *Robert Rutland's* James Madison, the Founding Father (*1987*) *is a readable biography of the most important constitution maker.*

For postwar political and economic problems, see Jackson T. Main, Political Parties Before the Constitution (*1937*); *Ronald Hoffman and Peter Albert, eds.,* Sovereign States in an Age of Uncertainty (*1918*); *E. James Ferguson,* The Power of the Purse (*1961*); *Peter Onuf,* The Origins of the Federal Republic (*1983*); *and David Szatmary,* Shays's Rebellion: The Making of an Agrarian Rebellion (*1980*).

Though several decades old, Jackson Main, The Anti-Federalists: Critics of the Constitution, 1781–1788 (*1961*), *is still important for an understanding of the Anti-Federalist opposition. See also Steven Boyd,* The Politics of Opposition: Antifederalists and the Acceptance of the Constitution (*1979*). *Dumas Malone et al.,* Rhetoric and the Founding (*1987*), *examines the relationship between language and meaning in the constitutional debates.*

TIME LINE

1784 Treaty of Fort Stanwix with the Iroquois

Spain closes Mississippi River to American navigation

1785 Treaty of Hopewell with the Cherokee

Land Ordinance for the Northwest Territory

Jay-Gardoqui negotiations

1786 Virginia adopts "Bill for Establishing Religious Freedom"

Annapolis convention calls for revision of the Articles of Confederation

1786–1787 Shays's Rebellion

1787 Northwest Ordinance

Constitutional Convention

Federalist Papers published by Hamilton, Jay, and Madison

1788 Constitution ratified

8

Creating a Nation

In October 1789, David Brown arrived in Dedham, Massachusetts. Born about 50 years before in Bethlehem, Connecticut, Brown served in the Revolutionary army and after the war shipped out on an American merchantman to see the world. His travels, as he later reported, took him to "nineteen different . . . Kingdoms in Europe, and nearly all the United States." For two years before settling in Dedham, he visited scores of Massachusetts towns, supporting himself as a day laborer while discussing the troubled state of public affairs with local townspeople.

Initially the people of Dedham took little notice of Brown, but he soon made his presence felt. Though he had little formal schooling, he was a man with powerful opinions and considerable natural ability. His reading and personal experience had persuaded him that government was a conspiracy of the rich to exploit farmers, artisans, and other common folk, and he was quick to make his opinions known.

"The occupation of government," Brown declared bluntly in one of his numerous pamphlets, "is to plunder and steal." The object of his wrath was the central government recently established under the new national constitution. The leaders of government, he charged, were engrossing the nation's western lands for themselves. "Five hundred [people] out of the union of five millions receive all the benefit of public property and live upon the ruins of the rest of the community." Brown warned that such policies would not last long, because no government could survive "after the confidence of the people was lost, for the people are the government."

In the highly charged political climate of the 1790s, Brown's radical language and exaggerated attacks on the new government's leaders brought a sharp response. In 1798, John Davis, the federal district attorney in Boston, issued a warrant for Brown's arrest on charges of sedition, while government-supported newspapers attacked him as a "rallying point of insurrection and disorder." Fearing arrest, Brown fled to Salem on the Massachusetts coast, but there he was caught and charged with intent to defame the government and aid the country's enemies. For want of $400 bail, he was clapped in prison.

In June 1799, Brown came before the U.S. Circuit Court, Justice Samuel Chase presiding. Chase was anything but judicial. Persuaded that critics of the administration were also enemies of the republic, Chase was determined to make Brown an example of what the government's opponents could expect. Confused and hoping for leniency, Brown pleaded guilty; for Chase, however, that made no difference. Ignoring Brown's plea, he directed the federal prosecutor to "examine the witness . . . that the degree of his guilt might be duly ascertained." Before sentencing him, Chase demanded that Brown provide the names of his accomplices and a list of subscribers to his writings. When Brown refused, protesting that he would "lose all my friends," Chase sentenced him to a fine of $480 and 18 months in jail. No matter that Brown could not pay the fine and faced the prospect of indefinite imprisonment.

In rendering judgment, Chase castigated Brown for the "vicious industry" with which he had circulated his "disorganizing doctrines and . . . falsehoods, and the very alarming and dangerous excesses to which he attempted to incite the uninformed part of the community." Not all citizens, Chase thought, should be allowed to comment on public affairs. For nearly two years, Brown languished in prison. Not until the Federalist party was defeated in the election of 1800 and the Jeffersonian Republicans had taken office was he freed.

David Brown discovered how easy it was for critics of the government to get into trouble during the 1790s, a decade of extraordinary political controversy. Even though the Revolutionary War was long past, the debate over Revolutionary principles and the struggle to create a republican political order continued. As Benjamin Rush, Philadelphia physician and Revolutionary patriot, explained: "The American War is over, but this is far from being the case with the American revolution. On the contrary, nothing but the first act of the great drama is closed. It remains . . . to establish and perfect our new forms of government."

Those efforts continued in the states, but with the new national government beginning to function, a government at least partially elected by the people and with substantially increased powers, patterns of national politics took clearer shape as well. As we have seen, the contest for ratification had generated fierce debate over the familiar concerns about power, political equality, and the proper role of the central government in a republican society. As the new government got under way during the 1790s, that debate heated up once again, catching countless people like David Brown in its toils.

Issues of domestic and foreign policy fueled the controversy as both citizens and political leaders tried to deal with the rapidly changing circumstances of national life. As the decade proceeded and the political debate escalated, Americans divided into two opposing political camps. The Federalists supported the presidential administrations of George Washington and John Adams; the Jeffersonian Republicans were the Federalists' increasingly vocal critics. Seldom has American political discourse been so virulent, and rarely has the survival of the republic seemed to hang more clearly in the balance.

In this chapter, we examine the new government's beginnings, initial controversies over the government's economic policies, the escalating debate fueled by the French Revolution and the outbreak of European war, and the polarizing political divisions between Federalists and Jeffersonian Republicans during the administration of John Adams. The chapter ends with the election of 1800, which brought Federalist defeat and Thomas Jefferson's election to the presidency.

LAUNCHING THE NATIONAL REPUBLIC

Once ratification of the Constitution was achieved, many Anti-Federalists seemed ready to give the new experiment a chance. They determined, however, to watch it closely and raise the alarm at the first sign of danger. It was not many months before those alarms were sounded.

Beginning the New Government

On April 16, 1789, George Washington started north from Virginia toward New York City to be inaugurated as the first president of the United States. The first electoral college convened under the Constitution had unanimously elected him to the nation's highest office. Nearly six years earlier, Washington had left the continental army camp believing that his years of public service were over. His feelings now were mixed as he set forth. "I bade adieu to Mount Vernon, to private life, and to domestic felicity," he confided to his diary, "and with a mind oppressed with more anxious and painful sensations than I have words to express, set out for New York . . . with the best disposition to render service to my country in obedience to its call, but with less hope of answering its expectations." Events would soon show that he had good reason for such forebodings.

Washington's journey through the countryside resembled a royal procession, for he was the object of constant adulation along the way. Local militias turned out to escort him. In villages and towns, guns boomed their salutes, children danced in the streets, church bells pealed, and dignitaries toasted his arrival. On April 23, the president-elect and his entourage reached the northern New Jersey shore, where awaited an elegant barge, festooned with flowers and attended by 11 ship's captains. People crowded the shore as Washington climbed aboard and, accompanied by a flotilla of boats, was rowed across the harbor to New York City. There, throngs of citizens and newly elected members of Congress greeted the weary traveler. Over the streets of the city stretched gaily decorated arches. During the

Commemorative ceramic pitchers were manufactured in Liverpool for export to America. Slogans on these pitchers popularized the principles of the new republic.

parade uptown to the governor's mansion, young women in white flowing robes preceded him, strewing flowers in his path. That night, bonfires illuminated the city.

Already the transition from the old Confederation Congress to the new government was under way. Back on October 2, the Congress had moved from its home in New York's City Hall so it could be redecorated and prepared for the new government's beginning. On October 10, the old Congress transacted its last official business and adjourned *sine die*. Before doing so, it set March 4, 1789, as the day for the new Congress to assemble.

Inaugural day was April 30. Shortly after noon, on a small balcony overlooking a Wall Street thronged with people, Washington took the oath of office. "It is done," exulted New York's chancellor, Robert Livingston. "Long live George Washington, President of the United States!" With the crowd roaring approval and 13 guns booming in the harbor, the president bowed his way off the balcony and into Federal Hall. The rest of the day and late into the night, celebrations filled the air.

Hopefulness and excitement surrounded the new government's beginning. But its first weeks were not easy, for so much had to be done and so many new decisions had to be made. It seemed especially important that the government start on a proper, republican footing. "Many things which appear of little importance in themselves and at the beginning," the president warned, "may have great and durable consequences from their having been established at the commencement of a new general government."

When Washington decided to address Congress, republican purists complained that it smacked too much of the English monarch's speech from the throne at the opening of Parliament. His appearance, moreover, confronted Congress with the question of how it should address the president in its reply and thus opened the sensitive issue of using titles in a republican government. Some congressmen pointed out that state governors and foreign ambassadors carried the title of "Excellency" and argued that the American president deserved a more exalted title than that. Vice-president Adams proposed "His Most Benign Highness." Others offered the even gaudier suggestion: "His Highness, the President of the United States, and Protector of the Rights of the Same." Both generated howls of outrage from those who thought titles had no place in a republic.

In the end, republican principles prevailed, and Congress settled on the simple and now familiar "Mr. President," but not before the House and Senate had spent days debating the matter. During these early years, every decision, no matter how trivial, seemed filled with significance, for people believed they were setting the direction and character of the new government for years to come. That belief gave special intensity to the politics of the time.

The Bill of Rights

Among the new government's first items of business were the amendments that several states had made conditions of their ratification. The government's supporters were eager to keep their promise that this would be done because it would reassure the fearful, weaken calls for a second constitutional convention, and build support for the new regime. After considerable debate, Congress reached agreement on 12 amendments and sent them on to the states, which ratified ten of them. These ten became the Bill of Rights. Among other things, they guaranteed freedom of speech, press, and religion; pledged the right of trial by jury, the right to bear arms, and the right to due process of law; and forbade both "unreasonable searches and seizures" and compulsion to testify against oneself in criminal cases. These constitutional amendments have protected individuals' basic rights throughout the nation's history.

During its first months in office, Washington's administration enjoyed almost universal support, both in Congress and among the people. The honeymoon, however, did not last long. Within a year, as the administration's policies took shape, differences sprang up as people moved into opposition on a variety of issues and for a variety of reasons. By the middle of the decade, opposition groups came together in a political coalition known as the Jeffersonian Republicans. As they did, the administration's remaining supporters rallied under the name of Federalists. By 1800, the Federalists were so reduced in number and so badly divided that their Jeffersonian opponents gained control of the government. The political conflict of this first decade revealed the fragility but also the resilience of this new government.

The People Divide

Disagreement began in January 1790, when Secretary of the Treasury Alexander Hamilton submitted the first of several major policy statements; the "Report on the Public Credit," to Congress. Seldom in the nation's history has a single official so dominated public affairs as Hamilton did during these first years. He was a man of extraordinary intelligence and ambition who preferred not to seek elective office but to act behind the scenes, where he could shape events beyond the public eye. His instincts for locating and seizing the levers of political power were unerring.

Hamilton was a nationalist and a proponent of America's economic development. Perhaps more clearly than anyone else among the nation's foun-

This imaginative scene of president-elect Washington's reception in Trenton, New Jersey, during his trip from Virginia to New York City for his first inauguration depicts the popular adulation that surrounded him as well as the sharply different political roles of men and women.

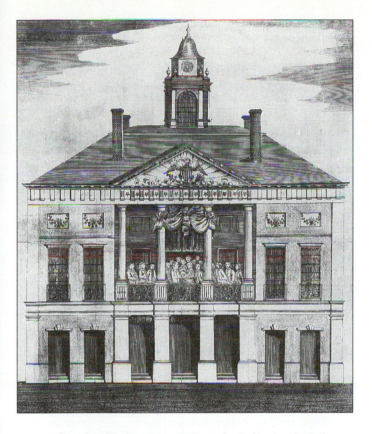

President Washington took the oath of office on the balcony of the recently refurbished Federal Hall. Its cornice was emblazoned with the arms of the United States, and its windows were topped with plaster friezes containing 13 arrows and an olive branch bound together.

his politics were profoundly conservative. He had supported the colonies' break with England but continued to be deeply impressed with England's political system, especially the stability of the monarchy and the confident governing style of the upper class. At bottom, Hamilton distrusted the people. He doubted their wisdom and feared their purposes. "The people," he asserted, "are turbulent and changing; they seldom judge or determine right." That stark belief guided much of what he did.

In the Philadelphia convention, Hamilton had urged that power be concentrated in the hands of the "rich and well-born" so that they could "check the unsteadiness" of the people. The Constitution that emerged he thought not "high-toned" enough to insure the nation's future. But he believed it was a considerable improvement over the Articles of Confederation and worked hard for its ratification. With that accomplished, he set about to find ways of giving it proper direction. His opportunity came when Washington named him secretary of the treasury. Recognizing the potential importance of his office, he determined to use it to build the kind of nation he envisioned.

Hamilton had five objectives: to stabilize the government's finances and establish its credit, to build and demonstrate its power, to tie the interests of the rich and well-born to the national government, to promote the country's commercial expansion overseas and its economic development at home, and to anchor the nation's foreign relations in a commercial and diplomatic alliance with England. All were essential to the nation's survival; each he believed, was closely tied to the others.

In his first "Report on the Public Credit," Hamilton recommended funding the remaining Revolutionary War debt by enabling the government's creditors to exchange their badly depreciated securities at full face value for new interest-bearing government bonds. The foreign debt, held chiefly in France and the Netherlands, Hamilton set at $11.7 million. The domestic debt, including back interest, he fixed at $40.4 million. Second, he proposed that the federal government assume responsibility for the $21.5 million in remaining state war debts. By these actions, he hoped to revive confidence in the government at home and abroad and tie business and commercial interests, which held most of the outstanding securities, firmly to the new government.

ders, he foresaw the country's future strength and was determined to promote its growth. The United States, he was fond of saying, was "a Hercules in the cradle." Domestic manufacturing and overseas commerce, he believed, were the ways to promote America's economic development and build national wealth. Competitive self-interest he thought the surest guide to behavior, whether of nations or of individuals.

The proper role of the new government, he argued, was to promote economic enterprise. The people he most admired were men of wealth, ambitious entrepreneurs eager to tie their own fortunes to America's rising empire. Hamilton regarded a close alliance between these people and government officials as essential to achieving American greatness.

If Hamilton's economic policies were liberal in looking forward to enhanced economic opportunity,

The proposal to fund the foreign debt aroused little controversy, but Hamilton's plans for handling the government's domestic obligations generated immediate opposition. In the House of Representatives, James Madison, Hamilton's recent ratification ally, protested the unfairness of funding depreciated securities at their face value, especially since speculators, anticipating Hamilton's proposals, had acquired most of them at a fraction of their initial worth. In addition, Madison and many of his southern colleagues knew that northern businessmen held most of the securities and that funding would little benefit the South.

Hamilton was not impressed. The speculators, he observed, "paid what the commodity was worth in the market, and took the risks." They should therefore "reap the benefit." If his plan served the interests of the wealthy, that was exactly as he intended, for it would further strengthen the tie between wealth and national power. After a bit of grumbling, Congress endorsed the funding plan.

Federal assumption of the remaining state debts, another important part of Hamilton's program, aroused even greater criticism. States with

Alexander Hamilton used both the office of secretary of the treasury and his personal relationship with President Washington to shape national policy during the early 1790s.

the largest remaining unpaid obligations, such as Massachusetts, thought assumption a splendid idea. But others, such as Virginia and Pennsylvania, which had already retired much of their debt, were not eager to help cover others' indebtedness as the assumption scheme demanded. Critics also pointed out that assumption would strengthen the central government at the expense of the states, for wealthy individuals would now look to it rather than the states for a return on their investments. Moreover, the federal government, with its increased need for revenue, would now have reason to exercise its newly acquired power of taxation. That was exactly what Hamilton intended.

Once again, Congress supported Hamilton's bill. Both Madison and Jefferson approved it as part of an agreement to move the seat of government from New York, first to Philadelphia and then, after 1800, to a special federal district on the Potomac River. Southerners, disturbed by the early growth of federal power, hoped that locating the government away from northern commercial centers would enable them to control its development and keep it more closely aligned with southern, agrarian interests.

Despite this congressional agreement, opposition to the funding and assumption scheme did not die, especially in the southern states. In December 1790, the Virginia assembly passed a series of resolutions, framed by that old republican Patrick Henry, warning that a monied aristocracy was taking control of the government, that agriculture was being subordinated to commerce, and that the government's powers were expanding dangerously. Nothing in the Constitution, the assembly protested, authorized Congress to assume the states' debts. Hamilton wrote privately to a friend upon hearing of the Virginia resolutions: "This is the first symptom of a spirit which must either be killed, or will kill the Constitution." The contest for control of the new government was now clearly joined.

In December 1790, Hamilton introduced the second phase of his financial program when he proposed a national bank capable of handling the government's financial affairs and pooling private investment capital for economic development. Though he was careful not to mention it publicly, he had the example of the Bank of England and its ties with the royal government clearly in mind.

Congressional opposition to the bank was largely sectional. Only one northern delegate voted against it; the rest of the opposition came from the

Overcoming opposition by Secretary of State Jefferson, Hamilton secured congressional approval of a national bank in 1791. The first bank building was erected in Philadelphia four years later.

South. It seemed obvious that the bank would serve far better the needs of the northern merchants and manufacturers than of southern agrarians. In February 1791, Congress approved the bank bill.

Before signing it, Washington asked his cabinet for advice. Following the constitutional doctrine of "implied powers"—the principle that the government possessed the authority to make any laws "necessary and proper" for exercising the powers specifically granted to it—Hamilton argued that Congress could charter such a bank under its power to collect taxes and regulate trade. Secretary of State Jefferson, however, disagreed and urged the president to veto the bill. He saw in Hamilton's argument a blueprint for the indefinite expansion of federal authority and argued instead that the Constitution should be construed narrowly and the government allowed only those powers specifically granted to it. Since the Constitution said nothing at all about chartering banks, the bill was unconstitutional and should be rejected.

Jefferson also opposed the bank because he feared the rapid development of commerce and domestic manufacturing that the bank was intended to promote. He opposed Hamilton's goal of a commercial republic filled with merchants and a de-

pendent laboring class and sought instead an agrarian republic populated by yeoman farmers committed to economic and political equality. Only among agrarians, "the chosen people of God," could republican liberty be sustained. To Jefferson's distress, Washington followed Hamilton's advice and signed the bank bill into law.

In December 1790, in his second "Report on the Public Credit," Hamilton broached the issue of federal taxation. He proposed a series of excise taxes, including one on the manufacture of distilled liquor. By this so-called Whiskey Tax he intended to signal the government's intention to use its new taxing authority to increase federal revenue. The power to tax and spend, Hamilton knew, was the power to govern. The Whiskey Tax became law in March 1791.

Finally, in his "Report on Manufactures," issued in December 1791, Hamilton called for a system of protective tariffs for American industry, bounties to encourage the expansion of commercial agriculture, and a network of federally sponsored internal improvements such as roadways and lighthouses. These were intended to stimulate commerce and bind the nation more tightly together. Neither the agrarian South nor northern seaport districts, however, wanted tariffs that might reduce trade and raise the cost of living. As a result, Congress never endorsed this report.

All the while, criticism of Hamilton's program continued to grow. In October 1791, opposition leaders in Congress established a newspaper, the *National Gazette,* and vigorously attacked the administration's program. Hamilton responded with a series of anonymous articles in the administration's paper, *The Gazette of the United States,* in which he directly attacked his cabinet colleague, Jefferson, accused him (inaccurately) of having opposed the Constitution, and charged him (also inaccurately) of fomenting opposition to the government. Alarmed at the division within his administration, Washington pleaded unsuccessfully for restraint.

Congressional criticism of Hamilton's policies reached a climax in January 1793 when Representative William Branch Giles of Virginia introduced

The Revolutionary generation found inspiration in the republican eras of ancient Greece and Rome. This bust of Thomas Jefferson, cast in the classical style, was completed in 1789 by the French sculptor Jean-Antoine Houdon.

a series of resolutions calling for an inquiry into the condition of the Treasury, accusing Hamilton of using the office for his own benefit and urging censure of the secretary's conduct. Hamilton vigorously defended both his policies and his personal conduct, and none of Giles's accusations passed the House. The month-long debate, however, showed just how bitter political discourse at the seat of government had become.

The debate was now spreading beyond the circle of governing officials in Philadelphia. Among ordinary Americans, Hamilton's financial program drew a mixed response. In northern towns and cities, artisans and other working people generally approved. Tied closely to the expansion of commerce and manufacturing, they supported efforts to improve credit and stimulate economic development. With their own economic circumstances improving, they seemed undisturbed by the special benefits that funding, assumption, and the bank brought to a few. Within several years, many of them would move into political opposition, but for the moment their support of the government was secure.

The Whiskey Rebellion

The farmers of western Pennsylvania provided the most dramatic expression of popular discontent with government policies. Its focus was the Whiskey Tax. Ever since the trouble with England 30 years before, Americans had been sensitive to taxation and suspicious of its connections with governmental power. The farmers of western Pennsylvania had special reason to dislike this particular tax. Their livelihood depended on their ability to transport surplus grain eastward across the mountains to market. To ship it in bulk was prohibitively expensive, so they distilled the grain and moved it in the more cost-efficient form of whiskey.

Hamilton's tax threatened to make this practice unprofitable. He knew that but cared little what the farmers thought; the government needed revenue, and the farmers would have to bear the cost. George Clymer, federal supervisor of revenue for Pennsylvania, was equally unsympathetic to the farmers and their situation. Referring to the "moral and personal weakness" of the lesser folk," Clymer publicly castigated the "sordid shopkeepers" who retailed Pennsylvania whiskey and the "greatly depraved" farmers who produced it. The farmers resented the

Federalists' arrogance as much as the tax and quickly made their resentment known.

Trouble was brewing by the summer of 1792 as angry farmers and their supporters gathered in mass meetings across western Pennsylvania. In August, a convention at Pittsburgh drew up a series of resolutions denouncing the tax and declaring that the people would prevent its collection. The convention's pronouncements echoed the Anti-Federalists' arguments against the Constitution. They had warned that once the central government secured the power to tax, a swarm of excise officers would descend like locusts on the people, consuming their property and offering nothing in return. If given the chance, one Anti-Federalist had warned, the central government would "monopolize every source of revenue . . . [and] demolish the state governments." To Pennsylvania's farmers, those predictions rang true. Like opponents of the Stamp Act in 1765, they decided that repression would follow if resistance did not soon begin.

Alarmed by the convention's resolutions, Washington quickly issued a proclamation warning against such "unlawful" gatherings and insisting on the enforcement of the excise. As tax collections began, the farmers took more direct action. They complained not only about the excise but also about the requirement that persons charged with evading the tax must stand trial in federal court. This seemed further evidence of the government's efforts to intimidate its critics. Moreover, the nearest federal court was hundreds of miles away, over the mountains, in Philadelphia.

In July 1794, federal marshal David Lennox, in company with John Neville, a local excise inspector, attempted to serve papers on several western farmers, commanding their appearance in court at Philadelphia. An angry crowd gathered and stood in the way. Soon 500 armed men surrounded Neville's home just outside Pittsburgh and, in a scene that echoed the Stamp Act riots of 1765, demanded his resignation. Learning that Neville had left, they ordered the dozen soldiers trapped in the house to lay down their arms and come out. Fearing for their safety, the soldiers refused, and for several hours the two sides exchanged rifle fire. After several men had been wounded, the soldiers finally surrendered, whereupon Neville's house was put to the torch. Similar episodes involving angry crowds, the erection of liberty poles as during the Revolution, and the hoisting of banners bearing such slogans as "Liberty and No Excise. O Whiskey!" erupted across

the state. At Parkinson's Ferry, a convention of over 200 delegates debated both armed resistance and secession from the United States.

Alarmed that the protests might spread through the entire whiskey-producing backcountry from New York to Georgia, Washington sternly ordered the insurgents home and called out troops from eastern Pennsylvania and surrounding states to restore order. For more than a year, Hamilton had been urging the use of force against protesters. He viewed the insurrection not as evidence of an unjust policy needing change but as a test of the administration's ability to govern. Firmly suppressing the rebellion, Hamilton explained, "will do us a great deal of good and add to the solidity of everything in this country." He eagerly volunteered to accompany a federal army west.

In late August, a force of nearly 13,000 men, larger than the average strength of the continental army during the Revolutionary War, moved toward western Pennsylvania. At its center was Colonel William McPherson's "Pennsylvania Blues," an upper-class and strongly Federalist cavalry regiment. At its head rode the president of the United States and the secretary of the treasury. Washington soon returned to Philadelphia, persuaded by his aides of the danger to his safety, but Hamilton pressed ahead. When later criticized for accompanying the army to Pittsburgh, he replied that he had "long since . . . learned to hold public opinion of no value." The battle that Hamilton had anticipated, however, never materialized for as the federal army approached, the "Whiskey Rebels" dispersed, their two chief leaders fleeing across the Ohio River. The federal army managed to take 20 prisoners. Two were convicted of high treason and sentenced to death. Later, in a calmer mood, Washington pardoned them both.

As people quickly realized, the "Whiskey Rebellion" had never threatened the government's safety. "An insurrection was announced and proclaimed and armed against," Jefferson scoffed, "but could never be found." Hamilton was merely pursuing his "favorite purpose of strengthening government" under "the sanction of a name [Washington's] which has done too much good not to be sufficient to cover harm also." Even as ardent a Federalist as Fisher Ames was uneasy at the sight of federal troops marching against American citizens. Though a government "by overcoming an unsuccessful insurrection becomes stronger," he noted, "elective rulers can scarcely ever employ the

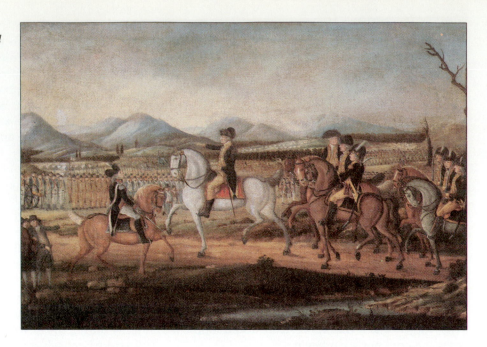

President Washington and Treasury Secretary Hamilton led a federal army of nearly 13,000 troops into the whiskey-producing region of western Pennsylvania in 1794. Rebelling farmers, protesting the government's excise tax on whiskey, dispersed as the army approached.

physical force of a democracy without turning the moral force, or the power of public opinion, against the government." Americans would soon have additional reason to ponder Ames's warning.

THE REPUBLIC IN A THREATENING WORLD

During the 1790s, because the nation was so new and the outside world so threatening, issues of foreign policy generated extraordinary excitement. This was especially so after the tumultuous events of the French Revolution and the accompanying European war burst upon the international scene. In the arguments over the revolution in France and its implications for the new American republic, the American people revealed once again how sharply they differed in values and beliefs.

The Promise and Peril of the French Revolution

France's revolution began in 1789 as an effort to reform an arbitrary monarchy weakened by debt and administrative decay. Pent-up demands for social justice, however, quickly outran the initial attempts at moderate, constitutional reform. By the early 1790s, France was embroiled in a genuinely radical social revolution. In January 1793, the mon-

arch, Louis XVI, was beheaded. While the rest of Europe watched in horror and fascination, the forces of revolution and reaction struggled for the nation's soul.

As the revolution grew and extended its attack on the aristocracy, the monarchy, and the Catholic church, the forces of conservatism across the Continent gathered in opposition, their fears fueled by the appeals of fleeing French aristocrats. Finding itself surrounded and facing assault by Austria and Prussia, France's revolutionary government launched a series of military thrusts into Belgium and Prussia. The result was a general declaration of war. By the end of 1793, Europe was locked in a deadly struggle between revolutionary France and a counterrevolutionary coalition led by Prussia and Great Britain.

For more than a decade, the French Revolution dominated European affairs. Before it was finished, it would transform the entire course of European history. The revolution cut like a ploughshare through the surface of American politics as well, dividing Americans more deeply against each other. Not only did it raise immediate threats to the nation's security, but it also captured people's imaginations and polarized the debate over what the American republic should be.

The outbreak of European war posed a number of thorny problems for Washington's administration. Both England and France wanted America's raw materials and were determined to prevent them from reaching the other. American merchants were eager to profit from trade with both sides. According to international law, neutral nations in time of war could continue to trade with belligerent powers, as long as it did not involve goods directly related to the war effort. Neither France nor England, however, was willing to tie itself down with legal formalities when locked in deadly combat. So both nations attempted to control American trade for their own advantage by stopping American ships headed for the other's ports and confiscating American cargoes.

America's relations with England were further complicated by its practice of impressing American sailors into service aboard ships of the Royal Navy to meet its growing demand for seamen. Washington faced the problem of upholding the country's neutral rights and protecting its citizens without getting drawn into the European war.

The old French alliance of 1778 compounded the government's dilemma. If still in effect, it seemed to require the United States to aid France, much as France had assisted the American states a decade and a half before. Persons sympathetic to the French cause argued that America's commitment still existed. Others, however, fearing the consequences of American involvement and the political infection that closer ties with revolutionary France might bring, insisted that the old treaty had been dissolved when the French monarchy collapsed.

The American people's intense reaction to the European drama further complicated the situation. Though an ocean away, Americans followed France's revolution with fascination, for they believed they had an important stake in its outcome. At first, virtually everyone supported the revolution as an extension of their own struggle for liberty. Even the swing toward social revolution did not immediately damp American enthusiasm.

By the mid-1790s, however, especially after France's revolutionary regime launched its attacks on organized Christianity, many Americans pulled back in alarm. This certainly did not resemble their own revolution. What connection could there possibly be between the principles of 1776 and the chaos of revolutionary France? "There is a difference between the French and the American Revolution," insisted the *Gazette of the United States.* "In America no barbarities were perpetrated—no men's heads were stuck upon poles—no mangled ladies bodies were carried thro' the streets in triumph.

. . . Whatever blood was shed, flowed gallantly in the field." The writer ignored the violence meted out by the supporters of monarchy in France and betrayed a selective memory of America's revolution. But the differences were indeed profound.

For the Federalists, revolutionary France now symbolized social anarchy and threatened the European order on which they believed America's commercial and diplomatic well-being depended. With increasing vigor, they castigated the revolution, championed England as the defender of European civilization, and sought ways of linking England and the United States more closely.

Many Americans, however, continued to support France. While decrying the revolution's excesses, they noted how deeply entrenched the forces of reaction had been and how difficult it was to root them out. Moreover, they believed that republican liberty would ultimately emerge from the turmoil. Jefferson wrote that although he regretted the shedding of innocent blood, he believed it necessary if true liberty were to be achieved. John Bradford, editor of the *Kentucky Gazette,* declared, "Instead of reviling the French republicans as monsters, the friends of royalty in this country should rather admire their patience in so long deferring the fate of their perjured monarch, whose blood is . . . considered . . . atonement for the safety of many guilty thousands that are still suffered to remain in the bosom of France." In Bradford's judgment, England was not a bastion of order but the defender of arbitrary privilege and despotism.

Citizen Genêt and the Democratic-Republican Societies

Popular associations known as the Democratic-Republican societies offered most vocal support for revolutionary France. As early as 1792, ordinary citizens began to establish "constitutional societies" for the purpose of "watching over the rights of the people, and giving an early alarm in case of governmental encroachments." During the government's first years, several dozen such societies formed to oppose Hamilton's financial program. Modeling themselves on the Sons of Liberty (see Chapter 5), they appealed to the people for support, and established networks of correspondence.

It was the French Revolution, however, that kindled democratic enthusiasm and stimulated the societies' growth. The arrival in April 1793 of Citizen Edmund Genêt, minister from the French republic

RECOVERING THE PAST

PATRIOTIC PAINTINGS

The questions that historians ask are limited only by their imagination and the historical evidence left behind for them to study. We have seen how historians use different kinds of written evidence, such as household inventories and Indian treaties, as well as material artifacts like tombstones and house designs. They also use visual evidence such as paintings and sculpture, for these too can provide insight into the life and culture of the past. With the proper mixture of care and ingenuity, historians can tease surprising amounts of information out of materials that at first glance seem silent and unrewarding.

Paintings offer unique insights into the past. They can tell us about the development over time of artistic styles and techniques. They also offer a window into the past for social and cultural historians, for they reveal how people lived and looked and did their work, as well as what the landscape and home furnishings were like.

During the Revolutionary era and the early national period, American artists employed painting and other visual arts to record the great events of the nation's founding. John Trumbull, for example, secured a commission from Congress in the early nineteenth century to prepare a series of historical canvasses. Grand in conception and scale, the four paintings that he completed—depicting the signing of the Declaration of Independence, the surrender of General Burgoyne at Saratoga and Lord Cornwallis at Yorktown, and Washington resigning his commission at the end of the war in 1783—now hang in the rotunda of the nation's capitol in Washington. Explained Trumbull in a letter to Thomas Jefferson: "The greatest motive I [have] had . . . for engaging in my pursuit of painting, has been the wish of commemorating the great events of our country's revolution."

The Founders were also popular subjects of the painter's brush. As a member of the Pennsylvania militia, Charles Willson Peale carried paint kits and canvas along with his musket as he followed George Washington during the war. Before it was over, he had completed four paintings of the general.

Although Washington left the presidency in 1797 amid a storm of controversy, his death in 1799 generated a surge of public mourning. During the first year after his death, countless sermons and eulogies celebrated him as "the Father of his Country," a man "first in war, first in peace, and first in the hearts of his countrymen." Everywhere people organized memorial processions and decked themselves out in black crepe, gold mourning rings, and funeral medals. In New York, an enterprising bookseller named Mason Weems quickly published a best-selling biography of the great hero. Complete with invented accounts of the cherry tree episode and the story of Washington throwing a silver dollar across the Delaware River, Weems's book went through 80 profitable editions over the next 100 years.

The Apotheosis of Washington, painted by an anonymous artist after an 1802 engraving by John Barralet and reproduced here, shows how Washington was mythologized during the years immediately following his death. Examine the painting carefully, for it is filled with a fascinating mixture of patriotic, religious, and cultural symbolism. Why is Washington depicted with his arms extended? Who is the woman standing at the left of the picture, and why are the children included? The bottom quarter of the picture is crowded with objects and human forms, each of them carefully chosen for what it might contribute to the painting's overall effect. Identify them and explain why they are there. Finally, why did the veneration of Washington in word and image take place?

Anonymous Chinese, The Apotheosis of Washington, after J. Barralet, 1802

to the United States, provided the spark. Genêt landed first at Charleston, South Carolina, to a tumultuous reception. His instructions were to woo public support and negotiate a commercial treaty with Washington's administration. It quickly became evident, however, that he had other plans as well. Immediately after his arrival in Charleston, he began commissioning American privateers to prey on British shipping in the Caribbean and enlisting American seamen for expeditions against Spanish Florida, both clear violations of American neutrality.

As he traveled northward toward Philadelphia, Genêt met enthusiastic receptions. His popularity, though, soon led him beyond the bounds of diplomatic propriety. When, at Washington's insistence, Secretary of State Jefferson warned Genêt that granting military commissions infringed American sovereignty and must stop, he threatened to appeal over the president's head to the people. In open defiance of diplomatic protocol, he urged Congress to reject Washington's recently issued neutrality proclamation and side with revolutionary France. That was the final straw. On August 2, the president demanded Genêt's recall, charging that his conduct threatened "war abroad and anarchy at home."

If Genêt had little success as a diplomat, he did fan popular enthusiasm for revolutionary France. In June 1793, with his open encouragement, the largest and most influential of the new societies, the Democratic Society of Pennsylvania, was founded in Philadelphia. It called immediately for the formation of similar societies elsewhere to join in supporting France and promoting "the spirit of freedom and equality" at home. People across the land, it declared, should join the effort to "erect the temple of *liberty* on the ruins of palaces and thrones." Washington and his colleagues might wonder if that challenge was also aimed at them.

Although a full network of popular societies never developed, about 40 organizations scattered from Maine to Georgia sprang up during the next several years. Federalist critics derided them as made up of "the lowest orders of mechanics, laborers and draymen, . . . butchers, tinkers, broken hucksters, and trans-Atlantic traitors." Working people—mechanics, artisans, and laborers in the cities, small farmers and tenants in the countryside—did provide the bulk of membership. The leaders, however, were individuals of acknowledged "respectability," such as doctors, lawyers, tradesmen, and landowners. They were united by a common dedication to what they called the "principles of '76" and a determination to preserve those principles against the "royalizing" tendencies of Washington's administration.

Lamenting the decline of republicanism, the societies worked actively for its reinvigoration. They organized public celebrations of the nation's birth, printed circulars, issued addresses to the people, and framed petitions to the president and Congress, almost all sharply critical of administration policies. They labeled Washington's proclamation of neutrality a "pusillanimous truckling to Britain, despotically conceived and unconstitutionally promulgated." Neutrality toward England and revolutionary France, they insisted, was irresponsible, for if Britain should succeed in Europe, America would again feel its wrath. Declared the New York society: "We firmly believe that he who is an enemy to the French revolution cannot be a firm republican; and therefore . . . ought not to be entrusted with the guidance of any part of the machine of government." Several of the societies openly urged the United States to enter the war on France's behalf.

The local societies took up other issues as well. In western areas, they agitated against the continuing British occupation of the frontier posts around the Great Lakes and berated Spain for closing the Mississippi. In the East, they castigated England for its "piracy" against American shipping. In the Carolinas, they demanded fuller representation for the growing backcountry in the state's assembly. And almost to a person they protested the Excise Tax, opposed the administration's overtures to England, and demanded that public officials, state and federal alike, attend to the people's wishes.

Finally, they campaigned for a press free from the political control of Federalist "aristocrats." "The greater part of the American newspapers," they protested, "seem to be lock, stock, and barrel in the hands of the anti-democrats." Declared William Manning, a Massachusetts farmer who had marched to the "Concord fight" in 1775 and continued to praise the principles for which he had fought: "A labouring man may as well hunt for pins in a haymow as to try to collect the knowledge necessary for him to have from such promiscuous piles of contradictions" as appeared in the Federalist press.

President Washington and his supporters were incensed by the societies' unwavering support of Genêt and their criticism of the government's domestic program. The "real design" of the societies, thundered the staunch Federalist Fisher Ames, was "to involve the country in war, to assume the reins of government and tyrannize over the people." As "nurseries of sedition," they were bent on revolutionizing America as the Jacobins had revolutionized France. Writing in the *Virginia Chronicle* of January 17, 1794, "Xantippe" berated Kentucky's Democratic Society as "that horrible sink of treason, that hateful synagogue of anarchy, that odious conclave of tumult, that frightful cathedral of discord, that poisonous garden of conspiracy, that hellish school of rebellion and opposition to all regular and well-balanced authority!" Such polemics illustrated how inflamed public discourse had become.

To Washington's supporters, the critics seemed dangerous radicals intent on spreading social revolution. In turn, those critics, now beginning to coalesce under the name of Jeffersonian Republicans, attacked the Federalists as defenders of special privilege, as antirepublicans eager to return the United States to monarchy and subject it once again to British control. The language of political attack on both sides was wildly exaggerated, but in the volatile political climate of the 1790s, when the nation was new and vulnerable, it was easy to believe the worst of one's opponents.

Jay's Controversial Treaty

Controversy over Jay's Treaty with England further heightened tensions at mid-decade. Alarmed by the worsening relations with England, Washington sent Chief Justice John Jay to London in the spring of 1794 with instructions to negotiate on a wide range of troublesome issues. Ever since the American Revolution, tension had been building over continued British occupation of the western posts and the failure of England to honor other clauses in the peace treaty of 1783. British interference with American neutral shipping and impressment of American seamen added to the rising tide of anti-English sentiment.

Early in 1795, Jay returned home with a treaty that resolved almost none of America's grievances. England finally agreed to vacate the western posts, but not for another year and then only if it had uninterrupted access to the fur trade on American soil south of the Great Lakes. Jay failed to secure compensation for American slaves the British carried off at the end of the Revolution. Nor would the British foreign minister offer guarantees against the future impressment of American seamen. England refused as well to compromise on the issue of neu-

tral rights, in effect declaring that it would decide what America's rights would be. Finally, England declined to open its West Indian possessions to American shipping.

When the terms of the treaty were made public, they triggered an explosion of protest. The administration's pleas that the agreement headed off an open breach with England and was the best that could be obtained failed to pacify the critics. In New York City, Hamilton was stoned when he defended the treaty at a noonday mass meeting. The "rabble," sniffed a Federalist newspaper, attempted "to knock out Hamilton's brains to reduce him to an equality with themselves." Southern planters were angry because the agreement brought no compensation for their slaves. Westerners complained that the British were not evacuating the posts, while merchants and sailors railed against Jay's capitulation on the West Indies trade and impressment. After a long and acrimonious debate, the Senate finally ratified the treaty by the narrowest of margins.

The administration made better progress on the still volatile issue of free transit out the mouth of the Mississippi River. In the Treaty of San Lorenzo, negotiated by Thomas Pinckney in 1795, Spain for the first time recognized the United States' boundaries under the peace treaty of 1783 (the Mississippi to the west and the 31st parallel to the south) and thus gave up all claim to U.S. territory. Spain also granted free navigation of the Mississippi and the right of American merchants to unload their goods on shore for transshipment for the next three years. Even on that issue, however, the future remained uncertain.

By mid-decade, political harmony had entirely disappeared, and the American people stood sharply divided on almost every significant issue of foreign and domestic policy. Frustrated by the president's growing dependence on Hamilton and increasingly estranged from administration policy, Jefferson resigned as secretary of state in July 1793. He soon joined politicians such as Madison and Albert Gallatin of Pennsylvania in open opposition to the Federalist administration. By 1796, the cabinet contained only the most ardent Federalists.

In September 1796, in what came to be called his Farewell Address, Washington announced that he would not accept a third term. He had long been contemplating retirement, for he was now 64 and was exhausted by the political controversy swirling about him. Even the Great Patriot was no longer immune to attack. The nadir of abuse had come in

July in an open letter published by that old revolutionary Thomas Paine in the Philadelphia *Aurora*. "As to you, sir," Paine fumed, "treacherous in private friendship . . . and a hypocrite in public life, the world will be puzzled to decide, whether you are an apostate or an imposter; whether you have abandoned good principles, or whether you ever had any." Seldom has an American president been subjected to such public abuse as was Washington during his final year in office.

FEDERALISTS VERSUS JEFFERSONIANS

By 1796, people's worst fears had been realized as bitter controversy surrounded the national government. That controversy intensified during the last half of the 1790s until it seemed to threaten the very stability of the country.

Heralded as the first president and worshiped by later generations, George Washington left office in 1797 amid vicious criticism.

The Election of 1796

The presidential election of 1796 reflected the political storms buffeting the nation. In 1792, Washington and Adams had been reelected without significant opposition. Four years later, the situation was vastly different.

With Washington out of the picture, the presidential contest quickly narrowed to John Adams and Thomas Jefferson. Both were now elder statesmen; Adams was 61 years old, Jefferson eight years his junior. Both had played distinguished and often intersecting roles during the Revolution.

Adams's eager intelligence and fierce patriotism had produced a stream of writings detailing the Americans' legal arguments against England and laying out the constitutional principles on which America's new governments should be based. Jefferson was no less ardent, and considerably more eloquent, in his defense of American liberties. He was also a more enthusiastic republican reformer. In Virginia, he called for the reform of inheritance laws, full separation of church and state, establishment of a public school system, and termination of the slave trade.

The paths of Jefferson and Adams had first crossed in the Continental Congress, where they became friends and earned each other's respect. Their bonds were fused more tightly when they shared in the electrifying task of drafting the Declaration of Independence. During the 1780s, they came together once again in Europe, where Adams negotiated crucial Dutch loans, helped frame the treaty of peace with England, and served as first U.S. minister to Great Britain while Jefferson served as minister to France. While abroad, they corresponded frequently and exchanged family visits. They joined forces a third time during the early 1790s, Adams as Vice-president (a position he described in frustration as "laborious" and "wholly insignificant") and Jefferson as Washington's first secretary of state.

Though they had worked closely together, Adams and Jefferson differed in many ways. Short, round, balding, and self-consciously neat, Adams contrasted sharply in physical appearance with the tall, angular, and frequently disheveled Jefferson. Intensely ambitious, though never able to acknowledge it, and deeply insecure about his contemporaries and the judgments of history, Adams struggled noisily with his public career. Perhaps in

This biting cartoon lampoons William Cobbitt, one of the Federalists' most acid-tongued pamphleteers. Cartoons became a part of the arsenal of the emerging political parties in the 1790s.

keeping with his Calvinist heritage, he often found reassurance in adversity. Jefferson, by contrast, charted his course more quietly and repeatedly sought the solace of private life.

They differed in intellect and vision as well. Jefferson's mind was more expansive and his interests far more encompassing. Politician and political theorist, he was also an avid naturalist, architect, and philosopher. Adams's interests were more tightly focused on legal and constitutional affairs. By the mid-1790s, they differed fundamentally in their visions of the national republic.

Though fearing Hamilton's ambition and distrusting his infatuation with England, Adams was a committed Federalist. He believed in a vigorous national government, was appalled by the French Revolution, and longed for political and social order. Jefferson, while firmly supporting the constitution, was alarmed by Hamilton's financial program, viewed France's revolution as a logical if chaotic extension of America's struggle for freedom, and sought to expand political democracy. By 1796, he had become the vocal leader of an increasingly articulate political opposition, the Jeffersonian Republicans.

The election of that year bound Jefferson and Adams in a strained alliance. With Washington gone, Adams became the Federalists' candidate. Though Jefferson did not officially oppose Adams, his fol-

lowers campaigned vigorously on Jefferson's behalf. In the election, Adams received 71 electoral votes and was declared president. Jefferson came in second with 68 and therefore, as specified in the Constitution, became vice-president. The narrowness of Adams's majority—his enemies often reminded him that he was only "a President of three votes"—gave indication of the Federalists' weakness and the growing strength of the Jeffersonians. Adams later recalled his inaugural day. "A solemn scene it was indeed, and it was made more affecting by the presence of the General [Washington], whose countenance was as serene and unclouded as the day. He seemed to enjoy a triumph over me. Methought I heard him say, 'Ay! I am fairly out and you fairly in! See which of us will be the happiest.' " The answer to that was not long in coming.

The War Crisis with France

Adams had no sooner taken office than he confronted a deepening crisis with France. Hoping to ease diplomatic relations between the two countries, he sent off a three-person commission to try to negotiate an accord.

When the commissioners arrived in Paris, three agents of the French foreign minister, Talleyrand, visited them and made it clear that the success of the negotiations depended on a prior loan to the French government and a $240,000 gratuity for them. The two staunchly Federalist commissioners, John Marshall and Charles Pinckney, indignantly rejected the demands and sailed home. The third commissioner, Elbridge Gerry, stayed behind, still hoping for an accommodation and alarmed by Talleyrand's intimation that if all three Americans left, France would declare war.

When Adams submitted a report to Congress on this so-called XYZ affair, Americans were outraged. The episode served the Federalists' purposes wonderfully well, and they made the most of it. Secretary of State Pickering urged an immediate declaration of war. Federalist congressmen thundered against the insult to American honor and demanded action. "Millions for defense, but not one cent for tribute" became their rallying cry. Adams now found himself an unexpected hero. When he attended the theater in Philadelphia, audiences cheered themselves hoarse with cries of "Adams and Liberty!" Caught up in the anti-French furor, the president lashed out at "enemies" at home and abroad. In response to the petitions of support that

Washington's vice-president, John Adams, narrowly gained election to the presidency in 1796. His administration was plagued by political turmoil.

flooded in, he warned that the country had never been in greater danger. "In the last extremity," he declared, "we shall find traitors who will unite with the invading enemy and fly within their lines."

For the moment, the Republicans were in disarray. Publicly they deplored the French government's behavior and pledged to uphold the nation's honor; they could do nothing else. But among themselves they talked with alarm about the Federalists' intentions. They had good reason for concern, because the Federalists quickly mounted a crash program to repel foreign invaders and roust out traitors in the country's midst.

The Alien and Sedition Acts

In May 1798, Congress created the Navy Department and called for the rapid development of a naval force to defend the American coast against French attack. In July, Congress unilaterally repealed the treaty of 1778, thus moving France and the United States closer to an open breach, and then approved a 10,000-man army. (The Federalists' original goal had been 50,000 men.) The army's stated mission was to defend the country against an expected French invasion. The Jeffersonians, however, feared otherwise. Given France's desperate struggle in Europe, its diversion of troops to North America seemed inconceivable. Moreover, memories of the speed with which the Federalists had used force against the Whiskey Rebels made the Jeffersonians wonder about the army's intended use now.

As criticism of the army bill mounted, Adams had second thoughts. He was still enough of a revolutionary to worry about the domestic dangers of standing armies. The navy, he believed, should be America's first line of defense, and he supported that part of the program. But the army alarmed him. "This damned army," he burst out, "will be the ruin of the country." He was further angered when some Federalists sought to make Alexander Hamilton the effective leader of the army. To the dismay of hardline Federalists, he delayed organization of the army by issuing only a few of the officers' commissions that Congress had authorized. Without officers, the troops could not be mobilized.

Fearful of foreign subversion and aware that French immigrants were active in the Jeffersonian opposition, the Federalist-dominated Congress moved in the summer of 1798 to curb the flow of aliens into the country. The Naturalization Act extended from 5 to 14 years the residence requirement

American anger over the XYZ affair is shown in this cartoon depicting the American commissioners Gerry, Pinckney, and Marshall spurning the bribery demands of a five-headed monster symbolizing the French Directory.

for citizenship, and the Alien Act authorized the president to expel "all such aliens as he shall judge dangerous to the peace and safety of the United States." Imprisonment and permanent exclusion from citizenship awaited individuals who were warned to leave but refused to go. Another bill, the Alien Enemies Act, empowered the president in time of war to arrest, imprison, or banish the subjects of any hostile nation without specifying charges against them or providing opportunity for appeal. The Federalist congressman Harrison Gray Otis explained that there was no need "to invite hordes of Wild Irishmen, nor the turbulent and disorderly of all parts of the world, to come here with a view to distract our tranquility."

The implications of these acts for basic political liberties were ominous, but the Federalists had not yet finished. In July 1798, Congress passed the Sedition Act, aimed directly at the Jeffersonian opposition. The bill made it a high misdemeanor, punishable by fine and imprisonment, for anyone,

citizen or alien, to conspire in opposition to "any measure or measures of the government" or to aid "any insurrection, riot, unlawful assembly, or combination." Fines and imprisonment were provided as well for persons who "write, print, utter, or publish . . . any false, scandalous and malicious writing" bringing the government, Congress, or the president into disrepute.

The Federalist moves stunned the Jeffersonians, for they threatened to smother political opposition. The Federalists left no room for doubts on the matter. With an open declaration of war, predicted Congressman James Lloyd of Delaware, "traitors and sedition mongers who are now protected and tolerated, would . . . be easily restrained or punished." The Federalists now equated preservation of their own political power with national survival.

Under the terms of the Alien Act, Secretary of State Pickering launched investigations intended to force the registration of all foreigners. The act's chilling effects were widespread. In July, Pickering noted approvingly that large numbers of aliens, especially persons of French ancestry, were leaving the country. Several prosecutions were started, but the individuals involved went into hiding before they could be caught. Prosecutions under the Sedition Act were more numerous. Twenty-five people, including David Brown of Dedham, were arrested and charged with violating the act. Fifteen were indicted, and ten were ultimately convicted, the majority of them Jeffersonian printers and editors.

In Congress, Vermont Representative Matthew Lyon, a cantankerous, acid-tongued Jeffersonian, soon learned the consequences of political opposition. Born in Ireland, Lyon came to America as a young indentured servant harboring undying enmity toward England and disrespect for privilege of all sorts. A veteran of the War for Independence, Lyon took his Revolutionary principles seriously.

Enjoying a modest political reputation following the war, Lyon was elected to Congress in 1796. During a particularly heated debate over the Sedition Act, he spat in the face of a Federalist opponent, Roger Griswold of Connecticut (the "Spitting Lion," the Federalists called him derisively). Two weeks later, Griswold exacted revenge by caning Lyon on the House floor. Later that year, Lyon was hauled into court, fined $1,000, and sentenced to four months in prison. His crime was making reference in a personal letter to President Adams's "unbounded thirst for ridiculous pomp, foolish adulation, and selfish avarice."

Local Reverberations

Luther Baldwin discovered how little it took even for ordinary people to get into trouble with Federalist authorities. On July 27, 1798, President and Mrs. Adams passed through Newark, New Jersey, on their way from Philadelphia to their home in Quincy, Massachusetts. As the chief magistrate entered Broad Street around 11 o'clock that morning, he was greeted by the firing of cannon, the ringing of church bells, and the cheers of the citizenry. The president's entourage did not stop but continued through town, the cannon booming a final 16-gun salute as he left.

Not all Newark's residents shared in the moment's enthusiasm. Luther Baldwin happened to be coming toward John Burnett's dram shop when one of the tavern's customers, noting that the cannon continued to fire after the president had passed by, observed, "There goes the President and they are firing at his a——." According to the Newark *Centinel of Freedom,* Baldwin, being "a little merry" with drink, replied that "he did not care if they fired thro' his a——." At that point, the Federalist tavernkeeper cried out that Baldwin had spoken sedition, whereupon "a considerable collection gathered—and the . . . Federalists, being much disappointed that the president had not stopped that they might have had the honor of kissing his hand, bent their malice on poor Luther and the cry was, that he must be punished."

Within two months, the local grand jury indicted Baldwin on charges of sedition. The following year, he was haled before the federal Circuit Court. After changing his plea from not guilty to guilty, Baldwin was convicted of speaking "seditious words tending to defame the President and Government of the United States," fined, assessed court costs, and committed to jail until both fine and fees were paid.

Baldwin's trial gave the local Jeffersonians a field day. The New York *Argus* confessed "astonishment . . . on hearing the peculiarity of the expressions for which so formal a trial was instituted. . . . Can the most enthusiastic Federalists and Tories suppose that those who are opposed to them would feel any justification in firing at such a disgusting target as the a——of J. A.?" But the Jeffersonians saw danger as well in the Federalists' use of informers and their zealous overreaction. "When cognizance is taken of such a ridiculous expression," the *Argus* concluded, every Republican could see "the extraordinary malignancy of the federal faction."

Passage of the Alien and Sedition Acts generated a firestorm of protest. The Virginia and Kentucky assemblies challenged the Federalist laws most directly. The Kentucky Resolutions, drafted by Jefferson and passed on November 16, 1798, declared that the national government had violated the Bill of Rights. Faced with the arbitrary exercise of federal power, the resolutions continued, each state "has an equal right to judge by itself . . . infractions . . . [and] the mode and measure of redress." Nullification was the "rightful remedy" for unconstitutional laws. The Virginia Resolutions, written by Madison and passed the following month, asserted that when the central government threatened the people's liberties, the states "have the right and are in duty bound to interpose for arresting the progress of the evil." It would not be the last time that state leaders would claim authority to set aside a federal law.

The Kentucky and Virginia resolutions received little support elsewhere. Neither state, moreover, attempted to obstruct enforcement of the acts. Still, the resolutions indicated the depth of popular opposition to the Federalists' program. As the Federalists pressed ahead, some Jeffersonians prepared for open conflict. The Virginia assembly called for the formation of a state arsenal at Harpers Ferry, reorganization of the militia, and a special tax to pay for these preparations. In Philadelphia, armed Federalist patrols walked the streets to protect government officials from angry crowds. The turmoil prompted President Adams to smuggle arms into his residence as a precaution. As 1799 began, the country seemed on the brink of upheaval.

Within a year, however, the cycle turned again, this time decisively against the Federalists. The break came with Adams's dramatic decision to send a new emissary to France. Adams's son, John Quincy Adams, was in Europe and sent his father assurances that Talleyrand, wishing to avoid war, was ready to negotiate an honorable accord. Adams seized the opening eagerly. He was alarmed at the political furor consuming the nation and feared that war with France "would convulse the attachments of the country." Opposition to the war program was spreading rapidly, even among some of the administration's supporters. "The end of war is peace," Adams explained, "and peace was offered me." Moreover, he had concluded that his only chance of reelection lay in fashioning a peace coalition out of both parties.

Adams's cabinet knew nothing of his intentions. When he told them of the new mission, they were enraged, for the entire Federalist war program depended on the credibility of the French crisis. When Secretary of State Pickering repeatedly ignored the president's orders to send the new commissioners on their way, Adams dismissed him and personally ordered the commissioners to depart. By year's end, they had secured an agreement releasing the United States from the 1778 alliance and providing for the restoration of peaceful relations between the two nations.

The "Revolution of 1800"

As the election of 1800 approached, the Federalists were in disarray. They had squandered the political advantage handed them by France in 1798 and now, with peace a reality, stood before the nation charged with the unconstitutional exercise of

French foreign minister Talleyrand's willingness to negotiate with the United States enabled Adams to avert war in 1800, a decision that enraged extremists within Adams's own Federalist party.

federal power, the suppression of political dissent, and the intention of using the federal army against American citizens. The Federalists never recovered.

The party, moreover, was bitterly divided. The Hamiltonians were furious at Adams's "betrayal" and demanded that he not seek reelection in 1800. The only chance for the Federalists' survival was for Adams to decline the presidency after his term ended. When Adams did not withdraw, the Hamiltonians plotted his defeat.

Emotions continued to run high as the election approached. Fisher Ames berated the Federalists' opponents as "fire-eating salamanders, poison-sucking toads," and the Jeffersonians returned the abuse in kind. Both sides fully believed that the republic's survival hung in the balance. The election, Jefferson declared, would "fix our national character" and "determine whether republicanism or aristocracy" would prevail. The Federalists saw the choice as between republicanism and "anarchy." In Virginia, rumors of a slave insurrection briefly interrupted the feuding. But the scare passed quickly, and Federalists and Jeffersonians were soon at each others' throats once again.

Election day was tense throughout the nation but passed without serious interruption. As the results were tallied, it became clear that the Jeffersonians had handed the Federalists a decisive defeat. The presidential outcome was surprisingly close. When the electoral votes were counted, the two Republican candidates, Jefferson and the New Yorker Aaron Burr, each had 73, so tightly disciplined had the Jeffersonians become. Adams followed with 65. His peace initiative had been effective but was too late to overcome the excesses of the Federalists' war program.

Because of the tie vote, the election was thrown into the House of Representatives where a deadlock quickly developed. In spite of considerable pressure from Jefferson's supporters, Burr refused to give way. The Federalist caucus decided to back Burr, believing him less a Francophile than Jefferson and more sympathetic to Federalist principles. Hamilton, however, distrusted Burr. He believed Jefferson

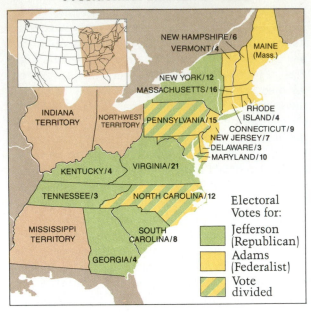

Presidential Election of 1800

Remembered later as the man who shot Alexander Hamilton in a duel in 1804, Aaron Burr came within a few votes of defeating Thomas Jefferson for the presidency in 1800.

dangerous but was even more fearful of Burr's ambition. In part through Hamilton's backstairs maneuvering, the House finally elected Jefferson, ten states to four, on the thirty-sixth ballot. (Seeking to prevent a recurrence of such a crisis, the new Congress soon passed and the states ratified the Twelfth Amendment, providing for separate electoral college ballots for president and vice-president.) The magnitude of the Federalists' defeat was more evident in the congressional elections, where they lost their majorities in both House and Senate.

The election's outcome revealed the strong sectional divisions now evident in the country's politics. The Federalists remained dominant in New England because of regional loyalty to Adams, the importance of the area's commercial ties with England, and fears, fed by ministers and politicians alike, that the Jeffersonians intended to import social revolution. From Maryland south, Jeffersonian control was almost as complete. South Carolina was the exception. There, the white society's fears of the black majority smothered every tendency toward political division, and the Federalists remained solidly in control. But elsewhere, loyalty to Jefferson, strong anti-British and pro-French sentiment, and suspicion of the commercially oriented Federalists kept power in the hands of the Jeffersonians.

In the middle states, Federalists and Jeffersonians were more evenly balanced because eco-

nomic and social differences in the mid-Atlantic region were greater and the issues of foreign and domestic policy cut across society in more complicated ways. As a result, political activity in these states was most intense, and the election most fiercely fought. This sectional pattern would continue to shape American politics.

The distinctions between the Federalists and Jeffersonians were grounded in socioeconomic divisions as well. The Federalists were strongest among merchants, manufacturers, and commercial farmers located within easy reach of the coast—groups that had supported the Constitution in 1787 and 1788. "Here [in Connecticut] as everywhere," claimed one Federalist leader, "the men of talents, information, and property . . . are found among the Federalists." The Jeffersonians concurred with such claims. In his state, one Pennsylvanian conceded, the Federalists commanded the support of "everything that considers itself a part of the natural aristocracy," including "nearly all the lawyers, nearly all the merchants, most of the patrons, [and]

many of the physicians." In both New York City and Philadelphia, the Federalists were strongest in the wards where assessments were highest, houses largest, and addresses most fashionable.

The Jeffersonians drew their strength from different segments of the population. They counted most of the old Anti-Federalists among their numbers and found their major support among agriculturalists in both North and South. But they had significant support in urban areas as well. Their opposition to Federalist elitism, support for revolutionary France, and defense of republican liberty attracted countless urban workers and artisans, many of whom had once been staunch Federalists. They attracted as well individuals who felt threatened by the Federalists' domestic programs, people such as Irish and French immigrants and religious minorities—Baptists, Jews, and Catholics—restive under the lingering religious establishments.

The political alignment of 1800 resembled but did not duplicate the Federalist–Anti-Federalist division of 1786–1789. The Jeffersonian coalition was much broader than the Anti-Federalists' had been, for it included countless individuals, from urban workers to leaders such as Madison and Jefferson, who had supported the Constitution and helped set the new government on its feet. Unlike the Anti-Federalists, the Jeffersonians were ardent supporters of the Constitution. They had no desire to return to the Articles but called for proper management of the new government consistent with the principles of liberty, political equality, and a strong dependence on state authority. Nationally, the Jeffersonians now enjoyed a clear political majority. Their coalition would dominate American politics well into the nineteenth century.

CONCLUSION
Toward the Nineteenth Century

The election of 1800 was a remarkable outcome to more than a decade of political crisis. The series of events had begun in the late 1780s with the intensifying debate over the Articles of Confederation and the movement toward a stronger central government. Then had come the heated contest over ratification of the new Constitution. Scarcely had the new government gotten under way than divisions began to form, first in Congress, then, increasingly, among the people. Hamilton's domestic policies first generated opposition, but it was foreign affairs—the French Revolution, the European war, Jay's Treaty, and the prospect of a war with France—that galvanized political energies and set the Federalist and Jeffersonians vehemently against each other.

After the election of 1800, control of the federal government passed for the first time from one political party to another, not easily but peacefully and legally. "The Revolution of 1800," the Jeffersonians called it—"as real a revolution in the principles of our government as that of 1776 was in its form." The future would show whether the Jeffersonians were correct. But for the moment the crisis had passed, the Federalists had been defeated, and the government was in new hands.

Recommended Reading

Important discussions of politics in the states during the heated decade of the 1790s include Alfred Young, The Democratic Republicans of New York: The Origins, 1763–1797 *(1967); Richard Beeman,* The Old Dominion and the New Nation, 1788–1801 *(1972); Norman Risjord,* Chesapeake Politics, 1781–1800 *(1978); and Charles Steffen,* The Mechanics of Baltimore: Workers and Politics in the Age of Revolution, 1763–1812 *(1984).*

For cogent discussions of the ideological debates between Federalists and Jeffersonians, see Joyce Appleby, Capitalism and a New Social Order: The Republican Vision of the 1790s *(1984); Lance Banning,* The Jeffersonian Persuasion: The Evolution of a Party Ideology *(1978); and John Zvesper,* Political Philosophy and Rhetoric: A Study of the Origins of American Party Politics *(1977).*

Party development during the 1790s can be followed in John Hoadley, Origins of American Political Parties, 1789–1803 *(1986); Richard Hofstadter,* The Idea of a Party System *(1970); William Nisbet Chambers,* Political Parties in a New Nation: The American Experience, 1776–1809 *(1963); and Merrill Peterson,* Thomas Jefferson and the New Nation *(1970).*

The Bill of Rights and the problem of civil liberties are treated by Bernard Schwartz, The Great Rights of Mankind *(1977); James M.*

Smith, Freedom's Fetters: The Alien and Sedition Laws and American Civil Liberties *(1956); and Leonard Levy,* Legacy of Suppression: Freedom of Speech and Press in Early American History *(1960).*

For a fuller understanding of foreign policy issues, turn to Harry Ammon, The Genêt Mission *(1973); Jerald Combs,* The Jay Treaty *(1970); Alexander DeConde,* The Quasi-War: The Politics and Diplomacy of the Undeclared War with France, 1797–1801 *(1966); Felix Gilbert,* To the Farewell Address: Ideas of Early American Foreign Policy *(1961); and Daniel Lang,* Foreign Policy in the Early Republic *(1985).*

Wiley Sword, President Washington's Indian War, 1790–1795 *(1985), describes the government's efforts to quash the Indians of the Old Northwest, and Thomas Slaughter explains the character of backwoods revolt in* The Whiskey Rebellion: Frontier Epilogue to the American Revolution *(1986). Aleine Austin,* Matthew Lyon: "New Man" of the Democratic Revolution, 1749–1822 *(1981), traces the meaning of political equality in the life of an ardent Jeffersonian.*

TIME LINE

1789 George Washington inaugurated as first president
Outbreak of French Revolution

1790 Slave trade outlawed in all states except Georgia and South Carolina
Hamilton's "Reports on the Public Credit"

1791 Bill of Rights ratified
Whiskey tax and national bank established
Hamilton's "Report on Manufactures"

1792 Washington reelected

1793 Outbreak of war in Europe
Washington's Neutrality Proclamation
Jefferson resigns from cabinet
Controversy over Citizen Genêt's visit

1794 Whiskey Rebellion in Pennsylvania

1795 Controversy over Jay's Treaty with England

1796 Washington's Farewell Address
John Adams elected president

1797 XYZ affair in France

1798 Naturalization Act; Alien and Sedition Acts
Virginia and Kentucky Resolutions

1798–1800 Undeclared naval war with France

1799 Trials of David Brown and Luther Baldwin

1801 Jefferson elected president by House of Representatives

9

Politics and Society in the Early Republic

IN June 1799, a middle-aged Seneca named Handsome Lake, living on a tiny reservation in western New York, began to preach a message of hope and redemption to his people. Like so many of his tribe, Handsome Lake had been beaten down by the experiences of the preceding 30 years. As a young warrior in 1776, he had joined England in the fight against American independence. Wounded on several occasions, his spirit broken by the American victory, he had watched helplessly as the Senecas' land was taken and his people were confined on reservations. Handsome Lake's own life had crumbled as well. On several occasions, alcohol and depression brought him close to death.

As he lay on his bunk, scarcely breathing, Handsome Lake experienced a vision. Out of that vision and others like it, he fashioned a message of renewal for the Seneca people. The Great Spirit, he explained, had given him two "gospels" to share with them. The first was a religious or apocalyptic gospel. In it Handsome Lake preached the imminence of the world's destruction; the dangers of spiritual sins such as witchcraft, abortion, and drunkenness; and the promise of salvation through the rituals of *Gaiwiio,* a new form of worship combining Christian elements with the great ceremonies of the Senecas' traditional religious calendar.

Handsome Lake also preached a social gospel, offering guidance for the reconstruction of Seneca life. Here again he called for a mingling of old ways and new. Drawing ideas from the federal officials who encouraged his revival movement and the example of nearby Quaker missionaries, Handsome Lake emphasized the importance of temperance, peace, land retention, acculturation, and domestic morality.

Though in time his dictatorial manner alienated many supporters, his message inspired a dramatic revitalization of the Seneca nation. In 1800, the Seneca people were hungering for leadership. The traumatic changes of the late eighteenth century had run their course, their lives had stabilized, and they could again imagine a better future. Handsome Lake offered them hope and renewed pride. His gospels, moreover, originated in a vision transmitted by the Great Spirit. In Seneca culture, no source of truth was more

powerful or certain. He also commanded the attention of his people because he had shared with them the humiliation of defeat and the poverty of reservation life. Finally, his gospels had effect because they were supported by other tribal leaders, especially his half sister Gayantgogwus, who spoke for the tribal women before the Great Council, and Cornplanter, political leader of the community and Handsome Lake's half brother.

Revitalization was one strategy of survival Native Americans followed during the early nineteenth century. There were others, including armed resistance. Most Native Americans lived at the margins of white society, near the frontiers of settlement, which pushed steadily westward. Their relations with white settlers and with state and national governments reveal much about the nation's early history—its dynamic expansion, commercial and agrarian values, and definitions of republican liberty.

Other changes as well transformed American life between 1800 and 1828. After their victory over the Federalists in 1800, the Jeffersonian Republicans reshaped the national government and implemented their vision of an expanding, agrarian republic. The Jeffersonians also reconstructed America's diplomatic relations with Europe and the rest of the Western Hemisphere. As Americans struggled to make the nation secure, they also worked to create a new cultural identity consistent with their republican values.

Finally, American politics continued to evolve during the years of Jeffersonian ascendency. At the local level, this meant the increasing democratization of political life. Nationally, these years brought the collapse of the Federalist-Jeffersonian party system of the 1790s and set the stage for the dramatically new political era that Andrew Jackson's election to the presidency in 1828 would usher in.

RESTORING REPUBLICAN LIBERTY

The Jeffersonians entered office in March 1801 with several objectives in mind: calming the political storms that had threatened to rend the country, consolidating their recent victory, purging the government of Federalist impurities, and setting it on a proper republican course. They set about these tasks with eager determination.

The Jeffersonian Republicans Take Control

The government had moved from Philadelphia to the new capital in the District of Columbia in November 1800, while John Adams was still president. When the politicians arrived in Washington, they were stunned by its primitiveness and isolation. In New York and Philadelphia, where the national government had met since 1789, politicians could find comfortable (though expensive) accommodations, enjoy the companionship of merchants and others, and keep abreast of news brought into those busy ports by ships from around the Atlantic world.

The new capital, however, was little more than a swampy clearing on the banks of the Potomac River, lost among the woods of Maryland and northern Virginia.

Congress, boasting that the new governmental community would become "the Rome of the New World," had commissioned a Frenchman, Pierre L'Enfant, to develop a plan for the capital. Aided by a black American mathematician and surveyor, Benjamin Banneker, L'Enfant produced a magnificent design, replete with central plazas and broad boulevards radiating outward from a government center anchored by the Capitol and the presidential mansion. At the time Adams moved there, however, little of the grand design had materialized. The Capitol wing containing the House chamber was finished, but the Senate chamber was still under construction. The president's mansion also remained unfinished.

Congress had expected that income from the sale of residential and commercial plots would pay for the government's resettlement. After an initial flurry of interest, however, sales sagged and people stopped coming. As late as 1820, Washington re-

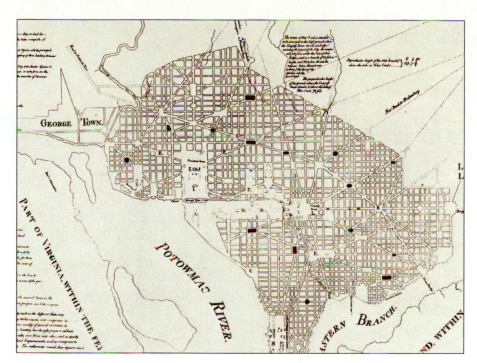

Pierre L'Enfant's grand design for the new capital city of Washington was published in the Columbian Magazine of march 1792. Ten years later, however, little of the plan had been completed.

mained a sleepy town of only 10,000 inhabitants. Congressmen complained constantly about the heat, poor accommodations, and isolation from family and home community. They also fled the capital at every opportunity to tend to their personal and financial affairs, and many refused to stand for reelection.

In keeping with his desire to rid the government of Federalist embellishments, Jefferson planned a simple inauguration. What might have been an awkward encounter was eased when an embittered President Adams slipped out of Washington early on the morning of inauguration day. Shortly before noon on March 4, the president-elect walked to the Capitol from his temporary lodgings at a nearby boardinghouse. "His dress," noted one observer, "was, as usual, that of a plain citizen, without any distinctive badge of office." Jefferson read his short inaugural address in a voice so low that some in attendance had difficulty hearing. Chief Justice John Marshall, a Virginian but a staunch Federalist as well, administered the oath of office, and a company of militia fired a 16-gun salute.

Though simple, the inauguration was filled with significance. The last years of Adams's presidency had been tempestuous, and people were uncertain what the new administration would bring. This was the first time in the nation's brief history that control of the government had shifted from one political

party to another. Some wondered if the change could be accomplished peacefully. Mrs. Samuel Harrison Smith, Washington resident and political observer, described the occasion's drama: "I have this morning witnessed one of the most interesting scenes a free people can ever witness," she wrote a friend. "The changes of administration, which in every . . . age have most generally been epochs of confusion, villainy, and bloodshed, in this our happy country take place without any species of distraction or disorder." Many Americans shared her sense of relief and pride.

In his inaugural speech, Jefferson enumerated "the essential principles of republican government" that would guide his administration: "equal and exact justice to all," support of the states as "the surest bulwarks against anti-republican tendencies," "absolute acquiescence" in the decisions of the majority, supremacy of civil over military authority, reduction of government spending, "honest payment" of the public debt, freedom of the press, and "freedom of the person under the protection of the *habeas corpus.*" Though Jefferson never mentioned the Federalists by name, his litany of principles reverberated with the dark experience of the 1790s. His followers could rest assured that the government was finally in safe, republican hands.

The president spoke also of political reconciliation. Everyone, Federalists and Jeffersonians alike,

Washington boasted few of the comforts to be found in the nation's earlier capitals of New York City and Philadelphia. This view of Georgetown, a neighboring settlement, in 1800 gives a vivid impression of the area's newness.

he declared, must "unite in common efforts for the common good." "Every difference of opinion," he explained, "is not a difference of principle. We have called by different names brethren of the same principles. We are all republicans—we are all federalists."

Not all his followers welcomed that final flourish, for many were eager to root the Federalists out and scatter them to the political winds. Memories of the 1790s were still too fresh, the stakes too high, and differences of principle too great to talk about reconciliation. Jefferson, however, was not naive. His goal was to absorb the moderate Federalists, isolate the extremists, and destroy the Federalist party as a political force. That was essential, he believed, to the continuing supremacy of his own party and the safety of the republic. His strategy worked, for never again did the Federalists regain control of the national government.

Cleansing the Government

Having swept both houses of Congress as well as the presidency in 1800, the Jeffersonians claimed a mandate to cleanse the government of Federalist officeholders. They were especially outraged by a flurry of last-minute appointments President Adams had pushed through the lame-duck Federalist Con-

gress during the closing days of his administration in an effort to reward party loyalists and deny the Jeffersonians full control.

Jefferson decided to withhold the commissions not yet delivered; but what about the Federalists already in place? In Connecticut, where the Jeffersonian party was still struggling to take hold, his supporters demanded control of federal appointments such as collector of customs and inspectors of the port of New Haven. A letter signed by the state's Jeffersonian leaders bluntly told the president, "Even if it should be judged good policy in all other States, to retain the Federalists . . . yet in this State . . . such a policy [would bring] only the certain ruin of republicanism." Jefferson reluctantly agreed that "a general sweep" of Federalist officeholders was necessary. By July 1803, only a third of appointive federal officials were Federalists; by 1808, virtually all government personnel were solid Republicans.

The Judiciary and the Principle of Judicial Review

Having lost Congress and the presidency, the Federalists turned to the judiciary for protection against the expected Jeffersonian onslaught. Late in Adams's administration, the Federalists had introduced a new Judiciary Act calling for more circuit courts, judges and the attendant array of federal marshals, attorneys, and clerks. Congress passed the bill in February 1801, just before adjourning. This blatant effort to pack the judiciary aroused the Jeffersonians' wrath. "The Federalists," observed Jefferson bitterly, "defeated at the polls, have retired into the Judiciary, and from that barricade . . . hope to batter down all the bulwarks of Republicanism."

A Federalist judiciary was especially obnoxious because during the 1790s, Federalist judges had expanded their jurisdiction by invoking principles of English common law. The Jeffersonians protested that the common law was a product of monarchic government and was incompatible with republican liberty. "The revolution [of 1800]," declared Representative William Branch Giles, "is incomplete so long as that strong fortress [the judiciary] is in possession of the enemy." Something had to be done.

In January 1802, Senator John Breckenridge of Kentucky introduced a bill calling for repeal of the Judiciary Act of 1801. A staunch opponent of common law, he was also angry because in the land controversies wracking his state, federal district courts had consistently ruled against Kentucky settlers and in favor of absentee Virginia landlords. The law of 1801, moreover, was a "wanton waste of the public treasure. . . . The time will never arrive," Breckenridge asserted, "when America will stand in need of 38 federal judges."

Even more than political patronage and special interests, the controversy centered on the issue of judicial review, the doctrine that it was the federal courts' responsibility to judge the constitutionality of laws and executive behavior. The Federalists insisted that the real issues were the judiciary's security from political attack and its ability to oppose democratic excesses. Gouverneur Morris, Federalist senator from New York, declared that an independent judiciary was necessary "to save the people from their most dangerous enemy, themselves." The Constitution, he explained, had provided for a judicial branch to "stop you short" if you "trench upon the rights of your fellow citizens, by passing an unconstitutional law."

The Jeffersonians responded by asking who would "check the courts when they violate the Constitution?" Granting the courts sole power to nullify legislation would give them "the absolute direction of the Government." Each branch of the government—executive and legislative as well as judicial—must have the right to decide on the validity of an act. Some among the Jeffersonians also argued that judges should be elected by the people rather than appointed, so that they could be held more closely accountable.

Congressional debate over repeal of the Judiciary Act generated wide public attention, for it raised issues of fundamental importance and offered a vivid contrast between Federalist and Jeffersonian notions of republican government. The House was deluged with petitions supporting and opposing repeal. Opposition came from 225 Philadelphia merchants and "sundry counsellers at law" in New Jersey, while support was voiced at public meetings in Baltimore and elsewhere.

In February 1802, by a strict party vote, Congress repealed the Judiciary Act. "Should Mr. Breckenridge now bring forward a resolution to repeal . . . the Supreme Court of the United States," declared the editor of the *Washington Federalist,* "we should only consider it a part of the system to be pursued. . . . Such is democracy." Jeffersonians, for their part, declared jubilantly that democracy had been saved.

The Jeffersonians also sought to purge several highly partisan Federalist judges from the bench. In March 1803, the House of Representatives voted to impeach federal District Judge John Pickering of New Hampshire. The grounds were not "high crimes and misdemeanors" as the constitution required but erratic judicial behavior, especially the Federalist diatribes with which Pickering regularly assaulted defendants and juries. In their rush to remove Pickering, the Jeffersonians asserted that impeachment was not a criminal process and thus did not require evidence of a crime. Declared Representative William Branch Giles of Virginia, it is "nothing more than a declaration by Congress" that an individual holds "dangerous opinions" that, if allowed to go into effect, "will work the destruction of the Union." Although these phrases echoed the language of repression used by Federalists a half decade before, the Senate convicted Pickering, again by a strict party vote.

Spurred on by success, the Jeffersonians brought impeachment charges against Supreme Court Justice Samuel Chase, one of the most notorious Republican baiters. The indictment charged Chase with "intemperate and inflammatory political harangues," delivered "with intent to excite the fears and resentment of the . . . people . . . against the Government of the United States." The trial, however, revealed that Chase had committed no impeachable offense. He was acquitted on every count and returned triumphantly to the bench.

Chase was a sorry hero, but constitutional principles are often established in the defense of less than heroic people. Had Chase's impeachment succeeded, Chief Justice Marshall would almost certainly have been next, and that would surely have precipitated a political and constitutional crisis. Sensing the danger, the Jeffersonians pulled back, content to allow time and the regular turnover of personnel to cleanse the courts of Federalist control.

Repeal of the Judiciary Act did not settle the issue of judicial review. That came in several trailblazing Supreme Court decisions. In *Marbury* v. *Madison* (1803), Chief Justice Marshall laid down in unmistakable terms the principle of exclusive judicial review. "It is emphatically the province and duty of the judicial department," he declared, "to say what the law is." In another landmark decision, *McCulloch* v. *Maryland* (1819), the court struck down as unconstitutional a Maryland law taxing the Baltimore branch of the Second Bank of the United States. No state, explained Chief Justice Marshall, possessed the right to tax a nationally chartered bank, for "the power to tax involves the power to destroy." In the *McCulloch* decision, Marshall also affirmed the constitutionality of the bank's congressional charter and laid down the constitutional argument for broad congressional authority. Let congressional intent "be within the scope of the Constitution," he wrote, "and all means which are appropriate . . . which are not prohibited, but consist with the letter and spirit of the Constitution, are constitutional." These two decisions established some of the most fundamental principles of American constitutional law.

John Marshall, appointed chief justice of the United States by President Adams in 1801, served in that position for 34 years. Under his leadership, the Supreme Court established some of the most basic principles of American constitutional law.

Dismantling the Federalist War Program

The Jeffersonians had regarded the Federalists' war program as a threat to republican liberty, so they moved quickly to dismantle it. Rather than wait for repeal of the hated Sedition Act, Jefferson simply stopped prosecutions under it and freed its victims. In 1802, the act silently lapsed. The Jeffersonians, however, were not thoroughgoing civil libertarians. More than a few Federalist newspaper editors felt the government's displeasure during the early nineteenth century. But Jefferson never duplicated the Federalists' campaign to stifle dissent.

Jefferson handled the Alien Acts similarly, not bothering to seek their repeal but dismantling the Federalists' inspection system and allowing enforcement to lapse. In 1802, Congress passed a new and more liberal naturalization law, restoring the requirement of 5 rather than 14 years of residence for citizenship. The Federalists' provisional army also fell before the Jeffersonians' attack. By 1802, land forces numbered only 3,400, most of them assigned to "Indian duty" in the West. No longer would federal troops intimidate American citizens. The excise tax came under fire as well. Jefferson wanted to end it immediately, but Secretary of the Treasury Albert Gallatin argued that its revenues could help reduce the national debt. Jefferson agreed to leave it in place until it expired in 1802.

Finally, the Jeffersonians sought ways to reduce the size of the federal government. An active, expanding government they thought dangerous because it required revenue, generated taxes, added to the number of officeholders, and increased governmental power. The central government, Jefferson declared in his first message to Congress in 1801, was "charged with the external and mutual relations only of these states. The principal care of our persons, our property, and our reputation, constituting the great field of human concerns," should be left to the states because they were more closely attuned to the people's needs and could be held more closely accountable.

The government inherited by the Jeffersonians was tiny by modern standards. In 1802, the fourteenth year of its existence, it had fewer than 3,000 civilian employees from the lowest clerk to the president. That amounted to one federal public official for every 1,914 citizens, compared with one for approximately every 62 citizens today. There were only 300 officials in Washington, half of them congressmen. Even so, Jefferson wrote his son-in-law that after carefully surveying government personnel, his administration was "hunting out and abolishing multitudes of useless offices, striking off jobs, etc., etc." As late as 1816, the government employed only 5,000 civilians, more than two-thirds of them in the post office.

In terms of domestic policy, the federal government did little more than deliver the mail, deal with Native Americans, and administer the public lands. Congress ordinarily sat only during the winter months, nor were the president or his cabinet around for much of the summer. "This government, if put to the test," declared one congressman, "is by no means calculated to endure . . . [because] it is a government not having a common feeling and a common interest with the governed." He may have overstated, but not by much.

Not everything the Jeffersonians did was consistent with strict notions of limited government. As the nation grew, so did pressures for a federal program of internal improvements. That reflected in part the growing political influence of the West, for the new states forming beyond the Appalachians were strongly nationalist in sentiment and sought closer ties of trade and communication with the East. The government responded by launching construction of several western routes, including the National Road (in 1811) connecting Cumberland, Maryland, with Wheeling, on the Ohio River. The states, however, carried the major responsibility for internal improvements.

Federal Revenues and Expenditures, 1790–1820 (in thousands of dollars)

Year	Revenues		Expenditures	
1790	Customs	4,399	Military	634
	Other	19	Interest on	
		4,418	public debt	2,349
			Other	1,426
				4,409
1800	Customs	9,081	Military	6,010
	Internal revenue	809	Interest on	
	Other	793	public debt	3,375
		10,683	Other	1,466
				10,851
1810	Customs	8,583	Military	3,948
	Internal revenue	7	Interest on	
	Sale of public lands	697	public debt	2,845
	Other	793	Other	1,447
		10,080		8,240
1820	Customs	15,006	Military	7,018
	Internal revenue	106	Interest on	
	Sale of public lands	1,636	public debt	5,126
	Other	2,769	Other	9,324
		19,517		21,468

Note: In constant dollars, the revenue of the federal government in 1987 was over $730 billion and its expenditures were nearly $950 billion.
Source: U.S. Bureau of the Census.

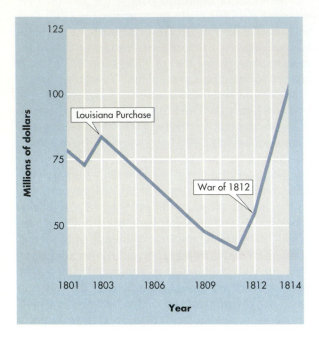

National Debt, 1801–1814

Louisiana Purchase

War of 1812

Millions of dollars

Year

Source: *Historical Statistics of the United States.*

The Jeffersonians were successful as well in reducing the national debt. In spite of the extraordinary costs of the Louisiana Purchase (1803), the debt dropped from $83 million in 1801 to $57 million a decade later. Renewed prosperity following the Panic of 1819 brought what one Senate committee described as "the serious inconvenience of an overflowing Treasury." Though the Jeffersonians may not have "revolutionized" the government as they claimed, they clearly changed its character and direction.

BUILDING AN AGRARIAN REPUBLIC

The Jeffersonians did far more than reverse Federalist initiatives; they worked vigorously to implement their own vision of an expanding, agrarian republic. That vision was mixed and inconsistent, for the Jeffersonian party was an amalgam of different and often conflicting groups: southern patricians determined to maintain a privileged, slavery-based agrarian order; lower- and middle-class southern whites generally committed to black slavery though lacking their own personal slaves, resentful of the patricians' social pretensions, and ardent proponents of political equality; northern artisans bringing to the Jeffersonian party a fierce dedication to honest toil, political autonomy, and their own economic interests; and western farmers devoted to working the land and living free. In time, under the pressure of domestic and foreign affairs, this diversity would help splinter the Jeffersonian party. For the moment, however, these groups found unity not only against their common Federalist enemies but also in a set of broadly shared principles. Those principles guided Jeffersonian policies for over two decades, through the presidential administrations of Jefferson (1801–1808), James Madison (1809–1816), and James Monroe (1817–1824).

The Jeffersonian Vision

Political liberty, the Jeffersonians believed, could survive only under conditions of broad economic and social equality. When wealth and social power became consolidated in the hands of a few, so did political power, and when power increased, liberty was threatened. The central task of Jeffersonian statecraft was thus to maintain an open and roughly equal society. The task was believed difficult because as societies grew in wealth and power, equality eroded and liberty was snuffed out. England offered ample evidence of that. Even in France, where the Jeffersonians had expected the cycle of oppression to be broken, the story was much the same. By 1799, the French Revolution had ended in Napoleon's dictatorship, and France's dream of republican liberty lay shattered.

The Jeffersonians, however, continued to believe that America, if properly guided, could escape Europe's fate. The Federalists had sought to build the American nation through commerce, manufacturing, and a strong central government and had regarded the resulting economic and social inequalities as both inevitable and good. The Jeffersonians' strategy for securing America's future was fundamentally different. They suspected commercial wealth, feared concentrated power, and distrusted social inequality. The central actor in the Jeffersonians' social and political drama was neither merchant nor banker but the independent yeoman farmer—self-reliant, secure in person and possessions, enterprising and yet filled with concern for the public good. Such people exemplified the qualities essential to republican citizenship.

The Jeffersonian vision threatened to become clouded, however, because industriousness generated wealth, and wealth bred inequality. In short, economic and social development threatened to destroy the social bases of republicanism. Human nature could not be changed, but the economic and social environment might be arranged to minimize concentrations of wealth, damp personal ambitions, and thus preserve republican liberty.

The solution of the problem of economic and social development, the Jeffersonians believed, lay in rapid territorial expansion. Land, constantly expanding and readily available to the nation's yeoman citizens, would offer opportunity to a restless people, draw them out of the cities and off the crowded lands of the East, and preserve the social equality that republican liberty required. While promoting habits of thrift and industry, the agrarian life would neither stimulate personal ambitions nor encourage the competition that in more crowded, commercial regions inflamed passions and set people against each other. Instead, exposure to the ordered regularity of nature would cleanse and calm the human spirit. Thus the republic's growth across the North American continent would delay, if not prevent, the cyclic process of growth, maturity, and decay through which all past societies had traveled.

The urgency of expanding America's land base was boosted by the arguments of an English clergyman and political economist named Thomas Malthus. In 1798, Malthus published an essay that jolted Europeans and Americans alike. Observing the growing population and increasingly crowded condition of his native England, Malthus offered ominous predictions about the future of English society and, by implication, other societies as well.

Given the remarkable fecundity of human beings, Malthus argued, population increased more rapidly than agricultural production. "The power of population," he wrote in characteristically stark prose, "is definitely greater than the power in the earth to produce subsistence for man." Optimistic Enlightenment notions of the steadily improving quality of human life, he warned, were a delusion, for the future would be filled with increasing misery and exploitation as population outran food. The future was most clear in Europe, where land was limited and poverty widespread, but the same fate awaited America. Talk of its "perpetual youth" was nonsense.

Jefferson took Malthus's warnings seriously but refused to believe that the Englishman correctly understood how America's vast reservoir of land would enable its people to escape Europe's fate. "The differences of circumstance between this and the old countries of Europe," Jefferson explained, "will . . . produce . . . a difference of result. There . . . the quantity of food is fixed . . . [while] supernumerary births add only to mortality. Here the immense extent of uncultivated and fertile lands enables every one who will labor, to marry young, and to raise a family of any size. Our food, then, may increase geometrically with our laborers, and our births, however multiplied, become effective."

Rapid and continuing national expansion was thus indispensable to the Jeffersonian vision of the agrarian republic. Occupation of the West was also essential to secure America's borders against continuing threats from England, France, and Spain. The rapid sale of new public lands would in addition provide revenue for reducing the national debt. Finally, the Jeffersonians calculated that the creation of new western states would strengthen their political control and assure the Federalists' demise.

The Windfall Louisiana Purchase

Securing the agrarian republic by rapid territorial expansion was the Jeffersonians' fundamental goal. It explains Jefferson's most dramatic accomplishment, his purchase of the vast Louisiana Territory in 1803.

In 1800, at the urging of Napoleon, who was eager to rebuild France's New World empire, Spain ceded the vast trans-Mississippi region known as Louisiana to France. When Jefferson learned of the secret agreement in 1801, he was profoundly disturbed. His fears were well grounded, for in October 1802, the Spanish commander at New Orleans, which Spain had retained, closed the Mississippi River to American commerce, thus depriving westerners of the major outlet for their agricultural produce. Spain's action caused consternation both in Washington and in the West. Especially upsetting were rumors that Spain would soon transfer New Orleans to France. "The day that France takes New Orleans," Jefferson wrote, "we must marry ourselves to the British fleet and nation."

In January 1803, the president sent his young associate James Monroe to Paris with instructions to purchase New Orleans and West Florida, which contained Mobile, the only good harbor on the Gulf Coast, and the mouths of several rivers that drained the southern interior. Congress appropriated $2 mil-

RECOVERING THE PAST

Of the several exploring ventures President Jefferson sent into the trans-Mississippi West, the Lewis and Clark expedition (1803–1806) was the most important. It proved the feasibility of an overland route to the Pacific, produced scientific information about the fauna and flora of the region, established contact with the Native Americans of the area, and helped stimulate westward expansion. Many of the place names the explorers gave to rivers and other natural features are still used today.

During their travels, Meriwether Lewis, William Clark, and others in their party kept extensive jour-

Lewis and Clark's map of the Missouri River, 1804

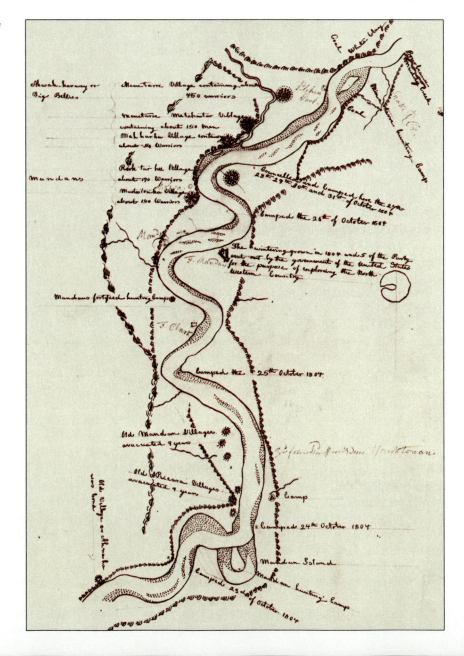

nals in which they recorded their experiences and observations. These journals provide a vivid account of the expedition, including information on the landscape through which the explorers passed and the people they encountered. The journals also reveal a great deal about the attitudes and expectations of the explorers themselves.

The accompanying selection from one of the journals not only reveals the diverse and beautiful topography of the American West in what is now Montana but also illustrates the value of journals to historians. What can you learn from this short excerpt about Lewis's attitude toward the land?

As suggested by Lewis's concern to acquire the data necessary to fix his latitude and longitude, the expedition produced many maps. These cartographic records tell us a great deal about the experience and perceptions of the explorers, as well as about the regions through which they passed.

Examine the map shown here. It is an example of the sketch maps that William Clark drew as the expedition made its way across the land. The map represents about a 30-mile stretch along the Missouri River in what is today west-central North Dakota. After the expedition was over, these detailed studies were used to prepare large, composite maps of the entire region that were far more accurate than any that had been made before.

Mapmaking has changed dramatically since Clark's early efforts. Over the years, as technology and map design have changed, we have vastly improved our knowledge of the earth's topography, as well as our ability to represent the earth's rounded surface on a map's flat plane. Today, the most detailed and accurate maps are drawn from high-resolution photos taken by satellites.

To imagine Clark's mapmaking difficulties, as well as to appreciate his accomplishment, try this experiment. Without consulting anything but your own memory, try to draw a map of the region you passed through on your way to college. Include the major topographical and other interesting features on the route also indicate the groups of people you met or passed near. Alternatively, draw a map of the area around your hometown, including the major features, inhabitants, and travel routes. Make your scale as accurate as possible to aid others who will depend on your map for their own travels.

Now consider how Clark's maps were created and how the data they contain were gathered and put on paper. How accurate do you suppose they are? How accurate would they have had to have been to be useful to people in the early nineteenth century? Examine the content of the map. What information does it contain? What are its dominant features, and why are they emphasized? What is missing that you might have expected to find on such a map? How would a modern map of the same region differ?

Finally, consider the impact of the expedition's maps and journals. What effect did Lewis and Clark's explorations have on the course of American history? How did they change the map of the United States (literally and figuratively)?

Meriwether Lewis's Journal

July 27th 1805.—We arrived at 9. A.M. at the junction of the S.E. fork of the Missouri and the country opens suddonly to extensive and beatifull plains and meadows which appear to be surrounded in every direction with distant and lofty mountains; supposing this to be the three forks of the Missouri I halted the party on the Lard shore for breakfast. and walked up the S.E. fork about ½ a mile and ascended the point of a high limestone clift from whence I commanded a most perfect view of the neighbouring country. . . . Believing this to be an essential point in geography of this western part of the Continent I determined to remain at all events untill I obtained the necessary data for fixing it's latitude Longitude &c.

In this 1803 panorama by Boqueto de Woiserie, the American eagle extends its wings over New Orleans following the Louisiana Purchase.

lion for the purchases, but Jefferson authorized Monroe to go as high as $10 million if necessary.

When Monroe arrived, he found French Foreign Minister Talleyrand ready to sell all of Louisiana. The recent failure to crush the black rebellion against the French in Haiti led by Toussaint L'Ouverture, had deprived Napoleon of the military base necessary to mount an effective occupation of Louisiana; nor did he any longer need those lands to provide food for Haitian slaves. Expecting a renewed war with England at any moment, moreover, Napoleon was eager to concentrate French troops in Europe. In addition, he feared American designs on Louisiana and knew he would not be able to keep American settlers away. In an effort to cut his losses, Napoleon decided to get what he could from the eager Americans and vacate North America.

In April, the deal was struck. For $15 million, the United States obtained all of Louisiana, nearly 830,000 square miles, in one stroke doubling the nation's size. It was a magnificent acquisition that would profoundly shape the nation's future. So important was Louisiana to Jefferson that he brushed aside complaints that the Constitution did not give the president authority to purchase additional territory. He urged Congress to ignore "metaphysical subtleties" and "throw themselves on their country for doing for them, unauthorized, what we know they would have done for themselves had they been in a situation to do it." Some within Jefferson's party questioned the constitutionality of Jefferson's act, but the public's response was overwhelmingly favorable, and Congress readily approved the purchase.

The Federalists, however, reacted with alarm to the acquisition. They feared that the new states ultimately to be carved from Louisiana would be staunchly Jeffersonian and that rapid expansion of the frontier would "decivilize" the nation. In New England, Federalist extremists talked of forming a northern confederacy and seceding from the Union. Their conspiracy included plans to enlist the support of Vice-President Aaron Burr, now in open conflict with Jefferson because of his refusal to step aside in Jefferson's favor in the election of 1800. The secessionist scheme failed because it lacked public support and because key Federalist leaders, including Alexander Hamilton, refused to endorse it. Within another decade, however, New England would again echo with threats of disunion.

The nation's expansion did not stop with Louisiana. In 1810, American adventurers fomented a revolt in Spanish West Florida, captured the fort at Baton Rouge, proclaimed an independent republic, and sought annexation by the United States. In May 1812, over vigorous Spanish objections, Congress formally annexed West Florida. In 1819, pressured by southern expansionists and facing a rising tide of rebellion throughout its Latin American colonies, Spain ceded East Florida as well in the Adams-Onis treaty. As part of that agreement, the United States for the first time extended its territorial claims beyond Louisiana to include the Pacific Northwest. This impressive accomplishment set the stage for the final surge of continental expansion during the 1840s.

Exploring and Opening the Trans-Mississippi West

If America's vast new domain was to serve the needs of the agrarian republic, it would have to be explored and made ready for settlement. In the summer of 1803, Jefferson dispatched an expedition led by his personal secretary, Meriwether Lewis, and William Clark, a young army officer, to explore the Far Northwest, make contact with the Native Americans there, and bring back scientific information about the area. For nearly 2½ years, the intrepid band of explorers, assisted by the Shoshoni woman

Sacajawea, made its way across thousands of miles of unmapped and hostile terrain—up the Missouri River, through the Rockies via the Bitterroot Valley and Lolo Pass, down the Columbia to the Pacific coast, and back again, finally reemerging at St. Louis in September 1806. Lewis and Clark's reports of their journey fanned American interest in the trans-Mississippi West, established an American presence in the region, and demonstrated the feasibility of an overland route to the Pacific.

In 1805 and 1806, Lieutenant Zebulon Pike explored the sources of the Mississippi as far as Leech Lake in northern Minnesota. He followed that trek with an equally bold venture into New Mexico and Colorado, where he explored and named the peak that bears his name. Although interest in western exploration waned after 1807 while the government was preoccupied with foreign affairs and the War of 1812, it revived in 1815. Over the next decade, the government established a string of military posts

Exploring the Trans-Mississippi West, 1804–1807

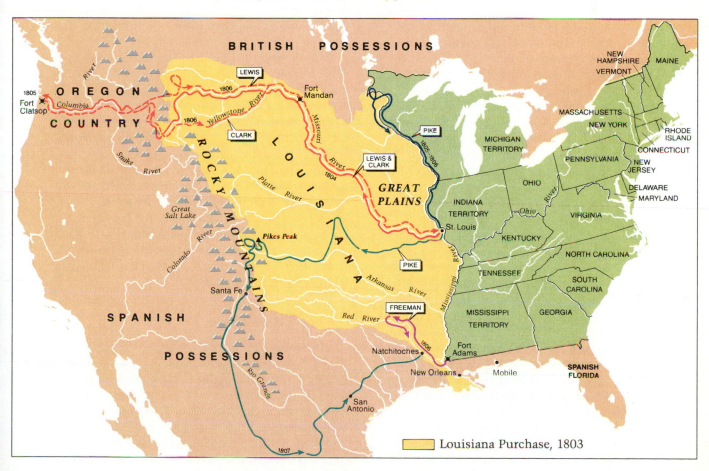

Louisiana Purchase, 1803

from Fort Snelling, at the confluence of the Minnesota and Mississippi rivers, to Fort Atkinson on the Missouri and Fort Smith on the Arkansas. They were intended to secure the American frontier, promote the fur trade, and support white settlement.

The Jeffersonians' agrarian vision also guided federal land policy. In the Land Act of 1796, the Federalists had set the minimum price for federal land at $2 per acre and the standard purchase at 640 acres. Their primary objective had been to produce government revenue. The Jeffersonians desired revenue to reduce the national debt, but they were even more interested in settling people on the land. High prices and large purchase requirements hindered that objective.

In 1801, the Republican Congress passed a new Land Act that reduced the minimum purchase to 320 acres, established a four-year credit system, and provided 8 percent discounts for cash sales. In addition, Congress established new land offices at Chillicothe, Marietta, and Steubenville, Ohio. Over the next year and a half, settlers, speculators, and land companies purchased nearly 400,000 acres of federal land, more than four times as much as during the entire 1790s. The amounts increased geometrically in the following decade.

The transfer of federal land into private hands was not tidy. Ownership was often confused in a tangle of conflicting titles, and the liberal credit system established in 1801 encouraged widespread speculation. In 1819, Secretary of the Treasury William Crawford reported that the government had disposed of $44 million worth of land since 1789 but had actually taken in only half that amount. In an effort to rectify that problem, the Land Act of 1820 abolished the credit system but further reduced the purchase price to $1.25 and the minimum purchase to 80 acres. During the 1820s, several additional principles were added to federal land policy: preemption, which for the first time enabled squatters to secure title to land, and pricing graduation, whereby lands that did not readily sell were offered at less than the established price or even given away. All were efforts to speed the transfer of public land into private hands.

Once again, northeastern Federalists, anxious about the West's growing political power and concerned that eastern labor costs would rise as workers sought new opportunities beyond the mountains, opposed these policies. Senator Samuel Foot of Connecticut even proposed a moratorium on the sale of public lands, an idea that Congress quickly rejected.

In the early nineteenth century, few activities of the federal government were as important to the American people as the expansion, exploration, and sale of public lands. Though it frequently proved wasteful and inefficient, fostered widespread speculation, and contributed to the Panic of 1819, federal land policy effectively served the Jeffersonians' goal of expanding the agrarian republic.

INDIAN-WHITE RELATIONS IN THE EARLY REPUBLIC

As white settlers surged across the interior, they found a land already occupied by Native American peoples. By 1800, white settlement, disease, and warfare had decimated Native Americans along the Atlantic coast. Powerful tribes, however, still controlled much of the trans-Appalachian interior. North of the Ohio River, the Shawnee, Delaware, Miami, and Potawatomi were allied in a Western confederacy capable of mustering several thousand warriors. South of the Ohio lived five major tribal groups: the Cherokee, Creek, Choctaw, Chickasaw, and Seminole. Together these southern tribes totaled nearly 60,000 people.

The years from 1790 to the 1820s brought a decisive shift in Indian-white relations throughout the trans-Appalachian interior. In 1790, the region was aflame with raids and warfare. As the pressures of white expansion increased, tribal groups devised various strategies of resistance and survival. Handsome Lake led the Seneca toward cultural revitalization. The Cherokee followed a path of peaceful accommodation. Others, like the Shawnee and the Creek, rose in armed resistance. None of the strategies was altogether successful, for by the 1820s the balance of power in the interior had shifted, and the Indians faced a bleak future of continued acculturation, military defeat, or forced migration to lands west of the Mississippi.

Land and Trade

Between 1790 and 1820, the government established policies that would guide Indian-white relations for the rest of the century. Federal policymakers attempted to protect Native Americans from exploitation by unscrupulous traders and aggressive settlers and to Christianize and civilize them in preparation for their admission into white society. Yet the overriding goal of territorial expansion, combined with officials' sensitivity to the demands of western settlers for Indian land, created irresistible pressure to move the Indians out of the white settlers' way.

The acquisition of Native American land was the main objective of federal Indian policy. By 1790, the government had given up its earlier "conquest" theory, recognized Indian rights to the soil, and declared that land transfers would henceforth be accomplished through treaty agreements. Those new principles had been made explicit in the Treaty of Fort Harmar, concluded with the Iroquois and Northwestern Confederacy in 1789. In the Intercourse Act of 1790, the government also stipulated that Congress must approve land treaties made between states and Indian tribes—a requirement that few states would bother to observe.

Responsibility for the management of Indian affairs rested with the War Department. Henry Knox, Washington's first secretary of war, laid out the government's basic positions in 1789. A just nation, he explained, should "reject every proposition to benefit itself by the injury of any neighboring community, however contemptible and weak." The In-

dians, he continued, "being the prior occupants of the soil, possess the right of the soil." It should not be taken from them "unless by their free consent, or by the right of conquest in case of just war." To dispossess them for any other reason would violate "the fundamental laws of nature and . . . justice." Maintaining "the right of conquest in case of just war" provided a gigantic loophole in the protection of Native American rights during the century ahead. Few of the land treaties negotiated after 1789, moreover, represented the "free consent" of Native American people. Still, Knox had established a new, more humane principle, the acquisition of Native American land by formal treaty agreement.

The new treaty-based strategy was effective. Native American leaders were frequently willing to cede land in return for trade goods, yearly annuity payments, and assurances that no further demands would be made on them. When tribal leaders proved reluctant, they could often be persuaded to cooperate by warnings about the inevitable spread of white settlement, or more tractable chieftains could

Indian Land Cessions, 1750–1830

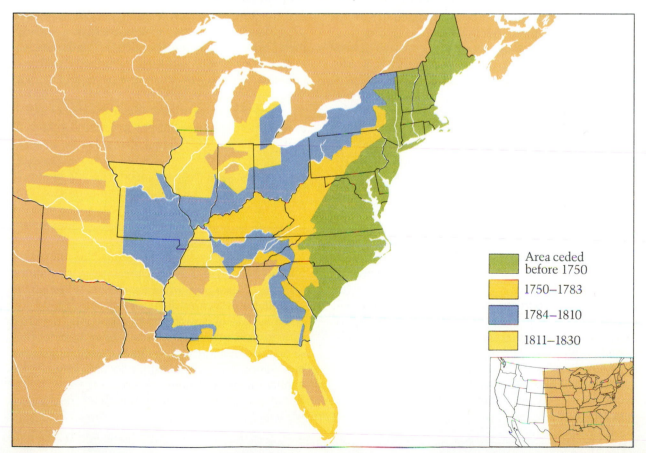

Area ceded before 1750

1750–1783

1784–1810

1811–1830

be found. In these ways, state and national governments gained title to vast areas of tribal land throughout the trans-Appalachian interior.

The continuing loss of land disastrously affected Native Americans. It brought the decline of hunting, one of the Indians' major means of subsistence and an essential way for young boys to demonstrate their manhood. The loss of land also altered the balance of tribal power. As tribes were forced to migrate west, moreover, they frequently intruded on the lands of other Native Americans, thus generating conflict.

Regulating the fur trade also concerned the national government. By 1790, most trans-Appalachian tribes served as intermediaries for hunters farther to the west. Handsome profits from the trade encouraged private companies such as John Jacob Astor's American Fur Company (1808) to expand operations into the interior. Access to western trade was also a point of contention between England and the United States in the Great Lakes region. Both Native Americans and whites entered willingly into the trade. In return for furs, which they had in abundance, the Indians secured highly valued goods such as blankets, guns, rum, and ironware. White traders acquired valuable furs in exchange for relatively inexpensive trade items. Both sides used the trade to cement diplomatic relations with each other.

The trade served white society very well. It had severe costs, however, for Native Americans. Trade goods frequently transmitted deadly diseases such as smallpox and measles. Trade generated patterns of dependence as well, for it offered the only certain supplies of rum, firearms, and other goods increasingly important to Indian life. As the demand for furs and pelts increased, moreover, Native Americans overtrapped their hunting grounds, forcing them to reach farther west for fresh sources of supply. That process disturbed long-standing tribal patterns of trade and diplomatic relations.

In 1790, in an effort to increase profits, prevent fraud and misdealing, and cement peaceful relations with tribal groups, Congress required the licensing of all private traders. The law proved ineffective, however, for enforcement was difficult, and the potential profits from unscrupulous behavior were too tempting for many traders to resist. In 1796, Congress created a system of government trading posts, or "factories," where Indians could come for fair treatment. The system lasted until 1822 but never supplanted private traders as Congress had expected.

Civilizing a "Savage" People

Another major objective of federal Indian policy was to civilize and Christianize the Native Americans and ultimately assimilate them into white society. In the trans-Appalachian West, where whites and Native Americans struggled openly for survival, most people believed that Indians would always remain "savage" and thus unsuited for republican citizenship. They regarded Indians as impediments to be moved out of white settlement's way. Different attitudes, however, were evident in the East, where the Indian "problem" seemed more distant. There, clergymen and government officials, newspaper editors and ordinary citizens displayed greater sympathy for the Native Americans' well-being.

Policymakers and church officials often distinguished between the capacities of blacks and Native Americans for republican citizenship. Perhaps because the bias against blackness was so deeply rooted in American culture and slavery was so much a part of American life, blacks were almost uniformly regarded as destined to perpetual subordination. The color of Native Americans was not so dark or so filled with cultural significance. Indians, moreover, were the country's original inhabitants and had lived free if "uncivilized" lives. While fearing the Indians' "savagery," white Americans admired their "bravery" and "independence," their stoicism in the face of pain, and their "simplicity" of life— qualities deemed important among republican citizens.

Even the most enthusiastic advocates of Indian assimilation believed the process would take generations. Language, religion, dress, family arrangements, social customs—all the Indians' "savage" ways would have to be replaced by white modes of living. Given time and the right circumstances, however, Native Americans might eventually share the blessings of republican liberty, American civilization, and Christianity.

A policy of assimilation seemed to offer hope for the Indians' survival in the face of continuing warfare, disease, and white expansion. Although the assimilationists cared deeply about the physical and spiritual fate of Native American people, they had little sympathy for Indian society or culture, for they demanded that Native Americans cease being Indian and adopt the ways of white society instead. Assimilation or continuing destruction were the alternatives posed by even the most benevolent whites.

Few government officials or other white Americans saw any reason to understand Native American customs, such as the Choctaw ceremonial dance shown in this painting by George Catlin.

Education and Christianization were the major instruments of assimilationist policy. After the Revolution, mission activity increased dramatically as Moravian, Quaker, Baptist, Congregationalist, and Dutch Reformed churches launched mission efforts of their own or joined together in bodies such as the Society for Propagating the Gospel Among Indians (1787). Together they sent scores of missionaries to live among the Indians, preach the gospel, and teach the benefits of white civilization. Among them was a Baptist missionary named Isaac McCoy. Born in Pennsylvania and entirely self-educated, McCoy moved to Indiana, where from 1817 to 1829 he ministered to the Shawnee tribe. John Stewart, a freeborn mulatto who was part Indian, was another. From 1815 to his death in 1821, he preached to the Wyandotte near Sandusky, Ohio. Among the most selfless were Quaker missionaries who labored with the Iroquois in New York, attempting to inspire conversion and improve the conditions of Iroquois life.

The missionaries' greatest success occurred where Indians had succumbed to white control or when missionaries blended Indian beliefs with the basic tenets of Christianity. Even so, most Native Americans remained aloof, for the chasm between Christianity and their own religions was wide (see Chapter 1), and the missionaries' denigration of Indian culture was obvious.

Education was the other weapon of the assimilationists. In 1793, Congress appropriated $20,000 to promote literacy, agriculture, and vocational instruction. Church groups established schools as well, believing that literacy would help Native Americans read the Scriptures and increase the likelihood of conversion. In 1819, the government handed over to the churches full responsibility for Indian education. Because federal officials thought that Christianity and civilization went hand in hand, they encouraged missionaries to teach their Indian students religious doctrine as well as reading, writing, and vocational skills.

Strategies of Survival: The Cherokee

Faced with the steady loss of land and autonomy, Native Americans devised various strategies of resistance and survival. During the early years of the nineteenth century, Handsome Lake led the Iroquois through a process of cultural revitalization. The Cherokee followed a different path of accommodation. Their goal was the redefinition of Cherokee life through a combination of white and Native American ways.

As the nineteenth century began, the Cherokee still controlled millions of acres in Tennessee, Georgia, and the western Carolinas. Their land base, however, was shrinking. By 1800, more than 40 Cherokee towns had disappeared, and over two-thirds of all Cherokee families had been forced to move into the increasingly crowded settlements that remained.

Southern state governments, responding to the demands of their white constituents for Indian lands, put increasing pressure on tribal autonomy. In 1801, the Tennessee legislature unilaterally expanded the boundaries of several counties to include Cherokee land and then claimed that the Indians fell under the authority of state law. As violence escalated along the borders between white and Indian settlements, state authorities demanded that Native Americans accused of horse stealing and other crimes be handed over for trial in state courts. The Cherokee, declaring that they had their own system of justice and distrusting the state courts with their all-white juries and exclusion of Indian testimony, rejected white demands.

In Cherokee councils, a group of full-blood leaders argued for armed resistance. Better to stand and fight than follow the false path of accommodation. Others, however, including mixed-bloods such as John Ross, pointed out the futility of fighting and argued that accommodation offered the only hope for survival. In the early 1800s, following a bitter struggle for tribal control, the accommodationists won out.

Their first goal was to bring the tribe's scattered villages under a common government, the better to defend their freedom and prevent the further loss of land. In 1808, the Cherokee National Council adopted a written legal code combining elements of white and Indian law, and in July 1827, the Cherokee devised a written constitution patterned after those of nearby states, complete with executive, legislative, and judicial branches of government. They accompanied it with a bold declaration of their standing as an independent nation holding full sovereignty over their lands in Tennessee, North Carolina, Alabama, and Georgia.

Their action alarmed southern whites, for it directly challenged state authority. White concerns proved well founded. In 1829, the Cherokee government formalized the "blood law," making it an offense punishable by death for any tribe member to transfer land to white ownership without the consent of tribal authorities.

Meanwhile, the process of social and cultural accommodation, encouraged by Cherokee leaders such as Ross and promoted by white missionaries and government agents, went forward. Missionaries opened a school for Cherokee youth on the Hiwanee River in 1804 and established a boarding school near present-day Chattanooga 12 years later. They stepped up their religious activities as well, baptizing Cherokee into the Christian faith.

As the Cherokee changed from a mixed hunting, gathering, and farming economy to one based predominantly on settled agriculture, many of them moved from traditional town settlements onto individual farmsteads. Others established sawmills and gristmills, country stores and blacksmiths' shops. In contrast to traditional Cherokee practices of sharing and the communal ownership of property, notions of private property took hold.

The majority of Cherokee people continued to inhabit crude log cabins no more than 15 by 25 feet and live a hand-to-mouth existence. Some however, prospered, especially mixed-bloods who learned English and understood how to deal with white society. A few of the most successful lived as well as upper-class whites. Joseph Vann, known as "Rich Joe," accumulated hundreds of acres of fertile land, scores of black slaves, and an assortment of mills, stores, and river ferries. While most Cherokee continued to wear hip-length buckskin shirts and moccasins, the families of people such as Vann and John Ross dressed in cloth trousers, leather shoes, long dresses, and fancy hats.

Changes in the Cherokee economy altered relations with blacks as well. Since the mid-eighteenth century, the Cherokee had held a few blacks in slave-like conditions. During the early nineteenth century, however, Cherokee slavery expanded and became

Major Tribes of the Old Southeast, c. 1820

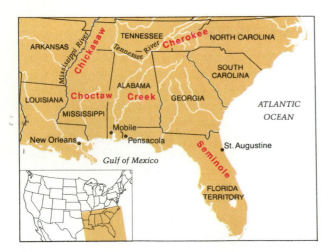

more harsh. By 1820, there were nearly 1,300 black slaves in the Cherokee nation. A Cherokee law of 1824 forbade intermarriage and prohibited blacks from owning livestock. Three years later, a tribal court declared that "negroes and descendants of white or Indian men by negro women who may have been set free" could not vote in tribal elections or "hold any office of profit, honor or trust under this government."

Such changes came about primarily because the spread of cotton cultivation increased the demand for slave labor among Cherokee as well as whites. As accommodation to white society increased, moreover, the ownership of slaves became a mark of social standing, and Cherokee assertions of black inferiority were a way of making common cause with whites.

By 1820, the strategy of peaceful accommodation had brought obvious rewards. Tribal government was stronger, the standard of living higher, and the sense of Cherokee identity reasonably secure. In the end, however, the Cherokee's success proved their undoing, for as their self-confidence grew, so did the hostility of southern whites, who were increasingly impatient to get them out of the way. That hostility would soon erupt in a final campaign to remove the Cherokee from their land forever (see Chapter 13).

Patterns of Armed Resistance: The Shawnee and the Creek

Not all tribes of the interior proved so accommodating to white expansion. Faced with growing threats to their political and cultural survival, the Shawnee and Creek nations rose in armed resistance. Conflict was smoldering as the nineteenth century began; it burst into open flame during the War of 1812.

In the late 1780s, the tribes of the Old Northwest, led by chieftains such as Joseph Brant of the Mohawk, Little Turtle of the Miami, and Blue Jacket of the Shawnee, had launched a series of devastating raids across Indiana, Ohio, and western Pennsylvania, creating panic among white settlers and openly challenging the federal government's control of the region. In September 1790, a force of 1,500, dispatched by President Washington to quell the uprising, fell into an ambush in northwestern Ohio, losing nearly 200 men. The following year, another army of 6,000 troops met a similar fate. Buoyed by their victories, the Shawnee and their allies followed

Sequoyah, who sat for this portrait in 1838, devised the Cherokee alphabet, which formed the basis for the first written Indian language in North America.

up with a furious assault, virtually clearing northern and central Ohio of white settlement.

Faced with two humiliating defeats, Washington determined to smash the Indians' resistance. In the autumn of 1793, General Anthony Wayne led a third army of conquest into the Ohio wilderness. The following year, Wayne's army clashed with over 2,000 Indian warriors in the decisive Battle of Fallen Timbers. This time the Americans won a complete victory. After the smoke of battle had cleared, Wayne wrung from the assembled chiefs an agreement ceding the southern two-thirds of Ohio. In return, he offered $20,000 in trade goods and a $10,000 annual annuity. It was the largest single transfer of Indian land yet, and it opened the heart of the Old Northwest to white control.

In subsequent years, additional treaties further reduced the Indians' land base, driving the Shawnee and Delaware, the Miami and Wyandotte more tightly in upon each other. A turning point came with the Treaty of Fort Wayne in 1809, which opened to white settlement 3 million additional acres of Delaware and Potawatomi land in Indiana. Shortly afterward, two Shawnee leaders, the brothers Tecumseh and Elskwatawa, the latter known to whites

Major Tribes of the Old Northwest, c. 1809

as "the Prophet," began to travel among the region's tribes warning of their common dangers and forging an alliance against the invading whites. In 1809, they established headquarters at an ancient Indian town named Kithtippecanoe in northern Indiana. Soon it became a gathering point for Native Americans from across the entire region as they responded to the messages of cultural pride, land retention, and pan·Indian resistance presented by the Shawnee brothers.

Between 1809 and 1811, Tecumseh carried his message of Indian nationalism and military resistance south to the Creek and the Cherokee. His speeches rang with bitter denunciations of white Americans. "The white race is a wicked race," he told his listeners. "Since the days when the white race first came in contact with the red men, there has been a continual series of aggressions. The hunting grounds are fast disappearing, and they are driving the red men farther and farther to the west. The mere presence of the white men is a source of evil. . . . The only hope . . . is a war of extermination against the paleface." The southern tribes refused to join, but by 1811, over 1,000 fighting men had gathered at Kithtippecanoe.

Alarmed by the Indians' growing militancy, the governor of the Indiana Territory, William Henry Harrison, decided to act. Mustering a force of 1,000 soldiers, Harrison surrounded the Indian stronghold at Kithtippecanoe. He carried with him full authority from the secretary of war to do whatever was necessary to secure the frontier. At dawn on November 7, 1811, some 400 Indian warriors assaulted Harrison's lines. For hours the battle raged, and by day's end, Harrison counted over 150 warriors dead and countless others wounded. Before retiring to the territorial capital at Vincennes, he burned Kithtippecanoe to the ground.

Over the next several months, Tecumseh's followers, taking advantage of the recent outbreak of the War of 1812 between the United States and England and aided by British troops from Canada, carried out devastating raids across Indiana and southern Michigan. Together they crushed American armies at Detroit and Fort Nelson and followed up with forays against Fort Wayne. At the Battle of the Thames near Detroit, the tide finally turned, for there Harrison inflicted a grievous defeat on a combined British and Indian force. Among those slain was Tecumseh.

The American victory at the Thames signaled the collapse of Tecumseh's confederacy and an end to Indian resistance in the Old Northwest. Beginning in 1815, American settlers surged once more across Ohio and Indiana, only now they pressed on unimpeded into Illinois and Michigan. The balance of power in the Old Northwest had permanently shifted.

To the south, the Creek challenged white intruders with similar militancy. As the nineteenth century began, white settlers were pushing onto Creek lands in northwestern Georgia and central Alabama. While some Creek leaders urged accommodation, others, called Red Sticks, prepared to fight. The embers of this smoldering conflict were fanned into flame by an aggressive Tennessee militia commander named Andrew Jackson. Citing Creek atrocities "which bring fresh to our recollection the influence . . . that raised the scalping knife and tomahawk against our defenseless women and children," Jackson in 1808 urged President Jefferson to endorse a campaign against the Creek. The Tennessee militia, Jackson reported, "pant for the orders of our government to punish a ruthless foe."

Bristling at their treatment by Georgia and Alabama, the Red Sticks carried out a series of violent frontier raids in the spring and summer of 1813, killing and scalping two white families and taking one woman captive. They capped their campaign with an assault on Fort Mims on the Alabama River, where they killed as many as 500 people, women and children among them. News of that tragedy raised bitter cries for revenge. The Tennessee legislature denounced the "horrid and inhuman murders" and called for proper "atonement," while frontier editors warned that "when the tomahawk and the scalping knife are drawn in the cabins of our peaceful and unsuspecting citizens, it is time, high time to prepare . . . for defense."

At the head of 5,000 Tennessee and Kentucky militia, augmented by Cherokee, Choctaw, and Chickasaw warriors eager to punish their traditional Creek enemies, Jackson launched his long-awaited attack. As he moved south, the ferocity of the fighting grew. David Crockett, one of Jackson's soldiers, later reported that the militia volunteers shot down the Red Sticks "like dogs." The Indians gave like measure in return.

The climactic battle of the Creek War came in March 1814 at Horseshoe Bend, on the Tallapoosa River in central Alabama. There, in the fortified town of Tohopeka, 1,000 Creek warriors made their stand against 1,400 state troops and 600 Indian allies. While American cannonfire raked the Creek defenses, the allied Indians crossed the river to cut off retreat. In the battle that followed, over 800 Native Americans died, more than in any other single battle in the history of Indian-white warfare. Jackson followed up his victory with a scorched-earth sweep through the remaining Red Stick towns. With no hope left, Red Eagle, one of the few remaining Red Stick leaders, walked alone into Jackson's camp and addressed the American commander:

> General Jackson, I am not afraid of you. I fear no man, for I am a Creek warrior. I have nothing to request in behalf of myself; you can kill me if you desire. But I come to beg you to send for the women and children of the war party, who are now starving in the woods. . . . I am now done fighting. The Red Sticks are nearly all killed. If I could fight you any longer I would most heartily do so. Send for the women and children. They never did you any harm. But kill me, if the white people want it done.

The war against the Creek was finished, and Jackson allowed Red Eagle to return home.

But the general was not quite done. He had fulfilled his vow to march to the Hickory Ground, the most sacred spot of the Creek nation. There he constructed Fort Jackson, where, in August 1814, he exacted his final revenge. Making clear that he held the entire Creek nation responsible for the Red Sticks' insurgency, he seized 22 million acres of their land, nearly two-thirds of their domain. Before his Indian-fighting days were over, Jackson would acquire for the United States through treaty and military conquest nearly three-fourths of Alabama and Florida, a third of Tennessee, and a fifth of both Georgia and Mississippi.

Just as Tecumseh's death had signaled the end of Indian resistance in the North, so the Creek's defeat at Horseshoe Bend broke the back of Indian defenses in the South. With all possibility of armed resistance gone, the Native Americans of the Old Southwest gave way before the swelling tide of white settlement.

A FOREIGN POLICY FOR THE AGRARIAN REPUBLIC

During the early decades of the nineteenth century, the Jeffersonians struggled to fashion a foreign policy appropriate for the expanding agrarian republic. They had several major goals: protecting American interests on the high seas during a period of European war, clearing America's western territories of foreign troops and influence, and breaking free from the country's historic dependence on Europe. Those goals were not easily accomplished; yet by the 1820s, aided by changes taking place across the Atlantic, the Jeffersonians had fashioned a new relationship with Europe. In the Monroe Doctrine of 1823, they projected as well a momentous new role for the United States within the Americas.

Jeffersonian Principles

Jeffersonian foreign policy was first of all based on the doctrine of "no entangling alliances" with Europe that Washington had articulated in his Farewell Address of 1796. In the Jeffersonians' minds, England was still the prime enemy, but France was now suspect as well. By the time the Jeffersonians took office, the French Revolution had run its course and ended in the consulate of Napoleon. While some Jeffersonians still harbored hopes for French liberty, most were sobered by Napoleon's dictatorial rule. They no longer needed Federalist warnings to believe that France should be held at arm's length.

Second, the Jeffersonians emphasized the importance of overseas commerce to the security and prosperity of the agrarian republic. The slave populations of the West Indies and the crowded cities of Europe offered crucial markets for American agricultural exports. Without those markets, what incentive would there be for American farmers to occupy the West and make it bloom?

Overseas commerce was almost as important for what it brought in return. The American ships that carried away agricultural commodities fetched back European manufactured goods. The Federalists had nurtured domestic manufacturing by offering tariff protection against European competition. The Jeffersonians, however, hoped to keep large-scale manufacturing in Europe, since they feared the concentrations of wealth and the dependent working classes that domestic manufacturing would bring.

Maintaining peace was a third major goal of Jeffersonian foreign policy. The Jeffersonians were not pacifists, but they pursued peace with special urgency because they feared war's effects on republican liberty. Not only did war kill people and destroy property but it also inflamed politics, stifled freedom of speech, disrupted the economy, increased the public debt, and expanded governmental power. The Jeffersonians understood the dangers lurking throughout the Atlantic world and knew that protecting the nation's interests might require force. Between 1801 and 1805, Jefferson dis-

patched naval vessels to the Mediterranean to defend American commerce against the Barbary States (Algiers, Morocco, Tripoli, and Tunis). War, however, was a policy of last resort. The Jeffersonians' handling of the crisis leading into the War of 1812 against Great Britain illustrates how eagerly, and in this case how futilely, they sought to avoid conflict.

Struggling for Neutral Rights

After a brief interlude of peace, European war resumed in 1803. Once again England and France seized American shipping. England's overwhelming naval superiority made its attacks especially serious. British impressment of American seamen and continued occupation of the Great Lakes posts also increased tension between the two nations.

In the *Essex* decision of 1805, a British court declared that European powers could not open their colonies to trade with neutral nations during war if such trade was prohibited during times of peace. The clear intention was to end the American practice of carrying cargoes from the French and Spanish West Indies to American ports, reloading them, and then shipping them to Europe as American neutral goods. Following the *Essex* decision, British seizures of American shipping increased dramatically. As they did, American anger grew as well.

When England disregarded American protests over such "unprovoked aggression," the Jeffersonians decided on a strategy of economic coercion. In April 1806, Congress passed the Non-Importation Act prohibiting the importation of English goods that could be produced domestically or acquired elsewhere. On May 16, in one of several orders in council, Britain replied by declaring a full blockade of the European coast. Threatened by Britain's action, Napoleon answered with the Berlin Decree, forbidding all commerce and communication with the British Isles. Americans were further angered by Britain's refusal to deal in good faith on issues of impressment and the reopening of the West Indian trade.

During 1807, the pressure on American shipping increased as Britain and France escalated their economic warfare against each other. Tension between England and the United States reached the breaking point in June, when the British warship *Leopard* stopped the American frigate *Chesapeake* off the Virginia coast. The British captain claimed that four *Chesapeake* crew members were British deserters and demanded their surrender. When the

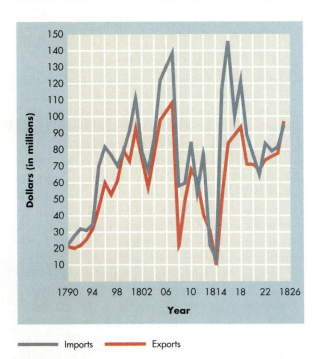

American Foreign Trade, 1790–1825

Dollars (in millions) / Year

Imports — Exports

Source: U.S. Bureau of the Census.

The tranquility of Crowninshield wharf in Salem, Massachusetts, gives evidence of the ships idled and docks emptied by Jefferson's embargo.

American commander refused, the *Leopard* opened fire, killing 3 men and wounding 18, and removed the alleged deserters. After the *Chesapeake* limped back into port with the story, cries of outrage rang across the land.

Fearing the approach of war and recognizing that the United States was not prepared to confront England, Jefferson decided to withdraw American ships from the Atlantic. In December 1807, Congress passed the Embargo Act, forbidding all American vessels from sailing for foreign ports. It was one of Jefferson's most ill-fated decisions.

The embargo had relatively little effect on England. British shipping actually profited from the withdrawal of American competition, and British importers supplied their agricultural needs from Latin America. Moreover, as word of the impending embargo spread, American merchantmen left port in order to escape confinement, while ships bound for the United States changed course and docked in Canada or the West Indies so that they could continue to sail.

The embargo's domestic impact, however, was far-reaching. American exports fell 80 percent in a year, and imports dropped by more than half. New England was hardest hit. In ports such as Salem, Boston, and Providence, depression settled in as ships rocked idly at the wharves and thousands of workers went unemployed.

Up and down the coast, communities dependent on overseas commerce for their livelihood openly challenged the embargo and opposed efforts to enforce it. Federalists, eager to embarrass the administration, were behind much of the opposition, but Republicans also resisted. The government's efforts to police the embargo proved futile, for it could not effectively patrol either the Atlantic coast or the long Canadian border, across which large quantities of American goods were smuggled.

In an effort to uphold federal authority, the government acted with an increasingly heavy hand. At Plattsburgh, New York, on Lake Champlain, federal officials declared martial law and sent in federal troops in an effort to stop smuggling into Canada. The result was guerrilla skirmishing as local citizens fired on U.S. revenue boats, recaptured confiscated goods, and ignored curfews. Equally ominous was the government's use of federal marshals to seize private goods on the suspicion that they might be smuggled abroad.

Throughout the Northeast, bitterness threatened to escalate into open rebellion. Town meetings attacked the embargo, while state legislatures questioned its constitutionality. Connecticut's governor, in words reminiscent of the Virginia and Kentucky Resolutions, warned that whenever Congress exceeded its authority, the states were duty-bound "to interpose their protecting shield between the rights and liberties of the people and the assumed power of the general government." A leading Massachusetts Federalist openly proposed a New England nullifying convention.

In the election of 1808, the Federalists rebounded after nearly a decade of decline. James Madison handily succeeded Jefferson in the presidency, but the Federalist candidates, C. C. Pinckney and Rufus King, garnered 47 electoral votes. Their party also made gains in Congress and recaptured several state legislatures.

Faced with the embargo's ineffectiveness abroad and its disastrous consequences at home, Congress repealed the measure in 1809, replacing it with the Non-Intercourse Act, which reopened trade with everyone except England and France and authorized the president to resume commerce with either of them that ceased its hostile behavior. It proved equally futile and was also soon repealed.

In 1810, Congress tried another tactic. In Macon's Bill No. 2, it authorized the president to reopen trade with France and Great Britain, then reinstitute an embargo against either of them that continued to attack American shipping. It was an ingenious attempt to shape French and English behavior, but it proved too clever by half. Napoleon, sensing an opportunity to drive a further wedge between England and the United States, informed the American government—falsely, as eventually became clear—that he had repealed France's trade restrictions. Madison rose to the bait, reopened trade with France, and set a date for halting all commerce with England unless it rescinded its restrictions as well. England, however, angry at France's duplicity and stung by Madison's threat, stepped up its campaign of impressment and confiscation while American war fever continued to grow.

The War of 1812

The most vocal calls for war came from the West and the South. The election of 1810 had brought to Congress a new group of western and southern leaders, firmly Republican in their party loyalty but impatient with the administration's bumbling policy and convinced of the need for tougher measures. The War Hawks, they were called, and an impressive group they proved to be: Henry Clay and Richard Johnson of Kentucky, John Calhoun and Langdon Cheves from South Carolina, Felix Grundy of Tennessee, and Peter Porter from western New York.

For too long, the War Hawks cried, the United States had tolerated Britain's presence on American soil, encouragement of Tecumseh's confederation, and attacks on American commerce. Their language echoed as well with talk of territorial expansion, north into Canada and south into Florida.

Most of all, these young, nationalistic War Hawks resented English arrogance and America's continuing humiliation. No government, they warned, could long survive unless it protected its people's interests and upheld the nation's honor. Members of the first post-Revolutionary generation of political leaders to occupy national office, they took responsibility for facing down England and completing the struggle for American independence. Their overriding goals were to secure the republic and demonstrate the Republican party's ability to govern.

Responding to the growing pressure, Madison finally asked Congress for a declaration of war on June 1, 1812. Opposition came entirely from the New England and Middle Atlantic states—ironically, the regions British policies affected most adversely—while the South and West voted solidly for war. Seldom had sectional alignments been sharper.

Seldom also had American foreign policy proved more ineffective. Madison decided to set economic coercion aside just as it seemed about to succeed, for the revival of the American trade embargo under Macon's bill, together with the increasing effectiveness of Napoleon's continental blockade, was creating havoc in the English economy. By the spring of 1812, the British government was under increasing pressure to seek accommodation. In an effort to make England's position clear, Foreign Secretary Castlereagh suspended the orders in council. His move was too late, for three days later, unaware of Castlereagh's action, the United States declared war.

The war itself was a curious affair, for its causes were uncertain and its goals unclear. England successfully fended off several American forays into Canada. In spite of American braggadocio, Canada proved secure. As the war progressed, England launched a series of attacks across the Canadian border, along the Gulf Coast, and inland from the Atlantic. The British navy once again blockaded American coastal waters, while British landing parties launched punishing attacks up and down the East Coast. On August 14, a British force occupied Washington, torched the Capitol and the president's house (which became known as the White House after being repaired and whitewashed), and sent the president, Congress, and a panic-stricken American army fleeing into Virginia. England, however, did not press its advantage, for it was preoccupied with Napoleon's armies in Europe and wanted to end the American quarrel. Throughout the contest, the American government struggled to coordinate the war effort, but with limited success, for it was too weak, the country too large, and communication too slow.

Emotions ran high among both the war's Federalist critics and Republican supporters. In Baltimore, on the night of June 22, 1812, a Republican crowd demolished the printing office of the *Federal-Republican,* a local Federalist newspaper. The at-

tack reflected not only partisan politics but also Republican working-class animosity toward Federalist "aristocrats" and the eagerness of working people for war-related jobs.

In late July, after copies of the *Federal-Republican* again appeared on Baltimore's streets, a mob of 1,000 men and women once more surrounded the paper's office. This time, 50 armed Federalists

The War of 1812

A British cartoon shows President Madison spilling official papers as he flees the burning capital, while citizens react with sarcastic comments during the British attack on Washington in 1814.

were there to defend it. When the Federalist defenders opened fire, the crowd rolled up a cannon and sent a round of grapeshot into the building. Several people lay dead on both sides before the militia finally arrived to cart the Federalists off to the safety of jail.

The bloody encounter was not over yet, however, for on the following night, a crowd reassembled in front of the city jail, brushed aside the mayor's pleas to disperse, and seized ten prisoners, including James Lingan, an old Revolutionary War general. The enraged mob beat Lingan and several others to death and left the bodies, stripped of their fine clothing, sprawling in the street.

Though the Baltimore riots were not duplicated elsewhere, emotions ran high throughout the country. In Federalist-dominated New England, organized opposition to the war veered toward outright disloyalty. The governors of Massachusetts and Connecticut refused to furnish troops or supplies, while New England merchants continued a brisk, illegal trade into Canada.

In December 1814, delegates from the five New England states met at Hartford, Connecticut, to debate proposals for secession. Cooler heads prevailed, but before adjourning, the Hartford Convention asserted the right of a state "to interpose its authority" against "unconstitutional" acts of the government. Now it was New England's turn to play with the nullification fire. The Federalist gathering also prepared a list of constitutional amendments designed to reshape the union to New England's liking. As the war dragged on, Federalist fortunes soared in the Northeast, while elsewhere bitterness grew over New England's disloyalty.

Before the war ended, American forces won several impressive victories, among them Commander Oliver Hazard Perry's defeat of the British fleet on Lake Erie in 1813. The most dramatic American triumph was Andrew Jackson's smashing victory in

1815 over an attacking British force at New Orleans. It had nothing to do with the war's outcome, however, for it occurred after preliminary terms of peace had already been signed.

Tiring of the contest and increasingly concerned about affairs in Europe, Lord Castlereagh offered to negotiate. Madison accepted eagerly, and on Christmas Eve in 1814, at Ghent, Belgium, the two sides reached agreement. The treaty resolved almost nothing, for it ignored impressment, blockades, neutral rights, and American access to Canadian fisheries. Nor did it address England's concern about military control of the Great Lakes or its proposal for a neutral Indian buffer state around them. England did finally agree to evacuate the western posts, but other than that, the treaty simply ended the conflict, provided for an exchange of prisoners and the restoration of conquered territory, and called for several joint commissions to deal with the remaining disputes.

The war did leave its mark on the American nation. It made Andrew Jackson a military hero and established him as a national political leader of major importance. The American people, moreover, regarded the contest as a "Second War of American Independence." Jackson's resounding victory at New Orleans enabled them to believe that they had whipped the British once again. Moreover, the republic now seemed finally secure. No longer would Americans have to worry about the vulnerability of their republican "experiment" to outside attack.

The years following 1815 brought an end to America's colonial-like dependence on Europe. In part that was because the United States was now economically stronger and more self-reliant and was focusing increasingly on tasks of internal development—occupying the continent, industrializing the economy, and reforming American society.

America's diplomatic reorientation was also speeded by changes in Europe, where industrialization, social change, and national unification absorbed governmental energies. Following the end of the Napoleonic wars in 1815, Europe entered nearly a century free from general conflict. In the past, European wars had involved the American people; in the twentieth century, they would do so again. For the remainder of the nineteenth century, however, that fateful link was missing. Finally, the focus of European colonialism was shifting away from the Americas to Africa and Asia. From the 1820s on, Europe left the Americas relatively alone. All these circumstances combined to end the United States' historic subordination to Europe and free it for the task of developing its own continental empire.

The Hartford Convention

Resolved. That the following amendments of the constitution of the United States be recommended to the states. . . .

First. Representatives and direct taxes shall be apportioned among the several states . . . according to their respective numbers of free persons . . . excluding Indians not taxed, and all other persons.

Second. No new state shall be admitted into the Union by Congress . . . without the concurrence of two thirds of both houses.

Third. Congress shall not have power to lay any embargo on the ships or vessels of the citizens of the United States, in the ports or harbours thereof, for more than sixty days. . . .

Fifth. Congress shall not make or declare war, or authorize acts of hostility against any foreign nation, without the concurrence of two thirds of both houses, except such acts of hostility be in defence of the territories of the United States when actually invaded.

Sixth. No person who shall hereafter be naturalized, shall be eligible as a member of the senate or house of representatives of the United States, nor capable of holding any civil office under the authority of the United States.

Seventh. The same person shall not be elected president of the United States a second time; nor shall the president be elected from the same state two terms in succession.

The Battle of Lake Erie, in which the American fleet under Commodore Oliver Hazard Perry defeated the British, was one of several spectacular victories in the War of 1812.

The United States and the Americas

While disengaging from Europe, the Jeffersonians fashioned new policies for Latin America that would guide the United States' hemispheric relations for years to come. Prior to 1800, the American people gave little thought to Europe's Latin American colonies. The Caribbean islands were of interest because of their trade, but Central and South America were not.

When those colonies began their struggles for independence from Spain and Portugal in 1808, however, Americans voiced support. It was flattering to have leaders such as Simón Bolívar hold the United States up as a model for Latin American liberation, and North Americans were happy to see European colonialism weakened further. What is more, Latin American independence promised increased trade.

In 1818, Henry Clay, congressman from Kentucky proposed that the United States recognize the newly independent governments of Colombia, Mexico, Chile, and Argentina. Initially, President Monroe was slow to act, primarily for fear of disrupting efforts to secure Florida from Spain. In March 1822, he finally sent Congress a message proposing formal recognition of the new Latin American republics. Congress quickly agreed, and over the next several years, the United States established diplomatic relations with seven Latin American nations.

Though Latin American independence seemed to offer advantages to the United States, it raised one troublesome question. What would the United States do if Spain or Portugal attempted to reestablish colonial control? It was more than a hypothetical question, for in November 1822, the Holy Alliance (France, Austria, Russia, and Prussia) talked of a plan to help Spain regain its American colonies. Prospects of a resurgent Spanish empire alarmed Great Britain as well. In August 1823, the British foreign secretary, George Canning, broached the idea of Anglo-American cooperation to thwart Spain's intentions.

Secretary of State John Quincy Adams opposed the idea. Son of the former Federalist president, Adams had joined the Jeffersonian camp some years before as part of the continuing exodus from the Federalist party. Adams inherited from his father a deep suspicion of English purposes in the New World. He also shared the new spirit of nationalism so evident following the War of 1812. The United States, Adams declared, should not "come in as a cockboat in the wake of the British man-of-war." He urged independent action based on two principles: a sharp separation between the Old World and the New, and the United States' dominance in the Western Hemisphere.

Monroe soon agreed that the United States should issue its own policy statement. In his annual message of December 1823, he outlined a new Latin American policy. Though known as the Monroe Doctrine, its content was of Adams's devising.

Monroe asserted four basic principles: (1) the

American continents were closed to new European colonization, (2) the political systems of the Americas were separate from those of Europe, (3) the United States would consider as dangerous to its peace and safety any attempts to extend Europe's political influence into the Western Hemisphere, and (4) the United States would neither interfere with existing colonies in the New World nor meddle in the internal affairs of Europe.

When Monroe issued his doctrine, it amounted to little more than a statement of principles. Europeans ignored it, and the United States had neither economic nor military power to enforce it. By the end of the nineteenth century, however, when the country's economic and military power had increased, it would become clear what a fateful turning point in the history of the Americas Monroe's declaration had been.

CULTURE AND POLITICS IN TRANSITION

The event-filled years of the early republic that brought changes in government, Indian-white relations, and diplomatic contacts with Europe and the Americas had important consequences for cultural and political life as well. Some people argued that breaking America's historic pattern of colonial subordination required fashioning a new, distinctively republican cultural identity. Yet they disagreed over the extent to which Anglo-European standards of art should prevail, as well as whether American culture should grow out of the experience of ordinary Americans or a social elite. Jeffersonians and Federalists differed almost as sharply over definitions of republican culture as they did over republican politics.

During the early nineteenth century, American politics continued to evolve as well. By the 1820s, the Federalist-Jeffersonian party system that had taken shape during the 1790s was in disarray, new patterns of political alignment were forming, and the very character of political life was changing.

The Tensions of Republican Culture

Many among the Revolutionary generation had believed that with independence, would come an outpouring of republican cultural creativity. This did not occur, in part because America's commercial spirit and growing preoccupation with the practical tasks of national development drained energy

from literature and the arts. In the expanding world of early nineteenth-century America, commerce and technology counted for more than literature or painting. Novelists such as Charles Brockden Brown and Susanna Haswell Rowson found only limited audiences, and painters such as Gilbert Stuart and Thomas Sully turned to portraiture to make a living. The painter and naturalist Charles Willson Peale met with financial success only after opening his remarkable natural history museum in Philadelphia, complete with the bones of an ancient mammoth, "the LARGEST of terrestrial beings," the "ninth wonder of the world!!!"

In their effort to forge an American cultural identity, artists and writers frequently turned to American themes. Jonathan Trumbull recorded the great events of the nation's founding on a series of massive canvases depicting the Battle of Bunker Hill, Cornwallis's surrender, and the Declaration of Independence. The poet Joel Barlow confected a sprawling epic poem, *The Vision of Columbus* (1787), in which he traced the flight of liberty to America's shores and waxed enthusiastic over the nation's boundless future. Noah Webster sought in his *Spell-*

John Quincy Adams, son of John and Abigail Adams and secretary of state under President Monroe, developed the basic principles of the famous Monroe Doctrine.

ing Book (1783) and *American Dictionary of the English Language* (1828) to standardize American styles of spelling and pronunciation and rid them of English affectations. By midcentury, schoolchildren and adults had purchased nearly 15 million copies of Webster's "speller."

Sharp disagreement arose over the continuing suitability of English cultural standards for republican America and the connections between culture and social class. The conservative Connecticut Wits—a group of Federalist poets and essayists including Timothy Dwight, David Humphries, and Lemuel Hopkins—consciously employed English Augustan literary styles in their satires on public education, popular religion, and what they called Jeffersonian mob rule. Many Americans, however, rejected English cultural standards just as they had rejected English politics and spurned the arts as

During the first half century following independence, the fine arts were frowned upon as inconsistent with proper republican simplicity and irrelevant to the practical tasks of building the nation, requiring many artists to device other means of a livelihood. Self-portrait of the Artist in His Museum *shows Charles Willson Peale unveiling his popular Natural History Museum in Philadelphia.*

artifacts of wealth, social privilege, and moral decadence. That belief was deeply rooted in republican values and in the historic sponsorship of high culture by monarchs and aristocrats in Europe. Viewed in this way, painting, sculpture, and imaginative literature seemed incompatible with republican simplicity, social equality, and moral virtue.

Politics in Transition

By the 1820s, the Federalist-Jeffersonian party system was in shambles. The Federalist party, its reputation damaged by charges of disloyalty during the War of 1812 and its continuing antidemocratic image, lay shattered as a national political force. Even in New England, long the bastion of Federalist strength, the party was in retreat.

The Jeffersonian Republicans stood triumphant, their ranks swollen by fresh recruits in the East and the admission of new states in the West. The Jeffersonians' success, however, proved their undoing, for no single party could contain the nation's growing diversity of economic and social interests, sectional differences, and individual ambitions. Divided among themselves, the Jeffersonians found it increasingly difficult to sustain the original Jeffersonian vision and even to govern effectively.

Following the War of 1812, largely in response to growing pressures from the West and Northeast, the government launched a Federalist-like program of national economic development. Wartime disorganization of the currency demonstrated the need for a new national bank to replace the First Bank of the United States, whose charter had expired in 1811. In March 1816, President Madison signed a bill creating a second bank, intended to stimulate economic expansion and regulate the loose currency-issuing practices of the country's countless state-chartered banks. In his final message to Congress in December 1816, Madison called for a tariff to protect the country's infant industries. Congress responded with the first truly protective tariff in American history, a set of duties on imported woolen and cotton goods, iron, leather, hats, paper, and sugar.

The administration's program of national economic development drew sharp criticism from so-called Old Republicans, who regarded themselves as keepers of the Jeffersonian conscience. Speaking in opposition to the bank bill in 1816, Congressman John Randolph of Virginia warned that "the question

The House of Representatives, depicted in this 1821 painting by Samuel F. B. Morse, later inventor of the telegraph, rang with debate over the Missouri Compromise and other explosive issues.

is whether . . . we are willing to become one great consolidated nation; . . . whether the state governments are to be swept away; or whether we . . . still . . . regard their integrity and preservation as part of our policy." Thirty-three Old Republicans voted against the bank bill. Over the next decade, their strength dwindled, even as their cries of alarm became increasingly shrill.

Madison also recommended construction of a federally subsidized network of roads and canals to speed economic development and enhance national security but warned of the need for a constitutional amendment authorizing such action. Unwilling to delay, Representatives John Calhoun and Henry Clay pushed an internal improvements bill through Congress. In the end, Madison vetoed the bill on constitutional grounds, but proposals for federal programs of national development would not die. By the early 1820s, Henry Clay and others, taking up the name National Republicans, were proposing an ambitious "American system" of tariffs and internal improvements.

The Specter of Sectionalism

Sectional tensions added to the growing disorganization of American politics around 1820. Congressional debates over the tariff, internal improve-

ments, and the national bank reverberated with the clash of sectional interests, while New England's opposition to the War of 1812 continued to fester. The Missouri crisis of 1819–1820 ultimately revealed how deep-seated sectional rivalries had become.

Ever since 1789, politicians had labored to keep the explosive issue of slavery safely beneath the surface of political life, for they recognized how quickly it could jeopardize national unity. Their fears were borne out in 1819 when Missouri applied for admission to the Union and raised anew the question of slavery's expansion. In the Northwest Ordinance of 1787, Congress had limited slavery north of the Ohio River while allowing its expansion to the south. But what about the vast new territory west of the Mississippi?

Seizing the opportunity to deal with that question, Senator Rufus King of New York demanded that Missouri prohibit slavery before entering the Union. His proposal triggered a fierce debate over slavery and Congress's authority to prevent its spread. Southerners were adamant that Congress could not close the trans-Mississippi West to their slave property and were determined to maintain the senate's balance between slave and free states. Already by 1819, the North's more rapidly growing population had given it a 105 to 81 advantage in the House of Representatives. Equality in the Senate offered the only sure protection of southern interests. Northerners vowed to keep the trans-Mississippi West open to free labor. That meant closing it to slavery.

For nearly three months, Congress angrily debated the issue. During much of the time, free blacks listening intently to northern antislavery speeches filled the House gallery. "This momentous question," worried the aged Jefferson, "like a fire-bell in the night, [has] awakened and filled me with terror." Northerners were similarly alarmed. The Missouri question, declared the editor of the New York *Daily Advertiser,* "involves not only the future character of our nation, but the future weight and influence of the free states. If now lost—it is lost forever."

In the end, compromise prevailed. Missouri gained admission as a slave state while Maine came in as a counterbalancing free state, and a line was drawn west from Missouri at latitude 36° 30′ to the Rocky Mountains dividing the lands that would be open to slavery from those that would not. For the moment, the explosive issue of slavery's expansion had been put to rest, but before long it would set North and South even more violently against each other.

A New Style of Politics

By the 1820s, basic patterns of political behavior were changing. Most evident was the surge of voter participation in state and local elections. Women, blacks, and Native Americans continued to be excluded, but white men flocked to the polls in unprecedented numbers. In the New Hampshire gubernatorial election of 1814, participation soared as high as 81 percent of eligible voters, and on one occasion in Alabama, to over 90 percent.

The flood of voters resulted in part from removal of property-holding and taxpaying restrictions on the franchise. The constitutions of Indiana (1816), Illinois (1818), and Alabama (1819) provided for universal white male suffrage, and older states such as Connecticut and New York abolished property requirements as well.

Equally important were the growing strength of democratic beliefs; the increasingly active role of state governments in building roads, selling public lands, and dealing with Native Americans; and the continuing drive of urban artisans and rural farmers to claim political power. Involved as well was the appearance of a new generation of political lead-

Missouri Compromise of 1820

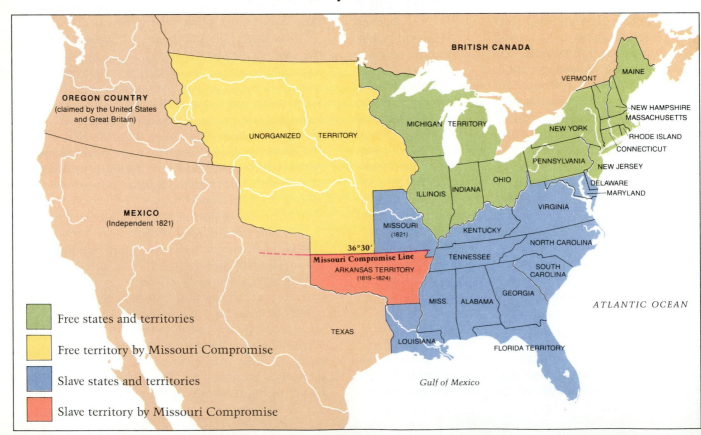

Free states and territories

Free territory by Missouri Compromise

Slave states and territories

Slave territory by Missouri Compromise

Part street theater, part governmental process, electoral politics generated excitement—at least for white males—during the early nineteenth century, as this Philadelphia scene reveals.

ers—men such as Martin Van Buren of New York, Levi Woodbury of New Hampshire, and Lewis Cass of Ohio—who accepted the legitimacy of party activity and perfected their skills in the techniques of mass politics. Even some of the younger Federalists, learning from their elders' political defeat, followed along. By the 1820s, politicians of every persuasion vied for voters' support through registration drives, party conventions, and popular campaigning.

Collapse of the Federalist-Jeffersonian Party System

The final collapse of the Federalist-Jeffersonian party system came with the presidential election of John Quincy Adams in 1824. For the first time since 1800, when the "Virginia dynasty" of Jefferson, Madison, and Monroe began, there was competition for the presidency from every major wing of the Jeffersonian party. Of the five candidates, Adams of Massachusetts and Henry Clay of Kentucky advocated strong federal programs of economic development. William Crawford of Georgia and Andrew Jackson of Tennessee clung to traditional Jeffersonian principles of limited government, agrarianism, and states' rights. In between stood John Calhoun of South Carolina, just beginning his fateful passage from nationalism to southern nullification.

A medical problem virtually eliminated Crawford from the campaign, while Calhoun, acknowl-

edging limited support, withdrew to become the vice-presidential partner of both Adams and Jackson. When none of the remaining candidates received an electoral majority, the election, as in 1800, moved into the House of Representatives. There an alliance of Adams and Clay supporters gave the New Englander the election, even though he had trailed Jackson in electoral votes, 84 to 99. The Jacksonians' charges of a "corrupt bargain" gained credence when Adams appointed Clay secretary of state.

Adams's ill-fated administration revealed the disarray in American politics. His stirring calls for federal road and canal building, standardization of weights and measures, establishment of a national university, promotion of commerce and manufacturing, and government support for science and the arts quickly fell victim to sectional conflicts, political factionalism, and his own open scorn for the increasingly democratic politics of the day.

Against the advice of his political advisers, Adams declined an invitation from the Maryland Agricultural Society to attend its annual cattle show, explaining disapprovingly that "from cattle shows to other public meetings for purposes of . . . exposures of public sentiment, the transition is natural and easy." In the political climate of the 1820s, that attitude was political suicide. Within a year of Adams's inauguration, his administration had foundered. For the rest of his term, politicians jockeyed for position in the political realignment that was under way.

CONCLUSION
The Passing of an Era

During the first quarter of the nineteenth century, Americans dramatically reshaped the geographic and political dimensions of their republic. The nation's territory more than doubled in size. Safely in control of the federal government, the Jeffersonians labored to set it on a proper republican course. In the process, they fashioned domestic policies designed to promote agrarian expansion and foreign policies that transformed the country's relations with Europe and the Americas. They also sought, less successfully, to reconcile Native American rights with national expansion.

The 1820s brought an end to the era of founding and another turning point in the nation's development. The transition was dramatized on July 4, 1826, the fiftieth anniversary of American independence, when two of the remaining Revolutionary patriarchs, John Adams and Thomas Jefferson, died within a few hours of each other. "The sterling virtues of the Revolution are silently passing away," wrote George McDuffie of South Carolina, "and the period is not distant when there will be no living monument to remind us of those glorious days of trial." A new and different era was at hand.

Recommended Reading

Drew McCoy, The Elusive Republic (*1980*), *describes the importance of agrarian expansion for the Jeffersonians. For Jeffersonian politics and government, see also Noble Cunningham,* The Process of Government Under Jefferson (*1978*); *James Young,* The Washington Community, 1800–1828 (*1966*); *Richard Buel,* Securing the Revolution (*1972*); *Daniel Jordan,* Political Leadership in Jefferson's Virginia (*1983*); *and Andrew Cayton,* The Frontier Republic: Ideology and Politics in the Ohio Country, 1780–1825 (*1986*). *Discussions of the Federalists can be found in James Broussard,* The Southern Federalists, 1800–1816 (*1978*); *Linda Kerber,* Federalists in Dissent (*1970*); *and David H. Fischer,* The Revolution of American Conservatism: The Federalist Party in the Era of Jeffersonian Democracy (*1965*). *Steven Watts,* The Republic Reborn: War and the Making of Liberal America, 1790–1820 (*1987*), *traces the change from Revolutionary republicanism to capitalism.*

Bernard Sheehan, Seeds of Extinction: Jeffersonian Philanthropy and the American Indian (*1973*), *describes the intellectual bases of early Indian policy. Robert Berkhofer discusses white attitudes toward Indians in* The White Man's Indian (*1978*). *See also Reginald Horsman,* Expansion and American Indian Policy, 1783–1812 (*1967*), *and William McLoughlin,* Cherokees and Missionaries, 1789–1839 (*1984*).

Foreign policy issues and the politics surrounding them are portrayed by Bradford Perkins, Prologue to War: England and the United States, 1805–1812 (*1961*); *Reginald Horsman,* The War of 1812 (*1969*) *and* The Diplomacy of the New Republic, 1776–1815 (*1986*); *Roger Brown,* The Republic in Peril, 1812 (*1964*); *and Ernest May,* The Making of the Monroe Doctrine (*1975*).

On politics and the Supreme Court, see Charles Haines, The Role of the Supreme Court in American Government and Politics, 1789–1835 (*1944*); *R. Kent Newmyer,* The Supreme Court Under Marshall and Taney (*1968*); *and Richard Ellis,* The Jeffersonian Crisis: Courts and Politics in the Young Republic (*1971*).

Donald Jackson, Thomas Jefferson and the Stony Mountains: Exploring the West from Monticello (*1981*), *discusses Jefferson's fascination with the West. For problems of cultural nationalism, see Neil Harris,* The Artist in American Society: The Formative Years, 1790–1860 (*1966*); *Joseph Ellis,* After the Revolution: Profiles of Early American Culture (*1979*); *Emory Elliott,* Revolutionary Writers; Literature and Authority in the New Republic, 1725–1810 (*1985*), *and David Simpson,* The Politics of American English (*1986*).

The following books provide perspective on the 1820s; George Dangerfield, The Era of Good Feelings (*1949*); *S. F. Bemis,* John Quincy Adams (*1951*); *and Glover Moore,* The Missouri Controversy (*1953*).

TIME LINE

1789 Treaty of Fort Harmar
Knox's reports on Indian affairs

1790s Second Great Awakening begins

1794 Battle of Fallen Timbers

1795 Treaty of Greenville

1796 Congress establishes Indian Factory System

1800 Capital moves to Washington

1801 Thomas Jefferson elected president
Judiciary Act
New Land Act

1802 Judiciary Act repealed

1803 *Marbury* v. *Madison*
Louisiana Purchase

1803–1806 Lewis and Clark expedition

1803–1812 Napoleonic Wars resume
British impress American sailors

1804 Jefferson reelected

1805–1807 Pike explores the West

1806 Non-Importation Act

1807 Embargo Act
Chesapeake-Leopard affair
Congress prohibits slave trade

1808 James Madison elected
Cherokee legal code established

1809 Tecumseh's confederacy formed
Non-Intercourse Act

1810 Macon's Bill No. 2

1811 Battle of Kithtippecanoe

1812 Madison reelected
West Florida annexed
War declared against Great Britain

1813 Battle of the Thames

1813–1814 Creek War

1814 Treaty of Ghent
Battle of Horseshoe Bend

1814–1815 Hartford Convention

1815 Battle of New Orleans
U.S. establishes military posts in trans-Mississippi West

1816 James Monroe elected
Second United States Bank chartered

1819 Adams-Onis Treaty with Spain
Spain cedes East Florida to U.S.
McCulloch v. *Maryland*

1820 Land Act
Missouri Compromise

1822 Diplomatic recognition of Latin American republics

1823 Monroe Doctrine Proclaimed

1824 John Quincy Adams elected

1827 Cherokee adopt written constitution

10

The Preindustrial Republic

In April 1795, Ben Thompson started north from Queen Anne's County, Maryland, for New York City. Since Ben knew little about making a living beyond farming, he first supported himself by common labor on the city's docks. Ben, however, was ambitious and resourceful. He listened carefully to the ship's captains who talked enthusiastically about life at sea while they recruited men for their crews. Ben was lucky, for he arrived in New York just as American overseas commerce, stimulated by renewed war in Europe, was entering a decade of unprecedented prosperity. Sailors were in demand, pay was good, and few questions were asked.

For five years, Ben sailed the seas. Several times his ship narrowly escaped capture by British and French men-of-war. Having enough of travel, he returned to New York, gathered his meager savings together, and hired out as an apprentice to a ship's carpenter.

About the same time, Phyllis Sherman left her home in Norwalk, Connecticut. She also headed for New York, where she took a job as a maid in the household of one of the city's wealthy merchants. As fate would have it, Phyllis and Ben met, fell in love, and, in the spring of 1802, were married.

There is little of note in all this, except that Ben and Phyllis were former slaves and were married in the new African Methodist Episcopal Zion Church. Ben had set aside his slave name, Cato, as a sign of liberation, while Phyllis kept the name her master had given her. Ben was doubly fortunate, for his master had allowed him to buy his freedom and move north just as cotton production was beginning to spread through the Chesapeake region. In another few years, he would have faced greater trouble securing his freedom. Phyllis had been freed as a child when slavery ended in Connecticut. As she grew up, she tired of living as a servant with her former owner's family and longed for the companionship of other blacks. She had heard that there were people of color in New York City, and she was correct. In 1800, it contained 6,300 blacks, more than half of them free.

Though life in New York was better than either Ben or Phyllis had known before, it was hardly easy. Along with most blacks, and many white families as well, they shared only marginally in the commercial prosperity and struggled just to get along. In 1804,

they watched helplessly as yellow fever carried off their daughter and many of their friends. And while they found support in the expanding black community and solace in their church, they constantly encountered the disdain of the city's white majority. They had to be on guard, moreover, because slave ships still moved in and out of the port, and runaways from the South were pursued in the city's streets. New York still contained 2,800 slaves, a fact that continually reminded them of their tenuous freedom.

Still, they persevered. All around them they heard white Americans talking about social equality and economic opportunity, and like other Americans, white and black, they struggled to understand what those words meant for them. Like others, Ben and Phyllis also tried to deal with the economic and social forces that were beginning to change their community. Though they scarcely understood it, they were living in a time of transition between two contrasting ways of life—the rural, preindustrial world of the eighteenth century and the increasingly urban, industrial world of nineteenth-century America.

During the nineteenth century, industrialization, urbanization, large-scale immigration, and westward expansion would revolutionize American economic and social life. These transformations and their consequences make up the essential story of nineteenth-century America. By the 1820s, the effects of economic and social change were already becoming evident, though they had not yet carried far enough to displace earlier ways of life. In economic and social affairs, as in government and politics, the years of the early republic were years of beginnings, of transitions between old ways of life and new. If we are to understand this nineteenth-century transformation, we must first understand the world that was transformed.

In this chapter, we first examine the underlying economic changes that between 1790 and 1828 began to remake American life. We turn next to a discussion of preindustrial society and how people lived in its distinctive regions and local communities. Finally, we examine the new ways in which the American people were beginning to think about their republican society and their first efforts at republican social reform.

THE PREINDUSTRIAL ECONOMY

In early nineteenth-century America, most people earned their livings much like their parents before them. The economy still depended on overseas trade, and agriculture, which occupied over 80 percent of the people, differed little from decades earlier. Change, however, was afoot: in commerce, where merchants began operating on a larger scale; in agriculture, where cotton became the South's new staple crop; and especially in manufacturing, where merchant capitalists began to reorganize industries, redefine the nature of work, and seek profits by producing for an expanding market.

The Return of
Commercial Prosperity

On August 14, 1801, the merchant ship *Arabella,* captain Charles Adams in command, left New York bound for Liverpool, England. The hold of the *Arabella* was filled with a cargo of flour from Pennsylvania, tobacco from the Chesapeake, and sugar from the West Indies. Adams and his crew were uneasy as the coast dropped out of sight because the North Atlantic was a dangerous as well as profitable place for American merchantmen.

Danger and profit both arose from the same circumstance—European war. That had often been the case during the colonial period, given Europe's insistent demand for America's staple commodities and the colonies' role as pawns in the European game of power politics. It was little different now that independence had been achieved.

We saw in Chapter 8 how powerfully the outbreak of European war in 1793 had affected American politics. It had equally important consequences for the economy. In 1790, the nation's merchants were still struggling to rebuild overseas trade to its pre-Revolution levels. By the end of the decade, however, American commerce was booming, and the country was in the midst of prosperity undreamed of but a few years before.

In part, the newfound prosperity stemmed from actions of the national government taken under the direction of Secretary of the Treasury Hamilton. He had quickly implemented his policies of funding and assumption to establish American credit and restore the confidence of investors, both foreign and domestic. The Federalists, moreover, worked hard to rebuild commercial ties with England, America's traditional trading partner.

Decisions made in the capitals of Europe, rather than in America, however, lay behind the country's surging commercial expansion. England and France,

The street bustle created by renewed commercial prosperity is vividly illustrated in this street scene of New York by Francis Guy.

locked in deadly struggle, sought North America's raw materials, especially its foodstuffs and naval stores. Each was anxious to keep American goods out of the hands of the other. As Europe's war-induced demand for American commodities grew, the price of those goods increased. As prices rose, so did profits and so, in turn, did the willingness of American merchants to risk capture on the high seas.

According to established practice, neutral nations in time of war could trade with the belligerents as long as two conditions were met. First, the goods that were exchanged could not include arms or other war matériel; second, the trade connections must predate the outbreak of hostilities. American commerce met both those conditions. Both England and France, however, were determined to control America's trade for their own advantage. To back up that determination, each sent armed cruisers to prowl the Atlantic and intercept American merchant ships believed headed for the other's ports.

For nearly two decades following 1793, England and France continued their desperate struggle. The losses in American ships and cargoes during those years were alarmingly high and included the *Arabella,* which ran afoul of a British cruiser off southern France and was lost to its owners. The costs of doing business in the North Atlantic were further increased by escalating insurance rates and the high wages needed to lure American sailors into the risky trade.

The profits waiting for cargoes that got through, however, more than compensated for the risks. And so American exports surged upward, more than tripling in value between 1793 and 1807. These swollen trade earnings financed the importation of an increasing volume of European manufactured goods. Stimulated by this direct trade and the replacement of European ships by neutral American vessels throughout the Atlantic, American tonnage increased dramatically. By 1800, American bottoms were carrying an astonishing 92 percent of all commerce between America and Europe. Between 1790

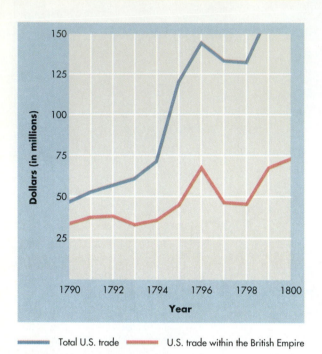

U.S. Trade, 1790–1800

Total U.S. trade   U.S. trade within the British Empire

Source: U.S. Department of the Treasury.

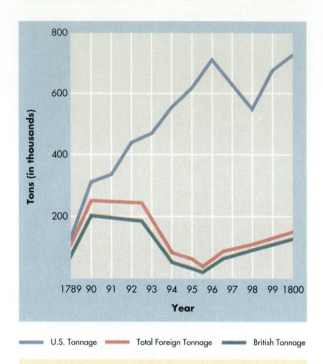

U.S. Foreign Trade Tonnage, 1789–1800

U.S. Tonnage   Total Foreign Tonnage   British Tonnage

Source: U.S. Department of the Treasury.

and 1808, ships sailing under American registry rose from 355,000 tons to over a million tons. The freight earnings from this expanded fleet added further to the country's newfound prosperity.

The main beneficiaries were the merchants who built the ships, gathered the cargoes, and dispatched them to the waiting markets in Europe. As the nineteenth century began, men such as E. H. Derby of Salem, John Jacob Astor of New York, and Stephen Girard of Philadelphia were amassing impressive fortunes. But America's booming commerce benefited others as well, especially in the ports, where overseas trade affected nearly everyone. The expansion of commerce stimulated insurance and banking activities, for ships had to be protected and financed. By 1800, some 33 insurance companies were in operation. State-chartered banks proliferated even more rapidly.

The dramatic increase in commerce also brought the shipbuilding industry out of its long doldrums. Employment for rope and sail makers, ship carpenters, and metalsmiths boomed. Even sailors found advantage, for work was steady and

wages high. As merchants' profits and the wages of artisans and other workers increased, so did their spendable income, and so, as a result, did the fortunes of tavernkeepers, grocers, and landlords.

Though America's prosperity was most evident in the ports, its effects radiated into the surrounding countryside, where the cargoes of agricultural and forest goods and the provisions required by the ships' crews were produced. Not everyone benefited equally; some Americans—blacks, unskilled laborers, and others living at the bottom of society—did not benefit at all. But the nation as a whole was thriving. Not within living memory had times been so good.

In spite of the prosperity, however, escape from England's empire had not fundamentally changed the realities of American economic life. Its export trade continued to depend on European demand for America's raw materials. American consumers, moreover, still preferred English and European manufactured goods to cruder American products. As yet, the United States had insufficient population, investment capital, manufacturing capability, trans-

Wholesale Price Index, 1788–1800

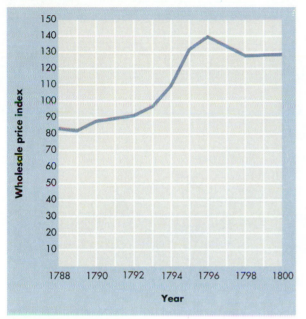

Note: 1821–1825 = 100

Source: U.S. Bureau of the Census.

portation systems, and levels of labor productivity to support its own internally generated economic development. Not until the second quarter of the nineteenth century would it finally escape this colonial-like dependence on Europe and develop the capacity for self-sustained economic growth.

While commerce continued in its traditional channels, a few merchants experimented with new forms of business organization, notably incorporation. It had two chief advantages. First, a charter of incorporation from a state government often brought certain legal privileges, such as the exclusive right to carry on certain activities for a number of years or special tax incentives. Second, corporations could sell stock and thus accumulate capital for investment. Between 1776 and 1800, the states chartered some 300 commercial, banking, and manufacturing enterprises. That was a striking change from the eighteenth-century practice of reserving charters almost exclusively for towns, colleges, and philanthropic organizations.

Most merchants, however, still operated their business individually or in simple partnerships.

Even the largest mercantile houses employed no more than a half dozen clerks. Moreover, they usually marketed their goods in familiar, informal ways. In New York, the merchant community developed a more centralized auction system for selling cargoes, but merchants elsewhere continued to depend on their own personal ties with wholesalers and shopkeepers.

As we shall see, many of the profits generated by the new prosperity would soon be put to new and innovative uses. The commercial activity that produced them, however, remained firmly rooted in the past.

Agriculture in the North

During the early years of the republic, the vast majority of Americans drew their living from the land. In 1800, fully 83 percent of the labor force was engaged in agriculture; as late as 1820, that figure had hardly changed. For American farmers, the dimensions of economic life—planting and harvesting, buying and selling—remained largely unaltered.

In the North, many farmers produced an agricultural surplus, which they exchanged in nearby markets for commodities such as tea, sugar, window glass, or tools. During the early nineteenth century, more agriculturalists came within the market's reach. In southern New England, along the Hudson River in New York, and in southeastern Pennsylvania, access to urban and European markets stimulated production for commercial sale. In New England, where the soil was poor, farmers turned fields into pasture and switched to more profitable dairying and livestock raising. New York and Pennsylvania farmers cultivated the land more intensively, virtually ending the earlier practice of allowing worn-out fields a fallow period to recover their fertility. During the eighteenth century, the rural landscape had looked cluttered and unkempt, with areas still covered by timber and fallow lands lapsing back into brush. Now, however, the countryside was clean and orderly, with most of the fields under regular cultivation and their boundaries marked by permanent hedges or stone walls.

The wills and estate inventories of farmers around the turn of the century indicate that many of them enjoyed new comforts. After 1800, farm families were much more likely than 50 years before to possess table linens and china bowls, store-bought furniture and fancy clothes. But this prosperity was

Merchant ships, such as the one depicted in this 1800 scene of a bustling Philadelphia wharf, brought renewed prosperity during the 1790s.

modest because agricultural opportunities remained limited. As the term *surplus* indicates, most farmers still took to market only what was left over after they had first met their family's needs. As late as 1820, no more than 25 percent of agricultural output was available for export. The rest was consumed on the country's farms or used in local exchange.

Custom dictated that farm families strive for self-reliance. "The great effort," reported a European traveler, "was for every farmer to produce anything he required within his own family; and he was esteemed the best farmer, to use a phrase of the day, 'who did everything within himself.'" Self-improvement meant primarily the acquisition of land rather than money or consumer goods. The goal of most farmers was to achieve a "pleasing competence" and transmit family farms intact to their children.

Across much of the country, cash still played only a small part in economic exchanges. "Instead of money going incessantly backwards and forwards into the same hands," declared an observant Frenchman in 1790, people "supply their needs in the countryside by direct reciprocal exchanges. The tailor and the bootmaker go and do the work of their calling at the home of the farmer . . . who most frequently provides the raw material for it and pays for the work in goods. . . . They write down what

they give and receive on both sides, and at the end of the year they settle a large variety of exchanges with a very small quantity of coin."

Most farms were not large. By 1800, the average size in the longer-settled areas of New England and the Middle Atlantic states was no more than 100 to 150 acres, down substantially from 50 years before. Even the cargoes of wheat exported from Philadelphia and Baltimore came from the surpluses of small producers, not from large-scale farmers.

Northern farms were not only small but limited in productivity as well, even in southeastern Pennsylvania, probably the richest and most productive area in the North. Unlike New England, where settlement had concentrated in town centers and farmers worked in the surrounding fields, the people of southeastern Pennsylvania lived on isolated farmsteads. A combination of circumstances contributed to their prosperity: the people's industriousness, fertile and well-watered lands, a lengthy growing season, and a burgeoning demand for wheat in Philadelphia and abroad. In spite of the slowness and high costs of wagon transport, grain from as far inland as 100 miles found its way profitably to market. Few persons held real wealth in the region, but most lived in reasonable comfort. During the eighteenth century, people had called it "the best poor man's country" in America.

As the nineteenth century began, however,

economic opportunity was actually declining in southeastern Pennsylvania. The average farm was no larger than 125 acres, barely above the margin of profitability. This resulted from the growing population and the continuing division of farm property from fathers to sons. By 1800, nearly 20 percent of the taxpayers were single freemen, clear evidence that young men were finding it harder to establish themselves on the land before taking a wife. Moreover, in certain areas of the region as many as 30 percent of the married taxpayers were landless. Some worked in the region's towns, but more were tenants and rural laborers. Declining productivity plagued inhabitants as well. Long and continuous cropping had robbed the soil of its fertility, and as population increased, farmers were forced to bring marginal land under cultivation.

Although some of the region's farmers showed interest in new, "scientific" theories of fertilization, crop rotation, and selective animal breeding, most farmers changed their ways only slowly. One disillusioned soul spoke bitterly of those "who turn a deaf or incredulous ear to all instructions; who condemn new things because they are new; . . . who keep themselves aloof and warn others of the specious and dangerous novelty." Among farmers of that time, tradition died hard.

In an effort to compensate for declining yields, most followed the self-defeating strategy of keeping their fields under constant cultivation. They continued to sow their grain broadcast and plant their corn in widely separated hills, one worker hoeing open a hole and another following behind to drop in the kernels and close the soil with his heel. Farmers knew that fertilizing with manure increased crop yields, but few had enough animals to produce a sufficient supply.

Nor had agricultural technology changed significantly from a century before. Farmers still worked the land with crude, wooden plows that required several yoke of oxen and two or three men to use and frequently broke when run against the rocks and tree stumps that dotted the fields. In 1807, Charles Newbold of Burlington, New Jersey, patented a cast-iron plow, but it was expensive and dulled easily. Not until the 1830s did efficient metal plows come into general use.

The costs of agricultural labor limited output as well. As landlessness increased, more people offered to work for wages, and farmers depended increasingly on hired help. But only the more prosperous could afford it. At planting and harvest time, moreover, when extra labor was most needed, the cost increased. On most farms, the acreage under cultivation was limited by the family's ability to plant and harvest the crop.

One mark of increasing commercialization was greater dependence on livestock and dairying. Most

As the population grew and settlement expanded, widlerness land was cleared for farms, while whites and Native Americans sought ways of living together.

Growth of Towns in Southeastern Pennsylvania, c. 1800

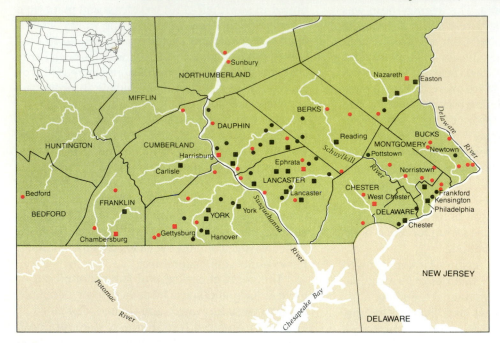

farmers, however, owned only a few animals—perhaps several horses, four or five cattle, some pigs, and a flock of chickens. Few farmers knew much about scientific breeding; even fewer practiced it. Animals typically grazed together in common fields or were allowed to forage for themselves in the countryside. Even in winter, many farmers neither sheltered their animals nor provided them with fodder. An animal's hardiness was valued as highly as its weight or productivity. One observer remarked, "It is a very pitiable sight to go about our country and see the condition of multitudes of cattle and sheep which fill almost every farmer's yard in the spring of the year. The severity of our winters [and] bad management are . . . the cause of so much poverty among our cattle."

By 1820, Pennsylvania's farmers were producing considerably more than 50 years before, but that was because there were more of them cultivating more land, not because there had been significant changes in the agricultural economy. It would be another several decades before the North's agricultural revolution got solidly under way.

The South Embraces Cotton

As the eighteenth century ended, southern agriculture was still in disarray. Falling prices, worn-out lands, and the destruction wrought during the

Revolutonary War had left the Chesapeake's tobacco economy in shambles. The extensive loss of slaves added to the region's economic woes.

Even before the Revolution, Virginia and Maryland planters had begun to diversify their crops in an effort to escape dependence on tobacco and bolster their sagging fortunes. Those efforts continued during the 1780s and 1790s. As agriculture became diversified, so did the rest of the region's economy, for grain required milling, packaging, and transporting before it could be exported. At the same time, grain absorbed fewer man-days of labor than tobacco, thus freeing slaves for other employment.

As the new century began, southern planters turned back to single-crop agriculture, only this time the crop was cotton. Planters in both the Chesapeake and South Carolina had experimented with cotton before the Revolution, but their efforts increased after the war. They were most successful in cultivating the long-staple variety. Its silky fibers were highly valued and could easily be separated from the cotton's seeds. The delicate long-staple plant, however, grew only where soil and climate were right—on the sea islands off the coast of Georgia and South Carolina.

There was an alternative—the hardier short-staple variety, which could be successfully cultivated across large areas of the South. Its fibers, however, clung tenaciously to the plant's sticky,

Although the cotton gin, invented in 1793, simplified one step of cotton processing, much of the work on a plantation continued to be done with rudimentary tools by slave labor. Here Benjamin Latrobe sketches An Overseer Doing His Duty.

green seeds and could be separated from them only with great difficulty. A slave could clean no more than a pound of short-staple cotton a day.

Demand for cotton of all sorts was growing, especially in England, where new textile factories, with their weaving and spinning machines, created an insatiable appetite for the crop. Demand and supply began to come together in 1793 when Eli Whitney, a Yankee schoolteacher seeking employment in the South, set his mind to the problem of short-staple cotton and its seeds. Within a few days, he had designed a functioning model of what he called a "cotton gin." In conception it was disarmingly simple, nothing more than a box containing a roller, equipped with wire teeth, designed to pull the fibers through a comblike barrier, thus stripping them from the seeds. A hand crank activated the mechanism. The implications of Whitney's invention were immediately apparent, for with this crude device a slave could clean up to 50 pounds of short-staple cotton per day.

During the next several decades, southern cotton production soared. In 1790, the South produced only 3,135 bales. By 1800, output had grown to 73,145 bales, and by 1820, it had mushroomed to 334,378. In 1805, cotton already accounted for 30 percent of the country's agricultural exports; by 1820, it exceeded half. Across both the old, coastal South and the newly developing interior states of Tennessee, Alabama, and Mississippi, cotton was becoming king. The growing demand of England's textile mills provided the stimulus, but a portentous combination of factors made possible the South's dramatic response: wonderfully productive virgin soil; a long and steamy growing season; the availability of ample, well-trained slave labor; and the long experience of southern planters with the production and marketing of staple crops.

As we shall see in later chapters, the swing to cotton marked a momentous turning point for both the South and the nation. Perhaps most important, it breathed new life into the institution of slavery,

Agricultural Productivity in 1800 and 1986				
	Wheat		Cotton	
	Worker-Hours per Acre	Yield per Acre	Worker-Hours per Acre	Yield per Acre
1800	56.0	15 bushels	185	147 pounds
1987*	2.6	37 bushels	5	581 pounds

* The 1986 data actually represents a 1982–1986 average.
Source: U.S. Bureau of the Census.

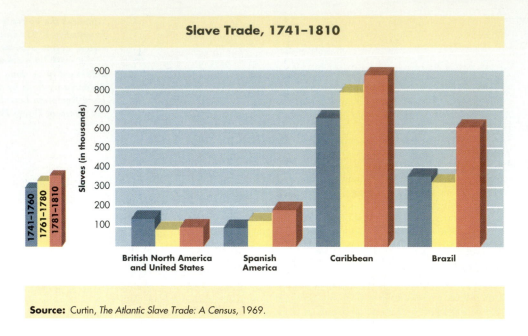

Slave Trade, 1741–1810

Slaves (in thousands)

900
800
700
600
500
400
300
200
100

1741–1760
1761–1780
1781–1810

British North America and United States · Spanish America · Caribbean · Brazil

Source: Curtin, *The Atlantic Slave Trade: A Census,* 1969.

for as cotton production increased, so did the value of prime fieldhands. Some of the escalating demand for slave labor was met from overseas. In 1803 alone, Georgia and South Carolina imported 20,000 new slaves as southern planters and northern merchant-suppliers rushed to fill the need before the slave trade finally ended in 1807. Much of the labor demand, however, would be met by natural reproduction and the internal slave trade that moved blacks from the worn-out lands of the Chesapeake to the booming "black belt" of the Deep South.

Preindustrial Manufacturing

Economic change was more noticeable in the manufacturing sector during the early nineteenth century. The majority of American goods continued to be produced at home or in small shops by artisans and their journeyman apprentices. Merchant capitalists, however, seeking investment opportunities for profits earned in overseas trade, began to buy into and consolidate industries such as textiles and shoes. Development of the factory system that would revolutionize manufacturing still lay in the future, but the early nineteenth century brought the first steps toward industrialization.

How much of the American work force was involved in manufacturing is difficult to determine, since most people did a variety of jobs. In the rural North, for example, farmers augmented their income by running gristmills, building cabinets, or repairing wagons. Farm women contributed as well by making clothes for sale or exchange with neighbors. "Almost all the farmers of the United States," declared one European visitor, "combine some trade with agriculture." In older regions, where the land was worn and farms were small, such work was essential for survival. Elijah Norton of Westhampton, Massachusetts, observed that he could "carry on his farm" only by making shoes for his neighbors in return for their labor.

Unlike later years, when industry grew larger and became concentrated in the cities, manufacturing in preindustrial America was small in scale and widely decentralized. The rural landscape was dotted with small enterprises—grain mills and sawmills, potash works and iron forges—that employed three or four workers and served people in the immediate vicinity. In the South, planters trained some of their slaves as artisans and set them to work producing commodities needed on the plantation.

In the shops of both North and South, artisans made goods much as they had for decades—slowly, by hand, and with the simplest of tools. Where more than human power was required, as in milling grain or sawing wood, waterwheels provided it. Not only was manufacturing small in scale, it was intensely personal as well. Artisans who made items for sale to their neighbors took pride in the quality of their work. To offer shoddy goods was to risk losing the community's confidence and with it the chance to make a reasonable living.

In the small shops of preindustrial America, labor and management were closely aligned. Artisans occupied both roles, working side by side with their journeymen helpers but also managing the enterprise. They owned their shops, which were often attached to their houses; hired their help; and made their living from profits rather than wages. Though artisans worked hard, they controlled their work schedule and tempo, often keeping irregular hours and stopping work when their stock of finished goods became too large or other activities enticed them away.

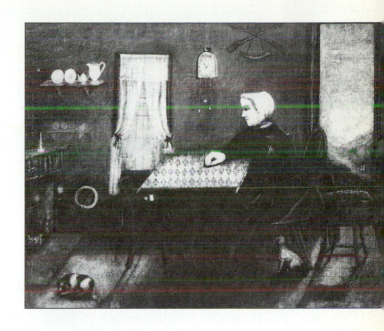

In the economy of the early republic, women continued to produce clothing and other household goods in traditional ways.

Rural Industry in the North, c. 1800

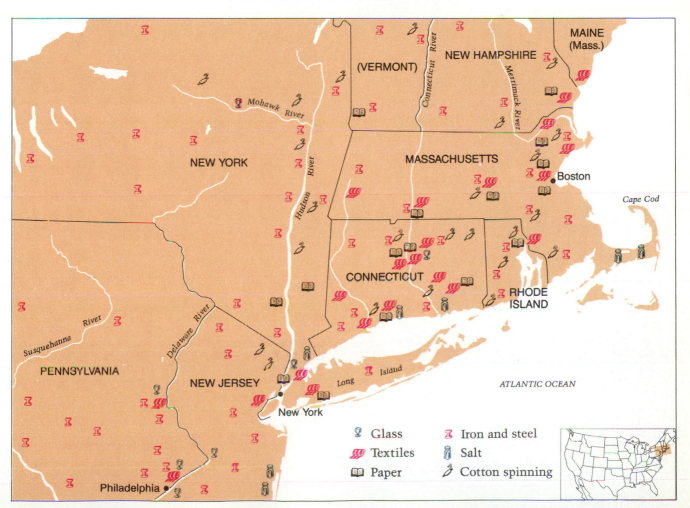

🍷 Glass		🛠 Iron and steel	
〰 Textiles		🧂 Salt	
📖 Paper		✂ Cotton spinning	

INNOVATION

The decades between 1790 and 1830 witnessed the first stirrings of a revolution in industrial technology that during the rest of the nineteenth century would transform the American economy and shape the working lives of millions of Americans. The nation's earliest experiments in industrial technology were fashioned out of wood, not iron. Though wooden machinery often broke down, required continuous maintenance, and frequently caught fire from friction, it was cheap to construct, easily repaired, and readily fabricated by experienced craftsmen. Wooden machinery, moreover, was especially well suited to the small scale of American manufacturing. The early republic was still part of the "wooden age," when, in addition to tools and machines, wood was the major source of fuel, construction material for ships and wagons, and important chemicals such as potash and turpentine.

Many Americans in the young republic were enthusiastic about technology's promise for the nation's future. Observed Tench Coxe, an ardent promoter of American economic development, "Machines, ingeniously constructed, will give us immense assistance." Robert Fulton, inventor of one

Samuel Slater in the 1830s

of the earliest steamboats, explained how technological progress would strengthen American republicanism. "Every order of things, which has a tendency to remove oppression and meliorate the condition of man, by directing his ambition to useful industry," he proclaimed in a speech before Congress in 1810, "is, in effect, republican." Fulton's comments reflected a widely held belief that technology, representing the practical application of

Samuel Slater's textile mill at the Pawtucket Falls in Rhode Island

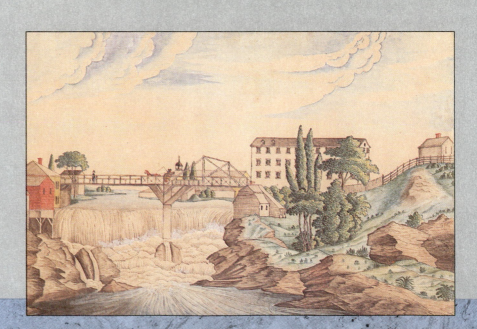

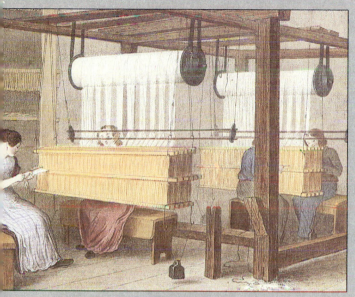

Textile workers attending cotton looms

Cotton dust filled the air, and the leather belts that transmitted power from the factory's waterwheels to the machinery frequently caught workers' hair or clothing, with awful results. Tending the machines, moreover, required repetitive and deadening labor, a fact that led factory managers to fill their work force with children—who were docile and commanded low wages.

Samuel Slater staffed his first factory entirely with youngsters between 7 and 12. By 1820, children comprised an estimated 47 percent of the labor force in Connecticut and 55 percent in Rhode Island. The children's workweek in the Connecticut mills ranged from 72 to 84 hours. In response to such obvious exploitation, the Connecticut legislature passed a law requiring instruction in reading, writing, and arithmetic for all children working in factories. The law, however, simply made child labor more acceptable.

Not until the middle of the nineteenth century would factories replace homes and shops as producers of most American textiles, and it would be another 30 years before most nonagricultural workers spent their days at factory labor. The awesome transformation of manufacturing technology, however, had its beginnings many years earlier, in the primitive wooden machinery of early America.

reason and science, would foster human progress. Franklin's lightning rod seemed to sanction that belief. The impact of industrial technology on people's lives, however, was not altogether beneficial.

In 1789, an enterprising immigrant mechanic named Samuel Slater arrived in New York. Familiar with British textile technology, he brought with him detailed knowledge of mechanical carding machines that combed cotton fibers into alignment suitable for spinning and the Arkwright spinning frame, capable of fashioning 48 uniform cotton threads at a time. Powered by waterwheels and placed in the fledgling textile factories that dotted the New England countryside in increasing numbers from the 1790s on, these machines helped spur a startling growth in the American textile industry. In 1800, an estimated 1,000 wage earners labored in the nation's textile factories. By 1830, the number had climbed to 55,000.

Though the new machines increased the output of cotton cloth, they created an unhealthy environment for the workers who tended them. Not only were the early textile factories deafeningly noisy because of the pounding machines and clacking wooden gears, but they were dangerous as well.

48-spindle spinning frame built by Samuel Slater in Pawtucket, 1790

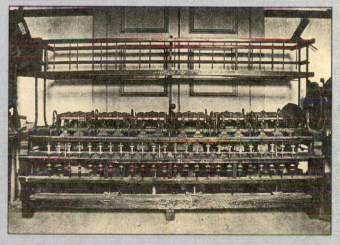

Processions of craftsmen were common in the early nineteenth-century cities. This Procession of Vietuallers of Philadelphia *shows many craft images such as rolling ships and banners with craft symbols.*

Merchant Capitalism and the Putting-Out System

During the first several decades of the nineteenth century, the decentralized, artisan-based manufacturing system slowly began to change. Already by the 1820s, industrial consolidation hinted of the more rapid and dramatic transformation that lay ahead. The explanation for these changes is to be found, once again, in America's continuing involvement with Europe.

In an attempt to prevent the United States from becoming more deeply embroiled in the ongoing European war, President Jefferson in 1807 declared an embargo, cutting off American trade across the Atlantic (see Chapter 9). The effect was immediate and far-reaching. In one year, the value of American exports declined nearly 80 percent.

When the embargo was lifted in 1809, American trade gradually recovered. In 1812, however, Britain and the United States once again went to war. During the next three years, while Britain blockaded the coast and captured nearly 1,400 American merchantmen, overseas trade sank to its lowest level in recorded history. Even after the war's end, American commerce languished, largely because England's new Corn Laws prohibited the importation of American grain.

The consequences of these trade disruptions for American manufacturing were immense. With prospects for profits from overseas trade drastically reduced, merchants sought other investment opportunities. Domestic manufacturing was attractive, especially since the embargo had also prevented the importation of British manufactured goods. As the domestic demand for American goods increased and prices rose, the shift in investment from commerce to manufacturing grew apace.

Merchants brought organizational skills as well as ambition and surplus capital to American manufacturing. They used all three to consolidate America's decentralized, inefficient industries. The merchant capitalists' strategy was to gain control of the raw materials from which goods were fashioned—leather in the case of shoes; cotton, flax, and wool for textiles—and arrangements for marketing the finished products. Some steps in the manufacturing process they farmed out to workers in shops and homes, paying them on a piecework basis, a practice that came to be called the "putting-out" system. Other steps they consolidated in their own central shops. Their wealth, connections, and organizational skills allowed them to absorb smaller producers and increase their control over different industries. The shoe industry attracted the special attention of the merchant capitalists because of its large potential market and suitability for consolidation.

The development of the early shoe industry in Lynn, Massachusetts, illustrates the merchant capitalists' techniques and the operation of the system. During the eighteenth century, Lynn's farmers learned to augment their income by making shoes. By 1800, Lynn had become a center of shoe production, the town's many small shops turning out one pair of shoes for every five people in the country.

At first, individual shopkeepers commissioned shoemakers to fill specific orders, which the shopkeepers then sold. But seeing the vast potential in shoe manufacturing, merchant capitalists soon began to take control of the industry. In the years following 1805, they developed central shops where the leather was cut into pieces and then put out to hundreds of workers, many of them women laboring at home, who sewed the pieces together. The completed uppers were then returned to the central shops, checked, and sent out again, this time to male workers who attached the soles. The finished shoes were then gathered, inspected, and packed for shipment.

The process was efficient and turned a hand-some profit for the merchant capitalists who managed it. It had serious implications, however, for the master craftsmen who had formerly dominated the trade. With manufacturing increasingly under the control of the merchants and focused around the central shops, the masters lost both their own independence and their influence over their journeyman apprentices.

A few, such as Chris Robinson, prospered under the new system. In 1818, he made shoes in a 10-foot-long shop attached to the back of his home. Within four years, he was able to build a new shop measuring 16 by 28 feet. A decade later, now with a partner, Robinson erected a wooden factory on one side of the town common. Among artisans, however, Robinson was the exception. Most shoemakers either entered the central shops or continued to work at home, no longer as independent producers but as dependent wage earners. Less and less often did they make important production decisions; those were reserved for the "bosses" who ran the enterprise. Moreover, the workers could be "turned away" for bringing in unsatisfactory work and thus deprived of their livelihood. By the 1820s, shoemaking in Lynn was no longer controlled by individual artisans.

In the early nineteenth century, older cities like Philadelphia continued to grow but were as yet little changed by industrialization.

Panic and Depression

Following the end of America's second war with England, consolidation under the limited system of merchant capitalism slowed, British goods again flooded American markets, and the manufacturing boom collapsed. In 1815, the value of imported goods zoomed upward to $113 million, and the next year rose over $30 million more. Because England's industrial revolution was further along and its factories were more efficient, its products sold competitively in the United States, even with the added costs of transportation across the Atlantic. The American shoe industry survived, but hundreds of others did not.

In 1819, the economy suffered a severe financial panic. Only a few commercial banks had existed anywhere in the country in 1790. By 1818, stimulated by commercial prosperity and the growth of manufacturing, the number had risen to 392. Many, however, were insufficiently capitalized and irresponsibly managed. Caught up in the commercial and manufacturing booms, their directors extended credit and printed money without retaining sufficient specie (coined money) in their vaults to cover their obligations. It was a financial system waiting to collapse, and in 1819 it did when the Bank of the United States, which had been rechartered by Congress in 1816, forced the state banks to redeem their note issue in specie. Many could not meet the demands, thus triggering a sequence of bank failures and the collapse of credit.

The panic, devastating by itself, was followed by a depression that generated an unprecedented stream of bankruptcies and shattered fortunes. Across New England and the Middle Atlantic states, businesses failed and unemployment soared. In Massachusetts, wages plummeted in less than a year from $1.50 per day to 53 cents, while in upstate New York the daily pay of unskilled turnpike workers dropped from 75 cents to 12 cents. Philadelphia businesses that at the end of the war had employed 9,700 workers had only 2,100 in 1819. In the trans-Appalachian West, land sales plummeted from $13.6 million in 1818 to $1.7 million the following year. William Greene, secretary to the governor of Ohio, reported in 1820 that "the greater part of our mercantile citizens are in a state of bankruptcy," while "the citizens of every class are uniformly delinquent in discharging even the most trifling of debts." In the South, farms and plantations stood abandoned as cotton and tobacco exports fell.

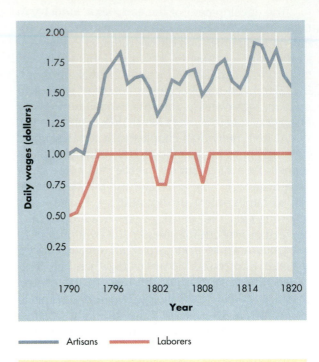

Average Daily Wages in Philadelphia, 1790–1820

Artisans ——— Laborers ———

Source: U.S. Bureau of the Census.

By the early 1820s, recovery was under way, and the stage had been set for the second and more dramatic phase of America's epic industrial revolution. The panic and depression, however, demonstrated how destabilizing that transformation could be and how powerfully its effects would be felt in the lives of individual Americans.

An Ideology of Expectant Capitalism

During the colonial period, circumstances had damped the economic ambitions of many Americans. English mercantilism had stressed the subordination of colonial to British enterprise and the supremacy of the common good over individual economic interests. More important, limited opportunities curbed economic incentives for most Americans living outside the coastal ports. While many colonists, especially southern tobacco and rice planters and northern merchants, accumulated significant wealth, ordinary Americans did not, nor did they expect to. Given the realities of daily life, farmers, artisans, and other workers hoped for what was often called a "pleasing mediocrity."

Attitudes began to change, however, late in the eighteenth century. Among artisans and commercial farmers as well as merchants and planters, earlier preoccupation with the limits of economic opportunity gave way to a newly expansive economic spirit. Several developments accounted for the change. The break with England enhanced Americans' sense of economic freedom and autonomy. Beyond that, they increasingly shared the attitudes toward economic affairs that Adam Smith elevated to an ideology in his *Wealth of Nations*. Published in England in 1776, Smith's tract launched an assault on the restrictive, controlling assumptions of mercantilism. It argued that economic behavior like physical nature, was governed by consistent and knowable laws. Smith asserted that individual self-interest was the only reliable guide to human behavior and that the public good was best served by the free and unregulated play of individual ambition in the marketplace. Government, Smith explained, should not control economic affairs but should act only to guarantee the free working of supply and demand. Smith's doctrines suited the circumstances of the new republic wonderfully, for they emphasized the importance of international free trade, provided a rationale for the rapid exploitation of the continent and the new capitalist endeavors, and

explained, in terms congenial with republican principles, that government's task was to nurture individual opportunity.

The booming prosperity at the turn of the century also fanned American imaginations and convinced people that economic opportunity was real. Not all Americans shared in this newly expansive spirit. Black slaves had little reason for enthusiasm, and many American farmers continued to labor in an agricultural world of constraints. Most women, moreover, continued to be closely dependent on the men around them. Still, countless Americans found their circumstances improved and believed that economic opportunities were expanding.

The new spirit was fed, finally, by the accelerating pace of westward settlement. In 1790, only 100,000 white settlers lived in the nation's interior beyond the Appalachian Mountains. By 1800, their numbers had swollen to nearly a million; by 1820, to over 2 million.

They came by wagon along Zane's Trace and other tortuous routes into Kentucky and Tennessee and clambered aboard flatboats at Pittsburgh to float down the Ohio River to destinations at Wheeling, Marietta, Louisville, and Cincinnati. The human tide seemed to grow with each passing year. "Genesee fever" brought thousands of settlers surging onto the rich lands of western New York. A traveler in 1797 counted 500 wagons a day on the road west

Growth of Trans-Appalachian White Population, 1790–1820

	1790	1800	1810	1820
Old Northwest				
Ohio	—	45,365	230,760	581,434
Indiana	—	5,641	24,520	147,178
Illinois	—	—	12,282	55,211
Michigan	—	—	4,762	8,896
Total	—	51,006	272,324	792,719
Old Southwest				
Kentucky	73,677	220,955	406,511	564,317
Tennessee	35,691	105,602	261,727	422,823
Alabama	—	1,250	9,046	127,901
Mississippi	—	7,600	31,306	75,448
Total	109,368	335,407	708,590	1,190,489
Trans-Mississippi West				
Louisiana	—	—	76,556	153,407
Arkansas	—	—	1,062	14,273
Missouri	—	—	19,783	66,586
Total	—	—	97,401	234,266

Source: U.S. Bureau of the Census.

RECOVERING THE PAST

CENSUS RETURNS

From the seventeenth century to the twentieth, the American population has changed dramatically, not only in size and geographic distribution but also in density, in birth, death, and fertility rates, in marriage age, and in family size. In the early nineteenth century, for example, the average life expectancy of white Americans was about 45 years, and men tended to outlive women. In our own time, the average life expectancy has reached 74, and women on the average live longer than men. Population characteristics have differed as well across regions, urban and rural settings, and among racial, ethnic, and class groups.

Changes in the demographic traits of the American population have had powerful effects on the nation's social and economic development. For example, the changing size and makeup of the labor force has helped shape economic production, and the changing proportions of older and younger citizens affect consumer habits and place different demands on health care and educational systems. When mortality rates have been high, as was often the case in the early centuries of American history, families were rendered more unstable and birthrates increased as parents tried to compensate by having more children. As mortality declined during the nineteenth century, so too did birthrates and family size.

Demographic information can also tell us a great deal about the life experiences of ordinary Americans. Indeed, demographic data is often the major source of historical information about otherwise anonymous individuals. In recent years, historians have paid increasing attention to the analysis of populations, their characteristics during different periods, and their change over time.

Two kinds of demographic data have proved most important. One consists of birth, death, and marriage records, often found in church or town registers. These record the basic demographic events in people's lives. If they are complete and continuous enough, they allow historians to trace the life course of individuals and to reconstruct patterns of family and community life over time.

Here we offer an example of the second kind of demographic data, a census. The material is from the federal census of 1820. Article 1, Section 2 of the Constitution called for an enumeration (or counting) of the nation's population within three years after the first meeting of Congress and then every ten years "in such manner as they shall by law direct." The first decennial census was taken in 1790. The information was necessary to determine the periodic reapportionment of the House of Representatives and the allocation of direct taxes to the states.

Compared with modern census inquiries, the first federal censuses were simple and collected a limited amount of information. The 1790 census, for example, gathered data under the following headings only: "Name of Head of Family," "Free White Males, 16 Years and Upward," "Free White Males, Under 16," "Free White Females," "All Other Free Persons," and "Slaves." As the nation grew, however, the demand for information increased. In 1820, Congress for the first time called for the collection of economic data. In the decades following, the categories of both social and economic data were expanded.

Here we see aggregate data from the 1820 federal census for two Ohio counties and the city of Cincinnati. Ashtabula County, settled mostly by immigrants from New England, is in the northeastern part of the state, along Lake Erie. Hamilton County is in the southwestern part of Ohio, near Cincinnati, across the Ohio River from Kentucky.

Examine the census headings. Why do you think this information was collected? How did these three local populations compare in terms of race, gender, and place of birth? How can you explain the differences? Why are there no slaves? What can you discover about the ways people earned their living in these localities? How would the federal census of 1990 compare with the census of 1820?

1820 Federal Census: Selected Districts in Ohio

ASHTABULA COUNTY

1. Free white males	3,878
2. Free white females	3,493
3. Foreigners not naturalized	16
4. Number of persons engaged in agriculture	1,499
5. Number of persons engaged in commerce	19
6. Number of persons engaged in manufacturing	271
7. Male slaves	0
8. Female slaves	0
9. Free male colored persons	3
10. Free female colored persons	1
11. All other persons except Indians not taxed	7
Total*	7,382

HAMILTON COUNTY

1. Free white males	16,262
2. Free white females	14,869
3. Foreigners not naturalized	303
4. Number of persons engaged in agriculture	4,127
5. Number of persons engaged in commerce	389
6. Number of persons engaged in manufacturing	1,548
7. Male slaves	0
8. Female slaves	0
9. Free male colored persons	328
10. Free female colored persons	305
11. All other persons except Indians not taxed	0
Total*	31,764

CITY OF CINCINATTI

1. Free white males	4,919
2. Free white females	4,290
3. Foreigners not naturalized	241
4. Numbers of persons engaged in agriculture	99
5. Number of persons engaged in commerce	313
6. Number of persons engaged in manufacturing	753
7. Male slaves	0
8. Female salves	0
9. Free male colored persons	219
10. Free female colored persons	214
11. All other persons except Indians not taxed	0
Total*	9,642

* The totals exclude categories 3 through 6, since the people listed in them are also included in the other categories.

from Albany. "The woods are full of new settlers," wrote an observer near Batavia, New York, in 1805. "Axes are resounding, and the trees literally falling about us as we passed." By 1812, some 200,000 souls lived in the western part of the state, where scarcely 30,000 had lived 20 years before.

Every spring, when the water was high and settlers were eager to go west and plant their new land, the Ohio was crowded with flatboats carrying people, animals, and a few valued family possessions downriver. "America is breaking up and going west!" exclaimed the British traveler Morris Birkbeck. To many people at the time, it certainly seemed so.

Settlers were drawn by the promotions of countless speculators seeking fortunes in the sale of western land. Between 1790 and 1820, land companies hawked vast areas of New York, Ohio, Kentucky, and Alabama to prospective settlers back east. The Holland Land Company, financed by a consortium of Dutch bankers, bought 2.5 million acres of prime land in western New York and another 1.5 million in Pennsylvania. Many of the most extravagant ventures failed, their plans too ambitious for the surging tide of settlement to fulfill. But many succeeded, returning handsome profits to their investors. Individual settlers shared in the speculative fever, going into debt to buy extra land so that they might sell it at a premium when population increased and land prices rose. For years, land had offered the promise of economic security. In the expanding re-

public, it stimulated economic ambitions as well.

Even the panic and depression of 1819–1821 failed to damp for long the exuberance of America's expansionary capitalist faith. Out of the depression came not despair and greater caution but renewed and even more reckless ambition. Indicative of this was the move in many states to ease bankruptcy laws so that entrepreneurs come upon hard times were not put in jail but were left free to try their fortunes again. Before long, bankruptcy would lose much of its earlier stigma.

By the 1820s, the American economy stood poised at a historic divide. Behind it lay the traditional world of preindustrial America; ahead loomed the emerging industrial world of the future. The details of that new order were not yet clear, but its outlines were coming into view.

THE NATURE OF PREINDUSTRIAL SOCIETY

Just as America's preindustrial economy differed from the later industrial order, so did the preindustrial society of the early republic. During the nineteenth century, the combined forces of industrialization, urban growth, large-scale immigration, and westward expansion would transform American social life. By the 1820s, enough had changed to

Important Routes Westward

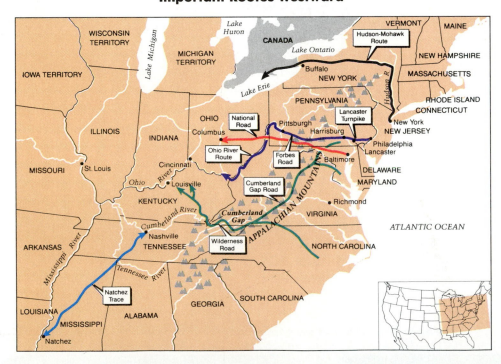

make clear that a new social order was in the making. At the same time, the traditional social relationships defined by family, community, class, gender, and race were slow to alter, considerably slower than ways of producing and marketing goods. If the future was increasingly on people's minds, the past was still evident in their daily lives.

It requires imagination on our part to understand that preindustrial society, so different was it from our own. We must do so, however, if we are to grasp the revolutionary changes that the nineteenth century would bring.

A Nation of Regions

Were we to be transported back to that preindustrial world, much about it would seem strange and unfamiliar. Probably nothing would impress us more than the smallness of American communities and the isolation of people from each other. In the early nineteenth century, community and region were much more real to most Americans than any sense of nationhood.

The country was divided first by distinct and separate regions. The regional differences between North and South that originated in the colonial period persisted and even increased during the early nineteenth century. The northern states continued down the path of economic diversification, with mixed farming, commerce, fishing, and manufacturing. The North's denser population and relatively broad distribution of wealth generated a growing demand for consumer goods. Moreover, the kinds of commodities produced in the North—grain, dried fish, forest and manufactured goods—created jobs and stimulated support industries. The production of dried fish, for example, required boats and nets, salt and barrels, sails and docks. Finally, the region's topography, combining agricultural lands, rapidly flowing rivers, and easy access to the sea, promoted economic diversification.

The South, by contrast, focused increasingly on the cultivation and export of cotton. Unlike many of the commodities produced in the North, cotton generated few economic "linkages," for it required little processing and stimulated few local industries. The South's relative advantage lay in expanding its staple-crop agriculture rather than in economic diversification.

As the two regions' economies diverged, so did their societies. In the North, wealth was not equally distributed, but the free-labor system did reward most people for their work. In the South, the slave-labor system produced a dramatically uneven distribution of wealth, for the masters reaped the profit from their slaves' labor. In white society, class differences were expanding. As cotton took hold, people without slaves or with access only to marginal lands fell rapidly behind.

America's regional diversity now included the vast area of Trans-Appalachia as well. During the first years of settlement on that rapidly moving frontier, life was hard as settlers struggled to clear the land and get their first crops in the ground. Their task was made more difficult because they initially shied away from the "oak openings" and prairie lands, believing that heavily forested areas were most fertile.

As population increased, however, and the rich virgin soil began to bloom, Trans-Appalachia began to grow. North of the Ohio River, settlement followed the grid pattern prescribed in the Northwest Ordinance of 1787, while south of the Ohio people distributed themselves more randomly across the land, much as their ancestors had done back east. Above the Ohio, mixed, free-labor agriculture quickly appeared as farmers worked to reproduce the life they had known in Pennsylvania or New England. In short order, towns such as Columbus and Cincinnati emerged to provide services and cultural amenities for the surrounding population. In Kentucky and Tennessee, mixed agriculture also took hold, but it was soon challenged by the spread of slave-based cotton.

As people continued to spill into the region, they established churches and courts, schools and even colleges (Transylvania University, founded in Lexington, Kentucky, in 1780, was the first college west of the Appalachians). Even so, Trans-Appalachia retained a reputation for its rough and colorful quality of life. Life could be depressingly lonesome for families lost in the hollows of the Cumberland Mountains of eastern Tennessee. In the river towns along the Ohio River, by contrast, boatmen and gamblers, con men and speculators gave civic life a raucous quality; and everywhere the transiency, youthfulness, and predominant maleness of the population kept society unsettled.

The constant drama of migration and the grandeur of the natural surroundings fed people's imaginations. No characters were more famous in popular folklore than westerners like Daniel Boone, who fought the Indians, explored the country, and founded frontier settlements. None were more colorful than the mythical riverman, Mike Fink, who boasted that he "was half man, half alligator" and

By 1800, Cincinnati had become an important port on the Ohio River between Pittsburgh and Louisville and was providing services for surrounding farms.

could "whip his weight in grizzly bears." And nothing revealed more graphically the West's rawness than the slashing, eye-gouging, ear-biting, no-holds-barred "rough and tumble" brawls that regularly erupted.

A Nation of Communities

If regional identify was important in Americans' lives, social existence centered even more tightly on communities, for most people spent their years—growing up and marrying, raising families and dying—within the physical and social boundaries of their localities. In the early republic, the social world of most Americans was intimate and self-contained.

The point is best made by noting what we would find missing were we to visit the nation's villages and farms around 1800. We would note first the absence of communication systems such as today join people closely together. The written word was the only means of communicating across space.

Newspapers and the mail provided the major information links between communities. From 1790 to 1820, both systems expanded greatly. Ninety-two newspapers circulated, mostly in towns along the Atlantic coast, as the new government got under way. By 1820, the number had risen to 512, and they were now widely scattered through the interior. The number of post offices and the flow of mail increased even more dramatically. When Washington was inaugurated, only 75 post offices existed in the entire nation; 30 years later, there were nearly 8,500. Over those same three decades, the number of letters sent through the postal system increased ninefold.

Improvements in communication, however, were not as dramatic as these figures at first suggest. Though newspapers were more numerous, they still had limited distribution, primarily because of the high costs of production. As late as 1820, the average circulation was only 800. Most papers, moreover, appeared only once or twice a week; not until mid-century would new, high-speed presses reduce printing costs sufficiently to make possible the production of cheap, mass-circulation papers. Though the flow of mail grew significantly and the average cost of mailing a letter declined, it still cost 25 cents to send a letter 30 miles or more. At a time when the daily wage averaged about a dollar, that was prohibitively expensive for most people.

Overland travel also improved during these years. In 1800, it took two days to go by horseback or coach from New York to Philadelphia, four days to Boston, and more than a week to Pittsburgh in western Pennsylvania. By 1820, those travel times had been halved, especially north of Virginia and east of the Appalachians, where the roads were better. Beginning in the 1790s, a flurry of turnpike construction began in the Northeast. The first one of any length opened between Philadelphia and Lancaster, Pennsylvania, in 1794. It immediately proved profitable, and soon dozens of similar projects were under way. By 1811, New York had chartered 137 turnpike companies and the New England states 200 more. In 1806, Congress authorized construction of the National Road westward from Cumberland, Maryland. By 1818, it had penetrated as far as Wheeling on the Ohio River and had reduced travel time along its length from eight days to three.

Even the turnpikes, though, would seem crude to the modern traveler, for most of them amounted to little more than dirt roadways with the bushes trimmed back along the sides and the tree stumps cut off at 16 inches, just low enough for most wagon axles to clear. Turnpikes, moreover, were few; most often people had to make their way along crude pathways or rutted wagon trails that wound across the countryside, following the path of least topographic resistance. In the summer, travel along these byways raised clouds of choking dust; in the spring, they dissolved into mud. People often preferred to travel in the winter if the weather was mild, for sleds and sleighs moved more easily than wagons. In the mountainous areas of western Pennsylvania, whole hillsides were denuded of trees cut by anxious travelers to drag behind their wagons as makeshift brakes on the jolting ride downhill. The usual pace of travel, whether on foot or horseback, was no more than 3 or 4 miles an hour. At that rate, a trip of 25 miles filled a day, and even that was impossible if there were mountains to cross or rivers to ford.

The contrast with modern communications is staggering. When George Washington died in December 1799 in Alexandria, Virginia, it took 5 days for the news to reach Philadelphia, 11 days to get as far as Boston, and over three weeks to penetrate west to Lexington, Kentucky. By contrast, when President Kennedy was assassinated in 1963, fully 68 percent of the American people heard the news *within half an hour.*

Improvements in transportation were also beginning to speed communication and travel. By 1810, steamboats were appearing along the Atlantic coast and on the Ohio and Mississippi rivers. In 1807, Robert Fulton had launched his 160-ton sidewheeler *Clermont* on the Hudson River and demonstrated the feasibility of steam travel. Four years later, the

The turnpike system, begun in the 1790s, reduced travel time through the countryside. Tree stumps were cut low enough to clear under a wagon's axles, and log roads were built over streams and swamps. Here an express coach makes its way through the forest.

New Orleans, a crude sternwheeler built at Pittsburgh, made the first successful run over the falls of the Ohio River at Cincinnati and down the Mississippi to New Orleans. Following the War of 1812, new shallow-draft hulls and more powerful engines brought a surge of steamboat construction in fast-growing river towns such as Pittsburgh, Louisville, and Cincinnati. Within a few decades, steamboats would revolutionize transportation on the nation's vast interior river system. For a moment, however, most westerners still depended on flatboats to carry them downstream and keelboats for the laborious task of poling upriver.

Also missing from America's preindustrial communities were regional and national organizations such as today knit localities together. Churches, schools, fire companies, laboring men's associations, militia companies—all were tightly bounded by the local community and had but tenuous connections with similar groups elsewhere. During the second quarter of the nineteenth century, political parties, religious denominations, reform societies, and countless other groups would begin to bring American communities into closer contact. That process of organization building was a fundamental part of America's national development. But in the early years of the republic, the organizational as well as informational boundaries of community life were tightly drawn.

Lives of Intimacy and Quietness

Life in preindustrial communities was intimate and highly personal. The vast majority of America's 5.2 million people in 1800 lived on farms and plantations or in villages of no more than a few hundred souls. Only ten places in the entire country were home to as many as 5,000 people. The two largest, New York and Philadelphia, at about 60,000, were the size of present day Port Arthur, Texas. All the towns of 2,500 or more taken together accounted for only 7 percent of the population.

In these rural and small-town settings, people encountered each other frequently. They went to church together, shared the joys of birth and the sorrows of death, exchanged goods, and gossiped at village stores. The continuity of local populations also contributed to this dense and intensely personal network of social relations. As the nineteenth century proceeded, the geographic mobility of the American people increased. The accelerating migration westward was one major cause, but the movement of people from countryside to town also contributed to it. This intraregional traffic was especially heavy in New England, where young men and women, finding it increasingly difficult to get a start on the crowded and rock-strewn soil, sought opportunity in Boston and emerging mill towns such as Waltham, Lowell, and Pawtucket. But it was evident in the Middle Atlantic states as well. Between 1790 and 1820, the nation's cities grew at a rate nearly twice that of the population as a whole, something entirely new in the American experience. Part of the increase came from immigration, now beginning again after a quarter century's interruption. Much of it, though, resulted from movement from the surrounding countryside.

Most people, however, did not move far or often during their lifetimes. Prior to 1820, persistence rates—people's tendency to stay in the same community over a decade's time—had changed little from the eighteenth century. As a result, generational continuity, family stability, and extended kin networks continued to characterize community life. In the intimate communities of preindustrial America, people encountered faces, voices, and patterns of behavior that were reassuringly familiar.

Life in the communities of preindustrial America was remarkably quiet as well. We who live in an environment filled with the relentless noise of engines and machinery, portable tape decks and piped-in Muzak would be amazed, perhaps even unnerved, by the quietness of that bygone day. In the world of preindustrial America, silence, not sound, was the regular accompaniment of daily life.

When the enveloping silence was interrupted, it was by the pealing of church bells or the clopping of horses' hoofs or the unmagnified sounds of human voices conversing. People labored to the accompaniment of a waterwheel's creaking or the pang of a blacksmith's hammer or the clacking of a hand loom—nothing more. Out in the endless countryside where most Americans lived, the sounds were nature's own—the wind blowing in the trees, a summer thunderstorm, the lowing of a cow, the call of a catbird seeking its mate.

The slowness and unscheduled character of life's pace would impress a modern visitor as well. Difficulties of transportation were in part responsible, for every trip required effort and was subject to interruption by a storm, a lame horse, a dying wind. It was common experience for storekeepers not to know when their new goods would arrive, for families to be uncertain whether relatives were coming for a visit, and for merchants to wonder if their cargoes had reached their destination. In the face of such uncertainties, it made little sense for people to try to schedule their lives closely.

Work patterns were similarly deliberate and informal. Since most Americans gained their living from the land, they were bound by the unhurried cycle of the seasons. Planting, cultivating, and harvesting followed regularly, one upon the other, but they could not be speeded by human effort. At harvest time, the tempo of farm life picked up, for wheat and other grains could spoil if left too long in the field. Corn, however, could wait, and root crops could even survive a frost.

Farm families worked hard. When not tending their crops, men found more than enough to do repairing the barn, shoeing a horse, or rooting out tree stumps from a field. Farm women also worked long and difficult hours cultivating the garden, raising children, preserving food, and making clothes. Though the hours were long and arduous, the pace was slow, and schedules were almost nonexistent.

Nonagricultural work patterns, at least outside the few factories, would also seem to us slow and inefficient. Working by hand with the simplest tools and for limited markets, artisans gave little thought to maximizing output. Instead, they worked when there were orders to fill and closed their shops when there were none. Seldom did either craftsmen or merchants keep regularly scheduled hours, nor did their customers expect that of them.

Nothing illustrates life's unscheduled pace more vividly than the ways people reckoned time. For most Americans, life went on in the absence of clocks and timepieces. Not until the 1830s did they become cheap enough for most families to own. Nor did most communities have public clocks, either on church towers or public buildings, to show and chime the hours. There was no use for them, for in the early nineteenth century, standard time did not exist. Even in the same community, clocks often told widely different times, and no one seemed to mind. Most people were content to estimate the time of day by the position of the sun. At night, they simply waited for the dawn. The tolling of a bell might indicate when church was to begin or a town meeting to convene, but estimates were generally sufficient for organizing life. Days, months, and seasons of the year were meaningful measures of human activity; hours and minutes often were not.

Lives of Difficulty and Trial

As modern visitors to the communities of preindustrial America, we would be impressed as well

The pace of rural life in the early nineteenth century, though far from leisurely, was largely determined by the rhythms of nature.

by the rigors of daily life. Though most Americans were better off than their colonial ancestors, their lives were hardly comfortable. They lacked virtually all the conveniences of housing and diet that we take for granted today, and disease and death were their constant companions.

Most people's housing offered limited space and few amenities. Its quality varied enormously from place to place and class to class. The wealthy lived comfortably enough, for they could afford fine townhouses or elegant plantation mansions. Most Americans, however, could not. For southern slaves, frontier settlers, and the urban poor, housing meant cramped and filthy spaces; dirt floors; small window openings, often lacking glass; and only the roughest and most rudimentary furniture. For the urban poor, even firewood was often too expensive to buy, forcing them to scavenge their neighborhoods for waste materials to burn.

Even the wealthy depended on fireplaces or stoves for heat and had no indoor plumbing. After dark, people used candles and firelight for illumination. During the winter months, when the sun set early and the nights were cold, evening activities were curtailed and people sought warmth in bed.

People's diet was limited as well. Farm and small-town families enjoyed regular access to fresh fruits and vegetables, dairy products, domestic animals, and wild game. In the cities, many families still maintained small garden plots, a few chickens, perhaps even a cow. But as the cities grew and land values increased, that became increasingly difficult. Ice for refrigeration was often scarce; as a conse-

quence, every city dweller knew the familiar taste of sour milk and the smell of rancid butter. Each city had its vegetable stands to which farmers brought their produce and markets where the meat of animals driven in from the countryside was sold. But prices were high and supplies often uncertain. Thus fresh meats and vegetables, like milk and butter, were but occasional parts of most urban dwellers' diets. Far more common were bread, potatoes, onions, and salt pork.

Even in the countryside, fresh fruits and vegetables disappeared during the winter months, and people turned to the dried fruits and root vegetables they had stored away. Coffee, sugar, and spices were expensive enough that most people could enjoy them only occasionally.

Alcohol was a central part of the diet. During the early nineteenth century, the consumption of alcohol, especially in the form of distilled spirits, skyrocketed. In 1790, the annual per capita consumption of spirits stood at about 2.6 gallons. By 1830, Americans were consuming 5.2 gallons of hard liquor for every man, woman, and child in the nation, nearly triple today's rate. Whiskey was the most popular drink, with hard cider close behind. In 1820, there were over 1,000 licensed distilleries in New York alone. Not until midcentury, after large numbers of Germans had entered the country and brewing techniques had changed, did the consumption of beer begin to grow.

Then, as now, drinking patterns differed across social boundaries. Among whites, the heaviest drinking was done by young, lower-class males.

Drinking rates were high as well among the foreign-born and people living in the West. The consumption of alcohol was lowest among middle-aged, native born New England farmers.

Women drank less extravagantly than men but still consumed from an eighth to a quarter of the nation's liquor. Ideals of femininity discouraged public tippling; women were supposed to show restraint, consistent with their higher virtue and delicacy. Still, many women found solace in the private consumption of alcohol-based medicines ostensibly taken for their health. On some occasions women imbibed publicly. Eastern upper-class women frequently drank in mixed company at dinner parties, while at frontier dances the whiskey bottle was "passed pretty briskly from mouth to mouth, exempting neither age nor sex." Even infants were often taught to imbibe. Wrote one traveler, "I have frequently seen fathers wake their child of a year from a sound sleep to make it drink rum or brandy."

Improvements in distilling contributed to the increase in liquor consumption. From 1802 to 1815, the federal government issued more than 100 patents for distilling devices. The rapid opening of the West, where farmers grew corn and turned it into whiskey before sending it east to market, was a factor as well. As output increased, prices dropped, further promoting consumption. In the early 1820s, whiskey sold at retail for as little as 25 cents per gallon.

As the consumption of alcohol grew, so did public concern. Washington thought that distilled spirits were "the ruin of half the workmen in this country," while Jefferson feared that raw whiskey was "spreading through the mass of our citizens." Anne Royall, who spent much of her life crisscrossing the country in stage coaches, observed, "When I was in Virginia, it was too much whiskey—in Ohio, too much whiskey—in Tennessee, it is too, too much whiskey!" By the 1830s, concern would change to alarm. As we shall see in Chapter 13, nothing aroused more zeal among reformers during the second quarter of the nineteenth century than demon rum.

Birth, Death, and Disease

The quality of life in early nineteenth-century America was also affected by the constant presence of disease and death. High infant mortality, the rigors of daily life, limitations of diet, and the risks of medical care resulted in dramatically shorter life spans than we enjoy today. At the turn of the century, only half the people could expect to live to age 45. Unlike today, women on the average died sooner than men, their bodies weakened by the rigors of frequent childbirth. Though birthrates were declining, white women could expect to give birth to four to eight children, and immigrant and black women averaged even more. Male physicians, such as Dr. William Shippen of Philadelphia, were increasingly overseeing the birth process. Whether that made childbirth less risky is uncertain. It did, however, reduce the role of female midwives and increasingly remove birthing from the realm of shared female experiences.

Disease constantly threatened human life. Medical knowledge had improved little over a century's time. Germ theories of infection were still unknown, and hospitals and well-trained physicians were few. Most Americans, especially among the lower classes, depended for health care on home remedies and prayer. That was probably not all bad, considering that the standard medical treatment for most diseases included bleeding, purging, and blistering.

Diseases such as diphtheria and tuberculosis took a steady toll of human life, and epidemics of smallpox and yellow fever periodically raced through the population with devastating results. Today, through programs of inoculation and public health, we have largely eliminated disease epidemics. In the early nineteenth century, however, they visited men, women, and children with terrifying regularity.

During the 1790s, yellow fever struck the coastal cities repeatedly. The most devastating attack hit Philadelphia in 1793. Within months, nearly 10 percent of the city's population died. Those who could afford to flee the city did so, seeking refuge in the surrounding countryside. Those who could not stayed in their homes, venturing out only as necessary to secure food and water. No one could feel safe from the dreaded disease, though the poor and the elderly fared worst because they could not as readily escape and were physically more vulnerable. Blacks also died in large numbers when the Free African Society, responding to appeals from the mayor, supplied nurses and men for burial duty. The common belief that blacks were naturally immune to the fever's ravages turned out to be tragically false.

The authorities made efforts to deal with the devastation by setting up hospitals to hold the sick and establishing quarantines to restrict movement in and out of the cities. After the crisis passed, city officials took steps to improve sanitation by cleaning the streets of their usual filth. Garbage, however, continued to litter the streets, animals still roamed freely in the cities, the collection of human excrement remained sporadic, and the wells from which people drank were often polluted. Disease-carrying mosquitoes continued to take their toll. Yellow fever returned to Philadelphia in 1796 and 1797 and hit hard at other seaboard cities as well.

Disease and death, then, were regular visitors to community and family life. Scarcely anyone could expect more than a few years to pass without suffering the loss of a family member or close friend.

Patterns of Wealth and Poverty

One of the defining features of any society is its pattern of social class—that is, the way in which wealth and thus power and status are distributed among its people. During the nineteenth century, class distinctions increased as early industrialization redrew the contours of economic and social life.

As the century began, property was already unequally distributed across gender and racial lines. Women continued to hold far less property than men. The large majority of blacks, moreover, were slaves; for them, ownership of anything more than the smallest items of personal property was beyond reach. Though the condition of free blacks was better, they too held little of the country's wealth.

Among white males, property was most broadly shared in rural areas of the North, where free-labor and family-farm agriculture predominated, and least so in the South, where control of slave labor and the best land permitted tobacco, rice, and cotton planters to monopolize the region's wealth.

The class structure was also sharply drawn in the ports where merchant capitalists controlled the sources of commercial and manufacturing wealth, while small artisans, sailors, and unskilled workers lived at the margins of the economy, their lives taken up almost entirely by a struggle for survival. Perhaps the most even distribution of property existed on the edges of settlement in the trans-Appalachian frontier, but that was an equality of want. As that region developed, differences in wealth appeared there as well.

Taking the country as a whole, the pattern of wealth distribution had not changed much from pre-Revolutionary times. In 1800, the top 10 percent of property holders controlled about 42 percent of the nation's wealth, very close to what it had been 50 years before. By 1850, that figure would reach 70 percent as industrialization reshaped economic life and separated capital from labor.

When the century opened, not many Americans were truly rich. Even the wealthiest, such as the Boston merchant Francis Lowell and the South Carolina planter Charles Manigault, could not match the grandeur of English landed aristocrats or the great London merchants. Nor did their wealth begin to approach the fortunes accumulated by America's captains of industry during the last half of the nineteenth century. Neither did America contain a large, destitute underclass such as could be found in the cities and countryside of Europe. By comparison with England and France, property in the United States was broadly distributed.

In a world where neither medicine nor hygiene could be depended on to save lives, death was a frequent presence in family life.

Poverty, however, existed and was increasing. In the South, it was most evident among slaves and poor whites living on the sandy pine barrens of the backcountry. In the North, the port cities housed growing numbers of the poor. The commercial prosperity of the 1790s was widely shared, but it did not benefit everyone. In Boston, for example, artisans and shopkeepers, who together had owned 20 percent of the city's wealth in 1700, held scarcely half that much as the nineteenth century began.

In the centers of commercial bustle, substantial numbers of people struggled to survive, their task actually made more difficult by the inflation of rent and food prices that prosperity brought. The commercial recession following Jefferson's embargo in 1807 hit the urban poor with particular force, for they felt the effects of unemployment most directly. Winter seasons regularly brought hard times for many as shipping slowed and jobs disappeared. During the winter months of 1805, New York's mayor, De Witt Clinton, worried publicly about the fate of 10,000 impoverished New Yorkers and asked the state legislature for help. During the winter of 1814–1815, relief agencies assisted nearly one-fifth of the city's population.

Even in rural New England and southeastern Pennsylvania, a lower class of transient and propertyless people was growing. The "strolling poor," they were called—men, and sometimes women, unable to secure land of their own and thus forced to roam the countryside searching for work.

Three other groups were conspicuous among the nation's poor. One consisted of old Revolutionary War veterans like Long Bill Scott, who had found poverty as well as adventure in the war. Just how many there were is not known, but state and federal governments were peppered with petitions from grizzled veterans describing their misery and asking for relief. Women and children also suffered from poverty. Annual censuses of almshouse residents in New York City from 1816 to 1821 consistently listed more women and children than men.

Nothing more clearly illustrated poverty's grip or the vulnerability of many Americans to economic hard times than the depression of 1819–1821. Hardest hit were the West and South, where land speculation had been rampant and wildcat banking the most uncontrolled. When the financial bubble burst and depression settled in, a tide of foreclosures swept across the West, destroying the livelihoods of farmers and speculators alike. Residents of the port cities felt the harsh grip of depression as well, as commerce slowed, banks collapsed, and businesses shut down, leaving thousands without employment.

Poverty was a continuing reality in the early nineteenth century. And for every American who actually suffered its effects, there were several others living just beyond its reach, their margin of safety alarmingly thin.

PERFECTING REPUBLICAN SOCIETY

During the Revolutionary era, politics had preoccupied the American people. There was concern as well, however, about the proper functioning of republican society. Between 1790 and 1828, Americans turned their thoughts to issues of social change and reform, for if their experiment was to succeed, society would have to be republicanized as well. Behind their reformist efforts lay a cluster of beliefs regarding the unique character of the American people.

The Youthfulness of America

The reformist impulse that emerged in the 1790s had roots deep in the colonial past. From the first days of colonial settlement, European immigrants had thought of America as a place free of Old World social rigidities and open to new ways of life. Separation from England convinced Americans that they were casting off the burden of their European past and launching a new and glorious future. They called their new society *novus ordo seclorum,* a new order of the ages. That motto expressed their sense of new beginnings and their belief that reason rather than habit or tradition would now guide America's social development.

These attitudes appeared in the growing emphasis on youthfulness that characterized American attitudes during these years. America, people repeatedly insisted, was a "young" and "rising" republic, a "new nation" taking its place among the "old" and "decadent" empires of Europe.

The emphasis on youthfulness reflected the widely shared belief that nations followed a cyclic course of birth, growth, maturity, decline, dissolution, and death, much like human beings. This cyclical theory of history helped explain America's birth as a new nation. England, aged and corrupted by its own power, had begun its decline, while the United States, youthful and vigorous, had entered its upward cycle of social development.

The Meaning of Social Equality

Equality was the second element of America's new social faith. By social equality, most people did not mean literal equality of social condition. They meant two other things instead.

The first was equality of opportunity. We have seen in Chapter 8 how reluctant the Federalists were to give up their familiar notions of social privilege. But we have also seen that it became increasingly difficult for them to support such doctrines openly. In a republican society, social differences should not be based on privilege or inherited position but on ability. For that to be true, society had to provide people with the opportunity to rise as far as their abilities and ambition would carry them. The emphasis on equality of opportunity was attractive to social democrats, for it spoke of setting privilege aside and giving everyone an equal chance. Social conservatives, however, could embrace it as well, for it could be used to justify existing social inequalities by implying that people who fell behind did not have the ability to succeed.

The doctrine of equal opportunity had little relevance for the actual life circumstances of many Americans. Slaves, women, and working-class men understood all too well the limits of opportunity in preindustrial America. But the principle was bold and inspiring for countless others.

Social equality had a powerful moral dimension as well, for it implied an equality of social worth among individuals, no matter what their wealth or social standing might be. Though Americans generally accepted inequalities of wealth and social position, they were much less willing to tolerate social pretension or the arrogant assumption that differences in social standing signified differences in people's value.

That attitude showed up vividly in an episode that took place in New York City in 1795. Thomas Burke and Timothy Crady, two recent Irish immigrants, operated a ferry across the East River between lower Manhattan and Brooklyn. One day in early November, Gabriel Furman, a merchant and Federalist alderman, arrived on the Brooklyn shore a bit before the scheduled departure time. Impatient to get across, Furman instructed the ferrymen to leave early. When they refused, he upbraided the "rascals" for their disrespect and threatened to have them arrested. Crady was especially angered by the alderman's arrogance. He and Burke, Crady exploded, "were as good as any buggers," and he threatened to use his boathook on anyone who tried

to arrest him. When the ferry landed on the Manhattan shore, Furman called the constable and had the two arrested, brandishing his cane at them as they were led off to jail, where they were charged with vagrancy. Their employer offered bail, but Furman refused to allow it, and so they remained 12 days in Bridewell prison awaiting trial.

Both Crady and Burke were eventually hauled before Mayor Varick and three other Federalist aldermen, sitting as the Court of General Sessions. There was no jury. The judges quickly decided to make examples of the two insolent Irishmen. "You rascals, we'll trim you," Varick allegedly said; "we'll learn you to insult men in office." The two ferrymen were not allowed to speak in their own behalf, nor were friendly witnesses permitted to testify. The magistrates quickly found the two guilty on charges of insulting an alderman and threatening the constable, sentenced them to two months at hard labor, and ordered 25 lashes for Crady as well.

Within a month, the two ferrymen had bolted from jail and disappeared into Pennsylvania, never to be heard from again. The episode, however, was not yet over, for a young Jeffersonian lawyer named William Keteltas took up the case and in time carried it all the way to the New York assembly. In a two-column newspaper account signed "One of the People," he castigated "the tyranny and partiality of the court" and concluded that Burke and Crady had been punished to "gratify the pride, the ambition and insolence of men in office." That, he argued, was intolerable in a republican society. The assembly, he charged, was protecting the mayor to save his reputation. But what of the ruined reputations of the ferrymen? Were they not just as important?

Before it was over, the incident generated wide public anger, and Keteltas earned a jail sentence for lambasting the legislature's failure to address the case. Over 2,000 citizens crowded the assembly chamber when Keteltas was sentenced and then carried him in a chair through the streets chanting "The Spirit of '76." Once released, he was paraded through the streets by a throng carrying American and French flags and a banner inscribed "What you rascal, insult your superiors?" In the early republic, notions of equal social worth spread rapidly.

The Doctrine of Individualism

The doctrine of individualism was the third element in America's new social faith. It asserted that society's basic purpose was to promote the interests of its individual members. That idea had been voiced during the colonial years, but it had been carefully balanced by the opposing view that individuals existed only as parts of a larger social order and must subordinate themselves to the general good.

Revolutionary republicanism, with its emphasis on public virtue, initially reinforced the doctrine that the public good outweighed individual interests. The Revolutionary experience, however, moved the balance in the other direction, in favor of an emphasis on the primacy of the free and unfettered individual. The stress on natural rights had that effect, as did the widespread questioning of authority that occurred.

Equality of opportunity and moral worth, individualism, and a belief that society could be shaped in ways to increase human liberty all combined to create a dramatically new social vision that Americans carried with them into the nineteenth century.

The Second Great Awakening and Social Reform

The early stages of the Second Great Awakening, a swelling tide of religious revivalism beginning in the 1790s that swept across the nation, catching thousands in its grasp, added urgency and moral sanction to the idea of social reform. The Awakening's theology, articulated most powerfully by itinerant Methodist and Baptist preachers who moved tirelessly across the land, was simple and

The popular revivalism of the Second Great Awakening rejected theological subtleties and emphasized the individual's direct and emotional encounter with God. This Anabaptist ceremony of baptism by immersion was painted by the Russian traveler Paul Svinin.

direct. In contrast with the intricate theological arguments of the First Great Awakening a half century before, it emphasized the immediacy of every believer's encounter with God, rejected predestination in favor of universal salvation, and proclaimed the responsibility of each individual for his or her own soul. Such beliefs were fully consistent with popular republicanism.

The Awakening took hold first among ordinary people in the farms and villages of the West. One of the most spectacular outpourings of religious enthusiasm occurred in 1801 at Cane Ridge, Kentucky, where for six frenetic days 10,000 people gathered to exalt God and wrestle with the Devil. With hundreds shouting at once, the uproar could be heard for miles around. "The noise," declared James Finley, an observer and participant, "was like the roar of Niagara." He counted as many as seven ministers preaching at once, while some of the people sang, others prayed, and still others cried out for mercy "in the most pitiable accents." "My heart beat tumultuously," recalled Finley, "my knees trembled, my lips quivered, and I felt as though I must fall to the ground." Stepping onto a log for a better view, he saw "at least five hundred swept down in a moment, as if a battery of a thousand guns had been opened upon them, and then immediately followed shrieks . . . that rent the very heavens." Finding it too much to endure, Finley fled to the surrounding woods, wishing he had stayed at home.

The Awakening reinforced Americans' sense of personal autonomy and new beginnings, for Salvation was a revolutionizing experience. Ministers urged hard work, thrift, and sobriety and brought about personal transformations in many of their frontier converts. Revivalism also rekindled broad millennialist hopes that America would become the perfect place for Christ's Second Coming. The Awakening's theology, moreover, emphasized human equality before God and stressed the duty of Christian believers to demonstrate their faith by doing good works in the world.

Alleviating Poverty and Distress

It was a heady brew, this new combination of social and religious beliefs that underlay early nineteenth-century social reform.

The alleviation of poverty was one goal of the early social reformers. Benjamin Rush of Philadelphia believed that poverty could be reduced permanently and proposed programs of education for the poor designed to achieve that end. Many Americans, however, taking a more limited view, continued to believe that poverty was inevitable, that its primary causes were hard drink and moral indolence, and that the most that could be done was to offer selective relief to deserving individuals. In New York City during the early decades of the century, private and public authorities established more than 100 charitable and relief agencies to aid orphans and widows, aged females and young prostitutes, immigrants and imprisoned debtors, juvenile delinquents and poverty-stricken seamen.

Most of these ventures distinguished between the "worthy poor," respectable folk who were victims of circumstance and merited assistance, and the "idle" or "vicious poor," who lacked character and thus deserved their fate. Many Americans thought such distinctions were real and discoverable. No matter that a New York commission in 1823 found only 43 able-bodied adults (37 women and 9 men) among the 851 inmates of the city's almshouses or that a census of homes for the indigent in 1813 listed people such as Susanne Wilson, a blind pauper, aged 76, who first entered the almshouse in 1761, or that another listing included a variety of disabled Revolutionary War veterans, abandoned infants, illegitimate children, and indigent immigrants recently arrived from Europe. New Yorkers had not yet connected pauperism with the changing conditions of urban, commercial life.

Poverty was not the only object of public and private reform. Both municipal authorities and private charities established orphanages for children, asylums for the insane, and hospitals for the sick. Most of these institutions were small and short-lived, but they provided a base for the more ambitious reform efforts to come.

Educating the Republic's Children

A virtuous republic required above all the education of its citizens so that they would be honest, hard-working, and civic-minded. Educating the "rising generation" of young Americans involved not just the three R's, but as Noah Webster explained, "an acquaintance with ethics and . . . the general principles of law, commerce, money and government"—in other words, the basic doctrines of republican society.

Except in New England, which had a long tradition of public schooling, education in the colonial era had been largely left to the family. Typically that meant that only the children of the well-to-do, who

could pay the costs of tutors or academies, received even the most rudimentary education.

Following the Revolution, however, state legislatures, led by Massachusetts in 1789, began for the first time to appropriate tax revenues for the support of free public education. In 1795, Governor George Clinton of New York complained that education was "confined to the children of the opulent" and urged state aid to common schools. Over the next five years, the legislature appropriated $50,000 a year to be divided among local school committees. Tax-shy legislatures and deep-seated devotion to local control often frustrated the efforts of educational reformers, but the new principle that the state had an obligation to educate its citizens had been declared. In the meantime, free charity schools, financed by churches and private philanthropists and organized to train the children of the poor in responsible republican citizenship, took up some of the slack.

Colleges were also affected by the new attention to education. When the Revolution began, only nine colleges existed in the colonies. By 1800, that number had increased to 25—including the first state universities in North Carolina (1789), Georgia (1801), and Virginia (1819)—and by 1820 to more than twice that many. In most of them, traditional education, based on classical languages and theology and designed primarily for the training of clergymen, was broadened to include geography, natural sciences, and European languages, subjects deemed more useful for republican leaders.

Zest for the diffusion of knowledge was also revealed in the founding of scientific organizations, natural history museums, and medical and philosophical societies. Drawing on the optimism of the Enlightenment, the new republic's intellectual leaders saw these organizations as instruments for improving American life. Boston's Academy of Arts and Sciences (1780), the New Jersey Society for the Promotion of Agriculture, Commerce, and Art (1781), and the Philadelphia Natural History Museum (founded in 1794 by Charles Willson Peale, one of the nation's most accomplished artists) were among the many organizations that sprang up between 1780 and 1820.

Women in Republican Society

Though women's lives did not change markedly during these early years, changes that helped set the stage for later, more dramatic breakthroughs did occur.

Ludwig Miller, who painted many watercolors of his life in York County, Pennsylvania, here shows himself giving a music lesson to the students of a coeducational Lutheran school in 1805.

Divorce was one area where women achieved more equal treatment. When a neighbor asked John Backus, a silversmith in Great Barrington, Massachusetts, why he kicked and struck his wife, John replied that it was partly owing to his education, for his father often treated his mother in the same manner. We do not know whether John's mother tolerated such abuse, but his wife did not. She complained of cruelty, desertion, and adultery and obtained a divorce. Her reaction was not unique, for around the turn of the nineteenth century, more and more women followed her example.

Many demonstrated their unwillingness to stay with a bad marriage by walking out. We know this from the increasing number of newspaper notices taken out by deserted husbands announcing that their wives had left bed and board. Some women filed directly for divorce. The process was not easy, for most states allowed divorce only on the ground of adultery, and South Carolina did not permit it at all. Moreover, women typically had to present detailed evidence of their husbands' infidelities and face the discomfort of an all-male court, while a wife's transgressions could be more easily established and might include disobedience as well as more serious offenses. Amos Bliss believed he had a valid complaint against his wife, Phebe, because, as his divorce petition stated, she "behaved herself

unfriendly and unsubjectedly toward him," had "linked herself in friendship with her father's family against him," and was "wasteful and careless of his provisions and goods." Marriage may have been a contract, but it remained a contract of unequals.

Still, divorce was becoming more available to women. In Massachusetts during the decade after independence, 50 percent more women than men filed for divorce, with almost exactly the same rate of success. Part of the explanation no doubt lies in the war's disruptions, which led larger numbers of men to desert their wives and thus larger numbers of women to take action. It is just as likely, however, that women shared the new notions of individualism and social equality and from them developed rising expectations of marriage. Finally, the increasingly sympathetic treatment of women's divorce petitions suggests that their complaints were being taken more seriously and that their status within the family had risen.

Changes also occurred in women's education. This was part of the general enthusiasm for educational reform, but it reflected a special concern for women's place in the new republic. Given women's role as keepers of public morality and nurturers of future citizens, their education was a subject of general concern. If the republic was to fulfill its destiny, young women would have to prepare for the responsibilities that motherhood would bring. During the 1790s, Judith Sargeant Murray published a series of essays, gathered under the title *The Gleaner,* in which she decried the antiegalitarian habit of assuming that a genteel education in music and needlework was superior to a practical one. She was also critical of parents who "pointed their daughters" toward marriage and dependence. "I would give my daughters every accomplishment which I thought proper," Murray wrote. "They should be enabled to procure for themselves the necessaries of life; independence should be placed within their grasp. A woman," she concluded, "should reverence herself."

Between 1790 and 1820, a number of female academies were established. Most, such as Susanna Rowson's Young Ladies Academy of Philadelphia, were located in northeastern cities. Timothy Dwight, the future president of Yale, opened his academy at Greenfield Hill in Connecticut to girls and taught them the same subjects he taught boys, at the same time and in the same room; but he was the exception. Most proposals for female education assumed that the curriculum should be different and less demanding than that for boys.

Benjamin Rush, in his essay "Thoughts upon Female Education" (1787), prescribed bookkeeping, reading, grammar, penmanship, geography, natural philosophy, vocal music ("because it soothes cares and is good for the lungs"), and history. But he argued that female education should be condensed so that young women could marry in a timely way. Traditionalists such as the Boston minister John Gardiner were decidedly less sympathetic. "Women of masculine minds," he warned, "have generally masculine manners, and a robustness of person ill calculated to inspire the tender passions." Even the *Lady's Magazine* counseled that while learning was the road to preferment for men, "consequences very opposite were the result of the same quality in women."

The prediction that intellect would unsex women was accompanied by the warning that educated women would abandon their proper sphere as mothers and wives. In the face of such attitudes, even Rush insisted to his bride that "from the day you marry you must have no will of your own. . . . The subordination of your sex to ours is enforced by nature, by reason, and by Revelation."

Even the most ardent supporters of female learning insisted that they sought education so that they might function more effectively within their traditional sphere. As Judith Sargeant Murray explained, the happiness of the nation depended on the happiness of families, and that was based in turn on women who are "properly methodical, and economical in their . . . expenditures of time." As "daughters of Columbia," educated women would "fill with honor the parts allotted to them." It was a lofty but limited vision of what women's place in the republic should be. Even that vision was restricted to white, urban, middle- and upper-class young ladies.

The Limits of Reform: Race and Slavery

Early nineteenth-century reform made only limited progress in ameliorating the twin evils of slavery and racism. Slavery's inconsistency with republican principles continued to be pointed out after 1790, but with much less urgency than before, while the prospects of further abolition became increasingly faint. In spite of Ben Thompson's experience, manumission of individual slaves by private owners slowed as well.

Thomas and Sarah Mifflin, a well-to-do Quaker couple, sat for this portrait by John Singleton Copley. Note that Mrs. Mifflin's hands are busy weaving thread into a strip of fringe, while her husband marks his place in the book he is reading. Literacy was not considered a necessity for most women until well into the nineteenth century.

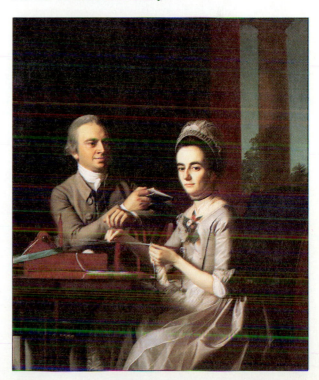

The reasons were several. The gradual abolition of slavery in the North soothed many consciences, while in the South, the spread of cotton increased the value of slave labor. Equally important in shaping white attitudes, however, were two slave rebellions, one bloody and successful on the Caribbean island of Hispaniola in 1791, the other, smaller, and unsuccessful but alarming nevertheless, near Richmond, Virginia, nearly a decade later.

Panic-stricken whites fleeing Hispaniola for their lives carried word to the North American mainland of the black Haitians' successful rebellion against a French colonial army of 25,000. The news spread terror, especially through the South, where rumors abounded that Haitian incendiaries would soon be landing. Immediately, southern whites tightened their black codes, cut the importation of new slaves from the Caribbean, and quizzed their slaves in an effort to root out malcontents and suspected Haitian revolutionaries. The bloody rebellion and the prospect of a nearby island nation governed by blacks frightened northern whites as well. Colonial rebellions were noble, but not when they set blacks against white authority.

A second shock followed in the summer of 1800, when another rebellion, this time just outside Richmond, was nipped in the bud. Gabriel Prosser, a 24-year-old free black, had devised a plan to arm 1,000 slaves for an assault on Richmond. Prosser and his immediate accomplices were all native-born Americans who spoke English, worked at skilled jobs that gave them considerable personal freedom (and thus opportunity to lay their plans), and knew enough about American independence to speak confidently of freedom and equality. A drenching downpour delayed the attack, giving time for several loyal, black house servants to sound the alarm before the conspirators could act. No white lives were lost, but blacks paid a heavy price, for alarmed white Virginians exacted their revenge. Scores of slaves and free blacks were arrested, and 25 suspects, including Prosser, were hanged at the personal order of Governor James Monroe.

The carnage saddened Thomas Jefferson. "There is strong sentiment that there has been hanging enough," he wrote to his young friend Monroe. "The other states and the world at large will forever condemn us if we indulge in a principle of revenge, or go one step beyond absolute necessity." In the midst of panic, however, necessity was hard to define, and the fateful steps had already been taken.

In the early nineteenth century, antislavery ap-

Blacks and Slavery, 1790–1820

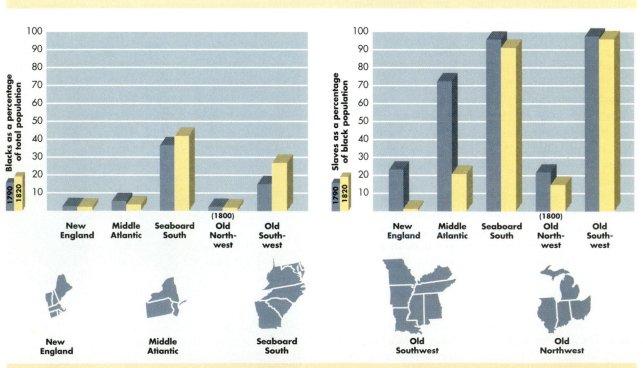

Source: U.S. Bureau of the Census.

In this watercolor of a black Methodist church meeting, Paul Svinin, a traveler from Russia, reveals his amazement at the physical emotion displayed by the worshipers. "African" churches and other organizations were rare before 1800 but grew steadily in the ensuing decades.

peals all but disappeared from the South, while proslavery arguments increased. Even religious groups that had once denounced slavery now ceased objecting to it. "A large majority of the people of the southern states," declared Congressman Peter Early of Georgia in 1806, "do not consider slavery as a crime. They do not consider it immoral to hold human flesh in bondage. Many deprecate slavery as an evil, as a political evil," he continued, "but not as a crime." White southerners at the time of the Civil War would be saying much the same thing.

In the North, antislavery attitudes were increasingly conciliatory toward slave owners and unsympathetic toward blacks. Most of slavery's critics assumed that private manumission was the only safe approach, that it should be gradual so as to avoid social turmoil, and that freed blacks should be relocated to colonies in Africa. The American Colonization Society, founded in 1816, typified these attitudes. Many of its supporters genuinely hated slavery but believed that the two races could never coexist without it. Others were slaveholders who saw in colonization a convenient way of reducing the free black population and eliminating troublesome bondsmen. The Colonization Society never sent many blacks abroad, but it did help allay white anxieties.

Nor did free blacks living in the North find their lives much improved by the first stirrings of republican reform. During the half century following independence, strong and growing black commu-

nities appeared in the northern ports. Emancipation in the North and the Upper South enabled increasing numbers of blacks to leave their masters' homes and establish their own households. The majority did so in the major cities of Boston, New York, Philadelphia, and Baltimore.

Fed by people like Phyllis Sherman coming in from the northern countryside and Ben Thompson making his way up from the South, black communities began to grow. On the eve of independence, 4,000 slaves and a few hundred free blacks had called the four port cities home; 50 years later, more than 30,000 free blacks did so.

The men who came sought employment as laborers or sailors, the women as domestics. They sought as well the companionship of other people of color. There were hundreds like Alexander Giles, a free black Philadelphia seaman who had been born in 1777 in nearby Kent County, Delaware, and Randall Shepherd, who had made his way north from Nansemond County, Virginia, in 1798.

The development of black neighborhoods was a result both of white discrimination and the black desire for community. In rural areas, free blacks lived in relative isolation and were largely defenseless against white hostility. In the cities, however, numbers provided some protection and greatly improved the chances of finding a marriage partner, establishing a family, and participating in the activities of community organizations. Family formation was eased by the fact that many of the migrants were women, thus correcting a long-standing urban imbalance.

Even so, the process of forming families often took years. After extricating themselves from their masters, former slaves typically established extended households that included relatives, friends, and boarders. As circumstances allowed, single family units were formed. In the northern cities by 1820, most blacks belonged to autonomous households.

As their numbers increased, blacks organized community institutions. In 1794, Richard Allen and Absalom Jones founded the first two black churches in Philadelphia. By 1813, the two congregations had over 1,800 members. "African" schools, mutual-aid societies, and fraternal associations followed, first in Philadelphia and Boston, more slowly in New York and Baltimore, where slavery lingered longer.

By 1820, a rich institutional and cultural life had taken root in the black neighborhoods of the port cities. White hostility, however, remained. Slavery's abolition actually increased rather than diminished white enmity in the North, in part because it pitted free blacks more directly against white laborers for employment, especially during the hard times following the embargo and the War of 1812. Working-class whites were unnerved as well by the growing black competition for cheap housing. Open expressions of violence against free blacks were infrequent during the early decades of the century, but even so, blacks found themselves increasingly segregated in residence, employment, and social life. Race, as well as gender and class, continued to separate Americans from each other and reveal the limits of America's new social faith.

CONCLUSION
Between Two Worlds

The years between 1790 and 1828 were years of transition between preindustrial America and the industrializing world of the nineteenth century. America's renewed commercial prosperity was grounded in traditional dependence on Europe, yet its profits financed the beginnings of industrialization. Northern agriculture remained largely unchanged, but the continuing spread of commercial agriculture would soon launch a revolution in farm productivity. Staple agriculture still dom-inated the South, but cotton would transform the region and powerfully affect the entire nation. Perhaps most important, separation from England, the surge of commercial prosperity, and the accelerating pace of westward expansion created a newly exuberant spirit of economic opportunity that would dominate the years ahead.

Region and locality still shaped people's lives, while differences of race, class, and gender remained largely unchanged. And yet old ways of life were giving way, and new ones were forming. Social ideals and expectations were changing most rapidly of all, as an emphasis on youthfulness and change, social equality and individualism, fanned by republican idealism and the Second Great Awakening, shaped Americans' attitudes toward social reform. Life in the early republic still echoed the past but pointed unmistakably toward the future.

Recommended Reading

Valuable information on America's preindustrial economy can be found in Stuart Bruchey, The Roots of American Economic Growth, 1607–1861 (1965); Curtis Nettels, The Emergence of a National Economy, 1775–1815 (1962); and Louis Hartz, Economic Policy and Democratic Thought: Pennsylvania, 1776–1860 (1948).

For illuminating discussions of merchant capitalism and early industrialization, see Jonathan Prude, The Coming of Industrial Order: Town and Factory Life in Rural Massachusetts, 1810–1860 (1983); Susan Hirsch, Roots of the American Working Class: The Industrialization of Crafts in Newark, 1800–1860 (1978); How-

ard Rock, Artisans of the New Republic: The Tradesmen of New York City in the Age of Jefferson (*1979*); *and Bruce Laurie,* Working People of Philadelphia, 1800–1850 (*1980*). *Early nineteenth-century agriculture is examined in Percy Bidwell and John Falconer,* History of Agriculture in the Northern United States, 1620–1860 (*1925*), *and James Lemon,* The Best Poor Man's Country: A Geographical Study of Early Southeastern Pennsylvania (*1972*).

Important information on the trans-Appalachian West can be found in Malcolm Rohrbough, The Trans-Appalachian Frontier: People, Societies, and Institutions, 1775–1850 (*1978*); *Richard Wade,* The Urban Frontier: The Rise of Western Cities, 1790–1830 (*1959*); *and Ray Billington,* Westward Expansion, *4th ed.* (*1974*). *Changes in transportation and communication are traced in Alan Pred,* Urban Growth and the Circulation of Information: The United States System of Cities, 1790–1840 (*1973*), *and Ronald Shaw,* Erie Water West: A History of the Erie Canal, 1792–1854 (*1966*).

On the Great Awakening, see John Bole, The Great Revival, 1787–1805 (*1972*) *and Donald Mathews,* Religion in the Old South (*1977*).

Themes of class and wealth are dealt with in Sean Wilentz, Chants Democratic: New York City and the Rise of the American Working Class, 1788–1850 (*1984*); *Robert Doherty,* Society and Power: Five New England Towns, 1800–1860 (*1977*); *Raymond Mohl,* Poverty in New York, 1783–1825 (*1971*); *and Toby Ditz,* Property and Kinship: Inheritance in Early Connecticut, 1750–1820 (*1986*).

Among important works on women are Nancy Cott, The Bonds of Womanhood: "Woman's Sphere" in New England, 1780–1835 (*1977*); *Lee Chambers-Schiller,* Liberty, a Better Husband (*1984*); *and Joan Jensen,* Loosening the Bonds: Mid-Atlantic Farm Women, 1750–1850 (*1987*). *On race and slavery, see Gerald Mullin,* Flight and Rebellion (*1972*); *Robert McColley,* Slavery and Jeffersonian Virginia (*1964*); *and Gary B. Nash,* Forging Freedom: The Formation of Philadelphia's Black Community, 1720–1840 (*1988*).

Books on early education include Carl Kaestle, Pillars of the Republic: Common Schools and American Society, 1780–1860 (*1983*); *Lawrence Cremin,* American Education: The National Experience, 1783–1876 (*1980*); *Howard Miller,* The Revolutionary College: American Presbyterian Higher Education, 1707–1837 (*1976*); *and Stephen Novak,* The Rights of Youth: American Colleges and Student Revolt, 1798–1815 (*1977*).

Two recent volumes provide splendid overviews of American society in the early republic: Jack Larkin, Reshaping Everyday Life, 1790–1840 (*1988*), *and Barbara Clark Smith,* After the Revolution: The Smithsonian History of Everyday Life in the Eighteenth Century (*1987*).

TIME LINE

1776 Adam Smith publishes *Wealth of Nations*

1790s Turnpike construction in Northeast
Yellow fever epidemics in cities
Female academies founded
Cotton production booms in the South

1791 Black rebellion begins in Haiti

1793 Eli Whitney invents the cotton gin
Europe embroiled in war

1794 First Afro-American churches founded

1800 Gabriel Prosser's Rebellion in Virginia

1807 Robert Fulton launches first steamboat
Cast-iron plow patented
U.S. slave trade ends

1807–1809 Trade embargo

1811 Successful steamboat trip from Ohio River to New Orleans

1812–1814 War with Great Britain

1817 American Colonization society formed

1819–1821 Depression

PART THREE

AN EXPANDING PEOPLE

1820 1877

During the first half of the nineteenth century, the young nation expanded rapidly. As Americans surged west across the Appalachians, secured vast new territories beyond the Mississippi, and, in the 1840s, pushed on to the Pacific coast, the population soared and became more diverse with the arrival of thousands of immigrants and the inclusion of western Indians and Mexicans. In the East, new modes of production laid the foundation for the material comfort that has come to characterize American life. But expansion sharpened regional differences, particularly between the North and the South, and the period ended with the most devastating conflict the nation has ever experienced.

Chapters 11, 12, and 13 cover roughly the same time period, and each chapter complements the other two. Chapter 11, "Currents of Change in the Northeast and the Old Northwest," investigates the economic and social transformations that affected work, social and family relations, and the rhythms of everyday life in these two regions. Chapter 12, "Slavery and the

Old South," considers the South's distinctive economic and social system, which, based as it was on slavery, raised questions about the special virtue of the nation and the meaning of justice and equality.

In Chapter 13, "Shaping America in the Antebellum Age," we focus on economic and social changes that sharpened the familiar tension between narrowly defined self-interest and social concerns. Some Americans sought to counteract the selfish tendencies of their age by establishing utopian societies; others tried to preserve ideals and virtue through reform activities or religious experiments. Still others sought to shape their world through politics. The election of Andrew Jackson as president marked the advent of the second American party system and of a lively political culture firmly rooted in new economic and social conditions. Yet while more white Americans than ever were politically active, they disagreed on the competing claims of liberty and power.

Chapter 14, "Moving West," shows the power of American

expansionism and the limited meaning many Americans gave to terms like *liberty* and *equality*. During the decade of the 1840s, war and diplomacy won vast new territories, peopled mostly by Mexicans and Native Americans. As settlers to new frontiers sought to re-create familiar institutions and patterns, these earlier inhabitants found themselves excluded from most of the promises of American life.

Territorial expansion not only illustrated the limitations of political and social ideals, but it also instigated angry political debates. The expansion of slavery into the West threatened the political balance of power between the North and the South and raised the question of where power and authority lay to decide the future of the West. These questions—which are addressed in Chapters 15, 16, and 17—could not be easily resolved.

Chapter 15, "The Union in Peril," traces the disintegration of the second party system and the eruption of civil war in Kansas. By 1850, two cultures and two societies jostled uneasily in one union, unable to agree on most of the important questions of the day. Secession and civil war soon followed. Chapter 16, "The Union Severed," examines the Civil War and the unanticipated results of the conflict. For example, although the war ended slavery, emancipation itself proved to be problematic. Also unexpected was the transformation of northern and southern society and the new conflicts that emerged. Chapter 17, "The Union Reconstructed," explores how Americans tried to resolve these and the many other dilemmas of the postwar period. With the return of the South to the Union, how would the political system on the local and national level be arranged? What would traditional ideals mean for white southerners, black freedmen, and white northerners?

1820

Political and Diplomatic	Social and Economic	Cultural and Technological

1820

1820 Monroe reelected
    Missouri Compromise
1823 Monroe Doctrine
1824 Clay's "American System"
1825 John Quincy Adams chosen
    president by House of
    Representatives
    Texas (Mexican territory) opened
    to settlement by U.S. citizens
1828 Andrew Jackson elected
    president
	1822 Denmark Vesey slave
	    conspiracy
	1824 New Harmony founded
	1827 Mechanics' Union of Trade
	    Association founded in
	    Philadelphia
	1828 Tariff of Abominations
	1829 Workingmen's party founded in
	    New York
		1823 James Fenimore Cooper, *The Pioneers*
		1824 Hudson River school of
		    landscape painting
		1825 Erie Canal completed
		1827 *Freedom's Journal* (first Negro
		    newspaper)

1830

1830 Webster-Hayne debate
    Indian Removal Bill
1832 Jackson reelected
    South Carolina nullification crisis
    Black Hawk War
1833 Force Bill
1834 Whig party formed
    Seminole Wars
1836 "Gag rule"
    Texas declares independence
    Battles of the Alamo and San
    Jacinto
    Martin Van Buren elected
    president
1838 Cherokee removal
	1830 Joseph Smith founds Mormon
	    church
	1831 Nat Turner's slave rebellion
	1832 Jackson vetoes U.S. Bank
	    Charter
	1832–1836 U.S. Bank funds removed
	    to state banks
	1833 American Anti-Slavery Society
	    founded
	    Oberlin College founded
	1834 Lowell mill girls strike
	    National Trades Union founded
	    1836 Specie circular
	    Mount Holyoke Female
	    Seminary founded
	1837 Panic of 1837
	1838–1844 Depression
		1830 First commercial steam
		    locomotive, *Tom Thumb*
		1831 William Lloyd Garrison begins
		    publishing *The Liberator*
		1832 Samuel F. B. Morse invents
		    telegraph
		1834 Cyrus McCormick patents
		    reaper
		1836 Ralph Waldo Emerson, *Nature*
		1837 Emerson, *The American Scholar*
		    John Deere invents first steel
		    plow
		    George Catlin paints *Gallery of Indians*
		1838 Morse code devised
		1839 Charles Goodyear produces
		    vulcanized rubber

1840

1840 William H. Harrison elected
    president
    Liberty party formed
1841 Harrison dies; John Tyler
    becomes president
1842 Webster-Ashburton Treaty
1844 James K. Polk elected president
    Boundary dispute over Oregon
    Treaty of commerce and
    friendship with China
1845 United States annexes Texas
    1846 Mexican War begins
    Wilmot Proviso
    Oregon boundary settled
1848 Zachary Taylor elected president
    Free-Soil party formed
    Treaty of Guadalupe Hidalgo
	1840 Independent Treasury Act
	1840s Great migration to Oregon
	    over Oregon Trail
	1841 Brook Farm founded
	1847 Irish potato famine immigration
	1848 Oneida community founded
	    Women's rights convention,
	    Seneca Falls, New York
	1849 California gold rush

		1843 Edgar Allan Poe short stories
		1844 Morse sends first telegraph
		    message
		1845 *Narrative of Frederick Douglass*
		1846 Herman Melville, *Typee*
		    Elias Howe invents sewing
		    machine

| Political and Diplomatic | Social and Economic | Cultural and Technological |

1850

1850 Taylor dies, Millard Fillmore becomes president
Compromise of 1850
1852 Franklin Pierce elected president
1853 Gadsden Purchase
1854 Republican party formed
Know-Nothing party formed
Ostend Manifesto
Kansas-Nebraska Act
1855 William Walker overthrows Nicaraguan government
1856 James Buchanan elected president
1857 Dred Scott decision
Lecompton Constitution
1858 Lincoln-Douglas debates
1859 Raid on Harpers Ferry; John Brown hanged

1851 Maine prohibition law
Fort Laramie Treaty
1852 Massachusets passes first school attendance law

1855 First oil business in U.S.
1857 Panic of 1857

1850 Nathaniel Hawthorne, *The Scarlet Letter*
1851 Melville, *Moby Dick*
Isaac Singer perfects sewing machine
1852 Harriet Beecher Stowe, *Uncle Tom's Cabin*
Otis invents passenger elevator
1854 Henry David Thoreau, *Walden*
1855 Walt Whitman, *Leaves of Grass*
1857 Central Park, New York City, designed
Atlantic Monthly founded

1860

1860 Abraham Lincoln elected president
South Carolina secedes
1861 Confederate States of America formed
Civil War begins
First Battle of Bull Run
1862 Battles of Shiloh, Bull Run, and Antietam
1863 Emancipation Proclamation
Battles of Gettysburg and Vicksburg
1864 Sherman's march through Georgia
Lincoln reelected
1865 Lee surrenders; Civil War ends
Lincoln assassinated; Andrew Johnson becomes president
Thirteenth Amendment
1866 Civil Rights Act
1868 Impeachment attempt against Johnson
Ulysses S. Grant elected
Fourteenth Amendment

1860 Pony Express begins
1861 First federal income tax
1862 Homestead Act
Morrill Land-Grant College Act
Morrill tariff
1864 Sand Creek, Colorado, massacre

1865 Freedmen's Bureau established
Union Stockyards opened in Chicago
1865–1866 Black codes
1867 Ku Klux Klan formed

1861 Mathew Brady begins photographing Civil War
1864 Pullman creates sleeping car

1870

1870 Fifteenth Amendment
1870–1871 Force Acts
1872 Grant reelected
1875 Civil Rights Act
1877 Rutherford B. Hayes becomes president

1873 Financial panic and depression

11

Currents of Change in the Northeast and the Old Northwest

In the fall of 1845, 15-year-old Mary Paul informed her father that she had decided to leave northern Vermont for employment in the Lowell textile mills. Despite her youth, Mary had already held a job as a domestic servant for a farming family near her hometown of Barnard. But she disliked the position. Her mistress, Mrs. Angell, was difficult and sometimes refused to speak to her. Years later, when Mary reflected on the shabby way in which many hired girls were treated, she was doubtless recalling her own experience with the Angell family.

Lowell, with its thousands of jobs and bustling economy, offered Mary both the chance to escape haughty mistresses and "degrading" housework and also the opportunity to be economically independent. Lowell also represented a sophisticated city life that the country-bred girl found alluring. As she explained to her father, she "could earn more to begin with [in Lowell] than I can any where about here. I am in need of clothes which I cannot get if I stay about here and for that reason I want to go to Lowell."

By November, Mary was settled in the mill town, living in "a very good boarding place" and working in a spinning room under a "first rate" overseer. Her situation pleased her, and she planned to stay "a year certain, if not more." As time passed, even the long hours, the regimented pace of work, and the risk of accidents, some of them fatal, did not diminish her enthusiasm.

Over the next few years, Mary worked intermittently in Lowell. Though she kept returning to the mills, her later experiences were not as positive as her initial encounter. In 1848, after a six-month break, she returned to Lowell to discover that all the mills "seem to be very full of help." Finally, she secured a place in the dressing rooms of the Tremont Corporation, where she prepared yarn for the weaving process. "It is *very* hard work indeed," Mary reported, "and sometimes I think I shall not be able to endure it. I never worked so hard in my life but perhaps I shall get used to it."

Not only was the work difficult, but Mary found that the companies were planning to reduce wages. "The companies pretend they are losing immense sums every *day* and therefore they are obliged to lessen wages," she reported, "but this seems perfectly absurd to me for they are constantly making *repairs* and it seems to me that this would not be if there were really any danger of their being obliged to *stop* the mills."

Mary Paul's experience in the Lowell mills was shared by many other Americans who found that economic change brought new opportunities and new uncertainties. On the whole, Mary seemed to have benefited from her contact with the new industrial world of work. Since her family did not require her financial assistance, she was free to spend her earnings as she wished. When she tired of regimented mill life, she returned home to Vermont or tried some new job—making coats in Vermont, housekeeping in New Hampshire, even joining a utopian community in New Jersey. In 1857, after 12 years of independence, she married Isaac Guild, a marbleworker. She retired from the wage labor work force to live as wife and mother in Lynn, Massachusetts.

This chapter explores the economic changes in the Northeast and the Old Northwest that not only transformed the economy between 1820 and 1860, as Mary Paul discovered, but also shaped social, cultural, and political life. Though most Americans still lived in rural settings rather than in factory towns or cities, economic growth and the new industrial mode of production affected them through the creation of new goods, opportunities, and markets. In urban communities and factory towns, the new economic order ushered in new forms of work, new class arrangements, and new forms of social strife.

After discussing the factors that fueled antebellum growth, the chapter turns to the industrial world, where so many of the new patterns of work and life appeared. An investigation of urbanization reveals shifting class arrangements and values as well as rising social and racial tensions. Finally, an examination of rural communities in the East and on the frontier in the Old Northwest highlights the transformation of these two sections of the country. Between 1840 and 1860, industrialization and economic growth increasingly knit them together.

ECONOMIC GROWTH

Between 1820 and 1860, the American economy entered a new and more complex stage of development as it moved away from its reliance on agriculture as the major source of growth toward an industrial and technological future. In this period of general national expansion, real per capita output grew an average of 2 percent annually between 1820 and 1840 and slightly less between 1840 and 1860. This means that per capita income doubled over the 40-year period.

Though expanding, the economy was also unstable, lurching from periods of boom (1822–1834, mid-1840s–1850s) to periods of bust (1816–1821, 1837–1843). As never before, Americans faced dramatic and recurrent shifts in the availability of jobs and goods and in prices and wages. Particularly at risk were working-class Americans, a third of whom lost their jobs during years of depression. Moreover, because regional economies were increasingly linked, problems in one area tended to affect conditions in others.

Expansion and Immigration

What accounted for this new phase of growth and economic development? The United States, of course, had abundant natural resources, enormously increased by the Louisiana Purchase in 1803. An expanding population, soaring from 9 million in 1820 to over 30 million in 1860, represented the new workers, new households, and new consumers so essential to economic development. As the accompanying chart shows, until the 1840s, most of the growth in population came from natural increase. But as the size of American families gradually shrank—in 1800, the average white woman bore seven children; by 1860, the number had declined to five—foreign immigration took up the slack. This influx of European laborers as well as European capital and technological ideas helped to shape American growth.

Immigration from Europe to the American continent had begun in the early seventeenth century, of course, but it occurred on an unprecedented scale after 1840. During the 1820s, some 128,502 foreigners came to American shores. In the 1850s, the trickle became a torrent as more than 2.8 million migrated to the United States. Most of the newcomers were young European men who represented a cheap pool of labor for American employers.

This vast movement of people, which began in the 1840s and continued throughout the nineteenth century, resulted from dramatic changes in European life: a population explosion between 1750 and 1845 and the introduction of new farming and in-

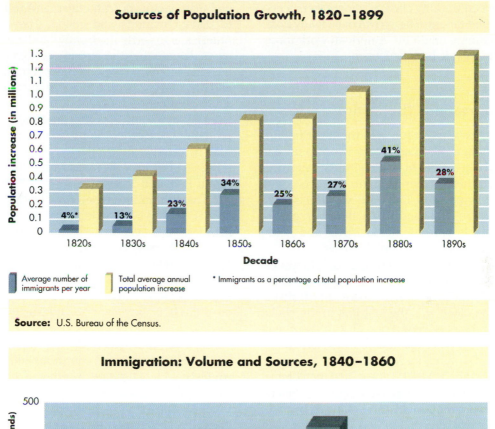

Sources of Population Growth, 1820–1899

- Average number of immigrants per year
- Total average annual population increase
- * Immigrants as a percentage of total population increase

Source: U.S. Bureau of the Census.

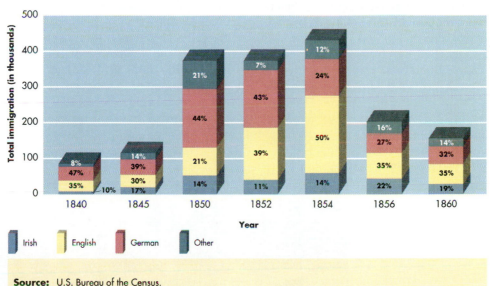

Immigration: Volume and Sources, 1840–1860

- Irish
- English
- German
- Other

Source: U.S. Bureau of the Census.

dustrial practices that uprooted many people from their traditional means of livelihood. Agricultural disaster also played a major role in driving the Irish from their homeland. Potatoes formed the foundation of the Irish diet. In 1845, a terrible blight attacked and destroyed the potato crop. Years of devastating famine followed. One million Irish died of starvation between 1841 and 1851; another million and a half emigrated. While not all chose the

United States as their destination, the Irish were the most numerous of all newcomers to America in the two decades preceding the Civil War. They usually arrived almost penniless in eastern port cities.

Germans, the second largest group of immigrants during this period (1,361,506 arrived between 1840 and 1859), were not fleeing from desperate circumstances in their homeland. Some had sufficient resources to go west and buy land. Others joined the urban working class as shoemakers, cab-inetmakers, and tailors. The arrival of so many non-British newcomers made the American work force more diverse than it had ever been.

Transportation: The Critical Factor

Improved transportation was the most impor-tant factor behind economic and geographic ex-pansion. Early in the century, high freight rates dis-couraged production for distant markets, and primitive transportation hindered western settle-ment. During the 1820s and 1830s, however, canal-building projects revolutionized travel and com-merce and made migration much easier.

The Erie Canal, completed in 1825, illustrates the impact of better and cheaper transportation. Stretching 363 miles between Albany and Buffalo, New York, the canal was the last link in the chain of waterways binding New York City to the Great Lakes and the Northwest. It carried travelers along at the pace of 4 miles an hour for only 4 cents a mile. Transportation rates tumbled, and the volume of trade and production increased. By 1837, the ca-nal was carrying over 665,000 tons annually; by mid-century, it carried about 2 million tons a year.

The Erie Canal and hundreds of other newly constructed canals bound the country together in a new way. Canals provided farmers, merchants, and manufacturers with cheap and reliable access to distant markets and goods. They encouraged Americans to settle the frontier and cultivate virgin lands. Eventually, the strong economic and social ties the waterways fostered between the Northwest and the East led people living in the two regions to share political outlooks.

Even at the height of the canal boom, politicians, promoters, and others, impressed with Britain's suc-cess with railways, supported the construction of railroads. But only 73 miles of track were laid be-tween 1828 and 1830.

The first trains jumped their tracks and spewed sparks, setting nearby fields ablaze. Technical dif-ficulties were eventually resolved. By 1840, there were 3,000 miles of track, most in the Northeast. Another 5,000 miles were laid during the 1840s, and by the end of the 1850s, total mileage soared to 30,000. Like the canals, the new railroads strength-ened the links between the Old Northwest and the East.

As the railroads followed—or led—settlers westward, they exerted enormous influence. Their routes could determine whether a city, town, or even homestead survived. The railroad transformed Chicago from a small settlement into a bustling com-mercial and transportation center. In 1850, the city contained not one mile of track, but within five years, 2,200 miles of track serving 150,000 square miles terminated in Chicago.

The Erie Canal, most famous of the many canals built between 1820 and 1840, boosted commerce and production across New York State.

Inland Freight Rates, 1785–1865

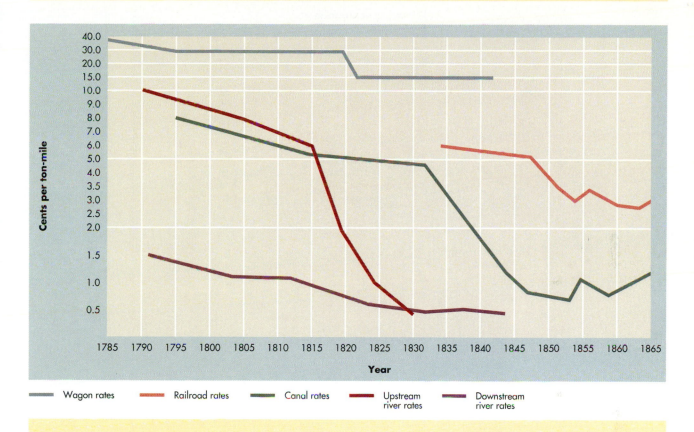

Source: North, *Growth and Welfare in the American Past*, 1974.

The dramatic rise in railroad construction in the two decades before the Civil War contributed to faster economic growth after 1839. Goods, people, commercial information, and mail flowed ever more predictably, rapidly, and cheaply. In 1790, an order from Boston took two weeks to reach Philadelphia; in 1836, it took only 36 hours.

Improved transportation stimulated agricultural expansion and regional specialization. Farmers began to plant larger crops for the market, concentrating on those most suited to their soil and climate. By the late 1830s, the Old Northwest had become the country's granary, while New England farmers turned to dairy or produce farming. By 1860, American farmers were producing four to five times as much wheat, corn, cattle, and hogs as they had in 1810. Their achievements meant plentiful, cheap food for American workers and more income for farmers to spend on the new consumer goods.

Capital Investment

Internal improvements, the exploitation of natural resources, and the cultivation of new lands all demanded capital. Much of it came from European investors. Between 1790 and 1861, over $500 million flowed into the United States from Europe. Foreign investors from Europe, adding to funds brought by immigrant families, financed as much as a third of all canal construction and bought about a quarter of all railroad bonds.

American mercantile capital fueled growth as well. As Chapter 10 suggested, the merchant class prospered in the half century after the Revolution. Now merchants invested in schemes ranging from canals to textile factories. Many ventured into the production of goods and became manufacturers themselves.

Prosperous Americans eagerly sought oppor-

Growth of the Railroads, 1850–1860

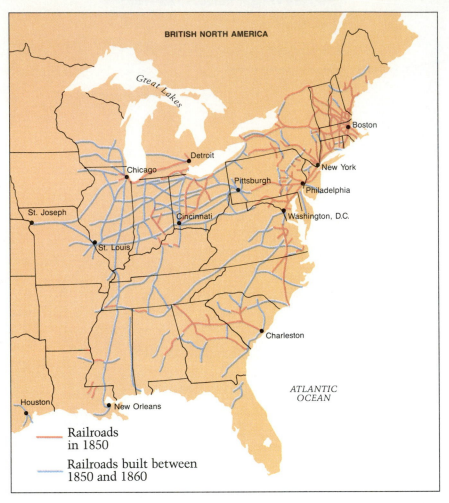

Railroads
in 1850

Railroads built between
1850 and 1860

tunities to put their capital to work. Two New Yorkers, Arthur Bronson and Charles Butler, exemplify the speculative spirit nurturing economic development. Intrigued by the Northwest's investment possibilities, Bronson and Butler made a careful tour of the region in 1833. They encountered "scenes, & things which we never dreamed of before leaving home, & which then should have revolted at." But despite primitive conditions, both men saw wonderful opportunities. Detroit, Butler concluded, "is destined to be a very great city," while Chicago "presents one of the finest fields in America for industry & enterprise." Each man channeled funds into western projects. Bronson's investments ranged from Ohio banks to farmland in Wisconsin Territory, Illinois, Michigan, Ohio, and Indiana to real estate in Chicago and Detroit, all in addition to his holdings in New York ironworks and banks.

Bronson's investment in banks indicated his understanding of their role in stimulating economic growth. He also actively promoted life insurance companies, which, unlike commercial banks, lent money on a long-term basis. These financial institutions, he realized, served as intermediaries, funneling into economic enterprises the capital of people with neither the time nor the expertise to invest their money themselves.

The Role of Government

Local and state government enthusiastically supported economic growth. States often helped new ventures raise capital by passing laws of incorporation, by awarding entrepreneurs special privileges such as tax breaks or monopolistic control, by underwriting bonds for improvement projects, which increased their investment appeal, and by providing loans for internal improvements. New York, Pennsylvania, Ohio, Indiana, Illinois, and Virginia publicly financed almost 75 percent of the canal systems in their states between 1815 and 1860.

The national government also encouraged economic expansion by cooperating with states on some internal improvements such as the National Road linking Maryland and Illinois. Federal tariff policy shielded American products, and the second U.S. Bank provided the financial stability investors required. So widespread was the enthusiasm for growth that the line separating the public sector from the private often became unclear.

The law also helped to promote aggressive economic growth. Judicial decisions created a new understanding of property rights. The case of *Palmer* v. *Mulligan,* decided by the New York State Supreme Court in 1805, laid down the principle that property ownership included the right to develop property for business purposes. Land was increasingly defined as a productive asset for exploitation, not merely subsistence, as earlier judicial rulings had suggested.

Investors and business operators alike wanted to increase predictability in the conduct of business. Contracts lay at the heart of commercial relationships, but contract law hardly existed in 1800. A period of rapid development ensued. A series of important Supreme Court decisions between 1819 and 1824 established the basic principle that contracts were binding. In *Dartmouth College* v. *Woodward,* the Court held that a state charter could not be modified unless both parties agreed and declared in *Sturges* v. *Crowninshield* that a New York law allowing debtors to repudiate their debts was unconstitutional.

The Innovative Mentality

As the discussion of the links between law and economic growth suggests, economic expansion depends on intangible factors as well as more obvious ones such as improved transportation. The entrepreneurial mentality that encouraged investment, new business ventures, and land speculation was just such a component of antebellum economic development.

Europeans often recognized another intangible factor when they described Americans as energetic and open to change. As one Frenchman explained in 1834, "All here is circulation, motion, and boiling

agitation. Experiment follows experiment; enterprise succeeds to enterprise." An American observer agreed. "Every man seems born with some steam engine within him, driving him into an incessant and restless activity of body and mind . . . every head and every hand busy, with a thousand projects, and only one holiday—the 4th of July—working from morning till night with the most intense industry."

Others described an American mechanical "genius." The American was "a mechanic by nature," one Frenchman insisted. "In Massachusetts and Connecticut, there is not a labourer who had not invented a machine or tool." This observer exaggerated, since many American innovations drew on British precedents, but every invention attracted scores of imitators. In 1854, the government patent office issued 56 patents for harvesting implements and 39 for seed planters; the next year, it issued 40 for sewing machines.

Mechanically minded Americans prided themselves on developing efficient and productive tools and machines. The McCormick harvester, the Colt revolver, Goodyear vulcanized rubber products, and the sewing machine were developed, refined, and developed further. Such improvements cut labor costs and increased efficiency. By 1840, the average American cotton textile mill was about 10 percent more efficient and 3 percent more profitable than its British counterpart.

While the shortage of labor in the United States stimulated technological innovations that replaced humans with machines, the rapid spread of education after 1800 also contributed to innovation and increased productivity. By 1840, most whites were literate. In that year, public schools nationwide were educating 38.4 percent of white children between the ages of 5 and 19.

White Secondary School Enrollment, 1840–1860 *Percent of white population between 5 and 19 years of age*			
	1840	1850	1860
New England	81.4	76.1	73.8
Middle Atlantic	54.7	61.9	61.3
North Central	29.1	52.4	69.4
South Atlantic	16.2	29.7	31.4
South Central	13.4	31.0	38.6
Nationwide	38.4	50.4	57.0

Source: Niemi, *U.S. Economic History* (1975).

The belief that education spurred economic growth helped to foster enthusiasm for public education, particularly in the Northeast. The development of the Massachusetts common school illustrates the connections many saw between education and progress.

Although several states had decided to use tax monies for education by 1800, Massachusetts moved first toward mass education by mandating in 1827 that taxes pay the whole cost of the state's public schools. Several years later, the state set up a permanent elementary education fund and in 1836 forbade factory managers to hire children who had not spent 3 of the previous 12 months in school. Despite the legislation, the Massachusetts school system did not function well. School buildings were often run-down and even unheated. Because school curricula were virtually nonexistent, students often lounged idly at their desks.

Under the leadership of Horace Mann, the reform of state education for white children began in 1837. Mann and others sought to strengthen public education by introducing graded schools, uniform curricula, and teacher training; by reducing the power of local districts over their schools; and by attracting more students. His campaigns made the Massachusetts system a model for reformers everywhere. For the first time in American history, primary education became the rule for most children between 5 and 19 in most parts of the country outside the South. Consequently, a whole new career, mostly for women emerged.

Mann believed that education promoted inventiveness. It "had a market value." Businessmen often agreed. Prominent industrialists in the 1840s believed that education produced workers who could handle complex machinery without undue supervision and were superior employees—reliable, punctual, industrious, and sober. Manufacturers valued education not merely because of its intellectual content but also because it encouraged habits essential to a disciplined and productive work force.

Ambivalence Toward Change

While supporting education as a means to economic growth, many Americans also firmly believed in its social value. Public schools could mold student character and promote "virtuous habits" and "rational self-governing" behavior. Many school activities sought to teach good habits. Students learned facts by rote because memory work and recitation taught them discipline and concentration. Nineteenth-century schoolbooks reinforced the classroom message. "It is a great sin to be idle," children read in one 1830 text, while another encouragingly pointed out, "He who rises early and is industrious and temperate will acquire health and riches." A third warned "Poverty is the fruit of idleness."

The concern with education and character indicate that as much as Americans welcomed economic progress, they also feared its results. The much-heralded improvements in transportation that facilitated trade and settlement caused some to wonder whether civilization might disintegrate as people moved far from their place of birth and from familiar institutions. Others worried that rapid change undermined the American family and would turn children into barbarians. Schools, which taught students to be deferential, obedient, and punctual, could counter the worst by-products of change. Schools served as much as a defense against change as its agents. Fear and confidence were two sides of the coin of economic transformation.

This early photograph of the Emerson School for Young Ladies suggests some of the ways in which schools tried to impart norms of obedience, deference, and orderly behavior.

Other signs of cultural uneasiness appeared. In the eighteenth century, Benjamin Franklin popularized the importance of hard work in his celebrated *Poor Richard's Almanack*. In the 1830s, popularizers restated Franklin's message. As the publishing revolution lowered costs and speeded the production of printed material, these authors poured out tracts, stories, and manuals on how to get ahead. Claiming that hard work and good character led to success, they touted the virtues of diligence, punctuality, temperance, and thrift. These habits probably did assist economic growth. Slothful workers are seldom productive. Industry and perseverance often pay off. But the success of early nineteenth-century economic ventures frequently depended on the ability to take risks, to think daringly. The emphasis given to the safe but stolid virtues suggests that the fear of social disintegration ran through antebellum society. New notions about women's duties and responsibilities, discussed later in this chapter, show a similar concern. By insisting on the necessity of responsible behavior, publicists hoped to counter unsettling effects of change and ensure the dominance of middle-class values.

The Advance of Industrialization

Significant economic growth between 1820 and 1860 resulted from the reorganization of production. As we saw in Chapter 10, before industrialization, individual artisans fashioned goods with hand tools. Many American families also fabricated necessary articles; as late as 1820, Americans made two-thirds of all their clothes at home.

Factory production reorganized work by breaking down the manufacture of an article into discrete steps. At first, manufacturers often relied on the putting-out system (see Chapter 10). Eventually, they centralized all the steps of production under one roof, where hand labor gradually gave way to power-driven machinery such as wooden "spinning jennies." Often they sought the help of British immigrants who had the practical experience and technical know-how no American possessed. In 1789, William Ashley and Moses Brown, Rhode Island merchants, hired 21-year-old Samuel Slater, a former apprentice with an English cotton textile firm, to devise a water-powered yarn-spinning machine. Slater did that, but he also developed a machine capable of carding, or straightening the cotton fibers. Within a year, Ashley and Brown's spinning mill had begun operations in Pawtucket, Rhode Is-

land. Its initial work force consisted of nine children, ranging in age from 7 to 12. Ten years later, their number had grown to over 100.

As factory workers replaced artisans and home manufacturers, the volume of goods rose, and prices dropped dramatically. The price of a yard of cotton cloth fell from 18 cents to 2 cents over the 45 years preceding the Civil War.

The transportation improvements that provided the opportunity to reach large markets after 1820 encouraged the reorganization of the production process and the use of machinery. The simple tastes and rural character of the American people suggested the wisdom of manufacturing inexpensive, everyday goods like cloth and shoes rather than luxuries for the rich.

Between 1820 and 1860, textile manufacturing became the country's leading industry. Textile mills sprang up across the New England and the Middle Atlantic states, regions that contained swift-flowing streams to power the mills, capitalists eager to finance the ventures, children and women to tend the machines, and numerous cities and towns with ready markets for cheap textiles. Early mills were small affairs, containing only the machines for carding and spinning. The thread was then put out to home workers to be woven into cloth. The early mechanization of cloth production did not replace home manufacture but supplemented it.

Already underway, however, were experiments that would further transform the industry. Closeted in the attic of a Boston house in 1813, Francis Cabot Lowell, a merchant, and Paul Moody, a mechanic, worked to devise a power loom capable of weaving cloth. Lowell's study of mechanical looms during his earlier tour of English and Scottish cotton factories guided their work. Eventually, they succeeded, and the loom they devised was soon installed in a mill at Waltham, Massachusetts, capitalized at $300,000 by Lowell and his Boston Associates.

The most important innovation of the Waltham operation was Lowell's decision to bring all the steps of cotton cloth production together under one roof. The Waltham mill thus differed from mills in Rhode Island and Great Britain, where spinning and weaving were separate operations. By centralizing the entire manufacturing process and work force in one factory, cloth for the mass market could be produced more cheaply and more profitably. In 1823, the Boston Associates expanded their operations to East Chelmsford on the Merrimack River, a town they renamed Lowell.

Most New England mills followed the Lowell system. In the Middle Atlantic states, the textile industry was more varied. Philadelphia became a center for fine textiles, while Rhode Island factories produced less expensive materials. Maryland manufacturers, like those in Philadelphia, focused on quality goods. The cumulative impact of the rise of the textile industry was to supplant the home production of cloth, even though some women would continue to spin and weave for their families for some years to come, and hand-loom weavers would survive for another generation. In the process, Americans were transformed from a people clad in earth-colored homespun into a nation decked out in gayer, more colorful clothing.

Textile mills helped to account for the increasingly industrial character of the Northeast. Although the majority of the South's cotton still went to England, an increasing share flowed to northeastern mills. But other manufacturing concerns, such as shoemaking, also contributed to the region's economy. By 1860, fully 71 percent of all manufacturing workers lived in this region of the country.

Other important manufacturing operations reached west and south from New England. The processing of wheat, timber, and hides using power-driven machinery was common in most communities of 200 families or more. Although a third of them were clustered in Philadelphia, paper mills were widespread. The iron and metalworking industry stretched from Albany, New York, south to Maryland and west to Cincinnati.

EARLY MANUFACTURING

Industrialization created a more efficient means of producing more goods at much lower cost than had been possible in the homes and small shops of an earlier day. Philadelphian Samuel Breck's diary reveals some of the new profusion and range of goods. "Went to town principally to see the Exhibition of American Manufactures at the Masonic Hall," he noted in 1833. "More than 700 articles have been sent. Among this great variety, I distinguished the Philadelphia porcelains, beautiful Canton cotton, made at York in this state, soft and capacious blankets, silver plate, cabinet ware, marble mantels, splendid pianos and centre tables, chymical drugs, hardware, saddlery, and the most beautiful black broadcloth I ever saw."

The Impact of Industrialization

Two examples illustrate how industrialization transformed American life. Before the nineteenth century, local printing shops depended on manual labor to produce books, newspapers, and journals. The cost of reading material was high enough to make a library a sign of wealth. Many literate families of moderate means had little in their homes to read other than a family Bible and an almanac.

Between 1830 and 1850, however adoption and improvement of British inventions revolutionized the printing and publishing industries. Like other changes in production, the transformation of pub-

This calico factory, located in Manchester, New Hampshire, produced colorful fabrics for American consumers. In 1854, fully 1,250 of the 2,000 workers were female.

lishing involved not only technological but also managerial and marketing innovations. A $2.5 million market in 1830, the book business quintupled by 1850.

As books and magazines dropped in cost and grew in number, far more people could afford them. No longer dependent solely on the words of the "better sort" for information, people could now form their views on the basis of what they read. Books and magazines spread norms, values, and ideas to households all over the country. Even on the frontier, pioneer women could study inexpensive ladies' magazines and books of domestic advice while their husbands kept up with the latest political news or theories about scientific farming and their children learned their letters from McGuffey readers. The proliferation of printed matter had an enormous impact on people's stock of information, values, tastes, and use of leisure time. It also contributed to the rising literacy rate among white Americans.

Just as printed materials wrought great changes in American life, the making of inexpensive timepieces affected its pace and rhythms. Before the 1830s, when few Americans could afford a clock, it was difficult to make exact plans. But the production of timepieces soared in the 1830s, and by midcentury, inexpensive, mass-produced ones could be found everywhere. As one observer of frontier life pointed out, "In Kentucky, in Indiana, in Illinois, in Missouri, and here in every dell in Arkansas, and in cabins where there was not a chair to sit on, there was sure to be a Connecticut clock." Free of nature's irregular divisions of the day, Americans could decide how to use their time and coordinate their activities. Clocks encouraged a more disciplined use of time and undergirded the economic changes taking place. Timepieces, for example, were essential for the successful operation of railroads, which ran on schedules.

Clocks also imposed a new rhythm in many workplaces. For some Americans, the clock represented a form of oppression rather than liberation. An early mill song put it directly: "The factory bell begins to ring / And we must all obey, / And to our old employment go / Or else be turned away."

A New England Textile Town

To understand the process of industrialization and its impact on work and the work force, let us examine Lowell, the "model" Massachusetts textile town, and Cincinnati, a bustling midwestern indus-

trial center. Though there were similarities between the process of industrialization in these two communities, significant differences also existed. The example of Cincinnati shows that industrialization was often an uneven and complex process, while Lowell points out the importance of women like Mary Paul in the early manufacturing work force.

Lowell was a new town, planned and built expressly for industrial purposes in the 1820s. Planners gave most attention to the shops, mills, and workers' housing, but the bustling town had a charm that prompted visitors to see it as a model factory community. In 1836, Lowell, with 17,000 inhabitants, aspired to become the "Manchester of America." It was the country's most important textile center.

By 1830 women composed nearly 70 percent of the Lowell textile work force, with men and children filling the remaining positions. The women who came to Lowell for jobs were the first women to labor outside their homes in large numbers. They were also among the first Americans to experience the full impact of the factory system.

Lowell's planners realized the difficulty of persuading men to leave farming for mill work but saw that they might recruit unmarried women relatively cheaply for a stint. Unlike mill owners farther south, they decided not to depend on child labor. By hiring women who would work only until marriage, they hoped to avoid the depraved and depressed work force so evident in Great Britain. New England factory communities, they hoped, because of their special arrangements, would become models for the world.

Working and Living in a Mill Town

Mary Paul was typical of the young women drawn to work in Lowell and other New England textile towns. As the planners had anticipated, most were unmarried and young. In 1830, more than 63 percent of Lowell's population was female, and most was between the ages of 15 and 29.

These women, from New England's middling rural families, came to the mills for a variety of reasons, but desperate poverty was not one of them. The decline of home manufacture deprived many women, especially daughters in farming families, of their traditional productive role. Mill work offered them the possibility of economic independence. As Sally Rice from Vermont explained, "I am almost nineteen years old. I must of course have something of my own before many more years have passed

Lowell, Massachusetts, planned and built in the 1820s as the site for textile manufacturing, was hailed as a model industrial community.

over my head. And where is that something coming from if I go home and earn nothing." Mill work paid women relatively well in the 1820s and 1830s. Domestic servants' weekly wages hovered around 75 cents and seamstresses' 90 cents, while in the mid-1830s women could make between $2.40 and $3.20 a week in the mill. The lure of the "privileges" of the new environment also drew young women to Lowell.

Few considered their decision to come to Lowell a permanent commitment. Most young women were like Mary Paul and Sally Rice. They came to work for a few years, felt free to go home or to school for a few months, and then returned to mill work. Once married—and the majority of women did marry—they left the mill work force forever.

New manufacturing work was regimented and exhausting. The day began at dawn or even earlier and ended about 7 in the evening. The standard schedule was 12 hours a day, six days a week, with only a half hour for breakfast and lunch. The clock tower atop the attractive four- to six-story brick mills symbolized the new control of work.

Within the factory, the organization of space facilitated production. In the basement was the waterwheel, the source of power. Above, successive floors were completely open, each containing the machines necessary for the different steps of cloth making: carding, spinning, weaving, and dressing. Elevators moved materials from one floor to another. On a typical floor, rows of machines stretched

the length of the low room, tended by operatives who might watch over several machines at the same time. From his elevated desk at the end of the room, the overseer watched the workers. The male supervisor and two or three children roamed the aisles to survey the work and to help out. The rooms were noisy, poorly lit, and badly ventilated. Overseers, believing that humidity would prevent threads from breaking, often nailed the windows shut.

Although machines, not operatives, did the basic work of production, workers had to ensure that their machines worked properly. The lowest-paid women workers who watched over the spinning frames and drawing frames were responsible for piecing together broken yarn once the machines had automatically halted. The better-paid weavers made skillful interventions in the production process, repairing warp yarns and rapidly replacing shuttle bobbins when they ran out of yarn so that production would slow down only momentarily. "I can see myself now," recalled Harriet Robbins, "racing down the alley, between the spinning frames, carrying in front of me a bobbin-box bigger than I was . . . so as not to keep the spinning-frames stopped long."

Involving an adaptation to a completely new work situation, mill work also entailed an entirely new living situation for women operatives. The companies provided substantial quarters for their overseers and housing for male workers and their families. Hoping to attract respectable females to

Lowell, the mill owners also constructed company boardinghouses where women workers had to live. Headed by female housekeepers, the boardinghouse maintained strict rules, including a 10 o'clock curfew. Owners wanted a respectable and well-rested work force. Little personal privacy was possible in the crowded 2- to 3½-story buildings. Normally, four or six girls shared a small room, which contained little more than the double beds in which they slept together.

Amid such intimate working and living conditions, young women formed close ties with one another and developed a strong sense of community. Strong group norms dictated acceptable behavior, clothing, and speech and shared leisure activities at lectures, night classes, sewing and literary circles, and church. At work, experienced operatives initiated newcomers into the mysteries of tending machines, stood in for each other, and shared work assignments.

The factory bell set the daily schedule for hundreds of workers. Morning starting times varied with the seasons; in midwinter, work began at 7 A.M., but in the summer, workers had to arrive by 5.

TIME TABLE OF THE LOWELL MILLS,

To take effect on and after Oct. 21st, 1851.

The Standard time being that of the meridian of Lowell, as shown by the regulator clock of JOSEPH RAYNES, 43 Central Street

	From 1st to 10th inclusive.				From 11th to 20th inclusive.				From 21st to last day of month.			
	1st Bell	2d Bell	3d Bell	Eve.Bell	1st Bell	2d Bell	3d Bell	Eve.Bell	1st Bell	2d Bell	3d Bell	Eve.Bell
January,	5.00	6.00	6.50	*7.30	5.00	6.00	6.50	*7.30	5.00	6.00	6.50	*7.30
February,	4.30	5.30	6.40	*7.30	4.30	5.30	6.25	*7.30	4.30	5.30	6.15	*7.30
March,	5.40	6.00		*7.30	5.20	5.40		*7.30	5.05	5.25		6.35
April,	4.45	5.05		6.45	4.30	4.50		6.55	4.30	4.50		7.00
May,	4.30	4.50		7.00	4.30	4.50		7.00	4.30	4.50		7.00
June,	"	"		"	"	"		"	"	"		"
July,	"	"		"	"	"		"	"	"		"
August,	"	"		"	"	"		"	"	"		"
September,	4.40	5.00		6.45	4.50	5.10		6.30	5.00	5.20		*7.30
October,	5.10	5.30		*7.30	5.20	5.40		*7.30	5.35	5.55		*7.30
November,	4.30	5.30	6.10	*7.30	4.30	5.30	6.20	*7.30	5.00	6.00	6.35	*7.30
December,	5.00	6.00	6.45	*7.30	5.00	6.00	6.50	*7.30	5.00	6.00	6.50	*7.30

* Excepting on Saturdays from Sept. 21st to March 20th inclusive, when it is rung at 20 minutes after sunset.

YARD GATES,

Will be opened at ringing of last morning bell, of meal bells, and of evening bells; and kept open Ten minutes.

MILL GATES.

Commence hoisting Mill Gates, Two minutes before commencing work.

WORK COMMENCES,

At Ten minutes after last morning bell, and at Ten minutes after bell which "rings in" from Meals.

BREAKFAST BELLS,

During March "Ring out"........at....7.30 a. m.........."Ring in" at 8:05 a. m.
April 1st to Sept. 20th inclusive.....at....7 00 " " .... " " at 7.35 " "
Sept. 21st to Oct. 31st inclusive....at....7.30 " " .... " " at 8.05 " "
Remainder of year work commences after Breakfast.

DINNER BELLS.

"Ring out"......................12.30 p. m........."Ring in".... 1.05 p. m.

In all cases, the *first stroke* of the bell is considered as marking the time.

Female Responses to Work

Although mill work offered better wages than other occupations open to women, all female workers had limited job mobility. The small number staying in the mills for more than a few years did receive increases in pay and promotions to more responsible positions. A top female wage earner took home 40 percent more than a newcomer. But she never could earn as much as male employees, who at the top of the job ladder earned 200 percent more than men at the bottom. Because only men could hold supervisory positions, economic and job discrimination was an integral part of the early American industrial system.

Job discrimination generally went unquestioned, for most female operatives accepted sexual differences as part of life. But the sense of sisterhood, so much a part of the Lowell work experience, supported open protest, most of it focused against a system that workers feared was turning them into a class of dependent wage earners. Lowell women's critique of the new industrial order drew on both the sense of female community and the Revolutionary tradition.

Trouble broke out when hard times hit Lowell in February 1834. Falling prices, poor sales, and rising inventories prompted managers to announce a 15 percent wage cut. This was their way of protecting profits—at the expense of their employees. The mill workers sprang into action. Petitions circulated, threatening a strike. Meetings followed. At one lunchtime gathering, the company agent, hoping to end the protests, fired an apparent ringleader. But, as the agent reported, "she declared that every girl in the room should leave with her," then "made a signal, and . . . they all marched out & few returned the ensuing morning." The strikers roamed the streets appealing to other workers and visited other mills. In all, about a sixth of the town's work force turned out.

Though this work stoppage was brief and failed to prevent the wage reduction, it demonstrated women workers' concern about the impact of industrialization on the labor force. Strikers, taunted as unfeminine for their "amazonian display," refused to agree that workers were inferior to bosses. Pointing out that they were daughters of free men, strikers sought to link their protest to their fathers' and grandfathers' efforts to throw off the bonds of British oppression during the Revolution.

Let oppression shrug her shoulders,
And a haughty tyrant frown,
And little upstart Ignorance,
In mockery look down.
Yet I value not the feeble threats
Of Tories in disguise,
While the flag of Independence
O'er our noble nation flies.

The women viewed threatened wage reductions as an unjust attack on their economic independence and also on their claim to equal status with their employers. Revolutionary rhetoric that once held only political meaning took on economic overtones as Lowell women confronted industrial work.

During the 1830s, wage cuts, long hours, increased work loads, and production speed-ups, mandated by owners' desires to protect profits, constantly reminded Lowell women and other textile workers of the possibility of "wage slavery." In Dover, New Hampshire, 800 women turned out and formed a union in 1834 to protest wage cuts. In the 1840s, women in several New England states agitated for the ten-hour day, while petitions from Lowell prompted the Massachusetts legislature to hold the first government hearing on industrial working conditions.

The Changing Character of the Work Force

Most protest efforts met with limited success. The short tenure of most women mill workers prevented permanent labor organizations. Protests mounted in hard times often failed because mill owners could easily replace striking workers. Increasingly, owners found that they could do without the Yankee women altogether. The waves of immigration that deposited so many penniless foreigners in northeastern cities in the 1840s and 1850s created a new pool of labor. The newcomers were desperate for jobs and would accept lower wages than New England farm girls. Gradually, the Irish began to replace Yankee women in the mills. Representing only 8 percent of the Lowell work force in 1845, the Irish composed nearly half the workers by 1860.

As the ethnic makeup of the work force changed, so did its gender composition. More men came to work in the mills. By 1860, some 30 percent of the Lowell workers were male. All these changes made the women expendable and increased the costs of going "against the mill."

It was easy for New England women to blame the Irish for declining pay and worsening conditions. Gender no longer unified women workers, not only because there were more men in the mills but also because Irish women and New England women had little in common. The Irish mill girl who started working as early as age 13 to earn money for her family's survival had a different perspective on work than the older Yankee women who were earning money for themselves. Segregated living conditions further divided the work force and undermined the likelihood of united worker actions in the 1850s.

Lowell itself changed as the Irish crowded into the city and New England women gradually left the mills. With owners no longer feeling the need to continue paternalistic practices, boardinghouses disappeared. A permanent work force, once a nightmare to owners, had become a reality by 1860, and Lowell's reputation as a model factory town faded away.

Work in textile mills was often tedious and repetitive. Although women were paid less than men, they often welcomed the opportunity to live independently and to earn their own money.

Factories on the Frontier

Cincinnati, a small Ohio River settlement of 2,540 in 1810, grew to be the country's third largest industrial center by 1840. With a population of 40,382, it contained a variety of industries at different stages of development. Cincinnati manufacturers who turned out machines, machine parts, hardware, and furniture were quick to mechanize for increased volume and profits. Other trades like carriage making and cigar making moved far more slowly toward mechanization before 1860. Alongside these concerns, artisans like coopers, blacksmiths, and riverboat builders still labored in small shops using traditional hand tools. The new and the old ways coexisted in Cincinnati, as they did in most manufacturing communities.

No uniform work experience prevailed in Cincinnati. The size of the shop, the nature of work, the skills required, and the rewards all varied widely. In 1850, most Cincinnati workers worked in small or medium-size shops, but almost 20 percent labored in factories with over 100 employees. Some craftsmen continued to use a wide array of skills as they produced goods in time-honored ways. Others used their skills in new factories, but they tended to focus on more specialized and limited tasks. In furniture factories, for example, machines did the rough work of cutting, boring, and planing while some artisans worked exclusively as varnishers, others as carpenters, and still others as finishers. No single worker made a chair from start to finish. But all used some of their skills and earned steady wages. Though in the long run machines threatened to replace them, these skilled factory workers often had reason in the short run to praise the factory's opportunities.

Less fortunate was the new class of unskilled factory laborers who performed limited operations at their jobs either with or without the assistance of machinery. In the meatpacking industry, for example, workers sat at long tables. Some cleaned the ears of the hogs, others scraped the bristles, others had the unenviable task of gutting the dead animals. While owners in the industry profited from efficient new operations, workers received low wages and had little job security. Since they had no skills to sell, they were easily replaced and casually dismissed during business slowdowns.

Many of Cincinnati's female residents were "outworkers" who worked in small shops or at home as seamstresses for the city's growing ready-to-wear clothing industry. Manufacturers purchased the cloth, cut it into basic patterns, and then contracted the work out to be finished.

Like many other urban women, Cincinnati women sought employment of this kind because they could not count on husbands or fathers earning enough to support the family and because outwork allowed them to labor at home. Middle-class domestic ideology prescribed that home was the proper sphere for women, not the workplace. Many working men supported these views because they feared female labor would undercut their wages and destroy order in the family. Outwork, then, allowed poor married women both to supplement their family income and honor social norms.

Paid by the piece, female outworkers were among the most exploited of Cincinnati's workers. Long days spent sewing in darkened rooms not only often failed to bring an adequate financial reward but also led to bad health—ruined eyes and curved spines.

The successful marketing of sewing machines in the 1850s contributed to worsening working conditions and lower pay. Since the sewing machine made stitching easier, the pool of potential workers increased and the volume of work that bosses expected grew. As tasks were further subdivided, work also become more monotonous. As one Cincinnati citizen observed, "as many as 17 hands" were employed on a single pair of pants.

Cincinnati employers claimed that the new industrial order offered great opportunities to most of the city's male citizens. Manufacturing work encouraged the "manly virtues" so necessary to the "republican citizen." Not all Cincinnati workers agreed. Like workers in Lowell and other manufacturing communities, Cincinnati's laborers rose up against their bosses in the decades before the Civil War.

Changing Occupational Distribution 1820–1860			
	1820	1840	1860
Agriculture	78.8%	63.1%	52.9%
Mining	0.4	0.6	1.6
Construction	—	5.1	4.7
Manufacturing	2.7	8.8	13.8
Trade	—	6.2	8.0
Transport	1.6	1.8	2.0
Service	4.1	5.0	6.4
Other	12.4	9.4	10.6

Source: U.S. Bureau of the Census.

THE SEWING MACHINE

In 1860, *Godey's Lady's Book* hailed the sewing machine as the "queen of inventions," crediting it not only with the power to transform the work of American women but also with the ability to "do a hundred times more toward clothing the indigent and feeble than the united fingers of all the [world's] charitable and willing ladies." Like many innovations, the marvelous device was the result of work by several inventors on both sides of the Atlantic. Their interest in a sewing machine was one response to the profusion of manufactured fabrics that were now readily available.

One of the first significant American design breakthroughs came in 1846, when Massachusetts machinist Elias Howe patented a machine with an eyepointed needle and a moving shuttle. Both became standard features of the commercial sewing machine. While Howe was in England trying to sell his machine, Isaac Singer, a onetime mechanic and cabinetmaker, also worked to solve some of the problems connected with the sewing machine, secured a patent in 1851, and began to manufacture and market his machines.

Elias Howe with his sewing machine competing and winning against five seamstresses

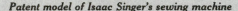

Patent model of Isaac Singer's sewing machine

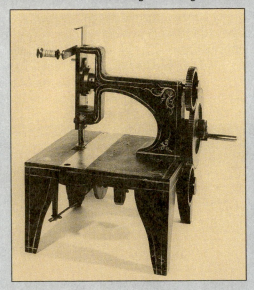

The basic Singer machine was both practical and complex. Special features made the machine relatively easy to operate, but also contributed to its cost. Clothing and shoe manufacturers quickly acquired the machines for their businesses because they could afford to pay the high price and because they recognized their obvious benefits. The introduction of the sewing machine stimulated a period of expansion. By 1858, in the city of Troy, New York, alone, 3,000 machines were turning out men's shirts and collars. Larger and more important than the clothing industry, the shoe industry had an immense demand for sewing machines, the first application of technology to the shoe manufacturing process. By 1860, one female worker, using a machine, was able to stitch together enough shoe uppers to keep 20 shoemakers busy.

Despite their marketing success with clothing and shoe manufacturers, sewing machine makers dreamed of selling their wares to the many

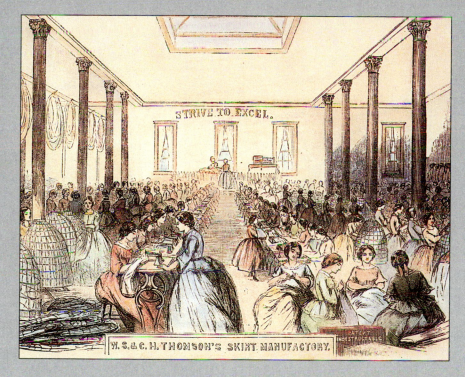

STRIVE TO EXCEL.

W. S. & C. H. THOMSON'S SKIRT MANUFACTORY.

thousands of women who were sewing by hand for their families. The sewing machine's purchase price, however, was too high for many family budgets. In 1856, Singer's partner, Edward Clark, came up with the novel idea of allowing buyers to pay for their machines in installments. A woman could put $5 down and pay the rest of the purchase price and interest over several months. The plan succeeded brilliantly. The very next year, sales of Singer machines almost tripled. Clark then hit upon another marketing concept—the trade-in. The Singer Company offered $50 for "old Sewing Machines of any kind" that could be used to finance a new machine. Sales took another leap upward. Profits produced by these innovative schemes allowed improvements in the production of sewing machines that halved prices by 1859.

As sewing machines entered American households, they relieved women of their most time-consuming domestic chore, sewing by hand. Harriet Kidder, the mother of five, welcomed her new "very valuable household article," which made "sewing a

pleasure rather than a toil." The calico dress that once demanded over six hours of handsewing now could be finished in less than an hour.

Some women ended up doing more and fancier sewing than they had done without their new machines. If one calico dress took only an hour, why not make several? Ruffles, pleats, tucks, and other embellishments could all be made with the machine, and women's fashions reflected the ornamental possibilities now within reach. Sewing machines also transformed other sewing tasks. Quilting became more elaborate, and many quilters during the second half of the nineteenth century used their machines to create complex works of art.

Many women did not have the luxury of using their machines to sew elaborate clothes or complex quilts. Instead, sewing machines became their means of support. For these women, technology brought a new form of drudgery rather than a liberation from toil. As their experience suggests, technological innovations could have both positive and negative consequences for those who used them.

By 1848, Cincinnati had become a bustling commercial and industrial center. There were few visible signs of its frontier past so evident in the picture in Chapter 10.

The workingman's plight, as Cincinnati labor leaders analyzed it, stemmed from his loss of independence. Even though a manufacturing job provided a decent livelihood for some people, the new industrial order was changing the nature of the laboring class itself. A new kind of worker had emerged. Rather than selling the products of his skills, he had only his raw labor to sell. His "wage slavery," or dependence on wages, promised to be lifelong. The reorganization of work signaled the end of the progression from apprentice to journeyman to master and undermined traditional skills. Few workers could expect to rise to the position of independent craftsman. Most would only labor for others, just as slaves labored for their masters. Nor would wages bring to most that other form of independence, the ownership of shop and home. The expression "wage slavery" contained a deep truth about the changed conditions of many American workingmen.

Workers also resented the masters' attempts to control their lives. In the new factories, owners insisted on a steady pace of work and uninterrupted production. Artisans who were used to working in spurts, stopping for a few moments of conversation or a drink, disliked the new routines. Those who

took a dram or two at work found themselves discharged. Even outside the workplace, manufacturers attacked Cincinnati working-class culture. Crusades to abolish volunteer fire companies and to close down saloons, both attacked as nonproductive activities, suggested how little equality the Cincinnati worker enjoyed in an industrializing society.

The fact that workers' wages in Cincinnati, as in other cities, rose more slowly than food and housing costs compounded discontent over changing working conditions. The working class sensed it was losing ground at the very time the city's rich were visibly growing richer. In 1817, the top tenth of the city's taxpayers owned over half the wealth, while the bottom half possessed only 10 percent. In 1860, the share of the top tenth had increased to two-thirds, while the bottom half's share had shrunk to 2.4 percent. Cincinnati workers may not have known these exact percentages, but they could see growing social and economic inequality in the luxurious mansions the city's rich were building and in the spreading blight of slums.

In the decades before the Civil War, Cincinnati workers formed unions, turned out for fair wages, and rallied in favor of the ten-hour day. Like the Lowell mill girls, they cloaked their protest with the mantle of the Revolution. Striking workers staged parades with fifes and drums and appropriated patriotic symbols to bolster their demands for justice and independence. Although they did not see their bosses as a separate or hostile class, labor activists insisted that masters were denying workers a fair share of profits. This unjust distribution doomed them to economic dependency. Since the republic depended on a free and independent citizenry, the male workers warned that their bosses' policies threatened to undermine the republic itself.

Only in the early 1850s did Cincinnati workers begin to suspect that their employers formed a distinct class of parasitic "nonproducers." Although most strikes still revolved around familiar issues of better hours and wages, signs appeared of the more hostile labor relations that would emerge after the Civil War.

As elsewhere, skilled workers were in the forefront of Cincinnati's labor protest and union activities. But their victories proved temporary. Depression and bad times always harmed labor organizations and canceled out employers' concessions. Furthermore, Cincinnati workers did not readily unite to protest new conditions. The uneven pace of industrialization meant that these workers, unlike the Lowell mill girls, had no common working experience. Moreover, growing cultural and ethnic diversity compounded differences in the workplace. By 1850, almost half the people in the city were foreign-born, most of them German, whereas only 22 percent had been in 1825.

As the heterogeneity of the American people increased, ethnic and religious tensions simmered. Immigrants, near the bottom of the occupational ladder, faced limited job choices and suspicion of their faith, habits, and culture. Protestant workers frequently felt that they had more in common with their Protestant bosses than with Catholic Irish or German fellow workers. These tensions exploded in Cincinnati in the spring of 1855. Americans attacked barricades erected in German neighborhoods, crying out death threats. Their wrath visited the Irish as well. Ethnic, cultural, and social differences often drove workers apart and concealed their common grievances. In many cases, disunity served economic progress by undermining workers' efforts for higher pay, shorter hours, and better working conditions, thus enabling businesses to maximize productivity and profits while minimizing the cost of labor.

URBAN LIFE

Americans experienced the impact of economic growth most dramatically in the cities. In the four decades before the Civil War, the rate of urbanization in the United States was faster than ever before or since. In 1820, about 9 percent of the American people lived in cities (defined as areas containing a population of 2,500 or more). Forty years later, almost 20 percent of them did. Older cities like Philadelphia and New York mushroomed, while new cities like Cincinnati, Columbus, and Chicago sprang up "as if by enchantment." Although urban growth was not confined to the East, it was most dramatic there. By 1860, more than a third of the people living in the Northeast were urban residents, compared to only 14 percent of westerners and 7 percent of southerners. Although the majority of northerners still lived on farms or in small farm towns, the region was clearly urbanizing.

The Process of Urbanization

Three distinct types of cities—commercial centers, mill towns, and transportation hubs—emerged during these years of rapid economic growth. Commercial seaports like Boston, Philadelphia, and Baltimore expanded steadily and developed diversified manufacturing to supplement the older functions of importing, exporting, and providing services and credit, although the lack of waterpower limited industrial development. New York replaced Philadelphia as the country's largest and most important city. With the completion of the Erie Canal, New

Ten Largest Cities in the United States, 1810 and 1860	
1810	1860
1. New York	1. New York
2. Philadelphia	2. Philadelphia
3. Baltimore	3. Baltimore
4. Boston	4. Boston
5. Charleston	5. New Orleans
6. New Orleans	6. Cincinnati
7. Salem	7. St. Louis
8. Providence	8. Chicago
9. Richmond	9. Buffalo
10. Albany	10. Newark

Source: U.S. Bureau of the Census.

York merchants gained control of much of the trade with the West. By 1840, they had also secured the largest share of the country's import and export trade.

Access to waterpower fueled the development of a second kind of city like Lowell, Massachusetts; Trenton, New Jersey; and Wilmington, Delaware. Situated inland along the waterfalls and rapids that provided the power to run their mills, these cities burgeoned as American industry, especially the production of textiles, expanded in the decades before the Civil War.

Between 1820 and 1840, one-quarter of the increase in urban population occurred west of the Appalachian Mountains, where a third type of city arose. Louisville, Cleveland, and St. Louis were typical of cities that had served as transportation service and distribution centers from the earliest days of frontier settlement. Chicago acted as "grand depot, exchange, counting-house, and metropolis" for its hinterlands. Like most of these western cities, Chicago was a commercial rather than an industrial center. In the 1850s, selling lumber to prairie farmers who needed it for fences and housing was one of Chicago's most significant commercial activities.

As the number of urban dwellers grew, their needs helped to generate economic growth. City dwellers rarely had gardens or animals, so they had to purchase their food. This encouraged farmers to turn to commercial farming. Cities also provided a growing market for other products, including shoes, clothing, furniture, and carriages. The iron industry sold more than a half million cast-iron stoves yearly, mainly to city dwellers, while city governments purchased cast-iron pipes for sewers and the water supply and city merchants erected cast-iron buildings.

Until 1840, the people eagerly crowding into cities came mostly from the American countryside. Then ships began to spill their human cargoes into seaboard cities, and a growing number of immigrants began their lives anew in the United States. Immigrants who could afford to leave the crowded port cities for the interior, many of them Germans and Scandinavians, did so. But the penniless had little choice but to remain in eastern cities and search for work there. By 1860, fully 20 percent of the people living in the Northeast were immigrants; in some of the largest cities, they and their children comprised more than half the population. The Irish, fleeing famine and poverty at home, were the largest foreign group in the Northeast.

A look at Philadelphia reveals the character, rhythms, rewards, and tensions of urban life during the antebellum period. The city was one of the giants of the age. An inland port, a bustling mercantile city, a center of shops producing textiles, metals, and a host of other products, Philadelphia stood second only to New York. Though William Penn's "green country town" boasted an attractive appearance and an orderly plan, the expanding nineteenth-century city merited little praise. Speculators interested only in profit relied on the grid pattern as the cheapest and most efficient way to divide land for development. They built monotonous miles of new streets, new houses, new alleys, with "not a single acre left for public use, either for pleasure or health," as merchant Samuel Breck observed.

Not all citizens enjoyed the benefits of urban life. Overwhelmed by rapid growth, city governments provided few of the services we consider essential today, and usually only to those who paid for them. Poor families devoted many hours to securing necessities that affluent citizens had at their fingertips. Water is a case in point. By 1801, Philadelphia had constructed a system of waterworks that drew water from the Schuylkill River, then pumped it through wooden pipes to street hydrants. Only by paying a special fee could Philadelphians have water brought into their homes, so most of the city's residents went without. In the 1820s, the city expanded the water system by constructing the Fairmount waterworks, but the more abundant supply of water again benefited those who could afford to pipe it into their homes.

In 1849, Isaac Parrish's report on the sanitary conditions in Philadelphia lamented some of the consequences. "There is . . . a general absence of bathing apparatus, and even of hydrants," he wrote, "in the houses of the poorer classes, and especially in confined courts and alleys of the populous districts of the city." An earlier inspection, carried out by Mathew Carey in 1837, had pointed to an even more basic problem: 253 persons crowded into 30 tenements without even one privy. The ability to pay for services determined not only comfort but health.

Class Structure in the Cities

The drastic differences in the quality of urban life reflected the growing economic inequality that characterized Philadelphia and other American cities. In sharp contrast to the colonial period, the first

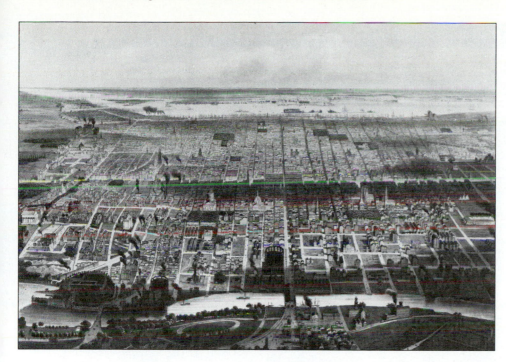

Philadelphia's grid pattern, a source of order in Penn's original design, was expanded and exploited by developers with little thought to attractiveness or availability of services.

half of the nineteenth century witnessed a dramatic rise in the concentration of wealth in the United States. The pattern was most extreme in cities.

Because Americans believed that profits belonged to the people who worked for them and because affluent Americans possessed so many advantages in the rush for riches, the well-to-do profited handsomely from this period of growth, while workers lost ground. The merchants, brokers, lawyers, bankers, and manufacturers of Philadelphia's upper class gained control of more and more of the city's wealth. By the late 1840s, the wealthiest 4 percent of the population held about two-thirds of the wealth. The economic pattern was similar in other American cities, as the accompanying table indicates.

This widening gap between the upper class and the working class did not translate into mass suffering because more wealth was being generated. But the growing inequality hardened class lines, nourished social tensions, and contributed to the labor protests of the antebellum period.

Between 1820 and 1860, Philadelphia's working class, like Cincinnati's, was transformed. As preindustrial ways of producing goods yielded to factory production, some former artisans and skilled workers climbed into the middle class, becoming businessmen, factory owners, mill supervisors, and shopkeepers. Urban growth provided many oppor-

tunities. Perhaps 10 to 15 percent of Philadelphians in each decade before the Civil War improved their occupations and places of residence. But downward occupational mobility also increased. Fed by waves of immigrants, the lower class was growing at an accelerating rate. Moreover, within the working class itself, the percentage of unskilled wage earners living in poverty or on its brink increased from 17 percent to 24 percent between 1820 and 1860. At the same time, the proportion of craftsmen, once the heart of the laboring class, shrank from 56 percent to 47 percent.

The Urban Working Class

As with so much else in urban life, housing reflected social and economic divisions. The poorest rented quarters in crowded, flimsily constructed shacks, shanties, and two-room houses. Because much of the worst housing was in back alleys or even in backyards, more substantial houses fronting the main streets concealed it. Many visitors did not even realize slums lay behind the rows of brick housing, nor did they know of the uncollected garbage, privy runoffs, and fetid decay in the dark, unpaved alleys. In his diary, Philadelphia shopkeeper Joseph Sill left a description of living conditions at the bottom. "In the afternoon," he wrote, "Mrs. S & I went to the lowest part of the City to see some poor

Wealth Distribution in Three Eastern Cities in the 1840s

Level of Wealth	Percentage of Population	Approximate Noncorporate Wealth Owned	Percentage Noncorporate Wealth
Brooklyn in 1841			
$50,000 or more	1%	$10,087,000	42%
$15,000 to $50,000	2	4,000,000	17
$4,500 to $15,000	9	5,730,000	24
$1,000 to $4,500	15	2,804,000	12
$100 to $1,000	7	1,000,000	4
Under $100	66	—	—
New York City in 1845			
$50,000 or more	1	85,804,000	40
$20,000 to $55,000	3	55,000,000	26
Boston in 1848			
$90,000 or more	1	47,778,500	37
$35,000 to $90,000	3	34,781,800	27
$4,000 to $35,000	15	40,636,400	32
Under $4,000	81	6,000,000	4

Source: Pessen, *Wealth, Class, and Power Before the Civil War* (1973).

persons who had call'd upon us for Charity. We found one woman, with two children, & expecting soon to be confined, living in a cellar, part of which was unfloored, & exhibited much wretchedness; but it was tolerably clean. Her husband is a Weaver, & had his loom in the Cellar, but has only occasional work."

What the Sills witnessed during their visit to the weaver's family was not just poverty but the transformation of working-class family life. Men could no longer be sure of supporting their wives and children, even when they were employed, and felt that they had lost much of their authority and power in the family. Some found their wives no longer subservient or seemingly careless with their hard-earned money. One woman angered her husband by failing to give a clear account of what she had done with the grocery money. "He said if she did not give him a full account . . . he would kill her or something like that." The squabble over grocery money ended in murder. This family was an extreme case, but family violence that spilled out onto the streets was not uncommon in working-class quarters.

Middle-Class Life and Ideals

Although the Sills ventured into the world of the working class, their life could not have been more different. Members of the comfortable middle class like the Sills profited from the dramatic increase in wealth in antebellum America. They lived in pleasantly furnished houses, enjoying more peace, more privacy, and more comfort than the less affluent. Franklin stoves gave warmth in winter, and iron cookstoves made cooking easier. Conveniences like Astral lamps made it possible to read after dark. Bathing stands and bowls ensured higher standards of cleanliness. Rugs muffled sounds and kept in the heat.

The houses of the city's elite were spacious and filled with new conveniences. Samuel Breck's house in 1839 was elegant and luxurious, with "parlours 14 feet high, . . . furnaces, water closet and shower and common bath up stairs, marble mantels and fireplaces in dressing rooms." Costing $22,500, Breck's "spendid house" represented the sum an ordinary Philadelphia textile factory operative might expect to earn in 75 years of work.

For the urban middle and upper class, the rewards of economic success included residential comfort, choice, and stability. But working-class renters moved often, from one cramped lodging to another. This common pattern of repeated mobility made it difficult to create close-knit neighborhoods in urban settings.

As the gap between classes widened, new middle-class norms emerged. They suited the rhythms of middle-class urban life, but they also affected working people and rural Americans.

The changing economy nourished new expectations about middle-class family life. In the seventeenth and eighteenth centuries, American families usually operated as an economic unit. Even though men and women, adults and children were hardly equal, they all performed complementary tasks in the family's struggle to get ahead. Better transportation, new products, and the rise of factory production and large businesses changed the family economy. Falling prices for processed and manufactured goods like soap, candles, clothing, and even bread made it unnecessary for women, except on the frontier, to continue making these items at home. As men increasingly involved themselves in a money economy, whether through commerce or market farming, women's and children's contributions to the family economy became relatively less significant. Although middle-class women and children still worked in their homes as their husbands left to "bring home the bacon," they often neither produced vital goods nor earned money. Even the rhythm of their lives, oriented to housework rather than the demands of the clock, separated them from the bustling commercial world where their husbands now labored. By 1820, the notion emerged that the sexes occupied separate spheres.

While men pursued success in the public world, what were women's responsibilities? Sarah Hale, editor of the popular magazine *Godey's Lady's Book,* and Catharine Beecher, well-known lecturer and writer, argued that woman's sphere was at home. There she would work not as producer but as housekeeper, creating a clean, wholesome, and private setting for family life.

But women were more than housekeepers; they also served as their families' moral and cultural guardians. Arguing that women had different characters from men, that they were innately pious, virtuous, unselfish, and modest, publicists extended the argument developed during the Revolutionary era. By training future citizens and workers to be obedient, moral, patriotic, and hardworking, mothers would ensure the welfare of the republic. Just as important, they would preserve important values in a time of rapid change. Wives were responsible for helping husbands cope with the temptations and tensions of the new, fast-paced economic order. As one preacher explained, a wife was the guardian angel who "watches over" her husband's interests, "warns him against dangers, comforts him under trial; and by . . . pious, assiduous, and attractive deportment, constantly endeavors to render him more virtuous, more useful, more honourable, and more happy."

This view, characterizing women as morally superior to and different from men, had important consequences for many women's lives. The physical separation of the male and female worlds and the shift in women's status often meant that women shared more with one another than with men, even their husbands. Similar social experiences and perspectives made female friendships central for many women, the source of comfort, security, and happiness.

They also experienced both pleasure and frustration in their role as housekeepers. Now that most domestic production had disappeared from the household, the task of creating a comfortable and attractive home became primary. But new standards of cleanliness, order, and beauty were often impossible to achieve. Moreover, efforts to create a perfect home often worked against harmonious family life.

Although the concept of domesticity seemed to confine women to the domestic sphere and to emphasize the private nature of family life, it actually prompted women to take on activities in the outside world. If women were the guardians of morality, why should they not carry out their tasks in the public sphere? This reasoning lay behind the tremendous growth of voluntary female associations in the early decades of the nineteenth century. Initially, most involved religious and charitable activities. Women supported orphanages, paid for and distributed religious tracts and Bibles, established Sunday schools, and ministered to the poor. The associations provided women with congenial companions and suitable tasks for their "moral character." Sometimes the women recognized special interests that men did not share. In the 1830s, as we shall see in Chapter 13, women added specific moral concerns

FAMILY PAINTINGS

Although paintings are often admired and studied for artistic reasons alone, their value as historical documents should not be overlooked. In an age before the camera, paintings, sketches, and even pictures done in needlework captured Americans at different moments of life and memorialized their significant rituals. Paintings of American families in their homes, for example, reveal both an idealized conception of family life and the details of its reality. In addition, the paintings provide us with a sense of what the houses of the middle and upper classes (who could afford to commission art) were like.

Artists trained in the European tradition of realism painted family scenes and portraits, but so did many painters who lacked formal academic training, the so-called primitive artists. Their art was abstract in the sense that the artists tended to emphasize what they knew or felt rather than what they actually saw.

Some primitive artists were women who had received some drawing instruction at school. They often worked primarily for their own pleasure. Other artists were craftsmen, perhaps house or sign painters, who painted pictures in their leisure time. Some traveling house decorators made a living by making paintings and wall decorations. Many primitive paintings are unsigned, and even when we know the painter's identity, we often know little more than a name and perhaps a date. Primitive artists flourished in the first three-quarters of the nineteenth century, eventually supplanted by the camera and inexpensive prints.

We see here a painting of the Sargent family done by an unknown artist around 1800. Though not an exact representation of reality, it does convey what the artist and the buyer considered important. Like any piece of historical evidence, this painting must be approached critically and carefully. Our questions focus on four areas: (1) the individual family members and their treatment, (2) the objects

Anonymous, **The Sargent Family,** *1800*

H. Knight, The Family at Home, *1836*

associated with each, (3) the implied or apparent relationship between family members, and (4) the domestic environment. The painting gives us an idealized version of what both the painter and the subjects felt ought to be as well as what actually was.

First, study the family itself. Describe what you see. How many family members are there, and what is each one doing? What seems to be the relationship between husband and wife? Why do you think Mr. Sargent is painted with his hat on? Who seems to dominate the painting, and how is this dominance conveyed (positioning, attitude or facial expression, eye contact, clothing)? What can you conclude about different "spheres" and roles for men and women?

Why do you think the artist painted two empty chairs and included a ball and a dog in this scene of family life? What do these choices suggest about attitudes toward children and their upbringing? What seems to be the role of the children in the family? What does the painting suggest about how this family wished to be viewed? How do your con-

clusions relate to information discussed in this chapter?

Take a look at the room in which the Sargents are gathered. Make an inventory of the objects and furnishings in it. The room seems quite barren in comparison to present-day interiors. Why? Why do you think the chairs are placed near the window and door? What kind of scene does the window frame?

The Family at Home, painted by H. Knight in 1836, is a more detailed painting showing a larger family gathering almost 40 years later. Similar questions can be asked about this painting, particularly in relationship to the different treatment of boys and girls and the positioning and objects associated with each sex. There are many clues about the different socialization of male and female children. The family's living room can be contrasted to the Sargent family's room to reveal some of the changes in the home brought about by industrialization.

Finally, how do these nineteenth-century homes and sex roles differ from those in colonial New England and the Chesapeake?

like the abolition of slavery to their missionary and benevolent efforts. As these women took on more active and controversial tasks, they often clashed with men and with social conventions about "woman's place."

Domesticity described norms, not the actual conduct of middle-class women. Obviously not all women were pious, disinterested, selfless, virtuous, cheerful, and loving. But these ideas influenced how women thought of themselves and promoted "female" behavior by encouraging particular choices. Domestic ideals helped many women make psychological sense of their lives.

The new norms, effectively spread by the publishing industry, influenced rural women and urban working women. The insistence on marriage and service to family discouraged married women from entering the work force. Those who had to work often bore a burden of guilt. Many took in poorly paid piecework so that they could remain at home. Though the new feminine ideal may have seemed noble to middle-class women in cities and towns, it created difficult tensions in the lives of working-class women.

As family roles were reformulated, a new view of childhood emerged. Working-class children still worked or scavenged for goods to sell or use at home, but middle-class children were no longer expected to contribute economically to the family. Middle-class parents now came to see childhood as

a special stage of life, a period of preparation for adulthood. In a child's early years, mothers were to impart important values, including the necessity of behaving in accordance with gender prescriptions. Harsh punishments lost favor. As Catharine Beecher explained, "Affection can govern the human with a sway more powerful than the authority of reason or [even] the voices of conscience." Schooling also prepared a child for the future, and urban middle-class parents supported the public school movement.

Children's fiction, which poured off the printing presses, also socialized children. Stories pictured modest youngsters happily making the correct choices of playmates and activities, obeying their parents, and being dutiful, religious, loving, and industrious. Occasionally, as in *The Child at Home* (1833), the reader could discover the horrible consequences of wrongdoing. The young girl who refused to bring her sick mother a glass of water saw her promptly die. Heavy-handed moralizing made sure that children got the proper message.

The growing publishing industry helped to spread new ideas about family roles and appropriate family behavior. Novels, magazines, etiquette and child-rearing manuals, and schoolbooks all carried the message from northern and midwestern centers of publishing to the South, to the West, and to the frontier. Probably few Americans lived up to the new standards established for the model parent or

Erastus Salisbury Field (1805–1900), an accomplished folk artist, painted this middle-class family in Ware, Massachusetts, in 1839. His portrait suggests different family roles and the domestic comfort that characterized middle-class family life.

child, but the standards increasingly influenced them.

New notions of family life supported the widespread use of contraception for the first time in American history. Since children required so much loving attention and needed careful preparation for adulthood, many parents desired smaller families. The declining birthrate was evident first in the Northeast, particularly in cities and among the middle class. Contraceptive methods included abortion, which was legal in many states until 1860. This medical procedure terminated perhaps as many as a third of all pregnancies. Other birth control methods included coitus interruptus and abstinence. The success of these methods for family limitation suggests that many men and women adopted the new definitions of the female sex as naturally affectionate but passionless and sexually restrained.

Mounting Urban Tensions

The social and economic changes transforming American cities in the half century before the Civil War produced urban violence on a scale never before witnessed in America, not even during the Revolution. Festering ethnic and racial tensions often triggered mob actions that lasted for days. American cities were slow to establish a modern police force (London had organized one in 1829). Most still had the traditional constable-and-watch system. The night watch lit city streetlights and patrolled the streets to preserve order and arrest suspicious persons. During the day, constables investigated health hazards, carried out court orders, and apprehended criminals against whom complaints had been lodged. Neither group tried to prevent crimes or discover offenses. Neither wore uniforms. Certainly neither was able to "prevent a tumult." Each chaotic event made the London model more attractive.

Racial tensions contributed to Philadelphia's disorders. An unsavory riot in August 1834 revealed other important sources of social antagonism as well as the inability of its police force to control disorder.

One hot August evening, several hundred white Philadelphians wrecked a building on South Street that contained the "Flying Horses," a merry-go-round patronized by both blacks and whites. A general melee followed. As the *Philadelphia Gazette* reported, "At one time it is supposed that four or five hundred persons were engaged in the conflict,

with clubs, brickbats, paving stones, and the materials of the shed in which the flying horses were kept." Spurred by the taste of blood, the white mob moved into the center of the crowded, racially mixed neighborhood, where they continued their orgy of destruction, looting, and intimidation of black residents. Similar mayhem followed on the next two nights. Intermittent rioting broke out the succeeding night as well, but the presence of 300 special constables, a troop of mounted militia, and a company of infantry prevented the violence from reaching the pitch of the previous nights.

An investigation following the riots revealed that the white mob had caused at least $4,000 of damage to two black churches and more than 36 private homes. At least one black had been killed, and numerous others had been injured. As one shocked eyewitness reported, "The mob exhibited more than fiendish brutality, beating and mutilating some of the old, confiding and unoffending blacks with a savageness surpassing anything we could have believed men capable of."

Many rioters bragged that they were "hunting the nigs." Riots, however, are complicated events, and this racial explanation does not reveal the range of causes underlying the rampage of violence and destruction. The rioters were young and generally of low social standing. Many were Irish. Some had criminal records. A number of those arrested, however, were from "a class of mechanics of whom better things are expected": weavers, house painters, a cabinetmaker, a carpenter, a blacksmith, and a plasterer. No professional people or businessmen seem to have been involved. Accompanying the rioters, however, were onlookers who egged the mob on. As one paper reported, these onlookers "countenanced" the operations of the mob "and in one or two instances coincided with their conduct by clapping." The rioters revealed that in the event of "an attack by the city police, they confidently counted" on the assistance of these bystanders.

The mob's composition hints at some of the reasons for participation. Many of the rioters were at the bottom of the occupational and economic ladder and competed with blacks for jobs. This was particularly true of the newly arrived Irish immigrants, who were attempting to replace blacks in low-status jobs. Subsequent violence against blacks suggested that economic rivalry was an important component of the riot. "Colored persons, when engaged in their usual vocations," the *Niles Register* observed, "were repeatedly assailed and maltreated. . . . Parties of white men have insisted that no blacks shall be employed in certain departments of labor."

If blacks threatened the dream of advancement of some whites, this was not quite the complaint of the skilled workers. These men were more likely to have experienced the negative impact of a changing economic system that was undermining the small-scale mode of production. The dream of a better life seemed increasingly illusory as their declining wages drew them closer to unskilled workers than to the middle class. Like other rioters, they were living in one of the poorest and most crowded parts of the city. Their immediate scapegoats were blacks, but for them the real but intangible villain was the economic system itself. Trade union organizing and a general strike a year later would highlight the grievances of this group.

Urban expansion also figured as a factor in the racial violence. Most of the rioters lived either in the riot area or nearby. All had experienced the overcrowded and inadequate living conditions caused by the city's rapid growth. The racial tensions generated by squalid surroundings and social proximity go far to explain the outbreak of violence. The same area would later become the scene of race riots and election trouble and became infamous for harboring criminals and juvenile gangs. The absence of middle- or upper-class participants did not mean that these groups were untroubled

during times of growth and change. But their material circumstances cushioned them from some of the more unsettling forces.

The city's police force proved unable to control the mob, thus prolonging the violence. Philadelphia, like other eastern cities, was in the midst of creating its police force. In 1833, a small force had been added to the constable-and-watch system. The new force was supposed to deter crime by walking the city streets. But their small size rendered them powerless in the face of the angry mob. Only continued rowdiness, violence, and riots would convince residents and city officials in Philadelphia (and in other large cities) to support an expanded, quasi-military, preventive police force in uniforms. By 1855, most sizable eastern cities had established such forces.

Finally, the character of the free black community itself was a factor in producing those gruesome August events. Not only was the community large and visible, but it also had created its own institutions and its own elite. Whites resented "dressy blacks and dandy coloured beaux and belles" returning from "their proper churches." The mob vented its rage against black affluence by targeting the solid brick houses of middle-class blacks and robbing them of silver and watches. Black wealth threatened the notion of the proper social order held by many white Philadelphians and seemed unspeakable when whites could not afford life's basic necessities or lacked jobs.

This 1827 broadside mockingly describes a Boston riot in which "a great number de white Trucker-man got angry . . . I spose so many bad girl who lib here" in the black section of town. The broadside's tone and its content suggest how hazardous urban life could be for blacks.

The Black Underclass

Events in Philadelphia showed how hazardous life for free blacks could be. Few enjoyed the rewards of economic expansion and industrial progress. Northern whites, like southerners, believed in black inferiority and depravity and feared black competition for jobs and resources. Although northern states had passed gradual abolition acts between 1780 and 1803 and the national government had banned slaves from entering new states to be formed out of the Northwest Territory, nowhere did any government extend equal rights and citizenship or economic opportunities to free blacks in their midst.

For a time in the early nineteenth century, some blacks living in the North were permitted to vote, but they soon lost that right. Beginning in the 1830s, in part because of the influx of fugitive slaves and manumitted blacks without property or jobs, Pennsylvania, Connecticut, and New Jersey disenfranchised blacks. New York allowed only those with three years' residence and property valued at $250 or more to vote. Only the New England states (with the exception of Connecticut), which had tiny black populations, preserved the right to vote regardless of color. By 1840, fully 93 percent of the northern free black population lived in states where law or custom prevented them from voting.

Other black civil rights were also restricted. In five northern states, blacks could not testify against whites or serve on juries. In most states, the two races were thoroughly segregated. Blacks increasingly endured separate and inferior facilities in railway cars, steamboats, hospitals, prisons, and other asylums. In some states, they could enter public buildings only as personal servants of white men. They sat in "Negro pews" in churches and took communion only after whites had left the church. Although most Protestant religious denominations in the antebellum period split into northern and southern branches over the issue of slavery, most northern churches were not disposed to welcome blacks as full members.

As the Philadelphia riot revealed, whites were driving blacks from their jobs. In 1839, *The Colored American* blamed the Irish. "These impoverished and destitute beings . . . are crowding themselves into every place of business . . . and driving the poor colored American citizen out." Increasingly after 1837, these "white niggers" became coachmen, stevedores, barbers, cooks, house servants—all occupations blacks had once held.

Educational opportunities for blacks were also severely limited. Only a few school systems admitted blacks, in separate facilities. The case of Prudence Crandall illustrates the lengths to which northern whites would go to maintain racial segregation. In 1833, Crandall, a Quaker schoolmistress in Canterbury, Connecticut, announced that she would admit "young colored ladies and Misses" to her school. The outraged townspeople, fearful that New England would become the "Liberia of America," tried all sorts of persuasion and intimidation to induce Crandall to abandon her project.

Nonetheless, Crandall opened the school. Hostile citizens harassed and insulted students and teachers, refused to sell them provisions, and denied them medical care and admission to churches. Ministers preached against Crandall's efforts, and local residents poured manure in the school's well, set the school on fire, and knocked in walls with a battering ram. Crandall was arrested, and after two trials—in which free blacks were declared to have no citizenship rights—she finally gave up and moved to Illinois.

Crandall would not have found the Old Northwest much more hospitable. The fast-growing western states were intensely committed to white supremacy and black exclusion. In Ohio, the response to talk of freeing the slaves was to pass "black laws" excluding them from the state. Said one Ohioan, "The banks of the Ohio would be lined with men with muskets to keep off the emancipated slaves." In 1829 in Cincinnati, where evidence of freedom papers and $500 bond was demanded of blacks who wished to live in the city, white rioters ran nearly 2,000 blacks out of town.

As an Indiana newspaper editor observed in 1854, informal customs made life dangerous for blacks. They were "constantly subject to insults and annoyance in traveling and the daily avocations of life; [and] are practically excluded from all social privileges, and even from the Christian communion." An Indiana senator proclaimed in 1850 that a black could "never live together equally" with whites because "the same power that has given him a black skin, with less weight or volume of brain, has given us a white skin with greater volume of brain and intellect." A neighboring politician, Abraham Lincoln of Illinois, would not have disagreed with this assessment.

RURAL COMMUNITIES

Although the percentage of families involved in farming fell from 72 percent to 60 percent between 1820 and 1860, Americans remained a rural people. Agriculture persisted as the country's most significant economic activity, and farm products still made up most of the nation's exports. The small family farm still characterized eastern and western agriculture.

Even though farming remained the dominant way of life, agriculture changed in the antebellum period. Vast new tracts of land came under cultivation in the West. Railroads, canals, and better roads pulled rural Americans into the orbit of the wider world. Some crops were shipped to regional markets; others, like grain, hides, and pork, stimulated industrial processing. Manufactured goods, ranging from cloth to better tools, flowed in return to farm families. Like city dwellers, farmers and their families read books, magazines, and papers that exposed them to new ideas. Commercial farming encouraged different ways of thinking and acting and lessened the isolation so typical before 1820.

Farming in the East

During the antebellum period, economic changes created new rural patterns in the Northeast. Marginal lands in New England, New York, and Pennsylvania, cultivated as more fertile lands ran out, yielded discouraging returns. Gradually after 1830, farmers abandoned these farms, forest reclaimed farmland, and the New England hill country began a slow decline. By 1860, almost 40 percent of people who had been born in Vermont had left their native state. A popular song of the 1840s captured the pattern of flight. "Come, all ye Yankee farmers who wish to change your lot, / Who've spunk enough to travel beyond your native spot. / And leave behind the village where Pa and Ma do stay, / Come follow me, and settle in Michigan, yea, yea."

Farmers who did not migrate west had to transform their production. By the 1830s, eastern farmers were realizing that they could not compete with western grain. Therefore, they sought new agricultural opportunities created by better transportation and growing urban markets.

One of the demands was for fresh milk. By the 1830s, some eastern cities had grown so large that

milk was turning sour before it reached central marketplaces. To meet the desire for milk, several cities, including New York City, started urban dairies where cows often fed on garbage and slop from distilleries and breweries. As railroad lines extended into rural areas, however, farmers living as far away as Vermont and upper New York State discovered that they could ship cooled milk to urban centers. In 1842 and 1843, the Erie Railroad carried 750,000 gallons of milk to New York City. As they turned to dairy farming, these farmers eventually drove the unsavory city dairies out of business. City residents had fresher and cheaper milk and drank more of it as a result.

Urban appetites encouraged other farmers to cultivate fruit and vegetables. Every city was surrounded by farmers growing produce for urban consumption. Railroads also prompted farmers miles away to turn to specialized farming. Upper New York State farmers began to raise and ship apples, while New Jersey and Delaware farmers became famous for their peaches. Thus in July 1837, a Boston housewife could buy at the central market a wide variety of fresh vegetables and fruits, ranging from peas, summer squash, and cauliflower to grapes, cherries, and raspberries. Cookbooks began to include recipes calling for fresh ingredients.

As northern farmers adopted new crops, they began to consider farming as a scientific endeavor. After 1800, northern farmers started using manure as fertilizer rather than disposing of it as a smelly nuisance. By the 1820s, some farmers were rotating their crops and planting new grasses and clover to restore fertility to the soil. These techniques recovered worn-out wheat and tobacco lands in Maryland and Delaware for livestock farming. Calculation began to replace "habit and prejudice . . . the powerful opponents of improvement."

Farmers in the Delaware River valley were leaders in adopting new methods, but interest in scientific farming was widespread. By 1860, American farmers had developed thousands of special varieties of plants for local conditions. Many improvements resulted from experimentation, but farmers also enjoyed more and better information. New journals like the *New England Farmer*, the *Farmers' Register*, and the *Cultivator* informed readers of modern farming practices, fertilizers, scientific breeding, and methods for treating fruits and vegetables. Following New York's lead in 1819, many states established agricultural agencies to propagate new ideas. Although wasteful farming practices did not dis-

Competition from western farmers and improved transportation to urban markets made it profitable for eastern farmers to produce perishables such as eggs, milk, vegetables, and fruit. Note the live chickens, which are also packed in a crate for the trip to market.

appear, they became less characteristic of the Northeast. Improved farming methods contributed to increased agricultural output and helped to reverse a 200-year decline in farm productivity in some of the oldest areas of settlement. The increased use of a tool called the cradle increased farmers' ability to harvest grain and made it possible to cultivate more acres than before. A "scientific" farmer in 1850 could often produce two to four times as much per acre as in 1820.

Farmers in the fertile area around Northampton, Massachusetts, illustrate the American farmer's adjustment to new economic conditions. As early as 1800, better roads, a turnpike, and stage routes reduced rural isolation. Canal improvements and then railroads strengthened new contacts. With markets ever more accessible, farmers began to change ag-

ricultural patterns. Rather than raising crops and animals for home use or for local barter, farmers started to cultivate crops "scientifically" in order to increase profits. Farming was becoming a business. At home, women found themselves freed from many of their traditional tasks. Peddlers brought goods to the door. The onerous duty of making cloth and clothing disappeared with the coming of inexpensive ready-made cloth and even ready-made clothes in the 1820s. Daughters liberated from the chores of home manufacturing went off to the mills or earned money by taking in piecework from local merchants.

As the rhythms of rural life in the Connecticut River valley quickened, attitudes also changed. Cash transactions replaced the exchange of goods. Country stores became more reluctant to accept wood, rye, corn, oats, and butter as payment for goods instead of cash. Some farmers adopted the ethic of getting ahead, although their motive was not entrepreneurial but rather a desire to provide for family material comfort.

Traditional attitudes did not wither completely, however. Some farmers continued to be content with making a living rather than chasing a profit. "Reason's whole pleasure, all the joys of sense / Lie in three words, health, peace and competence" remained the motto for some valley farmers.

One of these old-fashioned farmers, Moses Goodell, was described by his son as "always . . . too honest to get along in the world and get very rich. . . . He managed somehow to just about hold his own, but I suppose it has been tight work for the past few years." Some farmers prospered as they became involved in the market economy; others, like Goodell, just got along. Wealth inequality increased near Northampton, as it did elsewhere in the rural Northeast.

Frontier Families

Many people who left the North during these years headed for the expanding frontier. After the War of 1812, Americans flooded into the Old Northwest. Early communities dotted the Ohio River, the link to the South. Concentrating on corn and pork, settlers sent their products down the Ohio and Mississippi rivers to southern buyers. In 1820, less than one-fifth of the American population lived west of the Appalachians; by 1860, almost half did, and Ohio and Illinois had become two of the nation's most populous states.

By 1830, Ohio, Indiana, and southern Illinois were heavily settled, but Michigan, northern Illinois, Wisconsin, and parts of Iowa and Missouri were still frontier. Chicago had only 250 residents. Conditions were often primitive, as Charles Butler and Arthur Bronson discovered during their 1833 trip. Their hotel in Michigan City, Indiana was "a small log house, a single room, which answered the purpose of drawing room, sitting room, eating room & sleeping room; in this room some eleven or twelve persons lodged in beds & on the floor."

During the 1830s land sales and settlement boomed in the Old Northwest. Changes in federal land policy, which reduced both prices and the minimum acreage a settler had to buy, helped to stimulate migration, as the accompanying chart shows. Eastern capital also contributed to the boom with

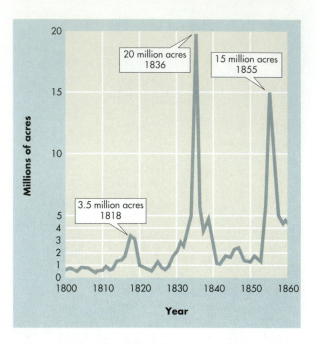

Western Land Sales, 1800–1860

20 million acres
1836

15 million acres
1855

3.5 million acres
1818

Millions of acres

Year

Source: Riegel and Athern, *America Moves West,* 1971.

loans, mortgages, and speculative buying. Speculators frequently bought up large tracts of land from the government, then subdivided them and sold parcels off to settlers.

Internal improvement schemes after 1830 also contributed to new settlement patterns and tied the Old Northwest firmly to the East. Erasmus Gest, who as a 17-year-old had worked on canal projects in Indiana, recalled the settlers' enthusiasm for improvements: "We Engineers were favorites with the People wherever we went."

Wheat for the eastern market rather than corn and hogs for the southern market became increasingly important with the transportation links eastward. Between 1840 and 1860, Illinois, southern Wisconsin, and eastern Iowa turned into the country's most rapidly growing grain regions. In the 1850s, these three states accounted for 70 percent of the increase in national wheat production.

Although the Old Northwest passed rapidly through the frontier stage between 1830 and 1860, its farming families faced severe challenges. Catharine Skinner, who moved from New York to Indiana with her husband when she was 24, described her rigorous existence. "We are poor and live in the woods where deers roam plentifully and the wolf is occasionally heard," she wrote to her sister in 1849. "We are employed in honest business and trying to do the best we can; we have got 80 acres of land in the woods of Indiana, a very level country; we have got two acres cleared and fenced and four more pirty well under way; we have got about five acres of wheat in the ground; we raised corn enough for our use and to fat our pork . . . we have a cow so that we have milk and butter and plenty of corn bread but wheat is hard to be got in account of our not having money."

The Skinners were typical. Western farms were small, for there were limits to what a family with hand tools could manage. A family with two healthy men could care for about 50 acres. In wooded areas, it took several years to get even that much land under cultivation, for only a few acres could be cleared in a year. The Skinners' target was to clear 10 acres during the first 12 months, if, as Catharine said, "health permit." At this rate, it could take ten years for settlers in forested areas to get a farm in full operation. On the prairies, the typical settler would need only half that time.

Catharine Skinner mentioned the shortage of money and described her family as "poor." Although money was in short supply in the Northwest, she probably overstated her family's poverty. It took capital to begin farming—a minimum initial investment of perhaps $100 for 80 acres of government land, $300 for basic farming equipment, and another $100 or $150 for livestock. To buy an already "improved" farm cost more, and free bidding at government auctions could drive the price of unimproved federal land far above the minimum price. Once farmers moved onto the prairies of Indiana and Illinois, they needed an initial investment of about $1,000 since they had to buy materials for fencing, housing, and, expensive steel plows. If farmers invested in the new horse-drawn reapers, they could cultivate more land, but all their costs also increased.

Opportunities in the Old Northwest

It was possible to begin farming with less, however. Some farmers borrowed from relatives, banks, or insurance companies like the Ohio Life Insurance and Trust Company. Others rented land from farmers who had bought more acres than they could manage. Tenants who furnished their own seeds and animals could expect to keep about a third of the yield. Within a few years, some saved enough to buy their own farms. Even those without any capital could work as hired hands. Since labor was scarce, they earned good wages. In Indiana, German settler Jacob Schramm hired men "to help with heavy labors of lumbering and field work, ditch-digging, and so on." Five to ten years of frugal living and steady work for men like Schramm would bring the sum needed to get started.

Probably about a quarter of the western farm population consisted of young men laboring as tenants or hired hands. Although they stood on the bottom rung of the agricultural ladder, their chances of moving up and joining the rural middle class were favorable. Widespread ownership of land characterized western rural communities. Lucinda Easteen knew as much when she told her younger sister to come to Illinois, where "you can have a home of your own, but never give your hand or heart to a lazy man."

Rural communities, unlike the cities, had no growing class of propertyless wage earners, but inequalities nevertheless existed in the Old Northwest. In Butler County, Ohio, for example, 16 percent of people leaving wills in the 1830s held half of the wealth. By 1860, the wealthiest 8 percent held half the wealth. In a Wisconsin frontier county in 1860, the richest tenth owned 40 percent of all property. While wealth was not as concentrated in rural areas as in the cities, a few residents benefited more from rapid economic development than others.

Nevertheless, the Northwest offered many American families the chance to become independent producers and to enjoy "a pleasing competence." The rigors of frontier life faded with time. As Catharine Skinner wrote to her sister from her new Illinois home in 1850, "We here have meetings instead of hearing the hunters gun and the woo[d]man's ax on the sabbath."

Commercial farming brought new patterns of family life. As one Illinois farmer told his wife and daughter, "Store away your looms, wheels, [and] warping bars . . . all of your utensils for weaving cloth up in the loft. The boys and I can make enough by increasing our herds." Many farm families had money to spend on new goods. As early as 1836, the *Dubuque Visitor* was advertising the availability of ready-made clothing and "Calicoes, Ginghams, Muslins, Cambricks, Laces and Ribbands." The next year the *Iowa News* told of the arrival of "Ready Made Clothing from New York."

CONCLUSION

The Character of Progress

Between 1820 and 1860, the United States experienced tremendous growth and economic development. Transportation improvements facilitated the movement of people, goods, and ideas. Larger markets stimulated both agricultural and industrial production. There were more goods and ample food for the American people. Cities and towns were established and thrived. Visitors constantly remarked on the amazing bustle and rapid pace of American life. The United States was, in the words of one Frenchman, "one gigantic workshop, over the entrance of which there is the blazing inscription 'NO ADMISSION HERE, EXCEPT ON BUSINESS.'"

Although the wonders of American development dazzled foreigners and Americans alike, economic growth had its costs. Expansion was cyclic, and financial panics and depression punctuated the era. Industrial profits were based partly on low wages to workers. Time-honored routes to economic independence disappeared, and a large class of unskilled, impoverished workers appeared in American cities. Growing inequality characterized urban and rural life, prompting some labor activists to criticize new economic and social arrangements. But workers, largely still unorganized, did not speak with one voice. Ethnic, racial, and religious diversity divided Americans in new and troubling ways.

Yet a basic optimism and sense of pride also characterized the age. To observers, however, it frequently seemed as if the East and the Old Northwest were responsible for the country's achievements. During these decades, many noted that the paths between the East, Northwest, and South seemed to diverge. The rise of King Cotton in the South, where slave rather than free labor formed the foundation of the economy, created a new kind of tension in American life, as the next chapter will show.

Recommended Reading

Two useful introductions to economic change during this period are Stuart Bruchey, The Roots of American Economic Growth, 1607–1861 *(1965), and Albert W. Niemi,* U.S. Economic History: A Survey of the Major Issues *(1975).*

The significance of changes in transportation forms the basis for George R. Taylor, The Transportation Revolution, 1815–1860 *(1951). Thomas C. Cochran provides an overview of industrial development in* Frontiers of Change: Early Industrialism in America *(1981), while technological innovation is the subject of Nathan Rosenberg,* Technology and American Economic Growth *(1972), and David J. Jeremy,* Transatlantic Industrial Revolution: The Diffusion of Textile Technology Between Britain and America, 1790–1830 *(1981).*

A number of useful studies focus on economic change in individual communities. Thomas Dublin gives a picture of life and work in Lowell in Women at Work: The Transformation of Work and Community in Lowell, Massachusetts, 1826–1860 *(1979). He has also edited primary sources in* Farm to Factory: Women's Letters, 1830–1860 *(1981). Alan Dawley portrays the reorganization of work in the shoe industry in* Class and Community: The Industrial Revolution in Lynn *(1976). Essays on Philadelphia can be found in Allen F. Davis and Mark H. Haller, eds.,* The Peoples of Philadelphia: A History of Ethnic Groups and Lower-Class Life, 1790–1940 *(1973). Steven J. Ross deals with a midwestern city in* Workers on the Edge: Work, Leisure, and Politics in Industrializing Cincinnati, 1788–1890 *(1985). See also Sean Wilentz,* Chants Democratic: New York City & The Rise of the American Working Class, 1788–1850 *(1984); Anthony F.C. Wallace,* Rockdale, The Growth of an American Village in the Early Industrial Revolution *(1978), and Gary B. Nash,* Forging Freedom: The Formation of Philadelphia's Black Community, 1720–1840 *(1988).*

Alexis de Tocqueville analyzes American society in the 1830s in Democracy in America (1957 ed.). Edward Pessen shows the growth of inequality in four cities in Riches, Class, and Power Before the Civil War (1973). Changes in middle-class housing are described in Russell Lynes, The Domesticated Americans (1957). Mary P. Ryan focuses on the middle-class family in Cradle of the Middle Class: The Family in Oneida County, New York, 1790–1865 (1981), while Christine Stansell focuses on lower-class urban women in City of Women: Sex and Class in New York, 1789–1860 (1986). For a more complete understanding of family life, see Tamara K. Hareven, ed., Family and Kin in Urban Communities, 1700–1930 (1977), and Robert V. Wells, Revolutions in Americans' Lives: A Demographic Perspective of the History of Americans, Their Families, and Their Society (1982). Immigrant life is described in Stephan Thernstrom, ed., Harvard Encyclopedia of American Ethnic Groups (1980).

For an understanding of the midwestern frontier, two useful overviews are Paul W. Gates, The Farmer's Age: Agriculture, 1815–1860 (1960), and Clarence Danhof, Changes in Agriculture: The Northern United States, 1820–1870 (1969). John Denis Haeger explores the role of eastern capital in western development in The Investment Frontier: New York Businessmen and the Economic Development of the Old Northwest (1981). Don H. Doyle provides an excellent community study in The Social Order of a Frontier Community: Jacksonville, Illinois, 1825–1870 (1978), as does John Mack Faragher in Sugar Creek: Life on the Illinois Prairies (1986).

TIME LINE

1805	*Palmer* v. *Mulligan*
1816	Second U.S. Bank
1817	New York Stock Exchange
1819	*Dartmouth College* v. *Woodward*
1820	Lowell founded by Boston Associates
	Land Act of 1820
	The expression "woman's sphere" becomes current
1824	*Sturges* v. *Crowninshield*
1824–1850	Construction of canals in the Northeast
1825–1856	Construction of canals linking the Ohio, the Mississippi, and the Great Lakes
1828	Baltimore and Ohio Railroad begins operation
1830	Preemption Act
1830s	Boom in the Old Northwest
	Increasing discrimination against free blacks
	Public education movement spreads
1833	Philadelphia establishes small police force
1834	Philadelphia race riots
	Lowell work stoppage
1837	Horace Mann becomes secretary of Massachusetts Board of Education
1837–1844	Financial panic and depression
1840	Agitation for ten-hour day
1840s–1850s	Rising tide of immigration
1841	Distributive-Preemption Act

12

Slavery and the Old South

As a young slave boy, Frederick Douglass was sent by his master to live in Baltimore. When he first met his mistress, Sophia Auld, she appeared to be "a woman of the kindest heart and finest feelings." He was "astonished at her goodness" as she began to teach him to read. Her husband, however, ordered her to stop because Maryland law forbade teaching slaves to read. A literate slave was "unmanageable," utterly "unfit. . .to be a slave." From this episode Douglass learned to set inverse goals from Master Auld's wishes. "What he most dreaded, that I most desired . . . and the argument which he so warmly urged, against my learning to read, only served to inspire me with a desire and determination to learn."

In the seven years he lived with the Aulds, young Frederick used "various strategems" to teach himself to read and write. In the narrative of his early life, written after his dramatic escape to the North, Douglass acknowledged that his master's "bitter opposition" had been as beneficial to him as Mrs. Auld's "kindly aid" in achieving his eventual freedom.

Most slaves did not, like Douglass, escape to freedom. But all were as inextricably tied to their masters as Douglass was to the Aulds. Nor could whites in antebellum America escape the pervasive influence of slavery. Otherwise decent people were often compelled by the "peculiar institution" to act inhumanely. After her husband's interference, Sophia Auld, Douglass observed, was transformed from an angel into a demon by the "fatal poison of irresponsible power." Her formerly tender heart turned to "stone" when she ceased teaching him. "Slavery proved as injurious to her," Douglass wrote, "as it did to me."

Such was also the case in Douglass's relationship with Mr. Covey, a slavebreaker to whom he was sent in 1833 to have his will broken. Covey succeeded for a time, Douglass reported, in breaking his "body, soul, and spirit" by brutal hard work and discipline. But one hot August day in 1833, the two men fought a long, grueling battle, which Douglass won. His victory, he said, "rekindled the few expiring embers of freedom, and revived within me a sense of my own manhood." Although it would be four more years before his escape to the North, the young man never again felt like a slave. The key to Douglass's successful resistance to Covey's power

was not just his strong will, nor even a magical root he carried in his pocket, but rather his knowledge of how to jeopardize Covey's reputation and livelihood as a slavebreaker. The oppressed survive by knowing their oppressors.

As Mrs. Auld and Covey discovered, as long as some people were not free, no one was free. Douglass observed, "You cannot outlaw one part of the people without endangering the rights and liberties of all people. You cannot put a chain on the ankle of the bondsman without finding the other end of it about your own necks." After quarreling with a house servant, one plantation mistress complained that she "exercises dominion over me—or tries to do it. One would have thought . . . that I was the Servant, she the mistress." Many whites lived in constant fear of a slave revolt. A Louisiana planter recalled that he had "known times here when there was not a single planter who had a calm night's rest; they then never lay down to sleep without a brace of loaded pistols at their sides." In slave folktales, the clever Brer Rabbit usually outwitted the more powerful Brer Fox or Brer Wolf, thus reversing the roles of oppressed and oppressor.

Slavery, then, was an intricate web of human relationships as well as a labor system. After showing the economic growth and development of the Old South, in which slavery and cotton played vital roles, this chapter will emphasize the daily lives and relationships of masters and slaves who, like Douglass and the Aulds, lived, loved, learned, worked, and struggled with one another in the years before the Civil War.

erhaps no issue in American history has generated quite as many interpretations or as much emotional controversy as slavery. As American attitudes toward that institution have changed over the years, three interpretive schools have developed, each adding to our knowledge of the "peculiar institution." The first saw slavery as a relatively humane and reasonable institution in which plantation owners took care of helpless, childlike slaves. The second depicted slavery as a harsh and cruel system of oppressive exploitation. The third, and most recent, interpretation described the slavery experience from the perspective of the slaves, who did indeed suffer brutal treatment in slavery but who also survived with individual self-esteem and a sense of community and culture.

The first and second interpretive schools emphasized workaday interactions among masters and slaves, while the third focused on life in the slave quarters from sundown to sunup. In a unique structure, this chapter follows these masters and slaves through their day, from morning in the Big House through hot afternoon in the fields to the slave cabins at night. But although slavery was the crucial institution in defining the Old South, many other social groups and patterns contributed to the tremendous economic growth of the South from 1820 to 1860. We will look first at these diverse aspects of antebellum southern life.

BUILDING THE COTTON KINGDOM

Many myths obscure our understanding of the vast region of the antebellum South. It was not a monolithic society filled only with large cotton plantations worked by hundreds of slaves. The realities of the South and slavery were much more complex. Large-plantation agriculture was dominant in the antebellum South, but most southern whites were not even slaveholders, much less large planters. Most southern farmers lived not in mansions but in dark, cramped, two-room cabins. Cotton was a key cash crop in the South, but it was not the only crop grown there. Some masters were kindly, but many were not; some slaves were contented, but most were not.

There were many Souths, encompassing several geographic regions, each with different economic bases and social structures and each reflecting its own cultural and political values. The older Upper South of Virginia, Maryland, North Carolina, and Kentucky grew different staple crops from those grown in the newer, Lower or "Black Belt" South that stretched from South Carolina to eastern Texas.

Within each state, morever, the economies differed between flat, coastal areas and inland, upcountry forests and pine barrens. A still further diversity existed between these areas and the Appalachian highlands of northern Alabama and Georgia, eastern Tennessee and Kentucky, and western Virginia and North Carolina. Finally, the cultural and economic life of New Orleans, Savannah, Charleston, and Richmond differed dramatically from rural areas of the South.

Although the South was diverse, agriculture dominated its industry and commerce. In 1859, a Virginia planter complained about a neighbor who was considering abandoning his farm to become a merchant. "To me it seems to be a wild idea," the planter wrote in his diary, hoping that his friend would "give it up and be satisfied to farm." Southerners placed a high value on agricultural labor. Slavery was primarily a labor system intended to produce wealth for landowners. Although slavery in older areas was paternalistic, with masters and slaves owing mutual obligations to each other, increasingly it became a capitalistic enterprise intended to maximize productivity and profits.

Economic Expansion

In the 20 years preceding the Civil War, the South's economy grew slightly faster than the North's. Personal income in 1860 was 15 percent higher in the South than in the prosperous states of the Old Northwest. If the South had become an independent nation in 1860, it would have ranked as one of the wealthiest countries in the world in per capita income. One dramatic technological breakthrough, the cotton gin, was fundamental to this economic growth. The cotton gin had two momentous effects: first, it tied the southern economy to cotton production for a century; second, it allowed the expansion of slavery into vast new territories.

As we learned in Chapter 10, most cotton farmers planted "long staple" cotton prior to the invention of Eli Whitney's cotton gin in 1793. After the cotton gin, the "short staple" variety, which could grow anywhere in the South, predominated. But only large plantation owners could afford to buy gins and purchase the fertile bottomlands of the Gulf states. Thus the plantation system spread with the rise of cotton.

Since cotton could be grown all over the South after the perfection of the cotton gin, men rushed westward to fresh, fertile lands. Large-scale farming increased, demanding more and more slave labor. As a valuable capital resource, slaves received a degree of care and protection. But despite the abolition of slavery in the North and occasional talk of emancipation in the South, slavery became more deeply entrenched, seemingly a permanent part of southern life. Any doubts whispered about ending it could be dispelled by one word: *cotton*.

Although corn was a larger crop than cotton in total acreage, cotton was the largest cash crop and for that reason was called "king." In 1820, the South became the world's largest producer of cotton, and from 1815 to 1860 cotton represented more than half of all American exports. The economic growth spurred on by cotton helped not only the South but also the North and the Midwest. Northern merchants gained by shipping, insuring, and marketing southern cotton. Western farmers found a major market for their foodstuffs. Cotton was the mainstay of the southern economy, but it was also a crucial link in the national economy.

The supply of cotton from the South grew at an astonishing rate. Cotton production soared from 461,000 bales in 1817 to 1.35 million bales in 1840.

Frederick Douglass, photographed here in about 1855, spent his life working for freedom and improved opportunities for blacks after his own escape to freedom as a young man in 1838.

A cotton "boom" started in 1849 when output reached 2.85 million bales and continued until 1860, when production peaked at 4.8 million bales. In the period from 1817 to 1860, cotton production jumped over tenfold. This rapid growth was stimulated by world demand, especially from English textile mills. The availability of new lands, a self-reproducing supply of cheap slave labor, and low-cost steamboat transportation down the Mississippi River to New Orleans helped to keep cotton king.

White and Black Migrations

Southerners migrated southwestward in huge numbers between 1830 and 1860 to grow more and more cotton. Seeking profits from the worldwide demand for cotton, they pushed the southeastern Indians and the Mexicans in Texas out of the way and were still moving into Texas as the Civil War began. The migration process made many planters rich.

Southern cotton growers, like northern grain farmers, followed parallel migration paths westward. While New Englanders moved into the upper Midwest, southerners migrated from the coastal states westward into the lower Midwest and the Lower South. By the 1830s, the center of cotton

The Varied Economic Life in the South

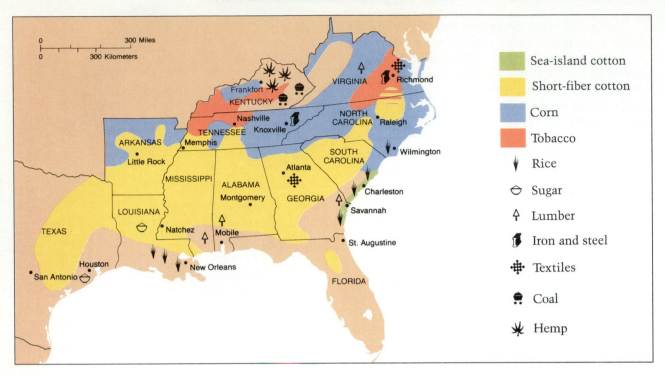

production had shifted from South Carolina and Georgia to Alabama and Mississippi. This process continued in the 1850s as southerners forged into Arkansas, Louisiana, and eastern Texas. As they moved, they carried their values and institutions, including slavery, with them. Usually, a father and his sons would go west first, find land and clear it, plant some corn, and begin to raise a cabin. Leaving the sons to finish, the father would return east, where his wife and daughters had been managing the farm, pack up the household, and bring it to the new home. Thus in November 1835, one extended family of nearly 50 persons left South Carolina for Alabama. "We bade adieu to friends," a daughter wrote, "and left the old homestead never to look upon it again."

Not only were these migrating southern families attracted by the pull of fresh land and cheap labor, but they were also pushed westward by worsening economic conditions and other pressures in the older Atlantic states. Beginning in the 1820s, the states of the Upper South underwent a long depression affecting tobacco and cotton prices. Moreover, years of constant use had exhausted their lands, and families with numerous children struggled to give each child an inheritance or financial

help to start a family or a career. In a society that valued land ownership, farm families had several choices. One was to move west. Another was to stay and diversify. Therefore, the older states of the Upper South continued to shift to grains, mainly corn and wheat. Because these crops required less labor than tobacco, slave owners, especially those with pressing debts, began to sell some of their slaves.

The internal slave trade from Virginia "down the river" to the Old Southwest thus became a multimillion-dollar "industry" in the 1830s. Between 1830 and 1860, an estimated 300,000 Virginia slaves were transported south for sale. One of the busiest routes was from Alexandria, Virginia, almost within view of the nation's capital, to a huge depot near Natchez, Mississippi. Although most southern states attempted occasionally to outlaw or control the traffic in slaves, these efforts were poorly enforced and usually short-lived. Besides, the reason for outlawing the slave trade was generally not humanitarian but rather originated in a fear of a rapid increase in the slave population, especially of "wicked" slaves sent south because they were considered unmanageable. Alabama, Mississippi, and Louisiana all banned the importation of slaves after the Nat Turner revolt in Virginia in 1831 (described later in

Southern Cotton Production, 1821–1859

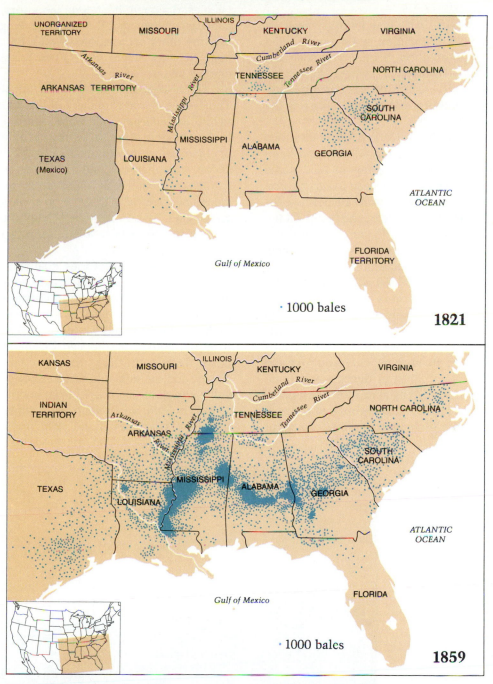

this chapter). But all three states permitted the slave trade again during the profitable 1850s.

Congress formally ended the external slave trade on January 1, 1808, the earliest time permitted by the Constitution. The British Navy, however, was primarily responsible for stopping this traffic in slaves from Africa and the West Indies. Enforcement by the United States was weak, and many thousands of blacks continued to be smuggled to North America until the end of the Civil War. The tremendous increase in the slave population was the result not of this illegal trade but of natural reproduction, often encouraged by slave owners eager for more laborers and salable human property.

The Dependence on Slavery

The rapid increase in the number of slaves, from 1.5 million in 1820 to 4 million in 1860, paralleled the growth of the southern economy and its dependence on the slave labor system. Economic growth and migration southwestward changed the geographic distribution of slaves, thus hindering the cause of abolition.

Although most slaves worked on plantations and medium-size farms, they could be found in all segments of the southern economy. In 1850, some 75 percent of all slaves were engaged in agricultural labor: 55 percent growing cotton, 10 percent tobacco, and 10 percent rice, sugar, and hemp. Of the remaining one-fourth, about 15 percent were domestic servants, and the remainder were in mining, lumbering, construction, and industry.

The 300,000 slaves in 1850 who were not domestics or agricultural laborers worked as lumberjacks and turpentine producers in Carolina and Georgia forests; gold, coal, and salt miners in Virginia and Kentucky; boiler stokers and deckhands on Mississippi River steamships; toilers on road and railroad construction gangs in Georgia and Louisiana; textile laborers in Alabama cotton mills; dockworkers in Savannah and Charleston; and tobacco and iron workers in Richmond factories. A visitor to Natchez in 1835 observed slaves working as "mechanics, draymen, hostelers, labourers, hucksters, and washwomen, and the heterogeneous multitude of every other occupation, who fill the streets of a busy city—for slaves are trained to every kind of manual labour."

Slaves were also used in the industrial sector. The Tredegar Iron Company of Richmond decided in 1847 to shift from white labor "almost exclusively" to slave labor in order to destroy the potential power of organized white workers to strike. Tredegar's decision, though local, had enormous future implications. Although black and white workers have sometimes been able to agree on class issues, racial animosities based on white perceptions of threats to their job security by black workers continue to this day.

Whether in iron factories, coal mines, or cotton fields, slavery was profitable as a source of labor and as a capital investment. In 1859, the average plantation slave produced $78 in cotton earnings for his master annually while costing only about $32 to be fed, clothed, and housed. Despite maintenance costs, debts from the purchase of land and more slaves, and the unstable price of cotton, the "crop value per slave" increased from about $15 in 1800 to $125 in 1860. Slaves were also a good investment. In 1844, a "prime field hand" sold for $600. A cotton

Slaves were found in nearly every kind of labor in the South. These Virginia dockworkers were photographed about 1860 in Alexandria, Virginia, by Mathew Brady.

Concentration of Slavery, 1820–1860

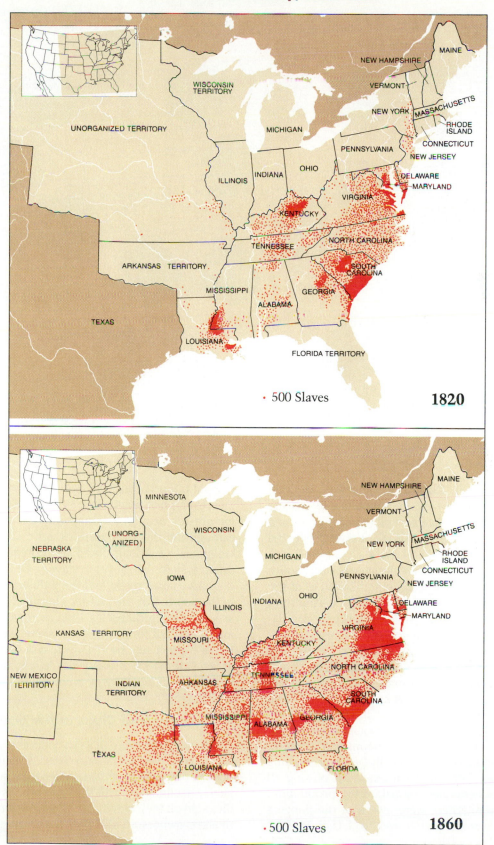

• 500 Slaves

1820

• 500 Slaves

1860

Population Patterns in the South: Whites, Slaves, and Free Blacks, by State, 1860

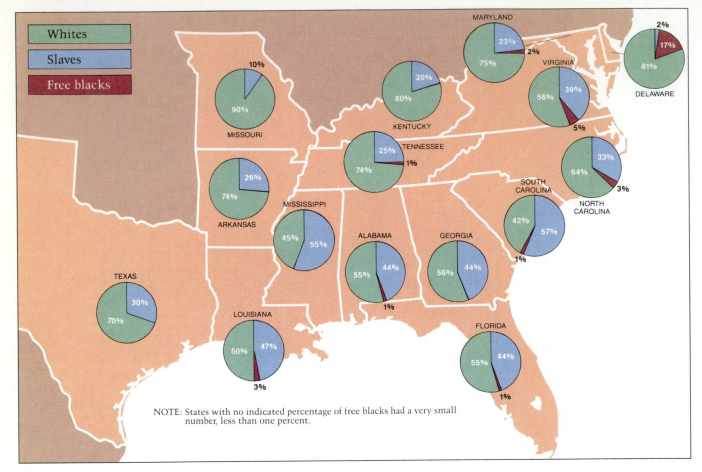

Whites

Slaves

Free blacks

MARYLAND
23%
75%
2%

VIRGINIA
56% 39%
5%

DELAWARE
2%
17%
81%

MISSOURI
10%
90%

KENTUCKY
20%
80%

TENNESSEE
25%
74%
1%

NORTH CAROLINA
33%
64%
3%

ARKANSAS
26%
74%

MISSISSIPPI
45% 55%

SOUTH CAROLINA
42% 57%
1%

ALABAMA
55% 44%
1%

GEORGIA
56% 44%

TEXAS
30%
70%

LOUISIANA
50% 47%
3%

FLORIDA
55% 44%
1%

NOTE: States with no indicated percentage of free blacks had a very small number, less than one percent.

boom beginning in 1849 raised this price by 1860 to $1,800. A slave owner could prosper by buying slaves, working them for several years, then selling them for a profit. The rising price of slaves reflected the optimism of the planter class.

The economic growth of the slaveholding South was impressive, but it was limited because of the dependence on slavery. Generally, agricultural growth leads to the rise of cities and industry, facilitating sustained economic growth. In the planter-dominated antebellum South, however, agricultural improvements did not lead to industrialization and urbanization. In 1860, the South had 35 percent of the country's population and only 15 percent of its manufacturing establishments. On the eve of the Civil War, one southerner in 14 was a city dweller, compared to one of every three people in the North. The South would be economically backward as long as the whites with capital insisted on putting all their business energies toward cotton production.

Some southerners were aware of the dangers of following a single path to wealth. J. D. B. De Bow

created a journal in 1846 dedicated to trade, commerce, and manufacturing. *De Bow's Review* called for greater economic independence in the South through the diversification of agriculture, the development of industry, and an improved transportation system. A believer in slavery, De Bow thought that slave labor could fuel the industrial revolution in the South. But the planter class had little enthusiasm for such plans. As long as money could be made through an agricultural slave system, plantation owners saw no reason to risk capital in new areas. One effect of this attitude was to block the economic opportunity of other white southerners.

Slavery and Class in the South

Slavery was more than an economic institution, for it also served social purposes. Although the proportion of southern white families that owned slaves slowly declined from 40 to 25 percent as some families sold off their slaves to cotton planters, the ideal of slave ownership still permeated all classes and determined the hierarchical character of the southern social structure. At the top stood the planter aristocracy, much of it new wealth, elbowing its way among the old established families like the Byrds and Carters of Virginia. Some 10,000 rich families owned 50 or more slaves in 1860; about 3,000 of these owned over 100. Below them was a slightly larger group of small planters who held from 10 to 50 slaves. But the largest group, 70 percent of all slaveholders in 1860, comprised 270,000 middle-level farm families with fewer than ten slaves. The typical slaveholder worked a small family farm of about 100 acres with eight or nine slaves, perhaps members of the same family. The typical slave, however, was more likely to be in a group of 20 or more other slaves on a large farm or small plantation.

In 1841, a young, white North Carolinian, John Flintoff, went to Mississippi to fulfill his dream of wealth and prestige. Beginning as an overseer managing an uncle's farm, he bought "a negro boy 7 years old" even before he owned any land. After several years of unrewarding struggle, Flintoff married and returned to North Carolina. There he finally bought 124 acres and a few more cheap, young blacks, and by 1860 he had a modest farm with several slaves growing corn, wheat, and tobacco. Although he never became as prosperous as he had dreamed, his son went to college, and his wife, he reported proudly, "has lived a *Lady*."

Slavery was a powerful force in the lives of middle-level farmers like John Flintoff, who had only a few slaves, and even for those who owned none. Upward economic mobility, social prestige, and political influence were determined by ownership of slaves. Many whites like John Flintoff hoped to purchase one slave, perhaps a female who would bear children, and then climb the economic and social ladder of southern society. White southerners therefore supported slavery whether they owned slaves or not.

They also defended the institution because it gave them a sense of superiority over at least one group and a sense of kinship, if not quite equality, with other whites. Although there was always a small element of southern society that believed in emancipation, most southerners did not. A small Alabama farmer told a northern visitor in the 1850s that if the slaves were given their freedom, "they'd all think themselves just as good as we. . . . How would you like to hev a nigger feelin' just as good as a white man." Another said that he wished "there warn't no niggers here" and did not know anybody who favored freeing them.

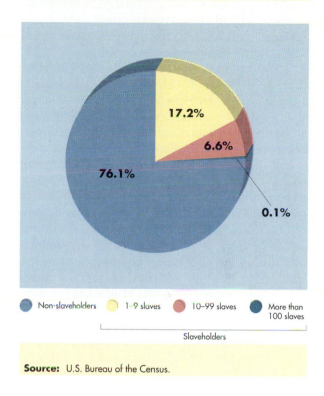

White Class Structure in the South, 1860

17.2%
6.6%
76.1%
0.1%

Non-slaveholders   1–9 slaves   10–99 slaves   More than 100 slaves

Slaveholders

Source: U.S. Bureau of the Census.

The Nonslaveholding South

Below Flintoff and other middling farmers lived the majority of white southerners, who owned no slaves but were equally, or even more, antiblack. Newton Knight, for example, worked a harsh piece of land cut out of the pines of southern Mississippi. He and his wife lived in a crude log cabin, scratching out their livelihood by growing corn and sweet potatoes and raising chickens and hogs. A staunch Baptist given to fits of violence, Knight had once killed a black.

The 75 percent of southern whites who, like Newton Knight and his family, owned no slaves were scattered throughout the South. Many were Scots-Irish. Most lived in the foothills of the mountains and worked generally poorer land than the large planters. They did not need to be near commercial centers because they were largely self-sufficient. Working together as a family, they raised mostly corn and wheat, hogs, enough cotton for their own clothes and a little cash, and subsistence vegetable crops. These farmers maintained a household economy, making soap, shoes, candles, whiskey, coarse textiles, and ax handles and trading hogs, eggs, small game, or home-made items for cash and other goods. They lived in two-room log houses separated by a "dog run." Cooperation with neighbors brightened the yeoman farmer's drab and isolated life. Families gathered at corn huskings and quilting parties, logrolling and wrestling matches, and political stump and revivalist camp meetings.

In many ways the yeoman farmers were the solid backbone of the South. In 1860 in North Carolina, 70 percent of the farmers held less than 100 acres, while in Mississippi and Louisiana, reputedly large plantation states, more than 60 percent of the farms were under 100 acres. Fiercely proud of their independence, the yeoman farmers had a share of political power, voting overwhelmingly for Andrew Jackson. Although some resented the tradition of political deference to "betters," these farmers were not yet ready to challenge planters for political power. Yeoman farmers fought with the Confederacy during the Civil War; but some, like Newton Knight, refused to fight against the Union and ended up organizing a guerrilla band of Unionists in southern Mississippi.

Another little-known group of southern whites were the herdsmen who raised hogs and other livestock. Living among the plantations and small farms, they supplied bacon and pork to local slaveholders (who often thought hog growing was beneath their dignity) and drove herds of hogs to stockyards in Nashville, Louisville, and Savannah. The South raised two-thirds of the nation's hogs. In 1860, the value of southern livestock was $500 million, twice that of cotton. Although much of the corn crop fed the hogs, many herdsmen preferred to let their stock roam loose in the woods. As one South Carolinian explained, "We raise our hogs by allowing them to range in our woods, where they get fat . . . on acorns," which he and others considered a better diet for bacon and pork than corn. However valuable the total size of the hog business, individual hog herdsmen did not stand very high on the southern social ladder.

Below them were the poor whites of the South, about 10 percent of the population. Often sneeringly called "hillbillies," "dirt eaters," "crackers," or "poor white trash," they lived in isolated, inhospitable areas of the South where they eked out a living from the poor soil of pine barrens, sand hills, and marshes. Although they grew a little corn and vegetables, their livelihood came mostly from fishing, hunting small game, and raising a few pigs. Some made corn whiskey, and many hired themselves out as farmhands for an average wage, with board, of about $14 per month. Because of poor diet and bad living conditions, these poor whites often suffered from diseases such as hookworm and malaria. This, and the natural debilitation of heat and poverty, led to their reputation as lazy, shiftless, and illiterate. An English visitor, Fanny Kemble, described them as "the most degraded race of human beings claiming an Anglo-Saxon origin that can be found on the face of the earth."

The poor whites were kept poor in part because the slave system allowed the planter class to accumulate a disproportionate amount of land and political power. High slave prices made entry into the planter class increasingly difficult, thus increasing class tensions within the South. Because the larger planters dominated southern life and owned the most slaves, an understanding of the character of slavery and the relationships between masters and slaves is best accomplished by looking at plantation life during a typical day from morning to night.

MORNING: MASTER IN THE BIG HOUSE

It is early morning on the southern plantation. Imagine four scenes. In the first, William Waller of Virginia and a neighbor are preparing to leave with 20 choice slaves on a long trip to the slave market in Natchez, Mississippi. Waller is making this "intolerable" journey, as he calls it, to sell some of his

Southern yeoman farm families lived self-sufficient lives of relative isolation. Gatherings such as this quilting party provided welcome social contact as well as the means to create a uniquely female American work of useful art.

slaves in order to ease his heavy debts. Although he "loaths the vocation of slave trading," he must recover some money out of a "sense of duty" to see his family "freed from my bondage" of indebtedness. To ease his conscience, he intends to supervise the sale personally, thus securing the best possible deal not only for himself but also for his departing slaves.

On another plantation, owned by James Hammond of South Carolina, the horn blows an hour before daylight to awaken the slaves for work in the fields. Hammond rises soon after, ever aware that "to continue" as a wealthy master, he must "draw the reign tighter and tighter" to hold his slaves "in complete check." He is as good as his word, recommending that "in general 15 to 20 lashes will be sufficient flogging" for most offenses but that "in extreme cases" the punishment "must not exceed 100 lashes in one day."

On an Alabama plantation, Hugh Lawson is up early, writing a sorrowful letter to Susanna Clay, telling her of the death of a "devotedly attached and faithful" slave, Jim. "I feel desolate," Hugh writes, "my most devoted friend is gone and *his place* can never be supplied by another." As Lawson pens his letter, a female slave has already awakened and "walked across a frosty field in the early morning and gone to the big house to build a fire" for her mistress. As the mistress wakes up to a warming house, she says to the slave, a grown woman responsible for the welfare of two families, "Well, how's my little nigger today?"

In a fourth household, this one a medium-size farm in upcountry Georgia, not far from Hammond's huge plantation, Charles Brock wakes up at dawn and joins his two sons and four slaves to work his modest acreage of grains and sweet potatoes, while Brock's wife and a female slave tend the cows that provide milk and butter. On small and medium-size family farms with five or fewer slaves, blacks and whites commonly worked together, as one observer noted, with "the axe of master and man [slave] falling with alternate strokes . . . [and] ploughing side by side."

As these scenes suggest, slavery thoroughly permeated the lives of southern whites. For the slaves, morning was a time for getting up and going to work. But for southern whites, morning involved contact with slaves in many ways: as burdens of figuring profit and loss, as objects to be kept obedient and orderly, as intimates and fellow workers, and as ever-present reminders of fear, hate, and uncertainty.

The Burdens of Slaveholding

Robert Francis Withers Allston (1801–1864) was a major rice planter in the Georgetown district of South Carolina, a low, swampy, mosquito-infested tidal area where four rivers empty into Winyah Bay. It was a perfect spot for growing rice, but so unhealthy that few whites wanted to live there. The death rate among slaves was appallingly high. In 1840, a total of 18,274 slaves toiled in the Georgetown district, but only 2,193 whites, many for only part of the year. Robert was the fifth generation of Allstons to live in this inhospitable land. By 1860, he owned seven plantations along the Peedee River, totaling some 4,000 acres, in addition to another 9,500 acres of pasture and timberland. He held nearly 600 slaves, 236 of whom worked at the home plantation, Chicora Wood. The total value of his land and slaves in the 1850s was approximately $300,000. Rich in land and labor, he nevertheless had large mortgages and outstanding debts.

Allston was an enlightened, talented, public-spirited man. Educated at West Point but also trained in the law, he did far more than practice agriculture. He served in the South Carolina state senate for 24 years and as governor from 1856 to 1858. His political creed, he wrote in 1838, was one of "virtue and purity" based on "the principles of Thomas Jefferson." The core of his conviction was "a plain, honest, commonsense reading of the Constitution," which for Allston clearly meant the constitutionality of slavery and nullification and the illegitimacy of abolitionism and the United States Bank.

Allston also reflected Jefferson's humane side. He was an ardent reformer, advocating liberalization of South Carolina's poor laws; an improved system of public education open to rich and poor alike; humanitarian care of the deaf, blind, insane, and other disabled persons; and the improvement of conditions on the reservations of the Catawba Indians. He was active in the Episcopal church and gave money generously to support ministerial students.

In 1832, Allston married Adele Petigru, an equally enlightened and hardworking person. She participated fully in the management of the plantation and ran it while Robert was away on politics. In a letter to her husband, written in 1850, Adele demonstrated her diverse interests by reporting on family affairs and the children's learning, sickness among the slaves, the status of spring plowing, the building of a canal and causeway, her supervision of the bottling of some wine, and current politics. After Robert's death during the Civil War, she assumed control of the Allston plantations, which had been abandoned when Union troops moved through the area. Eventually, she had to sell most of the estate at auction, holding on only to Chicora Wood, which she managed with a daughter until her death in 1896.

State politics lured Robert from his land for part of each year, but he was by no means an absentee owner. Except when away to escape the worst periods of mosquitoes and heat, the Allstons were fully engaged in the operation of their plantations. Managing thousands of acres of rice required not only an enormous investment in labor and equipment but also careful supervision of both the slaves and an elaborate irrigation system. Although Robert Allston's acreage and slave population were larger than those of most big planters and he grew rice rather than cotton, his concerns were typical.

Allston's letters frequently expressed the serious burdens of owning slaves. Although he was careful to distribute enough cloth, blankets, and shoes to his slaves and to give them sufficient rest, the sickness and death of slaves, especially young fieldworkers, headed his list of concerns. "I lost in one year 28 negroes," Allston complained, "22 of whom were task hands." He tried to keep slave families together but sold slaves when necessary. In a letter to his son Benjamin, he expressed concern over the bad example set by a slave driver who was "abandon'd by his hands" because he had not worked with them the previous Sunday. In the same letter Allston urged Benjamin to keep up the "patrol duty," less to guard against runaway slaves, he said, than to restrain the excesses of "vagabond whites." Clearly, the planter class felt a duty to control lower-class whites as well as black slaves.

Other planters shared Allston's concerns, seeing slavery as both a duty and a burden. A Louisiana planter, in financial difficulty, wrote how much he dreaded "the miserable occupation of seeing to negroes, and attending to their wants and sickness and to making them do their duty—and after all have no prospect of being paid for my trouble." Many planters insisted that they worked harder than their slaves to feed and clothe them and to make their lives "as comfortable as possible." Some accepted this as part of their responsibility, while others complained loudly. R. L. Dabney of Virginia exclaimed that "there could be no greater curse inflicted on us than to be compelled to manage a parcel of Negroes." Curse or not, Dabney and other planters profited from their burdens, a point they seldom admitted.

Their wives experienced other kinds of burdens. "The mistress of a plantation," wrote Susan Dabney Smedes, "was the most complete slave on it." Southern women were expected to adhere to the cult of domesticity both by improving their husbands' morals, which often meant restraining them from excessive cruelty toward slaves, and by beautifying their parlors. Moreover, plantation mistresses suffered under a double standard of morality. They were expected to act as chaste ladies, while their husbands had virtually unrestricted sexual access to slave women. "God forgive us, but ours is a monstrous system," Mary Boykin Chesnut wrote in her diary. "Like the patriarchs of old, our men live all in one house with their wives and their concubines; and the mulattoes one sees in every

Robert F. W. Allston married Adele Petigru in 1832. They shared the work of managing the rice plantation; after Robert's death in the Civil War, his widow continued to run the plantations in the face of the freedmen's resistance.

Agreement to Purchase Slaves, January 25, 1859

Agreed to purchase from Dr. Forster Forty one Negroes of Mrs. Withers of the "remainder" from the Estate of the late Francis Withers, to be deliver'd in all this week at $500. Titles to Ben Allston his Bond and mine payable in 8, 10, 12 yrs. secured by mortgage of the property, viz

$1000	1	Andrew	38	yrs.		$1000	19	Paris	35	
						800	20	Hannah	33	
800	2	Serena	36			800	21	Frank	16½	
400	3	Jos.	10			500	22	William	14	
300	4	Judy	8			350	23	Caty	9	
200	5	Henry	5			300	24	Michael	6	
						150	25	Eleanor	3½	
1000	6	Jack	30			50	26	Dandy	1	
800	7	Patience	27	pregnant						
400	8	Daniel	11			800	27	Strophon	50	
300	9	Prince	9			700	28	Lucy	18	
250	10	Phyllis	5			500	29	Judy	14	
200	11	Bess	3½							
						1000	30	Toney	38	an indifferent carpenter
800	12	James*	28	carpenter, Drinks, delicate						
						800	31	Betty	35	
800	13	Hagar	24	pregnant, near time of delivery		800	32	Daniel	16½	3 years with Bricklayers to mix mortar
1200	14	Joe	39	carpenter and cooper		200	33	Francis	4½	
						100	34	Caesar	1½	
800	15	Levi	50							
500	16	Betsey†	40	delicate		500	35	O Sary	50	cook and washer
400	17	Murria‡	18			1000	36	Israel	31	
400	18	Toby	14			800	37	Esther	28	
						100	38	William	1½	
						800	39	Dinah	18½	
						500	40	Quash	14½	
						300	41	William	9	

* Has Epileptic attacks produced by drink, would be valuable if kept from drink.
† With this family there is the incumbrance of an old man of 80 years, father of Betsey.
‡ Murria is half witted.
Notes: Prices are from a second list, as are some of the remarks concerning individuals. The horizontal lines probably separate family groups.
Source: This and other material on the Allstons is from *The South Carolina Rice Plantation As Revealed in the Papers of Robert F. W. Allston,* ed. J. H. Easterby (1945).

family partly resemble the white children. Any lady is ready to tell you who is the father of all the mulatto children in everybody's household but her own. Those, she seems to think, drop from the clouds."

Chesnut called the sexual dynamics of slavery "the sorest spot." There were others. Together with female slaves, plantation mistresses had to tend to the food, clothing, health, and welfare of not just their husbands and children but the plantation slave population as well. Adele Allston, we saw, added plantation management to these duties. The son of a Tennessee slaveholder remembered his mother and grandmother as "the busiest women I ever saw." One woman, who spent the night sitting up to attend a slave birth, complained to a northern visitor: "It is the slaves who own me. Morning, noon, and night, I'm obliged to look after them, to doctor them, and attend to them in every way." The plantation mistress, then, served many roles: as a potential humanizing influence on men; as a tough, resourceful, responsible manager of numerous plantation affairs; as a coercer of slaves and perpetuator of the system; and sometimes as a victim herself.

Justifying Slavery

The behavior of Douglass's mistress, Sophia Auld, suggests another way in which slavery victimized southern women. Whether they acted humanely or not, slavery burdened slaveholders. Increasingly attacked as immoral, they felt compelled to justify their institution. Until the 1830s, their defense explained slavery as a "necessary evil." After the abolitionists stepped up their attack in that decade, however, the justification shifted to defending slavery, in John C. Calhoun's words, as "a positive good." Various arguments were used: biblical, historical, constitutional, scientific, and sociological.

The biblical justification was based in part on the curse of Canaan, the son of Ham, who was condemned to eternal servitude because his father had looked on Noah's nakedness. Furthermore, in various places both the Old and New Testaments admonished servants to obey their masters and accept their earthly lot. Southern apologists also cited historical arguments. Slavery had existed throughout history. In fact, the greatest civilizations—Egypt, Greece, and Rome—had all built their strength and grandeur in part on slave labor. No less a figure than Aristotle taught that in society men of superior talents would become masters over those who were inferior.

A third argument justified slavery on legal grounds. Southerners pointed out that the United States Constitution did not forbid slavery. In fact, although slavery was not mentioned specifically, three passages in the original document clearly implied its constitutionality. First, slaves, called "all other Persons," were counted as three-fifths of a person for purposes of representation. Second, the overseas slave trade was protected from congressional abolition for 20 years. Third, the Constitution mandated the return of runaway slaves from one state to another.

A fourth justification was scientific. Until the 1830s, most white southerners believed that blacks were degraded not by nature but by environment. The retarded mental and moral development of Africans, the argument went, derived from the special conditions and circumstances of African climate

and American slavery. But with the "positive good" defense in the 1830s, southern ethnologists increasingly argued that blacks had been created separately (a theory called "polygenesis") and were an inherently inferior race. Through a study of cranial shapes and sizes, called "niggerology" by one doctor, southern scientists maintained that in the black "the animal parts of the brain preponderate over the moral and intellectual, which explains why he is deficient in reason, judgement and forecast." Therefore, the destiny of the inferior Africans was to serve the superior Caucasians (the "Adamic race") in work. At best, the patriarchal slave system would domesticate uncivilized blacks. As Allston put it, "The educated master is the negro's best friend upon earth."

Allston's point suggested a paternalistic sociological defense of slavery. George Fitzhugh, a leading advocate of this view, argued that "the Negro is but a grown child and must be governed as a child." Therefore, he needed the paternal guidance, restraint, and protection of his white masters. What would happen, apologists asked, if the slaves were freed? Many southerners believed that chaos would ensue. Allston wrote that emancipation "cannot be contemplated," for it would lead to "giving up our beautiful country to the ravages of the black race and amalgamation with savages." Fitzhugh was a little less direct. He compared the treatment of southern slaves favorably to that of free blacks and of free laborers working in northern factories. These "wage slaves," he argued, worked as hard as slaves, yet with their paltry wages they had to feed, clothe, and shelter themselves. Southern masters took care of all these necessities. Emancipation, therefore, would be heartless and unthinkable, a burden to both blacks and whites.

Southern apologists for slavery faced the difficult intellectual task of justifying a system that ran counter to the main ideological directions of nineteenth-century American society: the expansion of individual liberty, mobility, economic opportunity, and democratic political participation. Moreover, the southern defense of slavery had to take into account the 75 percent of white families who owned no slaves and who envied those who did. Because of the potential for class antagonisms among whites, wealthy planters developed a justification of slavery that deflected class differences by maintaining that all whites were superior to all blacks but equal to one another. The theory of democratic equality among whites, therefore, was made consistent with racism and the holding of slaves.

However couched in the language of science, law, history, or religion, the underlying motive of these various justifications, though rarely admitted, was that slavery was profitable. As the southern defense of slavery intensified in the 1840s and 1850s, it aroused greater opposition from northerners and from slaves themselves. Although slavery was cruel in many ways, perhaps its worst feature was not physical but psychological: to be enslaved at all and barred from economic advancement in a nation that put a high value on freedom and equality of opportunity. "One of the grossest frauds committed upon the down-trodden slave," Douglass wrote, was to encourage drunkenness during holidays so that slaves would be disgusted with freedom and would look forward to marching back to the field.

NOON: SLAVES IN HOUSE AND FIELDS

It is 2 o'clock on a hot July afternoon on the plantation. The midday lunch break is over, and the slaves are returning to their work in the fields. Lunch was the usual fare of cornmeal and pork. The slaves return to work slowly and listlessly, not because of innate laziness but because of a lack of stamina resulting from deficient diet and the suffocating heat and humidity. Douglass remembered that "we worked all weathers. . . . It was never too hot, or too cold" for toiling in the fields. Mary Reynolds of Louisiana recalled that she hated most having to pick cotton "when the frost was on the bolls," which made her hands "git sore and crack open and bleed."

Daily Toil

The daily work schedule for most slaves, whether in the fields or the Big House, was long and demanding. Aroused by a bell or horn before daybreak, they worked on an average day 14 hours in the summer and 10 hours in the winter. During harvest time, it was not uncommon to work for 18 hours. Depending on the size of the work force and the crop, the slaves were organized either in gangs or according to tasks. The gangs, usually of 20 to 25, worked their way along the cotton rows under the watchful eye and quick whip of a driver. Ben Simpson, a Georgia slave, remembered vividly how his master would use a "great, long whip platted out

of rawhide" to hit a slave in the gang who would "fall behind or give out."

Under the task system, each slave had a specific task to complete daily. This system gave slaves the incentive to work hard enough to finish early, but it meant that the quality of their work was scrutinized constantly. An overseer's weekly report to Robert Allston in 1860 noted that he had "flogged for hoeing corn bad Fanny 12 lashes, Sylvia 12, Monday 12, Phoebee 12, Susanna 12, Salina 12, Celia 12, Iris 12." The black slave driver, George Skipwith, was no less rigorous in his expectations of work from fellow slaves. In 1847, he reported to his master that several slaves working under him "at a reasonable days work" should have plowed 7 acres apiece but had only done 1½. Therefore, George proudly reported, "I gave them ten licks a peace upon their skins [and] I gave Julyann eight or ten licks for misplacing her hoe."

An average slave was expected to pick 130 to 150 pounds of cotton per day. The work on sugar and rice plantations was even harder. Sugar demanded constant cultivation and the digging of drainage ditches in snake-infested fields. At harvest time, cutting, stripping, and carrying the cane to the sugar house for boiling was exhausting. In addition, huge quantities of firewood had to be cut and carried. Working in the low-country rice fields was worse: slaves spent long hours standing in water up to their knees.

House slaves, most of them women, had relatively easier assignments than the field slaves, though they were usually called on to help with the harvest. Their usual work was in or near the Big House as housemaids, cooks, seamstresses, laundresses, coachmen, drivers, gardeners, and mammies. Slaves did most of the artisanal work on the plantation; many became skilled carpenters, blacksmiths, stonemasons, weavers, mechanics, and millers. More intimacy between whites and blacks occurred near the house. House slaves ate and dressed better than their fellow slaves in the fields.

But there were also disadvantages. House slaves were watched more closely, were on call at all hours of the day and night, and were more often involved in personality conflicts in the white household. As one house servant put it, "We were constantly exposed to the whims and passions of every member of the family." This meant everything from assignment to petty jobs to insults, spontaneous angry whippings, and sexual assault. The most feared punishment for a house slave, however, other than sale to the Deep South, was to be sent to the fields.

Slave Health

Although slave owners had an interest in keeping their slaves healthy by providing adequate care, slaves led sickly lives. Home was a crude, one-room log cabin with a dirt floor; some such houses were well made, but most were full of cracks and holes. Pesky mosquitoes came in at night, making sleep difficult in the summer months. Most cabins had a fireplace for heat and cooking. Typical furnishings included a table, some stools or boxes to sit on, an iron pot and wooden dishes, and perhaps a bed. Some slaves slept on the ground on mattresses of corn shucks, using burlap bags for blankets. The cabins were crowded, with usually more than one family living in each. Slave clothing was shabby and uncomfortable. Usually, each man was issued two cotton shirts and two pairs of cotton or woolen pants each fall and spring and a pair of stout shoes once a year. Women were given cotton and woolen cloth twice a year with which to make their own and their children's clothes.

Studies on the adequacy of slave diet disagree, some showing that the food most slaves ate was deficient in calories and vitamins, others claiming that the energy value of the slave diet exceeded that of free whites in the general population. Compared to Latin American slavery, where the ratio of male slaves to white residents was much higher than in the United States, American slaves were well fed. Once a week, each slave was issued an average ration of a peck of cornmeal, 3 to 4 pounds of salt pork or bacon, some molasses, and perhaps some sweet potatoes. The main regimen, however, was "corn, at every meal, from day to day, and week to week." This bland fare was supplemented for some slaves, with the master's permission, by vegetables grown in a small garden and by fishing or hunting small game.

Most slaves, however, rarely enjoyed fresh meat, dairy products, fruits, or vegetables. To make up for these deficiencies, they sometimes stole from the master's kitchen, gardens, and barnyard. Such offenses were frequent, and just as frequently punished. A Louisiana planter told a neighbor, "I beg to regrets that two of my men have been found guilty of killing one of your calves," and another complained of many acts of theft committed by "famished negroes." Inadequate diet, moreover, led some slaves to become dirt eaters, which gave them worms and "swollen shiny skin, puffy eyelids, pale palms and soles." Others suffered regularly from skin disorders, cracked lips, and sore eyes. Many slaves, like poor whites, came down with vitamin deficiency diseases such as rickets, pellagra, beriberi, scurvy, and even mental illness.

Women slaves especially suffered weaknesses caused by vitamin deficiency, hard work, and disease, as well as those associated with the menstrual cycle and childbirth. Women were expected to do the same tasks in the fields as the men, in addition to cooking, sewing, child care, and traditional female jobs in the quarters when the fieldwork was finished. "Pregnant women," the usual rule stated, "should not plough or lift but must be kept at moderate work until the last hour" and were given a three-week recovery period after giving birth. But these guidelines were more often violated than honored. Infant mortality of slave children under 5 years of age was twice as high as for white children.

Life expectancy for American slaves was longer than for those in Latin America and the Caribbean,

Slaves survived nobly despite hard work, ill health, a deficient diet, and poor living conditions. Female slaves had a double burden of work and caring for their families but managed to develop networks of support.

but not very high for either blacks or whites in the antebellum South (21.4 for blacks and 25.5 for whites in 1850). In part because of poor diet and climate, slaves were highly susceptible to epidemic diseases. Despite some resistance as a result of the sickle-cell trait, many slaves still contracted and died from malaria, yellow fever, cholera, and other diseases caused by mosquitoes or bad water, especially in the dangerous low-lying rice fields of the Georgia coast and the sugar fields of Louisiana. Slaves everywhere suffered and died from intestinal ailments in the summer and respiratory diseases in the winter. An average of 20 percent (and sometimes 50 to 60 percent) of the slaves on a given plantation would be sick at one time, and no overseer's report was complete without an account of sickness and the number of days of lost labor.

The relatively frequent incidence of whippings and other physical punishments aggravated the poor physical condition of the slaves. Many slaveholders offered rewards—a garden plot, an extra holiday, hiring oneself out, or passes—as inducements for faithful labor. For punishments they would withhold these privileges rather than resort to the lash. But southern court records, newspapers, plantation diaries, and slave memoirs reveal that sadistic slave punishments were frequent and harsh.

The slave William Wells Brown reported that on his plantation the whip was used "very frequently and freely" for inadequate or uncompleted work, stealing, running away, and even insolence and lying. Whippings ranged from 10 to 100 strokes of the lash, occasionally even more. Former slaves described a good owner as one who did not "whip too much" and a bad owner as one who "whipped till he'd bloodied you and blistered you." Slaveholders had many theories on the appropriate kind of lash to inflict sufficient pain and punishment without damaging a valuable laborer. Other forms of punishment included isolation and confinement in stocks and jails during leisure hours, chains, muzzling, salting lash wounds, branding, burning, and castration.

Nothing testifies better to the physical brutality of slavery than the advertisements for runaways that slaveholders printed in antebellum newspapers. In searching for the best way to describe the physical characteristics of a missing slave, slave owners unwittingly condemned their own behavior. One Mississippi slave had "large raised scars . . . in the small of his back and on his abdomen nearly as large as a person's finger." Another, a Georgia female, was "considerably marked by the whip." Still

An Overseer's Report

W. Sweet to Adele Petigru Allston

N[ightin]gale hall, 14th September, 1864.

DEAR MADAM I comence my harvest on last saterday on Boath Plantations the weather is very fin for harvest so far I will Bring some Rice in to the Barn yard at N[ightin]gale hall to Day and at ganderloss to morrow. I think that I will make about 2 Barrels of Syrrup on Each Place I finish grinding at ganderloss to Day I will not finish at Nightingale hall until the last of next weeak. litle Dianah was confined with a boy child on the 9 I am very sorry to say to you that one of Prisilia children a boy name July Dide on 12th with fits a[nd] fever I have had a grea[t] deal of fever among the children But not much among the grone negroes. old Rose is Stil quite sick mr Belflowers sent toney to mee on friday last I have concluded to let toney wife stay whare she is for a while as I understand that she is Pregnant and will not Be much survice in the harvest if I am Rong for soe Doing Pleas let mee know. the negroes all sends thare love to you an family my self and family is very un well.

N[ightin]gale hall

8th September	all hands hoing Bancks and grinding shugar cain no sick
9th September	all hands hoing Bancks grind shugar cain no sick
10th September	all hands cu[tt]ing Rice grinding shugar cain no sick
12th September	all hands harvesting grinding shugar cain 3 women with sick children
13th September	all hands harvesting grinding shugar cain 3 women with sick children
14th September	all hands harvesting grinding shugar cain 1 woman with sick child

Source: The South Carolina Rice Plantation As Revealed in the Papers of Robert F. W. Allston, ed. J. H. Easterby (1945).

another, who according to his North Carolina master had a "remarkably bad temper," was described by the "marks of the lash upon his back." Slaves who were branded were even easier to identify in these advertisements. One fugitive, Betty, was described as recently "burnt . . . with a hot iron on the left side of her face." "I tried to make the letter M" her master admitted in his diary.

Slave Law and the Family

One can almost imagine Betty's master agonizingly applying his brand. Complicating master-slave relationships was the status of slaves as both persons and property, a legal and psychological ambiguity the South never resolved. On the one hand, the slaves had names, personalities, families, and wills of their own. This required dealing with them as fellow humans. On the other hand, they were items of property, purchased and maintained to perform specific profit-making tasks. As a Kentucky court put the problem in 1836, "Although the law of this state considers slaves as property, . . . it recognizes their personal existence, and, to a qualified extent, their natural right."

This ambiguity led to confusion in the laws governing treatment of slaves. Until the early 1830s, some southern abolitionist activity persisted, primarily in the Upper South. Slaves had slight expectations that they might be freed, if not by state action, then by individual manumission. But along with this ray of hope, they suffered careless and often brutal treatment in matters of food, housing, work load, and punishments. This confusion changed with the threatening convergence in 1831 of Nat Turner's revolt and William Lloyd Garrison's publication of the abolitionist *Liberator*. After 1831, the South tightened up the slave system. Laws prohibiting manumission were passed, and the slaves' expectation of freedom other than by revolt or escape vanished. At the same time, laws protecting them from overly severe treatment were strengthened, and material conditions generally improved.

But whatever the law said, the practice was always more telling. Treatment varied with individual slaveholders and depended on their mood and other circumstances. This was especially true with regard to the slave family. Most planters, like Robert Allston, generally encouraged their slaves to marry and did all they could to keep families intact. They believed that families made black males more docile and less inclined to revolt or run away. But some masters failed to respect slave marriages or broke them up because of financial problems. This tendency was supported by southern courts and legislatures, which did not legally recognize slave marriages or the right to family unity. As a North Carolina supreme court justice said in 1853, "Our law required no solemnity or form in regard to the marriage of slaves."

Adding to the pain of forced breakup of the slave family was the sexual abuse of black women. Although the frequency of such abuse is unknown, the presence of thousands of mulattoes in the antebellum era is testimony to this practice. White men in the South abused black slave women in several ways: by offering gifts for sexual "favors," by threatening those who refused with physical punishment or the sale of a child or loved one, by purchasing concubines, or by rape. As Frederick Douglass put it, the "slave woman is at the mercy of the fathers, sons or brothers of her master."

Because of the need to obtain cheap additional slaves for the work force, slaveholders encouraged young slave women to bear children, whether married or not. If verbal prodding and inducements such as less work and more rations did not work, masters would choose mates and foist them on slave women. Massa Hawkins, for example, selected Rufus to live with 16-year-old Rose Williams, as she recalled many years later. She resisted the attempted liaison with unmistakable clarity: "I puts de feet 'gainst him and give him a shove and out he go on de floor 'fore he knew what I's doin'." When Rufus persisted, Rose took a poker and "lets him have it over de head." Hawkins then threatened Rose with a "whippin' at de stake" or sale away "from my folks." This was too much for her. "What am I's to do? So I 'cides to do as de massa wish and so I yields."

Unlike the case of Rose and Rufus, however, slaves usually chose their own mates on the basis of mutual attraction during an uneasy courtship complicated by the threat of white interferences. As among poor whites, premarital intercourse was frequent, but promiscuous behavior was rare. Most couples maintained affectionate, lasting relationships. This too led to numerous sorrows in slavery. Members of slave families had to witness the flogging or physical abuse of a loved one and were powerless to intervene. William Wells Brown remembered that "cold chills ran over me and I wept aloud" when he saw his mother whipped for being late into the fields for work. For this reason, some slaves preferred to marry a spouse from a plantation other than their own.

Although motherhood was the key event in a

slave woman's life, bearing children and the double burden of work and family responsibilities challenged her resourcefulness. New mothers often had to choose between taking their babies into the fields to be fed or to leave them with others. Some masters would provide time off for nursing mothers, but the more common practice was for them to work in the fields with their newborn infants lying nearby, wrapped in cloth to protect them from the sun. Although children were sometimes denied proper physical care and emotional support by the absence of their parents during the working day, the slaves adapted. Woman developed networks of mutual support, looking after each other's children, meeting together to sew, quilt, cook, or do laundry, and attending births, caring for the sick and dying, and praying together.

The most traumatic problem for slaves was the separation of families, a haunting fear rarely absent from slave consciousness. Although many slaveholders had both moral and economic reasons to maintain families, inevitably they found themselves destroying them. One study, compiling 30 years of data from three Deep South states, shows that masters dissolved one-third of all slave marriages. Even then, the slaves tried to maintain contact. When Abream Scriven informed his wife, Dinah, of his sale to a trader in New Orleans, he had no idea where he would be sold but promised to "write and let you know where I am. . . . My Dear Wife for you and my Children my pen cannot Express the griffe I feel to be parted from you all." Two Missouri slave women, when told they might be sent to Texas, begged their master to reconsider, pleading that "to be separated from our husbands forever in this world would make us unhappy for life."

There was much basis in fact for the abolitionists' contention that slavery was a harsh, brutal system. However, two points need to be emphasized. First, although slavery was a barbarous institution that led otherwise decent human beings to commit inhumane acts, many slaveholders throughout the South were neither sadistic nor cruel but did what they could to provide decent care and humane treatment for their slave laborers, out of both economic self-interest and Christian morality. Second, despite the travail of slavery, whether under relatively kind or cruel masters, the slaves endured with dignity, communal sensitivity, and even some joy. If daytime in the fields describes a view of slavery at its worst, nighttime in the quarters, as examined from the black perspective, reveals the slaves' survival powers and their capacity to mold an African-American culture under slavery.

NIGHT: SLAVES IN THEIR QUARTERS

It is near sundown, and the workday is almost over. Some of the slaves begin singing the gentle spiritual "Steal Away to Jesus," and others join in. Or perhaps they sing, "Dere's a meeting here tonight." To the unwary overseer or master, the humming, soothing sound of the song suggests happy slaves, content with their earthly lot and looking

The breakup of families and friendships was an ever-present fear for slaves, who might be sold for purely economic reasons as well as in retribution for uncooperative behavior.

forward to deliverance in heaven, "in the sweet bosom of Jesus." To the slaves, however, the songs are a signal that, as an ex-slave, Wash Wilson, put it, they are to "steal away to Jesus" because "dere gwine be a 'ligious meetin' dat night." When evening arrived on the plantation, after a hard day of work in the hot sun or in the Big House, the slaves returned to their own quarters. There, as Wilson said, "sometimes us sing and pray all night."

In the slave quarters, away from white masters, overseers, and the burdens of daily work, an elaborate black community helped the slaves make sense out of their lives. In family life, religion, song, dance, the playing of musical instruments, and the telling of stories, the slaves both described their experiences and sought release from hardship and suffering. However burdensome their lives from sunup to sundown, after work the slaves experienced enjoyment and a sense of self-worth, hope, and group identity in their quarters.

Black Christianity

As suggested by the scene Wash Wilson described, Christian worship was an indispensable part of slave life in the quarters. The revivals of the early nineteenth century led to an enormous growth of Christianity among black Americans. Some independent black Baptist and Methodist churches, especially in border states and cities, served both slaves and free blacks and occasionally even whites. These separate churches had to steer a careful path to maintain their freedom and avoid white interference. But the vast majority of southern blacks were slaves, attending plantation missions set up by their masters.

Robert Allston built a prayer house for his slaves, reporting with pride that they were "attentive to religious instruction, and greatly improved in intelligence and morals." For the slaveholders, religion often represented a form of social control. Despite the presence of illiterate but eloquent slave preachers on the plantation, who frequently played a prominent role in administering baptisms, weddings, and funerals, white masters sought to direct the purposes of religion to their own ends. Black religious gatherings were usually forbidden unless white observers were present or white preachers led them. Whether in slave or white churches (where blacks sat in the back), preachers often delivered sermons from the text "Servants, obey your masters." These sermons emphasized the importance of work, obedience, honesty, and respect for the master's property. One former slave complained that "all that preacher talked about was for us slaves to obey our masters and not to lie and steal."

As the comment suggests, there were limits to the effectiveness of paternal control. Although some slaves accommodated themselves to the master's brand of Christianity and patiently waited for heavenly deliverance, others rebelled and sought earthly liberty. Not far from Allston's plantation, several slaves were discovered (and imprisoned) for singing "We'll soon be free / We'll fight for liberty / When de Lord will call us home." Douglass had an illegal Sabbath school on one plantation, where he and others risked being whipped while learning about Christianity and how to read. "The work of instructing my dear fellow-slaves," he wrote, "was the sweetest engagement with which I was ever blessed."

In religious schools and meetings like these, the slaves created an "invisible" church. On Sunday morning, they sat dutifully through the master's service and waited for the "real meetin'," and "real preachin'," later that night. Sarah Fitzpatrick, an Alabama slave, recalled that the slaves wanted so much to "go to church by de'selves" that they were willing to sit through the "white fo'ks' . . . service in de mornin'." But when evening came, "a'ter dey clean up, wash de dishes, an' look a'ter ever'thing," the slaves would "steal away" to the nearby woods for their own service.

Long into the night they would sing, dance, shout, and pray. "Ya' see," Sarah explained, "niggers lack ta shout a whole lot an' wid de white fo'ks al'round 'em, dey couldn't shout jes' lack dey want to." But at night they could, taking care to deaden the sound to keep the whites away. One method was to hang a curtain from the trees. Another, an African custom, was to turn over a pot to "catch the sound." Another African form, the frenetic dancing of the ring shout, survived in adapted form. Dance, forbidden by Methodists, was transformed into the "ecstatic shout," praising the Lord. The religious ceremony itself, with its camp meeting features, relieved the day's burdens and expressed communal religious values. "At night," another ex-slave recalled with pride, "was when the darkies really did have they freedom of spirit."

Although many of the expressive forms were African, the message reiterated over and over in the invisible slave church was the Christian theme of suffering and deliverance from bondage. Slaves identified with the children of Israel and with the

Exodus story, as well as with the suffering of Jesus and the inner turmoil of an unconverted "trebbled spirit." "We prayed a lot to be free," Anderson Edwards recalled, but the freedom the slaves sought was a complex blend of a peaceful soul and escape from slavery. Nothing illustrated both the communal religious experience and these mixed Christian themes of suffering and redemption better than slave spirituals.

The Power of Song

A group of slaves gathers in the dark of night in the woods behind their quarters to sing and shout together:

O brothers, don't get weary
O brothers, don't get weary
O brothers, don't get weary
We're waiting for the Lord.
We'll land on Canaan's shore
We'll land on Canaan's shore
When we land on Canaan's shore
We'll meet forever more.

Then, after moaning of being stolen from Africa and sold in Georgia, with families "sold apart," they sing:

There's a better day a-coming,
Will you go along with me?
There's a better day a-coming,
Go sound the jubilee!

Music was a crucial form of expression in the slave quarters on both secular and religious occasions. The slaves were adept at creating a song, as one slave woman recalled, "on de spurn of de moment." Jeanette Robinson Murphy described a process of spontaneous creation that, whether in rural church music or urban jazz, describes black music to this day. "We'd all be at the 'prayer house' de Lord's day," she said, when all of a sudden, perhaps even in the midst of a white preacher's sermon, "de Lord would come a-shinin' thoo dem pages and revive dis ole nigger's heart, and I'd jump up dar and den and holler and shout and sing and pat, and dey would all cotch de words and I'd sing it to some ole shout song I'd heard 'em sing from Africa, and dey'd all take it up and keep at it, and keep a-addin' to it, and den it would be a spiritual."

Although the spirituals were composed for many purposes, they reiterated one basic Christian theme: a chosen people, the children of God, were held captive in bondage but would be delivered. The titles and lyrics reveal the message: "We Are de People of de Lord," "To the Promised Land I'm Bound to Go," "Go Down, Moses," "Who Will Deliver Po' Me?" What they meant by "deliverance" was not always clear and often had a double meaning: freedom in heaven and freedom in the North. Where, exactly, was the desired destination of "Oh Canaan, sweet Canaan / I am bound for the land of Canaan"? Was it heaven? A vague symbol for freedom "anyplace else but here"? A literal reference to the end of the underground railroad? For different slaves, and at different times for the same person, it meant all of these.

"The songs of the slave," Douglass wrote, "represent the sorrows of his heart." Indeed, they often expressed the sadness of broken families and the burdens of work and were filled with images of trouble, toil, and homelessness. But they also expressed joy, triumph, and deliverance. Each expression of sorrow usually ended in an outburst of eventual

Religious meetings provided an outlet for emotions hidden all day from the overseer. At the Christmas holidays, music and dancing continued day and night.

affirmation and justice. "O nobody knows a who I am" resolved itself on "judgment morning" when one heard the "bells a-ringing in my soul." The sadness of "Nobody knows the trouble I've seen" was lightened by happening upon some juicy berries hanging down "just as sweet as de honey in de comb." And the deep sorrow of "Sometimes I feel like a motherless chile," as terrible a situation as any person could endure, was transformed later in the song into "Sometimes I feel like / A eagle in de air. . . . / Gonna spread my wings an' / Fly, fly, fly."

Slave songs did not always contain hidden meanings. Sometimes slaves gathered simply for music, to play fiddles, drums, and other instruments fashioned by local artists in imitation of West African models. Some musicians were so talented that whites invited them to perform at ceremonies and parties. But most played for the slave community. Sacred and secular events such as weddings, funerals, holiday celebrations, family reunions, and a successful harvest were all occasions for a communal gathering, usually with music. So too was news of external events that affected their lives—a crisis in the master's situation, a change in the slave code, the outcome of a battle during the Civil War, or emancipation itself.

The Enduring Family

The role of music in births, weddings, funerals, and other milestones of family life suggests that the family was central to life in the slave quarters. Although the pain of sexual abuse and family separation was a real or potential part of the experience of all slaves, so was the hope for family continuity. The study of naming practices, for example, shows that children were connected to large extended families. In the records of one plantation for the century from 1760 to the eve of the Civil War, some 175 men, women, and children were found to be linked by blood and marital ties, respecting taboos against marrying first cousins.

The benefits of family cohesion were those of any group: love, protection, education, moral guidance, the transmission of culture, and the provision of status, role models, and basic support. All of these existed in the slave quarters. As the slaves gathered together at the end of the working day, parents passed on to their children the family story, language patterns and words, recipes, folktales, religious and musical traditions, and strong impressions of strength and beauty. In this way they preserved

cultural tradition, which enhanced the identity and self-esteem of parents and children alike. Parents taught their children how to survive in the world and how to cope with life under slavery. As the young ones neared the age when they would work full time in the fields, their parents instructed them in the best ways to pick cotton or corn, how to avoid the overseer's whip, whom to trust and learn from, and ways of fooling the master.

Opportunities existed on many plantations for fathers, and mothers as well, to improve the welfare of the family by working extra to earn money to buy scarce items like sugar or clothing, by hunting and fishing to add protein to the diet, or by working a small garden to grow vegetables. J. W. C. Pennington proudly recalled helping his "father at night in making straw hats and willow-baskets, by which means we supplied our family with little articles of food, clothing and luxury."

Slaves were not always totally at the mercy of abusive masters and overseers. Occasionally, one family member could intervene to prevent the abuse of another. When emotional appeals for mercy did not work, or when the subtle magical effects of the

Despite separation, sale, and sexual abuse by white masters, the slave family endured and provided love and support to all its members. This 1862 photograph shows five generations of a slave family, all born on the plantation of J. J. Smith of Beaufort, South Carolina.

conjurer's bag of herbs hung around the neck did not suffice, some slaves resorted to physical force. In 1800, a slave called Ben shot and killed a white man for living with Ben's wife, and another slave killed an overseer in 1859 for raping his wife. Female slaves, too, risked the consequences of resistance to protect themselves or family members from harm. When Cherry Loguen was attacked by a knife-wielding would-be rapist, she picked up a stick and knocked him out. And when an Arkansas overseer tried to make an example of a slave woman named Lucy, according to her son, "she jumped on him and like to tore him up."

The love and affection that slaves had for each other was sometimes a liability. Many slaves, women especially, were reluctant to run away because they did not want to leave their families. Those who fled were easily caught because, as an overseer near Natchez, Mississippi, told a northern visitor, they "almost always kept in the neighborhood, because they did not like to go where they could not sometimes get back and see their families."

As these episodes suggest, violence, sexual abuse, and separation constantly threatened the stability of slave families. But despite these serious restraints, slave parents served as protectors, providers, comforters, transmitters of culture, and role models for their children. The slave family, though constantly endangered, played a crucial role in helping blacks adapt to slavery and achieve a sense of self-esteem.

RESISTANCE AND FREEDOM

Songs, folktales, and other forms of cultural expression enabled slaves to articulate their resistance to slavery. For example, Old Jim was going on a "journey" to the "kingdom" and, as he invited others to "go 'long" with him, he taunted his owner: "O blow, blow, Ole Massa, blow de cotton horn / Ole Jim'll neber wuck no mo' in de cotton an' de corn." From refusal to work it was a short step to outright revolt. In another song, "Samson," the slaves clearly stated their determination to abolish the house of bondage: "An' if I had-'n my way /I'd tear the buildin' down! /. . . And now I got my way / And I'll tear this buildin' down." Every hostile song, story, or event, like Douglass's victory over Covey, was an act of resistance by which the slaves asserted their dignity and gained a measure of freedom. Some

escaped slavery altogether to achieve such autonomy as was possible for free blacks in the antebellum South.

Forms of Black Protest

One way slaves protested the burdensome demands of continuous forced labor was in various "day to day" acts of resistance. These ranged from breaking tools to burning crops, barns, and houses, from stealing or destroying animals and food to defending fellow slaves from punishment, from self-mutilation to deliberate work slowdowns, and from poisoning masters to feigning illness. Slave women, aware of their childbearing value, were adept at missing work on account of "disorders and irregularities," as a frustrated Virginia planter put it, "which cannot be detected by exterior symptoms." He went on to complain that "you dare not set her to work, and so she will lay up till she feels like taking the air again; and plays the lady at your expense." Two favorite techniques were to pretend sickness during periods when the overseers were driving the hardest and to misplace tools or deliberately leave them in the fields so that they would have to be "hunted all over the place when wanted."

Overseers also suffered from these acts of disobedience, for their job depended on productivity, which in turn depended on the goodwill of the slave workers. No one knew this better than the slaves themselves, who adeptly played on the frequent struggle between overseer and master. Often the conflicts were ended by firing a bad overseer and hiring a more suitable replacement. Many slaveholders eventually resorted to using black drivers rather than overseers, but this created other problems.

The slave drivers were "men between," charged with the tricky job of getting the master's work done without alienating fellow slaves or compromising their own values. Although some drivers were as brutal as white overseers, many became leaders and role models for other slaves. A common practice of the drivers was to appear to punish without really doing so. Solomon Northrup reported that he "learned to handle the whip with marvellous dexterity and precision, throwing the lash within a hair's breadth of the back, the ear, the nose, without, however, touching either of them." As he did this, the "punished" slave would howl in pretended pain and complain loudly to his master about his harsh treatment.

RECOVERING THE PAST

FOLKTALES

A frequent activity of family life in the slave quarters was telling stories. The folktale was an especially useful and indirect way in which older slaves could express hostility toward their masters, impart wisdom to the young, teach them how to survive, portray and mock their own weaknesses, and entertain themselves. Thus folktales reveal to historians a great deal about the slaves' view of their experience.

Although the tales took many forms, perhaps the best known were the "Brer Rabbit" animal stories. The trickster rabbit, who existed originally in African folklore, was weak, careless, and looked down on by the other animals. Like the slaves, he was a victim. But he was also clever, boastful, and full of mischief, and he knew how to use his cunning to outwit stronger foes, usually by knowing them better than they knew him, a psychological necessity for all who are oppressed.

In one story, the powerful Brer Tiger took all the water and food for himself during a time of terrible famine, leaving the weaker animals miserable. Brer Rabbit, however, turned things around. He played on Brer Tiger's fears that he would be blown away by a "big wind," secretly manufactured by the rabbit. The tiger was so afraid of the wind (perhaps the winds of revolt?) that he begged Brer Rabbit to tie him "tightly" to a tree to keep from being blown away. Brer Rabbit was happy to oblige, after which all the creatures of the forest were able to share the cool water and juicy pears.

In another folktale, Brer Rabbit fell into a well but then got out by tricking Brer Wolf into thinking it was more desirable to be in the cool bottom of the well than outside where it was hot. As the wolf lowered himself down in one bucket, Brer Rabbit rose up in the other, laughingly saying as he passed Brer Wolf, "Dis am life; some go up and some go down." In these stories, the slaves vicariously outwitted their more powerful masters and even reversed roles. The tiger was bound to the tree while Brer Rabbit and the other creatures were free, not to take revenge but simply to survive. In telling these stories, the slaves revealed much about their experience under slavery and their aspirations for freedom.

The accompanying excerpt is from perhaps the most famous animal tale, "The Tar Baby Tricks Brer Rabbit." This version is by William J. Faulkner, who after he retired as minister and dean of men at Fisk University, gathered and recorded the folktales he had heard in his youth in South Carolina as told by an ex-slave, Simon Brown. Rev. Faulkner opposed telling the stories in dialect because he believed readers formed stereotyped judgments from the dialect and missed the significance of the tale itself.

As you read the folktale, ask yourself what the message of the story is, how it reveals what slavery was like, and how it might have provided a sense of identity and self-worth for the slaves who heard it. We enter the story as an angry Brer Wolf has decided on a plan to catch the lazy Brer Rabbit, who refused to help the wolf build a well and has been fooling him by drinking from the well while Brer Wolf was asleep.

When you have finished reading the story, consider the following questions: What did you learn about slavery from this story? Did violence work for Brer Rabbit, or did it only make things worse? Notice the resourcefulness and survival instincts of the rabbit. He was in a terrible fix, but he got out. What finally worked? How do you interpret the ending? Brer Rabbit is returned to the briar patch, "the place where I was born." But is the briar patch, with all its thorns, scratches, and roots, Africa or slavery? Or what?

Finally, reflect on the stories *you* heard as a child or now find yourself telling others. What are they? How do they express the realities, flaws, values, and dreams of the American people? The basic question to ask of the folktales and stories that we tell is a question we could ask as well of the songs we sing, the art we make, the rhythms we move to, and the jokes we tell: What do they tell us about ourselves and our values? In answering these questions, we deepen the knowledge of our own history.

Brer Wolf studied and studied to find a way to catch Brer Rabbit. He scratched his head, and he pulled his chin whiskers until by and by he said, "I know what I'll do. I'll make me a tar baby, and I'll catch that good-for-nothing rabbit."*

And so Brer Wolf worked and worked until he had made a pretty little girl out of tar. He dressed the tar baby in a calico apron and carried her up to the well, where he stood her up and fastened her to a post in the ground so that nobody could move her. Then Brer Wolf hid in the bushes and waited for Brer Rabbit to come for some water. But three days passed before Brer Rabbit visited the well again. On the fourth day, he came with a bucket in his hand.

When he saw the little girl, he stopped and looked at her. Then he said, "Hello. What's your name? What are you doing here, little girl?"

The little girl said nothing.

This made Brer Rabbit angry, and he shouted at her, "You no-mannered little snip, you! How come you don't speak to your elders?"

The little girl still said nothing.

"I know what to do with little children like you. I'll slap your face and teach you some manners if you don't speak to me," said Brer Rabbit.

Still the little girl said nothing.

And then Brer Rabbit lost his head and said, "Speak to me, I say. I'm going to slap you." With that, Brer Rabbit slapped the tar baby in the face, and his right hand stuck.

"A-ha, you hold my hand, do you? Turn me loose, I say. Turn me loose. If you don't, I'm going to slap you with my left hand. And if I hit you with my left hand, I'll knock the daylights out of you."

But the little girl said nothing. So Brer Rabbit drew back his left hand and slapped the little girl in her face, bim, and his left hand stuck.

"Oh, I see. You're going to hold both my hands, are you? You better turn me loose. If you don't, I'm going to kick you. And if I kick you, it's going to be like thunder and lightning!" With that, Brer Rabbit drew back his right foot and kicked the little girl in the shins with all his might, blap! Then his right foot stuck.

"Well, sir, isn't this something? You better turn my foot loose. If you don't, I've got another foot left, and I'm going to kick you with it, and you'll think a cyclone hit you." Then Brer Rabbit gave that little girl a powerful kick in the shins with his left foot, blip! With that, his left foot stuck, and there he hung off the ground, between the heavens and the earth. He was in an awful fix. But he still thought he could get loose.

So he said to the little girl, "You've got my feet and my hands all stuck up, but I've got one more weapon, and that's my head. If you don't turn me loose, I'm going to butt you! And if I butt you, I'll knock your brains out." Finally then, Brer Rabbit struck the little girl a powerful knock on the forehead with his head, and it stuck, and there he hung. Smart old Brer Rabbit, he couldn't move. He was held fast by the little tar baby.

Now, Brer Wolf was hiding under the bushes, watching all that was going on. And as soon as he was certain that Brer Rabbit was caught good by his little tar baby, he walked over to Brer Rabbit and said, "A-ha, you're the one who wouldn't dig a well. And you're the one who's going to catch his drinking water from the dew off the grass. A-ha, I caught the fellow who's been stealing my water. And he isn't anybody but you, Brer Rabbit. I'm going to fix you good."

"No, sir, Brer Wolf, I haven't been bothering your water. I was just going over to Brer Bear's house, and I stopped by here long enough to speak to this little no-manners girl," said Brer Rabbit.

"Yes, you're the one," said Brer Wolf. "You're the very one who's been stealing my drinking water all this time. And I'm going to kill you."

"Please, sir, Brer Wolf, don't kill me," begged Brer Rabbit. "I haven't done anything wrong."

"Yes, I'm going to kill you, but I don't know how I'm going to do it yet," growled Brer Wolf. "Oh, I know what I'll do. I'll throw you in the fire and burn you up."

"All right, Brer Wolf," said Brer Rabbit. "Throw me in the fire. That's a good way to die. That's the way my grandmother died, and she said it's a quick way to go. You can do anything with me, anything you want, but please, sir, don't throw me in the briar patch."

"No, I'm not going to throw you in the fire, and I'm not going to throw you in the briar patch. I'm going to throw you down the well and drown you," said Brer Wolf.

"All right, Brer Wolf, throw me down the well," said Brer Rabbit. "That's an easy way to die, but I'm surely going to smell up your drinking water, sir."

"No, I'm not going to drown you," said Brer Wolf. "Drowning is too good for you." Then Brer Wolf thought and thought and scratched his head and pulled his chin whiskers. Finally he said, "I know what I'm going to do with you. I'll throw you in the briar patch."

"Oh, no, Brer Wolf," cried Brer Rabbit. "Please, sir, don't throw me in the briar patch. Those briars will tear up my hide, pull out my hair, and scratch out my eyes. That'll be an awful way to die, Brer Wolf. Please, sir, don't do that to me."

"That's exactly what I'll do with you," said Brer Wolf all happy-like. Then he caught Brer Rabbit by his hind legs, whirled him around and around over his head, and threw him way over into the middle of the briar patch.

After a minute or two, Brer Rabbit stood up on his hind legs and laughed at Brer Wolf and said to him, "Thank you, Brer Wolf, thank you. This is the place where I was born. My grandmother and grandfather and all my family were born right here in the briar patch."

And that's the end of the story.

---

* Tar was often spread on fences by masters to catch slaves who, out of hunger or mischief, would sneak into fields and orchards to steal food. Tar stuck on the hands would betray the "guilty" slave.

Working with tools and machinery enabled slaves to engage in silent protests by misplacing tools or sabotaging equipment. Note the cotton press and gin in the background. Slave women were particularly adept at missing work by pretending to be sick.

Another form of resistance was to run away. So many blacks ran off that a southern doctor coined a new word, *drapetomania,* which meant "the disease causing negroes to run away." The typical runaway was a young male, who ran off alone and hid out in a nearby wood or swamp. He left to avoid a whipping or because he had just been whipped, to protest excessive work demands, or, as one master put it, for "no cause" at all. But there was a cause—the need to experience a period of freedom away from the restraints and discipline of the plantation. Many runaways would sneak back to the quarters at night for food, and after a few days, if not tracked down by hounds, they would return, perhaps to be whipped but also perhaps with some concessions for better treatment in the future.

Some slaves left again and again. Remus and his wife Patty ran away from their master, James Battle, in Alabama. They were caught and jailed three times, but each time they escaped again. Battle urged the next jailer to "secure Remus well." Some runaways, called "Maroons," hid out for months and years at a time in communities of runaway slaves. Several Maroon colonies were located in the swamps and mountains of the South, especially in Florida, where Seminole and other tribes befriended them. In these areas, blacks and Indians, sharing a common hostility to local whites, frequently intermarried, though sometimes southeastern Indians were hired to track down runaway slaves.

The means of escape were manifold: forging passes, posing as master and servant, disguising one's sex, sneaking aboard ships, and pretending loyalty until taken by the master on a trip to the North. One slave even hid in a large box and had himself mailed to the North. The underground railroad, organized by abolitionists, was a series of safe houses and stations where runaway slaves could rest, eat, and spend the night before continuing. Harriet Tubman, who led some 300 slaves out of the South on 19 separate trips, was the railroad's most famous "conductor." It is difficult to know exactly how many slaves actually escaped to the North and Canada, but the numbers were not large. One estimate suggests that in 1850 about 1,000 slaves (out of over 3 million) attempted to run away, and most of them were returned. Nightly patrols by white militiamen, an important aspect of southern life, reduced the chances for any slave to escape and probably deterred many slaves from even trying to run away.

Other ways in which slaves sought their freedom included petitioning Congress and state legislatures, bringing suit against their masters that they were being held in bondage illegally, persuading masters to provide for emancipation in their wills, and purchasing their own freedom by hiring out to do extra work at night and on holidays.

Slave Revolts

The ultimate act of resistance, of course, was rebellion. Countless slaves committed individual acts of revolt. In addition, there were hundreds of conspiracies whereby slaves met to plan a group escape and often the massacre of whites. Most of these conspiracies never led to action, either because circumstances changed or the slaves lost the will to follow through or, more often, because some fellow slave—perhaps planted by the master—betrayed the plot. Such spies thwarted the elaborate conspiracies of Gabriel Prosser (Richmond, Virginia, 1800) and Denmark Vesey (Charleston, South Carolina, 1822). Both resulted in severe reprisals by whites, including mass executions of leaders and the random killing of innocent blacks. The severity and intensity of the white response indicated the enormous fear southern whites had of a slave revolt.

Only a few organized revolts, in which slaves threatened white lives and property, ever actually took place. Latin American slaves challenged their masters more often than their North American counterparts. Weaker military control, easier escape to rugged interior areas, the greater imbalance of blacks to whites, and the continued dependence of Latin American slaveholders on the African slave trade for their supply of mostly male workers explain this pattern. Nearly 80 percent of the Africans imported into Brazil in the 1830s and 1840s were male, and as late as 1875, only one in six Brazilian slaves

was recorded as married. The imbalance of males to females (156 to 100 in Cuba in 1860, for example, compared to a near one-to-one ratio in the United States) weakened family restraints on violent revolts.

The most famous slave revolt in North America, led by Nat Turner, occurred in Southampton County, Virginia, in 1831. Turner was an intelligent, skilled, unmarried, religious slave who had experienced many visions of "white spirits and black spirits engaged in battle." He believed that he was "ordained for some great purpose in the hands of the Almighty."

On a hot August night, Turner and a small band of fellow slaves launched their revolt. They intended, as Turner said, "to carry terror and devastation" throughout the country. They crept into the home of Turner's master, Joseph Travis, who Nat said was "a kind master" with "the greatest confidence in me," and killed the entire family. Before the revolt was finally put down, 55 white men, women, and children had been murdered and as many blacks killed in the aftermath. Turner hid in a hole in the woods for two weeks before he was apprehended and executed, but not before dictating a chilling confession to a white lawyer. The Nat

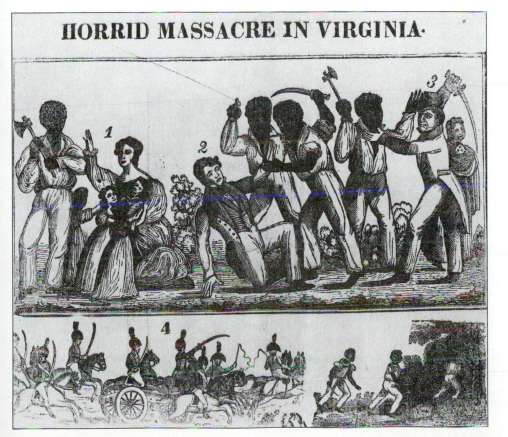

HORRID MASSACRE IN VIRGINIA.

Nat Turner's Revolt in 1831, the most famous American slave uprising, left 55 whites dead as Turner's band carried "terror and devastation" throughout Southampton County, Virginia.

Turner revolt was a crucial moment for southern whites. A Virginia legislator said that he suspected there was "a Nat Turner . . . in every family." Rarely thereafter would slaveholders go to sleep without the Southampton revolt in mind.

The fact that Turner was an intelligent and trusted slave, with "no cause to complain" of his master's treatment, and yet led such a terrible revolt suggests again how difficult it is to generalize about slavery and slave behavior. Slaves, like masters, had diverse personalities and changeable moods, and their behavior could not be easily predicted. Sometimes humble and deferential, at other times obstinate and rebellious, the slaves made the best of a bad situation and did what they needed to do to survive and achieve a measure of self-worth.

Free Blacks: Becoming One's Own Master

No matter how well they coped with their bondage, the slaves obviously preferred freedom. As Frederick Douglass said of the slave, "Give him a *bad* master, and he aspires to a *good* master; give him a good master, and he wishes to become his *own* master." When Douglass himself had successfully forged a free black's papers as a seaman and sailed from Baltimore to become his own master in the North, he found "great insecurity and loneliness." Apart from the immediate difficulties of finding food, shelter, and work, he realized that he was a fugitive in a land "whose inhabitants are legalized kidnappers" who could at any moment seize and return him to the South. Apart from this fear, which haunted blacks in the North, what was life like for the 11 percent of the total black population who in 1860 were not slaves?

Between 1820 and 1860, the number of free blacks in the United States doubled, from 233,500 to 488,000. This rise resulted from natural increase, successful escapes, "passing" as whites, purchasing freedom, and a continuation of some manumissions despite legal restriction in most states after the 1830s. Some free blacks passed into the white population, while others migrated to Canada or the West Indies. The free black population actually decreased from 13.2 percent in 1820 to a little more than 11 percent in 1860. Thus the number of American blacks who were slaves grew faster than those who were free. More than half the free blacks lived in the South, most (85 percent in 1860) in the Upper South, where the total number of slaves had declined slightly.

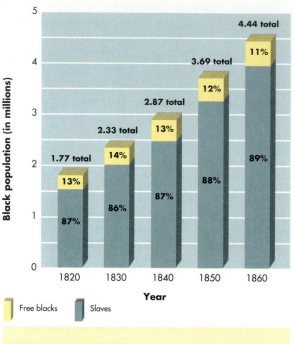

Growth of Black Population: Slave and Free, 1820–1860

Black population (in millions)

Year

Free blacks   Slaves

Source: U.S. Bureau of the Census.

Since free blacks represented a constant reminder of freedom to slaves and feared reenslavement themselves, they were found least frequently in the Black Belt of the Lower South. They lived, rather, away from the dense plantation centers, scattered on impoverished rural farmlands and in small towns and cities. One-third of southern free blacks lived in cities such as Baltimore, Richmond, Charleston, and New Orleans. In part because it took a long time to buy their freedom, they tended to be older, more literate, and more skilled than other blacks. A great many were light-skinned women, reflecting the favored privileges these blacks received from slaveholders. In 1860, over 40 percent of free blacks were mulattoes (compared to 10 percent of the slaves).

Most southern free blacks were poor, laboring as farmhands, day laborers, or woodcutters. In the cities, they lived in appalling poverty and worked in factories. A few skilled jobs, such as barbering, shoemaking, and plastering, were reserved for black men; they were barred from more than 50 other trades. Women worked as cooks, laundresses, and domestics. The 15 percent of free blacks who lived in the Lower South were divided into two distinct castes. Most were poor. But in New Orleans, Charleston, and other southern cities, a small, mixed-blood class of free blacks emerged as an elite group, closely connected to white society and removed from the mass of poor blacks. A handful even owned land and slaves. One white observed that these blacks were "respectable" and enjoyed "their rights."

Most free blacks, however, had no such privileges. "We reside among you . . . surrounded by the freest people and most republican institutions in the world," a Baltimore black paper said in 1826, pointing out that free blacks were not yet citizens and enjoyed "none of the immunities of freedom. . . . Though we are not slaves, we are not free." Southern state laws seriously limited the mobility, rights, and opportunities of free blacks. In most states, they could not vote, bear arms, buy liquor, assemble, speak in public, form societies, or testify against whites in court.

One reason for these restrictions was that urban white southerners feared the influence of free blacks, who mixed with whites in working-class grogshops, gambling halls, and brothels. Richmond police closed one house of ill fame where "men and women of diverse colors . . . congregate for most unhallowed purposes." Efforts were made to confine the free blacks to certain sections of the city or, increasingly by the 1850s, to compel them to leave the city, county, or state altogether. Those who stayed had trouble finding work, were required to carry licenses and freedom papers to be surrendered on demand, and often needed a white guardian to approve their actions.

However threatening free blacks were to southern standards of separatism and white supremacy, whites were even more afraid of contact between free blacks and slaves. Black ghettos were created by a combination of black needs to be together and white aversion to racial intermingling. As in the slave quarters of the plantation, blacks in cities developed a strong sense of identity and community life. Free blacks and slaves often worked together in factories and fields, attended the same churches and places of entertainment, and sometimes even married.

The center of urban black community was the church. Martin Delaney wrote to Douglass in 1849 that "among our people . . . the Church is the Alpha and Omega of all things." The church not only performed the usual religious ritual functions and guarded moral discipline and community values but also provided and promoted education, social insurance, fraternal associations, and picnics, concerts, and other forms of recreation. Besides the church, black community identity and pride revolved around the African schools and various burial and benevolent societies for self-help and protection against poverty, illness, and other disasters. Like their counterparts among whites, these societies grew and took on a new and significant social importance in the two decades before the Civil War. A young minister, Henry M. Turner, later bishop of the African Methodist Episcopal church, proudly claimed in the 1850s, "We, as a race, have a chance to be Somebody, and if we are ever going to be a people, now is the time."

Churches for free blacks, rare before 1800, became a major source of social as well as religious activity by the 1840s.

In part because free blacks were becoming more of a "people," they faced a crisis of extinction in the 1850s. Growing prosperity and the worsening conflict between North and South over slavery in the territories caused many white southerners to be even more concerned than usual with the presence of free blacks in their midst. North Carolina whites complained in 1852 that free blacks were "a perfect nuisance" because they attempted "in divers ways to equalize themselves with [the] white population." Pressures increased in the late 1850s either to deport the free blacks or to enslave them. In the wake of increasing threats to their already precarious free status, some black leaders not surprisingly began to look more favorably on migration to Africa. That quest was interrupted, however, by the outbreak of the Civil War, rekindling in Douglass and others the "expiring embers of freedom."

CONCLUSION

Douglass's Dream of Freedom

Frederick Douglass eventually won his freedom by forging a free black sailor's pass and escaping through Chesapeake Bay to New York. In a real sense, he wrote himself into freedom. The *Narrative of the Life of Frederick Douglass,* "written by himself" in 1845, was a way of both exposing the many evils of slavery and of creating his own identity, even to the point of choosing his own name. Ironically, Douglass had learned to value reading and writing, we recall, from his Baltimore masters, the Aulds. This reminds us again of the intricate and subtle ways in which the lives of slaves and masters were tied together in the antebellum South. Our understanding of the complexities of this relationship is enhanced as we consider the variations of life in the Big House in the morning, in the fields during the afternoons, in the slave quarters at night, and in the degrees of freedom blacks achieved through resistance, revolt, and free status.

In a poignant moment in his *Narrative,* Douglass described his dreams of freedom as he looked out at the boats on the waters of Chesapeake Bay as a boy. Contrasting his own enslavement with the boats he saw as "freedom's swift-winged angels," Douglass vowed to escape: "This very bay shall yet bear me into freedom. . . . There is a better day coming." As we will see later, southern white planters also bemoaned their lack of freedom relative to the North and made their own plans to achieve independent status through secession. Meanwhile, as that struggle brewed beneath the surface of antebellum life, many other Americans were dismayed by various evil aspects in their society, slavery among them, and sought ways of shaping a better America. We turn to these other dreams in the next chapter.

Recommended Reading

Gavin Wright provides a difficult but thorough analysis of the economic development of the Old South in The Political Economy of the Cotton South: Households, Markets, and Wealth in the Nineteenth Century *(1978). For a spirited argument of the economics of slavery, read the controversial* Time on the Cross: The Economics of American Negro Slavery *(1974), by Robert* Fogel and Stanley Engerman, *and two highly critical rejoinders, Herbert Gutman and Richard Sutch,* Slavery and the Numbers Game *(1975), and Paul David et al.,* Reckoning with Slavery: A Critical Study of the Quantitative History of American Negro Slavery *(1976). Nonagricultural slaves are dealt with in Robert Starobin,* Industrial Slavery in the Old South *(1970), and Richard Wade,* Slavery in the Cities *(1964). The most readable story of the lives of nonslaveholding whites in the South is an old one,*

Frank Owsley's Plain Folk in the Old South *(1949). For the Allston family story, see* The South Carolina Rice Plantation As Revealed in the Papers of Robert F. W. Allston, *ed. J. H. Easterby (1945).*

The standard picture of slavery from the point of view of its defenders is in two works by Ulrich B. Phillips, American Negro Slavery *(1919) and* Life and Labor in the Old South *(1929). A brilliant study of racism in America, including excellent chapters on the southern justification of slavery, is George Fredrickson,* The Black Image in the White Mind: The Debate on Afro-American Character and Destiny, 1817– 1914 *(1971). A fascinating insight into the life of southern white women is Catharine Clinton,* Plantation Mistress *(1983). For a stunning portrayal of female slaves in the plantation South, see Deborah Gray White,* Arn't I a Woman? *(1985). A remarkable new work that treats both white and slave women is Elizabeth Fox-Genovese,* Within the Plantation Household *(1988).*

Of the many collections of primary source documents about slavery, the best is Willie Lee Rose, A Documentary History of Slavery in North America *(1976). The four best surveys of slavery are Kenneth Stampp,* The Peculiar Institution *(1956); Eugene Genovese,* Roll, Jordan, Roll: The World the Slaves Made *(1974); Nathan I. Huggins,* Black Odyssey: The Afro-American Ordeal in Slavery *(1977); and John Blassingame,* The Slave Community, *rev. ed. (1979). Various aspects of slave culture and life in the quarters are treated brilliantly in Charles Joyner,* Down by the Riverside: A South Carolina Slave Community *(1984); Herbert Gutman,* The Black Family in Slavery and Freedom, 1750–1925 *(1976); Lawrence Levine,* Black Culture and Black Consciousness: Afro-American Folk Thought from Slavery to Freedom *(1977); Sterling Stuckey,* Slave Culture: Nationalist Theory and the Foundation of Black America *(1987); and Albert Raboteau,* Slave Religion: The "Invisible Institution" in the Antebellum South *(1978). Frederick Douglass's experiences are told in three separate autobiographies,* Narrative of the Life of Frederick Douglass *(1845),* My Bondage and My Freedom *(1855), and* Life and Times of Frederick Douglass *(1881). A good recent biography is* Slave and Citizen: The Life of Frederick Douglass *(1980), by Nathan I. Huggins.*

The definitive work on free blacks in the South is Ira Berlin, Slaves Without Masters: The Free Negro in the Antebellum South *(1976); see also two fascinating books by Michael P. John-* *son and James L. Roark,* No Chariot Down: Charleston's Free People of Color on the Eve of the Civil War *(1984) and* Black Masters: A Free Family of Color in the Old South *(1984). Slave resistance and revolt are described in Vincent Harding,* There Is a River: The Black Struggle for Freedom in America *(1981), but a superb way to experience both slavery and the struggle for freedom is by reading an old classic, Harriet Beecher Stowe's* Uncle Tom's Cabin *(1852).*

TIME LINE

1787 Constitution adopted with proslavery provisions

1793 Eli Whitney invents cotton gin

1800 Gabriel Prosser conspiracy in Virginia

1808 External slave trade prohibited by Congress

1820 South becomes world's largest cotton producer

1822 Denmark Vesey's conspiracy in Charleston

1830s Southern justification of slavery changes from a necessary evil to a positive good

1831 Nat Turner's slave revolt in Virginia

1845 *Narrative of the Life of Frederick Douglass* published

1850s Cotton boom

1851 Indiana state constitution excludes free blacks

1852 Harriet Beecher Stowe publishes best-selling *Uncle Tom's Cabin*

1860 Cotton production and prices peak

13

Shaping America in the Antebellum Age

On November 19, 1836, as the second term of President Andrew Jackson neared its end, 30-year-old Marius Robinson and Emily Rakestraw were married near Cincinnati, Ohio. Two months after their wedding, he went on the road to speak against slavery and to organize abolitionist societies throughout Ohio. Emily stayed in Cincinnati to teach in a school for free blacks. During their ten-month separation, they exchanged affectionate letters that reflected their love and work.

Writing after midnight from Concord, Ohio, Marius complained of "the desolation of loneliness" he felt without her. Emily responded that she felt "about our separation just as you do" and confessed that her "womanish nature" did not much enjoy self-denial. In their letters each imagined "the form and features" of the other and chided the other for not writing more often. Each voiced concern for the responsibilities and burdens of the other's work. Each expressed comfort and support, doubted his or her own abilities ("a miserable comforter I am"), and agreed that in their separation, as Marius put it, "we must look alone to God."

With such love for each other, what prompted this painful separation so early in their marriage? Emily wrote of their duty "to labor long in this cause so near and dear to us both," together if they could but apart if so decreed by God. Marius, who had experienced a series of conversions inspired by the revivalist Charles G. Finney and his abolitionist disciple Theodore Dwight Weld, described the reason for their separation: "God and humanity bleeding and suffering demand our services apart." Thus motivated by a strong religious commitment to serve others, these two young reformers dedicated themselves to several social causes: the abolition of slavery, equal rights and education for free blacks, temperance, and women's rights.

Their commitments cost more than separation. When Emily went to Cincinnati to work with other young reformers, her parents disapproved. When she married Marius, who already had a reputation as a "rebel," her parents disowned her altogether. Emily wrote with sadness that her sisters and friends also "love me less . . . than they did in by-gone days." Marius responded that he

wished he could "dry your tears" and sought to heal the rift. Although Emily's family eventually accepted their marriage, there were other griefs. Teaching at the school in Cincinnati was demanding, and Emily could not get rid of a persistent cough. Furthermore, the white citizens of the city resented the school and the young abolitionist people in their midst, treating them with contempt. Earlier in the year, Marius had escaped an angry mob by disguising himself and mingling with the crowd that came to sack the offices of a reformist journal edited by James G. Birney. Emily, meanwhile, tirelessly persisted in the work of "our school" while worrying about the health and safety of her husband on the road.

She had good reason for concern, for Marius's letters were full of reports of mob attacks, disrupted meetings, stonings, and narrow escapes. At two lectures near Granville, Ohio, he was "mobbed thrice, once most rousingly," as he faced crowds of "the veriest savages I ever saw" armed with clubs, cudgels, and intense hatred for the people speaking against slavery. In June, he was dragged from the home of his Quaker host and beaten, tarred, and feathered. Never quite recovering his health, Marius spent half a year in bed, weak and dispirited. For nearly ten years after that, the Robinsons lived quietly on an Ohio farm, only slightly involved in the abolitionist movement. Despite the joyous birth of two daughters, they felt lonely, restless, and guilt-ridden, "tired of days blank of benevolent effort and almost of benevolent desires."

The work of Emily and Marius Robinson represents one response by the American people to the rapid social and economic changes of the antebellum era described in Chapters 11 and 12. In September 1835, a year before the Robinsons' marriage, the *Niles Register* commented on some 500 recent incidents of mob violence and social upheaval. *"Society seems everywhere unhinged,* and the demon of 'blood and slaughter' has been let loose upon us. . . . [The] character of our countrymen seems suddenly changed."* How did Americans adapt to these changes? In a world that seemed everywhere "unhinged" and out of control, in which old rules and patterns no longer provided guidance, how did people maintain some sense of control over their lives? How did they seek to shape their altered world? How could they both adopt the benefits of change and reduce the accompanying disruptions?

One way was to embrace the changes fully. Thus some Americans became entrepreneurs in new industries; invested in banks, canals, and railroads; bought more land and slaves; and invented new machines. Others went west or to the new textile mills, enrolled in common schools, joined trade unions, specialized their labor both in the workplace and the home, and celebrated the practical benefits that resulted from modernization. Marius Robinson eventually went into life insurance, though he and Emily never fully abandoned their reformist efforts and idealism.

But many Americans were uncomfortable with the character of the new era. Some worried about the unrestrained power and selfish materialism symbolized by the slavemaster's control over his slaves. Others feared that institutions like the U.S. Bank represented a "monied aristocracy" capable of undermining the country's honest producers. Seeking positions of leadership and authority, these critics of the new order tried to shape a nation that retained the benefits of economic change without sacrificing humane principles of liberty, equality of opportunity, and community virtue. This chapter examines four ways in which the American people responded to change by attempting to influence their country's development: party politics, religious revivalism, utopian communitarianism, and social reform.

THE POLITICAL RESPONSE TO CHANGE

At the heart of American politics was the concern for the continued health of the republican experiment. As American society changed, so too did the understanding of what measures were necessary to maintain that health. In the late 1850s, a Maine newspaper warned that the preservation of the nation's freedom depended on the willingness of its citizens to go to the polls. It was, in fact, "the positive duty of every citizen of a Republic to vote." This insistence on voting as crucial to the well-being of the country was new. Before the 1820s, politics was primarily the business of the social and economic elite. Even though many states were removing voting restrictions in the early nineteenth century, the majority of white men did not trouble themselves with political matters. But the trauma of the Panic of 1819 and the spirited presidential campaign for

Andrew Jackson helped to create widespread interest in politics. For many Americans, political participation became an important way of asserting and supporting important values and promoting their vision of the republic.

Changing Political Culture

The presidency of Andrew Jackson was a crucial factor in bringing politics to the center of many Americans' lives. Styling himself as the people's candidate in 1828, Andrew Jackson derided the Adams administration as corrupt and aristocratic and promised a more democratic political system with the interests of the people at its center. To this end, he told voters that he intended to "purify" and "reform the Government," purging all "who have been appointed from political considerations or against the will of the people." Then as today, many Americans believed the campaign rhetoric. Four times more men turned out to vote in the election of 1828 than had gone to the polls four years earlier. They gave Jackson a resounding 56 percent of their ballots. No other president in the century would equal that percentage of popular support.

Despite campaign rhetoric and his image as a democratic hero, Jackson was not personally very democratic, nor did the era he symbolized involve any significant redistribution of wealth. Jackson himself owned slaves, defended slavery, and condoned mob attacks on abolitionists like Marius Robinson in the mid-1830s. He disliked Indians and ordered the forcible removal of the southeastern Indian nations to west of the Mississippi River in blatant disregard of the treaty rights of the Cherokee and a Supreme Court decision that protected their Georgia lands. And belying promises of widening opportunity, the rich got richer during the Jacksonian era, and most farming and urban laboring families did not prosper.

But the nation's political life had changed in important ways. The old system of politics based on elite coalitions bound together by ties of family and friendship and dependent on the deference of voters to their "betters" largely disappeared. In its place emerged a competitive party system, begun early in the republic but now oriented toward widespread voter participation and state and local politics. Party organizations bent on mobilizing large numbers of citizens became key to political victory. The major parties grew adept at raising money, selecting and promoting candidates, and bringing vot-

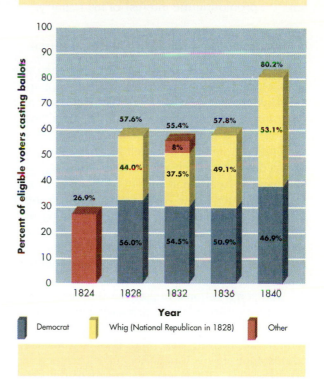

More Americans Vote for President, 1824–1840

Percent of eligible voters casting ballots

Year	Democrat	Whig (National Republican in 1828)	Other	Total
1824			26.9%	
1828	56.0%	44.0%		57.6%
1832	54.5%	37.5%	8%	55.4%
1836	50.9%	49.1%		57.8%
1840	46.9%	53.1%		80.2%

Democrat   Whig (National Republican in 1828)   Other

ers to the polls. A new "democratic" style of political life emerged as parties sponsored conventions, rallies, and parades to encourage political participation and identification. Party politics became a central preoccupation for many adult white males. In the North, even women turned out for political rallies and speeches and rode on floats at party parades.

A rough-and-ready style of political activity emerged as parties catered to popular emotions and ethnic prejudices. Party-subsidized newspapers regularly indulged in scurrilous attacks on political candidates. The language of politics became contentious and militaristic. Jackson's rhetoric exemplified the new trends. He described an opponent as an "enemy" who waged "war against the cause of the people." He reminded Americans that "those who are not for us are against us." Politicians pictured elections as battles or campaigns. Party leaders concerned themselves with the discipline of their party's "rank and file." Strong party identification was part of the new national political culture. James Buchanan complained in 1839 about a colleague who urged politicians "to rise above mere party, and to go for our country." Instead, Buchanan said, "in supporting my party, I honestly believe I am . . . promoting the interest of my country."

Jackson's Path to the White House

The early career of Andrew Jackson gave few hints of his future political importance. Orphaned at 14, young Jackson was rowdy, indecisive, and often in trouble. As a law student he was a "most roaring, rollicking, game-cocking, horse-racing, card-playing, mischievous fellow." Despite these preoccupations, which also included dueling, Jackson passed the bar and set out at the age of 21 to seek his fortune in the West. Settling in the frontier town of Nashville, the tall, redheaded young man built up a successful law practice in Tennessee and went on to become attorney general. Eventually, he became a substantial landowner and a prominent citizen of Nashville.

Jackson's national reputation stemmed mainly from his military exploits, primarily against American Indians. As major general of the Tennessee militia, he proved able and popular. Jackson's troops admired his toughness and nicknamed him "Old Hickory." His savage victory over the Creek nation in the South in 1813 and 1814 brought notoriety and an appointment as major general in the U.S. Army. But his victory over the British at New Orleans in 1815 and his image as a savior made him into a national hero. His tour of the country after the war suggested political ambitions. As early as 1817, resolutions supporting a Jackson bid for the presidency began to appear in several states.

Although Jackson's aggressive military forays into Spanish Florida in 1818 bothered rival politicians and added to his reputation for scandal, these actions increased his popularity and his interest in the presidency. Jackson recognized that his greatest appeal lay with ordinary people, whom he cultivated. At the same time, he realized the importance of effective political backing. Careful political maneuvering in Tennessee in the early 1820s brought him election as U.S. senator and nomination for the presidency in 1824.

In the 1824 election, Jackson won both the popular and electoral votes but lost in the House of Representatives to John Quincy Adams. When Henry Clay threw his support to Adams and was named secretary of state, Jackson condemned this deal as a "corrupt bargain." Soon after the 1824 election, a rumor surfaced in Washington that "a

Party is forming itself to oppose Mr. Adams' administration." Jackson's loss convinced him of the importance of having an effective political organization. He felt confident of his strength in the West, and support by Adams's vice-president, John C. Calhoun, helped him in the South. Jackson organized his campaign by setting up loyal committees and newspapers in many states and by encouraging efforts to undermine Adams and Clay. His candidacy got a strong boost in 1826 when a New York senator, Martin Van Buren, swung to his side.

The loose coalition promoting Jackson's candidacy, which began to call itself the Democratic party, was a mixed lot, drawing in politicians of diverse views from all sections of the country. Jackson proved masterful in playing down his position on controversial issues. He concealed his dislike of banks and paper money and told supporters that he believed in a tariff that held to a "middle and just course," a position vague enough to offend no one. He did, however, make clear his intentions of reforming government by throwing out of office anyone who was incompetent or who failed to represent the will of the people. Democratic newspapers picked up this theme and presented Jackson as a politician who would cleanse government of corruption and privileged interests.

The campaign between Jackson and Adams in 1828 degenerated into a nasty but entertaining contest. The Democrats organized barbecues, mass rallies, and parades to whip up enthusiasm. They gave out buttons and hats with hickory leaves attached. Amid the hoopla, few people discussed issues. Both sides engaged in slanderous personal attacks. Supporters of Adams and Clay, who called themselves National Republicans, claimed that Jackson was "an adulterer, a gambler, a cockfighter, a brawler, a drunkard, and a murderer." His wife, Rachel, was maligned as common and immoral.

The Jacksonians in turn charged Adams with bribing Clay for his support in 1824. They described him as a "stingy, undemocratic" aristocrat determined to destroy the people's liberties. Worse yet, Adams was an intellectual. Jackson, by contrast, was the hero of the Battle of New Orleans, a point underlined by an unprecedented campaign trip to celebrate the anniversary of his victory there. Jackson's campaign slogans emphasized the differences between himself as an energetic, military doer ("a man who can fight") and Adams as a weak, ineffectual thinker ("A man who can write"). "Who do you want," one slogan asked, "John Quincy Adams, who

Public criticism of Andrew Jackson began early in his career. This 1824 caricature lists the causes of his indigestion as the "Seven Deadly Sins," while a pack of newspapers join him in his misery.

quotes law, or Andy Jackson, who makes law?" The question left little doubt as to how proud Americans would vote.

Jackson's supporters in Washington worked to ensure his election by devising a tariff bill to win necessary support in key states. Under the leadership of Van Buren, who hoped to replace Calhoun as Jackson's heir apparent, the Democrats in Congress put together enough votes to pass what opponents called the "Tariff of Abominations." The tariff arbitrarily raised rates to protect New England textiles, Pennsylvania iron, and some agricultural goods, thereby winning voters in those states where the Democrats needed more support. John Randolph of Virginia sneered that the tariff "referred to manufactures of no sort or kind but the manufacture of a President of the United States."

The efforts of Jackson and his party paid off as he won an astonishing 647,286 ballots, about 56 percent of the total. Organization, money, effective publicity, and a popular style of campaigning had brought the 60-year-old Jackson to the presidency. Jackson's arrival in Washington in February 1829

was quiet and unassuming. A young army lieutenant from North Carolina saw "about half past 10 o'clock a plain carriage drawn by two horses followed by a single black servant. . . . This carriage contained the President Elect, and in this manner did the man enter the capital of the U.S. as a plain citizen."

However plain his entrance to the capital, Jackson's presidency would contain drama enough. His inauguration on a mild March 4 horrified many Americans. Washington was packed for the ceremonies. Daniel Webster noted that "persons have come five hundred miles to see General Jackson, and they really seem to think that the country is to be rescued from some dreadful danger." When Jackson appeared on the steps of the Capitol to take the oath of office, wild and unrestrained cheering broke out. Few in the crowd heard the short address or the oath, but many hoped to shake the new president's hand, and Jackson was all but mobbed as he tried to make his way to his horse.

The White House reception soon got completely out of hand. A throng of people, "from the highest and most polished, down to the most vulgar and gross," Justice Joseph Story observed, poured into the White House with muddy boots to overturn furniture in a rush for food and punch. Jackson was forced to leave by a side door. In an effort to stop the melee, the wine and ice cream were carried out to the lawn. The guests followed, many of them diving out through the windows. The inauguration, Story concluded, illustrated "the reign of King Mob." Another observer called it "a proud day for the people." These contrasting views on the events of the inauguration captured the essence of the Jackson era. For some they symbolized the excesses of democracy; for others they represented democratic fulfillment.

Old Hickory's Vigorous Presidency

Although Jackson had taken vague positions on important issues during the campaign, as president he needed to confront many of them. His decisions, often controversial, helped to sharpen what it meant to be a Democrat and what it meant to be Democracy's opponent.

A few key convictions—the principle of majority rule, the limited power of the national government, the obligation of the national government to defend the interests of the nation's average people against the machinations of the "monied aristocracy"— guided Jackson's political behavior as president. Because he saw himself as the people's most authentic representative (only the president was elected by all the people), Jackson intended to be an effective, vigorous executive. More than any previous president, Jackson used presidential power in the name of the people and justified his actions by popular appeals to the electorate.

Jackson asserted his power most dramatically through use of the veto. The six preceding presidents had used the veto only nine times, most often against measures that they had believed unconstitutional. Jackson, however, argued that he had "undoubted right . . . to withhold . . . assent from bills on other grounds than their constitutionality." In effect, he forced Congress to consider his position on legislative issues. In all, Jackson vetoed 12 bills during his eight years in office.

One of the abuses Jackson had promised to correct was what he described as an undemocratic and corrupt system of government officeholding. Too often "unfaithful or incompetent" men held on to their offices for years, making a mockery of the idea of representation. Jackson proposed to throw these scoundrels out and to establish a system of rotation of office. Because the duties of public office were so "plain and simple," he argued, ordinary men were fit to govern.

Jackson's rhetoric was more extreme than his actions. He did not engage in wholesale replacement of officeholders with his own supporters. In the first year and a half of his presidency, he removed 919 officeholders of a total of 10,093, fewer than one in ten. Most of these were for good reason—corruption or incompetence. Nor were the new Democratic appointees especially plain, untutored, or honest; they were in fact much like their predecessors. Still, Jackson's rhetoric helped to create a new kind of responsive democratic political culture that would prevail for most of the nineteenth century.

Jackson's Indian policy of forcible removal and relocation westward also defined white American practice for the rest of the century. In the opening decades of the nineteenth century, the vast landholdings of the five "civilized nations" of the Southeast (the Cherokee, Choctaw, Chickasaw, Seminole, and Creek) had been seriously eroded by the pressures of land-hungry whites supported by successful military campaigns led by professional Indian fighters such as General Jackson. The Creeks lost 22 million acres in southern Georgia and central Alabama as a result of their defeat by Jackson at Horseshoe Bend in 1814. Land cessions to the government

and private sales accounted for even bigger losses: Cherokee tribal holdings, for example, of more than 50 million acres in 1802 had dwindled to only 9 million 20 years later.

The trend was bolstered by a Supreme Court decision in 1823 declaring that Indians could occupy but not hold title to land in the United States. Recognizing that their survival was threatened, the tribes acted to end the pattern. By 1825, the Creek, Cherokee, and Chickasaw had each resolved to restrict land sales to government agents. The Cherokee, who had already assimilated many elements of white culture including clothing, agricultural practices, and slaveholding (see Chapter 9), established a police force to prevent local leaders from selling off tribal land piecemeal. Tribal determination to resist pressure confronted white resolve to gain these southern lands for cotton planting and mining. Jackson's election in 1828 boosted efforts to relocate the tribes west of the Mississippi.

In his first annual message to Congress in 1829, Jackson made clear his imposing political presence by recommending removal of the southeastern tribes. The democratic majority he spoke for were white. Appealing at first more to sympathy than to force, Jackson argued that because the Indians were "surrounded by the whites with their arts of civi-

As depicted in this Robert Cruickshank lithograph, All Creation Going to the White House, *the first inauguration of Andrew Jackson in 1829 was the scene of wild festivities, a harbinger of the excesses in American life and politics in the ensuing years.*

lization," it was inevitable that the "resources of the savage" would be destroyed, dooming the Indians to "weakness and decay." Removal was justified, Jackson claimed, by both "humanity and national honor." He also endorsed the paramount right of state laws over the claims of either Indians or the federal government.

With the president's position clear, the crisis soon came to a head in Georgia. In 1829, the Georgia legislature declared the Cherokee tribal council illegal and its laws null and void in Cherokee territories and announced that the state had jurisdiction over both the tribe and its lands. In the following year, the Cherokee were forbidden to defend their interests by bringing suits against whites into the Georgia courts or even by testifying in such cases. Without legal recourse on the state level, the Cherokee carried their protests to the Supreme Court. In 1832, Chief Justice Marshall supported their position in *Worcester* v. *Georgia,* holding that the Georgia law was "repugnant to the Constitution" and did not apply to the Cherokee nation.

Legal victory could not, however, suppress white land hunger. With Jackson's blessing Georgians defied the Court ruling. By 1835, harassment, intimidation, and bribery had persuaded a minority of chiefs to sign a removal treaty. That year, Jackson informed the Cherokee, "You cannot remain where you are. Circumstances . . . render it impossible that you can flourish in the midst of a civilized community." Despite the president's pronouncement and the treaty, most Cherokee refused to leave their lands. Therefore, in 1837 and 1838, the United States Army searched and seized the terrified Indians and gathered them in stockades prior to herding them west to the "Indian Territory" in Oklahoma. An eyewitness described how the Cherokee trek began:

> Families at dinner were startled by the sudden gleam of bayonets in the doorway and rose to be driven with blows and oaths along the weary miles of trail that led to the stockade. Men were seized in their fields, or going along the road, women were taken from their [spinning] wheels and children from their play. In many cases, on turning for one last look as they crossed the ridge they saw their homes in flames, fired by the lawless rabble that followed on the heels of the soldiers to loot and pillage.

The removal, the $6 million cost of which was deducted from the $9 million awarded the tribe for its eastern lands, brought death to perhaps a quarter of the 15,000 who set out. The Cherokee remember this event as the "Trail of Tears." Other southern

and some northwestern tribes between 1821 and 1840 shared a similar fate. The Chickasaw suffered as high a death rate as the Cherokee during their removal, while such nations as the Seminole and the Sac and Fox fought to avoid deportation. Most nations were in the end removed. Although both Jackson and the Removal Act of 1830 had promised to protect and forever guarantee the Indian lands in the west, within a generation those promises, like others before and since, would be broken.

Indian removal left the eastern United States open for the enormous economic expansion described in Chapters 11 and 12. On the question of internal improvements to support that expansion, Jackson also imposed his enormous will.

During the 1828 campaign, Jackson had waffled on the question of internal improvements. Like most Americans, he recognized their economic importance and as president wished "to see them extended to every part of the country." But Jackson believed that the national government should not infringe on states' rights. When proposals for federal support for internal improvements seemed to rob local and state authorities of their proper function, he opposed them. In 1830, he vetoed the Maysville Road bill, which would have authorized the use of federal funds to build a road in Henry Clay's Kentucky. But projects of national significance, like the building of lighthouses or river improvements, were different matters. In fact, Jackson supported an annual average of $1.3 million in internal improvements while he was in office.

In a period of rapid economic change, tariffs were a matter of heated debate. New England and the Middle Atlantic states, the center of manufacturing operations, favored protective tariffs. But the South had long opposed such tariffs because they made it more expensive for southerners to buy manufactured goods from the North or abroad. In addition, they feared that high tariffs would lead to reductions in trade harmful to the export of southern cotton and tobacco. Feelings against the "Tariff of Abominations" ran particularly high in South Carolina. Some of that state's leaders saw the tariff as the prime cause of the economic depression that hung over their state (it actually stemmed from the opening of new fertile lands in the West). In addition, some worried that the federal government might eventually interfere with slavery, a frightening prospect in a state where slaves outnumbered whites.

Vice-President Calhoun, a brilliant political thinker, provided the appropriate theory to counteract the power of the federal government and to protect minority rights. "We are not a nation," he once remarked, "but a Union, a confederacy of equal and sovereign states." In 1828, the same year as the hateful tariff, Calhoun published an anonymous essay, *Exposition and Protest,* which presented the doctrine of nullification as a means by which southern states could protect themselves from harmful national action. He argued that when federal laws were deemed to overstep the limits of constitutional authority, a state had the right to declare that legislation null and void and to refuse to enforce it.

Two years later, Calhoun's doctrine was aired in a Senate debate over public land policy. South Carolina's Robert Hayne defined nullification and, in the name of liberty, urged western states to adopt the doctrine. In a speech spread over two days, Daniel Webster eloquently responded. The federal government, he maintained, was far more than an agent of the states. It was "made for the people, made by the people, and answerable to the people." No state legislature, therefore, could ever be sovereign over the people. Aware that nullification raised the specter of "a once glorious Union . . . drenched . . . in fraternal blood," Webster cried out in his powerful closing words that the appropriate motto for the nation was not "Liberty first and Union afterwards, but Liberty and Union, now and forever, one and inseparable!"

The drama was reenacted a month later at a Jefferson birthday dinner when President Jackson declared himself on the issue. Despite his support of states' rights, Jackson did not believe that any state had the right to reject the will of the majority or to destroy the Union. Knowing that the supporters of nullification hoped to use the gathering to win adherents, Jackson rose for a toast, held high his glass, and said, "Our Union—it must be preserved." Not to be outdone, Calhoun followed with his toast: "The Union—next to our liberty most dear." The split between them widened over personal as well as ideological issues, and in 1832 Calhoun resigned as vice-president. Final rupture came in a collision over the tariff and nullification.

In 1832, following Jackson's recommendation of a "middle course" for tariff revisions, Congress modified the tariff of 1828 by retaining high duties on goods such as wool, woolens, iron, and hemp and lowering other rates to an earlier level. Many southerners felt injured. In a special convention later that year in South Carolina, the delegates adopted an Ordinance of Nullification, declaring that the offending tariffs of 1828 and 1832 were null and void in that state. None of the duties would be collected. Furthermore, the South Carolina legislature voted funds for a volunteer army and threatened secession if the federal government should try to force the state to comply.

South Carolina's actions represented a direct attack on the concepts of federal union and majority rule. Jackson responded with appropriate force. To the "ambitious malcontents" in South Carolina, as he called the nullifiers, he issued a proclamation that stated emphatically that "the laws of the United States must be executed. . . . Disunion by armed force is *treason*. . . . The Union will be preserved and treason and rebellion promptly put down."

Jackson's proclamation stimulated an outburst of patriotism and popular support all over the country. No other southern states supported nullification, and several state legislatures denounced it. South Carolina stood alone. When Jackson asked Congress for legislation to enforce tariff duties (the Force Bill of 1833), the crisis neared resolution. Tariff revisions, engineered by Henry Clay and supported by Calhoun, called for reductions over a ten-year period. South Carolina quickly repealed its nullification of the tariff laws but saved face by nullifying the Force Bill at the same time, an act that Jackson ignored. The crisis was over, but left unresolved were the constitutional issues it raised. Was the Union permanent? Was secession a valid way to protect minority rights? Debate on such questions would trouble Americans for three decades.

Jackson's Bank War and "Van Ruin's" Depression

As the people's advocate, Jackson could not ignore the Second Bank of the United States, which had been chartered for 20 years in 1816. The fate of the bank was an issue generating intense feelings in a period of economic change. Jackson believed the bank threatened the people's liberties and called it a "monster." But the bank was not as irresponsible as Jacksonians imagined.

Guided since 1823 by the aristocratic Nicholas Biddle, the Philadelphia bank and its 29 branches performed many useful financial services and generally played a responsible economic role in an expansionary period. As the nation's largest commercial bank, the U.S. Bank was able to shift funds to different parts of the country as necessary and to influence state banking activity. It restrained state banks from making unwise loans by insisting that they back their notes with specie (gold or silver coin) and by calling in its own loans to these institutions. The bank accepted federal deposits, made commercial loans, and bought and sold government bonds. Businessmen, state bankers needing credit, and nationalist politicians such as Webster and Clay, who were on the bank's payroll, all favored the bank.

Other Americans, however, led by the president, distrusted the bank. Businessmen and speculators in western lands resented the bank's careful control over state banking and wanted cheap, inflated money. Some state bankers, especially in New York and Baltimore, were jealous of the power and position of the Philadelphia bank. Southern and western farmers regarded the bank, which dealt with

"Old Hickory," the nickname Jackson earned in his early military career, is a reference to America's toughest hardwood. As president, Jackson continued his uncompromising tactics.

paper rather than landed property, as fundamentally immoral, and others thought it was unconstitutional and should be abolished.

Jackson had long opposed the U.S. Bank both for personal reasons (a near financial disaster in his own past) and because he and his advisers believed it was the chief example of a special privilege monopoly that hurt the common man—farmers, craftsmen, and debtors. Jackson called the bank an "irresponsible power" and a threat to the republic. Its power and financial resources, he thought, allowed the bank to become a "vast electioneering engine" with the "power to control the Government and change its character."

Aware of Jackson's persisting hostility, Clay and Webster persuaded Biddle to ask Congress to recharter the bank in 1832, four years ahead of schedule. They reasoned that in an election year, Jackson would not risk a veto. The bill to recharter the bank swept through Congress and landed on the president's desk one hot, muggy day in July. Many in his own party pressed for "a milk & water half way veto," which would make possible another attempt to recharter the bank at a less embarrassing time. But Jackson refused to listen. "The bank . . . is trying to kill me," he told Van Buren, *"but I will kill it."*

Jackson determined not only to veto the bill but also to carry his case to the public. His veto message, which condemned the bank as undemocratic, un-American, and unconstitutional, was meant to stir up emotions among voters. He presented the bank as a dangerous monopoly that helped the rich by providing them with special privileges and harmed "the humble members of society . . . who have neither the time nor the means of securing . . . favors to themselves." He also pointed to the high percentage of foreign investors in the bank. Jackson's veto message turned the issue of rechartering the bank into a struggle between the people and the aristocracy. His oversimplified analysis made the bank into a symbol of all that was worrisome to many Americans in a time of change.

The furor over the bank helped to clarify party differences. In the election of 1832, the National Republicans, now becoming known as Whigs to show their opposition to "King Andrew," nominated Henry Clay. Biddle and the Whigs spent thousands of dollars trying to ensure Clay's election over Jackson, whom they labeled a "tyrant." Democratic campaign rhetoric pitted Jackson, the people, and democracy against Clay, the bank, and aristocracy. The Anti-Masons, the first third party in American political life and the first to hold a nominating convention, revealed real issues more clearly than the two major parties. The anti-Masonic movement, which began in upstate New York, expressed popular resentments against the elitist Masonic order (Jackson was a member) and other secret societies. At a deeper level, anti-Masonry reflected tensions over commercialization as new groups vied with old families for political power.

When the ballots were counted, Jackson had once again won handsomely, garnering 124,000 more popular votes than the combined total for Clay and the Anti-Mason candidate, William Wirt, who said of Jackson, "He may be President for life if he chooses."

Although the election results suggest that the bank issue actually harmed Jackson, he interpreted the election as a victory for his bank policy and made plans to finish his war with Biddle. The bank still had four years before the charter expired. Jackson announced that "the hydra of corruption is only scotched, not dead" and declared that it must be killed. He and his advisers decided to weaken the bank by transferring $10 million in government funds to state banks. Although two secretaries of the treasury balked at the removal request as financially unsound, Jackson persisted until he found one, Roger Taney, willing to remove the funds. And when Chief Justice John Marshall, a Whig, died in 1835, Jackson replaced him with Taney. Businessman Samuel Breck was disgusted with Jackson's "folly and wickedness in taking the *public money from the U.S. Bank,* to place [it] for political purposes in the weaker state banks."

Jackson's war with Biddle and the bank had serious economic consequences. A wave of speculation in western lands and ambitious new state internal improvement schemes in the mid-1830s led to rising land prices and a flood of paper money. Even Jackson was concerned, and he determined to curtail irresponsible economic activity. In July 1836, he issued the Specie Circular, announcing that the government would accept only gold and silver in payment for public lands. Panicky investors rushed to change paper notes into specie, while banks started to call in loans. The result was the Panic of 1837. Although Jackson was blamed for this rapid monetary expansion followed by sudden deflation in the mid-1830s, international trade problems with Britain and China probably contributed more to the panic and to the ensuing seven years of depression than Jackson's erratic policies.

Whatever the primary cause, Jackson stuck his successor, Martin Van Buren, who was elected in 1836 over a trio of Whig opponents, with an economic crisis. Van Buren had barely taken the oath of office in 1837 when banks and businesses began to collapse. His term as president was marked by a depression so severe that it brought him the unfortunate nickname "Martin Van Ruin." As New York banks suspended credit and began calling in loans, an estimated $6 million was lost on defaulted debts. In 1838, a wealthy merchant and mayor of New York, Philip Hone, wrote in his diary that half his friends were deeply in debt. By 1840, he noted, his three grown sons were out of work and "business of all kinds [was] completely at a stand."

As Hone knew well, however, the laboring poor suffered most in a depression. By the fall of 1837, one-third of America's workers were unemployed, and thousands of others found only sporadic, part-time work. For those fortunate enough to retain their jobs, wages fell by 30 to 50 percent within two years. Meanwhile, the price of necessities like flour, pork, and coal nearly doubled. As winter neared in late 1837, a journalist estimated that 200,000 in New York City were "in utter hopeless distress with no means of surviving the winter but those provided by charity." Not surprisingly, they took to the streets, demanding, "Bread! Meat! Rent! Fuel! Their prices must come down!" One worker told newspaperman Horace Greeley that most laborers called "not for the bread and fuel of charity, but for Work!"

The pride of workers was damped as soup kitchens and bread lines grew faster than jobs. Moreover, the depression destroyed the trade union movement begun a decade earlier, leaving laboring families isolated and defenseless. Many employers hastened the process of killing trade unionism by imposing longer hours, cutting wages and piece rates, and dividing workers. One New England hat manufacturer offered to hire only those untouched by "the moral gangrene of Trades' Union principles." As the hardships of the depression grew worse, violence increased. In 1842, when Philadelphia textile employers lowered wages below subsistence levels, angry hand-loom weavers broke machinery, destroyed cloth, and wrecked the homes of Irish strikebreakers. Job competition, poverty, and ethnic animosities led to violent clashes in other eastern cities as well, as we saw in Chapter 11.

"How is it," a Philadelphia mechanic asked in 1837, that in a country as rich as the United States so many people were "pinched for the common necessaries of life . . . [and] bowed down with gloom and despair?" President Van Buren's responses to the social misery behind this question were sympathetic but limited. His independent government subtreasury system, intended to fill credit and currency needs in the absence of a national bank, actually made things worse by deflationary policies and did not last long. An executive order in 1840 declaring a ten-hour day for federal employees affected few workers. Although these measures were inadequate, political participation, as well as church membership, reached new heights during the depression, as Americans sought to alleviate their "gloom and despair."

The Second American Party System

By the mid-1830s, a new two-party system and a lively participatory national political culture had emerged in the United States. The parties had taken shape amid the conflicts of Jackson's presidency and mirrored the growing diversity of a changing nation. Although both parties included wealthy and influential, even despotic leaders, the Democrats had the better claim that they were the party of the common man with strength in all sections of the country.

Whigs represented greater wealth than Democrats and were strongest in New England and in areas settled by New Englanders across the Upper Midwest. In an appeal to businessmen and manufacturers, Whigs generally endorsed Clay's American System, which meant that they favored a national bank, federally supported internal improvements, and tariff protection for industry. Many large southern cotton planters joined the Whig party because of its position on bank credit and internal improvements. Whigs ran almost evenly with Democrats in the South for a decade, and artisans and laborers belonged equally to each party. The difficulty in drawing clear regional or class distinctions between Whigs and Democrats suggests that other factors, such as ethnic, religious, and cultural background, also influenced party choice. Because each party offered its own vision of the good society and notions on the role of government in private lives, broad cultural and social perspectives helped to determine party affiliation.

The Second American Party System

	Democrats	Whigs
Leaders:	Andrew Jackson John C. Calhoun Martin Van Buren Thomas Hart Benton	Henry Clay Daniel Webster John Quincy Adams William Henry Harrison
Political tradition:	Republican party (Jefferson, Madison)	Federalist party (Hamilton, John Adams)

Major Political Beliefs

State and local autonomy Against monopoly and privilege Low land prices and tariffs Leave people alone	National power U.S. Bank, high tariff Internal improvements Reform America

Primary Sources of Support

	Democrats	Whigs
Region:	South and West	New England, Middle Atlantic, Upper Midwest
Class:	Middle-class and small farmers, pockets of northeastern urban laborers and artisans	Big southern planters and wealthy businessmen, pockets of middling farmers in Midwest and South, artisans
Ethnicity:	Scots-Irish, Irish, French, German, and Canadian immigrants	English, New England old stock
Religion:	Catholics, frontier Baptists and Methodists, free thinkers	Presbyterians, Congregationalists, Quakers, moralists, reformers

In the Jeffersonian tradition, the Democrats espoused liberty and local rule. They wanted freedom from legislators of morality, from special privilege, and from too much government. For them, the best society was one in which all Americans were free to follow their own individual interests. Those who wanted to maintain religious or ethnic traditions found a home in the Democratic party. The Scots-Irish, German, French, and Irish Catholic immigrants, as well as free thinkers and labor organizers, tended to be Jacksonians. Although they zealously promoted their social vision, Democrats were less moralistic than Whigs. Especially on matters like temperance and slavery, their religious background generally taught the inevitability of sin and evil in the world. Therefore, Democrats sought to keep politics separate from moral issues.

By contrast, for many Whigs the line between reform and politics was hazy. Indeed, politics seemed an appropriate arena for cleansing society of sin. Calling themselves the party of law and order, most Whigs did not think Americans needed more freedom but rather they needed to learn to use the freedom they already had. If all men were to vote, they required "a system of general education" that would teach them to use their political privileges. Old-stock New England Yankee Congregationalists and Presbyterians were usually Whigs. So were Quakers and evangelical Protestants, who believed that positive government action could change moral behavior and eradicate sin. Whigs supported a wide variety of reforms, such as temperance, antislavery, public education, and strict observance of the Sabbath, as well as government action to promote economic development.

Party identification played an increasingly large part in the lives of American men. The flamboyant new electioneering styles and techniques were designed to recruit new voters into the political process and to ensure continued loyalty. Party activities offered excitement, entertainment, and camaraderie. They offered a way to shape the changing world.

The election of 1840 illustrated the new style of political culture. Passing over Henry Clay, the Whigs nominated William Henry Harrison of Indiana, the aging hero of the Battle of Tippecanoe (Kithtippecanoe), fought nearly 30 years earlier. A Virginian, John Tyler, was nominated as vice-president to underline the regional diversity of the party. The Democrats had no choice but to renominate Van Buren, who conducted a quiet campaign. The Whig campaign, however, featured every form of popularized appeals for votes—barbecues, torchlight parades, songs, and cartoons. Political symbolism was exploited by posing Harrison (who lived in a mansion) in front of a rural log cabin with a barrel of hard cider. Jugs of cider and coonskin caps inscribed with clever slogans were lavishly dispensed to grateful voters.

The Whigs reversed conventional images by labeling Van Buren an aristocratic dandy and contrasting him to their simple candidate sitting in front of his cabin. Harrison reminded voters of General Jackson and they swept him into office, 234 electoral votes to Van Buren's 60. In one of the largest turn-

In the election of 1840, the Whigs "out-Jacksoned the Jacksonians" by playing to the popular political style of slogans, songs, and cider. They also touted their candidate as a backwoodsy Indian fighter while maligning the Democrat Van Buren as an aristocratic dandy.

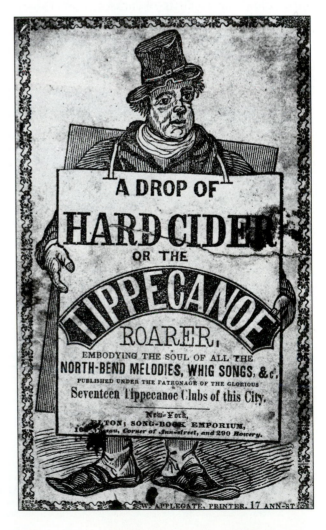

outs in American history, over 80 percent of eligible voters marched to the polls. Commenting on the defeat, a Democratic party journal acknowledged that the Whigs had out-Jacksoned the Jacksonians: "We taught them how to conquer us."

Concern over the new politics outlasted Harrison, who died only a month after taking office. One man complained during the campaign that he was tired of all the hoopla over "the Old Hero. Nothing but politics . . . mass-meetings are held in every groggery." His comment about the combination of politics and drinking was especially telling. For many Americans, usually Whigs and often women, it was precisely the excesses of Jacksonian politics, most notably intemperance and the inherent violence of slavery, that led them to seek other ways than politics of imposing order and morality on American society. To gain a measure of control over their lives and reshape their changing world, the American people turned also to religion, social reform, and utopianism.

RELIGIOUS REVIVAL AND REFORM

When the Frenchman Alexis de Tocqueville visited the United States in 1831 and 1832, he observed that he could find "no country in the whole world in which the Christian religion retains a greater influence over the souls of men than in America." What De Tocqueville was describing was a new and powerful religious enthusiasm among the American people. Religious commitment was the means by which some found certainty in a fast-changing world. Others were inspired by revivalism to refashion American society, either by founding model utopian communities or new religions or by tackling a particular social evil that needed reform. Like those reshaping American society through political parties in the 1830s, the religiously inspired social reformers also responded to the changing economic and ethnic character of the United States and had a national sense of the vital importance of their respective crusades.

Finney and the Second Great Awakening

From the late 1790s until the late 1830s, a wave of religious revivals that matched the intensity of the Great Awakening in the 1730s and 1740s swept through the United States. The camp meeting re-

vivals of the frontier at the turn of the century and the New England revivals sparked by Lyman Beecher took on a new emphasis and location after 1830. Led by the spellbinding Charles G. Finney, under whose influence Marius Robinson had been converted, revivalism shifted to upstate New York and the Old Northwest. Both areas had been experiencing profound economic and social changes, as the example of Rochester, New York, suggests.

By the 1830s, Rochester, like Lowell and Cincinnati, was a rapidly growing American city. Located on the recently completed Erie Canal, it was a flour-milling center for the rich wheat lands of western New York. The canal changed Rochester from a sleepy little village of 300 in 1815 to a bustling commercial and milling city of nearly 20,000 inhabitants by 1830. As in other cities, economic growth affected relationships between masters and workers, distancing them both physically and psychologically. As the gulf widened, the masters' control over their laborers weakened. Saloons and unions sprang up in workingmen's neighborhoods, and workers became more transient, following the canal and other opportunities westward.

Prominent Rochester citizens therefore invited Charles Finney to come to town in 1830 to deliver some sermons. What followed was one of the most successful revivals of the Second Great Awakening. "You could not go upon the streets," a convert recalled, "and hear any conversation, except upon religion." Finney preached nearly every night and three times on Sundays, converting first the city's business elite, often through their wives, and then many workers. For six months Rochester went through a citywide prayer meeting in which one conversion led to another.

The Rochester revival was part of the wave of religious enthusiasm in America that contributed to the tremendous growth of the Methodists, the Baptists, and other evangelical sects in the first half of the nineteenth century. By 1844, for example, the Methodist church had become the largest denomination in America, with over a million members. To bring large masses of people to accept Christ as their savior, revivalist preachers deemphasized doctrine in favor of emotion, softening strict Calvinist tenets such as predestination, original sin, and limited atonement.

Unlike Jonathan Edwards, who believed that revivals were God's miracles, Finney understood that the human "agency" of the minister was crucial in causing a revival. He even published a do-it-yourself

EUROPEANS' TRAVEL JOURNALS

The observations of Alexis de Tocqueville about American religion suggest that one source of recovering the American past is by reading the accounts of non-American visitors. In the 1830s and 1840s, a stream of Europeans came to the United States to see for themselves the development of American character and mass political participation in the age of Jackson. These notable visitors came from England, Scotland, France, Hungary, and the German states, as well as from Argentina and other newly independent nations in Latin America. Upon returning home, they wrote books about their travels, revealing their impressions of the character of the American people and institutions.

Obviously, these visitors did not all agree about the qualities they observed in Americans or whether the American style of democratic politics was a good or bad thing. Some saw the American people and their elected representatives as unsophisticated, uncultured, and undisciplined, less interested in the substance of a politician's speech, as Charles Dickens observed in 1842, than in "how long did he speak?" After a visit to Congress, Dickens described the dire condition of the handsome carpets in House chambers as a result of the prevalent habit of tobacco chewing and spitting among legislators. The Englishman noted the "universal disregard of the spittoon with which every honorable member is accommodated" and advised visitors not to look at the "squirted and dabbled upon" carpets or to pick up anything "with an ungloved hand." From many a European visitor's point of view, Americans were uncouth, violent, ill-mannered, more adept at handling a rifle than a fork.

Others, however, saw the United States as a model society that European nations should seek to imitate, while still others astutely observed the mixed, doubled-edged value of "democracy in America" for politics, the distribution of wealth, and personal character. Compare, for example, the accounts of patriotism, property, and politics in America by three European visitors in the 1830s. Alexis de Tocqueville, a French aristocrat and probably the most famous of the European observers of American life, visited the United States in 1831–1832 and published his impressions and insights in *Democracy in America* in 1835. A British feminist, Harriet Martineau, traveled in the United States in the mid-1830s and published *Society in America* in 1837, the same year as the Bohemian Francis Grund visited America and wrote *The Americans in Their Moral, Social, and Political Relations*.

All three celebrated democratic institutions in the United States, and all three explored the implications of democracy for individual freedom and equality of opportunity. But they did not come to the same conclusions. Summarize the major points of each observer and state their similarities and differences. What did they see as the most outstanding features of American life and politics? What did they note as the most dangerous flaws? Whether positive or negative in their overall assessment, how accurate and insightful do you think they were? Which one do you think was most perceptive in describing American life and politics and the character of the American people in the era of Andrew Jackson?

Alexis de Tocqueville, 1835

In my opinion, the main evil of the present democratic institutions of the United States does not arise, as is often asserted in Europe, from their weakness, but from their irresistible strength. I am not so much alarmed at the excessive liberty which reigns in that country, as at the inadequate securities which one finds there against tyranny. . . .

I do not say that there is frequent use of tyranny in America, at the present day; but I maintain that there is no sure barrier against it, and that the causes which mitigate the government there are to be found in the circumstances and the manners of the country, more than in its laws. . . .

I know of no country in which there is so little independence of mind and real freedom of discussion as in America. . . . In America, the majority raises formidable barriers around the liberty of opinion: within these barriers, an author may write what he pleases; but woe to him if he goes beyond them. . . . He is exposed to continued obloquy and persecution. His political career is closed forever, since he has offended the only authority which is able to open it to it. Every sort of compensation, even that of celebrity, is refused to him. Before publishing his opinions, he imagined that he held them in common with others; but no sooner has he declared them, than he is loudly censured by his opponents, whilst those who think like him, without having the courage to speak out, abandon him in silence. He yields at length, overcome by the daily effort which he has to make, and subsides into silence, as if he felt remorse for having spoken the truth.

Fetters and headsmen were the coarse instruments which tyranny formerly employed; but the civilization of our age has perfected despotism itself, though it seemed to have nothing to learn. Monarchs had, so to speak, materialized oppression: the democratic republics of the present day have rendered it as entirely an affair of the mind, as the will which it is intended to coerce. Under the absolute sway of one man, the body was attacked in order to subdue the soul; but the soul escaped the blows which were directed against it, and rose proudly superior. Such is not the course adopted by tyranny in democratic republics: there the body is left free, and the soul is enslaved. The master no longer says, "You shall think as I do, or you shall die"; but he says, "You are free to think differently from me, and to retain your life, your property, and all you possess; but you are henceforth a stranger among your people."

Harriet Martineau, 1837

One sunny October morning I was taking a drive, with my party, along the shores of the pretty Owasco Lake, in New York State, and conversing on the condition of the country with a gentleman who thought the political prospect less bright than the landscape. I had been less than three weeks in the country, and was in a state of something like awe at the prevalence of, not only external competence, but intellectual ability.

The striking effect upon a stranger of witnessing, for the first time, the absence of poverty, of gross ignorance, of all servility, of all insolence of manner, cannot be exaggerated in description. I had seen every man in the towns an independent citizen; every man in the country a land-owner. I had seen that the villages had their newspapers, the factory girls their libraries. I had witnessed the controversies between candidates for office on some difficult subjects, of which the people were to be the judges. With all these things in my mind, and with every evidence of prosperity about me in the comfortable homesteads which every turn in the road, and every reach of the lake, brought into view, I was thrown into a painful amazement by being told that the grand question of the time was "whether the people should be encouraged to govern themselves, or whether the wise should save them from themselves."

The confusion of inconsistencies was here so great as to defy argument; the patronage among equals that was implied; the assumption as to who were the wise; and the conclusion that all the rest must be foolish. This one sentence seemed to be the most extraordinary combination that could proceed from the lips of a republican. . . .

One of the most painful apprehensions seems to be that the poorer will heavily tax the richer members of society; the rich being always a small class. If it be true, as all parties appear to suppose, that rulers in general are prone to use their power for selfish purposes, there remains the alternative, whether the poor shall over-tax the rich, or whether the rich shall over-tax the poor: and, if one of these evils were necessary, few would doubt which would be the least.

But the danger appears much diminished on the consideration that, in the country under our notice, there are not, nor are likely to be, the wide differences in property which exist in old countries. There is no class of hereditary rich or poor. Few are very wealthy; few are poor; and every man has a fair chance of being rich. No such unequal taxation has yet been ordained by the sovereign people; nor does there appear to be any danger of it, while the total amount of taxation is so very small as in the United States, and the interest that every one has in the protection of property is so great.

A friend in the South, while eulogizing to me the state of society there, spoke with compassion of his northern fellow citizens, who were exposed to the risks of "a perpetual struggle between pauperism and property." To which a northern friend replied, that it is true that there is a perpetual struggle everywhere between pauperism and property. The question is, which succeeds. In the United States, the prospect is that each will succeed. Paupers may obtain what they want, and proprietors will keep that which they have.

Francis Grund, 1837

It often appeared to me as if the whole property of the United States was only held by the Americans in trust for their children, and that they were prepared to render a religious account of their stewardship. See with what willingness they labour to secure an independence to their children!—with what readiness they take a part in the national improvements of their country!—with what cheerfulness they quit an already fertilized soil and emigrate to the "far west" to make more room for their offspring! How ready they are to invest their fortunes in undertakings which can only benefit their progeny! Are these not proofs of a genuine patriotism? Is this not the most exalted love of country of which history furnishes us with a record? . . .

No class of society in the United States is opposed to republican institutions, as there is no political party whose permanent interests are opposed to the majority of the people. Neither is the policy of the United States likely to involve the country in a foreign war; and if in a national broil the republic should become a belligerent party, her political and geographical position is such, that she has little to fear from an enemy.

The Americans have kept good faith with all nations; and by the most unexampled economy discharged their national debt. Their credit is unrivalled; their honour unquestioned, and the most implicit confidence placed in their ability to fulfil their engagements. They have, thus far, received strangers with hospitality, and put no obstacles in the way of their progress. They have not monopolised a single branch of industry; but let foreigners and native citizens compete fairly for an equal chance of success. They have established liberty of conscience, and compelled no person to pay taxes for the support of ministers of a different persuasion from his own. They have abolished all hereditary privileges; but let all men start free and equal, with no other claims to preferment, than that which is founded on superiority of intellect. In short, they have made their country the market for talent, ingenuity, industry and every honest kind of exertion. It has become the home of all who are willing to rise by their own efforts, and contains within itself nearly half the enterprise of the world.

These are the true causes of the rapid growth of America, which, joined to her immense natural resources, must make her eventually the most powerful country on the globe. It is the principle of liberty, carried out in all its ramifications and details, which has produced these mighty results.

To what extent do these accounts still describe the American people and political styles a century and a half later? If you were to visit another society for several months, how accurate do you think you could be in assessing cultural values and national character? To what extent would you, like these early visitors to the United States, reflect your own values and national and class background as you analyzed another culture? What questions would you ask?

manual for other revivalists. Few, however, could match Finney's powerful preaching style. The hypnotic effect of his eyes and voice carried such power that he could dissolve an audience into tears. When he threw an imaginary brick at the Devil, people ducked. When his finger pointed the descent of a sinner into hell, people in the back row stood up to see the final disappearance. A former lawyer, Finney used logic as well as emotion to bring about conversions.

Most revivalists, especially in the South, sought individual salvation. The Finney revivals, however, were unique in that they nourished collective reform. Finney taught that humans were not passive objects of God's predestined plan but moral free agents who could choose good over evil, convince others to do the same, and thereby eradicate sin from the world. Conversion and salvation were not the end of religious experience but the beginning. Finney's idea of the "utility of benevolence" meant not only individual reformation but also the commitment to reform society. The Bible commanded humans, "Be ye therefore perfect even as your Father in heaven is perfect," and mid-nineteenth-century reformers took the challenge seriously. Eventually, a perfected millennial era of 1,000 years of peace, harmony, and Christian brotherhood on earth would bring the Second Coming of Christ.

The perfectionist thrust to revivalism fit America's sense of itself as a redeemer nation chosen by God to reform the entire world. Religious commitment fused with patriotic duty. The motivating impulse to reform in the 1830s, then, had many deep-rooted causes. These included the Puritan idea of American mission; the secular examples of founding fathers like Benjamin Franklin to do good, reinforced by Republican ideology and romantic beliefs in the natural goodness of human nature; the social activist tendencies in Whig political ideology; anxiety over shifting class relationships and the need to achieve some control over one's life as a result of the socioeconomic changes of recent years; family influence and the desire of young people to choose careers of principled service; and the direct influence of the Finney revivals in the early 1830s.

Reform and Politics

The reform impulse ultimately involved antebellum activists in the broader politics of the Jacksonian era. Reformers and party politicians, especially Whigs, both faced timeless dilemmas about how best to effect change. Does one, for example, try to change attitudes first and then behavior, or the reverse? Which is more effective, to appeal to

This 1839 painting of a camp meeting captures the religious fervor that many Americans turned to in the face of social and economic upheavals. These mass conversions led some believers to individual salvation and others to social reform.

Motivations and Causes of Reform in America, 1830–1850

- Changing relationships between men and women, masters and workers as a result of the market economy, growth of cities, and increasing immigration

- Finney and other religious revivals in the Second Great Awakening

- Social activist and ethical impulses of the Whig party

- Psychological anxieties over shifting class and ethnic relationships

- Family traditions and youthful idealism

- Puritan and Revolutionary traditions of the American mission to remake the world

- Republican ideology and Enlightenment emphasis on virtue and good citizenship

- Romantic literacy influences such as Transcendentalism

people's minds and hearts in order to change bad institutions or to change institutions first, assuming that altered behavior will change hearts and attitudes? Taking the first path, the reformer relies on education, on the moral suasion of sermons, tracts, literature, argument, and personal testimony. Following the second, the reformer acts politically and institutionally, seeking to pass laws, win elections, form unions, boycott tainted goods, and create or abolish institutions.

Reformers, moreover, have to decide whether to attempt to bring about limited, piecemeal practical change on a single issue or to take on many issues. Should they improve on a partly defective system or tear down the entire system in order to build a utopian new one? Reformers must further decide whether to use or recommend force and whether to enter into coalitions with less principled potential allies. They also face the difficult challenge of making sure that their own attitudes and actions are thoroughly consistent with the principles of behavior they would urge on others.

These challenging problems fill the lives of reformers with turmoil. Advocates of change in the status quo experience enormous pressures, recriminations, and economic or physical persecution from resisters (usually in the majority). As Marius and Emily Robinson understood, promoting change has its costs. What's more, reformers invariably do not agree on appropriate ideology and tactics, so they end up quarreling with one another as well as with representatives of the established order they wish to change. Although reformers suffer pressure to conform and to cease questioning things, their duty to themselves, their society, and God sustains their commitment.

The Transcendentalists

No one knew this better than Ralph Waldo Emerson, a Concord, Massachusetts essayist who was the era's foremost intellectual figure. Emerson's essays of the 1830s—"Nature," "American Scholar," and "Divinity School Address," among others—influenced the generation of reformist American intellectuals coming of age in midcentury and helped to inspire artists and writers. The small but influential group of New England intellectuals who lived near Emerson were called Transcendentalists because of their belief that truth was found beyond experience in intuition. Casting off the European intellectual tradition, Emerson urged Americans to look inward and to nature for self-knowledge, self-reliance, and the spark of divinity burning within all persons. "To acquaint a man with himself," he wrote, would inspire a "reverence" for self and others, which would then lead outward to social reform. "What is man born for," Emerson wrote, "but to be a Reformer?"

Inspired by self-reflection, the Transcendentalists asked troublesome questions about the quality of American life. They questioned not only slavery, an obvious evil, but also the obsessive competitive pace of economic life, the overriding concern for materialism, and the restrictive conformity of social life.

Although not considered Transcendentalists, Nathaniel Hawthorne and Herman Melville, two giants of midcentury American literature, also reflected these concerns in their fiction. Like Emerson, they were romantic in spirit, celebrating emotion over reason, nature over civilization, and virtue over self-interest. Hawthorne's great subject was the "truth of the human heart," which he portrayed as more authentic than the calculating minds of scientists and their schemes. In his greatest novel, *The Scarlet Letter* (1850), Hawthorne sympathetically told the story of a courageous Puritan woman's adultery and her eventual loving triumph over the narrowness of both cold intellect and intolerant social conformity.

Herman Melville dedicated his epic novel *Moby Dick* (1851) to Hawthorne. At one level a rousing story of whaling on the high seas in pursuit of the great white whale, *Moby Dick* was actually an immense allegory of good and evil, bravery and weakness, innocence and experience. In Melville's other novels, he continued this sea voyage setting for making a powerful statement on behalf of the lowly seaman's claims for freedom and just social relations against the tyranny of the ship captain. Like Emerson, Hawthorne and Melville mirrored the tensions of the age as they explored issues of freedom and control.

When Emerson wrote, "Whoso would be a man, must be a nonconformist," he described his friend Henry David Thoreau. No one thought more deeply about the virtuous natural life than Thoreau. On July 4, 1845, he went to live in a small hut by Walden Pond, near Concord. There he planned to confront "the essential facts of life"—to discover who he was and how to live well. When Thoreau left Walden two years later, he protested against slavery and the Mexican War by refusing to pay his taxes. He went to jail briefly and wrote an essay, "On Civil Disobedience" (1849), and a book, *Walden* (1854), which are still considered classic statements of what one person can do to protest unjust laws and wars and live a life of principle.

UTOPIAN COMMUNITARIANISM

Thoreau tried to lead an ideal solitary life. Other reformers sought to create perfect communities. Emerson noted in 1840 that he hardly met a thinking, reading man who did not have "a draft of a new community in his waistcoat pocket." One way to redeem a flawed society, one that seemed to be losing the cohesion and traditional values of small community life, was to create miniature utopian societies. These would offer alternatives to a world characterized by factories, foreigners, flawed morals, and greedy entrepreneurship.

Oneida and the Shakers

In 1831, as President Jackson and South Carolina neared their confrontation over the tariff and nullification, as Nat Turner planned his slave revolt in Virginia, and as the citizens of Rochester sought ways of controlling their workers' drinking habits,

a young man in Putney, Vermont, heard Charles Finney on one of his whirlwind tours of New England. John Humphrey Noyes was an instant, if unorthodox, convert.

Noyes believed that the act of final conversion led to absolute perfection and complete release from sin. However spiritually blessed, Noyes's earthly happiness was soon sorely tested. In 1837, a woman he loved rejected both his doctrine and his marriage offer. Despondent, Noyes wrote a friend that "when the will of God is done on earth as it is in heaven there will be no marriage." Among those who were perfect, he argued, all men and women belonged equally to each other. For Noyes, complete sharing in family relationships was a step toward perfect cooperation and shared wealth in socioeconomic relationships. Others called his heretical doctrines "free love" and socialism. Noyes recovered from his unhappy love affair and married a loyal follower. When she delivered four stillborn children within six years, Noyes revised even further his unconventional ideas about sex.

Leader of the Perfectionist community at Oneida, New York, John Humphrey ("Father") Noyes was one of the most revolutionary of the utopians. Under his strong and unorthodox leadership, the Oneida community prospered more and lasted longer than the scores of other communities that sprang up in the 1840s and 1850s.

In 1848, Noyes and 51 devoted followers founded a "perfectionist" community at Oneida, New York. Under his strong leadership, Oneida grew and prospered. Sexual life at the commune was subject to many regulations, including sexual restraint and male continence except under carefully prescribed conditions. In a system of planned reproduction, only certain spiritually advanced males (usually Noyes) were allowed to father children. Other controversial practices included communal child rearing, sexual equality in work, the removal of the competitive spirit from both work and play, and an elaborate program of "mutual criticism" at community meetings presided over by "Father" Noyes.

Though creating considerable tension, these unorthodox sexual and social rules gave Oneidans a sense of uniqueness. Wise economic decisions also bound community members in mutual prosperity. Forsaking the nostalgic agricultural emphasis that typified most other communes, Noyes opted for modern manufacturing. Oneida specialized at first in the fabrication of steel animal traps and later diversified into making silverware. Eventually abandoning religion to become a joint-stock company in which individual members held shares, Oneida thrived for many years and continues today as a silverware company.

Noyes greatly admired another group of communitarians, the Shakers, who also believed in perfectionism, the surrender of all worldly property to the community, and the devotion of one's labor and love to bringing about the millennial kingdom of heaven. But unlike the Oneidan experiments in reproduction, Shakers viewed sexuality as a sin and believed in absolute chastity, trusting in conversions to perpetuate their sect. Founded by an Englishwoman, Mother Ann Lee, who migrated to America in the late eighteenth century, Shaker conversions grew in the Second Great Awakening to a peak membership of around 6,000 souls by the 1850s. Centered at Mount Lebanon, New York, the Shakers established communities from Maine to Kentucky. They believed that God had a dual personality, male and female, and that Ann Lee was the female counterpart to the masculine Christ. The Shaker worship service featured frenetic dancing intended to release (or "shake") sin out through the fingertips. Shaker communities, some of which survived long into the twentieth century, were characterized by communal ownership of property, the equality of women and men, simplicity, and beautifully crafted furniture.

Other Utopias

In an era of disruptive economic and social change, over 100 utopian communities like Oneida and the Shaker colonies were founded. Some were religiously motivated; others were secular. Most were small and lasted only a few months or years. All eventually failed.

Pietist German-speaking immigrants founded the earliest utopian communities in America to preserve their language, spirituality, and ascetic life style. The most notable of these were the Ephrata colonists in Pennsylvania, the Harmonists in Indiana, the Zoar community in Ohio, and the Amana Society in Iowa. Some antebellum utopian communities focused less on otherwordly contemplation than on the regeneration of this world. In 1840, Adin Ballou founded Hopedale in Massachusetts as "a miniature Christian republic" based on the ethical teachings of Jesus. Hopedale's newspaper, *The Practical Christian*, advocated temperance, pacifism, women's rights, and other reforms.

Other communities, founded on the secular principles of reason inherited from the Enlightenment, responded more directly to the social misery and wretched working conditions accompanying the industrial revolution. These communities differed from religious ones in assuming that evil came from bad environments rather than individual acts of sin. They consequently believed that altered environments rather than new morals would eliminate or reduce poverty, ignorance, intemperance, and other ugly by-products of industrialism.

Robert Owen was the best known of the secular communalists. A Scottish industrialist who saw firsthand the miserable lives of cotton mill workers, he envisioned a society of small towns—"Agricultural and Manufacturing Villages of Unity and Mutual Cooperation"—with good schools and healthy work for all citizens. Unemployment, poverty, and vice would be unknown in Owen's model communities. In 1824, he chose the abandoned Pietist community of Harmonists in Indiana as the site for his first town in America. He called it New Harmony. But problems rather than harmony prevailed. Overcrowding, lazy and uncooperative members, Owen's frequent absences, splintered goals, and financial mismanagement ruined New Harmony within three years.

Brook Farm, founded by two Concord friends of Emerson, Bronson Alcott and George Ripley, was an experiment in integrating "intellectual and manual labor." Residents would hoe in the fields and shovel manure for a few hours each day and then study literature and recite poetry. Although the colony lasted less than three years, it produced some notable literature in a journal, *The Dial,* edited by Margaret Fuller. Hawthorne lived at Brook Farm for a short time and wrote a novel, *The Blithedale Romance* (1852), that criticized the naive optimism of utopian communitarians.

Whether secular or religious, the utopian communities all failed for similar reasons. Americans seemed ill-suited to communal living and work responsibilities and were unwilling to share either their property or their spouses with others. Nor was celibacy greeted with much enthusiasm. Other recurring problems included unstable leadership, financial bickering, the hostility of local citizens toward sexual experimentation and other unorthodox practices, the indiscriminate admission of members, and a waning of enthusiasm after initial settlement. Emerson pinned the failure of the communities on their inability to confront the individualistic impulses of human nature. As he said of Brook Farm, "It met every test but life itself." That could serve as an epitaph for all the utopian communities.

Millerites and Mormons

If utopian communities failed to bring about the millennium, an alternative hope was to leap directly past the thousand years of peace and harmony to the Second Coming of Christ. William Miller, a shy farmer from upstate New York, became so absorbed with the idea of the imminent coming of Christ that he figured out mathematically the exact time of the event: 1843, probably in March. A religious sect, the Millerites, gathered around him to prepare for Christ's return and the Day of Judgment.

A mixture of excitement and fear grew as the day of the predicted return came closer. Some people gave away all their worldly belongings, neglected business, put on robes, and flocked to high hills and rooftops to be nearest the blessed event. When 1843 passed without the expected end, Miller and his followers recalculated and set a series of alternative dates. Each new disappointment diminished Miller's followers, and he died in 1848 a discredited man. But a small Millerite sect, the Seventh-Day Adventists, had already taken root and continues to this day.

Other groups that emerged from the same religiously active area of upstate New York were more

successful. As Palmyra, New York, was being swept by Finney revivalism, young Joseph Smith, a recent convert, claimed to be visited by the angel Moroni. According to Smith, Moroni led him to golden tablets buried in the ground near his home. On these plates were inscribed more than 500 pages of *The Book of Mormon,* which described the one true church and a "lost tribe of Israel" missing for centuries. The book also predicted the appearance of an American prophet who would establish a new and pure kingdom of Christ in America. Smith published his book in 1830 and soon founded the Church of Jesus Christ of Latter-day Saints. His visionary leadership attracted thousands of ordinary people trying to escape what they viewed as social disorder, religious impurity, and commercial degradation in the 1830s.

Smith and a steadily growing band of converts migrated successively to Ohio and Missouri and then back to Illinois, where they met ridicule, persecution, and violence. The hostility stemmed in part from their active missionary work, in part from their beliefs and support for local Indian tribes, and in part from rumors of unorthodox sexual practices.

Despite external persecution and internal dissension caused by Smith's strong leadership style, the Mormons prospered and increased. Converts from England and northern Europe added substantially to their numbers. By the mid-1840s, Nauvoo, Illinois, with a thriving population of nearly 15,000 was the showplace of Mormonism. Smith petitioned Congress for separate territorial status and ran for the presidency in 1844. This was too much for the citizens of nearby towns. Violence escalated and culminated in Smith's trial for treason and his murder by a mob. Under the brilliant leadership of Smith's successor, Brigham Young, the Mormons headed westward in 1846 in their continuing search for the "land of promise."

REFORMING SOCIETY

The Mormons and the utopian communitarians had as their common goal, in Brigham Young's words, "the spread of righteousness upon the earth." Most persons, however, preferred to spread righteousness in a practical way by focusing on a specific social evil rather than by embracing whole new religions or joining utopian colonies.

"We are all a little wild here," Emerson wrote in 1840, "with numberless projects of social reform."

Religion, Reform, and Utopian Activity, 1830–1850

Mobilized in part by their increased participation in the political parties of Jacksonian America, the reformers created and joined all kinds of societies for social betterment. The reform ranks were swelled by thousands of women, stirred to action by the religious revivals and freed from domestic burdens by delayed marriage and smaller families. Organized in hundreds of voluntary societies, women such as Emily Rakestraw joined men such as Marius Robinson in directing their energies to numerous social issues. These included alcohol consumption; diet and health; sexuality; institutional treatment of the mentally ill, the disabled, paupers, and criminals; education; the rights of labor; slavery; and women's rights.

Temperance

On New Year's Eve in 1831, a Finney disciple, Theodore Dwight Weld, delivered a four-hour temperance lecture in Rochester. In graphic detail he described the awful fate of those who refused to stop drinking and urged his audience not only to cease their tippling but to stop others as well. Several were converted to abstinence on the spot. The next day, Elijah and Albert Smith, the largest providers of whiskey in Rochester, rolled their barrels out onto the sidewalk and smashed them. Cheering Christians applauded as the whiskey ran out into Exchange Street.

Americans in the nineteenth century drank heavily. One man observed that "a house could not

be raised, a field of wheat cut down, nor could there be a log rolling, a husking, a quilting, a wedding, or a funeral without the aid of alcohol." The corrosive effects of drinking were obvious: poverty, crime, illness, insanity, battered and broken families, and corrupt politics.

Early efforts at curbing alcohol consumption emphasized moderation. Forming local societies, groups of people agreed to limit how much they drank or to imbibe only beer and wine. Some societies even met in local taverns to toast their commitment to moderation. But under the influence of the Beecher and Finney revivals, the movement achieved better organization and clearer goals. The American Temperance Society, founded in 1826, was dedicated not just to moderation but to total abstinence. Within a few years, thousands of local and state societies had formed, though some refused to prohibit drinking of hard cider and communion wine.

Temperance advocates copied successful revival techniques. Fiery lecturers expounded on the evil consequences of drink and urged group pressure on the weak-willed. Mass meetings were accompanied by a deluge of graphic and sometimes gory temperance tracts. Who would not cringe at descriptions of drinkers: "Some are killed instantly; some die a lingering, gradual death; some commit suicide in fits of intoxication; and some are actually burnt up." One "intemperate man," it was claimed, died when his "breath caught fire by coming in contact with a lighted candle." The accumulated pressure of both written and oral testimony, capped off

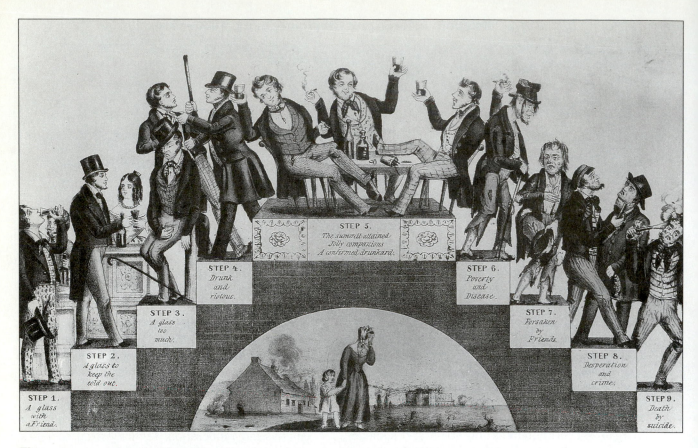

The temperance movement of the 1830s and 1840s used the tactics of religious revivalists to scare drinkers into taking the "teetotal" pledge. Who could resist this poignant 1846 portrayal of the **The Drunkard's Progress?**

by a sermon like Weld's, was intended to convince people to take the "teetotal" pledge.

By 1840, disagreements over goals and methods split the temperance movement into many separate organizations. In depression times, when jobs and stable families were harder to find than whiskey and beer, laboring men and women moved more by practical concerns than religious fervor joined the crusade. The Washington Temperance Society, founded in a Baltimore tavern in 1840, was enormously popular with unemployed young workers and grew to an estimated 600,000 members in three years. The Washingtonians, arguing that alcoholism was a disease rather than moral failure, changed the shape of the temperance movement. They replaced revivalist techniques with those of the new party politics by organizing parades, picnics, melodramas, and festivals to encourage people to take the pledge.

Tactics in the 1840s also shifted away from moral suasion to political action. Temperance societies lobbied for local option laws, which allowed communities to prohibit the sale, manufacture, and consumption of alcohol. The Maine law in 1851 was the first in the nation. Fifteen other states followed with similar laws before the Civil War. Despite weak enforcement, the per capita consumption of alcohol declined dramatically in the 1850s. Interrupted by the Civil War, the movement did not reach its ultimate objective until passage of the Eighteenth Amendment to the Constitution in 1919.

The temperance crusade reveals the many practical motivations that attracted Americans to join reform societies. For some, as in Rochester, temperance provided an opportunity for the Protestant middle classes to exert some control over laborers, immigrants, and Catholics. For perfectionists, abstinence was a way of practicing self-control and reaching moral perfection. For many women, the temperance effort was a respectable way to control the behavior of drunken men who beat wives and daughters. For many young men, especially after the onset of the depression of 1837, a temperance society provided entertainment, fellowship, and contacts to help their careers. In temperance societies as in political parties, Americans found jobs, purpose, support, spouses, and relief from the loneliness and uncertainty of a changing world.

Health and Sexuality

It was a short step from the physical and psychological ravages of drink to other potentially harmful effects on the body. Reformers were quick to attack excessive eating, use of stimulants of any kind, and, above all, the evils of too much sexual activity. Many endorsed a variety of special diets and exercise programs for maintaining good health. Some promoted panaceas for all ailments. One of these was hydropathy: clients sojourned at one of 70 special resorts for bathing and water purges of the body. Many of these resorts especially attracted women who not only found an escape from daily drudgery in the home but also found cures for chronic and untreated urogenital infections. Other panaceas, including hypnotism, phrenology (the study of bumps on the head), and various "spiritualist" seances, sought to cure problems of the mind.

Another movement concerned sexual purity. In 1834, Sylvester Graham, a promoter of proper diet and hygiene, delivered a series of lectures on chastity, later published as a manual of advice. To those "troubled" by sexual desire, the inventor of the Graham cracker recommended taking "more active exercise in the open air" and using "the cold bath under proper circumstances." Women especially, not as "passionless" as the Victorian stereotype suggested, were advised to remain pure and to "have intercourse only for procreation." Although females learned to control sexuality for their own purposes, as we shall see, male "sexual purity" advocates urged sexual restraint to protect various male interests. One doctor argued that women ought not to be educated because blood needed for the womb would be diverted to the head, thus breeding "puny men."

The authors of antebellum "health" manuals advocated abstinence from sexual activity as vehemently as they recommended abstinence from alcohol. The body, they argued, was a closed energy system in which each organ had particular and limited functions to perform. Semen was to be saved for reproductive purposes and should not be used for pleasure in either masturbation or intercourse. Such use, maintained the manuals on sexual purity, would lead to enervation, disease, insanity, and death. Some argued further that the "expenditure" of sperm meant a loss of needed energy from the economy. To drain energy away from business to sex was both wasteful and contributory to Jacksonian social disorder.

Humanizing the Asylum

In their effort to restore order to American society, some reformers preferred to work not for private influence over individuals but toward public changes in institutions. They wanted to transform such social institutions as asylums, almshouses, prisons, schools, and even factories. In many ways, Horace Mann, who led the struggle for common schools in Massachusetts (see Chapter 11), was a typical antebellum reformer. He blended dedicated idealism with a canny, practical sense of how to institutionalize educational improvements in one state: teacher training schools, higher teachers' salaries, and compulsory attendance laws.

Other reformers were less successful in achieving their goals. This was especially true of the treatment of society's outcasts. In the colonial era the family or the local community cared for orphans, paupers, the insane, and even criminals. Beginning early in the nineteenth century, various states built asylums, houses of refuge, reform schools, jails, and other institutions to uplift and house social victims. In some of these institutions, such as prisons and almshouses, the sane and insane, children and hardened adult criminals were thrown together in terrible conditions. In 1843, Dorothea Dix, a frail New Englander, horrified the Massachusetts legislature with her famous report that imprisoned insane persons in the state were subject to "the extremest state of degradation and misery." They were confined in "cages, closets, stalls, pens! Chained, naked, beaten with rods, and lashed into obedience!" Dix recommended special hospitals or asylums where the insane could be "humanly and properly controlled" by trained attendants.

Many perfectionist reformers like Dix believed that special asylums could reform society's outcasts. Convinced that bad institutions corrupted basically good human beings, they reasoned that reformed institutions could rehabilitate them. In 1853, Charles Loring Brace started a Children's Aid Society in New York City that was a model of change through effective education and self-help. Reformers like Dix and Brace, as well as Samuel Gridley Howe and Thomas Gallaudet, who founded institutions for the care and education of the blind and deaf, achieved remarkable results.

But all too often, results were disappointing. Prison reformers believed that a properly built and administered penitentiary could bring a hardened criminal "back to virtue." They argued intensely over the most appropriate structural design for rehabilitating criminals. Some preferred the rectangular prison at Auburn, New York, with its tiny cells and common work rooms, while others pointed to the Pennsylvania star-shaped system, where each inmate was in solitary confinement, though in a fairly modern cell. Whichever system was preferred, prison reformers assumed that by putting "penitents" into isolated cells to study the Bible and reflect on their wrongdoing, they would eventually decide to become good citizens. In practice, many criminals simply went mad or committed suicide. The institutions built by well-intentioned reformers became dumping places for society's outcasts. By midcentury, American prisons and mental asylums had become the impersonal, understaffed, overcrowded institutions we know today.

Working-Class Reform

Efforts to improve the institutional conditions of life in the United States were not all initiated and led by middle-class reformers on behalf of the less fortunate. For working-class Americans, the social institution most in need of transformation was the factory. Workers, many of whom were involved in other issues such as temperance, peace, and abolitionism, took it upon themselves to improve their own lives. As labor leader Seth Luther told a meeting of New England mechanics and laborers, "We must take our business into our own hands. Let us awake." And awake they did, forming both trade unions and

workingmen's parties as Andrew Jackson neared the presidency.

Between 1828 and 1832, dozens of workingmen's parties were formed, advocating such programs as free, tax-supported schools, free public lands in the West, equal rights for the poor, and the elimination of all monopolistic privilege. Trade union activity began in Philadelphia in 1827 as skilled workers organized journeymen carpenters, plasterers, printers, weavers, tailors, and other tradesmen. That same year, 15 unions combined into a citywide federation, a process followed in other cities. The National Trades Union, founded in 1834, was the first attempt at a national labor organization.

The trade unions fared better than the labor parties, in part because Jacksonian Democrats attracted many laboring men's votes and in part because trade union programs were more immediately practical. They included shorter hours, wages that would keep pace with rising prices, and ways (such as the closed shop) of warding off the competitive threat of cheap labor. In addition, both workers and their middle-class interlocutors called for the abolition of imprisonment for debt and of compulsory militia duty, both of which often cost workers their jobs; free public education; improved living conditions in workers' neighborhoods; and the right to organize. Discouraged by decisions of New York State courts, which denied the right to organize in 1835 and again in 1836, workers argued that unions were necessary to "resist the oppressions of avarice" and compared themselves to the Americans who dumped British tea in Boston harbor in 1773.

Thus strengthened by a Revolutionary tradition, by increasing political influence, and by a trade union membership of near 300,000, workers struck some 168 times between 1834 and 1836. Over two-thirds of the strikes were for higher wages or, as with the mill workers in Lowell, to avert wage cuts (see Chapter 11). The remaining strikes were for shorter hours. Identifying with the "blood of our fathers" shed on the battlefields of the American Revolution, Boston tradesmen struck in 1835 for a ten-your day. They failed, but their attempt heralded the subsequent resurgence of a successful ten-hour-day movement in many states in the 1850s. The Panic of 1837 and the ensuing depression dashed the hopes and efforts of American workers. But the organizational work of the 1830s promised that the labor movement would reemerge with greater strength later in the century.

ABOLITIONISM AND WOMEN'S RIGHTS

As American workers struggled in Lowell and other eastern cities for better wages and hours in 1834, Emily and Marius Robinson arrived in Cincinnati to fight for their causes. They had been attracted there, along with scores of other young idealists, by the newly founded Lane Seminary, a school to train abolitionist leaders. Financed by two wealthy New York brothers, Arthur and Lewis Tappan, Lane soon became a center of reformist activity. When nervous local residents persuaded President Lyman Beecher to crack down on the students, 40 "Lane rebels," led by Theodore Weld, fled to Oberlin in northern Ohio. As the Robinsons remained behind to marry and continue their reform work in southern Ohio, the group in the north turned Oberlin College into the first institution in the United States open equally to women and men, blacks and whites. Thus the movements to abolish slavery and to grant equal rights to women and free blacks were joined.

These movements also united elements of both practical reform and utopian perfectionism. The goals of the struggle to abolish slavery and subtle forms of racism and sexism often seemed as distant and unrealizable as the millennium itself. Yet antislavery and feminist advocates persisted in their efforts to abolish what they believed were concrete, visible, institutionalized social wrongs. Whether seeking to eliminate coercion in the cotton fields or in the kitchen, they faced the dual challenge of pursuing distant and elusive goals while at the same time achieving practical changes in everyday life.

Tensions Within Antislavery

Although the antislavery movement had a smaller membership than temperance reform, it revealed more clearly the difficulties of trying to achieve significant social change in America. As a young man of 22, William Lloyd Garrison passionately desired to improve, if not to perfect, the flawed world in which he lived. He was also ambitious and said that his name would "one day be known to the world." He was right. On January 1, 1831, eight months before Nat Turner's revolt, Garrison published the first issue of *The Liberator,* soon to become the leading antislavery journal in the United States. "I am in earnest," he wrote. "I will not equivocate—AND *I WILL BE HEARD."* After first organizing the New England Anti-Slavery Society with a group of blacks and whites in a church basement in Boston, in 1833 Garrison and 62 others established the American Anti-Slavery Society.

Until Garrison's publication, most people opposed to slavery, other than blacks, had advocated gradual emancipation by individual slave owners. Many joined the American Colonizationist Society, founded in 1816, which sent a small number of man-

William Lloyd Garrison was one of the most uncompromising abolitionists, which made him unpopular even among other reformers.

umitted slaves to Liberia, on the west coast of Africa. But these efforts proved inadequate and essentially racist in intent. Colonizationists seemed less interested in ending slavery (more new slaves were born in a week than were sent to Africa as free persons in a year) than in ridding the country of free blacks.

Garrison opposed the moderation and gradualism of the colonizationists. "I do not wish to think, or speak, or write, with moderation," he wrote. "No! no! tell a man whose house is on fire to give a moderate alarm; tell him to moderately rescue his wife from the hands of the ravisher." For Garrison, compromise was unthinkable. There would be "no Union with slaveholders," he cried, condemning the Constitution that perpetuated slavery as *a covenant with death, an agreement with Hell."* The American Anti-Slavery Society called for the immediate and total abolition of slavery. After his successful escape from slavery, Frederick Douglass agreed, saying, "Power concedes nothing without a demand. It never did and it never will." But the abolitionists did not always agree, splitting into factions over ideological differences between colonizationists, gradualists, and immediatists.

Abolitionists also differed over the tactics of ending slavery. Their primary method was moral suasion, by which they sought to convince slaveholders and their supporters that slavery was a sin. In an outpouring of sermons, petitions, resolutions, pamphlets, and speeches, abolitionists tried to overwhelm slaveholders with moral guilt to get them to free their slaves as an act of repentance. But as Marius wrote to Emily Robinson. "The spirit of slavery is not confined to the South." His Ohio trip suggests that northerners were equally guilty in providing the support necessary to maintain the slave system.

The abolitionists were unrestrained in their efforts. By 1837, they had flooded the nation with over a million pieces of antislavery literature. Their writing described slave owners as "mansteals" who gave up all claim to humanity. A slaveholder, Garrison wrote, led a life "of unbridled lust . . . of haughty domination, of cowardly ruffianism, of boundless dissipation, of matchless insolence, of infinite self-conceit, of unequalled oppression, of more than savage cruelty." In 1839, Weld published *American Slavery As It Is,* which described in gory detail every conceivable form of inhumane treatment of the slaves.

Other abolitionists preferred more direct methods than moral suasion. The main alternative lay in such political action as bringing antislavery petitions before Congress and forming third parties. Another tactic was to employ economic influence by boycotting goods made by slave labor. A fourth approach, although rare, was to call for slave rebellion, as did two northern blacks, David Walker in a pamphlet in 1829 and Henry Highland Garnet in a speech at a convention of black Americans in 1843.

Disagreement among abolitionists over tactics heightened ideological differences and helped to splinter the movement. Garrison's unyielding personal style and his commitment to even less popular causes such as women's rights offended many abolitionists. In 1840, at its annual meeting in New York, intended as a unity convention to heal growing divisions, the American Anti-Slavery Society split into two groups. Several delegates walked out when a woman, Abby Kelley, was elected to a previously all-male committee. One group, which supported multiple issues and moral suasion, stayed with Garrison; the other followed James Birney and the Tappans into the Liberty party and political action on the single issue of slavery.

Class differences and race further divided abolitionists. Northern workers, though fearful of the job competition implications of emancipation, nevertheless saw their "wage slavery" as similar to chattel slavery. Both violated fundamental republican values of freedom and equality. Strains between northern labor leaders and middle-class abolitionists, who minimized the seriousness of workingmen's concerns, were similar to those between white and black antislavery forces. Whites like Wendell Phillips decried slavery as a moral blot on American society, while blacks like Douglass were more concerned with the effects of slavery and discrimination on black people. Moreover, white abolitionists tended to see slavery and freedom as absolute moral opposites: a person was either slave or free. Blacks, however, knew that there were degrees of freedom and that discriminatory restrictions on freedom existed for blacks in the North just as did relative degrees of servitude in the South.

Furthermore, black abolitionists themselves experienced prejudice, not just from ordinary northern citizens but also from their white abolitionist colleagues. Many antislavery businessmen refused to hire blacks. The antislavery societies usually provided less than full membership rights for blacks, permitted them to do only menial tasks rather than form policy, and perpetuated black stereotypes in their literature. One free black, in fact, described a white abolitionist as one who hated slavery, "especially that slavery which is 1000 to 1500 miles away," but who hated even more "a man who wears a black skin."

The celebrated conflict between Garrison and Douglass reflected these tensions. The famous runaway slave was one of the most effective orators in the movement. But after a while, rather than simply describing his life as a slave, Douglass began skillfully to analyze abolitionist policies. Garrison warned him that audiences would not believe he had ever been a slave, and other whites told him to stick to the facts and let them take care of the philosophy.

Douglass gradually moved away from Garrison's views, endorsing political action and sometimes even slave rebellion. Garrison's response, particularly when Douglass came out for the Liberty party, was to denounce his independence as "ungrateful . . . and malevolent in spirit." In 1847, Douglass started his own journal, the *North Star,* later called *Frederick Douglass's Paper.* In it he expressed his appreciation for the help of that "noble band of white laborers" but declared that it was time for those who "suffered the wrong" to lead the way in advocating liberty.

Moving beyond Garrison, a few black nationalists, like the fiery Martin Delany, totally rejected white American society and advocated emigration and a new destiny in Africa. Most blacks, however, agreed with Douglass to work to end slavery and discrimination in the United States. They believed that for better or worse, their home was America and not some distant land they had not known for generations.

These black leaders were practical. David Ruggles in New York and William Still in Philadelphia led black vigilance groups that helped fugitive slaves escape to Canada or to safe northern black settlements. Ministers, writers, and orators such as Douglass, Henry Highland Garnet, William Wells Brown, Samuel Cornish, Lewis Hayden, and Sojourner Truth lectured and wrote journals and slave narratives on the evils of slavery. They also organized a National Negro Convention Movement, which began annual meetings in 1830. These blacks met not only to condemn slavery but also to discuss concrete issues of discrimination facing free blacks in the North.

Flood Tide of Abolitionism

Black and white abolitionists, however, agreed more than they disagreed and usually worked together well. They supported each other's publications. The first subscribers to Garrison's *Liberator* were nearly all black, and an estimated 80 percent of the readers of Douglass's paper were white. Weld and Garrison often stayed in the homes of black abolitionists when they traveled. Black and white "stations" cooperated on the underground railroad, too, passing fugitives on from hiding places in a black church to a white farmer's barn to a Quaker meetinghouse to a black carpenter's shop.

The two races worked together fighting discrimination as well as slavery. When David Ruggles was dragged from the "white car" of a New Bedford, Massachusetts, railway in 1841, Garrison, Douglass, and 40 other protesters organized what may have been the first successful integrated "sit-in" act of civil disobedience in American history. Blacks and whites also worked harmoniously in protesting segregated schools. After several years of joint boycotts and legal challenges in Massachusetts, in 1855 that state became the first to outlaw segregated public education. Almost exactly 100 years later, the Supreme Court would begin the desegregation of schools throughout the country.

White and black abolitionists were united perhaps most closely by defending themselves against the attacks of people who regarded them as dangerous fanatics bent on disrupting an orderly society. As abolitionists organized to rid the nation of slavery, they aroused many, northerners as well as southerners, who were eager to rid the nation of abolitionists. Mob attacks like the one on Marius Robinson in Ohio in 1836 occurred frequently in the mid-1830s. Abolitionists were stoned, dragged through streets, ousted from their jobs and homes, and reviled by northern mobs, often led or encouraged by leading citizens. Theodore Weld, known as "the most mobbed man in the United States," could hardly finish a speech without disruption. Douglass endured similar attacks, and Garrison was saved from a Boston mob only by being put in jail. In 1837, an antislavery editor in Illinois, Elijah Lovejoy, was murdered and his printing press destroyed.

Antiabolitionsts were as fervid as the abolitionists themselves and equally determined to publicize their cause. "I warn the abolitionists, ignorant and infatuated barbarians as they are," growled one South Carolinian, "that if chance shall throw any of them into our hands, they may expect a felon's death." One widely circulated book in 1836 described opponents of slavery, led by the "gloomy, wild, and malignant" Garrison, as "crack-brained enthusiasts" and "female fanatics" with "disturbed minds." President Jackson joined in, denouncing the abolitionists in his annual message in 1835 as "incendiaries" who deserved to have their "unconstitutional and wicked" activities broken up by mobs. The president went on to urge Congress to ban antislavery literature from the U.S. mails. A year later, southern Democratic congressmen, with the crucial support of Van Buren, succeeded in passing a "gag rule" to stop the flood of abolitionist petitions in Congress.

By the 1840s, despite factionalism and opposition, the antislavery movement had gained significant strength in American life. Many northerners, including many workers otherwise unsympathetic to the goal of ending slavery, decried the mob violence, supported the right of free speech, and denounced the South and its northern defenders as undemocratic. The gag rule, interference with the mails, and the killing of Lovejoy seemed proof of the growing pernicious influence of slave power. Former president John Quincy Adams, who had returned to Washington as a congressman, devoted himself for several years to the repeal of the gag rule, which he finally achieved in 1844. In this way, he kept the matter in the public eye until the question of slavery in the territories became the dominant national political issue of the 1850s (see Chapter 15). Meanwhile, black and white abolitionists continued their struggle, using many different tactics without knowing that the only one that would work, and indirectly at that, would be civil war.

Women's Rights

As a young teacher in Massachusetts in 1836, Abby Kelley circulated petitions for the local antislavery society. She came to reform from revivalism and in 1837 wrote, " 'Tis a great joy to see the world grow better. . . . Indeed I think endeavors to improve mankind is the only object worth living for." A year later, she braved the threats of an angry crowd in Philadelphia by delivering an abolitionist speech to a convention of antislavery women. Her speech was so eloquent that Weld told her that if

she did not join the movement full time, "God will smite you." Before the convention was over, a mob, incensed by both abolitionists and women speaking in public, attacked with stones and torches and burned the hall to the ground.

After a soul-searching year, Kelley left teaching to devote all her efforts to antislavery and women's rights. When she married Stephen Foster, she retained her own name and went on lecture tours of the West while her husband stayed home to care for their daughter. Other young women were also defining unconventional new relationships while illustrating the profound difficulty of both fulfilling traditional roles and speaking out for change. Angelina and Sarah Grimké, two demure but outspoken Quaker sisters from Philadelphia who had grown up in slaveholding South Carolina, went to New England in 1837 to lecture to disapproving audiences on behalf of abolitionism and the rights of women. After the tour, Angelina married Theodore Weld and stopped her public speaking to show that she could also be a good wife and mother. At the same time, she and Sarah, who moved in with her, undertook the task of compiling most of the research and doing most of the writing for Weld's book attacking American slavery.

Young couples like the Robinsons, Kelley and Foster, and Grimké and Weld, while pursuing reform, also experimented with equal private relationships in an age that assigned distinctly unequal roles to husbands and wives. The cult of domesticity told women that their sphere was the home, where they served as guardians of piety and virtue, influencing their husbands and children to lead morally upright lives in a harsh, changing economic world. As one clergyman said, although women were not expected to "step beyond the threshold" of the home, their ethical influence would be "felt around the globe." Given moral responsibilities like this, it is not surprising that many women joined the perfectionist movement to cleanse America of its sins. Active in every reform movement, women discovered the need to improve their own condition.

To achieve greater personal autonomy in the antebellum era, American women pursued several paths. The choice depended on class, cultural background, and situation. Thus in 1834, the Lowell textile workers went on strike to protest wage reductions while at the same time looking to marriage as an escape from mill work. Catharine Beecher argued that it was by accepting marriage and the home as woman's sphere and by mastering domestic duties there that women could best achieve power and autonomy. In another form of "domestic feminism," American wives exerted considerable control over their own bodies by convincing their husbands to practice abstinence, coitus interruptus, and other forms of birth control.

Other women found an outlet for their role as moral guardians by attacking the sexual double standard. In 1834, a group of Presbyterian women formed the New York Female Moral Reform Society. Inspired by revivalism, they visited brothels and opened up a house of refuge in an effort to convert prostitutes to evangelical Protestantism. They went even further, seeking to limit men's sexual behavior

by trying to close houses of prostitution and by publicly identifying men who visited them. Within five years, 445 auxiliaries of the Female Moral Reform Society had blossomed.

The Lowell mill workers and New York moral reformers generally accepted the duties—and attractions—of the cult of female domesticity. Other women, usually from upper-middle-class families, did not. They sought control over their lives by working directly for more legally protected equal rights with men. Campaigns to secure married women control of their property and custody of their children involved many of them. Others, like Kelley and the Grimkés, labored in the abolitionist movement and garnered not only valuable experience in

This marriage certificate from 1848, detailing the respective marital requirements of husband and wife, makes clear male dominance and female subservience ("the wife hath not power of her own body"). In that same year, women's rights activists began their long struggle for equality at Seneca Falls, New York.

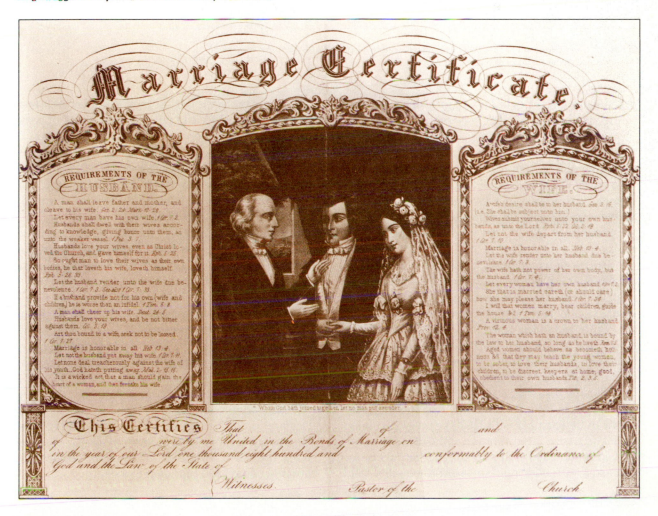

Elizabeth Cady Stanton (1815–1902) and Lucretia Mott (1793–1880) were the leaders of the 1848 gathering for women's rights at Seneca Falls, New York.

organizational tactics but also a growing awareness of the striking similarities between the oppression of women and that of slaves. As they collected antislavery signatures and spoke out in churches and public meetings, they continually faced denials of their right to speak or act politically. American women "have good cause to be grateful to the slave," Kelley wrote, for in "striving to strike his iron off, we found most surely, that we were manacled *ourselves.*"

The more active women became in antislavery activities, the more hostility they encountered, especially from clergymen, who quoted the Bible to justify female inferiority and servility. Sarah Grimké was criticized once too often for her outspoken views. She struck back in 1837 with a series called *Letters on the Condition of Women and the Equality of the Sexes,* claiming that "men and women were CREATED EQUAL" and that "whatever is *right* for man to do, is *right* for woman." Arguing that men ought to be satisfied with 6,000 years of dominion based on a false interpretation of the creation story, Grimké concluded that she sought "no favors for my sex. I surrender not our claim to equality. All I

ask of our brethren is, that they will take their feet from off our necks and permit us to stand upright on that ground which God designed us to occupy."

Male abolitionists were divided about women's rights. At the World Anti-Slavery Convention in 1840, attended by many American abolitionists, the delegates refused to let women participate. Two upstate New Yorkers, Elizabeth Cady Stanton and Lucretia Mott, were compelled to sit behind curtains and not even be seen, much less be permitted to speak. When they returned home, they resolved to "form a society to advocate the rights of women." In 1848, in Seneca Falls, New York, their intentions, though delayed, were fulfilled in one of the most significant protest gatherings of the antebellum era.

In preparing for the meeting, Mott and Stanton drew up a list of women's grievances. They discovered that even though some states had awarded married women control over their property, they still had none over their earnings. Modeling their Declaration of Sentiments on the Declaration of Independence, the women at Seneca Falls proclaimed it a self-evident truth that "all men and women are created equal" and that men had usurped women's freedom and dignity. A man, the Declaration of Sentiments charged, "endeavored in every way he could, to destroy [woman's] confidence in her own powers, to lessen her self-respect, and to make her willing to lead a dependent and abject life." The remedy was expressed in 11 resolutions calling for equal opportunities in education and work, equality before the law, and the right to appear on public platforms. The most controversial resolution called for women's "sacred right to the elective franchise." The convention approved Mott and Stanton's list of resolutions.

Throughout the 1850s, led by Stanton and Susan B. Anthony, women continued to meet in annual conventions, working by resolution, persuasion, and petition campaign to achieve equal political, legal, and property rights with men. The right to vote, however, was considered the cornerstone of the movement. It remained so for 72 years of struggle until 1920, when passage of the Nineteenth Amendment made woman suffrage part of the Constitution. The Seneca Falls convention was crucial in beginning the campaign for equal public rights. The seeds of gaining psychological autonomy and self-respect, however, were sown in the struggles of countless women like Abby Kelley, Sarah Grimké, and Emily Robinson. The struggle for that kind of liberation continues today.

CONCLUSION

Perfecting America

Advocates for women's rights and temperance, abolitionists, and other reformers carried on very different crusades from those waged by Andrew Jackson against Indians, nullificationists, and the U.S. Bank. In fact, Jacksonian politics and antebellum reform were often at odds. Most abolitionists and temperance reformers were anti-Jackson Whigs. Jackson and most Democrats repudiated the passionate moralism of reformers.

Yet both sides shared more than either side would admit. Reformers and political parties were both organized rationally. Both mirrored new tensions in a changing, growing society. Both had an abiding faith in change and the idea of progress yet feared that sinister forces jeopardized that progress. Whether ridding the nation of alcohol or the national bank, slavery or nullification, mob violence or political opponents, both forces saw these responsibilities in terms of patriotic duty. Whether inspired by religious revivalism or political party loyalty, both believed that by stamping out evil forces, they could shape a better America. In this effort, they turned to politics, religion, reform, and new life styles. Whether politicians like Jackson and Clay, religious community builders like Noyes and Ann Lee, or reformers like Garrison and the Grimkés, these antebellum Americans sought to remake their country politically and morally as it underwent social and economic change.

As the United States neared midcentury, slavery emerged as the most divisive issue. Against much opposition, the reformers had made slavery a matter of national political debate by the 1840s. Although both major political parties tried to evade the question, westward expansion and the addition of new territories to the nation would soon make avoidance impossible. Would new states be slave or free? The question increasingly aroused the deepest passions of the American people. For the pioneer family, the driving force behind the westward movement, however, questions involving their fears and dreams seemed more important. We turn to this family and that movement in the next chapter.

Recommended Reading

For sharply different interpretations of Andrew Jackson and party politics during his presidency, see Arthur Schlesinger, The Age of Jackson (1945), which is laudatory and Edward Pessen, Jacksonian America: Society, Personality, and Politics, rev. ed. (1979), which is not. Richard McCormick, The Second Party System: Party Formation in the Jacksonian Era (1966), and Richard Latner, The Presidency of Andrew Jackson: White House Politics, 1829–1837 (1979), are the definitive works on those topics. See also Richard Ellis, The Union at Risk: Jacksonian Democracy, States Rights, and The Nullification Crisis (1987); Ronald Formisano, The Transformation of Political Culture (1983); and Jean Baker, Affairs of Party (1983). Two highly readable works on Jackson's popular appeal are Robert Remini, Andrew Jackson (1966), and John William Ward, Andrew Jackson: Symbol for an Age (1955). For longer treatments, see two books by Robert Remini, Andrew Jackson and the Course of American Freedom, 1822–1832 (1981) and Andrew Jackson and the Course of American Democracy (1984). Jackson's political opponents are best understood by reading biographies of his major rivals: Clement Eaton, Henry Clay and the Art of American Politics (1957); Richard Current, Daniel Webster and the Rise of National Conservatism (1955), and Irving H. Bartlett, Daniel Webster (1978); and Margaret Coit, John P. Calhoun: American Portrait (1950).

The best single volume on antebellum religion and reform is Ronald Walters, American Reformers, 1815–1860 (1978), which replaces the old but still worthwhile Freedom's Ferment (1944), by Alice Felt Tyler. Delightfully fascinating accounts of revivalism are in Bernard Weisberger, They Gathered at the River (1958), and William McLoughlin, Modern Revivalism: From Charles G. Finney to Billy Graham (1959). Paul Johnson, A Shopkeeper's Millennium: Society and Revivals in Rochester, New York, 1815–1837 (1978), details the social impact of both economic change and revivalism in one community. There is no better way to understand the Transcendentalists than to read their writings, either in a collection by Perry Miller, ed., The Transcendentalists (1957), or by reading Thoreau's Walden and the essays, journals, and letters of Thoreau and Emerson.

The standard work on utopian communities is Arthur Bestor, Backwoods Utopias (1950), but John Humphrey Noyes's History of American Socialisms (1870) is indispensable. A critical look at Brook Farm is found in Nathaniel Hawthorne's novel, The Blithedale Romance (1852). For the early years of Mormonism, read Fawn Brodie, No Man Knows My History: The Life of Joseph Smith, Mormon Prophet (1945).

On the temperance crusade, see Ian Tyrrell, Sobering Up: From Temperance to Prohibition in Antebellum America, 1800–1860 (1979), and W. J. Rorabaugh, The Alcoholic Republic: An American Tradition (1979). The experience of most efforts at institutional reforms is superbly analyzed in David Rothman, The Discovery of the Asylum: Social Order and Disorder in the New Republic (1971). Working class reformers are the focus in Edward Pessen, Most Uncommon Jacksonians: The Radical Leaders of the Early Labor Movement (1967).

TIME LINE

1824 New Harmony established

1825 John Quincy Adams chosen president by the House of Representatives

1826 American Temperance Society founded

1828 Calhoun publishes *Exposition and Protest*
Jackson defeats Adams for the presidency
Tariff of Abominations

1828–1832 Rise of workingmen's parties

1830 Webster-Hayne debate and Jackson-Calhoun toast
Joseph Smith publishes *The Book of Mormon*

1830 Indian Removal Act

1830–1831 Charles Finney's religious revivals

1831 Garrison begins publishing *The Liberator*

1832 Jackson vetoes U.S. Bank charter
Jackson reelected
Worcester v. *Georgia*

1832–1833 Nullification crisis

1832–1836 Removal of funds from U.S. Bank to state banks

1833 Force Bill
Compromise tariff
Calhoun resigns as vice-president
American Anti-Slavery Society founded

1834 New York Female Moral Reform Society founded
National Trades Union founded
Whig party established

1835–1836 Countless incidents of mob violence

1836 "Gag rule"
Specie circular
Van Buren elected president

1837 Financial panic and depression
Sarah Grimké publishes *Letters on the Equality of the Sexes*
Emerson's "American Scholar" address

1837–38 Cherokee "Trail of Tears"

1840 William Henry Harrison elected president
American Anti-Slavery Society splits
World Anti-Slavery Convention
Ten-hour day for federal employees

1840–1841 Transcendentalists found Hopedale and Brook Farm

1843 Dorothea Dix's report on treatment of the insane

1844 Joseph Smith murdered in Nauvoo, Illinois

1846–1848 Mormon migration to the Great Basin

1847 First issue of Frederick Douglass's *North Star*

1848 Oneida community founded
First women's rights convention at Seneca Falls, New York

1850 Nathaniel Hawthorne, *Scarlet Letter*

1851 Maine prohibition law
Herman Melville, *Moby Dick*

1853 Children's Aid Society established in New York City

1854 Thoreau publishes *Walden*

1855 Massachusetts bans segregated public schools

14

Moving West

By the 1840s, the frontier was retreating across the Mississippi. As Americans contemplated the lands west of the great river, they debated the question of expansion. Some, like Michigan's senator Lewis Cass, saw the Pacific Ocean as the only limit to territorial expansion. Cass believed that the West represented not only economic opportunity for Americans but political stability for the nation as well. People crowded into cities and confined to limited territories endangered the republic, he told fellow senators in a speech. But if they headed west to convert "the woods and forests into towns and villages and cultivate fields" and to extend "the dominion of civilization and improvement over the domain of nature," they would find rewarding personal opportunities that would ensure political and social harmony.

Cass's arguments supporting the righteousness and necessity of westward expansion were echoed again and again in the 1840s. Thousands of men seconded his sentiments by volunteering to join American forces in the war against Mexico in the summer of 1845. Largely untrained, dressed in fanciful uniforms, and called by names like Eagles, Avengers, and Tigers, the companies hurried south. But before long these supporters of expansion saw the ugly side of territorial adventures: insects, bad weather, poor food, and unsanitary conditions. They discovered that such illnesses as the "black vomit" (yellow fever), dysentery, and diarrhea could kill more men than Mexican bullets. As a member of the American occupying army, Henry Judah also experienced the hostility of conquered peoples. In his diary, he reported, "It is dangerous to go out after night . . . Four of our men were stabbed today." Not only, he wrote, was a man "by the name of Brown" stabbed in the back, but an "infernal villain cut his throat."

Like Henry Judah, Thomas Gibson, a captain of Indiana volunteers, also paid some of the costs of winning new territories. Less than a month after Cass's speech, he wrote to his wife, Mary, in Charlestown, Indiana. Although glad to report news of an American victory, he described a battlefield "still covered with [Mexican] dead" where "the stench is most horrible." Indiana friends had been killed, and Gibson himself had narrowly escaped. "The ball struck me a glancing blow on the head and knocked me down,

but it did not harm me." As for the rest, the weather was foul, and so too was the food—"hard biscuit full of bitter black bugs."

Despite the harsh realities of war, Gibson did not challenge the enterprise. He bragged to Mary that "our little army could go out tomorrow in a fair field of battle and whip fifty thousand of the best Mexican troops that

ever were on a field of battle. One thing is certain, we would be willing to try it."

Like other wives and family members at home, Mary was less interested in heroics than in the simple truth: was Tommy dead or alive? As she anxiously awaited news, she wrote of her great hope: "May God bless you and send you home." Yet even with all her worries and

prayers for the war's rapid conclusion, she could not escape the heady propaganda for national expansion. She had heard that Indiana soldiers had "shode themselves great cowards by retreating during battle," and she disapproved. "We all would rather you had stood like good soldiers," she told her husband.

445

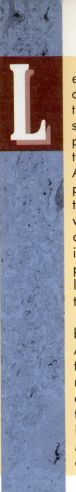

ewis Cass, Henry Judah, Thomas and Mary Gibson, and thousands of other Americans played a part in the nation's expansion into the trans-Mississippi West. The differences and similarities in their perspectives and in their responses to territorial growth unveil the complex nature of the western experience. Lewis Cass's speech illustrates the hold the West had on people's imagination and how some Americans linked expansion to individual opportunity and national progress. His reference to its riches reminds us of the gigantic contribution western resources made to national development and wealth. Yet his assumption that the West was vacant points to the costs of white expansion for Mexican-Americans and Native Americans. The Gibsons' letters show similar preconceptions and racial prejudices. They also portray the winning of the West on a human level: the anxieties, deprivation, enthusiasm, and optimism felt by those who fought for and settled in the West.

This chapter concerns movement into the trans-Mississippi West between 1830 and 1865. First, we will consider how and when Americans moved west, by what means the United States acquired the vast territories that in 1840 belonged to other nations, and the meaning of "Manifest Destiny," the slogan used to defend the conquest of the continent west of the Mississippi River. Then, we explore the nature of life on the western farming, mining, and urban frontiers. Finally, the chapter examines responses of Native Americans and Mexican-Americans to expansion and illuminates the ways in which different cultural traditions intersected in the West.

Until the 1840s, most Americans lived east of the Mississippi. The admission of new states between 1815 and 1840 symbolized the steady settlement of the eastern half of the continent. As frontier log cabins gave way to brick and clapboard houses, farmers cleared and planted land earlier settlers had ignored. Roads replaced tracks, and new churches, schools, stores, and banks attested to the march of settlement toward the Mississippi. By 1860, some 4.3 million Americans had moved west of the great river.

Foreign Claims and Possessions

With the exception of the Louisiana Territory, Spain held title to most of the trans-Mississippi region in 1815. Spanish holdings stretched south to Mexico and west to the Pacific and included present-day Texas, Arizona, New Mexico, Nevada, Utah, western Colorado, California, and small parts of Wyoming, Kansas, and Oklahoma. When Mexico won its independence from Spain in 1821, it inherited these lands and the 75,000 Spanish-speaking inhabitants and numerous Native Americans living there.

To the north of California was the Oregon country, a vaguely defined area extending from California to Alaska. Both Great Britain and the United States claimed the Oregon country on the basis of explorations in the late eighteenth century and fur trading in the early nineteenth. Joint occupation, agreed on in the Convention of 1818 and the Occupation Treaty of 1827, temporarily avoided settling the boundary question.

Traders, Trappers, and Cotton Farmers

Americans made commercial forays into the trans-Mississippi West long before the great migrations of the 1840s and 1850s and were familiar with some of its people and terrains. As early as 1811, Americans engaged in the fur trade in Oregon, and within ten years, fur trappers and traders were actively exploiting the resources of the Rocky Mountain region. Each summer, traders from St. Louis, the center of the fur trade, met with mountain men and Indians at a selected rendezvous in the wilderness to exchange their goods for beaver pelts. By the mid-1830s, trappers had almost exterminated the beaver, and the Rocky Mountain system disintegrated. But trade in bison robes prepared by the Plains tribes flourished in the area around the upper Missouri River and its tributaries until after 1860.

With the collapse of the Spanish Empire in 1821, American traders were able to penetrate the Southwest. Each year, caravans from "the States" followed the Santa Fe Trail over the plains and mountains, loaded with weapons, tools, and brightly colored calicoes. The 40,000 inhabitants of New Mexico proved eager buyers, exchanging precious metals and furs for manufactured goods. Eventually, some "Anglos" settled there. Their economic activities helped to prepare the way for military conquest later.

To the south, in Texas, land for cotton rather than trade attracted settlers and squatters in the 1820s. The lure of cheap land drew more Americans to the area than to any other. By 1835, almost 30,000 Americans were living in Texas, the largest group of Americans living outside the nation's boundaries at that time.

On the Pacific, a handful of New England traders carrying sea-otter skins to China anchored in the harbors of Spanish California in the early nineteenth century. By the 1830s, as the near extermination of the animals ruined this trade, a commerce based on California cowhides and tallow developed. New England ships tied up in California ports while hides were collected from local ranches in exchange for clothes, boots, hardware, and furniture manufactured in the East.

Among the earliest easterners to settle in the trans-Mississippi West were tribes from the South and the Old Northwest whom the American government forcibly relocated in present-day Oklahoma and Kansas. Ironically, some of these eastern tribes acted as agents of white civilization by introducing cotton, the plantation system, and schools. Other tribes triggered conflicts that weakened the western tribes with whom they came into contact. The Cherokee, Shawnee, and Delaware forced the Osages out of their Missouri and Arkansas hunting grounds, while tribes from the Old Northwest successfully claimed hunting areas long used by Kansas plains tribes. These disruptions foreshadowed white incursions later in the century.

The facts that much of the trans-Mississippi West lay outside U.S. boundaries and that the government had guaranteed Indian tribes permanent possession of some western territories did not curtail American economic activities. By the 1840s, a growing volume of published information fostered dreams of possession. Government reports by explorers Zebulon Pike and John C. Frémont, among others, provided detailed information about the interior, while guidebooks and news articles described the routes that such fur trappers as Jim Bridger, Kit Carson, and Jedediah Smith had mapped out. Going west was clearly possible. Lansford Hastings's *Emigrants' Guide to Oregon and California* (1845) provided not only the practical information that emigrants would need but also the encouragement that heading for the frontier was the right thing to do.

In his widely read guide, Hastings minimized the importance of Mexican and British sovereignty. California, as a Mexican possession, presented a problem, he conceded, but Oregon did not. "So far from having any valid claim to any portion of it," Hastings argued, Great Britain "had no right even to occupy it." Furthermore, American settlers were already trickling into the Pacific Northwest, bringing progress with them. Surely the day could not be far distant, he wrote approvingly, "when genuine Republicanism and unsophisticated Democracy shall be reared up . . . upon the now wild shores, of the great Pacific," to replace "ignorance, superstition, and despotism."

Hastings's belief that Americans would obtain rights to foreign holdings in the West came true within a decade. In the course of the 1840s, the United States, through war and diplomacy, acquired Mexico's territories in the Southwest and on the Pacific (1,193,061 square miles, including Texas) as well as title to the Oregon country up to the 49th parallel (another 285,580 square miles). Later, with the Gadsden Purchase in 1853, the country incorporated another 29,640 square miles of Mexican territory.

Manifest Destiny

What explained the feverish desire to expand? Bursts of florid rhetoric accompanied territorial growth, and Americans used the slogan "Manifest Destiny" to justify and account for it. The phrase, coined in 1845 by John L. O'Sullivan, editor of the *Democratic Review,* referred to the conviction that the country's superior institutions and culture gave Americans a God-given right, even an obligation, to spread their civilization across the entire continent. Lewis Cass, Henry Judah, the Gibsons, Lansford Hastings, and most other Americans agreed.

This sense of uniqueness and mission was a legacy of early Puritan utopianism and the republicanism of the Revolutionary era. By the 1840s, however, an argument for territorial expansion merged with the belief that the United States possessed a unique civilization. The successful absorption of the Louisiana Territory, rapid population growth, and advances in transportation, communication, and industry bolstered the idea of national superiority and the notion that the United

States could successfully absorb new territories. Publicists of Manifest Destiny proclaimed that the nation must.

WINNING THE TRANS-MISSISSIPPI WEST

Manifest Destiny justified expansion but did not cause it. Concrete events in Texas triggered the national government's determination to acquire territories west of the Mississippi River.

The Texas question originated in the years when Spain held most of the Southwest. Although some settlements such as Santa Fe, founded in 1609, were almost as old as Jamestown, the Spanish considered the sparsely populated and underdeveloped Southwest primarily a buffer zone for Mexico. The main centers of Spanish settlement, in coastal California, southern Arizona, New Mexico, the Rio Grande basin, and the San Antonio River valley, were geographically distant from one another and thousands of miles from Mexico City. While these

United States Territorial Expansion by 1860

John Gast's 1872 painting captures the perspective of white emigrants on the meaning of Manifest Destiny and the westward movement.

northern borderlands formed a weak defensive perimeter of the Spanish Empire, their legal status was recognized internationally in the Transcontinental Treaty. Moreover, in its treaty negotiations with Spain in 1819, the United States accepted a southern border excluding Texas, to which the Americans had vague claims stemming from the Louisiana Purchase.

Annexing Texas, 1845

By the time the treaty was ratified in 1821, Mexico had won its independence from Spain. The new nation inherited the borderlands, their people, and their problems. Mexicans soon had reason to wonder whether the American disavowal of any claim to Texas in the Transcontinental Treaty would last, for political leaders like Henry Clay began to cry out for "reannexation." Fear about American expansionism, fueled by several attempts to buy Texas and by continuing aggressive American statements, permeated Mexican politics.

In 1823, the Mexican government determined to strengthen border areas by increasing population. To attract settlers, it offered land in return for token payments and pledges to become Roman Catholics and Mexican citizens. Stephen F. Austin, who gained rights to bring 300 families into Texas,

was among the first of the American *empresarios,* or contractors, to take advantage of this opportunity. His call for settlers brought an enthusiastic response, as Mary Austin Holley recalled. "I was a young thing then, but 5 months married, my husband . . . failed in Tennessee, proposed to commence business in New Orleans. I ready to go anywhere . . . freely consented. Just then Stephen Austin and Joe Hawkins were crying up Texas—beautiful country, land for nothing etc.—Texas fever rose then . . . there we must go. There without much reflection, we did go." Like the Holleys, most of the American settlers came from the South, and some brought slaves. By the end of the decade, some 15,000 white Americans and 1,000 slaves lived in Texas, far outnumbering the 5,000 Mexican inhabitants.

Mexican officials soon questioned the wisdom of their invitation. Few American settlers became Catholics, and they remained more American than Mexican. Some of the settlers were malcontents who disliked Mexican laws and customs and limitations on their economic and commercial opportunities. In late 1826, a small group of them raised the flag of rebellion and declared the Republic of Fredonia. Although settlers like Austin assisted in putting down the brief uprising, American newspapers hailed the rebels as "apostles of democracy" and called Mexico "an alien civilization."

Mexican anxiety grew apace. Secretary of Foreign Relations Lucas Alámán accused American settlers of being advance agents of the United States. "They commence by introducing themselves into the territory which they covet," he told the Mexican Congress, "grow, multiply, become the predominant party in the population. . . . These pioneers excite . . . movements which disturb the political state of the country . . . and then follow discontents and dissatisfaction."

In 1829, the Mexican government altered its Texas policy. Determined to curb American influence, the government abolished slavery in Texas. The next year, it forbade further emigration from the United States, and officials began to collect customs duties on goods crossing the Louisiana border. But little changed in Texas. American slave owners freed their slaves and then forced them to sign life indenture contracts. Emigrants still crossed the border and continued to outnumber Mexicans.

Tensions escalated to the brink of war. In October 1835, a skirmish between the colonial militia and Mexican forces signaled the beginning of hostilities. Sam Houston, onetime governor of Tennessee and army officer, became commander in chief of the Texas forces. Although Texans called the war with Mexico a revolution, a Vermont soldier perhaps more accurately observed, "It is in fact a rebellion."

Mexican dictator and general Antonio López de Santa Anna, hurried north to crush the rebellion with an army of 6,000 conscripts. Although he had a numerical advantage, many of his soldiers were Mayan Indians who had been drafted unwillingly, spoke no Spanish, and were exhausted by the long march. Supply lines were spread thin. Nevertheless, Santa Anna and his men won the initial engagements of the war: the Alamo at San Antonio fell to him, taking Davy Crockett and Jim Bowie with it. So too did the fortress of Goliad, to the southeast.

As he pursued Houston and the Texans toward the San Jacinto River, carelessness proved Santa Anna's undoing. Although fully anticipating an American attack, the Mexican general and his men settled down to their usual siesta on April 21, 1836, without posting an adequate guard. As the Mexicans dozed, the Americans attacked. With cries of "Remember the Alamo! Remember Goliad!" the Texans overcame the army, captured its commander in his slippers, and won the war within 20 minutes. Their casualties numbered only 2, while 630 Mexicans lay dead.

The Evolution of Texas

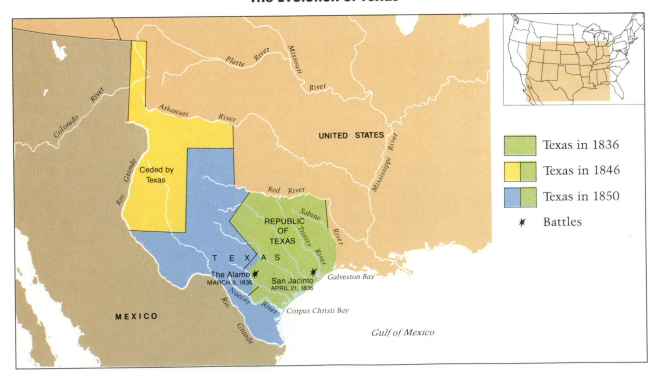

With the victory at San Jacinto, Texas gained its independence. Threatened with lynching, Santa Anna saw little choice but to sign the treaty of independence setting the republic's boundary at the Rio Grande. When news of the disastrous events reached Mexico City, however, the Mexican Congress repudiated "an agreement carried out under the threat of death." Mexico maintained that Texas was still part of Mexico.

The new republic started off shakily. It was financially unstable, unrecognized by its enemy, rejected by its friends. Although Texans immediately sought admission to the Union, their request failed. Jackson, whose agent in Texas had reported that the republic was so weak that "her future security must depend more upon the weakness and imbecility of her enemy than upon her own strength," was reluctant to act quickly. Many northerners violently opposed annexation of another slave state. The Union was precariously balanced, with 13 free and 13 slave states. Texas would upset that equilibrium in favor of the South. Petitions poured into Congress in 1837 opposing annexation, and John Quincy Adams repeatedly denounced the idea. Annexation was too explosive a political issue to pursue; debate finally died down and then disappeared.

For the next few years, the Lone Star Republic led a precarious existence. Mexico refused to recognize its independence but could send only an occasional raiding party across the border. Texans skirmished with Mexican bands, did their share of border raiding, and suffered an ignominious defeat in an ill-conceived attempt to capture Santa Fe in 1841. Diplomatic maneuvering in European capitals for financial aid and recognition were only moderately successful. Financial ties with the United States increased, however, as trade grew and many Americans invested in Texas bonds and lands.

Texas became headline news again in 1844. "It is the greatest question of the age," an Alabama expansionist declared, "and I predict will agitate the country more than all the other public questions ever have." He was right. Although President John Tyler (who assumed office after Harrison's sudden death) reopened the question of annexation, hoping that Texas would ensure his reelection, the issue exploded. It brought to life powerful sectional, national, and political tensions. Southern Democrats insisted that the South's future hinged on the annexation of Texas. "Now is the time to vindicate and save our institutions," John C. Calhoun insisted. His supporters hoped that by exploiting the Texas issue, Calhoun would win the White House.

Elected by a narrow margin in 1844, James K. Polk was a staunch expansionist. Although he would have preferred to avoid war with Mexico, he was determined to win broad territorial concessions from that nation.

Other wings of the Democratic party capitalized more successfully on the issue, however. Lewis Cass, Stephen Douglas of Illinois, and Robert Walker of Mississippi vigorously supported annexation, not because it would expand slavery, a topic they carefully avoided, but because it would spread the benefits of American civilization. Their arguments, classic examples of the basic tenets of Manifest Destiny, put the question into a national context of expanding American freedom. So powerfully did they link Texas to Manifest Destiny and avoid sectional issues that their candidate, James Polk of Tennessee, secured the Democratic nomination in 1844. Polk called for "the reannexation of Texas at the earliest practicable period" and the occupation of the Oregon Territory. Manifest Destiny had come of age.

Whigs tended to oppose annexation, fearing slavery's expansion and the growth of southern power with the addition of another slave state. They accused the Democrats of exploiting Manifest Destiny, more as a means of securing office than of bringing freedom to Texas.

The Whigs were right that the annexation issue would bring victory to the Democrats. Polk won a close election in 1844. But by the time he took the oath of office in March 1845, Tyler had resolved the question of annexation. In his last months in office, Tyler pushed through Congress a joint resolution admitting Texas to the Union. Unlike a treaty, which required the approval of two-thirds of the Senate and which Tyler had failed to win in 1844, a joint resolution needed only majority support. Nine years after its revolution, Texas finally became part of the Union. The agreement gave Texas the unusual right to divide into five states if it chose to do so.

War with Mexico, 1846–1848

When Mexico learned of Texas's annexation, it promptly severed diplomatic ties with the United States. It was easy for Mexicans to interpret the events from the 1820s on as part of a gigantic American plot to steal Texas. During the war for Texas independence, American papers, especially those in the South, had enthusiastically hailed the efforts of the rebels, while southern money and volunteers had aided the Texans in their struggle. Now that the Americans had gained Texas, would they want still more?

In his inaugural address in 1845, President Polk pointed out "that our system may easily be extended to the utmost bounds of our territorial limits, and that as it shall be extended the bonds of our Union, so far from being weakened will become stronger." What were those territorial limits? Did they extend into the territory the Mexican government considered as its own?

Polk, like many other Americans, failed to appreciate how the annexation of Texas humiliated Mexico and increased pressures on its government to respond belligerently. Aware of its weakness, the president anticipated that Mexico would grant his grandiose demands: a Texas bounded by the Rio Grande rather than the Nueces River 150 miles to its north, as well as California and New Mexico.

Even before the Texans could accept the long-awaited invitation to join the Union, rumors of a Mexican invasion were afloat. As a precautionary move, Polk ordered General Zachary Taylor to move "on or near the Rio Grande." By October 1845, Taylor and 3,500 American troops had reached the Nueces River. The positioning of an American army in Texas did not mean that Polk actually expected war. Rather, he hoped that a show of military force, coupled with secret diplomacy, would bring the desired concessions. In November, the president sent his secret agent, John L. Slidell, to Mexico City with instructions to secure the Rio Grande border and to buy Upper California and New Mexico. When the Mexican government refused to receive Slidell, an angry Polk decided to force Mexico into accepting American terms. He ordered Taylor south of the Rio Grande. To the Mexicans, who insisted that the Nueces River was the legitimate boundary, their presence constituted an act of war. Democratic newspapers and expansionists enthusiastically hailed Polk's provocative decision; the Whigs opposed it.

It was only a matter of time before an incident occurred to serve as the American justification for hostilities. In late April, the Mexican government

Public opinion was divided over the war in Mexico. This Currier & Ives print gloats over the U.S. victory at Buena Vista, but many Americans felt that the United States had no right to the lands it was fighting for.

declared a state of defensive war. Two days later, a skirmish broke out between Mexican and American troops, resulting in 16 American casualties. When Polk received Taylor's report, he quickly drafted a war message for Congress. The president claimed that Mexico had "passed the boundary of the United States . . . invaded our territory and shed American blood upon American soil." "War exists," he claimed, and, he added untruthfully, "notwithstanding all our efforts to avoid it, exists by act of Mexico."

Although Congress declared war, the conflict bitterly divided Americans. Many Whigs, including Abraham Lincoln, questioned the accuracy of Polk's initial account of the events, and their opposition grew more vocal as time passed. Lincoln called the war one "of conquest brought into existence to catch votes." The American Peace Society revealed sordid examples of army misbehavior in Mexico, while Frederick Douglass accused the country of "cupidity and love of dominion." Many workers also were critical of the war.

Debate continued as American troops swept into Mexico and advanced toward the capital. Although the Mexicans were also fighting Indian tribes on their northern border, the government refused to admit defeat and negotiate an end to the hostilities. The war dragged on and on. The *American Review,* a Whig paper, proclaimed that the conflict was a "crime over which angels may weep." In 1847, a month after General Winfield Scott took Mexico City, Philadelphian Joseph Sills wrote in his diary, "There is a widely spread conviction . . . that it is a wicked & disgraceful war."

Yet Polk enjoyed the enthusiastic support of expansionists. Thomas Gibson's men, like most other soldiers, were eager volunteers. Some expansionists even urged permanent occupation of Mexico. Illinois Democratic senator Sidney Breese told the Senate, "The avowed objects of the war . . .

The Mexican War, 1846–1848

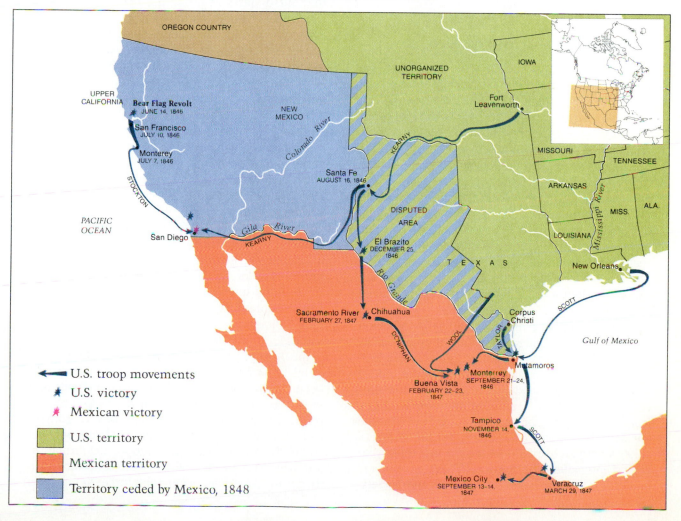

[were] to obtain redress of wrongs, a permanent and honorable peace, and indemnity for the past and security for the future." To secure these goals, Breese could even contemplate permanent occupation with "great ultimate good" to the United States, to Mexico, "and to humanity."

Inflated rhetoric did not win the war, however. In the end, chance helped draw hostilities to a close. Mexican moderates approached Polk's diplomatic representative, Nicholas Trist, who accompanied the American army in Mexico. In Trist's baggage were detailed, though out-of-date, instructions outlining Polk's requirements: the Rio Grande boundary, Upper California, and New Mexico. Although the president had lost confidence in Trist and had ordered him home in chains, Trist stayed in Mexico to negotiate an end to the war. Having obtained most of Polk's objectives, Trist returned to Washington to an ungrateful president. Apparently Polk had wanted more territory from Mexico for less money. Firing him from his job at the State Department, Polk denounced Trist as an "impudent and unqualified scoundrel."

California and New Mexico

Although Texas and Mexico dominated the headlines, Polk made it clear from the early days of his presidency that California and New Mexico were part of any resolution of the Mexico crisis. Serious American interest in California dated only from the late 1830s. A few Americans, mostly traders and shopkeepers, had settled in California during the 1820s and 1830s, but they constituted only a small part of the population. Many had married into Californio families and taken Mexican citizenship. But gradual recognition of California's fine harbors, its favorable position for the China trade, and the suspicion that other countries, especially Great Britain, had designs on the region nourished the conviction that it must become part of the United States.

In 1842, a comic dress rehearsal for rebellion occurred when a United States naval commodore, Thomas Catsby Jones, believing that war had broken out with Mexico, sailed into Monterey, forced the Mexican commander to surrender, and proclaimed California's annexation. When Jones learned of his error, he apologized and watched the Mexican flag hoisted once more. Yet the arrival of 1,500 American overland emigrants in a three-year period intensified the friction. These newcomers had little interest in blending into Californio society.

They and their families wanted an American California. As one resident realized, "The American population will soon be sufficiently numerous to play the Texas game."

In 1845, Polk appointed Thomas Larkin, a successful American merchant in Monterey, as his confidential agent. Larkin had clear instructions should Californians decide to break with Mexico. "While the President will make no effort and use no influence to induce California to become one of the free and independent states of the Union," wrote Polk's secretary of state, James Buchanan, to Larkin, "yet if the people should desire to unite their destiny with ours, they would be received as brethren." Polk's efforts to purchase California suggested that he was sensitive to the fragility of American claims to the region. But Santa Anna, who bore the burden of having lost Texas, was in no position to sell. Thus in 1846, a few armed American settlers rose up against Mexican "tyranny" and established the "Bear Flag Republic."

New Mexico was also on Polk's list. Ties with the United States began in the 1820s, when American traders began to bring their goods to Santa Fe. Economic profits stimulated American territorial appetites. As the oldest and largest Mexican group in North American (60,000 out of 75,000), however, New Mexicans had little desire for annexation. The unsuccessful attempt by the Texans to capture Santa Fe in 1841 and border clashes in the two following years did not enhance the attractiveness of their Anglo neighbors. But standing awkwardly in the path of westward expansion and further isolated from Mexico by the annexation of Texas in 1846, New Mexico's future as a Mexican province was uncertain.

In June 1846, shortly after the declaration of war with Mexico, the Army of the West, led by Colonel Stephen W. Kearney, left Fort Leavenworth, Kansas, for New Mexico. Kearney had orders to occupy Mexico's northern provinces and to protect the lucrative Santa Fe trade. Two months later, the army took Santa Fe without a shot, although one eyewitness noticed the "surly countenances" and the "wail of grief . . . above the din of our horses' tread." New Mexico's upper class, who had already begun to intermarry with American merchants and send some sons to colleges in the United States, readily accepted the new rulers. However, ordinary Mexicans and Pueblo Indians did not take conquest so lightly. After Kearny departed for California, resistance erupted in New Mexico. Californios also fought the American occupation force. Kearny was wounded, and the first appointed American governor of New Mexico was killed. In the end, however, superior American military strength won the day. By January 1847, both California and New Mexico were firmly in American hands.

The Treaty of Guadalupe Hidalgo, 1848

Negotiated by Trist and signed on February 2, 1848, the Treaty of Guadalupe Hidalgo dictated the fate of most people living in the Southwest. The United States absorbed the region's 75,000 Spanish-speaking inhabitants and its 150,000 Native Americans and increased its territory by 529,017 square miles, almost a third of Mexico's extent. Mexico received $15 million and in 1853 would receive another $10 million for large tracts of land in southern Arizona and New Mexico (the Gadsden Purchase). In the treaty, the United States guaranteed the civil and political rights of former Mexican citizens and their rights to land and also agreed to satisfy all American claims against Mexico.

If the territorial gains were immense, some costs were equally huge: 13,000 American lives lost, mostly to diseases such as measles and dysentery, and $97 million expended for military operations. Although sporadic violence would continue for years in the southwest as Mexicans protested the new status quo, the war was over, and the Americans had won.

The Oregon Question, 1844–1846

Belligerence and war secured vast areas of the Southwest and California for the United States. In the Pacific Northwest, the presence of mighty Great Britain rather than the weak, crisis-ridden Mexican government suggested more cautious tactics. There diplomacy became the means for territorial gains.

Despite the disputed nature of claims to the Oregon Territory, Polk assured the inauguration day crowd huddled under umbrellas that "our title to the country of Oregon is 'clear and unquestionable,' . . . already our people are preparing to perfect that title by occupying it with their wives and children." Polk's words reflected American confidence that settlement carried the presumption of possession. But the British did not agree. As the London *Times* warned, "Ill regulated, overbearing, and aggressive . . [Polk's] pretensions amount, if acted upon, to the clearest *causa belli* which has yet arisen between Great Britain and the American Union."

Though the British considered the president's speech belligerent, Polk was correct in saying that Americans had not hesitated to settle the disputed territories. Between 1842 and 1845, the number of Americans in Oregon grew from 400 to over 5,000. Most located south of the Columbia River in the Willamette valley. By 1843, these settlers had written a constitution and soon after elected a legislature. At the same time, changing conditions set the stage for an eventual compromise. British interests in the area were declining as the fur trade dwindled. Attractive commercial opportunities elsewhere were opening up; New Zealand and other colonies lured English settlers away from the Pacific Northwest.

Polk's flamboyant posture and the expansive American claims made mediation difficult, however. The Democratic platform and the slogan that had helped elect Polk laid claim to a boundary of 54°40′. In fact, Polk was not willing to go to war with Great Britain for Oregon. Privately, he considered reasonable a boundary at the 49th parallel, which would extend the existing Canadian-American border to the Pacific and secure the harbors of Puget Sound for the United States. But Polk could hardly admit this to his Democratic supporters, who had so enthusiastically shouted "Fifty-four forty or fight" during the recent campaign.

The Oregon Country

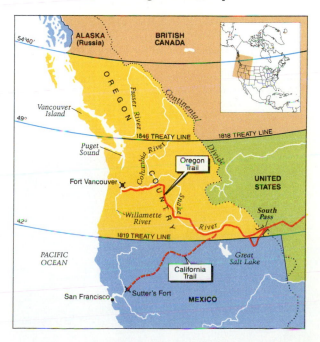

Soon after his inaugural, Polk offered his compromise to Great Britain. But his tone offended the British minister, who rejected the offer at once. Polk compounded his error by gracelessly withdrawing the suggestion. In his year-end address to Congress in 1845, the president created more diplomatic difficulties. Urging the protection of American settlers in Oregon, he again publicly claimed that Oregon belonged to the United States. In addition, he asked Congress to give Britain the one-year notice required by previous agreements to terminate joint occupation there.

Discussions about Oregon occupied Congress for months in early 1846. Debate, however, gradually revealed deep divisions about Oregon and the possibility of war with Great Britain. Despite slogans, most Americans did not want to fight for Oregon and preferred to resolve the crisis diplomatically. As war with Mexico loomed, this task became more urgent.

The British, too, were eager to settle. In June 1846, the British agreed to accept the 49th-parallel boundary if Vancouver Island remained British. Polk took the unorthodox step of forwarding this proposal to the Senate for a preliminary response. Within days, the Senate overwhelmingly approved the compromise. Escaping some of the responsibility for retreating from slogans by sharing it with the Senate, Polk ended the crisis just a few weeks before the declaration of war with Mexico.

As these events show, Manifest Destiny was an idea that supported and justified expansionist policies. It corresponded, at the most basic level, to what Americans believed, that expansion was both

Despite the questionable claim the United States had to the Oregon Territory, thousands of U.S. citizens settled there in the 1840s. They were eager to re-create familiar patterns of life, as this photo of Oregon City suggests.

necessary and right. As early as 1816, American geography books pictured the nation's western boundary at the Pacific and included Texas. Poems, essays, and stories about winning the West, enlivened with illustrations of covered wagons and Indian fighters, were standard reading fare. Popular literature typically described Indians as a dying race that had failed in the basic tasks of cultivating the soil and conquering the wilderness. Mexicans were dismissed as "unjust and injurious neighbor[s]." Only whites could make the wilderness flower. Thus as lands east of the Mississippi filled up, Americans automatically called on familiar ideas to justify expansion.

GOING WEST

After diplomacy and war clarified the status of the western territories, Americans lost little time in moving there. What had been a trickle of emigrants became a flood. During the 1840s, 1850s, and 1860s, thousands of Americans left their homes for the frontier. By 1860, California alone had 380,000 settlers.

Some chose to migrate by sea. Although the trip was expensive, one could sail from Atlantic or Gulf Coast ports around South America to the West Coast or take ship for Panama, cross the isthmus by land, and then continue by sea. Most emigrants, however, chose land routes. In 1843, the first large party succeeded in crossing the plains and mountains to Oregon. More followed. Between 1841 and 1867, some 350,000 traveled over the overland trails to California or to Oregon, while others trekked part of the way to intermediate points like Colorado and Utah.

The Emigrants

Most of the emigrants who headed for the Far West, where slavery was prohibited, were white and American-born. They came from the Midwest and the Upper South. A few free blacks made the trip as well. Pioneer Margaret Frink remembered seeing "a Negro woman . . . tramping along through the heat and dust, carrying a cast iron black stove on her head, with her provisions and a blanket piled on top . . . bravely pushing on for California." Emigrants from the Deep South usually selected Arkansas or Texas as their destination, and many brought their slaves with them. By 1840, over 11,000 slaves toiled in Texas and 20,000 in Arkansas.

Western Population Advance, 1830–1850

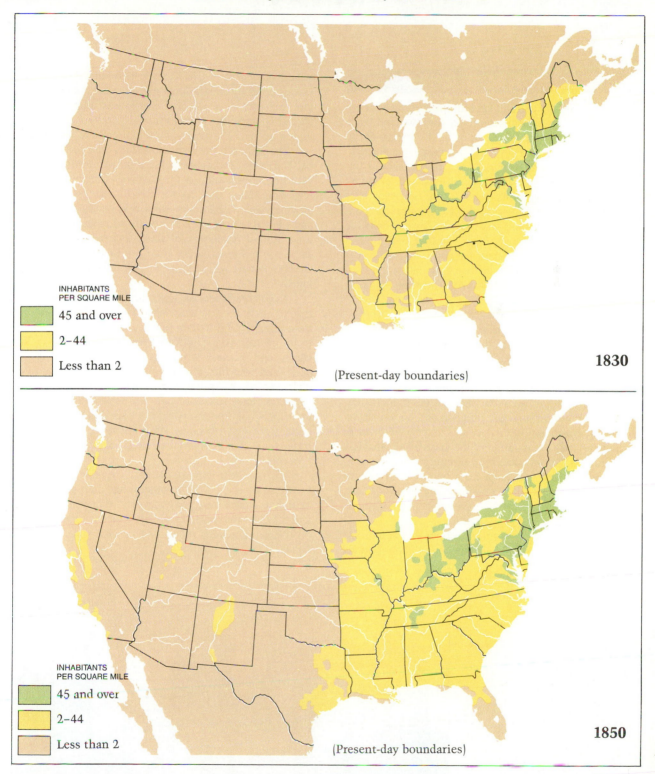

INHABITANTS
PER SQUARE MILE

45 and over

2–44

Less than 2

1830

(Present-day boundaries)

INHABITANTS
PER SQUARE MILE

45 and over

2–44

Less than 2

1850

(Present-day boundaries)

RECOVERING THE PAST

PERSONAL DIARIES

Nineteenth-century journals kept by hundreds of ordinary men and women traveling west on the overland trails constitute a rich source for exploring the nature of the westward experience. They are also an excellent example of how private sources can be used to deepen our understanding of the past. Diaries, journals, and letters all provide us with a personal perspective on major happenings. Since these sources tend to focus on the concrete, they convey some sense of the texture of daily life in the nineteenth century, daily routines and amusements, clothing, habits, and interactions with family and friends. They also provide evidence of the varied concerns, attitudes, and prejudices of the writers, thus providing a test of commonly accepted generalizations about individual and group behavior.

Like any historical source, diaries, journals, and letters must be used carefully. If possible, it is important to note the writer's age, sex, class, and regional identification. Although this information may not always be available, some of the writer's background can usually be deduced from what he or she has written. It is also important to consider for what purpose and for whom the document was composed. This information will help to explain the tone or character of the source and what has been included or left out. It is, of course, important to avoid generalizing too much from one or even several similar sources. Only after reading many diaries, letters, and journals is it possible to make valid generalizations about life in the past.

Here we present excerpts from two travel journals of the 1850s. Few of the writers considered their journals to be strictly private. Often they were intended as a family record or as information for friends back home. Therefore, material of a personal nature has often been excluded. Nineteenth-century Americans referred to certain topics, such as pregnancy, only indirectly or not at all.

The first excerpts come from Mary Bailey's 1852 journal. Mary was 22 when she crossed the plains to California with her 32-year-old doctor husband. Originally a New Englander, Mary had lived in Ohio for six years before moving west. The Baileys were reasonably prosperous and were able to restock necessary supplies on the road west. Robert Robe was 30 when he crossed along the same route a year earlier than the Baileys, headed for Oregon. Robert was a native of Ohio and a Presbyterian minister.

As you read these excerpts, notice what each journal reveals about the trip west. What kinds of challenges did the emigrants face on their journey? Do these correspond to the picture you may have formed from novels, television, and movies? What kinds of work needed to be done, and who did it? Can you see any indication of a division of work based on sex? What kinds of interactions appear to have occurred between men and women on the trip? What does the pattern tell us about nineteenth-century society? How does the painting of the "emigrant train" reinforce the journal accounts of men's and women's roles?

Each of these journals should be read in its entirety, but these short excerpts do suggest that men and women, as they traveled west, may have had different concerns and different perspectives on the journey. In what ways do the two accounts differ, and in what ways are they similar?

Benjamin Franklin Reinhardt,
The Emigrant Train Bedding
Down for the Night, 1867

Journal of Mary Stuart Bailey

Wednesday, April 13, 1852

Left our hitherto happy home in Sylvania amid the tears of parting kisses of dear friends, many of whom were endeared to me by their kindness shown to me when I was a stranger in a strange land, when sickness and death visited our small family & removed our darling, our only child in a moment, as it were. Such kindness I can never forget. . . .

Friday, 21st [May]

Rained last night. Slept in the tent for the first time. I was Yankee enough to protect myself by pinning up blankets over my head. I am quite at home in my tent.

12:00 Have traveled in the rain all day & we are stuck in the mud. I sit in the wagon writing while the men are at work doubling the teams to draw us out. . . .

Sunday, 23rd.

Walked to the top of the hill where I could be quiet & commune with nature and nature's God. This afternoon I was annoyed by something very unpleasant & shed many tears and felt very unhappy. . . .

Thursday, 4th [June]

Very cold this morning after the shower. . . . We stopped on the banks of the Platte to take dinner. I am sitting on the banks of the Platte with my feet almost in the water. Have been writing to my Mother. How I wish some of my own relations with me. . . .

Sunday, 4th [July]

Started at 3 o'clock to find feed or know where it was. Had to go 4 or 5 miles off the road. Found water & good grass. Camped on the sand with sage roots for fuel. It is wintery, cold & somewhat inclined to rain, not pleasant. Rather a dreary Independence Day. We speak of our friends at home. We think they are thinking of us. . . .

Monday, 12th.

Stayed in camp another day to get our horse better. He is much improved. It is cold enough. Washed in the morning & had the sick headache in the afternoon. . . .

Thursday, 12th [August]

Very warm. Slept until we stopped to take breakfast. Mr. Patterson starts as soon as light & stops in the heat of the day to rest the animals. We do not have much time to do anything except 4 or 5 hours in the middle of the day. . . .

Friday, 17th [September]

Have been confined ever since Monday with ague in my face which is very much swollen. Have suffered very much. We are now in Carson Valley. Plenty of trees but the country is very barren.

Saturday, 18th.

Very pleasant, delightful weather. Feel much better today. We are not stirring this afternoon. We have heard of a great deal of suffering, people being thrown out on the desert to die & being picked up & brought to the hospital. . . .

Tuesday, November 8th

Sacramento city has been nearly consumed. The Dr. has had all his instruments & a good deal of clothing burned, loss not exceeding $300. It really seems as though it was not right for us to come to California & lose so much. I do not think that we shall be as well off as at home.

Source: Sandra L. Myres, ed., Ho for California! Women's Overland Diaries from the Huntington Library (San Marino, Calif.: Henry E. Huntington Library, 1980).

Journal of Robert Robe

[May] 19. [1851] A fine day. The first spent in travelling on the plains of the Platte river.

20. Continue our journey up the Platte valley which I would judge to be here some 12 miles wide on this side of the river. The only game seen here are the antelope and wolf beside some wild fowl.

21. A rainy morning started early passed on old Pawnee village in ruins. The houses are constructed by placing timbers in forks and upon these without placing upright poles then rushes bound with [illegible] and finally earth. Chimney in center. Day became more & more rainy and wound up with a storm which beggared description.

22. Bluff approach the river—travelling less monotonous river finely skirted with timber.

23. Roads very muddy in afternoon. Today our wagon severed itself from our former companions & joined a company of Californians.

24. Before starting a trader direct from Ft. Kearney arrived at our camp. He informs us it is yet 25 miles thither. Travelling is by no means dangerous a waggon of provisions passing with only three guards. In the afternoon passed the entrance of the Independence Weston & St. Jo roads. Emigrants became more numerous.

25. Passed Fort Kearney this morning and after a short drive encamped. Having conversed with some of the soldiers I find they consider life very monotonous.

26. Roads heavy—short drive—a storm.

27. High Bluffs on the opposite side of river approach and present a beautiful appearance. At night a fearful storm.

28. Roads heavy nothing singular.

29. Have arrived in the region abounding in Buffalo. At noon a considerable herd came in sight. The first any of us had ever seen. Thus now for the chase—the horsemen proved too swift in pursuit and frightened them into the Bluffs without capturing any—the footmen pursued however and killed three pretty good success for the first.

30. Nothing remarkable today.

31. Game being abundant we resolved to rest our stock and hunt today—Started in the morning on foot. Saw probably 1000 Buffalo. Shot at several and killed one. Where ever we found them wolves were prowling around as if to guard them. Their real object is however no doubt to seize the calves as their prey. Saw a town of Prairie dogs, they are nearly as large as a gray squirrel. They bark fiercely when at a little distance but on near approach flee to their holes. Wherever they are we see numerous owls. After a very extensive ramble and having seen a variety of game we returned at sunset with most voracious appetites.

June 1. The Bluffs become beautifully undulating losing their precipitous aspect and the country further back is beautifully rolling prairie.

2. In the evening camped beside our old friends Miller and Dovey. They had met with a great loss this morning their 3 horses having taken fright at a drove of buffalo and ran entirely away. Some of our company killed more buffalo this evening & a company went in the night with teams to bring them in.

3. Spent the forenoon in an unsuccessful search for the above mentioned horses. In the afternoon pursued & caught our company after

4. Crossed the south fork of the Platte at 2 P.M.

Source: Pacific Northwest Quarterly 19 [January 1928]: 52–63.

Many American families who headed west to newly acquired territories had migrated as children or young people to earlier frontier areas.

The many pioneers who kept journals during the five- to six-month overland trip captured the human dimension of emigrating. Their journals, usually their only contribution to the historical record, focused on day-to-day events and expressed some of the thoughts and emotions experienced on the long journey west. One migrant, Lodisa Frizzell, described her feelings at parting in 1852:

> Who is there that does not recollect their first night when started on a long journey, the well known voices of our friends still ring in our ears, the parting kiss feels still warm upon our lips, and that last separating word FAREWELL! sinks deeply into the heart. It may be the last we ever hear from some or all of them, and to those who start . . . there can be no more solemn scene of parting only at death.

Most emigrants traveled with family and relatives. Only during the gold rush years did large numbers, usually young men, travel independently. Migration was a family experience, mostly involving men and women from their late twenties to early forties. A sizable number of them had recently married. And for most, migration was a familiar experience. Like other geographically mobile Americans, emigrants to the Far West had earlier moved to other frontiers, often as children or as newlyweds. The difference was the vast distance to this frontier and the seemingly final separation from home.

Migrants' Motives

What led so many Americans to sell most of their possessions and embark on an unknown future thousands of miles away? Many believed that frontier life would offer rich opportunities. A popular folksong expressed this widespread conviction:

> Since times has been hard, I'll tell you sweetheart,
> I've a notion to leave off my plow and my cart,
> Away to Californy a journey pursue,
> To double my fortunes as other men do.

The kinds of opportunities emigrants expected varied widely. Thousands sought riches in the form of gold. Others anticipated making their fortune as merchants, shopkeepers, and peddlers. Some intended to speculate in land, acquiring large blocks of public lands and then selling them later to settlers at a handsome profit. The possibility of professional rewards gained from practicing law or medicine on the frontier attracted still others.

Most migrants dreamed of bettering their life by cultivating the land. As one settler explained, "The motive that induced us to part with pleasant associates and dear friends of our childhood days, was to obtain from the government of the United States a grant of land that 'Uncle Sam' had promised." Federal and state land policies made the acquisition of land increasingly alluring. Preemption acts during the 1830s and 1840s gave "squatters" the right to settle public lands before the government offered them for sale and then allowed them to purchase these lands at the minimum price once they came on the market. At the same time, the amount of land a family had to buy shrank to only 40 acres. In 1862, the Homestead Act went further by offering 160 acres of government land free to citizens or future citizens over 21 who lived on the property, improved it, and paid a small registration fee. Oregon's land policy, which predated the Homestead Act, was even more generous. It awarded a single man 320 acres of free land and a married man 640 acres provided he occupied his claim for four years and made improvements.

Some emigrants hoped the West would restore them to health. Settlers from the Mississippi valley wished to escape the region's debilitating agues and fevers. Doctors advised those suffering the dreaded tuberculosis that the long out-of-doors trip and the western climate might cure them. Even invalids grasped at the advice offered by one doctor in 1850, who urged them to "attach themselves to the companies of emigrants bound for Oregon or Upper California."

Others pursued religious or cultural missions in the West. Missionary couples like David and Catherine Blaine, who settled in Seattle when it was a frontier outpost, determined to bring Protestantism and education west. Stirred by the stories they had heard of the "deplorable morals" on the frontier, they willingly left the comforts of home to evangelize and educate westerners. Still others, like the Mormons, made the long trek to Utah to establish a society in conformity with their religious beliefs.

Not everyone who dreamed of setting off for the frontier could do so, however. Unlike the moves to earlier frontiers, the trip to the Far West involved considerable expense. The sea route, while probably the most comfortable, was the most costly. Guidebooks estimated that the trip around Cape Horn came to $600 per person. For the same sum, four people could make the overland trip. And if the emigrants sold their wagons and oxen at the journey's end, the final expenses might amount to only $220. Clearly, however, the initial financial outlay was considerable enough to rule out the trip for the very poor. Despite increasingly liberal land pol-

icies, migration to the Far West (with the exception of group migration to Utah) was a movement of middle-class Americans.

The Overland Trails

The trip started for most emigrants in the late spring when they left their homes and headed for starting points in Iowa and Missouri: Council Bluffs, Independence, Westport, St. Joseph. There companies of wagons gathered, and when grass was up for the stock, usually by the middle of May, they set out. Emigrant trains first followed the valley of the Platte River. Making only 15 miles a day, they slowly wound their way through the South Pass of the Rockies, heading for destinations in California or Oregon.

Emigrants found the first part of the trip novel and even enjoyable. The Indians, one woman noted, "proved better than represented"; some even helped emigrants cross rivers swollen by spring rains. The scenery, with its spring and early summer flowers, was new. Familiar chores were a challenge out in the open. The traditional division of labor known at home persisted. Generally, men did the

Overland Trails to the West

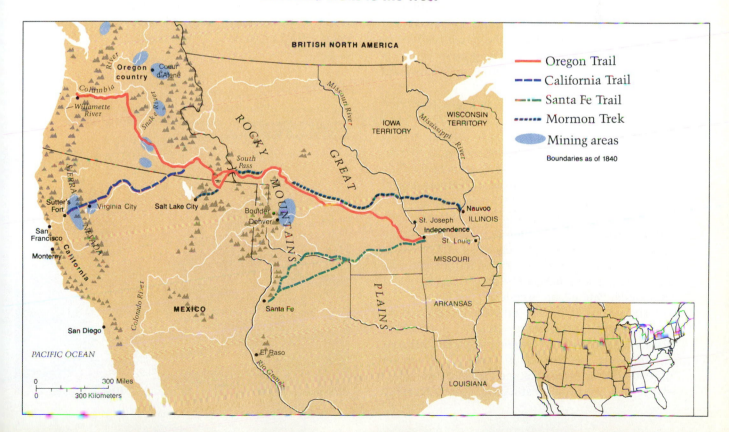

Oregon Trail
California Trail
Santa Fe Trail
Mormon Trek
Mining areas

Boundaries as of 1840

"outdoor" work. They drove and repaired the wagons, ferried cattle and wagons across rivers, hunted, and stood guard at night. Women labored at domestic chores, caring for children, cooking meals, and washing clothes. As they had at home, women procured small treats, trading with each other and with Indians for buffalo meat, fish, or moccasins. Young children stayed out of the way in wagons, while older brothers and sisters walked and lent a hand to their elders. Many of the children later remembered the trip as an exciting adventure. Sometimes a day off from traveling provided a chance for fun. Wagon trains might stop to observe the Sabbath, allowing men and animals time to rest and women an opportunity to catch up on the laundry.

As the trip lengthened, difficulties multiplied. Cholera often took a heavy toll. Conflict with Indians became a problem only in the 1850s and made emigrants jumpy during the second half of the trip. (Between 1840 and 1860, Indians killed about 400 emigrants, most during the second half of the trip; the emigrants themselves killed at least that many Indians.) Traveling grew more arduous as deserts and mountains replaced rolling prairies.

Since emigrants had to cross the final mountain ranges of the Sierras and the Cascades before the first snowfall, there was a pressing need to push ever onward. Animals weakened by constant travel, poor feed, and bad water sickened, collapsed, and often died. As families faced the harsh realities of travel, they had to lighten their wagons by throwing out possessions lovingly brought from home. Food grew scarce.

The familiar division of responsibilities often broke down. Women found themselves driving wagons, loading them, even helping to drag them over rocky mountain trails. Their husbands worked frantically with the animals and the wagons as the time of the first snowfall drew closer. Tempers frayed among tired, overworked, and anxious families. Finally, five or six months after setting out, emigrants arrived, exhausted and often penniless, in Oregon or California. As one wrote on a September day in 1854, her journey had ended "which for care, fatigue, tediousness, perplexities and dangers of various kinds, can not be excelled."

The strains of the trip led some groups to draw up rules and elect officers. This did not prevent dissension, however. Many companies split because of arguments over the pace of travel or the number of rest stops or because some changed their minds about their eventual destination. Family harmony

often collapsed under the strain of increased work loads, the irritations of travel, and crises of sickness and even death. Mary Power, who with her husband and three children crossed in 1853, revealed exasperation and depression in her journal: "I felt my courage must fail me, for there we were in a strange land, almost without anything to eat, [with] a team that was not able to pull an empty wagon." In a letter she was even more candid: "I felt as though myself and the little ones were at the mercy of a madman." Men too lost nerve as they confronted the hazards of travel. Oregon-bound John Minto described coming upon a father of four, "lying on his back upon a rock, taking the rain in his face, seemingly given up all thought of manly struggle," while the cry of Indians sent some men in another train into their wagons to hide.

LIVING ON THE FRONTIER

When emigrants finally reached their destinations, their feelings ranged from acute disappointment to buoyant enthusiasm. But whether elated or depressed, they had no choice but to start anew. As they turned toward building a new life, they naturally drew on their experiences back east. "Pioneers though we are, and proud of it, we are not content with the wilds . . . with the idleness of the land, the rudely construct[ed] log cabin," one Oregon settler explained. "Pioneers are not that kind of folks."

The adventure of travel turned into a nightmare for many as the terrain grew rougher, animals weaker, and food scarcer in the second half of the journey.

The Agricultural Frontier

Pioneer farmers faced the urgent task of establishing their homesteads and beginning farming. First, the family had to locate a suitable claim. Clearing the land and constructing a crude shelter followed. Only then could crops be planted. Since emigrants brought few of their possessions west, their work was more difficult. A young Oregon bride who set up housekeeping in the 1840s with only a stew kettle and three knives was not unusual. A letter from Sarah Everett to her sister-in-law in the East told the tale of hardship. Pleased with a gift of pretty trimmings, Sarah confessed, "I am a very old woman. My face is thin sunken and wrinkled, my hands bony and withered and hard—I shall look strangely I fear with your nice undersleeves and coquettish cherry bows." Sarah was 29 years old.

After months of intense interaction with other travelers, families were now alone on their claims. The typical frontier household consisted of parents with one to four children. Although frontier families might interact with nearby Indians, cultural biases made close friendships difficult. No wonder the pioneers often felt lonely and thought longingly of old friends. No wonder either that women helped men with their work and men assisted their wives in domestic chores such as washing.

For several years, such isolation was the rule. One pioneer remembered, "We were . . . 'all told,' eleven families within a radius of six or eight miles, widely separated by our holdings and three hundred and twenty acres to each family. In those days anyone residing within twenty miles was considered a neighbor." But the isolation usually ended within a few years as most areas attracted new emigrants and old settlers seeking better claims.

As rural communities grew, settlers worked to establish schools, churches, and clubs. These organizations drew together people from different places and backgrounds and helped mold them into a new community. They also served to redefine acceptable forms of behavior and remind members of conventional standards and beliefs.

The determination to reestablish familiar institutions was most apparent in politics and law. In Oregon, for example, the pioneers set up a political system based on eastern models before the status of the territory was resolved. Before permanent schools or churches existed, men resumed the familiar political rituals of voting, electioneering, and talking politics. They were also going to court to resolve controversies and to ensure law and order.

Although modern movies and novels suggest that violence was a part of everyday life on the frontier, this was not true on the farming frontier. Courts, rather than rough-and-ready vigilante groups, usually handled the occasional violence.

Setting up a common school system was more difficult and less urgent in the eyes of many frontier communities than beginning political life. Few settlers initially thought education important enough to tax themselves for permanent public schools. There were some schools, of course. But most operated sporadically and only for students who could pay at least part of the fees.

Various obstacles hindered organized religion. Although settlers often attended early church services no matter what the denomination, community growth proved a mixed blessing. When confirmed believers gathered in their own churches, they often discovered to their dismay that the congregation was too small to sustain the new church financially. Nor were converts plentiful, for many settlers had grown out of the habit of regular churchgoing. In early Seattle, Catherine and David Blaine were shocked. "Observation and experience have taught us since we left home," David remarked, "the unwelcome lesson that separation from gospel influences has rendered them quite indifferent to gospel truth." Catherine believed, "This is an awfully wicked country."

The chronic shortage of cash on the frontier retarded the growth of both schools and churches. Until farmers could send their goods to market, they had little cash to spare. Geographic mobility also contributed to institutional instability. Up to three-quarters of the population of a frontier county might vanish within a ten-year period as emigrants left to seek better land. Some farmed in as many as four locations until they found a satisfactory claim. Institutions relying on continuing personal and financial support suffered accordingly.

Yet even if their efforts to re-create familiar institutional life often faltered, settlers did not lose sight of their goals. Newspapers, journals, and books, which circulated early on the frontier, reinforced familiar values and norms and kept determination strong. As more and more settlers arrived, the numbers willing to support educational, religious, and cultural institutions grew. In the end, as one pioneer pointed out, "We have a telegraph line from the East, a daily rail road train, daily mail and I am beginning to feel quite civilized. And here ended my pioneer experience." Only 16 years had passed since she had crossed the Plains.

Although the belief in the frontier's special economic and social opportunities encouraged emigration, the dream was often illusory. Western society rapidly acquired a social and economic structure similar to that of the East. Frontier newspapers referred to leading settlers as the "better" sort, giving voice to an emerging world of social and economic distinctions. The appearance of workers for hire and tenant farmers also pointed to real economic differences and hinted at the difficulties those on the bottom would face as they tried to improve their situation.

Their widespread geographic mobility also indicates that many found it difficult to capitalize on the benefits of homesteading. Census data show that those who moved were generally less successful than the core of stable residents, who became the community's economic and social leaders. Of course, those on the move may have believed that fortune would finally smile on them at their next stop. But one wife was not so hopeful. When her husband announced that they were to move once again, she commented, "Perhaps I was not quite so enthusiastic as he. I seemed to have heard all this before."

The Mining Frontier

On the mining frontier, tales of prospectors who had reportedly struck it rich fueled the fantasies of fortune hunters. News of the discovery of gold in 1848 in California swept the country like "wildfire," according to one Missouri emigrant. Thousands raced to cash in on the bonanza. Within a year, California's population ballooned from 14,000 to almost 100,000. By 1852, that figure had more than doubled.

Like migrants to the agricultural frontier, the forty-niners were mostly young (in 1850, over half the people in California were in their twenties). Unlike pioneers headed for the rural frontier, however, the gold seekers were unmarried, predominantly male, and heterogeneous. Of those pouring into California in 1849, about 80 percent came from the United States, 8 percent from Mexico, and 5 percent from South America. The rest came from Europe and Asia. Few were as interested in settling the West as they were in extracting its precious metals and returning home rich.

California was the first and most dramatic of the western mining frontiers. But others sprang up. Rumors of gold propelled between 25,000 and 30,000 emigrants, many from California, to British Columbia in Canada in 1858. A year later, news of gold strikes in Colorado set off another frantic rush for fortune. Precious metals discovered in the Pacific Northwest early in the decade and in Montana and Idaho a few years later kept dreams alive and prospectors moving. In the mid-1870s, yet another discovery of gold, this time in the Black Hills of North Dakota, attracted hordes of fortune seekers.

The discovery of gold or silver spurred immediate, if usually short-lived, growth. In contrast to the agricultural frontier, where early settlers were isolated and the community expanded gradually, the mining frontier came to life almost overnight. Mining camps, ramshackle and often hastily constructed, soon housed hundreds or even thousands of miners and people serving them. Merchants, saloonkeepers, cooks, druggists, gamblers, and prostitutes hurried into boom areas as fast as prospectors. Usually about half of the residents of any mining camp were there to relieve the miners of their profits, not to prospect themselves.

Given the motivation, character, and ethnic diversity of those flocking to boomtowns and the feeble attempts to set up local government in what were perceived as temporary communities, it was hardly surprising that mining life was often disorderly. Racial antagonism between American miners and foreigners, whom they labeled "greasers" (Mexicans), "chinks" (Chinese), "keskedees" (Frenchmen), and lesser "breeds," led to ugly riots and lynchings. Miners had few qualms about eliminating Indians and others who interfered with the race for riches. Fistfights, drunkenness, and murder occurred often enough to become part of the lore of the gold rush. Wrote one woman, "In the short space of twenty four days, we have had murders, fearful accidents, bloody deaths, a mob, whippings, a hanging, an attempt at suicide, and a fatal duel."

Miners went west to get rich, not to advance civilization; and they usually made no pretense of upholding eastern manners.

If mining life was usually not this violent, it tolerated behavior that would have been unacceptable farther east. Miners were not trying to re-create eastern communities but to get rich. Married men, convinced of the raucous and immoral character of mining communities, hesitated to bring wives and families west. As one declared, "I would much prefer that a wife of mine should board in a respectable bawd house in the city of New York than live anywhere in the city of San Francisco."

Although the lucky few struck it rich or at least made enough money to return home with pride intact, miners' journals and letters reveal that many made only enough to keep going. Wrote one, "Everybody in the States who has friends here is always writing for them to come home. Now they all long to go home. . . . But it is hard for a man to leave . . . with nothing. . . . I have no pile yet, but you can bet your life I will never come home until I have something more than when I started." The problem was that easily mined silver and gold deposits soon ran out. Although Chinese miners proved adept at finding what early miners overlooked, the remaining rich deposits lay deeply embedded in rock or gravel. Extraction required cooperative efforts, capital, technological experience, and expensive machinery. Eventually, mining became a corporate industrial concern, with miners as wage earners. As early as 1852, the changing nature of mining in California had transformed most of the shaggy miners into wage workers.

Probably 5 percent of early gold rush emigrants to California were women and children. Many of the women also anticipated getting "rich in a hurry." Because there were so few of them, the cooking, nursing, laundry, and hotel services women provided had a high value. When Luzena Wilson arrived in Sacramento, a miner offered to pay her $10 for a biscuit. That night, Luzena dreamt she saw "crowds of bearded miners striking gold from the earth with every blow of the pick, each one seeming to leave a share for me." Yet it was wearying work, and some wondered if the money compensated for the exhaustion. As Mary Ballou thought it over, she decided, "I would not advise any Lady to come out here and suffer to toil and fatigue I have suffered for the sake of a little gold." As men's profits shrank, so too did those of the women who served them.

Some of the first women to arrive on the mining frontier were prostitutes. They rejected the hard labor of cooking and washing that "respectable" women performed, hoping that the sex ratio would make their profession especially profitable. Pros-

Although there were only a few women on the early mining frontier, they often found that the predominantly male environment offered them good opportunities to earn money.

titutes may have comprised as much as 20 percent of California's female population in 1850, and they probably vastly outnumbered respectable women in early mining camps. During boom days, they made good money and sometimes won a recognized place in society. But prostitutes always ran risks in a disorderly environment. They were more often the victims of murder and violence than the recipients of courtesy.

The Mexicans, South Americans, Chinese, and small numbers of blacks seeking their fortunes in California soon discovered that while they contributed substantially to California's growth, racial discrimination flourished vigorously in the land of golden promise. At first, American miners hoped to force foreigners out of the gold fields altogether. But an attempt to declare mining illegal for all foreigners failed. A high tax on foreign miners proved more successful. Thousands of Mexicans left the mines, while the Chinese found other jobs in San Francisco and Sacramento. As business stagnated in mining towns, however, white miners had second thoughts about the levy and reduced it. By 1870, when the tax was declared unconstitutional, the Chinese, who had paid 85 percent of it, had "contributed" $5 million to California for the right to prospect. The hostility that led to this legislation also fed widespread violence against the Chinese and Mexicans.

Black Americans found that their skin color placed them in a situation akin to that of foreigners. Deprived of the vote, forbidden to testify in civil or criminal cases involving whites, excluded from the bounties of the state's homestead law, blacks led a precarious existence. When news arrived of the dis-

Photographed in the 1870s, the near ghost town of Ophir City, Nevada, attests to the boom-and-bust pattern of the mining frontier and the ramshackle nature of many mining communities.

covery of gold in British Columbia in the late 1850s, hundreds of blacks as well as thousands of Chinese left the state hoping that the Canadian frontier would be more hospitable than California.

Alluring as the mining frontier was, men's and women's fantasies of dazzling riches rarely came true. The ghost towns of the West testify to the typical pattern: boom, bust, decay, death. The empty streets and rotting buildings stood as symbols of dashed hopes and disappointed dreams.

Yet gold had a huge impact on the West as a whole. Between 1848 and 1883, California mines supplied two-thirds of the country's gold. This gold transformed San Francisco from a sleepy town into a bustling metropolis. It fueled the agricultural and commercial development of California and Oregon as miners provided a market for goods and services. Gold built harbors, railroads, and irrigation systems not just in California and Oregon but all over the West. Though few people made large fortunes, both the region and the nation profited from gold.

The Mormon Frontier

In the decades before 1860, many emigrants heading for the Far West stopped to rest and buy supplies in Salt Lake City, the heart of the Mormon state of Deseret. There they encountered a society that seemed familiar and orderly, yet foreign and shocking. Visitors admired the attractively laid out town with its irrigation ditches, gardens and tidy houses. But as they noted the decorous nature of everyday life, they gossiped about polygamy and searched for signs of rebellion in the faces of Mormon women. Emigrants who opposed slavery were fond of equating the position of the Mormon wife with that of the black slave. They were amazed that so few Mormon women seemed interested in escaping from the bonds of plural marriage.

Violent events had driven the Mormons to the arid Great Basin area. Joseph Smith's murder in 1844 marked no end to the persecution of his followers. By the fall of 1846, angry mobs had chased the last of the "Saints" out of Nauvoo, Illinois. As they struggled to join their advance groups at temporary camps in Iowa, Smith's successor, Brigham Young, realized that flight from the United States represented the best hope for survival. The Saints must create the kingdom of God anew, somewhere in the West, far removed from the United States, that "Babylon" of corruption and injustice.

The Mexican war unexpectedly furthered Mormon plans. At first, most Mormons probably agreed with Hosea Stout, who was glad "to learn of the war," hoping it "might never end until the States were entirely destroyed, for they had driven us into the wilderness, and now were laughing at our calamaties." But Brigham Young realized that war might provide capital needed for the new Mormon kingdom. By raising 500 Mormon young men for Kearney's Army of the West, Young acquired vital resources. The battalion's advance pay bought wagonloads of supplies for starving and sick Mormons strung out along the trail between Missouri and Iowa and helped finance the impending great migration.

Young selected the Great Basin area, technically part of Mexico, as the best site for his future kingdom. It was arid and remote, 1,000 miles from its nearest "civilized" neighbors. But if irrigated, Mormom leaders concluded it might prove as fertile as the fields and vineyards of ancient Israel.

In April 1847, Young led an exploratory expedition of 143 men, 3 women, and 2 children to this promised land. In late July, after reaching Salt Lake, Young exclaimed, "This is the place." Before returning to Iowa to prepare Mormons for the trip to Utah, he announced his land policy. Settlers would receive virtually free land on the basis of a family's size and its ability to cultivate it. After Young left, the expeditionary group followed his directions to construct irrigation ditches and begin planting.

The following months and years tested Young's organizational talents and his followers' cooperative abilities. By September 1847, fully 566 wagons and 1,500 of the Saints had made the arduous trek to Salt Lake City. Still more Mormons came the next year, inspired by visions of a new Zion in the West. Their trip was also a collective venture, planned and directed by church leaders. By 1850, the Mormon frontier had attracted over 11,000 settlers. Missionary efforts in the United States and abroad, especially in Great Britain and Scandinavia, drew thousands of converts to the Great Basin. The church emigration society and a loan fund facilitated the journey for many who could never have otherwise undertaken the trip. By the end of the decade, over 30,000 Saints lived in Utah, not only in Salt Lake City but also in more than 90 village colonies Young had planned. Though hardship marked these early years, the Mormons thrived. As one early settler remarked, "We have everything around us we could ask."

Non-Mormon or "Gentile" emigrants passing through Utah found much that was recognizable. The government had familiar characteristics. Most Mormons were farmers; many of them came originally from New England and the Midwest and shared many of the same customs and attitudes. But outsiders perceived profound differences, for the heart of Mormon society was not the individual farmer living on his own homestead but the cooperative village.

Years of persecution had nourished a strong sense of group identity and acceptance of church leadership. Organized by the church leaders, who made the essential decisions, farming became a collective enterprise. All farmers were allotted land. All had irrigation rights, for water did not belong to individuals but to the community. During Sunday services, the local bishop might give farming instructions to his congregation along with his sermon. As Young explained, "I have looked upon the community of Latter-day Saints in a vision and beheld them organized as the great family of heaven, each person performing his several duties in his line of industry, working for the good of the whole more than for individual aggrandizement." In this vast communal effort, every Mormon was expected to work for success, men and women alike. "We do not believe in having any drones in the hive," one woman said tartly.

The church was omnipresent in Utah; in fact, nothing separated church and state. Despite familiar governmental forms, church leaders occupied all important political posts. Brigham Young's Governing Quorum contained the high priests of the church, who made both religious and political decisions.

When it became clear that Utah would become a territory, Mormon leaders drew up a constitution that divided religious and political power. But once in place, powers overlapped. As one Gentile pointed out, "This intimate connection of church and state seems to pervade everything that is done. The supreme power in both being lodged in the hands of the same individuals, it is difficult to separate their two official characters, and to determine whether in any one instance they act as spiritual or merely temporal officers."

The Treaty of Guadalupe Hidalgo officially incorporated Utah into the United States but little affected political and religious arrangements. Brigham Young became territorial governor. Local bishops continued to act as spiritual leaders as well as civil magistrates in Mormon communities. Mormons had come to Utah to establish a kingdom rather than a republic. Their motives dictated the unique politicoreligious nature of the Utah experience.

Other aspects of the Mormon frontier were distinctive. Mormon policy toward the Indian tribes was remarkably enlightened. As one prominent

When they were driven out of Nauvoo, Illinois, the Mormons left behind the fine temple they had constructed for the rites of their new faith.

Mormon pointed out, "It has been our habit to shoot Indians with tobacco and bread biscuits rather than with powder and lead, and we are most successful with them." After two expeditions against the Timpanagos and Shoshone in 1850, Mormons concentrated on converting rather than killing Native Americans. Mormon missionaries learned Bannock, Ute, Navajo, and Hopi languages in order to bring the faith to these tribes. They also encouraged Native Americans to ranch and farm.

While most Gentiles could tolerate some of the differences they encountered on the Mormon frontier, few could accept polygamy and the seemingly immoral extended family structure that plural marriage entailed. Although Joseph Smith and other church leaders had secretly practiced polygamy in the early 1840s, Brigham Young only publicly revealed the doctrine in 1852, when the Saints were safely in Utah. Smith believed that the highest or "celestial" form of marriage brought special rewards in the afterlife. Since wives and children contributed to these rewards, polygamy was a means of sanctification. From a practical standpoint, polygamy served to incorporate into Mormon society single female converts who had left their families to come to Utah.

Although most Mormons accepted the doctrine and its religious justification, some found it hard to follow. One woman called it "a great trial of feelings." Actually, relatively few families were polygamous. During the 40-year period in which Mormons practiced plural marriage, only 10 to 20 percent of Mormon families were polygamous. Few men had more than two wives. Because of the expense of maintaining several families and the personal strains involved, usually only the most successful and visible Mormon leaders practiced polygamy.

Polygamous family life was a far cry from the lascivious arrangement outsiders fantasized. Since jealousy among wives could destroy the institution of plural marriage, Mormon leaders minimized the role of romantic love and sexual attraction in courtship and marriage. Instead, they encouraged marriages founded on mutual attachment, with sex for the purposes of procreation rather than pleasure.

To the shock of outsiders, Mormon women did not consider themselves slaves but rather highly regarded members of the Mormon community. Whether plural wives or not, they saw polygamy as the cutting edge of their society and defended it to the outside world. Polygamy was preferable to monogamy, which left the single woman without the economic and social protection of family life and forced some of them into prostitution, Brenda Pratt explained. "Polygamy . . . tends directly to the chastity of women, and the sound health and morals . . . of their children."

Although they faced obvious difficulties, many plural wives found rewards in polygamy. Without the constant presence of husbands, they had an unusual opportunity for independence. Many treated husbands when they visited as revered friends; their children, not their spouses, provided them with day-to-day emotional satisfaction. Occasionally, plural wives lived together and shared domestic work, becoming close friends. As one such wife put it, "We three . . . loved each other more than sisters" and would "go hand in hand together down till eternity."

Although the Mormon frontier seemed alien to outsiders, it succeeded in terms of its numbers, its growing economic prosperity, and its group unity. Long-term threats loomed for this community, however, once the area became part of the United States. Attacks on Young's power as well as heated verbal denunciations of polygamy proliferated. Efforts began in Congress to outlaw polygamy. In the years before the Civil War, Mormons withstood these assaults on their way of life. But as Utah became more connected to the rest of the country, the tide would turn against them.

The Urban Frontier

Many emigrants went west not to claim farmland or to pan for gold but rather to settle in cities like San Francisco, Denver, and Portland. There they hoped to find business and professional opportunities or, perhaps, the chance to make a fortune by speculating in town lots.

Cities were an integral part of frontier life and, in some cases, preceded agricultural settlement. Some communities turned into bustling cities as they catered to the emigrant trade. St. Joseph, Missouri, outfitted families setting out on the overland journey. Salt Lake City offered weary pioneers headed for California an opportunity to rest and restock. Portland was the destination of many emigrants and became a market and supply center for homesteaders.

Some cities grew so rapidly that they have been called "instant cities." San Francisco and Denver turned into cities almost overnight; in a mere 12 years, San Francisco's population zoomed from 812 to 56,802. The discovery of precious metals sent thousands of miners with diverse demands and desires to and through these places. And once the strike ran out, many miners returned to these cities to make a new start. Still other places supplied frontier farmers and served as their markets. They only gradually acquired urban characteristics.

Commercial life bustled on the urban frontier, offering residents a wide range of occupations and services. As a Portland emigrant remarked in 1852, only a few years after that community's beginning, "In many ways life here . . . was more primitive than it was in the early times in Illinois and Missouri. But in others it was far more advanced. . . . We could get the world's commodities here which could not be had, then, or scarcely at all, in the interior of Illinois or Missouri."

Young, single men seeking their fortunes made up a disproportionate share of the urban population. Frontier Portland had more than three men for every woman. Predictably, urban life was often noisy, rowdy, and occasionally violent. The presence of so many young men could not help but affect urban family life. Mothers worried about their children falling into bad company. Some attempted to reform the atmosphere by pressing for Sunday store closings or prohibition. Other women, of course, enjoyed all the attention that came with the presence of so many young men. As one observed with gusto, "There is plenty of men here. They cast sheeps eyes at Lib and Lucy's girl but have not popt the question yet." Eventually the sex ratio became balanced, but as late as 1880, fully 18 of the 24 largest western cities had more men than women.

Although western cities began with distinctive characters, they soon resembled eastern cities. As a western publication boasted, "Transport a resident of an Eastern city and put him down in the streets of Portland, and he would observe little difference between his new surroundings and those he beheld but a moment before in his native city."

The history of Portland suggests the common pattern of development. In 1845, Portland was only a clearing in the forest, large enough for four streets and 16 blocks. Speculation in town lots was lively. By the early 1850s, Portland had grown into a small trading center with a few rough log structures and muddy tracks for streets. As farmers poured into Oregon, the city became a regional commercial center. More permanent structures were built, giving the city an "eastern" appearance.

The belief that urban life in the West abounded with special opportunities initially drew many young men to Portland and other western cities.

Many of them did not find financial success there. Opportunities were greatest for newcomers who brought assets with them. These residents became the elite of the community. By the 1860s, when the city's population had reached 2,874, Portland's Social Club symbolized the emergence of that city's elite. Portland's businessmen, lawyers, and editors controlled an increasing share of the community's wealth and set its social standards. Their elaborate parties, summer trips, and exclusive clubs showed how far Portland had come from its raw frontier beginnings.

CULTURES IN CONFLICT

Looking at westward expansion through the eyes of white emigrants provides only one view of the frontier experience. An entry from an Oregon Trail journal suggests other perspectives. On May 7, 1864, Mary Warner, a bride of only a few months, described a frightening event. That day, a "fine-looking" Indian had visited the wagon train and tried to buy her. Mary's husband, probably uncertain how to handle the situation, played along, agreeing to trade his wife for two ponies. The Indian generously

Frontier cities soon came to resemble cities in the East, as this view of San Francisco in 1853 suggests. Only four years after the gold rush, the shantytown had been replaced by a city with board sidewalks, kerosene streetlamps, and a circulating library with books in English, French, and Spanish.

offered three. "Then," wrote Mary, "he took hold of my shawl to make me understand to get out [of the wagon]. About this time I got frightened and really was so hysterical [that] I began to cry." Everyone laughed at her, she reported, though surely the Indian found the whole incident no more amusing than she had.

This ordinary encounter on the overland trail only begins to hint at the social and cultural differences separating white Americans moving west and the peoples with whom they came into contact. Confident of their values and rights, emigrants had little regard for those who had lived in the West for centuries and no compunction in seizing their lands. Many even predicted that the Indian race would disappear from the continent, a just reward for tribal "degeneracy."

Confronting the Plains Tribes

During the 1840s, white Americans, for the first time, came into extensive contact with the powerful Plains tribes, whose culture differed from that of the more familiar eastern Woodlands tribes. Probably a quarter million Native Americans occupied the area from the Rocky Mountains to the Missouri River and from the Platte River to New Mexico. Nearest the Missouri and Iowa frontier lived the "border" tribes—the Pawnee, Omaha, Oto, Ponca, and Kansa. These Indians, unlike other Plains tribes, lived in villages and raised crops, though they supplemented their diet with buffalo meat during the summer months. On the Central Plains lived the Brulé and Oglala Sioux, the Cheyenne, the Shoshone, and the Arapaho, aggressive tribes who followed the buffalo and often raided the border tribes. In the Southwest were the Comanche, Ute, Navajo, and some Apache bands, while the Kiowa, Wichita, Apache, and southern Comanche claimed northern and western Texas as their hunting grounds.

Although there were differences between these tribes, they shared certain characteristics. Most had adopted a nomadic way of life after the introduction of horses in the sixteenth century increased their seasonal mobility from 50 miles to 500 miles. Horses allowed Indian braves to hunt the buffalo with such

Indian Tribes in 1840

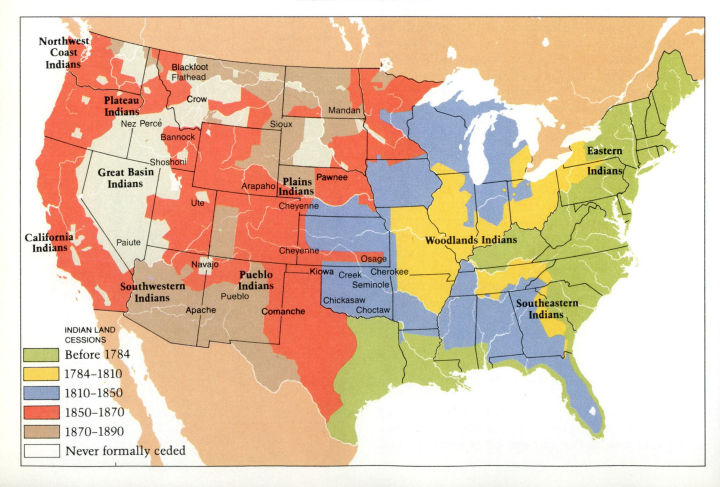

INDIAN LAND CESSIONS

- Before 1784
- 1784–1810
- 1810–1850
- 1850–1870
- 1870–1890
- Never formally ceded

Artists were fascinated by Plains Indian life, which they captured in sketches and paintings. Most anticipated that native culture would disappear with the coming of whites to the West.

success that tribes [with the exclusion of the border groups] came to depend on the beasts for food, clothing, fuel, tepee dwellings, and trading purposes. Because women were responsible for processing buffalo products, some men had more than one wife to tan skins for trading.

Mobility also increased tribal contact and conflict. War played a central part in the lives of the Plains tribes. No male became a fully accepted member of his tribe until he had proved himself in battle. But tribal warfare was not like the warfare of white men. Indians sought not to exterminate their enemies or to claim territory but rather to steal horses and to prove individual prowess. They considered it braver to touch an enemy than to kill or scalp him.

This pattern of conflict on the Plains discouraged political unity. Moreover, individual tribes were loosely organized. Chiefs enjoyed only limited authority over their followers. As Chief Low Horn, a Blackfoot, explained, chiefs "could not restrain their young men . . . their young men were wild, and ambitious, in their turn to be braves and chiefs. They wanted by some brave act to win the favor of their young women, and bring scalps and horses to show their prowess."

Armed with guns, mounted on fast ponies, and skilled in warfare and raiding, the Plains tribes, though disunified, posed a fearsome obstacle to white expansion. They had signed no treaties with the United States and had few friendly feelings toward whites. Their contact with white society had brought gains through trade in skins, but the trade had also brought alcohol and destructive epidemics of smallpox and scarlet fever.

When the first emigrants drove their wagons across the plains and prairies in the early 1840s, relations between Indians and whites were peaceable. But the intrusion of whites set in motion an environmental cycle that eventually drew the two groups into conflict. Indian tribes depended on the buffalo but respected this source of life. The Teton Sioux performed rituals to ensure a continuing supply of the animals, while hunters often ritualistically apologized to the Great Unseen Buffalo for slaughtering what the tribe needed.

Whites, however, fed their oxen and horses on the grass both the Indians' ponies and the buffalo needed. And they adopted the "most exciting sport," the buffalo hunt. As the great herds began to shrink, Native American tribes began to battle one another for hunting grounds and food. The powerful Sioux swooped down into the hunting grounds of their enemies and mounted destructive raids against the Pawnee and other smaller tribes. In an 1846 petition to President Polk, the Sioux explained that "for several years past the Emigrants going over the Mountains from the United States, have been the cause that Buffalo have in great measure left our hunting grounds, thereby causing us to go into the Country of Our Enemies to hunt, exposing our lives daily for the necessary subsistence of our wives and Children and getting killed on several occasions." Despite their difficulties, the Sioux had "all along treated the Emigrants in the most friendly manner, giving them free passage through our hunting grounds."

The Sioux requested compensation for damages caused by whites. When the president denied their request, they tried to extract taxes from the emigrants passing over their lands. Emigrants were outraged at what they considered Indian effrontery. After all, the United States had won these lands. Frontier newspapers printed letters denouncing the Sioux, demanding adequate protection for travelers and some chastening of the "savages." However, little was done to relieve the suffering of the tribes bearing the brunt of Sioux aggression, the dismay of the Sioux at the white invasion, or the fears of the emigrants themselves.

The discovery of gold in California, which lured over 20,000 across the Plains in 1849 alone, became the catalyst for federal action. The vast numbers of gold seekers and their animals wrought such devastation in the Platte valley that it rapidly became a wasteland for the Indians. The dreaded cholera that whites carried with them spread to the Indians, killing thousands.

To meet the crisis, government officials devised a two-pronged plan. The government would construct a chain of forts to protect emigrants and, simultaneously, call the tribes to a general conference. Officials expected that in return for generous presents, Indians would end tribal warfare and limit their movements to prescribed areas. They instructed tribes to select chiefs to speak for them at the conference.

The Fort Laramie Council, 1851

In 1851, the council convened at Fort Laramie. As many as 10,000 Indians, hopeful of ending the destruction of their way of life and eager for the promised presents, gathered at the fort. Tribal animosities simmered, however. Skirmishes occurred on the way to the fort, and the border tribes, fearful of the Sioux, declined to participate. The Comanche, Kiowa, and Apache also refused to come since their enemies, the Sioux and the Crow, were to be there.

At the conference, whites told the gathered tribes that times had changed. In the past, "you had plenty of buffalo and game . . . and your Great Father well knows that war has always been your favorite amusement and pursuit. He then left the question of peace and war to yourselves. Now, since

the settling of the districts West of you by the white men, your condition has changed." There would be compensation for the destruction of their grass, timber, and buffalo and annual payments of goods and services. But in return, the tribes had to give up their rights of free movement. The government drew tribal boundaries, and chiefs made promises to stay within them. In most cases, some tribal lands were sold.

The Fort Laramie Treaty was the first agreement between the Plains tribes and the United States government. It expressed the conviction of whites that Indians must stay in clearly defined areas apart from white civilization.

But this system of isolation and its purported benefits were still in the future. During the conference, ominous signs appeared that more trouble would precede any "resolution" of Indian-white affairs. Sioux chief Black Hawk told whites, "You have split the country and I do not like it." His powerful tribe refused to be restricted to lands north of the Platte, for south of the river lay their recently conquered lands. "These lands once belonged to the Kiowas and the Crows," one Sioux explained, "but we whipped those nations out of them and in this we did what the white men do when they want the lands of the Indians." The words suggested that Indians, despite agreements, would not willingly abandon their traditional way of life for confinement. In the following years, it would become evident that Americans and Sioux had conflicting interests south of the Platte. Elsewhere in the trans-Mississippi West, other tribes, like the fierce Navajo of New Mexico, also resisted white attempts to confine them.

Overwhelming the Mexicans

In the Southwest, in Texas, and in California, Americans contended with a Spanish-speaking population. Expansionist Lewis Cass expressed Americans' scorn for these people. Speaking in a congressional debate on the annexation of New Mexico, Cass stated, "We do not want the people of Mexico, either as citizens or as subjects. All we want is a portion of territory . . . with a population, which would soon recede, or identify itself with ours." Americans regarded Mexicans as lazy, ignorant, and cunning, the "dregs of society." Although Mexicans easily recognized such cultural arrogance, they lacked the numbers to fend off American aggression.

Although Anglo-Mexican interaction differed from place to place, few Anglos heeded the Treaty of Guadalupe Hidalgo's assurances that Mexicans would have citizens' rights and the "free enjoyment of their liberty and property." The greatest numbers of Spanish-speaking people lived in New Mexico, and, of all former Mexican citizens, they probably fared the best. Most were of mixed blood, living marginally as ranch hands for rich landowners or as farmers and herdsmen in small villages dominated by a *patron* or headman. As the century wore on, Americans produced legal titles and took over lands long occupied by peasant farmers and stock raisers. But despite economic reversals, New Mexicans survived carrying their rural culture well into the twentieth century.

Light-skinned upper-class landowners fared better. Even before the conquest, rich New Mexicans had protected their future by establishing contracts with American businessmen and by sending their sons east to American schools. When the United States annexed New Mexico, this substantial and powerful class contracted strategic marriage and business alliances with the Anglo men who slowly trickled into the territory. During the 1850s, they maintained their influence and prestige and their American connections. Only rarely did they bother with the plight of their poor countrymen. Class outweighed ethnic or cultural considerations.

In Texas, the Spanish-speaking residents, only 10 percent of the population in 1840, shrank to a mere 6 percent by 1860. Although the upper class also intermarried with Americans, they lost most of their power as Germans, Irish, French, and Americans poured into the state. Poor, dark-skinned Hispanics clustered in low-paying and largely unskilled jobs.

In California, the discovery of gold radically changed the situation for the Californios. In 1848, there were 7,000 Californios and about twice as many Anglos. By 1860, the Anglo population had ballooned to 360,000. Hispanic-Americans were hard pressed to cope with the rapid influx of outsiders. At first, Californios and several thousand Mexicans from Sonora joined Anglos and others in the gold fields. But competition there fed antagonism and finally open conflict. Posters warned foreigners out of the gold fields. In Anglo eyes, one Hispanic was much like another, even if one claimed to be a Californio with political rights and another a Sonoran. Taxes and terrorism ultimately succeeded in forcing most Spanish speakers out of the mines and established the racial contours of the new California.

Other changes were even more disastrous. In 1851, Congress passed the Gwinn Land Law, supposedly a measure for validating Spanish and Mexican land titles. The law violated the pledge contained in a Statement of Protocol accompanying the Treaty of Guadalupe Hidalgo that stated the government "did not in any way" intend to annul the grants of lands made by Mexico, for it forced California landowners to defend what was already theirs and encouraged squatters to settle on land in the hopes that the Californios' titles would prove false. It took an average of 17 years to establish clear title to land. The process was slow and unfamiliar. As one woman explained, her mother had been "totally unprepared for the problems that came with American rule. Not only was the language foreign to her, but also the concept of property taxes, mortgages and land title regulations." Landowners found themselves paying American lawyers large fees, often in land, and borrowing at high interest rates to pay for court proceedings. A victory at court often turned into a defeat when legal expenses forced owners to sell their lands to pay debts. In the south, where Anglos judged land less valuable than in the mining north, the process of dispossession was slower. But by the early 1860s, the ranching class there had also lost most of its extensive holdings.

Many working-class Hispanic-Americans lived marginal existences in California's growing towns and cities. Others became cowboys on American ranches or lived on their own small ranches in the

The population explosion California experienced as a result of the gold rush threatened the Californios' way of life as well as their possession of the land.

backcountry. For them, the coming of the Anglos presented not opportunity but oppression. By 1870, the average Hispanic-American worker's property was worth only about a third of its value of 20 years earlier. As newspaper editor and champion of the Mexican-American cause Francisco Ramírez pointed out in the Los Angeles newspaper *El Clamor Publico* in 1856, "California has fallen into the hands of the ambitious sons of North America who will not stop until they have satisfied their passions, by driving the first occupants of the land out of the country, villifying their religion and disfiguring their customs."

Western movies and novels have played a large role in forming images of the nineteenth-century West. Cowboys, sheriffs, outlaws, and bandits gallop across screens and pages. One of these outlaws, a sombrero-clad rider, merits a closer look in the context of American expansion into the Southwest.

As the career of Tiburcio Vásquez, a notorious *bandido* in southern California, suggests, some Hispanics felt that they could protest events only through violence:

> My career grew out of the circumstances by which I was surrounded. . . . As I grew to manhood I was in the habit of attending balls and parties given by the native Californians, into which the Americans, then beginning to become numerous, would force themselves and shove the native born men aside, monopolizing the dance and the women. This was about 1852. A spirit of hatred and revenge took possession of me. I had numerous fights in defense of my countrywomen. The officers were continually in pursuit of me. I believed we were unjustly and wrongfully deprived of the social rights that belonged to us.

What Anglos called crime, Vásquez called self-defense.

CONCLUSION
Fruits of Manifest Destiny

Like Lewis Cass, many nineteenth-century Americans were convinced that the country had merely gained western territories to which it was entitled. Although the process of acquiring the western half of the continent was swift, the prospect of winning the West loomed large in the imagination of the American people for many years. A number of western settlers became folk heroes. All white Americans could be thankful for the special opportunities, the new chance for success, that the West seemed to offer.

The expanding nation did gain vast natural wealth in the trans-Mississippi West. But only a small fraction of the hopeful emigrants heading for the frontier realized their dreams of success. And the move west had a dark side as Americans clashed with Mexicans and Native Americans in their drive to fulfill their "Manifest Destiny."

Recommended Reading

Ray Allen Billington gives two overviews of the move west in America's Frontier Heritage *(1966) and* The Far Western Frontier, 1830–1860 *(1965). Gilbert C. Fite treats agriculture in* The Farmer's Frontier, 1865–1900 *(1966). The cities of the West are the subject of* The Urban West at the End of the Frontier *(1978) by Lawrence H. Larson.*

Frederick Merk explores Manifest Destiny in Manifest Destiny and Mission in American History *(1963), while Norman A. Graebner presents a collection of documents with a helpful introduction in* Manifest Destiny *(1968). Gene Brack provides the Mexican side of American expansion in* Mexico Views Manifest Destiny, 1821–1846 *(1975). Robert W. Johanssen treats the Mexican War in* To the Halls of Montezuma: The Mexican War in the American Imagination *(1985). The diplomatic maneuvering for control* of Oregon is the subject of David Pletcher, The Diplomacy of Annexation: Texas, Oregon, and the Mexican War (1973).

George Pierre Castile treats cultural conflict in North American Indians: An Introduction to the Chichimeca (1979). Robert A. Trennert portrays relations during a crucial period in Alternative to Extinction: Federal Indian Policy and the Beginnings of the Reservation System, 1846–1851 (1975). Peter Nabakov has edited a collection of Indian responses, Native American Testimony: An Anthology of Indian and White Relations (1978).

Julie Roy Jeffrey compensates for the neglect of women in older frontier studies in Frontier Women: The Trans-Mississippi West, 1840–1880 (1979). Sandra Myres edited women's diaries in Ho for California! Women's Overland Diaries from the Huntington Library (1980), while John Mack Faragher provides an interpretation of the trail experience in Women and Men on the Overland Trail (1978). See also John D. Unruh, Jr., The Plains Across: The Overland Emigrants and the Trans-Mississippi West, 1840–1860 (1979). For details of the mining frontier, consult Rodman W. Paul, California Gold: The Beginning of Mining in the Far West (1974). Although there were not many blacks on the frontier, William Loren Katz studies them in The Black West (1971). As for the Mormons, see Richard L. Bushman's Joseph Smith and the Beginnings of Mormonism (1984). Studies of Mexicans include Leonard Pitt, The Decline of the Californios: A Social History of the Spanish-speaking Californians, 1846–1890 (1970); Paul Rodman's essay in John G. Clark, ed., The Frontier Challenge: Responses to the Trans-Mississippi West (1971); Robert J. Rosenbaum, Mexicano Resistance in the Southwest: "The Sacred Right of Self-preservation" (1981); M. S. Meir and Feliciano Rivera, The Chicanos: A History of Mexican-Americans (1972); and Alfredo Mirande and Evangeline Enriquez, La Chicana: The Mexican-American Woman (1979).

TIME LINE

1803–1806	Lewis and Clark expedition
1818	Treaty on joint U.S.-British occupation of Oregon
1819	Spain cedes Spanish territory in United States and sets transcontinental boundary of Louisiana Purchase, excluding Texas
1821	Mexican independence Opening of Santa Fe Trail Stephen Austin leads American settlement of Texas
1821–1840	Indian removals
1830	Mexico abolishes slavery in Texas
1836	Texas declares independence Battles of the Alamo and San Jacinto
1840s	Emigrant crossings of Overland Trail
1844	James Polk elected president
1845	"Manifest Destiny" coined United States annexes Texas and sends troops to the Rio Grande Americans attempt to buy Upper California and New Mexico
1846	Mexico declares defensive war United States declares war and takes Santa Fe Resolution of Oregon question
1847	Attacks on Veracruz and Mexico City Mormon migration to Utah begins
1848	Treaty of Guadalupe Hidalgo
1849	California gold rush begins
1850	California admitted to the Union
1851	Fort Laramie Treaty
1853	Gadsden Purchase
1862	Homestead Act

15

The Union in Peril

The autumn of 1860 was a time of ominous rumors and expectations. The election was held on November 6 in an atmosphere of crisis. In Springfield, Illinois, Abraham Lincoln, taking coffee and sandwiches prepared by "the ladies of Springfield," waited as the telegraph brought in the returns. By 1 A.M., victory was certain. He reported later, "I went home, but not to get much sleep, for I then felt, as I never had before, the responsibility that was upon me." And with good cause. He and the American people faced the most serious crisis since the founding of the Republic.

Lincoln won an unusual four-party election with only 39 percent of the popular vote. He had appealed almost exclusively to northern voters in a blatantly sectional campaign, defeating his three opponents by carrying every free state except New Jersey. Of the candidates, only Illinois senator Stephen Douglas campaigned actively in every section of the country. For his efforts he received the second highest number of votes. Douglas's appeal, especially in the closing days of the campaign, was "on behalf of the Union," which he feared—correctly—was in imminent danger of splitting apart.

Other Americans sensed the mood of crisis that fall and faced their own fears and responsibilities. A month before the election, plantation owner Robert Allston wrote his oldest son, Benjamin, that "disastrous consequences" would follow from a Lincoln victory. Although his letter mentioned the possibility of secession, he dealt mostly with plantation concerns: a new horse, the mood of the slaves, ordering supplies from the city, instructions for making trousers on a sewing machine. After Lincoln's election, Allston corresponded with a southern colleague about the need for "an effective military organization" to resist "Northern and Federal aggression." In this shift from sewing machines to military ones, Robert Allston prepared for what he called the "impending crisis."

Frederick Douglass, however, greeted the election with characteristic optimism. Not only was this an opportunity to "educate . . . the people in their moral and political duties," he said, but "slaveholders know that the day of their power is over when a Republican President is elected." But no sooner had Lincoln's victory been determined than Douglass's hopes turned sour. He

noted that Republican leaders, in their desire to keep southern border states from seceding, sounded more antiabolitionist than antislavery. They vowed not to touch slavery in areas where it already existed, which included the District of Columbia, and they promised to enforce the hated Fugitive Slave Act and to put down slave rebellions. Slavery would in fact, Douglass bitterly concluded, "be as safe, and safer" with Lincoln than with a Democrat.

Michael Luark, an Iowa farmer, was not so sure. Born in Virginia, Luark was a typically mobile nineteenth-century American. After growing up in Indiana, he followed the mining booms of the 1850s to Colorado and California before returning to the Midwest to farm. Luark sought a good living and resented all the furor over slavery. He could not, however, avoid the issue. Writing in his diary on the last day of 1860, Luark looked ahead to 1861 with a deep sense of fear. "Startling" political changes would occur, he predicted, perhaps even the "Dissolution of the Union and Civil War with all its train of horrors." He blamed abolitionist agitators, perhaps reflecting his Virginia origins. On New Year's Day, he expressed his fears that Lincoln would let the "most ultra sectional and Abolition" men disturb the "vexed Slavery question" even further, as Frederick Douglass wanted. But if this happened, Luark warned, "then farewell to our beloved Union of States."

Within four months of this diary entry, the guns of the Confederate States of America fired on a federal fort in South Carolina, and the Civil War began. Luark's fears, Douglass's hopes, and Lincoln's and Allston's preparations for responsibility all became realities. The explanation of the peril and dissolution of the Union forms the theme of this chapter.

uch a calamitous event had numerous causes, large and small. The reactions of Allston, Douglass, and Luark to Lincoln's election suggest some of them: moral duties, sectional politics, growing apprehensions over emotional agitators, and a concern for freedom and independence on the part of blacks, white southerners, and western farmers. But as Douglass understood, by 1860 it was clear that "slavery is the real issue, the single bone of contention between all parties and sections. It is the one disturbing force, and explains the confused and irregular motion of our political machine."

This chapter analyzes how the momentous issue of slavery disrupted the political system and eventually the Union itself. We will look at how four major developments between 1848 and 1861 contributed to the Civil War: first, a sectional dispute over the extension of slavery into the western territories; second, the breakdown of the political party system; third, growing cultural differences in the views and life styles of southerners and northerners; and fourth, intensifying emotional and ideological polarization between the two regions over losing their way of life and sacred republican rights at the hands of the other. A preview of civil war, bringing all four causes together, occurred in 1855–1856 in Kansas. Eventually, emotional events, mistrust, and irreconcilable differences made conflict inevitable. The election of Lincoln was the spark that touched off the conflagration of civil war, with all its "train of horrors."

SLAVERY IN THE TERRITORIES

Senator Lewis Cass (Chapter 14) was wrong when he confidently proclaimed that the western territories were areas of individual freedom where civilization would advance and political and social harmony would prevail. As many migrants and residents discovered, personal costs attended the American march westward. White migrations destroyed both the safety and the cultural integrity of Native Americans and Mexicans whose land stood in the way. They also brought Yankees and slaveholders into a costly collision.

The North and the South had managed to contain their differences over slavery, with only occasional difficulties, during the 60 years after the Constitutional Convention. Political compromise in 1787 had resolved the questions of the slave trade and how to count slaves for congressional representation. But although slavery threatened ("like a fireball in the night," Jefferson had said) to upset the uneasy sectional harmony in 1820, the Missouri Compromise had established a workable way of balancing the admission of free and slave states to the Union and had also defined a geographic line (36° 30') to determine future decisions. In 1833, compromise had defused South Carolina's nullification of the tariff, and the gag rule in 1836 had kept divisive abolitionist petitions to end slavery off the floor of Congress.

Each apparent resolution, however, raised the level of emotional conflict between North and South and put off an ultimate settlement of the slavery question to another time. One reason these compromises were temporarily successful was the existence of a two-party system with intersectional membership. Whigs and Democrats lived on both sides of the Mason-Dixon line. The party system encouraged developing party loyalties as an "antidote," as Van Buren put it, to sectional allegiance. Whigs and Democrats expressed their differences over cultural and economic issues, sometimes passionately, but the volatile issue of slavery was largely kept out of political campaigns and congressional debates. This changed in the late 1840s, and the change would prove catastrophic to the Union.

Free Soil or Constitutional Protection?

When the Mexican War broke out in 1846, it seemed likely that the United States would acquire new territories in the Southwest. Would they be slave or free? To an appropriations bill to pay for the war, David Wilmot, a congressman from Pennsylvania, added a short amendment declaring that "neither slavery nor involuntary servitude shall ever exist" in any territories acquired from Mexico. The debates in Congress over the Wilmot Proviso were significant because legislators voted not as Whigs and Democrats but as northerners and southerners.

A Boston newspaper prophetically observed that Wilmot's resolution "brought to a head the great question which is about to divide the American people." When the Mexican War ended, several solutions were presented to deal with this question of slavery in the territories. The first was the "free soil" idea of preventing any extensions of slavery. But did Congress have the power or right to do so? Two precedents suggested that it did. One was the Northwest Ordinance, which had prohibited the entry of slaves into states created in the Upper Midwest, and the other was the Missouri Compromise.

Supporters of "free soil" had mixed motives, making moral, economic, and political arguments for the Wilmot Proviso. For some, slavery was a moral evil to be attacked and destroyed because it trampled on principles of liberty and equality. But for many northern white farmers looking to move westward, the threat of economic competition with an expanding system of large-scale slave labor was even more serious. Neither did they wish to compete for land with free blacks. As Wilmot put it, his proviso was intended to preserve the area for "the sons of toil, of my own race and own color." Other northerners supported the Wilmot Proviso as a means of restraining what seemed to them the growing political power and "insufferable arrogance" of the "spirit and demands of the Slave Power."

Opposed to the free-soil position were the arguments of Senator John C. Calhoun of South Carolina, expressed in several resolutions introduced in the Senate in 1847. Not only did Congress lack the constitutional right to exclude slavery from the territories, Calhoun argued, but it had a positive duty to protect it. The Wilmot Proviso, therefore, was unconstitutional, as was the Missouri Compromise and any other federal act that prevented slaveholders from taking their slave property into the territories of the United States. Noting the rapid flow of immigrants to the North and the rapidity with which such slave states as Delaware were selling their remaining slaves to the Deep South, Calhoun argued that the South's political position was perilous.

Economic, political, and moral considerations stood behind the Calhoun position. Many southerners hungered for new cotton lands in the West and Southwest, even in Central America and the Caribbean. Politically, southerners feared that northerners wanted to trample on *their* liberties, namely, the right to protect their institutions against destructive abolitionists. Southern leaders saw the Wilmot Proviso as a moral issue that raised questions about basic republican principles. One congressman called it "treason to the Constitution," and Senator Robert Toombs of Georgia warned that if Congress passed the proviso, he would favor disunion rather than "degradation."

Popular Sovereignty and the Election of 1848

With such divisive potential, it was natural that many Americans sought a compromise solution to keep slavery out of politics. Polk's secretary of state, James Buchanan of Pennsylvania, proposed that the Missouri Compromise line be extended through the lands acquired from Mexico to the Pacific Ocean. But this was a way of avoiding thorny questions concerning the morality of slavery and the constitutionality of congressional authority. "Popular sovereignty" was another way of begging these issues. This doctrine, as promulgated by Senator Lewis Cass, left the decision of whether to permit slavery in a territory to the local territorial legislature, an idea that appealed to the American democratic belief in local self-government. But popular sovereignty left many details unanswered, such as at what point in the process toward statehood a territorial legislature could decide to permit or forbid slavery. Cass preferred to leave such questions ambiguous, reasoning that both northern and southern politicians would conclude that popular sovereignty favored their interests.

The Democratic party, attracted to the idea that popular sovereignty could mean all things to all people, nominated Cass for president in 1848. He denounced abolitionists and the Wilmot Proviso but otherwise avoided the issue of slavery. The Democrats, however, recognized the growing importance of sectional feeling by printing two campaign biographies of Cass, one for the South and one for the North.

The Whigs found an even better way to hold the party together by evading the slavery issue. Passing over Henry Clay, they nominated the Mexican War hero, General Zachary Taylor, a Louisiana slaveholder. Taylor compared himself to Washington as a "no party" man who was above politics. This was nearly the only thing he stood for. Southern Whigs supported Taylor because they thought he might understand the burdens of slaveholding, while northern Whigs were pleased that he took no stand on the Wilmot Proviso.

The evasions of the two major parties disappointed Calhoun, who tried to create a new unified southern party. His "Address to the People of the Southern States" rehearsed the history of northern attempts to destroy slavery. Threatening secession, Calhoun called for a united effort against further attempts to interfere with the southern right to extend slavery. But only 48 of 121 southern representatives signed the address, and his effort failed. Calhoun's argument, however, raised the specter of secession and disunion.

Warnings also issued from the North. A faction of Democrats in New York bolted the party to support Van Buren, a Cass foe for several years, for president. At first, the split had more to do with internal state politics than moral principles, but it soon involved the question of slavery in the territories. Disaffected "conscience" Whigs from Massachusetts, unhappy with a slaveholder as their party standard-bearer, were also interested in a third-party alternative. These groups met in Buffalo, New York, to form the Free-Soil party and nominate Van Buren as president. The platform of the new party, composed of an uneasy mixture of ardent abolitionists and racist opponents of free black mobility into western lands, pledged to fight for "free soil, free speech, free labor and free men."

General Taylor won the election easily, largely because defections from Cass in New York and Pennsylvania to the Free-Soilers cost the Democrats the electoral votes from those states. Although weakened, the two-party system survived, and purely sectional parties were prevented. Both major parties essentially retained the popular votes they had received in 1844. The Free-Soilers helped elect local candidates opposed to the expansion of slavery but received only about 10 percent of the popular vote and no electoral votes.

The Compromise of 1850

Taylor won the election by avoiding slavery issues, but as president he could no longer do so. As he was inaugurated in 1849, four compelling issues faced the nation. The rush of some 80,000 unruly gold miners to California qualified that territory for admission to the Union. But California's entry as a free state would upset the balance between slave and free states in the Senate that had prevailed since 1820.

The unresolved status of the Mexican cession in the Southwest posed a second problem. The longer the area was left unorganized, the louder local inhabitants called for an application of either the Wilmot Proviso or the Calhoun doctrine of protecting the extension of slavery. The boundary between Texas and the New Mexico Territory was also in dispute, with Texas claiming lands all the way to Santa Fe. This increased northern fears that Texas might be divided into five or six slave states.

The existence of slavery and one of the largest slave markets in North America in the nation's capital was a third problem, especially to abolitionists. Fourth, Southerners resented the lax federal enforcement of the Fugitive Slave Act of 1793. They called for a stronger act that would end the protection northerners gave runaway slaves as they fled along the underground railroad to Canada.

Although Taylor was a newcomer to politics (he had never even voted in a presidential election before 1848), he tried to tackle these problems in a statesmanlike, if evasive, manner. He thought he could sidestep the conflict over slavery in the territories by inviting California and New Mexico to apply immediately for statehood, presumably as free states. But it was not long before his efforts had alienated both southern supporters like Calhoun and mainstream Whig leaders like Clay and Webster.

Early in 1850, therefore, the old compromiser, Henry Clay, sought to regain control of the Whig party by proposing solutions to the divisive issues before the nation. With Webster's support, Clay introduced a series of resolutions in an omnibus pack-

The Compromise of 1850

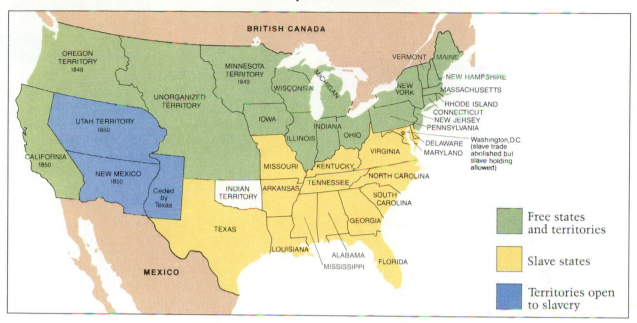

age intended to settle these issues once and for all. The stormy debates, great speeches, and political maneuvering that followed provided a crucial and dramatic moment in American history. Yet despite some 70 speeches on behalf of the compromise, the Senate defeated Clay's Omnibus Bill. As new bills were proposed, the tired and disheartened 73-year-old Clay left Washington, hoping to regain his strength. He never did. Into the gap stepped a new compromiser, Senator Stephen Douglas of Illinois, who understood that Clay's resolutions had a better chance of passing if voted on individually rather than as a package. Under Douglas's leadership, and with the support of Millard Fillmore, who succeeded to the presidency upon Taylor's untimely death, a series of bills was finally passed.

The so-called Compromise of 1850 put Clay's resolutions, slightly altered, into law. First, California entered the Union as a free state, upsetting the balance of free and slave states, 16 to 15. Second, the territorial governments of New Mexico and Utah were organized by letting the people of those territories decide for themselves whether to permit slavery. The Texas–New Mexico border was settled in a compromise that denied Texas the disputed area. In turn, the federal government compensated Texas with $10 million to pay off debts owed to Mexico. Third, the slave trade, but not slavery itself, was abolished in the District of Columbia.

Fourth, the Fugitive Slave Act went into effect. This most controversial part of the compromise contained many provisions that offended northerners. One denied a jury trial to the alleged fugitive, establishing special commissioners to decide special cases. (A commissioner received $5 for setting a fugitive free but $10 for returning a fugitive to his or her owner.) Another provision compelled all northern citizens to assist in the enforcement of the act by hunting down runaway slaves and turning them in.

Consequences of Compromise

The Compromise of 1850 was the last attempt to keep slavery out of politics. How well it succeeded in doing so is debatable. The intersectional party system was severely tested but for a while was preserved. Voting behavior on the several bills varied, with legislators following sectional lines on some issues and party lines on others. Douglas had good reason to feel pleased, celebrating the acts of 1850 as a "final settlement" of the slavery question.

The Compromise of 1850, however, only delayed more serious sectional conflict. It added two new ingredients to American politics. The first hinted at the realignment of parties along sectional lines. Political leaders as different as Calhoun, Webster, Van Buren, and New York senator William Sew-

SENATE SPEECHES

The history of average, anonymous Americans can be recovered in letters, diaries, folktales, and other nontraditional sources. But in times of political conflict with enormous implications for all Americans, as in the years before the Civil War, historians turn to more conventional sources such as congressional speeches. Recorded in the *Congressional Globe*, these speeches are a revealing means of recovering the substance, tone, and drama of political debate.

Despite the cynical view of American politics held by some European visitors, the mid-nineteenth century was an era of giants in the United States Senate: Daniel Webster, Henry Clay, Thomas Hart Benton, John C. Calhoun, William Seward, and Stephen Douglas. When Congress debated a major issue, such as the tariff, nullification, or the extension of slavery, large crowds would pack the Senate galleries. The speeches would then be quickly printed and widely distributed. These spectacular oratorical encounters provided mass entertainment and political instruction. Such was the case with the Senate speeches over the Compromise of 1850. The three principal figures early in the debates were Clay (Kentucky), Calhoun (South Carolina), and Webster (Massachusetts), each of whom delivered a great address crowning a long, distinguished career.

Born within five years of each other as the American Revolution was ending (1777–1782), each man began his political career in the House of Representatives in the War of 1812 era. Each served a term as secretary of state; in addition, Clay was speaker of the House and Calhoun secretary of war and vice-president. Each served for over a decade in the Senate (Clay, 13 years; Calhoun, 15 years; Webster, 19 years). Each was a party leader, Clay and Webster of the Whigs and Calhoun of the Democrats. During their 40 years of public service, they represented strong nationalistic positions as well as their various states and sections. All three were candidates for president between 1824 and 1844. All three spent most of their careers in the political shadow of Andrew Jackson, and all three had serious conflicts with him.

Henry Clay

February 5–6, 1850

I have seen many periods of great anxiety, of peril, and of danger in this country, and I have never before risen to address any assemblage so oppressed, so appalled, and so anxious; and sir, I hope it will not be out of place to do here, what again and again I have done in my private chamber, to implore of Him who holds the destinies of nations and individuals in His hands, to bestow upon our country His blessing, to calm the violence and rage of party, to still passion, to allow reason once more to resume its empire. . . .

Mr. President, it is passion, passion—party, party, and intemperance—that is all I dread in the adjustment of the great questions which unhappily at this time divide our distracted country. Sir, at this moment we have in the legislative bodies of this Capitol and in the States, twenty old furnaces in full blast, emitting heat, and passion, and intemperance, and diffusing them throughout the whole extent of this broad land. Two months ago all was calm in comparison to the present moment. All now is uproar, confusion, and menace to the existence of the Union, and to the happiness and safety of this people. . . .

Sir, when I came to consider this subject, there were two or three general purposes which it seemed to me to be most desirable, if possible, to accomplish. The one was, to settle all the controverted questions arising out of the subject of slavery. . . . I therefore turned my attention to every subject connected with this institution of slavery, and out of which controverted questions had sprung, to see if it were possible or practicable to accommodate and adjust the whole of them. . . .

We are told now, and it is rung throughout this entire country, that the Union is threatened with subversion and destruction. Well, the first question which naturally rises is, supposing the Union to be dissolved,—having all the causes of grievance which are complained of,—How far will a dissolution furnish a remedy for those grievances? If the Union is to be dissolved for any existing causes, it will be dissolved because slavery is interdicted or not allowed to be introduced into the ceded territories; because slavery is threatened to be abolished in the District of Columbia, and because fugitive slaves are not returned, as in my opinion they ought to be, and restored to their masters. These, I believe, will be the causes; if there be any causes, which can lead to the direful event to which I have referred. . . .

Mr. President, I am directly opposed to any purpose of secession, of separation. I am for staying within the Union, and defying any portion of this Union to expel or drive me out of the Union.

Many years of political and ideological conflict with each other not only sharpened their oratorical skills but also led to mutual respect. Webster said of Calhoun that he was "the ablest man in the Senate. He could have demolished Newton, Calvin, or even John Locke as a logician." Calhoun said of Clay, "He is a bad man, but by god, I love him." And "Old Man Eloquent" himself, John Quincy Adams, said of Webster that he was "the most consummate orator of modern times."

March 4, 1850

Having now, Senators, explained what it is that endangers the Union, and traced it to its cause, and explained its nature and character, the question again recurs—How can the Union be saved? To this I answer, there is but one way by which it can be—and that is—by adopting such measures as will satisfy the States belonging to the Southern section, that they can remain in the Union consistently with their honor and their safety. . . .

But can this be done? Yes, easily; not by the weaker party, for it can of itself do nothing—not even protect itself—but by the stronger. The North has only to will it to accomplish it—to do justice by conceding to the South an equal right in the acquired territory, and to do her duty by causing the stipulations relative to fugitive slaves to be faithfully fulfilled—to cease the agitation of the slave question, and to provide for the insertion of a provision in the Constitution, by an amendment, which will restore to the South, in substance, the power she possessed of protecting herself, before the equilibrium between the sections was destroyed by the action of this Government. . . .

But will the North agree to this? It is for her to answer the question. But, I will say, she cannot refuse, if she has half the love of the Union which she professes to have, or without justly exposing herself to the charge that her love of power and aggrandizement is far greater than her love of the Union. At all events, the responsibility of saving the Union rests on the North, and not on the South. . . . If the question is not now settled, it is uncertain whether it ever can hereafter be; and we, as the representatives of the States of this Union, regarded as governments, should come to a distinct understanding as to our respective views, in order to ascertain whether the great questions at issue can be settled or not. If you, who represent the stronger portion, cannot agree to settle them on the broad principle of justice and duty, say so; and let the States we both represent agree to separate and part in peace. If you are unwilling we should part in peace, tell us so, and we shall know what to do.

March 7, 1850

MR. PRESIDENT: I wish to speak to-day, not as a Massachusetts man, nor as a Northern man, but as an American, and a member of the Senate of the United States. It is fortunate that there is a Senate of the United States; a body not yet moved from its propriety, not lost to a just sense of its own dignity and its own high responsibilities, and a body to which the country looks, with confidence, for wise, moderate, patriotic, and healing counsels. It is not to be denied that we live in the midst of strong agitations, and are surrounded by very considerable dangers to our institutions and government. The imprisoned winds are let loose. . . .

I speak to-day for the preservation of the Union. "Hear me for my cause." I speak to-day, out of a solicitous and anxious heart, for the restoration to the country of that quiet and that harmony which make the blessing of this Union so rich, and so dear to us all. . . . I shall bestow a little attention, Sir, upon these various grievances existing on the one side and on the other. I begin with complaints of the South. . . . and especially to one which has in my opinion just foundation; and that is, that there has been found at the North, among individuals and among legislators, a disinclination to perform fully their constitutional duties in regard to the return of persons bound to service who have escaped into the free States. In that respect, the South, in my judgment, is right, and the North is wrong. Every member of every Northern legislature is bound by oath, like every other officer in the country, to support the Constitution of the United States; and the article of the Constitution which says to these States they shall deliver up fugitives from service is as binding in honor and conscience as any other article. . . .

Peaceable secession! Peaceable secession! The concurrent agreement of all the members of this great republic to separate! A voluntary separation, with alimony on one side and on the other. Why, what would be the result? Where is the line to be drawn? What States are to secede? What is to remain American? What am I to be? An American no longer? Am I to become a sectional man, a local man, a separatist, with no country in common with the gentlemen who sit around me here, or who fill the other house of Congress? Heaven forbid! Where is the flag of the republic to remain? Where is the eagle still to tower? or is he to cower, and shrink, and fall to the ground?

It was therefore a momentous event when they each prepared speeches and met for one last encounter early in 1850. Clay was over 70 years old and in failing health, but he came out of retirement to try to keep the Union together. He defended his compromise proposals in a four-hour speech spread over two days, February 5 and 6. The Senate galleries were so packed that listeners were pushed into hallways and even into the rotunda of the Capitol. Copies of his speech were in such demand that over 100,000 were printed.

A month later, on March 7, the scene was repeated as Webster rose to join Clay in defending the compromise. Three days earlier, although too ill to deliver the speech himself, Calhoun had "tottered into the Senate" on the arm of a friend to hear James Mason of Virginia read his rejection of the compromise. Within a month, Calhoun was dead. Clay and Webster followed him to the grave two years later, and Senate leadership passed on to Seward, Douglas, and a new generation of Senate giants.

As you read the excerpts from each speech, try to imagine yourself sitting in the gallery overlooking the Senate floor, listening to each man and absorbing the drama of the moment. How do the oratorical styles differ? Which specific passages make the best substantive points in support of each man's argument? Which passages convey the most emotional power? Which speaker is most persuasive to you? Why? To what extent do the three agree on the fugitive slave issue? What can you infer about the personality of these men from their speeches?

ard all flirted with or committed themselves to new parties. Second, although repudiated by most ordinary citizens, ideas like secessionism, disunion, and a "higher law" than the Constitution entered more and more political discussions. Some people wondered whether the question of slavery in the territories could be compromised away the next time it arose.

Others were immediately upset. The new fugitive slave law angered many northerners because it brought the evils of slavery right into their midst. The owners of runaway slaves hired agents, labeled "kidnappers" in the North, to hunt down fugitives. In a few dramatic episodes, most notably in Boston, literary and religious intellectuals led mass protests to resist slave hunters' efforts to return alleged fugitives to the South. When Senator Webster supported the law, New England abolitionists denounced him as "indescribably base and wicked." Theodore Parker called the new law "a hateful statute of kidnappers," and Ralph Waldo Emerson said it was "a filthy law" that he would not obey.

Frederick Douglass would not obey it either. As a runaway slave himself, he was threatened with arrest and return to the South until friends overcame his objections and purchased his freedom. Douglass still risked harm by his strong defiance of the Fugitive Slave Act. Arguing the "rightfulness of forcible resistance," he urged free blacks to arm themselves and even wondered whether it was justifiable to kill kidnappers. "The only way to make the Fugitive Slave Law a dead letter," he said in Pittsburgh in 1853, "is to make a half dozen or more dead kidnappers." Douglass raised money for black fugitives, hid runaways in his home, and helped hundreds escape to Canada.

Other northerners, white as well as black, increased their work for the underground railroad in response to the fugitive slave law. Several states passed "personal liberty laws" that prohibited the use of state officials and institutions in the recovery of fugitive slaves. But most northerners complied with the law. Of some 200 blacks arrested in the first six years of the law, only 15 were rescued, and

The hypocrisy of the Fugitive Slave Act (part of the Compromise of 1850) and Henry Clay's mixed motives are the focus of this 1851 cartoon. Whites preach "The Blessings of Liberty" at a free black man they are holding back from freedom as Clay turns his back on the fugitive slave and talks to a northerner about the tariff.

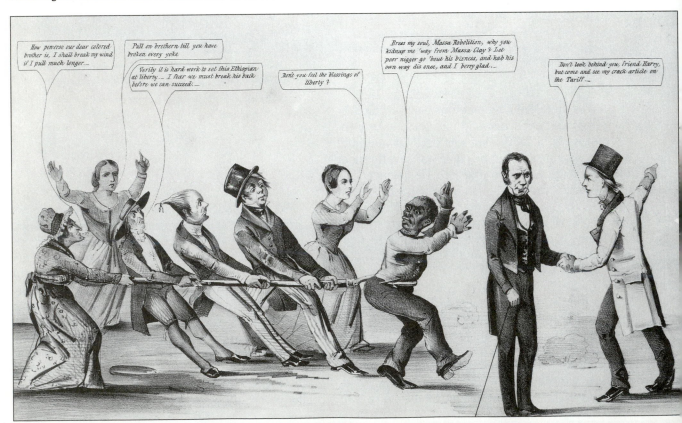

only 3 of these by force. Failed rescues, in fact, had more emotional impact than successful ones. In two cases in the early 1850s (Thomas Sims in 1851 and Anthony Burns in 1854), angry mobs of abolitionists in Boston, reminiscent of the pre-Revolutionary days of the Tea Party, failed to prevent the forcible return of blacks to the South. These celebrated cases aroused the antislavery emotions of more northerners than the abolitionists had been able to do in a thousand tracts and speeches.

But the spoken and written word also fueled emotions over slavery in the aftermath of 1850. In an Independence Day speech in 1852, Douglass wondered, "What, to the American slave, is your 4th of July?" It was, he said, the day that revealed to the slave "the gross injustice and cruelty to which he is the constant victim." To a slave, the American claims of national greatness were vain and empty; the "shouts of liberty and equality" were "hollow mockery . . . mere bombast, fraud, deception, impiety, and hypocrisy." Douglass's speeches, like those of another ex-slave, Sojourner Truth, took on an increasingly strident tone in the early 1850s.

At a women's rights convention in Akron, Ohio, in 1851, Truth made one of the decade's boldest statements for minority rights. The convention was attended by clergymen, who kept interrupting the proceedings to heckle female speakers. Up stood Sojourner Truth. She pointed to her many years of childbearing and hard, backbreaking work as a slave, crying out in a repetitive refrain, "And ar'n't I a woman?" Referring to Jesus, she asked where he came from: "From God and a woman: Man had nothing to do with Him." Referring to Eve, she concluded, "If the first woman God ever made was strong enough to turn the world upside down all alone, these women together ought to be able to turn it back, and get it right side up again! And now they is asking to do it, the men better let them." Her brief speech silenced the hecklers.

As Truth spoke, another American woman, Harriet Beecher Stowe, was finishing a novel, *Uncle Tom's Cabin*, that would go far toward turning the world upside down and trying to right it again. As politicians were hoping the American people would forget slavery, Stowe's novel brought it to the attention of thousands. She gave readers an absorbing indictment of the horrors of slavery and its immoral impact on both northerners and southerners. Published initially in serial form, each month's chapter ended at a nail-biting dramatic moment. Readers throughout the North cheered Eliza's daring escape

The dangers of the Fugitive Slave Act are evident in this 1851 broadside published by Boston abolitionist Theodore Parker, which alerted the city's black community to the dangers posed by the new law.

across the ice floes on the Ohio River, cried over Uncle Tom's humanity and Little Eva's death, suffered under the lash of Simon Legree, and rejoiced in the reuniting of black family members.

Although outraging the South when published in full in 1852, *Uncle Tom's Cabin* became one of the all-time best-sellers in American history. In the first year, over 300,000 copies were printed, and Stowe's novel was eventually published in 20 languages. When President Lincoln met Stowe in 1863, he is reported to have said to her, with a twinkle in his eye, "So you're the little woman who wrote the book that made this great war!"

POLITICAL DISINTEGRATION

The response to *Uncle Tom's Cabin* and the Fugitive Slave Act indicated that politicians had congratulated themselves too soon for saving the Republic in 1850. Political developments, not all dealing with slavery, were already weakening the ability of political parties—and ultimately the nation—to withstand the passions slavery aroused.

The Apathetic Election of 1852

Political parties, then and now, thrive on their ability to convince voters that their party stands for moral values and economic policies crucially different from those of the opposition. In the period between 1850 and 1854, these differences were blurred, thereby undermining party loyalty. First, both parties scrambled to convince voters that they had favored the Compromise of 1850. In addition, several states rewrote their constitutions and remodeled their laws in the early 1850s, standardizing many political and economic procedures. One effect of these changes was to reduce the number of patronage jobs available for party victors to dispense. Another effect was to regularize the process, begun in the 1830s, for securing banking, railroad, and other corporate charters, removing the role formerly played by the legislature. Both of these weakened the importance of the party in citizens' lives.

The third development that weakened parties was economic. For almost a quarter of a century, Whigs and Democrats had disagreed over such issues as the tariff, money and banking systems, and government support for internal improvements. But economic conditions improved markedly in the early 1850s. In a time of prosperity, party distinctions over economic policies seemed less important. An ample money supply made the revenues of a high tariff less necessary. Moreover, in the rush for railroad charters during the boom of the early 1850s, local connections were more important than national party politics.

Economic issues persisted, but the battles were fought at the local rather than national level. Thus Georgia voters in 1851 disagreed over commercial banking laws, taxes for internal improvements, and, as an Augusta newspaper put it, "the jealousies of the poor who owned no slaves, against the rich slaveholder." In Indiana, where Congressman George Julian observed that people "hate the Negro with a perfect if not a supreme hatred," legislators rewrote the state constitution in 1851, depriving blacks of the rights to vote, attend white schools, and make contracts. Those who could not post a $500 bond were expelled from the state, and an 1852 law made it a crime for blacks to settle in

Indiana. In Massachusetts, temperance reform and a law limiting the working day to ten hours were hot issues. Fleeting political alliances developed around particular issues and local personalities. As a Baltimore businessman said, "The two old parties are fast melting away."

The election of 1852 illustrated the lessening significance of political parties. The Whigs nominated General Winfield Scott, another Mexican War hero, who they hoped would repeat Taylor's success four years earlier. With Clay and Webster both dead, party leadership had passed to Senator William Seward of New York, who wanted a president he could influence more successfully than the prosouthern Fillmore. Still, it took 52 ballots to nominate Scott over Fillmore, with serious costs to the party allegiance of southern Whigs. Democrats had their own problems deciding on a candidate. After 49 ballots, in which Cass, Douglas, and Buchanan each held the lead for a time, the party turned to the lackluster Franklin Pierce of New Hampshire as a compromise candidate.

The two parties offered little choice. Both played down issues so as not to widen intraparty divisions. Voter interest diminished. "Genl. Apathy is the strongest candidate out here," was the report from Ohio, while the Baltimore *Sun* remarked that "there is no issue that much interests the people." Democratic prospects were aided by thousands of new Catholic immigrants from Ireland and Germany. Eligible for naturalization and, therefore, the right to vote after only three years, they were influenced by party officials, usually Democrats, who bought their votes with bribes and drinks. Internal conflicts and defections seriously weakened the Whigs, and Pierce won easily, 254 to 42 electoral votes.

The Kansas-Nebraska Act

The Whig party's final disintegration came on a February day in 1854 when southern Whigs stood to support Stephen Douglas's Nebraska bill, thus choosing to be more southern than Whig. The Illinois senator had many reasons for introducing a bill organizing the Nebraska Territory (which included Kansas). As an ardent nationalist and chairman of the Committee on Territories, he was concerned for the continuing development of the West. As an Illinoisan in a period of explosive railroad building, he wanted the eastern terminus for a transcontinental railroad in Chicago rather than in rival

St. Louis. This meant organizing the lands west of Iowa and Missouri.

Politics also played a role. Douglas wanted to recapture the party leadership he had held when he led the fight to pass the Compromise of 1850. He also harbored presidential ambitions. Although he had replaced Cass as the great advocate of popular sovereignty, which won him favor among northern Democrats, he needed the support of southern Democrats. Many southerners, especially slaveholders from Missouri, just east of the Nebraska Territory, opposed the organization of the territory unless it were open to slavery. The problem, as Douglas knew well, was that the entire Nebraska Territory lay north of the line where slavery had been prohibited by the Missouri Compromise.

Douglas's bill, introduced early in 1854, recommended using the principle of popular sovereignty in organizing the Kansas and Nebraska territories. This meant that inhabitants could vote slavery in, thereby violating the Missouri Compromise. Douglas reasoned, however, that the climate and soil of the prairies in Kansas and Nebraska would never support slavery-based agriculture, and the people would decide to be a free state. Therefore, he could win the votes he needed for the railroad without also getting slavery. His bill, then,

ignored the Missouri Compromise, simply stating that the state or states created out of the Nebraska Territory would enter the Union "with or without slavery, as their constitution may prescribe at the time of their admission."

Douglas miscalculated. Northerners from his own party immediately attacked him and his bill as a "criminal betrayal of precious rights" and as part of a plot promoting his own presidential ambitions by turning free Nebraska over to "slavery despotism." The outrage among Whigs and abolitionists was even greater. Frederick Douglass branded the act a "hateful" attempt to extend slavery, the result of the "audacious villainy of the slave power."

But Stephen Douglas was a fighter. The more he was attacked, the harder he fought. Eventually his bill passed, but not without seriously damaging the political party system. What began as a railroad measure ended in reopening the question of slavery in the territories that Douglas and others had thought finally settled in 1850. What began as a way of avoiding conflict ended up in violence over whether Kansas would enter the Union slave or free. What began as a way of strengthening party lines over issues ended up destroying one party (the Whigs), planting deep, irreconcilable divisions in another (the Democrats), and creating two new ones (Know-Nothings and Republicans).

Expansionist "Young America"

The Democratic party was weakened in the early 1850s not only by the Kansas-Nebraska Act but also by an ebullient, expansive energy that led Americans to adventures far beyond Kansas. As republican revolutions erupted in Europe in 1848, Americans greeted them as evidence that the American model of free republican institutions was the wave of the future. Those dedicated to the idea of this continuing national mission, which ironically included the spread of slavery, were called "Young America." An early expression of the spirit of Young America was the enthusiastic reception given the exiled Hungarian revolutionary Louis Kossuth while on a tour of the United States in 1851.

President Pierce's platform in 1852 recalled the successful expansionism of the Polk years, declaring that the Mexican War had been "just and necessary." Many Democrats took their overwhelming victory as a mandate to continue adding territory to the Republic. A Philadelphia newspaper in 1853 described the United States as a nation bound on

In this 1852 political cartoon, a poor immigrant is accosted by Daniel Webster, Sam Houston, Stephen Douglas, and General Winfield Scott, each soliciting his vote. Partly to prevent such blatant political hustling, the American (Know-Nothing) party emerged, urging tighter restrictions on immigration and citizenship.

the "East by sunrise, West by sunset, North by the Arctic Expedition, and South as far as we darn please." Southward expansion into Latin America looked most attractive.

Many of Pierce's diplomatic appointees were southerners interested in adding new cotton-growing lands to the national domain. As ambassador to Mexico, for example, Pierce sent James Gadsden, a railroad man from South Carolina. Almost immediately, Gadsden negotiated with Mexican president Santa Anna for the acquisition of large parts of northern Mexico, including all of Lower California (the Baja Peninsula). Gadsden failed to get all the land he wanted, but he did manage to purchase a strip of desert along the southwest border in order to build a transcontinental railroad linking the Deep South with the Pacific Coast.

The failure to acquire more territory from Mexico legally did not discourage expansionist Americans from pursuing illegal means. During the 1850s,

Stephen Douglas's 1854 bill to allow Kansas and Nebraska to decide the slavery question for themsleves sparked violent controversy and led to the demise of the Whig party.

Texans and Californians staged dozens of raids (called "filibusters") into Mexico. The most daring adventurer of the era was William Walker, a 100-pound Tennesseean with a zest for danger and power. After migrating to southern California, Walker made plans to add slave lands to the country. In 1853, he invaded Lower California with fewer than 300 men and declared himself president of the independent Republic of Sonora. Although eventually arrested and tried in the United States, he was acquitted after eight minutes of deliberation.

Back Walker went, invading Nicaragua two years later. He overthrew the government, proclaimed himself to have been elected dictator, and issued a decree legalizing slavery. When the Nicaraguans, with British help, acted to regain control of their country, the United States Navy rescued Walker. After a triumphant tour in the South, he tried twice more to conquer Nicaragua. Walker came to a fitting end in 1860 when he was captured and shot by a Honduran firing squad after invading that country.

Undaunted by failures in the Southwest, the Pierce administration looked more seriously to the acquisition of Cuba, a Spanish colony many Americans thought destined to be a part of their country. One expansionist even suggested that Cuba physically belonged to the United States because it had been formed by alluvial deposits from the Mississippi River. "What God has joined together let no man put asunder," he said. The acquisition of Cuba was necessary, many maintained, as an extension of America's Manifest Destiny and as an ideal place for expanding the slave-based economy of the southern states.

A decade earlier, the Polk administration had offered $10 million for Cuba, but Spain had refused the offer. Unsuccessful efforts were then made to foment a revolution among Cuban sugar planters, who would then request annexation by the United States. One Latin adventurer organized an invasion of Cuba, launched from New Orleans in 1850. When his attempt failed, he was executed, and hundreds of captured comrades were sent to Spain. The citizens of New Orleans rioted in protest, storming the Spanish consulate, which forced an embarrassed Congress to pay an indemnity. A few years later, the former governor of Mississippi, with the support of his friend, Secretary of War Jefferson Davis, planned to raise $1 million and 50,000 troops to invade the island. The proposed expedition, intended to carve Cuba into several new slave states, was aborted.

Thousands of gun-toting Missourians crossed into Kansas in 1854 and 1855 in order to vote illegally for a proslavery territorial government.

Although President Pierce did not support these illegal efforts, his administration did want Cuba. Secretary of State William Marcy instructed the emissary to Spain, Pierre Soulé, to offer $130 million for Cuba. If that failed, Marcy suggested stronger measures. In 1854, the secretary arranged for Soulé and the American ministers to France and England to meet in Belgium to consider options. The result was the Ostend Manifesto, a document intended to pressure Spain to sell Cuba to the United States. It also provides a fascinating glimpse of American expansionist attitudes.

The manifesto argued that Cuba "belongs naturally" to the United States. Both geographically and economically, the fortunes and interests of Cubans and southerners were so "blended" that they were "one people with one destiny." Trade and commerce in the hemisphere would "never be secure" until Cuba was part of the United States. Moreover, southern slaveholders feared that a slave rebellion would "Africanize" Cuba, like Haiti, suggesting all kinds of "horrors to the white race" in the nearby southern United States. The American acquisition of Cuba was necessary, therefore, to "preserve our rectitude and self-respect."

If Spain refused to sell the island, the ministers threatened a revolution in Cuba with American sup-

port. If that should fail, the manifesto warned, "we should be justified in wresting it from Spain." Even Secretary Marcy was shocked when he received the document from Belgium, and he quickly rejected it. Like the Kansas-Nebraska Act, the Ostend Manifesto was urged most by Democrats who advocated the expansion of slavery. The outraged reaction of northerners in both cases divided and further weakened the Democratic party.

Nativism, Know-Nothings, and Republicans

Foreign immigration damaged an already enfeebled Whig party and created concern among many native-born Americans. To the average, hardworking Protestant American, the foreigners pouring into the cities and following the railroads westward spoke unfamiliar languages, wore funny clothes, drank alcohol freely in grogshops, and increased crime and pauperism. Still worse, they attended Catholic churches, where the Latin mass and eucharistic rituals offended those used to Protestant worship, and sent children to their own schools. Furthermore, they seemed content with a lower standard of living and would work for lower wages in worse conditions than American workers, thus threatening their jobs. Perhaps worst of all, many said, the new immigrants corrupted American politics.

Catholic immigrants preferred the Democratic party out of traditional loyalties and because Democrats were less inclined than Whigs to interfere with religion, schooling, drinking, and other aspects of personal behavior. It was mostly former Whigs, therefore, who in 1854 founded the American party to oppose the new immigrants. Members wanted a longer period of naturalization in order to guarantee the "vital principles of Republican Government" and pledged themselves never to vote for Irish Catholics for public office since it was assumed that their highest loyalty was to the pope in Rome. They also agreed to keep information about their order secret. If asked, they would say, "I know nothing." Hence, they were dubbed the Know-Nothing party.

The Know-Nothings were overwhelmingly a party of the middle and lower classes, workers who worried about their jobs and wages and farmers and small-town Americans who worried about disruptive new forces in their lives. As one New Yorker put it in 1854, "Roman Catholicism is feared more than American slavery." It was widely believed that Catholics slavishly obeyed the orders of their priests, who represented a church that had long been associated with European despotism. The opposition of the Catholic church to the revolutionary movements of 1848 in Europe intensified the fears of many Protestant Americans that a mass of Catholic voters deeply threatened their democratic order. In the 1854 and 1855 elections, the Know-Nothings gave anti-Catholicism a national political focus for the first time. They did so well that they threatened to replace the Whigs as the second major party.

Although the nativists argued that papism would subvert freedom and other republican values, others maintained that the slave power of the South was the chief danger. No sooner had the debates over Nebraska ended than a group of ex-Whigs and Free-Soilers met and formed the nucleus of another new party, called the Republican party. Although concerned about southern expansionism, as reflected in the Kansas-Nebraska Act debates, the Ostend Manifesto, and plans to build a transcontinental railroad from the South to California on land acquired in the Gadsden Purchase, the party's first challenge was to respond to popular sentiments by mobilizing sectional fears and ethnic and religious concerns.

Composed almost entirely of northerners, former "conscience" Whigs, and disaffected Democrats, the Republican party combined four main elements. The first group, led by William Seward, Senators Charles Sumner of Massachusetts and Salmon P. Chase of Ohio, and Congressman Joshua Giddings of Ohio and George Julian of Indiana, were fired by a moral fervor to prohibit slavery in the territories. They also sought to divorce the federal government from the support of slavery by freeing slaves in the District of Columbia, repealing the Fugitive Slave Act, and eliminating the internal slave trade. There were, however, limits to the idealism of most Republicans. A more moderate and larger group, typified by Abraham Lincoln of Illinois, opposed slavery in the western territories only but would not interfere with it where it already existed. This group also indicated that it would not support efforts to achieve equal rights for northern free blacks.

Republicans were anti-Catholic as well as antislavery. This third element of the party, reflecting the traditional Whig reformist impulse, felt responsible for cleansing America of its sins of intemperance, impiety, parochial schooling, and other forms of immorality. Another sin included voting for Democrats, who were accused of catering to "the grog shops, foreign vote, and Catholic brethren" by combining "the forces of Jesuitism and Slavery."

The fourth element of the Republican party, a Whig legacy from the American System of Henry Clay, included those who wanted the federal government to promote commercial and industrial development and the dignity of labor. This fourth group, like the antislavery and anti-Catholic elements, had a strong ideological faith that a system of free labor led to progress. At the heart of both the new party and the future of America were hardworking, middle-class, mobile, free white laborers—farmers, small businessmen, and independent craftsmen. As the Springfield *Republican* said in 1856, the Republican party's strength came from "those who work with their hands, who live and act independently, who hold the stakes of home and family, of farm and workshop, of education and freedom—these as a mass are enrolled in the Republican ranks."

The strengths of the Republican and Know-Nothing (American) parties were tested in 1856. Which party could best oppose the Democrats? The American party nominated Fillmore, who had strong support in the Upper South and border states. The Republicans chose John C. Frémont, a Free-Soiler from Missouri with virtually no political experience. The Democrats nominated James Buchanan of Pennsylvania, commonly known as "a northern man with southern principles." Frémont's strength in the North helped him carry several free states, while Fillmore won only Maryland. Buchanan, taking advantage of the divided opposition, won the election, but with only 45 percent of the popular vote.

After 1856, the Know-Nothings died out, largely because Republican leaders cleverly redirected nativist fears—and voters—into their broader program, but also because Know-Nothing secrecy, hatreds, and occasional violent attacks on Catholic voters damaged their image. The Know-Nothings represented a powerful current in American politics that would return each time social and economic changes seemed to threaten the nation. It became convenient to label certain people "un-American" and seek to root them out. Thus the Know-Nothing party disappeared after 1856, but nativism did not.

KANSAS AND THE TWO CULTURES

However appealing nativist issues were for many Americans, the problem of slavery was the issue that would not disappear. As Democrats sought ways of expanding slavery and other American institutions westward across the Plains and south into Cuba in the mid-1850s, Republicans wanted to halt the advance of slavery to prove to the world, as Seward said, that the American "experiment in self-government" still worked. In 1854, Lincoln worried that it was slavery that "deprives our republican example of its just influence in the world." The specific cause of his concern was the likelihood that slavery might be extended into Kansas as a result of the passage that year of Stephen Douglas's Kansas-Nebraska Act.

Competing for Kansas

During the congressional debates over the Kansas-Nebraska bill, Seward had accepted the challenge of slave-state senators to "engage in competition for the virgin soil of Kansas." The passage of the Kansas-Nebraska Act in 1854 opened the way for proslavery and antislavery forces to meet physically and to compete over whether Kansas would become a slave or free state. No sooner had the bill

Changing Political Party Systems and Leaders

First Party System: 1790s–1820s

Republican*	Federalist
Jefferson	Hamilton
Madison	John Adams
Monroe	

Transition: 1824 and 1828

Democrat-Republican	National Republican
Jackson	J. Q. Adams

Second Party System: 1830s–1850s

Democrat	Whig
Jackson	Clay
Van Buren	Webster
Calhoun	W. H. Harrison
Polk	

Third Party System: 1856–1890s

Democrat	Republican*
Douglas	Lincoln
Pierce	Seward
Buchanan	

* Note that the Republican party label begins in one tradition and ends up in the other.

passed Congress than Eli Thayer founded the Massachusetts Emigrant Aid Society to recruit free-soil settlers to go to Kansas. From New York, Frederick Douglass called for "companies of emigrants from the free states . . . to possess the goodly land." By the summer of 1855, about 1,200 New England colonists had migrated to Kansas.

One of the migrants was Julia Louisa Lovejoy, a Vermont minister's wife. As a Mississippi riverboat carried her into a slave state for the first time, she described the dilapidated plantation homes of the monotonous Missouri shore as reflecting "the blighting mildew of slavery." By the time Julia and her husband arrived in the Kansas Territory, she had concluded that "the inhabitants and morals" of slaveholding Missourians who had moved into Kansas were of "an *undescribably repulsive* and undesirable character." To Julia Lovejoy, northerners came to bring the "energetic Yankee" virtues of morality and economic enterprise to the drunken, unclean slaveholders of the Southwest.

Perhaps she had in mind David Atchison, Democratic senator from Missouri. Atchison believed that Congress had an obligation to protect slavery in the territories, thereby permitting Missouri slaveholders to move into Kansas. As early as 1853, he pledged himself "to extend the institutions of Missouri over the Territory at whatever sacrifice of blood or treasure." He described New England migrants as "negro thieves" and "abolition tyrants." He recommended to fellow Missourians that they defend their property and interests "with the *bayonet* and with *blood*" and, if need be, "to kill every God-damned abolitionist in the district."

Under Atchison's inflammatory leadership, secret societies sprang up in the Missouri counties adjacent to Kansas. They vowed to combat the Free-Soilers. One editor exclaimed that northerners came to Kansas "for the express purpose of stealing, running off and hiding runaway negroes from Missouri [and] taking to their own bed . . . a stinking negro wench." It was not slaveholders but New Englanders, he said, who were immoral, uncivilized, and hypocritical. Rumors of 20,000 such Massachusetts migrants spurred Missourians to action. Thousands poured across the border late in 1854 to vote in the first territorial election. Twice as many ballots were cast as the number of registered voters, and in one polling place only 20 of over 600 voters were legal residents.

The proslavery forces overreacted to their fear of the New England migrants and their intentions. The permanent population of Kansas consisted primarily of migrants from Missouri and other border states who were more concerned with land titles than slavery. They opposed any blacks—slave or free—moving into their state. As one clergyman put it, "I kem to Kansas to live in a free state and I don't want niggers a-trampin' over my grave."

In March 1855, a second election was held to select a territorial legislature. The pattern of border crossings, intimidation, and illegal voting was repeated. Atchison himself, drinking "considerable whiskey" along the way, led a band of armed men across the state line to vote and frighten would-be Free-Soil voters away. Not surprisingly, a small minority of eligible voters elected a proslavery territorial legislature. Free-Soilers, meanwhile, staged their own constitutional convention in Lawrence and created a Free-Soil government at Topeka. It banned blacks from the state. The proslavery legislature settled first in Shawnee Mission and then in Lecompton, giving Kansas two governments.

The struggle shifted to Washington, where President Pierce, who could have nullified the illegal election, did nothing. Congress debated the wrongs in Kansas and sent an investigating committee,

which further inflamed passions. Throughout 1855, the call to arms grew more strident. One proslavery newspaper invited southerners to bring their weapons and "send the scoundrels" from the North "back to whence they came, or . . . to hell, it matters not which." In South Carolina, Robert Allston wrote his son Benjamin that he was "raising men and money . . . to counteract the effect of the Northern hordes. . . . We are disposed to fight the battle of our rights . . . on the field of Kansas."

Both sides saw Kansas as a holy battleground for their version of moral right. An Alabama, Colonel Jefferson Buford, even sold his slaves to raise money to hire an army of 300 men to fight for slavery in Kansas, promising free land to his recruits. Both a Baptist and a Methodist minister blessed their departure from Montgomery. The Baptist promised them God's favor and gave each man a Bible. Northern Christians responded in kind. At Yale University, the noted minister Henry Ward Beecher presented 25 Bibles and 25 Sharps rifles to young men who would go fight for the Lord in Kansas. "There are times," he said, "when self-defense is a religious duty. If that duty was ever imperative it is now, and in Kansas." Beecher suggested that rifles would be of greater use than Bibles. Missourians dubbed them "Beecher's Bibles" and vowed, as one newspaper put it, "Blood for Blood! . . . for each drop spilled, we shall require one hundred fold!"

"Bleeding Kansas"

As civil war threatened in Kansas, a Brooklyn poet, Walt Whitman, heralded American democracy in his epic poem, *Leaves of Grass* (1855). Whitman identified himself as the embodiment of average Americans "of every hue and caste, . . . of every rank and religion." Ebulliently, Whitman embraced urban mechanics, southern woodcutters, planter's sons, runaway slaves, mining-camp prostitutes, and a catalog of others in his poetic celebration of "the word Democratic, the word En-Masse." At the same time, Whitman's faith in the American masses faltered in the mid-1850s. He worried that a knife plunged into "the breast" of the Union would bring on the "red blood of civil war."

Inevitably, as Whitman feared, blood flowed in Kansas. In May 1856, supported by a prosouthern federal marshall, a mob entered Lawrence, smashed the offices and presses of a Free-Soil newspaper, fired several cannonballs into the Free State Hotel, and destroyed homes and shops. Three nights later, motivated by vengeance and a feeling that he was doing God's will, John Brown led a small New England band, including four of his sons, to a proslavery settlement near Pottawatomie Creek. There they dragged five men out of their cabins and despite the terrified entreaties of their wives, hacked them to death with swords.

Violence also entered the halls of Congress. That same week, abolitionist senator Charles Sumner delivered a tirade that became known as "The Crime Against Kansas." He lashed out at the "murderous robbers" and "incredible atrocities of the Assassins and . . . Thugs" from the South. With nasty invective, he accused proslavery Senate leaders, especially Atchison and Andrew Butler of South Carolina, of cavorting with "the harlot, Slavery." Two days later, Butler's nephew, Congressman Preston Brooks, avenged the honor of his colleague by beating Sumner senseless with his cane as he sat at his Senate desk.

The sack of Lawrence, the massacre at Pottawatomie Creek, and the caning of Sumner set off a minor civil war, which historians have called "Bleeding Kansas." It lasted throughout the sum-mer. Crops were burned, homes were destroyed, fights broke out in saloons and streets, and night raiders tortured and murdered their enemies. For residents like Charles Lines, who just wanted to farm his land in peace, it was impossible to remain neutral. Lines hoped his neighbors near Lawrence would avoid "involving themselves in trouble." But when proslavery forces seized a mild-mannered neighbor, bound him, tortured him, and left him to die, Lines joined the battle. He wrote to a friend that "blood must end in the triumph of the right."

Even before the bleeding of Kansas began, the New York *Tribune* warned, "We are two peoples. We are a people for Freedom and a people for Slavery. Between the two, conflict is inevitable." As the moral rhetoric and violence in Kansas demonstrated, competing visions of two separate cultures for the future destiny of the United States were at stake. Despite many similarities between the North and the South, the gap between the two sides widened as the hostilities of the 1850s increased.

Northern Views and Visions

The North saw itself, as Julia Lovejoy suggested, as a prosperous land of bustling commerce and expanding, independent agriculture. Northern farmers and workers were self-made free men who believed in individualism and democracy. The "free

"Bleeding Kansas"

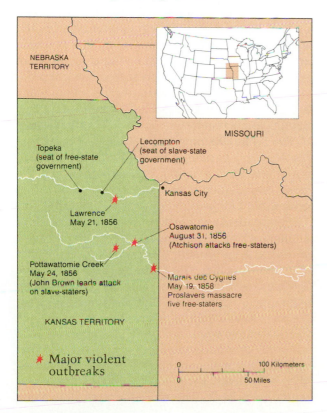

A preview of the Civil War occurred in Kansas. When a proslavery mob sacked Lawrence, leveling the Free State Hotel, a summer of violence followed, later known as "Bleeding Kansas."

labor system" of the North, as both Seward and Lincoln often said, offered equality of opportunity and upward mobility. Both generated more wealth. Although the North contained many growing cities, northerners revered the values of the small towns that spread from New England across the Upper Midwest. These values included a respect for the rights of the people, tempered by the rule of law; individual enterprise, balanced by a concern for one's neighbors; and a fierce morality rooted in Calvinist Protestantism. Northerners would regulate morality—by persuasion if possible but by legislation if necessary—to remove the sins of irreligion, illiteracy, and intemperance from American society. It was no accident that the ideas of universal public education and laws against the sale and consumption of alcohol both began in New England.

Northerners valued the kind of republican government that guaranteed the rights of free men, enabling them to achieve economic progress. Specifically, this meant supporting government action to promote free labor, industrial growth, some degree of immigration, foreign trade (protected by tariffs), and the development of railroads and free farm homesteads westward across the continent. Energetic mobility both westward and upward would dissolve state, regional, and class loyalties and increase the sense of nationhood. A strong Union could achieve national and even international greatness. These were the conditions, befitting a chosen people, that would, as Seward put it, spread American institutions around the world and "renovate the condition of mankind" These were also the ideological principles of the Republican party.

Only free men could achieve economic progress and moral society. Therefore, the worst sin in the northerner's view was the loss of one's freedom. Slavery was the root of all evil. It was, Seward said, "incompatible with all . . . the elements of the security, welfare, and greatness of nations." The South, then, represented the antithesis of everything that northerners saw as good. Southerners were unfree, backward, economically stagnant, uneducated, lawless, immoral, and out of harmony with the values and ideals of the nineteenth century. Julia Lovejoy's denunciation of slaveholding Missourians was mild. Her fellow migrants to Kansas described southerners as subhuman, unclean, and uncivilized. They were, as one put it, "drunken ourang-outans," "wild beasts" who drank whiskey, ate dirt, uttered oaths, raped slave women, and fought or dueled at the slightest excuse. In the popular language of the day, they were known as "Pukes."

The Southern Perspective

Epithets aside, southerners were a diverse people who, like northerners, shared certain broad values, generally those of the planter class. If in the North the values of economic enterprise were most important, southerners revered social values most. Like the English gentry they sought to emulate, they saw themselves as courteous, refined, hospitable, and chivalrous. By contrast, they saw northerners as coarse, ill-mannered, aggressive, materialistic "Yankees." In a society where one person in three was a black slave, racial distinctions and paternalistic relationships were crucial in maintaining order and white supremacy. Fear of slave revolt was ever present. The South had five times more military schools than the North. Northerners educated the many for economic utility, but southerners educated the few for grace and character. In short, the South saw itself as a genteel, ordered society guided by the aristocratic code of the gentleman planter.

Southerners agreed with northerners that sovereignty in a republic rested in the people, who created a government of laws to protect life, liberty, and property. But unlike people in the North, southerners believed that the democratic principle of self-government was best preserved in local political units such as the state. Southerners were ready to fight to defend their sacred rights against any tyrannical encroachment on their liberty, as they had in 1776. They saw themselves, in fact, as true revolutionary patriots. Like northerners, southerners cherished the Union. But they preferred the loose confederacy of the Jeffersonian past to the centralized nationalism Seward kept invoking.

To southerners, Yankees were in too much of a hurry—to make money, to reform the behavior of others, to put dreamy theories (like racial equality) into practice. Two images dominated the South's view of northerners: either they were stingy, hypocritical, moralizing Puritans, or they were grubby, slum-dwelling, Catholic immigrants. A Georgia paper combined both images in an 1856 editorial: "Free society! we sicken at the name. What is it but a conglomeration of greasy mechanics, filthy operatives, small-fisted farmers, and moonstruck theorists?" These northerners, the paper

These scenes illustrate the contrasting socioeconomic cultures of the antebellum North and South. Rochester in 1860 was a bustling industrial city, delivering manufactured goods to northern markets by canal boats and railroads, while the vital unit of southern commerce was the genteel individual plantation, with steamboats carrying cotton to port cities for trade with Europe.

said, "are devoid of society fitted for well-bred gentlemen."

Each side, then, saw the other threatening its freedom and infringing on its view of a proper republican society. Each saw the other imposing barriers to its vision for America's future, which included the economic systems described in Chapters 11 and 12. As hostilities increased, the views each section had of the other grew steadily more rigid and conspiratorial. Northerners saw the South as a "slave power," determined to foist the slave system on free labor throughout the land. Southerners saw the North as full of "black Republicanism," determined to destroy the southern way of life.

POLARIZATION AND THE ROAD TO WAR

Because of the national constituencies of the two major political parties, northern and southern cultural stereotypes and conspiratorial accusations had been largely held in check. But events in Kansas solidified the image of the Republicans as a northern party and seriously weakened the Democrats. Further events, still involving the question of slavery in the territories, soon split the Democratic party irrevocably into sectional halves: the Dred Scott decision of the Supreme Court (1857), the constitutional crisis in Kansas (1857), the Lincoln-Douglas debates in Illinois (1858), John Brown's raid in Vir-

ginia (1859), and Lincoln's election (1860). These incidents further polarized the negative images each culture held of the other and set the nation on the final road to civil war.

The Dred Scott Case

The events of 1857 reinforced the arguments of those who believed in a slave power conspiracy. Two days after James Buchanan's inauguration, the Supreme Court finally ruled in *Dred Scott* v. *Sandford*. The case had been pending before the Court for nearly three years, but the slave family of Dred Scott had been waiting longer for the decision. In 1846, Dred and Harriet Scott had filed suit in Missouri for their freedom. They argued that their master had taken them into Minnesota, Wisconsin, and other territories where the Missouri Compromise prohibited slavery, and therefore they should be freed. By the time the case reached the Supreme Court, the issue of slavery in the territories had become a heated political issue.

When the Court, which had a majority of southern judges, issued its decision, by a vote of 7 to 2, it made three rulings. First, since blacks were, as Chief Justice Roger Taney put it, "beings of an inferior order [who] had no rights which white men were bound to respect," Dred Scott was not a citizen and had no right to sue in federal courts. Justice Peter Daniel of Virginia was even more indelicate in his consenting opinion, saying that "the African Negro race" did not belong "to the family of nations" but rather was a subject for "commerce or traffic." The second ruling stated that the Missouri Compromise was unconstitutional because Congress did not have the power to ban slavery in a territory. And third, the fact that the Scotts had been taken in and out of free states did not affect their status. Despite two eloquent dissenting opinions, Dred and Harriet Scott remained slaves.

The implications of these decisions went far beyond the Scotts' personal freedom. The arguments about black citizenship insulted and infuriated many northerners. Frederick Douglass called the ruling "a most scandalous and devilish perversion of the Constitution, and a brazen misstatement of the facts of history." Many citizens worried about the few rights free blacks still held. Even more troublesome was the possibility hinted at in the decision that slavery might be permitted in the free states of the North, where it had long been banned. People who suspected a conspiracy were not calmed when Buchanan endorsed the Dred Scott decision as a final settlement of the right of citizens to take their "property of any kind, including slaves, into the common Territories . . . and to have it protected there under the Federal Constitution." One issue, however, remained unresolved by the Court. Could a territorial legislature write a constitution that permitted the introduction of new slaves? Rather than settling the political issue of slavery in the territories, as Buchanan had hoped, the Dred Scott decision threw it back into American politics. It opened up new questions and increased sectional hostilities.

Douglas and the Democrats

The Dred Scott decision and Buchanan's endorsement fed northern suspicions of a slave power conspiracy to impose slavery everywhere. Events in Kansas, which still had two governments, heightened these fears. In the summer of 1857, Kansas had still another election, with so many irregularities that only 2,000 out of a possible 24,000 voters participated. They elected a proslavery slate of delegates to a constitutional convention meeting at Lecompton as a preparation for statehood. The convention decided to exclude free blacks from the state, to guarantee the property rights of the few slaveholders in Kansas, and to ask voters to decide in a referendum whether to permit more slaves.

The proslavery Lecompton constitution, clearly unrepresentative of the wishes of the majority of the people of Kansas, was sent to Congress for approval. Eager to retain the support of southern Democrats, Buchanan endorsed it. Stephen Douglas challenged the president's power and jeopardized his own standing with southern Democrats by opposing it. Facing reelection to the Senate from Illinois in 1858, he needed to hold the support of the northern wing of his party. Congress sent the Lecompton constitution back to the people of Kansas for another referendum. This time they defeated it, which meant that Kansas remained a territory rather than becoming a slave state. While Kansas was left in an uncertain status, the larger political effect of the struggle was to split the Democratic party almost beyond repair.

The decision in 1857 to deny Dred Scott's suit for freedom was alarming even to those who took a moderate stance on the issue of slavery. This New York newspaper tells the sad story of Dred and Harriet Scott and their two daughters.

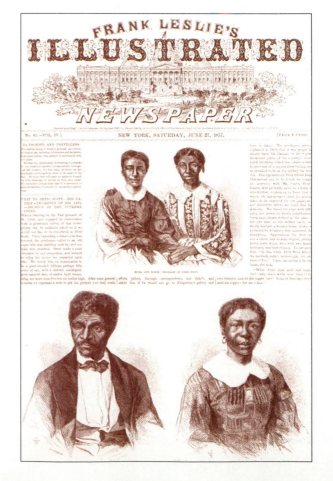

No sooner had Douglas settled the Lecompton question than he faced reelection in Illinois. Douglas's heroic opposition to the Lecompton constitution had restored his prestige in the North as an opponent of the slave power. This cut some ground out from under the Republican party claim that it was the only force capable of stopping the spread of southern power. Republican party leaders from the West, however, had a candidate who understood the importance of distinguishing Republican moral and political views from those of the Democrats.

Lincoln and the Illinois Debates

Although he was relatively unknown nationally and had not held elected office in several years, by 1858 Abraham Lincoln of Illinois had emerged to challenge William Seward for leadership of the Republican party. Lincoln's character was shaped on the midwestern frontier, where he had educated himself, developed mild abolitionist views, and dreamed of America's greatness.

Since Douglas was clearly the leading Democrat, the Senate election in Illinois appeared to be a preview of the presidential election of 1860. The other Douglass, Frederick, observed that "the slave power idea was the ideological glue of the Republican party." Lincoln's handling of this idea would be crucial in distinguishing him from Stephen Douglas. The Illinois campaign featured a series of seven debates between Lincoln and Douglas in different cities. With a national as well as a local audience, the debates provided a remarkable opportunity for the two men to state their views on the heated racial issues before the nation.

Lincoln set a solemn tone when he accepted the Republican senatorial nomination in Chicago in June. The American nation, he said, was in a "crisis" and building toward a worse one. "A House divided against itself cannot stand. I believe this government cannot endure, permanently half *slave* and half *free*." Lincoln said he did not expect the Union "to be dissolved" or "the house to fall" but rather that "it will become *all* one thing, or *all* the other." Then he rehearsed the history of the South's growing influence over national policy since the Kansas-Nebraska Act, which he blamed on Douglas. Lincoln stated his firm opposition to the Dred Scott decision, which he believed part of a conspiracy involving Pierce, Buchanan, Taney, and Douglas. People like himself, who opposed this conspiracy, wished to place slavery, he said, on a "course of ultimate extinction."

As he revealed in the debates with Stephen Douglas in 1858, Abraham Lincoln's views on slavery and black equality were at once more progressive than those of most Americans and sufficiently mainstream to win him the Republican party's presidential nomination in 1860.

In the ensuing debates with Douglas, Lincoln reiterated these themes, especially the controversial phrase about "ultimate extinction." He also expressed his views on race and slavery, formed from a blend of experience, principle, and politics. Although far from a radical abolitionist, in these debates Lincoln skillfully staked out a moral position not only in advance of Douglas but well ahead of his time.

Lincoln was also very much a part of his time. He believed that whites were superior to blacks and opposed equal rights for free blacks. He believed, furthermore, that the physical and moral differences between whites and blacks would "forever forbid the two races from living together on terms of social and political equality." He worried about the long-term implications and recommended "separation" and colonization in Liberia or Central America as the best solution to racial differences.

Lincoln differed from most contemporaries in his deep commitment to the humane principles of the equality and essential dignity of all human beings, including blacks. Douglas, by contrast, arguing against race mixing in a blatant bid for votes, continually made racial slurs. Lincoln believed not only that blacks were "entitled to all the natural rights . . . in the Declaration of Independence" but also that they had many specific economic rights as well, like "the right to put into his mouth the bread that his own hands have earned." In these rights, blacks were, Lincoln said, "my equal and the equal of Judge Douglas, and the equal of every living man."

Unlike Douglas, Lincoln hated slavery. At Galesburg, he said, "I contemplate slavery as a moral, social, and political evil." In Quincy, he said that the difference between a Republican and a Democrat was quite simply whether one thought slavery wrong or right. Douglas was more equivocal and dodged the issue in Freeport by pointing out that slavery would not exist if favorable local legislation did not support it. Douglas's moral indifference to slavery was clear in his admission that he did not care if a territorial legislature voted it "up or down." A white supremacist, Douglas was democratic enough to want white people to be able to create whatever type of society they wanted. Republicans did care, Lincoln affirmed, sounding a warning that by stopping the expansion of slavery, the course toward "ultimate extinction" had begun. Although barred by the Constitution from doing anything about slavery where it already existed, Lincoln said that since Republicans believed slavery to be wrong, "we propose a course of policy that shall deal with it as a wrong."

What Lincoln meant by "policy" was not yet clear, even to himself. However, in the debates he did succeed in affirming that the Republican party was the only moral and political force capable of stopping the slave power. It seems ironic now, though not at the time, that Douglas won the election. When he and Lincoln met again two years later, the order of their finish would be reversed. Elsewhere in 1858, however, Democrats did poorly, losing 18 congressional seats to the Republicans.

John Brown's Raid

Unlike Lincoln, John Brown was again prepared to act decisively against slavery. On October 16, 1859, he and a band of 22 men attacked a federal arsenal at Harpers Ferry, Virginia (now West Virginia). He hoped that the action might provoke a general uprising of slaves throughout the Upper South or at least provide the arms by which slaves could make their way to freedom. Although he seized the arsenal, federal troops soon overcame

him. Nearly half his men were killed, including two sons. Brown himself was captured, tried, and hanged for treason. So ended a lifetime of failures.

In death, however, he was not a failure. Brown's daring if foolhardy raid, and his impressively dignified behavior during his trial and speedy execution, unleashed powerful passions, further widening the gap between North and South. Northerners responded to his death with an outpouring of admiration and sympathy, for both the man and his cause. Memorial rallies, parades, and prayer meetings were held. Admirers wrote poems, songs, and speeches in his honor. Thoreau compared Brown to Christ and called him "an angel of light." Abolitionist William Lloyd Garrison, though a pacifist, was moved to wish "success to every slave insurrection" in the South. Ministers called slave revolt a "divine weapon" and glorified Brown's treason as "holy." Before the raid, Brown had consulted with Frederick Douglass, who later said that Brown had shown that slavery, "a system of brute force," could be ended only when "met with its own weapons."

Brown, Douglass pointed out, had also filled southerners with "dread and terror." Many concluded that northerners would stop at nothing, in-

The raid on Harpers Ferry by John Brown made him a hero to northern abolitionists. This portrait was painted by black artist David Bowser.

cluding armed force, to free the slaves. Brown's raid stimulated a wave of fear of slave revolts, led by hundreds of imaginary Nat Turners, throughout the South. This atmosphere of suspicion eroded freedom of thought and expression. A North Carolinian described a "spirit of terror, mobs, arrests, and violence" in his state. Twelve families in Berea, Kentucky, were evicted from the state for their mild abolitionist sentiments. A Texas minister who criticized the treatment of slaves in a sermon was given 70 lashes.

In response to the Brown raid, southerners also became more convinced, as the governor of South Carolina put it, that a "black Republican" plot in the North was "arrayed against the slaveholders." In this atmosphere of mistrust, southern Unionists lost their influence, and power became concentrated in the hands of those favoring secession. Only one step remained to complete the southern sense of having become a permanent minority within the United States: withdrawing to form a new nation. Senator Robert Toombs of Georgia, insistent that northern "enemies" were plotting the South's ruin, warned fellow southerners late in 1859, "Never permit this Federal government to pass into the traitorous hands of the black Republican party."

In the aftermath of John Brown's raid, passions fed by fear were unleashed throughout the South against northern sympathizers, and vice versa. A year later, the editor of a Massachusetts newspaper that expressed southern sympathies found himself the victim of the time-honored mob punishment of tarring and feathering.

The Election of 1860

The conflict between Buchanan and Douglas took its toll on the Democratic party. When the nominating convention met in Charleston, South Carolina, a hotbed of secessionist sentiments, it met for a record ten days without being able to name a presidential candidate. The convention went through 59 ballots, was disrupted twice by the withdrawal of southern delegates, and then adjourned for six weeks. Meeting again, this time in Baltimore, the Democrats acknowledged their irreparable division by naming two candidates in two separate conventions. Douglas represented northern Democrats, and John C. Breckenridge, Buchanan's vice-president, carried the banner of the proslavery South. The Constitutional Union party, made up of former southern Whigs and border-state nativists, claimed the middle ground of compromise and nominated John Bell, a slaveholder from Tennessee with mild views.

With Democrats split in two and a new party in contention, the Republican strategy aimed at keeping the states carried by Frémont in 1856 and adding Pennsylvania, Illinois, and Indiana. Seward, the leading candidate for the nomination, had been tempering his antislavery views to appear more electable. So had Abraham Lincoln, who seemed more likely than Seward to carry those key states. With some shrewd political maneuvering emphasizing Lincoln's "availability" as a moderate with widespread appeal, he was nominated by his party.

The Republican platform also reflected moderation, reducing attacks on slavery to oppose only its extension. Most of the platform spoke to the concerns of the several elements of the party: tariff protection, subsidized internal improvements, free labor, and a homestead bill. Above all, the Republicans, like southern Democrats, defended their view of what republican values meant for America's future. It did not include the kind of society of equal rights envisioned by Frederick Douglass. An English traveler in 1860 observed that in America "we see, in effect, two nations—one white and another

The Election of 1860

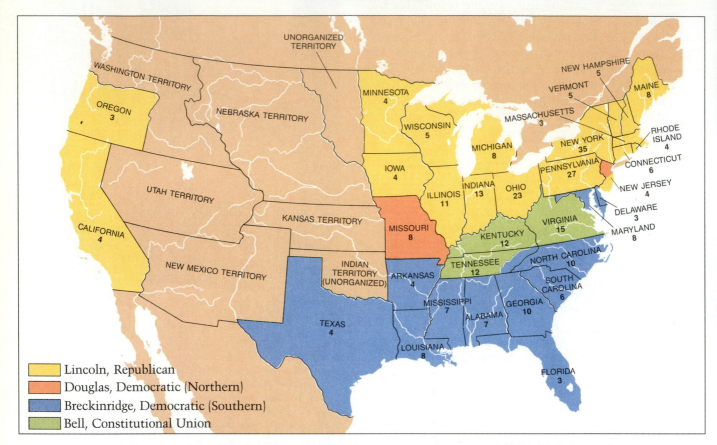

Lincoln, Republican
Douglas, Democratic (Northern)
Breckinridge, Democratic (Southern)
Bell, Constitutional Union

The Emerging Third Party System: Presidental Elections, 1852–1860

Year	Candidates	Party	Popular Vote	Electoral Vote
1852	FRANKLIN PIERCE	Democrat	1,601,474 (51%)	254
	Winfield Scott	Whig	1,386,578 (44%)	42
	John P. Hale	Free-Soil	156,149 (5%)	0
1856	JAMES BUCHANAN	Democrat	1,838,169 (45%)	174
	John C. Frémont	Republican	1,335,264 (33%)	114
	Millard Fillmore	American	874,534 (22%)	8
1860	ABRAHAM LINCOLN	Republican	1,866,352 (40%)	180
	Steven A. Douglas	Democrat	1,375,157 (29%)	12
	John C. Breckinridge	Democrat	847,953 (18%)	72
	John Bell	Constitutional Union	589,581 (13%)	39

Note: Winners' names appear in capital letters.

black—growing up together within the same political circle, but never mingling on a principle of equality."

The Republican moderate strategy for electoral victory worked exactly as planned, as Lincoln swept the entire Northeast and Midwest. Although receiving less than 40 percent of the popular vote nationwide, his triumph in the North was decisive. Even a united Democratic party could not have defeated him. With victory assured, Lincoln finished his sandwich and coffee on election night in Springfield and prepared for the consequences and awesome responsibilities of his election. They came even before his inauguration.

THE DIVIDED HOUSE FALLS

The Republicans overestimated the extent of Unionist sentiment in the South. They could not believe that the secessionists would prevail after Lincoln's victory. A year earlier, some southern congressmen had walked out in protest of the selection of an antislavery speaker of the House. A Republican leader, Carl Schurz, recalling this act, said that the southerners had taken a drink and then come back. After Lincoln's election, Schurz predicted, they would walk out, take two drinks, and come back again. He was wrong.

Secession and Uncertainty

On December 20, 1860, South Carolina seceded from the Union, declaring the "experiment" of putting people with "different pursuits and institutions" under one government a failure. By February 1, the other six Deep South states (Mississippi, Florida, Alabama, Georgia, Louisiana, and Texas) had seceded. A week later, delegates met in Montgomery, Alabama, created the Confederate States of America, adopted a constitution, and elected Jefferson Davis, a Mississippi senator and cotton planter, its provisional president. The divided house had fallen, as Lincoln had predicted it would. What was not yet certain, though, was whether the house could be put back together or whether disunion necessarily meant civil war.

The government in Washington had three options. The first was compromise, but the emotions of the time ruled out that possibility. Most proposed compromises were really concessions to the secessionist states. The second option, suggested by Horace Greeley, editor of the New York *Tribune*, was to let the seven states "go in peace," taking care not to lose the border states. But this was opposed by northern businessmen, who would lose profitable economic ties with the South, and by those who believed in an indissoluble Union. The third option was to compel secessionist states to return, which probably meant war.

Republican hopes that southern Unionism would assert itself and make none of these options necessary seemed possible in February 1861. The momentum toward disunion slowed, and no other southern states seceded. The nation waited and watched, wondering what Virginia and the border states would do, what outgoing President Buchanan

would do, and what Congress would do. Prosouthern and determined not to start a civil war in the last weeks of his already dismal administration, Buchanan did nothing. Congress made some feeble efforts to pass compromise legislation, waiting in vain for the support of the president-elect. And as Union supporters and cooperationists struggled with secessionists, Virginia and the border states, like the entire nation, waited for Abraham Lincoln.

Frederick Douglass waited too, without much hope. He wanted nothing less than "the complete and universal *abolition* of the whole slave system," as well as equal suffrage and other rights for free blacks. His momentary expectation during the presidential campaign, that Lincoln and the Republicans had the will to do this, had been thoroughly dashed. In November, the voters of New York State had defeated a referendum for black suffrage by more votes than a similar measure 14 years earlier. Moreover, Douglass saw northern politicians and businessmen "granting the most demoralizing concessions to the Slave Power."

In his despair, Douglass began to explore possibilities for emigration and colonization in Haiti, an idea he had long opposed. To achieve full freedom and citizenship in the United States for all blacks, he said in January 1861, he would "welcome the hardships consequent upon a dissolution of the Union." In February, Douglass said, "Let the conflict come." He opposed all compromises, hoping that with Lincoln's inauguration in March it would "be decided, and decided forever, which of the two, Freedom or Slavery, shall give law to this Republic."

Lincoln and Fort Sumter

As Douglass penned these thoughts, Lincoln began a long, slow train ride from Springfield, Illinois, to Washington, writing and rewriting his inaugural address. Lincoln's quietness in the period between his election and his inauguration had led many to wonder if he were not weak and indecisive. He was not. Lincoln was firmly opposed to secession and to any compromises with the principle of stopping the extension of slavery. He would neither conciliate secessionist southern states nor force their return.

But Lincoln believed in his constitutional responsibility to uphold the laws of the land, and on this significant point he would not yield. The focus of his attention was a federal fort in the harbor of

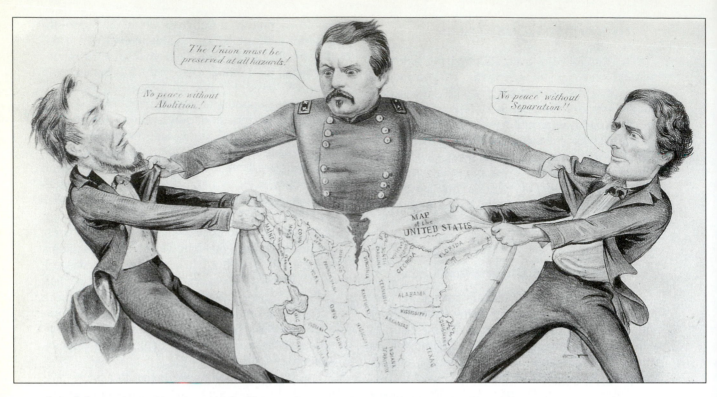

Appeals for a compromise to preserve the Union in the winter of 1860–1861 were in vain, according to this neutral cartoonist. The drawing shows equally guilty Abraham Lincoln and Jefferson Davis about to tear the map of the United States asunder.

Charleston, South Carolina. Major Robert Anderson, the commander of Fort Sumter, was running out of provisions and had requested new supplies from Washington. Lincoln would enforce the laws and protect federal property at Fort Sumter.

As the new president rose to deliver his inaugural address on March 4, he faced a tense and divided nation. Federal troops, fearing a Confederate attack on the nation's capital, were everywhere. Lincoln asserted his unequivocal intention to enforce the laws of the land, arguing that the Union was constitutionally "perpetual" and indissoluble. He reminded the nation that the "only substantial dispute" was that "one section of our country believes slavery is *right*, and ought to be extended, while the other believes it is *wrong*, and ought not to be extended." Still hoping to appeal to Unionist strength among southern moderates, Lincoln indicated that he would make no attempts to interfere with existing slavery or the law to return fugitive slaves.

Nearing the end of his address, Lincoln urged against rash actions and put the burden of initiating a civil war on the "dissatisfied fellow-countrymen"

who had seceded. As if aware of the horrible events that might follow, he said in an eloquent conclusion:

> I am loath to close. We are not enemies, but friends. We must not be enemies. Though passion may have strained, it must not break our bonds of affection. The mystic chords of memory, stretching from every battlefield, and patriot grave, to every living heart and hearthstone, all over this broad land, will yet swell the chorus of the Union, when again touched, as surely they will be, by the better angels of our nature.

Frederick Douglass was not impressed with Lincoln's "honied phrases" and accused him of "weakness, timidity and conciliation." Also unmoved, Robert Allston wrote his son from Charleston, where he was watching the developing crisis over Fort Sumter, that the Confederacy's "advantage" was in having a "much better president than they have."

On April 6, Lincoln notified the governor of South Carolina that he was sending "provisions only" to Fort Sumter. No effort would be made "to throw in men, arms, or ammunition" unless the fort were attacked. On April 10, Jefferson Davis directed

Major Causes and Events Leading to the Civil War		
Date	Event	Impact or Effect as Cause of Civil War
1600s–1860s	Slavery in the South	Major underlying pervasive cause
1700s–1860s	Development of two distinct socioeconomic systems and cultures	Further reinforced slavery as fundamental socioeconomic, cultural, moral issue
1787–1860s	States' rights, nullification doctrine	Ongoing political issue, less fundamental as cause
1820	Missouri Compromise (36°30′)	Background for conflict over slavery in territories
1828–1833	South Carolina tariff nullification crisis	Background for secession leadership in South Carolina
1831–1860s	Antislavery movements, southern justification	30 years of emotional preparation for conflict
1846–1848	Mexican War (Wilmot Proviso, Calhoun, popular sovereignty)	Options for slavery in territories issue
1850	Compromise of 1850	Temporary and unsatisfactory "settlement" of divisive issue
1851–1854	Fugitive slaves returned and rescued in North; personal liberty laws passed in North; Harriet Beecher Stowe's *Uncle Tom's Cabin*	Heightened northern emotional reactions against the South and slavery
1852–1856	Breakdown of Whig party and national Democratic party; creation of a new party system with sectional basis	Made national politics an arena where sectional and cultural differences over slavery were fought
1854	Ostend Manifesto and other expansionist efforts in Central America	Reinforced image of Democratic party as favoring slavery
	Formation of Republican party	Major party identified as opposing the expansion of slavery
	Kansas-Nebraska Act	Reopened "settled" issue of slavery in the territories
1856	"Bleeding Kansas"; Senator Sumner physically attacked in Senate	Foretaste of civil war (200 killed, $2 million in property lost) inflamed emotions and polarized North and South
1857	Dred Scott decision; proslavery Lecompton constitution in Kansas	Made North fear a "slave power conspiracy," supported by President Buchanan and the Supreme Court
1858	Lincoln-Douglas debates in Illinois; Democrats lose 18 seats in Congress	Set stage for election of 1860
1859	John Brown's raid and reactions in North and South	Made South fear a "black Republican" plot against slavery; further polarization and irrationality
1860	Democratic party splits in half; Lincoln elected president; South Carolina secedes from Union	Final breakdown of national parties and election of "northern" president; no more compromises
1861	Six more southern states secede by February 1; Confederate Constitution adopted February 4; Lincoln inaugurated March 4; Fort Sumter attacked April 12	Civil War begins

General P. G. T. Beauregard to demand the surrender of Fort Sumter. Davis told Beauregard to reduce the fort if Major Anderson refused.

On April 12, as Lincoln's relief expedition neared Charleston, Beauregard's batteries began shelling Fort Sumter, and the Civil War began. Frederick Douglass was about to leave for Haiti when he heard the news. He immediately changed his plans: "This is no time . . . to leave the country."

He announced his readiness to help end the war by aiding the Union to organize freed slaves "into a liberating army" to "make war upon . . . the savage barbarism of slavery." The Allstons had changed places, and it was Benjamin who described the events in Charleston harbor to his father. On April 14, Benjamin reported exuberantly "the glorious, and astonishing news that Sumter has fallen." With it fell America's divided house.

CONCLUSION:

The "Irrepressible Conflict"

Lincoln had been right. The nation could no longer endure half slave and half free. The collision between North and South, William Seward said, was not an "accidental, unnecessary" event but "an irrepressible conflict between opposing and enduring forces." Those forces had been at work for many decades but developed with increasing intensity after 1848 in the conflict over the question of the extension of slavery into the territories. Although economic, cultural, political, constitutional, and emotional forces all contributed to the developing opposition between North and South, slavery was the fundamental, enduring force that underlay all others, causing what Walt Whitman called "the red blood of civil war."

Recommended Reading

Easily the finest overall account of the political history of the 1850s is David Potter's superb narrative, The Impending Crisis, 1848–1861 *(1976), completed by Donald Fehrenbacher after Potter's death. The classic detailed account is Allen Nevins,* Ordeal of the Union, *4 vols. (1947–1950). Two recent studies, the first from a British point of view, are Bruce Collins,* The Origins of America's Civil War *(1981), and James McPherson,* Ordeal by Fire: The Civil War and Reconstruction *(1982). Four collections of stimulating essays on recent Civil War scholarship are Eric Foner, ed.,* Politics and Ideology in the Age of the Civil War *(1980); Robert Swierenga, ed.,* Beyond the Civil War Synthesis *(1975); Kenneth Stampp,* The Imperiled Union: Essays on the Background of the Civil War *(1980); and William E. Gienapp, Thomas B. Alexander, Michael F. Holt, Stephen E. Mazlish, and Joel H. Silbey,* Essays on American Antebellum Politics, 1840–1860 *(1982). Stampp has also compiled the most useful combination of primary and secondary sources representing differences of opinion,* The Causes of the Civil War, *rev. ed. (1974), a good book in which to explore various historical interpretations.*

Michael F. Holt, The Political Crisis of the 1850s *(1978), is the best overall work of "new politics" showing the breakdown of political parties as a major cause of the Civil War. An indispensable work on the ideas of the Republican party is Eric Foner,* Free Soil, Free Labor, Free Men: The Ideology of the Republican Party Before the Civil War *(1970). On ethnic and religious politics and the effects of nativism on political behavior, see Paul Kleppner,* The Third Electoral System, 1853–1892: Parties, Voters, and Political Cultures *(1979); Ronald Formisano,* The Birth of Mass Political Parties: Michigan, 1827–1861 *(1971); and Michael Holt,* Forging a Majority: The Formation of the Republican Party in Pittsburgh, 1848–1860 *(1969). For a monumental new synthesis and interpretation, see William E. Gienapp,* The Origins of the Republican Party, 1852–1856 *(1987). Specialized works on the effects of the issue of slavery in the territories on sectional rivalry and political parties are Hamilton Holman,* Prologue to Conflict: The Crisis and Compromise of 1850 *(1964); Thomas B. Alexander,* Sectional Stress and Party Strength *(1967); William J. Cooper,* The South and the Politics of Slavery *(1978); and Richard Sewell,* Ballots for Freedom: Antislavery Politics in the United States, 1837–1865 *(1976).*

On racism in the West, see Eugene Berwanger, The Frontier Against Slavery: Western Anti-Negro Prejudice and the Slavery Extension Controversy *(1967), and James Rawley,* Race and Politics: "Bleeding Kansas" and the Coming of the Civil War *(1969). The definitive work on the Dred Scott case is Donald Fehrenbacher,* Slavery, Law, and Politics: The Dred Scott Case in Historical Perspective *(1981). On the Buchanan administration and the Lincoln-Douglas debates, see Roy Nichols's classic,* The Disruption of American Democracy *(1948), and Harry Jaffa,* Crisis of the House Divided: An

Interpretation of the Lincoln-Douglas Debates (*1959*). *The final road to war after Lincoln's election in 1860 is detailed in Kenneth Stampp,* And the War Came (*1950*); *William Barney,* The Road to Secession (*1972*); *and Steven Channing,* Crisis of Fear: Secession in South Carolina (*1970*).

Reading biographies of major figures is an enjoyable and useful way to absorb the political and emotional crises of the 1850s. See Robert Johannsen, Stephen Douglas (*1973*); *Stephen Oates,* To Purge This Land with Blood: A Biography of John Brown (*1970*) *and* With Malice Toward None: The Life of Abraham Lincoln (*1982*). *A brilliant study of Lincoln's masterful prose is T. Harry Williams, ed.,* Abraham Lincoln: Selected Speeches, Messages, and Letters (*1957*). *The emotional flavor of the decade is captured in Harriet Beecher Stowe's novel,* Uncle Tom's Cabin (*1852*), *and Walt Whitman's poetry in* Leaves of Grass (*any edition*).

TIME LINE

1832 Nullification crisis

1835–1840 Intensification of abolitionist attacks on slavery
Violent retaliatory attacks on abolitionists

1840 Liberty party formed

1846 Wilmot Proviso

1848 Free-Soil party founded
Zachary Taylor elected president

1850 Compromise of 1850, including Fugitive Slave Act

1850–1854 "Young America" movement

1851 Women's rights convention in Akron, Ohio

1852 Harriet Beecher Stowe publishes *Uncle Tom's Cabin*
Franklin Pierce elected president

1854 Ostend Manifesto
Kansas-Nebraska Act nullifies Missouri Compromise
Republican and Know-Nothing parties formed

1855 Walt Whitman publishes *Leaves of Grass*

1855–1856 Thousands pour into Kansas, creating months of turmoil and violence

1856 John Brown's massacre in Kansas
Sumner-Brooks incident in Senate
James Buchanan elected president

1857 Dred Scott decision legalizes slavery in territories
Lecompton constitution in Kansas

1858 Lincoln-Douglas debates

1859 John Brown's raid at Harpers Ferry

1860 Democratic party splits
Four-party campaign
Abraham Lincoln elected president

1860–1861 Seven southern states secede

1861 Confederate States of America founded
Attack on Fort Sumter begins Civil War

16

The Union Severed

W e cannot escape history," Abraham Lincoln reminded Congress in 1862. "We of this Congress and this administration will be remembered in spite of ourselves. No personal significance, or insignificance, can spare . . . us. The fiery trial through which we pass, will light us down, in honor or dishonor, to the latest generation." Lincoln's conviction that Americans would long remember him and other major actors of the Civil War was correct. Jefferson Davis, Robert E. Lee, Ulysses S. Grant—these are the men whose characters, actions, and decisions have been the subject of continuing discussion and analysis, whose statues and memorials dot the American countryside and grace urban squares. Whether seen as heroes or villains, great men have dominated the story of the Civil War.

Yet from the earliest days, the war touched the lives of even the most uncelebrated Americans. From Indianapolis, 20-year-old Arthur Carpenter wrote to his parents in Massachusetts begging for permission to enlist in the volunteer army: "I have always longed for the time to come when I could enter the army and be a military man, and when this war broke out, I thought the time had come, but you would not permit me to enter the service . . . now I make one more appeal to you." The pleas worked, and Carpenter enlisted, spending most of the war fighting in Kentucky and Tennessee.

In that same year, in Tennessee, George and Ethie Eagleton faced anguishing decisions. Though not an abolitionist, George, a 30-year-old Presbyterian preacher, was unsympathetic to slavery and opposed to secession. But when his native state left the Union, George felt compelled to follow and enlisted in the 44th Tennessee Infantry. Ethie, his 26-year-old wife, despaired over the war, George's decision, and her own forlorn situation.

Mr. Eagleton's school dismissed—and what for? O my God, must I write it? He has enlisted in the service of his country—to war—the most unrighteous war that ever was brought on any nation that ever lived. Pres. Lincoln has done what no other Pres. ever dared to do—he has divided these once peaceful and happy United States. And Oh! the dreadful dark cloud that is now hanging over our country—'tis enough to sicken the heart of any one. . . . Mr. E. is gone. . . . What will become of me, left here without a home and relatives, a babe just nine months old and no George.

Both Carpenter and the Eagletons survived the war, but the conflict transformed each of their lives. Carpenter had difficulty settling down. Filled with bitter memories of the war years in Tennessee, the Eagletons moved to Arkansas. Ordinary people such as Carpenter and the Eagletons are historically anonymous. Yet their actions on the battlefield and behind the lines helped to shape the course of events, as their leaders realized, even if today we tend to remember only the famous and influential.

For thousands of Americans, from Lincoln and Davis to Carpenter and the Eagletons, war was both a profoundly personal and a major national event. Its impact reached far beyond the four years of hostilities. The war that was fought to conserve two political, social, and economic visions ended by changing familiar ways of political, social, and economic life in both North and South. War was a transforming force, both destructive and creative in its effect on the structure and social dynamics of society and on the lives of ordinary people. This theme underlies this chapter's analysis of the war's three stages: the initial months of preparation, the years of military stalemate between 1861 and 1865, and, finally, resolution.

ORGANIZING FOR WAR

The Confederate bombardment of Fort Sumter on April 12, 1861, and the surrender of Union troops the next day ended the uncertainty of the secession winter. The North's response to Fort Sumter was a virtual declaration of war as President Lincoln called for state militia volunteers to crush southern "insurrection." His action pushed several slave states (Virginia, North Carolina, Tennessee, Arkansas) off the fence and into the southern camp. Other states (Maryland, Kentucky, and Missouri) agonizingly debated which way to go. The "War Between the States" was now a reality.

Many Americans were unenthusiastic about the course of events. Southerners like George Eagleton only reluctantly followed Tennessee out of the Union. When he enlisted, he complained of "the disgraceful cowardice of many who were last winter for secession and war . . . but are now refusing self and means for the prosecution of war." Robert E. Lee of Virginia was equally hesitant to resign his federal commission but finally decided that he could not "raise [a] hand against . . . relatives . . . children . . . home." Whites living in the southern uplands (where blacks were few and slave holders were heartily disliked and envied), yeomen farmers in the Deep South (who owned no slaves), and many residents of border states were dismayed at secession and war. Many would eventually join the Union forces.

In the North, large numbers had supported neither the Republican party nor Lincoln. Irish immigrants who feared the competition of free black labor and southerners now living in Illinois, Indiana, and Ohio harbored misgivings about the war. Indeed, northern Democrats at first blamed Lincoln and the Republicans almost as much as the southern secessionists for the nation's crisis.

Nevertheless, the days following Fort Sumter and Lincoln's call for troops saw an outpouring of support on both sides, fueled in part by relief at decisive action, in part by patriotism and love of adventure, in part by unemployment. Northern blacks and even some southern freedman proclaimed themselves "ready to go forth and do battle," while whites like Carpenter enthusiastically flocked to enlist. In some places, workers were so eager to join up that trade unions collapsed. Sisters, wives, and mothers set to work making uniforms. A New Yorker, Jane Woolsey, described the drama of those early days "of terrible excitement."

> Outside the parlor windows the city is gay and brilliant with excited crowds, the incessant movement and music of marching regiments and all the thousands of flags, big and little, which suddenly came fluttering out of every window and door. . . . In our little circle of friends, one mother has just sent away an idolized son; another, two; another, four. . . . One sweet young wife is packing a regulation valise for her husband today, and doesn't let him see her cry.

The war fever produced so many volunteers that neither northern nor southern officials could handle the throng. Northern authorities turned aside offers from blacks to serve. Both sides sent thousands of

The First Michigan Regiment, mustering in Detroit to board trains to Washington, received an enthusiastic farewell.

white would-be soldiers home. The conviction that the conflict would rapidly come to a glorious conclusion fueled the eagerness to enlist. "We really did not think that there was going to be an actual war," remembered Mary Ward, a young Georgia woman. "We had an idea that when our soldiers got upon the ground and showed, unmistakably that they were really ready and willing to fight . . . the whole trouble would be declared at an end." Lincoln's call for 75,000 state militiamen for only 90 days of service and a similar enlistment term for Confederate soldiers supported the notion that the war would be short.

The Balance of Resources

Despite the bands, parades, cheers, and confidence, the oucome of the approaching civil conflict was much in doubt. Statistics of population and industrial development suggested that the North would win. But Great Britain had also enjoyed enormous statistical advantages in 1775 and yet had lost the War of American Independence. Many of the North's assets would become effective only with

time. The military stalemate in 1861 and 1862 proved that in the short term, North and South were evenly matched.

In the North, state militia volunteers called up in April 1861 supplemented the small federal army of 16,000. Probably a quarter of the regular army officers, however, had followed Lee's example and resigned. The Confederate army, authorized in March 1861, could count on the service of able military men like Robert E. Lee, Joseph E. Johnston, and Albert Sidney Johnston. Its president, Jefferson Davis, was an 1828 graduate of West Point.

The North's white population greatly exceeded that of the South, giving the appearance of a military advantage. Yet in the early days of war, the armies were not unevenly matched. Almost 187,000 Union troops bore arms in July 1861, while just over 112,000 men marched under Confederate colors. Even if numerically inferior, southerners believed that their population would prove the superior fighting force because it was more accustomed to outdoor life and the use of firearms. Many northerners feared that southerners were better natural warriors. True or not, slaves could carry on vital work behind the lines, freeing most adult white males to serve the Confederacy. Slavery, southerners thought, would prove to be "a tower of strength . . . at the present crisis."

The Union also enjoyed impressive economic advantages. In the North, 1 million workers in 110,000 manufacturing concerns produced goods valued at $1.5 billion annually, while 110,000 southern workers in 18,000 manufacturing concerns produced goods valued at only $155 million a year. The North had one factory for every southern industrial worker, and 70 percent of the nation's railroad tracks were in the North. Producing 17 times as much cotton cloth and woolen goods, 32 times as many firearms, and 20 times as much pig iron as the South, the North could clothe and arm troops and move them and their supplies on a scale that the South could not match. But to be effective, northern industrial resources had to be mobilized for war. That would take time, especially since the government did not intend to direct production. Furthermore, the depleted northern treasury made the government's first task the raising of funds to pay for military necessities.

The South traditionally depended on imported manufactured goods from the North and from Europe. If Lincoln cut off that trade, the South would face the enormous task of creating its industry almost from scratch. Moreover, its railroad system was organized to move cotton, not armies and supplies. Yet the agricultural South did have important resources of food, draft animals, and, of course, cotton, which southerners believed would secure British and French support. Finally, in choosing to wage a defensive war, the South could tap regional loyalty and would enjoy protected lines of supply and support. Union forces, embarked on an expensive war of conquest, their extended supply lines always vulnerable to attack, would be less mobile and secure than southern troops. The Union had to win a war of conquest and occupation. The South merely had to survive until its enemy tired and gave up.

The Border States

Uncertainty over the war's outcome and divided loyalties produced indecision in the border states. When the seven states of the Deep South seceded during the winter of 1860–1861, the border states adopted a wait-and-see attitude. Delaware identified

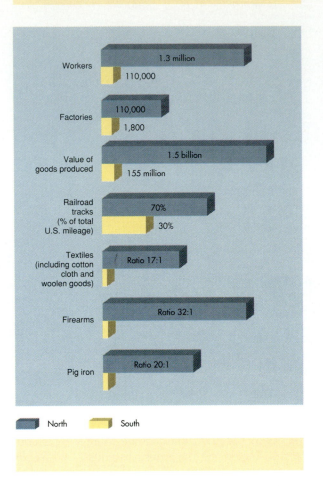

Resources for War: North versus South

	North	South
Workers	1.3 million	110,000
Factories	110,000	1,800
Value of goods produced	1.5 billion	155 million
Railroad tracks (% of total U.S. mileage)	70%	30%
Textiles (including cotton cloth and woolen goods)	Ratio 17:1	
Firearms	Ratio 32:1	
Pig iron	Ratio 20:1	

■ North   □ South

with the Union camp, but the others vacillated. Their decisions were critically important to both North and South.

The states of the Upper South could provide natural borders for the Confederacy along the Ohio River, access to its river traffic, and vital resources, wealth, and population. The major railroad link to the West ran through Maryland and western Virginia. Virginia boasted the South's largest ironworks, while Tennessee was the region's principal source of grain. Missouri provided the road to Kansas and the West and was strategically placed to control Mississippi River traffic. It was difficult to imagine the long- or short-term success of the confederacy without the border states.

For the North, every border state that elected to remain loyal was a psychological triumph for the idea of Union. Nor was the North indifferent to the

Secession of the Southern States

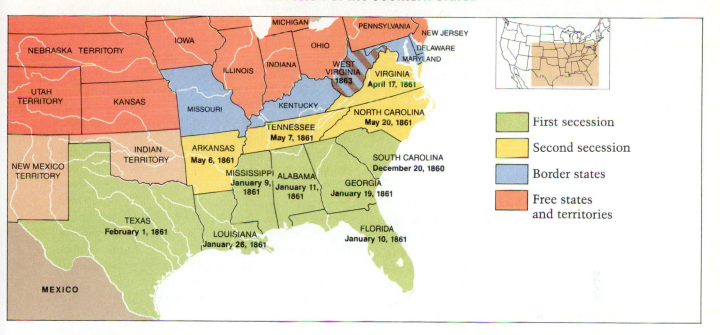

Legend:
- First secession (green)
- Second secession (yellow)
- Border states (blue)
- Free states and territories (red)

economic and strategic advantages of keeping the border states with the Union. Lincoln's call for troops precipitated decisions in several states, however. Between April 17 and May 20, 1861, Virginia, Arkansas, Tennessee, and North Carolina joined the Confederacy.

The significance of border-state loyalty was soon dramatized in Maryland. Slave-owning tobacco and wheat planters from the state's southern counties and eastern shore favored secession. Confederate enthusiasts abounded in Baltimore. But in the western and northern parts of the state, small farmers, often of German background, opposed slavery and supported the Union cause.

On the morning of April 19, the 6th Massachusetts Regiment arrived in Baltimore headed for Washington. Because the regiment had to change railroad lines, the soldiers set out across the city on foot and in horsecars. As they marched through the streets, a mob of some 10,000 southern sympathizers, flying Confederate flags, attacked them with paving stones, then bayonets and bullets. Finally, as a contemporary explained, "the patience of their commander was . . . exhausted. He cried out in a voice, which was heard even above the yells of the mob, 'Fire!' . . . A scene of bloody confusion followed." In the commotion, would-be secessionists burned the railroad bridges connecting Baltimore to the North and to the South. Washington

found itself cut off from the rest of the Union, an island in the middle of hostile territory.

Lincoln took stern measures to secure Maryland. The president agreed temporarily to route troops around Baltimore. In return, the governor called the state legislature into session at Frederick, a center of Union sentiment in western Maryland. This action and Lincoln's swift violation of civil rights damped secessionist enthusiasm. Hundreds of southern sympathizers, including 19 state legislators and Baltimore's mayor, were arrested and languished in prison without trial. Although the chief justice of the United States, Roger B. Taney, challenged the legality of the president's action and issued a writ of habeas corpus for the release of John Merryman, a southern supporter, Lincoln ignored him. A month later, Taney ruled in *Ex parte Merryman* that if the public's safety was endangered, only Congress had the right to suspend a writ of habeas corpus. By then, Lincoln had secured Maryland for the Union.

Though Lincoln's quick and harsh response ensured Maryland's loyalty, he was more cautious elsewhere. Above all, he had to deal with slavery prudently, for any hasty action would push border states into the waiting arms of the Confederacy. Thus when General John C. Frémont, in a burst of enthusiasm, issued an unauthorized declaration of emancipation in Missouri in August 1861, Lincoln revoked the order and recalled the general. As the president explained, he expected a chain reaction if certain key states left the Union. "I think to lose Kentucky is nearly the same as to lose the whole game. Kentucky gone, we cannot hold Missouri, nor, as I think, Maryland. These all against us, and the job on our hands is too large for us." In the end, after some fighting and much maneuvering, Kentucky and Missouri, like Maryland, stayed in the union.

Challenges of War

The tense weeks after Fort Sumter spilled over with unexpected challenges. Neither North nor South could handle the floods of volunteers. Both faced enormous organizational problems as they readied for war. In the South, a nation-state had to be created and its apparatus set in motion. Everything from a constitution and governmental departments to a flag and postage stamps had to be devised. As one onlooker observed, "The whole country was new. Everything was to be done—and to be made."

In February 1861, the original seceding states sent delegates to Montgomery, Alabama, to begin work on a provisional framework and to select a provisional president and vice-president. The delegates swiftly wrote a constitution, much like the federal constitution of 1787 except in its emphasis on the "sovereign and independent character" of the states and its explicit recognition of slavery. The provisional president, Jefferson Davis of Mississippi, tried to put together a geographically and politically balanced cabinet with a moderate face for the outside world. He succeeded in creating a balanced cabinet, but it had few of his friends and, more serious, few men of political stature. As time passed, it turned out to be unstable as well. In a four-year period, 14 men held six positions.

Davis's cabinet appointees faced the formidable challenge of creating government departments from scratch. They had to hire employees and initiate administrative procedures with woefully inadequate resources. The president's office was in a hotel parlor. The Confederate Treasury Department was housed in a room in an Alabama bank "without furniture of any kind; empty . . . of desks, tables, chairs or other appliances for the conduct of business." Treasury Secretary Christopher G. Memminger bought furniture with his own money; operations lurched forward in fits and starts. In those early

days, when an army captain came to the treasury with a warrant from Davis for blankets, he found only one clerk. After reading the warrant, the clerk offered the captain a few dollars of his own, explaining, "This, Captain, is all the money that I will certify as being in the Confederate Treasury at this moment." Other departments faced similar difficulties.

Inheriting the federal government, Lincoln never had to set up a postal system or decide whether laws passed before 1861 were valid. Without administrative experience, however, the new president, like his Confederate counterpart, faced organizational problems. Military officers and government clerks daily left the capital for the South. The treasury was empty. The Republicans had won their first presidential election, and floods of office seekers who had worked for Lincoln now thronged into the White House looking for rewards.

Nor could Lincoln, who did not know many of the "prominent men of the day," easily select a cabinet. Finally, he appointed important Republicans from different factions of the party to cabinet posts whether they agreed with him or not. Most were almost strangers to the president. Several scorned him as a bumbling backwoods politician. Treasury

Jefferson Davis, named provisional president of the Confederacy in 1861, faced the difficulties of setting up a new government while preparing for war.

Secretary Salmon P. Chase actually hoped to replace Lincoln as president in four years' time. Soon after the inauguration, Secretary of State William Seward sent Lincoln a memo condescendingly offering to oversee the formulation of presidential policy.

Lincoln and Davis

A number of Lincoln's early actions illustrated that he was no malleable backcountry bumbler. As his Illinois law partner, William Herndon, pointed out, Lincoln's "mind was tough—solid—knotty—gnarly, more or less like his body." In his reply to Seward's memo, the president firmly indicated that he intended to run his own administration. After Sumter, he swiftly called up the state militias, expanded the navy, and suspended habeas corpus. He ordered a naval blockade of the South and approved the expenditure of funds for military purposes, all without congressional sanction, since congress was not in session. As Lincoln told legislators later, "The dogmas of the quiet past are inadequate to the stormy present. . . . As our case is new, so must we think anew, and act anew . . . and then we shall save our country." This willingness to "think anew" was a valuable personal asset, even though some critics called his expansion of presidential power despotic.

By coincidence, Lincoln and his rival, Jefferson Davis, were born only 100 miles apart in Kentucky. However, the course of their lives diverged radically. Lincoln's father had migrated north and eked out a simple existence as a farmer in Indiana and Illinois. Abraham had only a rudimentary formal education and was largely self-taught. Davis's family, however, had moved south to Mississippi and become cotton planters. Davis grew up in comfortable circumstances, went to Transylvania University and West Point, and fought in the Mexican War before his election to the U.S. Senate. In recognition of his social, political, and economic prominence, Davis served as secretary of war under Franklin Pierce (1853–1857). Tall and distinguished-looking, he appeared every inch the aristocratic southerner.

Although Davis had not been eager to accept the presidency, he had loyally responded to the call of the provisional congress in 1861 and worked tirelessly as the chief executive of the Confederacy until the war's end. His wife, Varina, observed that "the President hardly takes time to eat his meals and works late at night." Some contemporaries suggested that Davis' inability to let subordinates han-

dle details explained this schedule. Others observed that he was sickly, reserved, humorless, too sensitive to criticism, and hard to get along with. But Davis, like Lincoln, found it necessary to "think anew." He reassured southerners in his inaugural address that his aims were conservative, "to preserve the Government of our fathers in spirit." Yet under the pressure of events, he moved toward creating a new kind of South.

CLASHING ON THE BATTLEFIELD, 1861–1862

The Civil War was the most brutal and destructive conflict in American history. Much of the bloodshed resulted from the application of the theories of Henri Jomini, a French military historian, to the battlefield. Jomini's ideas were enshrined in the curriculum of West Point, where many of the Union and Confederate officers had studied the art of war.

Jomini argued that an army seized victory by concentrating its infantry attack at the weakest point in the enemy's defenses. At the time Jomini wrote, this offensive strategy made military sense. The artillery, stationed well outside the range of enemy fire, could prepare the way for the infantry attack by bombarding enemy lines. By 1861, however, the range of rifles had increased from 100 yards to 500 yards, in part because the new French minié bullet traveled with tremendous velocity and accuracy. It was no longer possible to position the artillery close enough to the enemy to allow it to soften up the opposing line in preparation for the infantry charge. During the Civil War, then, enemy fire mowed down attacking infantry soldiers as they ran the 500 fatal yards to the front lines. Battles based on Jomini's theories produced a ghastly crop of dead men.

War in the East

The war's brutal character only gradually revealed itself. The Union commanding general, 70-year-old Winfield Scott, at first pressed for a cautious, long-term strategy, known as the Anaconda Plan. Scott proposed weakening the South gradually through blockades on land and at sea until the northern army was strong enough for the kill. The excited public, however, hungered for action and quick victory. So did Lincoln, who knew that the longer the war lasted, the more embittered the South and the

North would both become, making reunion ever more difficult. Under the cry of "Forward to Richmond!" 35,000 partially trained men led by General Irwin McDowell headed out from Washington in sweltering July weather.

On July 21, 1861, only 25 miles from the capital at Manassas Creek, or Bull Run, as it is also called, inexperienced northern troops confronted 25,000 raw Confederate soldiers commanded by Brigadier General P. G. T. Beauregard, a West Point classmate of McDowell's. Although sightseers, journalists, and politicians accompanied the Union troops, expecting only a Sunday outing, the encounter at Bull Run was no picnic. The course of battle swayed back and forth before the arrival of 2,300 fresh Confederate troops, brought by trains, decided the day. Union soldiers and sightseers fled toward Washington in terror and confusion. An English journalist, William Russell, described the troops as they poured into Washington on July 22:

> I saw a steady stream of men covered with mud, soaked through with rain . . . pouring irregularly, without any semblance of order, up Pennsylvania Avenue toward the Capitol. . . . I perceived they belonged to different regiments . . . mingled pell-mell together. . . . Hastily [I] . . . ran downstairs and asked an officer . . . a pale young man who looked exhausted to death and who had lost his sword . . . where the men were coming from. "Where from? Well, sir, I guess we're all coming out of Virginny as far as we can, and pretty well whipped too. . . . I know I'm going home. I've had enough of fighting to last my lifetime."

"Pretty well whipped" the Union forces certainly were. Yet inexperienced Confederate troops had lost their chance to turn the rout into the quick and decisive victory they sought. As General Joseph E. Johnston pointed out, his men were disorganized, confused by victory, and not well enough supplied with food to chase the Union army back toward Washington.

In many ways, the Battle of Bull Run was prophetic. Victory would be neither quick nor easy. As the disorganization and confusion of both sides suggested, the armies were unprofessional. And it was becoming obvious that bravado would not win the war. Then, too, both sides faced problems with short-term enlistments. Finally, logistic problems connected with mass armies plagued both sides. The Civil War put more men in the field than any previous American engagement. Supplying and moving so many men and ensuring adequate communication, especially during battle, were tasks of

Realizing the benefits of an early victory, Lincoln (center) urged his generals to move into action as soon as troops had received the most basic training.

an unprecedented kind. It was hardly surprising that the armies floundered trying to meet these logistic challenges.

Robert Allston, the prominent South Carolina rice planter, viewed the battlefield at Bull Run and decided it had been a "glorious tho bloody" day. For the Union, however, the loss at Bull Run was sobering. Replacing McDowell with 34-year-old General George McClellan, Lincoln began his search for a northern commander capable of winning the war. McClellan, formerly an army engineer, confronted the task of transforming the Army of the Potomac into a fighting force. Short-term militias went home. When Scott retired in the fall of 1861, McClellan became general in chief of the Union armies.

McClellan had considerable organizational ability but no desire to be a daring leader on the battlefield. Convinced that the North must combine military victory with efforts to persuade the South to return to the Union, he sought to avoid unnecessary and embittering loss of life and property. He intended to win the war "by maneuvering rather than fighting."

In March 1862, pushed by an impatient Lincoln, McClellan finally led his army of 130,000 toward Richmond, now the Confederate capital. By late June, his army was close enough to hear Richmond's church bells pealing. But just as it seemed that victory was within grasp, Lee counterattacked and slowly drove the Union forces away from the city. Finally, orders came from Washington: Abandon the Peninsula campaign.

Other Union defeats followed in 1862 as commanders came and went. In September, the South took the offensive with a bold invasion of Maryland. But after a costly defeat at Antietam, in which more than 5,000 soldiers were slaughtered and another 17,000 wounded on the grisliest day of the war, Lee withdrew his army to Virginia. Victory eluded both sides. The war in the East was stalemated.

War in the West

The early struggle in the East focused on Richmond, the Confederacy's capital and one of the South's most important railroad, industrial, and munitions centers. But the East was only one of three theaters of actions. Between the Appalachian Mountains and the Mississippi lay the western theater, the states of Kentucky, Tennessee, Mississippi, and Alabama. At its edge lay the Mississippi, with its vital river trade and its great port, New Orleans. Here both George Eagleton and Arthur Carpenter served. Beyond lay the trans-Mississippi West— Louisiana, Arkansas, Missouri, Texas, and the Great Plains—where Native American tribes joined the conflict on both sides.

In the western theater, the Union had two strategic objectives: the domination of Kentucky and eastern Tennessee, the avenues to the South and West, and control of the Mississippi River in order to split the South in two. Major campaigns sought strategic points along rivers and railroads.

It was in the western theater that Ulysses S. Grant rose to prominence. Working in his family's leather store in Illinois when the war broke out, Grant had lackluster military credentials. Although he had attended West Point and served creditably in the Mexican War, his career in the peacetime army was undistinguished and ended in resignation. But soon after Fort Sumter, Grant enlisted as a

Eastern Theater of the Civil War, 1861–1862

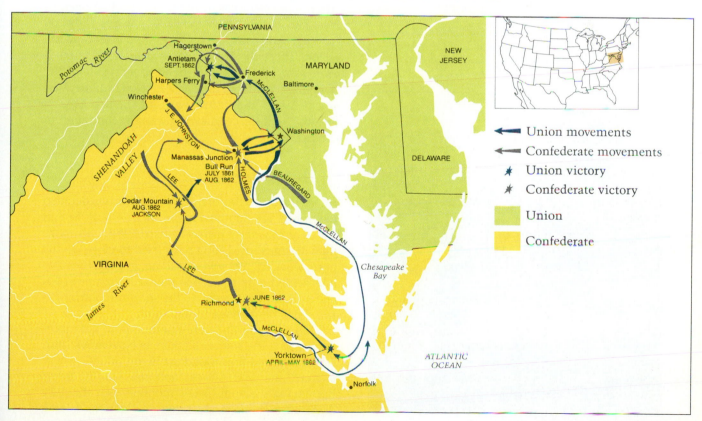

colonel in an Illinois militia regiment. Within two months, he was a brigadier general.

Grant's military genius consisted of an ability to see beyond individual battles to larger goals. In 1862, he realized that the Tennessee and Cumberland rivers were the paths for the successful invasion of Tennessee. A premature Confederate invasion of Kentucky allowed Grant to bring his forces into that state without arousing sharp local opposition. Assisted by gunboats, Grant was largely responsible for the capture of Fort Henry and Fort Donelson, key points on the rivers, in February 1862. His successes there raised fears among Confederate leaders that southern mountaineers, loyal to the Union, would rush to Grant's support.

Despite Grant's grasp of strategy, his army was nearly destroyed by a surprise Confederate attack at Shiloh Church in Tennessee. The North won this battle, but victory proved enormously costly. In that two-day engagement, the Union suffered over 13,000 casualties, while 10,000 Confederates lay dead or wounded. More men fell in this single battle than in the American Revolution, the War of 1812, and the Mexican War combined. Because neither army offered sufficient care on the battlefield, untreated wounds caused many of the deaths. A full day after the battle had ended, nine-tenths of the wounded

General Lee's 1862 invasion of Maryland ended with the battle of Antietam. Here the horse of a dead Confederate officer, stripped of saddle and bridle, lies dead on the battlefield.

still lay in the rain. Many died of exposure; others drowned in the downpour. Those who survived the weather had infected wounds by the time they received medical attention. Though more successful than efforts in the East, such devastating Union campaigns failed to bring decisive results. Western plans were never coordinated with eastern military activities. Victories there did not force the South to its knees.

The war in the trans-Mississippi West was a sporadic, far-flung struggle for the control of the manpower and natural resources of this vast area. California was one prize that lured both armies into the Southwest. Confederate troops from Texas held Albuquerque and Santa Fe briefly in 1862. Volunteer soldiers from the Colorado mining fields, joined by Mexican-Americans and other soldiers, drove the Texas Confederates from New Mexico. A Union force recruited in California arrived after the Confederates were gone. They spent the remainder of the Civil War years fighting the Apache and the Navajo and with brutal competence crushed both Native American nations.

Farther east was another prize, the Missouri River, which flowed into the Mississippi River, bordered Illinois, and affected military campaigns in Kentucky and Tennessee. Initially, Confederate troops were successful here, as they had been in New Mexico. But in March 1862, at Pea Ridge in northern Arkansas, the balance tilted in favor of the Union. There the Union forces defeated a Confederate army of 16,000 that included a brigade of Native Americans from the Five Civilized Nations. Missouri entered the Union camp for the first time in the war, and fierce guerrilla warfare continued in the region.

Naval Warfare

At the beginning of the war, Lincoln had decided to strangle the South with a naval blockade. But an effective blockade proved elusive. With no more than 33 ships, the Union navy tried to close up 189 ports along a 3,500-mile coastline. In 1861, the navy intercepted only about one blockade runner in ten and in 1862 one in eight. In the short run, the blockade did little damage to the South.

More successful were operations to gain footholds along the southern coast. In November 1861, a Union expedition took Port Royal Sound, where it freed the first slaves, and the nearby South Carolina sea islands. A few months later, the navy defeated a Confederate force on Roanoke Island,

North Carolina. By gaining fueling stations and other important coastal points, the navy increased the possibility of making the blockade effective. The Union's greatest naval triumph in the early war years was the capture of New Orleans in 1862. The loss of the South's greatest port seriously weakened the Confederacy. The success of this amphibious effort stimulated other joint attempts to cut the South in two.

The Confederate leadership, recognizing that the South could not match the Union fleet, concentrated on developing new weapons like torpedoes and formidable ironclad vessels, a concept already successfully tested by the French navy. Since the Union fleet consisted primarily of wooden ships, iron ships might literally crash through the Union blockade.

The *Merrimac* was one key to southern naval strategy. Originally a U.S. warship sunk as the federal navy hurriedly abandoned the Norfolk Navy Yard early in the war, the Confederates raised the vessel and covered it with heavy iron armor. Rechristened the *Virginia,* the ship steamed out of Norfolk in March 1862, heading directly for the Union ships blocking the harbor. Using its 1,500-pound ram and guns, the *Virginia* drove a third of the ships aground and destroyed the squadron's

Many deaths resulted from inadequate care for the wounded and sick soldiers of both armies. This wounded soldier receives water from a canteen rather than medical attention.

Trans-Mississippi Campaign of the Civil War

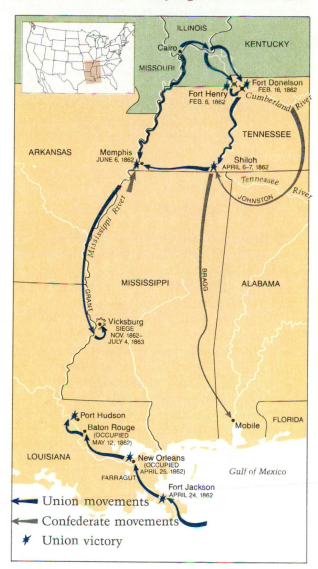

largest ships. Victory was short-lived. The next day, the *Virginia* confronted the *Monitor,* a newly completed Union iron vessel. Their duel was inconclusive, and the *Virginia* withdrew. It was burned during the evacuation of Norfolk that May. Southern attempts to buy ironclad ships abroad faded and with them southern hopes of evading the northern noose.

Though technological innovation failed to break the blockade, the Confederate navy's policy of harming northern commerce was more successful. Confederate raiders, many of them built in England wreaked havoc on northern shipping. In its two-year career, the raider *Alabama* destroyed 69 Union merchant vessels valued at more than $6 million.

But while such blows were costly to the North, they did not seriously damage its overall war effort.

Throughout the first two years of conflict, both sides achieved victories, but the war remained deadlocked. Although the South was far from being defeated, the North was as far from giving up or accepting southern independence. The costs of war, in manpower and supplies, far exceeded what either side had anticipated. The need to replace lost men and supplies thus loomed ever more serious at the end of 1862.

Cotton Diplomacy

Both sides in the Civil War realized that attitudes in Europe could be critical. European diplomatic recognition of the Confederacy would give the nation credibility in the eyes of the rest of the world. Furthermore, European loans and assistance might bring the South victory just as French and Dutch aid had helped the American colonies win their independence. If the European nations refused to recognize the South, however, the fiction of the Union was kept alive, undermining Confederate chances for long-term survival. The European powers, of course, consulted their own national interests. Neither England nor France, the two most important nations, wished to back the losing side. Nor did they wish to upset Europe's delicate balance of power by hasty intervention in American affairs. One by one, therefore, the European states declared a policy of neutrality.

Southerners were sure that cotton would be their trump card. English and French textile mills needed cotton, and southerners believed that their owners would eventually force government recognition of the Confederacy and an end to the North's blockade. But a glut of cotton in 1860 and 1861 left foreign mill owners oversupplied. As stockpiles dwindled, European industrialists found cotton in India and Egypt. The conviction that cotton was "the king who can shake the jewels in the crown of Queen Victoria" proved false.

Union Secretary of State Seward sought above all else to prevent diplomatic recognition of the Confederacy. Since the North had its own economic ties with Europe, the Union was not as disadvantaged as southerners thought. Seward daringly threatened Great Britain with war if it interfered in what he insisted was an internal matter. Some called his boldness reckless, even mad. Nevertheless, his policy succeeded. Even though England allowed the

Iron ships were an innovation used by both navies. Here the Confederate Virginia *(stubbornly called the* Merrimac *by northerners) confronts the Union* Monitor.

construction of Confederate raiders in its ports, it did not intervene in American affairs in 1861 or 1862. Nor did the other European powers. Unless the military situation changed dramatically, the Europeans were willing to sit on the sidelines.

Common Problems, Novel Solutions

As the conflict dragged on into 1863, unanticipated problems appeared in both the Union and the Confederacy, and leaders devised novel approaches to solve them. War acted as a catalyst for changes that no one could have imagined in the heady spring days of 1861.

The problem of fighting a long war was partly monetary. Both treasuries had been empty initially, and the war proved extraordinarily expensive. Neither side considered trying to finance the war by imposing direct taxes. Such an approach violated custom and risked alienating support. Nevertheless, each side was so starved for funds that it initiated taxation on a small scale. Ultimately taxes financed 21 percent of the North's war expenses (but only 1 percent of southern expenses). Both treasuries also tried borrowing. Northerners bought over $2 billion worth of bonds, but southerners proved reluctant to buy their government's bonds.

As in the American Revolution, the unwelcome solution was to print paper money. In August 1861, the Confederacy put into circulation $100 million in crudely engraved bills. Millions more followed the next year. Five months later, the Union issued $150 million in paper money, soon nicknamed "greenbacks" because of their color. Although financing the war with paper money was unexpected, the resulting inflation was not. Inflation was particularly troublesome in the Confederacy, but a "modest" 80 percent increase in food prices brought Union city families near starvation and contributed to urban unhappiness during the war.

Both sides confronted similar manpower problems as initial enthusiasm for the war evaporated. Soldiering, it turned out, was nothing like the militia parades and outings familar to most American males. Young men were shocked at the deadliness of diseases that accompanied the army wherever it went and unprepared for the boredom of camp life. As one North Carolina soldier explained, "If anyone wishes to become used to the crosses and trials of this life, let him enter camp life." None were prepared for the vast and impersonal destruction of the battlefield, which made a mockery of values like courage and honor. It was with anguish that Robert Carter of Massachusetts saw bodies tossed into trenches "with not a prayer, eulogy or tear to distinguish them from so many animals." Those in the service longed to go home. The swarm of volunteers disappeared. Rather than fill their military quotas from within, rich northern communities began offering bounties of $800 to $1,000 to outsiders who would join up.

Arthur Carpenter's letters give a good picture of life in the ranks and a young man's growing disillusionment with the war. As Carpenter's regiment moved into Kentucky and Tennessee in the winter of 1862, his enthusiasm for army life evaporated. "Soldiering in Kentucky and Tennessee," he complained, "is not so pretty as it was in Indianapolis. . . . We have been half starved, half frozen, and half drowned. The mud in Kentucky is awful." Soldiering often meant marching over rutted roads carrying 50 or 60 pounds of equipment with insufficient food, water, or supplies. One blanket was not enough in the winter. In the summer, stifling woolen uniforms attracted lice and other vermin. Poor food, bugs, inadequate sanitation, and exposure invited disease. Carpenter marched through Tennessee suffering from diarrhea and then fever. His regiment left him behind in a convalescent barracks in Louisville, which he fled as soon as he could. He feared the hospital at least as much as the sickness. "99 Surgeons out of a hundred," he wrote his parents, "would not know whether his patient had the horse distemper, lame toe, or any other disease."

Confederate soldiers, even less well supplied than their northern counterparts, complained similarly. In 1862, a Virginia captain described what General Lee called the best army "the world ever saw":

> During our forced marches and hard fights, the soldiers have been compelled to throw away their knapsacks and there is scarcely a private in the army who has a change of clothing of any kind. Hundreds of men are perfectly barefooted and there is no telling when they can be supplied with shoes.

In such circumstances, desertion was common. An estimated one of every nine men enlisting in the Confederate armies and one of every seven in the Union armies deserted.

As the manpower problems became critical, both governments resorted to the draft. Despite the sacrosanct notion of states' rights, the Confederate Congress passed the first conscription act in American history in March 1862. Four months later, the Union Congress also approved a draft measure. Both laws sought to encourage men already in the army to reenlist and to stimulate volunteers rather than to force men to serve. Ultimately, over 30 percent of the Confederate army and 6 percent of the Union forces were draftees.

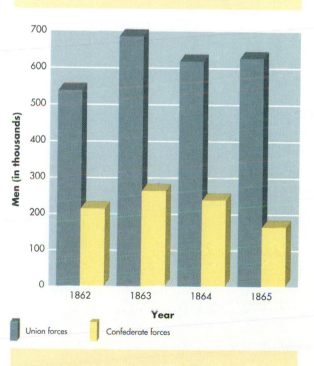

Men Present for Duty in the Civil War

The Confederacy relied more heavily on the draft than the Union did because the North's initial manpower pool was larger and growing. During the war, 180,000 foreigners of military age poured into the northern states. Some came specifically to claim bounties and fight. Immigrants made up at least 20 percent of the Union army.

Necessary though they were, draft laws were very unpopular. The first Confederate conscription declared all able-bodied men between 18 and 35 eligible for military service but allowed numerous exemptions and the purchase of substitutes. Critics complained that the provision entitling every planter with more than 20 slaves to one exemption from military service favored rich slave owners. Certainly the legislation fed class tension in the South and encouraged disloyalty and desertion among the poorer classes, particularly among southern mountaineers. The advice one woman shouted after her husband as he was dragged off to the army was hardly unique. "You desert again, quick as you kin. . . . Desert, Jake!" The law, as one southerner pointed out, "aroused a spirit of rebellion."

These advertisements from a Virginia newspaper include two for substitutes, indicating the advantages money provided for those who wished to avoid military service.

Northern legislation was neither more popular nor fair. The 1863 draft allowed the hiring of substitutes, and $300 bought an exemption from military service. Workers, already suffering from inflation, resented the ease with which moneyed citizens could avoid army duty. In July 1863, the resentment boiled over in New York City in the largest civil disturbance of the nineteenth century.

The three-day riot came only a month after a work stoppage on the New York waterfront. The process of selecting several thousand conscripts began on a weekend in early July. By Monday, workers opposed to the draft were parading through the streets. Several Irish members of the Black Joker Volunteer Fire Company whose names had been listed were determined to go further than peaceful protest by destroying draft records and the Enrollment Office. Events spun out of control as a mob also burned the armory, plundered the houses of the rich, and looted jewelry stores. Blacks, whom the Irish hated as economic competitors and the cause of the war, became special targets. Mobs beat and lynched blacks and even burned the Colored Orphan Asylum. More than 100 people died in the violence. There was much truth in the accusation that the war on both sides was a rich man's war but a poor man's fight.

Political Dissension, 1862

As the war continued, rumbles of dissension grew louder. On February 24, 1862, the Richmond *Examiner* summarized many southerners' frustration. "The Confederacy has had everything that was required for success but one, and that one thing it was and is supposed to possess more than anything else, namely Talent." As victory proved elusive, necessitating unpopular measures like the draft, criticism of Confederate leaders mounted. Jefferson Davis's vice-president, Alexander Stephens of Georgia, became one of the administration's bitterest accusers. Public criticism reflected private disapproval. Wrote one southerner to a friend, "Impeach Jeff Davis for incompetency & call a convention of the States. . . . West Point is death to us & sick Presidents & Generals are equally fatal."

Because the South had no party system, dissatisfaction with Davis and his handling of the war tended to be factional, petty, and personal. No party mechanism existed to channel or curb irresponsible criticism. Detractors rarely felt it necessary to offer programs in place of Davis's policies. Davis suffered personally from the carping comments of his detractors. More important, the Confederacy suffered. Without a party leader's traditional weapons and rewards, Davis had no mechanism to generate enthusiasm for his war policies.

Although Lincoln has since become a folk hero, at the time many northerners derided his performance and eagerly looked forward to a new president in 1864. Peace Democrats, called Copperheads, claimed that Lincoln betrayed the Constitution and that working-class Americans bore the brunt of his policy of conscription. Immigrant workers in eastern cities and those who lived in the southern parts of the Midwest had little sympathy for abolitionism or blacks, and they supported the antiwar stance of the Copperheads. Even Democrats favoring the war effort found Lincoln arbitrary and tyrannical. Fearing his expansion of presidential power, they also worried that extreme Republicans would push Lincoln into making the war a crusade for the abolition of slavery. Some Republicans judged Lincoln indecisive and inept. William Herndon, his former law partner, was one of the many who lashed out against the president. "Does he suppose he can crush—squelch out this huge rebellion by pop guns filled with rose water?" he asked indignantly. "He ought to hang somebody and get up a name for will or decision."

Republicans split gradually into two factions. The moderates favored a cautious approach toward winning the war. They feared the possible consequences of emancipating the slaves, confiscating Confederate property, or arming blacks. The radicals, however, urged Lincoln to make emancipation a wartime objective. They hoped for a victory that would revolutionize southern social and racial arrangements. The reduction of the congressional Republican majority in the fall elections of 1862 made it imperative that Lincoln not only listen to both factions but also to the Democratic opposition.

THE TIDE TURNS, 1863–1865

Hard political realities as well as Lincoln's sense of the public's mood help explain why he delayed an emancipation proclamation until 1863. Like congressional Democrats, many northerners supported a war for the Union but not one for emancipation. Not only did many, if not most, whites see blacks as inferior, but they also suspected that emancipation would trigger a massive influx of former slaves who would steal white men's jobs and political rights. Race riots in New York, Brooklyn, Phil-

adelphia, and Buffalo dramatized white attitudes. In Cincinnati, Irish dockworkers attacked blacks who were offering to work for less pay with the cry, "Let's clear out the niggers." Arthur Carpenter's evaluation of blacks was typical of many northern soldiers confronting blacks for the first time. In December 1861, he wrote to his parents:

> No one who has ever seen the nigger in all its glory on the southern plantations . . . will ever vote for emancipation. . . . If emancipation is to be the policy of the war (and I think it will not) I do not care how quick the country goes to pot. The negro never was intended to be equal with the white man.

The Emancipation Proclamation, 1863

If the president moved too fast on emancipation, he risked losing the allegiance of people like Carpenter, offending the border states, and increasing the Democrats' chances for political victory. Moreover, he had at first hoped that pro-Union sentiment would emerge in the South and compel its leaders to abandon their rebellion. But if Lincoln did not move at all, he would alienate abolitionists and lose the support of radical Republicans, which he could ill afford.

For these reasons, Lincoln proceeded cautiously. At first, he hoped the border states would take the initiative. In the early spring of 1862, he urged Congress to pass a joint resolution offering federal compensation to states beginning a "gradual abolishment of slavery." Border-state opposition killed the idea and indicated reluctance to believe, as Lincoln did, that the "friction and abrasion" of war would finally end slavery. Abolitionists and northern blacks, however, greeted Lincoln's proposal with "a thrill of joy."

That summer, Lincoln told his cabinet he intended to emancipate the slaves. Secretary of State Seward urged the president to delay any general proclamation until the North won a decisive military victory. Otherwise, he warned, Lincoln would appear to be urging racial insurrection behind the Confederate lines to compensate for northern military bungling.

Lincoln followed Seward's advice, using that summer and fall to prepare the North for the shift in the war's purpose. To counteract white racial fears of free blacks, he promoted various schemes for establishing free black colonies in Haiti and Panama. Seizing unexpected opportunities, he lay the groundwork for the proclamation itself. In August, Horace Greeley, the influential abolitionist editor of the New York *Tribune,* printed an open letter to Lincoln attacking him for failing to act on slavery. In his reply, Lincoln linked the idea of emancipation to military necessity. His primary goal, he wrote, was to save the Union:

> If I could save the Union without freeing *any* slave, I would do it; and if I could save it by freeing *all* the slaves, I would do it; and if I could do it by freeing some and leaving others alone, I would also do that. What I do about Slavery and the colored race, I do because I believe it helps to save this Union.

If Lincoln attacked slavery, then, it would only be because emancipation would save white lives, preserve the democratic process, and win the conflict for the Union.

In September 1862, the Union victory at Antietam gave Lincoln the opportunity to issue a preliminary emancipation proclamation. It stated that unless rebellious states (or parts of states in rebellion) returned to the Union by January 1, 1863, the president would declare their slaves "forever free." Although supposedly aimed at bringing the southern states back into the Union, Lincoln never expected the South to lay down arms after two years of bloodshed. Rather, he was preparing northerners to accept the eventuality of emancipation on the grounds of necessity. Frederick Douglass greeted the president's action with jubilation. "We shout for joy," he wrote, "that we live to record this righteous decree."

Not all northerners shared Douglass's joy. In fact, the September proclamation probably harmed Lincoln's party in the fall elections. As one Democratic ditty put it:

> "De Union!" used to be de cry—
> For dat we want it strong;
> But now de motto seems to be,
> "De nigger, right or wrong."

Although the elections of 1862 weakened the Republicans' grasp on the national government, they did not destroy it. Still, cautious cabinet members begged Lincoln to forget about emancipation. His refusal demonstrated his vision and humanity, as did his efforts to reduce racial fears. "Is it dreaded that the freed people will swarm forth and cover the whole land?" he asked. "Are they not already in the land? Will liberation make them any more numerous? Equally distributed among the whites of the whole country, and there would be but one colored to seven whites. Could the one, in any way, greatly disturb the other?"

Finally, on New Year's Day, 1863, Lincoln issued the final Emancipation Proclamation as he had promised. It was "an act of justice, warranted by the Constitution upon military necessity." Thus what had started as a war to save the Union now also became a struggle that, if victorious, would free the slaves. Yet the proclamation had no immediate impact on slavery. It affected only slaves living in the unconquered portions of the Confederacy. It was silent about slaves in the border states and in parts of the South already in northern hands. These limitations led Elizabeth Cady Stanton and Susan B. Anthony to establish the woman's Loyal National League to lobby Congress to emancipate all southern slaves.

Though the Emancipation Proclamation did not immediately liberate southern slaves from their masters, it had a tremendous symbolic importance. On New Year's Day, blacks gathered outside the White House to cheer the president and tell him that if he would "come out of that palace, they would hug him to death." They realized that the proclamation had changed the nature of the war. For the first time, the govenment had committed itself to freeing slaves. Jubilant blacks could only believe that the president's action heralded a new era for their race. More immediately, the proclamation sanctioned the policy of accepting blacks as soldiers into the military. Blacks also hoped that the news would reach southern slaves, encouraging them either to flee to Union lines or to subvert the southern war effort by refusing to work for their masters.

Diplomatic concerns also lay behind the Emancipation Proclamation. Lincoln and his advisers anticipated that the commitment to abolish slavery would favorably impress foreign powers. European statesmen, however, did not abandon their cautious stance toward the Union. The English prime minister called the proclamation "trash." But important segments of the English public who opposed slavery now came to regard any attempt to help the South as immoral. Foreigners could better understand and sympathize with a war to free the slaves than they could with a war to save the Union. In diplomacy, where image is so important, Lincoln had created a more attractive picture of the North. The Emancipation Proclamation became the North's symbolic call for human freedom.

Unanticipated Consequences of War

The Emancipation Proclamation was but another example of the war's surprising consequences. Innovation was necessary for victory. In the final two years of the war, both North and South experimented on the battlefields and behind the lines in desperate efforts to conclude the conflict successfully.

One of the Union's experiments involved using black troops for combat duty. Blacks had offered themselves as soldiers in 1861 but had been turned away. They were serving as cooks, laborers, teamsters, and carpenters in the army, however, and composed as much as a quarter of the navy. But as white casualties mounted, so did the interest in black service on the battlefield. The Union government allowed states to escape draft quotas if they enlisted enough volunteers and allowed them to count southern black enlistees on their state rosters. Northern governors grew increasingly interested in black military service. One piece of doggerel reflected changing attitudes:

> Some tell us 'tis a burnin' shame
> To make the naygers fight;
> And that the thrade of bein' kilt
> Belongs but to the white:
> But as for me, upon my soul!
> So liberal are we here.
> I'll let Sambo be murthered instead of myself
> On every day in the year.

Beyond white self-interest lay the promises of the Emancipation Proclamation and the desire to prove blacks' value to the Union. Black leaders like Frederick Douglass pressed for military service. "Once let the black man get upon his person the brass letter, U.S., let him get an eagle on his button, and a musket on his shoulder and bullets in his pocket," Douglass believed, "there is no power on earth that can deny that he has earned the right to citizenship." By the war's end, 186,000 blacks (10 percent of the army) had served the Union cause, 134,111 of them escapees from slave states.

Enrolling blacks in the Union army was an important step toward citizenship and acceptance of blacks by white society. But the black experience in the army highlighted some of the obstacles to racial acceptance. Black soldiers, usually led by white officers, were second-class soldiers for most of the war, receiving lower pay ($10 a month as compared to $13), poorer food, often more menial work, and fewer benefits than whites. "If we are good enough to fill up white men's places and fight, we should be treated then, in all respects, the same as the white man," one black soldier protested. Yet even whites who were working to equalize black and white pay often considered blacks inferior.

The army's racial experiment had mixed results. But the faithful and courageous service of black troops helped modify some of the most demeaning white racial stereotypes of blacks. The black soldiers, many of them former slaves, who conquered the South felt a sense of pride and dignity as they performed their duties. Wrote one, "We march through these fine thoroughfares where once the slave was forbid being out after nine P.M. . . . Negro soldiers!—with banners floating."

The faith in Jomini's military tactics was another wartime casualty. The infantry charge, so valued at the war's beginning, resulted in horrible carnage. As skepticism in the value of the charge increased, military leaders realized the importance of the strong defensive position. Although Confederate soldiers criticized General Lee as "King of Spades" when he first ordered them to construct earthworks, the epithet evolved into one of affection as it became obvious that earthworks saved lives. Union commanders followed suit. By the end of 1862, both armies dug defensive earthworks and trenches whenever they interrupted their march.

Black soldiers, some from southern states, were accepted for combat duty in the Union army as the war progressed. Here the First Carolina Volunteers gather to celebrate emancipation on January 1, 1863.

Gone, too, was the courtly idea that war involved only armies. Early in the war, many officers tried to protect civilians and their property. In the Richmond campaign, General McClellan actually posted guards to prevent stealing. Such concern for rebel property soon vanished, and along with it went chickens, corn, livestock, and, as George Eagleton noted with disgust, even the furnishings of churches, down to the binding of the Bible in the pulpit. Southern troops, on the few occasions when they came North, also lived off the land. War touched all of society, not just the battlefield participants.

Changing Military Strategies: 1863–1865

In the early war years, the South's military strategy combined defense with selective maneuvers. Until the summer of 1863, the strategy seemed to be succeeding, at least in the eastern theater. But an occasional victory over the invading northern army, such as at Fredericksburg in December 1862, did not change the course of the war. Realizing this, Lee reviewed his strategy and concluded, "There is nothing to be gained by this army remaining quietly on the defensive." Unless the South won victories in the North, he believed, it could not gain the peace it so desperately needed.

In the summer of 1863, Lee led the Confederate Army of Northern Virginia across the Potomac into Maryland and southern Pennsylvania. His goal was a victory that would threaten both Philadelphia and Washington. He even dreamed of capturing a northern city. Such spectacular feats would surely bring diplomatic recognition and might even force the North to sue for peace.

At Gettysburg on a hot and humid July 1, Lee came abruptly face to face with a Union army led by General George Meade. During three days of fighting, the fatal obsession with the infantry charge returned as Lee ordered costly assaults that probably lost him the battle. On July 3, Lee sent three divisions, about 15,000 men in all, against the Union center. The assault, known as Pickett's Charge, was as futile as it was gallant. At 700 yards, the Union artillery opened fire. One southern officer described the scene: "Pickett's division just seemed to melt away in the blue musketry smoke which now covered the hill. Nothing but stragglers came back."

Lee's dreams of victory died that hot week, with grave consequences for the southern cause. Fighting in the eastern theater dragged on for another year and a half, but Lee's Gettysburg losses were so heavy that he could never mount another southern offensive. Instead, the Confederacy committed itself to a desperate defensive struggle. Gettysburg marked the turn of the military tide in the East.

Despite the Gettysburg victory, Lincoln was dissatisfied with General Meade, who had failed to finish off Lee's demoralized and exhausted army as it retreated. His disappointment soon faded with news of a great victory at Vicksburg in the western theater. The commander, Ulysses S. Grant, would soon solve Lincoln's leadership problem. His July 4 triumph at Vicksburg was thus doubly significant. Vicksburg represented the completion of the Union campaign to gain control of the Mississippi River and to divide the South. Grant's successful capture of the city illustrated the boldness and flexibility that Lincoln sought in a commander.

By the summer of 1863, the military situation finally looked promising for the North. The Union controlled much of Arkansas, Louisiana, Mississippi, Missouri, Kentucky, and Tennessee. In March 1864, Lincoln recognized Grant as the commander to conclude the war and appointed him general in chief of the Union armies. Grant planned for victory within a year. "The art of war is simple enough," he reasoned. "Find out where your enemey is. Get at him as soon as you can. Strike at him as hard as you can, and keep moving on."

As an outsider to the prewar military establishment, Grant had no difficulty rejecting conventional military wisdom. "If men make war in slavish observance of rules, they will fail," he asserted. He sought no one decisive engagement. Rather, he proposed a grim campaign of annihilation, using the North's superior resources of men and supplies to wear down and defeat the South. Although Grant's plan entailed large casualties on both sides, he justified the strategy by arguing that "now the carnage was to be limited to a single year."

A campaign of annihilation involved the destruction not only of enemy armies but also of the resources that fueled the southern war effort. Although the idea of cutting the enemy off from needed supplies was implicit in the naval blockade, economic or "total" warfare was a relatively new and shocking idea. Grant, however, "regarded it as humane to both sides to protect the persons of those found at their homes, but to consume everything that could be used to support or supply armies." Following this policy, he set out after Lee's army in Virginia. General William Tecumseh Sherman, who

The Tide Turns, 1863–1865

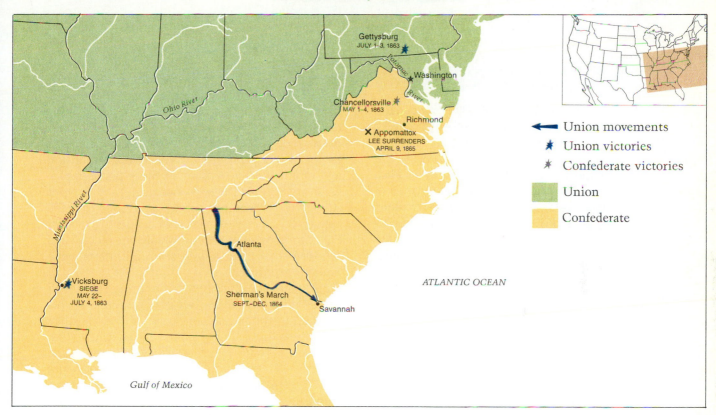

pursued General Joseph Johnston from Tennessee toward Atlanta, further refined this plan.

The war, Sherman believed, must also be waged in the minds of civilians. His desire was to make southerners "fear and dread" their foes. Therefore, his campaign to seize Atlanta and his march to Savannah spread destruction and terror. Ordered to forage "liberally" on the land, his army left desolation in its wake. "Reduction to poverty," Sherman asserted, "brings prayers for peace." A Georgia woman described in her diary the impact of Sherman's march:

> There was hardly a fence left standing all the way from Sparta to Gordon. The fields were trampled down and the road was lined with carcasses of horses, hogs and cattle that the invaders, unable either to consume or to carry away with them, had wantonly shot down, to starve out the people. . . . The dwellings that were standing all showed signs of pillage, and on every plantation we saw . . . charred remains.

This destruction, with its goal of total victory, showed once more how conflict produced the unexpected. The war that both North and South had hoped would be quick and relatively painless was ending after four long years with great cost to both sides. But the bitter nature of warfare during that final year threatened Lincoln's hopes for reconciliation.

CHANGES WROUGHT BY WAR

As bold new tactics emerged both on and off the battlefield, both governments took steps that changed their societies in surprising ways. Of the two, the South, which had left the Union to conserve a traditional way of life, experienced the more radical transformation.

A New South

The expansion of the central government's power in the South, starting with the passage of the 1862 Conscription Act, continued in the last years of the war. Secession grew out of the concept of states' rights, but, ironically, winning the war depended on central direction and control. Many southerners denounced Davis as a tyrant and a des-

RECOVERING THE PAST

PHOTOGRAPHY

The invention of photography in 1839 expanded the visual and imaginative world of nineteenth-century Americans. For the first time, Americans could visually record events in their own lives and see the images of people and incidents from far away. Photographs, of course, also expand the boundaries of the historian's world. As photographic techniques became simpler, more and more visual information about the nineteenth century was captured. Historians can use photographs to discover what nineteenth-century Americans wore, how they celebrated weddings and funerals, and what their families, houses, and cities looked like. Pictures of election campaigns, parades, strikes, and wars show the texture of public life. But historians can also study photographs, as they do paintings, to glean information about attitudes and norms. The choice of subjects, the way in which people and objects are arranged and grouped, and the relationships between people in photographs are all clues to the social and cultural values of nineteenth-century Americans.

Some knowledge of the early history of photography helps to place the visual evidence in the proper perspective. The earliest type of photograph, the daguerreotype, was not a print but the negative itself on a sheet of silver-plated copper. The first daguerreotypes required between 15 and 30 minutes for the proper exposure. This accounts for the stiff and formal quality of many of these photographs. Glass ambrotypes (negatives on glass) and tintypes (negatives on gray iron bases), developed after the daguerreotype, were easier and cheaper to produce. But both techniques produced only one picture and required what to us would seem an interminable time for exposure.

A major breakthrough came in the 1850s with the development of the wet-plate process. In this process, the photographer coated a glass negative with a sensitive solution, exposed the negative (that is, took the picture), then quickly developed it. The new procedure required a relatively short exposure time of perhaps five seconds out of doors and one minute inside. Action shots, however, were still not feasible. The entire process tied the photographer to the darkroom. Traveling photographers carried their darkrooms with them. The advantage of the wet-plate process was that it was possible to make

Mathew Brady, *Confederate Captives, Gettysburg.*

Mathew Brady, *Burial Party at Cold Harbor*.

many paper prints from one negative, opening new commercial vistas for professional photographers.

Mathew Brady, a fashionable Washington photographer, realizing that the camera was "the eye of history," asked Lincoln for permission to record the war with his camera. He and his team of photographers left about 8,000 glass negatives, currently stored in the Library of Congress and the National Archives, as their record of the Civil War. Shown here are two photographs, one of three Confederate soldiers captured at Gettysburg, the other of the battlefield of Cold Harbor in Virginia.

In the first photograph, study and describe the three soldiers. How are they posed? What kind of clothes are they wearing? What about their equipment? What seems to be their physical condition? Using this photograph as evidence, what might you conclude about the southern soldier—his equipment, uniforms, shoes? How well fed do the men in the picture appear? What attitudes are conveyed through their facial expressions and poses? Finally, what kind of mood was the northern photographer trying to create? What might a northern viewer con-

clude about the South's war effort after looking at this picture?

The second picture was taken in April 1865, about a year after the battle at Cold Harbor. In the background, you can see two Union soldiers digging graves. In the foreground are the grisly remains of the battle as shot by the photographer. What do you think is the intent of the photograph? The choice of subject matter shows clearly that photography reveals attitudes as well as facts. What attitude toward war and death is conveyed in this picture? Why is the burial party taking place a full year after the battle? What does this tell us about the nature of civil warfare? Notice that the soldiers ordered to undertake this ghastly chore are black, as was customary. What might this scene suggest about the experience of black soldiers in the Union army?

These photographs just begin to suggest what can be discovered from old photographs. Your local historical society and library probably have photograph collections available to you. In addition, at home or in a relative's attic you may find visual records of your own family and its history.

pot because he recognized the need for the central government to take the lead. Despite the accusations, the Confederate Congress cooperated with him and established important precedents. In 1863, it enacted a comprehensive tax law and an impressment act that allowed government agents to requisition food, horses, wagons, and other necessary war materials, often for only about half their market price. These were prime examples of the central government's power to interfere with private property. Government impressment of slaves for war work in 1863 affected the very form of private property that had originally driven the South from the Union.

The Conscription Act of 1862 did not solve the Confederate army's manpower problems. By 1864, the southern armies were only a third the size of the Union forces. Hence in February 1864, an expanded conscription measure made all white males between the ages 17 and 50 subject to the draft. By 1865, the necessities of war had led to the unthinkable: arming slaves as soldiers. Black companies were recruited in Richmond and other southern towns. However, because the war soon ended, no blacks actually fought for the Confederacy. In a message sent to Congress in November 1964, Davis speculated on some of the issues involved in arming slaves. "Should a slave who had served his country" be retained in servitude, he wondered, "or should his emancipation be held out to him as a reward for faithful service, or should it be granted at once on the promise of such service . . . ?" The war fought by the South to preserve slavery ended in the contemplation of emancipation.

Southern agriculture also changed under the pressure of war. Earlier, the South had imported food from the North, concentrating on the production of staples such as cotton and tobacco for market. Now, more and more land was turned over to food crops. Some farmers voluntarily shifted crops, but others responded only to state laws reducing the acreage permitted for cotton and tobacco cultivation. These measures never succeeded in raising enough food to feed southerners adequately. But they contributed to a dramatic decline in the production of cotton, from 4.5 million bales in 1861 to 300,000 bales in 1864.

The South had always depended on imported manufactured goods. Even though some blockade runners were able to evade the Union ships, the noose tightened after 1862. The Confederacy could not, in any case, rely on blockade runners to arm and equip the army. Thus war triggered the expansion of military-related industries in the South. Here, too, the government played a crucial role. The war and navy offices directed industrial development, awarding contracts to private manufacturing firms like Richmond's Tredegar Iron Works and operating other factories themselves. The number of southerners working in industry rose dramatically. In 1861, the Tredegar Iron Works employed 700 workers; two years later, it employed 2,500, more than half of them black. The head of the Army Ordnance Bureau reflected on the amazing transformation. "Where three years ago we were not making a gun, pistol nor a sabre, no shot nor shell . . . we now make all these in quantities to meet the demands of our large armies." At the end of the war, the soldiers were better supplied with arms and munitions than with food.

Although the war did not transform the southern class structure, relations between the classes began to change. The pressures of the struggle undermined the solidarity of whites, which was based on racism and supposed political unanimity. Draft resistance and desertion reflected growing alienation from a war perceived as serving only the interests of upper-class plantation owners. More and more yeoman families suffered grinding poverty as the men went off to war and government officials and armies requisitioned needed resources. A poor farmer from Georgia, Harlan Fuller, explained his family's situation in the spring of 1864. Fuller was 50 but now eligible for the draft. "I am liable at any time to be taken away from my little crops leaving my family almost without provisions & no hope of making any crop atal. I have sent six sons to the war & now the seventh enrolled he being the last I have no help left atal." This new poverty was an ominous hint of the decline of the yeoman farming class in postwar years.

The Victorious North

Although changes in the South were more noticeable, the Union's government and economy also responded to the demands of war. Like Davis, Lincoln was accused of being a dictator. Although he rarely tried to control Congress, veto its legislation, or direct government departments, Lincoln did use executive power freely. He violated the writ of habeas corpus by suspending the civil rights of over 13,000 northerners, who languished in prison without trials; curbed the freedom of the press because of supposedly disloyal and inflammatory articles; established conscription; issued the Emancipation Proclamation; and removed army generals. Lincoln argued that this vast extension of presidential power was temporarily justified because, as president, he was responsible for defending and preserving the Constitution.

Many of the wartime changes in government proved more permanent than Lincoln had imagined. The financial necessities of war helped to revolutionize the country's banking system. Ever since Andrew Jackson's destruction of the Bank of the United States, state banks had served American financial needs. Treasury Secretary Chase found this banking system inadequate and chaotic and proposed to replace it. In 1863 and 1864, Congress passed banking acts that established a national currency issued by federally chartered banks and backed by government bonds. The country had a federal banking system once again.

The northern economy also changed under wartime demands. The need to feed soldiers and civilians stimulated the expansion of agriculture and new investment in farm machinery. With so many men off soldiering, farmers were at first short of labor. McCormick reapers, however, performed the work of four to six men, and farmers began to buy them. During the war, McCormick sold 165,000 of his machines. Northern farming, especially in the Midwest, was well on the way to becoming mechanized. Farmers not only succeeded in growing enough grain to feed civilians and soldiers but gathered a surplus to export as well.

The war also selectively stimulated manufacturing. Although it is easy to imagine that northern industry as a whole expanded during the Civil War, in fact the war retarded overall economic growth. War consumed rather than generated wealth. Between 1860 and 1870, the annual rate of increase in real manufacturing value added was only 2.3 percent, in contrast with 7.8 percent for the years between 1840 and 1860 and 6 percent for the period 1870 to 1900. Some important prewar industries, like cotton textiles, languished without a supply of southern cotton.

However, industries that produced for the war machine, especially those with advantages of scale, expanded and made large profits. Each year, the Union army required 1.5 million uniforms and 3 million pairs of shoes; the woolen and leather industries grew accordingly. Meatpackers and producers of iron, steel, and pocket watches all profited from wartime opportunities. Cincinnati was one city that flourished from supplying soldiers with everything from pork to soap and candles.

On the Home Front, 1861–1865

In numerous, less tangible ways, the war transformed northern and southern society. The very fact of conflict established a new perspective for most civilians. War news vied with local events for their attention. They read newspapers and national weekly magazines with a new eagerness. The use of the mails increased dramatically as they corresponded with faraway relatives and friends. Wrote one North Carolina woman, "I never liked to write letters before, but it is a pleasure as well as a relief now." Distant events became almost as real and vivid as those at home. The war helped to make Americans less parochial, integrating them into the larger world.

For some Americans, like John D. Rockefeller and Andrew Carnegie, war brought army contracts and unanticipated riches. The New York *Herald* reported that New York City had never been "so gay, . . . so crowded, so prosperous," as it was in March 1864. Residents of Cincinnati noted people who "became suddenly immensely wealthy, and in their fine equipages, with liveried servants, rolled in magnificence along the city streets." In the South, blockade runners made fortunes slipping luxury goods past Union ships.

For the majority of Americans, however, war meant deprivation. The war effort gobbled up a large part of each side's resources, and ultimately ordinary people suffered. To be sure, the demand for workers ended unemployment and changed employment patterns. Large numbers of women and blacks entered the work force, a phenomenon that would be repeated in all future American wars. But while work was easy to get and wages appeared to increase, real income actually declined. Inflation, especially destructive in the South, was largely to blame. By 1864, eggs sold in Richmond for $6 a dozen; butter brought $25 a pound. Strikes and union organizing pointed to working-class discontent.

Low wages compounded the problem of declining income and particularly harmed women workers. Often forced into the labor market because husbands could save little or nothing from small army stipends, army wives and other women took what pay they could get. As more women entered the work force, employers cut costs by slashing wages. In 1861, the Union government paid Philadelphia seamstresses 17 cents per shirt. At the height of inflation, three years later, the government reduced the piecework rate to 15 cents. Private employers paid even less, about 8 cents a shirt. Working women in the South fared no better. War may have brought prosperity to a few Americans, North and South, but for most it meant trying to survive on an inadequate income.

Economic dislocation caused by the war reduced the standard of living for civilians. Shortages and hardships were severe in the South, which bore the brunt of the fighting. Most white southerners did without food, manufactured goods, and medicine during the war. Farming families who had no slaves to help with work in the fields fared poorly. As one Georgia woman explained, "I can't manage a farm well enough [alone] to make a suporte." Conditions were most dismal in cities, where carts brought in vital supplies since trains were reserved for military use. Hunger was rampant. Food riots erupted in Richmond and other cities; crowds of hungry whites broke into stores to steal food. The very cleanliness of southern cities pointed to urban hunger. As one Richmond resident noted, everything was so "cleanly consumed that no garbage or filth can accumulate."

Thousands of southerners who fled as Union armies advanced suddenly found themselves homeless. "The country for miles around is filled with refugees," noted an army officer in 1862. "Every house is crowded and hundreds are living in churches, in barns and tents." Caught up in the effort of mere survival, worried about what had happened to homes and possessions left behind and whether anything would remain when they returned, these southerners must have wondered if the cause was worth their sacrifices. Life was probably just as agonizing for those who chose to stay put when Union troops arrived. Virginia Gray, an Arkansas woman, wrote in her diary of her fear of the "Feds" and the turmoil they caused when they suddenly appeared and then disappeared.

White flight also disrupted slave life. Even the arrival of Union forces could prove a mixed blessing. White soldiers were unknown quantities, and as Carpenter's letter suggested, they might be hostile to blacks whom they were supposed to be liberating. One slave described the upsetting arrival of the Yankees at his plantation in Arkansas: "Them folks stood round there all day. Killed hogs . . . killed cows. . . . Took all kinds of sugar and preserves. . . . Tore all the feathers out of the mattresses looking for money. Then they put Old Miss and her daughter in the kitchen to cooking." So frightened was this slave's mother that she hid in her bed, only to be roused by the lieutenant, who told her, "We ain't a-going to do you no hurt. . . . We are freeing you." But the next day, the Yanks were gone and the Confederates back. "Pa was 'fraid of both" and resolved the problem by hiding out in the cotton patch.

Newspaper engravings provided civilians with images of the conflict. This colored lithograph by Currier & Ives was produced a generation after the war, but it is very much like the journalistic images of the time. The picture shows a black regiment, the 54th Massachusetts, storming Fort Wagner, South Carolina.

Wartime Race Relations

The journal kept by Emily Harris in South Carolina conveys some of the character of life behind the lines. She revealed not only the predictable story of shortages, hardships, and the psychological burdens of those at home but also the subtle social changes the war stimulated. Emily and her husband David lived on a 500-acre farm with their seven young children and ten slaves. When David went to war, Emily had to manage the farm, even though David worried that she would be "much at a loss with the . . . farm and the negroes."

Emily's early entries establish two themes that persist for the years she kept her diary. She was worried about how David would survive the "privation and hardships" of army life and was also anxious about her own "load of responsibilities." Her December 1862 entry provides a poignant picture of a wife's thoughts. "All going well as far as I can judge but tonight it is raining and cold and a soldier's wife cannot be happy in bad weather and during a battle." The dozens of tasks she had to do depressed her. "I shall never get used to being left as the head of affairs," she wrote in January 1863. "I am not an independent woman nor ever shall be." As time passed and the war went badly, the dismal news and mounting list of casualties heightened her concern about David's safety.

Her relations with her slaves compounded Emily's problems. As so many southerners discovered, war transformed the master-slave relationship. Because Emily was not the master David had been, her slaves gradually began to take unaccustomed liberties. At Christmas in 1864, several left the farm without her permission; others stayed away longer than she allowed. "Old Will" boldly requested his freedom. Worse yet, she discovered that her slaves had helped three Yankees who had escaped from prison camp.

The master-slave relationship was crumbling, and Emily reported in her journal the consequences for whites. "It seems people are getting afraid of negroes." Although not admitting to fear, she revealed that she could no longer control the blacks, who were increasingly unwilling to play a subservient role.

Understanding what was at stake, slaves, in their own way, often worked for their freedom. Said one later, "Us slaves worked den when we felt like it, which wasn't often." Emily's journal entry for February 22 confessed "a painful necessity." "I am re-

duced," she said, "to the use of a stick but the negroes are becoming so impudent and disrespectful that I cannot bear it." A mere two weeks later she added, "The Negroes are all expecting to be set free very soon and it causes them to be very troublesom."

Similar scenes occurred throughout the South. Insubordination, refusal to work, and refusal to accept punishment marked the behavior of black slaves, especially those who worked as fieldhands. The thousands of blacks (probably 20 percent of all slaves) who fled toward Union lines after the early months of the war were proof of the changing nature of race relations and the harm slaves could do to the southern cause.

Women and the War

If Emily Harris's journal reveals that she was sometimes overwhelmed by her responsibilities and shocked by the changes in dealings with her slaves, it also illustrates how the war affected women's lives. Nineteenth-century ideology promoted women's domestic role and minimized their economic importance. But the war made it impossible for many women to live according to conventional norms of behavior. So many men on both sides had gone off to fight that women had to find jobs and had to carry on farming operations. During the war years, southern women who had no slaves to help with the farmwork and northern farm wives who labored without the assistance of husbands or sons carried new physical and emotional burdens.

Women also participated in numerous war-related activities. In both North and South, they entered government service in large numbers. In the North, hundreds of women became military nurses. Under the supervision of Drs. Emily and Elizabeth Blackwell; Dorothea Dix, superintendent of army nurses; and Clara Barton, northern women nursed the wounded and dying for low pay or even for none at all. They also attempted to improve hospital conditions by attacking red tape and bureaucracy. The diary of a volunteer, Harriet Whetten, revealed the activist attitude of many others:

I have never seen such a dirty disorganized place as the Hospital. The neglect of cleanliness is inexcusable. All sorts of filth, standing water, and the embalming house near the Hospital. . . . No time had to be lost. Miss Gill and I set the contrabands at work making beds & cleaning.

Although men largely staffed southern military hospitals, Confederate women also played an important part in caring for the sick and wounded in their homes and in makeshift hospitals behind the battle lines. Grim though the work was, many women felt that they were participating in the real world for the first time in their lives.

Women moved outside the domestic sphere in other forms of volunteer war work. Some women gained administrative experience in soldiers' aid societies and in the United States Sanitary Commission. Many others made bandages and clothes, put together packages for soldiers at the front, and helped army wives and disabled soldiers find jobs. Fund-raising activities realized substantial sums. By the end of the war, the Sanitary Commission had raised $50 million for medical supplies, nurses' salaries, and other wartime necessities.

Many of the changes women experienced during war years ended when peace returned. Jobs in industry and government disappeared when the men came to reclaim them. Women turned over the operation of farms to returning husbands. But for women whose men came home maimed or not at all, the work had not ended. Nor had the discrimination. Trying to pick up the threads of their former lives, they found it impossible to forget what they had done to help the war effort. At least some of them were sure they had equaled their men in courage and commitment.

The Election of 1864

In the North, the election of 1864 brought some of the transformations of wartime into the political arena. The Democrats, seeking to regain power by capitalizing on war weariness, nominated General George McClellan for president. The party proclaimed the war a failure and demanded an armistice with the South. During the campaign, Democrats accused Lincoln of arbitrarily expanding executive power and denounced sweeping economic measures such as the banking bills. Arguing that the president had transformed the war from one for Union into one for emancipation, they tried to inflame racial passions by insinuating that if the Republicans won, a fusion of blacks and whites would result.

Although Lincoln easily gained the Republican renomination because of his tight control over party machinery and patronage, his party did not unite behind him. Lincoln seemed to please no one. His veto of the radical reconstruction plan for the South, the Wade-Davis bill, led to cries of "usurpation." The Emancipation Proclamation did not sit well with conservatives. In August 1864, a gloomy Lincoln told his cabinet that he expected to lose the election. As late as September, some Republicans actually hoped to reconvene the convention and select another candidate.

Sherman's capture of Atlanta in September 1864 and the march through Georgia to Savannah helped swing voters to Lincoln. In the end, Republicans had no desire to see the Democrats oust their party. Lincoln won 55 percent of the popular vote and swept the electoral college.

Why the North Won

In the months after Lincoln's reelection, the war drew to an agonizing conclusion. Sherman moved north from Altanta to North Carolina, while Grant pummeled Lee's forces in Virginia. The losses Grant would sustain were staggering: 18,000 in the Battle of the Wilderness, over 8,000 at Spotsylvania, and another 12,000 at Cold Harbor. New recruits stepped forward to replace the dead. On April 9, 1865, Grant accepted Lee's surrender at Appomattox. Southern soldiers and officers were allowed to return home with their personal equipment after promising to remain there peaceably. The war was finally over.

Technically, the war was won on the battlefield and at sea. But Grant's military strategy succeeded because the Union's manpower and economic resources could survive staggering losses of men and equipment while the Confederacy's could not. As Union armies pushed back the borders of the Confederacy, the South lost control of territories essential for their war effort. Finally, naval strategy eventually paid off because the North could build enough ships to make its blockade work. In 1861, fully 90 percent of the blockade runners were slipping through the naval cordon. By the war's end, only half made it.

The South had taken tremendous steps toward meeting war needs. But despite the impressive growth of manufacturing and the increasing acreage devoted to foodstuffs, the southern army and the southern people were poorly fed and poorly clothed. As one civilian realized, "The question of bread and meat . . . is beginning to be regarded as a more serious one even than that of War." Women working alone or with disgruntled slaves on farms could not produce enough food. Worn-out farm equipment was not replaced. The government's impressment of slaves and animals cut production. The half million blacks who fled to Union lines also played their part in pulling the South down in defeat.

New industries could not meet the extraordinary demands of wartime, and advancing Union forces destroyed many of them. A Confederate officer in northern Virginia observed, "Many of our soldiers are thinly clothed and without shoes and in addition to this, very few of the infantry have tents. With this freezing weather, their sufferings are indescribable." Skimpy rations, only a third of a pound of meat for each soldier a day by 1864, weakened the Confederate force, whose trail was "traceable by the deposit of dysenteric stool" it left behind. By that time, the Union armies were so well supplied that soldiers often threw away heavy blankets and coats as they advanced.

The South's woefully inadequate transportation system also contributed to defeat. Primitive roads deteriorated and became all but impassable without repairs. The railroad system, geared to the needs of cotton, not war, was inefficient. When tracks wore out or were destroyed, they were not replaced. Rails were too heavy for blockade runners to bother with, and as the Confederate railroad coordinator observed in 1865, "Not a single bar of railroad iron has been rolled in the Confederacy since the war, nor can we hope to do better." Thus food intended for the army rotted awaiting shipment. Supplies were tied up in bottlenecks and soldiers went hungry. Food riots in southern cities pointed to the hunger, anger, and growing demoralization of civilians.

Damage to southern railroads, whether due to battle, sabotage, or simple wear and tear, could not be repaired. The transportation breakdown led to food riots in southern cities and contributed to the defeat of the Confederacy.

Ironically, measures the Confederacy took to win the war undermined its own war effort. Conscription, impressment, and taxes all contributed to resentment and sometimes open resistance. They fueled class tensions already strained by the poverty war brought to many yeoman farmers and led some of them to assist the invaders or to join the Union army. The many southern governors who refused to contribute men, money, and supplies on the scale Davis requested implicitly condoned disloyalty to the cause. The belief in states' rights and the sanctity of private property that gave birth to the Confederacy also helped kill it.

It is tempting to compare Lincoln and Davis as war leaders. There is no doubt that Lincoln's humanity, his awareness of the terrible costs of war, his determination to save the Union, and his eloquence set him apart as one of this country's most extraordinary presidents. Yet the men's personal characteristics were probably less important than the differences between the political and social systems of the two regions. Without the support of a party behind him, Davis failed to engender enthusiasm or loyalty. Even though the Republicans rarely united behind Lincoln, they uniformly wanted to keep the Democrats from office. Despite all the squabbles, Republicans tended to support Lincoln's policies in Congress and back in their home districts. Commanding considerable resources of patronage, Lincoln was able to line up federal, state, and local officials behind his party and administration.

Just as the northern political system provided Lincoln with more flexibility and support, its social system also proved more able to meet the war's extraordinary demands. Although both societies adopted innovations in an effort to secure victory, northerners were more cooperative, disciplined, and aggressive in meeting the organizational and production challenges of wartime. In the southern states, old attitudes, habits, and values impeded the war effort. Southern governors, wedded to states' rights, refused to cooperate with the Confederate government. North Carolina, the center of the southern textile industry, actually kept back most uniforms for its own regiments. At the war's end, 92,000 uniforms and thousands of blankets, shoes, and tents still lay in its warehouses. When Sherman approached Atlanta, Georgia's governor would not turn over the 10,000 men in the state army to Confederate commanders. Even slaveholders whose property had been the cause for secession resisted the impressment of their slaves for war work.

In the end, the Confederacy collapsed, exhausted and bleeding. Hungry soldiers received letters from their families revealing desperate situations at home. They worried and then slipped away. By December 1864, the Confederate desertion rate has passed 50 percent. Replacements could not be found. Farmers hid livestock and produce from tax collectors. Many southerners felt their cause was lost and resigned themselves to defeat. But some fought on till the end. One northerner described them as they surrendered at Appomattox:

> Before us in proud humiliation stood the embodiment of manhood: men whom neither toils and sufferings, nor the fact of death, nor disaster, nor hopelessness could bend from their resolve; standing before us now, thin, worn, and famished, but erect, and with eyes looking level into ours, waking memories that bound us together as no other bond.

The Costs of War

The long war was over, but the memories of that event would fester for years to come. About 3 million American men, a third of all free males between the ages of 15 and 59, had served in the army. Each would remember his own personal history of the war. For George Eagleton, who had worked in army field hospitals, the history was one of "Death and destruction! Blood! Blood! Agony! Death! Gaping flesh wounds, broken bones, amputations, bullet

Diseases in the Civil War	
Early diseases affecting soldiers	Childhood diseases like mumps, measles. Usually not fatal.
Later diseases affecting soldiers	Dysentery, typhoid, diarrhea, malaria, usually caused by bad food, water, and sanitation, exposure, or mosquitoes. Often fatal.

and bomb fragment extractions." Of all wars Americans have fought, none has been more deadly. The death rate during this war was over five times as great as the death rate during World War II. About 360,000 Union soldiers and another 258,000 Confederate soldiers died, about a third of them because their wounds were either improperly treated or not treated at all. Disease claimed more lives than combat. Despite the efforts of men like Eagleton and the women army nurses, hospitals could not handle the scores of wounded and dying. "Glory is not for the private soldier, such as die in the hospitals," reflected one Tennessee soldier, "being eat up with the deadly gangrene, and being imperfectly waited on."

Thousands upon thousands of men would be reminded of the human costs of war by the injuries they carried with them to the grave, by the missing limbs that marked them as Civil War veterans. About 275,000 on each side were maimed. Another 410,000

However much he may have wished for the homecoming, nearly every soldier found readjustment to civilian life after years on the march difficult.

(195,000 northerners and 215,000 southerners) would recall their time in wretchedly overcrowded and unsanitary prison camps. The lucky ones would remember only the dullness and boredom. The worst memory was of those who rotted in prison camps, such as Andersonville in Georgia, where 31,000 Union soldiers were confined. At the war's end, over 12,000 graves were counted there.

Some Americans found it hard to throw off wartime experiences and adjust to peace. As Arthur Carpenter's letters suggest, he gradually grew accustomed to army life. War provided him with a sense of purpose. When it was over, he felt aimless. A full year after the war's end, he wrote, "Camp life agrees with me better than any other." Many others had difficulty returning to civilian routines and finding a new focus for life. Even those who adjusted successfully discovered that they looked at life from a different perspective. The experience of fighting, of mixing with all sorts of people from many places, of traveling far from home had lifted former soldiers out of their familiar local world and widened their vision. Fighting the war made the concept of national union real.

An Uncertain Future

What, then, had the war accomplished? On the one hand, death and destruction. Physically, the war devastated the South. Historians have estimated a 43 percent decline in southern wealth during the war years, exclusive of the value of slaves. Great cities like Atlanta, Columbia, and Richmond lay in ruins. Fields lay weed-choked and uncultivated. Tools were worn out. A third or more of the South's stock of mules, horses, and swine had disappeared. Two-thirds of the railroads had been destroyed. Thousands were hungry, homeless, and bitter about their four years of what now appeared a useless sacrifice. Over 3 million slaves, a vast financial investment, were free.

On the other hand, the war had resolved the question of union and ended the debate over the relationship of the states to the federal government. During the war, Republicans seized the opportunity to pass legislation that would foster national union and economic growth: the Pacific Railroad Act of 1862, which set aside huge tracts of public land to finance the transcontinental railroad; the Homestead Act of 1862, which was to provide yeoman farmers cheaper and easier access to the public domain; the Morrill Act of 1862, which established support for agricultural (land-grant) colleges; and the banking acts of 1863 and 1864.

The war had also resolved the issue of slavery, the thorny problem that had so long plagued American life. Yet uncertainties outnumbered certainties. What would happen to the former slaves? When blacks had fled to Union lines during the war, commanders had not known what to do with them. Now the problem became even more pressing. Were blacks to have the same civil and political rights as whites? In the Union army, they had been second-class soldiers. The behavior of Union forces toward liberated blacks in the South showed how deep the stain of racism went. One white soldier, caught stealing a quilt by a former slave, shouted, "I'm fighting for $14 a month and the Union"—not to end slavery. Would blacks be given land, the means for economic independence? What would be their relations with their former owners?

What, indeed, would be the status of the conquered South in the nation? Should it be punished for the rebellion? Some people thought so. Should southerners keep their property? Some people thought not. There were clues to Lincoln's intentions. As early as December 1863, the president had announced a generous plan of reconciliation. He was willing to recognize the government of former Confederate states established by a group of citizens equal to 10 percent of those voting in 1860, as long as the group swore to support the Constitution and

Ruined buildings and mourning women were common sights in Richmond as the war came to an end. This photograph gives a vivid sense of the devastation of the South in 1865.

to accept the abolition of slavery. He began to restore state governments in three former Confederate states on that basis. But not all northerners agreed with his leniency, and the debate continued.

In his 1865 inaugural address, Lincoln urged Americans to harbor "malice towards none . . . and charity for all." "Let us strive," he urged, "to finish the work we are in; to bind up the nation's wounds . . . to do all which may achieve a just and lasting peace." Privately, the president said the same thing. Generosity and goodwill would pave the way for reconciliation. On April 14, he pressed the point home to his cabinet. His wish was to avoid persecution and bloodshed.

That same evening, only five days after the surrender at Appomattox, the president attended a play at Ford's Theatre. There, as one horrified eyewitness reported,

> a pistol was heard and a man . . . dressed in a black suit of clothes leaped onto the stage apparently from the President's box. He held in his right hand a dagger whose blade appeared about 10 inches long. . . . Every one leaped to his feet, and the cry of 'the President is assassinated' was heard—Getting where I could see into the President's box, I saw Mrs. Lincoln . . . in apparent anguish.

John Wilkes Booth, a southern sympathizer, had killed the president.

CONCLUSION

An Uncertain Future

As the war ended, many Americans grieved for the man whose decisions had so marked their lives for five years. "Strong men have wept tonight & the nation will mourn tomorrow," wrote one eyewitness to the assassination. Many more wept for friends and relations who had not survived the war but whose actions had in one way or another contributed to its outcome. Perhaps not all Americans realized how drastically the war had altered their lives, their futures, their nation. It was only as time passed that the war's impact became clear to them. And it was only with time that they recognized how many problems the war had left unsolved. It is to these years of Reconstruction that we turn next.

Recommended Reading

Good general introductions are Peter J. Parrish, The American Civil War *(1985); David Donald,* Liberty and Union *(1978); and James McPherson,* Battle Cry of Freedom: The Civil War Era *(1988). Careful studies of the Confederacy during the war include Clement Eaton,* A History of the Southern Confederacy *(1954); Emory M. Thomas,* The Confederate Nation, 1861–1865 *(1979); and Paul D. Escott,* After Secession: Jefferson Davis and the Failure of Confederate Nationalism *(1978). For economic matters, consult David Gilchrist and W. David Lewis, eds.,* Economic Change in the Civil War Era *(1965).*

The military aspects of the war can be followed in T. Harry Williams, The History of American Wars *(1981); Russell F. Weigley,* The American Way of War: A History of U.S. Military Strategy and Policy *(1973); and Richard E. Beringer, Herman Hattaway, Archer Jones, and William N. Still, Jr.,* Why the South Lost the Civil War *(1986). Michael Barton analyzes soldiers' diaries in* Goodmen: The Character of Civil War Soldiers *(1981), while Gerald F. Linderman shows the impact of war on soldiers' beliefs and values in* Embattled Courage: The Experience of Combat in the American Civil War *(1987). Other views of the war from the soldier's perspective include Bell Wiley's two* volumes, The Life of Johnny Reb (*1943*) and The Life of Billy Yank (*1952*), and Henry S. Commager, ed., The Blue and the Gray: The Story of the Civil War as Told by Participants, *2 vols.* (*1950*).

Eric Foner's essays, collected in Politics and Ideology in the Age of Civil War (*1980*), *are valuable for understanding the political context of the Civil War. Also helpful are David Donald,* Lincoln Reconsidered (*1966 ed.*); James Rawley, The Politics of Union: Northern Politics During the Civil War (*1974*), *and Joel Silbey,* A Respectable Minority: the Democratic Party in the Civil War Era (*1977*). *Cullom Davis and colleagues have edited a series of provocative essays on the Union's complex president,* The Public and Private Lincoln: Contemporary Perspectives (*1979*). *Also helpful is John L. Thomas, ed.,* Abraham Lincoln and the American Political Tradition (*1986*). *For a biography, see Stephen B. Oates,* With Malice Towards None: The Life of Abraham Lincoln (*1977*).

Benjamin Quarles studies southern blacks in The Negro in the Civil War (*1968 ed.*), *while Leon F. Litwack illuminates changing race relations in* Been in the Storm So Long: The Aftermath of Slavery (*1979*). *A good primary source is James M. McPherson, ed.,* The Negro's Civil War (*1965*). *The strength of white racism is portrayed in George M. Frederickson,* The Black Image in the White Mind (*1971*), *and in C. Vann Woodward,* American Counterpoint: Slavery and Racism in the North-South Dialogue (*1971*).

The experience of women is treated in Mary E. Massey's Bonnet Brigades (*1966*). *Although Mary Boykin Chesnut's diary was actually written after the war, her vivid account,* Mary Chesnut's Civil War (*1981*), *is well worth consulting. Southern Unionists are explored in Phillip Shaw Paludan's* Victims: A True Story of the Civil War (*1981*).

Novels about the Civil War include Stephen Crane, The Red Badge of Courage (*any ed.*), *and MacKinlay Kantor,* Andersonville (*1955*).

TIME LINE

1861 Lincoln calls up state militia and suspends habeas corpus
First Battle of Bull Run
Union blockades the South

1862 Battles at Shiloh, Bull Run, and Antietam
Monitor and *Virginia* battle
First black regiment authorized by Union
Union issues greenbacks
South institutes military draft
Pacific Railroad Act
Homestead Act
Morrill Land-Grant College Act

1863 Lincoln issues Emancipation Proclamation
Congress adopts military draft
Battles of Gettysburg and Vicksburg
Union Banking Act
Southern tax laws and impressment act
New York draft riots
Southern food riots

1864 Sherman's march through Georgia
Lincoln reelected
Union Banking Act

1865 Lee surrenders at Appomattox
Lincoln assassinated; Andrew Johnson becomes president
Congress passes Thirteenth Amendment, abolishing slavery

17

The Union Reconstructed

In April 1864, one year before Lincoln's assassination, Robert Allston died of pneumonia. His daughter, Elizabeth, was left with a "sense of terrible desolation and sorrow" as the Civil War raged around her, and she and her mother took over the affairs of their many rice plantations. With Yankee troops moving through coastal South Carolina in the late winter of 1864–1865, Elizabeth's sorrow turned to "terror" as Union soldiers arrived seeking liquor, firearms, and hidden valuables. The Allston women endured an insulting search and then fled. In a later raid, Yankee troops encouraged the Allston slaves to take furniture and other household goods from the Big Houses, some of which the blacks returned when the Yankees were gone. But before they left, the Union soldiers, in their role as liberators, gave the keys to the crop barns to the semifree slaves.

When the war was over, Adele Allston took an oath of allegiance to the United States and secured a written order commanding the blacks to relinquish these keys. She and Elizabeth made plans to return in the early summer of 1865 to resume control of the family plantations, thereby reestablishing white authority. She was assured that although the blacks had guns and were determined to have the means to a livelihood, "no outrage has been committed against the whites except in the matter of property." But property was the key issue. Possession of the keys to the barns, Elizabeth wrote, would be the "test case" of whether former masters or their former slaves would control land, labor and its fruits, and even subtle aspects of interpersonal relations.

Not without some fear, Adele and Elizabeth Allston rode up in a carriage to their former home, Nightingale Hall, to confront their ex-slaves. To their surprise, a pleasant reunion took place. The Allston women greeted the blacks by name, inquired after their children, and caught up on the affairs of those with whom they had lived closely for many years. A trusted black foreman handed over the keys to the barns. This harmonious scene was repeated elsewhere.

But at Guendalos, a plantation owned by a son absent during most of the war fighting with the Confederate army, the Allston women met a very different situation. As their carriage ar-

rived and moved slowly toward the crop barns, a defiant group of armed ex-slaves lined both sides of the road, following the carriage as it passed by. Tension grew when the carriage stopped. A former black driver, Uncle Jacob, was unsure whether to yield the keys to the barns full of rice and corn, put there by black labor. Mrs. Allston insisted. As Uncle Jacob hesitantly began to hand the keys to her, an angry young man shouted out: "Ef yu gie up de key, blood'll flow." Uncle Jacob slowly slipped the keys back into his pocket.

The tension increased as the blacks sang freedom songs and brandished hoes, pitchforks, and guns in an effort to discourage anyone from going to town for help. Two blacks, however, left the plantation to find some Union military officers to come settle the issue of the keys, most likely on the side of the Allstons. As Adele and Elizabeth waited, word finally arrived that the Union officers, who were difficult to locate, would no doubt be found the next day and would come to Guendalos. The Allstons spent the night safely, if restlessly, in their house. Early the next morning, they were awakened by a knock at the unlocked front door. Adele slowly opened the door, and there stood Uncle Jacob. Without a word, he gave her the keys.

The story of the keys reveals most of the essential human ingredients of the Reconstruction era. Despite defeat and surrender, southern whites were determined to resume control of both land and labor. Rebellion aside, the law, property titles, and federal enforcement were generally on the side of the original owners of the land. The Allston women were friendly to the blacks in a genuine but maternal way and insisted on the restoration of the deferential relationships that existed before the war. Adele and Elizabeth, in short, both feared and cared for their former slaves.

The black freedmen likewise revealed mixed feelings toward their former owners. At different plantations, they demonstrated a variety of emotions: anger, loyalty, love, resentment, and pride. Respect was paid to the person of the Allstons but not to their property and crops. The action of the blacks indicated that what they wanted was not revenge but economic independence and freedom.

In this encounter between former slaves and their mistresses, the role of the northern federal officials is most revealing. The Union soldiers, literally and symbolically, gave the keys of freedom to the blacks but did not stay around long enough to guarantee that freedom. Although encouraging the freedmen to plunder the master's house and take possession of the crops, in the crucial encounter northern officials had disappeared. Understanding the limits of northern help, Uncle Jacob handed the keys to land and liberty back to his former owner. The blacks at Guendalos knew that if they wanted to ensure their freedom, they had to do it themselves.

The goals of the groups at the Allston plantations were in conflict. The theme of this chapter is the story of what happened to people's various dreams as they sought to form new social, economic, and political relationships during Reconstruction.

For much of the twentieth century, under the influence of historians and Hollywood filmmakers, pro-southern, Reconstruction was seen as a disgraceful period in which vindictive northern Radical Republicans imposed a harsh rule of evil carpetbaggers, scalawags, and illiterate blacks on the helpless, defeated South. *Gone with the Wind* reflects this view. In 1935, the brilliant black scholar, W. E. B. Du Bois, challenged this interpretation, suggesting instead that an economic struggle over land and the exploitation of black workers was the crucial focus of Reconstruction. Other historians have shown the beginnings of biracial cooperation and political participation in some southern states and the eventual violent repression of the freedmen's dreams of land, schooling, and votes.

This chapter reflects this later interpretation, enriched by an awareness of the ambiguity of human motives and behavior. Amid devastation and divisions of class and race, Civil War the survivors sought to put their lives back together again. Victorious but variously motivated northern officials, defeated but defiant southern planters, and impoverished but hopeful black freedmen—all had strong needs and dreams. In no way could all fulfill their conflicting goals, yet each had to try. This situation guaranteed that the Reconstruction era would be divisive, leaving a mixed legacy of human gains and losses.

THE BITTERSWEET AFTERMATH OF WAR

"There are sad changes in store for both races," the daughter of a Georgia planter wrote in her diary early in the summer of 1865, adding, "I wonder the Yankees do not shudder to behold their work." In order to understand the bittersweet nature of Reconstruction, we must look at the state of the nation in the spring of 1865, shortly after the assassination of President Lincoln.

The United States in 1865

The "Union" was in a state of constitutional crisis in April 1865. The status of the 11 states of the former Confederate States of America was unclear. They had claimed the right to secede, were successful for a time, but finally had failed. The North had denied the South's constitutional right to secede but needed four years of civil war and over 600,000 deaths to win the point. Were the 11 states part of the Union or not? Lincoln's official position had been that the southern states had never left the Union, which was "constitutionally indestructible." As a result of their rebellion, they were only "out of their proper relation" with the United States. The president, therefore, as commander in chief, had the authority to decide on the basis for setting relations right and proper again.

Lincoln's congressional opponents argued that by declaring war on the Union, the Confederate states had broken their constitutional ties and reverted to a kind of prestatehood status like territories or "conquered provinces." Congress, there-

---

Conflicting Goals During Reconstruction

Victorious Northern ("Radical") Republicans

- Justify the war by remaking southern society in the image of the North
- Political but not physical or economic punishment of Confederate leaders
- Continue programs of economic progress begun during the war: high tariffs, railroad subsidies, national banking
- Maintain the Republican party in power
- Help the freedmen make the transition to full freedom by providing them with the tools of citizenship (suffrage) and equal economic opportunity

Northern Moderates (Republicans and Democrats)

- Speedy establishment of peace and order, reconciliation between North and South
- Leniency, amnesty, and merciful readmission of southern states to the Union
- Perpetuate the primacy of land ownership, free labor, market competition, and other capitalist values
- Local self-determination of economic and social issues, limited interference by the national government
- Limited support for black suffrage

Old Southern Planter Aristocracy (Ex-Confederates)

- Protection from black uprising and excessive freedom
- Amnesty, pardon, and restoration of confiscated lands
- Restore traditional plantation-based market-crop economy with blacks as cheap labor force
- Restore traditional political leaders in the states
- Restore traditional paternalistic race relations as basis of social order

New "Other South": Yeoman Farmers and Ex-Whigs (Unionists)

- Speedy establishment of peace and order, reconciliation between North and South
- Recognition of loyalty and economic value of yeoman farmers
- Create greater diversity in southern economy: capital investments in railroads, factories, and the diversification of agriculture
- Displace the planter aristocracy with new leaders drawn from new economic interests
- Limited rights and powers to freedmen; suffrage granted only to the educated few

Black Freedmen

- Physical protection from abuse and terror by local whites
- Economic independence through land ownership (40 acres and a mule) and equal access to trades
- Educational opportunity and the development of family and cultural bonds
- Equal civil rights and protection under the law
- Political participation through the right to vote

fore, which decided on the admission of new states, should resolve the constitutional issues and assert its authority over the reconstruction process. In this conflict between Congress and the president was a powerful struggle between two branches of the national government. As has happened during nearly every war, the executive branch took on broad powers necessary for rapid mobilization of resources and domestic security. Many people believed, however, that Lincoln went far beyond his constitutional authority. As soon as the war was over, Congress sought to reassert its authority, as it would do after every subsequent war.

In April 1865, the Republican party ruled victorious and virtually alone. Although less than a dozen years old, the Republicans had made immense achievements in the eyes of the northern public. They had won the war, preserved the Union, and freed the slaves. Moreover, they had enacted most of the old Federalist-Whig economic programs on behalf of free labor and free enterprise: a high protective tariff, a national banking system, broad use of the power to tax and to borrow and print money, generous federal appropriations for internal improvements, the Homestead Act for western farmers, and an act to establish land-grant colleges to teach agricultural and mechanical skills. Alexander Hamilton, John Quincy Adams, and Henry Clay might all have applauded. Despite these achievements, the Republican party was still an uneasy grouping of former Whigs, Know-Nothings, Unionist Democrats, and antislavery idealists.

The Democratic party, by contrast, was in shambles. Republicans depicted southern Democrats as rebels, murderers, and traitors, northern Democrats as weak-willed, disloyal, and opposed to economic growth and progress. Nevertheless, it had been politically important in 1864 for the Republicans to show that the war was a bipartisan effort. A Jacksonian Democrat and Unionist from Tennessee, the tactless Andrew Johnson, had therefore been nominated as Lincoln's vice-president. In April 1865, he headed the government.

The United States in the spring of 1865 was a picture of stark economic contrasts. Northern cities hummed with productive activity while southern cities lay in ruins. Northern factories pounded out railroad tracks and engines, steel, textiles, farm implements, and building materials. Southern factory chimneys stood silent above the rubble. Roadways and railroad tracks laced the North, while in the South railroads and roads lay in ruins. Southern financial institutions were bankrupt, while northern

The United States in 1865: Crisis at the End of the Civil War

- Military casualties
  360,000 Union soldiers dead
  260,000 Confederate soldiers dead
  620,000 Total dead
  375,000 seriously wounded and maimed
  995,000 casualties nationwide in a total male population of 15 million (nearly 1 in 15)
- Physical and economic crisis
  The South devastated, its railroads, industry, and some major cities in ruins, its fields and livestock wasted
- Constitutional crisis
  Eleven ex-Confederate states not a part of the Union, their status unclear and uncertain
- Political crisis
  Republican party (entirely of the North) dominant in Congress; a former Democratic slaveholder from Tennessee, Andrew Johnson, in the presidency
- Social crisis
  Nearly 4 million black freedmen throughout the South face challenges of survival and freedom, along with thousands of hungry demobilized white southern soldiers and displaced white families
- Psychological crisis
  Incalculable resentment, bitterness, anger, and despair throughout North and South

banks flourished. Northern farms, under increasing mechanization, were more productive than ever before, and free farmers took pride that they had amply fed the Union army and urban workers throughout the war. They saw the Union victory as evidence of the superiority of free over slave labor. By contrast, southern farms and plantations, especially those that had lain in the path of Sherman's march, were like a "howling waste." Said one resident, "The Yankees came through . . . and just tore up everything."

Despite pockets of relative wealth, the South was largely devastated as soldiers demobilized and returned home in April 1865. Rare was the family, North or South, that had not suffered a serious casualty in the war. Missing limbs and suffering from hunger (a half million southern whites faced starvation), the ragtag remains of the Confederate army experienced widespread sickness and social disorder as they traveled home. Yet, as a later southern writer, Wilbur Cash, explained, "If this war had smashed the Southern world, it had left the essential Southern mind and will . . . entirely unshaken." Many southerners wanted nothing less than to resist Reconstruction and restore their old world. Others, the minority who had remained quietly loyal to the Union, dreamed of a postwar period not of defiance and old values but of reconciliation and new ones.

Whatever the extremes of southern white attitudes, the dominant social reality in the spring of 1865 was that nearly 4 million former slaves were on their own, facing the challenges of freedom. After an initial reaction of joy and celebration, expressed in jubilee songs, the freedmen quickly became aware of their continuing dependence on former owners. A Mississippi woman stated the uncertainty of her new status this way:

> I used to think if I could be free I should be the happiest of anybody in the world. But when my master come to me, and says—Lizzie, you is free! it seems like I was in a kind of daze. And when I would wake up in the morning I would think to myself, Is I free? Hasn't I got to get up before day light and go into the field of work?

For Lizzie and 4 million other blacks, everything—and nothing—had changed.

Hopes Among Freedmen

Throughout the South in the summer of 1865, there were optimistic expectations in the old slave quarters. As Union soldiers marched through Richmond, prisoners in slave-trade jails chanted: "Slavery chain done broke at last! Gonna praise God till I die!" The slavery chain, however, was not broken all at once but link by link. After Union soldiers

Both white southerners and their former slaves suffered in the immediate aftermath of the Civil War, as illustrated by this engraving from **Frank Leslie's Illustrated Newspaper.**

swept through an area, Confederate troops would follow, or master and overseer would return, and the slaves learned not to rejoice too quickly or openly. "Every time a bunch of No'thern sojers would come through," recalled one slave, "they would tell us we was free and we'd begin celebratin'. Before we would get through somebody else would tell us to go back to work, and we would go." Another slave recalled celebrating emancipation "about twelve times" in one North Carolina county. So former slaves became cautious about what freedom meant.

Gradually, the freedmen began to express a vision of what life beyond bondage and the plantation might be like. The first thing they did to test the reality of freedom was to leave the plantation, if only for a few hours or days. "If I stay here I'll never know I am free," a South Carolina woman said, and off she went to work as a cook in a nearby town. Some former slaves cut their ties entirely, leaving cruel and kindly masters alike. Some returned to an earlier master, but others went to towns and cities for work and to find schools, churches, and association with other blacks, where they would be safe from whippings and retaliation.

Many freedmen left the plantation in search of members of their families. The quest for a missing spouse, parent, or child, sold away years before, was a powerful force in the first few months of emancipation. Advertisements detailing these sorrowful searches filled black newspapers. For those who found a spouse or who had been living together in slave marriages, freedom meant getting married legally. Wedding ceremonies involving many couples were common in the first months of emancipation. Legal marriage was important morally, but it also served such practical purposes as establishing the legitimacy of children and gaining access to land titles and other economic opportunities. Marriage also meant special burdens for black women who took on the now familiar double role as housekeeper and breadwinner. For many newly married blacks, however, the initial goal was to create a traditional family life, resulting in the widespread withdrawal of women from plantation field labor.

Another way in which freedmen demonstrated their new status was by choosing surnames; names associated with the concept of independence, such as Washington, were common. As an indication of the mixed feelings the freedmen had toward their former masters, some would adopt their master's name, while others would pick "any big name 'ceptin' their master's." Emancipation changed black

Many freed blacks, like these young people photographed in Richmond, Virginia, gravitated to urban centers for work or to find members of their family.

manners around whites as well. Masks were dropped, and old expressions of humility—tipping a hat, stepping aside, feigning happiness, addressing whites with titles of deference—were discarded. For the blacks, these were necessary symbolic expressions of selfhood; they proved that things were now different. To whites, these behaviors were seen as acts of "insolence," "insubordination," and "puttin' on airs."

However important were choosing names, dropping masks, moving around, getting married, and testing new rights, the primary goal for most freedmen was the acquisition of their own land. "All I want is to git to own fo' or five acres ob land, dat I can build me a little house on and call my home," a Mississippi black said. Only through economic independence, the traditional American goal of controlling one's own labor and land, could former slaves prove to themselves that emancipation was real.

During the war, some Union generals had placed liberated slaves in charge of confiscated and abandoned lands. In the Sea Islands off the coast of South Carolina and Georgia, blacks had been working 40-acre plots of land and harvesting their own crops for several years. Farther inland, most freedmen who received land were the former slaves of Cherokees and Creeks. Some blacks held title to these lands. Northern philanthropists had organized others to grow cotton for the Treasury Department to prove the superiority of free labor over slavery. In the Davis Bend section of Mississippi, thousands of ex-slaves worked 40-acre tracts on leased lands formerly owned by Jefferson Davis. In this highly successful experiment, they made profits sufficient to repay the government for initial costs, then lost the land to Davis's brother.

Many freedmen expected a new economic order as fair payment for their years of involuntary work on the land. "It's de white man's turn ter labor now," a black preacher in Florida told a group of fieldhands. Whites would no longer own all the land, he went on, "fur de Guverment is gwine ter gie ter ev'ry Nigger forty acres of lan' an' a mule." Other freedmen were willing to settle for less: One in Virginia offered to take only one acre of land—"Ef you make it de acre dat Marsa's house sets on." Another was more guarded, aware of how easy the power could shift back to white planters: "Gib us our own land and we take care ourselves; but widout land, de ole massas can hire us or starve us, as dey please." However cautiously expressed, the freedmen had every expectation, fed by the intensity of their dreams, that the promised "forty acres and a mule" was forthcoming. Once they obtained land, family unity, and education, they looked forward to civil rights and the vote.

The White South's Fearful Response

White southerners had equally mixed goals and high expectations at the war's end. Yeoman farmers and poor whites stood side by side with rich planters in bread lines as together they looked forward to the restoration of their land and livelihood. Suffering from "extreme want and destitution," as a Cherokee County, Georgia, resident put it, white southerners responded with feelings of outrage, loss, and injustice. "I tell you it is mighty hard," said one man, "for my pa paid his own money for our niggers; and that's not all they've robbed us of. They have taken our horses and cattle and sheep *and everything.*" Others felt the loss more personally, as former slaves they thought were faithful or for whom they felt great affection suddenly left. "Something dreadful has happened dear Diary," a Florida woman wrote in May 1865. "My dear black mammy has left us . . . I feel lost, I feel as if someone is dead in the house. Whatever will I do without my Mammy?"

A more dominant emotion than sorrow, however, was fear. The entire structure of southern society was shaken, and the semblance of racial peace and order that slavery had provided was shattered.

Many white southerners could hardly imagine a society without blacks in bondage. It was the basis not only of social order but of a life style the larger slaveholders, at least, had long regarded as the perfect model of gentility and civilization. Having lost control of all that was familiar and revered, whites feared everything from losing their cheap labor supply to having to sit next to blacks on trains.

The mildest of their fears was the inconvenience of doing various jobs and chores they had rarely done before, like housework. A Georgia woman, Eliza Andrews, complained that it seemed to her "a waste of time for people who are capable of doing something better to spend their time sweeping and dusting while scores of lazy negroes that are fit for nothing else are lying around idle." Worst yet was the "impudent and presumin' " new manners of former slaves, as a North Carolinian put it. Many worried that the rude behavior meant that blacks wanted social equality.

The worst fears of southern whites were rape and revenge. Impudence and pretensions of social equality, some thought, would lead to intermarriage, which in turn would produce mulattoes, "Africanization," and the destruction of the purity of the white race. The presence of black soldiers touched off fears of violence and revenge. Although demobilization occurred rapidly after Appomattox, a few black militia units remained in uniform, parading with guns in southern cities. Acts of violence by black soldiers against whites, however, were rare.

Believing that their world was turned upside down, the former planter aristocracy tried to set it right again. Their goal was to restore the old plantation order and appropriate racial relationships. The key to reestablishing white dominance were the "black codes" that state legislatures passed in the first year after the end of the war. Many of the codes granted freedmen the right to marry, sue and be sued, testify in court, and hold property. But these rights were qualified. Complicated passages in the codes explained under exactly what circumstances blacks could testify against whites or own property (mostly they could not) or exercise other rights of free persons. Some rights were denied, including racial intermarriage and the right to bear arms, possess alcoholic beverages, sit on trains except in baggage compartments, be on city streets at night, or congregate in large groups.

Many of the alleged rights guaranteed by the black codes—testimony in court, for example—were passed to induce the federal government to

The Promise of Land: 40 Acres

To All Whom It May Concern

Edisto Island, August 15th, 1865
George Owens, having selected for settlement forty acres of Land, on Theodore Belab's Place, pursuant to Special Field Orders, No. 15, Headquarters Military Division of the Mississippi, Savannah, Ga., Jan. 16, 1865; he has permission to hold and occupy the said Tract, subject to such regulations as may be established by proper authority; and all persons are prohibited from interfering with him in his possession of the same.

By command of
   R. SAXTON
      Brev't Maj. Gen.,
      Ass't. Comm.
      S.C., Ga., and Fla.

withdraw its remaining troops from the South. This was a crucial issue, for in many places marauding groups of whites were assaulting and terrorizing virtually defenseless freedmen. In one small district in Kentucky, for example, a government agent reported in 1865:

Twenty-three cases of severe and inhuman beating and whipping of men; four of beating and shooting; two of robbing and shooting; three of robbing; five men shot and killed; two shot and wounded; four beaten to death; one beaten and roasted; three women assaulted and ravished; four women beaten; two women tied up and whipped until insensible; two men and their families beaten and driven from their homes, and their property destroyed; two instances of burning of dwellings, and one of the inmates shot.

Freedmen clearly needed protection and the right to testify in court against whites.

For white planters, the violence was another sign of social disorder that could be eased only by restoring a plantation-based society. More significantly, they needed the freedmen's labor. The crucial provisions of the black codes were thus intended to regulate the freedmen's economic status. "Vagrancy" laws provided that any blacks not "lawfully employed," which usually meant by a white employer, could be arrested, jailed, fined, or hired out to a man who would assume responsibility for their debts and future behavior. The codes regulated the work contracts by which black laborers worked in the fields for white landowners, including severe penalties for leaving before the yearly contract was fulfilled and rules for proper behavior, attitude, and manners. Thus southern leaders sought to reestablish their dominance. Although thwarted in perpetuating slavery or even in a program for gradual emancipation, many southerners believed, like this Texan, that "we will be enabled to adopt a coercive system of labor." A Kentucky newspaper was more direct: "The tune . . . will not be 'forty acres and a mule,' but . . . 'work nigger or starve.'"

NATIONAL RECONSTRUCTION

The black codes passed by southern legislatures supported these intentions. The question facing the national government in 1865 was whether it would use its power to support the black codes and the reimposition of racial intimidation in the South or to uphold the newly sought rights of the freedmen. Would the federal government side with the democratic reform impulse in American history, which stressed human rights and liberty, or with the forces emphasizing property, order, and self-interest? Although the primary drama of Reconstruction took place in the conflict between white landowners and black freedmen over land and labor in the South,

the struggle over Reconstruction policy among politicians in Washington played a significant role in the local drama, as well as the next century of American history.

The Presidential Plan

After an initially tough stand calling for punishment of the defeated Confederates for "treason," President Johnson soon adopted a more lenient policy. On May 29, 1865, he issued two proclamations setting forth his reconstruction program. Like Lincoln, he maintained that the southern states had never left the Union. His first proclamation continued Lincoln's policies by offering "amnesty and pardon, with restoration of all rights of property" to all former Confederates who would take an oath of allegiance to the Constitution and the Union of the United States. There were exceptions: ex-Confederate government leaders and rich rebels whose taxable property was valued at over $20,000. In this latter exception Johnson revealed his old Jacksonian hostility to wealthy aristocratic planters and his preference for leadership by self-made yeoman farmers like himself. Any southerners not covered by the amnesty proclamation could, however, apply for special individual pardons, which Johnson granted to nearly all applicants. By the fall of 1865, only a handful remained unpardoned.

The black codes, widespread violence against freedmen, and President Johnson's veto of the Civil Rights Bill gave rise to the sardonic question "Slavery Is Dead?

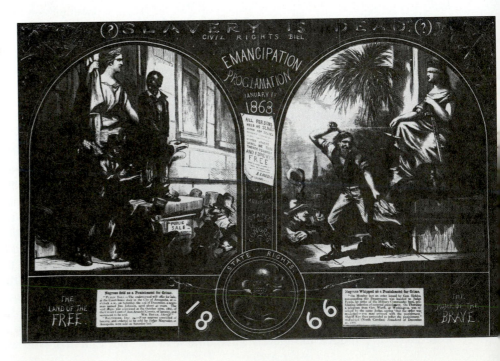

Johnson's second proclamation accepted the reconstructed government of North Carolina and laid out the steps by which other southern states could reestablish state governments. First, the president would appoint a provisional governor, who would call a state convention representing "that portion of the people of said State who are loyal to the United States." This included those who took the oath of allegiance or were otherwise pardoned. The convention should ratify the Thirteenth Amendment, which abolished slavery, void secession, repudiate all Confederate debts, and then elect new state officials and members of Congress.

Under this lenient plan, each of the southern states successfully completed reconstruction and sent newly elected members to the Congress that convened in December 1865. Southern voters defiantly elected dozens of former officers and legislators of the Confederacy, including a few not yet pardoned. Some state conventions hedged on ratifying the Thirteenth Amendment, and some asserted their right to compensation for the loss of slave property. No state convention provided for black suffrage, and most did nothing to guarantee civil rights, schooling, or economic protection for the freedmen.

Less than eight months after Appomattox, the southern states were back in the Union, the freedmen were returning to work for their former masters under annual contracts, and the new president seemed firmly in charge. Reconstruction of the southern states seemed to be over. But northern Republicans were far from satisfied with President Johnson's efforts. Georges Clemenceau, a young French newspaper reporter covering the war, wondered if the North, having made so many "painful sacrifices," would "let itself be tricked out of what it had spent so much trouble and perseverance to win."

Congressional Reconstruction

As they looked at the situation late in 1865, northern leaders painfully saw that almost none of their postwar goals—moral, political, or psychological—were being fulfilled. The South seemed far from reconstructed and was taking advantage of the president's program to restore the power of the prewar planter aristocracy. The freedmen were receiving neither equal citizenship nor economic independence. And the Republicans were not likely to maintain their political power and stay in office. Would the Democratic party and the South gain by postwar elections what they had been unable to achieve by civil war?

A song popular in the North in 1866 posed the question: "Who shall rule this American Nation?"—those who would betray their country and "murder the innocent freedmen" or those "loyal millions" who had shed their "blood in battle"? The answer was obvious. Congressional Republicans, led by Congressman Thaddeus Stevens of Pennsylvania and Senator Charles Sumner of Massachusetts, thus

Promised Land Restored to Whites

Richard H. Jenkins, an applicant for the restoration of his plantation on Wadmalaw Island, S. C., called "Rackett Hall," the same having been unoccupied during the past year and up to the 1st of Jan. 1866, except by one freedman who planted no crop, and being held by the Bureau of Refugees, Freedmen and Abandoned Lands, having conformed to the requirements of Circular No. 15 of said Bureau, dated Washington, D. C., Sept. 12, 1865, the aforesaid property is hereby restored to his possession.

. . . The Undersigned, Richard H. Jenkins, does hereby solemnly promise and engage, that he will secure to the Refugees and Freedmen now resident on his Wadmalaw Island Estate, the crops of the past year, harvested or unharvested; also, that the said Refugees and Freedmen shall be allowed to remain at their present houses or other homes on the island, so long as the responsible Refugees and Freedmen (embracing parents, guardians, and other natural protectors) shall enter into contracts, by leases or for wages, in terms satisfactory to the Supervising Board.

Also, that the undersigned will take the proper steps to enter into contracts with the above described responsible Refugees and Freedmen, the latter being required on their part to enter into said contracts on or before the 15th day of February, 1866, or surrender their right to remain on the said estate, it being understood that if they are unwilling to contract after the expiration of said period, the Supervising Board is to aid in getting them homes and employment elsewhere.

asserted their own policies for reconstructing the nation. Many southerners believed that the Republican Congress wanted to transform the South in the North's image and to punish it by providing numerous political and economic rights for the freedmen. Although some congressional leaders did indeed have strong punitive and political motivations, as well as a strong sense of responsibility to set the freedmen on their feet, the vast majority of Republicans were moderates. Although branded as "radicals," only for a brief period in 1866 and 1867 did "radical" rule prevail.

Rejecting Johnson's notion that the South had already been reconstructed, Congress asserted its constitutional authority to decide on its own membership and refused seats to the newly elected senators and representatives from the old Confederate states. Congress then established the Joint Committee on Reconstruction to investigate conditions in the South. Its report documented disorder and resistance and the appalling treatment and conditions of the freedmen. Even before the report was made final in 1866, Congress passed a civil rights bill to protect the fragile rights of the blacks and extended for two more years the Freedmen's Bureau, an agency providing emergency assistance at the end of the war. President Johnson vetoed both bills, arguing that they were unconstitutional and calling his congressional opponents "traitors."

Johnson's growing anger forced moderates into the radical camp, and Congress passed both bills over his veto. Both, however, were watered down by weakening the power of enforcement. Southern civil courts, therefore, regularly disallowed black testimony against whites, acquitted whites charged with violence against blacks, sentenced blacks to compulsory labor, and generally made discriminatory sentences for the same crimes. In this judicial climate, racial violence erupted with discouraging frequency.

In Memphis, for example, a race riot occurred in May 1866 that typified race relations during the Reconstruction period. In the months prior to the riot, local Irish policemen frequently unleashed unprovoked brutality on black Union soldiers stationed at nearby Fort Pickering. A Memphis newspaper suggested that "the negro can do the country more good in the cotton field than in the camp" and criticized what it called "the dirty, fanatical, niggerloving Radicals of this city" who thought otherwise.

In this inflamed atmosphere, a street brawl erupted between the police and some recently discharged but armed black soldiers. After some fighting and an exchange of gunfire, the soldiers went back to their fort. That night, white mobs, led by prominent local officials (one of whom urged the mob to "go ahead and kill the last damned one of the nigger race"), invaded the black section of the city. With the encouragement of the Memphis police, the mobs engaged in over 40 hours of terror, killing, beating, robbing, and raping virtually helpless residents and burning houses, schools, and churches. When it was over, 48 persons, all but two of them black, had died in the riot. The local Union army commander took his time intervening to restore order, arguing that his troops had "a large amount of public property to guard [and] hated Negroes too." A congressional inquiry found that in Memphis, blacks had "no protection from the law whatever."

A month later, Congress proposed to the states the ratification of the Fourteenth Amendment, the single most significant act of the Reconstruction era. The first section of the amendment sought to provide permanent constitutional protection of the civil rights of freedmen by defining them as citizens. States were prohibited from depriving "any person of life, liberty, or property, without due process of law," and all persons were guaranteed "the equal protection of the laws." In section 2, Congress granted black male suffrage in the South by making blacks whole persons eligible to vote (thus can-

A white mob burned this freedmen's school during the Memphis riot of May 1866.

celing the Constitution's "three-fifths" clause). States that denied this right would have their "basis of representation reduced" proportionally. Other sections of the amendment denied leaders of the Confederacy the right to hold national or state political office (except by act of Congress), repudiated the Confederate debt, and denied claims of compensation by former slave owners for their lost property.

President Johnson urged the southern states not to ratify the Fourteenth Amendment, and ten states immediately rejected it. Johnson then went on the campaign trail in the midterm election of 1866 to ask voters to throw out the radical Republicans. Vicious name calling and other low forms of electioneering marked this first political campaign since the war's end. The president exchanged insults with hecklers and lashed out against his opponents. Democrats in both the South and the North appealed openly to racial prejudice in calling for the defeat of those who had passed the Fourteenth Amendment. The nation would be "Africanized," they charged, with black equality threatening both the marketplace and the bedroom.

Republican campaigners, in turn, called Johnson a drunkard and a traitor. Bitter Civil War memories were revived as Republicans "waved the bloody shirt" in telling voters that Democrats were traitorous rebels or draft dodgers, while Republicans were patriotic saviors of the Union and courageous soldiers. Governor Oliver P. Morton of Indiana described the Democratic party as "a common sewer and loathsome receptacle, into which is emptied every element of treason . . . inhumanity and barbarism which has dishonored the age." Although the electorate was moved more by self-interest on other issues than by the persuasive power of these speeches, the result of the election was an overwhelming victory for the Republicans. The mandate was clear. The presidential plan of reconstruction in the seceded states had not worked, and Congress must suggest another.

Therefore, early in 1867, three Reconstruction Acts were passed. The first divided the southern states into five military districts in which military commanders had broad powers to maintain order and protect the rights of property and persons. Congress also defined a new process for readmitting a state. Qualified voters, which included blacks and excluded unreconstructed rebels, would elect delegates to state constitutional conventions, which then would write new constitutions guaranteeing black suffrage. After the new voters of the states had ratified the constitutions, elections would be held to choose governors and state legislatures. When a state ratified the Fourteenth Amendment, its representatives to Congress would be accepted, thus completing readmission to the Union.

The President Impeached

At the same time as it passed the Reconstruction Acts, Congress also approved bills to restrict the powers of the president and to establish the dominance of the legislative branch over the executive. The Tenure of Office Act, designed to protect the outspoken secretary of war, Edwin Stanton, from removal by Johnson, limited the president's appointment powers. Other measures restricted his power as commander in chief. Johnson behaved exactly as congressional Republicans had anticipated, vetoing the Reconstruction Acts, issuing orders to limit military commanders in the South, and removing cabinet and other government officials sympathetic to Congress's program. The House Judiciary Committee investigated, charging the president with "usurpations of power" and of acting in the "interests of the great criminals" who had led the southern rebellion. It was evident, however, that Johnson was guilty only of holding principles, policies, and prejudices different from those of congressional leaders, and moderate House Republicans defeated the impeachment resolutions.

In August 1867, Johnson finally dismissed Stanton and asked for Senate consent. When the Senate refused, the president ordered Stanton to surrender his office, which he refused, barricading himself inside. This time the House rushed impeachment resolutions to a vote, charging the president with "high crimes and misdemeanors" as detailed in 11 offenses while in office, mostly focusing on alleged violations of the Tenure of Office Act. The three-month trial in the Senate early in 1868 featured impassioned oratory. Radical Republicans declared the president "guilty of all, and infinitely more." Evidence was skimpy, however, that Johnson had committed any crime that justified his removal. With seven moderate Republicans joining Democrats against conviction, the effort to find the president guilty as charged fell short of the two-thirds majority required by a single vote.

The moderate Republicans, satisfied with the changes wrought by the Civil War, may have feared the consequences of removing Johnson, for the next man in line for the presidency, Senator Benjamin Wade of Ohio, was a leading radical Republican.

Wade had endorsed women's suffrage, rights for labor unions, and civil rights for blacks in both southern and northern states. As the moderate or regular Republicans gained strength in 1868 through their support of the presidential election winner, Ulysses S. Grant, radicalism lost much of its power within Republican ranks. Not for another 100 years would a president again face removal from office through impeachment.

Congressional Moderation

The impeachment crisis revealed that most Republicans were more interested in protecting themselves than the freedmen and in punishing Johnson rather than the South. Congress's political battle against the president was not matched by an idealistic resolve on behalf of the rights and welfare of the freedmen. As early as the state and local elections of 1867, it was clear that voters preferred moderate reconstruction policies. It is important to look not only at what Congress did during Reconstruction but also at what it did not do.

With the exception of Jefferson Davis, Congress did not imprison Confederate leaders, and only one person, the commander of the infamous Andersonville prison camp, was put to death. Congress did not insist on a long-term probationary period before southern states could be readmitted to the Union. It did not reorganize southern local governments. It did not mandate a national program of education for the 4 million ex-slaves. It did not confiscate and redistribute land to the freedmen, nor did it prevent President Johnson from taking land away from freedmen who had gained possessory titles during the war. It did not, except indirectly, provide economic help to black citizens.

What Congress did do, and that only reluctantly, was grant citizenship and suffrage to the freedmen. At the end of the Civil War, northerners were no more prepared than southerners to make blacks equal citizens. Between 1865 and 1869, several states held referendums proposing black suffrage. Voters in Kansas, Ohio, Michigan, Missouri, Wisconsin, Connecticut, New York, and the District of Columbia (by a vote of 6,521 to 35!) all turned the proposals down. Only in Iowa and Minnesota (on the third try, and then only by devious wording) did northern whites grant the vote to blacks.

Black suffrage gained support, however, after the election of 1868, when General Grant, a military hero regarded as invincible, barely won the popular vote in several states. Congressional Republicans, who had twice rejected a suffrage amendment, took another look at the idea as a way of adding grateful black votes to party rolls. After a bitterly contested fight, repeated in several state ratification contests, the Fifteenth Amendment, forbidding all states to deny the vote to anyone "on account of race, color, or previous condition of servitude," became part of the Constitution in 1870. A black preacher from Pittsburgh observed that "the Republican party had done the Negro good, but they were doing themselves good at the same time."

For political reasons, therefore, Congress gave blacks the vote but not the land, the opposite priority of what the freedmen wanted. Almost alone, Thaddeus Stevens argued that "forty acres . . . and a hut would be more valuable . . . than the . . . right to vote." But Congress never seriously considered his plan to confiscate the land of the "chief rebels" and to give a small portion of it, divided into 40-acre plots, to the freedmen, for it went against deeply held beliefs of the Republican party and the American people in the sacredness of private property. Moreover, the idea of a large propertyless class of cheap black laborers attracted northern business interests concerned with the development of southern industry and with investing in southern land.

Although most Americans, in the North as well as the South, opposed confiscation and did not want blacks to become independent landowners, Congress passed an alternative measure. Proposed by George Julian of Indiana, the Southern Homestead Act of 1866 made public lands available to blacks and loyal whites in five southern states. But the land was of poor quality and inaccessible. No transportation, tools, or seed were provided, and most blacks who might have wanted to take advantage of the offer had only until January 1, 1867, to claim their land. But that was nearly impossible for most because they were under contract with white employers until that date. Only about 4,000 black families even applied for the Homestead Act lands, and fewer than 20 percent of them saw their claims completed. The record of white claimants was not much better. Congressional moderation, therefore, left the freedmen economically weak as they faced the challenges of freedom.

Women and the Reconstruction Amendments

One casualty of the Fourteenth and Fifteenth amendments was the goodwill of the women who had been petitioning and campaigning for suffrage for two decades. They had hoped that grateful male legislators would recognize their support for the Union effort during the war and the suspension of their own demands in the interests of the more immediate concerns of preserving the Union, nursing the wounded, and emancipating the slaves. During the war, for example, the Woman's Loyal League, headed by Elizabeth Cady Stanton and Susan B. Anthony, gathered nearly 400,000 signatures on petitions asking Congress to pass the Thirteenth Amendment. They were therefore shocked to see the wording of the Fourteenth Amendment, which for the first time inserted the word *male* in the Constitution in referring to a citizen's right to vote.

Stanton and Anthony campaigned actively against the Fourteenth Amendment, despite the pleas of those who, like Frederick Douglass, had long supported woman suffrage and who also declared that this was "the Negro's hour." When the Fifteenth Amendment was proposed, they wondered why the word *sex* could not have been added to the "conditions" no longer a basis for denial of the vote. Largely abandoned by radical reconstructionists and abolitionist activists, they had few champions in Congress, however, and lost that battle too.

Disappointment over the suffrage issue was one of several reasons that led to a split in the women's movement in 1869. Anthony and Stanton continued their fight for a national amendment for woman suffrage and a long list of other rights, while other women concentrated their hopes on securing the vote on a state-by-state basis.

LIFE AFTER SLAVERY

Union army major George Reynolds boasted to a friend late in 1865 that in the area of Mississippi under his command, he had "kept the negroes at work, and in a good state of discipline." Clinton Fisk, a well-meaning white who helped to found a black college in Tennessee, told freedmen in 1866 that they could be "as free and as happy" working again for their "old master . . . as any where else in the world." For many blacks such pronouncements sounded familiar, reminding them of white preachers' exhortations during slavery to work hard and obey their masters. Ironically, though, both Fisk and Reynolds were agents of the Freedmen's Bureau, the crucial agency intended to ease the transition from slavery to freedom for the 4 million ex-slaves.

				Reconstruction Amendments				
Amendment	Substance	Date of Congressional Passage	Outcome of Ratification Process	Finally Implemented and Enforced
---	---	---	---	---
Thirteenth	Prohibited slavery in the United States	January 1865	Ratified by 27 states, including 8 southern states, by December 1865	Immediately, although economic freedom came by degrees
Fourteenth	1. Defined equal national citizenship 2. Reduced state representation in Congress proportional to number of disfranchised voters 3. Denied former Confederates the right to hold office	June 1866	Rejected by 12 southern and border states by February 1867; radicals made readmission depend on ratification; ratified in July 1868	Civil Rights Act of 1964
Fifteenth	Prohibited denial of vote because of race, color, or previous servitude	February 1869	Ratification by Virginia, Texas, Mississippi, and Georgia required for readmission; ratified in March 1870	Voting Rights Act of 1965

The Freedmen's Bureau

Never in American history has one small agency—underfinanced, understaffed, and under-supported—been given a harder task than was the Bureau of Freedmen, Refugees and Abandoned Lands. Its purposes and mixed successes symbolize, as well as those of any other institution, the tortuous course of Reconstruction.

The activities of the Freedmen's Bureau included issuing emergency rations of food and providing clothing and shelter to the homeless, hungry victims of the war; establishing medical care and hospital facilities; providing funds for transportation for the thousands of freedmen and white refugees dislocated by the war; helping blacks search for and put their families back together; and arranging for legal marriage ceremonies. The bureau also served as a friend in local civil courts to ensure that the freedmen got fair trials. Although not initially empowered to do so, the agency was responsible for the education of the ex-slaves. To bureau schools came many idealistic teachers from various northern Freedmen's Aid societies.

In addition to these many activities, the largest task of the Freedmen's Bureau was to serve as an employment agency, tending to the economic well-being of the blacks. This included settling them on abandoned lands and getting them started with tools, seed, and draft animals, as well as arranging work contracts with white landowners. As we shall see, in the area of work contracts, the Freedmen's Bureau served more to "reenslave" the freedmen as impoverished fieldworkers than to set them on their way as independent farmers.

Although some agents were idealistic young New Englanders eager to help slaves adjust to freedom, others were Union army officers more concerned with social order than social transformation. Working in a postwar climate of resentment and violence, Freedmen's Bureau agents were constantly accused of partisan Republican politics, corruption, and partiality to blacks by local white residents. But even the best-intentioned agents would have agreed with General O. O. Howard, commissioner of the bureau, in a belief in the traditional nineteenth-century American values of self-help, minimal government interference in the marketplace, the sanctity of private property, contractual obligations, and white superiority. The bureau's work served to uphold these values.

On a typical day, these overworked and underpaid agents would visit courts and schools in their district, supervise the signing of work contracts, and handle numerous complaints, most involving contract violations between whites and blacks or property and domestic disputes among blacks. One agent sent a man, who had complained of a severe beating, back to work with the advice, "Don't be sassy [and] don't be lazy when you've got work to do." Another, reflecting his growing frustrations, complained that the freedmen were "disrespectful and greatly in need of instruction." Although helpful in finding work for the freedmen, more often than not the agents found themselves defending white landowners by telling the blacks to obey orders, to trust their employers, and to sign and live by disadvantageous contracts.

Despite mounting pressures to support white landowners, personal frustrations, and even threats on their lives, the agents accomplished a great deal. In little more than two years, the Freedmen's Bureau issued 20 million rations (nearly one-third to poor whites), reunited families and resettled some 30,000 displaced war refugees, treated some 450,000 cases of illness and injury, built 40 hospitals and hundreds of schools, provided books, tools, and furnishings—and even some land—to the freedmen, and occasionally protected their economic and civil rights. Black historian W. E. B. Du Bois wrote an epitaph for the bureau that might stand for the whole of Reconstruction: "In a time of perfect calm, amid willing neighbors and streaming wealth," he wrote, it "would have been a herculean task" for the bureau to fulfill its many purposes. But in the midst of hunger, sorrow, spite, suspicion, hate, and cruelty, "the work of any instrument of social regeneration was . . . foredoomed to failure."

The Freedmen's Bureau had fewer resources in relation to its purpose than any agency in the nation's history. Harper's Weekly published this engraving of freemen lining up for aid in Memphis in 1866.

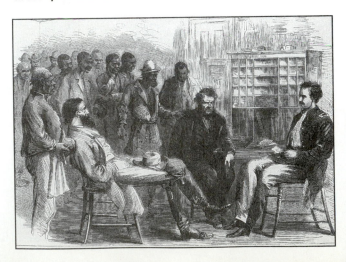

Economic Freedom by Degrees

The economic failures of the Freedmen's Bureau, symbolic of the entire congressional program, forced the freedmen into a new economic dependency on their former masters. Although the planter class did not lose its economic and social power in the postwar years, the character of southern agriculture went through some major changes. First, a land-intensive system replaced the labor intensity of slavery. Land ownership was concentrated into fewer and even larger holdings than before the Civil War. From South Carolina to Louisiana, the wealthiest tenth of the population owned about 60 percent of the real estate in the 1870s. Second, these large planters increasingly concentrated on one crop, usually cotton, and were tied into the international market. This resulted in a steady drop in food production (both grains and livestock) in the postwar period. Third, reliance on one-crop farming meant that a new credit system emerged whereby most farmers, black and white, depended on local merchants (often in competition with large landowners) for renting seed, farm implements and animals, provisions, housing, and land. These changes affected race relations and class tensions among whites.

This new system, however, took a few years to develop after emancipation. At first, most freedmen signed contracts with white landowners and worked in gangs in the fields as farm laborers very much as during slavery. Watched over by superintendents, who still used the lash, they toiled from sunrise to sunset for a meager wage and a monthly allotment of bacon and meal. All members of the family had to work to receive their rations. The freedmen resented this new form of semiservitude, preferring small plots of land of their own to grow vegetables and grains. Moreover, they wanted to be able to send their children to school and insisted on "no more outdoor work" for women. What the freedmen wanted, a Georgia planter correctly observed, was "to get away from all overseers, to hire or purchase land, and work for themselves."

Many blacks therefore broke contracts, ran away, engaged in work slowdowns or strikes, burned barns, and otherwise expressed their displeasure with the contract labor system. One white landowner expressed his frustration over having "to bargain and haggle with our servants about wages." In the Sea Islands and rice-growing regions of coastal South Carolina and Georgia, where slaves had long held a degree of autonomy, resistance was especially strong. On the Heyward plantations, near those of the Allstons, the freedmen "refuse work at any price," a Freedman's Bureau agent reported, and the women "wish to stay in the house or the garden all the time." The former Allston slaves also refused to sign their contracts, even when offered livestock and other favors, and in 1869, Adele Allston was forced to sell much of her vast landholdings.

Blacks' insistence on autonomy and land of their own was the major impetus for the change from the contract system to tenancy and sharecropping. As a South Carolina freedman put it, "If a man got to go crost de riber, and he can't git a boat, he take a log. If I can't own de land, I'll hire or lease land, but I won't contract." Families would hitch a team of mules to their old slave cabin to drag it to their assigned plot of land as far away from the Big House as possible. The sharecroppers were given seed, fertilizer, farm implements, and all necessary food and clothing to take care of their families. In return, the landlord (or a local merchant) told them what to grow and how much and took a share—usually half—of the harvest. The half retained by the cropper, however, was usually needed to pay for goods bought on credit (at huge interest rates) at the landlord's store. Thus the sharecroppers were semiautonomous but remained tied to the landlord's will for economic survival.

Under the tenant system, farmers had only slightly more independence. In advance of the harvest, a tenant farmer promised to sell his crop to a local merchant in return for renting land, tools, and other necessities. He was also obligated to purchase goods on credit (at higher prices than whites paid) against the harvest from the merchant's store. At "settling up" time, the income from the sale of the crop was matched with debts accumulated at the store. It was possible, especially after an unusually bountiful season, to come out ahead and eventually to own one's own land. But tenants seemed rarely to do so; they remained in debt at the end of each year and were then compelled to pledge the next year's crop. World cotton prices remained low, and while large landowners still enjoyed profits through their large scale of operation, sharecroppers rarely received much money. When they were able to pay off their debts, landowners frequently altered the loan agreements. Thus a system of debt peonage replaced slavery, ensuring a continuing cheap labor supply to grow cotton and other staples in the South. Only a very few blacks became independent landowners—about 2 to 5 percent by 1880, but closer to 20 percent in some states by 1900.

These changes in southern agriculture affected yeoman and poor white farmers as well as the freedmen. This raised the threat, always troubling to the planter class, of a coalition between poor black and pro-Unionist white farmers. As a yeoman farmer in Georgia said in 1865, "We should tuk the land, as we did the niggers, and split it, and giv part to the niggers and part to me and t'other Union fellers." But confiscation and redistribution of land was no more likely for white farmers than for the freedmen. Whites, too, were forced to concentrate on growing staples, to pledge their crops against high-interest credit from local merchants, and to face the inevitability of perpetual indebtedness. In the upcountry piedmont area of Georgia, for example, the number of whites who worked their own land dropped from nine in ten before the Civil War to seven in ten by 1880. During the same period, the production of cotton doubled.

Larger planter's reliance on cotton meant fewer food crops, which necessitated greater dependence on local merchants for provisions. In 1884, Jephta

A Freedmen's Work Contract

State of South Carolina
Darlington District
Articles of Agreement

This Agreement entered into between Mrs. Adele Allston Exect of the one part, and the Freedmen and Women of The Upper Quarters plantation of the other part *Witnesseth*:

That the latter agree, for the remainder of the present year, to reside upon and devote their labor to the cultivation of the Plantation of the former. And they further agree, that they will in all respects, conform to such reasonable and necessary plantation rules and regulations as Mrs. Allston's Agent may prescribe; that they will not keep any gun, pistol, or other offensive weapon, or leave the plantation without permission from their employer; that in all things connected with their duties as laborers on said plantation, they will yield prompt obedience to all orders from Mrs. Allston or his [sic] agent; that they will be orderly and quiet in their conduct, avoiding drunkenness and other gross vices; that they will not misuse any of the Plantation Tools, or Agricultural Implements, or any Animals entrusted to their care, or any Boats, Flats, Carts or Wagons; that they will give up at the expiration of this Contract, all Tools & c., belonging to the Plantation, and in case any property, of any description belonging to the Plantation shall be willfully or through negligence destroyed or injured, the value of the Articles so destroyed, shall be deducted from the portion of the Crops which the person or persons, so offending, shall be entitled to receive under this Contract.

Any deviations from the condition of the foregoing Contract may, upon sufficient proof, be punished with dismissal from the Plantation, or in such other manner as may be determined by the Provost Court; and the person or persons so dismissed, shall forfeit the whole, or a part of his, her or their portion of the crop, as the Court may decide.

In consideration of the foregoing Services duly performed, Mrs. Allston agrees, after deducting Seventy five bushels of Corn for each work Animal, exclusively used in cultivating the Crops for the present year; to turn over to the said Freedmen and Women, one half of the remaining Corn, Peas, Potatoes, made this season. He [sic] further agrees to furnish the usual rations until the Contract is performed.

All Cotton Seed Produced on the Plantation is to be reserved for the use of the Plantation. The Freedmen, Women and Children are to be treated in a manner consistent with their freedom. Necessary medical attention will be furnished as heretofore.

Any deviation from the conditions of this Contract upon the part of the said Mrs. Allston or her Agent or Agents shall be punished in such manner as may be determined by a Provost Court, or a Military Commission. This agreement to continue till the first day of January 1866.

Witness our hand at The Upper Quarters this 28th day of July 1865.

Sharecroppers and tenant farmers, though more autonomous than contract laborers, remained dependent on the landlord for their survival.

Dickson of Jackson County, Georgia, purchased over $50 worth of flour, meal, meat, syrup, and peas and corn from a local store, an almost unthinkable situation 25 years earlier, when he would have needed to buy almost no food to supplement his homegrown fare. Fencing laws seriously curtailed the livelihood of poor whites raising pigs and hogs, and restrictions on hunting and fishing reduced the ability of poor whites and blacks alike to supplement their income and diet.

In the worn-out flatlands and barren mountainous regions of the South, poor whites thus faced diminishing fortunes in the era of Reconstruction. Their antebellum heritage of poverty, ill health, and isolation worsened in the years after the war. A Freedmen's Bureau agent in South Carolina de-

Changes on the Barrow Plantation, 1860–1881

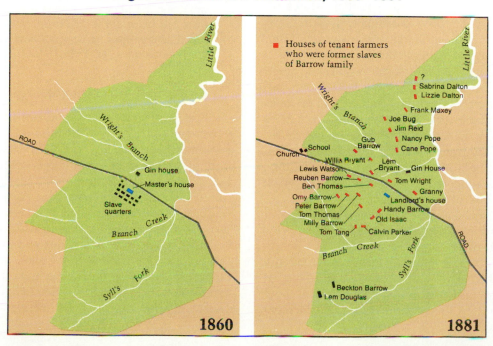

Sharecropping in the South, 1880

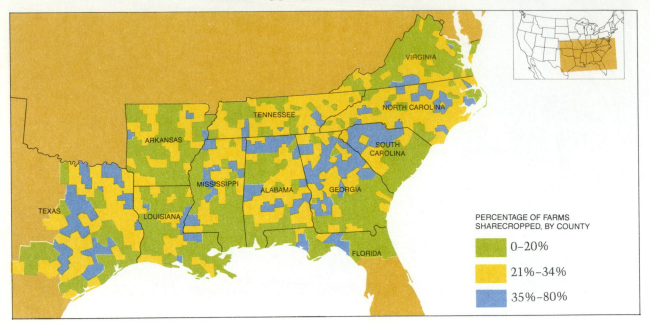

PERCENTAGE OF FARMS
SHARECROPPED, BY COUNTY

- 0–20%
- 21%–34%
- 35%–80%

scribed the poor whites in his area as "gaunt and ragged, ungainly, stooping and clumsy in build." They lived a marginal existence, hunting, fishing, and growing corn and potato crops that, as a North Carolinian put it, "come up *puny,* grow *puny,* and mature *puny.*" Many poor white farmers, in fact, were even less productive than black sharecroppers. Some became farmhands, earning $6 a month (with board) from other farmers. Other fled to low-paying jobs in urban cotton mills, where they would not have to compete against blacks.

The cultural life of poor southern whites reflected both their lowly position and their pride. Their religion was emotional and revivalistic, centering on the camp meeting. Music and folklore often focused on debt and chain gangs, as well as on deeds of drinking prowess. In backwoods clearings and bleak pine barrens, men and women told tall tales of superhuman feats and exchanged folk remedies for bad health. In Alabama, there were over 90 superstitious sayings for calling rain. Aesthetic expression, in quilt making and house construction, for example, reflected a marginal culture in which everything was saved and put to use.

In part because their lives were so hard, poor whites persisted in their belief in white superiority. As a federal officer reported in 1866, "The poorer classes of white people . . . have a most intense hatred of the Negro, and swear he shall never be reckoned as part of the population." Many poor whites, therefore, joined the Ku Klux Klan and other southern white terror groups that emerged between 1866 and 1868. But however hard life was for poor whites, blacks were far more often sentenced to chain gangs for the slightest crimes and were bound to a life of debt, degradation, and dependency. The high hopes with which the freedmen had greeted emancipation turned slowly to resignation and disillusionment. Felix Haywood, a former Texas slave, recalled:

> We thought we was goin' to be richer than white folks, 'cause we was stronger and knowed how to work, and the whites . . . didn't have us to work for them anymore. But it didn't turn out that way. We soon found out that freedom could make folks proud but it didn't make 'em rich.

Black Self-help Institutions

Felix Haywood understood the limitations of government programs and efforts on behalf of the freedmen. It was clear to many black leaders, therefore, that since white institutions could not fulfill the promises of emancipation, black freedmen would have to do it themselves. Fortunately, the tradition of black community self-help survived in the organized churches and schools of the antebellum free Negro communities and in the "invisible" cultural institutions of the slave quarters. Religion, as usual, was vital. Emancipation brought an explosion in the growth of membership in black churches. The Negro Baptist church grew from

150,000 members in 1850 to 500,000 in 1870. The various branches of the African Methodist Episcopal church increased fourfold in the decade after the Civil War, from 100,000 to over 400,000 members.

Black ministers continued their tradition of community leadership. Many led efforts to oppose discrimination, some by entering politics. Over one-fifth of the black officeholders in South Carolina were ministers. Most preachers, however, focused on traditional religious themes of sin, conversion, and salvation. An English visitor to the South in 1867 and 1868, after observing a revivalist preacher in Savannah arouse nearly 1,000 people to "sway, and cry, and groan," noted the intensity of black "devoutness." Despite some efforts by urban elite blacks to restrain the emotionalism characteristic of black worship, most congregations preferred their traditional forms of religious expression. One black woman, when urged to pray more quietly, complained: "We make noise 'bout ebery ting else . . . I want ter go ter Heaben in de good ole way."

The freedmen's desire for education was as strong as for religion. A school official in Virginia echoed the observation of many when he said that the freedmen were "down right crazy to learn." A Mississippi farmer vowed, "If I nebber does do nothing more, I shall give my children a chance to go to school, for I consider education next best ting to liberty." The first teachers of these black children were unmarried northern women, the legendary "Yankee schoolmarms." Sent by groups such as the American Missionary Association, these idealistic young women sought to convert blacks to Congregationalism and to white moral values of cleanliness, discipline, and dutiful work. In October 1865, Esther Douglass found "120 dirty, half naked, per-fectly wild black children" in her schoolroom near Savannah, Georgia. Eight months later, she reported that "their progress was wonderful." They could read, sing hymns, and repeat Bible verses and had learned "about right conduct which they tried to practice."

Glowing reports like this one changed as white teachers grew frustrated with crowded facilities, limited resources, local opposition, and the absenteeism that resulted from the demands of fieldwork. In Georgia, for example, only 5 percent of black children went to school for part of any one year between 1865 and 1870; this contrasted with 20 percent of white children. Furthermore, blacks increasingly preferred their own teachers, who could better understand former slaves. To ensure the training of black preachers and teachers, northern philanthropists founded Howard, Atlanta, Fisk, Morehouse, and other black universities in the South between 1865 and 1867.

Black schools, like churches, became community centers. They published newspapers, provided training in trades and farming, and promoted political participation and land ownership. A black farmer in Mississippi founded both a school and a society to facilitate land acquisition and better agricultural methods. These efforts made black schools objects of local white hostility. A Virginia freedman told a congressional committee that in his county, anyone starting a school would be killed and that blacks were "afraid to be caught with a book." In 1869, in Tennessee alone, 37 black schools were burned to the ground.

White opposition to black education and land ownership stimulated the rise of black nationalism and separatism. In the late 1860s, Benjamin "Pap"

Along with equal civil rights and land of their own, what the freedmen most wanted was education. Despite white opposition and limited facilities for black schools, one of the most positive outcomes of the Reconstruction era was education in freedmen's schools.

Singleton, a former Tennessee slave who had escaped to Canada, observed that "whites had the lands and . . . blacks had nothing but their freedom." Singleton urged them to abandon politics and migrate westward. He organized a land company in 1869, purchased public property in Kansas, and in the early 1870s took several groups from Tennessee and Kentucky to that prairie state to establish separate black towns. In following years, thousands of "exodusters" from the Lower South bought some 10,000 acres of infertile land in Kansas. There they faced both natural and human obstacles to their efforts to develop self-sufficient communities. Most were forced eventually to disband and seek relief.

By the 1880s, despairing of ever finding economic independence in the United States, Singleton and other nationalists urged emigration to Canada and Liberia. Other black leaders, notably Frederick Douglass, continued to assert that suffrage would eventually lead to full citizenship rights within the United States.

RECONSTRUCTION IN THE STATES

Douglass's confidence in the power of the ballot seemed warranted in the enthusiastic early months under the Reconstruction Acts of 1867. With President Johnson neutralized, national Republican leaders were finally in a position to accomplish their political goals. Local Republicans, taking advantage of the inability or refusal of many southern whites to vote, overwhelmingly elected their delegates to state constitutional conventions in the fall of 1867. With guarded optimism and a sense of the "sacred importance" of their work, black and white Republicans turned to the task of creating new state governments.

Republican Rule

Despite popular belief, the southern state governments under Republican rule were not dominated by illiterate black majorities intent on "Africanizing" the South by passing compulsory racial intermarriage laws, as many whites feared. Nor were these governments unusually corrupt or financially extravagant. Nor did they use massive numbers of federal troops to enforce their will. By 1869, only 1,100 federal soldiers remained in Virginia, and most federal troops in Texas guarded the frontier against Mexico and hostile Indians. Without the support of a strong military presence, then, these new state governments tried to do their work in a climate of economic distress and increasingly violent harassment.

A diverse combination of political groups made up the new governments elected under congressional Reconstruction. Labeled the "black and tan" governments by their opponents to suggest domination by former slaves and mulattoes, they were actually predominantly white, with the one exception of the lower house of the South Carolina legislature. One part of the new leadership consisted of an old Whiggish elite class of bankers, industrialists, and others interested far more in economic growth and sectional reconciliation than in radical social reforms. A second group consisted of northern Republicans who headed south out of motives similar to those prompting migration southward in our own time. These included capitalists seeking economic investment in land, railroads, and new industries; retired Union veterans seeking a warmer climate for health purposes; and missionaries and teachers pursuing an outlet for their idealism in the Freedmen's Bureau schools. Such people were unfairly labeled "carpetbaggers."

Moderate blacks made up a third group participating in the Republican state governments. A large percentage of black officeholders were mulattoes, many of them well-educated preachers, teachers, and soldiers from the North. Others, such as John Lynch of Mississippi, were self-educated tradesmen or representatives of the small landed class of southern blacks. In South Carolina, for example, of some 255 black state and federal officials elected between 1868 and 1876, two-thirds were literate and one-third owned real estate. Only 15 percent owned no property at all. This class composition meant that black leaders often supported land policies that largely ignored the economic needs of the black masses.

These black politicians were more interested in pursuing a political agenda of gaining access to government influence and education than an economic agenda of land redistribution or state aid to black peasants. They fashioned their political goals squarely in the American republican tradition. Black leaders reminded whites that they, too, were southerners and Americans, attached both to the land of the South and to the white families they had lived with for generations: "The dust of our fathers mingles with yours in the same grave yards. . . . This is your country, but it is ours too." Because of this intermingled past, blacks sought no revenge or reversal of power, only, as an 1865 petition said, "that the same laws which govern white men shall govern black men [and that] we be dealt with as others are—in equity and justice."

The primary accomplishment of Republican rule in the South was in eliminating the undemocratic features of earlier state constitutions. All states provided universal men's suffrage and loosened requirements for holding office. The basis of state representation was made fairer by apportioning more legislative seats to the interior regions of southern states. Social legislation included the abolition of automatic imprisonment for debt and laws for the relief of poverty and care of the handicapped. The first divorce laws in many southern states were passed, as were laws granting property rights to married women. Penal laws were modernized by reducing the list of crimes punishable by death, in one state from 26 to 5.

Republican governments undertook the task of financially and physically reconstructing the South, overhauling tax systems, and approving generous railroad and other capital investment bonds. Harbors, roads, and bridges were rebuilt. Hospitals, asylums, and other state institutions were established. Most important, the Republican governments provided for a state-supported system of public schools, absent before in most of the South. As in the North, these schools were largely segregated, but for the first time, rich and poor, black and white alike had access to education. As a result, black school attendance increased from 5 to over 40 percent and white from 20 to over 60 percent by the 1880s. All of this cost money, and the Republicans did indeed greatly increase tax rates and state debts. All in all, the Republican governments "dragged the South, screaming and crying, into the modern world."

These considerable accomplishments were achieved in the midst of opposition like that ex-

pressed at a convention of Louisiana planters, which labeled the Republican leaders "the lowest and most corrupt body of men ever assembled in the South." There was some corruption, to be sure, but mostly in land sales, fraudulent railway bonds, and construction contracts, the kind of graft that had become a way of life in American politics, South and North, in the aftermath of the Civil War. Given their lack of experience with politics, the black role was remarkable. As Du Bois put it, "There was one thing that the White South feared more than negro dishonesty, ignorance, and incompetence, and that was negro honesty, knowledge, and efficiency."

Despite its effectiveness in modernizing southern state governments, the Republican coalition did not last very long. In fact, as the map indicates, Republican rule lasted for different periods of time in different states. In some states, Virginia, for example, the Republicans ruled hardly at all. Situated in the shadow of Washington, conservatives in Virginia professed their agreement with Congress's Reconstruction guidelines while doing as they pleased. As one of the states most devastated by the war, Virginia looked almost immediately to northern investors to rebuild its cities and to develop industry. Blacks and whites alike flocked to the cities for work. In South Carolina, the unwillingness of black leaders to use their power to help black laborers contributed to their loss of political control to the Democrats. Class tensions and divisions among blacks in Louisiana helped to weaken that Republican regime as well.

Republican rule lasted the longest in the black-belt states of the Deep South, where the black population was equal to or greater than the white. In Louisiana, Reconstruction began with General Ben Butler's occupation of New Orleans in 1862. Although he insisted on granting civil rights to blacks, he was quickly replaced by a succession of Repub-

Despite threats of white reprisals, black freemen proudly voted in Republican state governments under the Congressional Reconstruction Plan of 1867.

lican governors in the late 1860s more interested in graft, election laws, and staying in office than in the rights and welfare of poor black Louisianans. Alabama received a flood of northern capital to develop the rich coal, iron ore, and timber resources of the northern third of the state. Republican rule in Alabama, as in other states, involved a greater role for towns and merchants, the endorsement of generous railroad bonds, and an emergent class structure that replaced the old planter aristocracy with a new industrial one.

Violence and "Redemption"

A Georgia newspaper in 1868 charged that Republican rulers would "see this fair land drenched in blood from the Potomac to the Rio Grande rather than lose their power." In fact, it was the Democrats who used racial violence, intimidation, and coercion to restore their power. As one southern editor put it, "We must render this either a white man's government, or convert the land into a Negro man's cemetery." The Ku Klux Klan was only one of several secret organizations that used force and violence against black and white Republicans to drive them from power. The cases of North Carolina and Mississippi are representative in showing how conservative Democrats were able to regain control.

After losing a close election in North Carolina in 1868, conservatives waged a concentrated campaign of terror in several counties in the piedmont area. If the Democrats could win these counties in 1870, they would most likely win statewide. In the year prior to the election, several prominent Republicans were killed, including a white state senator, whose throat was cut, and a leading black

Union League organizer, who was hanged in the courthouse square with a sign pinned to his breast: "Bewar, ye guilty, both white and black." Scores of citizens were flogged, tortured, fired from their jobs, or forced to flee in the middle of the night from burning homes and barns. The courts consistently refused to prosecute anyone for these crimes. Local papers, in fact, charged that "disgusting negroes and white Radicals" had committed the crimes. The conservative campaign worked. In the election of 1870, some 12,000 fewer Republicans voted in the two crucial counties than had voted two years earlier, and the Democrats swept back into power.

In the state election in Mississippi in 1875, Democrats used similar tactics, openly announcing that "the thieves . . . , robbers, and scoundrels, white and black," in power "deserve death and ought to be killed." In what was called the Mississippi Plan, local Democratic clubs organized themselves into armed militias, marching defiantly through black areas, breaking up Republican meetings, and provoking riots to justify the killing of hundreds of blacks. Armed men were posted during voter registration to intimidate Republicans. At the election itself, anyone still bold enough to attempt to vote was either helped by gun-toting whites to cast a Democratic ballot or driven away from the polls with cannon and clubs. Counties that had earlier given Republican candidates majorities in the thousands, in 1875 managed a total of less than a dozen votes!

Democrats called their victory "redemption." As conservative Democratic administrations resumed control of each state government, Reconstruction came to an end. Redemption resulted from a combination of the persistence of white southern

Return to the Union During Reconstruction

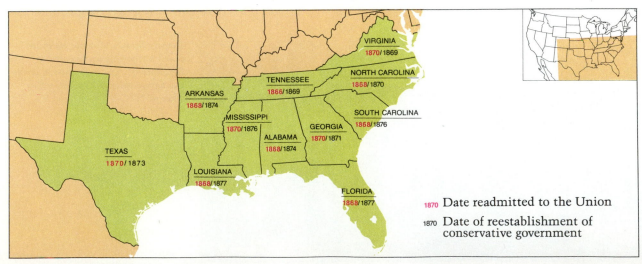

VIRGINIA 1870/1869
NORTH CAROLINA 1868/1870
TENNESSEE 1866/1869
ARKANSAS 1868/1874
SOUTH CAROLINA 1868/1876
MISSISSIPPI 1870/1876
GEORGIA 1870/1871
ALABAMA 1868/1874
TEXAS 1870/1873
LOUISIANA 1868/1877
FLORIDA 1868/1877

1870 Date readmitted to the Union
1870 Date of reestablishment of conservative government

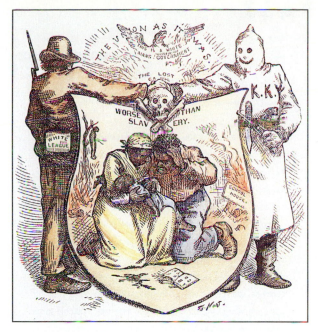

As shown in this Thomas Nast cartoon, Worse than Slavery, *to restore "a white man's government" and redeem the noble "lost cause," white groups such as the Ku Klux Klan and the White Leagues used every form of terror, violence, and intimidation.*

resistance, including violence and other coercive measures, and a loss of will to persist in the North. Albion Tourgée summed up the Reconstruction era in his novel *A Fool's Errand* (1879): "The spirit of the dead Confederacy was stronger than the mandate of the nation to which it had succumbed in battle."

Congress and President Grant did not totally ignore the violence in the South. Three Force Acts, passed in 1870 and 1871, gave the president strong powers to use federal supervisors to make sure that citizens were not prevented from voting by force or fraud. The third act, known as the Ku Klux Klan Act, declared illegal secret organizations that used disguise and coercion to deprive others of equal protection of the laws. Congress created a joint committee to investigate Klan violence, which reported in 1872 in 13 huge volumes of horrifying testimony. Grant, who had supported these measures, delivered special messages to Congress proclaiming the importance of the right to vote, issued proclamations condemning lawlessness, and sent some additional troops to South Carolina. However, as reform Republicans realized that black voters supported Grant, they lost interest in defending those voters. Regular Republicans were also not

very supportive, since many felt that they could do without black voters. Both groups were much more concerned with northern issues. In 1875, Grant's advisers told him that Republicans might lose important Ohio elections if he continued to protect blacks. Thus he decided that year to reject appeals by Mississippi blacks that troops be stationed in their state to guarantee free elections. Grant declared instead that he and the nation "had tired of these annual autumnal outbreaks."

The success of the Mississippi Plan in 1875, imitated a year later in South Carolina and Louisiana, indicated that congressional reports and presidential proclamations did little to stop the reign of terror against black and white Republicans throughout the South. The Force Acts were wholly inadequate and were themselves weakly enforced. Although there were hundreds of arrests, all-white juries were reluctant to find their fellow citizens guilty of crimes against blacks. The U.S. Supreme Court backed them. In two decisions in 1874, the Court threw out cases against whites found guilty of preventing blacks from voting and declared key parts of the Force Acts unconstitutional. In Hamburg, South Carolina, in 1876, several blacks were killed in a riot that started in a courtroom when a white mob came to provide its own form of "justice" to some black militiamen who had been arrested for parading on Independence Day. Although the Ku Klux Klan's power was officially ended, the attitudes (and tactics) of Klansmen would continue long into the next century.

Reconstruction, Northern Style

The American people, like their leaders, were tired of battles over the freedmen and were shifting their attention to other matters than fulfilling idealistic principles. Frustrated with the difficulties of trying to transform an unwilling South and seemingly ungrateful blacks, the easiest course was to give blacks their citizenship and the vote and move on to something else. After the interruptions of civil war and its aftermath, most Americans were primarily interested in starting families, finding work, and making money. This meant firing furnaces in the new steel plant in Wheeling, West Virginia, pounding in railroad ties for the Central Pacific in the Nevada desert, struggling to teach in a one-room schoolhouse in Vermont for $23 a month, or battling heat, locusts, and railroad rates on a family homestead in Kansas.

At both the individual and national levels, Re-

RECOVERING THE PAST

NOVELS

We usually read novels, short stories, and other forms of fiction for pleasure, for the enjoyment of plot, style, symbolism, and character development. "Classic" novels such as *Moby Dick, Huckleberry Finn, The Great Gatsby,* and *The Invisible Man,* to name a few American examples, are not only written well but also explore timeless questions of good and evil, of innocence and knowledge, or of noble dreams fulfilled and shattered. Often we enjoy novels because we find ourselves identifying with one of the major characters. Through that person's problems, joys, relationships, and search for identity we gain insights about our own.

We can also read novels as historical sources, for they reveal much about the attitudes, dreams, fears, life styles, and ordinary everyday experiences of human beings in a particular historical period. They also show how people reacted to and felt about the major events of that era. We must be careful, however, to note the date when a novel was written, especially if different from the period written about. The novelist, like the historian, is a product of time and place and has an interpretive point of view.

Consider the two novels about Reconstruction quoted here. Neither is reputed for great literary merit, yet both reveal much about the various interpretations and impassioned attitudes of the post–Civil War era. *A Fool's Errand* was written by Albion Tourgée, a northerner; *The Clansman,* by Thomas Dixon, Jr., a southerner.

Tourgée was a young northern teacher and lawyer who fought with the Union army at several major battles during the Civil War. After the war, he moved to North Carolina, partly for health reasons and partly to begin a legal career. He became a judge and was an active Republican, supporting black suffrage and helping to shape the new state constitution and the codification of North Carolina laws in 1868. With jurisdiction over eight counties, Tourgée earned a reputation as one of the fairest judges in the state. Because he boldly criticized the Ku Klux Klan for its campaign of terror against blacks, his life was threatened many times. When the fearless judge finally left North Carolina in 1879, he published an autobiographical novel about his experiences.

A Fool's Errand

Albion Tourgée (1879)

When the second Christmas came, Metta wrote again to her sister:

"The feeling is terribly bitter against Comfort on account of his course towards the colored people. There is quite a village of them on the lower end of the plantation. They have a church, a sabbath school, and are to have next year a school. You can not imagine how kind they have been to us, and how much they are attached to Comfort. . . . I got Comfort to go with me to one of their prayer-meetings a few nights ago. I had heard a great deal about them, but had never attended one before. It was strangely weird. There were, perhaps, fifty present, mostly middle-aged men and women. They were singing in a soft, low monotone, interspersed with prolonged exclamatory notes, a sort of rude hymn, which I was surprised to know was one of their old songs in slave times. How the chorus came to be endured in those days I can not imagine. It was—

'Free! free! free, my Lord, free!
An' we walks de hebben-ly way!'

"A few looked around as we came in and seated ourselves; and Uncle Jerry, the saint of the settlement, came forward on his staves, and said, in his soft voice,

" 'Ev'nin', Kunnel! Sarvant, Missus! Will you walk up, an' hev seats in front?'

"We told him we had just looked in, and might go in a short time; so we would stay in the back part of the audience.

"Uncle Jerry can not read nor write; but he is a man of strange intelligence and power. Unable to do work of any account, he is the faithful friend, monitor, and director of others. He has a house and piece of land, all paid for, a good horse and cow, and, with the aid of his wife and two boys, made a fine crop this season. He is one of the most promising colored men in the settlement: so Comfort says, at least. Everybody seems to have great respect for his character. I don't know how many people I have heard speak of his religion. Mr. Savage used to say he had rather hear him pray than any other man on earth. He was much prized by his master, even after he was disabled, on account of his faithfulness and character."

The "fool's errand" in the novel is that of the northern veteran, Comfort Servosse, who like Tourgée seeks to fulfill humane goals on behalf of both blacks and whites in post–Civil War North Carolina. His efforts are thwarted, however, by threats, intimidation, a campaign of violent "outrages" against Republican leaders in the county, and a lack of sup-

The Clansman

Thomas Dixon, Jr. (1905)

At noon Ben and Phil strolled to the polling-place to watch the progress of the first election under Negro rule. The Square was jammed with shouting, jostling, perspiring negroes, men, women, and children. The day was warm, and the African odour was supreme even in the open air. . . .

Phil and Ben passed on nearer the polling-place, around which stood a cordon of soldiers with a line of negro voters two hundred yards in length extending back into the crowd.

The negro Leagues came in armed battalions and voted in droves, carrying their muskets in their hands. Less than a dozen white men were to be seen about the place.

The negroes, under the drill of the League and the Freedman's Bureau, protected by the bayonet, were voting to enfranchise themselves, disfranchise their former masters, ratify a new constitution, and elect a legislature to do their will. Old Aleck was a candidate for the House, chief poll-holder, and seemed to be in charge of the movements of the voters outside the booth as well as inside. He appeared to be omnipresent, and his self-importance was a sight Phil had never dreamed. He could not keep his eyes off him. . . .

[Aleck] was a born African orator, undoubtedly descended from a long line of savage spell-binders, whose eloquence in the palaver houses of the jungle had made them native leaders. His thin spindle-shanks supported an oblong, protruding stomach, resembling an elderly monkey's, which seemed so heavy it swayed his back to carry it.

The animal vivacity of his small eyes and the flexibility of his eyebrows, which he worked up and down rapidly with every change of countenance, expressed his eager desires.

He had laid aside his new shoes, which hurt him, and went barefooted to facilitate his movements on the great occasion. His heels projected and his foot was so flat that what should have been the hollow of it made a hole in the dirt where he left his track.

He was already mellow with liquor, and was dressed in an old army uniform and cap, with two horse-pistols buckled around his waist. On a strap hanging from his shoulder were strung a half-dozen tin canteens filled with whiskey.

port from the so-called wise men in Congress. Historians have verified the accuracy, down to the smallest details, of the events in Tourgée's novel. While exposing the brutality of the Klan, Tourgée features loyal southern Unionists, respectable planters ashamed of Klan violence, and even guilt-ridden poor white Klansmen who try to protect or warn intended victims. In the end, his analysis of the ultimate failure of Reconstruction blames the shortsightedness and incompleteness of the northern congressional program even more than southern violent resistance.

In the year of Tourgée's death, 1905, another North Carolinian published a novel with a very different analysis of Reconstruction and its fate. Thomas Dixon was born during the Civil War. He was a lawyer, North Carolina state legislator, Baptist minister, lecturer, and novelist. *The Clansman,* subtitled "A Historical Romance of the Ku Klux Klan," reflects turn-of-the-century attitudes most white southerners still had about Republican rule during Reconstruction. According to Dixon, once the "Great Heart" Lincoln was gone, a power-crazed, vindictive radical Congress, led by scheming Austin Stoneman (Thaddeus Stevens), sought to impose corrupt carpetbagger and brutal black rule by bayonet on a helpless South. Only through the inspired leadership and redemptive role of the Ku Klux Klan was the South saved from the horrors of rape and revenge.

Dixon dedicated *The Clansman* to his uncle, a Grand Titan of the Klan in North Carolina during the time when two crucial counties were being transformed from Republican to Democratic through intimidation and terror. No such violence shows up in Dixon's novel. Although *The Clansman* clearly twisted the truth of many historical events, it is an accurate and faithful representation of a dominant attitude southerners—and northerners as well—had about those events. When the novel was made the basis of D. W. Griffith's film classic, *Birth of a Nation,* in 1915, these attitudes were firmly imprinted on the twentieth-century American mind.

Both novels convey the events and attitudes of the era by creating clearly defined heroes and villains. Both include exciting chase scenes, narrow escapes, daring rescues, and tragic, heart-rending deaths. Both include romantic subplots in which a young white southern man falls in love with a young white northern woman. In each novel, however, the author's primary purpose was to convey his views of the politics of Reconstruction. The romantic elements were added, like sugarcoating around a pill, to make readers enjoy the medicine the novelist wanted them to take. Examining brief excerpts is a poor substitute for reading the novels in their entirety. Notice the obvious differences of style and attitude in the descriptions of Uncle Jerry and Old Aleck.

These two scenes vividly contrast family life during Reconstruction in the North and South. For most white northerners, as shown in this 1868 Currier & Ives print, the end of the Civil War meant renewing the good life of genteel middle-class values. For many black freedmen, however, family life was constantly threatened by the intrusion of Klan violence.

construction, northern style, meant the continuation of the enormous economic revolution of the nineteenth century. Although failing to effect a smooth transition from slavery to freedom for ex-slaves, Republican northerners were able to accelerate and solidify their program of economic growth and industrial and territorial expansion.

As Klansmen met in dark forests to plan their next raid in North Carolina in 1869, the Central Pacific and Union Pacific railroads met at Promontory Point, Utah, linking the Atlantic and the Pacific by rail. As cotton production increased again in the postbellum South, so did the making of iron and steel in the North and the settlement of the mining, cattle, and agricultural frontiers in the West. But also, as black farmers were "haggling" over work contracts with white landowners in Georgia, white workers were organizing and joining the National Labor Union in Baltimore. As Elizabeth and Adele Allston demanded the keys to their crop barns in the summer of 1865, the Boston Labor Reform Association was demanding that "our . . . education, morals, dwellings, and the whole Social System" needed to be "reconstructed." If the South would not be reconstructed, labor relations might be.

The years between 1865 and 1875 featured not only the rise (and fall) of Republican governments in the South but also the spectacular rise of working-class activity and organization. Stimulated by the Civil War to improve working conditions in northern factories, such groups as trade unions, labor reform associations, and labor parties flourished, culminating in the founding of the National Labor Union

in 1866. Before the depression of 1873, an estimated 300,000 to 500,000 American workers had enrolled in some 1,500 trade unions, the largest such increase in the nineteenth century. This growth would inevitably affect class tensions. In 1876, hundreds of freedmen in the rice region along the Combahee River in South Carolina went on strike to protest a 40-cent-per-day wage cut, clashing with local sheriffs and white Democratic rifle clubs. A year later, also over wage cuts, thousands of railroad workers in Pittsburgh, St. Louis, Omaha, and other northern cities went out in a nationwide wave of strikes, clashing with local police and the National Guard.

As economic relations changed, so did the Republican party. Heralded by the moderate tone of the state elections of 1867 and the national election of Grant in 1868, the Republicans changed from the party of moral reform to one of material interest. In the continuing struggle in American politics between "virtue and commerce," self-interest was again winning. No longer willing to support an agency like the Freedmen's Bureau, Republican politicians had no difficulty backing huge grants of money and land to the railroads. As blacks were told to go to work and help themselves, the Union Pacific was being given subsidies of between $16,000 and $48,000 for each mile of track laid across western plains and mountains. As Susan B. Anthony and others were tramping through the snows of upstate New York with petitions for rights of suffrage and citizenship, Boss Tweed and others were defrauding the citizen-taxpayers of New York of millions of dollars in boondoggles. As Native Americans in the

Great Plains struggled to preserve their sacred Black Hills from greedy gold prospectors and U.S. soldiers, urban, state, and federal officials in the East were "mining" public treasuries by means of various forms of graft.

By 1869, the year financier Jay Gould almost succeeded in cornering the gold market, the nation was increasingly defined by materialistic "go-getters" and by sordid grasping for wealth and power. Henry Adams, descendant of two presidents, was living in Washington, D.C., during this era. As he wrote later in his autobiography, *The Education of Henry Adams* (1907), he had high expectations in 1869 that Grant, like another "great soldier" and president, George Washington, would restore moral order and peace. But when Grant announced the members of his cabinet, a group of Army cronies and rich friends to whom he owed favors, Adams felt betrayed, complaining that "a great soldier might be a baby politician."

Ulysses Grant himself was an honest man, but his judgment of others was flawed. His administration featured a series of scandals that touched several cabinet officers and relatives and even two vice-presidents. Under Grant's appointments, outright graft, as well as loose prosecution and generally negligent administration, flourished in a half dozen departments. Most scandals involved large sums of public money. The Whiskey Ring affair, for example, cost the public millions of dollars in lost tax revenues siphoned off to government officials. Gould's gold scam received the unwitting aid of Grant's Treasury Department and the knowing help of his brother-in-law.

Nor was Congress pure in these various schemes. Crédit Mobilier figured in the largest of several scandals in which construction companies for transcontinental railroads (in this case a dummy company) received generous bonds and work contracts in exchange for giving congressmen gifts of money, stocks, and railroad lands. An Ohio congressmen described the House of Representatives in 1873 as "an auction room where more valuable considerations were disposed of under the speaker's hammer than any place on earth." Henry Adams spoke for many Americans when he said that Grant's administration "outraged every rule of decency."

In *Democracy* (1880), a novel written about Washington life during this period, Adams's main character, Mrs. Madeleine Lee, sought to uncover "the heart of the great American mystery of democracy and government." What she found were corrupt legislators and lobbyists in an unprincipled pursuit of power and wealth. "Surely something can be done to check corruption?" Mrs. Lee asked her friend one evening. "Are we forever to be at the mercy of thieves and ruffians? Is a respectable government impossible in a democracy?" The answer she heard was hardly reassuring: "No responsible government can long be much better or much worse than the society it represents."

The election of 1872 marked the decline of public interest in moral issues. A "liberal" faction of the Republican party, unable to dislodge Grant and disgusted with his administration, formed a third party with a reform platform and nominated Horace Greeley, editor of the New York *Tribune,* for president. The liberal Republicans advocated free trade, which meant lower tariffs and fewer grants to railroads; honest government, which meant civil service reform; and noninterference in southern race relations, which meant the removal of federal troops from the South. Democrats, lacking notable presidential candidates, also nominated Greeley, even though he had spent much of his earlier career assailing Democrats as "rascals." Despite his wretched record, Grant easily won a second term. Greeley was beaten so badly, he said, that "I hardly knew whether I was running for the Presidency or the Penitentiary."

The End of Reconstruction

Soon after Grant's second inauguration, a financial panic, caused by overconstruction of railroads and the collapse of some crucial eastern banks, created a terrible depression that lasted throughout the mid-1870s. In times of hardship, economic issues dominated politics, further pulling attention away from the plight of the freedmen. As Democrats took control of the House of Representatives in 1874 and looked toward winning the White House in 1876, politicians talked about such issues as new scandals in the Grant administration, unemployment and various proposals for public works expenditures for relief, the availability of silver and greenback dollars, and high tariffs.

No one, it seemed, talked much about the rights and conditions of southern freedmen. In 1875, a guilt-ridden Congress passed Senator Charles Sumner's civil rights bill, intended to put teeth into the Fourteenth Amendment. But the act was not enforced and was declared unconstitutional by the Supreme Court eight years later. Congressional Reconstruction, long dormant, had ended. The election of 1876 sealed the conclusion.

As their nominee for president in 1876, the Republicans turned to a former governor of Ohio, Rutherford B. Hayes, partly because of his reputation for honesty, partly because he had been an officer in the Union army (a necessity for post–Civil War candidates), and partly because, as Henry Adams put it, he was "obnoxious to no one." The Democrats chose Governor Samuel J. Tilden of New York, who achieved national recognition as a civil service reformer in breaking up the corrupt Tweed Ring.

Tilden won a majority of the popular vote and appeared to have enough electoral votes for victory. Twenty more electoral votes were disputed, all but one in the Deep South states of Louisiana, South Carolina, and Florida, where some federal troops still remained on duty and where Republicans still controlled the voting apparatus. Democrats, however, had applied various versions of the Mississippi Plan to intimidate voters. To resolve the disputed electoral votes, Congress created a special electoral commission consisting of five senators, five representatives, and five Supreme Court justices, eight of whom were Republicans and seven Democrats. The vote in each disputed case was 8 to 7 along party lines. Hayes was given all 20 votes, enough to win, 185 to 184.

Outraged Democrats threatened to stop the Senate from officially counting the electoral votes, thus preventing Hayes's inauguration. The country was in a state of crisis, and some Americans wondered if civil war might break out again. But unlike the 1850s, when passions over slavery erupted, compromise was possible between northerners and southerners mutually interested in modernization of the southern economy through capital investments. They focused on a Pacific railroad linking New Orleans with the West Coast. Northern investors wanted the government to help pay for the railroad, while southerners who hoped that it would revive their economy wanted northern dollars but not northern political influence. This meant no social agencies, no federal enforcement of the Fourteenth and Fifteenth amendments, and no military occupation, not even the small symbolic presence left in 1876.

As the inauguration date approached and newspapers echoed outgoing President Grant's call for "peace at any price," the forces of mutual self-interest concluded the "compromise of 1877." The Democrats agreed to suspend resistance to the counting of the electoral votes, and on March 2, Rutherford B. Hayes was declared president. In exchange for the presidency, Hayes ordered the last

As early as 1868, three white groups—here stereotyped as apelike northern Irish workers, unrepentant ex-Confederates, and rich northern capitalists—joined hands to bring Republican Reconstruction to an end almost before it began. The immigrant's vote, the Kluxer's knife, and the capitalist's dollars would restore "a white man's government" on the back of the freedman, still clutching the Union flag and reaching in vain for the ballot box. No single image better captures the story of the end of Reconstruction than this Thomas Nast cartoon.

remaining troops out of the South, appointed a former Confederate general to his cabinet, supported federal aid to bolster economic and railroad development in the South, and announced his intentions to let southerners handle race relations themselves. He then went on a goodwill trip to the South, where he told blacks in an Atlanta speech that "your rights and interests would be safer if this great mass of intelligent white men were let alone by the general government." The message was clear: Hayes would not enforce the Fourteenth and Fifteenth amendments, thus initiating a pattern of executive inaction not broken until the middle of the twentieth century. But the immediate crisis was averted, officially ending the era of Reconstruction.

CONCLUSION
A Mixed Legacy

In the 12 years between Appomattox and Hayes's inauguration, the diverse dreams of victorious northern Republicans, defeated white southerners, and hopeful black freedmen conflicted. There was little chance that all could be realized, yet each group could point to a modest fulfillment of its goals. The compromise of 1877 cemented the reunion of South and North, thus providing new opportunities for economic development in both regions. The Republican party achieved its economic goals and preserved its political hold on the White House, though not Congress, with two exceptions, until 1932. The ex-Confederate states were brought back into the Union, and southerners retained their firm control of southern lands and black labor, though not without struggle and some changes. To the extent that the peace of 1877 was preserved "at any price," that price was paid by the freedmen.

In 1880, Frederick Douglass summarized Reconstruction for the freedmen:

> Our Reconstruction measures were radically defective. . . . To the freedmen was given the machinery of liberty, but there was denied to them the steam to put it in motion. They were given the uniform of soldiers, but no arms; they were called citizens, but left subjects; they were called free, but left almost slaves. The old master class . . . retained the power to starve them to death, and wherever this power is held there is the power of slavery.

Douglass went on to say that it was a wonder to him "not that freedmen have made so little progress, but, rather, that they have made so much; not that they have been standing still, but that they have been able to stand at all." Indeed, despite their liabilities, the freedmen had made admirable gains in education and in economic and family survival. Although sharecropping and tenancy were harsh systems, black laborers organized themselves to achieve a measure of autonomy and opportunity in their lives that could never be diminished. Moreover, the three great Reconstruction amendments to the Constitution, despite flagrant violation over the next 100 years, held out the promise that the rights of equal citizenship and political participation would yet be fulfilled.

Nevertheless, given the potential for reconstructed relations in the postwar period, there was an underlying tragedy to Reconstruction, as a short story by W. E. B. Du Bois, written a few years later, makes sadly clear. Two boyhood playmates, both named John, one black and one white, are sent from the fictional town of Altamaha, Georgia, north to school to prepare for leadership of their respective communities, the black John as a teacher and the white John as a judge and possible governor of the state. While they were away, the black and white people of Altamaha, each race thinking of its own John and not of the other, except with "a vague unrest," waited for "the coming of two young men, and dreamed . . . of new things that would be done and new thoughts that all would think."

After several years, both Johns returned to Altamaha, but a series of tragic events shattered the hopes and dreams of a new era of racial justice and harmony. Neither John understood the people of the town, and each was in turn misunderstood. Black John's school was closed because he was teaching ideals of liberty. Heartbroken and discouraged as he walked through the forest near town, he surprised the white John in an attempted rape of his sister. Without a word, black John picked up a fallen limb and with "all the pent-up hatred of his great black arm" smashed his boyhood friend to death. Within hours he was lynched.

Du Bois's story capsulizes the human cost of the Reconstruction era. The black scholar's hope for reconciliation by "a union of intelligence and sympathy across the color-line" was smashed in the tragic encounter between the two Johns. Both young men, each once filled with glorious dreams, lay dead under the pines of the Georgia forest. Dying with them were hopes that interracial harmony, intersectional trust, and equal opportunities and rights for the freedmen might be the legacies of Reconstruction. Conspicuously absent in the forest scene was the influence of the victorious northerners. They had turned their attention to other, less noble causes.

Recommended Reading

The best overviews of the Reconstruction era are John Hope Franklin, Reconstruction After the Civil War *(1961); Kenneth Stampp,* The Era of Reconstruction, 1865–1877 *(1965); and the brilliant new work by Eric Foner,* Reconstruction: America's Unfinished Revolution, 1863–1877 *(1988). A recent collection of essays on the issues of the era can be found in Morgan Kousser and James M. McPherson, eds.,* Region, Race, and Reconstruction: Essays in Honor of C. Vann Woodward *(1982).*

The fullest, most moving account of the black experience in the transition from slavery to freedom is Leon Litwack's massive and sensitive work, Been in the Storm So Long: The Aftermath of Slavery *(1980). See also Willie Lee Rose,* Rehearsal for Reconstruction *(1964), an account of the earliest adjustments to freedom in the Sea Islands. The southern white response to emancipation is described in James Roark,* Masters Without Slaves: Southern Planters in the Civil War and Reconstruction *(1977), and Dan T. Carter,* When the War Was Over: The Failure of Self-reconstruction in the South, 1865–1867 *(1985).*

The economy of the South and the freedmen's experience with land and labor are described in Roger Ransom and Richard Sutch, One Kind of Freedom: The Economic Consequences of Emancipation *(1977); Robert Higgs,* Competition and Coercion: Blacks in the American Economy, 1865–1914 *(1977); and Eric Foner,* Nothing but Freedom: Emancipation and Its Legacy *(1983). An excellent work showing the white experience with tenancy in the changing economy of the South is Stephen Hahn,* The Roots of Southern Populism *(1983). The northern labor movement is described in David Montgomery,* Beyond Equality: Labor and the Radical Republicans, 1862–1872 *(1967). For an excellent view of the New South, see C. Vann Woodward,* Origins of the New South, 1877–1913 *(1951). The Freedmen's Bureau has been the subject of several studies, the best of which are Peter Kolchin,* First Freedom *(1972); Claude*

Oubré, Forty Acres and a Mule: The Freedmen's Bureau and Black Land Ownership *(1978); and Donald Nieman,* To Set the Law in Motion: The Freedmen's Bureau and the Legal Rights of Blacks, 1865–1868 *(1979). Continuing racial prejudice in the South and North is the subject of C. Vann Woodward,* The Strange Career of Jim Crow, *3d rev. ed. (1974), and Rayford Logan,* The Betrayal of the Negro, *rev. ed (1965). See also W. E. B. Du Bois's* Black Reconstruction *(1935) and* The Souls of Black Folk *(1903).*

Northern politics during Reconstruction have been widely discussed. See LaWanda Cox and John Cox, Politics, Principles, and Prejudice, 1865–1866 *(1963); Eric McKitrick,* Andrew Johnson and Reconstruction *(1960); David Donald,* The Politics of Reconstruction *(1965); and Michael Les Benedict,* A Compromise of Principle: Congressional Republicans and Reconstruction, 1963–1869 *(1974). Southern politics is best seen in Michael Perman,* Reunion Without Compromise: The South and Reconstruction, 1865–1868 *(1973) and* The Road to Redemption: Southern Politics, 1869–1879 *(1984). Grant's presidency and the abandonment of the freedmen by northern Republicans can be traced in William McFeeley,* Grant: A Biography *(1981), and William Gillette,* Retreat from Reconstruction, 1969–1879 *(1979). The campaign of violence that ended the Republican governments in the South is told with gripping horror in Allen Trelease,* White Terror: The Ku Klux Klan Conspiracy and Southern Reconstruction *(1971), and in George C. Rable,* But There Was No Peace: The Role of Violence in the Politics of Reconstruction *(1984). The end of Reconstruction is the subject of C. Vann Woodward's classic little book* Reunion and Reaction *(1956).*

Five novels written at different times and representing different interpretations of the story of Reconstruction are Albion Tourgée, A Fool's Errand *(1879); Thomas Dixon,* The Clansman *(1905); W. E. B. Du Bois,* The Quest of the Silver Fleece *(1911); Howard Fast,* Freedom Road *(1944); and Ernest Gaines,* The Autobiography of Miss Jane Pittman *(1971).*

1865 Civil War ends
Lincoln assassinated; Andrew
Johnson becomes president
Johnson proposes general amnesty
and reconstruction plan
Racial confusion, widespread
hunger, and demobilization
Thirteenth Amendment ratified
Freedmen's Bureau established

1865–1866 Black codes
Repossession of land by whites and
freedmen's contracts

1866 Freedmen's Bureau renewed and
Civil Rights Act passed
over Johnson's veto
Southern Homestead Act
Ku Klux Klan formed
Tennessee readmitted to Union

1867 Reconstruction Acts passed over
Johnson's veto
Impeachment controversy
Freedmen's Bureau ends

1868 Fourteenth Amendment ratified
Impeachment of Johnson fails
Ulysses Grant elected president

1868–1870 Ten states readmitted under
congressional plan

1869 Georgia and Virginia reestablish
Democratic party control

1870 Fifteenth Amendment ratified

1870s–1880s Black "exodusters" migrate to
Kansas

1870–1871 Force Acts
North Carolina and Georgia
reestablish Democratic control

1872 General Amnesty Act
Grant reelected president

1873 Crédit Mobilier scandal
Panic causes depression

1874 Alabama and Arkansas reestablish
Democratic control

1875 Civil Rights Act
Mississippi reestablishes
Democratic control

1876 Hayes-Tilden election

1876–1877 South Carolina, Louisiana, and
Florida reestablish Democratic
control

1877 Compromise of 1877; Rutherford B.
Hayes assumes presidency and
ends Reconstruction

1880s Tenancy and sharecropping prevail
in the South
Disfranchisement and segregation
of southern blacks begins

APPENDIX

THE UNANIMOUS DECLARATION OF THE THIRTEEN UNITED STATES OF AMERICA

When, in the course of human events, it becomes necessary for one people to dissolve the political bonds which have connected them with another, and to assume, among the powers of the earth, the separate and equal station to which the laws of nature and of nature's God entitle them, a decent respect to the opinions of mankind requires that they should declare the causes which impel them to the separation.

We hold these truths to be self-evident: That all men are created equal; that they are endowed by their Creator with certain unalienable rights; that among these are life, liberty, and the pursuit of happiness; that, to secure these rights, governments are instituted among men, deriving their just powers from the consent of the governed; that whenever any form of government becomes destructive of these ends, it is the right of the people to alter or to abolish it, and to institute new government, laying its foundation on such principles, and organizing its powers in such form, as to them shall seem most likely to effect their safety and happiness. Prudence, indeed, will dictate that governments long established should not be changed for light and transient causes; and accordingly all experience hath shown that mankind are more disposed to suffer, which evils are sufferable, than to right themselves by abolishing the forms to which they are accustomed. But when a long train of abuses and usurpations, pursuing invariably the same object, evinces a design to reduce them under absolute despotism, it is their right, it is their duty, to throw off such government, and to provide new guards for their future security. Such has been the patient sufferance of these colonies; and such is now the necessity which constrains them to alter their former systems of government. The history of the present King of Great Britain is a history of repeated injuries and usurpations, all having in direct object the establishment of an absolute tyranny over these states. To prove this, let facts be submitted to a candid world.

He has refused his assent to laws the most wholesome and necessary for the public good.

He has forbidden his governors to pass laws of immediate and pressing importance, unless suspended in their operation till his assent should be obtained; and, when so suspended, he has utterly neglected to attend to them.

He has refused to pass other laws for the accommodation of large districts of people, unless those people would relinquish the right of representation in the legislature, a right inestimable to them, and formidable to tyrants only.

He has called together legislative bodies at places unusual, uncomfortable, and distant from the depository of their public records, for the sole purpose of fatiguing them into compliance with his measures.

He has dissolved representative houses repeatedly, for opposing, with manly firmness, his invasions on the rights of the people.

He has refused for a long time, after such dissolutions, to cause others to be elected; whereby the legislative powers, incapable of annihilation, have returned to the people at large for their exercise; the state remaining, in the mean time, exposed to all the dangers of invasions from without and convulsions within.

He has endeavored to prevent the population of these states; for that purpose obstructing the laws for naturalization of foreigners; refusing to pass others to encourage their migration hither, and raising the conditions of new appropriations of lands.

He has obstructed the administration of justice, by refusing his assent to laws for establishing judiciary powers.

He has made judges dependent on his will alone, for the tenure of their offices, and the amount and payment of their salaries.

He has erected a multitude of new offices, and sent hither swarms of officers to harass our people and eat out their substance.

He has kept among us, in times of peace, standing armies, without the consent of our legislatures.

He has affected to render the military independent of, and superior to, the civil power.

He has combined with others to subject us to a jurisdiction foreign to our constitution, and unacknowledged by our laws, giving his assent to their acts of pretended legislation:

For quartering large bodies of armed troops among us;

For protecting them, by a mock trial, from punishment for any murders which they should commit on the inhabitants of these states;

For cutting off our trade with all parts of the world;

For imposing taxes on us without our consent;

For depriving us, in many cases, of the benefits of trial by jury;

For transporting us beyond seas, to be tried for pretended offenses;

For abolishing the free system of English laws in a neighboring province, establishing therein an arbitrary government, and enlarging its boundaries, so as to render it at once an example and fit instrument for introducing the same absolute rule into these colonies;

For taking away our charters, abolishing our most valuable laws, and altering fundamentally the forms of our governments;

For suspending our own legislatures, and declaring themselves invested with power to legislate for us in all cases whatsoever.

He has abdicated government here, by declaring us out of his protection and waging war against us.

He has plundered our seas, ravaged our coasts, burned our towns, and destroyed the lives of our people.

He is at this time transporting large armies of foreign mercenaries to complete the works of death, desolation, and tyranny already begun with circumstances of cruelty and perfidy scarcely paralleled in the most barbarous ages, and totally unworthy the head of a civilized nation.

He has constrained our fellow-citizens, taken captive on the high seas, to bear arms against their country, to become the executioners of their friends and brethren, or to fall themselves by their hands.

He has excited domestic insurrection among us, and has endeavored to bring on the inhabitants of our frontiers the merciless Indian savages, whose known rule of warfare is an undistinguished destruction of all ages, sexes, and conditions.

In every stage of these oppressions we have petitioned for redress in the most humble terms; our repeated petitions have been answered only by repeated injury. A prince, whose character is thus marked by every act which may define a tyrant, is unfit to be the ruler of a free people.

Nor have we been wanting in our attentions to our British brethren. We have warned them, from time to time, of attempts by their legislature to extend an unwarrantable jurisdiction over us. We have reminded them of the circumstances of our emigration and settlement here. We have appealed to their native justice and magnanimity; and we have conjured them, by the ties of our common kindred, to disavow these usurpations, which would inevitably interrupt our connections and correspondence. They, too, have been deaf to the voice of justice and of consanguinity. We must, therefore, acquiesce in the necessity which denounces our separation, and hold them, as we hold the rest of mankind, enemies in war, in peace friends.

We, therefore, the representatives of the United States of America, in General Congress assembled, apppealing to the Supreme Judge of the world for the rectitude of our intentions, do, in the name and by the authority of the good people of these colonies, solemnly publish and declare, that these United Colonies are, and of right ought to be, FREE AND INDEPENDENT STATES; that they are absolved from all allegiance to the British crown, and that all political connection between them and the state of Great Britian is, and ought to be, totally dissolved; and that, as free and independent states, they have full power to levy war, conclude peace, contract alliances, establish commerce, and do all other acts and things which independent states may of right do. And for the support of this declaration, with a firm reliance on the protection of Divine Providence, we mutually pledge to each other our lives, our fortunes, and our sacred honor.

Preamble

We the people of the United States, in order to form a more perfect union, establish justice, insure domestic tranquillity, provide for the common defense, promote the general welfare, and secure the blessings of liberty to ourselves and our posterity, do ordain and establish this Constitution for the United States of America.

Article I

Section 1 All legislative powers herein granted shall be vested in a Congress of the United States, which shall consist of a Senate and a House of Representatives.

Section 2 The House of Representatives shall be composed of members chosen every second year by the people of the several States, and the electors in each State shall have the qualifications requisite for electors of the most numerous branch of the State Legislature.

No person shall be a Representative who shall not have attained to the age of twenty-five years, and been seven years a citizen of the United States, and who shall not, when elected, be an inhabitant of that State in which he shall be chosen.

Representatives and direct taxes shall be apportioned among the several States which may be included within this Union, according to their respective numbers, *which shall be determined by adding to the whole number of free persons, including those bound to service for a term of years and excluding Indians not taxed, three-fifths of all other persons.* The actual enumeration shall be made within three years after the first meeting of the Congress of the United States, and within every subsequent term of ten years, in such manner as they shall by law direct. The number of Representatives shall not exceed one for every thirty thousand, but each State shall have at least one Representative; *and until such enumeration shall be made, the State of New Hampshire shall be entitled to choose three, Massachusetts eight, Rhode Island and Providence Plantations one, Connecticut five, New York six, New Jersey four, Pennsylvania eight, Delaware one, Maryland six, Virgina ten, North Carolina five, South Carolina five, and Georgia three.*

When vacancies happen in the representation from any State, the Executive authority thereof shall issue writs of election to fill such vacancies.

The House of Representatives shall choose their Speaker and other officers; and shall have the sole power of impeachment.

Section 3 The Senate of the United States shall be composed of two Senators from each State, *chosen by the legislature thereof,* for six years; and each Senator shall have one vote.

Immediately after they shall be assembled in consequence of the first election, they shall be divided as equally as may be into three classes. The seats of the Senators of the first class shall be vacated at the expiration of the second year, of the second class at the expiration of the fourth year, and of the third class at the expiration of the sixth year, so that one-third may be chosen every second year; *and if vacancies happen by resignation or otherwise, during the recess of the legislature of any State, the Executive thereof may make temporary appointments until the next meeting of the legislature, which shall then fill such vacancies.*

No person shall be a Senator who shall not have attained to the age of thirty years, and been nine years a citizen of the United States, and who shall not, when elected, be an inhabitant of that State for which he shall be chosen.

The Vice-President of the United States shall be President of the Senate, but shall have no vote, unless they be equally divided.

The Senate shall choose their other officers, and also a President *pro tempore,* in the absence of the Vice-President, or when he shall exercise the office of President of the United States.

The Senate shall have the sole power to try all impeachments. When sitting for that purpose, they shall be on oath or affirmation. When the President of the United States is tried, the Chief Justice shall preside; and no person shall be convicted without the concurrence of two-thirds of the members present.

Judgment in cases of impeachment shall not extend further than to removal from the office, and disqualification to hold and enjoy any office of honor, trust or profit under the United States: but the party convicted shall nevertheless by liable and subject to indictment, trial, judgment and punishment, according to law.

Section 4 The times, places and manner of holding elections for Senators and Representatives shall be prescribed in each State by the legislature thereof; but the Congress may at any time by law make or alter such regulations, except as to the places of choosing Senators.

The Congress shall assemble at least once in every year, and such meeting *shall be on the first Monday in*

---

* The Constitution became effective March 4, 1789.
NOTE: Any portion of the text that had been amended appears in italics.

December, unless they shall by law appoint a different day.

Section 5   Each house shall be the judge of the elections, returns and qualifications of its own members, and a majority of each shall constitute a quorum to do business; but a smaller number may adjourn from day to day, and may be authorized to compel the attendance of absent members, in such manner, and under such penalties, as each house may provide.

Each house may determine the rules of its proceedings, punish its members for disorderly behavior, and with the concurrence of two-thirds, expel a member.

Each house shall keep a journal of its proceedings, and from time to time publish the same, excepting such parts as may in their judgment require secrecy; and the yeas and nays of the members of either house on any question shall, at the desire of one-fifth of those present, be entered on the journal.

Neither house, during the session of Congress, shall, without the consent of the other, adjourn for more than three days, nor to any other place than that in which the two houses shall be sitting.

Section 6   The Senators and Representatives shall receive a compensation for their services, to be ascertained by law and paid out of the treasury of the United States. They shall in all cases except treason, felony and breach of the peace be privileged from arrest during their attendance at the session of their respective houses, and in going to and returning from the same; and for any speech or debate in either house, they shall not be questioned in any other place.

No Senator or Representative shall, during the time for which he was elected, be appointed to any civil office under the authority of the United States, which shall have been created, or the emoluments whereof shall have been increased, during such time; and no person holding any office under the United States shall be a member of either house during his continuance in office.

Section 7   All bills for raising revenue shall originate in the House of Representatives; but the Senate may propose or concur with amendments as on other bills.

Every bill which shall have passed the House of Representatives and the Senate, shall, before it becomes a law, be presented to the President of the United States; if he approve he shall sign it, but if not he shall return it with objections to that house in which it originated, who shall enter the objections at large on their journal, and proceed to reconsider it. If after such reconsideration two-thirds of that house shall agree to pass the bill, it shall be sent, together with the objections, to the other house, by which it shall likewise be reconsidered, and, if approved by two-thirds of that house, it shall become a law. But in all such cases the votes of both houses shall be determined by yeas and nays, and the names of the persons voting for and against the bill shall be entered on the journal of each house respectively. If any bill shall not be returned by the President within ten days (Sundays excepted) after it shall have been presented to him, the same shall be a law, in like manner as if he had signed it, unless the Congress by their adjournment prevent its return, in which case it shall not be a law.

Every order, resolution, or vote to which the concurrence of the Senate and House of Representatives may be necessary (except on a question of adjournment) shall be presented to the President of the United States; and before the same shall take effect, shall be approved by him, or being disapproved by him, shall be repassed by two-thirds of the Senate and House of Representatives, according to the rules and limitations prescribed in the case of a bill.

Section 8   The Congress shall have power:

To lay and collect taxes, duties, imposts, and excises, to pay the debts and provide for the common defense and general welfare of the United States; but all duties, imposts and excises shall be uniform throughout the United States;

To borrow money on the credit of the United States;

To regulate commerce with foreign nations, and among the several States, and with the Indian tribes;

To establish an uniform rule of naturalization, and uniform laws on the subject of bankruptcies throughout the United States;

To coin money, regulate the value thereof, and of foreign coin, and fix the standard of weights and measures;

To provide for the punishment of counterfeiting the securities and current coin of the United States;

To establish post offices and post roads;

To promote the progress of science and useful arts by securing for limited times to authors and inventors the exclusive right to their respective writings and discoveries;

To constitute tribunals inferior to the Supreme Court;

To define and punish piracies and felonies committed on the high seas and offenses against the law of nations;

To declare war, grant letters of marque and reprisal, and make rules concerning captures on land and water;

To raise and support armies, but no appropriation of money to that use shall be for a longer term than two years;

To provide and maintain a navy;

To make rules for the government and regulation of the land and naval forces;

To provide for calling forth the militia to execute the laws of the Union, suppress insurrections, and repel invasions;

To provide for organizing, arming, and disciplining the militia, and for governing such part of them as may be employed in the service of the United States, reserving to the States respectively the appointment of the officers, and the authority of training the militia according to the discipline prescribed by Congress;

To exercise exclusive legislation in all cases whatsoever, over such district (not exceeding ten miles square) as may, by cession of particular States, and the acceptance of Congress, become the seat of government of the United States, and to exercise like authority over all places purchased by the consent of the legislature of the State, in which the same shall be, for erection of forts, magazines, arsenals, dockyards, and other needful buildings;—and

To make all laws which shall be necessary and proper for carrying into execution the foregoing powers, and all other powers vested by this Constitution in the government of the United States, or in any department or officer thereof.

Section 9   *The migration or importation of such persons as any of the States now existing shall think proper to admit shall not be prohibited by the Congress prior to the year 1808; but a tax or duty may be imposed on such importation, not exceeding $10 for each person.*

The privilege of the writ of habeas corpus shall not be suspended, unless when in cases of rebellion or invasion the public safety may require it.

No bill of attainder or ex post facto law shall be passed.

No capitation or other direct tax shall be laid, unless in proportion to the census or enumeration herein before directed to be taken.

No tax or duty shall be laid on articles exported from any State.

No preference shall be given by any regulation of commerce or revenue to the ports of one State over those of another; nor shall vessels bound to, or from, one State be obliged to enter, clear, or pay duties in another.

No money shall be drawn from the treasury, but in consequence of appropriations made by law; and a regular statement and account of the receipts and expenditures of all public money shall be published from time to time.

No title of nobility shall be granted by the United States: and no person holding any office of profit or trust under them, shall, without the consent of the Congress, accept of any present, emolument, office, or title, of any kind whatever, from any king, prince, or foreign state.

Section 10   No State shall enter into any treaty, alliance, or confederation; grant letters of marque and reprisal; coin money; emit bills of credit; make anything but gold and silver coin a tender in payment of debts; pass any bill of attainder, ex post facto law, or law impairing the obligation of contracts, or grant any title of nobility.

No States shall, without the consent of Congress, lay any imposts or duties on imports or exports, except what may be absolutely necessary for executing its inspection laws: and the net produce of all duties and imposts, laid by any State on imports or exports, shall be for the use of the treasury of the United States; and all such laws shall be subject to the revision and control of the Congress.

No State shall, without the consent of Congress, lay any duty of tonnage, keep troops or ships of war in time of peace, enter into any agreement or compact with another State, or with a foreign power, or engage in war, unless actually invaded, or in such imminent danger as will not admit of delay.

Article II

Section 1   The executive power shall be vested in a President of the United States of America. He shall hold his office during the term of four years, and, together with the Vice-President, chosen for the same term, be elected as follows:

Each State shall appoint, in such manner as the legislature thereof may direct, a number of electors, equal to the whole number of Senators and Representatives to which the State may be entitled in the Congress; but no Senator or Representative, or person holding an office of trust or profit under the United States, shall be appointed an elector.

The electors shall meet in their respective States, and vote by ballot for two persons, of whom one at least shall not be an inhabitant of the same State with themselves. And they shall make a list of all the persons voted for, and of the number of votes for each; which list they shall sign and certify, and transmit sealed to the seat of government of the United States, directed to the President of the Senate. The President of the Senate shall, in the presence of the Senate and House of Representatives, open all the certificates, and the votes shall then be counted. The person having the greatest number of votes shall be the President, if such number be a majority of the whole number of electors appointed; and if there be more than one who have such majority, and have an equal number of votes, then the House of Representatives shall immediately choose by ballot one of them for President; and if no person have a majority, then from the five highest on the list said house shall in like manner choose the President. But in choosing the President the votes shall be taken by States, the representation from each State having one vote; a quorum for this purpose shall consist of a member or members from two-thirds of the States, and a majority of all the States shall be necessary to a choice. In every case, after the choice of the President, the person having the greatest number of votes of the electors shall be the Vice-President. But if there should remain two or more who have equal votes, the Senate shall choose from them by ballot the Vice-President.

The Congress may determine the time of choosing the electors and the day on which they shall give their votes; which day shall be the same throughout the United States.

No person except a natural-born citizen, *or a citizen of the United States at the time of the adoption of this Constitution,* shall be eligible to the office of President; neither shall any person be eligible to that office who shall not have attained to the age of thirty-five years, and been fourteen years a resident within the United States.

In case of the removal of the President from office or of his death, resignation, or inability to discharge the powers and duties of the said office, the same shall devolve on the Vice-President, and the Congress may by law provide for the case of removal, death, resignation, or inability, both of the President and Vice-President, declaring what officer shall then act as President, and such officer shall act accordingly, until the disability be removed, or a President shall be elected.

The President shall, at stated times, receive for his services a compensation, which shall neither be increased nor diminished during the period for which he shall have been elected, and he shall not receive within that period any other emolument from the United States, or any of them.

Before he enter on the execution of his office, he shall take the following oath or affirmation:—"I do solemnly swear (or affirm) that I will faithfully execute the office of the President of the United States, and will to the best of my ability preserve, protect and defend the Constitution of the United States."

Section 2 The President shall be commander in chief of the army and navy of the United States, and of the militia of the several States, when called into the actual service of the United States; he may require the opinion, in writing, of the principal officer in each of the executive departments, upon any subject relating to the duties of their respective offices, and he shall have power to grant reprieves and pardons for offenses against the United States, except in cases of impeachment.

He shall have power, by and with the advice and consent of the Senate, to make treaties, provided two-thirds of the Senators present concur; and he shall nominate, and by and with the advice and consent of the Senate, shall appoint ambassadors, other public ministers and consuls, judges of the Supreme Court, and all other officers of the United States, whose appointments are not herein otherwise provided for, and which shall be established by law: but Congress may by law vest the appointment of such inferior officers, as they think proper, in the President alone, in the courts of law, or in the heads of departments.

The President shall have power to fill up all vacancies that may happen during the recess of the Senate, by granting commissions which shall expire at the end of their next session.

Section 3 He shall from time to time give to the Congress information of the state of the Union, and recommend to their consideration such measures as he shall judge necessary and expedient; he may, on extraordinary occasions, convene both houses, or either of them, and in case of disagreement between them, with respect to the time of adjournment, he may adjourn them to such time as he shall think proper; he shall receive ambassadors and other public ministers; he shall take care that the laws be faithfully executed, and shall commission all the officers of the United States.

Section 4 The President, Vice-President and all civil officers of the United States shall be removed from office on impeachment for, and on conviction of, treason, bribery, or other high crimes and misdemeanors.

Article III

Section 1 The judicial power of the United States shall be vested in one Supreme Court, and in such inferior courts as the Congress may from time to time ordain and establish. The judges, both of the Supreme and inferior courts, shall hold their offices during good behavior, and shall, at stated times, receive for their services a compensation which shall not be diminished during their continuance in office.

Section 2 The judicial power shall extend to all cases, in law and equity, arising under this Constitution, the laws of the United States, and treaties made, or which shall be made, under their authority—to all cases affecting ambassadors, other public ministers and consuls;—to all cases of admiralty and maritime jurisdiction;—to controversies to which the United States shall be a party;—to controversies between two or more States;—*between a State and citizens of another State;*—between citizens of different States;—between citizens of the same State claiming lands under grants of different States, and between a State, or the citizens thereof, and foreign states, citizens or subjects.

In all cases affecting ambassadors, other public ministers and consuls, and those in which a State shall be party, the Supreme Court shall have original jurisdiction. In all the other cases before mentioned, the Supreme Court shall have appellate jurisdiction, both as to law and fact, with such exceptions, and under such regulations, as the Congress shall make.

The trial of all crimes, except in cases of impeachment, shall be by jury; and such trial shall be held in the State where said crimes shall have been committed;

but when not committed within any State, the trial shall be at such place or places as the Congress may by law have directed.

Section 3 Treason against the United States shall consist only in levying war against them, or in adhering to their enemies, giving them aid and comfort. No person shall be convicted of treason unless on the testimony of two witnesses to the same overt act, or on confession in open court.

The Congress shall have power to declare the punishment of treason, but no attainder of treason shall work corruption of blood, or forfeiture except during the life of the person attainted.

Article IV

Section 1 Full faith and credit shall be given in each State to the public acts, records, and judicial proceedings of every other State. And the Congress may by general laws prescribe the manner in which such acts, records, and proceedings shall be proved, and the effect thereof.

Section 2 The citizens of each State shall be entitled to all privileges and immunities of citizens in the several States.

A person charged in any State with treason, felony, or other crime, who shall flee from justice, and be found in another State, shall on demand of the executive authority of the State from which he fled, be delivered up, to be removed to the State having jurisdiction of the crime.

No person held to service or labor in one State, under the laws thereof, escaping into another, shall, in consequence of any law or regulation therein, be discharged from such service or labor, but shall be delivered up on claim of the party to whom such service or labor may be due.

Section 3 New States may be admitted by the Congress into this Union; but no new State shall be formed or erected within the jurisdiction of any other State; nor any State be formed by the junction of two or more States, or parts of States, without the consent of the legislatures of the States concerned as well as of the Congress.

The Congress shall have power to dispose of and make all needful rules and regulations respecting the territory or other property belonging to the United States; and nothing in this Constitution shall be so construed as to prejudice any claims of the United States, or of any particular State.

Section 4 The United States shall guarantee to every State in this Union a republican form of government, and shall protect each of them against invasion; and on application of the legislature, or of the executive (when the legislature cannot be convened), against domestic violence.

Article V

The Congress, whenever two-thirds of both houses shall deem it necessary, shall propose amendments to this Constitution, or, on the application of the legislatures of two-thirds of the several States, shall call a convention for proposing amendments, which, in either case, shall be valid to all intents and purposes, as part of this Constitution, when ratified by the legislatures of three-fourths of the several States, or by conventions in three-fourths thereof, as the one or the other mode of ratification may be proposed by the Congress; provided *that no amendments which may be made prior to the year one thousand eight hundred and eight shall in any manner affect the first and fourth classes in the ninth section of the first article; and* that no State, without its consent, shall be deprived of its equal suffrage in the Senate.

Article VI

All debts contracted and engagements entered into, before the adoption of this Constitution, shall be as valid against the United States under this Constitution, as under the Confederation.

This Constitution, and the laws of the United States which shall be made in pursuance thereof; and all treaties made, or which shall be made, under the authority of the United States, shall be the supreme law of the land; and the judges in every State shall be bound thereby, anything in the Constitution or laws of any State to the contrary notwithstanding.

The Senators and Representatives before mentioned, and the members of the several State legislatures, and all executive and judicial officers, both of the United States and of the several States, shall be bound by oath or affirmation to support this Constitution; but no religious test shall ever be required as a qualification to any office or public trust under the United States.

Article VII

The ratification of the conventions of nine States shall be sufficient for the establishment of this Constitution between the States so ratifying the same.

Done in Convention by the unanimous consent of the States present, the seventeenth day of September in the year of our Lord one thousand seven hundred and eighty-seven and of the Independence of the United States of America the twelfth. In witness whereof we have hereunto subscribed our names.

Amendments to the Constitution*

Amendment I [1791]

Congress shall make no law respecting an establishment of religion, or prohibiting the free exercise
thereof; or abridging the freedom of speech, or of the
press; or the right of the people peaceably to assemble,
and to petition the government for a redress of grievances.

Amendment II [1791]

A well-regulated militia being necessary to the security of a free State, the right of the people to keep and
bear arms shall not be infringed.

Amendment III [1791]

No soldier shall, in time of peace, be quartered in
any house without the consent of the owner, nor in time
of war, but in a manner to be prescribed by law.

Amendment IV [1791]

The right of the people to be secure in their persons,
houses, papers, and effects, against unreasonable
searches and seizures, shall not be violated, and no
warrants shall issue but upon probable cause, supported
by oath or affirmation, and particularly describing the
place to be searched, and the persons or things to be
seized.

Amendment V [1791]

No person shall be held to answer for a capital or
otherwise infamous crime, unless on a presentment or
indictment of a grand jury, except in cases arising in
the land or naval forces, or in the militia, when in actual
service in time of war or public danger; nor shall any
person be subject for the same offense to be twice put
in jeopardy of life or limb; nor shall be compelled in
any criminal case to be a witness against himself, nor
be deprived of life, liberty or property, without due process of law; nor shall private property be taken for public
use without just compensation.

Amendment VI [1791]

In all criminal prosecutions, the accused shall enjoy
the right to a speedy and public trial, by an impartial
jury of the State and district wherein the crime shall

---

* The first ten amendments are known as the Bill of Rights.

have been committed, which district shall have been
previously ascertained by law, and to be informed of
the nature and cause of the accusation; to be confronted
with the witnesses against him; to have compulsory
process for obtaining witnesses in his favor, and to have
the assistance of counsel for his defense.

Amendment VII [1791]

In suits at common law, where the value in controversy shall exceed twenty dollars, the right of trial
by jury shall be preserved, and no fact tried by a jury
shall be otherwise reexamined in any court of the United
States, than according to the rules of the common law.

Amendment VIII [1791]

Excessive bail shall not be required, nor excessive
fines imposed, nor cruel and unusual punishments inflicted.

Amendment IX [1791]

The enumeration in the Constitution, of certain
rights, shall not be construed to deny or disparage others
retained by the people.

Amendment X [1791]

The powers not delegated to the United States by
the Constitution, nor prohibited by it to the States, are
reserved to the States respectively, or to the people.

Amendment XI [1798]

The judicial power of the United States shall not
be construed to extend to any suit in law or equity,
commenced or prosecuted against one of the United
States by citizens of another State, or by citizens or
subjects of any foreign state.

Amendment XII [1804]

The electors shall meet in their respective States,
and vote by ballot for President and Vice-President, one
of whom, at least, shall not be an inhabitant of the same
State with themselves; they shall name in their ballots
the person voted for as President, and in distinct ballots
the person voted for as Vice-President, and they shall
make distinct lists of all persons voted for as President,
and of all persons voted for as Vice-President, and of
the number of votes for each, which lists they shall sign
and certify, and transmit sealed to the seat of government of the United States, directed to the President of

the Senate;—the President of the Senate shall, in the presence of the Senate and House of Representatives, open all the certificates and the votes shall then be counted;—the person having the greatest number of votes for President shall be the President, if such number be a majority of the whole number of electors appointed; and if no person have such majority, then from the persons having the highest numbers not exceeding three on the list of those voted for as President, the House of Representatives shall choose immediately, by ballot, the President. But in choosing the President, the votes shall be taken by States, the representation from each State having one vote; a quorum for this purpose shall consist of a member or members from two-thirds of the States, and a majority of all the States shall be necessary to a choice. And if the House of Representatives shall not choose a President whenever the right of choice shall devolve upon them, before *the fourth day of March* next following, then the Vice-President shall act as President, as in the case of the death or other constitutional disability of the President.

The person having the greatest number of votes as Vice-President shall be the Vice-President, if such number be a majority of the whole number of electors appointed; and if no person have a majority, then from the two highest numbers on the list the Senate shall choose the Vice-President; a quorum for the purpose shall consist of two-thirds of the whole number of Senators, and a majority of the whole number shall be necessary to a choice. But no person constitutionally ineligible to the office of President shall be eligible to that of Vice-President of the United States.

Amendment XIII [1865]

Section 1 Neither slavery nor involuntary servitude, except as a punishment for crime whereof the party shall have been duly convicted, shall exist within the United States, or any place subject to their jurisdiction.

Section 2 Congress shall have power to enforce this article by appropriate legislation.

Amendment XIV [1868]

Section 1 All persons born or naturalized in the United States, and subject to the jurisdiction thereof, are citizens of the United States and of the State wherein they reside. No State shall make or enforce any law which shall abridge the privileges or immunities of citizens of the United States; nor shall any State deprive any person of life, liberty, or property, without due process of law; nor deny to any person within its jurisdiction the equal protection of the laws.

Section 2 Representatives shall be apportioned among the several States according to their respective numbers, counting the whole number of persons in each State, excluding Indians not taxed. But when the right to vote at any election for the choice of Electors for President and Vice-President of the United States, Representatives in Congress, the executive and judicial officers of a State, or the members of the legislature thereof, is denied to any of the male inhabitants of such State, being twenty-one years of age and citizens of the United States, or in any way abridged, except for participation in rebellion, or other crime, the basis of representation therein shall be reduced in the proportion which the number of such male citizens shall bear to the whole number of male citizens twenty-one years of age in such State.

Section 3 No person shall be a Senator or Representative in Congress, or Elector of President and Vice-President, or hold any office, civil or military, under the United States, or under any State, who, having previously taken an oath, as a member of Congress, or as an officer of the United States, or as a member of any State legislature, or as an executive or judicial officer of any State, to support the Constitution of the United States, shall have engaged in insurrection or rebellion against the same, or given aid or comfort to the enemies thereof. Congress may, by a vote of two-thirds of each house, remove such disability.

Section 4 The validity of the public debt of the United States, authorized by law, including debts incurred for payment of pensions and bounties for services in suppressing insurrection or rebellion, shall not be questioned. But neither the United States nor any State shall assume or pay any debt or obligation incurred in aid of insurrection or rebellion against the United States, or any claim for the loss of emancipation of any slave; but all such debts, obligations, and claims shall be held illegal and void.

Section 5 The Congress shall have power to enforce, by appropriate legislation, the provisions of this article.

Amendment XV [1870]

Section 1 The right of citizens of the United States to vote shall not be denied or abridged by the United States or by any State on account of race, color, or previous condition of servitude.

Section 2 The Congress shall have power to enforce this article by appropriate legislation.

Amendment XVI [1913]

The Congress shall have power to lay and collect taxes on incomes, from whatever source derived, without apportionment among the several States, and without regard to any census or enumeration.

Amendment XVII [1913]

Section 1 The Senate of the United States shall be composed of two Senators from each State, elected by the people thereof, for six years; and each Senator shall have one vote. The electors in each State shall have the qualifications requisite for electors of [voters for] the most numerous branch of the State legislatures.

Section 2 When vacancies happen in the representation of any State in the Senate, the executive authority of such State shall issue writs of election to fill such vacancies: Provided that the legislature of any State may empower the executive thereof to make temporary appointments until the people fill the vacancies by election as the legislature may direct.

Section 3 The amendment shall not be so construed as to affect the election or term of any Senator chosen before it becomes valid as part of the Constitution.

Amendment XVIII [1919]

Section 1 After one year from the ratification of this article the manufacture, sale, or transportation of intoxicating liquors within, the importation thereof into, or the exportation thereof from the United States and all territory subject to the jurisdiction thereof, for beverage purposes, is hereby prohibited.

Section 2 The Congress and the several States shall have concurrent power to enforce this article by appropriate legislation.

Section 3 This article shall be inoperative unless it shall have been ratified as an amendment to the Constitution by the legislatures of the several States, as provided by the Constitution, within seven years from the date of the submission thereof to the States by the Congress.

Amendment XIX [1920]

Section 1 The right of citizens of the United States to vote shall not be denied or abridged by the United States or by any State on account of sex.

Section 2 The Congress shall have power to enforce this article by appropriate legislation.

Amendment XX [1933]

Section 1 The terms of the President and Vice-President shall end at noon on the 20th day of January, and the terms of Senators and Representatives at noon on the 3d day of January, of the years in which such terms would have ended if this article had not been ratified; and the terms of their successors shall then begin.

Section 2 The Congress shall assemble at least once in every year, and such meeting shall begin at noon on the 3d day of January, unless they shall by law appoint a different day.

Section 3 If, at the time fixed for the beginning of the term of the President, the President-elect shall have died, the Vice-President-elect shall become President. If a President shall not have been chosen before the time fixed for the beginning of his term, or if the President-elect shall have failed to qualify, then the President-elect shall act as President until a President shall have qualified, and the Congress may by law provide for the case wherein neither a President-elect nor a Vice-President-elect shall have qualified, declaring who shall then act as President, or the manner in which one who is to act shall be selected, and such persons shall act accordingly until a President or Vice-President shall have qualified.

Section 4 The Congress may by law provide for the case of the death of any of the persons from whom the House of Representatives may choose a President whenever the right of choice shall have devolved upon them, and for the case of the death of any of the persons from whom the Senate may choose a Vice-President whenever the right of choice shall have devolved upon them.

Section 5 Sections 1 and 2 shall take effect on the 15th day of October following the ratification of this article.

Section 6 This article shall be inoperative unless it shall have been ratified as an amendment to the Constitution by the legislatures of three-fourths of the several States within seven years from the date of its submission.

Amendment XXI [1933]

Section 1 The eighteenth article of amendment to the Constitution of the United States is hereby repealed.

Section 2 The transportation or importation into any State, Territory, or Possession of the United States for delivery or use therein of intoxicating liquors, in violation of the laws thereof, is hereby prohibited.

Section 3 This article shall be inoperative unless it shall have been ratified as an amendment to the Constitution by conventions in the several States, as provided in the Constitution, within seven years from the date of submission thereof to the States by the Congress.

Amendment XXII [1951]

Section 1 No person shall be elected to the office of President more than twice, and no person who has held the office of President, or acted as President, for more than two years of a term to which some other person was elected President shall be elected to the office of President more than once. But this article shall not apply to any person holding the office of President when this article was proposed by the Congress, and shall not prevent any person who may be holding the office of President, or acting as President, during the term within which this article becomes operative from holding the office of President or acting as President during the remainder of such term.

Section 2   This article shall be inoperative unless it shall have been ratified as an amendment to the Constitution by the legislatures of three-fourths of the several States within seven years from the date of its submission to the States by the Congress.

Amendment XXIII [1961]

Section 1   The District constituting the seat of Government of the United States shall appoint in such manner as the Congress may direct:

A number of electors of President and Vice-President equal to the whole number of Senators and Representatives in Congress to which the District would be entitled if it were a State, but in no event more than the least populous State; they shall be in addition to those appointed by the States, but they shall be considered for the purposes of the election of President and Vice-President, to be electors appointed by a State; and they shall meet in the District and perform such duties as provided by the twelfth article of amendment.

Section 2   The Congress shall have the power to enforce this article by appropriate legislation.

Amendment XXIV [1964]

Section 1   The right of citizens of the United States to vote in any primary or other election for President or Vice-President, for electors for President or Vice-President, or for Senator or Representative in Congress, shall not be denied or abridged by the United States or any State by reason of failure to pay any poll tax or other tax.

Section 2   The Congress shall have the power to enforce this article by appropriate legislation.

Amendment XXV [1967]

Section 1   In case of the removal of the President from office or of his death or resignation, the Vice-President shall become President.

Section 2   Whenever there is a vacancy in the office of the Vice-President, the President shall nominate a Vice-President who shall take office upon confirmation by a majority vote of both houses of Congress.

Section 3   Whenever the President transmits to the President pro tempore of the Senate and the Speaker of the House of Representatives his written declaration that he is unable to discharge the powers and duties of his office, and until he transmits to them a written declaration to the contrary, such powers and duties shall be discharged by the Vice-President as Acting President.

Section 4   Whenever the Vice-President and a majority of either the principal officers of the executive departments or of such other body as Congress may by law provide, transmit to the President pro tempore of the Senate and the Speaker of the House of Representatives their written declaration that the President is unable to discharge the powers and duties of his office, the Vice-President shall immediately assume the powers and duties of the office as Acting President.

Thereafter, when the President transmits to the President pro tempore of the Senate and the Speaker of the House of Representatives his written declaration that no inability exists, he shall resume the powers and duties of his office unless the Vice-President and a majority of either the principal officers of the executive department[s] or of such other body as Congress may by law provide, transmit within four days to the President pro tempore of the Senate and the Speaker of the House of Representatives their written declaration that the President is unable to discharge the powers and duties of his office. Thereupon Congress shall decide the issue, assembling within forty-eight hours for that purpose if not in session. If the Congress, within twenty-one days after receipt of the latter written declaration, or, if Congress is not in session, within twenty-one days after Congress is required to assemble, determines by two-thirds vote of both Houses that the President is unable to discharge the powers and duties of his office, the Vice-President shall continue to discharge the same as Acting President; otherwise, the President shall resume the powers and duties of his office.

Amendment XXVI [1971]

Section 1   The right of citizens of the United States, who are eighteen years of age or older, to vote shall not be denied or abridged by the United States or by any State on account of age.

Section 2   The Congress shall have power to enforce this article by appropriate legislation.

States of the United States

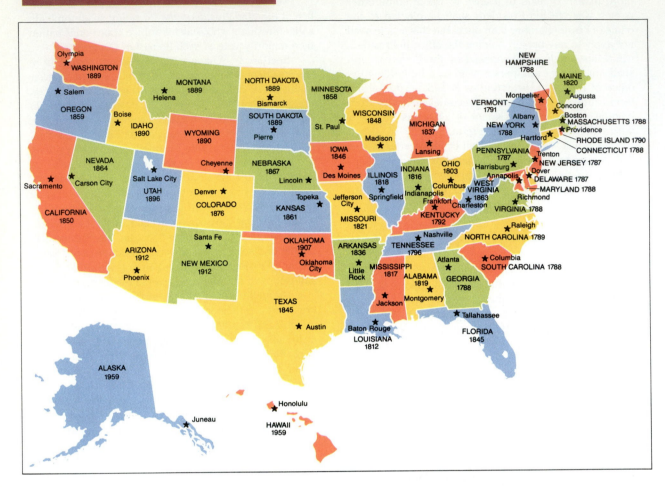

State	Date of Admission	State	Date of Admission
Delaware	December 7, 1787	Michigan	January 16, 1837
Pennsylvania	December 12, 1787	Florida	March 3, 1845
New Jersey	December 18, 1787	Texas	December 29, 1845
Georgia	January 2, 1788	Iowa	December 28, 1846
Connecticut	January 9, 1788	Wisconsin	May 29, 1848
Massachusetts	February 6, 1788	California	September 9, 1850
Maryland	April 28, 1788	Minnesota	May 11, 1858
South Carolina	May 23, 1788	Oregon	February 14, 1859
New Hampshire	June 21, 1788	Kansas	January 29, 1861
Virginia	June 25, 1788	West Virginia	June 19, 1863
New York	July 26, 1788	Nevada	October 31, 1864
North Carolina	November 21, 1789	Nebraska	March 1, 1867
Rhode Island	May 29, 1790	Colorado	August 1, 1876
Vermont	March 4, 1791	North Dakota	November 2, 1889
Kentucky	June 1, 1792	South Dakota	November 2, 1889
Tennessee	June 1, 1796	Montana	November 8, 1889
Ohio	March 1, 1803	Washington	November 11, 1889
Louisiana	April 30, 1812	Idaho	July 3, 1890
Indiana	December 11, 1816	Wyoming	July 10, 1890
Mississippi	December 10, 1817	Utah	January 4, 1896
Illinois	December 3, 1818	Oklahoma	November 16, 1907
Alabama	December 14, 1819	New Mexico	January 6, 1912
Maine	March 15, 1820	Arizona	February 14, 1912
Missouri	August 10, 1821	Alaska	January 3, 1959
Arkansas	June 15, 1836	Hawaii	August 21, 1959

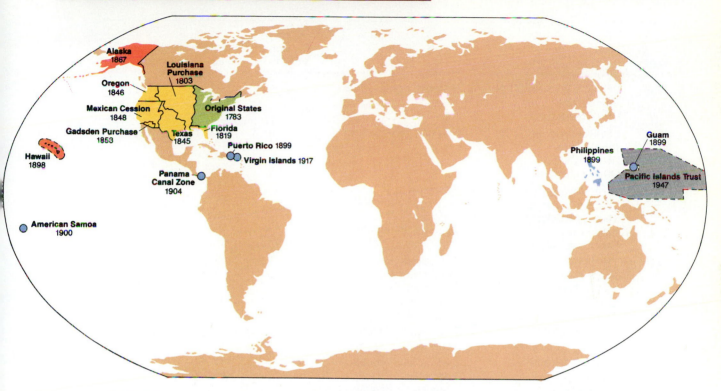

Date	Territory	Area (sq. mi.)	Cumulative Total (sq. mi.)
1793	Original states	888,685	888,685
1803	Louisiana Purchase	827,192	1,715,877
1819	Florida	72,003	1,787,880
1845	Texas	390,143	2,178,023
1846	Oregon	285,580	2,463,603
1848	Mexican Cession	529,017	2,992,620
1853	Gadsden Purchase	29,640	3,022,260
1867	Alaska	589,757	3,612,017
1898	Hawaii	6,450	3,618,467
1899	Philippines	115,600	3,734,067
1899	Puerto Rico	3,435	3,737,502
1899	Guam	212	3,737,714
1900	American Samoa	76	3,737,790
1904	Panama Canal Zone	553	3,738,343
1917	Virgin Islands	133	3,738,476
1947	Pacific Islands Trust	8,489	3,746,965
	All others	46	3,747,011

Year	Candidates	Parties	% of Popular Vote*†	Electoral Vote‡	% Voter Participation†
1789	GEORGE WASHINGTON	No party designations		69	
	John Adams			34	
	Other candidates			35	
1792	GEORGE WASHINGTON	No party designations		132	
	John Adams			77	
	George Clinton			50	
	Other candidates			5	
1796	JOHN ADAMS	Federalist		71	
	Thomas Jefferson	Democratic-Republican		68	
	Thomas Pinckney	Federalist		59	
	Aaron Burr	Democratic-Republican		30	
	Other candidates			48	
1800	THOMAS JEFFERSON	Democratic-Republican		73	
	Aaron Burr	Democratic-Republican		73	
	John Adams	Federalist		65	
	Charles C. Pinckney	Federalist		64	
	John Jay	Federalist		1	
1804	THOMAS JEFFERSON	Democratic-Republican		162	
	Charles C. Pinckney	Federalist		14	
1808	JAMES MADISON	Democratic-Republican		122	
	Charles C. Pinckney	Federalist		47	
	George Clinton	Democratic-Republican		6	
1812	JAMES MADISON	Democratic-Republican		128	
	DeWitt Clinton	Federalist		89	
1816	JAMES MONROE	Democratic-Republican		183	
	Rufus King	Federalist		34	
1820	JAMES MONROE	Democratic-Republican		231	
	John Quincy Adams	Independent Republican		1	
1824	JOHN QUINCY ADAMS	Democratic-Republican	30.5	84	26.9
	Andrew Jackson	Democratic-Republican	43.1	99	
	Henry Clay	Democratic-Republican	13.2	37	
	William H. Crawford	Democratic-Republican	13.1	41	
1828	ANDREW JACKSON	Democratic	56.0	178	57.6
	John Quincy Adams	National Republican	44.0	83	
1832	ANDREW JACKSON	Democratic	54.5	219	55.4
	Henry Clay	National Republican	37.5	49	
	William Wirt	Anti-Masonic	8.0	7	
	John Floyd	Democratic		11	
1836	MARTIN VAN BUREN	Democratic	50.9	170	57.8
	William H. Harrison	Whig		73	
	Hugh L. White	Whig	49.1	26	
	Daniel Webster	Whig		14	
	W. P. Mangum	Whig		11	
1840	WILLIAM H. HARRISON	Whig	53.1	234	80.2
	Martin Van Buren	Democratic	46.9	60	
1844	JAMES K. POLK	Democratic	49.6	170	78.9
	Henry Clay	Whig	48.1	105	
	James G. Birney	Liberty	2.3	0	
1848	ZACHARY TAYLOR	Whig	47.4	163	72.7
	Lewis Cass	Democratic	42.5	127	
	Martin Van Buren	Free-Soil	10.1	0	

Year	Candidates	Parties	% of Popular Vote*†	Electoral Vote‡	% Voter Participation†
1852	FRANKLIN PIERCE	Democratic	50.9	254	69.6
	Winfield Scott	Whig	44.1	42	
	John P. Hale	Free-Soil	5.0	0	
1856	JAMES BUCHANAN	Democratic	45.3	174	78.9
	John C. Frémont	Republican	33.1	114	
	Millard Fillmore	American	21.6	8	
1860	ABRAHAM LINCOLN	Republican	39.8	180	81.2
	Stephen A. Douglas	Democratic	29.5	12	
	John C. Breckinridge	Democratic	18.1	72	
	John Bell	Constitutional Union	12.6	39	
1864	ABRAHAM LINCOLN	Republican	55.0	212	73.8
	George B. McClellan	Democratic	45.0	21	
1868	ULYSSES S. GRANT	Republican	52.7	214	78.1
	Horatio Seymour	Democratic	47.3	80	
1872	ULYSSES S. GRANT	Republican	55.6	286	71.3
	Horace Greeley	Democratic	44.0	0°—§	
1876	RUTHERFORD B. HAYES	Republican	48.0	185	81.8
	Samuel J. Tilden	Democratic	51.0	184	
1880	JAMES A. GARFIELD	Republican	48.5	214	79.4
	Winfield S. Hancock	Democratic	48.1	155	
	James B. Weaver	Greenback-Labor	3.4	0	
1884	GROVER CLEVELAND	Democratic	48.5	219	77.5
	James G. Blaine	Republican	48.2	182	
1888	BENJAMIN HARRISON	Republican	47.9	233	79.3
	Grover Cleveland	Democratic	48.6	168	
1892	GROVER CLEVELAND	Democratic	46.0	277	74.7
	Benjamin Harrison	Republican	43.0	145	
	James B. Weaver	Populist	8.5	22	
1896	WILLIAM McKINLEY	Republican	51.1	271	79.3
	William J. Bryan	Democratic	46.7	176	
1900	WILLIAM McKINLEY	Republican	51.7	292	73.2
	William J. Bryan	Democratic; Populist	45.5	155	
1904	THEODORE ROOSEVELT	Republican	56.4	336	65.2
	Alton B. Parker	Democratic	37.6	140	
	Eugene V. Debs	Socialist	3.0	0	
1908	WILLIAM H. TAFT	Republican	51.6	321	65.4
	William J. Bryan	Democratic	43.1	162	
	Eugene V. Debs	Socialist	2.8	0	
1912	WOODROW WILSON	Democratic	41.9	435	58.8
	Theodore Roosevelt	Progressive	27.4	88	
	William H. Taft	Republican	23.2	8	
	Eugene V. Debs	Socialist	6.0	0	
1916	WOODROW WILSON	Democratic	49.4	277	61.6
	Charles E. Hughes	Republican	46.2	254	
	Allan L. Benson	Socialist	3.2	0	
1920	WARREN G. HARDING	Republican	60.4	404	49.2
	James M. Cox	Democratic	34.2	127	
	Eugene V. Debs	Socialist	3.4	0	
1924	CALVIN COOLIDGE	Republican	54.0	382	48.9
	John W. Davis	Democratic	28.8	136	
	Robert M. La Follette	Progressive	16.6	13	
1928	HERBERT C. HOOVER	Republican	58.2	444	56.9
	Alfred E. Smith	Democratic	40.9	87	

Year	Candidates	Parties	% of Popular Vote*†	Electoral Vote‡	% Voter Participation†
1932	FRANKLIN D. ROOSEVELT	Democratic	57.4	472	56.9
	Herbert C. Hoover	Republican	39.7	59	
1936	FRANKLIN D. ROOSEVELT	Democratic	60.8	523	61.0
	Alfred M. Landon	Republican	36.5	8	
1940	FRANKLIN D. ROOSEVELT	Democratic	54.8	449	62.5
	Wendell L. Willkie	Republican	44.8	82	
1944	FRANKLIN D. ROOSEVELT	Democratic	53.5	432	55.9
	Thomas E. Dewey	Republican	46.0	99	
1948	HARRY S TRUMAN	Democratic	49.5	303	53.0
	Thomas E. Dewey	Republican	45.1	189	
	J. Strom Thurmond	States' Rights	2.4	39	
	Henry A. Wallace	Progressive	2.4	0	
1952	DWIGHT D. EISENHOWER	Republican	55.1	442	63.3
	Adlai E. Stevenson	Democratic	44.4	89	
1956	DWIGHT D. EISENHOWER	Republican	57.4	457	60.6
	Adlai E. Stevenson	Democratic	42.0	73	
1960	JOHN F. KENNEDY	Democratic	49.7	303	64.0
	Richard M. Nixon	Republican	49.6	219	
	Harry F. Byrd	Independent	0.7	15	
1964	LYNDON B. JOHNSON	Democratic	61.1	486	61.7
	Barry M. Goldwater	Republican	38.5	52	
1968	RICHARD M. NIXON	Republican	43.4	301	60.6
	Hubert H. Humphrey	Democratic	42.7	191	
	George C. Wallace	American Independent	13.5	46	
1972	RICHARD M. NIXON	Republican	60.7	520	55.5
	George S. McGovern	Democratic	37.5	17	
1976	JIMMY CARTER	Democratic	50.0	297	54.3
	Gerald R. Ford	Republican	48.0	240	
1980	RONALD REAGAN	Republican	50.8	489	53.0
	Jimmy Carter	Democratic	41.0	49	
	John B. Anderson	Independent	6.6	0	
1984	RONALD REAGAN	Republican	58.7	525	52.9
	Walter F. Mondale	Democratic	40.6	13	
1988	GEORGE BUSH	Republican	54.0	426	50.1
	Michael Dukakis	Democratic	46.0	111	

* Candidates receiving less than 2.5 percent of the popular vote have been omitted. Hence the percentage of popular vote may not total 100 percent.
† Prior to 1824, most presidential electors were chosen by state legislators rather than by popular vote.
‡ Before the Twelfth Amendment was passed in 1804, the electoral college voted for two presidential candidates; the runner-up became the vice-president.
§ Greeley died before the electoral college met. His votes were divided among four other candidates.

Washington, 1789–1797

Vice-President	John Adams	1789–1797
Secretary of State	Thomas Jefferson	1790–1793
	Edmund Randolph	1794–1795
	Timothy Pickering	1795–1797
Secretary of Treasury	Alexander Hamilton	1789–1795
	Oliver Wolcott	1795–1797
Secretary of War	Henry Knox	1789–1794
	Timothy Pickering	1795–1796
	James McHenry	1796–1797
Attorney General	Edmund Randolph	1789–1793
	William Bradford	1794–1795
	Charles Lee	1795–1797
Postmaster General	Samuel Osgood	1789–1791
	Timothy Pickering	1791–1794
	Joseph Habersham	1795–1797

John Adams, 1797–1801

Vice-President	Thomas Jefferson	1797–1801
Secretary of State	Timothy Pickering	1797–1800
	John Marshall	1800–1801
Secretary of Treasury	Oliver Wolcott	1797–1800
	Samuel Dexter	1800–1801
Secretary of War	James McHenry	1797–1800
	Samuel Dexter	1800–1801
Attorney General	Charles Lee	1797–1801
Postmaster General	Joseph Habersham	1797–1801
Secretary of Navy	Benjamin Stoddert	1798–1801

Jefferson, 1801–1809

Vice-President	Aaron Burr	1801–1805
Secretary of State	James Madison	1801–1809
Secretary of Treasury	Samuel Dexter	1801
	Albert Gallatin	1801–1809
Secretary of War	Henry Dearborn	1801–1809
Attorney General	Levi Lincoln	1801–1805
	Robert Smith	1805
	John Breckinridge	1805–1806
	Caesar A. Rodney	1807–1809
Postmaster General	Joseph Habersham	1801
	Gideon Granger	1801–1809
Secretary of Navy	Robert Smith	1801–1809

Madison, 1809–1817

Vice-President	George Clinton	1809–1812
	Elbridge Gerry	1813–1817
Secretary of State	Robert Smith	1809–1811
	James Monroe	1811–1817
Secretary of Treasury	Albert Gallatin	1809–1813
	George W. Campbell	1814
	Alexander J. Dallas	1814–1816
	William H. Crawford	1816–1817
Secretary of War	William Eustis	1809–1812
	John Armstrong	1813–1814
	James Monroe	1814–1815
	William H. Crawford	1815–1817
Attorney General	Caesar A. Rodney	1809–1811
	William Pinckney	1811–1814
	Richard Rush	1814–1817
Postmaster General	Gideon Granger	1809–1814
	Return J. Meigs, Jr.	1814–1817
Secretary of Navy	Paul Hamilton	1809–1813
	William Jones	1813–1814
	Benjamin W. Crowninshield	1814–1817

Monroe, 1817–1825

Vice-President	Daniel D. Tompkins	1817–1825
Secretary of State	John Quincy Adams	1817–1825
Secretary of Treasury	William H. Crawford	1817–1825
Secretary of War	George Graham	1817
	John C. Calhoun	1817–1825
Attorney General	Richard Rush	1817
	William Wirt	1817–1825
Postmaster General	Return J. Meigs, Jr.	1817–1823
	John McLean	1823–1825
Secretary of Navy	Benjamin W. Crowninshield	1817–1818
	Smith Thompson	1818–1823
	Samuel L. Southard	1823–1825

John Quincy Adams, 1825–1829

Vice-President	John C. Calhoun	1825–1829
Secretary of State	Henry Clay	1825–1829
Secretary of Treasury	Richard Rush	1825–1829
Secretary of War	James Barbour	1825–1828
	Peter B. Porter	1828–1829

Attorney General	William Wirt	1825–1829
Postmaster General	John McLean	1825–1829
Secretary of Navy	Samuel L. Southard	1825–1829

Jackson, 1829–1837

Vice-President	John C. Calhoun	1829–1833
	Martin Van Buren	1833–1837
Secretary of State	Martin Van Buren	1829–1831
	Edward Livingston	1831–1833
	Louis McLane	1833–1834
	John Forsyth	1834–1837
Secretary of Treasury	Samuel D. Ingham	1829–1831
	Louis McLane	1831–1833
	William J. Duane	1833
	Roger B. Taney	1833–1834
	Levi Woodbury	1834–1837
Secretary of War	John H. Eaton	1829–1831
	Lewis Cass	1831–1837
	Benjamin F. Butler	1837
Attorney General	John M. Berrien	1829–1831
	Roger B. Taney	1831–1833
	Benjamin F. Butler	1833–1837
Postmaster General	William T. Barry	1829–1835
	Amos Kendall	1835–1837
Secretary of Navy	John Branch	1829–1831
	Levi Woodbury	1831–1834
	Mahlon Dickerson	1834–1837

Van Buren, 1837–1841

Vice-President	Richard M. Johnson	1837–1841
Secretary of State	John Forsyth	1837–1841
Secretary of Treasury	Levi Woodbury	1837–1841
Secretary of War	Joel R. Poinsett	1837–1841
Attorney General	Benjamin F. Butler	1837–1838
	Felix Grundy	1838–1840
	Henry D. Gilpin	1840–1841
Postmaster General	Amos Kendall	1837–1840
	John M. Niles	1840–1841
Secretary of Navy	Mahlon Dickerson	1837–1838
	James K. Paulding	1838–1841

William Harrison, 1841

Vice-President	John Tyler	1841
Secretary of State	Daniel Webster	1841
Secretary of Treasury	Thomas Ewing	1841
Secretary of War	John Bell	1841
Attorney General	John J. Crittenden	1841
Postmaster General	Francis Granger	1841
Secretary of Navy	George E. Badger	1841

Tyler, 1841–1845

Vice-President	None	
Secretary of State	Daniel Webster	1841–1843
	Hugh S. Legaré	1843
	Abel P. Upshur	1843–1844
	John C. Calhoun	1844–1845
Secretary of Treasury	Thomas Ewing	1841
	Walter Forward	1841–1843
	John C. Spencer	1843–1844
	George M. Bibb	1844–1845
Secretary of War	John Bell	1841
	John C. Spencer	1841–1843
	James M. Porter	1843–1844
	William Wilkins	1844–1845
Attorney General	John J. Crittenden	1841
	Hugh S. Legaré	1841–1843
	John Nelson	1843–1845
Postmaster General	Francis Granger	1841
	Charles Wickliffe	1841
Secretary of Navy	George E. Badger	1841
	Abel P. Upshur	1841
	David Henshaw	1843–1844
	Thomas W. Gilmer	1844
	John Y. Mason	1844–1845

Polk, 1845–1849

Vice-President	George M. Dallas	1845–1849
Secretary of State	James Buchanan	1845–1849
Secretary of Treasury	Robert J. Walker	1845–1849
Secretary of War	William L. Marcy	1845–1849
Attorney General	John Y. Mason	1845–1846
	Nathan Clifford	1846–1848
	Isaac Toucey	1848–1849
Postmaster General	Cave Johnson	1845–1849
Secretary of Navy	George Bancroft	1845–1846
	John Y. Mason	1846–1849

Taylor, 1849–1850

Vice-President	Millard Fillmore	1849–1850
Secretary of State	John M. Clayton	1849–1850
Secretary of Treasury	William M. Meredith	1849–1850
Secretary of War	George W. Crawford	1849–1850
Attorney General	Reverdy Johnson	1849–1850
Postmaster General	Jacob Collamer	1849–1850
Secretary of Navy	William B. Preston	1849–1850
Secretary of Interior	Thomas Ewing	1849–1850

Fillmore, 1850–1853

Vice-President	None	
Secretary of State	Daniel Webster	1850–1852
	Edward Everett	1852–1853
Secretary of Treasury	Thomas Corwin	1850–1853
Secretary of War	Charles M. Conrad	1850–1853
Attorney General	John J. Crittenden	1850–1853
Postmaster General	Nathan K. Hall	1850–1852
	Samuel D. Hubbard	1852–1853
Secretary of Navy	William A. Graham	1850–1852
	John P. Kennedy	1852–1853
Secretary of Interior	Thomas M. T. McKennan	1850
	Alexander H. H. Stuart	1850–1853

Pierce, 1853–1857

Vice-President	William R. King	1853–1857
Secretary of State	William L. Marcy	1853–1857
Secretary of Treasury	James Guthrie	1853–1857
Secretary of War	Jefferson Davis	1853–1857
Attorney General	Caleb Cushing	1853–1857
Postmaster General	James Campbell	1853–1857
Secretary of Navy	James C. Dobbin	1853–1857
Secretary of Interior	Robert McClelland	1853–1857

Buchanan, 1857–1861

Vice-President	John C. Breckinridge	1857–1861
Secretary of State	William L. Marcy	1857
	Lewis Cass	1857–1860
	Jeremiah S. Black	1860–1861
Secretary of Treasury	James Guthrie	1857
	Howell Cobb	1857–1860
	Philip F. Thomas	1860–1861
	John A. Dix	1861
Secretary of War	John B. Floyd	1857–1861
	Joseph Holt	1861
Attorney General	Jeremiah S. Black	1857–1860
	Edwin M. Stanton	1860–1861
Postmaster General	Aaron V. Brown	1857–1859
	Joseph Holt	1859–1861
	Horatio King	1861
Secretary of Navy	Isaac Toucey	1857–1861
Secretary of Interior	Jacob Thompson	1857–1861

Lincoln, 1861–1865

Vice-President	Hannibal Hamlin	1861–1865
	Andrew Johnson	1865
Secretary of State	William H. Seward	1861–1865
Secretary of Treasury	Samuel P. Chase	1861–1864
	William P. Fessenden	1864–1865
	Hugh McCulloch	1865
Secretary of War	Simon Cameron	1861–1862
	Edwin M. Stanton	1862–1865
Attorney General	Edward Bates	1861–1864
	James Speed	1864–1865
Postmaster General	Horatio King	1861
	Montgomery Blair	1861–1864
	William Dennison	1864–1865
Secretary of Navy	Gideon Welles	1861–1865
Secretary of Interior	Caleb B. Smith	1861–1865
	John P. Usher	1863–1863

Andrew Johnson, 1865–1869

Vice-President	None	
Secretary of State	William H. Seward	1865–1869

Secretary of Treasury	Hugh McCulloch	1865–1869
Secretary of War	Edwin M. Stanton	1865–1867
	Ulysses S. Grant	1867–1868
	Lorenzo Thomas	1868
	John M. Schofield	1868–1869
Attorney General	James Speed	1865–1866
	Henry Stanbery	1866–1868
	William M. Evarts	1868–1869
Postmaster General	William Dennison	1865–1866
	Alexander W. Randall	1866–1869
Secretary of Navy	Gideon Welles	1865–1869
Secretary of Interior	John P. Usher	1865
	James Harlan	1865–1866
	Orville H. Browning	1866–1869

Grant, 1869–1877

Vice-President	Schuyler Colfax	1869–1873
	Henry Wilson	1873–1877
Secretary of State	Elihu B. Washburne	1869
	Hamilton Fish	1869–1877
Secretary of Treasury	George S. Boutwell	1869–1873
	William A. Richardson	1873–1874
	Benjamin H. Bristow	1874–1876
	Lot M. Morrill	1876–1877
Secretary of War	John A. Rawlins	1869
	William T. Sherman	1869
	William W. Belknap	1869–1876
	Alphonso Taft	1876
	James D. Cameron	1876–1877
Attorney General	Ebenezer R. Hoar	1869–1870
	Amos T. Akerman	1870–1871
	George H. Williams	1871–1875
	Edwards Pierrepont	1875–1876
	Alphonso Taft	1876–1877
Postmaster General	John A. J. Creswell	1869–1874
	James W. Marshall	1874
	Marshall Jewell	1874–1876
	James N. Tyner	1876–1877
Secretary of Navy	Adolph E. Borie	1869
	George M. Robeson	1869–1877
Secretary of Interior	Jacob D. Cox	1869–1870
	Columbus Delano	1870–1875
	Zachariah Chandler	1875–1877

Hayes, 1877–1881

Vice-President	William A. Wheeler	1877–1881
Secretary of State	William M. Evarts	1877–1881
Secretary of Treasury	John Sherman	1877–1881
Secretary of War	George W. McCrary	1877–1879
	Alexander Ramsey	1879–1881
Attorney General	Charles Devens	1877–1881
Postmaster General	David M. Key	1877–1880
	Horace Maynard	1880–1881
Secretary of Navy	Richard W. Thompson	1877–1880
	Nathan Goff, Jr.	1881
Secretary of Interior	Carl Schurz	1877–1881

Garfield, 1881

Vice-President	Chester A. Arthur	1881
Secretary of State	James G. Blaine	1881
Secretary of Treasury	William Windom	1881
Secretary of War	Robert T. Lincoln	1881
Attorney General	Wayne MacVeagh	1881
Postmaster General	Thomas L. James	1881
Secretary of Navy	William H. Hunt	1881
Secretary of Interior	Samuel J. Kirkwood	1881

Arthur, 1881–1885

Vice-President	None	
Secretary of State	Frederick T. Frelinghuysen	1881–1885
Secretary of Treasury	Charles J. Folger	1881–1884
	Walter Q. Gresham	1884
	Hugh McCulloch	1884–1885
Secretary of War	Robert T. Lincoln	1881–1885
Attorney General	Benjamin H. Brewster	1881–1885
Postmaster General	Timothy O. Howe	1881–1883
	Walter Q. Gresham	1883–1884
	Frank Hatton	1884–1885
Secretary of Navy	William H. Hunt	1881–1882
	William E. Chandler	1882–1885
Secretary of Interior	Samuel J. Kirkwood	1881–1882
	Henry M. Teller	1882–1885

Cleveland, 1885–1889

Vice-President	Thomas A. Hendricks	1885–1889
Secretary of State	Thomas F. Bayard	1885–1889
Secretary of Treasury	Daniel Manning Charles S. Fairchild	1885–1887 1887–1889
Secretary of War	William C. Endicott	1885–1889
Attorney General	Augustus H. Garland	1885–1889
Postmaster General	William F. Vilas Don M. Dickinson	1885–1888 1888–1889
Secretary of Navy	William C. Whitney	1885–1889
Secretary of Interior	Lucius Q. C. Lamar William F. Vilas	1885–1888 1888–1889
Secretary of Agriculture	Norman J. Colman	1889

Benjamin Harrison, 1899–1893

Vice-President	Levi P. Morton	1889–1893
Secretary of State	James G. Blaine John W. Foster	1889–1892 1892–1893
Secretary of Treasury	William Windom Charles Foster	1889–1891 1891–1893
Secretary of War	Redfield Proctor Stephen B. Elkins	1889–1891 1891–1893
Attorney General	William H. H. Miller	1889–1891
Postmaster General	John Wanamaker	1889–1893
Secretary of Navy	Benjamin F. Tracy	1889–1893
Secretary of Interior	John W. Noble	1889–1893
Secretary of Agriculture	Jeremiah M. Rusk	1889–1893

Cleveland, 1893–1897

Vice-President	Adlai E. Stevenson	1893–1897
Secretary of State	Walter Q. Gresham Richard Olney	1893–1895 1895–1897
Secretary of Treasury	John G. Carlisle	1893–1897
Secretary of War	Daniel S. Lamont	1893–1897
Attorney General	Richard Olney Judson Harmon	1893–1895 1895–1897
Postmaster General	Wilson S. Bissell William L. Wilson	1893–1895 1895–1897
Secretary of Navy	Hilary A. Herbert	1893–1897
Secretary of Interior	Hoke Smith David R. Francis	1893–1896 1896–1897
Secretary of Agriculture	J. Sterling Morton	1893–1897

McKinley, 1897–1901

Vice-President	Garret A. Hobart Theodore Roosevelt	1897–1899 1901
Secretary of State	John Sherman William R. Day John M. Hay	1897–1898 1898 1898–1901
Secretary of Treasury	Lyman J. Gage	1897–1901
Secretary of War	Russell A. Alger Elihu Root	1897–1899 1899–1901
Attorney General	Joseph McKenna John W. Griggs Philander C. Knox	1897 1897–1901 1901
Postmaster General	James A. Gary Charles E. Smith	1897–1898 1898–1901
Secretary of Navy	John D. Long	1897–1901
Secretary of Interior	Cornelius N. Bliss Ethan A. Hitchcock	1897–1899 1899–1901
Secretary of Agriculture	James Wilson	1897–1901

Theodore Roosevelt, 1901–1909

Vice-President	Charles W. Fairbanks	1905–1909
Secretary of State	John M. Hay Elihu Root Robert Bacon	1901–1905 1905–1909 1909
Secretary of Treasury	Lyman J. Gage Leslie M. Shaw George B. Cortelyou	1901–1902 1902–1907 1907–1909
Secretary of War	Elihu Root William H. Taft Luke E. Wright	1901–1904 1904–1908 1908–1909
Attorney General	Philander C. Knox William H. Moody Charles J. Bonaparte	1901–1904 1904–1906 1906–1909
Postmaster General	Charles E. Smith Henry C. Payne Robert J. Wynne George B. Cortelyou George von L. Meyer	1901–1902 1902–1904 1904–1905 1905–1907 1907–1909

Secretary of Navy	John D. Long	1901–1902
	William H. Moody	1902–1904
	Paul Morton	1904–1905
	Charles J. Bonaparte	1905–1906
	Victor H. Metcalf	1906–1908
	Truman H. Newberry	1908–1909
Secretary of Interior	Ethan A. Hitchcock	1901–1907
	James R. Garfield	1907–1909
Secretary of Agriculture	James Wilson	1901–1909
Secretary of Commerce and Labor	George B. Cortelyou	1903–1904
	Victor H. Metcalf	1904–1906
	Oscar S. Straus	1906–1909
	Charles Nagel	1909

Taft, 1909–1913

Vice-President	James S. Sherman	1909–1913
Secretary of State	Philander C. Knox	1909–1913
Secretary of Treasury	Franklin MacVeagh	1909–1913
Secretary of War	Jacob M. Dickinson	1909–1911
	Henry L. Stimson	1911–1913
Attorney General	George W. Wickersham	1909–1913
Postmaster General	Frank H. Hitchcock	1909–1913
Secretary of Navy	George von L. Meyer	1909–1913
Secretary of Interior	Richard A. Ballinger	1909–1911
	Walter L. Fisher	1911–1913
Secretary of Agriculture	James Wilson	1909–1913
Secretary of Commerce and Labor	Charles Nagel	1909–1913

Wilson, 1913–1921

Vice-President	Thomas R. Marshall	1913–1921
Secretary of State	William Jennings Bryan	1913–1915
	Robert Lansing	1915–1920
	Bainbridge Colby	1920–1921
Secretary of Treasury	William G. McAdoo	1913–1918
	Carter Glass	1918–1920
	David F. Houston	1920–1921
Secretary of War	Lindley M. Garrison	1913–1916
	Newton D. Baker	1916–1921
Attorney General	James C. McReynolds	1913–1914
	Thomas W. Gregory	1914–1921
	A. Mitchell Palmer	1919–1921
Postmaster General	Albert S. Burleson	1913–1921

Secretary of Navy	Josephus Daniels	1913–1921
Secretary of Interior	Franklin K. Lane	1913–1920
	John B. Payne	1920–1921
Secretary of Agriculture	David F. Houston	1913–1920
	Edwin T. Meredith	1920–1921
Secretary of Commerce	William C. Redfield	1913–1919
	Joshua W. Alexander	1919–1921
Secretary of Labor	William B. Wilson	1913–1921

Harding, 1921–1923

Vice-President	Calvin Coolidge	1921–1923
Secretary of State	Charles E. Hughes	1921–1923
Secretary of Treasury	Andrew W. Mellon	1921–1923
Secretary of War	John W. Weeks	1921–1923
Attorney General	Harry M. Daugherty	1921–1923
Postmaster General	Will H. Hays	1921–1922
	Hubert Work	1922–1923
	Harry S. New	1923
Secretary of Navy	Edwin Denby	1921–1923
Secretary of Interior	Albert B. Fall	1921–1923
	Hubert Work	1923
Secretary of Agriculture	Henry C. Wallace	1921–1923
Secretary of Commerce	Herbert C. Hoover	1921–1923
Secretary of Labor	James J. Davis	1921–1923

Coolidge, 1923–1929

Vice-President	Charles G. Dawes	1925–1929
Secretary of State	Charles E. Hughes	1923–1925
	Frank B. Kellogg	1925–1929
Secretary of Treasury	Andrew W. Mellon	1923–1929
Secretary of War	John W. Weeks	1923–1925
	Dwight F. Davis	1925–1929
Attorney General	Harry M. Daugherty	1923–1924
	Harlan F. Stone	1924–1925
	John G. Sargent	1925–1929
Postmaster General	Harry S. New	1923–1929
Secretary of Navy	Edwin Denby	1923–1924
	Curtis D. Wilbur	1924–1929
Secretary of Interior	Hubert Work	1923–1928
	Roy O. West	1928–1929

Secretary of Agriculture	Henry C. Wallace	1923–1924
	Howard M. Gore	1924–1925
	William M. Jardine	1925–1929
Secretary of Commerce	Herbert C. Hoover	1923–1928
	William F. Whiting	1928–1929
Secretary of Labor	James J. Davis	1923–1929

Hoover, 1929–1933

Vice-President	Charles Curtis	1929–1933
Secretary of State	Henry L Stimson	1929–1933
Secretary of Treasury	Andrew W. Mellon	1929–1932
	Ogden L. Mills	1932–1933
Secretary of War	James W. Good	1929
	Patrick J. Hurley	1929–1933
Attorney General	William D. Mitchell	1929–1933
Postmaster General	Walter F. Brown	1929–1933
Secretary of Navy	Charles F. Adams	1929–1933
Secretary of Interior	Ray L. Wilbur	1929–1933
Secretary of Agriculture	Arthur M. Hyde	1929–1933
Secretary of Commerce	Robert P. Lamont	1929–1932
	Roy D. Chapin	1932–1933
Secretary of Labor	James J. Davis	1929–1930
	William N. Doak	1930–1933

Franklin D. Roosevelt, 1933–1945

Vice-President	John Nance Garner	1933–1941
	Henry W. Wallace	1941–1945
	Harry S Truman	1945
Secretary of State	Cordell Hull	1933–1944
	Edward R. Stettinius, Jr.	1944–1945
Secretary of Treasury	William H. Woodin	1933–1934
	Henry Morgenthau, Jr.	1934–1945
Secretary of War	George H. Dern	1933–1936
	Henry A. Woodring	1936–1940
	Henry L. Stimson	1940–1945
Attorney General	Homer S. Cummings	1933–1939
	Frank Murphy	1939–1940
	Robert H. Jackson	1940–1941
	Francis Biddle	1941–1945
Postmaster General	James A. Farley	1933–1940
	Frank C. Walker	1940–1945
Secretary of Navy	Claude A. Swanson	1933–1940
	Charles Edison	1940
	Frank Knox	1940–1944
	James V. Forrestal	1944–1945

Secretary of Interior	Harold L. Ickes	1933–1945
Secretary of Agriculture	Henry A. Wallace	1933–1940
	Claude R. Wickard	1940–1945
Secretary of Commerce	Daniel C. Roper	1933–1939
	Harry L. Hopkins	1939–1940
	Jesse Jones	1940–1945
	Henry A. Wallace	1945
Secretary of Labor	Frances Perkins	1933–1945

Truman, 1945–1953

Vice-President	Alban W. Barkley	1949–1953
Secretary of State	James F. Byrnes	1945–1947
	George C. Marshall	1947–1949
	Dean G. Acheson	1949–1953
Secretary of Treasury	Fred M. Vinson	1945–1946
	John W. Snyder	1946–1953
Secretary of War	Robert P. Patterson	1945–1947
	Kenneth C. Royall	1947
Attorney General	Tom C. Clark	1945–1949
	J. Howard McGrath	1949–1952
	James P. McGranery	1952–1953
Postmaster General	Frank C. Walker	1945
	Robert E. Hannegan	1945–1947
	Jesse M. Donaldson	1947–1953
Secretary of Navy	James V. Forrestal	1945–1947
Secretary of Interior	Harold L. Ickes	1945–1946
	Julius A. Krug	1946–1949
	Oscar I. Chapman	1949–1953
Secretary of Agriculture	Clinton P. Anderson	1945–1948
	Charles F. Brannan	1948–1953
Secretary of Commerce	Henry A. Wallace	1945–1946
	W. Averell Harriman	1946–1948
	Charles Sawyer	1948–1953
Secretary of Labor	Lewis B. Schwellenbach	1945–1948
	Maurice J. Tobin	1948–1953
Secretary of Defense	James V. Forrestal	1947–1949
	Louis A. Johnson	1949–1950
	George C. Marshall	1950–1951
	Robert A. Lovett	1951–1953

Eisenhower, 1953–1961

Vice-President	Richard M. Nixon	1953–1961
Secretary of State	John Foster Dulles	1953–1959
	Christian A. Herter	1959–1961
Secretary of Treasury	George M. Humphrey	1953–1957
	Robert B. Anderson	1957–1961
Attorney General	Herbert Brownell, Jr.	1953–1958
	William P. Rogers	1958–1961

Postmaster General	Arthur E. Summerfield	1953–1961
Secretary of Interior	Douglas McKay Fred A. Seaton	1953–1956 1956–1961
Secretary of Agriculture	Ezra Taft Benson	1953–1961
Secretary of Commerce	Sinclair Weeks Lewis L. Strauss Frederick H. Mueller	1953–1958 1958–1959 1959–1961
Secretary of Labor	Martin P. Durkin James P. Mitchell	1953 1953–1961
Secretary of Defense	Charles E. Wilson Neil H. McElroy Thomas S. Gates, Jr.	1953–1957 1957–1959 1959–1961
Secretary of Health, Education and Welfare	Oveta Culp Hobby Marion B. Folsom Arthur S. Flemming	1953–1955 1955–1958 1958–1961

Kennedy, 1961–1963

Vice-President	Lyndon B. Johnson	1961–1963
Secretary of State	Dean Rusk	1961–1963
Secretary of Treasury	C. Douglas Dillon	1961–1963
Attorney General	Robert F. Kennedy	1961–1963
Postmaster General	J. Edward Day John A. Gronouski	1961–1963 1963
Secretary of Interior	Stewart L. Udall	1961–1963
Secretary of Agriculture	Orville L. Freeman	1961–1963
Secretary of Commerce	Luther H. Hodges	1961–1963
Secretary of Labor	Arthur J. Goldberg W. Willard Wirtz	1961–1962 1962–1963
Secretary of Defense	Robert S. McNamara	1961–1963
Secretary of Health, Education and Welfare	Abraham A. Ribicoff Anthony J. Celebrezze	1961–1962 1962–1963

Lyndon Johnson, 1963–1969

Vice-President	Hubert H. Humphrey	1965–1969
Secretary of State	Dean Rusk	1963–1969
Secretary of Treasury	C. Douglas Dillon Henry H. Fowler	1963–1965 1965–1969
Attorney General	Robert F. Kennedy Nicholas de B. Katzenbach Ramsey Clark	1963–1964 1965–1966 1967–1969

Postmaster General	John A. Gronouski Lawrence F. O'Brien Marvin Watson	1963–1965 1965–1968 1968–1969
Secretary of Interior	Stewart L. Udall	1963–1969
Secretary of Agriculture	Orville L. Freeman	1963–1969
Secretary of Commerce	Luther H. Hodges John T. Connor Alexander B. Trowbridge Cyrus R. Smith	1963–1964 1964–1967 1967–1968 1968–1969
Secretary of Labor	W. Willard Wirtz	1963–1969
Secretary of Defense	Robert S. McNamara Clark M. Clifford	1963–1968 1968–1969
Secretary of Health, Education and Welfare	Anthony J. Celebrezze John W. Gardner Wilbur J. Cohen	1963–1965 1965–1968 1968–1969
Secretary of Housing and Urban Development	Robert C. Weaver Robert C. Wood	1966–1969 1969
Secretary of Transportation	Alan S. Boyd	1967–1969

Nixon, 1969–1974

Vice-President	Spiro T. Agnew Gerald R. Ford	1969–1973 1973
Secretary of State	William P. Rogers Henry A. Kissinger	1969–1973 1973–1974
Secretary of Treasury	David M. Kennedy John B. Connally George P. Shultz William E. Simon	1969–1970 1971–1972 1972–1974 1974
Attorney General	John N. Mitchell Richard G. Kleindienst Elliot L. Richardson William B. Saxbe	1969–1972 1972–1973 1973 1973–1974
Postmaster General	Winton M. Blount	1969–1971
Secretary of Interior	Walter J. Hickel Rogers C. B. Morton	1969–1970 1971–1974
Secretary of Agriculture	Clifford M. Hardin Earl L. Butz	1969–1971 1971–1974
Secretary of Commerce	Maurice H. Stans Peter G. Peterson Frederick B. Dent	1969–1972 1972–1973 1973–1974
Secretary of Labor	George P. Shultz James D. Hodgson Peter J. Brennan	1969–1970 1970–1973 1973–1974
Secretary of Defense	Melvin R. Laird Elliot L. Richardson James R. Schlesinger	1969–1973 1973 1973–1974

Secretary of Health, Education and Welfare	Robert H. Finch	1969–1970
	Elliot L. Richardson	1970–1973
	Caspar W. Weinberger	1973–1974
Secretary of Housing and Urban Development	George W. Romney	1969–1973
	James T. Lynn	1973–1974
Secretary of Transportation	John A. Volpe	1969–1973
	Claude S. Brinegar	1973–1974

Ford, 1974–1977

Vice-President	Nelson Rockefeller	1974–1977
Secretary of State	Henry A. Kissinger	1974–1977
Secretary of Treasury	William E. Simon	1974–1977
Attorney General	William Saxbe	1974–1975
	Edward H. Levi	1975–1977
Secretary of Interior	Rogers C. B. Morton	1974–1975
	Stanley K. Hathaway	1975
	Thomas S. Kleppe	1975–1977
Secretary of Agriculture	Earl L. Butz	1974–1976
	John A. Knebel	1976–1977
Secretary of Commerce	Frederick B. Dent	1974–1975
	Rogers C. B. Morton	1975–1976
	Elliot L. Richardson	1976–1977
Secretary of Labor	Peter J. Brennan	1974–1975
	John T. Dunlop	1975–1976
	William J. Usery, Jr.	1976–1977
Secretary of Defense	James R. Schlesinger	1974–1975
	Donald H. Rumsfeld	1975–1977
Secretary of Health, Education and Welfare	Caspar W. Weinberger	1974–1975
	Forrest David Mathews	1975–1977
Secretary of Housing and Urban Development	James T. Lynn	1974–1975
	Carla Anderson Hills	1975–1977
Secretary of Transportation	Claude S. Brinegar	1974–1975
	William T. Coleman, Jr.	1975–1977

Carter, 1977–1981

Vice-President	Walter F. Mondale	1977–1981
Secretary of State	Cyrus R. Vance	1977–1980
	Edmund S. Muskie	1980–1981
Secretary of Treasury	W. Michael Blumenthal	1977–1979
	G. William Miller	1979–1981
Attorney General	Griffin B. Bell	1977–1979
	Benjamin R. Civiletti	1979–1981
Secretary of Interior	Cecil D. Andrus	1977–1981

Secretary of Agriculture	Bob S. Bergland	1977–1981
Secretary of Commerce	Juanita M. Kreps	1977–1979
	Philip M. Klutznick	1979–1981
Secretary of Labor	F. Ray Marshall	1977–1981
Secretary of Defense	Harold Brown	1977–1981
Secretary of Health, Education and Welfare	Joseph A. Califano, Jr.	1977–1979
	Patricia Roberts Harris	1979
Secretary of Health and Human Services	Patricia Roberts Harris	1979–1981
Secretary of Education	Shirley M. Hufstedler	1979–1981
Secretary of Housing and Urban Development	Patricia Roberts Harris	1977–1979
	Moon Landrieu	1979–1981
Secretary of Transportation	Brock Adams	1977–1979
	Neil E. Goldschmidt	1979–1981
Secretary of Energy	James R. Schlesinger	1977–1979
	Charles W. Duncan	1979–1981

Reagan, 1981–1989

Vice-President	George Bush	1981–1989
Secretary of State	Alexander M. Haig, Jr.	1981–1982
	George P. Shultz	1982–1989
Secretary of Treasury	Donald T. Regan	1981–1985
	James A. Baker	1985–1988
	Nicholas F. Brady	1988–1989
Attorney General	William French Smith	1981–1985
	Edwin Meese	1985–1988
	Richard Thornburgh	1988–1989
Secretary of Interior	James G. Watt	1981–1983
	William C. Clark	1983–1985
	Donald P. Hodel	1985–1989
Secretary of Agriculture	John R. Block	1981–1985
	Richard E. Lyng	1985–1989
Secretary of Commerce	Malcolm Baldrige	1981–1987
	C. William Verity, Jr.	1987–1989
Secretary of Labor	Raymond J. Donovan	1981–1985
	William E. Brock	1985–1987
	Ann D. McLaughlin	1987–1989
Secretary of Defense	Caspar W. Weinberger	1981–1987
	Frank C. Carlucci	1987–1989
Secretary of Health and Human Services	Richard S. Schweiker	1981–1983
	Margaret M. Heckler	1983–1985
	Otis R. Bowen	1985–1989

Secretary of Education	Terrel Bell	1981–1985
	William J. Bennett	1985–1988
	Lauro F. Cavazos	1988–1989
Secretary of Housing and Urban Development	Samuel R. Pierce, Jr.	1981–1989
Secretary of Transportation	Andrew L. Lewis, Jr.	1981–1983
	Elizabeth Hanford Dole	1983–1987
	James H. Burnley	1987–1989
Secretary of Energy	James B. Edwards	1981–1982
	Donald P. Hodel	1982–1985
	John Herrington	1985–1989

Bush, 1989–

Vice-President	Dan Quayle	1989–
Secretary of State	James A. Baker	1989–
Secretary of Treasury	Nicholas F. Brady	1989–
Attorney General	Richard Thornburgh	1989–
Secretary of Interior	Manuel Lujan, Jr.	1989–

Secretary of Agriculture	Clayton K. Yeutter	1989–
Secretary of Commerce	Robert A. Mosbacher	1989–
Secretary of Labor	Elizabeth Hanford Dole	1989–
Secretary of Defense	Richard Cheney	1989–
Secretary of Health and Human Services	Louis Sullivan	1989–
Secretary of Education	Lauro F. Cavazos	1989–
Secretary of Housing and Urban Development	Jack Kemp	1989–
Secretary of Transportation	Samuel K. Skinner	1989–
Secretary of Energy	James D. Watkins	1989–
Secretary of Veterans Affairs	Edward J. Derwinski	1989–

Supreme Court Justices

Name	Service	Appointed by	Name	Service	Appointed by
John Jay	1789–1795	Washington	Rufus W. Peckham	1896–1909	Cleveland
James Wilson	1789–1798	Washington	Joseph McKenna	1898–1925	McKinley
John Blair	1789–1796	Washington	Oliver W. Holmes	1902–1932	T. Roosevelt
John Rutledge	1790–1791	Washington	William R. Day	1903–1922	T. Roosevelt
William Cushing	1790–1810	Washington	William H. Moody	1906–1910	T. Roosevelt
James Iredell	1790–1799	Washington	Horace H. Lurton	1910–1914	Taft
Thomas Johnson	1791–1793	Washington	Charles E. Hughes	1910–1916	Taft
William Paterson	1793–1806	Washington	Willis Van Devanter	1910–1937	Taft
John Rutledge*	1795	Washington	Joseph R. Lamar	1911–1916	Taft
Samuel Chase	1796–1811	Washington	**Edward D. White**	1910–1921	Taft
Oliver Ellsworth	1796–1799	Washington	Mahlon Pitney	1912–1922	Taft
Bushrod Washington	1798–1829	J. Adams	James C. McReynolds	1914–1941	Wilson
Alfred Moore	1799–1804	J. Adams	Louis D. Brandeis	1916–1939	Wilson
John Marshall	1801–1835	J. Adams	John H. Clarke	1916–1922	Wilson
William Johnson	1804–1834	Jefferson	**William H. Taft**	1921–1930	Harding
Henry B. Livingston	1806–1823	Jefferson	George Sutherland	1922–1938	Harding
Thomas Todd	1807–1826	Jefferson	Pierce Butler	1923–1939	Harding
Gabriel Duval	1811–1836	Madison	Edward T. Sanford	1923–1930	Harding
Joseph Story	1811–1845	Madison	Harlan F. Stone	1925–1941	Coolidge
Smith Thompson	1823–1843	Monroe	**Charles E. Hughes**	1930–1941	Hoover
Robert Trimble	1826–1828	J. Q. Adams	Owen J. Roberts	1930–1945	Hoover
John McLean	1829–1861	Jackson	Benjamin N. Cardozo	1932–1938	Hoover
Henry Baldwin	1830–1844	Jackson	Hugo L. Black	1937–1971	F. Roosevelt
James M. Wayne	1835–1867	Jackson	Stanley F. Reed	1938–1957	F. Roosevelt
Roger B. Taney	1836–1864	Jackson	Felix Frankfurter	1939–1962	F. Roosevelt
Philip P. Barbour	1836–1841	Jackson	William O. Douglas	1939–1975	F. Roosevelt
John Catron	1837–1865	Van Buren	Frank Murphy	1940–1949	F. Roosevelt
John McKinley	1837–1852	Van Buren	**Harlan F. Stone**	1941–1946	F. Roosevelt
Peter V. Daniel	1841–1860	Van Buren	James F. Byrnes	1941–1942	F. Roosevelt
Samuel Nelson	1845–1872	Tyler	Robert H. Jackson	1941–1954	F. Roosevelt
Levi Woodbury	1845–1851	Polk	Wiley B. Rutledge	1943–1949	F. Roosevelt
Robert C. Grier	1846–1870	Polk	Harold H. Burton	1945–1958	Truman
Benjamin R. Curtis	1851–1857	Fillmore	**Frederick M. Vinson**	1946–1953	Truman
John A. Campbell	1853–1861	Pierce	Tom C. Clark	1949–1967	Truman
Nathan Clifford	1858–1881	Buchanan	Sherman Minton	1949–1956	Truman
Noah H. Swayne	1862–1881	Lincoln	**Earl Warren**	1953–1969	Eisenhower
Samuel F. Miller	1862–1890	Lincoln	John Marshall Harlan	1955–1971	Eisenhower
David Davis	1862–1877	Lincoln	William J. Brennan, Jr.	1956–	Eisenhower
Stephen J. Field	1863–1897	Lincoln	Charles E. Whittaker	1957–1962	Eisenhower
Salmon P. Chase	1864–1873	Lincoln	Potter Stewart	1958–1981	Eisenhower
William Strong	1870–1880	Grant	Byron R. White	1962–	Kennedy
Joseph P. Bradley	1870–1892	Grant	Arthur J. Goldberg	1962–1965	Kennedy
Ward Hunt	1873–1882	Grant	Abe Fortas	1965–1969	Johnson
Morrison R. Waite	1874–1888	Grant	Thurgood Marshall	1967–	Johnson
John M. Harlan	1877–1911	Hayes	**Warren E. Burger**	1969–1986	Nixon
William B. Woods	1880–1887	Hayes	Harry A. Blackmun	1970–	Nixon
Stanley Matthews	1881–1889	Garfield	Lewis F. Powell, Jr.	1972–1988	Nixon
Horace Gray	1882–1902	Arthur	William H. Rehnquist	1972–1986	Nixon
Samuel Blatchford	1882–1893	Arthur	John Paul Stevens	1975–	Ford
Lucious Q. C. Lamar	1888–1893	Cleveland	Sandra Day O'Connor	1981–	Reagan
Melville W. Fuller	1888–1910	Cleveland	**William H. Rehnquist**	1986–	Reagan
David J. Brewer	1889–1910	B. Harrison	Antonin Scalia	1986–	Reagan
Henry B. Brown	1890–1906	B. Harrison	Anthony Kennedy	1988–	Reagan
George Shiras	1892–1903	B. Harrison			
Howell E. Jackson	1893–1895	B. Harrison			
Edward D. White	1894–1910	Cleveland			

Note: **Chief Justices appear in bold type.**
* Acting Chief Justice; Senate refused to confirm appointment.

Population of the United States

Year	Number of States	Population	% Increase	Population per Square Mile
1790	13	3,929,214		4.5
1800	16	5,308,483	35.1	6.1
1810	17	7,239,881	36.4	4.3
1820	23	9,638,453	33.1	5.5
1830	24	12,866,020	33.5	7.4
1840	26	17,069,453	32.7	9.8
1850	31	23,191,876	35.9	7.9
1860	33	31,443,321	35.6	10.6
1870	37	39,818,449	26.6	13.4
1880	38	50,155,783	26.0	16.9
1890	44	62,947,714	25.5	21.2
1900	45	75,994,575	20.7	25.6
1910	46	91,972,266	21.0	31.0
1920	48	105,710,620	14.9	35.6
1930	48	122,775,046	16.1	41.2
1940	48	131,669,275	7.2	44.2
1950	48	150,697,361	14.5	50.7
1960	50	179,323,175	19.0	50.6
1970	50	203,235,298	13.3	57.5
1980	50	226,545,805	11.5	64.1
1989	50	248,251,000	9.4	68.6

Population of the United States

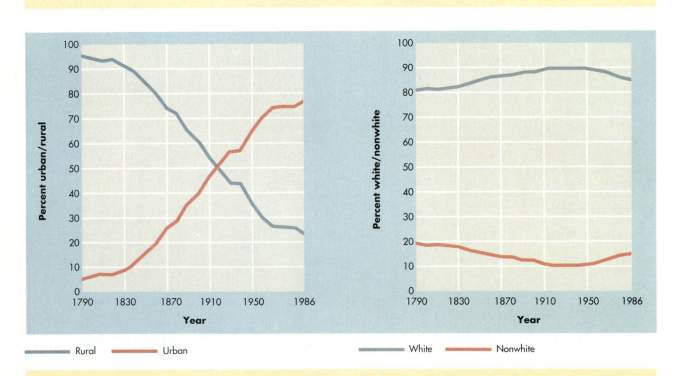

Source: U.S. Bureau of the Census estimates.

A–28

Demographic Contours of the American People

Year	Life Expectancy from Birth White	Life Expectancy from Birth Black	Age at First Marriage Male	Age at First Marriage Female	Number of Children Under 5 per 1,000 Women Age 20–44	Age Distribution (%) Under 15	Age Distribution (%) 15–59	Age Distribution (%) Over 59
1800					1,342			
1810					1,358			
1820					1,295			
1830					1,145			
1840					1,085			
1850					923	41.5	54.3	4.1
1860					929	40.5	55.1	4.3
1870					839	39.2	55.8	5.0
1880					822	38.1	56.3	5.6
1890			26.1	22.0	716	35.5	58.0	6.2
1900	47.6	33.0	25.9	21.9	688	34.4	59.0	6.4
1910	50.3	35.6	25.1	21.6	643	32.1	61.0	6.8
1920	54.9	45.3	24.6	21.2	604	31.8	60.6	7.5
1930	61.4	48.1	24.3	21.3	511	29.4	62.1	8.5
1940	64.2	53.1	24.3	21.5	429	25.0	64.5	10.4
1950	69.1	60.8	22.8	20.3	589	26.9	61.0	12.2
1960	70.6	63.6	22.8	20.3	737	31.1	55.7	13.2
1970	71.7	64.1	22.5	20.6	530	28.5	57.4	14.1
1980	74.4	68.1	23.6	21.8	440	22.6	61.6	15.7
1986	75.4	69.6	24.6*	22.8*	531	21.6	61.4	17.0

* 1984 figures.

Demographic Contours of the American People

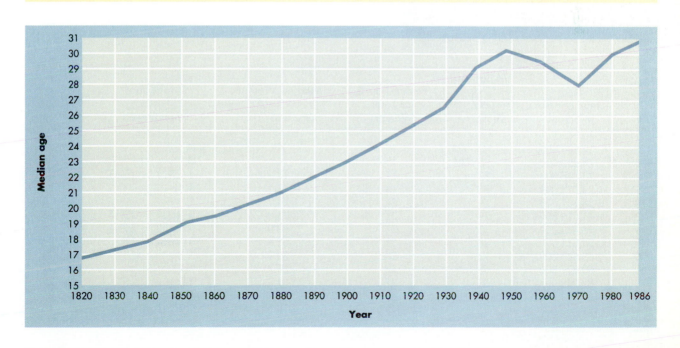

National Origins of U.S. Immigrants, 1821–1987

Year	Total Immigrants	Total Europe No. (%)	Europe North and West No. (%)	Europe East and Central No. (%)	Europe South and Other No. (%)	Western Hemisphere No. (%)	Asia No. (%)	Other No. (%)
1821–1830	144	99 (69.2)	96 (67.1)	——	3 (2.1)	12 (8.4)	——	32 (22.4)
1831–1840	599	496 (82.8)	490 (81.8)	——	1 (1.0)	33 (5.5)	——	70 (11.7)
1841–1850	1,713	1,599 (93.3)	1,592 (92.9)	2 (0.1)	5 (0.3)	62 (3.6)	——	53 (3.1)
1851–1860	2,598	2,453 (94.4)	2,432 (93.6)	3 (0.1)	21 (0.8)	75 (2.9)	42 (1.6)	29 (1.1)
1861–1870	2,315	2,065 (89.2)	2,032 (87.8)	12 (0.5)	21 (0.9)	167 (7.2)	65 (2.8)	19 (0.8)
1871–1880	2,812	2,272 (80.8)	2,070 (73.6)	127 (4.5)	76 (2.7)	405 (14.4)	124 (4.4)	11 (0.4)
1881–1890	5,247	4,738 (90.3)	3,778 (72.0)	624 (11.9)	331 (6.3)	425 (8.1)	68 (1.3)	16 (0.3)
1891–1900	3,688	3,559 (96.5)	1,641 (44.5)	1,210 (32.8)	704 (19.1)	41 (1.1)	70 (1.9)	18 (0.5)
1901–1910	8,795	8,136 (92.5)	1,909 (21.7)	3,914 (44.5)	2,313 (26.3)	361 (4.1)	246 (2.8)	53 (0.6)
1911–1920	5,736	4,376 (76.3)	998 (17.4)	1,916 (33.4)	1,463 (25.5)	1,141 (19.9)	195 (3.4)	23 (0.4)
1921–1930	4,107	2,477 (60.3)	1,302 (31.7)	591 (14.4)	587 (14.3)	1,516 (36.9)	99 (2.4)	16 (0.4)
1931–1940	528	348 (65.9)	205 (38.8)	58 (11.0)	85 (16.1)	160 (30.3)	15 (2.8)	5 (0.9)
1941–1950	1,035	622 (60.1)	492 (47.5)	48 (4.6)	82 (7.9)	355 (34.3)	32 (3.1)	26 (2.5)
1951–1960	2,516	1,328 (52.8)	445 (17.7)	611 (24.3)	272 (10.8)	996 (39.6)	151 (6.0)	40 (1.6)
1961–1970	3,322	1,239 (37.3)	394 (11.9)	419 (12.6)	426 (12.8)	1,579 (47.6)	445 (13.4)	58 (1.9)
1971–1980	4,384	801 (18.3)	188 (4.3)	246 (5.6)	368 (8.4)	1,929 (44.0)	1,634 (37.3)	19 (0.4)
1981–1987	4,068	446 (11.0)	156 (3.9)	199 (4.9)	91 (2.2)	1,580 (38.9)	1,902 (46.7)	140 (3.4)

Note: Numbers are given in thousands.

The American Work Force

Year	Total Number of Workers	Males as % of Total Workers	Females as % of Total Workers	Married Women as % of Female Workers	% of Labor Force Unemployed	% of Workers in Labor Unions
1870	12,506,000	85	15	NA	NA	NA
1880	17,392,000	85	15	NA	NA	NA
1890	23,318,000	83	17	13.9	4 (1894 = 18%)	NA
1900	29,073,000	82	18	15.4	5	3
1910	38,167,000	79	21	24.7	6	6
1920	41,614,000	79	21	23.0	5 (1921 = 12%)	12
1930	48,830,000	78	22	28.9	9 (1933 = 25%)	7
1940	53,011,000	76	24	36.4	15 (1944 = 1%)	27
1950	59,643,000	72	28	52.1	5	25
1960	69,877,000	68	32	59.9	5.4	26
1970	82,049,000	63	37	63.4	4.8	25
1980	108,544,000	58	42	59.7	7.0	23
1986	117,835,000	55	45	58.5	7.0	18

Note: NA = not available.

The American Farmer

Year	Farm Population (in thousands)	% of Total Population	Number of Farms (in thousands)	Total Acres (in thousands)	Average Acreage per Farm
1850	NA	NA	1,449	293,561	203
1860	NA	NA	2,044	407,213	199
1870	NA	NA	2,660	407,735	153
1880	21,973	43.8	4,009	536,082	134
1890	24,771	42.3	4,565	623,219	137
1900	29,875	41.9	5,740	841,202	147
1910	32,077	34.9	6,366	881,431	139
1920	31,974	30.1	6,454	958,677	149
1930	30,529	24.9	6,295	990,112	157
1940	30,547	23.2	6,102	1,065,114	175
1950	23,048	15.3	5,388	1,161,420	216
1960	15,635	8.7	3,962	1,176,946	297
1970	9,712	4.8	2,949	1,102,769	374
1980	6,051	2.7	2,433	1,039,000	427
1986	5,226	2.2	2,212	1,008,000	456

Note: NA = not available.

The American Economy

Year	Gross National Product (GNP) (in $ billions)	Steel Production (in short tons)	Automobiles Registered	Foreign Trade (in $ billions) Exports	Imports
1790	NA	NA	NA	0.02	0.02
1800	NA	NA	NA	0.07	0.09
1810	NA	NA	NA	0.07	0.09
1820	NA	NA	NA	0.07	0.07
1830	NA	NA	NA	0.07	0.07
1840	NA	NA	NA	0.13	0.10
1850	NA	NA	NA	0.15	0.18
1860	NA	13,000	NA	0.40	0.36
1870	7.4*	77,000	NA	0.45	0.46
1880	11.2†	1,397,000	NA	0.85	0.76
1890	13.1	4,779,000	NA	0.91	0.82
1900	18.7	11,227,000	8,000	1.50	0.93
1910	35.3	28,330,000	458,300	1.92	1.65
1920	91.5	46,183,000	8,131,500	8.66	5.79
1930	90.7	44,591,000	23,034,700	4.01	3.50
1940	100.0	66,983,000	27,465,800	4.03	7.43
1950	286.5	96,836,000	40,339,000	10.82	9.13
1960	506.5	99,282,000	61,682,300	19.60	15.05
1970	992.7	131,514,000	89,279,800	42.70	40.19
1980	2,631.7	111,800,000	121,600,000	220.78	244.87
1986	4,235.0	81,600,000	135,700,000	217.30	370.00

Note: NA = not available.
* Figure is average for 1869–1878.
† Figure is average for 1879–1888.

The Federal Budget, 1940–1990

	National Defense	Human Resources	Physical Resources	Net Interest	Other	Undistributed Offsetting Receipts
1940	17.5	43.7	24.4	9.5	8.2	−3.4
1945	89.5	2.0	1.9	3.4	4.8	−1.5
1950	32.2	33.4	8.6	11.3	18.7	−4.3
1955	62.4	21.8	4.0	7.1	9.8	−5.1
1960	52.2	28.4	8.7	7.5	8.4	−5.2
1965	42.8	30.9	9.5	7.3	14.5	−5.0
1970	41.8	38.5	8.0	7.4	8.8	−4.4
1975	26.0	52.1	10.7	7.0	8.3	−4.1
1980	22.7	53.0	11.2	8.9	7.6	−3.4
1985	26.7	49.9	6.0	13.7	7.2	−3.5
1990 (est.)	26.3	52.1	5.2	14.8	5.3	−3.6

The Federal Debt

Year	Debt	Per Capita
1790	$75,463,000	$19
1800	82,976,000	16
1810	53,173,000	7
1820	91,016,000	9
1830	48,565,000	4
1840	3,573,000	0.20
1850	63,453,000	3
1860	64,844,000	2
1870	2,436,453,000	61
1880	2,090,909,000	42
1890	1,222,397,000	19
1900	1,263,417,000	16
1910	1,146,940,000	12
1920	24,299,321,000	230
1930	16,185,310,000	132
1940	42,967,531,000	326
1950	257,357,352,000	1,708
1960	286,330,761,000	1,596
1970	370,918,707,000	1,825
1980	914,300,000,000	4,035
1986	2,132,900,000,000	8,591

CREDITS

PART- AND CHAPTER-OPENING ILLUSTRATIONS

Part One *Dutch Seascape* (detail), thought to depict departure of Pilgrims from Delfthave on the *Speedwell*, attributed to W. Van de Velde, seventeenth century. Courtesy of the Pilgrim Society, Plymouth, Mass. **Chapter 1** The French, under Jean Ribault, discovering the River of May in Florida on May 1, 1564, engraving by Theodore De Bry, 1591, after a painting by Jacques Le Moyne, who accompanied the expedition in 1564. The Granger Collection. **Chapter 2** Detail of a painting by Gerard Soest, court painter to Charles II, depicting Cecil Calvert grasping a map of Maryland held by his grandfather, the second Lord Baltimore, 1669–1670. Enoch Pratt Free Library, Baltimore. **Chapter 3** Anonymous, *Slave Deck of the Albanoz*, n.d. National Maritime Museum, Greenwich, England. **Chapter 4** Joseph Beekman Smith, *Wesley Chapel on John Street, New York City—1768* (detail), completed 1817–1844 (based on earlier sketches). Courtesy of the Old John Street United Methodist Church, New York City. **Chapter 5** *A View of the Town of Concord* (April 1775), attributed to Ralph Earle. Concord Museum, Concord, Mass.

Part Two John Trumbull, *Surrender of Cornwallis at Yorktown* (detail), c. 1828. Copyright Yale University Art Gallery, New Haven, Conn. **Chapter 6** William Mercer, *Battle of Princeton*, c. 1786–1790. The Historical Society of Pennsylvania, Philadelphia. **Chapter 7** First page of the U.S. Constitution. John Feingersh/Stock, Boston. **Chapter 8**

George Ropes, *The Launching of the Ship Fame*, 1802. Courtesy of the Essex Institute, Salem, Mass. **Chapter 9** Thomas Coke Ruckle, *Fairview Inn or Three Mile House on Old Frederick Road* (detail), 1829(?). Collection of the Maryland Historical Society, Baltimore. **Chapter 10** John A. Woodside, *A Pennsylvania County Fair*, 1824. Courtesy Christie's, New York.

Part Three William Sidney Mount, *California News* (detail), 1850. The Museums at Stony Brook, N.Y., gift of Mr. and Mrs. Ward Melville, 1955. **Chapter 11** B. J. Harrison, *Fair of the American Institute at Niblo's Garden*, c. 1845. Museum of the City of New York. **Chapter 12** John Antrobus, *Negro Burial*, c. 1860. The Historic New Orleans Collection, Museum/Research Center. **Chapter 13** A. Wighe, *Trial by Jury*, 1849. Museum of Art, Rhode Island School of Design, gift of Edith Jackson Green and Ellis Jackson. **Chapter 14** Albert Bierstadt, *The Rocky Mountains, Lander's Peak*, 1863. The Metropolitan Museum of Art, Rogers Fund, 1907 (07.123). **Chapter 15** Theodor Kaufmann, *On to Liberty*, 1867. The Metropolitan Museum of Art, gift of Erving and Joyce Wolf, 1982 (1982.443.3). **Chapter 16** Winslow Homer, *The Sharpshooter* (detail), 1863. Private Collection. **Chapter 17** *The First Vote* (freedmen voting in the American South), engraving after the artist A. R. Waud, in *Harper's Weekly*, November 16, 1867. The Granger Collection.

TEXT ILLUSTRATIONS *(listed by page numbers)*

7 Native American Basketry. Museum of the American Indian, Heye Foundation, New York; photo Lee Boltin. **8** Hopewell culture, serpentine earthworks, near Cincinnati. Cahokia Mounds Museum Society. **12** Reconstructed view of Cahokia, painted by Valerie Waldorf. Cahokia Mounds Museum Society. **13** Pottery effigy vessels from Arkansas. Museum of the American Indian, Heye Foundation, New York. **15** Drawing of the city of Loanga, at the mouth of the Congo River. Granger Collection, New York. **16** LEFT: Fon culture, Dahomey, *Gou, God of War*. Musée de l'Homme, Paris. RIGHT: Bambara antelope headdresses, Senegambia. Collection Ernst Anspach; photo Ronald L. C. Kienhuis. **21** Lucas Cranach the Younger, *Epitaph of the Burgomasters of Myenburg*. The Bettmann Archive. **23** Reconstructed view of Tenochtitlán, by Ignacio Marquina. American Museum of Natural History, New York. **24** T. De Bry, Battle between the Spaniards and Indians at Cuzco, from *The Island of Pearls* (Frankfurt, 1590). Rare Book Collection, New York Public Library, Astor, Lenox & Tilden Foundations. **25** Fray Bernardo de Sahagún, woodcut of Aztecs suffering from smallpox, from *Historia de las Cosas de Nueva España*, sixteenth century. Biblioteca Medicea Laurenziana, Florence, Italy; photo Guido Sansoni. **29** George Gower, *Queen Elizabeth I* ("The Armada Portrait"). By kind permission of the Marquess of Tavistock and Trustees of Bedford Estates.

37 John White, *Secotan*, 1585–1587. Trustees of the British Museum. **38** Sidney King, conjectural mural of Jamestown, c. 1965. Courtesy Colonial National Historical Park, Jamestown, Va. **39** ABOVE: Title page of *Nova Britannia* . . . (London, 1609). BELOW: List of what New World Settlers should bring, from Edward Williams, *Virginia*, 2d ed. (London, 1605). Both, Rare Book Collection, New York Public Library, Astor, Lenox & Tilden Foundations. **40** Tabaco, or Henbane of Peru, from *Historia de las Cosas* John Gerarde, *The Herballe or Generall Historie of Plantes*, 1633. Courtesy of Dover Publications, Inc. **42** Tobacco production, from William Tatham, *An Historical and Practical Essay on the Culture of Tobacco*. Arents Collection, New York Public Library, Astor, Lenox & Tilden Foundations. **44** Early Chesapeake architecture, crude

earthfast clapboard church. Harold Wickliffe Rose Papers, Yale University Library, New Haven, Conn. **45** Anonymous portrait of John Winthrop, governor of the Massachusetts Bay Colony. American Antiquarian Society; photo Marvin Richmond. **48** Title page, William Hubbard, *The Present State of New-England, Being a Narrative of the Troubles with the Indians* . . . (Boston and London, 1677). Rare Book Collection, New York Public Library, Astor, Lenox & Tilden Foundations. **50** LEFT: Richard J. Stinely, plan of Rowley, Massachusetts, from David Grayson Allen, *In English Ways* (1982). By permission of University of North Carolina Press. RIGHT: John Walker, Sr., map of Chelmsford, 1591. Public Records Office, Chelmsford, Essex, England. **52** William Boardman House, Saugus, Mass., with floor plans. Society for the Preservation of New England Antiquities; photo Marcus Whiffen. **53** Reconstructed Chesapeake planter's house. Photo Julie Roy Jeffrey. **54** Page from a New England Primer. American Antiquarian Society. **58** Thomas Coram, *Mulberry Plantation*. Gibbes Art Gallery, Carolina Art Association. **61** Lenape wampum belt. Museum of the American Indian, Heye Foundation, New York. **63** Edward Hicks, *Penn's Treaty with the Indians*. National Gallery of Art, Washington, D.C.

71 LEFT: Diagram of "tight packing." National Maritime Museum, Greenwich, England. RIGHT: W. Ralph, *Negroes Just Landed from a Slave Ship*, 1808. Print Collection, New York Public Library, Astor, Lenox & Tilden Foundations. **73** Anonymous, *The Old Plantation*. Abby Aldrich Rockefeller Center for American Folk Art, Williamsburg, Va. **75** LEFT: John Singleton Copely, *Head of a Negro*. Detroit Institute of Arts, Founders Society, Gibbs-Williams Fund. RIGHT: John Greenwood, *Jersey Nanny*, 1784. Museum of Fine Arts, Boston, gift of Henry Lee Shattuck. **77** Paul Revere, engraving of King Philip. American Antiquarian Society; photo Marvin Richmond. **80** Joseph Tapping headstone. King's College Chapel Burial Ground, Boston. Photo Daniel Farber. **81** Betsy Shaw headstone, Plymouth, Mass. Photo Daniel Farber. **83** Charles A. Lawrence, *Boston's First Town House, 1657–1711*, 1930. The Bostonian Society. **86** Witch Hanging, from Ralph Gardner,

England's Grievance Discovered . . . (London, 1655). New York Public Library, Rare Book Collection. **89** *Le Champ d'Asile,* seventeenth-century French engraving. Eugene C. Barker Texas History Center, University of Texas, Austin.

97 Portraits of John Jacob Schmick and Johanna Schmick. Moravian Historical Society, Nazareth, Pa. **98** LEFT: Advertisement for recovery of a runaway indentured servant, *Pennsylvania Packet,* December 28, 1772. RIGHT: Advertisement for the sale of an Irish servant girl's time, *Pennsylvania Journal,* November 25, 1772. Both, Historical Society of Pennsylvania, Philadelphia. **102–103** Van Bergen Overmantel Homestead. New York Historical Association, Cooperstown. **106** Frontispiece of Benjamin Franklin's *Poor Richard's Almanack.* Historical Society of Pennsylvania, Philadelphia. **108** Anonymous, *The Cheney Family,* 1795. National Gallery of Art, Washington, D.C., gift of Edgar William and Bernice Chrysler Garbisch. **110** Richard J. Stinely, plot of tidewater landscape, from Rhys Isaac, *The Transformation of Virginia* (1983). By permission of University of North Carolina Press. **115** William Russell Birch, *Preparation for War to Defend Commerce* (detail), 1800. Athenaeum of Philadelphia, gift of Mrs. Charles Pearson. **118** Mason Chamberlin, *Portrait of Benjamin Franklin,* 1762. Philadelphia Museum of Art, Mr. and Mrs. Wharton Sinkler Collection. **119** ABOVE LEFT: Title page of first edition of Franklin's *Experiments and Observations on Electricity,* 1751. Granger Collection. BELOW LEFT: Apparatus for measuring current, illustration from a 1773 French edition of Franklin's *Experiments and Observations.* Harvard College Library. RIGHT: Illustration from D. Beck, *Kurzer entwurf der Lehre von der Elektricität* (Brief Sketch of the Doctrine of Electricity), Salzburg, 1787. Collection of Historical Scientific Instruments, Harvard University. **121** ABOVE: Joseph Badger, *Jonathan Edwards.* Yale University Art Gallery, New Haven, Conn., gift of Eugene Phelps Edwards. BELOW: John Wollaston, *George Whitefield.* The Bettmann Archive. **124** Anonymous, *Front View of Yale College and the College Chapel, New Haven, 1786.* Yale University Art Gallery, New Haven, Conn., gift of Jesse Lathrop Moss. **128** Henry Dawkins, *The Paxton Expedition,* Library Company of Philadelphia.

137 *A View of the Taking of Quebec, September 13, 1759,* printed for Robert Wilkinson & Bowles & Carver, London. Royal Ontario Museum, Toronto, Canada. **143** Anonymous American, *Patrick Henry Arguing the "Parson's Cause."* Virginia Historical Society, Richmond. **145** J. S. Barber, New Hampshire Stamp Master in Effigy, from *Interesting Events in the History of the U.S., 1829.* Metropolitan Museum of Art, New York, bequest of Charles Allen Munn. **147** Paul Revere, *A View of Part of the Town of Boston . . . 1768,* 1770. Henry Francis du Pont Winterthur Museum, Winterthur, Del. **148** Paul Revere, *The Boston Massacre,* 1770. American Antiquarian Society. **150** *The Bostonians Paying the Excise-Man.* Colonial Williamsburg Foundation. **151** *To the Delaware Pilots . . .* (signed) *The Committee for Tarring and Feathering, November 27, 1773,* broadside. Rare Book Collection, New York Public Library, Astor, Lenox & Tilden Foundations. **154** Paul Revere, *The Able Doctor, or America Swallowing the Bitter Draught,* 1774. Massachusetts Historical Society, Boston. **155** LEFT: Title page, Thomas Paine's *Common Sense,* 1776. Library of Congress. RIGHT: William Sharp, *Thomas Paine,* engraved after a painting by George Romney, 1793. New-York Historical Society, New York. **158** *A Society of Patriotic Ladies at Edenton in North Carolina,* printed for R. Sayer and J. Bennett, 1775. Colonial Williamsburg Foundation, Williamsburg, Va. **159** Charles Willson Peale, *Portrait of Benjamin Rush,* c. 1783–1786. Henry du Pont Winterthur Museum, Winterthur, Del.

173 Godefroy, *Journée de Lexington,* published in Nicholas Ponce, *Recueil d'Estampes.* Library of Congress. **179** *The Surrender of Earl Cornwallis . . . to General Washington and Count de Rochambeau,* engraving and etching by Thornton, based on a drawing by Hamilton, published in Edward Barnard, *History of England,* 1783. Library of Congress. **181** J. R. Smith, after George Romney, *Joseph Tayadaneega, Called the Brant,* 1779. Prints Division, New York Public Library, Astor, Lenox & Tilden Foundations. **182** Benjamin West, *Commissioners of the Preliminary Peace Negotiations with Great Britain,* c. 1783. Henry Francis du Pont Winterthur Museum, Winterthur, Del. **184** Anonymous, *A Real American Rifle Man,* 1780. Library of Congress. **187** Francois Xavier Habermann, *Représentation du Feu terrible a Nouvelle Yorck . . .* 177-(?). Library of Congress. **188** John Trumbull, The Tory's Day of Judgment, from *M'Fingal.* The Bettmann Archive. **190** Portrait of James Armistead

Lafayette, 1784. Virginia Historical Society, Richmond. **193** *Now fitting for a Privateer,* broadside, Beverly, Mass., September 17, 1776. American Antiquarian Society; photo Marvin Richmond. **195** Currency of the Continental Congress, issued 1779. American Antiquarian Society; photo Marvin Richmond. **196** *La Destruction de la Statue Royale a Nouvelle Yorck (Die Zerstörung der Königlichen Bilde Saule zu Neu Yorck),* 177-(?), hand-colored etching, Chez Basset, Paris. Library of Congress. **197** *A Representation of the Figures Exhibited and Paraded Through the Streets of Philadelphia on Saturday the 30th of September 1780.* American Antiquarian Society; photo Marvin Richmond. **199** Anonymous portrait, traditionally said to be Abigail Adams. New York State Historical Association, Cooperstown. **200** *The Female Patriot,* broadside, New York, May 30, 1770. Library of Congress. **202** Samuel Hill, A S.W. View of the State House in Boston, published in *Massachusetts Magazine,* July 1793. Stokes Collection, New York Public Library, Astor, Lenox & Tilden Foundations. **205** Old Statehouse of Pennsylvania, later called Independence Hall. Independence National Historic Park Collection, Philadelphia. **206** Anonymous, *A Correct View of the Old Methodist Church in John St.* Metropolitan Museum of Art, New York, The Edward W. C. Arnold Collection of New York Prints, Maps, and Pictures; bequest of Edward W. C. Arnold, 1954.

218 Bertrand, after Vauthier, *L'Amérique,* 181-(?). Library of Congress. **219** *Taxation Royal Tyranny,* broadside, Philadelphia, September 22, 1779. Library of Congress. **225** Anonymous, *General Daniel Shays and Colonel Job Shattuck,* 1787, published in *Bickerstaff's Boston Almanach,* 3d ed., 1787. National Portrait Gallery, Smithsonian Institution, Washington, D.C. **226** Paul Revere, silver bowl presented to General Wm. Shepard, c. 1787. Yale University Art Gallery, New Haven, Conn., Mabel Brady Garvan Collection. **227** Gilbert Stuart, *James Madison,* 1804. Mead Art Museum, Amherst College, Amherst, Mass. **228** Thomas Rossiter, *Constitutional Convention, 1787,* 186-(?). Independence National Historic Park Collection, Philadelphia. **230** Title page of Mercy Otis Warren, *Observations on the New Constitution,* 1788. Rare Book Collection, New York Public Library, Astor, Lenox & Tilden Foundations. **231** *The Federal Ship Hamilton,* from Martha Lamb, *History of New York City,* 1877. New York Public Library, Astor, Lenox & Tilden Foundations. **234** ABOVE: Samuel Jennings, *Liberty Displaying the Arts and Sciences,* 1792. Library Company of Philadelphia. **235** Quilt, initials C. A. C., 1853. National Gallery of Art, Washington, D.C. Index of American Design. **236** Chest; possibly made in Ohio, c. 1860. From the collection of the Henry Ford Museum and Greenfield Village, Dearborn, Michigan.

241 "Liverpool" china pitcher, New-York Historical Society, bequest of Mrs. J. Insley Blair. **242** S. H. Gimber, after J. L. Morton, *Washington's Reception on the Bridge at Trenton in 1789,* lithograph. Library of Congress. **243** Amos Doolittle, after Peter LaCour, *Federal Hall, the Seat of Congress* 1789. Stokes Collection, New York Public Library, Astor, Lenox & Tilden Foundations. **244** John Trumbull, *Alexander Hamilton.* Yale University Art Gallery, New Haven, Conn. **245** William Birch and Son, *Bank of the United States, in Third St., Philadelphia,* 1799. Library of Congress. **246** Jean-Antoine Houdon, *Bust of Thomas Jefferson,* 1789. New-York Historical Society, New York. **248** Attributed to Frederick Kimmelmayer, *Washington Reviewing the Western Army at Fort Cumberland, Maryland, October 18, 1794.* Metropolitan Museum of Art, New York, gift of Edgar William and Bernice Chrysler Garbisch. **251** Anonymous Chinese artist, after Barralet, *The Apotheosis of Washington,* after 1802. Peabody Museum, China Trade Gallery, Salem, Mass. **254** Joseph Wright, *George Washington,* 1790. Metropolitan Museum of Art, New York, bequest of Charles Allen Munn. **255** *Porcupine in Colors Just Betrayed.* Historical Society of Pennsylvania, Philadelphia. **256** William Winstanley, *John Adams,* 1798. Adams National Historical Site, Quincy, Mass.; photo George Dow. **257** *Cinque-têtes, or the Paris Monster,* c. 1798–1800. Huntington Library, San Marino, Cal. **259** Anonymous miniature, *Charles Maurice de Talleyrand-Périgord, Prince de Benevent.* New-York Historical Society, New York. **260** James Van Dyke, *Aaron Burr,* 1834. New-York Historical Society, New York. **261** Textile banner celebrating Jefferson's victory, 1800. National Museum of American History, Smithsonian Institution, Washington, D.C.

267 Andrew Ellicott, after Pierre L'Enfant, Plan of the District of Columbia, Intended for the Permanent Seat of Government of the U.S., 1792. Library of Congress. **268** George I. Parkyns, View of the

Suburbs of Washington, D.C., c. 1800. Library of Congress.
270 Chester Harding, *John Marshall,* 1828. Boston Athenaeum.
274 Lewis and Clark, Map of the Missouri River, October 22–31, 1804.
Joslyn Art Museum, Omaha, Neb., Maximilian Bodmer Collection,
Internorth Art Foundation, Center for Western Studies. **276** Boqueto
de Woiserie, *Under My Wings Everything Prospers,* view of New
Orleans from the plantation of Marginy, November 1803. Chicago
Historical Society. **281** George Catlin, *A Choctaw Eagle Dance.*
American Museum of Natural History, New York. **283** *Portrait of
Se-Quo-Yah, Cherokee,* after C. B. King, 1836–1844. National Museum
of Natural History, Smithsonian Institution, Washington, D.C.
287 George Ropes, *Crowninshield Wharf After the Embargo,* c. 1806.
Essex Institute, Salem, Mass. **290** S. W. Fores, *The Fall of Washington,
or Maddy in Full Flight,* London, 1814. Brown University Library,
Providence, R.I., Anne S. K. Brown Military Collection. **292** Ambrose
Louis Garneray, *The Battle of Lake Erie.* Chicago Historical Society.
293 Thomas Gimbrede, *John Quincy Adams,* 1826. National Portrait
Gallery, Smithsonian Institution, Washington, D.C. **294** Charles
Willson Peale, *The Artist in His Studio,* 1822. Pennsylvania Academy of
Fine Art, Philadelphia. **295** Samuel F. B. Morse, *Congress Hall: Old
House of Representatives, 1821.* Corcoran Gallery of Art, Washington,
D.C. **297** John L. Krimmel, *Election Day at the Statehouse,* c. 1815.
Historical Society of Pennsylvania, Philadelphia.

303 Francis Guy, *Tontine Coffee House, New York,* c. 1798. New-York
Historical Society, New York. **306** William Birch and Son, *Arch Street
Ferry, Philadelphia,* 1800. Stokes Collection, New York Public Library,
Astor, Lenox & Tilden Foundations. **307** McIntyre, Plan of an
American New-Cleared Farm, published in P. Campbell, *Travels in
North America,* 1793. Rare Book Division, New York Public Library,
Astor, Lenox & Tilden Foundations. **309** Benjamin Henry Latrobe, *An
Overseer Doing His Duty.* Maryland Historical Society.
311 Anonymous, *At the Loom,* c. 1795. Archives of American Art,
Downtown Gallery Papers, Smithsonian Institution, Washington, D.C.
312 ABOVE: *Portrait of Samuel Slater,* 1830. Courtesy Pawtucket (R.I.)
Library; photo Slater Mill Historic Site. BELOW: Slater's textile mill at
Pawtucket, R.I. Courtesy of the Rhode Island Historical Society,
Providence. **313** Reeding or Drawing In, no. 9 from the *Progress of
Cotton* series, lithograph by J. R. Barfoot. Yale University Art Gallery,
Mabel Brady Garvan Collection. BELOW: Samuel Slater's 48-spindle
spinning frame, built 1790. Photo (c. 1890) courtesy Slater Mill Historic
Site, Pawtucket, R.I. **314** Frederick Bourquin, after John L. Krimmel,
*White's Great Cattle Show and Grand Procession of the Victuallers of
Philadelphia,* 1815. Historical Society of Pennsylvania, Philadelphia.
315 William Birch, *Second Street North from Market Street, with Christ
Church, Philadelphia,* 1799. New York Public Library, Stokes Collection.
322 Strobridge, after A. J. Swing, *Cincinnati, 1800.* Cincinnati Historical
Society. **323** George Tattersall, Highways and Byways of the Forest,
from *American Western Sketches,* 1838. Museum of Fine Arts, Boston,
M. and M. Karolik Collection. **325** Anonymous, He that by the plough
would thrive . . . , c. 1810. Addison Gallery of American Art, Phillips
Academy, Andover, Mass., gift of Mrs. Evelyn Roberts; photo John
Woolf. **327** Prudence Punderson, *The First, Second, and Last Scene
of Mortality,* late eighteenth century. Connecticut Historical
Society, Hartford. **330** Pavel Petrovich Svinin, *A Philadelphia
Anabaptist Immersion During a Storm.* Metropolitan Museum of Art,
New York, Rogers Fund. **332** Lewis Miller, Ludwig Miller, teacher at
the Old Lutheran Schoolhouse in the year 1805, from *Sketches and
Chronicles,* 1805. Historical Society of York County, Pa. **333** John
Singleton Copley, *Thomas and Sarah (Morris) Mifflin,* 1743. Historical
Society of Pennsylvania, Philadelphia. **335** Pavel Petrovich Svinin,
Negro Methodist Meeting. Metropolitan Museum of Art, New York,
Rogers Fund.

346 Mary Keys, *Lockport on the Erie Canal,* 1832. Munson-Williams-
Proctor Institute, Museum of Utica, N.Y. **350** Southworth and Hawes,
The George Barrell Emerson School, c. 1840–1862. Metropolitan
Museum of Art, New York, gift of I. N. Phelps Stokes, Edward S. Hawes,
Alice Mary Hawes, and Marian Augusta Hawes. **352** The Manchester
Print Works at Manchester, N.H., from *Gleason's Pictorial,* 1854. Library
of Congress. **354** Pendleton, *Lowell, Massachusetts, 1834.* Worcester
Art Museum, Worcester, Mass., Goodspeed Collection. **355** Time
Table of the Lowell Mills, October 1851. Baker Library, Harvard
Business School, Cambridge, Mass. **356** Anonymous, *Drawing In.*
Museum of American Textile History, North Andover, Mass.
358 ABOVE: Isaac Singer supervising a demonstration of his

perpendicular-action sewing machine at his office in New York City,
c. 1853. BELOW: Patent model of Singer's sewing machine. Both,
Smithsonian Institution, Washington, D.C. **359** Workers in W. S. and
H. G. Thomson's skirt factory, New York, 1859. Granger Collection.
360 Photograph of the Ohio River at Cincinnati, 1848. Public Library
of Cincinnati and Hamilton County, Ohio. **363** Asselineau, after John
Bachman, *Panoramic View of Philadelphia,* c. 1855. Historical Society
of Pennsylvania, Philadelphia. **366** Anonymous, *The Sargent Family,*
1800. National Gallery of Art, Washington, D.C., gift of Edgar William
and Bernice Chrysler Garbisch. **367** H. Knight, *The Family at Home,*
1836. Hirschl & Adler Galleries. **368** Erastus Salisbury Field, *Joseph
Moore and His Family,* 1839. Museum of Fine Arts, Boston, M. and
M. Karolik Collection. **370** *Dreadful Riot on Negro Hill!* broadside,
1827. Library of Congress. **373** N. Currier, after L. Maurer, *Preparing
for Market,* 1856. Yale University Art Gallery, New Haven, Conn.,
Mabel Brady Garvan Collection.

381 *Frederick Douglass,* c. 1855, engraved portrait by J. C. Battre from
a daguerrotype. New York Public Library, Schomburg Center for
Research in Black Culture. **384** Mathew Brady, *Black Dockworkers,* c.
1860. National Archives. **388** Anonymous, *The Quilting Party,* after an
engraving in *Gleason's Pictorial,* after 1854. Abby Aldrich Rockefeller
Center for Folk Art, Williamsburg, Va. **390** Adele Petigru Allston and
Robert F. W. Allston. Both, South Caroliniana Library, Columbia,
S.C. **394** George Fuller, Interior of a Slave Cabin, January 28, 1858.
Private Collection. **397** Taylor, *The American Slave Market,* 1852.
Chicago Historical Society. **399** Christmas on the Plantation, *Frank
Leslie's Illustrated Newspaper,* December 16, 1857. New York Public
Library, Astor, Lenox & Tilden Foundations. **400** Slave family of five
generations, 1862, all born on plantation of J. J. Smith, Beaufort, S.C.,
photographed by T. H. Sullivan. Library of Congress. **404** George
Fuller, *Cotton Press and Gin,* February 2, 1858. Private Collection.
405 *Horrid Massacre in Virginia,* woodcut, 1831. Library of Congress.
407 Meeting in the African Church, *Frank Leslie's Illustrated
Newspaper,* April 30, 1853. Library of Congress.

415 *Symptoms of Indigestion,* 1824. Library Company of Philadelphia.
416 Robert Cruickshank, *All Creation Going to the White House,* 1829.
Library of Congress. **419** Old Hickory, figurehead, 1834. Museum of
the City of New York. **422** "A Drop of Hard Cider, or The Tippecanoe
Roarer," songbook cover, 1840. Cincinnati Historical Society.
426 J. Maze Burbank, *Religious Camp Meeting,* 1839. The Whaling
Museum, New Bedford, Mass. **428** *Portrait of John Humphrey Noyes,
Perfectionist.* The Granger Collection. **432** N. Currier, *The Drunkard's
Progress, from the First Glass to the Grave,* 1846. Museum of the City of
New York, Harry T. Peters Collection. **435** William Lloyd Garrison,
The Granger Collection. **439** N. Currier, *Certificate of Marriage,*
1848. Library of Congress. **440** LEFT: E. Decker, *Elizabeth Cady
Stanton.* RIGHT: *Lucretia Mott.* Both, Sophia Smith Collection, Smith
College, Northampton, Mass.

449 Jon Gast, *Westward the Course of Empire . . . ,* 1872. Library of
Congress. **451** Mathew Brady, *James Knox Polk,* 1849. Library of
Congress. **452** Currier & Ives, *Flight of the Mexican Army at the
Battle of Buena Vista, February 23, 1847.* Museum of the City of New
York. **456** Lorenzo Lorain, *Oregon City,* 1857. Oregon Historical
Society. **458** Benjamin Franklin Reinhart, *The Emigrant Train Bedding
Down for the Night,* 1867. Corcoran Gallery of Art, Washington, D.C.,
gift of Mr. and Mrs. Lansdell K. Christie. **460** Emigrant wagon, c.
1848. The Granger Collection. **462** *The Rigors of the Trail . . . the
End of a Long Day.* Denver Public Library, Western History
Department. **464** Charles Nahl, *Saturday Night at the Mines,* 1856.
Stanford University Museum of Art, gift of Mrs. Jane L. Stanford.
465 Mining, Auburn Ravine, American River, 1852. California State
Library, Sacramento. **466** William Henry Jackson, *Ophir City, Nevada,*
c. 1875. Denver Public Library, Western History Department.
467 C. C. A. Christensen, *The Nauvoo Temple, 1844.* Brigham Young
University Art Museum Collection, Provo, Utah. **469** Sacramento
Street, San Francisco, 1853. Bancroft Library, University of California,
Berkeley. **471** Alfred Jacob Miller, *Throwing the Lasso,* 1836. Yale
University Library, New Haven, Conn., Beinecke Rare Book and
Manuscript Collection. **473** Mission San Fernando Corridors with
Gen. Andrés Picos and daughter, by Edward Vischer, 1865. California
Historical Society, Ticor Collection of Historical Photographs,
Los Angeles.

484 *The Blessings of Liberty, or How to Hook a Gentleman ob (sic) Color,* 1851. Library of Congress. **485** *Caution! Colored People of Boston . . . ,* broadside, 1851. Library of Congress. **487** *Soliciting a Vote,* 1852. Library of Congress. **488** Mathew Brady, *Stephen Douglas,* c. 1858–1860. The Bettmann Archive. **489** Ferrying Missouri Voters to the Kansas Shore, from *Century Illustrated Magazine,* 1887, Kansas State Historical Society, Topeka. **493** *Ruins of the Free State Hotel, Lawrence, Kansas, 1856,* from a daguerrotype. State Historical Society, Topeka. **495** LEFT: G. G. Lange, *Rochester, New York,* 1860. Library of Congress. RIGHT: Calvert, *Sunny South,* c. 1850. The Bettmann Archive. **496** Front page, *Frank Leslie's Illustrated Newspaper,* June 27, 1857. New York Public Library, Astor, Lenox & Tilden Foundations. **497** Abraham Lincoln, c. 1860. The Bettmann Archive. **498** David Bowser, *John Brown,* Historical Society of Pennsylvania, Philadelphia. **499** Southern Sympathizer Tarred and Feathered in Haverhill, Massachusetts, from *Frank Leslie's Illustrated Newspaper,* August 31, 1861. New York Public Library, Astor, Lenox & Tilden Foundations. **502** *The True Issue,* cartoon. Library of Congress.

509 First Michigan Regiment musters in Detroit, May 11, 1861, before taking the train to Washington. Detroit Public Library. **512** Jefferson Davis, c. 1857. Museum of the Confederacy, Richmond, Va. **514** Alexander Gardner, *Lincoln with Pinkerton and Major General McClelland at Antietam, October 1862.* Library of Congress. **516** Killed at Antietam: Horse of a Confederate Officer. Library of Congress. **517** Wounded Zouave Receiving Water. National Archives, Office of the Chief Signal Officer. **518** J. G. Tanner, *Engagement Between the Monitor and the Merrimac.* National Gallery of Art, Washington, D.C. **520** Advertisements for Substitute Confederate Conscriptees, Virginia Historical Society, Richmond. **523** Emancipation Day at Smith's

Plantation Port Royal, S.C., from *Frank Leslie's Illustrated Newspaper,* January 24, 1863. New-York Historical Society, New York. **526** Mathew Brady, *Confederate Captives at Gettysburg.* National Archives. **527** Mathew Brady, *Burial Party at Cold Harbor, April 1965.* National Archives. **530** Currier & Ives, *The 54th Massachusetts Regiment Storming Fort Wagner, South Carolina . . . ,* 1890. Museum of the City of New York. **533** *A Relic of Pope's Retreat (Overturned Train).* Library of Congress. **534** Currier & Ives, *The Solider's Dream of Home.* Museum of the City of New York. **535** Ruins of Richmond, May 1865. Library of Congress.

543 The Desolate Home: A Picture of the Suffering of the South, from *Frank Leslie's Illustrated Newspaper,* February 23, 1867. Library of Congress. **544** Freedmen, Richmond, 1865. Library of Congress. **546** Slavery Is Dead? *Harper's Weekly,* January 12, 1867. Library Company of Philadelphia. **548** Burning of a Freedmen's School, *Harper's Weekly,* May 26, 1866. Library Company of Philadelphia. **552** Office of the Freedmen's Bureau, Memphis, from *Harper's Weekly,* June 2, 1866. Library of Congress. **555** Negro Home in the South: Sharecroppers. Brown Brothers. **557** Black Schoolchildren. Valentine Museum, Richmond, Va. **559** J. Kerst, "I shall discharge every Nigger who votes to adopt this Radical Yankee Constitution," from Trowbridge, *A Picture of the Desolate States,* 1868. Library of Congress. **561** Thomas Nast, *Worse than Slavery,* n.d. Library of Congress. **564** LEFT: Currier & Ives, "Middle Age," from *The Seasons of Life,* 1868. Museum of the City of New York. RIGHT: *A Visit from the Ku Klux Klan,* 1878. The Granger Collection. **566** Thomas Nast, "This is a White Man's Government," from *Harper's Weekly,* September 5, 1868. Library Company of Philadelphia.

INDEX

Credit. *See also* National debt
  installment buying, 359
  postrevolutionary pyramid, 223–225
Creek, 99, 100, 180, 218, 416
  War, 284–285
Crime, on mining frontier, 464
Crockett, Davy, 285, 450
Cuba, 20
  foreign relations, U.S., 488–489
Culpeper, John, 82
Currency
  Civil War, 518–519, 529
  colonial, 142
  Revolutionary War, 194
  Specie Circular of 1836, 420

Dabney, R. L., 390
Danforth, Thomas, 187
Daniel, Peter, 495–496
Dartmouth College v. *Woodward,* 349
Davenport, James, 122–123
Davenport, John, 48
Davies, Samuel, 123
Davis, Jefferson, 501, 502–503, 488, 506,
    509, 525, 544
  cabinet of, 512
  personal characteristics of, 513, 533
Davis, John, 239
Deane, Silas, 193
Death, Puritan attitude toward, 80–81
De Bow, J. D. B., 386
Declaration of Independence, 152–153,
    176, 197
Declaration of Indulgence, 83
Declaratory Act of 1766, 145
De Grasse, Comte, 179
Delancy, James, 158
Delaney, Martin, 407, 437
Delaware, 206, 232, 283, 372, 510
Delaware Indians, 9, 61, 137
Democratic party. *See also* Presidential
    elections; *specific names*
  immigrants in, 486, 490
  Jacksonian, 413, 414, 421, 422, 423,
    434
  Peace Democrats (Copperheads), 521
  in Reconstruction era, 542, 549, 560
  and slavery issue, 480, 487, 496, 499
  and westward expansion, 451, 453
Democrat-Republican societies, 249, 252
Denver, Colorado, 468
Depressions, 565
  of 1819, 316, 328
  of 1837, 420–421, 434
Derby, E. H., 304
Derby, Elias, 192
Description of New England (Smith), 45
De Soto, Hernando, 27
De Tocqueville, Alexis, 423, 424
Detroit, Michigan, 348
Dial, The, 430

Dickens, Charles, 424
Dickinson, John, 171
Dickson, Jephta, 554–555
Diet
  antebellum, 372
  preindustrial, 325
  of slaves, 394
Disease
  Black Death, 17, 22
  in Civil War, 519, 534
  in colonial period, 42, 51, 58
  among Native Americans, 4, 24–25,
    471
  in preindustrial society, 326–327
  in Revolutionary War, 185, 187
  among slaves, 394–395
  in westward migration, 462
District of Columbia. *See* Washington,
    D.C.
Divorce, 332, 559
Dix, Dorothea, 433, 531
Dixon, Thomas, Jr., 562, 563
Dominican Republic, 20
Donne, John, 40
Dorchester, Massachusetts, 34
Douglas, Stephen, 451, 480
  in election of 1860, 476, 499
  Kansas-Nebraska bill of, 486–487, 491
  and Lecompton constitution, 496
  Lincoln-Douglas debates, 497–498
Douglass, Esther, 557
Douglass, Frederick, 381, 407, 453, 487,
    491, 496, 523, 551
  and abolitionism, 436, 437
  defiance of Fugitive Slave Act, 484
  denunciation of slavery, 396, 399, 406,
    485
  as free black, 406, 408
  on Harpers Ferry raid, 498
  on Lincoln, 476–477, 501, 502, 503,
    522
  on Reconstruction, 567
  as slave, 378–379, 398
Draft, in Civil War, 519–520, 528
Drake, Francis, 29
Dred Scott v. *Sandford,* 495–496, 497
Drinker, Elizabeth, 186
Duane, James, 151, 203
Du Bois, W. E. B., on Reconstruction,
    540, 552, 559, 567
Dudley, Thomas, 46
Dunmore, Lord, 189
Durant, George, 82
Dutch West India Company, 55, 84
Dwight, Timothy, 294, 333
Dyer, Mary, 60

Eagleton, George and Ethie, 506, 507,
    524, 534
Early, Peter, 335
East India Company, 149, 150

Economic policy. *See also* Currency;
    Tariffs; Taxation
  in Jackson presidency, 418–421
  in Lincoln presidency, 518–519, 529
  in Madison presidency, 294–295
  in Washington presidency, 242–246
Economy. *See also* Agriculture; Depres-
    sions; Industry; Inflation; National
    debt; Trade; Unemployment
  antebellum, 486
    boom-bust cycles in, 344
    capital investment and, 347–348
    education and, 349–350
    entrepreneurial mentality and, 349
    fear of social disintegration and,
      350–351
    governmental role in, 348–349
    immigration and, 344–346
    industrialization and, 351–357
    in South, 381
    transportation and, 346–347, 351
    urbanization and, 361–362
  Civil War impact on, 528, 529–530,
    542
  colonial, 117, 138–139
  preindustrial, 302–320
  Revolutionary War impact on. *See*
    Revolutionary era, economy
  slavery impact on, 386
Ecuador, 23
Eddis, William, 188–189
Education. *See also* Colleges and univer-
    sities
  of blacks, 371, 437, 557, 559
  and economic growth, 350
  expansion of, 349
  on frontier, 463
  of Native Americans, 281, 282
  segregated, 437
  and school reform, 350
  and social reform, 331
  in South, 559
  of women, 332–333
Education of Henry Adams, The (Henry
    Adams), 564
Edwards, Jonathan, 121
Eighteenth Amendment, 432
Elections. *See* Presidential elections;
    Suffrage
Eliot, Jaret, 103
Eliot, John, 49, 78
Elizabeth I, Queen of England, 22, 28,
    36, 43
Elskwatawa, 283–284
Emancipation Proclamation, 521–522,
    532
Embargo Act of 1807, 287–288, 314, 328
Emerson, Ralph Waldo, 427, 428, 430,
    484
*Emigrants' Guide to Oregon and Califor-
    nia* (Hastings), 447
Employment. *See* Labor force